P9-DZN-977
0 00 30 0376462 2

ENCYCLOPEDIA OF AMERICAN LIVES

REFERENCE

The SCRIBNER ENCYCLOPEDIA *of*
AMERICAN LIVES

The SCRIBNER ENCYCLOPEDIA *of*

AMERICAN LIVES

VOLUME FIVE

1997–1999

KENNETH T. JACKSON
EDITOR IN CHIEF

KAREN MARKOE
GENERAL EDITOR

ARNOLD MARKOE
EXECUTIVE EDITOR

CHARLES SCRIBNER'S SONS

GALE GROUP

THOMSON LEARNING

New York • Detroit • San Diego • San Francisco
Boston • New Haven, Conn. • Waterville, Maine
London • Munich

Charles Scribner's Sons
An imprint of The Gale Group
300 Park Avenue South, 9th floor
New York, NY 10010

Library of Congress Cataloging-in-Publication Data

The Scribner encyclopedia of American lives / Kenneth T. Jackson,
    editor in chief ; Karen Markoe, general editor ; Arnold Markoe,
    executive editor.
        p.   cm.
    Includes bibliographical references and index.
    Contents: v. 1. 1981–1985
    ISBN 0-684-80492-1 (v. 1 : alk. paper)
    1. United States—Biography—Dictionaries. I. Jackson, Kenneth
    T. II. Markoe, Karen.   III. Markoe, Arnie.
CT213.S37   1998
920.073—dc21   98-33793
                                                                         CIP

ISBN 0-684-80663-0 (v. 5 : alk. paper)

1 3 5 7 9 11 13 15 17 19 20 18 16 14 12 10 8 6 4 2
PRINTED IN THE UNITED STATES OF AMERICA

The paper in this publication meets the minimum requirements of the American
National Standard for Information Services—Permanence of Paper for Printed
Library Materials, ANSI Z39.48–1992.

EDITORIAL *and* PRODUCTION STAFF

PREFACE

This fifth volume in the *Scribner Encyclopedia of American Lives (SEAL)* series contains the biographies of 345 persons who died in the three-year period between 1 January 1997 and 31 December 1999. It also includes cumulative name and occupations indexes containing the names of all the 1,964 biographees in the entire series.

The format of this book is alphabetical. Each essay in it appraises the circumstances and influences that shaped the life of an individual subject. Each entry also includes the full dates of birth and death, the full names and occupations of parents, the number of siblings, the educational institutions attended and degrees granted, the names of spouses and the dates of marriages and divorces, and the number of children. Wherever possible, the book also includes information on residences, cause of death, and place of burial. The length of articles was determined both by the relative significance of the subject and by the completeness of biographical material available.

In selecting a few hundred subjects from the many millions of Americans who died in 1997, 1998, and 1999, the editors followed a rigorous process. First, they compiled a list of several thousand candidates from a variety of sources. Second, they classified the names according to profession or occupation. Third, they submitted the lists to specialists or groups of specialists who helped to rank the potential biographees. The final list, however, is solely the responsibility of the editors, who weighed the relative significance of particular politicans and poets, chemists and criminals, business leaders and baseball players.

The 345 individuals who are profiled in this book obviously lived extraordinary lives and in conspicuous ways set themselves apart from the rest of us. Some won fame on the battlefield or in the halls of government. Others distinguished themselves by their books, their research efforts, or their creative genius. Still others became household names because of their achievements as performing artists or sports heroes. But taken together, these unusual individuals reflect the diversity of the nation they called home. They came from every race, ethnic group, socioeconomic class, and region of the United States. Many were born to privilege; others were born to poor parents. All took advantage of their natural gifts to leave a permanent mark on a continental nation. In general, the editors have included inviduals, such as Lawrence Stone, who made major professional or artistic contributions while living in the United States, whether or not they ever actually became American citizens.

Some of the choices of subjects were easy, and many of the names in this book, such as artist Willem de Kooning, slugging outfielder Joe DiMaggio, civil rights activist Eldridge Cleaver, comedian Henny Youngman, poet Denise Levertov, Congresswoman Bella Abzug, John F. Kennedy, Jr., Dr. Benjamin Spock, actor James Stewart, Nobel laureates Melvin Calvin and Glenn Seaborg, Senator Barry Goldwater, and such legends as Roy Rogers and Frank Sinatra will be familiar to almost everyone. But this volume also includes persons who were not much in the news during their lifetimes and who are only now receiving the recognition they deserve.

As is the case in any large-scale research effort, *SEAL* depended on the hard work and cooperation of hundreds of contributors, many new to this venture. We acknowledge again the diligent research efforts undertaken by our 230 writers. Resourceful photo editors located photographs for almost every subject. Happily, the editors of this volume all had worked together on similar ventures and chose to do so again. The result of this collaboration is a book that we trust will be useful, reliable, and enjoyable.

In particular, we wish to thank Alja K. Collar, Sarah Feehan, and Neil Schlager, who oversaw the administration and copy editing of this volume. We also wish to thank Richard H. Gentile, who has provided valuable insight and advice throughout our many years of collaboration. Finally, we wish to record our continuing gratitude to the publisher of Charles Scribner's Sons, Frank Menchaca, and the associate publisher, Timothy J. DeWerff, for their personal commitment to this project.

Kenneth T. Jackson, Editor in Chief
Karen E. Markoe, General Editor
Arnold Markoe, Executive Editor

CONTENTS

The SCRIBNER ENCYCLOPEDIA *of*
AMERICAN LIVES

A

ABZUG, Bella Savitzky (*b.* 24 July 1920 in New York City; *d.* 31 March 1998 in New York City), labor lawyer, civil liberties advocate, peace activist, and one of the first Jewish women elected to the U.S. House of Representatives, best known for her progressive causes, flamboyant style, Bronx accent, and large hats.

Abzug was born Bella Savitzky, the younger daughter of Emanuel and Esther Savitzky. Her father, who had emigrated from Russia, ran the Live and Let Live meat market in Manhattan. Her mother was a homemaker. Abzug excelled in the public schools of New York City. Elected president of her high school class and later student body president at Hunter College, she also found time to march in protest against the spread of Nazism in Europe and against British and American neutrality in the Spanish Civil War. Ironically, it was Abzug's faith that led to the development of her commitment to feminism. As she wrote in her 1972 autobiography, when she attended synagogue with her grandfather, she was offended that "women were consigned to the back rows of the balcony." Abzug received a B.A. degree in political science from Hunter College in 1942, and during World War II, she worked in a shipbuilding factory. On 4 June 1944 she married Maurice Abzug, a stockbroker and novelist, whom she had met on a bus in Miami on the way to a concert performance by violinist Yehudi Menuhin. They had two daughters.

Abzug received her LL.B. degree in 1947 from Colum-bia University and embarked on a private law practice. She became involved in the civil rights movement, defended many cases in the South, and earned threatening references in the editorials of Southern newspapers to the "white lady lawyer." While carrying her second child in 1952, Abzug defended a black man in Mississippi who was accused of raping the white woman with whom he claimed he had been having an affair. During the trial, she was threatened by members of the Ku Klux Klan and was forced to hide in the lady's room for hours. Although she lost the case, she was able to delay the man's execution for two years by twice appealing the conviction to the U.S. Supreme Court. These appeals were based on Abzug's arguments that her client had been unconstitutionally convicted by a jury from which African Americans were systematically excluded and that, in being sentenced to death for rape—a sentence virtually never given to a white man for the same crime—he had unconstitutionally received a "cruel and unusual punishment." Such arguments were nearly two decades ahead of their time. In the early 1970s the Warren and Burger Courts accepted both arguments in applying those provisions of the Bill of Rights guaranteeing a fair trail and prohibiting cruel and unusual punishment.

During the 1950s Abzug also defended teachers, writers, and actors accused of un-American activities by Senator Joseph McCarthy and helped draft legislation that was incorporated into the Civil Rights Act in 1954. During the 1960s Abzug juggled the demands of her Manhattan legal

Bella Abzug. PRINTS AND PHOTOGRAPHS DIVISION, LIBRARY OF CONGRESS

practice with her fight against nuclear testing. In 1961 Abzug helped found Women's Strike for Peace and often led that organization in its lobbying efforts before Congress and in demonstrations in Washington, D.C., and New York City. After the signing of the Test Ban Treaty in August 1963, she also helped to refocus the antinuclear movement into an antiwar movement as the United States became more involved in the conflict in Vietnam.

In the late 1960s Abzug's concerns about the war in Vietnam and the decay of American cities drew her even further into the political arena. She ran for the U.S. House of Representatives, winning the 1970 election comfortably by capitalizing on her ties with labor and campaigned with celebrities such as Barbra Streisand to win over the Jewish vote. In Congress, Abzug championed progressive causes, declaring, "We can change this country. I think we have the capacity to build the kind of humanistic society in which men and women can fully express their creativity and talents. That is what I would like to see woman power used for." Abzug's career could have easily ended with that one term, as the 1970 census cost New York State one of its seats in the House. The legislature in Albany reappor-

tioned its congressional seats by essentially merging Abzug's district into that of William Fitz Ryan, another progressive. She lost the primary, but when Ryan died three months later, Abzug was chosen to represent the Democrats in a general election held to replace him. She won with 56 percent of the vote, and two years later was reelected with a majority of 79 percent.

In 1976 Abzug announced her decision to run for the U.S. Senate, but this race was the beginning of the end of her career in elective politics. She lost the 1976 Democratic primary to Daniel Patrick Moynihan and failed the following year to win the mayoral primary against challenger Ed Koch. Her electoral career ended in 1978 when she lost to a Republican opponent in the race to fill Koch's Eighteenth Congressional District seat. Abzug's flamboyant, assertive style was used by critics to paint her as the caricature of a feminist. But her style also won her admirers. "I like her," the New York governor Nelson Rockefeller once said. "She's got balls."

Although no longer in Congress, Abzug continued her activism, serving as presiding officer of the National Commission on the Observance of International Women's Year and the National Women's Conference in 1977. She went on to act as cochair of President Jimmy Carter's President's National Advisory Council for Women in 1978. During the 1980s, Abzug served as a cable television commentator, a fellow at Harvard University's John F. Kennedy School of Government, and a popular speaker throughout the country. She cochaired the Women's Environmental Development Organization in 1991 and served as a senior adviser to the United Nations Conference on the Environment and Development in 1992. In that capacity Abzug joined the environmental organization Greenpeace in support of a worldwide ban of chlorine-based chemicals because of their suspected link to breast cancer.

As Abzug wrote in *Gender Gap: Bella Abzug's Guide to Political Power for American Women* (1984), "women can either learn to become political leaders and activists, or [they] can sit back and let a minority of men in government backed by powerful money and military interest . . . try to run the whole world." Certainly Abzug amply demonstrated her unwillingness to sit back and watch the world go by. Abzug continued her work as a pacifist and feminist until her death at age seventy-seven at Columbia-Presbyterian Medical Center in Manhattan after a long illness and heart surgery. She is buried in Mount Carmel Cemetery in Queens, New York.

Abzug identified a particular role and a higher degree of freedom for women in cleaning up "the mess" that had been made throughout the world: "I believe women will bring a new vision, with new perspectives as to how and what to change," she said in a 1997 interview. New York City's Mayor Koch said of Abzug, "History will remember her as the earth mother who really performed brilliantly in a whole host of issues, her struggle and successful fight to bring equality and power to women all over the world."

★

Abzug's works include *Bella! Ms. Abzug Goes to Washington* (1972), and with Kim Kelber, *Gender Gap: Bella Abzug's Guide to Political Power for American Women* (1984), which speak of the causes she believed in and the work she thought was important in Washington. Doris Faber, *Bella Abzug* (1976), aimed at young readers, gives a very good overview of Abzug's life. Abzug made many speeches in Congress and for the many causes that she championed. Nancy Kartawich's master's thesis, "An Analysis of the Frequency and Pattern of Arguments in Bella Abzug's Speeches to Women, 1971–1975" (Southern Illinois University, 1976), describes Abzug's speeches and their rhetoric. May Joy Breton, *Women Pioneers for the Environment* (1998), discusses Abzug's progressive causes. Obituaries are in the *Los Angeles Times* and the *New York Times* (both 1 Apr. 1998).

JOAN GOODBODY

ACKLEY, H(ugh) Gardner   (*b.* 30 June 1915 in Indianapolis, Indiana; *d.* 12 February 1998 in Ann Arbor, Michigan), professor of economics at the University of Michigan and economic adviser to Presidents John F. Kennedy and Lyndon B. Johnson.

H. Gardner Ackley, 1964. AP/WIDE WORLD/TRANSCENDENTAL

Ackley was one of three children. His father, Hugh M. Ackley, was a mathematics professor, and his mother, Margaret MacKenzie, was a high school Latin teacher. Ackley grew up in Kalamazoo, Michigan, attending local schools. Ackley graduated from Western Michigan Teacher's College (now Western Michigan University) in 1936 with a B.A. degree in English and history. When he accepted a one-year scholarship for graduate study at the University of Michigan at Ann Arbor, he was told that if he did well, he could be nominated for a teaching fellowship. He didn't want to teach, but he "did want to have something to do." Because the Great Depression had piqued his interest in economics, and because economics was a much less crowded field than either English or history, in the fall of 1936 Ackley began his career-long relationship with the Department of Economics at the University of Michigan.

Ackley's first year of graduate study convinced him that what he really wanted to do was work for the federal government, and a Doctor of Philosophy degree wasn't the usual preparation for that career. But a teaching fellowship for doctoral study was something he could depend on, and Ackley accepted the offer when it came. He received his M.A. degree in the spring of 1937 and, as a newly married doctoral student (he married Bonnie A. Lowry on 18 Sep-

tember 1936), spent the remainder of that year "trying to understand Keynes's *General Theory,*" which had just been published. By the summer of 1939 he was looking for a job, having completed all but the final revisions on his thesis. He accepted an offer from Ohio State University to teach there for the 1939–1940 academic year. Ackley's doctoral thesis, which resulted in his first published article, dealt with oligopoly (in which a few producers affect but do not control the market) theory and was notable for its pioneering use of Legrange multipliers (devices used in advanced calculus) in economics work. The University of Michigan granted Ackley his Ph.D. in February 1940. Around that time, a death among the university's economics faculty created an unanticipated opening, and the department offered him a job.

His return to the University of Michigan forced Ackley to become an economic historian which, he discovered, fit quite well with his interest in microeconomic theory. "I had a lot of fun sort of trying to think out what economic institutions were . . . and [trying] to pull together some ideas about how they'd evolved." During the 1940–1941 school year Ackley became involved with his first Washington project, a study of industrial location done by the National Resources Planning Board. When he was offered a job with the Office of Price Administration (OPA) in the spring of 1941, he accepted without hesitation. Ackley resigned his university position and moved his family (the first of two sons had been born in early 1941) to Washington, D.C., where they would live until 1946.

Initially assigned to OPA's copper branch, Ackley took charge of the scrap metal section with a staff of fifteen or twenty economists and business specialists. In a 1964 *Newsweek* interview, CEA colleague Walter Heller quipped, "Ackley is probably the first Ph.D. who ever dealt with junk, and he made it intellectually respectable." Ackley also spent the year from 1943 to 1944 working for the Office of Strategic Services.

In the summer of 1946, anticipating that many veterans would take advantage of the GI Bill to go to college, the University of Michigan contacted Ackley regarding his plans. He had many offers in the business sector, but in the end decided that his vocation was economics. He returned to Ann Arbor as assistant professor, was quickly promoted to associate professor (1947), and found himself teaching the economic department's course in Keynesian economics.

Ackley returned to Washington, D.C., in 1950 as a price control consultant and stayed through 1952 as assistant director and chief economist of the newly formed Office of Price Stabilization. When he returned to Ann Arbor in 1952 he was promoted to full professor; three years later he became department chairman. This position, too, became enjoyable, as Ackley was an active advocate for colleagues caught in McCarthy-era conflicts.

Ackley spent a sabbatical year in 1956 in Italy as a Fulbright scholar. Research he conducted during this year resulted in *Macroeconomic Theory* (1961), a standard economic textbook that has been translated into several languages. A second trip to Italy in 1961 as a Ford Foundation Faculty Research Fellow enabled Ackley to apply mathematics and statistics to economic theory in order to develop a mathematical model of the interrelationships among various factors in the Italian economy. Resulting publications, which he wrote in Italian, earned him Italy's highest honor, the Cavaliere del Gran Croce Italy (1969).

In the spring of 1962 President John F. Kennedy invited Ackley to join the Council of Economic Advisers (CEA), on the recommendation of its chairman, Walter Heller. It was a job Ackley "couldn't imagine any economist not accepting." Between 1962 and 1964 Ackley was the chief architect of the government's wage-price guidelines, which specified that salary increases should generally be held to 3.2 percent annually, and that industries with productivity rates above normal should cut prices. As chairman of the CEA from 1964 to 1968, Ackley fearlessly rebuked business and labor for price and wage increases that exceeded government guidelines. Particularly adept at explaining economic technicalities to non-specialists, Ackley became one of President Lyndon B. Johnson's most trusted economic advisers. When Ackley resigned from the CEA in 1968, President Johnson appointed him ambassador to Italy. Ackley served in this capacity until 1969, then returned to the University of Michigan as the Henry Carter Adams University Professor of Political Economy. The university further recognized his professional contributions by selecting him to receive its 1976 Distinguished Faculty Achievement Award and naming him professor emeritus upon his retirement in 1984.

Throughout his career Ackley served on many academic and governmental councils and committees, and was considered one of the leading macroeconomists of the time. Tall, trim and unassuming, Ackley was admired as much for his humility as for his economic acuity. Ackley died of Alzheimer's disease at age eighty-two.

★

The Gardner Ackley Papers (1937–1987) at the Bentley Historical Library at the University of Michigan contain reports, correspondence, and other records documenting Ackley's years in Washington, D.C., as well as his teaching career. Oral histories at the John F. Kennedy and Lyndon B. Johnson Presidential Libraries focus on Ackley's years with the CEA. Two oral histories at the Bentley Historical Library address his academic career: the Centennial History Project of the University of Michigan Department of Economics (1979) and the *Historica Critica* university history project (begun in 1985). Martin F. J. Prachowney, *The Kennedy-Johnson Tax Cut* (2000), analyzes Ackley's role in the CEA and claims to be the first truly critical study of 1960s fiscal policy. Obituaries are in the *Detroit News* (19 Feb. 1998) and *New York Times* (21 Feb. 1998).

MARILYN SAUDER MCLAUGHLIN

ADAMS, Charles Francis (*b.* 2 May 1910 in Boston, Massachusetts; *d.* 5 January 1999 in Dover, Massachusetts), business executive who led the Raytheon Company to become Massachusetts' largest industrial employer.

Adams was the second of two children of Charles Francis Adams and Frances Lovering, a homemaker. His father, a lawyer, financier, yachtsman, and longtime treasurer of Harvard College, became secretary of the navy under President Herbert Hoover and ultimately a director of some fifty-six corporations, including General Electric and American Telephone and Telegraph (AT&T). The first Charles Francis Adams, Adams's great-grandfather, was President Abraham Lincoln's masterly envoy to Great Britain and the son of John Quincy Adams and grandson of John Adams, both of whom were presidents of the United States. But Adams was not preoccupied with lineage; early in life he saw too many cousins become "so goddamned inhibited" worrying about whether they would become an-

Charles Francis Adams, 1961. AP/WIDE WORLD/TRANSCENDENTAL

other John Quincy Adams that he told himself, "Go ahead and do your own thing."

Still, family tradition played its part. After attending Saint Mark's School in Southborough, Massachusetts, from 1922 to 1928, Adams spent the next four years at Harvard College, where he participated in the U.S. Navy's Reserve Officer Training Corps and earned an A.B. degree in fine arts in 1932. Over the next two years he attended the Harvard Business School. On 16 June 1934 he married Margaret Stockton; they had three children. That year he also joined a Boston brokerage firm, Jackson and Curtis, where he became a partner in 1937. He walked to his first day of work with his father, who offered a word of advice: "You've inherited a reputation for honesty, but God help you if you ever lose that." The firm merged with another to become Paine, Webber, Jackson, and Curtis, and Adams remained as partner until 1947.

The Adams tradition was rooted strongly in public service. Before his father, he reflected, "no Adams had ever made any money. They married money." Indeed, it was marriage and not lineage that accounted for the odd coupling of Adams with the Raytheon Manufacturing Company, a scrappy little manufacturer of radio tubes. Raytheon

was founded near Boston after World War I and led for most of its life by Laurence Marshall. An early backer was the American financier J. P. Morgan, Jr., whose son had married Adams's sister. In 1938 Morgan needed someone close at hand to represent him on the Raytheon board, and he turned to Adams. Adams served as a director of Raytheon from 1938 to 1942. In 1940 Adams was called to active duty in the U.S. Navy. During World War II, he commanded destroyer escorts and participated in the invasions of Luzon and Iwo Jima in the Pacific theater. He attained the rank of commander and left active service in 1946. Meanwhile, Raytheon had become a leading manufacturer of radar parts and systems. Adams, greatly impressed with the shipboard equipment, thought that creating it must be "a fascinating field."

Back in Boston, Adams resumed his work for the brokerage firm and rejoined the Raytheon board. In 1947 the other directors asked him to become Raytheon's full-time executive vice president. He knew that it was stretching the norms of his class. As Adams put it, "Industry wasn't where people went in my time." But the brokerage business did not fully engage him, and he had no desire to "just fiddle around." The end of the war meant the wholesale cancellation of radar contracts, and Marshall boldly pushed development of dozens of new products. His vision quickly exceeded Raytheon's capacity, and the directors contemplated bankruptcy. Instead, they named Adams president in 1948.

Adams's father "thought it was madness" for someone with so few qualifications to lead a small technical company against giants like General Electric. But Adams was willing to take risks. The appeal was not in making money but rather in the opportunity to perform a public service— helping reverse Massachusetts' economic decline. Adams's initial contribution was to impose order by selecting among the many innovations already in the pipeline, providing organization for the creative chaos, and integrating newly acquired operations into the company. He continued the development of large Radarange microwave ovens through a period of disappointing restaurant sales. While selling off assets for badly needed cash, one vice president reported that he had verbally agreed to sell a warehouse but later received a far better offer. Adams reply was instinctive: "Your word and handshake—that's better than a contract."

In 1950 an engineering team originally hired by Marshall built a successful ground-to-air missile, the Lark. Adams actively sought more military contracts, and during the next decade Raytheon developed the Hawk and Sparrow missiles and guidance components for the underwater Polaris missile. Through internal development and acquisitions Raytheon expanded into household appliances (including smaller Radaranges for home use), textbook publishing, and road-building equipment. In 1959 the name of the firm was shortened to the Raytheon Company. Over the years Adams helped create an atmosphere of stability and profitability in which others could innovate, and he was not rank-conscious. He relied heavily for advice on the company's full-time engineers and also on an array of consultants from the Massachusetts Institute of Technology. His lack of technical training was not an impediment. "You could reduce engineering questions to practical questions if you tried hard enough," he said.

Adams served as Raytheon's president until 1960 and again from 1962 to 1964 and as its chairman from 1960 to 1962 and from 1964 to 1975, the second tenure coming after his initial replacement did not work out. During Adams's twenty-seven years of active leadership, Raytheon's sales grew fortyfold, and the company became the nation's eighty-second largest corporation. It served Massachusetts not only as a source of jobs but also as a reservoir of engineering talent on which newer technology firms could draw. For all Adams's successes, the opportunities lost during his tenure were even greater than those seized. He approved a crash program to develop the newly invented transistor for use in hearing aids, and by 1954 Raytheon was the world's largest producer. But when its germanium products were eclipsed by silicon, Adams cut his losses rather than invest in the newer technology. Likewise, for several years he encouraged a talented engineering team to develop a computer under government contract but then balked at supplying the millions of dollars needed to create a machine for business use. Reliance on military contracts was safer but cost Raytheon its lead in the two dominant technologies of the digital age.

Adams devoted increasing time to community service. In 1954 he replaced his late father on the board of trustees of the Woods Hole Oceanographic Institution and served as chairman from 1973 to 1985. Like his father, he led in the development of the United Way. He was a major force in creating a museum for Old Ironsides, the legendary warship launched during the presidency of John Adams. Adams's first wife died in 1972, and in October 1973 he married Beatrice Dabney Penati. Adams remained on Raytheon's board until 1997. Looking back, he was proudest of the company's "good reputation for integrity," in its way of doing business and the quality of its products and engineering. Adams died at age eighty-eight.

Adams extended the values and accomplishments of America's most distinguished family into another generation and another realm of activity. He rescued Raytheon from bankruptcy and led it to become a foundation of Massachusetts' high-technology resurgence and America's high-technology military capability.

★

There is no biography of Adams. The best overviews of his career are in Otto J. Scott's *Creative Ordeal: The Story of Raytheon* (1974), and Paul R. Ryan's "Charles Francis Adams: Honorary Oceanographer," *Oceanus* 28 (fall 1985). All of the Adams quotations are from an unpublished interview by Peter Eckstein (13 Jan. 1988), except the quotation on engineering questions, which is from a videotape, *Raytheon History—Charles F. Adams Interview* (Nov. 1998), from the company archives. Obituaries are in the *Boston Globe* (6 Jan. 1999) and *New York Times* (9 Jan. 1999).

PETER ECKSTEIN

ADAMS, Walter (*b.* 27 August 1922 in Vienna, Austria; *d.* 8 September 1998 in East Lansing, Michigan), economist and educator best known for his critiques of corporate power and advocacy of antitrust action.

Adams was the son of Edward Adams, an international linen and diamond merchant, and Ilona Schildkraut, a homemaker. In 1935 the family moved to Brooklyn, New York, where Adams attended New Utrecht High School. From 1938 to 1942 he was a student at Brooklyn College (now Brooklyn College of the City University of New York), graduating magna cum laude with a B.A. degree in economics. Adams entered military service in April 1943, which eventually led him to participation in the battles of Normandy and the Bulge during World War II, a battlefield commission, and an assignment as aide-de-camp to the commanding general of the Eleventh Armored Division. He attained the rank of first lieutenant, and in 1945 was awarded a Bronze Star Medal for heroic conduct. At the end of the war Adams returned to his wife, Pauline Gordon, whom he had married on 23 August 1943, and to his studies, earning a M.A. degree in 1946 and a Ph.D. in 1947, both from Yale University. After the birth of his only child, William James, in 1947, Adams became an assistant professor at Michigan State University (MSU) in East Lansing, where he taught economics until his retirement in 1993.

Interested in the New Deal's revival of antitrust law enforcement, Adams soon made undue economic concentration his specialty. In 1950 he edited *The Structure of American Industry,* a collaborative work exploring the differing degrees of concentration in some thirteen industries. The work became a leading textbook, eventually going through ten editions. Adams also began defending antitrust action in articles published in professional journals and law reviews. He became a consultant for Congress's new small business committees, and from 1953 to 1955 he served on the U.S. Attorney General's National Committee to Study the Antitrust Laws. There, he dissented from the endorsement of existing policy. Arguing that existing concentration could not be explained by technological or economic imperatives, he and Horace Gray published *Monopoly in America* (1957). Its cause was "unwise, discriminatory, privilege-creating governmental measures," and in the book the authors argued that changing such measures could lead to an effective competition capable of reconciling welfare and freedom far better than any regulatory commission or managerial elite. National progress required that corporate power be reduced, not regulated, and countervailed, or given a "soul."

From 1955 to 1969 Adams continued this general line of argument, both in articles and papers often reprinted in the *Congressional Record* and as an expert witness in congressional investigations of administered prices and monopolistic practice. He was, he said, a "philosophical populist" who admired "the Wayne Morses and Estes Kefauvers more than the Franklin Roosevelts and Dwight Eisenhowers of this world." In addition, he became known for his work with the historian John Garraty on a survey of American university programs overseas. This produced two critical studies, *From Main Street to the Left Bank* (1959) and *Is the World Our Campus?* (1960), which were greeted with strong criticism from the "International Programs bureaucracy," including charges that Adams was a covert "isolationist." Still, as a member of the U.S. Advisory Commission on International Educational and Cultural Affairs (1961–1969) and cochair of an international conference on the "brain drain" (1967), he continued to speak out. Such overseas programs, he believed, were obscuring the central mission and compromising the institutional neutrality of American universities.

By 1969 Adams had also gained recognition as a master teacher offering legendary courses and seminars that could "expand minds and change lives." Given this reputation, his name came to the fore as MSU trustees sought an interim president following the unexpected retirement of John Hannah. Initially, Adams scoffed at the idea, noting his anti-establishment record. But he finally agreed to serve until a permanent replacement for Hannah could be found and thus became Michigan State's thirteenth president, serving from 1 April 1969 to 1 January 1970. It was a time of turmoil marked by campus rebellions and confrontations, but Adams's unusual degree of accessibility helped him to isolate extremists and defuse tense situations with "love and laughter." In October 1969 he won further student support by leading a Vietnam peace march to the state capitol, and shortly thereafter over 17,000 students and nearly 1,000 faculty signed petitions urging him to change his mind about staying on. He refused, saying that administration was still not his "bag."

After 1970 Adams's teaching reputation kept growing. He became Michigan Professor of the Year (1985), one of *Rolling Stone* magazine's "ten best college professors"

(1991), and after retirement a distinguished visiting teacher at Trinity University. He found time as well to hold visiting professorships abroad and to serve as president of the American Association of University Professors (1972–1974), the Midwest Economic Association (1979–1980), and the Association of Social Economics (1980–1981). And continuing with his critiques of corporate power, he supported the congressional antitrust initiatives of the 1970s, sharply criticized the acceptance of massive mergers in the 1980s, and in collaboration with James Brock wrote two major works, *The Bigness Complex* (1986) and *Dangerous Pursuits* (1989). In these he argued against the "cult of size," maintaining that the new conglomerates were appallingly bureaucratic and incompetent. In addition, he and Brock published *Antitrust Economics on Trial* (1991), *Adam Smith Goes to Moscow* (1993), and *The Tobacco Wars* (1998), all in the form of plays intended primarily for the teaching of economics.

As a personality Adams combined a congenial disposition and striking self-assurance with a flair for argumentation, a passion for honesty, an irreverent and playful sense of humor, and considerable personal magnetism. Also adding color were such idiosyncrasies as his Brooklyn accent, cigar smoking, bow ties, and exceptionally enthusiastic support for MSU's athletic teams and marching band. As an economist he conceded the political dimensions of his work and remained suspicious of abstract theorizing, "value-free" pretensions, and any analysis that ignored power relationships. His critics saw him as mired in an outmoded stance, but for Adams the trouble was with the profession. Its "almost obsessive addiction to a mathematical-econometric methodology" amounted to "a formidable misallocation of intellectual resources." His optimistic search for an effective competition proved disappointing, but his work helped to keep alive concerns about concentrated power and hopes for another revival of antitrust legislation and litigation. Following his death at age seventy-six of pancreatic cancer, the practice field of the MSU marching band was renamed Walter Adams Memorial Field, and a memorial service ended with the band playing the Michigan State fight song. His body was cremated.

★

A collection of Adams's papers, primarily limited to his MSU presidency, is in the University Archives and Historical Collections Division of the Michigan State University Library. His other papers are still held by the family but are expected to go to the MSU Library. There is no biography, but Adams told the story of his MSU presidency in *The Test* (1971) and discussed his professional work in Walter Adams and James W. Brock, "Reflections on Our Collaboration," *American Economist* 41 (fall 1997): 22–26. On his contributions, see also James W. Brock and Kenneth G. Eizinga, eds., *Antitrust, The Market, and The State: The Con-*

tributions of Walter Adams (1991). The longest and best biographical sketches are in *Contemporary Authors,* vol. 170 (1999), and *Contemporary Authors, New Revision Series,* vols. 3 and 37 (1981, 1992). Also informative are Robert Bao, "Walter Adams, Spartan Extraordinaire," *MSU Alumni Magazine* (winter 1999); William Breit, "Remembering Walter," *Trinity* (winter 1998); Roger Spencer "A Road Less Traveled: The Institutionalist Walter Adams," *Challenge* (Jan.–Feb. 2001); and the tributes to Adams in the MSU college newspaper, the *State News* (9–10 Sept. and 26 Oct. 1998). Obituaries are in the *Detroit News* (10 Sept. 1998), *New York Times* (11 Sept. 1998), *Washington Post* (12 Sept. 1998), and *Chicago Tribune* (17 Sept. 1998).

ELLIS W. HAWLEY

ALFEREZ, Enrique ("Rique") (*b.* 4 May 1901 in San Miguel de Mezuital [now Miguel Auza, Zacatecas], Mexico; *d.* 13 September 1999 in New Orleans, Louisiana), artist, sculptor, and raconteur whose works grace public and private buildings and spaces in New Orleans and in other cities and collections in the Americas and Europe.

Alferez was the youngest of ten children of Longinus Alferez and Chlotilde Alferez Guzman. In partial compensation for service with Benito Juarez's republican forces

Enrique Alferez, 1995. AP/WIDE WORLD/TRANSCENDENTAL

against Emperor Maximilian's French troops, Longinus was awarded a grant by Juarez to study art in Europe. Longinus, who witnessed the slaughter of his eleven brothers, Juarez's companions, in 1867, was also given the "honor" of playing the drum roll at Maximilian's execution. When he returned to Mexico, Longinus supported his large family by sculpting religious statues. In 1913 during the Mexican Revolution, while the family was living in Durango, Mexico, young Alferez ran away from home after breaking a piece of school equipment. Unable to return home through the lines of Federal troops, Alferez joined the rebel general Francisco (Pancho) Villa, a friend of Alferez's maternal grandfather, who took the boy with him, first to carry water and find firewood and later as a mapmaker. When Alferez's commanding officer, a particularly vicious man, was murdered in 1923, Alferez traveled across the border using an American visa he had acquired in 1918. He found work retouching photographs in a photography studio in El Paso, Texas.

In El Paso, Alferez heard a lecture by sculptor Lorado Taft, who invited Alferez and another young Texas artist, Tom Lee, to come to the Art Institute of Chicago where Taft gave classes. Alferez was awarded a scholarship from the Kiwanis International and moved to Chicago in 1924 to join a group of students who lived and worked in Taft's studio. At the Art Institute, Alferez extended the training he received from his father. The innovative Bauhaus style, which emphasized functionality and good design in a streamlined aesthetic, suited Alferez's vision and craftsmanship. Working with architectural designer Norman BelGeddes, Alferez began his career in the United States by creating pieces to adorn skyscrapers built during Chicago's building boom of the late nineteenth and early twentieth centuries. He produced low relief sculptural designs for the face of a Michigan Avenue office building and carved decorative walnut elevator doors for the Palmolive Building.

Intending to work his way back to Mexico, Alferez left Chicago with his wife Evelyn Kelly and arrived in New Orleans in May 1929. Connections through architect Alex Norman led to a commission to sculpt five figures for the Church of the Holy Name of Mary Church in suburban Algiers, Louisiana. Almost at the same time, Alferez was hired to give classes at the New Orleans Arts and Crafts School. Tulane University also invited Alferez to join their expedition to the Yucatan, where they intended to reproduce the remains of the quadrangle of the nunnery in Uxmal for the 1933 Chicago World's Fair.

Alferez married Rosemarie Huth, an art student and the model for the statue of the Virgin Mary, in June 1931. Huth and Alferez had one daughter before divorcing. In the mid-1940s Alferez married model Judy Mosgrove, who later committed suicide. And on 20 July 1953 Alferez, now a widower, married Peggy Selway, with whom he had a second daughter.

While director of the New Orleans' Works Progress Administration (WPA) during the 1930s, Alferez produced a large body of sculpture for the city's public spaces, particularly for the Botanical Gardens of City Park. A prolific, intense, and witty craftsman, his work in metal, limestone, and cast stone provided New Orleans with fountains, bridges, light standards, and architectural ornaments. From 1936 to 1939 Alferez created two impressive reliefs for Charity Hospital: *Louisiana in Work and Play* in cast aluminum, and a second work of medical themes carved in limestone. *The Fountain of the Four Winds* at Lakefront Airport, sculpted in 1936 as a private commission, relied on WPA labor in its construction. The four, massive nude statues caused controversy when city officials objected to the explicit genitalia of the male figure of the North Wind. Alferez guarded the statue with a 30–30 rifle after city officials threatened to attack it with sledgehammers, but the piece was ultimately saved through the intervention of President Franklin and Mrs. Eleanor Roosevelt.

Although most of Alferez's work is apolitical, *St. George and the Dragon* (1940), carved in walnut for Christ Church Cathedral, represents the dragon's scales as swastikas. Eager to enlist in the U.S. Marine Corps in 1943, Alferez tried to persuade the recruiting officer of his sincerity by sculpting *Molly Marine,* a twelve-foot figure of cast concrete, fortified with marble and granite chips and painted to look like bronze. Alferez eventually joined the U.S. Army Transport Service and worked for the war effort by patrolling the Gulf of Mexico in a tugboat.

After World War II, Alferez lived in Greenwich Village in New York City where he made and sold leather goods. He returned to New Orleans in 1951 to accept a commission for *The Family,* a figure intended for the entrance of the New Orleans Municipal Courts Building. This oversized nude grouping of a seated mother, father, and child was cast in concrete and sheathed in aluminum. Responding to complaints from a neighboring clergyman, the piece was condemned as obscene, removed from public view, and later sold at auction for $600 more than the city had paid Alferez. Alferez considered *The Family* one of his best pieces and remained saddened and angered by its removal from public view.

Alferez continued to live and work in New Orleans for the rest of his life, with extended stays in Mexico, often at his home in Morelia where he had a foundry. He carved Old and New Testament figures for the doors of Saint Martin's Church in 1959, using rosewood he brought back from Vera Cruz. In the 1960s he produced several fountains with human and animal figures, and in 1967 created a wall, *Symbols of Communication,* for the *Times-Picayune* building. During the 1970s and 1980s Alferez, who worked long

hours all of his life, created an extensive collection of bronze figures, often graceful, female forms. These figures included *Fleeing Woman: Vietnam* (1970); *Woman in a Huipil* (1981); a number of mother and child figures, notably the *Mother and Child* (1983) at Touro Infirmary, New Orleans; and *Lovers on the Water,* which he started in 1970 and completed in 1984. Two large bronze figures, *David* and *The Lute Player,* were installed in front of the Louisiana Land and Exploration Building in New Orleans. In 1993 Alferez replaced his lost 1939 relief of Solomon at the Saint Bernard Parish Courthouse.

Alferez's long association with New Orleans and the wealth of his architectural, sculptural, and public art contributions brought him public recognition by the city in his last years. In 1980 a giant oak was designated the Alferez Oak. In 1983 a street near the Museum of Art was renamed for him. The city and mayor of New Orleans honored him in 1994 on his ninety-third birthday. Often sought out as a storyteller, Alferez polished his tales as carefully as he did his sculptures. A radiant, romantic man, whose life was spent with a passion for making beautiful things, Alferez thought artistic inspiration was "hokum. Work is work." Until illness made work impossible, Alferez worked every day, all day; his handmade tools an extension of his mind. He died of lung cancer at age ninety-eight, and his body was cremated.

★

Allgemeines Kunstlerlexikon (1984) is a primary source for artist biographies and includes a biography of Alferez. A biographical portrait of Alferez by Don Lee Keith, "Portrait of the Artist," appears in *Times-Picayune*'s Sunday magazine, *Dixie* (3 May 1981). Keith's "Sculptor Enrique Alferez, Cast in His Own Mold," in *Louisiana Cultural Vistas* (spring 1999), written shortly before Alferez's death, contains a portrait of the artist with photographs of his work and is enhanced with lengthy quotations. The *Times-Picayune* columnist Roger Green regularly reported on Alferez's installations and gallery shows, as did columnists in other newspapers. Alferez is cited in *Who's Who in Art* (1985 and 1999); Paula and Michael Gravez, *Dictionary of Texas Artists* (1999); and Randolph Delehanty, *Art in the American South* (1996). Howard Jacobs, *Charlie the Mole and Other Droll Stories* (1973), contains a somewhat exaggerated story of Alferez's adventure with a chimpanzee. A film biography of Alferez, *His Name Is Enrique Alferez, Sculptor* (1989), produced by B. Colman, and written and directed by M. Martinez as a production of the University of New Orleans, is valuable for the artist's recollections and accompanying views of his work. Alferez provided recollections of his experience with Pancho Villa in the PBS series *American Experience: The Hunt for Pancho Villa.* Obituaries are in the *New York Times* and *Times-Picayune* (both 15 Sept. 1999), and an editorial eulogizing Alferez appeared in the *Times-Picayune* (18 Sept. 1999).

WENDY HALL MALONEY

ALIOTO, Joseph Lawrence (*b*. 12 February 1916 in San Francisco, California; *d*. 29 January 1998 in San Francisco, California), antitrust attorney and businessman who as mayor of San Francisco exemplified the moderate liberalism of mainstream Democratic Party leaders active in urban affairs in the late 1960s and early 1970s.

Alioto was born and grew up in the Italian-American North Beach district of San Francisco. He was the only boy of four children in the family of Giuseppe Alioto, a fish wholesaler and proprietor of the International Fish Company, and Domenica Lazio, a homemaker. Alioto and his sisters Angelina, Stephanie, and Antoinette learned Italian as their first language, speaking it at home before they started school. Alioto began his education at the neighborhood public school, then transferred to Saints Peter and Paul Elementary School, a Catholic private school operated by the Salesians, an Italian order of Catholic priests. He graduated from Sacred Heart High School in 1933 and received his B.A. degree magna cum laude from Saint Mary's College in Moraga, California, in 1937. A leader in school affairs in high school and college and valedictorian of his class at Saint Mary's, Alioto excelled in debate and public speaking. A scholarship to the Catholic University of America School of Law took him to Washington, D.C., where he received his LL.B. degree in 1940.

Joseph Alioto, 1974. Sal Veder/Associated Press AP

After working as an intern at the prestigious San Francisco firm of Brobeck, Pfleger, and Harrison, Alioto served in Washington, D.C., as a special assistant in the antitrust division of the Justice Department. He and Angelina Genaro, the daughter of a Dallas wholesaler and distributor, were married on 2 June 1941. During World War II, Alioto went to work for the Board of Economic Warfare. He returned to San Francisco after the war, started a family that eventually included five boys and one girl, and opened a law practice specializing in private antitrust suits. In 1948 he represented the Society of Independent Motion Picture Producers, an organization established by Walt Disney, David O. Selznick, and Samuel Goldwyn, in a suit against United Detroit Theatres Corporation, a firm controlled by Paramount Pictures. Then in 1950 he represented Samuel Goldwyn separately in a suit against Twentieth Century–Fox's West Coast operation. The Fox West Coast case was settled in Goldwyn's favor, with $1.9 million in damages awarded in 1966. Alioto's successes in these and other antitrust cases during the late 1940s and 1950s brought him financial security, professional respect, and national recognition.

In 1959 Alioto became general manager of the California Rice Grower's Association, moving to the presidency of the organization in 1964. He successfully expanded its sales, particularly across the Pacific, and modernized production methods and transportation techniques.

Alioto also devoted considerable time and energy to public service in municipal government. From 1948 to 1954 he served as a member and as president of the Board of Education in San Francisco, and he chaired the San Francisco Redevelopment Agency from 1955 to 1959. As mayor of San Francisco for two terms, serving from January 1968 through December 1974, Alioto supported downtown redevelopment despite growing opposition to what opponents dubbed "the Manhattanization of San Francisco." He made the Transamerica Pyramid building in the financial district a pet project, and he championed the completion of the Embarcadero Center complex of offices and apartments that replaced the aging wholesale produce market adjacent to the waterfront.

Alioto opposed freeway construction; and in 1970 he convinced the federal government to move a section of Interstate Highway 280 away from a proposed lakefront site along city-owned property in San Mateo County. Always a supporter of labor unions, the mayor both insisted on the legitimacy of strikes by police and fire department employees and aggressively mediated settlements of the conflicts. He reached beyond moderate American Federation of Labor–Congress of Industrial Organizations (AFL-CIO) union leaders when making appointments to city commissions when he included members of the independent, left-wing dock workers and warehouse workers union, several of whom had been members of the Communist Party during the 1934 waterfront strike. He also appointed Black, Hispanic, and Asian officials to his administration and worked with both city agencies and private employers to establish recruitment programs for minority workers. During the student strike at San Francisco State College from 1968 to 1969, Alioto encouraged dissenting students to express their grievances, but he also refused to allow violence on the campus and authorized mass arrests by police tactical squad members as a strategy to maintain order.

Alioto's political career demonstrated his commitment to the moderate, centrist version of Democratic Party liberalism, particularly his belief in strong labor unions and his willingness to use the power of government to direct urban development and to expand economic and social opportunities for ethnic and racial minorities and the poor. The mayor strongly supported "law and order" and worked aggressively to counter the influence of New Left, Black Nationalist, and Asian-American and "Chicano" radicals. In 1968, during a raucous Democratic Party national convention in Chicago split by bitter feuds between right, moderate, and left-wing factions, Alioto spoke for the mainstream and introduced Hubert H. Humphrey (then vice president under Lyndon B. Johnson). Many party leaders and the press considered the San Franciscan a likely future national Democratic leader. However, his national—and state—prospects were shattered by a 23 July 1969 *Look* magazine article that accused Alioto of having connections with Mafia members. By the time the mayor won his suit for libel against the magazine, which included damages of $350,000, he had lost the 1974 primary campaign for the California gubernatorial election.

Alioto's marriage suffered due to his extensive political activities during the late 1960s and 1970s. After a highly publicized divorce, he married Kathleen Sullivan in 1978, and the couple went on to have two children.

Alioto continued to conduct successful, high-profile antitrust cases through the 1980s. In one of his many noteworthy victories, he successfully represented the Oakland Raiders against the National Football League's attempt to prevent the team from moving to Los Angeles. In 1992 the State Bar of California named Alioto "Antitrust Lawyer of the Year." At the same time, he was plagued by feuds with his son Joseph M. Alioto about their law practice and found it necessary to defend himself against numerous charges of unethical conduct. All such charges prior to the late 1990s were dismissed, but in 1997 the California State Bar Court suspended his license for two years, and that case was on appeal at the time of his death.

Diagnosed with prostate cancer in 1991, Alioto maintained an active public life, eventually dying of pneumonia at age eighty-one in his home and surrounded by family members.

★

There is no biography of Alioto, and the Alioto Manuscript Collection at the History Center of the San Francisco Public Library primarily relates to his two terms as the city's mayor from 1968 to 1976. Critical, generally negative, accounts of Alioto's mayoral administration can be found in John H. Mollenkopf, *The Contested City* (1983), Rufus Browning et al., *Protest Is Not Enough: The Struggle of Blacks and Hispanics for Equality in Urban Politics* (1984), and Chester Hartman, *The Transformation of San Francisco* (1984). Frederick M. Wirt provides a more balanced account in *Power in the City: Decision-Making in San Francisco* (1974). Obituaries are in the *New York Times* and *Los Angeles Times* (both 30 Jan. 1998) and *Washington Post* (31 Jan. 1998).

WILLIAM ISSEL

ALLIN, John Maury   (*b.* 22 April 1921 in Helena, Arkansas; *d.* 6 March 1998 in Jackson, Mississippi), twenty-third presiding bishop of the Episcopal Church, U.S.A., who was a pivotal supporter of Mississippi's efforts to rebuild black churches and an ardent opponent of ordaining women.

Allin was one of two sons of Richard Allin, an accountant, and Eudora Harper. He grew up in Helena, Arkansas, and at age eighteen entered the University of the South in Se-

Rt. Rev. John M. Allin, 1979. AP/WIDE WORLD/TRANSCENDENTAL

wanee, Tennessee, where he received both his B.A. degree in 1943 and his B.D. degree in 1945, the latter from Saint Luke's Seminary, a part of the University of the South. He was ordained a deacon in 1943 and a priest following his graduation in 1945. In his first assignment as a priest, he was appointed vicar of Saint Peter's Episcopal Church, a newly established mission in Conway, Arkansas, where he served from 1945 to 1949. It was there on 18 October 1949 that he married Frances Ann Kelly. In 1950 Allin became curate of Saint Andrews Church in New Orleans and also served as the Episcopal chaplain at Tulane University and other colleges in the area.

In 1952 Allin became rector of Grace Episcopal Church in Monroe, Louisiana, where he remained for six years until he moved to Vicksburg, Mississippi, to become president of All Saints Episcopal Junior College in 1958. He was elected bishop coadjutor of the diocese of Mississippi and was consecrated in 1961 at Saint James Church in Jackson, Mississippi. He also found time in 1960 to complete a M.Ed. degree from Mississippi College.

Mississippi in the 1960s was a hotbed of racial tension. It was at this time that Allin gained national attention as he mediated events that threatened to completely polarize the church. His was a voice of calm and reconciliation between the races. He became bishop of Mississippi in 1966 and founded a "Committee of Concern," an interracial group dedicated to the rebuilding of black churches that had been burned or bombed during this period of intense racial conflict. Allin had an uncanny ability to see beyond local tensions and bring a voice of reason to a very troubled time. At the same time, he served on the national level as a member of the Commission on Ecumenical Relations of the Episcopal Church. Thomas Tiler, who worked as a program director in the Mississippi diocese under Allin from 1966 to 1973, observed that Allin knew how to get different factions to come together at the same table, air their differences, and reach a solution or compromise. Overriding any rhetoric from opposing sides was the feeling that Allin had "prayed the situation through" and followed through with what he believed God would have wanted.

When Allin was elected presiding bishop of the Episcopal Church, U.S.A., in 1973, he was regarded as a religious conservative by the church. But in an interview for the *New York Times* after his election, he said that he viewed himself as a liberal, at least by Mississippi's standards. The diplomacy with which he approached racial conflicts in the Deep South worked well for him in his work for the church at the national level. His election to succeed Bishop John Hines was fiercely debated at the general convention of the church in Louisville, Kentucky, in October 1973. The objections centered not on Allin's civil rights activities but on his theological conservatism, which came under fire from liberals. In the end, Allin was elected

the twenty-third presiding bishop of the Episcopal Church, U.S.A., and he would find that his talent for reconciliation would be heavily taxed during his thirteen years as bishop.

Allin assumed leadership when factions within the church wanted to ordain women to the priesthood and to ordain black priests. The ordination of women had been narrowly approved by the Episcopal House of Bishops in New Orleans in 1972 but was rejected twice by the House of Deputies. The bishop of Philadelphia, however, ignored this proscription one month after the election of Allin and "illegally," according to the constitution of the Episcopal Church, ordained eleven women to the priesthood on 29 October 1973. The reaction of Allin was that these ordinations were contrary to the constitution and canons of the Episcopal Church, that the bishops who sanctioned these ordinations exceeded their authority, and that they did not speak for the entire church. However, he persuaded the House of Bishops to take no action against the bishops who had ordained the women. The matter was debated at the church's general convention in 1976, and the delegates voted to permit the ordination of women. In 1975 at a House of Bishops meeting in Port Saint Lucie, Florida, Allin offered his resignation as presiding bishop of the 3-million-member church because he could not accept the ordination of women. He asked the question in an address on 30 September 1977: "Can you accept a bishop who's unable to accept women in the role of priest? To date my conviction has remained unchanged and if it is determined by prayerful authority that this conviction prevents one from serving as bishop I will resign."

The issue of ordaining women continued to be a controversial one, but the church declined to accept his resignation and instead passed a resolution affirming his leadership and respecting his right to hold a personal conviction on the issue of ordaining women. It also adopted "a statement of conscience" under which no bishop, priest, or layperson should be penalized in any manner for opposing the ordination of women. In February 1989 the Episcopal Church consecrated the first female bishop.

In 1979, during Allin's tenure as bishop, there arose another controversy concerning the adoption of a new Book of Common Prayer for general usage. It was a long process and one that required extreme diplomacy. In one meeting about the prayer book reform, Allin told the group gathered that he was weary of the carping, and he insisted the church had more important matters to focus on than squabbling over liturgy.

Allin's effectiveness as presiding bishop might be questionable; however, change did occur during his tenure. When he was elected bishop in 1973, he found himself at the head of a church that was losing members and was torn by conflicting views on liturgical reform. By the time he retired in 1986, he had managed to slow the losses and restore the church's financial health. He had a gift for fund-raising, and one of his most successful efforts was one that began in the 1970s. Known as "Venture in Mission," it was an endeavor aimed at strengthening missionary work in the dioceses across the nation. Again he was criticized, but he pleaded to the bishops to support the program and to respond to the needs of human suffering. The program raised $150 million.

The central office of the Episcopal Church was located in New York City, and Allin and his family made their home in Greenwich, Connecticut. For six years they journeyed to Kennebunkport, Maine, and for three months Allin served as vicar of Saint Ann's Church, where President George Bush and his family were members. He also served as an honorary canon of the Cathedral of Saint John the Divine in New York City and as canon of Saint George's Cathedral in Jerusalem. Although busy, he served as chancellor of his alma mater, the University of the South. He was awarded an honorary doctorate from the University of the South.

Allin retired in 1986 but remained active and was named chaplain of the General Community of Transfiguration, an order of Episcopal nuns in Cincinnati, Ohio. Prior to his death, he and his family had moved back to Jackson. He died at age seventy-six after suffering a stroke and battling lung cancer. Allin was survived by Ann, his wife of forty-nine years, a son, three daughters, one brother, and twelve grandchildren. He is buried in Jackson. Following his death, the Mississippi legislature passed a bill that listed all of the many accomplishments of Allin and expressed deepest sympathy to his family. The bill was signed by the governor on 3 April 1998.

★

Allin's personal correspondence and papers are housed in the archives of the Episcopal Church at the University of Texas at Austin. Obituaries are in the *Washington Post* (8 Mar. 1998) and *New York Times* (9 Mar. 1998).

BETTY B. VINSON

AMORY, Cleveland ("Clip") (*b.* 2 September 1917 in Nahant, Massachusetts; *d.* 14 October 1998 in New York City), writer, social historian, animal rights activist and advocate, critic, and radio and television personality.

Amory was one of three children born to Robert Amory and Leonore Cobb, and was raised in Boston. His father, a successful textile manufacturer, came from a long line of prosperous merchants. As a result, the family was well known in Boston society. Amory attended Milton Academy (1931–1935) and Harvard College (1935–1939). In his senior year at Harvard, he served as editor of the *Harvard Crimson;* he graduated in 1939 with a B.A. degree.

Cleveland Amory. THE FUND FOR ANIMALS

Following his graduation, Amory worked as a reporter for the *Nashua Telegraph* in Nashua, New Hampshire, and the *Arizona Star* in Tucson, Arizona. Subsequently, he became managing editor of the *Prescott Evening Courier* in Prescott, Arizona. After these brief forays into newspaper work, Amory returned east to Philadelphia, Pennsylvania and assumed the associate editorship at the *Saturday Evening Post*. He held the editorship from 1939 to 1941, the youngest person ever to hold the position. Amory left the *Post* in 1941 to serve in World War II in Army Intelligence. In the same year, he married Cora Fields Craddock; they divorced in 1947 and Amory moved permanently to New York City. He married Martha Hodge, an actress and writer, on 31 December 1954; they divorced in 1977.

In 1943 Amory became a freelance writer, an occupation he continued throughout his life. His reputation as a social historian rests on his trilogy: *The Proper Bostonians* (1947), *The Last Resorts* (1952), and *Who Killed Society?* (1960). These books present a general and specific description of the Massachusetts social elite (among whom Amory includes himself as an "upper crustacean"), their recreational locations and habits, and their steady decline as a "society." Almost without exception, reviewers acknowledged Amory's thorough scholarship and astute analysis, and delighted in his wit. In a 1947 review of *The Proper Bostonians* in *Saturday Review of Literature,* Edward Weeks said of Amory that he "writes smooth and witty prose, is nicely judgmatic for a man still in his twenties, and by wide reading and adroit questioning has brought together a compilation of characters as rich as it is diverse."

By the time these books were published, Amory was entrenched in his animal rights endeavors, which consumed much of his time and energy until the day he died. Amory's desire to be an advocate for animals developed early in life with his love of his first pet, a dog, and a gift of the book *Black Beauty.* In addition, as a young journalist, Amory was sickened by the animal cruelty obvious in a bullfight he was covering. By the 1960s his campaign against inhumanity to animals was in full force. He founded the Fund for Animals in New York City in 1967 and served without pay as president until his death. The motto of the fund is "We speak for those who can't," and its commitment is "litigation, legislation, education, and confrontation." Marian Probst, Amory's assistant for thirty-seven years, told *People Weekly* in 1998 that his "angle was to always fight any kind of cruelty. He was the kind of guy who always swam upstream." Amory was a frequent critic of inhumanity to animals through the forums of radio, television, newspaper, magazines, and especially in his book *Man Kind? Our Incredible War on Wildlife* (1974), in which Amory lashed out at senseless killing for sport, profit, agriculture, or revenge. On 2 November 1974 Farley Mowat declared in *Saturday Review of Literature* that the book "is a case history of murderous insanity not only at the individual level, but also at the species level, and the species is Modern Man." *Man Kind?* prompted an editorial in the *New York Times* and also precipitated a television documentary on hunting, *The Guns of Autumn,* which appeared on the CBS network on 5 September 1975.

Amory and the Fund for Animals created a home for needy animals in Murchison, Texas, in 1980. Called the Black Beauty Ranch after the book that profoundly impressed Amory in his youth, the ranch became a haven for animals which, Amory said, needed to be "looked after" rather than "looked at." Many of the animals had been rescued by the fund's campaigns and others individually salvaged from misfortune. Amory's last book, *Ranch of Dreams* (1997), chronicles the founding of the ranch and describes the rescues of thousands of seals, burros, horses, goats, and other animals.

Amory's love for animals provided the subject of his most delightful and most popular books. The first, *The Cat Who Came for Christmas* (1987), chronicled his Christmas Eve 1978 rescue of an emaciated and injured stray cat in New York City, whom he christened Polar Bear. *The Cat Who Came for Christmas* sold 1.5 million copies, and its two sequels, *The Cat and the Curmudgeon* (1990) and *The Best*

Cat Ever (1993), were also best-sellers. The third book, written and published after Polar Bear's death in 1992, is a poignant story that retains Amory's spice and acerbity. Polar Bear's story makes good reading on its own, but all three books also reveal much of the author's life and his self-proclaimed curmudgeonry. For example, *The Cat Who Came for Christmas* describes Amory's agreement to assist the Duchess of Windsor with her autobiography, his weeks with the Duke and Duchess, and his eventual resignation from the commitment.

Throughout his years of writing animal biographies, social history, and an animal-rights activist book, Amory dispensed his satire through other media. He was social commentator on the NBC's *Morning Show* (later called *The Today Show)* with Dave Garroway from 1952 to 1963. He was a columnist for the *Saturday Review of Literature* (1952–1972) and chief critic for *TV Guide* (1963–1976). He was radio essayist on "Curmudgeon at Large" (1963–1973) and senior contributing editor of *Parade Magazine* from 1980 until his death. Selections from his syndicated newspaper column *Animail* were published under the title *Cleveland Amory's Animail* (1976).

Amory died at age eighty-one of an aneurysm after a full day's work at the Fund for Animals office. He was cremated, and his ashes are buried on the Black Beauty Ranch. His headstone stands beside the stone of his beloved Polar Bear.

For more than half a century, Amory served as the conscience of the public on issues of society's foibles and animal welfare. His reputation as author, radio and television personality, and critic of popular culture made him a long-standing celebrity. He informed and chastised with a sardonic yet highly entertaining wit. His careful research and his background and experience gave him stature, and his unfailing curmudgeonry endeared him to his public.

★

The manuscripts and papers of Amory are housed in the Boston Public Library. No full-length biography exists, but the trilogy of Polar Bear books contains much autobiographical information. *Contemporary Authors, New Revision Series,* vol. 29 (1990), provides biographical information, comment on the writings, and a 1988 interview with Amory, which was concerned primarily with the Fund for Animals. An interview with Marian Probst, Amory's assistant for thirty-seven years, appears in *People Weekly* (2 Nov. 1998). The *New York Times* obituary (16 Oct. 1998) provides a detailed short biography. Other obituaries are in the *Chicago Tribune, Los Angeles Times,* and *Washington Post* (all 16 Oct. 1998).

MARY BOYLES

ANDERSON, (Helen) Eugenie Moore (*b.* 26 May 1909 in Adair, Iowa; *d.* 31 March 1997 in Red Wing, Minnesota), first woman U.S. ambassador.

Moore was one of five children of Methodist minister Ezekiel Arrowsmith Moore and Flora Belle McMillen. She studied music at Stephens College in Columbia, Missouri, between 1926 and 1927, and at Simpson College in Indianola, Iowa, between 1927 and 1928. Anderson transferred to Carleton College in Northfield, Minnesota, in 1929 and attended until 1930, but received no degree.

On 9 September 1930, Moore married John Pierce Anderson, a Red Wing, Minnesota, artist and photographer she met at Carleton. (His father, Alexander P. Anderson, was a food technologist who invented the breakfast cereals Puffed Wheat and Puffed Rice.) They later had two children. Between 1930 and 1932, Anderson trained as a concert pianist and organist at the Juilliard Institute of Musical Art in New York City, where she and her husband were living. In 1932 they moved to Tower View, the Anderson family experimental farm in Red Wing.

In 1937 the Andersons toured Europe, where Anderson observed for the first time a "totalitarian state in action" on a visit to Germany. She continued her interest in world affairs at home, lecturing on behalf of the Minnesota League of Women Voters. Anderson entered Democratic politics to oppose what she considered Republican isolationism, the unwillingness to face the danger of war in Europe. She joined the Democratic-Farmer-Labor (DFL)

Eugenie M. Anderson. HARRY S. TRUMAN LIBRARY

Party in 1944, just after it was organized by Hubert H. Humphrey, who was then a professor at Macalester College in St. Paul, Minnesota. Anderson was elected vice-chairperson of the Executive Committee of the DFL Party two years later. As a result of her vigorous campaigning in 1948 on behalf of President Harry S. Truman and Senator Hubert H. Humphrey, she was nominated the U.S. ambassador to Denmark on 12 October 1949.

Although three women had served as U.S. ministers to foreign states prior to Anderson's appointment, the United States did not have embassies in those nations, and Anderson became the first woman to hold the higher rank of ambassador. The world's first woman to head a diplomatic mission was Aleksandra Mikhailovna Kollontai (1872–1952), who began representing the U.S.S.R. in Norway in 1924. Few other Soviet women subsequently attained that station.

In 1951 Anderson was the first woman to sign a treaty on behalf of the United States, when she arranged a trade and navigation agreement in Copenhagen. In the same year, she also negotiated the Greenland Treaty, which provided joint defense of the island. Anderson gave her first major speech as ambassador at Rebild Park in Aalborg, in Danish, on 4 July 1950. She remained as ambassador to Denmark until January 1953, when Republican Dwight D. Eisenhower became president. King Frederick IX awarded her the Grand Cross of the Order of the Danneborg, Denmark's highest honor and the highest award ever given a woman in Danish history. Anderson became so popular that Danes simply assumed that her son Hans's middle name was "Christian" (it was actually "Pierce").

After 1953 Anderson resumed her work in Minnesota politics, serving as the first female chairperson of the Minnesota Commission for Fair Employment Practices between 1955 and 1961. Anderson was also a member of the Democratic National Advisory Committee on Foreign Policy between 1957 and 1961. She belonged to the Minnesota Centennial Commission in 1958. Anderson campaigned for the DFL Senate nomination in 1958, but she lost to Eugene McCarthy. She supported Adlai E. Stevenson for president in 1952 and Hubert Humphrey for president in 1968, then backed Humphrey for senator in 1970.

In 1957 Anderson toured refugee camps in Eastern Europe as a member of the Zellerbach Commission, studying the problems of refugees from Iron Curtain nations. From 1959 to 1961, she served on the board of the American Association for the United Nations and on the United Nations (UN) Committee for Refugees. Between 1961 and 1962 Anderson was a vice-chairwoman of the Citizens' Committee for International Development. She lectured in India, the Far East, and many other nations from 1953 to 1962. She also made repeated visits to Scandinavia and the Middle East.

Senator Humphrey mentioned Anderson as a possible ambassador to President John F. Kennedy's presidential adviser, Ralph Dungan. Although the United States had previously sent only career diplomats to Iron Curtain countries, Anderson immediately impressed Dungan, and Kennedy subsequently appointed Anderson the envoy to Bulgaria, making her the first U.S. woman to serve as chief-of-mission in a Soviet-bloc country. She held the post between May 1962 and December 1964.

Anderson met Bulgarian premier Todor Zhivkov in November 1962, just nine days after he assumed the post. In a diplomatic dispatch to Washington, she judged him a "follower" rather than a "leader," perhaps because Zhivkov was self-deprecating, frequently referring to his inexperience and "poor abilities." His manner and bearing were those of a modest man. However, Zhivkov subsequently organized rock-throwing demonstrations at the U.S. embassy. And during a diplomatic reception in Bulgaria, Anderson found that the olive in her martini was a radio transmitter and the toothpick its antenna.

Anderson, however, was outspoken and not easily intimidated by heads of state. At one annual Plovdiv Fair, when police prevented her aides from passing out literature on life in the United States, Anderson grabbed a pile of pamphlets and handed them out herself. During a diplomatic reception in November 1962, President Dimitri Ganev referred to the "piratical actions" of the United States during the Cuban missile crisis, and Anderson walked out. In 1964 Anderson exited a session of the Bulgarian National Assembly when Zhivkov spoke about "American imperialists" in Southeast Asia.

Anderson learned to speak some Bulgarian, and became the first Westerner to appear on Bulgarian radio or television. She reached an agreement on war claims with Bulgaria in May 1963, after only a few months. Previous negotiators had been unable to settle these claims during two years of talks. Between August 1965 and September 1968 Anderson represented the United States in the United Nations Trusteeship Council, holding the rank of ambassador. Beginning with Eleanor Roosevelt, who served as chairperson of the UN Commission on Human Rights from 1946 to 1951, a woman had always held a top post at the U.S. mission to the United Nations, and Anderson replaced Marietta Tree in the Trusteeship Council. Between 1966 and 1967 Anderson served on the UN Committee for Decolonization, known as the Committee of Twenty-Four. Its members mostly dealt with African affairs. Anderson was also an alternate delegate to the UN General Assembly from 1965 to 1968, and in July 1966 she briefly replaced ambassador Arthur J. Goldberg as the U.S. representative on the UN Security Council, becoming the first woman to sit on the Security Council.

President Lyndon B. Johnson asked Anderson to visit Vietnam in 1967 to study the U.S. Revolutionary Development Program, a program for "rooting out the Viet Cong infrastructure and rooting in the government" in the South Vietnamese countryside. In September 1967 she was named senior adviser to the U.S. delegation at the United Nations, and in 1968 she was appointed a special assistant to Secretary of State Dean Rusk. In 1971 Anderson became the first female board member of the First National Bank of Minneapolis. Afterward, in her sixties, Anderson held various posts in Minnesota government. When she had spare time, she enjoyed music, reading, and art.

Anderson planned to write a thirty-chapter memoir of her experiences in Denmark titled "Mrs. Ambassador," but only three unpublished chapters were ever completed. Anderson died from pneumonia at the age of eighty-seven in Red Wing, where she is buried. She once remarked that diplomacy was "a natural field for women to use their inborn talents. Woman's role is human relations, to compose differences, to find ways to make people get along together." In 2000 just under 25 percent of the U.S. ambassadors to various nations were women.

★

Nineteen boxes of Anderson's papers for 1945 to 1973 are at the Minnesota Historical Society, which also has three files boxes on the Minnesota chapter of the Americans for Democratic Action, which Anderson chaired. See also Peggy Lamson, *Few Are Chosen: American Women in Political Life Today* (1968); and U.S. Department of State, *Foreign Relations of the United States, 1961– 1963: Eastern Europe; Cyprus; Greece; Turkey*, ed. James E. Miller (1994). Obituaries are in the *Minneapolis Star Tribune* (2 Apr. 1997) and *New York Times* (3 Apr. 1997). The Minnesota Historical Society has oral histories recorded by Anderson in 1971, and the JFK Library in Boston has sixty-four pages of interviews.

JOHN L. SCHERER

APPLEWHITE, Marshall Herff, Jr. ("Herff"; "Do") (*b.* 17 May 1931 in Spur, Texas; *d.* between 23 and 25 March 1997 in Rancho Santa Fe, California), leader of cult combining religion and UFOs who ended his life with thirty-eight others.

Applewhite was the son of Marshall Herff Applewhite, Sr., a Presbyterian minister, and Louise Applewhite. He had one sister, Louise, who was four years his senior. Applewhite's father relocated the family frequently in southern Texas, establishing churches and moving on. Applewhite graduated from Corpus Christi High School in Texas in 1948 and then attended Austin College in Sherman, Texas, graduating in 1952 with a philosophy degree. Charismatic, intelligent, and popular, he led the campus a cappella choir, the judiciary council, and an organization for prospective

Marshall Applewhite. Associated Press APTV

ministers. Herff then enrolled in the Union Theological Seminary of Virginia, but after a year he dropped out to pursue musical interests.

In the early 1950s Applewhite married Ann Pearce; they had two children. Their family was as peripatetic as Applewhite's had been in his youth. Applewhite was a Presbyterian church music director in Gastonia, North Carolina; an occupational therapist in a tuberculosis hospital in Colorado; the choir director at a Presbyterian school in Kingsville, Texas; and a singer and conductor in Houston and New York City. He served as a radio operator in the U.S. Army in 1954 and was honorably discharged in 1956. In the 1960s he received a master's degree in music from the University of Colorado.

Applewhite and his wife divorced in the early 1960s after he was forced to resign from the University of Alabama School of Music, in Tuscaloosa, for an affair with a male student. Applewhite lived in Houston from 1966 to 1970, becoming music department head at the University of St. Thomas, a Roman Catholic school, and singing with the Houston Grand Opera. He left St. Thomas on a "terminal leave of absence" due to "health problems of an emotional nature," according to a school spokesperson. Again, the real issue was homosexuality.

In 1971 Applewhite checked himself into a Houston psychiatric hospital. He told his sister he had suffered a heart blockage and a near-death experience; one friend

speculates that Applewhite had overdosed on drugs. Inarguably, he was depressed, upset over his homosexuality, and hearing voices. In the hospital he met his partner for the rest of her life, psychiatric nurse Bonnie Lu Trusdale Nettles, an ex-Baptist astrology enthusiast who told Applewhite that God had reserved him for a higher purpose. Nettles left her husband and four children and entered an asexual partnership with Applewhite.

Applewhite and Nettles renamed themselves "The Two," after the two witnesses promised in Revelations 11:1–14. They developed a complex philosophy that included elements of Christianity, gnostic New Age thought, reincarnation, and belief in visitations and help from UFOs. They also used terminology from the Bible and from the television show *Star Trek*. Other probable influences include Mormonism, Black Islam, Hinduism, Buddhism, theosophy, and Scientology. Applewhite and Nettles saw themselves as aliens sent by the Heavenly Kingdom to inhabit human forms and to warn mankind that Earth was about to be "recycled" and that only their followers would reach the "Level Above Human."

Applewhite and Nettles opened a metaphysical bookstore, the Christian Arts Center, in Houston, but it failed in 1973. They then traveled and gathered followers—a number of different sites, group names, and personal names resulted. One group in Los Angeles was called Guinea Pig: Applewhite was Guinea; Nettles was Pig. Other groups were called HIM (Human Individual Metamorphosis), TOA (Total Overcomers Anonymous), and the UFO Society. "Higher Source" was the group's business name; "Heaven's Gate," the name of their website, gained the most infamy.

Applewhite drew converts throughout the western United States, with stops in Illinois and Alabama. He and Nettles called themselves Him and Her, Bo and Peep (shepherds of their flock), Tweedle and Dee, Tiddly and Wink. They became best known as Do (Applewhite) and Ti (Nettles). The group's fluctuating size ranged from two dozen to hundreds. In 1974 Applewhite and Nettles readied their group for departure via UFO. When the predicted date passed uneventfully, the group dissolved and its leaders withdrew from publicity. Later that year Applewhite and Nettles were arrested for auto and credit card theft; otherwise, Applewhite and his followers were law-abiding, even ascetic and conservative.

All members of Applewhite's group lived by "the Process," which included celibacy; abstinence from alcohol, marijuana, and tobacco; regimented daily schedules; hard work and Bible study; a regulated, spartan diet; and uniform, asexual clothing and haircuts. Applewhite recruited intelligent, if often troubled, men and women; everyone took a new name and was strongly encouraged to terminate contact with family and friends. In 1985 Nettles died of cancer. Previously, the UFO voyages would be taken by the whole person; now the trip, which was imminent, would involve leaving their earthly "vehicles" behind. Applewhite spoke of Nettles's continued leadership, calling her his "older member" and "father."

In October 1996 Applewhite and the group settled in Rancho Santa Fe, a wealthy suburb of San Diego, renting a mansion at 18241 Colina Norte for a rumored $7,000 to $10,000 per month. The group founded its own computer consulting firm and website design company. Group members worked hard and well, often silently, in pairs. Yet the group's pronouncements grew direr. For example, members believed that the comet Hale-Bopp concealed a UFO that would take them from earth to the Heavenly Kingdom. Applewhite stated that he was dying of cancer, though an autopsy later found no fatal disease.

On 26 March 1997 thirty-nine bodies—twenty-one women and eighteen men, including Applewhite—were found in the mansion Applewhite's group had been renting; they had died, in planned groups, on 23, 24, and 25 March. They had eaten phenobarbital in pudding or applesauce, drunk vodka, then tied plastic bags over their heads. The bodies were eerily composed. Each wore uniform black clothing and was draped in purple cloth. A packed suitcase was beside each bed and five dollars and change in each pocket. Unlike at Jonestown, all had died willingly. The dead ranged in age from the twenties to seventy-two. Applewhite and seven followers were found to be surgically castrated, voluntarily.

Applewhite is buried in San Antonio, Texas, next to his father. After his death, his ex-wife and daughter chose anonymity, although his son addressed the press, saying he, his wife, and their two children were Christians "with the real tickets to heaven."

Heaven's Gate left a rich media legacy: public access television shows, videotapes, books, a website. At least one former member committed suicide in imitation of those at Rancho Santa Fe. Other members met in Rolla, Missouri, around that time, to plan life without Applewhite and Nettles. The suicidal group Applewhite led evoked anxiety about both cults and the possibly insidious influence of the burgeoning Internet and World Wide Web. The group was compared to the Peoples Temple, nearly a thousand of whose members died at Jonestown, Guyana, in 1978, and to Charles Manson's group; Applewhite himself compared them to the Branch Davidians at Waco. In the computer venues the group had used for self-promotion, many Christians posted sermons disavowing Applewhite's religion, calling him Jesus's opposite. Writers debate whether his followers chose freely, but all blame Applewhite's charismatic leadership and doomsday philosophy for their deaths.

★

Books on Applewhite, all written after his suicide, include Bill Hoffman and Cathy Burke, *Heaven's Gate: Cult Suicide in San Diego* (1997), and William Henry, *The Keeper of Heaven's Gate: The Religion Behind the Rancho Santa Fe Suicides* (1997). Some pieces appeared before the suicide, including Brad Steiger and Hayden Hewes, *UFO Missionaries Extraordinary* (1976), and Robert W. Balch, "Waiting for the Ships: Disillusionment and the Revitalization of Faith in Bo and Peep's UFO Cult," in *The Gods Have Landed,* ed. James R. Lewis (1995). Key articles written after the suicide are in the *San Francisco Chronicle* (29 Mar. 1997); *Maclean's* (7 Apr. 1997); *Newsweek* (7 Apr. 1997, 14 Apr. 1997); *U.S. News and World Report* (7 Apr. 1997, 30 Mar. 1998); *Washington Post* (28 Apr. 1997); *The Advocate* (29 Apr. 1997); and *Skeptical Enquirer* (July/Aug. 1997).

BERNADETTE LYNN BOSKY

ARCARO, George Edward ("Eddie") (*b.* 19 February 1916 in Cincinnati, Ohio; *d.* 14 November 1997 in Miami, Florida), National Museum of Racing Hall of Fame, "the Master" jockey who was the first to win five Kentucky Derbies, the second to win six Belmont Stakes, and the sole rider to win six Preaknesses and two Triple Crowns.

Arcaro was born to Pasquale Arcaro and Josephine Giancola, both of whom emigrated from Italy. His father was a cab driver. Arcaro weighed three pounds at birth and stopped growing at five feet, two inches. He dropped out of school when he was thirteen to work at a track as an exercise boy. He galloped horses at the old Latonia track, now Turfway Park, in Florence, Kentucky, earning $20 a month. Told he would never become a jockey, Arcaro moved to California and sought work at the Tanforan track near San Francisco. A trainer there, Clarence Davison, gave him some horses to ride. Arcaro rode his first race on 18 May 1931 at Bainbridge Park near Cleveland, Ohio, but lost forty-five races before riding his first winner, a claimer named Eagle Bird at Aqua Caliente in Tijuana, Mexico, on 14 January 1932. The following year, Arcaro moved to Fair Grounds in New Orleans and became the leading apprentice. He later moved to Chicago, where he was signed to his first contract by Warren Wright and began his long and prosperous relationship with Calumet Farm. In 1937 he married Ruth, a former model. They had two children.

Arcaro's first victory in a Triple Crown race came on Lawrin in the Kentucky Derby in 1938, only seven years after he was told he had no future as a jockey. As his career progressed he became known as a rider of uncommon strength and intelligence. He employed a distinctive style, sitting nearly motionless on his mounts, and made famous the practice of switching the whip from side to side in the stretch drive. Arcaro was a cofounder of the Jockeys Guild

Eddie Arcaro, 1945. AP/WIDE WORLD PHOTOS

in the 1940s and served as its president from 1949 until his retirement.

On 30 April 1941 Arcaro rode four winners out of five mounts at the Jamaica racetrack in New York City before leaving for Churchill Downs to ride Whirlaway in the Kentucky Derby. Whirlaway won, clocking a then-record of 2:01 for the 1¼-mile race. Arcaro and Whirlaway went on to win the Triple Crown, the first of two for Arcaro. In 1942 Arcaro had his license suspended after knocking fellow rider Vincent Nodarse off his mount during a race. In his appearance before chief steward Marshall Cassidy, Arcaro answered that "I was trying to kill the S.O.B." Arcaro spent part of his suspension working at Greentree's training base in South Carolina and figuring out how to mend his ways. "My trouble had risen from a desire to win; my honesty had not been impugned," he wrote in his 1951 memoir, *I Ride to Win!* "They [Greentree's owner, Helen Hay Whitney, and the trainer John Gaver] were eager to have me continue my association with them." Arcaro was the highest paid exercise rider in the country until the suspension was lifted at the request of the ailing Mrs. Whitney.

Arcaro may have learned patience, but he retained his greatest asset, his desire to win. The jockey Willie Shoemaker noted, "We were good friends. He was a great rider and he helped me when I first went to New York to ride

in 1951. He introduced me to horse owners and a lot of people. In his day, he was the strongest finisher there on a horse. He was very competitive. In the jockeys' room, he might have been your friend, but once that gate opened, you were on your own."

The horse Citation, with Arcaro aboard, won the Kentucky Derby in 1948. Arcaro recounted in his autobiography that he kept hearing the voice of Ben Jones, the father and training mentor of Jimmy Jones, saying, "The horse that Citation could not run down ha[s] not yet been born." He wondered, "Suppose Citation doesn't pick Coaltown up when I call on him?" But Ben Jones's words were borne out in a memorable Kentucky Derby stretch run. Citation sped past Coaltown to win by three-and-a-half lengths, igniting a sixteen-race winning streak. Citation went on to win the Preakness with ease. Then came the Belmont, where the speed of the track led Arcaro to say, "The only way I can lose this race is if I fall off my horse." That almost happened when Citation stumbled out of the gate, nearly throwing the jockey. But they regrouped, and Citation scored an eight-length win over Better Self in a time of 2:28 ⅕, tying Count Fleet's record for the 1½-mile Belmont.

Citation was one of Arcaro's two favorite horses to ride. Kelso was the other. "I believe Kelso was the best horse I ever rode," Arcaro said. "He was Horse of the Year five straight years [1960 to 1964], and that takes a lot of doing. And he hooked everybody, every place, on every kind of racetrack. He just was the best horse. Sprint, go a distance, run all day. He could do it all."

Inducted into racing's Hall of Fame in 1958, Arcaro rode his last race at the age of forty-five on 18 November 1961. On 4 April 1962, without fanfare, Arcaro formally announced his retirement. In 24,092 races, Arcaro had 4,779 wins, 3,807 seconds, 3,302 thirds, and earnings of $30,039,543. His record of 554 stakes victories stood for eleven years until Willie Shoemaker broke it in 1972. Arcaro led the jockeys' list in earnings in 1940, 1942, 1948, 1950, 1952, and 1955, and he topped the list in stakes earnings in 1940, 1941, 1946, 1948, and 1950 through 1955.

Arcaro was as good a businessman as he was a rider. He invested in oil, a chain of drive-in restaurants on the West Coast, and the wholesale saddlery business. After his retirement he and Ruth settled in South Florida, where Arcaro played golf daily—this was his favorite hobby during his riding years and became his main pastime during retirement. In retirement he also analyzed major races, including the Triple Crown, for network television and was a spokesman for the Golden Nugget Casinos. Ruth, his wife of over fifty years, died in 1988, and in 1997 Arcaro married a longtime family friend, Vera. He died at age eighty-one of liver cancer at his home near Miami.

Arcaro was a master at his craft of riding horses. Upon the jockey's death, Joe Hirsch, executive columnist for the

Daily Racing Form, wrote, "He was the best I ever saw. . . . You would think that I would have seen somebody better come along in all those years, but I haven't."

★

Arcaro's autobiography, *I Ride to Win!* (1951), describes his dedication to and early years in racing. Numerous interviews in newspapers, on television, and especially in *Blood-Horse* magazine give even more insight into Arcaro and his life. The book *Out in Front* (1971) by Vashti Brown, Jack Brown, and Margaret Lalor shows Arcaro and other athletes at their finest to influence the actions of children. The cover article in a 1948 issue of *Time,* and the articles "The Master: Eddie Arcaro 1916–17" and "Remembering Arcaro," *Blood-Horse* (both 22 Nov. 1997), and "The Master of Memory" and "What's Going On," *Blood-Horse* (both 8 Mar. 1986), let the reader understand this man and his love of riding. A documentary about the Triple Crown on Classic ESPN devoted one segment exclusively to Arcaro and his riding career. Obituaries are in the *Miami Herald* and *New York Times* (both 15 Nov. 1997).

JOAN GOODBODY

ARRINGTON, Leonard James (*b.* 2 July 1917 near Twin Falls, Idaho; *d.* 11 February 1999 in Salt Lake City, Utah), economist, historian, and religious leader best known for his scholarly writings on the history of the Church of Jesus Christ of Latter-day Saints (the Mormon Church) and for serving as a mentor to the New Mormon historians, active church members who apply the methodology of academic history to the study of the Mormon past.

Arrington was the third of eleven children (two girls and nine boys) of Noah Wesley Arrington and Edna Grace Corn, who owned and worked a farm near Twin Falls. Arrington worked on the family farm while attending local public schools (1923–1935). He then attended the University of Idaho (1935–1939), where he graduated Phi Beta Kappa with a B.A. degree in economics. In 1939 he enrolled in a Ph.D. program in economics at the University of North Carolina at Chapel Hill, studying there from 1939 to 1941 and 1949 to 1950, and earning his Ph.D. in 1952. At the university, he came under the influence of a group of southern regionalists, among them his adviser Milton S. Heath.

In 1941 Arrington began teaching at North Carolina State University in Raleigh. After trying unsuccessfully to enlist in the Army Air Forces when the United States entered World War II, he left North Carolina State in 1942 to work in the North Carolina Office of Price Administration. Drafted into the U.S. Army in March 1943, he served for three years in North Africa and Italy, collecting and analyzing statistics, administering price controls, and in-

Leonard J. Arrington, 1998. ASSOCIATED PRESS/MORMON CHURCH

terviewing Italian prisoners of war. He married Grace Fort of Raleigh on 24 April 1943; they had three children.

Discharged from the army in late 1945, he joined the economics faculty at Utah State Agricultural College (later Utah State University) in Logan in 1946. He took a leave from 1949 to 1950 to complete his dissertation at the University of North Carolina, where his professors encouraged him to study the Mormon people. A personal religious experience in 1950 led him to further define the scope and method of his dissertation. In his autobiography, *Adventures of a Church Historian* (1998), he described this event as "a peak experience [that] helped me to see that my research efforts were compatible with the divine restoration of the church."

After returning to Logan in September 1950, Arrington began conferring with other scholars, especially the history professor S. George Ellsworth, who helped to train him in historical methodology. Arrington started writing and publishing articles and books about the history of the Latter-day Saints. With the encouragement of William Mulder of the *Western Humanities Review,* he published his first article, "A Story of Mormon Desert Conquest," in a 1951 issue of the review. Harvard University Press published his

Great Basin Kingdom: An Economic History of the Latter-day Saints, 1830–1900 (1958), in which Arrington reshaped his dissertation to emphasize the contrast between the religiously motivated community building of the Mormon people and the self-interested actions of the robber barons during the late nineteenth century.

Although Arrington's early publications focused primarily on the economic life of the Latter-day Saints, as his career advanced, he broadened the scope of his work to write about the economic history of the West. These books and articles covered such topics as mining, railroads, labor, and the New Deal. Later works by Arrington primarily covered aspects of Mormonism, but he also wrote about such subjects as intellectual history, women's history, and the history of childhood. In addition to the acclaimed biography *Brigham Young: American Moses* (1985), Arrington wrote other works on such prominent Mormon and western leaders as General Charles C. Rich, Bishop Edwin D. Woolley, and the industrialist David Eccles.

In December 1965 Arrington and a group of like-minded colleagues, students, and lay people met at the American Historical Association conference in San Francisco to organize the Mormon History Association. He was elected as the association's first president. In recognition both of his work and his extraordinary ability, many professional associations called upon him for service. Arrington served as the president of the Western History Association (1968–1969), Agricultural History Society (1968–1970), Utah Academy of Sciences, Arts, and Letters (1975–1976), and American Historical Association–Pacific Coast Branch (1982–1983), and as the chair of the Utah Humanities Council. He was also elected to the Society of American Historians (1986). He taught on visiting appointments at the University of Genoa in Italy (1958–1959) and at the University of California at Los Angeles (1966–1967). In 1969 the Western History Association selected Arrington and Ellsworth as the founding editors of the *Western Historical Quarterly,* and he served as a coeditor until 1972.

Arrington's work won many prizes and other honors. He held honorary doctorates from the University of Idaho and Utah State University. He was given the governor's award in the humanities by the state of Utah, and his biography on Brigham Young won the prestigious Evans Biography Award.

Arrington's study and promotion of the history of the Latter-day Saints and his reputation as a religious and professional leader gained him recognition not only in historical circles, but in the highest councils of the Church of Jesus Christ of Latter-day Saints (LDS). He served in numerous capacities in the LDS, including as a branch president, Sunday school teacher, stake high councilman, and member of a stake presidency. In 1972 the church's First Presidency recognized Arrington as the church historian. He was the only professional historian and only person who was not a general authority to hold that position. He continued to serve as the church historian until 1980, when he was appointed as the director of the history division, a position he held until 1982. Under Arrington's supervision and with his support, his associates in the historical department, historians from various universities, and other scholars published numerous articles, books, and reports on the Latter-day Saints.

Concurrent with Arrington's call in 1972 to serve as the church historian, Brigham Young University appointed him to the newly endowed Lemuel Hardison Redd, Jr., Chair of Western American History and as the director (1972–1980) of the newly founded Charles Redd Center for Western Studies. He held the Redd chair and taught classes in Mormon and western American history until his retirement in 1987. In 1980 an agreement between the LDS General Authorities and the Brigham Young University administration led to the transfer of the history division to Brigham Young University and its renaming as the Joseph Fielding Smith Institute for Church History. Arrington served as the institute's director until his retirement.

From 1972 until his death Arrington lived in Salt Lake City. His first wife died in 1982. On 19 November 1983 he married Harriet Horne, who brought four stepchildren to the marriage. Arrington died of a heart attack at his home and is buried in Logan.

Arrington influenced research in Mormon history perhaps more than any other person in the twentieth century. In hundreds of articles and books, he demonstrated that a first-rate scholar could present the Mormon past fairly and creatively to Latter-day Saints, lay historians, and the community of scholars. With his collaboration, support, and tutelage, dozens of students and scholars published works on Mormon history, economic history, and western history. He patterned for a generation of scholars the role of a committed scholar and churchman. Arrington marked his professional and personal style by reaching out to historians, community leaders, and others, many of whom were not Latter-day Saints. He had an extraordinary facility for making all people feel comfortable in his presence and for drawing others into his circle.

★

Arrington's papers are housed in the Special Collections and Archives Department at the Milton R. Merrill Library, Utah State University. Arrington's autobiography, *Adventures of a Church Historian* (1998), traces his life with an emphasis on his professional career and includes a comprehensive bibliography. An obituary is in the *Salt Lake Tribune* (12 Feb. 1999).

THOMAS G. ALEXANDER

ASERINSKY, Eugene (*b*. 6 May 1921 in New York City; *d*. 22 July 1998 in Carlsbad, California), pioneer in sleep studies whose discovery of rapid eye movement (REM) sleep opened up new areas of study in the biology of sleep.

Aserinsky grew up in New York City and attended public schools. He then went to Brooklyn College, the University of Maryland, and Baltimore College to complete his undergraduate studies. He married Rita Goldman in 1942. They had three children. Aserinsky entered the U.S. Army in 1943 and served as a high-explosives handler in England with the Office of Strategic Services until 1945. After completing military duty, he was a supervisor for the U.S. Employment Service in Baltimore.

Aserinsky then attended dental school before beginning his doctoral studies at the University of Chicago in 1950. At Chicago, Aserinsky worked with Nathaniel Kleitman, a pioneer of sleep research, in the department of physiology. When a possible topic for Aserinsky's dissertation, blinking and the onset of sleep in children, proved to be unproductive, he began investigating eyelid movement during sleep. Working with the same group of infants he had observed during his investigation of blinking, Aserinsky discovered that there was an interval of complete "ocular quiescence" during each hour of sleep, a period that he labeled "no eye movement" (NEM). He mistakenly attributed the rapid eye movement that he observed when the infants slept to residual waking movement.

Having determined that the infants' sleep patterns included NEM periods, Aserinsky then tested adults to see if the same pattern appeared. He was the first sleep researcher to monitor a person's sleep behavior all night long. He carried out his first all-night observation with his eight-year-old son as the test subject, using an electrooculogram (EOG), a device for recording eye movement. During this observation, he found that a pattern of rapid eye movement recurred over the course of a night. What he had initially regarded as residual waking movement of the eye was actually part of the pattern of sleep. Uncertain of the machine's reliability, he ran the test for another night and found the same patterns of eye movement.

Aserinsky then added another piece of equipment, an electroencephalograph (EEG), and repeated the experiment with twenty adults. The results confirmed his previous observation. He also found that the period of eye movement was a period of brain wave activity. In a further test, Aserinsky noted that 75 percent of the subjects tested reported that they were dreaming when he awakened them during an episode of rapid eye movement. He initially called the period of vigorous ocular activity "jerky eye movement" (JEM) periods but later changed the designation to REM periods, the name by which the phenomenon is known today.

To ensure that Dr. Kleitman would accept his findings, Aserinsky convinced a fellow graduate student, William C. Dement (who went on to work in the field of sleep disorders), to film the phenomenon of REM. After much shooting and editing, Dement produced a three-minute documentary. Aserinsky described this research in his doctoral dissertation, "Ocular Motility During Sleep and Its Application to the Study of Rest-Activity Cycle and Dreaming," in 1953. Aserinsky's discoveries also appeared in a brief article in *Science* (4 September 1953), which he coauthored with Kleitman. In the article, REM sleep is characterized by increased physiological activity, including bodily movement and twitching and eye movement that is "rapid, jerky and binocularly symmetrical." REM sleep tends to lengthen through the night and accounts for 20 percent to 22 percent of a person's sleep time.

Aserinsky's career as a teacher began at the Northern Illinois College of Optometry, where from 1951 to 1952 he taught as a graduate student. After completing his doctorate in 1953, he worked for a year as a research associate physiologist in the School of Fisheries at the University of Washington. For most of his teaching career he was on the faculty of the Jefferson Medical College in Philadelphia. He began as an instructor in the department of physiology in 1954 and moved up through the ranks to full professor. He taught at Jefferson Medical College until 1976, where students voted him best teacher in 1972. He was also an adjunct professor in the department of physiology of West Virginia University from 1977 to 1987. After leaving Jefferson Medical College, he accepted an appointment as chair of the department of physiology in the School of Medicine at Marshall University, where students named him professor of the year in 1984. Aserinsky remained at Marshall until 1987, when he retired and moved to Escondido, California. He died as a result of an automobile accident in Carlsbad, California. He is buried at Eternal Hills Memorial Park in Oceanside, California.

Aserinsky's achievement in showing that REM sleep occurred and was part of the normal sleep cycle opened the door to further research into the biology of sleep, sleep disorders, and how the brain and nervous system function over the course of a sleep cycle. His studies made obsolete the previously accepted notion that the brain was inactive during sleep.

★

Details of Aserinsky's life and work appear in Bill Hayes, *Sleep Demons: An Insomniac's Memoir* (2001). Aserinsky described his major contribution to sleep research in "The Discovery of REM Sleep," in the *Journal of the History of the Neurosciences* 5 (Dec. 1996). See also Mark R. Opp and William C. Dement, "Dr. Aserinsky Remembered," *SRS Bulletin* 4 (spring 1999): 13–14. Information about Aserinsky's career is in *American Men and Women of Science,* 20th ed., vol. 1 (1999). An obituary is in the *Los Angeles Times* (25 July 1998).

ROBERT B. CAREY

ASHBURN, Don Richard ("Richie") (*b.* 19 March 1927 in Tilden, Nebraska; *d.* 9 September 1997 in New York City), a Hall of Fame outfielder with the Philadelphia Phillies for twelve years and a longtime broadcaster for the team after his playing career was over.

Ashburn was the fourth child of Neil Ashburn, a blacksmith and semiprofessional baseball player, and Genevieve Warner, a homemaker. The family lived in a tiny house in Tilden, Nebraska, a town of about 1,000 people. Sports, mostly baseball, were a focal point in the childhood of Ashburn and his three older siblings. Short and slight by sporting standards even as an adult, in childhood Ashburn found the only way he could play baseball growing up was to be the catcher. He ended up playing in that position through Little League and high school. Despite his size, he managed to be a good enough basketball player to receive a college scholarship to Norfolk Junior College in Nebraska. Then scouted heavily as a baseball prospect, the sixteen-year-old Ashburn was offered a contract by the Cleveland

Richie Ashburn, 1957. ASSOCIATED PRESS AP

Indians, but major league commissioner Kenesaw Mountain Landis voided the agreement and fined the team $500 for breaking minimum age rules. After Ashburn finished high school, the Chicago Cubs signed him, but a technicality voided that contract as well. He enrolled at Norfolk Junior College, but in February of 1945, after he had completed only one college semester, Phillies' scout Eddie Krajnik signed him to a contract. Ashburn eventually graduated from the University of Nebraska with a degree in elementary education.

In 1945 the left-swinging Ashburn began his professional baseball career as a catcher with the Eastern League's Utica Blue Sox in New York. Realizing his potential, manager Eddie Sawyer soon moved Ashburn to center field to take advantage of his speed, and he finished with a .312 batting average. Ashburn entered the army on the day Japan surrendered and World War II ended. He served for one year, then returned to Utica, where he batted .362 in the 1947 season. When Ashburn arrived in Philadelphia, Pennsylvania, in 1948, he discovered that the Phillies already had a center fielder in Harry "the Hat" Walker, the reigning National League batting champion. In 1947 Walker had hit .363, but an injury from spring training kept him out of the lineup until late May. Ashburn made the most of the opportunity, hitting close to .350 during the first half of the 1948 season. He compiled a twenty-three-game hitting streak, a rookie record, and played a superb defensive center field. Over a million ballots named Ashburn for the 1948 All-Star game, and he was the only rookie elected to the squad. He justified the fans' selection by collecting two hits and stealing a base. Ashburn was hitting .333 on 28 August 1948 when he fractured a finger sliding into second base and missed the rest of the season. His .333 average, though, was still good enough for second best in the National League and enough to help him win the *Sporting News* Rookie of the Year award.

Between 1948 and 1959 Ashburn excelled as the prototypical leadoff hitter and center fielder with the Phillies. On 6 November 1949 Ashburn married Nebraskan Herberta Cox; they had four daughters and two sons. The couple separated in 1977 but remained close for the remainder of Ashburn's life.

Ashburn was a sparkplug of the 1950 "Whiz Kids," who brought the Phillies their first pennant in thirty-five years, but it almost wasn't to be. After the Phillies had led the league standings for most of the season, the rival Brooklyn Dodgers roared back into the race. Finally, on 29 September, the Phillies traveled to Brooklyn's Ebbets Field needing to win one of the season's two remaining games to clinch the National League pennant. After Brooklyn won the first game, 7–3, it was Ashburn's time to shine. In the next and final game, in the bottom of the ninth with the score tied at 1–1, Brooklyn's Cal Abrams tried to score from second base on a hit to center by Duke Snider. The Dodger third base coach, Milt Stock, furiously waved Abrams in, but Ashburn quickly scooped up the ball and pegged a perfect strike to catcher Stan Lopata. Abrams was out by fifteen feet. The Phillies won the game in the tenth, on Dick Sisler's three-run homer, to take the pennant. The Phillies would later be swept by the powerful New York Yankees in the World Series.

The Phillies never really contended after 1950, but Ashburn put together one fine season after another. From 1948 to 1954 he led the National League in putouts, recording more than 500 per year in 1949 and 1951. He led the league in batting in 1955 with .338, and in 1958 with .350. By the opening of the 1955 season Ashburn had not missed a game for the Phillies since 6 June 1950 and had a consecutive game string of 731. Because of a sore knee suffered in spring training and a muddy field in Philadelphia, manager Mayo Smith decided not to risk further injury to Ashburn's knee. This snapped Ashburn's streak just 91 games short of the then–National League record held by Gus Suhr.

In 1959 Ashburn hit .266, only the second time since 1950 he had been below .300. The Phillies traded him to the Cubs on 11 January 1960 for pitcher John Buzhardt, infielder Alvin Dark, and third baseman Jim Woods. After two sub-.300 seasons, he was sold to the New York Mets for a reported $100,000 for their inaugural 1962 season. Ashburn hit .306 for the Mets, was voted the team's Most Valuable Player, and was their lone All-Star representative while playing for a team that lost a record 120 games. He retired after the 1962 season, becoming one of the few regulars to ever retire following a season in which he had batted over .300.

During his fifteen-year major league career, Ashburn twice won the National League batting title, finished second three times, and batted over .300 nine times. A lifetime .308 hitter, his career 1,198 walks and 2,574 hits helped him finish with a .397 on-base percentage. With an excellent eye at the plate, he led the league in walks on four separate occasions. His 1958 season marked the first time a leadoff hitter had paced the league in both average and bases on balls. Defensively, Ashburn set outfield marks with nine years of 400 or more putouts and four years with 500 or more.

After retiring from the game and first considering a run for U.S. Congress from Nebraska, Ashburn began a second career when he returned to Philadelphia and joined the Phillies' television and radio broadcasting team in 1963. He shared his perceptive commentary and wry sense of humor with Phillies fans for thirty-five years. While his professional life was a success, 1977 proved to be a tough year. His father passed away, and he separated from his wife, though they would remain close for the rest of his life.

Besides his broadcasting career, Ashburn also worked as a newspaper columnist, first for the *Philadelphia Evening Bulletin* and then for the *Philadelphia Daily News* from 1974 to 1991. He wrote the introduction to Allen Lewis's *The Philadelphia Phillies: A Pictorial History* (1981) and compiled a book called *Richie Ashburn's Phillies Trivia* (1983). Ashburn died of a heart attack at age seventy in his room at the Grand Hyatt Hotel in Manhattan, where he was staying during a Philadelphia series with the Mets. He is buried at Gladwyn Methodist Church Cemetery in Gladwyn, Pennsylvania.

A fleet-footed baseball player and a much-loved broadcaster, Ashburn was a fixture in Philadelphia for half a century. Because he played in an era that featured such stalwart center fielders as Willie Mays, Mickey Mantle, and Duke Snider, Ashburn was sometimes overlooked by fans. But after fifteen years of National Baseball Hall of Fame eligibility, Ashburn was finally elected to the Hall of Fame by the Veterans' Committee in 1995.

★

The only biography of Ashburn is Joe Archibald, *The Richie Ashburn Story* (1960), but because it was published after the 1959 season, it leaves almost forty years of his life uncovered. The best source for Ashburn research materials are his clipping files stored at the National Baseball Hall of Fame Library in Cooperstown, New York. These files include numerous newspaper and magazine stories published throughout his long career. A tribute to Ashburn was published in the *Philadelphia Inquirer* (10 Sept. 1997). An obituary is in the *New York Times* (10 Sept. 1997).

BILL FRANCIS

ASHMORE, Harry Scott (*b.* 28 July 1916 in Greenville, South Carolina; *d.* 20 January 1998 in Santa Barbara, California), Southern newsman and civil rights advocate who won a Pulitzer Prize for his editorial opposition to the attempt of Arkansas Governor Orval Faubus to block the racial integration of Little Rock's Central High School in 1957.

Ashmore, the younger of two sons of William Green Ashmore, a merchant, and Elizabeth Scott, grew up in Greenville, South Carolina. He came of age "in the era of political ferment following the election of Franklin D. Roosevelt." His family's comfortable middle-class existence ended abruptly when his father's shoe store went bankrupt in the early 1930s. Ashmore graduated from Greenville High School in 1933, where most of his activities were focused on writing. He was the class prophet for his senior class, served on the *Nautilus* staff (the yearbook), and was a writer for the *High News* (the school newspaper), which featured his column "More Ashes from Harry." He was able to at-

Harry S. Ashmore. PRINTS AND PHOTOGRAPHS DIVISION, LIBRARY OF CONGRESS

tend Clemson College in Clemson, South Carolina, from 1933 to 1937, then a tuition-free state military school, by waiting tables to earn room and board. He recalled that the "unsettling threat of poverty" he and most of his classmates experienced posed no serious challenge to their "Southern Way of Life."

After graduating from Clemson and securing a job as a reporter for the *Greenville Piedmont* in 1937, the young newsman detected signs of black social and political discontent but found they provoked little concern at the civic meetings he covered. Moving from the city to the county beat and later covering the statehouse for the *Greenville News,* Ashmore discovered that nowhere was the race issue part of the political agenda. While in Greenville, Ashmore met Barbara Edith Laier, a Boston native who was teaching at Furman University. The couple married on 2 June 1940. They had one daughter.

In 1941 Ashmore was selected as one of fifteen American newsmen to attend Harvard University as a Nieman Fellow. At this "fountainhead of the abolitionists movement," the southern reporter observed that mythology inspired by century-old sectional differences still influenced perception. Many of Ashmore's colleagues at Harvard assumed that "one could not be pro-Negro without being anti-South," a conviction Ashmore believed was "as firmly held among neoabolitionists as it was among the Daughters of the Confederacy."

Ashmore's sabbatical year was interrupted by Japan's attack on the U.S. naval base in Pearl Harbor. Commissioned an army reserve officer, Ashmore was ordered to Fort Benning, Georgia, in February 1942 for infantry training. When the 95th Division was activated, the twenty-six-year-old second lieutenant joined the unit and remained with it during its campaign through France to the Ruhr. By V-E (Victory in Europe) Day, Lieutenant Colonel Ashmore was an operations officer in the G-3 section of the division's general staff. After the end of the European war, he was reassigned to the Pentagon, where he served until the surrender of Japan.

While in Washington, Ashmore received an offer to join the staff of the *Charlotte News* as associate editor. Discharged shortly after V-J (Victory in Japan) Day, he assumed the position recently vacated by W. J. Cash, author of the influential *Mind of the South* (1941). In North Carolina, Ashmore found himself at odds with community and state leaders who resisted the first stirrings of the civil rights movement, but his editorials urging political justice for blacks aroused little indignation among readers as long as he did not advocate social equality. His stand did attract the attention of *Time* magazine, which characterized him as "one of the South's most realistic and readable editorial writers" and earned him promotion to editor. The new title brought no increase in income, a matter of concern since he had recently become a father.

Reluctant to leave the South on the eve of the region's most unsettled era since Reconstruction, Ashmore accepted an offer in 1947 to move to Little Rock, Arkansas, as editorial page editor of the *Arkansas Gazette.* Promoted to executive editor the next year, he immediately found himself embroiled in strife within the Democratic Party over President Harry Truman's proposal to secure civil liberties for black Americans. Ashmore's position put him near the center of political action in Arkansas, but the commotion subsided after Truman's election and civil rights faded from the headlines. Ashmore continued expressing his views on race relations in his editorials and articles, in public appearances, and on radio and television. In 1953 he was chosen by the Fund for the Advancement of Education to summarize the findings of forty-five scholars on biracial education in the South into language the public could understand. Advance copies of *The Negro and the Schools* (1954), Ashmore's first book, circulated among the justices of the United States Supreme Court before it ruled against segregation in *Brown* v. *Board of Education, Topeka.*

In 1955 Ashmore took a leave of absence to serve as personal assistant to former Illinois governor Adlai Stevenson, who was running for the U.S. presidency. His duties included placating southern congressmen threatening to bolt the party unless concessions were made on the race issue. When President Dwight D. Eisenhower was reelected, Ashmore returned to Little Rock in 1956 to face a new challenge.

In 1957 Arkansas governor Orval Faubus defied a federal court and ordered the National Guard to prevent nine black students from attending Central High School in Little Rock. Suddenly, the *Gazette* editor found himself in the center of a controversy of international significance. Throughout the crisis, the *Gazette* editorially opposed the action of the governor despite death threats and loss of circulation and advertising revenue. The paper's stand and Ashmore's editorials earned Pulitzer Prizes, and he received the Freedom House Award in 1958. Ashmore's second book, *Epitaph for Dixie* (1958), was published that same year. His call for the South to put its past behind it and rejoin the rest of the nation further antagonized southern firebrands. Actually, Ashmore was a gradualist who realized that southerners required time to come to terms with new values that were undermining their traditions.

Ashmore left the *Gazette* in 1959 to become a senior fellow at the Center for the Study of Democratic Institutions, a liberal think tank in Santa Barbara, California, established by his old friend, Robert Maynard Hutchins, former president of the University of Chicago. Hutchins had invited Ashmore to serve on the board of directors of the Fund for the Republic in 1954 and promoted the *Gazette* editor's career until his death in 1977. Ashmore's duties in Santa Barbara allowed him to continue writing. As a special features correspondent for the *New York Herald Tribune,* he undertook a variety of assignments and produced a series on blacks outside the South, which led to another book, *The Other Side of Jordan* (1960).

Ashmore accepted an offer in 1960 from Hutchins, the longtime chairman of the board of editors of *Encyclopedia Britannica,* to serve as editor in chief of the publication. After leaving *Britannica* in 1963, Ashmore devoted his attention to the efforts of the Center for the Study of Democratic Institutions to use Pope John XXIII's 1963 encyclical, *Pacem in Terris,* as a vehicle to ease world tension. He became principal organizer of a meeting to bring influential people from East and West together to discuss issues central to world harmony in a setting free of ideological rancor. Two thousand delegates from twenty nations met in New York City in February 1965. Neither they nor those who attended a second meeting convened two years later had much effect on the cold war or the conflict in Vietnam, but Ashmore's efforts did lead to trips to Hanoi, Vietnam. After a two-hour conversation with Ho Chi Minh in January 1967, Ashmore and Bill Baggs, editor of the *Miami News,* believed the North Vietnamese leader was willing to open negotiations to end the war in his country. When conflicting responses from officials in Washington persuaded Ashmore that the Johnson administration had sabotaged his peace effort, he published an account of the negotiations in an article in *Center Magazine* (1967).

From 1977 to 1978 Ashmore served as acting president of the Center of the Study of Democratic Institutions when Hutchins died. Ashmore remained in touch with former associates, wrote articles, op-ed pieces, and six more books, and contributed to the inaugural address of President William J. Clinton. He was still productive at age eighty-one, and on 9 January 1998 attended a dinner at the home of longtime friend and television correspondent Sander Vanocur. At the dinner, Ashmore suffered a massive stroke from which he never regained consciousness. His body was cremated, and his ashes were scattered in the Pacific Ocean near Santa Barbara.

Unlike his colleagues in broadcast journalism, Ashmore worked for most of his life in relative obscurity. Described as "a Southerner by birth and professional experience," Ashmore and a few other enlightened Southern editors challenged bigotry below the Mason-Dixon line. His editorial stand against Governor Faubus in 1957 focused national attention on a dramatic moment of his career, but Ashmore's legacy was a lifetime of thoughtful defense of civil liberty. For this defense, he received the Robert F. Kennedy Memorial Lifetime Achievement Award in 1996.

★

Correspondence and papers primarily related to the pre-California period of Ashmore's career were donated to the University of South Carolina. The University of Arkansas library in Little Rock also has a collection of Ashmore's papers covering his years with the *Gazette.* Material relating to his association with the Center for the Study of Democratic Institutions is in the Special Collections Department of the library at the University of California, Santa Barbara. Scattered letters and other materials are located in library collections of papers deposited by people with whom Ashmore corresponded. No detailed biography of Ashmore has been published, but two of his books, *Hearts and Minds: The Anatomy of Racism from Roosevelt to Reagan* (1982), and *Civil Rights and Wrongs: A Memoir of Racism and Politics, 1944–1996* (1997), contain autobiographical material. Nathania Sawyer's M.A. thesis, "Harry S. Ashmore: On the Way to Everywhere" (2001), in the library of the University of Arkansas, Little Rock, covers his life and career until his departure from the *Arkansas Gazette* in 1959. Biographical sketches appear in *Contemporary Authors,* vols. 15–16 (1966) and vol. 163 (1998). Obituaries are in the *New York Times* and *Arkansas Times Gazette* (both 22 Jan. 1998). A tribute from Sander Vanocur, "He Saw Folly of Racism Through Prism of Humor," appeared in the *Nieman Reports* (spring 1998).

BRAD AGNEW

AUTRY, (Orvon) Gene (*b.* 29 September 1907 in Tioga, Texas; *d.* 2 October 1998 in Studio City, California), singer, actor, and businessman who as a crooning cowboy wound up as one of the richest men in the United States.

Autry was the eldest of three children of Delbert Autry and Elnora Ozmont. His father went from job to job, frequently dealing in livestock. His paternal grandfather, a Baptist minister, taught him to sing at the age of five to augment his church choir. Autry continued to perform in local venues, purchasing his first guitar by mail order for $8 at age twelve. At age fifteen, Autry traveled for three months as a singer with the Fields Brothers Marvelous Medicine Show. He graduated from high school in Ravia, Oklahoma, in 1924, and despite a leaning toward a career in baseball, he obtained a steadier job with the railroad as a telegraph operator.

Most accounts of Autry's career stress the importance of his "discovery" by humorist Will Rogers. Apparently, Rogers stopped to send a telegram at the Chelsea, Oklahoma, railroad station in the summer of 1927 and found Autry passing the time at his post by strumming his guitar and singing. Impressed, Rogers encouraged the younger man to seek a job in radio. Months later, when the railroad began to cut its work force, Autry took that advice and went to New York City but was told to get more experience under his belt. He returned to Oklahoma, where he was billed on Tulsa's KVOO radio station as "The Oklahoma Yodeling Cowboy." Despite this nickname, Autry's music was in the style later called "country," then known as "hillbilly." His musical hero was the hillbilly great Jimmie Rodgers.

Autry signed a contract with Victor Records in 1929 and cut his first record. In 1931 he signed with the American Record Corporation, which distributed its recordings in large part through the Sears, Roebuck and Company department stores. This led to work on WLS, the Sears radio station in Chicago, where Autry was featured on *National Barn Dance*, the nation's most popular country program. He was also given his own WLS program, *Conqueror Record Time*. Sears began merchandising Gene Autry guitars and music. Autry added to the popularity of his radio work by touring to promote it, a practice he continued throughout his career.

Autry had his first hit song in 1931, "That Silver-Haired Daddy of Mine," which he cowrote with another former railroad employee, Jimmy Long. The record company gave Autry a gold-plated disc to celebrate the song's success, inaugurating a recording-industry tradition. As Autry began to establish a professional pattern, his personal life also became more settled. He married Long's niece Ina Mae Spivey, a teacher, on 1 April 1932; the couple had no children.

Gene Autry.

During the early 1930s, Autry cultivated the cowboy image for which he became known. Historians credit him with legitimating country music, his cowboy image fueling his mainstream appeal. Peter Stanfield noted, "Early publicity photographs of Autry show him not as a cowboy but as a slicked-up guitar picker in a suit, showing all the signs of a man trying to escape the confines of his class. Where the suit failed him the Stetson saved him; as a cowboy Autry transcended any notion of class."

Autry was approached by Mascot Studios (soon to be part of Republic Pictures) in 1934 to appear in a Ken Maynard western, *In Old Santa Fe*. The once-flourishing B-Western movie industry was stagnant and threatened by the newly implemented motion picture production code, which frowned on violence. Studio executives wanted to inject new (and wholesome) life into the genre.

Along with his wife and *National Barn Dance* comedian Smiley Burnette, Autry went to Hollywood and sang and called a square dance in Maynard's film. Mascot Studios then cast Autry and Burnette in small parts in a Maynard serial called *Mystery Mountain* (1935). Later that year they made Autry the star of his own serial, a bizarre blend of the Western and science fiction genres, entitled *The Phantom Empire*.

Autry had his first starring role in a 1935 feature film, *Tumbling Tumbleweeds*, which established the standard

Gene Autry formula. The film included an appearance by Roy Rogers, a box office rival, but lifelong friend of Autry's. Autry later noted, "Trying to single out one of my pictures is like trying to recall a particular noodle you enjoyed during a spaghetti dinner." In *Tumbleweeds*, as in most of the films that followed, the new actor played a character named Gene Autry, who sang and rode the range. Action alternated with humorous scenes featuring *National Barn Dance* alumni, particularly the broadly comedic Burnette and Pat Buttram, and, of course, with musical numbers. Autry's horse Champion almost always received second billing to the cowboy hero and attracted his own fan mail.

Autry appealed to many audiences. The characters who served as the love interests in the films were often working women who never hesitated to express their opinions, even if they did agree with Autry's character by the end of the story. In deference to the distaste of the actor's younger viewers for "mush," however, Autry seldom kissed his heroines. The plots of Autry pictures, which evoked a mythic rural past, frequently pitted small farmers and ranchers against corporate interests; film historian William K. Everson called the onscreen Autry a "spokesman for the rural victim of the depression." In 1940 Autry was voted fourth in box-office appeal by film exhibitors, following Mickey Rooney, Spencer Tracy, and Clark Gable. He cemented his popularity by continuing to record and by touring with stage shows and rodeos between pictures. A savvy marketer, Autry is said to have known many of the theater owners who showed his pictures. He once remarked, "When I started, they said I couldn't act. Other people said I couldn't sing, but I sure as hell could count."

The busy performer returned to radio in January 1940 with a weekly CBS program, *Melody Ranch*. Like his films, the show blended comedy and music and featured a short dramatic scene in which Autry embodied his "cowboy code." His ten commandments for cowboys included fair play; assistance to those in need; respect for "women, parents, and the nation's laws"; and patriotism.

As well as watching him on film, hearing him on records and the radio, and taking in personal appearances, fans could also purchase Autry merchandise (which ranged from musical instruments to games and cowboy gear) and read about their hero's exploits in a newspaper comic strip, *Gene Autry Rides!* In 1941 the small town of Berwyn, Oklahoma, changed its name to "Gene Autry" in homage to its favorite performer. Autry's actual birthplace, Tioga, Texas, refused the opportunity to do the same.

Autry interrupted his career in 1942 to enter the U.S. Army. Originally assigned to entertainment duty, he took flying lessons and served in the Air Transport Command in the China-Burma-India theater. Discharged in September 1945, he went back overseas to entertain troops. Upon his return to Hollywood, Autry resumed his radio program but came into conflict with Republic Pictures. He believed that his contract should have expired during the war, but the studio maintained that Autry's service time was excluded from the period of the contract. Autry launched a lawsuit against the studio, which he ultimately won, but being a savvy businessman, he agreed to make three more pictures for Republic while awaiting the outcome.

Autry founded his own movie-production company in 1947, and cooperated with Columbia Pictures on a deal in which Autry would have creative control over his films and would receive half of the profits. He continued to make films until 1953, when the B-Western had run its course. His ninety-third and final picture was *Last of the Pony Riders* (1953).

By the time *Last of the Pony Riders* was released, Autry had other irons in the fire. Sensing the coming demise of his genre, he entered television in 1950 with *The Gene Autry Show*. In this series, he and Champion (by then the third horse bearing that name) fought bad guys, made music, and inspired children in half-hour dramas that Autry produced himself with an eye to economy. The distributors of his films protested that young people who could see Autry for free on television might be unwilling to spend money at the box office for their hero's pictures. To make sure this did not happen, Autry wisely inserted brief promotional announcements in the programs, urging viewers to attend his latest releases.

The Gene Autry Show remained on CBS until 1956, when the cowboy's *Melody Ranch* radio program also left the airwaves. In the wake of his television success, Autry produced a number of other Western programs, including *The Range Rider* (1921–1952); *Annie Oakley* (1953–1956); and *The Adventures of Champion* (1955–1956), in which his trusty horse finally received top billing.

Autry had recorded songs throughout the 1940s and 1950s, and wrote or cowrote many of his hits, including "Mexicale Rose," "Here Comes Santa Claus," and his theme song, "Back in the Saddle Again." He produced his most successful recording in 1949. Impressed by the underdog theme of a new song, Ina Mae Autry suggested he sing "Rudolph the Red-Nosed Reindeer." The record sold 2.5 million copies the first year and proved a perennial holiday hit. At the time of Autry's death, his version was the second-best-selling recording in American history.

By the mid-1950s, however, Autry was performing less. "Look," he told Republic Pictures executives early in his career, "a cowboy, if he doesn't let his public down, is good until he's fifty years old." As he approached the half-century mark, the actor/singer began to diversify his investments. These grew to encompass radio stations, a movie lot, a Los Angeles television station, and hotels.

Autry, a lifelong baseball fan, decided to make sure that he would always have ball games to broadcast by purchasing the California Angels (later the Anaheim Angels) baseball team in 1961. Popular among players, he hoped that the team would make it to the World Series during his lifetime. It did not, but the sale of one-quarter of the team to the Walt Disney Company in 1995 (along with rights to purchase the remainder at Autry's death) made Autry even wealthier. For several years *Forbes* magazine counted Autry among the 400 richest Americans.

Autry's autobiography *Back in the Saddle Again* (written with Mickey Herskowitz) was published in 1978. In it Autry revealed that he had suffered from alcoholism. Ina Mae Autry, who had helped her husband maintain his cowboy costumes and had toured with him, died in 1980. On 19 July 1981 Autry married Jacqueline Ellam, a bank executive thirty-six years his junior, who had been a friend and business associate for many years. Jackie Autry helped her husband introduce his films to a new public in 1986 on cable television's Nashville Network under the title *Melody Ranch Theater*. She also helped spearhead his dream project, the Gene Autry Museum of Western Heritage, which opened in Los Angeles in 1988. The museum houses Autry's collection of Western memorabilia, as well as many of his personal and business files.

Autry died of lymphoma at age ninety-one in the Studio City section of Los Angeles. He is buried in Forest Lawn Memorial Park, in Hollywood Hills.

Although Autry was the only performer to have five stars on Hollywood's Walk of Fame—for films, recording, radio, television, and personal appearances—he never pretended to be the town's most talented performer. He remarked late in life, "I honestly never considered myself an actor. An actor would be someone like Paul Muni or Spencer Tracy. I was more of a personality." Nevertheless, he prospered by dint of a pleasant manner, a careful cultivation of his audience, and business savvy. His Western musicals combined feminine and masculine genres and were consistently underrated by critics, who—unlike several generations of American youngsters—had no idea what to make of them. Perhaps his most challenging role came off-screen, where he added a touch of shrewd entrepreneurialism to his likable, straightforward persona. His frequent sidekick Pat Buttram eventually joked, "Autry used to ride off into the sunset; now he owns it."

★

Aside from his autobiography *Back in the Saddle Again* (1978), and the materials at the Autry Museum, the best sources for information on Autry's life are the fan-oriented but detail-filled David Rothel, *Gene Autry Book* (1988), the *Current Biography* entry on the performer (1947), and two video profiles: Arts and Entertainment, *Gene Autry: America's Singing Cowboy* (1993), and KTLA, *Gene Autry: An American Hero* (1980). *Dun's Review* produced an outline of the cowboy tycoon's business interests (Aug.

1975). Edward Buscombe and Roberta Pearson, eds., *Back in the Saddle Again: New Essays on the Western* (1998), offers two chapters that touch on Autry: Peter Stanfield, "Dixie Cowboys and Blue Yodels: The Strange History of the Singing Cowboy"; and William Boddy, "Sixty Million Viewers Can't Be Wrong: The Rise and Fall of the Television Western." Obituaries are in the *New York Times* (3 Oct. 1998) and *Washington Post* and *Variety* (both 5 Oct. 1998). A memorial tribute to Autry and his friendly rival Roy Rogers is Peter Hogue, "Roy and Gene: Men from Music Mountain," *Film Comment* (Nov. 1998).

TINKY "DAKOTA" WEISBLAT

AXTON, Hoyt Wayne (*b.* 25 March 1938 in Duncan, Oklahoma; *d.* 26 October 1999 near Victor, Montana), songwriter, singer, and motion picture and television actor whose career spanned the last four decades of the twentieth century.

Axton was the older of two sons of John Thomas Axton, a naval officer, high school teacher, and coach, and Mae Boren, an English teacher turned songwriter. His early years were spent in southeastern Oklahoma before the family moved to Jacksonville, Florida, in 1949. There Axton manifested an interest in music, particularly after his mother cowrote Elvis Presley's hit "Heartbreak Hotel" (1956). When he saw her royalties, Axton thought, "Golly, you mean you can make a living doing this?" Before discovering the answer, he completed high school in 1956, earning All-State honors in football and an athletic schol-

Hoyt Axton. ROGER RESSMEYER/CORBIS

arship to Oklahoma State University. After giving college a brief try, he enlisted in the navy. Assigned to an aircraft carrier in the Pacific, he boxed his way to the heavyweight championship of his thirty-five-ship task force. Ashore, the young sailor married Mary Lou Sanino, a widow ten years his senior. They had no children.

In southern California, where he was stationed, folk music attracted Axton and many other aspiring performers to area coffeehouses. In 1961, after separating from the navy and his wife, he tried his fortune in New York City, but the next year he was back in California performing. Although frequently onstage, some of his contemporaries were more successful than the struggling balladeer. However, the Kingston Trio's recording of his cowritten "Greenback Dollar" reached twenty-one on the singles chart in 1963. He earned only $800 but claimed not to care about money.

While appearing in Chicago in 1962 (a year in which he had a brief affair that produced a son), Axton met Kathryn Hall Roberts, who became his second wife in July 1966. They had a son and a daughter, and Axton adopted Roberts's son from a previous relationship. The couple divorced in 1973. In 1966 Steppenwolf's recording of Axton's song "The Pusher" became a hit and was featured in the 1969 film *Easy Rider.* Axton performed his own and other writers' songs on several labels in the 1960s, but attracted little attention until the mid-1970s. His songs, recorded by others, continued to rise in the charts. "Joy to the World," released by Three Dog Night, remained number one for six weeks in 1971, and the same group's rendition of "Never Been to Spain" rose to number five in 1972. Three years later, Axton wrote "The No No Song," which Ringo Starr made a hit.

Success came at a price. Concerning his drinking and addiction to cocaine, Axton said, "I just got tired of bein' drunk and crazed." By the mid-1970s he appeared to have overcome his dependency on drugs. His daughter never saw him drunk, but in 1991 he sought treatment for addiction to marijuana and speed. Axton maintained that his songs sprang "solely from my own life." He drew on his cocaine addiction when he wrote "Snowblind Friend," recorded by Steppenwolf in 1967. Weight was another problem. He joked that his father had urged him to leave home because "boy, you eat too much."

Substantial debts and a demand for $100,000 in back taxes confronted the singer in the 1970s. Upset by the fees of his attorney, agent, and others, Axton said, "I fired all those people and took over myself." His financial difficulties inspired an album released in 1980, *Where Did the Money Go?* Axton's generosity contributed to his financial problems. He seldom turned down a needy friend. His third wife, Donna Roberts, whom he married in October 1980 and divorced in 1990, and with whom he had one

son, said he would throw $20 bills out the car window because it made people happy. His friends claimed that he embodied the lyrics of "Greenback Dollar," in which Axton wrote, "I don't give a damn about a greenback dollar. I spend it as fast as I can."

Songwriting and performing created other career opportunities. A producer from the television series *Bonanza* saw him at the Troubadour in Los Angeles and developed an episode featuring him. A role in a movie followed, but after seeing himself on the screen, Axton claimed, "I couldn't act my way out of a wet paper sack." Subsequent roles in *The Black Stallion* (1979), *Gremlins* (1984), and other movies earned critical acclaim. He also made frequent guest appearances on television series from the mid-1960s until the mid-1990s, including *Murder, She Wrote, Diff'rent Strokes, Growing Pains,* and *I Dream of Jeannie.* He felt his best performance was in *The Black Stallion,* for which he wrote his own lines. His television commercials for Pizza Hut, McDonald's, and Busch Beer projected a genuine warmth and believability.

Despite his success, Axton admitted, "Acting doesn't make my soul sing the way music does." During the 1970s and 1980s he did as many as 300 shows a year. In 1988 the performer said, "I like the traveling, the cheeseburgers and french fries, the starry nights, and rolling out of town in the dark." While filming *Disorganized Crime* (1989), Axton fell in love with the Bitterroot valley and moved to Montana in 1991, but not to retire. He explained, "I've got just a little longer drive to work now, that's all." He continued writing songs and appeared in or narrated at least eight more movies and television programs before suffering a stroke in July 1995.

Excessive weight and diabetes hampered Axton's recovery. He and Deborah Hawkins, who became his fourth wife in August of 1997, were arrested for possession of marijuana. Although they claimed it was used to ease pain associated with Axton's stroke, the couple received a fine and deferred sentences. The ailing songwriter again found himself heavily burdened with back taxes. Despite his problems, Axton lent his name and talent to raising money for the Missoula Boys and Girls Club. He continued writing songs and even appeared in the movie *King Cobra* in 1999. In October of that year he suffered a heart attack at his home and another while in surgery in Missoula. He died at home a few days later and is buried in Riverview Cemetery in Hamilton, Montana.

Axton seemed to have been unaffected by his celebrity. He described himself as "No big deal. I don't sell gold records and I don't pack concert halls. I'm a guy who can fill clubs, and that's OK." Generous with his time and money, he charmed even those who disapproved of the way he lived his life. The sheriff who arrested him on drug charges expressed distress that Axton died at what he considered "a young age" and called him "a good man. He had a big heart and a ton of talent and he did a lot of good things in his time."

★

No detailed biographies of Axton have been published, but the "Official Hoyt Axton Website" contains a biography and other information about his career. Mae Boren Axton devoted a chapter to her son in *Country Singers as I Know 'Em* (1973). Biographical sketches appear in *The New Country Music Encyclopedia* (1993), *The Guinness Encyclopedia of Popular Music,* 2d ed. (1995), *The Encyclopedia of Country Music* (1998), *The Virgin Encyclopedia of Country Music* (1998), and *Contemporary Musicians,* vol. 28 (2000).

Contemporary Theatre, Film, and Television, vol. 18 (1998), provides personal and professional information and lists Axton's credits in television, onstage, and in films, as well as his writings and recordings. See interviews with Axton by Gene Triplett, "Hoyt Axton Goes His Own Way," *Daily Oklahoman* (2 Apr. 1982), which explores his career in different periods, and Zach Dundas, "Joy to the World," *Missoula Independent* (19 Nov. 1998). Obituaries are in the *Los Angeles Times, New York Times, Missoulian, Tulsa World, Jacksonville Florida Times Union, Daily Oklahoman* (all 27 Oct. 1999), and *People Weekly* (15 Nov. 1999).

BRAD AGNEW

B

BANCROFT, Mary (*b.* 29 October 1903 in Cambridge, Massachusetts; *d.* 10 January 1997 in New York City), writer, translator, and key American spy in Switzerland during World War II.

Bancroft was the only child of Hugh Bancroft, a lawyer and later publisher of the *Wall Street Journal*, and Mary Agnes Cogan. Her mother died hours after her birth, and her paternal grandparents, members of a prominent Congregationalist family, took Mary to their Cambridge, Massachusetts, home to prevent her mother's Irish Catholic relatives from raising her. At age fifteen she went to live with her father, his second wife, and their three children in Boston, and transferred from the Cambridge School for Girls to the Winsor School in Brookline, Massachusetts, where she received her high school diploma in 1921.

As a child, Bancroft was fascinated by the news and in adolescence developed a kinship with her stepmother's stepfather, Clarence W. Barron, publisher of the *Wall Street Journal*. Barron taught her about politics, journalism, and finance, and his advice to "remember that facts are not the truth, but only indicate where the truth may lie" became a lasting influence.

After going to Europe in June 1921 and against her family's wishes, she entered Smith College in Northampton, Massachusetts, in 1922, but she found freshman courses boring and left after three months. With friends marrying, and wanting to maintain a popular social life, in 1923 Bancroft married Sherwin Badger, an old friend and a figure skating champion of the United States. They lived in Cuba for a year, then moved to Brookline. There they had a son, who died in infancy. To cope with their grief and foundering marriage, they moved to New York City, where Badger worked for the *Wall Street Journal* and Bancroft helped him with articles, wrote theater reviews, and later summarized world news for *Barron's*. Another son was born in 1928 and a daughter in 1930.

Bancroft soon fell in love with Leopold Mannes, a painter and composer, and divorced Badger in 1932. Her liaison with Mannes ended disappointingly, and in 1933 she met Jean Rufenacht, a Swiss businessman. Bancroft's father committed suicide, and Rufenacht's father died about the same time, which lent a fated tone to their relationship. The couple moved, with Bancroft's daughter, to Switzerland in 1934 and married in 1935. They eventually settled in Zurich. The couple divorced in 1947.

Rufenacht traveled frequently on business, so Bancroft had time to pursue the busy social life that she enjoyed. An attractive brunette with a frank and generous personality, Bancroft was a people person whom others found fascinating. But her extroversion was partly compensatory, and the sneezing fits and asthma that she suspected were related to her personal losses. The need for love led her to the Swiss psychiatrist Carl Gustav Jung, who eventually analyzed and cured her of her symptoms. Jung remained her confidant for years after her analysis ended, and she was interested in Jungian psychology throughout her life.

As World War II struck Europe, Bancroft stayed in

Switzerland with her family rather than return to the United States. She lectured, wrote about American life for Swiss newspapers, and did humanitarian work. Seeking to do more after the United States entered the war in 1941, she joined the American legation's Office of Coordinator of Information in Bern, where she wrote articles and analyzed German news and Nazi speeches and writings. In December 1942 Bancroft met Allen W. Dulles, chief of the Office of Strategic Services (OSS) bureau in Switzerland. Dulles recruited her to be a special agent, but from the start they were powerfully attracted to each other and quickly became lovers. Dulles's wife, Clover, recognized and approved of her husband's relationship with Bancroft and, after it ended, all three remained close lifelong friends.

Bancroft's job as an American spy involved making contacts with the refugees and agents pouring into neutral Switzerland, seeking those who might be helpful to the Allies. Her intelligence work with Yugoslavians helped steer the Allies from dealing with royalist underground army general Dragoljub Mihailovic toward Josip Broz Tito, whose Partisan movement was more aggressive against the Germans.

Bancroft's most important work began in May 1943, when Dulles asked her to work with Hans Bernd Gisevius, a top German intelligence officer and later key figure in the unsuccessful plot by Germans to assassinate Adolf Hitler on 20 July 1944. Dulles wanted to confirm that Gisevius was not a double agent and had Bancroft translate a book he had written about his Third Reich experiences. Her real job, however, was to build such a good relationship with Gisevius that he talked freely and she could assess his honesty. Bancroft's reports to Dulles were favorable and helped establish the credibility of the German resistance movement with the Allies.

As the war ended in 1945, Bancroft decided not to accept Dulles's offer to set up a German OSS mission with him and instead attended the Nuremberg trials, where Gisevius appeared as a witness for Dr. Hjalmar Schacht, a fellow conspirator. She remained in Zurich for seven years, writing articles for the Swiss weekly, *Die Weltwoche*, contributing to the books *Switzerland* (1949) and *Our Leave in Switzerland* (1950), and writing and translating for films.

In the fall of 1953 Bancroft moved to New York City, where she again built an active life for herself. She spoke on international topics for the Columbia Lecture Bureau; published a second novel, *The Inseparables* (1958); and in the 1960s produced translations for *Atlas: The Magazine of the World Press* and articles and book reviews for *Manhattan East*. She got involved in local New York politics, working for others and making her own unsuccessful runs for a state assembly seat in the 1960 Democratic primary and as a delegate to the 1964 Democratic National Convention. She was a trustee of the C. G. Jung Foundation of New York,

an active member of the related Analytical Psychology Club of New York, and from 1978 to 1986 was a contributing editor and writer for the Jungian journal *Psychological Perspectives*. Among her close friends were the filmmaker Woody Allen and Henry R. Luce, founder of Time, Inc.

Bancroft was a complex woman, born to wealth and convention, who, resisting her expected future and overcoming tragic losses, went on to influence history. Bancroft died of pneumonia at age ninety-three. Her ashes were buried in Groton Cemetery, Groton, Massachusetts. A memorial service was later held in New York City.

★

Bancroft's papers and manuscripts are at the Arthur and Elizabeth Schlesinger Library on the History of Women in America at Radcliffe College. Correspondence between Bancroft and Allen W. Dulles from 1946 to 1969 is also found in Dulles's papers in the Seeley G. Mudd Manuscript Library at Princeton University. Autobiographical works include *Upside Down in the Magnolia Tree* (1952), a fictionalized account of Bancroft's childhood, and her memoir, *Autobiography of a Spy* (1983). Bancroft wrote about her relationship with C. G. Jung, including his advice regarding her wartime activities, in "Jung and His Circle," *Psychological Perspectives* 6, no. 2 (fall 1975): 114–127; and "Zurich Days," in *Memories and Perspectives*, a special issue of the *Bulletin of the Analytical Psychology Club of New York* 37, no. 8 (Dec. 1975): 32–35. She recounted her experience as the sole guest on *The Dick Cavett Show* on 6 and 7 July 1981 in "Authentication," *Psychological Perspectives* 13, no. 1 (spring 1982): 28–30. Bancroft's intelligence work and romance with Dulles are covered in the following biographies: Leonard Mosley, *Dulles: A Biography of Eleanor, Allen, and John Foster Dulles and Their Family Network* (1978); Peter Grose, *Gentleman Spy: The Life of Allen Dulles* (1994); and James Srodes, *Allen Dulles: Master of Spies* (1999). Oral histories are "Mary Bancroft," a one-hour videotaped segment in George Wagner and Suzanne Wagner's series, *Remembering Jung: Conversations About C. G. Jung and His Work* (1980); and Frederick Peterson Jessup's *The Reminiscences of Mary Bancroft* (1980), Oral History Collection of Columbia University. Comprehensive obituaries are in the *New York Times* (19 Jan. 1997) and *Independent* (London) and *Times* (New Zealand) (both 25 Jan. 1997); shorter obituaries are in the *Washington Post* and *Saint Petersburg Times* (both 21 Jan. 1997).

MADELEINE R. NASH

BARNETT, A(rthur) Doak (*b.* 8 October 1921 in Shanghai, China; *d.* 17 March 1999 in Washington, D.C.), scholar of Chinese politics and economics who was a strong advocate for resuming normal relations between the United States and the People's Republic of China.

Barnett was the fourth and youngest child of Eugene Barnett and Bertha Smith. He was born in Shanghai, China,

A. Doak Barnett, 1966. AP/WIDE WORLD PHOTOS

where his father worked for the Young Men' Christian Association (YMCA). Barnett returned to the United States in the late 1930s and, after earning a B.A. degree summa cum laude in 1942 from Yale University, enlisted in the U.S. Marine Corps and served in the Pacific. He returned briefly to China with the American forces in 1945 and attained the rank of captain before his military service ended the next year.

Barnett earned an M.A. degree from Yale in international relations in 1947. From then until 1950, he was in China as a fellow of the Institute of Current World Affairs and occasionally worked as a reporter for the *Chicago Daily News*. Barnett traveled extensively through the shrinking areas of China that were still controlled by the embattled nationalists of Jiang Jieshi (Chiang Kai-shek) and had been in Beijing for most of a year when the city was captured by the Chinese Communists in 1949. Most of his reports to the institute were published together in 1963 as *China on the Eve of Communist Takeover*. Though honest and realistic about the shortcomings of the nationalists, he nevertheless sided with them.

With the expulsion of Americans from the Chinese mainland in the late 1940s and early 1950s, Barnett became a "China watcher," serving as public affairs officer in the American consulate in Hong Kong until 1951. For the next five years, he was an associate with the American Universities Field Staff in the same city and for the latter part of the decade served as director for the Ford Foundation in Hong Kong. He married Jeanne Hathaway Badeau on 22 November 1954; they had two daughters and a son.

Although he never earned a doctorate, Barnett began his academic career at Columbia University as professor of government and a China specialist in 1961. He joined the prestigious Brookings Institute as a senior fellow in 1969. Too young to have been tarred with the brush of having "lost China" (the U.S. "China lobby" blamed communist sympathizers in the State Department for the communist victory in China), and because of his apparent sympathies with the nationalist cause, Barnett was able to escape the hysteria that prematurely ended the careers of so many China specialists during the McCarthy era.

Aware of the international importance of the People's Republic of China, Barnett was an early member of the National Committee on U.S.–China Relations, serving as chair from 1968 to 1969. As chair he quietly lobbied for the resumption of normal relations between the two nations. He advised presidents (beginning with Richard Nixon), the National Security Council, Congress, and the State Department. Barnett was among those most responsible for Nixon's visit to the People's Republic of China in 1972, which resulted in more normal relations between the United States and China.

Following Nixon's visit, Barnett became a member of the newly established Committee on Scholarly Relations with the People's Republic of China, serving as vice chair from 1972 to 1975. He was also a member of the China Council of the Asia Society and was cochair from 1976 to 1979. In 1982 he joined the Johns Hopkins School of Advanced International Studies in Washington, D.C., as a professor. After retiring in 1989, Barnett continued as professor emeritus of China studies at the same institution.

The tragedy of Barnett's professional career was that, for more than two crucial decades beginning with the establishment of the People's Republic in China in 1949 to Nixon's visit (signaling a thaw in U.S.-Chinese relations) in 1972, the hostile political situation prevented his revisiting mainland China. Nevertheless, he was able to produce a number of scholarly works and was the author or editor of more than twenty books as well as numerous articles in professional journals.

Although in his late sixties, Barnett made an extensive trip to China in 1988, during which he strove to repeat the travels he had originally undertaken from 1947 to 1949. He traveled close to 18,000 miles throughout China. The communist government had labeled Barnett an "American imperialist" in 1949 because of his access to top nationalist officials, but on this trip he had access to ranking leaders of the new China.

The aim of Barnett's trip was to produce a volume demonstrating the changes that China had undergone over a period of forty years. After assessing the material collected from his observations and interviews, Barnett modified his goal to create a multivolume magnum opus. Only the first volume, titled *China's Far West: Four Decades of Change* (1993), was completed before his death at age seventy-seven in Washington, D.C., of lung cancer. He is buried at Rock Springs Church in Arlington, Virginia.

During an academic and public career that spanned almost half a century, Barnett garnered a number of prestigious grants, such as the Contemporary China Studies Committee research grant and the Council for Research in the Social Sciences research grant (both in 1964 and 1965). Barnett's lasting legacy, though, is far more vital. Largely through his efforts, a quarter of a century of vocal hostility between the United States and the People's Republic of China ended with President Nixon's visit to China in 1972. His work will continue through the efforts of the many students he inspired.

★

Most of Barnett's personal papers are at Columbia University. There are no full-length biographies of Barnett; however, autobiographical information can be found in several of his writings, including *China on the Eve of Communist Takeover* (1963) and *China's Far West* (1993). Obituaries are in the *New York Times* (19 Mar. 1999) and *Washington Post* (20 Mar. 1999).

ART BARBEAU

BATE, Walter Jackson (*b.* 23 May 1918 in Mankato, Minnesota; *d.* 26 July 1999 in Boston, Massachusetts), professor of English literature at Harvard University who was awarded Pulitzer Prizes for his biographies of John Keats and Samuel Johnson.

Bate was the second of five children born to William G. Bate, a high school principal, and Isabel Melick, a homemaker. When Bate was two years old, his father took a job as superintendent of schools and moved the family to Richmond, Indiana, where Bate learned to love reading and acting in school plays. At fifteen he discovered and became entranced by the work of the romantic poets William Wordsworth and John Keats. Bate's father encouraged him to read biographies and to pursue an Ivy League education. Bate attended Morton Senior High (now Richmond Senior High) and graduated in 1935.

Though the Great Depression was in full swing, Bate worked sixty-five hours a week washing milk bottles in a dairy and had managed to save $100 by the fall of 1935

Walter Jackson Bate, 1978. ASSOCIATED PRESS AP

when he arrived at Harvard University. Bate lived in a rooming house in Boston and frequently walked the six miles to classes in Cambridge to avoid paying five cents for the subway. Even though he worked thirty hours a week as a dishwasher, among other low-paying jobs, Bate graduated summa cum laude in 1939 with an A.B. degree. He received his M.A. degree a year later, and his Ph.D. in 1942. Although he was poor and ill-clothed compared to other students at Harvard, Bate was recognized for his brilliant mind and was encouraged by Harvard greats in English romanticism, Douglas Bush and Robert Hillyer.

The first of Bate's three Bowdoin Prizes was awarded for the best undergraduate thesis of 1939, and was published by Harvard University Press as *Negative Capability: The Intuitive Approach in Keats* that same year. His second Bowdoin Prize, for best master's thesis, was awarded in 1940 for his thesis on Jonathan Swift; and his third was awarded in 1942 for a chapter of his doctoral dissertation on John Keats. Bate's election to the Harvard Society of Fellows, also in 1942, afforded him the luxury of a stipend and five years of postdoctoral research. By 1945 Bate had revised and published his doctoral dissertation as a book, *The Stylistic Development of Keats*, and by 1947 he was appointed assistant professor.

Over the years, a course taught by Bate called "The Age of Johnson" became a popular offering, frequently attracting as many as 800 students per year. Bate was promoted to associate professor in 1949 and to full professor in 1956, having served as chair of the history and literature department during the 1955–1956 academic year; he was a Guggenheim Fellow in 1956. Bate served as chair of the English department from 1956 to 1962, was named Abbott Lawrence Lowell Professor of the Humanities in 1962, and received the Phi Beta Kappa Christian Gauss Prize for literary history and criticism in 1956 and again in 1964. Bate was given Harvard's highest academic honor, the Kingsley Porter University Professor chair in 1977; upon his retirement in 1986, he was named professor emeritus.

Bate's seminal work is *The Achievement of Samuel Johnson* (1955), which "stress[ed] the greatness of Johnson as a moralist, a critic of literature, and a humanist generally of perennial importance." Bate was responding to the New Critics, who believed that a subject must be studied apart from the subject's personal life or place in history. Bate was dedicated to "the ideal of a new kind of psychographic-intellectual biography of the writer's mind and style." After completing work on four volumes of the *The Yale Edition of Samuel Johnson* (1963–1968), Bate decided to write the definitive biography of Keats: "In it I hoped by coalescing biography with different critical approaches especially to concentrate on the most elusive problem to the biographer of genius—what in the character and circumstances of the man permitted him to achieve what he did." The biography, *John Keats,* was published in 1963 to great critical acclaim and was awarded the Pulitzer Prize for biography, the first Pulitzer ever awarded for a book with a non-American subject. *Samuel Johnson* (1977) secured a second Pulitzer Prize for Bate in 1978. Bate observed that Johnson created "literary biography," which Bate saw as "biography united with specific critical analysis of the writer's works and of the tone and character of his mind." The book also won a National Book Award and a National Book Critics Circle Award.

Bate continued to write after retiring from Harvard. In 1995 he recorded a series of seven videos for the Conrad Aiken Video Lecture Series, "A Life of Allegory," which were lectures on Samuel Johnson. Bate never married, as he was devoted to his career and spent the majority of his time teaching, researching, and writing about his beloved eighteenth-century poets. In addition to his residence in Cambridge, Bate owned a farm in Amherst, New Hampshire. A man of delightful, if sometimes self-effacing, humor, Bate once wrote that his "principal hobby has been farming. Unsuccessful farming, I hasten to add. For a few years I actually had a dairy farm of sorts, and then, after continued loss, decided to grow rocks." Following Bate's death at age eighty-one from cardiac arrest, family members scattered his ashes at his farm.

Bate's literary genius brought eighteenth-century English writers to the forefront of literary criticism, and his psychographic biographies are acknowledged as the pinnacle to which all others must aspire.

★

Biographical information about Bate can be found in Gregory S. Jay, ed., *Dictionary of Literary Biography,* vol. 67: *Modern American Critics Since 1955* (1988); and *Dictionary of Literary Biography,* vol. 103: *American Literary Biographers,* First Series (1991). For a collection of essays in honor of Bate, see J. Robert Barth and John L. Mahoney, *Coleridge, Keats and the Imagination: Romanticism and Adam's Dream: Essays in Honor of Walter Jackson Bate* (1993). Obituaries are in the *Boston Globe* (27 July 1999) and *Los Angeles Times* and *New York Times* (both 28 July 1999).

ELAINE MCMAHON GOOD

BATES, Clayton ("Peg Leg") (*b.* 11 October 1907 in Fountain Inn, South Carolina; *d.* 6 December 1998 in Fountain Inn, South Carolina), one-legged tap dancer and owner of one of the first integrated resorts in the Catskill Mountains of New York.

Bates was an only child, raised by his mother, Emma, after his father, a sharecropper, abandoned the family. By the age of five, Bates was already dancing for pennies and nickels. Bates and his mother moved to Greenville, South Carolina, where she worked as a nurse for a white family. In 1919, when Bates was twelve, his left leg and two fingers

Clayton "Peg Leg" Bates. CORBIS CORPORATION (BELLEVUE)

on his right hand were mangled in the auger of a cotton gin at a mill where he was working. Because there were no nearby hospitals for African Americans, the doctor amputated his leg on his mother's kitchen table.

Bates's uncle Whit Stewart whittled him a wooden peg leg, which is how he came upon his nickname, Peg Leg. Tapdancers make use of four "contacts" with the floor (heel and toe on each foot); Bates had to relearn each step and dance using just three contacts. His peg tip was covered with leather on the inside, for sound purposes, and rubber on the outside, for balance.

By age fifteen, with only a sixth-grade education, Bates was dancing regularly in amateur shows, carnivals, and county fairs. He moved on to minstrel shows and to vaudeville, and was soon performing in African-American theaters throughout the United States. Bates eventually danced at the old Lincoln and Lafayette theaters in New York City. At the Lafayette Theater in Harlem, Lew Leslie, the producer of the "Blackbirds" revues, saw Bates. At age twenty-one, Bates was signed to perform on Broadway in "Blackbirds of 1928." He worked with Mantan Moreland, Lloyd Mitchell, and Blue McAlister, and the group was booked as the "Four Bad Men of Harlem." Bates went on to travel to Paris with the revue in 1929.

Another performer with the show was the famous Bill "Bojangles" Robinson. He insisted that Bates, Moreland, Mitchell, and McAlister go on after his act, as the four were such a sensation that he felt they were too tough an act to follow. Bates became close friends with Robinson, who taught him many new routines.

Throughout the 1930s Bates appeared in major New York City theaters such as the Paramount, the Roxy, and the Apollo and played in Harlem clubs, including Connie's Inn, the Cotton Club, and Club Zanzibar. In 1938 and 1939 he gave command performances before King George VI of England. In 1938 he played the Tivoli circuit in Australia, the only African-American performer in the shows.

Bates also performed with many of the big bands of the 1930s, including those of Jimmy Dorsey, Duke Ellington, Cab Calloway, Count Basie, Louis Armstrong, and Erskine Hawkins. Unlike other tap dancers that performed with big bands, Bates did not become associated with any particular band; he had mastered many styles because he felt he had to surpass two-legged dancers.

Bates's signature step was the "Imitation American Jet Plane," in which he would jump five feet in the air and land on his peg leg, with his good leg sticking straight out behind him. A dapper dresser, Bates had peg legs made to match the color of whichever suit he was wearing.

Also during the 1930s Bates met Ed Sullivan, then a newspaper columnist, and danced in the opening act for the touring Ed Sullivan Revue. In the 1950s and early 1960s Bates performed on "The Ed Sullivan Show" over twenty times, more than any other tap dancer.

Early on Bates became determined to be financially independent. In 1951 Bates and his wife Alice, a former dancer whom he had married in 1936, purchased a sixty-acre turkey farm in Kerhonkson, New York, in the Catskill Mountains, and transformed it into the Peg Leg Bates Country Club. Because Bates was often denied a room to stay in at the hotels and resorts where he had performed, he wanted a place where African Americans could stay and enjoy the same comforts as whites, so he created his country club as one of the first integrated private establishments in the nation. Alice was the "brains" of the club, and Bates was the "personality and financier." After Alice died in 1987, Bates retired from running the club. He leased it in 1989 and then later sold it.

Bates performed frequently for the disabled, beginning in the 1940s in U.S. Army and Navy hospitals. Later in life he appeared before youth groups, senior citizens, and handicapped groups and gave inspirational talks about overcoming personal adversities.

Although in poor health, Bates returned to Fountain Inn on 5 December 1998 to perform and receive the Order of the Palmetto, South Carolina's highest honor. The event was part of a celebration of his life given by the Peg Leg Bates Foundation as part of its fund-raising efforts to purchase a life-size sculpture of Bates to be placed at the Fountain Inn city hall. The next day, Bates collapsed on his way to Mount Carmel AME Church. He died of a heart attack that same day and is buried next to his wife in Kerhonkson, New York. On 17 April 2001 the Peg Leg Bates statue was unveiled at Quillen Square in Fountain Inn.

More than a novelty act, Bates overcame racial segregation, poverty, and the loss of his leg to become one of the world's greatest tap dancers. His talent enabled him to travel the world and appear regularly on television. Although without a high school education, Bates successfully operated a resort in the Catskills and helped others to overcome adversity.

★

Valuable information about Bates's life and career is in *Contemporary Black Biography,* vol. 14 (May 1997). Bates's unique contribution to the history of tap dancing is discussed in Rusty E. Frank, *TAP! The Greatest Tap Dance Stars and Their Stories 1900–1955* (1990). For details about the Peg Leg Bates Country Club, see Michael Winerip, "A Legend and His Catskills Resort for Blacks," *New York Times* (15 July 1985). Obituaries are in the *New York Times* (8 Dec. 1998) and *New Bedford (Massachusetts) Standard-Times—South Coast Today* (9 Dec. 1998). A documentary film about Bates, *The Dancing Man: Peg Leg Bates* (1991), was made by Dave Davidson, Hudson West Productions and

South Carolina Educational Television, and distributed by PBS video, Alexandria, Virginia.

MICKEY DUBROW

BATES, Daisy Lee Gatson (*b.* 11 November 1912 [?1914] in Huttig, Arkansas; *d.* 4 November 1999 in Little Rock, Arkansas), civil rights activist and newspaper publisher who in 1957 advised and led the nine African-American students who enrolled at Central High School in Little Rock, Arkansas.

Bates was born in the small sawmill town of Huttig. Little is known of her parents. When Bates was about nine years old, she learned that her mother had been raped and murdered by three white men and that her father left the family after the tragedy. She was taken in and reared by neighbors Orlee and Susan Smith. The truth about her birth parents had a tremendous impact on Bates, who wrote, "so happy once, now I was like a little sapling which, after a violent storm, puts out only gnarled and twisted branches." Growing up in southern Arkansas meant she attended segregated schools that used handed-down textbooks from white schools. When Bates was fifteen, she met Lucious Christopher (L. C.) Bates, a journalist turned insurance agent

Daisy Bates, 1958. AP/WIDE WORLD PHOTOS

who made a sales call to her home. After a long courtship, the two married in 1941 and moved to Little Rock.

In 1942 Bates and her husband started a weekly newspaper called the *Arkansas State Press,* which provided in-depth reporting on racial violence and oppression and soon became a voice for civil rights. In 1952 Bates was elected president of the Arkansas branch of the National Association for the Advancement of Colored People (NAACP). Bates was also a strong advocate of desegregation. After the landmark 1954 *Brown* v. *Board of Education* decision, in which the U.S. Supreme Court ruled that segregation in schools was unconstitutional, she accompanied black students going to register in white schools. When the schools refused to admit them, she reported the event in her paper.

Arkansas Governor Orval Faubus was an adamant opponent of integration, as were 85 percent of the state's white residents, according to polls. Local officials purposely delayed progress. Recognizing the intensity of the opposition, the NAACP filed a suit to facilitate integration. In 1957 seventy-five black students were registered at Central High School in Little Rock, but that number was cut back by school authorities to the nine students who seemed the most emotionally mature and able to handle the potential acrimony. When the nine students attempted to enter the school on 4 September 1957, they were met by the Arkansas National Guard, sent by Governor Faubus to keep them out of the building. An angry crowd spit and taunted the students as they unsuccessfully attempted to enter the school. As Bates wrote, "most of the citizens of Little Rock were stunned as they witnessed a savage rebirth of passion and racial hatred that had lain dormant since Reconstruction days."

When President Dwight D. Eisenhower was forced to send in federal troops to protect the law and the students, it was Bates who received a call from the school superintendent advising her to bring the students to Central High on 25 September 1957. The students met at the Bates home, were picked up by a military convoy, and were successfully escorted to school. The National Guard remained on patrol throughout the school year. Bates stayed in close contact with the nine students, and word got out that anyone who harassed the African-American students would have to contend with her. Bates's activism earned her the animosity and contempt of most of Arkansas's white population.

Bates served as mentor and adviser to the nine students and in addition worked closely with their parents and with school authorities. Bates's role in the controversy did not go unnoticed; a rock was thrown into her window with a note attached, warning "Stone this time. Dynamite next." A cross was burned on her roof. Undaunted by the threats, Bates continued to work on behalf of the students. The group would typically gather at her home each morning to pray for the courage they needed to face the challenges of the day.

In October 1957 Bates was arrested for failing to provide the city clerk's office with specific information about the NAACP's records. She was tried in December 1957, found guilty, and fined $100. The U.S. Supreme Court overturned the conviction. By 1959 Bates and her husband were forced to close the *Arkansas State Press* due to flagging advertisements. She published her memoir, *The Long Shadow of Little Rock,* in 1962 and was the only woman to speak at the March on Washington in 1963. She had moved to Washington, D.C., to work for the Democratic National Committee and, later, for antipoverty programs during President Lyndon B. Johnson's administration.

Bates suffered a stroke in 1965 and returned to Little Rock, but she regained enough strength to work as a community development activist in Mitchellville, Arkansas. In 1968 she served as director of the Mitchellville Office of Economic Opportunity Self-Help Project. In that capacity she oversaw vast improvements, including a new water and sewer system, a new community center and swimming pool, and paved streets. In 1980 her husband died. She revived their newspaper in 1984 but sold it in 1987. Bates received more than 250 citations and awards for her life's work. In 1999 Bates suffered a series of strokes and died. She is buried at the Haven of Rest Cemetery in Little Rock.

Bates's traumatic childhood discovery shaped her response to a world of segregation, discrimination, and humiliation. In the Little Rock crisis, she played a critical role as liaison and protector of nine students who came to be known as "Daisy Bates's children" and established herself as the symbol of black defiance. Despite her sometimes bitter experiences fighting for civil rights, Bates remained optimistic that America would hold true to its promise of equality. In a 1986 interview she declared, "I would like to see before I die that blacks and whites and Christians can all get together."

★

Bates donated her papers to the University of Arkansas Libraries. Her memoir, *The Long Shadow of Little Rock* (1962), was reprinted in 1988 and won the American Book Award. Other sources on the Little Rock crisis include Virgil T. Blossom, *It Has Happened Here* (1959); Wilson and Jane C. Record, eds., *Little Rock, U.S.A.: Material for Analysis* (1960); Elizabeth Huckaby, *Crisis at Central High School: Little Rock, 1957–1958* (1980); and Tony Freyer, *The Little Rock Crisis: A Constitutional Interpretation* (1984). Entries on Bates are printed in *The African-American Almanac* (1989); Darlene Clark Hine, ed., *Black Women in America: An Historical Encyclopedia* (1993); and *Who's Who Among African Americans* (1996). An obituary is in the *New York Times* (5 Nov. 1999).

LIANN E. TSOUKAS

BATTEN, William Milford (*b.* 4 June 1909 in Reedy, West Virginia; *d.* 22 January 1999 in Hilton Head, South Carolina), business executive who transformed the J.C. Penney Company into a diversified mass merchandiser and later modernized the New York Stock Exchange.

Batten was the eldest of three children born to Lewis Allen Batten and Gurry Frances Goff, who ran a general store in Reedy, West Virginia. When Batten was three the family moved to nearby Parkersburg for better educational opportunities, and there Batten's father became a produce wholesaler. Batten's long association with J. C. Penney began in high school, when he took a part-time job as a shoe salesman in the local store. An outstanding student and athlete, Batten attended Ohio State University, where he ran the Beta Gamma Sigma fraternity house, led the student senate, and obtained a B.S. degree in economics in 1932. While there he also met Kathryn Clark, whom he married on 10 August 1935; together they had two children.

Turned down for a position at J. C. Penney during the height of the Great Depression, Batten borrowed against his life insurance to attend the University of Chicago, but family needs soon forced him to leave school. He temporarily accepted a job with the Kellogg Company and man-

William M. Batten, 1976. AP/WIDE WORLD/TRANSCENDENTAL

aged a nine-hole executive golf course. Not until February 1935 did he join J. C. Penney's Lansing, Michigan, store as a $70-a-month salesman, "enough to live on until you prove that you are worth more."

Hard work and managerial skill characterized Batten's career, but these were combined with an analytical ability so acute that he consistently walked a "fine line between getting promoted and getting fired." J. C. Penney's credo in the 1930s was "managementship," and the talented Batten was soon training all Lansing associates and running its daily operations. With the support of his manager, Batten's training program was presented to the company's central office, and in February 1940 he moved to New York City as director of training within the personnel department. He and Kathryn moved to the "Gold Coast" of northern Long Island, where they maintained a home for the next forty years. They were especially active in the Congregational Church of Manhasset. The couple later settled in Mill Neck.

Batten's administrative reforms were soon overshadowed by the onset of World War II, and he was recruited as an organizational planning consultant to the Office of the Quartermaster General. Commissioned as a major, Batten mobilized the 80,000 civilian employees of the Quartermaster Corps to effectively move supplies and equipment around the globe; he rejected the chance to manage Montgomery Ward after its seizure by the government. Leaving the service as a lieutenant colonel, Batten became personnel chief over J. C. Penney's 400 eastern stores from 1945 to 1951. His influence grew when, in 1951, he was appointed special assistant to President Al Hughes; he was appointed corporate vice president in 1953 and a board member in 1955.

In 1957 Batten put his career on the line by presenting a 150-page memo to J. C. Penney's Board of Directors. He argued that the 1,600 company stores, although successfully supplying the needs of small-town America on a cash-and-carry basis, would fail in the coming age of shopping malls. Suburbanization and credit cards were about to change American life, and Batten's fervor convinced the board (which still included James "Cash" Penney) to reinvent the company. The task fell to Batten, who was named president and chief executive officer (CEO) in 1958. Hughes graciously called his successor "the chief architect of the new Penney."

Batten made the company the anchor of hundreds of malls (King of Prussia in Valley Forge, Pennsylvania, was the first to take credit cards, and in 1963 issued the first Penney catalog), introduced credit cards, and overcame store manager resistance to catalog sales. Amazingly, J. C. Penney's internal credit card debate revolved around the ethics of offering them to homemakers who might be tempted to go into debt. Batten also hired the National

Cash Register Company (NCR) to create a point-of-sale computer system, which became standard for all of the company's department stores. By 1974 J. C. Penney's sales had quintupled to $6.9 billion as store locations grew to number more than 2,000, seriously challenging Sears' dominance in the marketplace.

The corporation became a major success story, and Batten, chairman of the board and CEO after 1964, won national acclaim. He served as president of the Economic Club of New York (1968) and The Business Council (1971–1972) headquartered in Washington, D.C.; chaired a record-setting Treasury Department savings bond campaign (1973); and traveled the nation on behalf of the Urban League. Banking leader Walter Wriston called him "wiser than a treeful of owls," and the J. C. Penney board insisted that he remain as CEO for five years beyond mandatory retirement age, until 1 October 1974.

Incapable of just relaxing at his home in John's Island, Florida, or in New York City, Batten in his retirement became "executive in residence" at San Jose State University and continued to hold several corporate directorships (AT&T, Boeing, Citicorp, Texas Instruments). When the bear market of 1974 produced great dislocations on Wall Street, investors blamed the specialist system, which allocated stocks to selected individuals. Batten, a member of the New York Stock Exchange (NYSE) Board of Directors since 1972, was asked to investigate the situation. His report, delivered in January 1976, recommended substantial changes in the securities trading system. When the chaotic investment atmosphere spurred the early resignation of James Needham, Batten became the second paid chairman of the NYSE on 19 May 1976. Some of his achievements there include a renegotiation of commission rates, the development of a futures exchange, the implementation of additional federal securities regulations in 1975, and the creation of a true national marketplace. Moreover, a $70 million renovation of the exchange floor tripled trading capacity. Batten, who described the trading floor as "like a store at Christmas time," earned $2 million for this endeavor, and the board extended his contract until 1984, when he retired for the second time.

A workaholic who considered business to be "fun," Batten became a fellow at the John F. Kennedy School of Government at Harvard University (1984–1986) and immersed himself in directorships. During his career, Batten received at least seven honorary degrees and was honored by such groups as Beta Gamma Sigma and the national Urban League. During his last years, he and his wife Kathryn traveled more, enjoyed their grandchildren, and relocated to Hilton Head, where Batten was an active member of the Hilton Head Country Club and the South Carolina Yacht Club. Succumbing to heart failure on 22 January

1999, he was buried at the First Presbyterian Church of Hilton Head in South Carolina.

★

There is no biography of Batten. Personal papers are in the hands of his family, but both J. C. Penney and the NYSE maintain archives that may be of use to researchers. "W. M. Batten: Architect of the New J. C. Penney" (1 Oct. 1974) and "In Memoriam: Mil Batten, 1909–1999" (1999) were issued by the company's communications department. His career at the NYSE is summarized in the "Report of the Chairman" within each *Annual Report*. An obituary is in the *New York Times* (23 Jan. 1999) and covers the highlights of a career often mentioned in its pages (see, for example, 28 Apr. 1975).

GEORGE J. LANKEVICH

BETTMANN, Otto Ludwig (*b.* 15 October 1903 in Leipzig, Germany; *d.* 1 May 1998 in Boca Raton, Florida), picture archivist, rare book librarian, and historian who founded the Bettmann Archive of print reproductions and photographs.

Bettmann, one of two sons of Dr. Hans Bettmann, an orthopedic surgeon and bibliophile, and Charlotte Frank, began in childhood to develop his interest in books, visual images, and music. At age ten he was using his father's darkroom; at age thirteen he assembled an album of pictures illustrating the history of medicine. Throughout his school years he studied the piano and organ. In 1923 he

Otto L. Bettmann, 1961. © BETTMANN/CORBIS

graduated from gymnasium (high school) and went on to study history at two separate universities, the University of Leipzig and the University of Freiburg in Breisgau. Bettmann received his Ph.D. at Leipzig in 1927. For the next year he worked as an assistant editor in the Leipzig music publishing house C. F. Peters. In the early 1930s, having received a diploma in librarianship from the university, he served as curator of rare books in the Staatliche Kunstbibliothek (state library) in Berlin. It was then that he developed a professional interest in pictures as documents of human history and began to build and organize his own collection of reproductions and photographs, especially in the fields of music, medicine, and art.

With the rise of the Nazis, Bettmann, a Jew, was dismissed from his library post and in 1935 emigrated to the United States. He arrived in New York City virtually penniless but with two trunks crammed with the 25,000 pictures he had managed to carry out of Germany. Bettmann was naturalized as a U.S. citizen in 1939. Intending to find an academic post, he became a businessman instead when, in order to make a living, he began to rent out material from his picture files to publishing firms for use as illustrations. Bettmann's first real break came in 1938. When Columbia Broadcasting System, Inc. (CBS) approached him seeking a picture that might relate to the transmission of sound, to be used for an advertisement, he turned up just the thing: a reproduction of a seventeenth-century drawing showing huge trumpets, shaped like snail shells, being blown in the rooms of a castle. The award-winning advertisement built on this image ran in *Fortune* magazine in January 1938. On 4 March of that same year Bettmann married Anne Clemens Gray (d. 1988), a widow with three children.

The Bettmann Archive was incorporated in 1941, with the founder as president. First housed in New York City in a two-room basement office on East Fifty-seventh Street, the collection was moved in 1961 to more spacious quarters on the same street. By then it had grown to more than a million pictures, filed, with elaborate indexing and cross-indexing, according to the over 2,000 subject categories Bettmann had devised. While Bettmann made frequent trips throughout the United States and abroad searching for items to add to the files, his staff of researchers handled rental requests coming in from commercial artists, art directors of advertising agencies, writers, editors, and publishers, and television studios. In 1966, with the aim of "putting windows on our picture house," he compiled the *Bettmann Portable Archive,* an anthology of small-scale reproductions of the most significant and usable images in each subject category; it was essentially an advertising catalogue of the archive's wares.

With his grave, scholarly mien, signature Vandyke beard and horn-rimmed spectacles, Bettmann resembled the stock image of a European psychoanalyst. A self-confessed workaholic, in addition to administering his growing and profitable company, he wrote and collaborated on many books, among them *A Pictorial History of Medicine* (1956). *In the Good Old Days—They Were Terrible* (1974) proved to be a best-seller. Its selection of drawings, cartoons, and prints recorded the historical reality of American life between the Civil War and World War I. Three years before his death, Bettmann returned to his favorite avocation, music, and completed *Johann Sebastian Bach as His World Knew Him* (1995), a loving tribute to his great Leipzig compatriot.

In 1981 the archivist sold his business to the Kraus-Thomson Organization in New York City, publishers and distributors of scholarly material. By then the Bettmann Archive, now housed at 902 Broadway, contained some 5 million works on paper, mostly of historical significance: reproductions of drawings, woodcuts, engravings, lithographs, posters, and cartoons, in addition to modern photographs. The holdings were more than tripled in 1990 by the acquisition of over 11 million news photos from the libraries of United Press International (UPI) and Reuters; work was then started to digitize the collection. In 1995 the combined holdings were purchased by Corbis, a private company owned by Bill Gates, founder and chairman of Microsoft Corporation.

After the sale of his business, Bettmann moved from his Sutton Place apartment in New York City to Boca Raton, Florida. There he continued to write and served as curator of rare books at Florida Atlantic University where, as an adjunct professor, he also taught classes in history and the graphic arts. He was a member of both the Special Libraries Association and the American Institute of Graphic Arts. Bettmann died of kidney failure and advanced age at the Boca Raton Community Hospital, survived by his three stepchildren as well as several grandchildren and great-grandchildren.

Many of the picture agencies established in the twentieth century were larger than Bettmann Archive, but Bettmann's company was an indispensable archival source in which researchers could find rare, offbeat images to illustrate almost any subject or idea. It was the personal creation of an acute businessman and impassioned bookman who, acknowledging the power of the visual media to make one "an immediate participant in [an] event," lamented the eclipse of the written word in which "the meaning of the event lies."

★

An account of Corbis's acquisition of the Kraus-Thomson Organization's combined holding of the Bettmann Archive and the UPI and Reuters libraries, as well as the controversial plans for storage and preservation of the archive, is given in the *New York*

Times (15 Apr. 2001). In addition to the books mentioned above, Bettmann wrote, with Bellamy Partridge, *As We Were: Family Life in America, 1850–1900* (1946); with John Durant, *A Pictorial History of American Sport* (1952); and with Paul Lang, *A Pictorial History of Music* (1960). Royalties from *The Delights of Reading: Quotes, Notes and Anecdotes* (1987), were donated to the Library of Congress. Bettmann's autobiography, *Bettmann, the Picture Man* (1992), is amply illustrated with family photographs and Bettmann Archive pictures, including several shots of the archive itself. An article in *Current Biography* (1961) gives an account of his earlier career. An obituary is in the *New York Times* (4 May 1998).

ELEANOR F. WEDGE

BIGGIE SMALLS. *See* Notorious B.I.G.

BING, Franz Josef Rudolf (*b.* 9 January 1902 in Vienna, Austria; *d.* 2 September 1997 in Yonkers, New York), opera manager and impresario who was general manager of the Metropolitan Opera House from 1950 to 1972.

Bing was the youngest of four children born in an upper-class family in what was then the Austro-Hungarian Em-

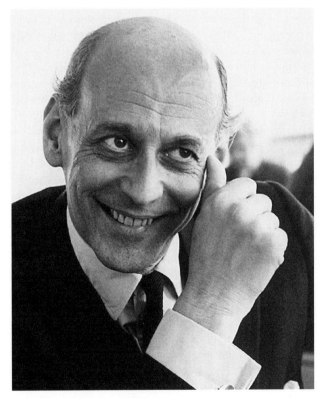

Rudolf Bing. © BETTMANN/CORBIS

pire; his parents were Ernst Bing, head of the Austro-Hungarian Steel and Iron Trust, and Stefanie Hoenigsvald. As a youth Bing enjoyed chamber music recitals at home and performances at the opera. His education came from English-speaking governesses and Viennese schools, but he never graduated and never completed the *Gymnasium* program of study. Bing studied literature and art history for one year with Frau Dr. Schwarzwald, a Polish educator, who also instructed such prominent family friends as Richard Strauss and Hugo von Hofmannsthal. In 1918 Bing began studying voice with Franz Steiner, described as Vienna's leading *Lieder* singer, and with Helge Lindberg, a prominent Finnish bass-baritone.

The postwar collapse of the Empire and of his father's business compelled Bing to find employment as a salesman, first with the bookstore Gilhofer and Ranschburg (1919) and, then after one year, with the Hugo Heller Bookstore. The latter housed one of Vienna's leading concert agencies. As Bing gradually began working with the agency, he perceived his career goal to be a music manager instead of a *Lieder* performer; an assignment in London further impressed him with the potential elegance of the managerial profession. In Vienna, Bing met Nina Schelemskaya-Schelesnaya, a Russian émigré, who danced with the Ellen Tels Ballet. They married on 7 December 1929. They had no children.

Bing left for Berlin in January 1927 to work with an artist booking agency, *Paritätischer Stellennachweis,* which was part of the *Deutsche Bühnenverein,* the umbrella organization of German theater managers. As head of the opera division, Bing visited more than eighty theaters throughout Germany. Hired the following spring (1928) by one of Berlin's leading stage actors, Carl Ebert, now *Generalintendant* (music director) of the *Hessisches Staatstheater* in Darmstadt, to assist as artistic and casting secretary (a position known as *Leiter des Betriebsbureaus*), Bing moved to Darmstadt in July. He returned to Berlin in 1930 to work on a motion picture with the American film producer Curtis Melnitz and German film director Max Reinhardt. Bing worked for six months on the film *L'homme qui assassine* (starring Conrad Veidt) but disliked the filmmaking business, and the film group fired him upon his acceptance of a position offered by Dr. Singer, the *Intendant* of the *Städtische Oper,* or suburban Berlin's Charlottenburg Opera. Again working under Carl Ebert (who soon replaced Dr. Singer), Bing learned how to plan an efficient "cover system," whereby an emergency roster (sometimes even two or more) of singers for leading parts in particularly challenging operas was established far in advance, with attention to rehearsal and potential performance scheduling.

After Hitler became German chancellor in January 1933, Ebert and Bing were fired because both were Social Democrats. Bing returned to Vienna and was offered a position under the auspices of the German Propaganda Min-

istry to start work in September 1933 in Teplitz-Schönau in the Sudetenland. Near the end of the year, he was once again forced to leave because of his political ideas. In 1934 Fritz Busch, now music director of the first summer Mozart festival proposed by John Christie (of Christie Unit Organ fame) and his wife, Canadian singer Audrey Mildmay, on the Christie estate in Glyndebourne, England, suggested Bing as personal assistant to the Christies. Bing earned promotion to stage manager and assistant producer for the second Glyndebourne Festival in early 1935. He became general manager of the annual festival, with year-round duties and an office in London. World War II temporarily halted the festival in 1940.

Tyrone Guthrie hired Bing to manage the southwestern English tour of the Sadler's Wells Ballet while based in Devon, and Guthrie wanted him to revive Sadler's Wells Opera, but the Old Vic board of trustees quashed the ongoing tour as well as the opera idea. Family members of the John Lewis Partnership, major contributors to Glyndebourne, offered Bing employment in one of their department stores, Peter Jones in London's Sloane Square. In one year he advanced from assistant to the director of selling for all John Lewis stores to the position of one of three divisional managers. In the fall of 1944 Bing reopened a London office in preparation for the first postwar Glyndebourne Festival to be held in 1946. From spring 1945, he worked as director of organization for the first Edinburgh International Festival of Music and Drama (1947); he was appointed the festival's artistic director in July 1947.

When Bing went to the Metropolitan Opera in New York City in March 1949 for discussions on behalf of the Glyndebourne Festival, he found himself in a whirlwind of meetings that ultimately, after a call-back a month later to the United States, resulted in a unanimous vote by the board on 25 May to appoint Bing as the Metropolitan Opera Association's general manager.

With his wife, Bing arrived in New York City on 3 November to observe Edward Johnson's final season (1949 to 1950) as general manager, and to learn first-hand about the operations of the Metropolitan. He began formulating the 1950–1951 season by scheduling operas and offering contracts. Bing remained in this illustrious and demanding position until the completion of the 1971–1972 season, running one of the most prestigious opera houses in the world. President Harry S. Truman signed a bill on 3 April 1952 granting him permanent residence status. Despite strikes that delayed the 1961–1962 and 1969–1970 seasons, Bing remained a man dedicated to the routine of preparing the "clock" for perfect functioning each performance. He was the elegant impresario in white tie who accompanied his wife to Box Thirteen, where they hosted heads of states or potential major donors. Bing received scores of awards and honors. He was named a Commander of the Order of the British Empire in January 1956, and on 9 November 1971 at Buckingham Palace, Queen Elizabeth II dubbed Bing a knight.

Upon the recommendation of Mayor John V. Lindsay, the New York Board of Higher Education approved Bing's appointment in February 1972 as Distinguished Visiting Professor of Music at the City University of New York's Brooklyn College. He was appointed director of college-community cultural affairs in December 1973. Bing resigned from Brooklyn College in May 1975, following his 1974 election to the board of Columbia Artists Management, Inc. (CAMI). He eventually worked on a Carnegie Hall concert series and the Community Concerts division. Bing assisted in CAMI's fiftieth anniversary gala at New York City's Plaza Hotel on 13 October 1980.

A sudden stroke on 28 January 1978 left his wife Nina an invalid, half-paralyzed and incapable of speech. The couple continued to live at the Essex House in Manhattan, their permanent address since 1949. About a year or two after Nina's death on 21 December 1983, Bing's health and immediate memory seemed to be declining.

Bing met Carroll Lee Douglass in the lobby of the Essex House in May 1986; their eventual courtship resulted in Bing's marriage on 9 January 1987 to the forty-seven-year-old, twice-divorced Douglass in a courthouse in Arlington, Virginia. Prior to the marriage, Paul C. Guth, an attorney in charge of Bing's legal matters for more than thirty years, initiated proceedings in New York courts to regulate his finances because Guth believed that Bing was stricken with Alzheimer's disease and was being financially manipulated by Douglass.

On 12 January 1987 Justice Arthur Blyn of the New York State Supreme Court froze Bing's assets and appointed Guth as conservator of his estate. Despite court orders to remain in the country and appear before the court on 27 January, Bing and Douglass traveled to Palm Beach and Fort Lauderdale, Florida, and then to Anguilla, British West Indies, where they arrived on 27 January. From spring through fall of that year, the press reported the couple's comings and goings in England and Scotland. Justice Blyn found Bing and Douglass in contempt of court on 13 May and upgraded Guth's status to "committee of the person and property" for Bing, who was now designated as "incompetent" instead of "impaired." The judge also allowed the start of annulment proceedings and ordered Douglass to convey Bing to court on 3 June.

Douglass returned with Bing to the Essex House in November. During 1988 the press reported on Douglass's unruly behavior, as well as her travel to Europe. Bing was removed from the Essex House on 12 May 1989 and taken to the Hebrew Home for the Aged in the Riverdale section of the Bronx. The New York State Supreme Court annulled the Bing-Douglass marriage on 6 September, based on their view that Bing was "incapable of understanding the nature and consequences" of the marriage.

Bing made a rare formal public appearance at the Metropolitan Opera Guild luncheon at the Waldorf-Astoria hotel on 2 April 1993 to celebrate the twenty-fifth anniversary of Lincoln Center. His health continued to decline, and during the last week of August 1997, respiratory distress prompted his removal to St. Joseph's Hospital in Yonkers, where he later died. A Sunday matinee gala to benefit the Metropolitan Opera Company's Pension Fund was held in Bing's honor on 25 January 1998.

Bing restored the vitality and worldwide reputation of the Metropolitan Opera, which had been dimmed somewhat by the Great Depression and World War II. He rearranged the subscription series format and increased subscription numbers, and he presented opening nights as glamorous nonsubscription fund-raising events. He also expanded the working season, reduced the number of operas performed, and increased rehearsal time. Bing included lighter fare such as *Die Fliedermaus* in the opera's repertoire; strengthened the presentation of grand operas (especially those of Guiseppe Verdi); hired the best directors and set designers from Broadway and the British and continental theatrical traditions; integrated the company when he hired ballerina Janet Collins during the 1952 season and singer Marian Anderson during the 1954–1955 season; and presented a roster that included most of the greatest conductors and opera stars on the world scene—regardless of race. He successfully operated the "cover system," utilized cable and broadcast television, and maintained the radio broadcasts of the Saturday matinees. Bing also supervised the move of the Metropolitan to Lincoln Center during the 1966–1967 season. Although not everyone agreed with Bing's "one-man democracy," he tried to keep everyone well balanced with his wit. As overseer of a massive artistic and financial entity that involved thousands of different categories of skilled individuals and groups, including more than a dozen unions, Bing had to engage in frequent power plays. Yet he assumed total responsibility for the maintenance of the highest professional standards by exercising fairness and consistency among all parties concerned.

★

The Sir Rudolf Bing collection in the special collections at the University of Boston includes some manuscripts, correspondence (1951–1974), photographs, and newspaper clippings. Bing wrote two professional reminiscences: *5000 Nights at the Opera* (1972), with the assistance of Martin Mayer, and *A Knight at the Opera* (1981). Some of Bing's writings in the *New York Times* include "American Export: Opera Stars" (26 Dec. 1954), "Rudolf Bing Interviews Rudolf Bing" (14 May 1967), and "Nobody Knows the Traubels I've Seen" (16 Apr. 1972). Bing wrote a tribute to Roberto Bauerin, *Opera News* (7 Feb. 1970). Major articles and interviews include Howard Taubman, "British Impresario to Head the Met," *New York Times* (2 June 1949); Harold C. Schonberg,

"Mr. Bing's Dream (Opera) House," *New York Times* (27 Oct. 1957); Howard Taubman, "The Bing Decade as Manager of the 'Met,'" *New York Times* (17 Apr. 1960); Martin Mayer, "Mr. Bing Makes the Met Go," *New York Times* (11 Oct. 1964); Robert Sabin, "Guest Editorial: 15 Years with Mr. Bing," *Musical America* (Nov. 1964); Frank Merkling, "The Importance of Bing: An Appraisal of the General Manager's First Fifteen Years," *Opera News* (17 Apr. 1965); much of the 22 April 1972 issue of *Opera News* serves as a salute to the retiring Bing, including cover, tributes, articles, and summaries of each season; Joan Higgins, "Sir Rudolf Bing: A Lion in Winter," *High Fidelity* (Nov. 1982); and Martin Mayer, "Sir Rudolf Bing, 1902–97," *Opera* (London) (Nov. 1997). Obituaries are in the *New York Times* and *Washington Post* (both 3 Sept. 1997), and the *Times* (London) (4 Sept. 1997).

MADELINE SAPIENZA

BIRD, Rose Elizabeth (*b.* 2 November 1936 in Tucson, Arizona; *d.* 4 December 1999 in Palo Alto, California), first woman to hold a cabinet post in California state government and the first woman to serve on the California Supreme Court.

Bird's father was a hat salesman who went bankrupt during the depression. In order to make ends meet, the family operated a chicken farm. In 1941 her parents separated, and

Rose Bird. AP/WIDE WORLD PHOTOS

her father died shortly afterward. In 1950 Anne Bird, her mother, moved Bird and her two older brothers to her home state of New York, where she worked in a plastics factory to support her children.

Bird excelled in school and earned a scholarship to Long Island University. She endured a two-hour commute, part of which she did on a bicycle, to the Brooklyn campus of the university, where she earned a B.A. degree magna cum laude in English and was named most outstanding senior in 1958. Upon graduation Bird worked briefly as a secretary and then decided to attend graduate school and study political science at the University of California, Berkeley, thinking it would help her in a career as a journalist. However, an internship in the California state legislature convinced her to enter law school. Bird believed that lawyers and not social scientists nor journalists could most influence public policy.

Bird graduated with honors from the University of California Berkeley's Boalt Hall School of Law in 1965. Her first job after graduation was as a clerk for the Nevada Supreme Court, although she wanted to become a litigator. At the time, almost no opportunities existed for women in the civil field. The few opportunities for women to become litigators existed in the criminal field, and Bird became the first woman to serve as deputy public defender in Santa Clara County, after she was turned down for the same job in Sacramento because the man who interviewed her believed women make poor trial attorneys. While a public defender, Bird also taught a course in criminal defense at Stanford Law School.

In 1974 Bird worked as a volunteer in Jerry Brown's gubernatorial campaign. After his election, Brown asked Bird to become an adviser on his transition team. Once in office, in 1975, Brown broke the tradition that a grower should head the state's department of agriculture, the largest state department at the time, and appointed Bird as its secretary. Bird underscored consumer protection and supported worker safety, health, and unionization. She was instrumental in banning a short-handled hoe that made farm workers spend their working days bowed in the fields. She also helped draft a labor bill that guaranteed secret-ballot union elections for agricultural workers and convinced the state legislature to pass it.

In 1977 Brown nominated Bird to the post of the chief justice of the California Supreme Court in an effort to make the state's judiciary more sensitive to ordinary people. Police groups, conservative politicians, and her foes in California's agribusiness immediately started to campaign against Bird by arguing that she would favor defendants. This campaign became permanent because California Supreme Court justices appointed by the governor had to be approved by the electorate in the immediate gubernatorial election and periodically thereafter. In 1978, the first time she stood for retention, Bird won 51.7 percent of the voters' approval.

The Bird Supreme Court of California strengthened clean water and air initiatives and advanced the rights of the poor, minorities, women, children, consumers, tenants, and criminal defendants. Bird sold the supreme court's limousine, considering it a luxury item, and she stayed at inexpensive hotels whenever she traveled on court business. She put an end to the annual meeting of supreme court justices in fancy resorts. Her cost-cutting and reform efforts incensed many in the state's judicial system who felt she was cheapening the profession.

Conservative groups continued their attacks against Bird by accusing her of being soft on crime and pointing to her votes to vacate the death sentence all sixty-one times that such a case arrived in her court. They launched nine unsuccessful recall attempts against her. In 1985, a year before Bird had to be reconfirmed by the electorate, efforts against her intensified. San Diego sheriff John Duffy used his deputies while on duty to distribute thousands of postcards that called for her resignation. Bird received thousands of postcards with abhorrent remarks and numerous death threats that continued for the rest of her life. During the same year, Republican governor George Deukmejian argued that the Bird court had hurt the state's economy because its rulings made the operation of corporations in California burdensome. After continuous high-profile attacks, California voters rejected Bird in 1986 by a margin of two to one.

After her defeat, Bird retreated from public life, taking care of her elderly mother in her home in Palo Alto. Soon after, her mother had to be placed in convalescent care. Bird visited her every day until 1991, when her mother died at age eighty-six. Bird never married nor did she have any children.

Bird was not offered a teaching job in a law school after her career in public office, as was customary. She instead volunteered for various charities. In 1993, while volunteering for a community law center in East Palo Alto, its staff asked her to make photocopies and file papers because they did not recognize her. Once they learned of her identity, the lawyers of the center wanted her to help them with the law, but Bird was no longer licensed because she could not afford the bar dues. With the exception of a lecture tour with conservative jurist Robert Bork and a one-semester teaching assignment at the University of Sidney in Australia, Bird stayed away from professional activities. In 1997 she was the recipient of the American Civil Liberties Union of Southern California's Conscience Award.

Bird had numerous health problems throughout her life. In 1976 she was diagnosed with breast cancer. Between 1976 and 1980 Bird underwent four operations on her left breast. In 1996 she had a mastectomy of her right breast. During her struggle with cancer, she refused chemotherapy and radiation and instead treated herself with large doses of vitamin C and an exclusive diet of uncooked fruit and vegetables. Bird succumbed to cancer in 1999 at age sixty-three.

Throughout her career, Bird blazed trails by attaining professional and political positions traditionally closed to women. She was a champion of the rights of ordinary people and tried to strengthen them whenever given a chance. In 1987, when asked how she wanted to be remembered, she replied: "That she cared and that she tried to be a good person."

★

Information about Bird can be found in Betty Medsger, *Framed: The New Right Attack on Chief Justice Rose Bird and the Courts* (1983), and Preble Stolz, *Judging Judges: The Investigation of Rose Bird and the California Supreme Court* (1981). Obituaries are in the *Los Angeles Times* (5 Dec. 1999) and *New York Times* and *Washington Post* (both 6 Dec. 1999).

THEMIS CHRONOPOULOS

BISHOP, Hazel Gladys (*b.* 17 August 1906 in Hoboken, New Jersey; *d.* 5 December 1998 in Rye, New York), cosmetics executive, stockbroker, and educator.

Bishop was one of two children born to Henry Bishop, a successful entrepreneur who simultaneously ran multiple businesses, manufacturing everything from awnings to sleds, and Mabel Billington. Whether it was exhibiting early motion pictures or popularizing his candy business, Henry was an expert publicist. To increase candy sales during the holiday season, he put Santa Claus atop an elephant that he paraded around town. Bishop and her brother were exposed from a young age to nearly incessant discussion of business in the family home. In time Bishop herself established several successful businesses.

In her youth, however, an entrepreneurial career was not her goal. After graduating from the Bergen School for Girls in Jersey City, New Jersey, she enrolled in the premedical program at Barnard College in New York City, receiving a B.A. degree in 1929, just months before the stock market crash. With the onset of the depression, Bishop was forced to abandon any thoughts of medical school. Although she enrolled in evening graduate courses at Columbia University, in 1930 she began working as a biochemical technician at the New York State Psychiatric Hospital and Institute. She remained there until 1935 when she obtained a position as research assistant in the laboratory of Dr. A. Benson Cannon, a celebrated dermatologist.

With the advent of World War II, Bishop put her chemistry background to work for companies supplying products to the military. In 1942 she joined the Standard Oil De-

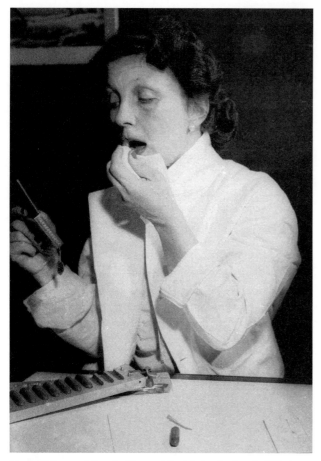

Hazel Bishop applying the kissproof lipstick she developed, 1951. Associated Press AP

paign which at the time, was said to be the largest of its
kind for a single beauty product. "Never again need you
be embarrassed by smearing friends, children, relatives,
husband, sweetheart," proclaimed an advertisement for the
lipstick. *Business Week* magazine put Bishop on its cover,
the first time a woman was so honored, but in a feature
story questioned whether the lipstick was "really kissproof,"
adding "If you ask Hazel Bishop that question, she will
giggle coyly and say: 'How kissproof it is, depends on the
degree of friction.'"

By imitating her father's example of publicizing a business and its product, Bishop was able to jump start sales.
By 1954 when Hazel Bishop, Inc. sold an impressive
$10,000,000 worth of long-lasting lipstick, the company's
founder was no longer involved in the business. Her departure was the result of a dispute with advertising executive Raymond Spector, who owned 92 percent of the
company's stock. Alleging that the company was being
mismanaged, Bishop sued and a 1954 settlement resulted
in a buyout of her share of the company, for a little under
$300,000. The agreement required Bishop to disassociate
herself completely from Hazel Bishop, Inc. by henceforth
disclosing that none of her other businesses were affiliated
with Hazel Bishop, Inc. One of those firms, H. B. Laboratories, Inc., manufactured chemicals for cleaning leather
while H. G. B. Products Corporation made an aerosol foot
product. Hazel Bishop's Perfemme, Inc. produced solid
perfume in lipstick style cases. Once again, imitating her
father's example, she publicized her line of four solid per-
fumes by giving each fragrance a distinctive case color and
such names as "Young Love," "Rejoyce," "Willing," and
"Young and Gay."

In 1954 Bishop was inducted as a Fellow of the American Institute of Chemists, an organization which she
served as national secretary from 1950 to 1960, and in 1981
she became a fellow of the New York Academy of Sciences.
In 1976 she was honored as Cosmetics Executive Woman
of the Year.

Beginning in 1962, Bishop, who once again found herself in a legal dispute, this time with her partner in H. B.
Laboratories, who ended up owning the Hazel Bishop
name, put her thorough knowledge of both chemistry and
cosmetics to use in a new career as a stockbroker with Bache
and Co. in New York City. Praised for having "a real flair
for analyzing portfolios," the five foot, three-and-one-half
inch Bishop was described as "a trim woman of fifty-six
with wide hazel eyes and the peach complexion of a teenager." To stay in shape she exercised regularly at the West
Side Tennis Club and at Top of One Swimming. Somewhat of an anomaly in the securities industry, she was one
of only 120 female registered representatives out of a total
of 1,800 people employed in that capacity at Bache and Co.
Among her clients were executives of chemical, cosmetic,

velopment Company as a senior organic chemist. Before
leaving this position to work for the Socony Vacuum Oil
Company in 1945, she played a role in creating specially
formulated aviation fuel for bombers. At Socony, petroleum
research remained her area of specialization. While studying and experimenting with petroleum by day, Bishop devoted her evenings to developing products for the cosmetics
industry. A remedy for pimples was one product which
came out of the closet-sized laboratory she created in the
kitchen of her Manhattan apartment, but it took second
place to a new formula for long-lasting lipstick. The result
of more than 300 experiments, the lipstick, containing a
sizable percentage of bromo acids known for their staining
ability, made its public debut in 1949 at a Barnard College
Fashion Show. In 1950 she abandoned her career at Socony
to devote her attention to her new cosmetics company,
Hazel Bishop, Inc.

From the moment it was introduced at New York City's
fashionable Lord and Taylor department store, the lipstick,
selling for $1 a tube, became an instant success, in part
because of an unprecedented $1.4 million advertising cam-

and drug companies, some of whom she met while touring their facilities in conjunction with a series of lectures she did for the American Chemical Society.

So enamored was she of her position as a stockbroker, as she neared her seventieth birthday, Bishop told a *New York Times* reporter in 1975 that she was not contemplating retiring. Having gone from Bache and Co. to Evans and Co. as a financial analyst, she had accumulated more than a dozen years experience in the brokerage business and was regarded as an investment and economics expert. During the *Times* interview she expressed concern about inflation but dismissed the possibility of a severe economic downturn. "I lived through the depression where pessimism was extreme," she told the *Times,* adding: "I don't think this present economic setback is of the same caliber. Besides, the national economy is structured in such a way—with unemployment benefits, welfare, and pensions—that I don't think it can happen." Commenting on the more widespread and equitable distribution of wealth in the United States, Bishop pointed out that "such lifestyle changing developments as home ownership and the enjoyment of leisure-creating appliances . . . have transformed our society."

Bishop continued to formulate her own foundation and lipstick. Her signature lip color was mostly red but "with a blue cast"; her advice to other women was to "use makeup to accentuate their most attractive feature. After the age of twenty-five or thereabouts, personality becomes an increasingly more attractive feature." In 1978 Bishop embarked upon yet another career as an adjunct faculty member at the Fashion Institute of Technology in New York City. Two years later, in 1980, she was appointed to the Revlon Chair in Cosmetics Marketing. At the time, Revlon chairman Michel Bergerac said of this multi-faceted woman, "It is really quite an achievement to carve one outstanding career in a lifetime. To succeed in business, in finance, and in academics in only part of a life is truly an amazing thing."

Bishop, who never married, ostensibly because she had devoted herself to her widowed mother during the years when she was likely to have wed, died at the age of ninety-two at the Osborn Retirement Community in Rye, New York. She is buried in Flower Hill Cemetery, in North Bergen, New Jersey. She was survived by a niece and two nephews.

In the course of her long life, Bishop, who was born at a time when few American women were college educated and an even smaller number chose to study science, excelled as a chemist before embarking upon other careers. By making maximum use of her intelligence, education, and promotional ability, Bishop charted new territory, both as an entrepreneur and as a stockbroker and financial analyst. Her last career as an educator was more traditional

but it represented an opportunity to impart what she had learned. The enthusiasm with which she embraced the chance to give back by teaching was entirely consistent with her decades of service to institutions such as the Women's Medical College of Pennsylvania, on whose board she served, and the Society of Women Engineers, which benefited from her active participation in various aspects of its work.

★

Bishop's papers are in the Arthur and Elizabeth Schlesinger Collection on the History of Women in America at Harvard University. A substantial article on Bishop's early career appears in *Current Biography* (1957). Additional information about her careers as an entrepreneur and stockbroker can be found in *Webster's Dictionary of American Women* (1996); *Liberty's Women* (1980); "Woman Chemist Hits Lipstick Jackpot," *Business Week* (17 Mar. 1951); *New York Times* (12 May 1963, 2 Jan. 1975, 12 Jan. 1975); *Business Week* (17 Mar. 1951); and "Hazel Bishop," *People Weekly* (11 Jan. 1999). Obituaries are in the *New York Times* (10 Dec. 1998) and the *Boston Globe* and *Newsday* (both 11 Dec. 1998).

MARILYN E. WEIGOLD

BLACKMUN, Harry Andrew (*b.* 12 November 1908 in Nashville, Illinois; *d.* 4 March 1999 in Arlington, Virginia), U.S. Supreme Court Justice who wrote the controversial *Roe v. Wade* (1973) abortion decision and supported other decisions that expanded freedom of speech, the right to privacy, and consumer protection.

Blackmun was the son of Corwin Manning Blackmun and Theo Huegal Ruetner, whose family owned a local flour-mill. He grew up in St. Paul, Minnesota, where his father, who had wanted to be a lawyer, worked in a bank before owning a grocery store and then a hardware store. Blackmun was a quiet, bookish child, something of a perfectionist in a home of devout Methodists. Classical music on the Victrola often enlivened an otherwise somber and serious mood. He also had a wry sense of humor. "Nothing pleased him more than to make me laugh at church while he sat there looking saintly," his sister recalled.

The Harvard Club of Minnesota awarded Blackmun a tuition scholarship to Harvard University. He majored in mathematics, graduating Phi Beta Kappa and summa cum laude in 1929 while working odd jobs to cover expenses, but he never quite felt he belonged there. Blackmun almost decided to go to medical school but opted for law school instead. After graduating from Harvard Law School in 1932, he served as law clerk to federal appellate Judge John B. Sanborn in St. Paul in 1932 and 1933 before entering law practice with the Minneapolis firm of Dorsey, Cole-

Harry A. Blackmun. ARCHIVE PHOTOS, INC.

man, Barker, Scott and Barber, where he specialized in tax and estate law. "He was thorough, meticulous and sometimes a little slow," recalled an associate. "But when he was finished, anything he wrote could be a treatise for law students." In 1950 Blackmun became the first general counsel to the Mayo Clinic in Rochester, Minnesota. He was active in community affairs and his years there, he frequently said, were his happiest: "I was able to have a foot in both camps—law and medicine."

Blackmun was appointed by President Dwight D. Eisenhower to the U.S. Court of Appeals for the Eighth Circuit in 1959 at the recommendation of Judge Sanborn. He developed a reputation as a diligent, methodical, and moderate judge, somewhat progressive on civil rights matters, less so on criminal issues. His favorite case, *Jackson* v. *Bishop* (1968), marked the first application of the Eighth Amendment to prison conditions and banned the use of whips for punishing prisoners in Arkansas.

In 1970 Blackmun was appointed to the U.S. Supreme Court. After Justice Abe Fortas resigned for ethical transgressions in 1969, the Democratic-controlled Senate refused to confirm federal judges Clement F. Haynesworth,

Jr., of South Carolina, and G. Harrold Carswell of Florida, mainly on grounds that they were too conservative on civil rights. Warren E. Burger, who had become Chief Justice in 1969, urged Blackmun's appointment, and on 14 April 1970 President Richard M. Nixon, with more relief than enthusiasm, nominated him. The Senate confirmed him 94–0 on 12 May 1970; Blackmun took to calling himself "old No. 3." He was expected to become a clone of the moderately conservative Burger, whom he had known since childhood, and he was initially paired as "Hip Pocket Harry." When an article called him a "white Anglo-Saxon Protestant Republican Rotarian Harvard Man from the suburbs," Blackmun observed, "It was the Rotarian part that really bugs me." He later noted that it took him "five years to become comfortable" at the Court. At first the enormity of the job and the Court's finality overwhelmed Blackmun, but he decided he had no choice but to do his best and hope it would all work out. Gradually, his true inner self emerged along with the belief that emotions play a proper part of judging. In 1973 Blackmun upheld the constitutionality of imposing a $50 fee on individuals filing for bankruptcy (*U.S.* v. *Kras*), by 1977 he talked of "the cancer of poverty" (*Beal* v. *Doe*), and in 1980 he spoke of the "atrocities and inhuman conditions of prison life in America [that] are almost unbelievable" (*U.S.* v. *Bailey*).

Roe v. *Wade* and its reception were central in his evolution. Writing for a 7–2 Court in 1973, Blackmun overturned a Texas statute that prohibited women from having, and their doctors from performing, most abortions. The state could not interfere with a woman's choice during the first trimester, and its "interest" became "compelling" enough to regulate abortion only when a fetus is capable of surviving outside the womb. After spending several weeks during the summer at the Mayo Clinic researching the medical aspects of abortion, Blackmun placed this time at roughly the start of the third trimester. The constitutional right of privacy, he concluded, was "broad enough to encompass a woman's decision whether or not to terminate her pregnancy."

The decision radically transformed American politics and more than any other single action, legal or otherwise, ignited the culture wars that came to dominate American politics. Critics had an endless field day with the opinion, vituperatively denouncing its reasoning and result. Many supporters had continuing problems locating its constitutional source. Blackmun gave no quarter. When the Court held in 1977 that poor women could not have an abortion funded with public money, he bristled in dissent: "There is another world 'out there,' the existence of which the Court, I suspect, either chooses to ignore or fears to recognize" (*Beal*). Even if it "goes down the drain," Blackmun said in 1986, "I'd still like to regard *Roe* v. *Wade* as a landmark in the progress of women." And in 1994 "It was a step that had to be taken as we go down the road toward the full emancipation of women." By then, he had hired more female law clerks than the rest of the justices combined.

"Think of any name," Blackmun said. "I've been called it." He read much of the nearly 90,000 pieces of hate mail he received over the years, even quoting from letters in speeches. The "hurt" lessened only gradually. Blackmun realized he would be remembered as "author of the abortion decision." "I knew it was a no-win case, but I didn't ask for the assignment," he said. "We all pick up tabs. I'll carry this one to my grave. So be it." A bullet was shot into Blackmun's Arlington, Virginia, apartment in 1985. Neither he nor his wife was injured, but thereafter armed guards protected him.

Tolerance was a recurring theme in Blackmun's opinions. "What the Court really has refused to recognize," he wrote in dissent in *Bowers* v. *Hardwick* (1986), concerning a law that was selectively enforced against homosexuals and criminalized sexual behavior by consenting adults in the privacy of their bedroom, "is the fundamental interest all individuals have in controlling the nature of their intimate associations with others." Blackmun also advocated an often expansive application of rules protecting minorities. In joining the Court's 1978 ruling in *Regents of the University of California* v. *Bakke* that race could be a factor in university admissions decisions, he pointedly noted, "In order to get beyond racism, we must first take account of race. There is no other way." Blackmun's opinion in *Virginia Pharmacy Board* v. *Virginia Consumer Council* (1976) gave constitutional protection for the first time to commercial speech—speech with a business purpose.

Each summer from 1979 to 1994 Blackmun served as comoderator of the Aspen Institute's justice and society summer seminar, directing the group's readings and discussion. They reinforced his developing perspective and he explicitly incorporated some of these works in his opinions. The interplay between law and science fascinated him. Scientific evidence must be both "relevant" and "reliable" in order to be admitted at trial, he held for the Court in *Daubert* v. *Merrell Dow Pharmaceuticals* (1993).

In 1984 Blackmun described the Court as "moving to the right where it wants to go by hook or crook." "I fear for the future," he wrote in a dissent in a 1989 abortion case. "The signs are evident and very ominous, and a chill wind blows." Blackmun started speaking of *Roe* "almost in the past tense," and in 1990 he strongly considered retiring but not, he said, as long as a Republican was in the White House to name his successor. Even if *Roe* were reversed, his consolation would be that it had helped a generation of women, he said in 1991.

Blackmun's spirits visibly lifted in 1992 when a plurality of the Court, in *Planned Parenthood* v. *Casey*, reaffirmed *Roe*'s "essential holding"—a woman's right to choose abortion in the first six months of pregnancy, before the fetus is able to live outside the womb. Even so, he wrote, "I am eighty-three years old. I cannot remain on the court forever." But the election of William J. Clinton that year as president led him to believe that his successor would share his views on the issue and that he could retire when he chose. In December 1993 Blackmun told Clinton that he planned to retire at the end of the Court's term, and his decision was announced in April 1994.

One major issue remained. For several years Blackmun had privately expressed increasing doubt about whether the death penalty could be fairly imposed, and he had drafted but not released an opinion to that effect. In March 1994 Blackmun repudiated his judicial acceptance of capital punishment and declared himself opposed in all circumstances. "The death-penalty experiment has failed," he wrote in *Callins* v. *Collins*, dissenting from the Court's refusal to hear a case. "I no longer shall tinker with the machinery of death." He believed that arbitrariness, inconsistency, subjectivity, unreliability, and racism infected the death penalty. The hope that these factors could be eliminated had proved to be a "delusion." "Despite what the politicians say," Blackmun observed in 1995, the death penalty "has no deterrent effect. It's solely a matter of retribution and revenge."

Blackmun labored prodigiously. Every morning at 8:05, he ate breakfast with his law clerks in the Court's public cafeteria. Only a late afternoon exercise break and meals interrupted his usual fifteen-hour workday. Blackmun did not unify the Court or build consensus. The bent of his mind was solitary and his struggles were internal: he spent hours daily working in a room in the justices's library. At first, unlike many justices, he wrote his opinions from scratch, but the demands of the Court's docket forced him gradually to abandon the practice. Blackmun wanted to show that justices "are ordinary people too." He was devoted to baseball, and in *Flood* v. *Kuhn* (1972), he upheld major league baseball's antitrust exemption. He named eighty-eight diamond luminaries ("the list seems endless"), but for years Blackmun was chagrined that he forgot New York Giants Hall of Fame right fielder Mel Ott (despite 511 home runs).

Blackmun retained an empathy for outsiders, perhaps because he always had a touch of insecurity and a soft spot for those living on what he called the "raw edges of existence." Blackmun never forgot that a widow raised Warren Burger and that his own favorite aunt was divorced when her husband was imprisoned for embezzlement. Blackmun wanted to drive his Volkswagen from Minnesota to Washington until the Secret Service quashed the idea, and at the Supreme Court he parked it next to the Chief Justice's limousine, silently staring at both cars, a bare glimmer of a smile on his lips. Occasionally, he mimicked his colleagues privately or criticized them by name publicly. This was done with affection, but his meaning was clear. "I hope you will be yourself," Blackmun said at a law school commencement, "human, even a little sentimental, possessed of a sense of humor and a sense of humility. . . . There are arrogant people in this world and arrogant lawyers and, what is worse, arrogant judges."

In 1941 Blackmun married Dorothy Clark whom he had met in a chance pairing at a mixed doubles tennis match on a municipal court. Ever cautious, he had waited four years to propose; they had three daughters. He did not shield his love, and they danced frequently at parties. There was a subdued poetry about him, especially as he aged. Slight, with a full head of gray hair, soft-spoken, reserved, and modest ("the shy person's Justice," one friend called him) yet sometimes prickly and ornery, Blackmun was self-effacing almost to a fault. He was rarely recognized when, dressed as usual in a pale cardigan, he stood alone at the top of the Court's steps before abortion cases watching protesters march. He happily celebrated a birthday at a polka barn, easily sang "Take Me out to the Ballgame," and had to control his emotions when hearing funeral marches. Abraham Lincoln was his hero.

On the Court and off, Blackmun gave justice a humane face. "Poor Joshua!" he wrote in *DeShaney* v. *Winnebago County Department of Social Services* (1989), dissenting from the majority's holding that a state had no constitutional duty to protect a child from brutality at his father's hands. "Faced with the choice, I would adopt a 'sympathetic' reading [of the Fourteenth Amendment], one which comports with dictates of fundamental justice and recognizes that compassion need not be exiled from the province of judging." Blackmun died at age ninety from complications following hip replacement surgery.

★

Blackmun's papers are in the Library of Congress. Information on Blackmun can also be found in John A. Jenkins, "A Candid Talk with Justice Blackmun," *New York Times Magazine* (20 Feb. 1983); Robert Siegel, ed., *The NPR Interviews* (1994); David M. O'Brien, *Storm Center* (1996); and Phillipa Strum, "Change and Continuity on the Supreme Court: Conversations with Justice Harry A. Blackmun," *University of Richmond Law Review* 34, no. 1 (Mar. 2000): 285. Obituaries are in the *Los Angeles Times, Minneapolis Star Tribune, New York Times, St. Paul Pioneer Press,* and *Washington Post* (all 5 Mar. 1999).

ROGER K. NEWMAN

BLOOM, Benjamin Samuel (*b.* 21 February 1913 in Lansford, Pennsylvania; *d.* 13 September 1999 in Chicago, Illinois), educator whose *Taxonomy of Educational Objectives* and research on learning formed the scientific basis for the Head Start early education program, the most durable element of President Lyndon B. Johnson's Great Society initiative.

Bloom was the fourth of five children born to Russian Jewish immigrant parents. His father, William Bloom, was a picture framer and his mother, Rose Gronesine, was a homemaker noted for her flower gardens. As a child, Bloom proved a voracious reader known for borrowing, reading, and returning books to the library on the same day. He attended public schools in Lansford. A talented swimmer and handball player, he graduated as the class valedictorian. He entered Pennsylvania State University in 1931 and graduated with a B.A. degree in February 1935 and an M.S. degree in June of the same year.

In 1935, during the Great Depression, Bloom worked as a researcher for the Pennsylvania State Relief Organization and immediately thereafter, from 1936 to 1938, for the American Youth Commission in Washington, D.C. There Bloom met Ralph W. Tyler, a renowned education specialist at Ohio State University. When Tyler was hired by the University of Chicago as a university examiner, Bloom followed him as a doctoral student in 1939 and also served as Tyler's assistant. Bloom was awarded a Ph.D. in 1942. One night in 1939, while both were studying in the education library, Bloom met Sophie Missenbaum, who was studying for her master's degree. A week later he proposed marriage. On 7 July 1940 they were married in Detroit; the couple had two sons.

After his graduation from the University of Chicago, Bloom remained at the university as an associate examiner and in 1944 he joined the university's education department. He rose from an instructor to the Charles H. Swift Distinguished Service Professor in a career that spanned more than fifty years at the University of Chicago. He was appointed as a university examiner in 1953 following Tyler's departure. Chicago was among those U.S. universities to follow the practice more common in Europe of using examinations prepared by professional examiners instead of by teaching faculty to certify student progress to graduation. Bloom worked with Tyler in developing objective, multidisciplinary, comprehensive examinations. These tests often contained more than 600 items and took four to six hours to complete. Tests that were rigorous and reliable were essential.

During this phase of his career, Bloom collaborated with examiners from other universities on *Taxonomy of Educational Objectives, Handbook I: The Cognitive Domain* (1956) and *Taxonomy of Educational Objectives, Handbook II: The Affective Domain* (1964). His principal coauthor in these two undertakings was David R. Krathwohl, an assistant to Bloom and later a professor at Michigan State University and Syracuse University in New York. Although both books were done collaboratively with a number of scholars, they quickly became known simply as Bloom's *Taxonomy,* the label originally attached to the first volume.

For more than forty years Bloom's *Taxonomy,* which was translated into more than thirty languages, aided teachers and administrators in creating educational experiences that emphasized higher-order thinking. The handbooks explained that educational goals should ascend a ladder of increasingly complex knowledge and skills (memorization, comprehension, knowledge application, analysis, synthesis, and evaluation). More than one million copies were distributed in China. Bloom's *Taxonomy* sold millions of copies and, at the end of the twentieth century, continued to be cited in hundreds of scholarly publications. In addition, it exercised a profound heuristic effect, spawning myriads of imitations and local applications worldwide. Neither Bloom nor Krathwohl derived any personal profits from the *Taxonomy*'s success, having decided early on to reinvest their book royalties to benefit research and students at their universities.

In 1959 Bloom left his position as a university examiner to study for a year at the Center for the Advanced Study in Behavioral Sciences at Stanford University in California. During this period he began working on the insightful *Stability and Change in Human Characteristics* (1964), which demonstrated the importance of early childhood learning in both the home and school settings. This richly empirical study showed the learner's critical "window of opportunity" was between infancy and age ten, thus indicating that enhanced home and school environments were absolutely critical to a child's learning. Bloom was successful both in conversations with President Johnson and in testimony before Congress in arguing for the establishment of the Head Start program, which required increased parental involvement and federal support for early childhood education for disadvantaged youth. This program was the most enduring and successful part of Johnson's War on Poverty. Also in 1964 Bloom, along with two of his University of Chicago colleagues, Allison Davis and Robert Hess, staged a major national conference that led to their collaboration on *Compensatory Education for Cultural Deprivation* (1965). Bloom still had Congress's ear, and this work helped to create Title I of the Elementary and Secondary Education Act, which benefited children through the third grade.

Bloom's early reputation as the creator of the *Taxonomy* took him to many parts of the world; later, he also traveled as a learning theorist. He conducted educational projects in India, Israel, and China. He personally recruited international graduate students to the University of Chicago. He was the cofounder in 1959 of the International Association for the Evaluation of Educational Achievement and in the 1960s conducted the first twelve-country study of mathematical attainment. In 1972 he was a founding member of the International Curriculum Association. He remained active in these organizations throughout his life.

In 1983 Bloom faced the mandatory retirement age at the University of Chicago. However, he kept his office at the university, where he continued to teach part-time. Bloom started a second career as an adjunct professor at Northwestern University in Evanston, Illinois, serving there until the 1990s. During this part of his career, Bloom turned his attention to talent development and mastery of learning. His study *Developing Talent in Young People* (1985), done with a team of eight researchers, looked at 120 highly accomplished athletes, musicians, artists, and scientists. Bloom noted that parental caring, excellent teaching, and learning that stressed accuracy were key to talent development.

Bloom died at age eighty-six at his home in Chicago from complications from Alzheimer's disease. He is buried in Oak Woods Cemetery in Chicago. In a career that spanned more than sixty years and seventeen books, Bloom distinguished himself nationally and internationally as a scholar, teacher, and public-policy advocate. The evidence that Bloom accumulated convinced him that all children could learn at much higher levels than previously thought possible, and that anything the smartest students learned could be learned by virtually all students.

Bloom concluded his 1985 book on talent development by saying, "No matter what the quality of initial gifts, each of the individuals . . . went through many years of special development under the care of attentive parents and . . . a remarkable series of teachers and coaches." This was a major theme for Bloom, confirming a lifetime of research. He believed that for all students to be superbly educated, the essential interventions of excellent teachers needed to be accompanied by the quintessential roles of caring parents, assisted by the creation of supportive social structures. In both his teaching and his scholarship, Bloom moved society through yesteryear's notion of education as a talent search for the few to a more contemporary vision of education as challenged by the vastness of individual human potential.

★

There is no biography of Bloom. An oral history and approximately fifty linear feet of archival materials are housed at the Department of Special Collections at the Regenstein Library at the University of Chicago. Biographical information may be found in Lorin W. Anderson, "Benjamin Bloom, Values and the Professoriate," in *Teachers and Mentors: Profiles of Distinguished Twentieth-Century Professors of Education,* ed. Craig Kridel (1996). See also a critical appraisal of Bloom's life and work in Lorin W. Anderson, "Benjamin S. Bloom: His Life, His Works, and His

Legacy," in *Educational Psychology: A Century of Contributions,* ed. B. J. Zimmerman and D. H. Schunk (2001). Obituaries are in the *New York Times* (15 Sept. 1999) and *Los Angeles Times* (17 Sept. 1999).

JOSEPH G. FLYNN

BONO, Salvatore Phillip ("Sonny") (*b.* 16 February 1935 in Detroit, Michigan; *d.* 5 January 1998 near South Lake Tahoe, California), entertainer and politician who gained fame as part of the singing duo Sonny and Cher and who later was elected to the U.S. House of Representatives.

Bono was the youngest of three children of Jean and Santo Bono, who had immigrated to Detroit from Montelepre, Sicily, in the early 1930s. Poverty-stricken, the family relocated to Los Angeles in 1942 to find work. Bono's father became employed as a construction worker, and his mother operated a beauty shop out of their home. In Los Angeles, the family lived in Hawthorne, a working-class neighborhood, where the children attended schools in the Inglewood district. Even though Bono had no formal musical training, he realized at an early age that music would be his way to a better life.

Sonny Bono, 1995. REUTERS/ARCHIVE PHOTOS, INC.

Before age twelve Bono started writing songs. As a teenager, he played conga drum in a combo that entertained classmates by jamming at a nearby recreation center after Friday night football games. During high school, he composed songs on a ukulele, stringing melodies together as he listened to his idol Frankie Laine on the radio. Playing his ukulele, Bono auditioned for Peter Potter's *Search for a Song,* a televised amateur talent show, and won first prize with his original tune "Ecstasy" (1952). After dropping out of high school, Bono moonlighted as a songwriter. By day he worked at various jobs to support himself; at night he peddled songs to record companies along Sunset Boulevard in Hollywood. In 1953 Bono and Jack Nitzsche composed "Needles and Pins," a song later recorded by Jackie DeShannon. His first break came when the rhythm and blues musician Johnny Otis hired him to sing backup and write songs for his company, Dig Records, in 1955. As luck would have it, Art Rupe, the owner of Specialty Records, hired him as an artist and repertoire man in 1957. The job included scouting talent, singing backup, songwriting, and pushing new records to local radio disc jockeys. At Specialty, Bono worked with the singers Sam Cooke and Little Richard while learning the business from the musicians Harold Battiste and Nitzsche. In February 1954 Bono married Donna Rankin. They had one child and divorced in 1962.

Shortly after Rupe fired Bono for promoting his own material, Bono met Cherilyn ("Cher") LaPiere Sarkisian on a blind date arranged by Nitzsche in April 1962. The alluring sixteen-year-old with long black hair worked as a salesgirl at a candy store. Meeting Cher marked a turning point in both their lives and the beginning of a tumultuous romance. Through Nitzsche, Bono gained an audience with the producer Phil Spector, who hired him to work in West Coast promotions for his label Philles Records. A risk-taker, the mecurial Spector had an ear for talent and flaunted a new mix of unconventional, rebellious pop music. Using girl groups and innovative recording techniques, Spector produced such hits as "He's a Rebel," "Da Doo Ron Ron," and "Be My Baby." His unique sound exposed the raw emotion of teenage love.

Bono suggested that Cher sing backup during recording sessions and began promoting her as a solo vocalist. While recording "Baby Don't Go," Cher, who was nervous and shy of the microphone, refused to continue. To reassure her, Bono sang by her side while holding her hand, and, with Spector's approval, the couple began recording duets. Their hits included "I Got You, Babe" in June 1965 and "The Beat Goes On," released in February 1967. The couple cut ten top forty singles, composed mostly by Bono. Their meteoric rise to fame took place through a lucrative record contract with Atlantic Records, appearances on Dick Clark's *American Bandstand* and the *Ed Sullivan Show,* and a trip to London. Record sales, which included the albums *Look at Us* (1965) and *The Wondrous World of Sonny and Cher* (1966), totaled forty million by late 1967, even though their sound had declined in popularity following the British rock group invasion, psychedelic rock, and the protest mantras of the late 1960s.

Consequently, Bono refashioned their singing act into a Las Vegas–style comedy routine. Impressed with their new look, the CBS executive Fred Silverman brought the couple to prime-time television. *The Sonny and Cher Comedy Hour* ran from 1971 to 1974 and showcased Cher in dazzling gowns and Sonny as a foppish straight man. Filled with biting sarcasm, the monologue often reflected the tension in their offstage relationship. They married on 27 October 1964 and had one daughter together in 1969. They separated in 1974 and divorced in 1975 amid a deluge of tabloid headlines.

As Cher rose to the status of a pop icon, Bono virtually disappeared from the public eye. With limited exposure in the press, minor roles in such B-grade films as *Escape to Athena* and *Hairspray,* and rare cameo appearances on television, it seemed that Bono's position in the entertainment industry had dwindled. His marriage to the actress Susie Coelho in 1981 ended in divorce in 1984. In 1983 Bono opened Bono's, a restaurant in Los Angeles, and a similar establishment in Houston, Texas. In 1984 he sold his share in the Houston location and opened another restaurant in Palm Springs, California. At the Los Angeles restaurant he met Mary Whitaker, a college student, in May 1984. The couple married in 1986 and made Palm Springs their home. They had two children. A reunion with Cher on *Late Night with David Letterman* in February 1987 proved to be bittersweet.

Unanswered questions concerning building codes in Palm Springs inspired Bono to run for mayor on the Republican ticket in 1988. Often seeking the advice of the actor Clint Eastwood, the mayor of Carmel, California, Bono won the election and used Palm Springs' city hall as a political base to launch an unsuccessful bid for the U.S. Senate in 1992. As the mayor of Palm Springs, Bono helped eliminate a $2.5-million city deficit and instituted the Palm Springs International Film Festival. Bolstered by the resurgence of the Republican Party in 1994, Bono gained a seat in the U.S. House of Representatives, representing the Forty-fourth Congressional District. In the House, he earned praise from conservatives for his voting record and ability as a fund-raiser and was reelected in 1996.

Skiing alone on the heavily wooded Orion Trail at the Heavenly Valley ski resort near the California-Nevada border, Bono died at age sixty-two from head injuries sustained after crashing into a pine tree. Ironically, the greatest tribute after his death came from Cher, who, quoted in the *New York Times* on 10 January 1998, said: "He was smart enough to take an introverted sixteen-year-old and a guy with a bad voice and turn them into the most successful, beloved couple of our generation." Bono is buried at Desert Memorial Park in Cathedral City, near Palm Springs.

★

Shortly after he met Cher in 1962, Bono began recording his thoughts and important happenings in a diary, lending a degree of historical accuracy to his autobiography *And the Beat Goes On* (1991). Obituaries are in the *New York Times* and *Los Angeles Times* (both 7 Jan. 1998).

JEAN W. GRIFFITH

BOWERMAN, William Jay ("Bill") (*b.* 19 February 1911 in Portland, Oregon; *d.* 24 December 1999 in Fossil, Oregon), track coach and shoe-design innovator who helped to change American exercise habits and was a cofounder of the Nike Corporation.

Bowerman's father, William Jay Bowerman, Sr., an attorney and politician, left his mother, Elizabeth Hoover, when their son was just two years old. Bowerman and his three siblings were raised in Fossil and Medford, Oregon, by his mother and aunts. He attended Medford High School, where he became involved in athletics. As an undergraduate at the University of Oregon during the early 1930s, Bowerman played football, basketball, and ran track under coach Bill Hayward. His plans for medical school after graduation in 1934 were scrapped when Bowerman decided instead to coach track and football at Medford High School. On 22 June 1936 he married Barbara Young; they had three sons.

After serving as an army officer in Italy during World War II, Bowerman returned to Oregon on V-J Day, disobeying orders to go with the army to Texas. When military police came to arrest him, Bowerman told them with his usual toughness that since the war was over, he had better things to do with his time. Discharge papers arrived a few days later. In 1949 Bowerman took a position as the University of Oregon's head track coach, where he soon gained a reputation as a demanding but inspiring trainer. He was also a technical innovator. To help his teams excel, Bowerman worked to develop lighter, faster running shoes, once estimating that shaving a single ounce off each shoe would translate into lifting 200 fewer pounds over the course of an average race.

Bowerman's ideas impressed Phil Knight, a middle-distance runner who had trained at Oregon during the late 1950s. Knight went on to graduate studies at the Stanford Business School, where his research focused on the possibilities of using low-priced, high-tech Japanese sports shoes to end the dominance of such German running shoe firms

University of Oregon track coach Bill Bowerman (*center*) with Vic Reeve and Dyrol Burleson, 1960. Asso-CIATED PRESS AP

as Adidas. Knight and Bowerman went into business together in 1964, each putting $500 into a company called Blue Ribbon Sports. They started by importing and marketing Japanese running shoes in the United States. The first year they sold 1,300 pairs.

During a track team trip to New Zealand in the winter of 1962 and 1963, Bowerman was introduced to a new form of exercise called "jogging," developed by a popular local coach, Arthur Lydiard. In each of the twelve New Zealand towns Bowerman visited, he found a local jogging club. Everywhere, Bowerman recalled, he found joggers, "fit beyond belief." When he returned to the University of Oregon in early 1963, Bowerman founded the first jogging club in the United States. Two hundred people came the first week. The second week, between two and five thousand showed up.

Bowerman and Knight began designing their own shoes in 1971 after a dispute with their original Japanese supplier. They renamed their company Nike, after the Greek goddess of victory, and adopted as a logo the familiar "swoosh," which had been designed by a student, Carolyn Davidson, for $35. Nike's first success came with the "waffle sole" shoe designed when Bowerman heated rubber compounds in his wife's waffle iron. Light and springy, waffle-sole shoes were introduced at the U.S. trials for the 1972 Olympics, held that year at Hayward Field at the University of Oregon. Helped by Bowerman's own reputation as a coach, Nike running shoes quickly caught the attention of leading athletes. Through the 1960s and early 1970s Bowerman's

Oregon track teams won four National Collegiate Athletic Association (NCAA) outdoor championships. Ten of his runners broke the four-minute mile. In 1972 Bowerman coached the U.S. Olympic team at Munich that won six gold medals. Athletes who benefited from Bowerman's coaching included Steve Prefontaine, Alberto Salazar, Mac Wilkins, Kenny Moore, Wade Bell, and Dyrol Burleson. Bowerman's methods were unorthodox, including kicking athletes off the team for excessive running (too much danger of injury), and branding them with hot keys in the sauna (a way of getting undivided attention). But his devotion to his athletes was intense, and no one who trained with Bowerman ever forgot him.

Bowerman was not happy with his team's performance at Munich. The combination of a deadly Palestinian terrorist raid and disappointments on the field—notably, Prefontaine's fourth-place finish in the 5,000 meter race—led Bowerman to call the Olympics the "worst experience I've had in my entire educational and athletic life." The next year he retired from coaching to concentrate on business interests. Phil Knight's marketing genius transformed running shoes from athletic wear to fashion statement, expanding the market far beyond the running track with savvy advertising and creative design. Nike controlled 50 percent of the American running shoe market by 1979. Just over a decade later, it became the first sportswear company to reach revenues of $3 billion. Slogans such as "Just Do It" and endorsements from superstars such as Michael Jordan helped to make Nike an American success story.

Bowerman shared in the company's financial success, but he paid a price. A glue he used in his early shoe design experiments contained hexane, a chemical whose fumes permanently damaged his neurological system. Bowerman was left with a limp and forced to wear a leg brace. Always a maverick, Bowerman refused induction into the National Track and Field Hall of Fame in 1981 because Bill Hayward, his track coach at Oregon, had never received the same honor. Bowerman retired from the Nike board of directors in early 1999. In October of that year, Nike announced it would use a silhouette of Bowerman wearing his signature Tyrolean hat on Nike running shoes. Bowerman died of natural causes at his home. After learning of his death, Nike chairman Phil Knight called Bowerman the biggest influence on his life after his parents: "He was for so many of us a hero, leader and most of all teacher," he said.

Bowerman helped to get America running and helped to launch one of the most successful companies of the late twentieth century. "Bowerman's way of teasing, humiliating or strangling men and problems into submission resulted not only in a distinguished line of champion athletes but in the education of a community, the beginning of a fitness movement and the creation of a company to serve that movement," wrote one of his trainees, writer Kenny Moore.

★

Runner Kenny Moore's memories of working with Bowerman can be found in "Muleskinner," a feature story in *Oregon Quarterly* (summer 1993). In the same issue, "Jogging into History," by Richard Leutzinger, includes a history of Bowerman's introduction of jogging into America. Obituaries are in the *Washington Post* (26 Dec. 1999), *New York Times* (27 Dec. 1999), *Daily Telegraph* (London) (29 Dec. 1999), and *Sports Illustrated* (24 Jan. 2000). Robert Towne's 1998 film *Without Limits* tells the story of runner Steve Prefontaine, and starred Donald Sutherland as Bill Bowerman.

THOMAS HAGER

BOWLES, Paul Frederic(k) (*b.* 30 December 1910 in New York City; *d.* 18 November 1999 in Tangier, Morocco), composer, writer, translator, and poet.

Bowles, an only child, was the son of Claude Dietz Bowles, a dentist and a tyrannical father whom he hated, and Rena Winnewisser, a former teacher. At age three, Bowles taught himself to read and write from cereal boxes and blocks. At age four, Bowles wrote a collection of animal stories and kept dozens of notebooks, creating imaginary worlds that he had no desire to inhabit, seeing himself only as a registering consciousness. Until he was five, Bowles never saw

Paul Bowles, 1983. AP/WIDE WORLD PHOTOS

another child; he was unaware, even, of the existence of school, until he was assigned to the second grade of the Model School in Jamaica, New York City. At age seven, he took music lessons in piano, ear training, and theory. At age eight, he wrote what he thought was an opera, which he called *Le Carré, An Opera in Nine Chapters* and played on a zither while reciting the words. "You can see how, even then, I got my arts mixed up," admitted Bowles. "What I liked particularly was popular music, so I tried to write Broadway-like tunes. Of course they were no good," Bowles told his composer friend Phillip Ramey in 1995.

At Jamaica High School, Bowles was the president of the poetry society and edited the literary magazine *The Oracle,* in which he published poetry and fiction. Bowles was still in high school when two of his poems were accepted by *transition*, an avant-garde review in Paris, France. Upon graduation from high school in 1928, he entered the University of Virginia in Charlottesville because the writer Edgar Allan Poe had gone there, but he ran away to Paris before finishing his first semester. At age eighteen, he was publishing dozens of poems in first-rate journals in Europe and the United States.

Upon his return to New York City in 1929, Bowles met Aaron Copland, who seemed to him "the ideal of what a composer should be because he knew exactly why he put down every note." They traveled to Berlin, Germany, together from Paris, then to Tangier, Morocco, upon the advice of the writer Gertrude Stein. In 1931 in Tangier, where Bowles later established his home, he composed a Sonata for Oboe and Clarinet, which premiered at the Aeolian Hall in London, England, in a concert of works also by Copland and Virgil Thomson. Of his Sonata no. 1 for Flute and Piano, composed in 1932 in Paris and Grenoble, France, Bowles wrote, "When I had finished writing this piece, I was fortunate in having the great French flautist René Le Roy at hand. He played it for me so that I knew exactly how it sounded. Usually there is no way of hearing a piece prior to public performance."

Upon Bowles's return to New York City in the spring of 1933, he wrote music for the Federal Theatre, film music, and theater scores for more than thirty Broadway plays, including Tennessee Williams's *The Glass Menagerie* (1945) and *Summer and Smoke* (1948). In 1936 a concert funded by the Federal Music Project featured his Concerto for Flute and Piano (1932); Trio for Violin, Violoncello, and Piano (1932); *Scènes d'Anabase* (1932), a chamber piece in five sections scored for tenor, oboe, and piano; Suite for Violin and Piano; and other piano pieces. The concert prompted Copland to declare that Bowles's music "comes from a fresh personality, music full of charm and melodic invention, at times surprisingly well made in an instinctive and nonacademic fashion. Personally I much prefer an 'amateur' like Bowles to your 'well-trained' conservatory product." Among Bowles's other important works were his first commissioned piece, Concerto for Two Pianos, Winds, and Percussion, performed in 1948 by Arthur Gold and Robert Fizdale at New York City's Town Hall, and *A Picnic Cantata* for four women's voices, two pianos, and percussion, which premiered in 1953. When described as a "self-confessed miniaturist, primarily a composer of brief, episodic pieces," Bowles replied, "For me, short, simple pieces were the most satisfying, perhaps because I didn't know how to appreciate long, complex ones. I wasn't certain how such pieces were made. . . . Music should engage the attention of the listener and make him more aware of what sound can do to him; it has to entertain," he insisted.

Bowles married the novelist and playwright Jane Auer on 21 February 1938, and she became the main influence in his writing of fiction as an adult. In 1947 the couple established more or less permanent residency in Tangier. Here Bowles wrote his first and most successful novel, *The Sheltering Sky* (1949), dedicated to his wife; *The Delicate Prey and Other Stories* (1950) was dedicated to his mother because she first read him the stories of Poe. A second novel, *Let It Come Down* (1952), appeared without a dedication, but his third novel, *The Spider's House* (1955), was dedicated to his father, who never acknowledged it. Later,

Bowles declared, "I don't know why I dedicated that book, or any book, to him; he had no interest in me whatsoever." Bowles considered his fourth novel, *Up Above the World* (1966), "the best written," although not his favorite. The novella *Too Far from Home* (1991) was published to accompany twenty-one watercolors painted in Mali by Miquel Barcelo. A subsequent edition appeared in 1994, with drawings by Marguerite McBey. Bowles also published two books of poems, *Scenes* (1968) and *Thicket of Spring* (1972).

Devoted to the folk music and art music indigenous to Morocco, Bowles made two extensive trips in August and September 1959 through northern and central Morocco to record the music of its people before it was irretrievably lost, a project supported by a Rockefeller grant and the Library of Congress. Bowles made over forty reel-to-reel tapes of native Moroccan music, which are housed in the central archive of the Library of Congress in Washington, D.C.

Bowles also was noted for his translations of several Moroccan writers, commencing with *A Life Full of Holes* (1964), by Larbi Layachi (a pseudonym for Driss ben Hamed Charhadi). Bowles went on to produce twelve books by Mohammed Mrabet, who recited his tales in Moghrebi. Bowles translated three books by Mohamed Choukri, the only literate Moroccan with whom he worked, and four books by Rodrigo Rey Rosa, a Guatemalan who wrote in Spanish. Bowles also translated Jean-Paul Sartre's 1946 play *No Exit*. Bowles devoted much of his late years to translating, which he could do in the evening when there were fewer demands from his increasingly ill wife, who suffered a series of immobilizing strokes from 1957 until her death in Malaga, Spain, in 1973. By then she was schizophrenic, blind, and unable to move or speak.

Later in life, Bowles returned to composing music, especially theater scores for a number of plays at the urging of Joseph A. McPhillips IV, the headmaster of the American School of Tangier, including a dramatization of his own short story, *The Garden* (1967); he also wrote scores for such classics as *Oedipus the King* (1966), *The Bacchae* (1969), *Caligula* (1978), *Hippolytus* (1992), *Salomé* (1993), and, two years before his death, *The Royal Hunt of the Sun* (1997), all produced by the American School of Tangier. Bowles died in Tangier from a respiratory infection. On 1 November 2000 his ashes were interred in Lakemont Cemetery, which overlooks Seneca Lake and the village of Glenora, New York, where Bowles spent his happiest summers as a child.

More than anything, Bowles wanted to be remembered as a composer, although he recognized that the general public knew him best as a writer. Shortly before his death, Bowles observed, "I think my best writing may lie in my short stories and tales. They were also the most fun to write." In 1991 he received the Rea Award for the Short

Story. The jurors' description of his work captured the essence of his contributions as both a writer and a composer: "Paul Bowles is a storyteller of the utmost purity and integrity. He writes of a world before God became man, a world in which men and women in extremis are seen as components in a large, more elemental drama. His prose is crystalline and his voice unique. Among living American masters of the short story, Paul Bowles is sui generis."

★

Bowles's unpublished correspondence resides chiefly at the Harry Ransom Humanities Research Center at the University of Texas at Austin, and in the Special Collections Department of the Hugh M. Morris Library of the University of Delaware in Newark. Important books include Bowles's autobiography, *Without Stopping* (1972); Millicent Dillon, *A Little Original Sin: The Life and Work of Jane Bowles* (1981); Allen Hibbard, *Paul Bowles: A Study of His Short Fiction* (1993); Gena Dagel Caponi, *Paul Bowles: Romantic Savage* (1994); Jeffrey Miller, ed., *In Touch: The Letters of Paul Bowles* (1994); Claudia Swann, ed., *Paul Bowles's Music* (1995); Paul Bowles, *Dear Paul, Dear Ned: The Correspondence of Paul Bowles and Ned Rorem* (1997); and Millicent Dillon, *You Are Not I: A Portrait of Paul Bowles* (1998). Obituaries are in the *New York Times* and *Guardian* (both 19 Nov. 1999).

VIRGINIA SPENCER CARR

BRADBURY, Norris Edwin (*b.* 30 May 1909 in Santa Barbara, California; *d.* 20 August 1997 in Los Alamos, New Mexico), scientist and administrator who helped assemble the first atomic bomb and who became the longest tenured director of the Los Alamos National Laboratory.

Bradbury was one of four children born to Edwin Perly and Elvira C. Norris. His father was a machinist at the California Institute of Technology and worked on the 200-inch Palomar telescope. His mother taught school until she had children and later worked for the Fontana, California, school board. Bradbury attended Hollywood High School and Chaffey Union High School (Ontario, California), graduating at age sixteen. He received a bachelor's degree in chemistry from Pomona College in 1929. In 1932 he received a Ph.D. in physics and mathematics from the University of California, Berkeley, where he focused on the mobility of ions in gases. After spending two years at the Massachusetts Institute of Technology on a National Research Council Fellowship, Bradbury joined the physics faculty at Stanford University, becoming a full professor in 1942. He married Lois Platt, with whom he had three sons, in 1933.

Bradbury was a member of the naval reserve, and in 1941 he was called to active duty and assigned to the Naval Proving Ground at Dahlgren, Virginia, where he worked

Norris Bradbury, 1963. ASSOCIATED PRESS AP

on projectile ballistics. In 1944 he accepted a transfer to the Manhattan Project's top-secret Los Alamos National Laboratory. At Los Alamos, Bradbury was assigned the difficult task of overseeing the assembly of the non-nuclear components of the plutonium implosion bomb, which was successfully detonated at the Trinity test site near Alamogordo, New Mexico, on 16 July 1945.

Shortly after the end of the war, J. Robert Oppenheimer resigned as the director of the laboratory. He recommended Bradbury as his successor. Bradbury accepted the position, intending to stay for only six months or until the passage of atomic energy legislation that would determine the laboratory's fate, whichever came first. Instead, he directed the facility for twenty-five years until his retirement in 1970.

Bradbury's first years as director were among his most difficult. The end of the war brought an exodus of military and civilian personnel from Los Alamos, which shrank from a wartime high of more than 3,000 people in July 1945 to approximately 1,000 people by January 1946. Many of the Los Alamos scientists wanted to return to their home institutions and rejoin academic life. Bradbury gave up any ideas of returning to academic life in order to help stem the outflow of scientists. His reasoning was simple: "You can't persuade anybody to work hard at something if you won't work hard at it yourself, and if I didn't believe in Los

Alamos, nobody else would either." Despite the initial drain of scientists and the lack of a definite postwar role for the laboratory, Bradbury succeeded in building the facility into a viable and productive research institution.

The primary postwar mission for the laboratory was the development of nuclear armaments for the U.S. cold war arsenal. In addition to advances in the technology of fission weapons, Bradbury led the development of the first thermonuclear, or fusion, bomb, which was successfully tested in 1952. Although he directed one of the world's premier weapons-development laboratories, Bradbury argued as early as 1955 for a halt to the nuclear arms race and was an advocate of the 1963 Limited Test Ban Treaty. He believed that a strong nuclear deterrent was necessary at the time, but hoped that eventually the realization that a nuclear war was unwinnable would lead to international agreements for nuclear disarmament. For Bradbury, the aim of the nuclear weapons business was to put itself out of business.

Under Bradbury's direction, the laboratory expanded beyond its mission to create nuclear armaments and undertook basic scientific research on nuclear energy as well as research on peaceful applications of nuclear energy, including nuclear medicine and reactors for nuclear power plants. Bradbury helped foster scientific creativity by shielding scientists from budget concerns and bureaucratic red tape. The expanded research opportunities and intellectual freedom that Bradbury provided helped the institution attract top scientists and led to important accomplishments. Frederick Reines and Clyde Cowan used detectors built at the laboratory to detect the neutrino, for which Reines won the 1996 Nobel Prize in physics. By the late 1960s weapons work was reduced from a majority of the laboratory's effort to only 25 to 30 percent.

Bradbury not only created a thriving intellectual community at the Los Alamos National Laboratory, he also took an active role in improving the town itself. As Los Alamos was transformed from a military base into a civilian community, Bradbury played a role in developing its housing, hospital facilities, and schools. He helped organize the first Cub Scout troop in Los Alamos, served on the board of education, and was president of the New Mexico Archaeological Society. His involvement in the archaeological society reflected his own interest in archaeology and geology, and he often explored remote areas of the state in his pickup truck. He also enjoyed spending time in his woodworking shop at home.

During his tenure as director, Bradbury managed to transform the laboratory from a temporary wartime installation into a leading scientific research institution. In doing so, he had to balance the needs of both scientists and politicians. The increasing connections among science, government, and industry in the postwar era brought a need

for scientists who were also effective administrators and lobbyists for science. The success of Los Alamos is a testament to Bradbury's ability to negotiate the often complex relationships between science and politics. A museum featuring exhibits related to the work conducted in Los Alamos was renamed the Norris E. Bradbury Science Museum in 1970. The institution, which was later officially named the Bradbury Science Museum, moved into a new building in downtown Los Alamos in 1993.

Bradbury received numerous awards and honors during his lifetime, including the navy's Legion of Merit (1945), Department of Defense Public Service Medal (1966), and the Enrico Fermi Award (1970). He was a member of the National Academy of Sciences and a fellow of the American Physical Society. Bradbury continued to live in Los Alamos after his retirement until his death from natural causes at age eighty-eight. His wife, Lois, passed away in January 1998.

★

For information about Bradbury, see Norris Bradbury, "Los Alamos—The First 25 Years," in L. Badash, J. Hirschfelder, and H. Broida, eds., *Reminiscences of Los Alamos, 1943–1945* (1980). Obituaries are in the *New York Times* (22 Aug. 1997) and *Independent* (London) (2 Sept. 1997).

J. CHRISTOPHER JOLLY

BRADLEY, Thomas ("Tom") (*b.* 29 December 1917 in Calvert, Texas; *d.* 29 September 1998 in Los Angeles, California), police officer, city council member, and five-time mayor of Los Angeles who transformed the city from a collection of suburban neighborhoods to a "world class" metropolis.

Bradley was the second of five surviving children of Lee Bradley and Crenner Hawkins. His parents were sharecroppers until the family moved to Los Angeles when Bradley was seven. In Los Angeles, Bradley's father worked as a cook, waiter, and railroad porter, among other odd jobs. Eventually, a discouraged Lee Bradley left his wife, who supported the family by working long hours as a domestic servant in numerous homes. Bradley stayed in touch with his father, but his mother was his major influence, delegating to him adult responsibilities, supporting his studiousness and love for reading, and giving him an example of courage and hope despite the family's poverty. After attending Rosemont Elementary and Lafayette Junior High, he enrolled at Polytechnic High in 1934, using the address of one of his mother's employers. Although 1 of 100 African Americans in a student body of 1,500 students, Bradley excelled in and out of the classroom. He was selected for the Ephebian Honor Society, which had previously been off-limits to African Americans, and was the first African

American to be elected student body president. He set the city track record for the quarter-mile and was All-City tackle in football. Bradley entered the University of California at Los Angeles (UCLA) on a track scholarship in 1937.

Now only 1 of 100 African Americans in 13,000 students at UCLA, Bradley commuted daily from his home in the impoverished central city to affluent Westwood. He took his studies seriously and ran on the mile relay team, but his time and attention also turned to other campus organizations and activities, notably Adeline Gunther's Religious Conference, which, he said later, reinforced his mother's teaching and values, and Kappa Alpha Psi, an African-American fraternity, which gave him opportunity for leadership as well as a network of lifelong supporters and friends. Bradley had also fallen in love with Ethel Arnold, a successful owner of beauty parlors, whom he had first met as a teenager at New Hope Baptist Church. In 1940, late in his junior year, he took the examination for city policeman and not only passed but did extremely well. Two things motivated Bradley's decision to join the police force before completing his degree. First, it was among the highest paying jobs an African American could then traditionally aspire to, and second, he wanted to marry Ethel, which he did on 4 May 1941. They had three children, one of whom died at birth.

Bradley was given the typical assignments of an African-American officer: youth and vice work in the ghetto. He performed his job conscientiously and was eventually chosen to establish a new community relations unit. Bradley made sergeant in 1946 and lieutenant in 1958, at the time one of only two African Americans in that rank. In 1950 the family moved into a white neighborhood with the help of a white friend who posed as the purchaser of their home.

In 1946 Bradley broadened his activities beyond his duties as a police officer and his family responsibilities. At nights and on weekends, he became well known in many areas of Los Angeles as a key member of various clubs and organizations, notably the Democratic Minority Conference and the California Democratic Council, a liberal reform group with a racially mixed membership. Attending Southwestern University School of Law at night for four years, Bradley earned his LL.B. degree and passed the bar exam in 1956. Just as Bradley was retiring from the police force in 1961 to join the law practice of Charles Matthews, a group of civic leaders who wanted an African American to finally join the city council urged Bradley to make himself available for appointment to a vacant seat. A surprised Bradley agreed. Although thousands signed a petition in his support, the council chose instead a wealthy Republican businessman. Despite this loss, Bradley found his new career.

Bradley became the people's choice for city councillor

Tom Bradley, 1966. PRINTS AND PHOTOGRAPHS DIVISION, LIBRARY OF CONGRESS

in the predominantly white Crenshaw tenth district, and he easily defeated the incumbent in 1963. He won reelection in 1967 and 1971, each time running unopposed. During ten years on the city council, Bradley supported parks and recreation, street lights and neighborhood safety, police integrity, housing, transportation, jobs, equal opportunity, and fiscal accountability. Bradley believed his responsibility was to represent all of Los Angeles, not just his own district. For example, although Watts was miles from Crenshaw, Bradley spoke out about conditions in Watts prior to the 1965 riots and about police brutality in the aftermath, and he led efforts to secure federal funds to revitalize the injured neighborhood. Concerned about earthquake faults and Southern California's beaches, he opposed offshore oil drilling across from the Pacific Palisades, another area far from his home district. Developing a vision for Los Angeles and eager to unite its many peoples, Bradley ran for mayor in 1969. After a stunning victory margin of 42 to 26 percent in the primary, he unexpectedly lost in the runoff to Mayor Sam Yorty, 53 to 47 percent. Bradley's team still had things to learn; his coalition was not yet firmly in place. Yorty's vigorous campaign did not shy from insinuation and playing on voters' fears. In spite of his defeat, Bradley quietly promised to enter another mayoral race.

By the time of Bradley's next run for mayor in 1973, the people of Los Angeles knew and respected Bradley, who was now fifty-five years old, for his wealth of experience. For this campaign, Bradley moved from a low-key to a more aggressive style, and he brought in media experts to augment his usual grassroots methods. Bradley had solidified and expanded his support base, a coalition of African-American, white liberal, Jewish, and increasingly, Latino and Asian voters. He defeated Yorty in the primary by 35 to 29 percent, with Jess Unruh, the powerful Democratic Speaker of the State Assembly, getting only 17 percent; on 29 May 1973, Bradley was elected mayor with 54 percent of the vote. Once in power, the progrowth and antipoverty Bradley coalition attracted powerful new members, including business, labor, and other minorities. Bradley served five terms as mayor of Los Angeles (1973–1993).

Mayor Bradley pursued the same progressive, antipoverty goals as he had as a city councillor. He systematically opened up city government and patronage to minorities and women. One of his first policy initiatives was a redevelopment plan that led to rapid physical and economic growth, both downtown and throughout the city. At a time when other cities were struggling, Los Angeles, with its modernized airport and thriving harbor, was developing into a "world class" city and a major portal on the "Pacific Rim" (favorite Bradley phrases). The 1984 Olympics were a symbolic high point for Los Angeles; Bradley would later call it "the major event of my life." Funded privately, the games took place without a hitch. They amounted to fifteen days of jubilation and produced a $250 million surplus.

Bradley was a presence and force beyond Los Angeles. Because of his stature and longevity as mayor of the second largest city in the United States, his travels to secure funding and commercial relationships, and his prominence as chief organizer of the 1984 Olympics, Bradley became known throughout the world. He served as cochair of the 1976 Democratic National Convention, and President Jimmy Carter offered him a cabinet post as head of the Department of Housing and Urban Development (HUD). Walter Mondale seriously considered Bradley as his running mate in the 1984 presidental campaign, for which Bradley made the prime-time speech nominating Mondale. Bradley twice ran for governor of California, losing to George Deukmejian by less than a percentage point in 1982 and by 61 to 37 percent in 1986.

There were signs of trouble in the mid-1980s during Bradley's fourth term as mayor. He narrowly avoided a runoff election in 1989. Rapid growth in Los Angeles had led to traffic jams, air pollution, airport congestion (including at the Tom Bradley International Terminal), expensive housing, and the disruption of once quiet neighborhoods. Meanwhile the city experienced financial stress due to President Ronald Reagan's administration's cutbacks and the downsizing of the defense industry, Proposition 13 property tax limitation, and the overloading of social services by newly arriving poor from other states and other countries. Bradley's coalition began to show cracks, as racial groups feuded and African Americans and Latinos accused him of neglect in favor of downtown and westside interests. Bradley even endured a financial scandal involving consulting fees and stock holdings from two banks with which the city did business. He admitted an "error in judgment" and paid a fine but eventually was cleared of conflict-of-interest charges. Bradley called the killing and destruction that occurred in 1992 following the acquittal of the white police officers charged with beating the African American Rodney King "the most painful experience of my life." But Bradley left office with the final successes of forcing the resignation of Daryl Gates, police chief and Bradley foe since 1977, and restoring civilian control of the police department. He then joined the law firm of Brobeck, Phleger, and Harrison and generally avoided politics. After a heart attack and triple bypass surgery in 1996, Bradley suffered a stroke which left him unable to speak clearly. He died of heart failure two years later at Kaiser Permanente West Los Angeles Medical Center. He is buried in Inglewood Park Cemetery in Inglewood, California.

Bradley's *Los Angeles Times* obituary read: "Bradley's entire life was a series of firsts, a primer on how to surmount institutionalized injustice." Bradley himself once said, "I have never let an experience with discrimination or prejudice embitter me. . . . My attitude was 'That's the other guy's problem, and I'm just going to keep pushing on.'"

Bradley was six feet, four inches tall, handsome, and of athletic build. He dressed neatly in a suit and tie and was noted for his dignity and personal presence, which commanded immediate respect. A courteous, soft-spoken man, Bradley listened carefully and gave his full attention to the person at hand. He knew and remembered, uncannily at times, what was going on around him, could get to the core of an issue, and could appreciate a variety of points of view—all of which made him a master at reconciliation and building consensus. He worked long hours, and defeat only strengthened his resolve. He had an iron will and great control of his emotions. Paradoxes emerge from the various descriptions of those who knew him: Bradley was cautious, yet he took risks; his demeanor was expressionless, "sphinx-like," yet he could light up a room with his smile and wit; Bradley's style was formal and cool, yet he was a man of warmth and compassion. Many remember him as an honorable and sincere gentleman who was dedicated to serving Los Angeles and respected by the whole community.

★

The Mayor Tom Bradley Administrative Papers (Collection 293) are in the Department of Special Collections, University Research Library, University of California, Los Angeles (including "The Impossible Dream," an oral history). J. Gregory Payne and Scott C. Ratzan published a biography, *Tom Bradley: The Impossible Dream* (1986). Raphael J. Sonenschein, *Politics in Black and White: Race and Power in Los Angeles* (1993), analyzes Bradley's entire political career but is short on personal detail. Obituaries are in the *Los Angeles Times, New York Times,* and *Washington Post* (all 30 Sept. 1998).

JAMES N. LOUGHRAN

BRANSCOMB, (Bennett) Harvie (*b.* 25 December 1894 in Huntsville, Alabama; *d.* 24 July 1998 in Nashville, Tennessee), international educator, theologian, and university chancellor who guided the twentieth-century expansion of Vanderbilt University in Nashville, Tennessee.

Branscomb was one of two children born to Lewis Capers Branscomb, a prominent Methodist minister in Bessemer, Alabama, and Nancy McAdory, a homemaker. Branscomb's mother already had tuberculosis when she married in 1891, and she died in 1897, when Branscomb was only three. His father then married Minnie Vaughn McGee, who had seven children. Branscomb attended Birmingham College (later named Birmingham-Southern College) in Birmingham, Alabama, and earned a B.A. degree in 1913. The following year he won a Rhodes scholarship to Oxford University in England, where he received First Honors in Theology and was the recipient of the coveted Greek Prize. At Oxford, Branscomb earned B.A. and M.A. degrees in biblical studies in 1917.

While attending Oxford, Branscomb and a fellow student, O. C. Carmichael, were among a group of American student volunteers who worked for President Herbert Hoover's Commission for Relief in Belgium. The two students smuggled a politically sensitive letter from Cardinal Mercier through the German lines during World War I, despite being searched by German troops. This letter to Belgian priests encouraged resistance to the German invasion and was published in the *Times* (London). For this they were awarded the Medaille du Roi Albert, Medaille de la Reine (Belgium). Carmichael was later Branscomb's predecessor as chancellor of Vanderbilt University.

After returning from Oxford, Branscomb served as a lieutenant in the field artillery, but the war ended before he saw action. Branscomb began his teaching career in 1919 at Southern Methodist University in Dallas as a New Testament scholar, which required mastery of Greek, Hebrew, and Latin. He served as adjunct professor of philosophy (1919–1920) and as associate professor (1920–1921) and full professor of New Testament studies (1921–1925). In Dallas he met Margaret Vaughan, the daughter of a judge in Greenville, Texas. Branscomb and Vaughan were married

Harvie Branscomb on the rue de Castiglione, Paris, 1949. AP/WIDE WORLD PHOTOS

on 15 June 1921; they had three children. While he was at Southern Methodist University, Branscomb championed the right of another junior faculty member to academic freedom, a right he continued to advocate in his future university positions. In 1923 Branscomb took a year's leave of absence to complete course work for a Ph.D. in philosophy from Columbia University in New York City.

In 1925 Branscomb moved to Duke University in Durham, North Carolina, to take a faculty position in theology. While at Duke, he served as Director of Libraries (1934–1941), chairman of the Division of Ancient Languages and Literatures (1937–1944), and dean of the university's divinity school (1944–1946). In 1940, under sponsorship of the Carnegie Corporation, he published *Teaching with Books,* demonstrating that libraries were primarily repositories for research materials and were little used in classroom teaching. He received the Order of the Southern Cross from the Brazilian government for his work in reorganizing the National Library of Brazil while serving as chairman of the American Library Association Mission to Brazil in 1945.

In 1946, at age fifty-one, Branscomb was appointed Vanderbilt University's chief executive, becoming the fourth chancellor to serve since the university's founding in 1873. He knew that Vanderbilt must be open not only to all types of ideas but also to all types of people. He stressed the idea that Vanderbilt could not hope to become a true national university unless it was willing to make changes, and that meant dealing with racial integration at a time when higher education in the South was strictly segregated. In 1947 President Harry S. Truman appointed Branscomb as the first chairman of the United States Advisory Commission for Education Exchange, which he led for four years. Under his imaginative and forceful leadership during the 1950s and early 1960s, Vanderbilt University experienced dynamic growth and began the transition from an excellent regional institution to one of national prominence. Branscomb was successful in transforming the selection process for nominees to the board of trustees to attract leaders of national as well as local institutions. He recruited Harold Vanderbilt, great-grandson of the university's founder, Cornelius Vanderbilt, to membership on the board. In an effort to hire and retain distinguished scholars and scientists for the university's faculty, Branscomb urged the board to reinforce the university's commitment to academic freedom, to raise faculty salaries, and to recruit well-known faculty.

During his seventeen-year tenure as chancellor, full-time enrollment reached a record level even as test scores and grades continued to rise. The university became a more diverse institution as students from around the country were drawn to Vanderbilt, and in 1952 the university opened its doors to minority students before other private universities in the South. By the time Branscomb retired, the number of full-time faculty had doubled and faculty salaries had almost tripled. The university's annual budget increased by more than 400 percent, and the endowment grew from $38 million in 1946 to $88 million in 1963. Branscomb rebuilt the medical school, which had been recommended for closure; it became one of the outstanding institutions of its kind in the nation. Between 1953 and 1962, the schools of engineering, divinity, and law all acquired their own buildings, and fifteen new residence halls were built, more than doubling the number of buildings that existed on the campus before his tenure. In 1963, Branscomb's final year as chancellor, Vanderbilt was ranked for the first time among the top twenty private institutions in the United States.

After he retired as chancellor, Branscomb continued to work with Vanderbilt, initiating the conversations that led to the development of the Mary Jane and Albert Werthan Chair of Jewish Studies at the divinity school. Branscomb

also remained active on the international education scene, serving the vice chairman of the U.S. delegation to the Unesco General Conference in Paris in 1964. The following year he chaired the U.S. delegation to the World Conference on the Eradication of Illiteracy, held in Tehran, Iran. Branscomb died at the age of 103 of natural causes and is buried in Nashville, Tennessee.

Branscomb's vision led Vanderbilt University to become one of the top institutions in America. He successfully directed the expansion of Vanderbilt, vastly improving the facilities. He developed a controversial open admissions policy and helped shape Vanderbilt's commitment to academic freedom and faculty support. Branscomb also shaped the lives of many students, refining their knowledge of life. As chancellor, Branscomb brought Vanderbilt to new levels of recognition, quality, and possibility.

★

Branscomb's papers are housed in the Rare Book, Manuscript and Special Collection Library at Duke University. He also wrote *Purely Academic: An Autobiography* (1978). Obituaries are in the *Washington Post* and *New York Times* (both 26 July 1998).

REED B. MARKHAM

BRENNAN, William J., Jr. (*b.* 25 April 1906 in Newark, New Jersey; *d.* 24 July 1997 in Arlington, Virginia), U.S. Supreme Court Justice who wrote important decisions expanding freedom of speech and press and separation of church and state and who advocated an expansive view of institutional rights.

Brennan was the second of eight children of William J. Brennan and Agnes McDermott, both emigrants from County Roscommon, Ireland. His father, whose own father was a member of Sinn Fein, rose from shoveling coal in a brewery to head the county trade union council and in 1917 won a seat on the Newark city commission, the equivalent of the city council. Brennan's father eventually became the police commissioner and then director of public safety, the city's most powerful public official, in charge of police, fire, and licensing. Brennan graduated with honors in 1928 from the University of Pennsylvania. His father had decided early that he would become a lawyer, representing unions and working-class interests. Brennan attended Harvard Law School instead of Columbia because the Boston police commissioner told his father it was "far from the New York City night spots." While at Harvard, Brennan served as president of the student Legal Aid Society. With the help of a scholarship that paid his third year tuition after the death of his father, Brennan graduated in the top 10 percent of his class in 1931.

He returned to Newark to join the corporate law firm of Pitney, Hardin, and Skinner. Becoming a partner in

William J. Brennan, Jr. PRINTS AND PHOTOGRAPHS DIVISION, LIBRARY OF CONGRESS

1937, Brennan specialized in the burgeoning field of labor relations, representing management, a position that often made him uncomfortable despite his adeptness in dealing with people. In court, recalled one rival, "he was a vigorous, overwhelmingly able, and above all gracious opponent." During World War II, Brennan served in military procurement and the labor manpower branch of Army ordnance. His refusal after Allied victory in the European Theater to furlough servicemen based on occupational preferences, fearing that to do so would undermine morale, resulted in heated Senate hearings. He was discharged at the rank of colonel and awarded the Legion of Merit. After the war, the firm's two senior partners died, and Brennan, now a name partner, found himself effectively running the business.

Brennan became deeply active in the movement to reform New Jersey's judiciary. Leading the effort was Arthur T. Vanderbilt who became the state's chief justice. At his urging, Brennan, in 1949, was offered a position on the superior court. Brennan initially resisted, citing a substantial drop in income. "I'm a child of the depression," he said. Only when the firm agreed that he could return if he wished did he accept the post. In eighteen months he substantially reduced the backlog of cases, and he was ap-

pointed to the appellate division of superior court in 1950. Named to the New Jersey Supreme Court in 1952, Brennan evinced a broad view of state constitutional provisions in a series of cases involving self-incrimination, double jeopardy, confessions, and freedom of speech. He was likely to become the next state chief justice.

In 1956, to his surprise, Brennan was appointed to the U.S. Supreme Court. President Dwight D. Eisenhower wanted a Roman Catholic, a Democrat, and a relatively young sitting judge. Brennan fit the criteria. A lecture he gave in Washington that May on judicial reform, substituting for Vanderbilt, impressed Attorney General Herbert Brownell, who urged Brennan's appointment to replace the retiring Sherman Minton. "There was very little opposition," Brownell recalled. "Vanderbilt's good recommendation"—that Brennan had "an ideal judicial concept"—"meant a great deal to Ike. That was so important." Brennan joined the Court in a recess appointment on 16 October 1956. After hearings during which he was the only witness, the Senate confirmed him by a voice vote on 19 March 1957 with only Joseph McCarthy, who had grilled him on pending internal security cases, voting no. The experience of having his fitness to serve questioned lingered in Brennan for several years.

On the Supreme Court Brennan immediately impressed his colleagues with his swift intelligence, hard work, and warm, unassuming personality. It took five years to feel fully confident about his views, he admitted. The self-assurance came through in Brennan's opinion for the Court in *Baker* v. *Carr* (1962), holding that cases challenging unequal legislative apportionment could be heard in federal court. It led directly to the "one person–one vote" reapportionment cases that transformed American politics and remains one of the most important court decisions in the nation's history. Brennan believed that individuals should have the greatest possible access to the federal courts. His opinion in *Bivens* v. *Six Unknown Named Agents* (1971) was the first to recognize a direct right to sue a federal official for violation of a constitutional right.

From the beginning, Brennan gave substantial deference to asserted governmental interests. He focused on the manner of regulation and usually found that it stifled speech or press. "Mistaken factfinding" could "penalize . . . legitimate utterance," he wrote in *Speiser* v. *Randall* (1958). As he put it, "on the First Amendment, I was already there." His opinion for the Court in *New York Times* v. *Sullivan* (1964) reconfigured the law of libel, protecting all speech about public affairs and public officials excepting only when the officials could show that a statement was deliberately false or published in reckless disregard of the truth. In order to ensure "uninhibited, robust, and wide-open" debate, free expression must have "breathing space." The right to criticize government, Brennan wrote, is "the central meaning of the First Amendment." The opinion stands as one of the great state papers on freedom.

Brennan stood at the midpoint of the liberal coalition during the constitutional revolution of the 1960s. He had "an instinct for accommodation," gladly incorporating his colleagues' suggestions in his opinions and freely offering changes in theirs. During the Court's liberal heyday, from 1962 to 1969, Brennan averaged only two dissents each term. He had an unusually close working relationship with Chief Justice Earl Warren; they frequently talked about securing and retaining a majority for their position. Holding up his hand, fingers outstretched, Brennan liked to explain to his clerks the "rule of five," the "most important in constitutional law": "it takes five votes around here to do anything."

"Law and social justice are inseparable," Brennan said in 1964. "Least of all should a judge forget that law *is* an instrument of social justice." In *Griswold* v. *Connecticut* (1965), involving the use of contraceptive devices, he successfully urged Justice William O. Douglas to apply by analogy the First Amendment's freedom of association provision in order to establish the constitutional right to privacy. Brennan's opinion in *Eisenstadt* v. *Baird* (1972) extended this right to unmarried people to receive information about birth control. His lengthy concurring opinion in *Abington* v. *Schempp* (1963), in which the Court prohibited Bible reading and devotional prayer in public schools, was his hardest case because of his lifelong Catholicism, he said. It also led to an abortive effort to excommunicate him.

Starting with *Roth* v. *U.S.* (1957), Brennan wrote a series of opinions narrowing the definition of obscene materials not protected by the First Amendment. By the mid-1960s he was uneasy with his handiwork, which depended on "indefinite concepts as 'prurient interest,' 'patent offensiveness' [and] 'serious literary value'"; but he did not know what could replace it. In 1973 Brennan dropped the effort entirely: "the concept of 'obscenity' cannot be defined with sufficient specificity and clarity" and "fail[s] to distinguish between protected and unprotected speech" (*Miller* v. *California*). It was a rare admission of failure for any judge.

There was "really a brand-new Constitution after the Civil War" because of the Fourteenth Amendment, Brennan said. The principle of equality "is the rock upon which our Constitution rests," and he viewed its pursuit as "the noblest mission of judges." In *Green* v. *New Kent County School Board* (1968) Brennan wrote for the Court that once-segregated school districts had an "affirmative duty" to desegregate schools. He strongly defended the use of affirmative action programs. Brennan led the Court in the 1970s in striking down official discrimination on the basis of sex, creating, in *Craig* v. *Boren* (1976), a new, "intermediate" level of scrutiny under the Fourteenth Amendment's equal protection clause.

The appointment of Warren Burger as Chief Justice in 1969 changed the Court. His awkwardness in personal relations and his bumbling inefficiency in presiding at the Court's conferences, both much more than his views, propelled Brennan to new and unexpected positions. At the same time his wife Marjorie, whom he married in 1929 after she convinced him to elope in Baltimore and with whom he had three children, was operated on for throat cancer. Brennan left the Court each afternoon to be with her. He came "very close to crumbling" under the pressure and nearly retired, he said. "But she wouldn't have any part of that." After a bout with throat cancer in 1978, which almost cost him his voice, and a mild stroke in 1979, from which he fully recovered, Brennan again considered retiring and teaching instead. But he rejected the idea because on the Court he could directly affect what was most important to him.

"What got me interested in people's rights and liberties," Brennan said, "was the kind of neighborhood I was brought up in. I saw all kinds of suffering—people had to struggle." He never forgot, at age ten, seeing his father carried into the house, bloodied and beaten by police working for a local business during a transit strike. The Court's cutback on seemingly established constitutional guarantees and refusal to extend some others in the mid-1970s led Brennan, in speeches and articles, to urge state courts to expand protection of individual rights based on state constitutions. "Without the independent protective force of state law," he wrote in the *Harvard Law Review* in 1977, "the full realization of our liberties cannot be guaranteed." This article encouraged a renaissance of interest in the importance of state constitutions.

Brennan was an optimist who appealed to the better side of people's nature. He struggled as a judge, he wrote, whether to rely simply on "reason" or to "go beyond sterile rationality and have government treat its citizens with dignity. . . . A judge who operates on the basis of reason alone risks cutting himself off from the wellspring from which concepts such as dignity, decency and fairness flow." The fundamental purpose of the Constitution, Brennan believed, was to protect people from arbitrary government power. Writing for the Court in *Goldberg* v. *Kelly* (1970), he held that a state could not cut off a welfare recipient's benefits without a hearing. Brennan considered this case as possibly "my most important decision in its practical significance," and it led to the "due process revolution," a series of decisions requiring that government must follow prescribed procedures in many contexts.

In 1972 Brennan joined the Court in striking down capital punishment laws in *Furman* v. *Georgia*. "Death stands condemned as fatally offensive to human dignity," he wrote. The Court's computer system, starting in 1975, automatically noted his dissents from the Court's refusal to hear capital punishment cases; this eventually totaled over 2,500 cases. When the Court upheld new death penalty laws in 1976, Brennan, in dissent, claimed that they treat "members of the human race as nonhumans, as objects to be toyed with and discarded." He thereafter dissented in every capital case that came before the Court, claiming that the death penalty was applied arbitrarily and in a racially discriminatory manner. "One day," Brennan confidently predicted, "the Court will outlaw the death penalty. Permanently."

In the 1980s and 1990s liberals lionized Brennan. "Our hero of the Constitution," went one accolade. "He is the rock on which it rests." In early 1983, three months after the death of his first wife, he married Mary Fowler, who had been his secretary since shortly after he joined the Court. A new spryness entered his step. He also acquired a brighter wardrobe and in his speeches even adopted some mannerisms of entertainers. A freshness of outlook remained with Brennan. In his eighties he spoke on law for outer space.

Brennan tried to be philosophical about the continued trend of adverse Court decisions in the 1980s. "Twists and turns, especially with majority doctrine," were to be expected, he noted, calling his dissents "damage control." "Save me!" he said only half-rhetorically. "Is there anybody else up there?" Conservatives ferociously attacked his vision and approach. The Constitution should be interpreted, they claimed, according to the original intentions of those who adopted and ratified it. Brennan shrugged off this criticism as "little more than arrogance cloaked as humility. . . . We current justices read the Constitution in the only way we can: as Twentieth Century Americans," he said in a 1985 speech. "The ultimate question must be, what do the words of the text mean in our time? . . . For the genius of the Constitution rests not in any static meaning it might have had in a world that is dead and gone, but in the adaptability of its great principles to cope with current problems and current needs."

No constitutional provision was more important to Brennan than the First Amendment. Its "enforcement gives us this society," he said. In *Texas* v. *Johnson* (1989), he granted for the Court constitutional protection to the act of burning the American flag as political protest. "We do not desecrate the flag by punishing its desecration, for doing so we dilute the freedom that this cherished document represents," Brennan wrote. It was his most controversial opinion. To his bemusement a neighbor soon placed a flag on Brennan's apartment door. Brennan retired after suffering a small stroke in July 1990. Brennan died at age ninety-one in suburban Arlington and is buried in Arlington National Cemetery.

Short, with large ears framing a round face frequently cracked by a smile, eyes twinkling, and with a gentle, two-fisted handshake, Brennan resembled a little leprechaun. He took delight in everyone he met, speaking warmly of adversaries as he criticized their views. A tireless worker with few hobbies, Brennan wrote 1,360 opinions, many of them on a card table at home that he set up after washing the dinner dishes. His writing was always lucid, if rarely brief, and devoid of legalese. He had the gift of ringing changes on a thought.

Brennan formulated doctrine in specific cases to focus, in his words, more on "the concrete human realities at stake" than on grand constitutional theory. His legacy is greater. He constructed a massive legal edifice that, as Justice David Souter, his successor whom he befriended and to whom he became unusually close, noted at his funeral, "is an enormously powerful defining force in the contemporary life of this republic." Brennan is universally recognized for his humanity and as one of the most powerful shapers of the American Constitution.

★

Brennan's papers are in the Library of Congress. Writings on him include Kim Isaac Eisler, *A Justice for All* (1993); Hunter R. Clark, *Justice Brennan: The Great Conciliator* (1995); and E. Joshua Rosenkranz and Bernard Schwartz, eds., *Reason and Passion* (1997). Selected opinions and speeches through 1966 are collected in Stephen J. Friedman, ed., *An Affair with Freedom: Justice William J. Brennan, Jr.* (1967). Other sources include Edward de Grazia and Roger K. Newman, *Banned Films* (1982); Jeffrey T. Leeds, "A Life on the Court," *New York Times Magazine* (5 Oct. 1986); Jack David and Robert B. McKay, eds., *The Blessings of Liberty* (1989); John P. Frank, "William J. Brennan, Jr.," *Arizona State University Law Journal* (winter 1990); Nat Hentoff, "The Constitutionalist," *New Yorker* (12 Mar. 1990); Herbert Brownell with John P. Burke, *Advising Ike* (1993); Stephen J. Wermiel, "The Nomination of Justice Brennan: Eisenhower's Mistake? A Look at the Historical Record," *Constitutional Commentary* (winter 1994–1995); David M. O'Brien, *Storm Center* (1996); and Wermiel, "Justice on a Grand Scale," *Newsweek* (4 Aug. 1997). Obituaries are in the *Chicago Tribune, Los Angeles Times, New York Times,* and *Washington Post* (all 25 July 1997).

ROGER K. NEWMAN

BRICKHOUSE, John Beasley ("Jack") (*b.* 24 January 1916 in Peoria, Illinois; *d.* 6 August 1998 in Chicago, Illinois), sports broadcaster for more than forty years who announced the plays on 5,300 Chicago Cubs and Chicago White Sox games, earning himself a place in the Major League Baseball Hall of Fame.

Brickhouse was the only child of John William ("Will") Brickhouse, a sideshow barker and frustrated actor from Clarksville, Tennessee, and Daisy James, a cashier in a Pe-

Jack Brickhouse, with his wife, Pat, at the dedication of a Chicago street in his name, 1990. © BETTMANN/ CORBIS

oria hotel cigar store who was from a Welsh immigrant family and was a coal miner's daughter. Brickhouse's parents separated soon after his birth and his father died in 1919 from pneumonia. Brickhouse's teenage mother wed Gilbert G. Schultze in 1920 and the family moved in with Daisy's mother, Mae, who also lived in Peoria. Brickhouse worked odd jobs after school to help support the family. At age eight he delivered food trays at Proctor Hospital, where Mae was a cook, and found "it was a good way to keep from getting hungry." Brickhouse progressed to selling newspapers and pencils in downtown office buildings. A clever salesman, he noticed that when he broke his wrist it improved sales, so he kept the cast on long after the injury had healed.

Brickhouse began his journalism career as a freshman at Peoria Manual High School. He reported the basketball team's win at the 1930 state championships for the school newspaper, *The Manual*, and became the paper's sports editor by his senior year. He debuted on radio in his junior year, playing the part of George Washington's half brother in a school radio drama. Knowing his voice could be heard "all the way to Pekin," ten miles south of Peoria, seemed "a miracle."

After graduating from Peoria Manual in 1933, Brickhouse began attending Bradley University in Peoria. The divorce of his mother and stepfather forced him to leave Bradley in the fall of 1933 because he lacked the $100 tuition. He took a job at the Hiram Walker distillery filling gin bottles and planned on joining the Civilian Conserva-

tion Corps, but entered an announcing contest at local radio station WMBD instead. Brickhouse didn't win the contest, but his earnestness impressed the station owner, Edgar Bill, who gave him a job as a switchboard operator and part-time announcer at $17 per week.

Billed as "the nation's youngest broadcaster," Brickhouse sold ads, swept the studio, emceed barn dances, and faked man-on-the-street interviews when passersby were few. His radio career progressed quickly, although not without mishaps. In his first sports broadcast, Brickhouse mistook an extra point for a field goal in football and, while interviewing John Barrymore, asked if the noted thespian had ever acted onstage. As the station's "Town Crier," Brickhouse covered church services and read comics over the air. By 1937 he was broadcasting minor league baseball and Bradley University basketball games. When the Bradley Braves basketball team finished the season 19–1, ranked thirteenth in the nation, they helped make Brickhouse a regional celebrity. As the station's sports editor, he broadcast University of Illinois football games and Golden Gloves boxing matches. With his career on the rise, Brickhouse married Nelda Teach, a local notary public, on 7 August 1939 in Bessemer, Michigan. Eight months later, the couple moved to Chicago where Brickhouse became a staff announcer for WGN at $55 per week. The couple had two daughters; one died at birth in 1947, and the other was born on 19 April 1949.

At WGN in Chicago, Brickhouse assisted Bob Elson in calling Cubs and White Sox baseball games, reading the news, covering DePaul basketball games, conducting man-on-the-street interviews, and announcing big band broadcasts. When Elson entered the U.S. Navy in the summer of 1942, Brickhouse became WGN's full-time baseball announcer. After the 1943 season he enlisted in the Marine Corps, but was discharged later that year after being diagnosed with tuberculosis. Brickhouse returned to WGN in January 1944 and broadcast the Republican and Democratic National Conventions from Chicago on the fifteen-station Mutual Radio Network. He prepared diligently, spoke easily, and his work was widely praised. In January 1945 he was Mutual's announcer at President Franklin Roosevelt's fourth inaugural ceremony. Later that year WJJD in Chicago lured Brickhouse into broadcasting the White Sox games for $450 per week. The job change meant Brickhouse missed his only opportunity to cover the Cubs in the World Series. In 1946 WMCA in New York City paid him $35,000 per year to broadcast New York Giants baseball games, and Paramount had him announce their newsreels. Brickhouse returned to Chicago in 1947 to broadcast Cubs games on the city's only television station, WBKB, and to announce the National Football League championship season of the Chicago Cardinals (later the St. Louis and then the Arizona Cardinals).

WGN hired Brickhouse back to announce the International Golden Gloves boxing tournament from Chicago Stadium on 5 March 1948, the station's first-ever television broadcast. On 16 April 1948 Brickhouse began a twenty-year run of calling Cubs and White Sox home games for WGN, continuing his coverage of Cubs games until 1981. For twenty-four years he also broadcast the Chicago Bears football games on WGN radio; their 1963 championship season was a personal highlight. Brickhouse sometimes broadcast wrestling and professional basketball, but baseball announcing built his national reputation and made him first in the hearts of Chicago's loyal sports fans.

In 1948 the Cubs and White Sox both finished in last place, a sign of things to come. In the four decades and 5,000 games that followed, the White Sox finished first only once, in 1959, before losing the World Series in six games. The Cubs, in the meantime, were setting records for futility, finishing in the second division every year between 1948 and 1966, a period in which Brickhouse's baritone could be heard heralding every Cub homer with his trademark, "Hey, hey!" These daytime games (because Wrigley Field lacked lights for night games) became a permanent part of Chicago summers for two generations of youngsters, many of whom developed a passion for their team and its announcer; these baseball-crazed kids knew Brickhouse loved the game as much as they did. Characteristic of this enthusiasm was his call on 12 May 1970 of the 500th career homer of Cubs Hall of Famer Ernie Banks. At the crack of the bat, Brickhouse exclaimed, "There's a fly ball. Deep to left. Back. Back. That's it! Hey, hey! He did it! Everyone on your feet! This is it! Weeee!"

Each season, inevitably, as the Cubs fell farther and farther from first place, Brickhouse would encourage fans. "It might take a minor miracle," he said after a particularly crushing defeat in 1969, "but minor miracles have happened before, and the Cubs are still in this thing." Brickhouse saw sports as entertainment and he preached hope. He rooted openly for the home team throughout the 1970s, even when greater objectivity in sports reporting increasingly became the standard. In 1983 he was awarded the Ford Frick Award for his outstanding contribution to Major League Baseball. Brickhouse also received the National Sportscasters and Sportswriters Award as outstanding Illinois sportscaster (five times); he was inducted into the National Sportscasters and Sportswriters Hall of Fame (1983), the broadcasting wing of the Major League Baseball Hall of Fame (1983), Chicago Cubs Hall of Fame (1983), and American Sportscasters Association Hall of Fame (1985). Brickhouse's 5,000th baseball broadcast on 5 August 1979 was a source of civic celebration. His busy work schedule, however, took its toll; in 1978 he and Nelda were divorced. On 22 March 1980 Brickhouse married the publicist Patricia Ettelson. He retired from play-by-play work at the end of the 1981 season, having broadcast more games, and easily more losses, than anyone in the history of baseball. In 1983 Brickhouse retired from WGN as the vice president and manager of sports. After undergoing a successful operation to remove a brain tumor in early 1998, Brickhouse died of cardiac arrest on 6 August 1998 at Saint Joseph Hospital in Chicago. He is buried in Chicago's Rosehill Cemetery.

At his 1983 induction into the broadcasting wing of the Major League Baseball Hall of Fame, Brickhouse told the crowd his unrealized dream: to call a Cubs–White Sox World Series with the score tied in the seventh and deciding game, when the game at Wrigley Field had to be suspended in extra innings on account of darkness. Fans going to that field after his death traveled down Jack Brickhouse Way, saw his star in the Walk of Fame just outside the ballpark, and read the words "hey, hey" just above the outfield ivy, permanently posted on each foul pole in loving tribute to a fan favorite and family friend.

★

Brickhouse wrote an autobiography, *Thanks for Listening!* (1986). See also the biography by Janice A. Petterchak and Jerome Holzman, *Jack Brickhouse: A Voice for All Seasons* (1996). Biographical collections on Brickhouse can be found at the Major League Baseball Hall of Fame in Cooperstown, New York, and at the Museum of Broadcast Communication in Chicago, where many of his most famous television calls are kept. The Tribune Company, which owns the Chicago Cubs and WGN, maintains a biographical file on Brickhouse. A series of articles on his life and career can be found in the *Chicago Tribune* (7 and 9 Aug. 1998). Obituaries are in the *New York Times* and *Chicago Tribune* (both 7 Aug. 1998).

BRUCE J. EVENSEN

BRIDGES, Lloyd Vernet, Jr. (*b.* 15 January 1913 in San Leandro, California; *d.* 10 March 1998 in Los Angeles, California), versatile actor of stage, screen, and television.

Bridges was the only child of Lloyd Bridges, a businessman, and Harriet Brown, a homemaker. The senior Bridges, who was in the hotel business, also owned a nickelodeon in San Francisco, where the young Bridges fell in love with movies. The family had a history of entertainers, including vaudeville performers and jugglers; Bridges's father had been a silent movie actor. Lloyd, Jr., first tasted fame in 1913, when President William Howard Taft awarded him a trophy for being America's fattest baby. At Petaluma High School the athletic Bridges was captain of the baseball and basketball teams.

Bridges's father did not want him to become an actor and insisted that he study law. At the University of California at Los Angeles (UCLA), Bridges studied pre-law and majored in political science. He also joined and became president of the University Dramatic Society. Through the society he met a fellow student Dorothy Simpson, whom

Lloyd Bridges, 1967. KOBAL COLLECTION

he married on 10 March 1938. The couple had four children: Beau, Gary, Jeff, and Lucinda.

Spotted in a student play at UCLA, Bridges was offered a role and made his professional stage debut in Berkeley, California, in *The Taming of the Shrew* in 1935. After graduating in 1936 from UCLA with a B.A. degree in political science, Bridges moved to the East Coast and worked in summer stock theater companies. To earn money he and Dorothy taught drama at the Cherry Lawn School in Darien, Connecticut. After two uneventful years in New York City, Bridges joined some actor friends in forming the Playroom Club, one of the first off-Broadway theater companies. The struggling actor made his Broadway debut in 1937 in a bit part in *Othello*. A producer from Columbia Pictures, Sidney Buchman, saw Bridges in a rerun of this play in 1941 and signed him to a studio contract that led to his screen debut in *The Lone Wolf Takes a Chance* (1941). In his four years with Columbia, Bridges made more than forty-five films, mostly in supporting roles. He won good reviews for his performance in *Sahara* (1943) opposite Humphrey Bogart.

The turning point in Bridges's film career came when he left Columbia and appeared in Lewis Milestone's *A Walk in the Sun* (1945). This was followed by impressive performances in such Stanley Kramer films as *Home of the Brave* (1949), a racially charged military film in which Bridges had a supporting role, and *High Noon* (1952), in which Bridges played a cowardly deputy who refuses to aid the sheriff, played by Gary Cooper. In the early 1950s Bridges was caught in the furor of anticommunist McCarthyism. He appeared as a friendly witness before the House Un-American Activities Committee and admitted that he had been a member of the Communist Party and a member of the Actor's Lab, a radical theater group of the 1940s. As a result of his admission, Bridges was blacklisted. His film career took a dip, so Bridges returned to Broadway, where he received good reviews for his appearance costarring with Katharine Hepburn in *The Rainmaker* (1956). But when he was offered a television series, Bridges landed the role that made his a household name.

In 1957 the television producer Ivan Tors, who had seen Bridges play a sponge diver in a minor movie called *16 Fathoms Deep* (1948), offered him the role of Mike Nelson, an ex-navy frogman turned private investigator and underwater adventurer, in a series called *Sea Hunt*. Although every American network had turned down the series, Tors offered it in syndication, and it drew a larger television audience than any of the network shows. The 156 episodes of the series were filmed at Marineland of the Pacific, an aquarium on the Palos Verdes Peninsula near Los Angeles, and Bridges learned to scuba dive for the role. Always believing family comes first, Bridges introduced his sons Beau and Jeff to the American television public in *Sea Hunt*. The series was so popular that, by the time he left in 1961, Bridges was making $1 million a year.

Bridges left the series because the producers refused to address environmental issues, such as pollution of the oceans. Following *Sea Hunt,* he attempted seven other series, most short-lived. Among those series were *The Lloyd Bridges Show* (1962–1963), *The Loner* (1965–1966), *San Francisco International Airport* (1970–1971), *Lloyd Bridges' Water World* (1972), *Joe Forrester* (1975–1976), *Paper Dolls* (1984), and *Capitol News* (1990). Bridges invited his sons and his daughter to take roles in several episodes of these series.

In the 1980s Bridges discovered his comedic side and made several films in which he parodied his own macho, serious screen image. The roles in these comedy spoofs included the hard-drinking air traffic controller in *Airplane* (1980) and its sequel *Airplane II* (1982), and the severe but bungling admiral in *Hot Shots!* (1991) and its sequel *Hot Shots! Part Deux* (1993).

Bridges underwent surgery for blocked coronary arteries in 1992 but continued to act. He made his last television appearance in 1997 as a cantankerous exercise coach on the series *Seinfeld.* In 1998 he made his final two films, *Jane Austen's Mafia* and *Meeting Daddy,* in which he starred with his son Beau. Bridges died of natural causes. His body was cremated, and his ashes were scattered in places unknown.

Bridges was an athletic actor who played a variety of roles in everything from summer stock to the Broadway stage to Hollywood films to television series. He appeared in more than 100 motion pictures and was the star of eight television series during his sixty-year career. He played the reliable tough hero, the authority figure, the villain, or the comic for over half a century. His underwater television series, *Sea Hunt,* made scuba diving popular in the 1950s. He authored a book, *Mask and Flippers: The Story of Skin Diving* (1960), and he wrote the foreword to another book, *The SIDS Survival Guide: Information and Comfort for Grieving Family and Friends and Professionals Who Seek to Help Them* (1956), in memory of his son Gary, who died of sudden infant death syndrome in 1947. Bridges also showed a strong interest in social causes, including world hunger and the environment, and often made public service announcements for these causes. In 1988 he headed a Cooperative for Assistance and Relief Everywhere, Inc. (CARE) mission on hunger in sub-Saharan Africa. Six years later the Bridges received UCLA's Ralph Bunche Peace Award.

★

A complete listing of Bridges's movies and major television appearances is in the *Internet Movie Database,* <http://us.imdb.com>. Details of his life and career are in *Current Biography Yearbook* (1990) and *Biography Index* (1999). Extensive obituaries are in the *New York Times* (11 Mar. 1998) and *London Daily Telegraph* (12 Mar. 1998).

JOHN J. BYRNE

BRIMSEK, Francis Charles ("Frankie") (*b.* 26 September 1915 in Eveleth, Minnesota; *d.* 11 November 1998 in Virginia, Minnesota), one of the first American-born stars of the National Hockey League (NHL), who twice won the Vezina Trophy as the league's best goaltender.

Brimsek, known as Frankie to his friends, was born to emigrant parents from Slovenia in 1915 (some sources say 1913). He was raised in Minnesota, where he became an avid fan of ice hockey. By the time he reached high school, from which he graduated in 1932, both he and his older brother John were playing for their school team. Brimsek became the team's goalie when John gave up goaltending to became a defenseman. During these years, followed by a stint from 1934 to 1935 with the Eveleth Players of the U.S. Junior Hockey Association, Brimsek became known

Frankie Brimsek, 1941. AP/WIDE WORLD PHOTOS

as "Kid Zero" because of his amazing ability to keep a clean sheet.

Brimsek, who stood five feet, nine inches tall and weighed 170 pounds during his professional career, continued his athletic development as he joined the Pittsburgh Yellowjackets of the Eastern Association Hockey League (EAHL). He played for the Yellowjackets from 1935 to 1937, during which time he tended goal in 101 games (53 victories) and began his climb to fame. In 1936 Brimsek was awarded the first of many honors when he received the EAHL's George L. Davis, Jr., Trophy for fewest goals scored against. In 1937 Brimsek left the Yellowjackets to play for the Providence Reds of the International American Hockey League (IAHL). During his first season with Providence, he tended goal in forty-eight games, winning twenty-five, including five shutouts. He was named to the first All-Star team in the IAHL in 1938. Providence, a farm team for the NHL's Boston Bruins, brought Brimsek to the attention of the Bruins management.

The next season Brimsek moved from Providence to the National Hockey League (NHL). Joining the Bruins at a time of transition, Brimsek faced unhappy fans when he replaced Cecil "Tiny" Thompson, the beloved Boston goaltender who, at age thirty-three, was ill with an eye ailment and nearing retirement. Thompson returned to the net. However, Bruins general manager Art Ross saw great promise in Brimsek, and after Thompson was traded to the Detroit Red Wings in November 1938, Brimsek became the Bruins' primary goalie. During Brimsek's first year with the Bruins, Ross said of his new goalie, "The kid had the fastest hands I ever saw—like lightning."

Brimsek's first game for the Bruins was a 2–0 loss, but it was followed by three straight shutouts. This shutout streak amounted to 231 minutes, 54 seconds, which broke Thompson's standing record of 224 minutes, 47 seconds, and remained a twentieth-century hockey record. After a loss, Brimsek again produced three straight shutouts, including one against the Red Wings with Thompson in the net. In an echo of his junior hockey nickname, these six shutouts in seven games prompted Boston fans to call Brimsek "Mr. Zero." During his career he was also occasionally known as the "Minnesota Icicle" and "Frigid Frankie." In his first season with the Bruins, Brimsek managed a 1.56 goals against average over forty-three games. Brimsek earned the Vezina Trophy as the league-leading goalie and the Calder Trophy as the outstanding rookie of the season. He was also the first American-born and first NHL rookie named to the All-Star first team. During the 1939 play-offs, Brimsek led the Bruins to the Stanley Cup for the first time in a decade with a 1.50 goals against average.

Brimsek's successes with the Bruins continued over the next several years; he was named to the All-Star second team in 1940, played successfully for the Stanley Cup again in 1941, and won a second Vezina Trophy in 1942. The United States' entry into World War II interrupted Brimsek's professional career. He joined the U.S. Coast Guard in 1942 and served overseas after a brief appearance as the goaltender for the Coast Guard Cutters, where he played in twenty-seven games, producing nineteen victories. He returned to the Bruins for the 1945–1946 season but never reached his prewar productivity again; Brimsek himself said that his legs had lost their strength as a result of his war duties. Despite performing worse than before the war, Brimsek was named to the All-Star second team for the first three seasons after his return to the NHL. Aware that he would soon have to retire, Brimsek sought and received a trade to the Chicago Black Hawks for the 1949–1950 season. Here, even though the team ended the season in last place, Brimsek had five shutouts. His statistics over the ten years he played in the NHL included a total of 514 games with 252 victories, 182 losses, and 80 ties, with an overall 2.7 career average of goals against. The total of his victories included forty-two shutouts.

Brimsek retired from hockey in 1950. After a brief time working for his brother in Chicago he became an engineer for the Canadian National Railway, where he served for twenty-five years. He was elected to Toronto's Hockey Hall of Fame in 1966 and was the first American so honored. He was inducted into the U.S. Hockey Hall of Fame in 1973, its inaugural year. Brimsek retired to Virginia, Minnesota, just five miles from his birthplace. He died at age eighty-three of a heart attack while preparing to shovel snow and is buried at Calvary Cemetery in Virginia.

Brimsek's stellar hockey career can be attributed to determination, luck, and a psychological understanding of the game and its players. He once described how he encouraged players to think he was going to make a save with the glove, for example, drawing their attention to the stick side, which is where he intended to make his play all along. As a record-setting and highly accurate goalie, Brimsek's speed and precision on the ice began a new era for the Bruins, who began a more aggressive form of play under his leadership.

★

Information about Brimsek and his career can be found in Stan and Shirley Fischler, *The Hockey Encyclopedia: The Complete Record of Professional Ice Hockey* (1983), and Ralph Hickock, *A Who's Who of Sports Champions: Their Stories and Records* (1995). Brimsek's career is reviewed in "Teams Often Came Up Blank vs. Brimsek," *Boston Globe* (1 Oct. 1999). An obituary is in the *New York Times* (13 Nov. 1998).

JAMES J. SULLIVAN III

BROWN, George Edward, Jr. (*b.* 6 March 1920 in Holtville, California; *d.* 15 July 1999 in Bethesda, Maryland), California congressman best known for his opposition to the Vietnam War and advocacy of federal support for science and space exploration.

Brown was one of four children of George Edward Brown, Sr., and Bird Alma Kilgore, who operated a restaurant together. He graduated from Holtville Union High School in 1935 and then attended El Centro Junior College and the University of California, Los Angeles (UCLA). His liberal idealism came to light when he headed the student housing association and took as a roommate an African American, becoming the first student to do so. His studies were interrupted by military service in World War II. As a Quaker, he had registered as a conscientious objector and was assigned to a Civilian Conservation Corps camp in Oregon. There he spoke out against the internment of Japanese Americans. Brown left the camp and entered the U.S. Army (curiously, given his initial objections); he served as a second lieutenant in the infantry from 1944 to 1946. After graduating from UCLA in 1946 with a B.S. degree in industrial physics, he worked for the city of Los Angeles as a civil engineer and an administrator. Brown married Iris Pauline Miller in 1942; they had three children. After divorcing Miller, Brown married Rowena Somerindyke in 1960. After her death in 1987, he married Patience Saunders, a marriage that lasted a little over a year. In 1989 he married Marta Macias.

Brown became interested in politics and won a seat on the city council of Monterey Park in 1954, serving for four years, during three of which he was mayor. He was elected to the California State Assembly in 1958 and pushed through a bill guaranteeing public employees' right to collective bargaining. Brown waged a successful campaign to represent the Twenty-ninth Congressional District in 1962, serving from 1963 to 1971. He ran for the U.S. Senate in 1970; in the primary he faced Representative John V. Tunney, son of Gene Tunney, the former boxing champion. Brown called Tunney the "lightweight son of the heavyweight champ." As a war protester Brown gained an early lead after the U.S. invasion of Cambodia. Tunney responded by smearing Brown as a radical, and Brown lost the election. Resilient, he made a comeback, winning the seat for the Thirty-eighth Congressional District two years after his defeat; this time he served from 1973 until his death in 1999. The district, which covered part of the inland empire of California, had its boundaries redrawn in the 1970s, 1980s, and 1990s, until at last it became the Forty-second Congressional District. The district became more and more conservative with redistricting, and Brown ran some very close races in the 1990s against Republican opponents.

In his first tour at the House, Brown showed his Quaker roots in his opposition to military spending projects. When the White House requested funds to build bomb shelters in 1963, he resolutely opposed the bill. At the well of the House he asserted that the "military wants a civil defense program because it creates a climate in which nuclear war becomes more credible, more reasonable, more acceptable to the American people." He opined that the building of fallout shelters would heighten the chances of a nuclear exchange "by helping to establish a psychological climate in which such a war becomes acceptable." Brown gained a reputation as an early and fierce opponent of the Vietnam War. During a debate over a supplemental appropriations bill for military operations in Vietnam in 1965, he could not contain his doubts. He said that President Lyndon B. Johnson's Vietnam policy was based on "the illusion that liberty, democracy, and the peace of mankind can be won by the slaughter of peasants in Vietnam."

George E. Brown, Jr., 1968. AP/WIDE WORLD PHOTOS

In the 1980s, fearing a militarization of space, Brown opposed President Ronald Reagan's Strategic Defense Initiative. He offered amendments to defense authorization bills to impose yearlong moratoriums on the testing of antisatellite missiles in space, as long as the Soviets refrained from doing so. He tried for a permanent conditional ban in 1988, but failed. Yet Brown did not always oppose military spending. Starting in 1980 he began voting for the production of the B-1 bomber, admitting that he probably would not have done so, except that there were veterans who backed the plane and two Air Force bases in his district.

Brown had a strong commitment to government involvement in the environment. As a state legislator he offered the first bill that would have banned the use of lead in gasoline. He proposed elimination of cars with internal combustion engines in 1969. He helped create the Environmental Protection Agency and fought efforts to cut its appropriations. He wanted to ban oil drilling off the coast of California and pushed for development of alternative fuels and solar energy. Brown believed strongly in government support of scientific and technological research. He backed the Office of Technology Assessment in the early 1970s and played an important role in reorganizing and strengthening the National Science Foundation in the 1960s and 1980s. In 1976 he was fundamental in creating the Office of Science and Technology in the executive office of the president, which was to advise him on these matters. He wrote laws that assisted international cooperation in science by setting up joint research programs among U.S., Russian, and Mexican scientists. He backed the National Aeronautics and Space Administration fighting efforts to put the international space station on the budgetary chopping block, but he scolded the agency for allowing technical problems and cost overruns. He failed in saving the superconducting supercollider from fiscal demise in 1993.

Brown had heart valve replacement surgery in May 1999 and seemed to recover. He was admitted once again to Bethesda Naval Hospital with a postoperative infection, from which he died at age seventy-nine. His body was cremated.

Brown will always be remembered for vociferous opposition to the Vietnam War and advocacy of peace. More significant for the future, he forcefully advocated peaceful uses of science and technology. In an interview for the *New York Times* not long before he died, he admitted that as a young man he had dreamed of a scientific utopia. As a political leader, he pursued his belief that science could improve the lot of humankind.

★

There is no full-scale biography and only short accounts of Brown's political career in *The Almanac of American Politics* (1999) and the Congressional Quarterly's annual *Politics in America* (1985, 1989, and 1999) and *Almanac*. See also the *Congressional Record*. An interview is in the *New York Times* (9 Mar. 1999). Obituaries are in the *New York Times, Los Angeles Times, Orange County Register, Washington Post,* and *Washington Times* (all 17 July 1999).

TRACY S. UEBELHOR

BROWN, Raymond Edward (*b.* 22 May 1928 in New York City; *d.* 8 August 1998 in Redwood City, California), Roman Catholic priest and theological educator who was one of the most productive and influential biblical scholars of the twentieth century.

Brown was one of two sons of Robert Harold Brown, a businessman active in real estate, construction, and insurance, and Loretta Sullivan, a homemaker. The family moved from New York City to Saint Petersburg, Florida, in 1944 and then to Miami Shores, Florida, in 1949. Brown attended All Hallows School in New York City, graduating in 1944. From 1945 to 1946 he attended Saint Charles College, a minor seminary, and later went to Gregorian University (1949–1950), but returned at the start of the Korean War. He received a B.A. degree from the Catholic University of America in Washington, D.C., in 1948 and an M.A. degree in 1949; he was ordained as a Roman Catholic priest on 23 May 1953 in Miami, for the diocese of Saint Augustine. He completed a doctoral program in theology at Saint Mary's Seminary and University in Baltimore in 1955; his dissertation examined the theory of the *sensus plenior* of Scripture, the divinely inspired "fuller sense" beyond what the human authors might have recognized. Brown also obtained an S.T.B from Saint Mary's in 1951, an S.T.L. in 1953, and an S.T.D. in 1955.

In 1951 he entered the Society of Saint Sulpice, a group of Catholic priests dedicated to theological education. During his doctoral program in Semitics at Johns Hopkins University in Baltimore (1954–1958), his mentor was William Foxwell Albright, a pioneer in studying the Bible in its ancient Near Eastern historical, linguistic, and archaeological contexts. In Brown's dissertation on "mystery" in Judaism and the New Testament, he was one of the first scholars to use the Dead Sea Scrolls in biblical research. From 1958 to 1959 in Jerusalem, he collaborated in preparing the official concordance to these scrolls, also known as the Qumran manuscripts.

Brown served as a professor of Sacred Scriptures at Saint Mary's Seminary and University from 1959 to 1971. There he established an international reputation through his two-volume commentary *The Gospel According to John* (1966, 1970), in which he showed how reading John's Gospel in its original Jewish and early Christian historical contexts could clarify and enrich its literary and theological understanding. He taught Bible studies at Union Theological Seminary in New York City and at Woodstock College outside Baltimore from 1971 to 1990, and became a professor emeritus at Union upon his retirement in 1990. At Union, a historically Protestant institution, he was the first tenured Catholic professor and was active in ecumenical affairs. There he wrote *The Birth of the Messiah* (1977; rev., 1993), in which he gave particular attention to the role of Old Testament texts in the New Testament narratives about Jesus' birth and infancy (Matt. 1:2 and Luke 1:2). He also prepared a large commentary on *The Epistles of John* (1982), in which he situated these letters in the early Christian movement known as the Johannine community or school.

Brown was a popular and effective teacher. In lectures and writings he was able to explain complex and often controversial issues in a clear manner. His custom was to state the question or problem, lay out the various arguments and scholarly positions, determine what best explained the biblical evidence, and draw the most plausible conclusion or suggest that the matter could not be resolved. Brown's primary methodology was historical criticism, that is, studying the Bible in its literary, historical, and theological dimensions. He sought to show how such study could illumine human existence and theology. But he was also sensitive to the limits of the historical-critical method, and he was not afraid to say that our knowledge is limited. His comprehensive approach to research was best seen in his major books. He not only worked carefully through the primary sources but also took it as his obligation to read all the modern scholarship. Language presented few obstacles, and he diligently tracked down the most obscure publications. Readers of his books could expect an accurate and fair presentation along with a judicious assessment of the work of other scholars.

In 1990 Brown retired from teaching to devote himself even more fully to biblical research, writing, and lecturing. While residing at Saint Patrick's Seminary in Menlo Park, California, he completed *The Death of the Messiah* (1994), a detailed literary and historical analysis of the New Testament accounts of the Passion and Crucifixion of Christ. His last major work was *An Introduction to the New Testament* (1997), a survey of the historical setting, content, and theological significance of each New Testament writing. Brown was the president of the Society of Biblical Literature, the Catholic Biblical Association, and the Society of New Testament Studies. He wrote his major works largely for professors, pastors, and other people with advanced theological training, while his small books made accessible to the general public his own work and that of other biblical scholars.

In his positions on controversial historical and theological matters (for example, on Jesus' virginal conception, self-consciousness, and Resurrection, as well as on the development of the early church), Brown provided balanced judgments. Although some biblical scholars considered him to be too conservative and others regarded him as liberal, most scholars and most Catholics (including a large number of bishops who relied on him for advice about the Bible) viewed him as moderate. He was twice appointed as a member of the Pontifical Biblical Commission, a small group of senior Catholic biblical scholars chosen by the Holy Vatican to provide advice on theological and historical topics pertaining to the Bible. Apart from his academic and church involvement, Brown was a stamp collector, an opera fan, a swimmer, and a reader of detective stories. He died of a heart attack at the age of seventy. He is buried in the Sulpician Cemetery in Catonsville, Maryland.

Brown's forty books include *Jesus God and Man* (1967); *Priest and Bishop: Biblical Reflections* (1970); *The Virginal Conception and Bodily Resurrection of Jesus* (1973); *The Community of the Beloved Disciple* (1979); with John P. Meier, *Antioch and Rome: New Testament Cradles of Catholic Christianity* (1983); and *The Churches the Apostles Left Behind* (1984). He served as the coeditor of *Peter in the New Testament* (1973), and *Mary in the New Testament: A Collaborative Assessment by Protestant and Roman Catholic Scholars* (1978), as well as *The Jerome Biblical Commentary* (1968), and *The New Jerome Biblical Commentary* (1990). He also contributed articles to the *Catholic Biblical Quarterly, New Testament Studies,* and *Theological Studies.* Brown's legacy as a biblical scholar lay in his efforts at bringing together critical biblical analyses and Catholic theology. His success is in doing so in an ecumenical context, and in his reverence for the Bible as Sacred Scripture.

★

Articles written about Brown include Daniel J. Harrington, "Raymond E. Brown: A Teacher for Us All," *America* 179, no. 2 (1998): 5–6; and Joseph A. Fitzmyer, "Raymond E. Brown, S.S. in Memoriam," *Union Seminary Quarterly Review* 52, no. 3 (1998): 1–18. Obituaries are in the *New York Times* (11 Aug. 1998) and the *Chicago Tribune* and *Los Angeles Times* (both 12 Aug. 1998).

DANIEL J. HARRINGTON

BROZEN, Yale (*b.* 6 July 1917 in Kansas City, Missouri; *d.* 4 March 1998 in San Diego, California), "Chicago school" free-market economist who was critical of government regulation and consultant to business, government agencies, and President Ronald Reagan's transition team.

Brozen was one of two children of Oscar Brozen and Sarah Sholtz. He received an A.A. degree from Kansas City Community College in 1936, going on to gain a B.S. degree from the Massachusetts Institute of Technology two years later. In 1939 he obtained a B.A. degree in economics from the University of Chicago, an M.A. degree in economics the following year, and a Ph.D. in economics in 1941. While working on his doctorate, he taught social sciences at the University of Florida at Gainesville. Immediately afterward Brozen enlisted in the U.S. Army Signal Corps, completing his wartime military service as director of the corps' radar and telephone maintenance training program. He also held an assistant professorship in social science (1941–1944) at the Illinois Institute of Technology in Chicago, receiving tenure as an associate professor in 1944. In the late 1940s Brozen began publishing scholarly articles in economics journals and college economics textbooks. Brozen was an associate professor at the University of Minnesota in Minneapolis during the 1946–1947 academic year. From 1947 to 1957 he was professor of engineering economics at Northwestern University, in Evanston, Illinois.

From 1957 to his retirement thirty years later Brozen was professor of economics at the University of Chicago. From 1960 to 1984 he was director of the Chicago Graduate School of Business program in applied economics, and from 1959 to his retirement he also directed the research and development administration. On 26 April 1962 Brozen married Lee Parsons; they had two children. His second marriage, to Katherine Hart, took place on 8 November 1985.

As a member of the "Chicago school" of economists, Brozen used both technical and nontechnical arguments to increase acceptance of free-market economics. Under the auspices of the Washington, D.C.–based American Enterprise Institute for Public Policy Research (AEI), a major conservative think tank, Brozen published *Automation: The Impact of Technological Change* (1963) and *Mergers in Perspective* (1982). He also edited more than fifty other publications for AEI, seeking out youthful talent from leading universities to write these works. Some of these economists, such as Sam Peltzman and Thomas Sowell, were to become famous in their own right. The majority of these publications, belonging to the Evaluative Studies Series, carried out rigorous empirical studies of the effects of government programs and policies, comparing them to their professed goals and investigating the causes of their successes or, more often, failures. Several studies dealt with transportation and housing programs and others with agricultural subsidies, the U.S. Postal Service, and affirmative action in college faculty hiring. Another series of studies dealt specifically with aspects of energy policy. The methods used in these studies later were used by such federal regulatory oversight agencies as the Council on Wage and Price Stability and the Office of Information and Regulatory Affairs.

In Brozen's own publications, including *Concentration, Mergers, and Public Policy* (1982) and *Is the Government the Source of Monopoly? and Other Essays,* published in 1980 under the auspices of the strongly libertarian Cato Institute, he demonstrated both theoretically and empirically that a high market share for a dominant firm, in the absence of government barriers to entry, is consistent with vigorous competition, thus challenging many arguments made in the U.S. Department of Justice's antitrust suits. Although Brozen was said by a colleague to have "never seemed to come across an antitrust suit he liked," unlike other libertarian economists, he never advocated the repeal of antitrust legislation. Writing in 1965 in *New Individualist Review,* a libertarian—to some critics almost anarchist—publication edited by University of Chicago students (Brozen was a faculty adviser), Brozen asserted that the name "liberalism" had been stolen "by latter-day reactionaries" because "it stands for the opposite of what they propose." To Brozen, liberalism stood for freedom and opposition to all forms of tyranny; thus he himself stands in the tradition of the nineteenth-century British philosophers John Stuart Mill and Herbert Spencer and, some would add, Thomas Jefferson.

Critics have characterized viewpoints like Brozen's as "rich men's anarchism" and have pointed out that he worked as a consultant for such large corporations as General Motors and American Telephone and Telegraph (AT&T) and for such business groups as the National Association of Manufacturers. In the early 1970s, while serving as a consultant for a public relations firm employed by the ITT Continental Baking Company, the makers of Wonder Bread, Brozen strongly criticized a charge of false advertising made by the Federal Trade Commission. The commission asserted that the claim that Wonder Bread "helps build strong bodies twelve ways" was deceptive because other bread makers also could make this claim. Brozen replied that to require ITT Continental Baking to mention the latter fact in its advertising would be to force a business to give free publicity to its competitor's products; he likened such a requirement to the Salem witch trials. In 1978, in an opinion article in the *New York Times,* Brozen called President Jimmy Carter's proposed budget "absolutely unprecedented and utterly irresponsible."

Brozen also edited *Advertising and Society* (1974) and *The Competitive Economy: Selected Readings* (1975). He was at various times a consultant to the U.S. Department of State, the Antitrust Division of the Department of Justice, and the National Science Foundation, and he served on President Ronald Reagan's transition team. He was a member of the Mont Pelerin Society, a highly exclusive organization of libertarian economists. In 1983 Emory University awarded him the National Prize for Scholarship in Law and Economics. After his retirement from the University of Chicago in 1987, Brozen moved to San Diego, where he died at age seventy of heart disease. He is buried in San Diego.

Although one colleague characterized Brozen as "never interested in being politically correct or powerful," another praised him for his sense of humor, passion, and humanity. Brozen was introverted and sometimes standoffish, but he cared passionately about people.

★

There is no biographical work on Brozen, and information about his early life is difficult to obtain. Some biographical information appears in Marvin H. Kosters and Robert B. Helms, "Reflections on Yale Brozen and His Role at the American Enterprise Institute," *AEI Announcements* (Apr. 1998). Obituaries are in the *Chicago Tribune* (6 Mar. 1998), *New York Times* (14 Mar. 1998), *Washington Post* (16 Mar. 1998), and *University of Chicago Magazine* (Apr. 1998).

STEPHEN A. STERTZ

BUNTING-SMITH, Mary Alice Ingraham ("Polly") (*b.* 10 July 1910 in Brooklyn, New York; *d.* 21 January 1998 in Hanover, New Hampshire), microbiologist, president of Radcliffe College, and founder of the Radcliffe Institute for Independent Study.

Bunting-Smith was born into a book-filled home where her parents assumed that she and her three siblings would lead interesting and productive lives. Her father, Henry Ingraham, was a lawyer and one of the founders of the Long Island College of Medicine. Her mother, Mary Shotwell, was the president of the Brooklyn Young Women's Christian Association (YWCA) and of the YWCA's national board. An energetic woman, Bunting-Smith's mother helped to start the United Service Organizations (USO) during World War II and in her seventies, as a member of the New York City Board of Education, helped to establish the City University of New York.

Bunting-Smith, who was called Polly from childhood to distinguish her from her mother, was an avid reader but a poor student. Her mother said that she may have wasted time in terms of marks, but never in terms of learning. Because of poor health Bunting-Smith did not attend classes regularly until high school, when she developed a fascination with the sciences. She majored in physics at her mother's alma mater, Vassar College in Poughkeepsie, New York, graduating Phi Beta Kappa in 1931. With a fellowship to study microbiology she entered the University of Wisconsin, where she received her M.S. degree in agricultural bacteriology in 1933. The following year she received her Ph.D. in agricultural bacteriology and agricultural chemistry. She remained at Wisconsin for one more year, working as a research assistant.

Mary Bunting-Smith, 1960. AP/WIDE WORLD PHOTOS

At the University of Wisconsin she met and became engaged to John Bunting, a medical student. While he was in his residency, she taught at Bennington College in Vermont as an instructor in genetics. On 22 June 1937 the two were married. Then, while her husband worked as a resident at the Johns Hopkins University in Baltimore for $6 a month, Bunting-Smith supported them by teaching physiology and hygiene at nearby Goucher College. When her husband finished his residency they moved to Connecticut, where Bunting taught at Yale Medical School and Bunting-Smith worked as a research assistant in Yale's bacteriology department. This part-time position allowed Bunting-Smith the freedom to continue with her own research.

From the time she was a doctoral student, Bunting-Smith researched the effects of radiation on bacteria, focusing on the bacterium *Serrata marcescens,* which changes from red to speckled to white over several generations. Her study of this species was supported by the U.S. Atomic Energy Commission (AEC) and brought her renown in the field of microbial genetics. She also received a research grant from the American Tuberculosis Association to study the genetics of the mycobacterium that causes tuberculosis. She published numerous papers on her work.

In 1940 the first of their four children was born. For the next six years Bunting-Smith busied herself with caring for them while becoming active in their Bethany, Connecticut, community. She was a 4-H leader, served on library and school boards, and initiated the building of a new regional high school. She was one of the organizers and directors of the Public Health Nursing Association. Bunting-Smith enjoyed these family and community activities but was also glad to return to her research. From 1946 to 1947, while her husband did postdoctoral research, she lectured in the botany department at Wellesley College in Wellesley, Massachusetts, and by 1948, with the family back at Yale, she resumed her research there while serving as a research assistant in the bacteriology department. In 1952 she began lecturing in the department.

In 1954 Bunting-Smith's life changed. Her beloved husband died suddenly of a brain tumor, and she was left with four children to support. Because she was a woman, she was not offered a faculty position at Yale but was given a full-time position as a researcher and lecturer in the bacteriology department. In 1955 she was offered the deanship of Douglass College, the women's branch of Rutgers, the State University of New Jersey. Douglass fascinated her. Full of young women who were the first of their families to go to college, they often had no idea why they were there, how able they were, or how much they could contribute. She set about increasing their self-confidence. One such project involved letting the students run their own multilingual course in poetry. "It was a dandy," she said. Bunting-Smith also started an innovative part-time study program for married women, making it a great success.

Busy as a mother and as a dean, Bunting-Smith also managed to teach as a full-time professor in the college's department of bacteriology and was an honorary professor in the Rutgers Institute of Microbiology. She was an engaging and spirited teacher who involved the students by asking them novel questions to get them thinking. She also continued her research for the AEC, with additional grants from the Rutgers Research Council and the U.S. Public Health Service. In 1958 she chaired the American Council on Education's Commission on the Education of Women.

In 1959 Radcliffe College, the undergraduate college for women affiliated with Harvard University in Cambridge, Massachusetts, asked her to become the college's fifth president. While reluctant to leave Rutgers, she felt Radcliffe offered her the best platform in the country to highlight what she had come to view as a national problem, a society that discouraged women from academic and career goals with what she called a "climate of unexpectation." Often women went to college just to find a husband. In an era of early marriages, lightened housework, and lengthened lives, Bunting-Smith felt women had an obligation to put their brains and education to creative use.

She was inaugurated as the president of Radcliffe on 19 May 1960 and went right to work. Describing herself as

a geneticist with nest-building experience, early on she eliminated the school's impersonal, institutional room-and-board dormitories, creating instead close-knit, residential communities in which faculty families, graduate students, and undergraduate students lived together in residential halls. She launched a $4.5 million drive to build a new library.

In 1961, after securing $150,000 in funding from the Carnegie Foundation and from other grants, she established the Radcliffe Institute for Independent Study. This project studied the psychological and cultural factors affecting women in society and supported female artists, scientists, and scholars, particularly those who had interrupted their careers to fulfill family obligations. In its first year the institute gave twenty women residential scholarships. In the next four decades more than 1,300 women benefited from the program, which inspired similar programs at universities and colleges throughout the United States. Renamed the Mary Ingraham Bunting Institute in 1978 in her honor, the institute was one of Bunting-Smith's major contributions to the advancement of women.

In her eleven years at Radcliffe, Bunting-Smith worked to integrate the college more completely with Harvard. Radcliffe students took classes with Harvard students, but were admitted to the school separately and had their own living quarters, administration, and trustees. Under Bunting-Smith's tenure, undergraduate women received Harvard degrees for the first time and were admitted to the Harvard Business School, and the graduate schools of the two institutions merged.

In 1964 she stepped down from her presidency for one year to become the first female director of the AEC. Bunting-Smith felt women often lacked professional motivation because they saw few opportunities for advancement, and said she accepted the AEC position to make one more opportunity visible. The late 1960s found her back at Radcliffe, where in those turbulent times she dealt with student protests for minority rights and against the Vietnam War. In 1972 she retired from Radcliffe and then served for three years as an assistant to the president of Princeton University in New Jersey, where she worked on coeducational issues.

During her career Bunting-Smith became a member of the American Academy of Arts and Sciences, the President's Committee on the Status of Women, the American Society for Microbiology, and the national science board of the National Science Foundation, as well as a vice president of the Peace Corps. In 1961 she received the Eminent Achievement Award of the American Women's Association and in 1962 the Gold Medal of the National Institute of Social Scientists. On a personal note, in 1979 she married Clement A. Smith, a pediatrician and a faculty member at Harvard. He died in 1988.

On 21 January 1998 Bunting-Smith died at her home in Hanover, New Hampshire, at age eighty-seven. As an advocate for women she worked to change a society that offered educated women few opportunities to use their talents. The Mary Ingraham Bunting Institute at Radcliffe remains a symbol of her belief in women and all they can accomplish. Radcliffe College President Linda S. Wilson remembered Bunting-Smith as a distinguished leader on the national landscape and in the educational institutions that she served.

★

"One Woman, Two Lives," *Time* (3 Nov. 1961), gives a broad background on college women during this era, highlights Bunting-Smith's beliefs and efforts on their behalf, and gives a biographical sketch of her life. Her merits as a scientist are described in Martha J. Bailey, *American Women in Science* (1994), and her work as an educator is cited in Frederick Ohles, Shirley M. Ohles, and John G. Ramsey, *Biographical Dictionary of Modern American Educators* (1997). Further biographical information is in *Current Biography Yearbook* (1967). Tributes to Bunting-Smith are in *Radcliffe Quarterly* (spring 1998), and the history and current information about the Mary Ingraham Bunting Institute can be found on the Radcliffe College website. An obituary is in the *New York Times* (23 Jan. 1998).

JULIANNE CICARELLI

BURROUGHS, William Seward (*b.* 5 February 1914 in St. Louis, Missouri; *d.* 2 August 1997 in Lawrence, Kansas), novelist best known for *Naked Lunch* (1959), a landmark of postmodernism.

Burroughs had a privileged upper-class childhood in St. Louis. His paternal grandfather was a graduate of Princeton University who perfected the adding machine by incorporating an oil cylinder and formed the Burroughs Corporation. His parents were listed in the St. Louis *Social Register* and his uncle Ivy Lee was the publicist and right-hand man for the industrialist and philanthropist John D. Rockefeller. Burroughs's father, Mortimer Perry, was retiring and ineffectual; he spent his time collecting and selling antiques. His mother, Laura Lee, a descendant of General Robert E. Lee, smothered her two sons with an overdeveloped sense of Victorian propriety. She wrote several pamphlets on floral decoration for Coca-Cola and ran the family antique business.

As a young man Burroughs saw himself as an unwholesome misfit, a detestable creep, a "walking corpse," as he described himself in one anecdote. Most of the family money had been lost in the Great Depression, but there was enough left to send Burroughs to the Los Alamos Ranch School in New Mexico, a preparatory school for

William S. Burroughs. AP/WIDE WORLD PHOTOS

sickly boys; Burroughs had suffered from insomnia and troubling dreams since childhood. Instead of riding horses, Burroughs read Guy de Maupassant, Charles Baudelaire, Oscar Wilde, and André Gide. He also kept a diary account of an infatuation with a male classmate, called "The Autobiography of a Wolf."

In 1932 Burroughs entered Harvard College in Cambridge, Massachusetts, where he heard the poet T. S. Eliot attack romanticism in one of his Norton lectures. Remote, laconic, with a dark interest in crime, Burroughs kept a pet ferret in his room to discourage visitors and a pistol in his drawer. After graduating from Harvard with an A.B. degree in 1936, he briefly studied medicine in 1937 at the University of Vienna in Austria. That same year he married Ilse Herzfeld Klapper to enable her to escape the Nazis. They never lived together and their marriage was dissolved in 1946.

Burroughs returned to the United States in 1937, living briefly in New York City. In 1938 he again entered Harvard to pursue a graduate degree. With his friend Kells Elvins, he wrote "Twilight's Last Gleamings," a story about the abuses of authority during the sinking of the *Titanic,* juxtaposing lines from patriotic songs with his depictions of the ship's captain ransacking passengers' jewels from the purser's safe and boarding the first lifeboat. The story was a paradigmatic expression of his vision of a collapsing United States. After leaving Harvard in 1938, Burroughs entered psychoanalysis. Despite his academic background, he then worked variously as a bartender, exterminator, and private detective in Chicago, attempting to encounter and observe criminals. During World War II he tried to join the newly formed and supersecret Office of Strategic Services (OSS), the forerunner of the Central Intelligence Agency. He had the proper credentials and appropriate family connections—his uncle Ivy Lee was a good friend of Colonel William Donovan, who organized the agency. Burroughs passed all of the intelligence tests, but his application was denied when, during his physical examination, he admitted to having sliced off the tip of a finger to experience the sensation. Later, he claimed that his application had been jinxed by a former Harvard professor who disliked him.

After serving for three months in the U.S. Army and being released for unspecified physical reasons with the intervention of his mother, Burroughs moved in the spring of 1943 to New York City. Through his St. Louis friend Lucien Carr, who was attending New York City's Columbia University, he met the writers Allen Ginsberg and Jack Kerouac, who were also studying at Columbia. The trio's friendship and association are seen by many literary critics and historians as the birth of the Beats. Soon the three young men were sharing an apartment on 115th Street and Broadway with several young women. One of them, Joan Vollmer Adams, a married woman with a husband at war and an infant daughter, fell in love with Burroughs. At this time, Burroughs also met Herbert Huncke, a Times Square hustler and addict who was also a recruiter for Alfred Kinsey, who later became famous as a sex researcher. Huncke introduced Burroughs to morphine, and Burroughs installed Huncke in an apartment on the Lower East Side so that he could observe Huncke's subterranean life.

Both Burroughs and Vollmer became addicted to drugs by the end of the war. They fled New York City in 1947 as a result of police interest in their drug activity and settled on a farm in New Waverly, Texas, where their son was born. In Texas, Burroughs observed how the agricultural bureaucracy conspired to provide migrant labor for the big farmers. The federal bureaucracy tripled under President Harry Truman, and its regulations troubled the individualistic Burroughs. He planned to grow opium but succeeded only in growing marijuana between rows of alfalfa. In 1948, when Burroughs became worried about the local authorities, he and his family moved to Algiers, just outside New Orleans, where police apprehended him on weapons

and drug charges. In 1949, while he was out on bail, Burroughs and Vollmer retreated south to Mexico City. His fascination with Mayan culture, in particular Mayan cruelty and control systems, was subsequently reflected in his writing, especially *Naked Lunch* (1959). In the late summer of 1951 Burroughs suffered a period of nightmarish depression. On 7 September, after a night of drinking and drug taking, he fatally shot Vollmer when she balanced a glass on her head and dared him to shoot it off.

Kerouac early on had encouraged Burroughs, and the two had collaborated on an unpublished novel in the apartment near Columbia in 1944, but Burroughs had become totally blocked as a writer. During the long course of his trial in Mexico City, while he was free on bail, he began writing *Queer,* an autobiographical exploration of what he knew about the world of homosexuality; the book was not published until 1986. He also wrote *Junkie: The Confessions of an Unredeemed Drug Addict,* a naturalistic, flat account of the drug underground he had observed in Huncke's Lower East Side apartment. Burroughs sent the manuscript of this book to Ginsberg in New York City , who showed it to Carl Solomon, an editor for Ace Books. Solomon persuaded Ace to publish it (in expurgated form) as a paperback original in 1953 under the pseudonym William Lee. The unexpurgated version was published as *Junky* in 1977.

Having fled Mexico in 1952, a week before a verdict of accidental death was announced in his trial, Burroughs traveled to the backwaters of Colombia and Peru in 1953 to experiment with a drug called *ayahuasca* or *yage,* which supposedly induced telepathic states. He described some of his terrifying experiences in letters to Ginsberg, which were later published as *The Yage Letters* (1963). His trip into an inferno reminiscent of Joseph Conrad's "Heart of Darkness" (1902) seemed like some sort of purgation or expiation. In 1954 he moved to Tangier, Morocco, where drugs and boys were cheap; he lived there until 1958. Under the influence of heroin and *kif,* a hashish confection, he began taking notes on his fantasies and on the process of his own decomposition. From 1955 to 1956, using a voice of savage parody, he worked on what became *Naked Lunch,* a series of disconnected "routines" that he sent as letters to Ginsberg in New York City. Instead of the benign sociological approach of *Junky,* he described the debilitations and terrors of addiction from the inside, from the disordered, schizophrenic perspective of the addict. The result was a startling departure in form, an antinovel juxtaposing a series of mordantly bizarre burlesque sketches, fragmented, discontinuous, and expressing a hallucinated and conspiratorial vision of state control with surreal hyperbole. Typed in part by Kerouac in Burroughs's hotel room in Tangier, the novel was first published by Maurice Girodias's Olympia Press in Paris and then, after his trial and vindication by the court system, by Grove Press in the United States in 1962.

Burroughs spent most of the 1960s in London, England, working on the three subsequent installments of the *Naked Lunch* tetralogy, *The Soft Machine* (1961), *The Ticket That Exploded* (1962), and *Nova Express* (1964). His writing became as dense as that of the Irish playwright Samuel Beckett, because of what Burroughs called the cut-up device, a process introduced to him by the painter Brion Gysin. Using this technique, he would splice the work of an earlier writer like Conrad directly into his text. Also while in London, Burroughs underwent a controversial form of drug treatment under John Yerby Dent, who used apomorphine to wean people off morphine. In the short run, the treatment was successful. In later years, Burroughs reverted to heroin.

Returning to New York City early in 1973, he took over Kurt Vonnegut's creative writing class at City College in the fall of 1974. In his own writing, Burroughs adopted a less-complicated technique and a return to narrative in novels like *The Wild Boys: A Book of the Dead* (1971) and *Exterminator!* (1973). In 1978 a group of his admirers organized the Nova Convention in New York City, a four-day festival held in his honor that featured rock musicians and performance artists such as Laurie Anderson. Burroughs had emerged as a cult figure; he was photographed by Richard Avedon, Andy Warhol, and Robert Mapplethorpe, his face a cool cipher in the crowd on the cover of the Beatles record album *Sergeant Pepper's Lonely Hearts Club Band* (1967). As the result of his friendship with his assistant James Grauerholz in 1981, Burroughs moved to Lawrence, Kansas. During the 1980s he was featured on the late-night television program *Saturday Night Live* and was the subject of a documentary film by Howard Brookner. He also appeared in a series of ads for Nike and the Gap, and played a priest in a role that he seemed to have written for himself in Gus van Sant's film *Drugstore Cowboy* (1989).

Burroughs was inducted into the American Academy and Institute of Arts and Letters in 1983, despite opposition led by the novelist Glenway Wescott. His supporters included Ginsberg, the novelist Mary McCarthy, and the biographer Leon Edel. Burroughs continued to write fiction throughout the 1980s, publishing futuristic novels like *Cities of the Red Night* (1981), *The Place of Dead Roads* (1984), and *The Western Lands* (1987). He also began painting, characteristically blasting the completed work with a double-barreled Rossi shotgun. Burroughs's reputation had begun as an underground phenomenon, but by the 1990s he was regarded as a major cultural force, influencing Kurt Cobain, Lou Reed, Patti Smith, and the entire punk rock music scene, for example, as much as writers such as Norman Mailer, Thomas Pynchon, Vonnegut, or Don DeLillo. He performed with rap groups and did a music video with

U2. Several groups, such as Steely Dan, derived their names from his work.

In 1991 David Cronenberg filmed his version of *Naked Lunch* for Hollywood. In 1995 some of Burroughs's "cut-ups" and collages were displayed at the Beat retrospective show at the Whitney Museum in New York. In 1996 his paintings were displayed in the Los Angeles County Museum of Art. Burroughs died at age eighty-three when one of his heart valves collapsed; he is buried in the Burroughs family plot at Bellfontaine Cemetery in St. Louis. A journal Burroughs kept in the last nine months of his life was edited by Grauerholz and published posthumously as *Last Words: The Final Journals of William S. Burroughs* (2000).

★

The Letters of William Burroughs, 1945–1959 (1993) is edited with a brilliant introduction by Oliver Harris. Ted Morgan's *Literary Outlaw: The Life and Times of William S. Burroughs* (1988) is an impressionistic biography. John Tytell's biographical portraits are in *Naked Angels: The Lives and Literature of the Beat Generation* (1976) and *Paradise Outlaws: Remembering the Beats* (1999). John Tytell's interview with Burroughs is reprinted in the *Dictionary of Literary Biography,* vol. 237 (2001). Conrad Knickerbocker's interview, "William Burroughs," appears in George Plimpton, ed., *Writers at Work: The Paris Review Interviews,* 3d series (1967). Burroughs's self-interviews are in Daniel Odier, ed., *The Job: Interviews with William S. Burroughs* (1970). His theoretical perspectives are considered in *The Third Mind* (1978), a book that he wrote with Brion Gysin, and in John Tytell's interview with Allen Ginsberg, "On Burroughs's Work: A Conversation with Allen Ginsberg," *Partisan Review* 41, no. 2 (1974): 253–262. An obituary is in the *New York Times* (4 Aug. 1997).

JOHN TYTELL

BUSCAGLIA, Felice Leonardo ("Leo") (*b.* 31 March 1924 in Los Angeles, California; *d.* 12 June 1998 in Lake Tahoe, Nevada), author, lecturer, and college professor known for his best-selling books on the subjects of love, personal growth, and human relationships.

Buscaglia was the youngest of four children of Tulio Bartolomeo Buscaglia, a waiter for most of his life, and Rosa Cagna, a homemaker. Soon after Buscaglia's birth, the family left Los Angeles and returned to Tulio and Rosa's hometown of Aosta, a small village at the foot of the Italian Alps. They came back to Los Angeles when Buscaglia was five years old. Because the boy spoke little English, he was mistakenly assigned to a class for the mentally retarded. He was inspired, however, by his "warm, pulsating, loving teacher" Miss Hunt, and upon being reassigned to the appropriate class, was "bored for the rest of my educational career." Although his family often faced financial hardship,

Leo Buscaglia. © SAGA 1992/FRANK CAPRI/ARCHIVE PHOTOS

during which he realized he did not enjoy administrative work, he left this job to teach in the USC department of special education as an assistant professor.

Shortly after joining the USC faculty, however, Buscaglia took a two-year leave of absence, spending most of his time in Asia, where he immersed himself in Eastern philosophy and religion. *The Way of the Bull: A Voyage* (1973), an account of his Asian travels, was a best-seller in which he analyzed Zen Buddhism and Hinduism and compared them to other religions. He was promoted to associate professor in 1968 and full professor in 1975, and in both 1970 and 1972 was voted the USC professor of the year. After one of his students committed suicide in 1969, however, he began to question the value of what he taught. In response, he offered a class called "Love 1A," a noncredit course that explored topics relating to personal growth, human relationships, and death. Buscaglia, who became known as "Dr. Love," taught this class for twelve years and it became the most popular course at USC, with a waiting list of as many as 600 students.

In 1972 the publisher Charles B. Slack heard Buscaglia give a lecture and offered to publish a book based on his "love class." The book, simply titled *Love* (1972), was intended for a mass audience rather than an academic one. Sales were slow at first, but it eventually became a best-seller, like the subsequent books based on his lectures: *Personhood: The Art of Being Fully Human* (1978), *Living, Loving, and Learning* (1982), and *Loving Each Other: The Challenge of Human Relationships* (1984). Other popular works by Buscaglia included *The Fall of Freddie the Leaf* (1982), a children's book that explored the topic of death; *Bus Nine to Paradise* (1986); *Seven Stories of Christmas Love* (1987); *A Memory for Tino* (1988); and *Papa, My Father: A Celebration of Dads* (1989). He also edited the textbook *The Disabled and Their Parents: A Counseling Challenge* (1975). A lover of food and cooking, he even wrote a cookbook, *Leo Buscaglia's Love Cookbook* (1994). Five titles by Buscaglia were once on the *New York Times* best-seller list at the same time, and altogether his books sold more than 10 million copies in twenty languages during his lifetime.

In the late 1970s and early 1980s Buscaglia became a celebrity when his lectures, including "Speaking of Love" and "The Art of Being Fully Human," were televised by the Public Broadcasting Service during their fundraising weeks. He was given the nicknames "Dr. Hug" and the "hug therapist" for his tradition of hugging audience members after his lectures. Although he remained a professor-at-large at USC, Buscaglia left their faculty in 1984 to focus on writing and lecturing. He also served from 1984 to 1998 as the president and chairman of the board of the Felice Foundation, an organization that aids and rewards those who have contributed to the betterment of society by helping others. It was inspired by a young Chinese refugee

their household was a nurturing and loving one, and Buscaglia later dedicated his book *Love* (1972) to his parents, the "best teachers of love, because they never taught me, they showed me." His father, who had only attended school until fifth grade, nevertheless valued education and required each child to share something learned during the day at the dinner table.

Buscaglia graduated from Roosevelt High School, in Los Angeles, but postponed entering college to serve in the U.S. Navy during World War II, from 1941 to 1944, as a medical corpsman second class. Upon his return to the United States, he enrolled at the University of Southern California (USC) in Los Angeles and decided to become a teacher. He earned an A.B. degree in English and speech in 1950, followed by an M.A. degree in 1954 and a Ph.D. in 1963, both in language and speech pathology. During his time in graduate school from 1950 to 1960, Buscaglia worked in the California public school system as a teacher and speech therapist. In 1960 he was appointed as the supervisor of special education programs in the Pasadena city schools, but after what he described as "five very unhappy years,"

named Wong whom Buscaglia helped in Hong Kong by paying for his English-language classes. Years later, when Wong was successfully employed and wanted to repay his debt, Buscaglia told him to help someone else with the money.

Buscaglia never married, explaining, "I think we have to make choices in life, and the choice for me was to embrace all personkind rather than concentrate on one single individual." Although he was raised as a Catholic and had a firm belief in God, Buscaglia avoided institutionalized religion. He died at home from a heart attack at age seventy-four, and his ashes were scattered over the Pacific Ocean, Lake Tahoe, and Lake Geneva.

Buscaglia's popular writings have been criticized by some as being trite and too simplistic. He believed, however, that teachers are guides rather than instructors and should persuade people to act upon what they already know. He felt that education was the process of helping a person discover what is unique to him or her and how to share that with others. In the midst of a materialistic and self-centered society, Buscaglia instead advocated a simple lifestyle based on the enjoyment of everyday pleasures and the selfless sharing of love.

★

Most of Buscaglia's books contain numerous personal anecdotes that provide a great deal of autobiographical information. For further concise biographical material, see *Current Biography* (1983), and *Contemporary Authors,* rev. ed. (1989), which also includes an interview with Buscaglia. Ursula Vils, "Leo Buscaglia and a Passion for Sharing," *Los Angeles Times* (22 Apr. 1985), provides background on his educational philosophy. For an interview that elaborates on the lessons that his father taught him, see Marian Christy, "Preaching the Language of Love," *Boston Globe* (11 June 1989). Obituaries are in the *New York Times, Washington Post, Los Angeles Times*, and *Chicago Tribune* (all 13 June 1998).

ARLENE R. QUARATIELLO

BYRD, Charlie Lee (*b.* 16 September 1925 in Suffolk, Virginia; *d.* 2 December 1999 in Annapolis, Maryland), jazz guitarist who popularized the bossa nova in North America.

Byrd was the eldest of four boys born to Newman Herbert Byrd and Mary Lee Holland, a homemaker. The family moved to Chuckatuck, near Norfolk, Virginia, when Byrd was very young. His father was an amateur musician who held various jobs, among them, automobile mechanic, retailer, and deputy sheriff. At the age of nine, Byrd learned to play guitar from his father, who played the mandolin and ran a general store where local musicians gathered. Byrd then taught his younger brothers how to play as well.

Charlie Byrd playing the guitar, with disc jockey Felix Grant, 1962. © BETTMANN/CORBIS

As a youngster, Byrd and the family band played on radio shows, and he also played at high school dances. During his teen years, Byrd was captivated by the jazz music he heard on the radio. He cited Les Paul and Charlie Christian as well as the gypsy guitar phenomenon Django Reinhardt as early influences.

Byrd went on to study business from 1941 to 1943 at Virginia Polytechnic Institute and State University in Blacksburg and completed an associates degree. Byrd was drafted into the U.S. Army in 1943, during World War II, and saw combat in Europe. He left active service in 1946 as a sergeant. After the war, he performed for troops in a Special Services band.

While stationed in Paris in 1945, Byrd sought out Reinhardt, one of the inventors of jazz guitar. Byrd got a chance to play with his idol, and the experience inspired him to study jazz theory and composition at Harnett National Music School in New York City from 1947 to 1949. He also studied classical guitar under Rey de la Torre and started playing jazz gigs with a number of different groups. On 23 April 1950 Byrd married Virginia ("Ginny") Marie Darpino; they had two children. That same year he went to Washington, D.C., to study with the noted classical guitarist Sophocles Papas. In the early 1950s he firmly established himself on the East Coast jazz scene and in 1954 went to Italy on a scholarship to study under the classical guitar master Andrés Segovia.

By 1957 Byrd was working frequently at the Showboat Lounge in Washington, D.C. He divided his sets into two parts: small-band jazz and solo pieces by the seventeenth-century organist and composer Girolamo Frescobaldi and the Brazilian musician Heitor Villa-Lobos and classical pieces by Johann Sebastian Bach. Byrd's first record, *Jazz Recital,* was released in 1957, and a succession of others followed, including a collection of sixteenth-century compositions called *Classical Byrd.* In the late 1950s he worked with Woody Herman, and together they made recordings that included a few samba songs. He formed the Charlie Byrd Trio in 1957, recorded with Columbia Records, and signed with the Riverside label for a string of successful albums. In 1958 Byrd also wrote the music for Tennessee Williams's production of *The Purification* at the Arena Stage in Washington, D.C.

Byrd's brother Gene ("Joe") joined him in his band after studying bass guitar at the Peabody Institute. They continued to play and record together for the next forty years. In 1959 Byrd was named *Downbeat's* "New Artist of the Year." In 1961 he wrote the score for the film *Dead to the World* and also went to Brazil as part of a twelve-week State Department tour of South America. There he was captivated by Brazilian music and recognized the strong connection between the bossa nova and American jazz. He felt that jazz musicians could improvise within the rhythm and mood of the material that had developed in Rio de Janeiro.

After his return to the United States, Byrd persuaded the saxophonist Stan Getz to listen to the music he had brought back. Six months later the duo recorded an album at All Souls Unitarian Church in Washington, D.C. That 1962 album, *Jazz Samba,* is credited with launching the bossa nova dance craze in America. It was one of the first and most successful jazz–bossa nova hybrid albums of the era, topping the jazz and pop charts in 1963. Getz won a Grammy award for his solo on the single "Desafinado" after Byrd's contribution was excised from the shortened version. Byrd brought a court action against Getz and the record company in 1964 for his share of the royalties on the album. The case was settled out of court in Byrd's favor in 1967.

Despite that dispute, *Jazz Samba* cemented Byrd's status as a guitarist. The precision of Byrd's technique and the expressive charm of his playing appealed to a wide audience. In the late 1960s he was invited several times to play at the White House for President and Mrs. Johnson.

Byrd wrote the score for the 1970 film *Bleep,* as well as music for many stage productions in the 1970s, among them the Broadway production of *The Conversation of Patrolman O'Connor.* In 1972 Byrd moved to Annapolis and became a fixture at Maryland Inn's King of France Tavern. Byrd formed the trio Great Guitars with Herb Ellis and

Barney Kessel in 1973. That same year Byrd wrote an instruction manual for the guitar called *Charlie Byrd's Melodic Method for Guitar* that became widely used.

After Byrd's wife Ginny died in 1974, he married Marguerite "Maggie" Johnson on 25 November 1975. The couple had one child before they divorced in 1989. Byrd's son from his first marriage died in an auto accident in 1976. In 1980 Byrd opened his own Washington, D.C., jazz club, called Charlie's Georgetown, which remained in business until 1986. In 1987 he helped form the Washington Guitar Quintet, which lasted more than five years. The Community Arts Alliance of Maryland named Byrd the first Maryland Arts Treasure on 27 May 1993. Byrd was also the principal composer of music for the syndicated cooking program *Great Chefs,* which lasted almost twenty years. He wrote music suitable to culinary themes, which ranged from New Orleans jazz to Caribbean rhythms. The show was retired from production at his death.

In 1994 Byrd played at the twenty-sixth Fujitsu-Concord Jazz Festival. On 22 February 1998 he married his longtime girlfriend, Rebecca Good. In April of 1998 the Brazilian government named him Knight of the Rio Branco, an honor usually given to prominent Brazilian citizens. Byrd continued to record up until his death. His last album, *For Louis,* a tribute to Louis Armstrong, was released posthumously in March of 2000. Throughout the 1990s Byrd battled cancer, and he died at the age of seventy-three at his home in Annapolis. He is buried in a private plot in Annapolis.

Before he died, Byrd donated his extensive library to the Peabody Institute of Johns Hopkins University in Baltimore. A personal friend of Byrd, Max Corzilius, set up a scholarship fund at the school for the study of guitar, which is supported by private donations and proceeds from annual tribute concerts in Byrd's name.

During his half-century career, Byrd recorded more than 100 albums in musical styles ranging from jazz to classical to bossa nova to rock. He ignited the bossa nova flame in the United States in the 1960s and brought the sound of Spanish guitar into the jazz world. The nylon string guitarist brought together the grace and precision of classical guitar, the harmonic and melodic hipness of modern jazz, and the infectious undulating pulse of the bossa nova.

★

Byrd's personal papers are in the Charlie Byrd Library at the Peabody Institute of Johns Hopkins University in Baltimore, Maryland. Articles about Byrd are in *Washington Magazine* (July 1999), *Guitar Player* (Apr. 2000), and *Capital* (16 Mar. 2001). Obituaries are in the *Baltimore Sun, Daily Press, Washington Post,* and *Los Angeles Times* (all 3 Dec. 1999), *New York Times* (4 Dec. 1999), and *Daily Variety* (7 Dec. 1999).

TIM MARTIN CROUSE

BYRNES, Robert Francis (*b.* 30 December 1917 in Waterville, New York; *d.* 19 June 1997 in Ocean Isle, North Carolina), Indiana University historian who founded and directed the Russian and East European Institute, a premier American center for study.

Byrnes was the fifth of nine children born to Michael Joseph Byrnes, a baker, and Pauline Albicker, a homemaker. As a boy in Waterville, Byrnes demonstrated talent as a student and an athlete and earned a full scholarship to Amherst College in Massachusetts. With ten dollars in his pocket, Byrnes arrived at Amherst. There he played on the baseball team and graduated in 1939 with a B.A. degree in history and Phi Beta Kappa honors. While at Amherst, Byrnes met Eleanor Frances Jewell, a student at the University of Massachusetts. They were married on 6 June 1942 and had seven children.

Byrnes was a graduate student in history at Harvard University when World War II erupted. He left Boston in 1944 and served in military intelligence in Washington, D.C., until 1945, when he took a teaching position at Swarthmore College in Swarthmore, Pennsylvania, for one year. Between 1946 and 1953, Byrnes had a post teaching Russian history at Rutgers University in New Brunswick, New Jersey. While he was teaching there he completed his Ph.D. for Harvard in 1947. Owing to the paucity of Russian scholars after World War II, however, Byrnes was part of a select group called to contribute to advanced study of that region. For this reason Byrnes left Rutgers periodically to work for the Russian Institute at Columbia University in New York City (1948–1950) and the Institute for Advanced Study in Princeton, New Jersey (1950–1951). During the Korean War, Byrnes went back to Washington, D.C., and worked for the Office of National Estimates of the Central Intelligence Agency (1951–1954). He then worked as director of research at the Mid-European Studies Center in New York City (1954–1955), becoming director in 1955.

In 1956 Byrnes accepted a position at Indiana University in Bloomington, where he spent the rest of his career. He was regarded as a devoted teacher, excellent scholar, and extraordinary institution builder. He served as chair of the department of history (1958–1965), was the founder and director of the Russian and East European Institute (1959–1962, 1971–1975), and was the founding director of the International Affairs Center (1965–1967). It was in the throes of the anticommunist hysteria of the McCarthy era that Byrnes was one of the key initiators of postwar Slavic studies. Working closely with Indiana University's president, Herman B. Wells, Byrnes successfully strove to build world-renowned programs at the university. He was also an integral force in the initial academic exchanges with the Soviet Union and Eastern Europe during the cold war. One of the agencies that was critical in promoting academic cooperation during the uneasiness of the cold war was the Inter-University Committee on Travel Grants. Byrnes helped frame the agency's policies and then chaired the organization between 1960 and 1969, sending American scholars and students to Eastern Europe and the Soviet Union to pursue academic study. Because of the political tension, Byrnes and the other pioneers of the committee were careful to keep the words "Soviet" and "Eastern Europe" out of the title of the committee.

Byrnes was an inspiring and warm teacher who typically held graduate seminars at his home in his book-filled study. He held his students to high standards but was fair and kind, and as a mentor, he helped shape numerous careers as well as lives. Undergraduates were drawn in large numbers to his surveys of Russian and Soviet history and his class on the historical roots of contemporary issues.

Byrnes excelled as a scholar. Although his first major publication, *Antisemitism in Modern France: The Prologue to the Dreyfus Affair* (1950), was in the area of French history, the remainder of his work focused on Slavic history and studies. He wrote two major monographs in Russian history, *Pobedonostsev: His Life and Thought* (1968) and *V.O. Kliuchevsky: Historian of Russia* (1995). He also edited several volumes of essays, including *After Brezhnev: Sources of Soviet Conduct in the 1980s* (1983) and *U.S. Policy Toward Eastern Europe and the Soviet Union: Selected Essays* (1989). As part of his commitment to building and documenting Slavic Studies, he published three books: *Soviet-American Academic Exchanges, 1958–1975* (1976), *Awakening American Education to the World: the Role of Archibald Cary Coolidge* (1982), and *A History of Russian and East European Studies in the United States* (1994). Byrnes also authored or coauthored more than one hundred book chapters and articles and served as editor of the *American Historical Review* in 1976.

According to his colleagues and friends, Byrnes's success was due to his character. In addition to his appreciation of art and music, he was an avid sportsman who played tennis and followed Indiana's sports teams religiously. He savored intellectual debate and could be argumentative and opinionated when discussing issues. Those who engaged with him, however, were rarely offended by his pugnaciousness. Byrnes enjoyed the process of debate and the stimulating exchange of information and opinion. He respected and supported those who could argue well and never was hostile or angry when someone expressed opposition. While attending a family reunion in North Carolina, Byrnes suffered a heart attack and died. He is buried in Bloomington.

Byrnes was an "idea man" with expertise and insight and the passion and intensity to turn his ideas into reality. His intellectual courage was evident as he crossed barriers and promoted exchange between cold war nations. His ability as an institution builder was obvious in the prestige and success attained by the Russian and East European

Institute as well as the other organizations that he founded, shaped, and directed. His scholarship, university, organizations, family, colleagues, students, and friends all profited from his devotion and intelligence. Byrnes left a legacy of academic excellence, institutional success, and personal grace. He lived by the same motto with which he signed all his correspondence: "Onward and upward."

★

No biography of Byrnes exists, but a memoriam is available at Indiana University's website at <http://www.indiana.edu/bfc/BFC/circulars/98-99/B6-99.htm>. An obituary is in the *New York Times* (3 July 1997).

LIANN E. TSOUKAS

C

CADMUS, Paul (*b*. 17 December 1904 in New York City; *d*. 12 December 1999 in Weston, Connecticut), artist known for meticulous figurative works ranging from biting social commentary to beautiful nudes recalling works of the Renaissance.

Cadmus's parents were an interesting and exotic mix. His father, Egbert Cadmus, traced his family to Dutch immigrants who came to America in 1710. Cadmus's mother, Maria Latasa, was of Basque origin, from a family that had lived in Cuba and then immigrated to Tampa, Florida. She moved to New York City to study at the National Academy of Design, where she met her husband. The couple had two children. The family lived at 103rd Street in New York City, and Cadmus attended public schools on the Upper West Side until 1919, when he entered the National Academy of Design. There had never been any question about his vocation. On holiday at the New Jersey shore, he had said at the age of nine, "I am going to be a marine painter, and Sister is going to be a portrait painter."

Cadmus's father worked as a commercial lithographer, and both of his parents were painters, so there was nothing but encouragement for his career choice. His principal instructor at the academy was Charles Hinton, who also had been a major instructor of his parents. Hinton had studied with Jean-Léon Gérome in Paris, who himself had been a student of the French painter Jean-Auguste-Dominique Ingres. In this way Cadmus always felt himself directly linked to the classical tradition of painting. In 1922 he was given the academy's Suydam Bronze Medal for the excellence of his work. Cadmus also studied printmaking and by 1923 was selling illustrations to the *New York Herald Tribune*. He completed the academy's curriculum in 1926.

In 1928 Cadmus found work as a layout artist at Blackman and Company, an advertising agency. He worked for Blackman from 1928 to 1931, while continuing his studies at the Art Students League in the evenings and on weekends. There, in 1926, he had met Jared French, who was working on Wall Street in a stockbroker's office. Cadmus and French soon became lovers. It was French who decided that they must save their money and go to Europe, which they managed to do in 1931 as the Great Depression was deepening. As they bicycled across Europe, Cadmus had the opportunity to see religious art, which was not familiar to him at the time. It was to have a lasting and major effect on the construction and perspective of much of his later painting. Of this period Cadmus said, "Jerry French . . . really got me started into painting pictures other that just direct painting from life . . . trying to be more like the Old Masters."

The two men settled in Majorca. Cadmus's first major painting on a U.S. theme, *YMCA Locker Room* (1933), was painted there and, despite its theme, owed much to Renaissance frescoes in its design. There he also painted his first picture using the U.S. Navy as a subject, *Shore Leave* (1933). Cadmus and French returned to the United States

Paul Cadmus. CORBIS BETTMANN

in October 1933, rented an apartment on St. Luke's Place in New York City that served as both living and studio space, and applied to the Public Works of Art Project (PWAP), recently established by the government to help artists. He painted *The Fleet's In!* for the PWAP in 1934; the work was included in an exhibition at the Corcoran Gallery in Washington, D.C. The depiction of drunken sailors, floozies, and a homosexual pickup angered Admiral Hugh Rodman, who wrote to the secretary of the navy and demanded that the painting be removed from the show. The U.S. press, loving a censorship scandal, spread the news and a reproduction of the picture. Cadmus later wrote that he owed the start of his career to the admiral who had tried to suppress his painting.

Throughout the period that he worked for the PWAP, Cadmus painted pictures that commented acerbically on such New York subjects as the habitués of Greenwich Village, the half-naked mobs at Coney Island, and, more homoerotically, young men at bathhouses. Meanwhile, his living arrangement with French in his studio space in Greenwich Village was interrupted in 1937 when French married Margaret Hoening. Cadmus continued to share much of his life with the couple for many years. His first one-person show was held in 1937 at the Midtown Galler-

ies in New York City. Also in the late 1930s Cadmus became friendly with Lincoln Kirstein, a wealthy young man who had founded, with George Balanchine, the School of American Ballet and a series of other ballet companies. Kirstein, who married Cadmus's sister, Fidelma, in 1941, admired Cadmus's work and asked him to design several ballets, including *Filling Station* (1938), for which he did sets and costumes, and *Afternoon of a Faun* (1953), for which he developed the concept for the set. Cadmus also became friendly with the photographer George Platt Lynes, and the two men frequently posed for each other. The result was many fine portraits of Cadmus and some excellent paintings of Platt Lynes with his ménage-à-trois partners Monroe Wheeler and Glenway Wescott.

The realistic piece *Herrin Massacre* (1940), about the killing of twenty-six strikebreakers in Illinois, ended Cadmus's social commentary painting. World War II had begun in Europe, and there was no mood of self-criticism in the United States. This work also signaled the end of Cadmus painting in a mixed technique of oil and tempera. From 1940 on he used only the more demanding technique of egg tempera. During World War II, Cadmus devoted himself to a genre of painting that placed him among a group of artists called magic realists. His young men on beaches or dancers in studio settings made no reference to the war except obliquely, with a feeling of hovering disaster and, at the end of the war, past catastrophe. Also at this time Cadmus began taking photographs on and around Fire Island, New York, and in Provincetown, Massachusetts, with Jared and Margaret French. They called themselves PaJaMa, utilizing the first two letters of their first names, and attributed these photographs to themselves as a group. Cadmus also began a relationship with a younger painter, George Tooker. Cadmus continued to paint beautiful egg tempera works into the 1950s, but the art world's new fascination with abstract expressionism dimmed public interest in his paintings. This never deterred Cadmus, who shifted to still life in the late 1950s. He continued to live in the Greenwich Village apartment on St. Luke's Place that he originally had shared with French. After 1950 Tooker was no longer in his life.

In 1964 Cadmus met Jon Andersson, a handsome young blond who was to become his muse for the latter part of his life. He created only one biting social satire painting, *Subway Symphony* (1975–1976), in this later period. Using acid-bright colors, Cadmus in this work interpreted the New York City subways as places of danger. One of his best paintings of the period, *Study for a David and Goliath* (1971), depicted a hovering and almost devilish Andersson above the artist's head, which looked decapitated. Cadmus continued to paint and draw every day throughout the remainder of his life. He died of a heart attack five days before his ninety-fifth birthday and his ashes were buried in Andersson's family plot in New Haven, Connecticut. By the time of his death, Lincoln Kirstein, who had provided a home in Weston, Connecticut, for Cadmus and Andersson in later years, had died, as had his beloved sister and his great love, Jared French.

Cadmus was awarded the Witkowsky Prize from the Art Institute of Chicago in 1945. His works are in the permanent collections of many major U.S. museums, including the Metropolitan Museum of Art, the Whitney Museum of American Art, and the Museum of Modern Art in New York City; the Fogg Art Museum of Harvard University in Cambridge, Massachusetts; and the National Museum of American Art of the Smithsonian Institution in Washington, D.C.

★

David Leddick, *Intimate Companions: A Triography of George Platt Lynes, Paul Cadmus, Lincoln Kirstein, and Their Circle* (2000), is a study of the ways in which the lives of these three men intertwined. Lincoln Kirstein, *Paul Cadmus,* rev. ed. (1992), is a comprehensive study of the art of Paul Cadmus. David Sutherland produced a videocassette, *Paul Cadmus: Enfant Terrible at Eighty* (1984). *Collaboration: The Photographs of Paul Cadmus, Margaret French, and Jared French* (1992), published by the Twelvetrees Press, collects the works of the PaJaMa group. An obituary is in the *New York Times* (15 Dec. 1999).

DAVID LEDDICK

Herb Caen, 1994. STEVEN LEWIS/ASSOCIATED PRESS AP

CAEN, Herb Eugene (*b.* 3 April 1916 in Sacramento, California; *d.* 1 February 1997 in San Francisco, California), newspaper columnist whose idiosyncratic, humorous style and "three-dot" format made him a San Francisco icon during a nearly six-decade career in journalism.

Caen (pronounced "cane") was one of two children of Lucien Caen, who ran a diner and pool hall, and Augusta Gross, a homemaker. He grew up in the California capital Sacramento, though he often claimed he was conceived in San Francisco when his parents visited in 1915. He began his journalism career while attending Sacramento High School (1932–1934), where he wrote a gossip column under the byline "Raisen' Caen" for the school paper. He also worked from 1932 to 1934 for the *Sacramento Union,* where he started full-time as a sportswriter after receiving his diploma. He attended Sacramento Junior College in 1934.

In 1936 Caen landed a job as radio columnist for the *San Francisco Chronicle.* When the paper scrapped the column, Caen told the editor Paul Smith he wanted to write a daily column on San Francisco. The column, "It's News to Me," debuted on 5 July 1938. Caen worked at the *Chronicle* almost continuously until 1997. From 1942 to 1945 he served in the U.S. Army Air Forces. Achieving the rank of

captain, he worked in communications and as an aerial reconnaissance photo analyst in England and France during World War II. From 1950 to 1958 he wrote for the rival *San Francisco Examiner.* In 1991 Caen dropped his column's frequency from six to five days a week, then later to three.

In 1941 Caen married Beatrice Matthews; they divorced in 1948. On 15 February 1952 he married Sally Gilbert; they divorced in 1959. Caen had no children from either marriage. On 9 March 1963 he married Maria Theresa Shaw, with whom he had one son before they divorced in 1982.

Over the years Caen's column evolved into a tapestry of news items, gossip, jokes, and prose poems to San Francisco, the city he loved. Written in Caen's breezy vernacular, items were strung together with "three-dot" ellipses, a format made famous by the gossip maven Walter Winchell. The following excerpt from a 1955 *Examiner* column is typical: "V's Lee Giroux dropped in last wk. to see Cress Weltner, the Pontiac dealer, and sold him a new television show. However, Weltner is a pretty fair salesman, too. Before Giroux could break away, Weltner had sold him a black and white Pontiac convertible." It took some time to get the hang of Caen's style, but once they formed the habit, generations of readers found it hard to break. *Chronicle* surveys showed that more people read Caen's column than the paper's front page.

Caen worked his beat tirelessly, collecting items as he made his rounds of the city's bars, restaurants, parties, and performances. In the mornings he entered his office and, with the help of an assistant, went through messages and took calls from a network of tipsters. Then he cranked out the next day's column on a Royal typewriter, which he used even after the rest of the newsroom converted to computers.

Although a mention in Caen's column meant one was somebody in San Francisco, the love notes Caen wrote to his adopted hometown hooked the readers. He waxed poetic about San Francisco's hills and fog, bridges and bay, romanticizing everything from the way the light played off the Financial District's skyscrapers to the city's rowdy street life. He was quoted by the Associated Press as saying: "I hadn't realized the depth of the narcissism in this city. To this day, I think people aren't all that crazy about the gossip and political stuff—they like the sentimental stuff the best."

In contrast to another great urban columnist of the era, Chicago's Mike Royko, who cultivated an image as a man of the people, Caen loved San Francisco high society. He lived in various places around San Francisco; his addresses were almost always fashionable, whether on downtown's Russian Hill and Nob Hill, or in Pacific Heights, with its commanding views of San Francisco Bay, Alcatraz, and the Golden Gate Bridge. He dropped names almost constantly in his column, and a few kind words could boost a play or a restaurant. His politics were old-fashioned liberalism. He was a union member and a Democrat, but in his later years confessed to befuddlement at the ins and outs of political correctness in San Francisco as some of his jokes rang hollow with women and members of minority groups. Nevertheless, he impacted San Francisco life. He is credited with coining the term "beatnik" and with bestowing the nicknames "Baghdad by the Bay" on San Francisco and "Berserkeley" on the university town across the bay.

In the late 1940s and the early 1950s Caen campaigned to save San Francisco's cable cars, which soon became the city's most recognizable symbol. In the 1960s he spoke out against the Vietnam War. During the fall of 1978, when San Francisco was hit with the mass suicides of the Rev. Jim Jones's People's Temple cult and the assassinations of Mayor George Moscone and Supervisor Harvey Milk, Caen's column served, in the words of *Examiner* columnist Rob Morse, as "civic psychotherapy." In 1994 he walked the picket line with union members during a strike against the *Chronicle,* and in 1995 his defense of his longtime friend Willie Brown helped lift the former Speaker of the California Assembly to victory in the San Francisco mayoral race.

The spring of 1996 was eventful for Caen. He was eighty years old in April, and he was awarded a special Pulitzer Prize for his "extraordinary and continuing contribution as a voice and a conscience of his city." Also in April he married his longtime companion Ann Moller. On 30 May 1996 Caen, who smoked for forty years, informed *Chronicle* readers that he had inoperable lung cancer. "In a lightning flash, I passed from the world of the well to the world of the unwell, where I will now dwell for what I hope is a long time," he wrote. On 14 June 75,000 people turned out for a city-sponsored Herb Caen Day, and the city renamed the sidewalk next to the waterfront Embarcadero in his honor. Caen filed intermittent columns for the remainder of his life.

Caen died of cancer at the California Pacific Medical Center in San Francisco, and his remains were cremated. Some 2,500 people attended Caen's memorial service at Grace Cathedral, where he was eulogized by a quintessentially San Francisco quartet: Mayor Brown; the *Chronicle* editor Bill German; the comedian Robin Williams; and the longtime Caen tipster "Strange de Jim," who appeared in the pulpit wearing a pillowcase over his head. Thousands more mourned Caen across the city, and dozens of saloons offered specials on Caen's beloved "vitamin V," a vodka martini with a twist, served in a wine glass.

★

Caen's columns are bound and filed in the Bancroft Library at the University of California, Berkeley. He wrote nine books, including *Baghdad-by-the-Bay* (1949), *Don't Call It Frisco* (1953), and *One Man's San Francisco* (1976). His friend Barnaby Conrad edited *The World of Herb Caen: San Francisco 1938–1997* (1997), a collection of vintage photographs interspersed with Caen's columns and remembrances by readers. The *Chronicle* and the *Examiner* both provided extensive coverage of Caen's life, death, and the week of mourning in San Francisco that followed his death (2 Feb.–9 Feb. 1997). This coverage is available on the Internet at <http://www.sfgate.com/columnists/caen/>. Obituaries are in the *Los Angeles Times, New York Times,* and *Washington Post* (all 2 Feb. 1997).

TIM WHITMIRE

CAFARO, William Michael (*b*. 23 May 1913 in Youngstown, Ohio; *d*. 22 April 1998 in Youngstown, Ohio), real estate tycoon and leader in shopping center development whose family-owned company is one of the ten largest firms in commercial real estate development.

One of seven children born to immigrant parents, Anthony Cafaro, an entrepreneur, and Flora Diana Cafaro, a homemaker, Cafaro grew up on the east side of Youngstown. As a boy he worked as a pin-setter at the Champion Bowling Alley and delivered newspapers. At seventeen he went to work at the tube mills of Republic Steel, eventually rising to the position of shift foreman. Having an insatiable appetite for knowledge, he attended Hall's Business College and returned to East High School to study Italian and learn typing. He married Alyce Prystash on 10 February 1934. The two shared their lives until her death in 1996.

Cafaro was the youngest of three brothers; the older two were in the service during World War II, and therefore he was exempt from serving in the armed forces during the war. After World War II, Cafaro assumed ownership and management of the family-owned business, the Ritz Bar and Supper Club, a popular neighborhood gathering place. He subsequently purchased other properties, including Warren Motors, a car dealership in Warren, Ohio. In 1949 he founded William M. Cafaro and Associates with his brother John, who was the firm's vice chairman until his death in 1987. The company's first major project was the Sharon Towne Center in Sharon, Pennsylvania. John oversaw construction while William managed the development and leasing responsibilities. The name of the firm was later changed to the Cafaro Company.

In 1965 Cafaro built the American Mall in Lima, Ohio, one of the first enclosed shopping malls in the country. Another Cafaro mall is the Eastwood Mall in Niles, Ohio, built in 1969 as one of the nation's first superregional malls. Other Cafaro malls followed. The success of the company was partly attributed to a high level of financial liquidity and low levels of debt. Also, the company never built malls in major metropolitan areas, concentrating instead on the middle market. Projects initially focused in Indiana, Pennsylvania, Ohio, and West Virginia, and later expanded to Kentucky, Oregon, Tennessee, Virginia, and Washington.

"Our business stems around family: my immediate family, our corporate structure, and the family relationships we have with every tenant," Cafaro stated. This belief was connected to the loyalty that Cafaro felt toward others, and it is reflected in the management philosophy of the firm, which required that one stand by one's word. Friends and business associates agreed that "His handshake is his bond." The reputation he gained for such integrity allowed the company to form close business ties to major retailers like Montgomery Ward, Sears, Wal-Mart, Target, T. J. Maxx, J. C. Penney, and Toys "R" Us, which served as anchor stores for the shopping centers Cafaro built.

The Cafaro Company continued to rise in value, as did Cafaro's personal fortune. In 1997 *Forbes* magazine listed Cafaro as 217th on its annual list of the 400 richest people in America, with a personal fortune valued at $800 million. He had been on the list since 1989. At one time Cafaro considered taking the company public and went as far as contacting a brokerage house. He reconsidered, however, and never regretted the decision.

Cafaro was long involved in Democratic party politics and counted presidents Harry S. Truman, John F. Kennedy, Lyndon B. Johnson, Jimmy Carter, and Bill Clinton among his friends. Deeply religious, he was an active member of Our Lady of Mount Carmel Parish. He helped found the National Shrine of Our Lady of Lebanon in North Jackson, Ohio, and founded the Youngstown Chapter of the Missionaries of the Sacred Heart. Other charitable endeavors included personal involvement with the construction of the Youngstown Osteopathic Hospital, which was renamed the Cafaro Memorial Hospital. He served on many corporate boards and was a board member of the Youngstown State University Education Foundation. In 1995 the university honored him by dedicating a newly constructed residence hall as Cafaro House.

Only four days before his death, Cafaro pledged $1 million to Wheeling Jesuit University in Wheeling, West Virginia, for a student center. Originally to be named after his wife, it became "The William and Alyce Cafaro Student Center." In 1970 the President of the Republic of Italy named Cafaro a "Knight of the Order of the Star of Italian Solidarity." The National Italian American Foundation (NIAF) awarded him a lifetime achievement award in 1996. President Clinton described him in a video address as "a master builder who has helped build his community through long work in religious and civic activities."

Cafaro's devotion to the business never wavered. He rarely traveled and once recalled that the worst trip he ever took was a 1967 vacation to Hawaii, which was cut short. In a 1992 interview he stated that visiting his malls and meeting the tenants was a vacation to him.

Cafaro died at his desk of an apparent heart attack at the age of eighty-four and is buried in Calvary Cemetery in Youngstown. His three children continue to run the company. His son Anthony has served as president, his son John as executive vice president, and his daughter, Flora, as vice president and assistant treasurer. Each had been active in the management of the firm for at least twenty-five years.

Cafaro was a pioneer in the development of retail commercial real estate. He was one of the first to see the economic possibilities of an industry that became the single largest source of product and merchandise in the current marketplace. The Cafaro Company developed more than seventy commercial properties, including strip, open, and enclosed malls, amounting to more than 37 million square feet of shopping center space. His philanthropy changed the lives of many people, especially in his hometown of Youngstown.

★

The Cafaro Company holds key biographical information about Cafaro. Articles about Cafaro include entries in the annual listing in the *Forbes* 400 richest people in America issue (1989–

1997), *Chain Store Age Executive* 68, no. 5 (May 1992), and *Sharon Herald* (12 Aug. 1998). Obituaries are in the *Charleston Gazette Online* (24 Apr. 1998), *New York Times* (25 Apr. 1998), *Seattle Times* (26 Apr. 1998), and *Chain Store Age* 74, no. 6 (June 1998).

JOCELYN BERGER

CALDERONE, Mary Steichen (*b.* 1 July 1904 in New York City; *d.* 24 October 1998 in Kennett Square, Pennsylvania), a leader in the movement to promote birth control and sex education in the twentieth century.

Calderone was the first daughter of Edward Steichen and Clara E. Smith. Her father, who had emigrated from Luxembourg as a small child and grown up in Milwaukee, Wisconsin, became one of the country's most important photographers, spending much of his life in New York and Europe. Her mother had been raised in the Ozark Mountains of Missouri and was a singer and musician. The parenting styles of the Steichens differed: Edward's lifestyle was bohemian, associating with avant-garde artists and excelling at photographing nudes, and Clara tended to worry about their daughters' moral values. In May 1915, when Mrs. Steichen moved to France with her younger daughter

Mary S. Calderone, 1969. J. HARRIS/ASSOCIATED PRESS AP

Kate, Mary chose to live with her father in New York City. Eventually Calderone's parents divorced.

As a child, Calderone attended the Brearley School, an exclusive but progressive private girls' school on New York City's Upper East Side. Later she continued her education at Vassar College, majoring in chemistry and graduating in 1925, after which she apprenticed as an actor with the American Laboratory Theater. In her twenties she wed fellow actor W. Lon Martin. Their marriage resulted in two children. After her divorce in 1933, Calderone decided to become a doctor and attended medical school at the University of Rochester in upstate New York, where she received her M.D. in 1939. A one-year residency followed at Bellevue Hospital, in New York City, after which she attended Columbia University School of Public Health, where she was awarded an M.P.H. degree in 1942.

At Columbia, she met Frank A. Calderone, a district health officer on the Lower East Side, and they married in 1941. He soon became deputy commissioner of health for New York City and later chief administrative officer for the World Health Organization; after retirement he ran a theater in Hempstead, Long Island. In 1979 they separated but did not divorce, and he died in 1987.

Calderone worked as school physician in suburban Great Neck, New York, from 1949 to 1953, and for much of her adult life she lived in Old Brookville, Long Island. After this assignment she became medical director of the Planned Parenthood Federation of America, assuming the position some years before the birth control pill became available (in 1960). In this capacity in 1964, she managed to persuade the recalcitrant American Medical Association that the country's physicians should disseminate information on reproduction and birth control and prescribe birth control measures to all patients who needed them; thus she helped to introduce birth control into mainstream America. According to Jane Brody in the *New York Times,* "Dr. Calderone did more than any other individual to convince both the medical profession and the public that human sexuality goes far beyond the sex act. She heralded it as a multifaceted and vital part of a healthy life that should not be hidden under a shroud of secrecy or limited to erotic expression. . . . [She was] indefatigable and fired by a zeal for sexual responsibility and realism."

A Quaker and a Democrat, Calderone was regarded during this difficult period not only as "the grandmother of modern sex education" but also as an "aging libertine." Moderates praised her call for "responsible sexuality," but the far right denounced her as immoral. On the left, some feminists considered her politically suspect. Her distinguished demeanor helped her to defend her causes against attacks by the Christian Crusade, the conservative John Birch Society, and the Moral Majority, who claimed that her promotion of sex education in schools encouraged premature sexual experience, undermining the role of parents.

In May 1964, with five colleagues, Calderone cofounded the Sex Information and Education Council of the United States (SIECUS). She became executive director of the organization and remained in that post until 1975. She then served as president of SIECUS until 1982.

Calderone wrote numerous articles for popular and professional periodicals, edited *Abortion in the United States* (1958), and wrote *Release from Sexual Tensions* (1960) and *Manual of Family Planning and Contraceptive Practice* (1964). Later she published two books dealing with children and sexuality, *The Family Book About Sexuality* (1981; with Eric W. Johnson) and *Talking with Your Child About Sex: Questions and Answers for Children from Birth to Puberty* (1982; with James W. Ramey).

Primarily as a result of her expertise as cofounder of SIECUS, Calderone lectured widely and from 1982 to 1988. She was an adjunct professor of the program in Human Sexuality at New York University and received fifteen major awards, including the Woman of Conscience Award from the National Council of Women in 1968; the Lifetime Achievement Award from the Schlesinger Library, Radcliffe/Harvard; the Browning Award for Prevention of Diseases from the American Public Health Association; the Margaret Sanger Award from the Planned Parenthood Federation of America; the Elizabeth Blackwell Award for Distinguished Services to Humanity; and the Humanist of the Year Award from the American Humanist Association. In addition she was granted twelve honorary degrees from colleges and universities.

Calderone remained active into her eighties. On 24 October 1998, she died at the Longwood nursing home after a decade of Alzheimer's disease. On 27 October 1999 a memorial service was held for her at her first alma mater, the Brearley School. In addition to her daughters, Calderone was survived by three grandchildren and three great-grandchildren.

★

Calderone's papers are housed in the Schlesinger Library at Radcliffe College. Lois N. Magner, ed., *Doctors, Nurses, and Medical Practitioners A Bio-Bibliographical Sourcebook* (1997), includes useful information on Calderone. Ellen More, a professor of history and medical humanities at the Institute for the Medical Humanities of the University of Texas Medical Branch in Galveston, has studied and written extensively on Calderone: "Inquiry: Sex Education: 'She was a queen.' Mary Steichen Calderone and the Politics of Sexuality," *Radcliffe Quarterly* (winter 2001); *Restoring the Balance: Women Physicians and the Profession of Medicine, 1850–1995* (1999; paperback, 2001); *Transgressions: Mary Steichen Calderone and the Cultural Politics of Sexuality in Postwar America* (forthcoming). An obituary is in the *New York Times* (25 Oct.

1998). The Mary S. Calderone Library, housed at SIECUS, collects materials related to human sexuality and comprehensive sexuality education. SIECUS is located at 130 W. 42nd St., Suite 350, New York, NY 10036.

VERNE MOBERG

CALVIN, Melvin (*b*. 8 April 1911 in Saint Paul, Minnesota; *d*. 8 January 1997 in Berkeley, California), biochemist who won the Nobel Prize in chemistry in 1961 for elucidating the chemical processes of photosynthesis.

Calvin was the son of Eastern European Jewish immigrants who came to the United States in the 1880s. Elias Calvin and Rose Irene Hervitz moved to Detroit when Melvin was a small child and opened a grocery store there; later, his father went to work at an automobile manufacturing plant. Melvin attended Detroit public schools and helped out in the family store in his free time. Familiarity with the various products the store carried led to an early curiosity about the physical composition of materials. Excited when his early intuitions about matter coincided with what he was learning in the classroom, Calvin resolved to become a scientist.

After graduating from Detroit's Central High School in 1927, Calvin entered the Michigan College of Mining and

Melvin Calvin. PRINTS AND PHOTOGRAPHS DIVISION, LIBRARY OF CONGRESS

Technology (now Michigan Technological University). To finance his education, he interrupted his studies after two years and worked at a brass factory in Detroit, where he gained experience in the practical applications of chemistry. This factory experience convinced Calvin that there was a demand for engineers versed in chemical processes. When he returned to school, he became the school's first chemistry major, receiving his B.S. degree in 1931.

Calvin next enrolled in the doctoral program in chemistry at the University of Michigan, where he earned a Ph.D. in 1935. His doctoral thesis was on the electron affinity of iodine and bromine. Through a Rockefeller Foundation fellowship, Calvin did two years of postgraduate work at the University of Manchester, England, under Michael Polanyi, a professor of physical chemistry. Calvin's work in photosynthesis began at Manchester, where he researched the organic molecules from which chlorophyll is derived.

Calvin became an instructor of chemistry at the University of California at Berkeley in 1937, becoming an assistant professor in 1941, associate professor in 1945, and full professor in 1947. He retired in 1980. During World War II Calvin served as an investigator for the National Defense Research Council and as a researcher for the Manhattan Project, which developed the first atomic bomb. Calvin married Marie Genevieve Jemtegaard, a social worker of Norwegian descent, in 1942; they had three children.

In the mid-1940s Calvin was appointed director of the Bio-Organic Chemistry Group at Berkeley's Lawrence Radiation Laboratory. This administrative post made it possible for him to organize the research on photosynthesis for which he is known. By this time, scientists had only a general understanding of the complex biochemical process by which green plants, in sunlight, take carbon dioxide from the air and convert it to carbohydrates and oxygen, which is then released into the air. Using analytical techniques developed during the war, including chromatography and radioisotope analysis, Calvin set out to reveal this process. Essential to Calvin's undertaking was carbon 14, a radioactive isotope of carbon that had been used in wartime nuclear research. Carbon 14 allowed Calvin to study the "dark" reactions of photosynthesis, those that occur in the absence of light. He traced these various reactions by exposing algae cells to carbon dioxide tagged with carbon 14, and then extracting the synthesized compounds. The cycle of photosynthetic reactions that he delineated is now known as the Calvin cycle. He published his findings in *Path of Carbon in Photosynthesis* (1957). His achievement was recognized in 1959 with election to the Royal Society of London, and in 1961 with the Nobel Prize in chemistry, as stated in the award-presentation speech, for "track[ing] the various steps of the path of carbon in photosynthesis and creat[ing] a clear picture of this complicated sequence

of reactions, reactions of immense importance for life on our planet."

After he received the Nobel Prize, Calvin established the Chemical Biodynamics Division (today the Structural Biology Division) of the Lawrence Radiation Laboratory, which he led until 1980, when the distinctive round building in which this division is housed was renamed for him. His time as director was noted for a record of interdisciplinary collaboration, which included biologists, chemists, and physicists, and for projects ranging from solar energy to carcinogenesis to brain chemistry to the composition of lunar rocks.

Throughout his career, Calvin participated in scientific endeavors outside academia. He was a delegate to the International Conference on Peaceful Uses of Atomic Energy in Geneva, Switzerland, in 1955, and a member of the President's Science Advisory Committee under both John F. Kennedy and Lyndon B. Johnson. Calvin served as chairman of the Committee on Science and Public Policy of the National Academy of Sciences from 1972 to 1975, and advised the National Aeronautics and Space Administration (NASA) on extraterrestrial research. From 1981 to 1985 Calvin served on the Energy Research Advisory Board of the Department of Energy. He was a member of the board of directors of the Dow Chemical Company from 1964. Calvin's numerous honors included the National Medal of Science, which he received from President George Bush in 1989.

Diminutive and balding, Calvin was described by associates as an approachable man with alert brown eyes and an easy laugh. He was known as an effective administrator, quick to make decisions, and as a talented lecturer, whose breadth of interests and roaming, inquisitive mind informed both his teaching and his research. He wrote eight books, including *The Theory of Organic Chemistry* (1941), and more than 500 scientific papers.

After his retirement, Calvin maintained a small research group on the Berkeley campus until 1996, continuing his studies on the evolution and principles of photosynthesis and its application to the production of renewable resources, among other subjects. He died at age eighty-five of a heart attack at Alta Bates Hospital in Berkeley.

Allan Laufer, of the Department of Energy's (DOE) Office of Basic Energy Sciences, told the *San Francisco Chronicle* in 1997 that Calvin's research in photosynthesis was "the cause of [the DOE] starting its solar photochemical energy conversion research. He showed [that] converting energy from the sun into useful forms was scientifically possible." Thus, Calvin's elucidation of the biochemical process vital to life may in turn affect the quality of life on Earth as alternatives to fossil fuels are increasingly sought.

★

Calvin's autobiography is *Following the Trail of Light: A Scientific Odyssey* (1992). George B. Kauffman, "Multidisciplinary Scientist—Melvin Calvin: His Life and Work," *Journal of Chemical Education* 73, no. 5 (May 1996): 412–416, highlights Calvin's broad range of inquiry and interdisciplinary approach. See also Glenn T. Seaborg and Andrew A. Benson's tribute in National Academy of Sciences, *Biographical Memoirs* 75 (1998). An oral history of the Bio-Organic Chemistry Group and its research into photosynthesis is at the Bancroft Library of the University of California at Berkeley; this collection includes transcripts of a series of interviews Calvin gave in the 1980s. Obituaries are in the *New York Times* and *San Francisco Chronicle* (both 10 Jan. 1997).

MELISSA A. DOBSON

CARAY, Harry (*b*. 1 March 1914 in St. Louis, Missouri; *d*. 18 February 1998 in Rancho Mirage, California), Hall of Fame sportscaster who covered major league baseball for more than fifty years and became one of the game's most colorful personalities.

Born Harry Christopher Carabina, Caray was the son of Christopher Carabina, a waiter, and Daisy Argint. Soon after Caray's birth, his father abandoned the family. When Caray was seven years old, his mother died and he even-

Harry Caray. CORBIS CORPORATION (BELLEVUE)

tually moved to Webster Groves, a St. Louis suburb, to live with an aunt. "The first thing I fell deeply, passionately, madly, and irrevocably in love with as a young boy was the game of baseball," Caray recalled years later. As a switch-hitting infielder for the Webster Groves High School baseball team, he was offered a tuition scholarship to play at the University of Alabama, but declined because he could not afford to pay room and board.

After high school, Caray worked as a bartender, waiter, and newspaper vendor. He played semiprofessional baseball for the Webster Groves Birds and was paid $15 to $20 a game. Although invited to try out for the St. Louis Cardinals' minor league organization, Caray was not offered a contract. "They took a good look at me," he wrote in his autobiography. "But I just didn't have the physical skills—the arm, the speed, the eyesight—to play ball professionally." Caray began working in the mid-1930s as an assistant sales manager for the Medart Manufacturing Company, which made sports equipment.

An avid Cardinals fan, Caray often attended games at Sportsman's Park in St. Louis or listened to radio broadcasts of the games. "One of the first things I noticed about baseball was how exciting it was at the ballpark—the scene, the aroma, the feeling," he told the *Sporting News* in 1987. "And I noticed how much different it came across on the radio, how the games sounded routine, almost boring. . . . That's what triggered me, I guess, when I figured it wasn't the games, it was the announcers."

Asserting that he could do better, in 1942 Caray demanded an audition for an announcing job at KMOX radio. The general manager of the St. Louis station was impressed enough to recommend him to WCLS-AM in Joliet, Illinois. It was there, at the suggestion of the station manager, that he shortened his last name to "Caray" because it "had a quicker sound." During the 1942 baseball season, he aired half-hour summaries of the Chicago Cubs and Chicago White Sox games, which he recreated from the Western Union sports ticker. "I'd take the scoring highlights and give them as much color, flavor, and authenticity as I could."

Caray became the sports director for KXOK-AM in Kalamazoo, Michigan, in 1943, and he provided play-by-play coverage for Western Michigan University football and basketball games and for a local semiprofessional baseball team. Drafted into the army later that year, he returned to St. Louis for induction but was rejected because of poor eyesight. "I couldn't see the scoreboard at Sportsman's Park, let alone the eye charts across the room," he said. Reclassified by the draft board as eligible for limited service, Caray resumed his broadcasting career.

Caray joined KXOK in St. Louis in 1944 as a staff announcer and hosted a nightly fifteen-minute sports talk show that often stirred controversy. "Every night," he recalled, "I'd be on the air blasting, ripping, praising, and slashing. I would editorialize, and I would break real scoops."

Following the 1944 World Series, Caray moved across town to become a sports announcer at KXOX. He made his debut on 17 April 1945 as the radio voice of the St. Louis Cardinals, with former Cardinals manager Gabby Street as the color analyst. At the time, two other local stations also aired the Cardinals games, and rival broadcasters Dizzy Dean and France Laux had much larger followings. But in the 1946 season, Caray and Street began reporting road games from the Western Union ticker in addition to their live coverage of home games. They expanded their listening audience as the Cardinals advanced to the 1946 National League pennant and outfielder Stan Musial came within a home run of winning the Triple Crown (awarded to the hitter who leads the league in home runs, batting average, and runs batted in). Cardinals owner Sam Breadon chose Caray and Street as the team's exclusive broadcasters in 1947.

As the announcer for the Cardinals through 1969, Caray became one of the best-known voices of the game. For his first two decades in St. Louis, the Cardinals were the southernmost team in the National League, and for many of his seasons, they were also the westernmost team. After the Anheuser-Busch company bought the franchise in 1953, Caray moved to KMOX, which became the flagship of a Cardinals network that eventually included 124 stations in fourteen states. When the Cardinals won the National League pennant in 1964, 1967, and 1968, Caray covered the World Series for NBC television. He won the *Sporting News* baseball announcer of the year award seven times. "Harry made the game different. He was excitable and he made baseball interesting," recalled Musial. "He loved life. He had fun and he loved baseball. He was always promoting the game."

Despite his vast popularity in St. Louis, Caray was fired after the 1969 baseball season. There was speculation that Caray had been romantically involved with the wife of August Busch III. "I preferred to have people believe the rumor than keep my job," he told *Inside Sports* in 1984. "I mean, think of it, I was so irresistible that a beautiful young starlet-type would go for me over the twenty-five-year-old billionaire heir to the crown."

Caray spent the 1970 season calling games in California for the Oakland Athletics, an exciting young team on the verge of becoming a dynasty. But his flamboyant style did not earn him a following in San Francisco's Bay Area, and he had an uneasy relationship with the team's owner, Charles O. Finley.

From 1971 through the 1981 season, Caray announced for the White Sox. He took a lower salary with a clause in his contract that provided he would get bonuses for attracting more people to the ballpark. When attendance increased 40 percent in Caray's first year, he collected a windfall, and management discontinued the bonus incentive. But he kept building attendance. On occasion he would strip to the waist and broadcast from the center-field bleachers. He waved a fishnet to catch foul balls from his broadcasting booth. In 1976 during the seventh-inning stretch, Caray began a tradition by leading fans in singing "Take Me out to the Ballgame." The White Sox owner, Bill Veeck, said that the announcer did much to boost his team's popularity. "It wasn't the players. It wasn't the marketing," said Veeck. "It was Caray."

Veeck sold the White Sox in 1981 to a group headed by Jerry Reinsdorf and Eddie Einhorn. Caray stayed on for the 1981 season under the new owners, but quit after a disagreement about their plan to put the White Sox on pay-per-view television.

Caray was the voice of the Cubs from 1982 through 1997. This move coincided with the emergence of WGN television as a superstation when it beamed its programming by satellite throughout the United States and abroad. Caray, with his oversized glasses that he described as picture windows, gained the largest following of his career as the Cubs announcer. Although the Cubs had losing records during most of Caray's tenure, they won division titles in 1984 and 1989. Caray was inducted into the broadcasters' wing of the Baseball Hall of Fame in 1989. "I always tried, in each and every broadcast, to serve the fans to the best of my ability," he said on this occasion. "In my mind, they are the unsung heroes of our great game." In 1994 Caray was inducted into the National Association of Broadcasters Hall of Fame.

Caray suffered a stroke in the winter of 1987 and missed the first six weeks of the season. When he returned to the broadcast booth on 19 May 1988, he received a phone call from President Ronald Reagan, himself a former Cubs broadcaster. After Caray fell and passed out before a Cubs game on 23 June 1994, he covered few road games but continued to call most home games.

Caray's personal life matched his turbulent career. He married three times, divorced twice, and fathered five children. He said that the biggest thrill of his career was on 13 May 1991 when his son Skip, the announcer for the Atlanta Braves, and grandson Chip, who was also a Braves announcer, worked a Cubs-Braves game with him. Chip joined WGN in December 1997 and was to have called the 1998 season with his grandfather.

Caray collapsed on 14 February 1998 at a restaurant in Rancho Mirage while having dinner with his third wife, Dutchie. He never regained consciousness and died four days later from brain damage resulting from cardiac arrest at the Eisenhower Medical Center. Caray is buried at All Saints Cemetery in Des Plaines, Illinois.

For more than fifty years, Caray was baseball's master showman and apostle of fun. He was witty, quick, full of enthusiasm, and often larger than life. Caray invented the trademark exclamations of "Holy Cow!" and "It might be! It could be! It is!" for home runs and other major events. A keen student of the game, he gained the respect of baseball fans for his blunt commentary on management mistakes and players who choked. "My style is a very simple one," he said in 1975. "Be entertaining, be informative and, of course, tell the truth. If you don't have the reputation for honesty, you can't keep the respect of the listener." After Caray's death, Bob Verdi of the *Chicago Tribune* wrote, "He wasn't a pretty face or golden throat, and he certainly didn't come from central casting. He was green grass and cold beer and bright sunshine. He was fun. He was a fan. He was the voice of summer, but summer will never be the same."

★

Caray wrote an autobiography with Bob Verdi, *Holy Cow!* (1989), which is as engaging as its subject. Curt Smith's *Voices of the Game: The Acclaimed Chronicle of Baseball Radio and Television Broadcasting, from 1921 to the Present,* rev. ed. (1992), includes a fine analysis of Caray's long career. Jonathan R. Laing profiled Caray on the front page of the *Wall Street Journal* (26 Sept. 1972). Caray was the cover subject of *USA Today Baseball Weekly* (25 Feb. 1998), and *TV Guide* (7 Mar. 1998). The *Chicago Tribune* (27 Feb. 1998) published a special supplement about Caray. Leigh Montville wrote a farewell tribute, "The Party's Over," *Sports Illustrated* (2 Mar. 1998). Obituaries are in the *New York Times, Chicago Sun-Times,* and *Chicago Tribune* (all 19 Feb. 1998).

STEVE NEAL

CARBERRY, John Joseph (*b.* 31 July 1904 in Brooklyn, New York; *d.* 17 June 1998 in Kirkwood, Missouri), member of the Roman Catholic hierarchy who attended all four sessions of Vatican Council II (1962–1965) and became a post-Conciliar spokesman for ecumenism, civil rights, and pro-life activities and a staunch defender of the traditional spiritual backbone of the Church.

Carberry was the youngest of ten children born to James J. Carberry, a clerk at King's County Court in Brooklyn, and Mary Elizabeth O'Keefe, a homemaker. In 1919, after attending Saint Boniface Elementary School in Brooklyn, he began studies for the priesthood at the Cathedral College of the Immaculate Conception, Brooklyn. In residence at the North American College from 1924 to 1930 in Rome while studying at the (Pope) Urban University of the Propagation of the Faith, he received a Ph.D. in philosophy in 1929 and S.T.D. (doctorate in sacred theology) in 1930.

Ordained a priest in Rome on 28 July 1929, Carberry

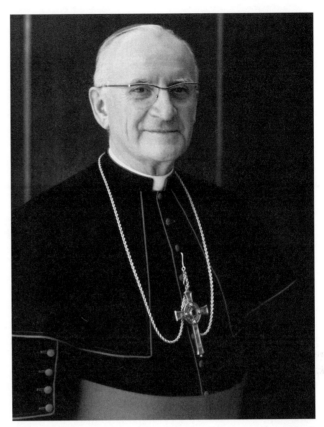

John J. Carberry, archbishop of St. Louis, on being named a cardinal, 1969. © BETTMANN/CORBIS

returned to New York, where he served on Long Island as an assistant pastor at Saint Peter's Church (1930–1931) in surburban Glen Cove and at Saint Patrick's Church (1934–1935) in Huntington. He studied at the Department of Canon Law at the Catholic University of America in Washington, D.C., where he earned a doctoral degree in canon law jurisprudence in 1934. He was loaned from the Diocese of Brooklyn to that of Trenton, New Jersey, to serve as secretary to Archbishop Moses E. Kiley and assistant chancellor. He also taught at Cathedral High School in Trenton from 1939 to 1940. Upon return to the Diocese of Brooklyn, Carberry taught at Saint Dominic's High School in Oyster Bay and then at Immaculate Conception Seminary in Huntington from 1941 to 1945. He served as officialis from December 1945 to August 1956 of the Tribunal of the Diocese of Brooklyn. Active as Director for Radio and Television for the diocese, he became known as Brooklyn's "radio priest." Pope Pius XII named him papal chamberlain in 1948 and domestic prelate in 1954. Carberry was elected in 1945 and 1955 to serve twelve-month terms as recording secretary and president, respectively, of the Canon Law Society of America.

Named coadjutor bishop of Lafeyette, Indiana, an area

consisting of close to 50,000 Roman Catholics, by Pope Pius XII, Carberry was consecrated a bishop in Brooklyn's Church (now Basilica) of Our Lady of Perpetual Help on 25 July 1956. Ten days later, he celebrated his first solemn Pontifical Mass at Saint Boniface Church. He was installed as coadjutor bishop in Saint Mary's Cathedral, Lafayette and served as officialis of the Tribunal of the Diocese and Vicar General until his installation as Bishop of Lafayette on 20 November 1957. Carberry chose "*Maria, Regina Mater*," or "Mary, Queen and Mother," as his motto. He convened Lafayette's first diocesan synod to discuss church law, the sacraments, and spiritual devotions. He established the Diocesan Council of Men and the Society for Priestly Vocations, undertook a diocesan census, and promoted rosary devotion. In 1962 Carberry was called to observe Vatican Council II in Rome. He diligently read the documents and taped commentaries from Rome for broadcast throughout the diocese. During its third session he addressed the Council on the "Declaration on Religious Liberty."

Carberry was named Bishop of Columbus, Ohio, on 20 January 1965, with its 170,000 Catholics. He called for involvement in the civil rights and ecumenical movements. In his first few years, he made his rounds throughout the diocese to explain the Council and its driving impetus of spiritual renewal. He also developed close ties with various Protestant and Jewish leaders, especially in efforts to improve housing, education, and racial justice. This collaboration helped establish the Inter-Church Board for Metropolitan Affairs (ICBMA) in 1966, the first time in the United States that a Catholic diocese was involved with a metropolitan church organization. Early joint successes included establishing the Catholic interracial justice program, Project Equality, and obtaining the first Christian chaplain within the Columbus jail system. For these and similar activities, Carberry received the Pastor of Pastors Award on 31 January 1968 from the Ohio Council of Churches.

In 1965 and 1966 the National Conference of Catholic Bishops (NCCB) elected Carberry committee chairman of its General Secretariat for Ecumenical and Interreligious Affairs. He was instrumental in monitoring the NCCB's Commission for Catholic-Jewish Relations and the ten-point *Guidelines for Catholic-Jewish Relations*. Named to the NCCB Committee on Ministry and Life of Priests, he was one of the six responsible for drafting the committee's affirmation of the celibate priesthood. In 1966 Francis Cardinal Spellman appointed Carberry vicar delegate of the Military Ordinariate for Ohio, West Virginia, Kentucky, Tennessee, Mississippi, and Alabama.

On 21 February 1968 Pope Paul VI appointed Bishop Carberry as Archbishop of St. Louis, with its 518,000 Catholics. During the installation at the Cathedral Basilica of St. Louis, Carberry paid tribute to his predecessor, "a pioneer in the race issue," the late Joseph Cardinal Ritter.

Carberry repeated his platform of working together with clergy, nuns and brothers, and laity "for the salvation of souls" and the honor and glory of God; reverence for the Church and Pope Paul VI; and "the fostering of deeper bonds" with non-Catholics. When tense debates resulted over Pope Paul VI's encyclical *Humanae Vitae* and its rejection of artificial birth control, Carberry supported the Holy Father by affirming the encyclical's "moral force." On 27 May 1969 Carberry was named a cardinal, one of four new American cardinals in the consistory of thirty-three new cardinals in Rome.

Cardinal Carberry continued to serve his St. Louis parish; he explored areas for adult religious education, issued guidelines on marriage and on teenage chastity, traveled twice to the St. Louis missions in South America, and addressed concerns for Vietnamese immigrants. In 1972 he established an Urban Services Apostolate, consisting originally of six priests to interact with inner-city parishes; in 1974 he appointed the first woman in the United States to be an assistant superintendent of a Catholic parochial school system; and in 1977 he permitted reception of communion by hand—something that he always opposed within the NCCB. When the U.S. Supreme Court decision in *Roe v. Wade* (1973) legalized abortion, Carberry became very active in the pro-life movement. He issued his pastoral letter and soon established an Archdiocesan Pro-Life Committee, the nation's first. During the 1976 presidential election year, he joined other prelates in rebuking presidential candidate Jimmy Carter for supporting his party's opposition to a constitutional amendment to ban abortion.

Carberry headed the NCCB committee that issued the pastoral letter *Behold Your Mother—Woman of Faith* in November 1973. He was one of the handful of prelates elected by the NCCB to serve as U.S. delegates to the World Synod of Bishops at the Vatican in 1971, 1974, and 1977. He was elected NCCB vice president in 1974 and served until 1977. He frequently traveled to Rome for such events as the archdiocesan Holy Year Pilgrimage, the canonization of Bishop John N. Neumann, and the conclaves to select successors to Popes Paul VI and John Paul I.

In November 1978 Carberry announced his intention to resign as Archbishop of St. Louis upon his seventy-fifth birthday, the following July. In October 1979 Carberry accompanied Pope John Paul II on his first papal visit to the United States. In November 1979 at the NCCB, Carberry voted against the inclusive language proposal to alter the English translation of the Bible for such words as "man" and "men," or "brothers" to "men and women," or "brothers and sisters." Carberry was honored on 7 December 1979 with the Patronal Medal from the Catholic University of America (in absentia, along with Mother Teresa of Calcutta) for "his singular efforts in promoting devotion to Mary." After the installation of his successor on 25 May

1980, Cardinal Carberry retained a chancery office and secretary. New organizational posts and more awards acknowledged his spiritual and civic concerns. He continued to accompany the Holy Father on several international visits.

After suffering a stroke in 1988 and experiencing difficulty in walking, Carberry was admitted to DePaul Health Center for tests and then to St. Agnes Home in Kirkwood, Missouri. He celebrated Mass every day and received telephone calls from the Pope and Mother Teresa as well as visits from specials guests, including members of the St. Louis Cardinals. Carberry's last public function was celebrating Mass at St. Agnes Home upon the twenty-fifth anniversary of the Archdiocesan Pro-Life Committee. The day of his death, Carberry, the eldest cardinal in the United States, took in some fresh air before resting in bed, where he died in his sleep at age ninety-three. Immediately following the Funeral Mass (22 June) at the Cathedral Basilica of St. Louis, he was entombed in the Cathedral Crypt.

Cardinal Carberry balanced his almost seventy years in the priesthood between a refined, sophisticated intellect and a deep spiritual commitment to his faith and Church. Known for being "totally unflappable," he upheld the Church's authority while being both gracious and good humored. Many times he relieved tense atmospheres by playing the violin or playing Irish tunes on his chromatic harmonica. In his three episcopal posts, he sought a better dialogue among the clergy, nuns and brothers, and laity, and he also fought against subjectivism, relativism, and secularism within the Church, adamantly upholding the Church's ultimate authority. He described himself as a "spiritual optimist," and his commitment to ecumenical efforts and social welfare persisted at local, state, and national levels. Cardinal Carberry served as a vital anchor for the church in America by stressing that the changing sociopolitical climate did not in the least diminish the Church's sacramental and spiritual foundation.

★

Works by Carberry include "The Juridical Form of Marriage: An Historical Conspectus and Commentary," J.C.D. diss., The Catholic University of America (1934); *Mary, Queen and Mother: Marian Pastoral Reflections* (1979); a pamphlet, *The Book of the Rosary* (1983); and Introduction to Catherine M. Odell, *Those Who Saw Her: Apparitions of Mary* (1988). Many of his writings, interviews, and pastoral letters, along with photographs, appear in the various diocesan newspapers, such as Brooklyn's *The Tablet,* Lafayette-in-Indiana's *Catholic Moment,* Columbus's *Catholic Times,* and the *St. Louis Review.* His address on "Mary's Pilgrimage of Faith," delivered at the Pontifical International Marian Congress in Zagreb, Yugoslavia, is a superior display of his message and style (13 Aug. 1971). The *New York Times* often published pieces on Carberry, including George Dugan, "Bishops Establish Ecu-

menical Body" (17 Nov. 1966); "Bishop for Everyone: John Joseph Carberry" (22 Feb. 1968); and Edward B. Fiske, "Synod Is Keeping Prelates on Run" (22 Oct. 1971). There are several articles concerning Carberry and Catholic-Jewish issues, such as Fisk, "Catholics Seek New Jewish Ties: Bishops' Guidelines Suggest Official and Lay Contacts and Prayer in Common"; a copy of the 2,000 word document issued by the Bishops' Committee for Ecumenical and Interreligious Affairs, chaired by Carberry, *Guidelines for Catholic-Jewish Relations,* is found in the same issue of the *New York Times* (16 Mar. 1967). Extensive multipaged sections on Carberry are in the *St. Louis Review* (29 Mar. 1968, 16 May 1969, 26 June 1998, and 10 July 1998); several different articles on Carberry are in *The Tablet* (27 June 1998). An obituary is in the *New York Times* (19 June 1998).

MADELINE SAPIENZA

CARL, Marion Eugene (*b.* 1 November 1915 near Hubbard, Oregon; *d.* 29 June 1998 in Roseburg, Oregon), military aviator who was the first U.S. Marine Corps ace in World War II and set speed and altitude records as a test pilot.

Carl was born on a farm in Oregon's Willamette Valley, the second of four children of Herman Lee Carl, a farmer, and Ellen Ellingsen, a homemaker and registered nurse. Raised on the family farm, he graduated from Hubbard High School in 1934 and then matriculated at Oregon State College (now Oregon State University), where he received a B.S. degree in mechanical engineering in 1938. Because enrollment in the Reserve Officer Training Corps was required at the land-grant college, Carl was commissioned as a second lieutenant in the U.S. Army Reserve Corps of Engineers. Interested in aviation, he seized the opportunity to enter flight training through the U.S. Marine Corps. After winning his wings at Pensacola, Florida, Carl accepted a commission as a second lieutenant in the corps in December 1939.

Assigned to Marine Fighter Squadron 221 (VMF-221), Carl saw early combat in World War II. Flying from Midway Island, he shot down a Mitsubishi Zero during the Battle of Midway of 4 June 1942, an action for which he received the first of two Navy Crosses. In August 1942 he joined VMF-223 shortly after the marines landed at Guadalcanal in the southwest Pacific. Carl spent three months in combat, becoming the Marine Corps' first ace, with five victories on 26 August 1942. He was credited with the destruction of 16.5 enemy aircraft. During an engagement on 9 September, Carl was forced to bail out of his heavily damaged F-4F4 Wildcat. He was picked up off the coast of Guadalcanal by friendly natives in a canoe and returned to battle five days later.

During a triumphant tour of the United States to pro-

Major Marion E. Carl with Navy Commander Turner F. Caldwell, Jr., in front of the Skystreak in which Carl set a world speed record of 650.6 miles per hour, 26 August 1947. ASSOCIATED PRESS AP

mote the sale of war bonds, Carl met Edna Theresa Kirvin, a model with the Power Agency. On 8 January 1943 they married. The lifelong happy union produced two children. Carl went back into combat in July 1943 as the commanding officer of VMF-223. Flying an F4U Corsair, he recorded two additional victories and ended the war with the Marine Corps' seventh-highest total of enemy aircraft destroyed (120). In January 1945, eight months before the defeat of Japan, Major Carl joined the first class of the new Naval Test Pilot School at the Naval Air Test Center in Patuxent River, Maryland. In August 1945 he became the first marine aviator to qualify in helicopters and later was designated Marine Helicopter Pilot Number One. Carl made an easy transition from rotary wings to jet power. During tests in November 1946 to determine whether the Lockheed P-80 would be suitable for carrier operations, he became the first marine aviator and the second American to land a jet fighter on an aircraft carrier.

Carl spent the summer of 1947 at Muroc Field (now Edwards Air Force Base) in California, testing the latest models of navy jet fighters and working to take away the world speed record from the U.S. Air Force. On 25 August he set a world speed record of 650.6 miles per hour in a Douglas D-558-1 Skystreak. Enamored of speed, both on the ground and in the air, Carl found test flying to be the closest experience to combat flying. Carl took command of VMF-122, the Marine Corps' first jet squadron, at Cherry Point, North Carolina, in September 1947. Two years later, he returned to Patuxent River for a second tour at the test center. While there, he suffered a broken back during a hard landing in a disabled aircraft and spent two months in a body cast. After recovering, Carl went on to become the first marine to qualify in rocket-powered aircraft. On 21 August 1953 he set an unofficial altitude record of 83,235 feet in a Douglas D-558–2 Skyrocket. This feat was considered unofficial because the aircraft was dropped from the belly of a B-29 rather than taking off from the ground.

Carl took command of Marine Photographic Squadron 1 (VMJ-1) in Korea from 1954 to 1956 and flew several hazardous reconnaissance missions over China. After graduating from the Air War College at Maxwell Air Force Base in Montgomery, Alabama, in 1959, Carl served in several senior positions at the Pentagon and at Marine Corps headquarters in Washington, D.C., becoming director of Marine Corps Aviation in 1962. Promoted to brigadier general in January 1964, Carl took command of the First Marine Brigade, which he led into Vietnam in 1965. He served in Hawaii as assistant wing commander of the First Marine Aircraft Wing from 1965 to 1966 and flew 12 fighter bomber and 114 helicopter combat missions in the expanding conflict. Carl was promoted to major general in August 1967. He commanded the Marine Corps Air Station (1966–1968) and the Second Marine Aircraft Wing (1968–1970) at Cherry Point, North Carolina, before becoming Inspector General of the Marine Corps in 1970. He retired on 10 July 1973, having accumulated more than 13,000 hours of flying time. Returning to his native Oregon, Carl briefly became involved in a wood-product business and a charter aircraft operation. A shotgun-wielding intruder murdered him while he was attempting to protect his wife. Carl is buried at Arlington National Cemetery in Arlington, Virginia, with full military honors.

Known for his aeronautical skills, personal modesty, and dedication to the Marine Corps, Carl was a "marine's marine" who would forever be associated with the battles that took place over the skies of Guadalcanal during the early days of World War II. Rear Admiral James D. Ramage considered him "one of the three finest Naval Aviators of the World War II generation," an assessment with which most of his contemporaries agreed.

★

Carl's papers are at the Marine Corps University Archives at Quantico, Virginia. Carl wrote his autobiography, *Pushing the En-*

velope: The Career of Fighter Ace and Test Pilot Marion Carl (1994) with the assistance of Barrett Tillman. For the aerial battles over Guadalcanal, see John B. Lundstrom, *The First Team and the Guadalcanal Campaign: Naval Fighter Combat from August to November 1942* (1994). An obituary is in the *New York Times* (30 June 1998).

WILLIAM M. LEARY

CARMICHAEL, Stokely (Kwame Touré) (*b.* 29 July 1941 in Port-of-Spain, Trinidad; *d.* 15 November 1998 in Conakry, Guinea), civil rights activist who popularized the rallying cry "Black Power!" in the 1960s.

Carmichael was the son of Adolphus Carmichael, a carpenter and taxi driver, and Mabel (also known as May Charles) Carmichael. When he was two, his parents moved to Harlem, New York, to better the family's fortunes, leaving Carmichael in the care of his two aunts and grandmother in Port-of-Spain. There, he received a traditional British education until, at age eleven, he joined his parents in Harlem. The family then moved to Morris Park, a white neighborhood in the East Bronx. Carmichael attended the prestigious Bronx High School of Science, moving in a white, liberal, middle-class circle he later reviled as phony. He graduated high school in 1960.

Rejecting scholarships from several predominantly white colleges, Carmichael chose to go to the predominantly African-American Howard University in Washington, D.C., in 1960. He had initially been indifferent to the civil rights sit-ins that began that year. "But one night when I saw those young kids on TV, getting back up on the lunch counter stools after being knocked off them, sugar in their eyes, ketchup in their hair—well, something happened to me. Suddenly I was burning." He joined the Nonviolent Action Group (NAG), a student organization involved in civil rights activity in the Washington, D.C., area that was loosely affiliated with the Student Nonviolent Coordinating Committee (SNCC). Following his freshman year he joined the Freedom Rides, the hazardous bus trips of African Americans and whites that challenged segregated interstate travel in the South. Arrested in Jackson, Mississippi, in 1961—the first of some three dozen arrests—Carmichael served seven weeks in Mississippi's infamous Parchman Penitentiary. Back at Howard, the tall, slim, handsome Carmichael became a leader of NAG, espousing the democratic socialist credo of Bayard Rustin, one of his mentors who believed that the racial question needed more of an emphasis on economic issues.

Carmichael graduated from Howard in 1964 with a B.A. degree in philosophy and became a full-time organizer for SNCC. He was chosen to direct the Council of Federated

Organizations (COFO) office in Mississippi's second congressional district, headquartered in Greenwood, for the Mississippi Freedom Summer Project that year. Then he devoted himself to SNCC's African-American voter registration project in Lowndes County, Alabama, where blacks were in the majority but politically powerless. He quickly gained a reputation as one of the most committed, fiery, radical organizers in the South, one both politically astute and able to communicate with less-educated African Americans on their own terms. The Alabama Democratic Party, led by the segregationist George Wallace, used the words "white supremacy" in its slogan. Rather than encourage African Americans to register as Democrats, Carmichael helped to form an independent party, the Lowndes County Freedom Organization, featuring a snarling black panther as its symbol.

In 1966 the winds of change were blowing through SNCC, and the charismatic Carmichael broke with tradition to challenge the reelection of John Lewis for the chair of the organization. Lewis personified SNCC's initial commitment to nonviolence and racial integration. Many in SNCC's Atlanta headquarters, however, now urged the expulsion of whites from the organization and the fostering of a potent racial consciousness among African Americans. Like them, Carmichael had been significantly affected by the appeal of Malcolm X's fiery rhetoric to discontented

Stokely Carmichael (Kwame Touré). ARCHIVE PHOTOS, INC.

African Americans, and by the theorist Franz Fanon's *The Wretched of the Earth* (1961), which depicted all African Americans as victims of white racist colonial oppression. The refusal of the Democratic Party to seat the Mississippi Freedom Democratic Party delegates at its nominating convention in Atlantic City, New Jersey, in 1964 had convinced Carmichael and others in SNCC that liberalism had failed to deliver on its promises of racial justice. It showed that the national conscience and the civil rights movement's white allies were unreliable; it indicated the need for racial power. The selection of Carmichael as the chair heralded a new course for SNCC, one that emphasized African-American consciousness and the building of African-American-controlled institutions.

Barely a month after his election, Carmichael shook the nation to its core by demanding "Black Power!" On 5 June 1966 James Meredith, who had integrated the University of Mississippi in 1962, set out to march from Memphis, Tennessee, to Jackson, Mississippi, to show African Americans that they need not fear registering to vote. Three blasts from a shotgun wounded Meredith. Carmichael, Martin Luther King, Jr., and Floyd McKissick of the Congress of Racial Equality (CORE), eager not to let a member of the Ku Klux Klan stymie Meredith's goal, decided to continue the March Against Fear. Carmichael saw it as an opportunity to show that SNCC was the cutting edge of the movement, and that he could best express the frustration of all whose hopes had been raised, but not fulfilled, by the civil rights movement. His moment came on 16 June in Greenwood, Mississippi, when, following yet another jailing, an angry Carmichael told a rally, "This is the twenty-seventh time I have been arrested—and I ain't going to jail no more. . . . The only way we gonna stop them white men from whippin' us is to take over. We been saying freedom for six years and we ain't got nothin'. What we gonna start saying now is Black Power!" As he shouted, "What do you want?" the crowd would roar "black power!" "Black Power!" "BLACK POWER!" Virtually overnight "Black Power" became the rallying cry of many African-American protesters.

Initially an inchoate, emotional response to frustration, and a vague hope that awakened African-American consciousness would somehow lead to a new social order, Black Power appealed to the many African Americans disillusioned by attempts to achieve change through nonviolent tactics and interracial alliances. Carmichael correctly sensed that the slogan appealed to discontented African Americans in the northern ghettos as well as in the rural South, and he kept repeating his call for racial self-determination, for building power bases in local communities to replace the civil rights alliance, for the cultural and political autonomy of African Americans. Few knew exactly what Black Power meant, but most whites and the old-guard leadership of the civil rights movement quickly con-

demned it as reverse racism, an incitement to antiwhite violence, a hateful and suicidal scheme for African-American separatism.

Belatedly, Carmichael began to construct an intellectual rationale for Black Power. Although never offering much in the way of concrete strategy, he stressed the need to foster in African Americans a greater sense of pride, confidence, and racial identity. "The most important thing that black people have to do is to begin to come together, and to be able to do that we must stop being ashamed of being black," he said. "We are black and beautiful." Less and less constrained by a concern for the sensibilities of whites, he preached African-American separatism "by any means necessary." While always denying being antiwhite, the connotations of racial retributions and antiwhite violence grew unmistakable.

To clarify his message, Carmichael coauthored *Black Power: The Politics of Black Liberation* (1967), with the Columbia University political scientist Charles V. Hamilton. They accused the civil rights movement of speaking only "to an audience of middle-class whites" and not to the African-American community, and they rejected "the old language of love and suffering." Denouncing racial integration as a concept "based on the assumption that there is nothing of value in the black community," and as a middle-class goal wanted only by "a small group of Negroes with middle-class aspirations," Carmichael and Hamilton claimed it to be "a subterfuge for the maintenance of white supremacy." Instead of civil rights, they urged African Americans "to define their own goals, to lead their own organizations . . . to resist the racist institutions and values of this society." They called "for black people in this country to unite, to recognize their heritage, and to build a sense of community." They espoused African-American economic and political empowerment, self-defense tactics, and racial pride. The time had come, they concluded, for African Americans to control the institutions of the communities where they lived, and to stop the exploitation of nonwhite people around the world.

The book did little to reassure either whites or the older generation of African Americans. Black Power ruptured the civil rights movement, helped ignite white backlash, and soon acquired as many different meanings as there were proponents, becoming linked with everything from the election of African-American politicians to the creation of a new value system, from African-American capitalism to revolution. For Carmichael it became a complete rejection of the values of U.S. society and of his own former NAG and SNCC ideals. "When you talk about black power, you talk about bringing this country to its knees," he liked to say. "When you talk of black power, you talk of building a movement that will smash everything Western civilization has created." His speeches grew increasingly provocative and his message, said Hamilton, associated "with riots and guns and 'burn, baby, burn.'"

In mid-1967 Carmichael and SNCC became a target of the Federal Bureau of Investigation (FBI) Counterintelligence Program, a secret plan "to expose, disrupt, misdirect, discredit, or otherwise neutralize the activities of black nationalist, hate-type organizations." Believing that Carmichael had the "necessary charisma" to be a new African-American symbolic leader, the FBI was especially interested in undermining his influence both within and outside SNCC. At the same time, with his term as the SNCC chair over, Carmichael announced he was "going back to the field to organize." Instead, he went on a four-month tour of the Third World.

Meeting with Fidel Castro in Cuba, Ho Chi Minh in North Vietnam, and Sékou-Touré and Kwame Nkrumah in Guinea, among many others, Carmichael publicly proclaimed that African Americans were urban guerrillas looking to the Cuban revolution for inspiration. He denounced the United States for racist imperialism in Vietnam, asserted that revolutionary violence was necessary for the liberation of African Americans, and insisted they must be provided with "an African ideology which speaks to our blackness—nothing else. It's not a question of right or left, it's a question of black."

The public expression of such views got Carmichael's passport confiscated and held for ten months and earned him an invitation to become the honorary prime minister of the Black Panther Party for Self-Defense (BPP). A militant Marxist, African-American revolutionary group founded in 1966 in Oakland, California, by Huey P. Newton and Bobby Seale, the BPP called for the arming of all African Americans, their exemption from the draft, the release of all African Americans from jail, and the payment of compensation to African Americans for centuries of exploitation by white America. Carmichael's ideology of separatism looked to alliances with the Third World rather than coalitions with poor whites; he also de-emphasized Marxist notions of class conflict and attempts to mobilize the poor by stressing common class interests. These were views that soon clashed with the BPP program of alliances with white radicals.

In mid-1968 SNCC expelled Carmichael and the BPP accepted his resignation. That same year he married the South African singer and political activist Miriam Makeba. In 1969 they left the United States to live in Conakry, Guinea. There, Carmichael changed his name to Kwame Touré, a combination of the names of Kwame Nkrumah, the first president of Ghana and father of Pan-Africanism, and of Sékou-Touré, the Marxist leader of Guinea. Kwame Touré founded the All-African People's Revolutionary Party, with the goal of liberating black people by unrelenting armed struggle. Hoping to see a single socialist state

for all of Africa, he insisted that oppressed African Americans return to Mother Africa rather than transform U.S. society. After his divorce from Makeba in 1979, he married Marlyatou Barry, a Guinean doctor. For the remainder of his years, the flamboyant Kwame Touré made periodic lecture tours in the United States, advocating socialism and Pan-Africanism, and criticizing capitalism, Israel, and U.S. imperialism.

Diagnosed with prostate cancer in 1996, Carmichael received financial help from the Nation of Islam leader Louis Farrakhan for his treatments in Cuba and at the Columbia–Presbyterian Medical Center in New York City. He returned to Africa, wishing "to sleep . . . in Guinea, eternally." Never compromising, always committed—to the end he answered his telephone, "Ready for the revolution!"—Carmichael died of what he claimed to be an assassination by "FBI-induced cancer." Carmichael wrote in his final communication, "Thirty years later, I still live in Guinea, working, studying, and struggling for the African Revolution. And I will continue to do so until the last second, of the last minute, of the last hour, of the last day." He is buried in Conakry, Guinea.

Carmichael is remembered as one of the bravest, most militant young African Americans who put his life on the line in the struggle for equal rights, and then became ever-more radical, a Marxist fighter for nonwhites opposed to U.S. interests abroad.

★

Carmichael's two books are *Black Power: The Politics of Black Liberation* (1967), with Charles Hamilton, and *Stokely Speaks: Black Power Back to Pan-Africanism* (1971). For discussions of his career, see Cleveland Sellers with Robert Terrell, *The River of No Return* (1973), and Clayborne Carson, *In Struggle, SNCC and the Black Awakening of the 1960s* (1981). An obituary is in the *New York Times* (18 Nov. 1998).

HARVARD SITKOFF

CARTER, Betty (*b.* 16 May 1929 in Flint, Michigan; *d.* 26 September 1998 in Brooklyn, New York), jazz singer and songwriter whose lifelong commitment to the bebop and postbop jazz idioms, and to the expansion of the vocalist's role in the jazz combo, earned her the hard-won designation of "musician" among jazz instrumentalists.

Carter was born Lillie Mae Jones and was raised on Detroit's West Side. Her father, James Taylor Jones II, worked as a press operator for the Ford Motor Company until his untimely death in 1946. Her mother was Bertha Cox. Carter was the eldest of three children and also had two older half-sisters from her father's previous marriage. She did not receive early exposure to jazz, which her strict Bap-

Betty Carter, 1990. ARCHIVE PHOTOS, INC.

tist parents considered the Devil's music, but she gained early musical experience singing alto in the church choir. Her father was a choir director at Chapel Hill Baptist Church. Receiving rudimentary piano instruction in 1944 and singing in assemblies at Northwestern High School furthered her musical development.

As the bebop style—swift tempos, complex harmonies, and extreme displays of virtuosity—arrived in Detroit in the mid-1940s, Carter absorbed the idiom and made a specialty of scat singing. Her successful appearance at the Paradise Theater's talent night competition in 1946 led her to acquire a booking agent, and she began singing professionally in Detroit and nearby cities. Important early opportunities included sitting in with bebop's great innovators, "Dizzy" Gillespie and Charlie Parker, when each brought their groups to Detroit in 1947.

In July 1948, after adopting the stage name Lorene Carter, the vocalist joined Lionel Hampton's big band and toured the United States with that group until January 1951. Exploiting the bebop craze, Hampton announced his young scat singer as Betty Bebop, a name she detested. Her earliest recordings are *Jubilee* broadcasts of Hampton's shows for the Armed Forces Recording Service in 1948 to 1949.

After moving to Manhattan in 1951, Carter soon established a reputation in the city's thriving jazz community as a singer who improvised. In 1957 she moved to nearby Newark, New Jersey, and in 1960 she began living with James Romeo Redding. The couple had two sons together. Carter received great exposure from touring on the same bill as Miles Davis in 1959 to 1960, Ray Charles in 1960 to 1962, and Sonny Rollins in 1963. The 1961 recording *Ray Charles and Betty Carter* gave her a minor hit with the single "Baby, It's Cold Outside." Despite these early successes, Carter fell into obscurity after 1964, as her pure jazz approach lost commercial viability. During this time she crystallized an approach to working with the jazz rhythm section—piano, bass, and drums—that characterized her sound thereafter.

In 1970 Carter formed Bet-Car Records, which enabled her to promote her work on college radio stations. Her move to Brooklyn, New York, with pianist Daniel Mixon in 1972 initiated a new direction in her creative life, leading to the composition of several new songs. She began to see more work in the ensuing years, leading to sold-out shows at San Francisco's Keystone Korner in 1975, as well as at venues in Boston and New York City. From 1976 on, she built a following in Europe, and appearances on *Saturday Night Live,* as well as at the Newport Jazz Festival in 1977 to 1979, gave her the critical publicity she needed to establish her importance as a key figure in the bebop revival. Her creative efforts from this period culminated in *The Audience with Betty Carter,* recorded live in 1979. In the early 1980s she began performing concerts with strings, a format she returned to intermittently throughout her career. Since the mid-1960s Carter had made a practice of hiring young talent, but as her career gained momentum during the 1980s, the youthfulness of her trios became a selling point.

The live recording of *The Carmen McRae–Betty Carter Duets* in 1987 led Carter to sign with Verve Records, which released her next five recordings. Television appearances, including one on *The Bill Cosby Show* on Thanksgiving 1988, and her recording, *Look What I Got,* which won a Grammy award in 1989, brought Carter a new level of celebrity. In 1992 the National Endowment of the Arts recognized her contribution with an American Jazz Masters Fellowship. The following year Carter initiated the *Jazz Ahead* program, a high-profile forum for emerging jazz stars to present their work, initially at the Brooklyn Academy of Music, and after 1997, at the Kennedy Center in Washington, D.C.

Carter was invited by President and Mrs. Clinton to perform at the White House several times in 1994 to 1996, and she was honored with the National Medal of Arts in September 1997. She received an honorary doctorate from Williams College in 1997 and from the New School for Social Research in 1998. In 1996 the singer toured Brazil, and in 1997 she performed in Bombay, Shanghai, and Beijing, as well as in public schools in Chicago, Detroit, Dallas, and Houston for the *Harman: How to Listen* music education outreach program. Carter's sudden death of pancreatic cancer at age sixty-nine stunned the jazz world. In the days following her death, the singer's family honored her with a private ceremony and cremation.

Unlike Ella Fitzgerald, Billie Holiday, and Sarah Vaughan, who made their mark when jazz was America's popular music, Carter achieved celebrity after the bop and neo-bop idioms she advocated had lost their commercial appeal. Although Carter was respected by her peers in the jazz world, she did not engender direct imitators. Her sound was too distinctive for others to emulate without sounding derivative, but her innovative recasting of the jazz singer's role into that of a fully interacting member of the small combo has influenced all subsequent vocalists who improvise. In addition to bringing the scat vocal to new heights, Carter reworked the melodies of popular songs, revealing new depths of expression in the songs' lyrics. In doing so, she not only built upon the model of jazz vocalism offered by Louis Armstrong and Billie Holiday but also extended the bebop practice of creating fresh compositions from the chord progressions of established songs.

Many important instrumentalists received early exposure in Carter's trios, including pianists John Hicks, Mulgrew Miller, Benny Green, Jacky Terrasson, and Cyrus Chesnut; bassists Walter Booker, Jr., Curtis Lundy, Michael Bowie, Dwayne Burno, and Ira Coleman; drummers Kenny Washington, Lewis Nash, Winard Harper, Gregory Hutchinson, and Clarence Penn; and saxophonists Don Braden and Mark Shim. By giving so many young musicians an essential proving ground in her trios and in her *Jazz Ahead* programs, Betty Carter did much to assure the future of the jazz tradition.

★

The Carter estate, administered by her eldest son, Myles Redding, holds all of her personal papers and many unreleased recordings. William R. Bauer, *Open the Door: The Life and Music of Betty Carter* (2002), considers the singer's professional career and creative life in depth. Several interviews appear in print, including those by Leothee Miller, "An Interview with Betty Carter," *Black Creation* 3/4 (1972); Arthur Taylor, *Notes and Tones* (1977); Barbara van Rooyen and Pawel Brodowsky, "Betty's Groove," *Jazz Forum* 57 (1979); Christopher Kuhl, "Betty Carter," *Cadence* (1985); and Gil Noble, "Special Moments with Betty Carter" (1993) from WABC-TV's *Like It Is*. Interview footage appears in several videotapes, including Chris White, *Jazz Talk* (1976); Michelle Parkerson, *but then . . . she's Betty Carter* (1980); Michael Cuscuna, *Call Me Betty Carter* (1981); Matthew Yaple, *Jazz Is Betty Carter* (1982). An obituary is in the *New York Times* (28 Sept. 1998).

WILLIAM R. BAUER

CASTANEDA, Carlos César Salvador Arana (*b.* 25 December 1925 in Cajamarca, Peru; *d.* 27 April 1998 in Los Angeles, California), author, anthropologist, and literary hoaxer known as the "Godfather of the New Age."

Born in Cajamarca, Peru, the only child and son of César Arana Burungaray, a Basque goldsmith, and Susana Castañeda Novoa, an aristocratic Spanish woman, Castaneda spent an adventurous childhood in the Andes. His intellectual parents were undemonstrative and reserved, frequently sending Castaneda off to live with his grandparents. He apparently thrived in academic environments, but was not a particularly good student, and progressed from one institution to the next. He attended P.S. 91 and San Ramon High School in Cajamarca, then moved to Lima, where he entered the National Fine Arts School. He did not finish high school until 1948, when he was twenty-three years old.

Small, slim, and young looking, Castaneda never grew taller than five feet, five inches tall or heavier than 140 pounds. His aristocratic features, curly black hair, and glib tongue made him popular with the ladies. His roommates in Lima, Carlos Reluz and Jose Bracamonte, remembered him in 1973 as a "big liar and a good friend," a witty fellow who lived off card games, horses, and dice, with an obsession for going to the United States. After impregnating a Chinese-Peruvian girl in early 1951, Castaneda decided it was time to leave Peru. He entered the United States through San Francisco later that year and disappeared for four years.

He enrolled in the Los Angeles Community College in 1955, and took courses in psychology and creative writing. By the time of his graduation in 1959, when he received an A.A. degree in psychology, he was also ready to apply for his U.S. citizenship, listing himself as Carlos César Arana Castaneda, after his mother. He befriended Margaret Runyon, a distant cousin of the writer Damon Runyon, in December 1955 and married her in a secret ceremony in Tijuana, Mexico, on 27 January 1960. Margaret had a son from a previous relationship; Castaneda was very fond of the boy as an infant and formally adopted him. Castaneda never admitted to the marriage north of the border, and he separated from Margaret six months later, but the two apparently remained more than friends for years. Margaret did not file for divorce until 1973.

Castaneda enrolled in undergraduate studies at the University of California, Los Angeles (UCLA) in 1959, received a B.A. degree in anthropology in 1962, and was in and out of college through 1973. From 1962 on, he was in UCLA's graduate program. He even did a short stint as a teacher at the University of California, Irvine campus in 1972. But the big event of these years was the publication of his *Teachings of Don Juan: A Yaqui Way of Knowledge* (1968). The paperback edition of Castaneda's first book sold over 300,000 copies and made him a celebrity. The sequel *A Separate Reality: Further Conversations with Don Juan* was published in 1971. Both books told the story of a hopelessly mundane young man, Castaneda, who came under the influence of the Yaqui *brujo* or sorcerer Don Juan Matus, who used the stimulant peyote and other reality-shattering techniques to teach him the "way of the warrior." These tales of drug-induced visions caught on big with the hippie counterculture of the time. The publishers ran the books as nonfiction, and Castaneda made it seem that anyone could get lucky and become a sorcerer.

Castaneda pulled off his best trick in March 1973 when he convinced UCLA to give him a Ph.D. in anthropology for a thesis about his experiences with Don Juan. Except for a fifty-word introduction and a different title, the thesis was identical to his third book, *Journey to Ixtlan: The Lessons of Don Juan* (1972). An analysis of the work by outraged scholars and skeptical reviewers briefly called the legitimacy of the whole UCLA anthropology program into question, but the controversy blew itself out in about a year. Castaneda said at the time, "Writing to get my Ph.D. was my accomplishment, my sorcery, and now I am at the apex of a cycle that includes the notoriety. But this is the last thing I will ever write about Don Juan." This proved to be another of his perpetual falsehoods, as he continued to write about Don Juan right up through his last book in 1997.

In 1973 Castaneda made the front cover of *Time* magazine and was dubbed the Godfather of the New Age. He always maintained that his books were true accounts of his adventures, and in spite of opposition from bona fide anthropologists like Robert Gordon Wasson and conclusive analysis and proof by Richard de Mille that the books were a mishmash of stolen ideas, they were accepted by an uncritical world as one of the great magical sagas of the twentieth century. The legend of a sorcerer in training was much more appealing than the reality of a scholarly hoaxer and intellectual con man.

By the mid-1970s Castaneda was already practicing what his imaginary teacher had told him about leaving no traces in the world. He refused to allow photographs or voice recordings to be made of him, dodged appointments, and generally made himself hard to find. *Time* wheedled him into allowing them to take some pictures, which showed a middle-aged man hiding his face behind his hands and hat. He granted several interviews over the next twenty years, but never allowed them to be recorded on tape—those who met him either had to take notes or rely on their memory. By all accounts he was a fascinating conversationalist and a great storyteller. The stories he told about his life often contradicted each other, but generally supported the myth that he was the sorcerer in training portrayed in his books.

After publishing his first three works about Don Juan, Castaneda wrote eight more books and amassed an estate valued at $20 million. Although he never repeated the phenomenal success of *The Teachings of Don Juan,* all of his books sold well and remained in print. In 1993 he started the Tensegrity movement, a cult of mystic passes and movements based on kung fu. These seminars and gatherings cost from $200 to $1,000 to attend. By late 1996 Castaneda knew he had liver cancer and began taking medication and losing weight. In July 1997 he submitted his last book, *The Active Side of Infinity,* which read like something written by a man who knew he would die soon. Castaneda died on 27 April 1998; his remains were cremated, and the location of his ashes is unknown. His corporation Cleargreen continued to promote Tensegrity after his death, and planned to issue more of Castaneda's writings posthumously.

The Godfather of the New Age responded to the spiritual yearning of the time in 1968 with his tales of drug-induced visions, offering a kind of legitimacy to users of psychedelics who were seeking a different reality. His impeccable elusiveness and splendid storytelling captured the imagination and loyalty of millions, no matter how many critics demonstrated that he made it all up. Castaneda's followers perpetuated the myth of Don Juan and the "way of the warrior" because his stories satisfied a kind of spiritual need that could not be met by the mundane truth.

★

For information about Castaneda's life and works, see Richard de Mille, *Castaneda's Journey: The Power and the Allegory* (1976); Victor Sanchez, *The Teachings of Don Carlos: Practical Applications of the Works of Carlos Castaneda* (1995); and de Mille, *The Don Juan Papers: Further Castaneda Controversies* (2001), <http://www.iuniverse.com>. Helpful articles on Castaneda include "Don Juan and the Sorcerer's Apprentice," *Time* (5 Mar. 1973), and Mick Brown, "Shaman or Sham?" *London Daily Telegraph* (1 Aug. 1998). Obituaries include J. R. Moehringer, "A Hushed Death for Mystic Author Carlos Castaneda," *Los Angeles Times* (19 June 1998), and Thomas Ropp, "Carlos Castaneda, A Mystery in Life, Death," *Arizona Republic* (20 June 1998).

KENNETH E. ST. ANDRE

CASTELLI, Leo   (*b.* 4 September 1907 in Trieste, Italy, then part of the Austro-Hungarian Empire; *d.* 21 August 1999 in New York City), art dealer whose galleries introduced most of the American post–abstract expressionist movements and secured their international recognition.

Born Leo Krauss, Castelli was the second of three children. His father, Ernest Krauss, was a banker of Hungarian birth; his mother came from an old Triestine family, the Castellis. During World War I, Castelli, his parents, and his siblings moved to Vienna. When Trieste became part of Italy in 1919, they returned and changed their surname to Castelli. As the child of wealth and privilege, Castelli received a sound education. He showed a special aptitude for languages and literature, and eventually spoke five languages interchangeably, including Italian, German, French, Romanian, and English. To please his father, Castelli studied law at the University of Milan and received his degree in 1924, but never practiced. Instead he took a post in an insurance firm, meanwhile enjoying a pleasant life "with lots of pretty girls, and tennis, and swimming," as he recalled. Short and wiry, Castelli was also an excellent skier and mountain climber.

Castelli's firm transferred him to Bucharest in 1932, where he met Ileana Schapira, daughter of Mihail Schapira, a wealthy Romanian industrialist. The couple, who shared an interest in modern art, were married in 1933. They moved to Paris about 1935 with their one-year-old daughter, and Castelli went to work for a branch of Banca d'Italia. Castelli opened the Galerie René Drouin with a friend in 1938 on the Place Vendôme. Unfortunately, the gallery's inaugural exhibition of surrealist art, which was held in the spring of 1939, proved to be its last until after World War II. When France fell to the Nazis, the Castellis (who were Jewish) fled to the South of France to escape the Nazis, and then, via North Africa and Spain, to the United States. They arrived in New York City in March 1941.

Castelli's father-in-law, who had come to America before his daughter's family, gave the Castellis an apartment in his townhouse at 4 East Seventy-seventh Street. Castelli was drafted into the U.S. Army in 1943 and assigned to military intelligence as an interpreter. His army service earned him United States citizenship.

Following his discharge, Castelli worked in his father-in-law's knit-goods business, but became an increasingly influential part of the New York City art world, attending gatherings at Peggy Guggenheim's Art of This Century gallery and frequenting the Museum of Modern Art (MOMA). He occasionally acted as an independent art dealer, representing his former partner, René Drouin, in New York City (for whom he sold several paintings by Wassily Kandinsky) and working with his friend, gallery owner Sidney Janis. Castelli helped finance the groundbreaking "Ninth Street Show" of abstract expressionist art in 1951, mounted by the Club, a group of artists, poets, and critics of which he was now a member.

Castelli opened his own gallery in 1957 in the living room of his home. There, he and his wife received friends and clients in an informal salon setting, first dealing in European and American works from their own collection, but soon deciding to concentrate on contemporary American artists. Later in 1957, upon viewing the Jewish Museum's exhibition "Artists of the New York School: The Second Generation," he had what he deemed the turning point of his career when he saw *Green Target,* a painting by Jasper Johns. He met Johns a few days later and was so overwhelmed by what he saw in the artist's studio that he immediately scheduled a gallery showing for him in January 1958. The exhibition sold out, with four of the paintings purchased by MOMA.

Castelli's first showing of Robert Rauschenberg, another second-generation abstractionist, followed in March 1958. The artist's work raised many eyebrows but produced no sales. Castelli himself bought one of the controversial pieces, *Bed,* for $1,200, promising to give it eventually to MOMA "in repayment for a debt of gratitude I owe the museum . . . for having been my great mentor." Thirty years later—at a time when there were no tax deductions for gifts to museums—he kept his promise, forfeiting the painting that was then worth $10 million.

Having established the careers of Johns and Rauschenberg, Castelli was often criticized for contributing to the demise of abstract expressionism. He refused to be indicted, however. That movement, he maintained, was already dead, "I just helped remove the bodies." Castelli was also falsely suspected of influencing the judges when his protégé Rauschenberg became the first American to win the grand prize in painting at the Venice Biennale. The charges, however, came to nothing. On the contrary, Castelli was re-

Leo Castelli, 1996. MARK LENNIHAN/ASSOCIATED PRESS AP

spected for unusually fair practices, refusing to drive up art prices artificially, and for his generosity to artists, to whom he paid regular stipends regardless of whether or not their paintings were sold. In such ways he inspired loyalty among his clients and his roster of artists that lasted for years.

What really set Castelli apart from other art dealers was his ability to intuit emerging art trends, a talent he attributed to having not only "a good eye, but also a good ear. . . . You hear things, feel vibrations, gauge reactions." For example, he had an epiphany in 1959 when he saw the protominimalist black paintings of Frank Stella, which he reported hit him "like a bolt of lightning." By 1960 Castelli represented Stella, paving the way for other minimalist sculptors like Donald Judd and Richard Serra.

Castelli remains best known for his association with pop art, which began in 1961 when he enthusiastically took on Roy Lichtenstein. Three years later, after some initial hesitation, he added Andy Warhol and James Rosenquist to his roster. Although Castelli had managed to mount the latter's ten-foot-by-eighty-six-foot *F-111* (a sensational icon of pop protest against the Vietnam War) on the walls of the Seventy-seventh Street gallery, he moved his operations to a much larger space downtown in 1971 in order to accommodate increasingly huge paintings and sculptures. His 420 West Broadway gallery was one of the first in the new Soho art center; it soon became a major gathering spot for the art world.

Castelli opened an annex nearby at 142 Greene Street in 1980. Over the next decade, he expanded operations further by associating with other galleries nationwide (thereby decentralizing the New York–based art market), and occasionally sharing artists with them. Thus, with the dealer Mary Boone, he put on the blockbuster shows that catapulted the neoexpressionist painters Julian Schnabel and David Salle to fame in 1981 and 1982, respectively.

For many years, Castelli's involvement with other women had threatened his marriage, and in 1960 he and his wife divorced. In 1963 he married Antoinette Fraissex du Bost, with whom he had a son; du Bost died in 1987. Castelli married Barbara Bertozzi, an Italian art historian fifty-five years his junior, in 1996. Bertozzi was instrumental in reorganizing Castelli's business, which was now declining because of increased competition and the defection of some of his artists to other galleries. She helped move the gallery to smaller quarters on East Seventy-ninth Street in 1999. Castelli died in his Fifth Avenue apartment just before his ninety-second birthday. He was survived by his wife and two children, one from each of his two earlier marriages.

Castelli's contributions to the art world were recognized in 1976 when he was given the New York City mayor's award for cultural contributions and, in 1987, the San Giusto d'Oro award, given by his native city to an illustri-

ous Triestine. In 1987 Castelli also was named a knight of the French Legion of Honor. Possessed of courtly old-world charm and an apparent passion for art that somewhat masked his business acumen, Castelli is widely regarded as one of the most influential dealers of his time, establishing modern American art as the preeminent presence in the international art world. His hard work and keen eye created a lucrative market and spurred the careers of many great late-twentieth-century American artists.

★

According to Mark Lasswell, "Leo in Winter," *New York* magazine (26 Jan. 1988), Castelli's gallery archives, including papers, photographs, and diaries assembled over forty years, were to be sold to the Getty Research Institute for the History of Art and the Humanities in Los Angeles, pending the settlement of his estate. Castelli contributed an autobiographical sketch to Laura de Coppet and Alan Jones, eds., *The Art Dealers: The Powers Behind the Scene Tell How the Art World Really Works* (1984). In the meantime, biographical information can be found in Calvin Tomkins, "A Good Eye and a Good Ear," *New Yorker* (26 May 1980; reprinted in Tomkins, *Post- to Neo-: The Art World of the 1980s* [1988]); a chapter in Tomkins, *Off the Wall: Robert Rauschenberg and the Art World of Our Time* (1980); Meryle Secrest, "Leo Castelli: Dealing in Leo Castelli Myths," *ARTnews* (summer 1982); *Current Biography* (1984); and Susan Brundage, ed., *Jasper Johns—35 Years—Leo Castelli*, with essay by Judith Goldman (1993). Information specifically about the dealer's business practices and philosophy is detailed in interviews with John Greenfield, "Sort of the Svengali of Pop," *New York Times Magazine* (8 May 1966); Carter Ratcliff, "The Marriage of Art and Money," *Art in America* (July 1988); Paul Taylor, "Leo Castelli in His 85th Year: A Lion in Winter," *New York Times* (16 Feb. 1992); Grace Glueck, "Leo Castelli Takes Stock of Thirty Years of Selling Art," *New York Times* (5 Feb. 1987); and Milton Esterow, "Leo Castelli," *ARTnews* (Apr. 1991). Obituaries are in the *New York Times* (29 Aug. 1999) and *ARTnews* (Oct. 1999).

ELEANOR F. WEDGE

CELEBREZZE, Anthony Joseph (*b.* 4 September 1910 in Anzi, Italy; *d.* 29 October 1998 in Cleveland, Ohio), first foreign-born mayor of Cleveland and first Italian-born member of a U.S. president's cabinet. President Lyndon B. Johnson appointed Celebrezze to the U.S. Court of Appeals on 27 July 1965, and he remained a judge in the Sixth Circuit until his death.

Celebrezze was the ninth of thirteen children and the only one born in Italy to Dorothy Marcoguiseppe and Rocco Celebrezze. His parents, naturalized citizens of the United States, had gone back to Italy in 1908 because of a depres-

Anthony Celebrezze, 1962. AP/WIDE WORLD/TRANSCENDENTAL

sion in the United States. While in Italy, Celebrezze's father was a shepherd. His father returned to the United States and worked as a railroad employee a few months before Celebrezze was born, but could not afford the fare for his pregnant wife. The family reunited in Cleveland in 1912.

Celebrezze grew up in the working-class neighborhood of Haymarket (near what is now Jacobs Field, Cleveland's major league baseball stadium), and at the age of six joined his elder brothers in hawking newspapers. A tough group of boys, they ousted all of the other children from the area, which became known as "Celebrezze's Corner." A stocky, rugged-looking young man with a powerful physique, Celebrezze played halfback on Central High School's football team in his senior year and also started boxing for money in local sports programs. As an older man, Celebrezze told others that his football experience prepared him for work in the federal judiciary because "the coach kept [me] on the bench for so long." After graduating from high school in 1929, Celebrezze went on to John Carroll University in Cleveland for a year and then transferred to Ohio Northern University in Ada. He worked his way through school and received an LL.B. degree from Ohio Northern in 1936.

After he passed the bar exam, he married Anne Marco, his high school sweetheart. The marriage took place on 7 May 1938; the couple had two children. Celebrezze's son, Anthony, Jr., became an Ohio senator as well as secretary of state and attorney general.

Celebrezze began his career in 1936 as a lawyer for the Ohio Bureau of Unemployment Compensation. He went into private practice in 1939 and, except for a period during World War II when he was a seaman in the U.S. Navy, maintained this practice until 1952. He won election to the Ohio state senate in 1950 and was reelected in 1952. While in the senate Celebrezze served on the judiciary, taxation, veterans affairs, civil defense, and federal relations committees. As a senator he enjoyed a close professional relationship with the Democratic governor Frank Lausche, who considered Celebrezze a confidant and often relied on him to do his bidding in the legislature.

In 1953, with strong support from Lausche, Celebrezze upset Albert S. Porter in the Democratic primary for mayor of Cleveland and went on to victory in November. He won reelection four times, becoming the first Cleveland mayor to be elected for five consecutive terms. He served until 1962. He formed the Cleveland Seaport Foundation in the spring of 1955 to promote the city as a world trade center. While Celebrezze was in office, more than $140 million was spent on vast urban renewal projects, including University Circle, a cultural, educational, and medical center. He also presided over projects to improve airports, highways, harbors, housing, and recreational facilities in the city. Despite these accomplishments, Celebrezze was unique among mayors in the United States in the 1950s in that he reduced the number of municipal employees during his tenure.

Celebrezze's varied accomplishments were widely recognized, and he received the Brotherhood Award of the National Conference of Christians and Jews (1955), an honorary L.H.D. from Wilberforce University in Ohio (1955), and the Order of Merit of the Republic of Italy (1955). Although he was defeated in his attempt to become governor of Ohio in 1958, Celebrezze's public service continued. He served as president of the American Municipal Association in 1958 and 1959, and as president and director of the U.S. Conference of Mayors in 1962. President Dwight D. Eisenhower appointed Celebrezze to the Advisory Commission on Intergovernmental Relations in 1959, and President John F. Kennedy reappointed him in 1962. President Kennedy bestowed even greater recognition on Celebrezze in July 1962, when he invited Celebrezze to join his cabinet as Secretary of Health, Education, and Welfare (HEW). The president sent Celebrezze's nomination to the U.S. Senate on 16 July 1962, and the appointment was confirmed just four days later. Celebrezze was sworn in on 31 July 1962. He served in the post until President Lyndon B. Johnson appointed him to the federal judiciary on 27 July 1965; Senate confirmation came on 19 August. After serving twenty-five years on the bench, Celebrezze assumed senior status in 1980.

As Secretary of HEW, Celebrezze oversaw 112 programs in 5 divisions: Public Health Service, Social Security Administration, Office of Education, Office of Vocational Rehabilitation, and the Food and Drug Administration. Celebrezze had been an early advocate of support for the physically handicapped and came out forcefully for federal aid to higher education and for medical care for the aged. In later years, while reflecting upon his life's work, Celebrezze seemed proudest of his efforts to persuade Congress to pass the Medicare bill in 1964. During his tenure he helped shepherd several other significant bills through Congress, including the Civil Rights Act of 1964 and the Clean Air Act of 1965, as well as the 1965 bill establishing the Head Start development program for nursery-age children. During Celebrezze's more than thirty years on the bench, he produced more than fourteen volumes of opinions, although none received extensive press coverage. He died at age eighty-eight of cancer of the esophagus and is buried in Holy Cross Cemetery in Brook Park, Ohio.

Celebrezze's alma mater, Ohio Northern University, named its law building's largest and grandest room the Anthony J. Celebrezze Moot Courtroom. Many friends and colleagues eulogized Celebrezze during his funeral service, which was held at Saint John the Evangelist Cathedral in Cleveland. Bishop Anthony M. Pilla lauded Celebrezze not only for leading an exemplary and productive life but also for being an honorable politician whose service was never tainted by scandal. Cleveland's Mayor Michael R. White acknowledged Celebrezze's outstanding accomplishments when he said, "Let us not forget that the good times we are experiencing today in Cleveland are due, in large part, to the diligence of Anthony J. Celebrezze. No mayor and no man has loved this city more."

★

Celebrezze's manuscripts relating to his years as mayor of Cleveland are housed at the Western Reserve Historical Society in Cleveland. No books or major articles have been written about him. Obituaries are in the Cleveland *Plain Dealer, Cincinnati Enquirer,* and *New York Times* (all 31 Oct. 1998).

LEONARD DINNERSTEIN

CHAFEE, John Hubbard (*b.* 22 October 1922 in Providence, Rhode Island; *d.* 24 October 1999 in Bethesda, Maryland), governor, secretary of the navy, and U.S. senator from Rhode Island noted for his bipartisanship and strong commitment to environmental protection and to expanding health care coverage.

A scion of one of Rhode Island's "five families" that ran the state until the 1930s, Chafee was the only son of four children of John Sharpe Chafee, an executive for a machine tool manufacturer, and Janet Hunter. He attended Deerfield Academy in Deerfield, Massachusetts, graduating in 1940. When the United States entered World War II, Chafee, then a sophomore at Yale College in New Haven, Connecticut, enlisted in the U.S. Marine Corps. He participated in the invasion of Guadalcanal, Solomon Islands (August 1942), the battle of Okinawa, Japan (April 1945), and the surrender of Japanese troops in China after the war. He was discharged with the rank of second lieutenant in December 1945. Chafee returned to Yale, receiving his B.A. degree in 1947. He then enrolled in Harvard Law School in Cambridge, Massachusetts, graduating in 1950. After being admitted to the Rhode Island bar and beginning a law practice in Providence, Chafee married Virginia Coates on 4 November 1950; they had six children.

Chafee, who had retained his reserve commission at the end of World War II, was recalled to active duty in March 1951 to fight in the Korean War. He commanded a rifle company, served as a tank battalion and weapons company officer, and worked in the U.S. Marine Corps legal office at Pearl Harbor, Hawaii. He was discharged with the rank of captain in 1953.

Chafee entered politics in 1956 facing long odds: he was Yankee blue blood, Episcopalian, and Republican in a state dominated by blue-collar, Roman Catholic, Democratic voters of French-Canadian, Portuguese, and Italian extraction. But Chafee was a tireless campaigner with an engaging personality. He won election to the state legislature (1957–1963) and also served three terms as Rhode Island's governor (1963–1969). As governor, he supported a comprehensive medical assistance program for the elderly, expanded vocational training programs, created state woodlands and waterfront parks, pushed construction of Interstate 95, and established the state's first junior college.

Chafee suffered several political and personal setbacks in 1968. His criticism of the Republican Party's civil rights record cost him the vice chair at the national convention. He preferred George W. Romney, then Nelson A. Rockefeller, to Richard M. Nixon as the party's presidential nominee, and opposed the selection of Spiro T. Agnew as Nixon's running mate. When one of Chafee's daughters died after being kicked by a horse, he stopped campaigning for several weeks leading up to the 1968 gubernatorial election. In November, Rhode Island voters turned Chafee out of office, rejecting his call for a personal income tax. But he did not remain in political limbo for long. To satisfy liberal eastern Republicans, Nixon appointed Chafee as secretary of the navy (31 January 1969 to 4 April 1972). In this position, Chafee focused on maintaining the combat readiness of the U.S. Navy and Marine Corps, while meet-

Senator John Chafee, 1994. ASSOCIATED PRESS AP

ing demands to downsize the military in accordance with the Nixon Doctrine at the end of the Vietnam War.

After a failed bid in 1972, Chafee won election to the U.S. Senate in 1976, becoming Rhode Island's first Republican senator in forty-six years. He was reelected in 1982, 1988, and 1994. He served as the chairman of the Senate Republican Conference, the third most powerful position in the Republican Party, from 1985 to 1990. In addition, throughout his senatorial career, Chafee served on committees that dealt with the issues of environmental protection, health care, Social Security, transportation, taxes, and trade; from 1995 to 1999 he chaired the Environment and Public Works Committee.

From the late 1970s through the 1990s, Chafee sponsored every major piece of environmental legislation. His accomplishments included passage of the Superfund Toxic Waste Cleanup Program (1980); the Coastal Barrier Resources Act (1982), which was renamed in Chafee's honor following his death; the Clean Air Act (1986); the National Estuary Program (1987); legislation against ocean dumping (1988); the Oil Spill Prevention and Response Act (1990); amendments strengthening both the Clean Air Act (1990) and the Safe Drinking Water Act (1995); and the expansion of the National Wildlife Refuge system. Chafee opposed any attempts to weaken environmental protection, particularly changes to the Clean Air Act and the Endangered Species Act. He also urged U.S. compliance with the Rio and Kyoto treaties on global climate change. Not surprisingly, Chafee received numerous major environmental award, including the League of Conservation Voters Lifetime Achievement Award (1999), and environmentalists were often his greatest campaign contributors.

Chafee also led every important effort to expand Medicaid, the federal health program for the poor, extending the program's coverage in the areas of maternal care, child health programs, and community health centers that cared for uninsured patients and the disabled. During the early 1990s Chafee led his party's task force on national health care insurance. He rejected the proposal by President William J. Clinton's administration to require employers to buy coverage for workers, instead favoring federal subsidies for those who could not afford health care coverage. His effort to craft a bipartisan compromise in 1994 fell victim to a Republican filibuster in the Senate.

Chafee's independence irked conservative Republican senators. To be sure, Chafee could be a stubborn partisan, as shown by his support for President George H. W. Bush's nomination of Clarence Thomas to the Supreme Court (1991) and his opposition to Clinton's economic stimulus package (1993). But Chafee paid dearly for opposing President Ronald W. Reagan's budget cuts on social programs during the 1980s and supporting abortion rights and gun control, when conservative Republicans ousted him as Senate conference chair in 1990 after a close vote won by Senator Thad Cochran of Mississippi. They also threatened to revoke his committee chair, but did not out of respect for the Senate seniority system. Undaunted, Chafee continued to defy Republican leaders through a bipartisan effort to balance the budget, support for a patients' bill of rights, and opposition to tax cuts. Chafee also acquitted President Clinton of both charges in Clinton's impeachment trial (1999). By then Chafee had become an isolated voice of moderation and bipartisanship in the Republican Party.

Chafee died of heart failure at age seventy-seven at Bethesda Naval Hospital, seven months after announcing his intention to retire from the Senate in 2001. He is buried in a private family plot in Kent County, Rhode Island.

In a political era dominated by fierce partisanship, Chafee was a consensus builder who placed principle ahead of party and ideology. Chafee's dignity, fairness, good will, lack of pretense, warmth, honesty, and steadfast integrity made him popular with colleagues in both parties. They praised his decency, civility, common sense, intelligence, pragmatism, and profound sense of responsibility. These traits, and Chafee's legacy on environmental protection, led Ron Wyden, the Democratic senator from Oregon, to call Chafee "the gold standard for public service."

★

Chafee's papers, which cover his tenure as Rhode Island governor, secretary of the navy, and U.S. senator, are located at the University of Rhode Island in Kingston. This collection, combined with committee reports, the *Congressional Quarterly Almanac,* and the *Congressional Record,* is especially helpful in studying his Senate career. For Chafee's years as a state legislator, one should rely on the *Providence Journal* archives. See also Matthew J. Smith, "Rhode Island Politics, 1956–1964: Party Realignment," *Rhode Island History* 35 (May 1976): 49–61. For Chafee's service in the Nixon cabinet, see Paul B. Ryan, "John Hubbard Chafee," in Paolo E. Coletta, ed., *American Secretaries of the Navy,* vol. 2 (1980). James Brady praises Chafee's service in the Korean War in *The Coldest War: A Memoir of Korea* (2000). For Chafee's impact on environmental protection, see Walter A. Rosenbaum, *Environmental Politics and Policy,* 4th ed. (1998). Nicholas Laham, *A Lost Cause: Bill Clinton's Campaign for National Health Insurance* (1996), covers Chafee's involvement in the national health insurance debate during the early 1990s. For Chafee's legacy, see U.S. Congress, *Memorial Tributes and Addresses: John H. Chafee, Late a Senator from Rhode Island* (1999). An obituary is in the *New York Times* (26 Oct. 1999).

DEAN FAFOUTIS

CHAMBERLAIN, Wilt(on) Norman (*b.* 21 August 1936 in Philadelphia, Pennsylvania; *d.* 12 October 1999 in Los Angeles, California), professional basketball player who revolutionized play through his tremendous scoring and rebounding.

Chamberlain was the sixth of nine children of William and Olivia Chamberlain. His father worked as a janitor and handyman for Curtis Publishing Company in Philadelphia, and his mother was a homemaker. The family owned a row house in the Haddington section of west Philadelphia. Chamberlain was of normal height and weight at birth, but by the time he was ten it was clear that he might grow as tall as his brother, who reached six feet, six inches in height. By the time Chamberlain entered Overbrook

Wilt Chamberlain in the locker room after he scored 100 points for the Philadelphia Warriors against the New York Knicks, 2 March 1962. ASSOCIATED PRESS AP

High School he was six feet, eleven inches tall and was considered the finest high school sports player in Philadelphia. During Chamberlain's three years in high school, Overbrook won the Public League title every year. Chamberlain also led his Young Men's Christian Association (YMCA) team to the national YMCA title one year. He averaged thirty-seven points per game and caused the National Basketball Association (NBA) to alter its definition of a territorial draft pick.

The NBA allowed teams to claim players from local colleges as territorial draft selections. Eddie Gottlieb, owner of the Philadelphia Warriors, persuaded his fellow owners to allow the rule to be changed to include local high school players, though they could not be signed until their college class graduated. This was one of many basketball rules that Chamberlain caused to be changed during his career. While in high school Chamberlain also established himself as an elite track-and-field competitor. He ran the 440-yard dash in 44.8 seconds, a high school record. It was not recognized, however, because it was set in a Police Athletic League meet rather than a high school championship competition. He also ran the 880-yard dash in under two minutes and competed in the shot put and the high jump.

Following high school, Chamberlain accepted a basketball scholarship to the University of Kansas in Lawrence, an institution steeped in basketball history. Their first basketball coach had been James Naismith, the inventor of basketball. He was succeeded by one of his former players, Forrest ("Phog") Allen, who was the Jayhawks coach for more than thirty-five years and was largely responsible for the inclusion of basketball as an Olympic sport starting in 1936. Impressed with the Kansas tradition of basketball, Chamberlain enrolled there in the fall of 1955. Chamberlain played on the freshmen team, which in accordance with league rules played only scrimmages against the varsity. As a sophomore, Chamberlain ascended to the varsity. When "Phog" Allen was forced to retire at age seventy, the freshmen coach, Dick Harp, became varsity coach.

Early in Chamberlain's career, the rule regarding when players could leave the free-throw line after shooting was changed. Previously, players had to wait until the ball hit the rim or backboard before leaving the line. Another rule modified the definition of offensive goaltending, which prevented a player from guiding a teammate's shot into the basket. Chamberlain had two outstanding years of varsity basketball at Kansas and was named first-team All-American both years, but there was frustration. He was often double- and triple-teamed—pitted against two or three players—and was fouled many times. The biggest frustration, however, was that Kansas did not win a national collegiate basketball title. In the 1957 National Collegiate Athletic Association (NCAA) championship game, Kansas lost in triple overtime to the University of North Carolina. The next year Kansas failed to win the Big Seven Conference and thus did not qualify for the NCAA tournament.

Chamberlain was bothered by the slowdown tactics and triple-teaming that college teams used to thwart him, and he decided to forgo his last year of college basketball eligibility and sign a one-year contract (1958–1959) with the Harlem Globetrotters. The year with the Trotters gave him a chance to learn to handle the ball well and to fulfill a longtime ambition to travel. He also grew to attain his height of seven feet, one inch. The next year he signed with the Philadelphia Warriors and took them from a 32–40 record of wins and losses to a record of 49–26 in 1959–1960. He led the league in points, scoring average, rebounding, field goals attempted, field goals made, free throws attempted, and minutes played. Chamberlain played nearly every minute of every game, a record he maintained throughout his professional career. Even more amazing was the fact that in his entire career, including high school, college, and professional basketball, Chamberlain never fouled out of a game. The Warriors improved vastly, and Chamberlain was voted both Rookie of the Year and Most Valuable Player (MVP) in the NBA, but the Warriors lost in the second round of the playoffs to the Boston Celtics and Bill Russell, a scenario that would be repeated almost yearly throughout Chamberlain's career.

In the 1960–1961 season the Warriors again finished second in the Eastern Division to the Celtics and lost in the first round of the playoffs to the Syracuse Nationals. Chamberlain led the league in eight major categories, including scoring average (38.4), rebound average (27.2)—both new NBA records—and points. These records, however, were only a prelude to Chamberlain's most amazing year for individual performance, 1961–1962. Possibly the most famous one-game record was set on 2 March 1962 in Hershey, Pennsylvania. On that night he scored 100 points in a 169–147 victory over the New York Knicks. He had thirty-six field goals and scored twenty-eight points on free throws out of thirty-two attempts. Because Chamberlain was only a 51 percent free-throw shooter for his career, this latter statistic was amazing. For the year Chamberlain was similarly impressive. He averaged 50.4 points per game, a record unlikely ever to be broken. He also led the league in at least nine other categories, including rebounding, but the Warriors were again eliminated from the playoffs by the Boston Celtics.

The next season the Warriors were sold to a California group, which moved them to San Francisco under the name the San Francisco Warriors. In California, the Warriors had one disappointing season, but the next year (1963–1964) they won the Western Division. Although Chamberlain continued to lead the league in scoring and many other categories, his team again lost to the Celtics in the playoffs, this time in the finals. Midway through the next season, the floundering Warriors traded Chamberlain back to Philadelphia to the 76ers, the former Nationals who had moved from Syracuse the previous year. In 1965–1966 the 76ers posted the best record in basketball but were defeated by the Celtics in the playoffs. Finally, in 1967, the 76ers lost only thirteen games (of eighty-one) and raced through the playoffs to win the title. Chamberlain's scoring in the playoffs was down (21.7 points per game), but he led the league in rebounding and achieved the victory that he had sought since entering the NBA.

A year later, after the 76ers lost in the playoffs to Boston, Chamberlain was traded to the Los Angeles Lakers, who took Boston to seven games before losing to them in the NBA finals. Meanwhile, Chamberlain sustained his first serious injury ever, and his knee problems kept him out of play for most of the season. He returned for the playoffs, but the Lakers lost in the finals to the New York Knicks. The next year the Lakers lost in the semifinals to the Milwaukee Bucks, led by Lew Alcindor (now Kareem Abdul-Jabbar) and Oscar Robertson. In 1971–1972 the Lakers compiled a thirty-three-game winning streak and lost only three games (of fifteen) in the playoffs, as Chamberlain won his second NBA championship.

Chamberlain signed a contract for 1973–1974 to be player-coach with the San Diego Conquistadors of the new American Basketball Association, but he was enjoined from playing because he had not played out his option with the Lakers. So he coached only, and San Diego finished last in the Western Division. The team folded the next year, and Chamberlain left professional basketball at age thirty-eight.

Chamberlain had invested in real estate, thoroughbred horses, and small businesses, and he was financially well off after retiring from basketball. His athletic career was not over, however. He was one of the first presidents of the International Volleyball Association, in which he also played. Chamberlain talked of becoming a heavyweight boxer or returning to basketball, but that did not materialize. In 1991 Chamberlain's autobiography aroused controversy and interest because of his claim that he had had sexual relations with more than 20,000 women. (Chamberlain never married.) He also wrote a book entitled *Who's Running the Asylum? Inside the Insane World of Sports Today* (1997). Chamberlain died of a heart attack at his home in the Bel Air section of Los Angeles. He was cremated, and the ashes were given to family members.

Some experts assert that Chamberlain was the greatest basketball player ever. In his professional career he won four MVP awards and led in scoring in seven consecutive seasons and in rebounding eleven times. He even led the league in assists one year. He retired as the all-time leader in total scoring, a record since broken by Kareem Abdul-Jabbar, who played six years longer. He also was second in scoring average (30.1) to Michael Jordan's 31.5. He is the all-time leader in rebounds, more than 2,000 more than his closest competitor. He is second all-time in field goals made (again behind Abdul-Jabbar), first in free throws attempted, and third in minutes played, averaging nearly forty-six minutes a game for his career. His single game records include most rebounds (55), most points (100), and most free throws in one game (28). His average of 50.4 points per game in the 1961–1962 season seems unassailable. He was voted to the First Team NBA seven times and named to the NBA All-Star team thirteen times; he scored more than sixty points in a game 32 times and more than fifty points on 118 occasions. Of the top ten all-time game scoring highs, Chamberlain has the top four. He was inducted into the Basketball Hall of Fame in 1978.

★

The few biographies of Chamberlain are addressed to the younger reader. George Sullivan's *Wilt Chamberlain* was published in 1966, but the 1970 printing has a note that highlights the 1967 championship. Chamberlain wrote an autobiography (of sorts), *A View from Above* (1991). An earlier autobiography, *Wilt: Just Like Any Other Seven-Foot Black Millionaire Who Lives Next Door* (1973), was coauthored with David Shaw. At his death the *Philadelphia Inquirer* published a thirty-page tribute (13 Oct. 1999). An obituary is in the *New York Times* (13 Oct. 1999).

MURRY R. NELSON

CHANDLER, Dorothy Buffum (*b.* 19 May 1901 in Lafayette, Illinois; *d.* 6 July 1997 in Hollywood, California), civic leader, philanthropist, and newspaper executive whose activities helped shape Los Angeles cultural and social life.

Chandler was the youngest of three children (she had an older brother and sister) of Charles Abel and Fern Smith Buffum. The family moved to southern California while she was a toddler, and her father and his brother opened the Long Beach Mercantile Co., which grew into an upscale chain of successful department stores known as Buffum's.

Chandler was valedictorian of Long Beach High School's graduating class of 1918. "Buff," as she was known to close friends throughout her life, enrolled at Stanford University, where she was voted a "Campus Queen" and met Norman Chandler (whose family owned the *Los Angeles Times,* of which he became publisher in 1944). They married on 30 August 1922; they soon had a daughter, Camilla, and a son, Otis, who succeeded his father as publisher of the *Los Angeles Times* in 1960. In the words of David Halberstam, within a few years of her marriage Chandler found herself "very underemployed, very unhappy." She fell into a severe depression in the 1930s, but

Dorothy Chandler, 1965. AP/WIDE WORLD/TRANSCENDENTAL

114

successfully underwent intense psychiatric treatment, an unusual step at the time. A transformed Chandler began her involvement with many civic, cultural, and community organizations, as well as a decades long involvement with the *Los Angeles Times.*

Chandler's formal association with the newspaper began in 1948, with her appointment as administrative assistant to her publisher-husband. In 1955 she became a director of the company, serving in that capacity until 1973. From 1969 to 1976 she served as assistant to the chairman of the board and oversaw the design and construction of the company's new corporate headquarters in 1973. An ardent advocate of women's rights, Chandler also worked with various editors to increase awareness of women's issues, and she launched the *Los Angeles Times* Women of the Year program in 1950. During its twenty-six-year existence, the program honored more than 200 women in southern California. Chandler seems never to have been formally involved in policy decisions concerning general news coverage or specific operations. But informally, counseling her husband and son during their tenures as *Los Angeles Times* publishers, she did play a role (overstated, according to some critics) in the transformation of the paper from what the *Economist* dubbed "a shoddy sheet of extreme right-wing viewpoint" into an open-minded, Pulitzer Prize–winning exemplar of American journalism.

Chandler's first notable volunteer efforts, in the 1940s, were on the boards of the Los Angeles Children's Hospital and the Southern California Symphony Association. But her career as a civic cultural leader began in earnest in 1950, when she led a drive to help save the financially troubled Hollywood Bowl. Her "Save the Bowl" fund-raising campaign enabled the bowl to reopen, complete its season, and end the year in profit. Chandler was elected to the Board of Trustees of Occidental College, was named to the University of California Board of Regents, and served on a 1950s presidential committee on higher education.

Chandler's greatest achievement was her drive to establish the Performing Arts Center of Los Angeles County, more commonly known as the Music Center. Her efforts began in 1955 with a benefit party that raised over $400,000. Over the next nine years she coordinated an extensive campaign that raised over $18 million. She also spearheaded a committee that managed to float an additional $13.7 million in bonds that were guaranteed by the county. Chandler marshaled an army of volunteers and proved so successful that *Advertising Age* dubbed her "the greatest fund-raiser since Al Capone." The three-theater Music Center complex was dedicated 6 December 1964 and completed in 1967. Fittingly, the central building, which became the home of the Los Angeles Philharmonic Orchestra, was named the Dorothy Chandler Pavilion.

Her intense fund-raising had important social side effects in Los Angeles. Chandler not only approached the long-established conservative "old money" families but also "new money" sources in the entertainment industry. According to her son, Chandler's determination and drive brought "people together who'd never been together and never expected to be together." In 1971 she became the first woman to be awarded the Stanford University Alumni Association's Herbert Hoover Medal for Distinguished Service, for setting "an example that inspired others to move boldly on behalf of the arts in cities throughout the country."

Chandler spent the final years of her life in the second-floor bedroom of her Los Angeles home, Los Tiempos, suffering from senile dementia. She was later moved to the Garden Crest Convalescent Home in Hollywood, where she died. Chandler was cremated and her ashes were scattered in the Pacific Ocean near the same spot as her husband's.

A woman of immense energy, Chandler threw herself into various cultural activities that benefited the cultural life of Los Angeles. Although she never gave up her regal manner or style of life, she did succeed in living up to her self-image as a "catalyst," bringing people together in pursuit of common goals.

★

There is no biography of Dorothy Buffum Chandler, but there is a great deal of information about her in David Halberstam, *The Powers That Be* (1979), and Dennis McDougal, *Privileged Son* (2001). Also useful is an article in *Current Biography* (1957) and a cover story in *Time* (18 Dec. 1964). Obituaries are in the *Los Angeles Times* (7 July 1997) and *New York Times* (8 July 1997).

DANIEL J. LEAB

CHERNE, Leo (*b.* 18 September 1912 in New York City; *d.* 12 January 1999 in New York City), businessman, economist, attorney, and publisher who transformed the International Rescue Committee into the largest secular agency in the world devoted to resettling refugees.

Cherne was one of two children of Russian Jewish immigrants Max and Dora Cherne. His father owned a photography store in the borough of the Bronx in New York City, and his mother was a homemaker. Cherne's first job was with the children's choir at the Metropolitan Opera. The pay was fifty cents a rehearsal, one dollar for a dress rehearsal, and $2.50 per performance. As a teenager, Cherne pursued an interest in journalism, working as an investigative reporter for the *New York Daily Mail*, writing stories about the dangerous substances used in the products dispensed in the city's speakeasies during Prohibition. He at-

Leo Cherne, 1975. ANDY LOPEZ/© BETTMANN/CORBIS

tended New York City public schools and New York University, and graduated in 1935 from New York Law School.

In 1935 Cherne answered an ad in a newspaper that led to a job with the Research Institute of America (RIA), a firm started by a former Bible salesman from Kansas named Carl Hovgard. With Hovgard, Cherne—who eventually became executive director of RIA—managed a newsletter and other publications geared to advising American business on New Deal regulations, particularly the new Social Security law. As American involvement in World War II loomed, RIA became known for its analysis of how a war would affect the American economy. At that time, Cherne began advising President Franklin D. Roosevelt, and he later advised Roosevelt's successors, all the way through President Ronald W. Reagan.

RIA's work attracted a mix of intellectuals and business leaders, including the writer Irving Stone and William Casey, who returned to the company after service in World War II with the Office of Strategic Services, the forerunner of the Central Intelligence Agency. Casey, a lifetime colleague and friend of Cherne's, later led the CIA. President Gerald Ford appointed Cherne to serve as chairman of the President's Foreign Intelligence Advisory Board.

RIA attracted the attention of much of the American elite. Attendees at its twenty-fifth anniversary dinner in 1960 at the Waldorf-Astoria in New York City included such luminaries as the former postmaster general James

Farley, the future Supreme Court justice Thurgood Marshall, the CBS network chief executive William Paley, and the former first lady Eleanor Roosevelt. RIA's access to decision makers, a process fostered in large part by Cherne, provided the company with the ability to forecast trends in the days before the widespread dissemination of inside information in Washington and business circles. An early *Saturday Evening Post* profile of Cherne and Hovgard noted that RIA's "most profitable commodity is prophecy and its batting average has been high."

During the postwar years, Cherne advised President Harry Truman on how best to reconstruct the devastated economies of Germany and Japan. He served for a short time with General Douglas MacArthur, advising the new government of Japan on developing a tax policy that would provide for a stable middle class sympathetic to Western-style democracy. Cherne had also become known as a public speaker, and his annual economic and political forecast talk at the Waldorf-Astoria drew thousands. At the time, he was a Democratic New Dealer who also was opposed to the growing threat of Soviet communism. Cherne participated in a 1953 radio program, "The Town Meeting of the Air," during which he challenged Senator Joseph McCarthy, the Wisconsin Republican, and his anti-Communist tactics, including the Senator's charge that General George C. Marshall was a Communist sympathizer.

Dedicated to containing Soviet aggression after World War II, Cherne became chairman of the International Rescue Committee (IRC) in 1951. He helped the agency, which was founded in 1933 by Albert Einstein and others to assist Jews fleeing Nazi Germany, move to address the emerging needs of refugees fleeing communism. Cherne lent support to Dr. Tom Dooley, an American physician who worked among Indo-Chinese refugees in the 1950s, and spearheaded the Vietnam Lobby, which supported Dooley's work and sought increased American aid to anti-communism in Vietnam. After the Hungarian revolt was suppressed by the Soviet Union in 1956, Cherne led a massive effort to resettle thousands of Hungarians in the United States. His work included a fund-raising pitch on the *Ed Sullivan Show* and a trip to Vienna, Austria, where he delivered $200,000 worth of medical supplies to refugees. After the end of the Vietnam War, IRC assisted in efforts to resettle Indo-Chinese refugees to the United States.

As the pressures of the cold war waned then came to an end during the 1990s, IRC shifted its focus to assisting refugees from various ethnic conflicts, including Rwanda and Kosovo. IRC, Cherne once said in an interview, is dedicated to helping those fleeing "dictatorships on the right, dictatorships on the left, and dictatorships of the nuts."

In 1936 Cherne married Julia Lopez; they had one child. The couple divorced in 1964, and in 1968 Cherne married Phyllis Abbott Brown, who had worked with him at RIA. She died in 1995.

Cherne held diverse interests. As a young man he wrote pop music and had a single hit, "I'll Never Forget," which made its debut on radio on 7 December 1941. Recuperating from a case of acute fatigue in 1954, Cherne took up sculpting. Without any formal training, he produced busts of many famous figures, including Albert Schweitzer, Winston Churchill, the author Boris Pasternak, the diplomat Ralph Bunche, and President John F. Kennedy. Cherne's bust of President Abraham Lincoln has been a fixture on the desks of many American presidents and is visible in numerous Oval Office addresses. His memorial to Ralph Bunche is on public display at the University of California at Los Angeles.

President Reagan awarded Cherne the United States Medal of Freedom in 1984 for his humanitarian efforts. "Although he has never held elected office, Mr. Cherne has had more influence on governmental policy than many members of Congress," noted Reagan at the award ceremony. In his retirement years, Cherne quietly advised various political and economic leaders and served as chairman emeritus of IRC (he left his full-time position there in 1991). He remained a regular guest on radio talk shows commenting on current events. Always a keen observer of social trends, Cherne noted: "The computer is incredibly fast, accurate, and stupid. Man is unbelievably slow, inaccurate, and brilliant. The marriage of the two is a force beyond comprehension."

Cherne died at age eighty-six in New York City from complications developed from a long struggle with upper-respiratory illnesses.

★

Cherne's papers are at Boston University Library. There is no definitive biography, but his role in various capacities is chronicled in numerous works. A critical view is offered by Eric Thomas Chester, *Covert Network: Progressives, the International Rescue Committee, and the CIA* (1995). Cherne's early work is detailed in the report of the Research Institute of America's twenty-fifth anniversary (1960), and in Irving Stone, *Evolution of an Idea* (1945). Cherne's assistance to Dr. Tom Dooley is detailed in James T. Fisher, *Dr. America, the Lives of Thomas A. Dooley* (1997). Cherne's work with the International Rescue Committee is described in articles in *Reader's Digest* (May 1986), and the *Washington Times* (15 July 1991). An obituary is in the *New York Times* (14 Jan. 1999).

PETER FEUERHERD

CHILES, Lawton Mainor, Jr. (*b.* 3 April 1930 in Lakeland, Florida; *d.* 12 December 1998 in Tallahassee, Florida), U.S. senator and Florida governor who launched his statewide political career with a 1,000-mile walk from the Florida Panhandle to the Keys.

Chiles was the son of Lawton Mainor Chiles, a railroad conductor, and Margaret Patterson, a homemaker. Chiles and his sister lived with their parents in Lakeland and attended the public schools there. After graduating from high school in 1948, Chiles entered the University of Florida in Gainesville, where he majored in business and was elected to the Florida Blue Key leadership fraternity. On 27 January 1951 he married Rhea May Grafton; they had four children. He entered the University of Florida College of Law in June 1951, before completing his undergraduate program. In 1952 he received a B.S. degree and a commission in the U.S. Army Reserves. He left law school for active service in 1952 and was an artillery lieutenant in Korea from 1953 to 1954. Upon discharge he resumed his law studies and received an LL.B. degree from the University of Florida in 1955.

Chiles practiced law in his native Lakeland, a small city in the citrus belt of central Florida, from 1955 to 1970. A Democrat in a state dominated by the Democratic Party, Chiles won a seat in the Florida House of Representatives in 1958 and held it until he ran for the Florida State Senate in 1966. In a time of great social change, Chiles staked out moderate positions in his strongly conservative district, urg-

Florida governor Lawton Chiles celebrating the state's $11.3 billion settlement with the tobacco industry, Tallahassee, 1997. MARK FOLEY/ASSOCIATED PRESS AP

ing acceptance of school desegregation and political reforms that undermined Florida's traditional, rural-based power structure. Earnest, soft-spoken, and amiable, Chiles was a bird-hunting, bass-fishing, football-loving, blue-eyed, fair-haired "good old boy," whom his constituents instinctively trusted. He appealed to their good nature, not their base instincts; he was a populist, but not a demagogue. His law practice brought him a decent income, but did not make him rich. In the 1960s he made shrewd investments in local real estate and in Lakeland's nascent Red Lobster restaurants, but the payoff was many years in coming. His successful campaigns for the Florida State Senate in 1966 and the U.S. Senate in 1970 were famously underfunded. Never seriously accused of graft or the misuse of public office, he was a credible spokesman for the common man.

When Chiles entered the 1970 race for a vacant U.S. Senate seat, he was popular among his state senate colleagues, but his name was recognized by barely 5 percent of Florida's voters. In a crowded Democratic primary, he distinguished himself and reaped a media bonanza by walking the length of Florida, 1,003 miles, in ninety-two days, chatting with tens of thousands of Floridians along the way; and by refusing all campaign contributions of more than $10. He came in second in the first primary with 26 percent of the vote, and garnered a stunning 66 percent to defeat the former Governor Farris Bryant in the runoff. In the general election, Chiles faced the Republican Congressman William C. Cramer, who tried to label him "Liberal Lawton," but the nickname that stuck was "Walkin' Lawton." Cramer, a key figure in the Republican Party's "southern strategy," had the strong support of President Richard Nixon's administration, but Chiles topped him with nearly 54 percent of the vote to win the senate seat.

In 1971 in Washington, D.C., Chiles, a former hawk on U.S. involvement in the Vietnam War, joined George McGovern and other U.S. Senate doves in offering unsuccessful resolutions to force the early withdrawal of U.S. forces from Southeast Asia. On matters of fiscal responsibility and environmental protection, Chiles's positions sometimes coincided with those of the Nixon administration; he opposed federal funding of the development of a supersonic airliner and fought to halt construction of the environmentally destructive cross-Florida barge canal. Environmental protection and fiscal responsibility became his trademark issues, along with the Government-in-the-Sunshine initiative to open the committee meetings of Congress and regulatory agencies to public scrutiny. His achievements during eighteen years in the U.S. Senate were unspectacular, but he served his constituents honestly and well and was twice reelected by substantial margins, even while maintaining strict limits on campaign contributions ($100 after 1970).

In the 1970s Chiles's power in the U.S. Senate was lim-

ited by his lack of seniority. Then, in 1980, the Republicans won control of the Senate and Chiles found himself among the minority in the upper chamber. In 1986 the Democrats regained control of the Senate and Chiles was designated chairman of its powerful budget committee. He worked diligently to achieve a bipartisan consensus on how to cut spending and balance the federal budget, goals avowed by President Ronald Reagan and both parties in Congress. But Chiles was undercut and federal spending accelerated as Democrats and Republicans alike insisted on funding their favorite projects.

"I began to see the president wasn't serious, the Speaker wasn't serious, the majority leader wasn't serious," Chiles lamented. "It was all a charade. I just wanted to scream, 'This is a fraud!' But," the three-term senator acknowledged, "I helped create it." He sank into a deep depression and chose not to stand for reelection in 1988. Chiles retired from the U.S. Senate on 3 January 1989.

Treated with a new drug for depression, Chiles overcame his illness and decided to run for governor of Florida in 1990 against the Republican incumbent, Bob Martinez. Chiles won handily, pledging to reinvent government. His ambitious health care and tax reform proposals, however, were turned down by the state legislature. Chiles also had to deal with the devastation of Hurricane Andrew in 1992 and bad publicity from a series of murders of foreign tourists. In 1994, when a huge influx of raft-borne immigrants from Cuba disturbed many Floridians, Chiles flew to Washington, D.C., with the Cuban exile leader Jorge Mas Canosa. There, they negotiated an agreement with President William Clinton for the reversal of the long-standing U.S. policy welcoming refugees from Cuba, thereby precluding a replay of the Berlin Wall scenario in the Florida Strait and, arguably, guaranteeing the survival of the communist regime in Havana, Cuba.

Reelected in 1994 with a margin of less than 1 percent, Chiles barely survived the Republican tide that swept Florida and the nation that year. His second term as governor was more successful than his first. He won state and federal funding for a huge Everglades restoration effort. The legislature approved $2.7 billion for his school-building program, and legal action his administration pursued against the tobacco industry yielded $11.3 billion. Barred from reelection in 1998 by term limits, he saw his chosen successor lose to Jeb Bush, the Republican who had almost defeated Chiles four years earlier.

Chiles died of a heart attack a few weeks before the end of his term, while working out in the exercise room of the governor's mansion. He is buried in Roselawn Cemetery in Tallahassee. Chiles's grassroots popularity was an asset for his party after his death. His name was invoked by Democrats in Florida in the presidential election of 2000, helping to produce an unusually large voter turnout that almost gave the state's electoral votes, and the presidency, to Democratic nominee Al Gore.

★

The Lawton Chiles papers are in Special Collections, University of Florida Libraries, Gainesville. For an early assessment of Chiles by a member of the Ralph Nader Congress Project, see Hilda Maness Lynch, *Lawton Chiles: Democratic Senator from Florida* (1972). Chiles is profiled near the end of his life in Robin Williams Adams et al., *The Fifty Most Important Floridians of the Twentieth Century* (1998). Obituaries are in the *Miami Herald* and *New York Times* (both 13 Dec. 1998). Oral history interviews of Chiles are available in the office of the Oral History Program, University of Florida, Gainesville.

NEILL MACAULAY

CHINO, Wendell (*b.* 25 December 1923 in Mescalero, New Mexico; *d.* 4 November 1998 in Santa Monica, California), president of the Mescalero Apache tribe who fought for Native American rights and led his tribe to be one of the wealthiest in the United States.

Chino was the son of Sam Chino. Born on the Mescalero reservation in New Mexico, situated on 720 square miles of land in the south central part of the state, Chino was educated in the Santa Fe Indian School. He attended Cen-

Wendell Chino, 1992. © PETER TUNLEY/CORBIS

tral College in Pella, Iowa, and the Cook Christian School in Phoenix. He was a 1951 graduate of Western Theological Seminary in Holland, Michigan, and was ordained that same year as a minister in the Dutch Reformed Church.

Chino became the Mescalero tribal business council chairman in 1955 and maintained that post until 1965, when the tribe adopted a new form of government, with a president and a council. In 1965 Chino became the first president of the Mescalero Apache Nation. Reelected sixteen consecutive times, he served as president until his death in 1998. As tribal president, Chino fought for greater self-determination and sovereignty for Indians, often using the American legal system to force the federal government to honor its treaties with Indian nations. Chino believed that Indian people should make decisions about Indian lands and affairs, a notion he described as "red capitalism."

Chino fostered a level of economic growth never before experienced by a Native American tribe. As one of his first independent acts as president of the Mescalero Apache Nation, he took advantage of expiring contracts with the Bureau of Indian Affairs for mining, lumber production, and water use to form companies that managed the resources and were controlled by the tribe. He also oversaw the construction of a sawmill and a plant for fabricating metal containers. Most profitably of all, he created a ski resort on the slopes of the 12,000-foot Sierra Blanca Mountain. The resort, known as the Inn of the Mountain Gods, generated consistent income and provided employment for the local population. Besides the usual amenities available at any first-class resort, the Inn of the Mountain Gods contained a casino. Chino expressed his pursuit of economic self-sufficiency for the Mescalero Apaches when he said, "The Zuni make jewelry, the Navajo make blankets, and the Apache make money."

As a result of Chino's economic leadership, he became recognized nationally. He was offered several opportunities for service in 1968. In April, Chino was a member of the U.S. delegation to the Sixth Inter-American Indian Congress, held at Pátzcuaro, Mexico, and was also appointed chairman of the New Mexico Commission of Indian Affairs. He served as president of the National Congress of American Indians and was appointed by President Lyndon B. Johnson to the National Council on Indian Opportunity, a new governmental body established to facilitate Indian participation in U.S. government decision making concerning Indian policy.

Chino strenuously opposed the Indian Gaming Regulatory Act of 1988. He felt that the act curtailed the tribe's sovereignty because it regulated an activity to be held within reservation land. Even after the Act was passed, Chino, among other leaders, fought its constitutionality in court. In New Mexico the contract between Indians and the legislature gave 16 percent of the revenue to the state.

Chino, however, refused to pay, alienating a number of other New Mexico Indian leaders.

Always seeking self-sufficiency, Chino applied to the Department of Energy for a grant to study the feasibility of building a Monitored Retrievable Storage (MRS) site to house nuclear waste on the reservation; the two-year study was to last from 1991 to 1993. Chino projected that the proposed, temporary storage site would earn the tribe $250 million in return for storing waste for forty years, until a permanent site could be built. The capacity of the MRS would provide storage for as much as 10,000 metric tons of spent nuclear fuel. Chino believed that such an arrangement would increase the tribe's living standard and economic autonomy by providing tribe members with training and high-paying technical jobs. Moreover, he believed that the storage facility would offer incentives for Mescaleros to stay on the reservation rather than look elsewhere for work. However, he faced steady opposition to his ideas from the state government of New Mexico, environmental groups, and some members of his tribe.

Because of mounting environmental pressure, the federal government withdrew the grant program in 1993. The Mescalero Apache Tribal Council then began working directly with thirty-three nuclear power plant officials, and in 1994 it signed a nuclear waste storage agreement with Northern States Power, a Minnesota utility, to negotiate the construction of a private nuclear waste storage facility on the reservation. This created even more controversy, as most tribal members were unaware of the negotiations and were concerned about negotiating with private companies. Sure of his following, Chino decided to put the agreement to a vote in a referendum on 31 January 1995. The proposition lost by a vote of 490–362. Chino requested a revote, however, and the proposition passed by a vote of 593–372 on 9 March 1995. On 26 April 1996, though, negotiations between the tribe and the power plant officials were broken off due to an inability to reach an understanding on several critical issues related to the project.

Many questions regarding Chino's leadership emerged from the referendum process. Chino had, for example, received gifts from the nuclear companies with whom he was negotiating, suggesting charges of bribery. The Mescalero voting system was also brought into question, as voting was done in pencil and counted, behind closed doors, by the Tribal Election Board, the members of which were all selected by Chino. Other irregularities involved hastily convened tribal council meetings, no financial reporting on the council's many enterprises, and suspected favoritism, as Chino seemed to have control over employment and housing on the reservation.

Chino died of a heart attack at age seventy-four while working out at the Pritikin Longevity Center in Santa Monica, California. Taken to the emergency room and revived, he suffered a second heart attack at the hospital and died. Chino's body was returned to New Mexico, and his funeral was held at the Mescalero Community Center on 9 November 1998. The public was invited to attend. He is buried at the Mescalero Cemetery.

Although often controversial, Chino proved to be an indefatigable fighter for Native American rights. A small, stoop-shouldered man with hearing aids and a booming voice, Chino transformed the 4,000 members of the Mescalero Apache tribe from poverty-stricken people to comparative economic contenders. In fact, personal per capita income on the reservation rose to $16,536, several times that of Native Americans on reservations with comparable natural resources.

★

Several newspapers published obituaries at Chino's death, in particular the *New York Times* (9 Nov. 1998) and *Independent* (London) (30 Nov. 1998). Whereas much newspaper coverage focuses on Chino's thoughts and actions, there is very little published on his life, especially his personal life.

Micaela Waldman

CLARKE, John Henrik (*b.* 1 January 1915 in Union Springs, Alabama; *d.* 16 July 1998 in New York City), historian, educator, scholar, author, activist, and editor who played a critical role in documenting African and African-American history.

Clarke was the son of John Clark, a sharecropper, and Willie Ella Mays Clark, a laundress. The oldest of nine children and the first to learn to read, Clarke was born John Henry Clark in Alabama but grew up in Georgia in a poor, landless, but nurturing family. When Clarke was four years old, a storm severely damaged the family farm, and his father decided to move the family to Georgia. When he was about seven years old, his mother died. Shortly after her death, Clarke's father went back to Union Springs, remarried, and then returned to Georgia.

A brilliant student who demonstrated academic prowess early in life, Clarke once amazed Mrs. Taylor, his English teacher, by seamlessly "reading" an essay, which the teacher realized later had been a blank piece of paper. Clarke attended and finished Fifth Avenue Grade School in Columbus and later attended Spencer High School for one summer. He worked before and after school to help support his family. As a teenager he held a series of jobs, including caddying for Dwight D. Eisenhower, Omar N. Bradley, and other officers at Fort Benning, Georgia.

Clarke decided to add an "e" to his family name Clark, and changed his middle name to "Henrik" after the Scandinavian rebel playwright Henrik Ibsen. In 1933 Clarke left

Georgia for New York City, where he hoped to pursue a career as a writer. He was motivated to leave Georgia in part because when his mother was dying of pellagra she was denied adequate hospital care and facilities because she was black. Another motivation for Clarke's journey was the Jim Crow laws in Georgia libraries—black people were not permitted to borrow books or utilize public libraries. Although Clarke was forbidden from borrowing library books, he would pretend to be getting them for whites and would forge their names and borrow the books for himself. His frustration heightened when his trick was discovered and he could no longer borrow books.

Upon arriving in New York, Clarke spent hours in the city's public libraries researching African history. He attended writing classes conducted by the Works Projects Administration (WPA) Writers Project in New York. Clarke was active in the Young Communist League, but was never a member of the Communist Party. His first act in the Young Communist League was with Henry Winston and family when he prevented them from being evicted from their home.

Clarke soon became a member of the Harlem History Club, which is where he developed relationships with Arthur Schomburg, Willis Higgins, and John Jackson, who became his mentors. Clarke had become a fan of Schomburg while still living in Georgia when he read Schomburg's essay, "The Negro Digs Up His Past." As a member of the Harlem History Club, Clarke was introduced to materials and books that he had never seen or heard of before, and learned much about black history and its political significance through his association with the Club's members, including Josef Ben Jochanan and William Leo Hansberry. Clarke's mission of researching African history later took him to libraries, museums, archives, and collections around the world.

In 1941 Clarke was drafted into the army and stationed in San Antonio, Texas, where he became a sergeant major. After returning to New York in 1945, Clarke did odd jobs to support himself and his research. Clarke soon enrolled at New York University, where he studied history and world literature from 1948 to 1952. He also took creative writing at Columbia University but did not earn a degree from either school. In 1949 he became an administrator at the New School for Social Research while also teaching African and African-American history in Harlem. Teaching in Harlem was a function of his grant through the school. From 1956 to 1958 he was both a student and a teacher at the New School, where he assisted in setting up the Center for African Studies. Between 1958 and 1959 he traveled to West Africa, lecturing on African history and continuing his study and research.

On 24 December 1961 Clarke married Eugenia Evans, a teacher. They had a daughter and a son. His devotion to intellectual pursuits consumed so much of his time, however, that it made family life difficult, and the marriage failed. Clarke also had a daughter, who later died, from an earlier marriage. On 21 September 1997 he married Sybil Williams.

In the 1960s Clarke became recognized as an authority on African history. He was mainly self-taught and had written and lectured extensively; his knowledge was recognized by many institutions, including Cornell University, Columbia University, and Hunter College, among others. At People's College, he earned a license to teach African and African-American history. Between 1962 and 1963 he taught these subjects at the adult continuing education program at Malverne High School in Malverne, New York. In 1964 Clarke became the director of the Heritage Teaching Program for Harlem Youth and Associated Community Teams (HARYOU-ACT), the first antipoverty program in Harlem. He was also a coordinator for the CBS television series *Black Heritage: The History of Afro-Americans*, which aired in 1968. In 1969 he left HARYOU-ACT to teach African and African-American history at New York University.

With the rise of black studies in the late 1960s, Clarke became a visiting professor in the Africana Studies and Research Center at Cornell University from 1970 to 1973. In September 1969 he was appointed lecturer at Hunter College, New York City, where he established the Department of Black and Puerto Rican Studies. In 1970 Clarke was promoted to associate professor. Before he retired in 1985, he also helped establish the black studies program at Cornell University.

Clarke became a respected scholar without earning a high school diploma, although he eventually earned a B.A. degree in 1992 and Ph.D. in 1994 from Pacific Western University in Los Angeles. Referred to as "a veritable walking library," Clarke was also the recipient of three honorary doctorates and was appointed Thomas Hunter Professor at Hunter College. Emeritus professorship was awarded to him in 1983. He also received the Carter G. Woodson medallion and the Phelps-Stokes Fund's Aggrey medal. A philosopher and activist, Clarke remained unafraid of controversy throughout his life. In 1993, for example, he suggested that Columbus Day should become "a day of mourning for the millions of Africans and Indians who died to accommodate the spread of European control over the Americas and the Caribbean Islands."

Of Clarke's 200 short stories, over fifty have been published. The best known of these, "The Boy Who Painted Christ Black," was translated into more than a dozen languages and made into a film by Home Box Office (HBO). Clarke published six books and edited many others, including *Ten Black Writers Respond* and *Harlem, U.S.A.* A staff member of five different publications, Clarke was cofounder and editor of the *Harlem Quarterly,* book review editor of the *Negro History Bulletin,* associate editor of *Freedomways Magazine,* and feature writer for the *Pittsburgh Courier.* He was a correspondent of *Ghana Evening News* and was the founding member of the Black Academy of Arts and Letters. One of Clarke's most notable contributions was the role he played in assuring the publication of American editions of three great humanists: Cheikh Anta Diop, Ngugi Wa Thiongo (James Ngugi), and John G. Jackson.

Clarke died of a heart attack on 16 July 1998 at St. Luke's–Roosevelt Hospital in New York City. He is buried in Green Acres Cemetery in Columbus, Georgia. He was survived by his wife, Sybil Williams Clarke, and his two children from a previous marriage. In November 2000 the New York City council renamed Harlem's 137th Street as Dr. John Henrik Clarke Place.

★

Clarke's papers are at the Schomburg Center for Research in Black Culture, Harlem, New York; Woodruff Library Center at Clark Atlanta University, Atlanta; and Africana Studies Center Library at Cornell University, Ithaca, New York. Biographies of Clarke are Barbara Eleanor Adams, *John Henrik Clarke: The Early Years* (1992), and Larry F. Crowe, *Reflections on the Life of Dr. John Henrik Clarke* (1998). Wesley Snipes directed a documentary film about Clarke, *John Henrik Clarke: A Great and Mighty Walk* (1997). Clarke's career is discussed in the *Atlanta Inquirer* (19 Feb. 2000) and *Amsterdam News* (26 July 2000). Obituaries are in the *New York Times* (20 July 1997) and *Black Scholar* 28, nos. 3–4 (1998).

NJOKI-WA-KINYATTI

CLEAVER, (Leroy) Eldridge (*b.* 31 August 1935 in Wabbaseka, Arkansas; *d.* 1 May 1998 in Pomona, California), author and revolutionary who gained notoriety as minister of information for the Black Panther Party from 1968 to 1971.

Cleaver was one of six children of Leroy Cleaver, a waiter and piano player, and Thelma Robinson Carver, an elementary school teacher. The family moved to Phoenix in 1945 when Leroy's father became a waiter for a railroad company. When he was assigned to the "Super Chief," which ran between Chicago and the West Coast, the family moved to California. They lived in the Watts section of Los Angeles, where Cleaver's best friends were Latinos.

Cleaver had his first brush with the law at age twelve, when he was arrested for stealing a bicycle. He was sent to reform school, where he converted to Catholicism in order to be more like his Latino friends. In 1954 he was imprisoned on a felony marijuana charge. Released in 1957, Cleaver continued in a life of crime as a rapist, who soon

Eldridge Cleaver, 1969. AP/WIDE WORLD PHOTOS

targeted white women and justified rape as an "insurrectionary act"; he also sold drugs and committed holdups. He was imprisoned for rape and assault with intent to kill in 1958.

While in prison, Cleaver was introduced to the teachings of Elijah Muhammad, leader of the Chicago-based Nation of Islam, a radical organization that advocated black separatism. Cleaver became a Black Muslim in 1958. When the Nation of Islam's two leaders, Malcolm X and Muhammad, split over philosophical differences in 1964, Cleaver sided with Malcolm X and left the group. Malcolm X was assassinated the following year, in February 1965. In an effort to deal with his grief, Cleaver began to write, focusing his rage at the condition of black American life. His work—shown by his lawyer Beverly Axelrod to editors at *Ramparts* and subsequently published in that left-wing magazine—attracted the attention of a variety of literary figures, including Norman Mailer, who petitioned for Cleaver's release from prison. Cleaver was paroled and these writings, heavily edited, were later published in book form as *Soul on Ice* (1968).

In February 1967 Cleaver met the leaders of the fledgling Black Panther Party for Self Defense, Bobby Seale and Huey P. Newton, and joined the organization, becoming minister of information. Shortly thereafter, on a trip to Fisk University, he met party member Kathleen Neal; they married in December of that year. When *Soul on Ice* was published the following February, Cleaver became an instant celebrity, and the book became required reading for recruits to the Black Panther Party (as well as high school and college students).

Soul on Ice was influential in its day because it articulated the anger and disenfranchisement of young African Americans. However, it was not a nihilistic treatise. Cleaver advocated replacing the corrupt government system with a black socialist government. At a time when Stokely Carmichael had taken the previously integrated Student Nonviolent Coordinating Committee (SNCC) in a separatist direction, Cleaver and the Black Panthers opposed only those whites who sided with "the oppressor."

In "Initial Reactions on the Assassination of Malcolm X," Cleaver expressed his admiration for Malcolm, explaining why he had followed him out of the Nation of Islam in 1964. Malcolm was important to African Americans, he explained, because he "articulated their aspirations better than any other man of our time." He had awakened "into self-consciousness . . . twenty million Negroes." Further, Malcolm rejected the "racist strait-jacket demonology of Elijah Muhammad," who taught that the white man is the "blue-eyed devil." Malcolm had also been in prison and had overcome his past.

"The White Race and Its Heroes" expressed Cleaver's sympathy with young whites who wanted to break with the racist past and join black radicals like himself in creating what he sometimes called "the Garden of Eden." The essay also explored why he thought young whites would reject past heroes of American history in favor of the exploited, "the wretched of the earth," as Frantz Fanon called them. The contradictions between the country's democratic principles of equality and freedom and the actual course of earlier American history, which Cleaver saw as tainted by slavery, exploitation, and genocide, made unreflective patriotism impossible. Cleaver believed it was recognition of the need to repair these critical flaws that drove students to the streets, to become Freedom Riders, and to make heroic sacrifices. Cleaver called such white American youths a generation "truly worthy of a black man's respect."

Soul on Ice also discussed the war in Vietnam. In "The Black Man's Stake in Vietnam," Cleaver stressed the importance of "intensifying the struggle" against the government while the army was busy overseas. In "Domestic Law and International Order," he compared the role of an army in war to the function of police in the ghetto, calling both "muscles of control and enforcement . . . for those in power."

In April 1968, two days after the assassination of Martin Luther King, Jr., Cleaver and several other Black Panthers were involved in a shoot-out with the Oakland, California, police. Cleaver was imprisoned for his role in the attack, which left him and at least one police officer wounded as well as the Black Panther member Bobby Hutton dead. The shoot-out violated Cleaver's parole, and he was jailed for two months until a judge ruled that he was being held unlawfully as a political prisoner. Released on a writ of habeas corpus, Cleaver taught a special sociology class at the University of California at Berkeley and ran for president of the United States on the Peace and Freedom Party ticket. Within a few months, however, a higher court overturned the judge's ruling, and Cleaver was ordered back to prison for parole violation. He fled the country for Cuba instead.

Cleaver's stay in Cuba was short—within six months he was sent to Algiers, Algeria. This may have been because Angela Davis and a group of black communists were soon to visit the island, and the party regulars didn't want them to hear Cleaver's complaints about their country's socialism. Cleaver's pregnant wife met him in Algeria; both of their children were born there. During Cleaver's three-year exile in Algiers, he served as head of the Black Panther's international section. Meanwhile, the Federal Bureau of Investigation (FBI) made a concerted effort to drive a wedge between Cleaver and the Black Panther founder Newton, who was in prison for the murder of a policeman in a 1967 shoot-out. The FBI capitalized on the distance between the two, using forged letters and anonymous accusations to create an atmosphere of distrust between them. In February 1971 Cleaver announced that he was leaving the party and would run the international section by himself. Two years later, however, the Algerian government withdrew its financial support, and Cleaver realized that he could no longer continue to live there. He moved his family to Paris.

In the United States, the Black Panther Party turned on Cleaver after the split, blaming him for the 1968 shoot-out that had killed Bobby Hutton and led to the imprisonment of so many other Black Panthers. Party members who had been arrested in connection with events of that day testified that the confrontation with the police had been entirely due to Cleaver's desire for action that night. And Cleaver himself admitted that he had provoked the shoot-out. When he finally returned to the United States in 1975, he was accused of betraying party members to the FBI.

Cleaver's decision to return to the United States was motivated by several factors. In part, he disliked living where he had little language proficiency, and he hoped to see his son play football rather than soccer in school. He was also disenchanted with communism and had become more appreciative of the American political system. He hoped that the passage of time had cooled the furor that had surrounded him and that he might even be released from his 1968 prison sentence. He returned in November and was placed in the federal corrections center in San Diego, then transferred to the Alameda County Courthouse in Oakland, where he was paroled in August 1976 after announcing that he was a "born again" Christian.

For a while Cleaver earned a living as an evangelist. Attacked as an opportunist by some, he eventually ran into trouble with Christian preachers for promoting his own ideas. He then founded the Cleaver Crusade for Christ and published a new collection of essays, *Soul on Fire* (1978). After the crusade folded, Cleaver created a new religion called Christlam, an amalgamation of the principles of Christianity and Islam; following that, he dabbled in the teachings of Sun Myung Moon. He then registered as a Republican and conducted a speaking tour to support conservative causes. After a stint as a tree surgeon, he became a Mormon. None of these schemes created the fame he had enjoyed in 1968.

By the 1980s, when the original wing of the Black Panther Party had virtually dissolved, Cleaver was once again using drugs. He was arrested for possession of cocaine in October 1987 and for theft from a residence in February 1988. He was also divorced in that year, following a long separation from his wife. During their seven years apart she attended Yale University, earning two degrees, but he fell into dissolution.

When Newton was murdered by a crack dealer in 1989, Cleaver reconciled with Bobby Seale and began to tour with him intermittently through the early and mid-1990s, speaking mostly on college campuses about the history and importance of the Black Panther Party. Cleaver died of undisclosed causes at age sixty-two while living in a religious halfway house in Pomona and trying to write his memoirs.

In its day, Soul *on Ice* was occasionally referred to as "the Red Book (after Chairman Mao's) of the Second American Revolution," as the counterculture/antiwar/pro–civil rights movement was sometimes labeled. When it was reprinted in 1992, in the new preface Ishmael Reed called Cleaver "a symbol of black manhood." He declared that the book is a "classic" because it is not just about the sixties, "*Soul on Ice is* the sixties. The smell of protest, anger, tear gas, and the sound of skullcracking billy clubs, helicopters, and revolution is present in its pages."

Although Cleaver's spotlight on the public stage extended only from February 1968, when *Soul on Ice* was published, to November 1968, when he went into exile, his name is still recognized. The Black Panther Party, with which he is strongly identified, remains a symbol of resistance from the tumultuous 1960s. In an era when many colorful figures vied for attention, Cleaver held his own.

★

The only full-length study of Cleaver's life is Kathleen Rout, *Eldridge Cleaver* (1991). Two Christian publications treated his life after his 1976 conversion: John Oliver, *Eldridge Cleaver Reborn* (1977), promoted Cleaver as an exhibit establishing the power of God to affect men's lives; George Otis, *Eldridge Cleaver: Ice and Fire!* (1977), also presented Cleaver as a sincere convert. Cleaver's other works may be found in anthologies and in original copies of the party publication *The Black Panther.* Some have been reprinted in collections like Philip Foner, ed., *The Black Panthers Speak* (1970), and *The Black Panther Leaders Speak* (1976) or *Off the Pigs!* (1976), both edited by Louis Heath. Obituaries are in the *Los Angeles Times, New York Times,* and *Washington Post* (all 2 May 1998).

KATHLEEN KINSELLA ROUT

CLIFFORD, Clark McAdams (*b.* 25 December 1906 in Fort Scott, Kansas; *d.* 10 October 1998 in Bethesda, Maryland), lawyer and Washington power broker who played a significant role in shaping American foreign and domestic policy in the post–World War II years while serving as an adviser to four presidents, but whose reputation was seriously damaged in his last years when he was indicted on charges of conspiracy and fraud in an international banking scandal.

Clifford was the son of Frank Andrew Clifford, an auditor and later a manager with the Missouri Pacific Railroad, and Georgia McAdams, a children's storyteller, who in the 1930s appeared nationally on CBS radio. Like his elder sister, he attended public schools in St. Louis, graduating from Soldan High School in 1922 at the age of fifteen. He spent a year working as a clerk in his father's office before enrolling at nearby Washington University, where he joined the tennis team and the theatrical society. After completing two years of undergraduate study in 1925, he transferred to the university's law school, where he earned an LL.B. degree in 1928 at the age of twenty-one, already displaying those qualities of intelligence, hard work, and sustained drive that would mark his rise to power and influence.

Finishing second among some 300 candidates in the state bar examinations in the summer following his graduation, Clifford became an associate that fall in the St. Louis firm of Holland, Lashly, and Donnell, working principally as defense counsel in criminal cases involving indigent men and women. He soon turned to corporate and labor law, becoming a skilled and successful litigator. He married Margery ("Marny") Pepperell Kimball on 3 October 1931; they had three daughters. In 1938 he became a full partner in the successor firm of Lashly, Lashly, Miller, and Clifford. By 1941 he was one of the most successful lawyers in St. Louis. He was active in the Democratic Party and, as he would all his life, cultivated friends in high places who would be helpful in furthering his career.

Clark Clifford. AP/WIDE WORLD PHOTOS

World War II changed Clifford's life, carrying him from the insular world of America's midland to the corridors of power in Washington, D.C. In the months after the Japanese attack on Pearl Harbor, Clifford was named Adjutant General of the Missouri State Guard with the rank of major, a position he held for fifteen months. Chafing at the narrowness of this assignment, he used his political contacts to secure in 1943 a commission as a lieutenant junior grade in the U.S. Navy. Assigned to the Office of the Chief of Naval Operations in Washington in 1944, he was sent to the West Coast to supervise the logistics of supplying troops in the South Pacific. By the following summer, with the temporary rank of lieutenant commander, he was in the White House as a temporary assistant to President Harry Truman's chief naval aide; by summer's end, both his rank and assignment were made permanent.

Over the next few months, Clifford impressed Truman with his skills and charm. Charged with organizing the president's weekly poker game, he was himself invited to sit in as a regular and gradually assumed more substantive duties, attending state dinners and assisting the president in negotiations over such matters as atomic energy. He became the chief naval aide in April 1946 with a captain's rank. When his naval service ended six months later, the president appointed him White House special counsel on 27 June 1946, with easy access to the Oval Office and a broad range of responsibilities that included drafting a substantial portion of President Truman's State of the Union messages in 1946 and 1947.

Among Clifford's first duties was writing a lengthy memorandum in September 1946 that became the foundation for America's postwar relations with the Soviet Union. He also planned the legal strategy that brought a nationwide coal strike to an end in December. Working closely with members of the administration, he helped draft the Marshall Plan (1947), the U.S.-funded effort that helped Western Europe rebuild its infrastructure; the Truman Doctrine, designed to curb the spread of communism in Greece and Turkey (1947); and the National Security Acts of 1947 and 1949, which reorganized the postwar military services, created both the National Security Council and the Central Intelligence Agency, and established the Department of Defense. In addition, Clifford played a major role in developing President Truman's Middle Eastern policy, which ultimately led to the creation and recognition of the state of Israel in 1948. In the same year, he assumed control of Truman's seemingly ill-fated presidential campaign, urging the president to run as a liberal committed to labor and minority rights when others in the Democratic Party were looking for an alternative candidate. He convinced the president to embark on the 22,000-mile, whistle-stop tour of America that many analysts believe helped secure Truman's upset victory over Thomas Dewey, the Republican standard bearer.

Having refused an offer from Missouri Democrats to run for the U.S. Senate in 1948, Clifford served another year as President Truman's special counsel. Unable to support his family on a government salary, he resigned in 1950 to practice law as a senior partner in the firm of Clifford and Miller. He quickly formed a client base representing some of the nation's wealthiest and most powerful corporations, including Standard Oil of California, Phillips Petroleum, E. I. du Pont de Nemours, the Pennsylvania Railroad, American Telephone and Telegraph, and several foreign governments. His specialty was tax law; additionally, he provided strategic advice for his clients in their dealings with Congress and government regulatory agencies.

Never a lobbyist in the usual sense of the word, Clifford worked quietly behind the scenes, using his connections within the federal government and in exclusive private clubs to shape legislation or blunt governmental authority in ways that protected his clients' personal and business interests. By the middle of the Eisenhower years, he was the man to see in Washington if there was a need for access to the highest levels of power. He was a commanding figure, tall and lean, a nondrinker with disciplined habits who never raised his voice and rarely showed anger. By all accounts, he was a man of integrity and credibility, the two character traits he held to be the most valuable in the conduct of his law practice. And he was rich, the first Washington lawyer to earn a million dollars a year.

In 1960 Clifford managed Stuart Symington's unsuccessful bid for the party's nomination and then smoothly transferred his allegiance to John F. Kennedy, preparing a memorandum on the problems his presidency might face and heading the transition team that prepared the way for the transfer of power in the White House. Over the next three years, Clifford, who was also the president's personal lawyer, offered counsel on a number of policy initiatives, notably on reorganizing the Department of Defense and on foreign policy.

He played a similar role in the administration of Lyndon Johnson, first directing the transition following Kennedy's assassination and then joining the president's inner circle of advisers. He served as a strategist in the presidential campaign of 1964. During the summer of 1967, as the Vietnam War escalated, he served as the president's emissary (with General Maxwell D. Taylor) to several nations in Asia and the Pacific. On 1 March 1968 Clifford succeeded Robert McNamara as Secretary of Defense. Initially perceived as a "hawk" supporting an aggressive stand against the North Vietnamese, Clifford soon became convinced that America had entered "a kind of bottomless pit," in which tens of thousands of American troops would die for no purpose. He urged Johnson to limit the troop buildup in Southeast Asia, halt the bombing of North Vietnam, and open peace negotiations with Hanoi. Before the year was over, he recommended that the president withdraw American troops from the conflict, an antiwar position that he held throughout the Nixon presidency and that, for a time, threatened the long-standing personal relationship between President Johnson and himself.

President Jimmy Carter, despite his anti-Washington platform, used Clifford as a consultant on domestic and foreign policy during his first year in office and sent him as an emissary abroad, notably to Greece and Turkey (1977) and to India (1980). In 1981 Clifford assumed the chairmanship of the First American Bank in Washington, an institution he had helped create on behalf of a group of Arab investors.

Clifford's memoirs, *Counsel to the President,* were published in 1991, the year he and his banking partner, Robert Altman, were indicted on New York State and federal charges of bank fraud, conspiracy, and other violations of the nation's banking laws, following a series of independent investigations into the operations of the First American Bank by a New York grand jury, a Congressional committee, and the Justice Department. The investigations, begun in January 1991, eventually determined that the Bank was, in fact, a front for the offshore Bank of Credit and Com-

mercial International (BCCI), which had been barred in 1971 from doing business in the United States and which, in July 1991, had been shut down in seventy countries for drug-money laundering and fraud. Clifford and Altman's Arab partners, it was alleged in all the indictments, were representatives of BCCI, a fact, it was charged, Clifford and Altman had deliberately withheld from banking authorities when they sought a charter for First American.

Claiming innocence, Clifford resigned from First American in early 1991, as did Altman, but his cherished reputation for probity was destroyed, and so was his health. After a protracted legal struggle, the criminal charges against him were dropped because of his age and his weakened condition following quadruple bypass surgery. Nonetheless, he and Altman paid $5 million as part of a negotiated settlement of civil suits brought by the Federal Reserve Board. They also abandoned their suit to recover $18.5 million in legal fees and First American stock stemming from court proceedings against BCCI, which paid over $500 million in fines to the United States government in 1992. Clifford declared himself vindicated when a New York trial jury acquitted Altman of all criminal charges after a four-month trial in 1993.

Clifford died in Bethesda of respiratory failure complicated by heart disease in 1998 and is buried in Arlington National Cemetery. Through his forty years of public service in Washington, he played a major role in shaping the postwar policies of the Truman administration and laying the foundation for America's cold war responses to the Soviet Union. He was the architect of major reforms in the military and a trusted insider for four presidents. As a lawyer, he was arguably the most influential power broker in Washington, D.C., for more than thirty years. Whether he was, in fact, guilty of the charges brought against him in the BCCI scandal, he was a willing captive to the belief that he was not a mere lobbyist protecting the special interest of America's wealthiest corporations—while he himself became rich in the bargain—but a statesman acting on principle in service to the public good.

★

Clifford's papers are in the Truman Presidential Museum and Library in Independence, Missouri; the John F. Kennedy Library in Boston, Massachusetts; the Lyndon Baines Johnson Library and Museum in Austin, Texas; and the Jimmy Carter Library in Atlanta, Georgia. His memoir with Richard Holbrooke, *Counsel to the President* (1991), covers his career up to the Reagan-Bush administration. The BCCI scandal and trial are the center of a biography by Douglas Frantz and David McKean, *Friends in High Places: The Rise and Fall of Clark Clifford* (1995). The *New York Times* reported the final disposition of the case against Clifford on 4 February 1998. An early profile appears in *Current Biography* (1968). An obituary is in the *New York Times* (11 Oct. 1998). Oral history tapes are deposited in the Truman and Johnson libraries. An hour-long interview on C-Span's "Booknotes" was broadcast 28 July 1991.

ALLAN L. DAMON

COCHRAN, Thomas Childs (*b.* 29 April 1902 in Brooklyn, New York; *d.* 2 May 1999 in Haverford, Pennsylvania), economic and business historian of the United States.

Cochran was the son of Thomas Cochran, a teacher, and Ethel Childs. He attended New York University (NYU), where he received a B.S. degree in 1923 and a master's degree in 1925. He then enrolled at the University of Pennsylvania, where he earned his Ph.D. in 1930. His dissertation, *New York in the Confederation: An Economic Study*, published in 1932 by the University of Pennsylvania Press, focused on economic developments. Cochran's chosen area of specialization bore subsequent fruit in a large and impressive series of works related to the economic development of the United States.

Before he had completed his doctorate, Cochran returned to NYU as an instructor in history in 1927. On 26 May 1938 he married Rosamund Beebe. After Beebe's death Cochran married Anne M. Witmer. He marched steadily up the academic ladder at NYU to become a professor of history in 1944. In 1950 he was lured back to the University of Pennsylvania, where he became Benjamin Franklin Professor of History in 1968. He retired from active teaching in 1972, when he was named Emeritus Benjamin Franklin Professor of History.

Cochran staked out a subspecialty within American economic history, the history of business. In 1942 he published his signature work jointly with William Miller, *The Age of Enterprise,* in which he set forth his enduring theme that business, not politics, was the real determinant of American history and culture. He followed this with his study of the Pabst Brewing Company, *The Pabst Brewing Company: The History of an American Business* (1948; rev., 1961), the first in a series sponsored by the NYU Graduate School of Business Administration and edited by Cochran. Cochran then spent a year at Harvard University as a visiting lecturer at the Research Center in Entrepreneurial History from 1948 to 1949, leading to his next major publication, *Railroad Leaders: The Business Mind in Action, 1845–1890* (1953).

As early as the 1940s Cochran participated in the activities of a variety of professional organizations, notably the Economic History Association (of which he was secretary-treasurer from 1942 to 1946 and president from 1958 to 1960), the National Bureau of Economic Research (of which he was a director from 1949 to 1952), and the Social Science Research Council (as a member of the council's committee on historiography from 1943 to 1964 and as a member of its executive committee from 1962 to 1965). He was president and chairman of the National Records Management Council from 1948 to 1950 as well as coeditor of the journal of the Economic History Association in 1945 and its editor from 1950 to 1955. Cochran was a member of the executive board of the Organization of American Historians from 1964 to 1966 as vice president and then as president of the organization. A member of the Council of the American Historical Association, he served as its president in 1972.

Cochran also held positions at a large number of universities, including visiting professor at the Research Center of Social Sciences at the University of Puerto Rico from 1955 to 1956; Pitt Professor at Clare College, Cambridge University, from 1965 to 1966; and visiting fellow at St. Antony's College, Oxford University, in 1970. Following his retirement he was Bailey Professor of History at the University of North Carolina from 1973 to 1974 and a visiting scholar at the Eleutherian Mills–Hagley Foundation in Wilmington, Delaware, from 1973 to 1975.

Cochran's ties to business led to appointments as a consultant to National City Bank from 1942 to 1943 and to the American Hawaiian Steamship Company from 1943 to 1945. He was a bicentennial consultant to St. Regis Paper Company from 1973 to 1974. Returning to his roots in the late 1970s, Cochran wrote *Pennsylvania: A Bicentennial History* in 1978.

Early in his career Cochran familiarized himself with related social sciences, especially economics but also sociology, psychology, and anthropology. In his writings he frequently used statistical data, particularly information compiled by the U.S. Census Bureau following World War II on historical statistics of the United States. From his intensive study of these statistics he concluded, contrary to the opinion of most specialists, that the Civil War had actually retarded American economic development. He pointed out that American economic growth after World War II was less vigorous than that of Europe. A convinced Keynesian, he believed private enterprise was by itself incapable of providing full employment for Americans, and in his later years he offered trenchant criticism of government and business policies.

Cochran's interest in the social sciences and what these related disciplines could contribute to understanding the historical development of the United States led to his participation in what came to be called the Norristown project. In 1951 Cochran, Dorothy S. Thomas, a professor of sociology, and Anthony F. C. Wallace, a professor of anthropology at the University of Pennsylvania, conducted a special seminar for graduate students on technological change and social adjustment, using Norristown, Pennsylvania, as the "laboratory."

Cochran believed the character of the entrepreneur was a product of the culture in which that entrepreneur lived. He studied Latin American economic development while visiting in Puerto Rico, and in collaboration with Ruben E. Reinz he investigated the fate of an Argentine company that had hired an American consultant to modernize its business practices. In both instances he found that Latin American culture, with its emphasis on social standing, did not fit well with American-style entrepreneurship, in which the economic success of the business was the standard of accomplishment.

Cochran was a leader of the movement in American history away from the political to emphasis on the social factors as the defining characteristics of the culture. The defining social factor in American history that differentiated American development from that of other nations was, Cochran maintained, the continuing migration of the population, always seeking new economic opportunities. Cochran's last work, *Challenges to American Values* (1985), explored the changing social attitudes of Americans over the nation's history since the earliest European colonists landed in 1607.

At age ninety-seven, Cochran died of a heart attack. Little is known about his personal life because he was reticent about sharing personal details during his lifetime.

★

Cochran published some thirty-eight articles in scholarly journals and about twenty in a wide variety of edited volumes, and he collaborated as author on an additional eight titles. Cochran is profiled in *Contemporary Authors, New Revision Series,* vol. 8 (1983), which cites most of his twenty-nine major works. One of Cochran's students, Harold Issadore Sharlin, edited a Festschrift for Cochran, *Business and Its Environment* (1983), which includes a complete chronological list of Cochran's numerous publications up to 1980. Obituaries are in the *New York Times* (15 May 1999) and *Washington Post* (18 May 1999).

NANCY M. GORDON

COMMAGER, Henry Steele (*b.* 25 October 1902 in Pittsburgh, Pennsylvania; *d.* 2 March 1998 in Amherst, Massachusetts), noted historian, educator, and activist who championed civil liberties, opposed McCarthyism and the Vietnam War, and was a prolific writer of both scholarly history and more popular articles.

Commager was one of three sons of James William Commager and Anna Elizabeth Dan. His parents divorced when the boys were young, and his mother died when he was nine. His two brothers went to live with an uncle, and Commager was sent to live with his maternal grandfather, Adam Dan, in Chicago. Dan, a minister and one of the

Henry Steele Commager. PRINTS AND PHOTOGRAPHS DIVISION, LIBRARY OF CONGRESS

founders of the Danish Lutheran Church in the United States, remained busy and distant from the boy. From the time he was fifteen, Commager worked in the University of Chicago Library to support himself. He received three degrees from the University of Chicago: a Ph.B. degree in 1923, an M.A. degree in 1924, and a Ph.D. in history in 1928. Commager married Evan Carroll on 3 July 1928; they had a son and two daughters. Commager's first wife died in 1968, and he married Mary E. Powlesland on 14 July 1979.

While still writing his dissertation in European history, Commager was hired in 1926 to teach American history at New York University in New York City. At the same time, he began reviewing books for the *New York Herald Tribune,* whose editors claimed that he wrote 234 reviews in a decade, a foreshadowing of Commager's prolific writing throughout his career. In the process of reviewing books he met Allan Nevins, his closest friend for the rest of his life. Nevins arranged a teaching position for Commager at New York's Columbia University in 1938. Commager left Columbia in 1956 for Amherst College in Massachusetts, where he taught until his retirement in 1971. Even in his late eighties, Commager taught one seminar a year to Amherst seniors. During his forty-five years in front of a class (sixty-five years, unofficially), he taught subjects in American constitutional and intellectual history.

Commager wrote or edited more than three dozen books, including several U.S. history survey textbooks he coauthored with noted historians. A handful of these works stand out as most significant. Beginning in 1928, Samuel Eliot Morison and Commager wrote *The Growth of the American Republic* (1930), which went through several editions in succeeding decades. In 1950 students at the City College of New York in Harlem criticized Morison's and Commager's use of the name "Sambo" for African Americans. Although Morison had authored the part of the volume with the offensive racial language, Commager's partnership in the book meant that criticism was aimed at him, too. In the 1930s Commager also published *Documents of American History* (1934), a compilation of primary historical documents, and *Theodore Parker* (1936), a biography of the nineteenth-century Unitarian minister. With Nevins, Commager wrote *The Pocket History of the United States* (1942), which later became *A Short History of the United States* (1945). Some of Commager's best work also appeared in *Majority Rule and Minority Rights* (1943), in which he suggested that judicial review was less democratic than the rule of a legislature; *The American Mind* (1950), a study of the national character; *Freedom, Loyalty, Dissent* (1954), a collection of his magazine essays opposing McCarthyism; *Freedom and Order* (1966), a volume of his essays on civil liberties and the rule of law; *The Defeat of America* (1974), a prophetic call to the nation to purge itself of the arrogance, corruption, violence, secrecy, racism, and hypocrisy associated with the Vietnam War; and *The Empire of Reason* (1977), a celebration of the virtues of the Enlightenment in Europe and America.

Commager fought three main battles in his life. The first was to establish that the United States had a definable identity and character. As part of the "American character school" of American studies, he wrote books such as *The American Mind* and *The Empire of Reason* to establish that, like Italy or France, the United States had a unique character. Although he believed that some American traits were brought from Europe, many of them he considered a result of the national experience. Like the historian Frederick Jackson Turner, Commager maintained that the environment and experiences of a nation formed its qualities and ideas.

In the twenty years after World War II, liberalism championed a universalism that embraced equality of opportunity and disparaged racism and discrimination, but a later generation decided that this mid-century philosophy was only a cover for the interests of the powerful. In the 1970s a younger generation of historians criticized Commager and other American character writers for assuming that the country had one mind or identity, for failing to acknowledge cultural diversity, and for using anecdotal instead of empirical evidence to construct their claims. By the 1980s Americans had resolved that ethnocentrism was a beneficial necessity.

In a second campaign, Commager fought for intellectual freedom generally, and specifically in the 1950s against the investigations initiated by Senator Joseph McCarthy and the resulting anticommunist scare. In a series of prominent magazine articles and in frequent speeches around the United States, Commager attacked the followers of McCarthy, whom he believed were enforcing intellectual conformity and outlawing the free exchange of ideas. Commager feared that anticommunism, domestically, could become a greater danger than communism. He believed the United States had to encourage originality and criticism instead of conformity, or it would become a second-rate nation with second-rate institutions stocked with people who did not read or question. If dissenters became afraid to speak, he warned, a group of second-class citizens would be created whose members would not voice their real opinions, even though the "only kind of advice a society needs is unpalatable advice." Commager asserted that, in order to learn by experience, children should be exposed to dangerous political ideas just as they were exposed to other dangers. A vaccination, after all, he maintained, was nothing more than exposure to the disease it protected against.

Commager was not sympathetic to Soviet communism. In fact, he was asked by the U.S. State Department to assist in proclaiming the ideals of U.S. democracy abroad. His opposition to McCarthyism was part of his larger commitment to intellectual freedom and civil liberties, which included his involvement in the American Civil Liberties Union and his essays in *Freedom and Order*. Despite his patriotism, Commager's criticism of immoderate anticommunism earned him a reputation as a dangerous radical among some elements of the citizenry, resulting in cancelled speaking engagements and warnings from the publishers of his high school textbook.

The third battle Commager fought was against the Vietnam War and the culture of government secrecy, arrogance, clandestine policies, and oppression that accompanied the cold war. One of the earliest critics of U.S. foreign policy in the 1960s, Commager in 1962 publicly questioned the assumptions that led to the Cuban Missile Crisis, and in 1964 was already warning the public about the dangers of involvement in Vietnam. As in his campaign against McCarthyism, he embarked on a series of prominent articles and a relentless barrage of public speeches and appearances on television and before Congress, hoping to bring the nation back to its moral balance at home and abroad. "This is not only a war we cannot win," he wrote of the conflict in Vietnam, "it is a war we must lose if we are to survive morally." Commager cautioned, "We engage in the deception of our own people," particularly under the leadership of President Richard Nixon. Further, he wrote, "Perhaps the most odious violation of justice is the maintenance of a double standard of one justice for blacks and another for whites, one for the rich and another for the poor, one for those who hold 'radical' ideas, and another for those who are conservative and respectable."

Clearly, Commager was one of the activist intellectuals who helped define the liberal reform agenda of his generation. He believed that it was his responsibility, whether by publishing magazine articles or standing at a podium, to address what his friend Nevins called that "one democratic public—the public to which Emerson and Lincoln spoke." Commager held a vision of the historian's role that recalled the public lives of nineteenth-century historians such as George Bancroft. A scholar should be a generalist, in this view, an exhorter as well as an interpreter. No less than a preacher, an historian should address the moral principles of life, the necessary commitments to justice and equality and opportunity, the responsibility that the powerful owe to the weak. The historian's badge was not a license to retreat to the archive away from the pain of the world but an obligation to join in current debates and to propose solutions that might be divined from the experience of history.

In 1971 Commager announced that he was "theoretically retiring," which meant that he sharply curtailed his teaching at Amherst College. During the 1970s and 1980s he continued to write books and magazine articles, and occasionally took to the op-ed pages of newspapers to point out the shortcomings of Ronald Reagan's presidential administration. Commager died of pneumonia at his home in Amherst at age ninety-five.

During his academic career, Commager was honored with visiting positions at Cambridge, Oxford, and other prestigious universities, and was awarded the Gold Medal of the American Academy of Arts and Letters in 1972. None of these laurels saved his scholarly position from erosion by criticism from a later generation of historians. Yet, in the end, he championed the principles he thought important. Commager fought to protect intellectual freedom and a common democratic culture. While other historians gravitated to the library, he spent part of his time fostering public debate and bringing history to his fellow citizens. Like Theodore Parker, the Unitarian minister he so admired, Commager was happy to stay his course in the face of hostility and indifference. The words the historian Richard Hofstadter once used about Charles Beard also apply to Commager's legacy: "Some scholars choose to live their lives, usefully enough, amid the clutter of professional detail. [He] aimed to achieve a wisdom commensurate with his passion, and to put them both in the public service. No doubt he would rather have failed in this than succeeded in anything else."

★

Commager's papers are in the special collections of the Robert Frost Library at Amherst College. The only biography of Commager is Neil Jumonville, *Henry Steele Commager: Midcentury Liberalism and the History of the Present* (1999). A few personal memories by colleagues can be found in Harold Hyman and Leonard Levy, eds., *Freedom and Reform* (1967), a Festschrift for Commager. An obituary is in the *New York Times* (3 Mar. 1998). Commager's oral history, "The Reminiscences of Henry Steele Commager" (1983), is in the Oral History Research Office, Columbia University.

NEIL JUMONVILLE

CORMACK, Allan MacLeod (*b.* 23 February 1924 in Johannesburg, South Africa; *d.* 7 May 1998 in Winchester, Massachusetts), physicist who won the Nobel Prize for his theoretical work on the development of the computerized axial tomography, or computer-assisted tomography (CAT), scanning system.

Cormack was the youngest of three children born to George Cormack, a civil service engineer, and Amelia MacLeod, a teacher, who immigrated to South Africa from Scotland just before World War I. Although the family moved frequently, they settled in Cape Town after Cormack's father's death in 1936. In that same year, Cormack began his studies at the Rondebosch Boys High School, where he became fascinated with astronomy. As a result of reading works by Sir Arthur Eddington and Sir James Jeans, and realizing that mathematics and physics played major roles in astronomy, he developed a keen interest in those subjects as well. Some of his extracurricular activities included debating, tennis, and acting.

When made aware of the uncertain future faced by astronomers at that time, however, Cormack decided to pursue a career in electrical engineering just as his father and brother had done. Fortunately, the head of the electrical engineering department at the University of Cape Town at that time, Professor B. L. Goodlet, had adopted a new curriculum that included an emphasis on physics and mathematics. Consequently, Cormack switched majors, earning a B.S. degree in physics (1944) and an M.S. degree in crystallography (1945). When not working in the laboratory, Cormack spent his spare time mountaineering or listening to music. Surprisingly, Cormack never earned a doctorate degree, although he received an honorary doctorate and the

Allan M. Cormack with his wife, Barbara, and daughter, Jean, on learning that he had won the Nobel Prize in medicine, 1979. AP/WIDE WORLD PHOTOS

rank of university professor, the highest academic level attainable, from Tufts University in 1980.

After the completion of his graduate education, Cormack became a research student at the Cavendish Laboratory, St. John's College at Cambridge University in England, under the tutelage of Professor Otto Robert Frisch, who had been working with helium-6. It was during a lecture in quantum mechanics that Cormack met an American student named Barbara Jeanne Seavey, whom he later married on 6 January 1950. Before doing so, however, it was necessary for him to find a full-time position; he was offered a lectureship at the University of Cape Town, which he accepted.

In 1950 Cormack returned to Cape Town with his new wife but felt professionally isolated and lonely because he was one of only a handful of nuclear physicists in all of South Africa. His former mentor, Professor R. W. James, then head of the physics department, helped him adapt to his environment and Cormack published several papers. In 1956 he served as a medical physicist in the radiology department of Groote Schuur Hospital in Cape Town. This was where he became interested in work that ultimately led to the discovery of the computerized axial tomography, or computer-assisted tomography (CAT), scanning system.

During Cormack's first sabbatical, he and his wife decided to go to the United States, where he spent time working at the Harvard cyclotron. His work on nucleon-nucleon scattering allowed him to begin a richly rewarding association with the professors Norman F. Ramsey and Richard

Wilson, as well as Joseph Palmieri, who was then a graduate student, and the cyclotron's director, Andreas Koehler.

While Cormack was still on sabbatical, the physics department chairman at Tufts University in Medford, Massachusetts, offered him a faculty position. Cormack remained at Tufts for the remainder of his career, with the exception of a short return to South Africa and occasional sabbatical leaves. From 1957 until his death, Cormack, his wife, and their three children resided in Winchester, Massachusetts, though they spent their summers near Lake Winnipesaukee, New Hampshire.

In 1963 and 1964 Cormack published the results of his work on problems associated with CAT scanning in the *Journal of Applied Physics*, but the articles attracted little response from other scientists. He continued to conduct research in the areas of nuclear and particle physics and to teach; he also became a naturalized citizen of the United States in 1966. From 1968 to 1976 he served as chairman of the physics department at Tufts. Although he spent a minimal amount of time on the CAT scanning problem during the 1960s, his interest in it was renewed in the early 1970s when a number of developments related to its technology occurred. Cormack then began devoting a great deal of his time to the theory of computerized axial tomography. His groundbreaking work led to his sharing the 1979 Nobel Prize in physiology or medicine with Sir Godfrey Newbold Hounsfield, an English engineer who actually developed the first commercially successful CAT scanner in 1972. The work of these two independent scientists is considered the most revolutionary advance in radiography since Wilhelm Conrad Röntgen discovered the X ray in 1895. The CAT technology provided images of internal structures of the human body that could not previously be seen, offering earlier and more definitive diagnoses of many diseases and conditions.

In addition to the Nobel Prize, Cormack also won the Ballou Medal from Tufts University (1978), the Medal of Merit from the University of Cape Town (1980), the Mike Hogg Medal from the University of Texas Cancer Center (1981), and the National Medal of Science (1990). He was also a member of the National Academy of Sciences, was named a fellow of the American Physics Society, an honorary member of the South African Institute of Physics, and a foreign associate of the Royal Society of South Africa. Cormack died at age seventy-four of cancer at his home in Winchester.

Vivacious, enthusiastic, amicable, and humorous are just some of the words Cormack's colleagues used to describe him. An administrator at Tufts called him a "modest genius." When not working, he enjoyed swimming and sailing in the summer and reading during the winter; he was interested in religious and political theory, the connections between animals and humans, and what people might learn as a result. Cormack was a family man who would never hesitate to help someone in need, and did so in such a kind manner that he truly exemplified what it means to be "a gentleman and a scholar."

★

Cormack wrote a short autobiographical sketch for the Nobel Foundation after he won the Nobel Prize in physiology or medicine in 1979; it can be found at the Nobel Foundation's website. An interview with Cormack is in *Technology of Our Times: People and Innovation in Optics and Optoelectronics* (1990). Newspaper biographies and tributes include "Allan MacLeod Cormack: 1924–1998," *Johannesburg Sunday Times* (24 May 1998), and "UCT Alumnus and Nobel Prize Winner Dies in U.S., aged 74," *Monday Paper* (18–25 May 1998). Obituaries are in the *New York Times, Los Angeles Times, Boston Globe,* and *Atlanta Journal* (all 9 May 1998), *Independent* (3 Aug. 1998), and *Scotsman* (Edinburgh, Scotland) (25 Apr. 2000).

ADRIANA C. TOMASINO

CRISP, Quentin (*b.* 25 December 1908 in Sutton, England; *d.* 21 November 1999 in Manchester, England), writer, actor, and wit who, late in life, became a cultural icon for the gay community with his unique view of life and lifestyle affectionately dubbed "Crisperanto."

Crisp was born Denis Charles Pratt but changed his name to Quentin Crisp in the 1920s (declaring that he "dyed"

Quentin Crisp. CORBIS BETTMANN

it). Despite his father's work as a solicitor and his mother's position as a nursery governess, the family struggled with their finances throughout his childhood, dismissing their live-in servants and frequently relocating to more affordable residences in London and the Home Counties in England. Crisp's family included a sister eight years older and two brothers, one older by seven years and the other by thirteen months.

Crisp attended a local prep school in Surrey and then won a scholarship to a public school, Denstone College, in Staffordshire. These years passed unhappily for Crisp; as he summarized his experiences in typical, self-deprecating fashion, "I discovered that my great gift was for unpopularity." After graduating, Crisp attended King's College, London, to study journalism; he left before completing his degree and subsequently enrolled in art classes at local colleges in Battersea, High Wycombe, and Regent Street.

For the next forty years, Crisp lived a bohemian lifestyle, primarily in Soho and Chelsea. Open about his homosexuality, Crisp adopted a flamboyant and feminine appearance shocking to British mores, with his hair dyed red or lavender and his face heavily made-up; as a result, he frequently suffered verbal and physical abuse from strangers. Moving from one profession to another, he worked as an electrical engineer's assistant, designed book covers and freelanced as a commercial artist, engaged briefly in prostitution, taught tap dancing, and posed nude as an artist's model. He wrote two books on graphic design, display, and color: *Lettering for Brush and Pen* (1936) and *Colour in Display* (1938). In 1943 he published *All This and Bevin Too,* a tale written in limericks that describes the unsuccessful attempts of a kangaroo to join the zoo. Crisp received public assistance after losing his jobs, a frequent occurrence in his life. Because of his homosexuality, Crisp was exempted from service during World War II. He was once arrested for solicitation, but the charges were dropped due to insufficient evidence.

Crisp's job as an artist's model provided the title for his 1968 autobiography, *The Naked Civil Servant,* and this book's publication sparked his slow but steady rise to fame. After it was made into a television film in 1975, featuring John Hurt in the eponymous role, Crisp himself began performing a one-man show, *An Evening with Quentin Crisp,* in London in 1975. He subsequently toured throughout Great Britain, Canada, and Australia; the show traveled to the Players Theater of New York in 1978, and Crisp won a special Drama Desk Award for Unique Theatrical Experience. Quickly enamored by Manhattan, Crisp obtained resident alien status in the United States in 1981 and lived at 46 East Third Street until his death.

Building upon his increasing exposure, Crisp landed small roles in several films, including *Hamlet* (1976), *The Bride* (1985), *Orlando* (1993), *Naked in New York* (1994), and *To Wong Foo, Thanks for Everything, Julie Newmar* (1995). He appeared as Lady Bracknell in an off-Broadway production of Oscar Wilde's *The Importance of Being Earnest* and in advertisements for Calvin Klein and Levi Strauss. Two documentary films—*Resident Alien* (1991) and *The Divine Mr. Crisp* (1994)—tell the story of Crisp's life, and he was interviewed in the Home Box Office (HBO) documentary *The Celluloid Closet* (1995) about the history of depictions of homosexuals in cinema. The pop star Sting paid tribute to Crisp with the song "An Englishman in New York," which fittingly contains the lyric "Be yourself, no matter what they say."

Crisp also published prodigiously after the success of *The Naked Civil Servant.* Further autobiographical writings appeared in *How to Become a Virgin* (1981) and *Resident Alien: The New York Diaries* (1996), and his film reviews and social commentaries regularly appeared in the periodicals *Christopher Street* and *New York Native.* Crisp's fictional works include *Love Made Easy* (1977) and *Chog: A Gothic Fable* (1979); he also penned nonfiction volumes on

life, lifestyle, and art, including *How to Have a Life-Style* (1975), *Doing It with Style* (1981), *Manners from Heaven: A Divine Guide to Good Behaviour* (1985), and *How to Go to the Movies: A Guide for the Perplexed* (1989).

As Crisp's fame grew throughout the 1970s until his death in the late 1990s, many gay activists were disheartened by his apolitical stances. Seeing in his steadfast nonconformity a condemnation of heterosexual values, gay liberationists attempted to lionize Crisp as a pioneering, homosexual freedom fighter. Crisp, however, refused to play the part of a post-facto sexual revolutionary, calling homosexuality an "illness" and deriding the response to the AIDS crisis as a "fad." Crisp flatly declared that "It's not normal to be gay, and I think it's very weird to think that it is." He was also severely criticized for his studied effeminacy, as the male gay rights movement of the 1970s prized masculinity in its efforts to claim masculine equality for gay men.

While touring a new run of his one-man show *An Evening with Quentin Crisp* in the Chorlton-cum-Hardy district of Manchester, England, at the age of ninety, Crisp suffered a heart attack. He died at the Manchester Royal Infirmary, leaving no immediate survivors. His remains were cremated and returned to New York City.

Crisp's contribution lies primarily in his striking wit and unflinching individuality. In his youth, he was physically attacked for failing to conform to heterosexuality; in his senescence, he was verbally assaulted for refusing to serve as the grande dame of a queer political agenda with which he felt at odds. In his typically self-deprecating words, his "whole life was an unsympathetic part played to a hostile audience." Throughout it all, Crisp lived freely as himself in a manner few can achieve and with a wit fewer can match. At the very least, he succeeded in his goal of "making the existence of homosexuality abundantly clear to the world's aborigines."

★

The New York Public Library mounted a 1998 exhibit, *Particular Voices: Robert Giard's Portraits of Gay and Lesbian Writers,* in which a portrait and some of Crisp's books and manuscripts were featured. Some of his papers are archived here. The primary biographical sources on Crisp are his autobiographical writings: *The Naked Civil Servant* (1968), *How to Become a Virgin* (1981), and *Resident Alien: The New York Diaries* (1996). Compilations of his witticisms can be found in *The Wit and Wisdom of Quentin Crisp* (1984) and *Quentin Crisp's Book of Quotations* (1989). Paul Bailey, *The Stately Homo: A Celebration of the Life of Quentin Crisp* (2000), combines anecdotes from Crisp's writings, interviews with his friends, and personal recollections of other confidantes. An obituary is in the *New York Times* (22 Nov. 1999).

TISON PUGH

D

DANILOVA, Alexandra Dionysievna ("Choura") (*b.* [?] February 1903 in Peterhof, Russia; *d.* 13 July 1997 in New York City), Russian-trained ballerina who was hailed as a *prima ballerina assoluta* and later became known for her teaching and choreography.

Danilova was the daughter of Dionis Danilov, a soldier in the Imperial Guard, and Claudia Gotovtzev. After her parents died when she was about two, Danilova went with her older sister, Elena, to live with their grandmother. Her grandmother died when she was four, and she alone was adopted by Lidia Gototsova of Saint Petersburg. At a very young age, Danilova decided she wanted to become a ballerina, and her "Aunt" Lidia applied on her behalf to the Maryinsky Theatre (Imperial Ballet) School, the feeder school for the Maryinsky (now Kirov) Ballet, which Danilova entered on 20 August 1911 when she was eight.

Like the other students, Danilova received academic as well as balletic instruction at the school. Within about a year she made her first appearance in the theater as a walk-on and was soon thereafter performing with other children as a dancer there. During the 1917 Russian revolutions, the school closed, reopening around 1918. Danilova returned to complete her training, which included instruction with Agrippina Vaganova, finished school in 1920, and then entered the Maryinsky Ballet (renamed the Soviet State Ballet) for the autumn season.

Although young, Danilova moved quickly from corps work to solos, partly because the company's artistic director, Feodor Lopukhov, believed she had talent and would someday be a ballerina. Her first solo piece was as Prayer in *Coppélia* in about 1921, but it was her performance in the title role of Lopukhov's version of Stravinsky's *Firebird* in 1922 that established her as a principal dancer.

Danilova also appeared regularly in the Youth Ballet, created by George Balanchine, a former schoolmate of Danilova's, to showcase his choreography. The State Ballet, disapproving of these choreographic endeavors, threatened to expel Danilova, who left the Youth Ballet in 1923, though not before dancing in the premieres of Balanchine's *Adagio, Marche Funèbre, Poème,* and, in 1924, *Invitation to the Dance.* Danilova, Balanchine, and others began to find impoverished, postrevolutionary Russia restrictive, so when the opportunity arose to tour Germany for the summer of 1924, they agreed. Although due back in Russia that autumn, they later accepted an invitation to dance in London in November; in December, Serge Diaghilev hired them to dance with his Ballets Russes.

By 1926 Balanchine had become the company's ballet master, as well as its principal choreographer, and it was during this period that he and Danilova began to live together, although they never married. While working with Diaghilev, Balanchine created a number of new ballets featuring Danilova, including *L'Enfant et les Sortilèges* (1925), *Barabou* (1925), *Jack in the Box* (1926), *The Triumph of Neptune* (1926), *Apollon Musagète* (1928), *The Gods Go A-Begging* (1928), and *Le Bal* (1929).

Unfortunately for the company, Diaghilev died sud-

Alexandra Danilova in *La Boutique Fantasque,* 1934. ALEX STEWART SASHA/© HULTON-DEUTSCH COLLECTION/CORBIS

denly in 1929. Balanchine soon left, but Danilova remained with the others for the opera season in Monte Carlo. In 1931 she was invited to dance in the musical *Waltzes from Vienna* in London. When she left for England, she and Balanchine separated amicably, with her declaring, "George and I had a perfect understanding. We both had a deep respect for art—that was our strongest bond, and it remained."

After Danilova finished *Waltzes,* she stayed in London, where she married Giuseppe Massera in about 1932. The marriage was doomed from the start. He was a ventilation engineer who "hated the ballet," and she "hated air-conditioning." They stayed together for about a year, and then, in 1933, she joined Colonel W. de Basil's Ballets Russes de Monte Carlo at the invitation of Leonide Massine, a principal dancer for the troupe, its chief choreographer, and the ballet master. While with this company, she became famous for her role as the Street Dancer in Massine's *Le Beau Danube,* in which her performance, Massine later said, was "like champagne."

Danilova first came to the United States in 1933 with the de Basil company, and after a month on Broadway she toured New York State. She said that most American audiences had never seen a ballet before, and although at first she longed to return to Paris, it soon seemed "small and insignificant" compared to the vastness and possibility of the United States. The company returned every year, and she always looked forward to these tours.

Around 1935 her erstwhile husband, Massera, died. In 1937, when Massine asked her to join him in a new Ballet Russe de Monte Carlo directed by Serge Denham, Danilova accepted. With this company she danced primarily with Frederic Franklin, appearing in the Massine premieres of *Capriccio Espagnol* (1939) and *Saratoga* (1941). When Balanchine became the chief company choreographer in about 1944, he again created new roles for her in his *Danses Concertantes* (1944) and *Night Shadow* (1946). Danilova was at the height of her dancing career, proclaimed by critics as *prima ballerina assoluta* (absolute).

In 1941 Danilova married a company soloist Casimir Kokitch while on tour in Los Angeles. Kokitch soon entered the army, and when he returned the marriage foundered. The couple separated around 1948, and Danilova "resigned" herself to a divorce. During World War II, the company came to the United States, and Danilova bought a house in New Jersey. She became a U.S. citizen in 1946. That same year she staged *Paquita,* and she and Balanchine rechoreographed the old Petipa ballet *Raymonda.* Nevertheless, by the end of the decade many of the company dancers, including Anton Dolin, Alicia Markova, and Maria Tallchief, had departed, and Danilova herself left the company in late 1951.

In 1952 Danilova made guest appearances with Dolin's and Markova's Festival Ballet in London and with the Slavenska-Franklin Ballet in New York City. She accepted an invitation to teach in Dallas but left to form a concert group called Great Moments of Ballet in 1956. This group toured throughout the United States, Asia, Canada, and South America until Danilova gave her farewell performance in September 1957 in Tokyo in *Raymonda.*

Danilova then taught at a ballet school in New York City and appeared in the musical *O, Captain!* in 1958; that same year she received the Capezio Dance Award. In late 1958 she was invited to choreograph the ballet in the Metropolitan Opera's *La Gioconda,* soon adding four more opera ballets to her choreographic repertoire. She mounted a full-length production of *Nutcracker* for the Washington Ballet in 1961 and later staged other productions for other companies.

In 1964 Balanchine asked Danilova to teach both classical technique and variations of established ballets at his School of American Ballet in New York City. While at the school, she appeared in the movie *Turning Point* (1977). She was the recipient of the 1984 Dance Magazine Award and in 1986 published her autobiography, *Choura: Memoirs of Alexandra Danilova*. She died of unpublished causes at age ninety-four.

As a performer, and especially in the particular roles she made her own, Danilova, small, impeccably groomed, and filled with what the dance writer John Gruen called an "intoxicating joie de vivre," was considered unrivaled. In 1977 Anthony Fay wrote in *Dance* magazine, "Danilova was a personality among personalities, a singular stylist, a blithe spirit, a great lady of the theatre." At a posthumous reception in September 1997 in her honor, the choreographer Donald Saddler added, "Wit, technical skill, and consummate artistry have united to make Alexandra Danilova one of the greatest ballerinas of all time."

Danilova was also, through her long dance and later teaching careers, a remarkable single thread from the apogee of Russian ballet to dance at the end of the twentieth century. She studied directly with Vaganova, Nicholas Legat, and Enrico Cecchetti; she knew many of the century's leading choreographers, including Michel Fokine, Massine, Bronislava Nijinska, Balanchine, and Agnes de Mille; she danced with most leading dancers of the age; and, as a teacher, she worked with Gelsey Kirkland, Suzanne Farrell, and Mikhail Baryshnikov. Fay concluded his article with this observation, "She has probably made more contributions to ballet in America . . . than any other ballerina . . . [and] her fans will always regard her as Alexandra the Great."

★

Although Danilova's class notebooks, personal correspondence, and other documents were given to the Library of Congress by her stepdaughter Kim Kokitch, the most complete information about her is in her autobiography, *Choura: Memoirs of Alexandra Danilova* (1986). Details about her early life can also be found in Eileen ("Pigeon") Crowle, "Alexandra Danilova: Her Early Years," *Dance* (Mar. 1956); Allyn Moss, "Alexandra Danilova," *Dance* (Mar. 1961); and John Gruen, *The Private World of Ballet* (1975). Her work with the various Ballets Russes companies is well described in Anthony Fay, "The Belle of the Ballets Russes: Alexandra Danilova," *Dance* (Oct. 1977); as a dancer with Balanchine in Robert Tracy, *Balanchine's Ballerinas* (1983); and as a teacher at his School of American Ballet in Jennifer Dunning, *But First a School* (1985). An obituary is in the *New York Times* (15 July 1997). The testimonials from her memorial service are in "Remembering Alexandra Danilova," *Ballet Review* (spring 1998).

SANDRA SHAFFER VANDOREN

DAVIES, John Paton, Jr. (*b.* 6 April 1908 in Kiating, Sichuan Province, China; *d.* 23 December 1999 in Asheville, North Carolina), career U.S. foreign service officer and China expert who became a prominent victim of McCarthyism.

Davies was the elder of two sons born to Baptist missionaries John Paton Davies, Sr., an American, and his Canadian-born wife, Helen MacNeill, a former singer and church soloist. Davies was born and raised in China, where as a teenager he attended the Shanghai American School, a missionary institution. He then spent two undergraduate years at the University of Wisconsin Experimental College, followed by successive years at Yenching University, Beijing, and Columbia University, which granted him a B.S. degree in 1931. Davies joined the Foreign Service the following year, then returned to China in 1933, where he served successively in Kunming, Beijing, Shenyang, and Hankou, before returning to Beijing. On 24 August 1942 Davies married Patricia Louise Grady, a *Washington Post* correspondent and the daughter of Henry F. Grady, the first American ambassador to India. The couple had seven children.

Immediately after the Japanese attack on the U.S. naval base in Pearl Harbor in December 1941, Davies became diplomatic aide and political adviser to U.S. General Joseph W. Stilwell, the new commander of the China-India-Burma theater. Until Stilwell's 1944 recall, Davies accompanied him through the Allied forces' initial defeat in Burma and subsequent retreat to China's temporary Nationalist capital, Chongqing. Thereafter, until 1945 Davies advised Patrick J. Hurley, presidential envoy and United States ambassador to China.

John Paton Davies, 1969. AP/WIDE WORLD PHOTOS

But Davies was much more than a desk-bound diplomat. In 1943 Davies and seventeen other American officials and journalists (among them Eric Sevareid) were forced to parachute from the plane during a flight from China to India when an engine failed. Once on the ground, Davies led the group to safety on a harrowing month-long trek through the jungle. He received the Medal of Freedom in 1948 for this heroic effort.

The U.S. government dispatched the Dixie Mission to Chinese Communist headquarters at Yan'an in 1944, due partly to Davies's insistence. Its purpose was to encourage Chinese Communist efforts to repel the Japanese invasion, but it also sought to evaluate Communist strength. Impressed by Communist discipline, austerity, and popular support, several of the Dixie Mission's members came to believe Mao Zedong would probably ultimately overthrow the Nationalist government, and Davies urged the United States, without abandoning Jiang Jieshi (Chiang Kai-shek), to cultivate the Chinese Communists.

Davies visited several times, fruitlessly relaying relatively cooperative messages from the Communist leader Mao Tsetung to top American officials. In late 1944 Davies assisted Ambassador Hurley's efforts to negotiate a truce and forge a coalition government that would include both Chinese Nationalists and Communists. Davies characterized China's civil war as a conflict incomprehensible to foreigners, from which the United States should remain aloof. When this became impossible, he recommended continuing American aid to the ruling Nationalist Kuomintang regime under Chiang Kai-shek, but also suggested that if, as he anticipated, the Communists eventually took power, the United States should cooperate with them to preclude a Sino-Soviet alliance.

Davies realized only later that he had underestimated the Communists' pro-Soviet leanings and that he had confused their popularity with a commitment to democracy. This led Hurley to suspect Davies of harboring pro-Communist sympathies. From 1945 onward Davies and other China specialists were denounced by the "China Lobby," a powerful group of industrialists and politicians that supported the Nationalist forces in Taiwan. After China fell to the Communists, Davies and his fellow China specialists also drew the ire of Senator Joseph R. McCarthy, the Republican junior senator who from the late 1940s to mid-1950s spearheaded an extremist campaign against those who were suspected of being pro-Communist.

Despite the cloud of suspicion that was beginning to surround him, Davies became first secretary at the U.S. embassy in Moscow in 1945. Two years later he was appointed deputy director of the policy planning staff. In contrast to the China Lobby's fears, his advice and analyses tended to be relatively hardline. Although he favored U.S. recognition of the People's Republic of China, he repeatedly condemned its pro-Soviet attitude, and in 1950 even suggested the United States exploit its nuclear superiority to force a showdown with the Soviet Union.

In July 1950, shortly after the Korean War began, Davies warned of the increasing probability that China might intervene in the conflict. He recommended that the United States inform the Chinese government that, should this occur, the United States would retaliate with a major bombing campaign against Chinese territory. In spring 1951, following the massive Chinese military intervention of November 1950, Davies helped arrange an unofficial Soviet-American dialogue that eventually helped bring about peace talks.

Davies underwent eight separate security investigations by the civil service loyalty review board between 1950 and 1953. Although each investigation cleared him, they failed to satisfy the China Lobby. McCarthyites insisted that Davies's proposal to recruit double agents from Americans friendly with the Chinese Communists proved that he was out to subvert his country's intelligence network. Davies joined the United States High Commission in Germany in 1951 as director of political affairs. In 1953 the new Eisenhower administration, apprehensive of McCarthyism but unable to force the senator's resignation, exiled Davies to diplomatic obscurity in Peru. A ninth security investigation in 1954, based partly upon testimony from Hurley, characterized Davies as disloyal, whereupon Secretary of State John Foster Dulles dismissed him, stating Davies had "demonstrated a lack of judgment, discretion, and reliability."

Davies, virtually unemployable in the prevailing political climate, established a furniture design and manufacturing business called Estilo in Lima, Peru, and wrote a weekly newspaper column. Returning to Washington in 1964, he published *Foreign and Other Affairs* (1964), a collection of his newspaper articles criticizing U.S. Latin American policy as insufficiently supportive of strong governments. It wasn't until 1969 that was he rehabilitated and his pension rights reinstated.

Davies and other old China hands, their reputations greatly restored by the impact of the Vietnam War and the new opening to China, testified before the Senate Foreign Relations Committee in 1971. In that same year Davies moved to Málaga, Spain, where he continued to write his newspaper columns. He also produced an autobiographical account of U.S. China policy, analyzing its persistent inability to influence China. Later in the 1970s Davies settled in Asheville, North Carolina, where he died of multiple organ failure in 1999. After a private funeral service, his remains were cremated. Davies was the most intellectual of the U.S. State Department China experts, whose post–World War II purging severely crippled the country's capacity to develop prudent and rational policies toward Asia.

★

Davies's personal papers are held by the Harry S. Truman Presidential Library at Independence, Missouri. His diplomatic reports and other official papers, including records on his investigation and eventual dismissal, are among Department of State records in National Archives II, College Park, Maryland. Many documents written by Davies are included in the relevant volumes of the Foreign Relations of the United States series, published by the U.S. Department of State, and Anna Kasten Nelson, ed., *The State Department Policy Planning Staff Papers*, 3 vols. (1983). Davies himself published *Foreign and Other Affairs* (1964), the memoir *Dragon by the Tail: American, British, Japanese, and Russian Encounters with China and One Another* (1972), and reflected further in Paul Gordon Lauren, ed., *The China Hands' Legacy: Ethics and Diplomacy* (1987). Eric Sevareid, in *Not So Wild a Dream* (1946), details Davies wartime heroism, and Maochun Yu, *OSS in China: Prelude to Cold War* (1997), describes Davies's wartime dealings with the Chinese Communists. Davies's truncated foreign service career is discussed in David Halberstam, *The Best and the Brightest* (1972); George F. Kennan, *Memoirs, 1950–1963* (1972); Ely Jacques Kahn, *The China Hands: America's Foreign Service Officers and What Befell Them* (1975); and James Fetzer, "The Case of John Paton Davies, Jr.," *Foreign Service Journal* 54 (1976): 15–22, 31–32. Informative sketches of Davies's role in successive presidential administrations are given in Eleanora W. Schoenebaum, ed., *Political Profiles: The Truman Years* (1978), and *Political Profiles: The Eisenhower Years* (1980). Obituaries are in the *Washington Post, New York Times,* and *Chicago Sun-Times* (all 24 Dec. 1999). Davies recorded several television interviews on U.S. China policy in the 1990s.

PRISCILLA ROBERTS

DAVIS, Martin S. (*b*. 5 February 1927 in New York City; *d*. 4 October 1999 in New York City), film executive responsible for transforming the diversified Gulf + Western Industries into the media conglomerate Paramount Communications.

Davis, an extremely private person when it came to discussing his background and family, was the son of a Polish immigrant father who worked as a real estate broker. When Davis left high school in 1943, two years short of graduation, to join the army, he lied about his age, only to be discharged when his deception was discovered. After completing high school in 1945, he reenlisted at age eighteen, just as the war was coming to an end. After returning to civilian life in 1946, Davis attended college, but a few semesters at City College of New York and New York University convinced him he could succeed in business without a degree.

Davis began working in the public relations division of

Martin S. Davis, 1991. NICK UT/ASSOCIATED PRESS AP

the Samuel Goldwyn Company's New York City office in 1946. Although he initially had no special interest in the movie industry, and saw this first job as nothing more than a paycheck, his attitude changed when, within two years, he was promoted to the assistant national director of advertising and publicity. Having mastered the art of publicizing movies, Davis left Goldwyn in 1955 to become the eastern publicity head at Allied Artists. Three years later he joined Paramount Pictures, the studio where he spent most of his career. Again, his rise was rapid, from the director of sales and marketing (1958–1961) to the head of publicity (1960–1965), and finally to positions as the executive vice president and chief operating officer (1965).

In 1965 Ernest Martin, a Broadway producer, and Herbert Siegel, the president of the talent agency General Artists Corporation, attempted to gain control of Paramount, charging that the studio had become such a gerontocracy, it could only survive with young (or relatively young) blood, which they intended to supply. Paramount's president, George Weltner, knew his studio could not remain freestanding for long, given its dismal grosses and mediocre films. But he was so alienated by the insurgents' contempt for seniority that he asked Davis to find an alternative buyer for Paramount.

The buyer was already on the Paramount board:

Charles Bluhdorn, who had built Gulf+Western Industries from a foundation of automobile replacement parts into a diversified corporation with interests in beef, sugar, citrus-fruit processing, paper products, and metals. In 1966 Paramount became a Gulf+Western subsidiary. That same year, Bluhdorn, who knew nothing about making movies, hired the former actor Robert Evans, who was soon elevated to the production head. Evans brought the journalist Peter Bart onboard, and together they were responsible for some of Paramount's greatest successes of the 1970s, such as *The Godfather* (1972) and *The Godfather, Part II* (1974).

Davis, who had become the senior vice president of Gulf+Western in 1970, was not involved in film production. He was known as Bluhdorn's hatchet man, and he saved Bluhdorn from public humiliation when the Securities and Exchange Commission (SEC) conducted an investigation of Gulf+Western because of the company's misleading financial reports, inflated stock prices, and Bluhdorn's habit of using Gulf+Western stock as collateral for personal loans. Davis was responsible for the SEC dropping its suit against Bluhdorn.

With Bluhdorn's death in 1984, Davis was elected the chief executive officer of Gulf+Western. He sold off subsidiaries that were not media centered (sugar operations, racetracks), keeping those that were (the publishing house Simon and Schuster, Paramount Pictures), and acquiring new ones (the publishing house Prentice Hall). By 1989 Davis had reduced Gulf+Western to a communications conglomerate (film, television, music publishing, a Canadian theater chain, educational and trade publishing). Thus a new corporate name was necessary: Paramount Communications. Having created Paramount Communications, Davis decided to extend his empire by making a bid for Time, Inc., which was planning to merge with Warner Communications. Davis failed to stop the merger, which resulted in the birth of Time Warner.

By turning Gulf+Western into a media conglomerate, Davis also made it a desirable takeover prospect. In 1993 Sumner Redstone, who owned the mini conglomerate Viacom and the theater chain National Amusements, succeeded in defeating Barry Diller in a bid for Paramount Communications, which then became a division of Viacom, joining other units such as MTV, VH1, Blockbuster Video, Showtime, Simon and Schuster, and United Paramount Network (known as the fifth network). Although Redstone had promised Davis a major role in the newly restructured company, he brought in Frank Biondi, an Ivy Leaguer like himself, as Viacom's president and chief operating officer. The Davis era was over.

Even though he lacked a college degree, Davis knew enough about finance to become in 1995 a cofounder and managing partner of Wellspring Capital Management, a New York City private investment firm. After suffering a heart attack, he died at age seventy-two at New York City's Roosevelt Hospital. His survivors were his second wife Luella and son Philip. His other son, Martin, Jr., had predeceased him.

Although many found Davis ruthless and unfeeling, he also had a philanthropic side. He was the chair of the New York chapter of the National Multiple Sclerosis Society and a trustee of Fordham University and Carnegie Hall. Above all, Davis should be remembered for having reduced Bluhdorn's bloated operation to a slick media conglomerate. By realizing that Gulf+Western's most valuable operations were media related, Davis succeeded in proving that less is more—a point that Bluhdorn, with his tendency toward excess, would never have appreciated.

★

Davis's interviews only dealt with his professional, never his personal, life. One of the better interviews is Paul Richter, "Sharpening the Focus," *Los Angeles Times* (12 Apr. 1989). Davis is also discussed at some length in Ken Auletta, *The Highwaymen: Warriors of the Information Superhighway* (1997), and Bernard F. Dick, *Engulfed: The Death of Paramount Pictures and the Birth of Corporate Hollywood* (2001). Obituaries are in the *New York Times* (6 Oct. 1999) and *Washington Post* (7 Oct. 1999).

BERNARD F. DICK

DAY, James Lewis (*b.* 5 October 1925 in East Saint Louis, Illinois; *d.* 28 October 1998 in Cathedral City, California), U.S. Marine Corps general who was awarded the Medal of Honor for valor during the battle for Okinawa, Japan, in May 1945.

Day was the son of James Almon Day, a bookkeeper, and Gayle Hamilton Moy. He grew up in Overland, Missouri, and attended Ritenour High School. In March 1943, at the age of seventeen, Day dropped out of high school to enlist in the U.S. Marine Corps. Following basic and advanced infantry training he joined the Twenty-second Marine Regiment as a private. In February 1944 Day first saw combat when his World War II regiment took part in the capture of Eniwetok in the Marshall Islands. Later that year he participated in the capture of Guam in the Mariana Islands.

In the largest U.S. operation in the Pacific phase of World War II, the Twenty-second Marines, part of the Sixth Marine Division, landed on Okinawa in the Ryukyu Islands on 1 April 1945. During the next six weeks Day, now a lance corporal in charge of a squad in the weapons company of the regiment's Second Battalion, experienced little action as the Sixth Division and three other U.S. divisions slowly pushed forward against the Japanese, defending the southern end of the island. In early May the

Major General James L. Day, USMC, wearing the Medal of Honor he was awarded on 20 January 1998. J. Scott Applewhite/Associated Press AP

Americans reached a group of local strong points, known as the Shuri Line, stretching eight miles across the island. They launched a general offensive against the Shuri defenses on 11 May, but quickly stalled as the Japanese ferociously defended every hill, ridge, and gulch and punished the attacking Americans with devastating cross fire from their interlocking redoubts.

The Sixth Marine Division was on the extreme west side of the U.S. front. In its path stood Sugar Loaf Hill and two other hills that together served as the western anchor of the Japanese defensive line. If these hills could be secured, the Americans would be able to neutralize the enemy's cross fire and punch through the Shuri defenses. The Japanese had put together an ingenious system of fortifications to defend the hills and were determined to counterattack every U.S. penetration. Moreover, they had registered the hills and the surrounding ground so they could pummel the Americans with murderous artillery and mortar fire. The Twenty-second Marines began the battle for Sugar Loaf on 11 May, assaulting it several times before pulling back after suffering heavy casualties.

Over the next days the Marines launched more attacks against Sugar Loaf. On 14 May, Day and seven members of his squad went into the fray in support of an attacking infantry company. With his squad and the remnants of another unit, Day made his way to a critical position in front of the U.S. line on the western slope of Sugar Loaf. During the following days, using rifles, grenades, and a machine gun to stop the Japanese, they held this position in the face of fierce artillery and mortar shelling and a dozen enemy counterattacks. Only Day and one other Marine survived. For a time Day virtually fought alone despite suffering severe shrapnel wounds and white phosphorus burns. By 17 May, when he came down from Sugar Loaf, Day had yielded no ground to the Japanese, and more than 100 enemy dead were counted in front of his position, some of them just a few feet away.

The battle for Sugar Loaf continued for two more days before it was firmly in U.S. hands. But by valiantly holding off the Japanese counterattacks, Day had made it easier for the Marines to seize the hill and ultimately open a seam in the Shuri Line. Immediately after the battle Day's battalion commander began to collect witness statements to support a recommendation that he be awarded the Medal of Honor. The battalion commander was killed several days later, however, and the paperwork for the recommendation fell through the cracks and never moved up the chain of command. Day himself was too modest to pursue the award and for years refused to countenance a campaign on his behalf by veterans of the battle. The paperwork eventually resurfaced in 1996, when copies were found in the files of a recently deceased marine. Authorities verified their authenticity and, in January 1998, President Bill Clinton awarded Day the Medal of Honor in a White House ceremony.

After World War II, Day remained in the marines and attained the rank of gunnery sergeant before being commissioned as a second lieutenant in 1952. He was then sent to Korea, where he saw action as a company grade officer while with the Seventh Marine Regiment. From 1954 to 1976 Day rose from captain to the rank of brigadier general while holding a variety of line and staff billets. These included two tours in Vietnam, the first from 1966 to 1967 as a battalion commander with the Ninth Marine Regiment, and the second from 1972 to 1973 as the operations officer of the Ninth Marine Brigade. He also attended the Army War College from 1971 to 1972.

Between 1976 and 1986 Day advanced to the rank of major general. Among other assignments, he served as commander of the First Marine Division, with additional duty as the commander of the I Marine Amphibious Force, and deputy chief of staff for training in the Marine Corps headquarters. At one time he held three simultaneous positions: commander of the Marine Corps Base, Camp S. D. Butler, Okinawa; deputy commander, Marine Corps Bases, Pacific; and Okinawa Area Coordinator. When he retired in 1986 Day was the last active-duty marine to have served as a combat infantryman in World War II, Korea, and Vietnam. In addition, he was the only Marine infantryman to have been wounded and decorated for valor in all three wars.

In retirement Day served as chancellor of the National University campus in Palm Springs, California, and was a partner in a Cathedral City construction company. During his last assignment on Okinawa, Day became involved with the Ryukyu-American Historical Research Society. After he left the marines, he was an honorary president of the society and played a prominent role in its efforts to return works of art and artifacts to Okinawa that had been removed by Americans during and after the war.

A tall, slim, retiring man, Day was married to Sally Aguayo. They had four children. Day died of a heart attack at age seventy-three. He is buried at Fort Rosecrans National Cemetery, in San Diego, California. Possessing thirty-one decorations and medals for valor in addition to the Medal of Honor, Day stood out for his courage under fire, and his role in helping the Americans triumph in the bloody struggle for Okinawa.

★

Day's exploits at Sugar Loaf are described in Joseph H. Alexander, *The Final Campaign: Marines in the Victory on Okinawa* (1996), "Vet to Get Top Medal Fifty-Three Years After Deeds," *Pacific Stars and Stripes* (19 Jan. 1998), and Malcolm McConnell, "Hero of Sugar Loaf Hill," *Reader's Digest* (Dec. 1998). The battle for Sugar Loaf is extensively discussed in George Feifer, *Tennozan: The Battle for Okinawa and the Atomic Bomb* (1992). An obituary is in the *New York Times* (4 Nov. 1998).

JOHN KENNEDY OHL

DE KOONING, Willem (*b.* 24 April 1904 in Rotterdam, the Netherlands; *d.* 19 March 1997 in East Hampton, New York), influential pioneer of abstract expressionism who remained committed in his art to the dual agendas of abstraction and figuration.

Willem de Kooning was one of two children of Leendert de Kooning, distributor of beer, wine, and soft drinks, and Cornelia Nobel, proprietor of a café bar frequented by sailors. When his parents divorced in June 1907, he was placed in his father's care. By all accounts a formidable woman, his mother fought the arrangement, and shortly thereafter de Kooning came to live with her. In 1908 both parents remarried and between them provided him with four half-siblings.

De Kooning attended grammar school until he was twelve. Late in life he recalled that one of his teachers believed he should attend the Rotterdam Academy of Fine Arts and Techniques, but his mother thought he should be

Willem de Kooning, 1968. ASSOCIATED PRESS AP

earning money. He began as an apprentice at the commercial arts and decorating firm, Jan and Jaap Giddings, where he received encouragement to pursue art. From 1917 to 1921 (and sporadically until 1924) de Kooning attended evening classes at the Rotterdam Academy. In 1920 he began to work for Bernard Romein, a sign and display designer for a local department store, who broadened his understanding of modern art. In 1924 he traveled with student friends to Brussels and Antwerp, Belgium, picking up odd commercial art jobs, attending the occasional art class, and visiting museums. He returned that year to complete his studies at the Rotterdam Academy, after which he decided to leave the Netherlands.

On 16 August 1926 de Kooning entered the United States illegally as a stowaway on the SS *Shelley*, leaving the ship when it docked in Newport News, Virginia. His route to New York was circuitous as he sailed to Boston, acquired legitimate papers, headed south again by train and ferry, and settled in Hoboken, New Jersey, in a Dutch Seaman's Home. As he began to learn English, he supported himself by painting houses. A year later de Kooning moved to New York City, living at first in a studio apartment in the West Forties. His was a peripatetic life: he moved constantly from one apartment to another, living sometimes with a friend, sometimes with a girlfriend. In 1936 de Kooning secured a Chelsea area loft at 156 West Twenty-second Street, where he remained until 1943.

De Kooning had no thoughts of being an artist when he arrived in the United States. Rather, he sought prosperity, which he believed was best accomplished through commercial art, an idea that first came to him as a young boy looking at slick ads in American magazines. But once in New York City, he discovered Greenwich Village and "a whole tradition in painting and in poetry." By the early 1930s, he had forged friendships with other artists, including John Graham, Mark Rothko, and, most importantly, Arshile Gorky, a close friend who influenced not only de Kooning's art but also his definition of how to be an artist.

At this time de Kooning described himself as a Sunday painter who worked at a variety of jobs. However, his participation in the mural division of the Works Progress Administration (WPA) from August 1935 through 1936 changed his attitude. Suddenly he was part of a cadre of artists working together, and he was for the first time able to support himself on a modest salary while painting full time. De Kooning began his first series of paintings in 1936—male figures set within a constricted space in compositions that seemed to evoke the sense of isolation and despair of the depression. The paintings were composites of his image with those of his friends.

In 1937 de Kooning met a young art student, Elaine Fried, sharing with her first his training, then his loft. They married on 9 December 1943 and by 1944 had moved to Greenwich Village. He also established a separate studio nearby. Shortly after their meeting, de Kooning began his first series of women (1937–1945). Both Elaine and her sister sat for the artist, who painted at first quiet, serene images. By 1940 de Kooning's women had become progressively more agitated and frenetic, as he distorted and flattened anatomical elements, shoulders and knees particularly, in resistance to the Renaissance understanding of space.

In 1946 de Kooning embarked on a series of black-and-white abstractions, considered among his finest achievements. He used commercial black enamel paint and often painted on paper that he later mounted onto canvas. To avoid a preconceived idea or subject, he sometimes began randomly, painting a word or number. He also adapted the concepts of collage by making paper drawings that he tore up and placed on the surface of the work. Before removing the paper template, he painted over both surfaces and sometimes left fragments in the paint film. After each spontaneous gesture de Kooning deliberated over the fresh strokes, incorporating free associations in the compositions but never letting go of conscious control.

When the Charles Egan Gallery exhibited ten of de Kooning's abstractions in April 1948, de Kooning achieved recognition and great critical acclaim within the art community. Alfred Barr purchased *Painting* (1948) for the Museum of Modern Art, and critics were enthusiastic, especially Thomas Hess. Hess and Harold Rosenberg were influential advocates of his work. De Kooning was invited by Josef Albers to teach at the famed Black Mountain College in Asheville, North Carolina, that summer. Albers also asked him to join the faculty at Yale University for the 1950 fall term.

De Kooning also achieved prominence among his colleagues, a diverse group of artists who came to be known as the abstract expressionists. His black-and-white abstractions were perhaps the first major statement of the artistic issues with which many of them had been grappling. "Indeed, his subject seems to be the crucial intensity of the creative process itself," wrote the perceptive critic of *ARTnews*, "which de Kooning has translated into a new and purely pictorial idiom." The critic's observations conveyed the meaning of the term "action painting" (coined by Rosenberg in 1952) as epitomized by both de Kooning and his friend and rival, Jackson Pollock.

De Kooning, Pollock, and Franz Kline formed the core of the hard-drinking, argumentative, downtown Cedar Tavern crowd, whereas the uptown intellectualizing group formed around Rothko, Adolph Gottlieb, and Barnett Newman. Recognizing that they shared certain philosophical and aesthetic concerns, both groups of artists launched a series of organized activities. In February 1949 de Kooning gave his first lecture at the short-lived Subjects of the Artist school, and he was one of the founding members of The Club, established that fall with the purpose of holding meetings, panels, lectures, and parties to socialize and discuss art. In April 1950 de Kooning joined his colleagues in a now legendary three-day roundtable discussion to codify their artistic goals. Eighteen painters, including de Kooning, and ten sculptors signed a letter of protest (published that May in the *New York Times*) to the Metropolitan Museum of Art about its acquisition policy for vanguard American art. A photograph of the painters, captioned as "the Irascible Eighteen," was published in the 15 January 1951 issue of *Life Magazine* and gave the artists a national identity.

During this period, de Kooning began his second series of women (1947–1949) but continued his all-over abstractions. In June 1950 the artist finished his monumental abstraction, *Excavation* (Chicago Art Institute). He immediately shipped it and three other paintings off to the Venice Biennial, to which he, Pollock, and Gorky, among others, had been invited. While the painting garnered acclaim as it traveled from Venice to New York, Chicago, São Paulo, Brazil, and then back to Chicago to enter the Art Institute's collection, de Kooning found himself at an impasse, believing that he had taken his abstractions as far as they could go. He began work on what was to become his most controversial painting, *Woman I,* the key work in his third series of women and one of the most widely reproduced images of the 1950s. He placed the seated figure in the canvas center and pasted on the face a cutout of a woman's smile taken from a magazine ad, thereby identifying a particular confluence between the high and low arts.

De Kooning's painting process—always lengthy and filled with great anxiety—took on new meaning in *Woman I:* he would start to paint, contemplate the composition, get fresh ideas, scrape back parts, and revise the work, only to begin again. The figure was shifted to the left and her cutout smile removed to become a toothy grin of multifarious meanings depicted in slashes of paint. Visible in the paint film are ghosts of earlier stages. Painting quickly with his characteristic wet-into-wet technique to capture what he defined as "not so much the particular flash or glimpse, but the emotion of it," de Kooning often changed the painting dramatically within just a few hours of work. He finally finished it shortly before it was exhibited, alongside five more paintings of women, at the Sidney Janis Gallery in March 1953, his third solo show.

This time de Kooning did not receive the same approbation he had enjoyed earlier, although *Woman I* was purchased for the collection of the Museum of Modern Art. Many of his colleagues believed he had abandoned abstraction. Pollock, for example, is reported to have said accusingly, "You're doing the figure, you're still doing the same goddamn thing." Most of the critics were baffled by the confrontational nature of the figures, baring their teeth in ferocious grins, and many associated the aggressiveness with de Kooning's presumed view of women. The artist was never happy with the reactions the painting fueled, and at times he attempted to define his intent. In 1960 he said "painting the *Women* is a thing in art that has been done over and over," adding, "it had to do with the idea of the idol, the oracle, and above all the hilariousness of it."

As de Kooning began a series of urban abstractions in 1955, his marriage to Elaine was foundering. They officially separated in 1956, the same year his only child was born to artist Joan Ward. In 1958 de Kooning moved his studio to a loft on Broadway Avenue and began his parkway series, which were inspired by the sensation of weekend drives. Using large strokes of bright color, he painted with a new sense of assuredness, finding completion much easier. Thirteen large abstractions were exhibited in 1959 in his sixth gallery solo show. Held at Sidney Janis, it was a huge commercial success, with nearly every work sold by the end of the first day. As the *Time* magazine reviewer noted, "young abstractionists in search of a style have acclaimed as their leader New York City's Dutch-born Willem de Kooning, 55." De Kooning had become a celebrity.

Financially secure but uncomfortable with his fame, de Kooning began to spend most of his time in East Hampton, Long Island, which he and Elaine had first visited in 1951. De Kooning purchased land in the Springs area of East Hampton in 1959. He started building his new studio and home in 1962, but moved to East Hampton permanently in June 1963 before the studio was completed. His daughter, an active part of his life, lived nearby with her mother. By 1967 Knoedler Gallery was representing de Kooning; he later changed galleries in order to remain with Xavier Fourcade, then director of Knoedler, until Fourcade's death in 1987.

De Kooning was deeply affected by the East Hampton light and a pastoral quality entered his work. In 1961 he began a new series of women that lasted through the decade. Painted in a lighter, almost hedonistic palette, de Kooning's figures merged with the landscape, the tension between abstraction and figuration nearly snapping. In 1975, after a foray into sculpture lasting six years, de Kooning started a series of monumental abstract landscapes in large-scale, nearly square formats. The figure was now subsumed within the landscape. Only the sensual essence of the figure remained as a kind of charged eroticism to the very paint itself.

De Kooning's reputation had a curious duality in his later years. He was the most famous survivor of an art movement that had brought international attention to New York. Yet his recent work, although commercially successful, was no longer received with the same kind of critical attention, a development he had clearly foreseen at his 1959 exhibition when he was quoted as saying, "There's no way of astonishing anyone any more. I'm selling my own image now." His awards during this period were numerous, starting in 1960 with his election to the National Institute of Arts and Letters. He received the Guggenheim International Award in 1964, the Presidential Medal of Freedom in 1964 (of which he was especially proud), and the National Medal of Arts in 1986. De Kooning was elected to the American Academy of Arts and Letters in 1978, the same year the Solomon R. Guggenheim Museum gave him an exhibition focusing on his East Hampton work.

De Kooning received many retrospectives, the first significant one in 1968, organized by Hess for the Museum of Modern Art. When it opened at the Stedelijk Museum in Amsterdam, he returned to the Netherlands for the first time since 1926 (he had become a U.S. citizen in 1962). His next major retrospective was held in 1983 at the Whitney Museum of American Art. Included were his most recent paintings, the sparest he had ever produced; the severely reduced forms were painted in brightly hued, elegant lines that recalled shapes he had painted decades earlier. Around this time, those closest to de Kooning, including Elaine, were aware that he was declining mentally. Elaine had come back into his life in 1975, when she had purchased a house nearby. She helped him recover from alcoholism and began promoting his work and reputation. Elaine died in 1989 at a point when de Kooning's suffering from Alzheimer's had become acute. That September his daughter and his lawyer became his co-conservators. De Kooning, who had been in seclusion for a number of years, died at age ninety-two in his Springs studio in East Hampton, New York. His remains were cremated. At the time of his death, his work of the 1980s was on view at the Museum of Modern Art, where a memorial tribute was held that September.

De Kooning, who alone of the abstract expressionists remained inspired by visual cues from his environment, produced icons of modern painting. In 1989 a de Kooning painting brought $20.7 million at auction, the highest price at the time for the work of a living artist. His impact on later generations was substantial. De Kooning's gestural abstraction was appropriated by a wide range of artists, in particular the second generation of abstract expressionists, and his recognition of the ironical uses of commercial art provided a catalyst to pop artists. Just two years after his death, *ARTnews* magazine named de Kooning one of twenty-five most influential artists in America.

Whether figurative or abstract, de Kooning's retained his characteristic spatial ambiguity, for his overriding concern in painting had to do with space—as both subject and aesthetic issue. "The idea of space is given him [the artist] to change if he can," stated de Kooning in 1949. "The subject matter in the abstract is *space*. He fills it with an attitude." Two years later, at a symposium at the Museum of Modern Art, de Kooning likened the handling of space in the painting process to the limitless reaches of artistic imagination. "If I stretch my arms next to the rest of myself and wonder where my fingers are—that is all the space I need as a painter."

★

Of the many books on de Kooning, three are particularly insightful, the first by Thomas B. Hess, *Willem de Kooning* (1959), which was the first monograph on any of the abstract expressionists. See also Harry F. Gaugh, *De Kooning* (1983), and especially Sally Yard, *Willem de Kooning* (1997), an outgrowth of her dissertation for Princeton University, published in 1986, "Willem de Kooning: The First Twenty-six Years in New York, 1927–1952." There are many exhibition catalogues, among the most detailed being Whitney Museum of American Art, *Willem de Kooning: Drawings, Paintings, Sculpture* (1983); Judith Zilczer, *Willem de Kooning, from the Hirshhorn Museum Collection* (1993); and National Gallery of Art, *Willem de Kooning: Paintings* (1994). Elaine de Kooning published her recollections in "De Kooning Memories," *Vogue* (Dec. 1983). Most of de Kooning's important essays and statements are in George Scrivani, ed., *The Collected Writings*

of Willem de Kooning (1988), which includes his 1960 interview with David Sylvester, published without the questions. New biographical material is in Edvard Lieber, *Willem de Kooning: Reflections in the Studio* (2000). The library of the Museum of Modern Art has an artist file on de Kooning as well as a three-volume collection of photographs, critical commentaries, and annotations compiled by William C. Agee in 1962. His obituary is in the *New York Times* (20 Mar. 1997).

LEIGH BULLARD WEISBLAT

DELANY, Sarah Louise ("Sadie") (*b.* 19 September 1889 in Lynch's Station, Virginia; *d.* 25 January 1999 in Mount Vernon, New York), educator and author best known for *Having Our Say* (1993), a memoir written with her sister Bessie that achieved worldwide acclaim.

Delany was the second of ten children born to Henry Beard Delany, a freed slave who became a renowned educator and America's first elected African-American Episcopal bishop, and Nanny James Logan, a college matron. Although her entire life was marked by achievement, it was

Sadie Delany *(left)*, with her sister Bessie, 1993. © JACQUES CHENET/ GAMMA LIAISON

not until she was over 100 years old that Delany gained worldwide fame, with the publication of *Having Our Say: The Delany Sisters' First 100 Years* (1993), a dual memoir written with her sister Annie Elizabeth ("Bessie") Delany and the journalist Amy Hill Hearth.

Delany grew up on the campus of Saint Augustine's School (now College) in Raleigh, North Carolina, an institution established by the Episcopal Church in 1867 to educate freed slaves. The Delany children attended classes taught by teachers in training at the college. The importance of education was stressed in the Delany household. Despite growing up in an era when few people, black or white, went to college, all ten Delany children went on to become college-educated professionals.

Delany graduated from Saint Augustine's in 1910. She saved money for college by working as a Jeanes Supervisor for Wake County, North Carolina. In *Having Our Say*, Delany explains that the position of Jeanes Supervisor "was named after a white man, named Jeanes, who started a fund to introduce domestic science to colored schools in many parts of the South." She also recalled in *Having Our Say* that she also took on many of the duties of the school superintendent, so that at age twenty-one, she was the de facto supervisor of all of the African-American schools in Wake County.

In 1916 she moved to Harlem in New York City and enrolled in a two-year domestic-science program at the Pratt Institute in Brooklyn. Upon her graduation from Pratt in 1918, she entered the Teachers College of Columbia University, where she earned a B.Sc. degree in 1920 and an M.Ed. degree in 1925.

Delany was hired by the New York City public school system in the fall of 1920 to teach at Public School 119, a predominantly African-American elementary school. To supplement her income, she sold homemade cakes and candies. The venture was so successful that she eventually rented a loft in Harlem's business district and opened Delany's Delights. She closed the shop when the Great Depression came and people had little money for chocolate confections.

In 1926 Delany moved to Theodore Roosevelt High School, making her the first African American to teach domestic science at the high school level in New York City. Before she retired in 1960, she also taught at Washington Irving High School in Manhattan and Girls' High School in Brooklyn.

Delany lived for most of her life with her younger sister Bessie, who, after receiving a doctorate from Columbia University's dental school in 1923, became only the second African-American woman licensed to practice dentistry in New York State. The two sisters moved from Harlem to suburban Mount Vernon in 1957. Neither ever married.

In September 1991 the journalist Amy Hill Hearth knocked on the door of the sisters' Mount Vernon home, hoping to write a story about the pair on the occasion of Bessie's 100th birthday. Their meeting was the beginning of a long-lasting and providential relationship that propelled the sisters into the homes and hearts of the U.S. public.

Hearth was not only charmed by the sisters; she recognized they were living witnesses to a full century of U.S. history and had a story worth sharing with the world. In 1991 she wrote about the sisters for the *New York Times*, and the 22 September story generated tremendous interest and elicited the attention of the publisher Kodansha America. The sisters then teamed with Hearth to write *Having Our Say*. In the book, the two sisters' narratives were interwoven with interstitial material by Hearth, and the three voices blended together in a powerful and poignant chronicle of the United States at its best and worst.

The sisters' distinct personalities emerged through their writings—saintly "Sweet Sadie" and bossy "Queen Bess." Each had a different method of dealing with the challenges of being an African-American woman in the segregated South and the pre–civil rights era North. While Bessie was known to fight racism head-on, Sadie preferred a more subtle approach, often "playing dumb" and smiling in the face of her oppressors. She received one job, she claimed, by deliberately missing the interview so that the school officials would not realize she was an African American. Instead, she pretended there had been a mix-up and showed up on the first day of classes. "Child, when I showed up that day—at Theodore Roosevelt High School, a white high school—they just about died. But my name was on the list to teach there, and it was too late for them to send me someplace else."

Having Our Say appeared on the *New York Times* hardcover best-seller list for twenty-eight weeks, and the paperback best-seller list for seventy-seven weeks. It was adopted as a high school and college text, and a companion study guide, written by Jannette L. Dates, was published. The memoir was adapted into a play, which had a nine-month run on Broadway, and was performed in over 120 cities in the United States and abroad. A television movie, starring Diahann Carroll as Sadie and Ruby Dee as Bessie, aired on CBS in 1999.

The sisters still had a few more things to say after the publication of their first book, so they teamed with Hearth to write *The Delany Sisters' Book of Everyday Wisdom* (1994). In this sequel, the sisters dispensed practical advice about everything from diet and nutrition to marriage and religion. "We're as old as Moses," they wrote in the book's prologue, "so maybe we have learned a few things along the way, and we'd like to pass them along."

After Bessie's death in 1995 at the age of 104, Sadie told interviewers that she wasn't sure she could go on living without the little sister who'd been by her side for over 100 years. She dealt with her grief by writing another book, *On My Own at 107: Reflections of a Life Without Bessie,* published in 1997. The book's publication made her America's oldest best-selling author. In the book, she paid tribute to her sister and wrote of "learning that I am a separate human being . . . for the first time in my life."

Delany died in her sleep of natural causes at the age of 109 and is buried in Mount Hope Cemetery in Raleigh. The two sisters left a $1 million bequest in honor of their father to fund a scholarship at Saint Augustine's College. One of the centenarian sweetheart's most quoted sayings was, "Life is short, and it's up to you to make it sweet." For Delany, who weathered more than 100 years of societal changes, overcoming racial and gender discrimination to become a pioneer in the New York City school system and a best-selling author, life was sweet indeed.

★

The library at Saint Augustine's College in Raleigh is home to a large collection of materials donated from the estates of Sadie and Bessie Delany. The North Carolina Museum of History in Raleigh also houses a collection of the sisters' personal belongings, including photographs, furnishings, clothing, and household items. The inspiration for *Having Our Say,* was the article by Amy Hill Hearth, "Two 'Maiden Ladies' with Century-Old Stories to Tell," *New York Times* (22 Sept. 1991). Other articles of note include Marjorie Rosen, "Free Spirits: The Sisters Delany Have Been Ahead of Their Time for a Century," *People Weekly* (22 Nov. 1993); Judith Newmark, "A 'Say' Worth Having: The Delany Sisters Had More Than Enough Stories to Fill a Play—and Three Books," *St. Louis Post-Dispatch* (2 Jan. 1997); and Sarah Booth Conroy, "Recalling the Sisters: A Best-Seller and Tony-Nominated Play Comes to TV," *Washington Post* (18 Apr. 1999). An obituary is in the *New York Times* (26 Jan. 1999).

BRENDA SCOTT ROYCE

DE MENIL, Dominique Schlumberger (*b.* 23 March 1907 in Paris, France; *d.* 31 December 1997 in Houston, Texas), heiress to the Schlumberger oil field service company fortune who was a world-famous art collector, philanthropist, and advocate for human rights.

De Menil was the daughter of Conrad Schlumberger, an inventor (and, with his brother Marcel, founder of the Société de Prospection Electrique, an early ancestor of Schlumberger, Ltd.), and Louise del Pech. De Menil received an undergraduate degree from the Sorbonne in 1927 and pursued graduate studies there in both mathematics and physics.

On 9 May 1931 she married Jean de Menil, with whom she had five children. The de Menils were equal partners

Dominique de Menil, 1987. WALT FRERCK/© BETTMANN/CORBIS

in all of their artistic and social concerns. After the fall of France to the German army during World War II, Dominique and Jean, who later changed his name to John, moved to Venezuela in 1941. There, John established Schlumberger as an overseas company free of Nazi-occupied France. The de Menils moved to Houston in 1942 and became U.S. citizens in 1962.

As early as the 1940s, the de Menils began to collect art. Approached by the University of St. Thomas, they provided the Philip Johnson master plan for the school's campus. They also founded the art department, and when its director, Jermayne McAgy, died in midterm, Dominique became acting director and lecturer. At age fifty-six she was an immediate success in her new career. In 1954 the de Menils founded the Menil Foundation, a nonprofit charitable organization of diverse interests. As members of the Contemporary Art Museum, they curated a Van Gogh retrospective, and they gave Max Ernst his first exhibition in a museum. Dominique was donor, president, and a trustee of the foundation.

In 1969, on the campus of Rice University, the de Menils founded the Rice Media Center, whose Film Series established itself with regular visits by such notable filmmakers as Jean-Luc Godard, Andy Warhol, and Roberto Rossellini. The same year, they founded the Institute for the Arts, also at Rice University, with Dominique serving as director until 1980. In 1971 they built the Rothko Chapel as a place of worship open to all religious traditions. The chapel features fourteen meditational works by Russian-born abstract artist Mark Rothko, commissioned by the de Menils in 1964, that constitute a holistic work involving architecture and lighting as well as the fourteen panels. They also expanded the art and art history departments at Rice University and created the Southwest Alternate Media Project in 1977, a direct offshoot of the Rice Media Center. As these media art centers became established, the legacy of the de Menils was set in motion. Their influence and support of film inspired generations of filmmakers.

By 1970 the de Menil art collection had grown to some 10,000 pieces, and John and Dominique saw the need to construct a museum to house it. Following John's death in 1973, Dominique undertook the task of building the museum. She visited other American art museums and chose Renzo Piano, Italian architect of the Pompidou Museum in Paris, to design the building. The Menil Collection Museum, which opened on 7 June 1987, is widely considered the definitive private art museum in the world—containing some 15,000 objects, with more than 100 works each by René Magritte and Max Ernst. The collection spans the chronological extremes of art, ranging from 20,000-year-old Paleolithic carvings to Jackson Pollock's abstract expressionism and Andy Warhol's pop art, and has four areas of emphasis: antiquities, Byzantine art, tribal arts, and twentieth-century art, with an especially impressive collection of surrealist art.

Resistant to labels, de Menil hated to be called a "collector," considering it too pretentious. "I don't even know what surrealism is," she remarked tartly. It was important to her that the building that housed the art be understated in style. "Works of art are like people," she said. "They either talk or they're mute. It depends upon what surrounds them." A very slight, graceful person with translucent skin and fine-spun silver hair, she herself had an understated elegance, preferring simple black slacks and silk blouses.

Determined to preserve the collection, de Menil never sold or loaned a piece of art from the Menil Collection Museum. At her direction, no more than 5 percent of the collection was to be shown at one time, in order to give museum-goers a fresh experience with each visit.

In 1995 de Menil opened the Cy Twombly Gallery, also designed by Piano, across the street from the Menil Collection, and in 1997, close to the Rothko Chapel, she built the Byzantine Fresco Chapel Museum, designed by her architect son François, to house rare thirteenth-century frescoes from Cyprus. As an expression of her passion for making great art accessible to everyone, admission to her

museums, all located within blocks of each other, is free. Grace Glueck of the *New York Times* called the de Menils "Houston's most rewardingly subversive citizens, bringing maverick ideas to the provinces about art, politics, and what to do with money."

Throughout their life in Houston, the de Menils supported human rights and political candidates with similar commitment. Dominique, increasingly dedicated to human rights, established in 1981 the Rothko Chapel Awards for "Commitment to Truth and Freedom." In 1986, in cooperation with Jimmy Carter, she created the Carter-Menil Human Rights Foundation, which awards a $100,000 prize every other year to organizations or individuals for their outstanding commitment to opposing human rights violations. In 1994 the Foundation awarded a special prize to the Institute of Applied Science, Oslo, Norway, for its efforts to bring peace between the Palestine Liberation Organization (PLO) and Israel.

The Association of Rice Alumni in 1973 awarded de Menil its Gold Medal for her contributions to the university. Additionally, she received honorary doctorates from Emory University, Harvard University, and Loyola University in New Orleans; the French Order of Arts and Letters (1984), the French Legion of Honor (1985), and Commander of Arts and Letters (1991); the Officers' Cross of the Order of Leopold I, from the King of Belgium; and the Commander's Cross of the Order of Merit of the Federal Republic of Germany. President Ronald Reagan awarded de Menil the United States Medal of the Arts (1986).

De Menil died in her sleep early on New Year's Eve morning in 1997. She was survived by her five children, ten grandchildren, and three great-grandchildren. She is buried at Forest Park Lawndale Cemetery in Houston. Tributes to de Menil abounded in Houston, where her gifts to the city, both tangible and intangible, defy tabulation, and where the Schlumberger oil business has long been headquartered. After her arrival in Houston in the early 1940s, she became the person most responsible for expanding the cultural horizons of her adopted city, and she is credited with the lasting cultural legacy of having established one of the best private collections in the world.

★

Numerous articles chronicle de Menil's life and work: Nancy Brown, "At Home in Houston," *Entre Nous* (15 Feb. 1957); "Mrs. De Menil to Receive Rice Alumni's Top Award," *Houston Chronicle* (14 Oct. 1973); "Awards Slated at Rice," *Houston Post* (14 Oct. 1973); Clifford Pugh, "The Magnificent Obsession—Dominique de Menil's Life in the Arts," *Houston Post* (31 May 1977); Marguerite Johnston, "The de Menils" [four-part series], *Houston Post* (Jan. 1977); Grace Glueck, "The de Menil Family—The Medici of Modern Art," *New York Times Magazine* (18 May 1986); Grace

Glueck, "Houston's Elegant Menil Collection," *New York Times* (26 May 1987); Patricia C. Johnson, "Art Patron Dominique de Menil—A Personal Vision Goes Public," *Houston Chronicle* (29 July 1990); Karl Kilian, "A Window into de Menil's Life of Touching Passion," *Houston Chronicle* (4 Jan. 1998); Mel White, "All Things de Menil," *National Geographic Traveler* (Mar./Apr. 1998); Patricia C. Johnson and Dan Feldstein, "Surreal Art, Real Worry," *Houston Chronicle* (23 May 1999); Bruce Westbrook, "Dominique de Menil—Her Legacy," *Houston Chronicle* (23 May 1999); and Patricia C. Johnson, "Menil and Glaser Reach Agreement over Dismissal," *Houston Chronicle* (9 July 1999). An obituary is in the *Houston Chronicle* (1 Jan. 1998).

JAMES AGUSTÍN CASTAÑEDA

DENVER, John (*b.* 31 December 1943 in Roswell, New Mexico; *d.* 12 October 1997 off the coast of Pacific Grove, California), singer and songwriter who attracted a massive following in the 1970s for his concerts, records, and television appearances, and thereafter used his celebrity to support political and humanitarian causes.

Denver was born Henry John Deutschendorf, Jr., the son of a career Air Force officer who worked primarily as a flight instructor but also occasionally as a test pilot. In 1961 his father set the world speed record for a B-58 bomber. His mother, Erma Louise Swope, was a homemaker. He had a younger brother, Ron. The family moved frequently during Denver's childhood, following his father's military postings. They spent a year in Japan (1949–1950), then moved to Tucson, Arizona.

At the age of eleven or twelve, Denver was given a guitar, a 1910 Gibson, by his grandmother and took lessons for a year. In 1957 the Deutschendorfs moved to Montgomery, Alabama, where Denver sang in his junior high school chorus and entertained friends by playing his guitar. The family moved to Fort Worth, Texas, in 1958, and he graduated from Arlington Heights High School in 1961.

Rejected for enrollment by the U.S. Air Force Academy because of poor eyesight, Denver instead enrolled at Texas Technological Institute, where he majored in architecture. But he also performed locally in a folk group called the Alpine Trio, and in the middle of his junior year in early 1964 his musical ambitions caused him to drop out and move to Los Angeles. Denver supported himself as a draftsman while signing up for open-mike nights at folk clubs. He eventually came to the attention of folk impresario Randy Sparks, founder of the New Christy Minstrels, who gave him an extended booking at his club, Ledbetter's, and arranged for him to cut a demonstration tape.

John Denver, 1985. AP/WIDE WORLD PHOTOS

Adopting his stage name at this point, Denver also worked in clubs in Texas and Arizona through mid-1965, when he went to New York City to audition for a place in the Mitchell Trio. Formerly called the Chad Mitchell Trio, the group was one of the major commercial folk acts of the day. Denver was selected to replace Chad Mitchell from among 250 applicants and joined the group in July 1965. On 9 June 1967 he married Ann Martell, a student he had met while performing with the trio at her college in Minnesota.

Denver remained with the trio until it dissolved in 1969, meanwhile gradually building a reputation as a solo performer and songwriter. He relaunched his solo career and signed a recording contract with RCA Victor in the summer of 1969. The label released his debut solo album, *Rhymes and Reasons,* that fall. Its sales were marginal, but at the same time, "Leaving on a Jet Plane," a Denver composition that had been covered by Peter, Paul, and Mary two years earlier, became an unexpected hit, reaching number one and selling a million copies. Denver's follow-up albums, *Take Me to Tomorrow* and *Whose Garden Was This?,* were also commercial failures, but he turned his career around in 1971 with the upbeat country-folk tune "Take Me Home, Country Roads," his own million-selling number-one hit, and *Poems, Prayers, and Promises,* the gold-selling album from which it came.

Aerie, Denver's fifth album, released later that year, also went gold, though it did not produce a major hit. But *Rocky Mountain High* and its title song, both of which peaked in *Billboard*'s top ten in early 1973, consolidated Denver's success. They also exemplified his appeal. At a time when popular music had many acoustic-guitar-playing, confessional singer-songwriters, Denver had an optimistic, nature-loving take on the style. With golden brown hair falling on his forehead, round, gold-rimmed glasses, and a perpetual smile, he frequently sang of the joys of the outdoors in the West. And he backed up that image by moving with his wife to Aspen, Colorado, and building a house with a view of the Rocky Mountains.

Denver's image was well suited to television, and he actively pursued guest shots on television, gaining experience by hosting a six-week variety series on the BBC in the spring of 1973. *Farewell Andromeda,* his seventh album, was not as popular as *Rocky Mountain High,* but in the fall of 1973 RCA released *John Denver's Greatest Hits.* Actually, he had only had two big hits up to this point, but RCA let him pick out an album's worth of his older material and rerecord it, thus reintroducing it to his audience. The tactic worked. "Sunshine on My Shoulders," salvaged from his third album, now became a number-one pop and country hit, and when "Annie's Song," the advance single from his next album, *Back Home Again,* followed it to the top of the charts in the spring of 1974, Denver had ascended to superstar status.

Denver signed a long-term contract with ABC to star in a series of television specials, which he used in turn to promote his records. In the spring of 1975 his double-LP concert recording, *An Evening with John Denver,* featuring the number-one single "Thank God I'm a Country Boy," was another massive hit, and he also topped the charts with his next single, "I'm Sorry," and album, *Windsong,* that fall, ranking him next to Elton John as the most popular musical performer of the year.

Personally, Denver was beginning to experience problems in his marriage owing to his extensive travel, though he and his wife had adopted a son in 1974 and a daughter in 1976. His interest in the outdoors led to an attraction to environmentalism, and his celebrity allowed him to befriend important scientists and thinkers, notably Jacques Cousteau (for whom he wrote the hit "Calypso") and R. Buckminster Fuller. In 1976 he founded the Windstar Foundation, an educational facility, to further his political interests, and increasingly devoted his time and money to philanthropic efforts. In 1977 he helped to establish the World Hunger Project and was appointed by President Jimmy Carter to the Commission on World Hunger.

Denver's record sales began to fall off after 1975, but his albums continued to go gold with regularity into the early 1980s, and he maintained a healthy following that attended his concerts around the world. In 1977 he costarred with George Burns in the comic film *Oh, God!,* which was a hit at the box office. He also acted occasionally in television movies and continued to make television specials.

Denver and his wife divorced in 1983. On 12 August 1988 he married the Australian singer/actress Cassandra Delaney, with whom he had a daughter in 1989. This marriage also ended in divorce.

Much of Denver's attention in the 1980s was given to charity and political work. Determined to break down cultural barriers between nations, he arranged to perform in the Soviet Union and tried to set up a tour of China, though he was not able to achieve that goal until 1992. Two years after that, he became the first American artist to perform in Vietnam since the end of the Vietnam War.

Denver's declining record sales led RCA to drop him in 1986, after which he continued to release records on his own Windstar label. In the early 1990s, as his second marriage collapsed, his emotional state suffered. On 21 August 1993, the night after the final hearing in his second divorce, he was arrested for drunk driving in Aspen but allowed to plead to a lesser charge. He was arrested again a year later after driving his car into a tree.

In the mid-1990s, however, Denver seemed to right himself. He published his autobiography, *Take Me Home,* in 1994, and in 1995 returned to a major record label, recording *The Wildlife Concert* for Sony's Legacy division as a benefit for the Wildlife Conservancy. His final recording, also for Sony, was *All Aboard* (1997), an album of train songs that won him his first Grammy Award, for Best Musical Album for Children. The award was given posthumously, as Denver was killed on 12 October 1997 when the recently purchased single-passenger experimental plane he was flying ran out of gas and crashed into Monterey Bay, off the coast of California. Denver was cremated, and the family transported his remains to Colorado, the state commemorated by Denver in *Rocky Mountain High*, for a memorial service. His ashes were scattered over the Rockies.

Denver went unappreciated by music critics accustomed to reviewing rock music who found his country-and folk-influenced pop style cloying and sentimental. His sunny countenance and repeated exclamations of "Far out!" made him seem a caricature to those who did not share his optimism during a cynical era. But a closer examination of his music reveals a haunting sense of loss, especially in his songs about separation from a loved one, while his celebrations of nature come off as heartfelt. And there was a growing sophistication in his work that tends to go unremarked because his later songs were less popular than his early ones. Denver was an enthusiast for a dizzying combination of self-help strategies, from Erhard Seminars Training (EST) to meditation, but these and his tireless activities to alleviate hunger and promote environmentalism are examples of his hopeful, forward-looking attitude. He aspired to go into space, and when the *Challenger* spacecraft, with its civilian crewmember, blew up in 1986, he wrote a song commemorating its flight, not its crash. His life exemplified that attitude.

★

Though flawed, the best source for information on Denver is his autobiography, *Take Me Home* (1994), written with Arthur Tobier. David Dachs, *John Denver,* and Leonore Fleischer, *John Denver—The Man and His Music* (both 1976), are popular biographies written at the height of his fame; they are necessarily incomplete and highly promotional. John Collis, *John Denver: Mother Nature's Son* (2000), is the first attempt at a serious biography. But Collis is an admittedly unsympathetic chronicler constructing a book out of press clippings and padding it with tangential material. (For example, Denver's birthplace of Roswell, New Mexico, provides an excuse for an irrelevant discussion of UFOs.) Denver's fans have weighed in with their own largely self-referential tributes: Roger Himes, *John Denver's Legacy: A Fire in His Heart and a Light in His Eyes* (1997); Javana Richardson, *A Tribute to John Denver: Poems, Prayers, and Promises* (1998); and a loving memoir of a one-night stand by stewardess Jeannie St. Marie, *John Denver and Me* (2000). An obituary is in the *New York Times* (14 Oct. 1997).

WILLIAM J. RUHLMANN

DICKERSON WHITEHEAD, Nancy (*b.* 19 January 1927 in Wauwatosa, Wisconsin; *d.* 18 October 1997 in New York City), pioneer woman news broadcaster on national network television.

Born Nancy Conners Hanschman, Dickerson was one of two daughters of Frederick R. Hanschman, a building contractor, and Florence Conners. She grew up in the suburbs of Milwaukee, Wisconsin, and attended Clarke College, a Catholic girls' school in Dubuque, Iowa, to study piano. Feeling insulated, she transferred to the University of Wisconsin; she applied to the medical school and then switched to an education major. She studied English, Spanish, and Portuguese and graduated in 1948 with a degree in education. That same year, she was chosen as a United Nations student delegate to Europe, and as she wrote in her auto-

Nancy Dickerson, 1964. © BETTMANN/CORBIS

biography, she went abroad "like a wild horse trying to break loose."

Returning to the United States, she took a teaching job in Milwaukee, but after two restless years she moved to Washington, D.C., where she was first employed as a registrar at Georgetown University, and then in 1951 as a typist for the Senate Foreign Relations Committee. Gradually, she expanded her duties to writing speeches and reports and setting up hearings. A willowy, stylish, single woman, she attracted senators from Lyndon Johnson to Joseph McCarthy, and dated John F. Kennedy, Henry M. Jackson, and Kenneth Keating.

In 1954 she learned that CBS was looking for "a man who knew Capitol Hill," and convinced the network that she could do the job. Dickerson became a producer of two CBS radio programs, the *Leading Question* and *Capitol Cloakroom,* and was later associate producer of the television news show *Face the Nation.* Needing to book prominent politicians as guests on these programs, she enlisted the help of her congressional friends. She scored a coup by arranging for Senator McCarthy to appear on *Face the Nation* just a week before his censure debate commenced.

Dickerson aspired to get out from behind the camera and appear on air as a correspondent, and she felt it was important to act quickly after turning thirty. At the time, broadcast journalism was almost entirely male-dominated, and male television executives regarded women's voices as too thin and high-pitched for news reporting. The only woman who appeared regularly on national news was the deep-voiced, professorial Pauline Frederick, who covered the United Nations first for ABC and later for NBC.

Dickerson took speech classes at Catholic University and suggested stories to her bosses that she might do without infringing on any other correspondent's territory. Meeting continued resistance, she decided that the only way she could get on the air was to report something no one else could get. She persuaded the notoriously camera-shy House Speaker Sam Rayburn to give her an interview, which when presented won rave reviews. In 1960 CBS News hired her as its first woman news correspondent. (CBS was the last of the three American networks to hire a woman as an on-air reporter.) Dickerson did general political news on television and a daily radio show, *One Woman's Washington,* aimed at female listeners. Concerned that her stylish clothes might distract audiences, she adopted a simple turtleneck with a suit as her trademark outfit.

In 1960 Dickerson covered the Democratic National Convention, where her personal friendships with both members of the ticket, Kennedy and Johnson, further boosted her standing at the network. The following January, Kennedy chatted with her while waiting in the Capitol Rotunda before his inauguration, and on the way out she

was the first reporter he spoke to after taking the oath of office. On 24 February 1962 she married businessman C. Wyatt Dickerson and dismayed CBS executives by taking his surname, since viewers had until this time known her by her maiden name. CBS identified her as Nancy Hanschman Dickerson for six months until viewers grew accustomed to her new name. She had two sons and three stepdaughters from the marriage.

The Dickersons purchased Merrywood, a sprawling estate in Virginia that had been the childhood home of Jacqueline Kennedy Onassis, and a spacious townhouse in Washington, where they entertained frequently. Regarded as a legendary hostess in Washington, she picked up news tips at these parties and maintained that knowing the right people was essential to a Washington reporter's job. Her son John Dickerson later observed that her socializing enabled her to overcome the "locker-room atmosphere" of Washington politics that favored her male colleagues.

Feeling that CBS did not use her talents sufficiently, Dickerson switched to NBC in 1963. NBC promised her more airtime, not only on the nightly *Huntley–Brinkley Report* but also on the morning *Today Show* and as anchor of a five-minute news report each afternoon. President Johnson especially appreciated Dickerson's ability to get members of his administration on *Today* because so many afternoon newspapers quoted from the morning program. At the 1964 Democratic National Convention in Atlantic City, New Jersey, Johnson awarded her with an exclusive interview. Alighting from his helicopter, he greeted her on camera: "Hello, Nancy, I've been watching you all day and you're doing a wonderful job." He then announced his selection of Senator Hubert Humphrey for vice president.

NBC president Robert Kintner had wanted more women correspondents on the air, but after his departure in 1966 producers of the *Huntley–Brinkley Report* began using Dickerson less frequently. Dickerson blamed the women's movement for triggering a backlash. So long as she was the sole woman correspondent, the men around her treated her well, but with more women competing for television news jobs, male anxiety rose. She complained loudly that the network had relegated her to covering "second-class stories." The stressful atmosphere of network news also brought out the worst in her. She acknowledged that raising a family of five children while working a full schedule, often on weekends, made her "excessively abrupt, even arrogant."

Dickerson left NBC in 1970, and in the following year formed the Dickerson Company to syndicate her own daily "column-on-the-air," *Inside Washington,* for local news programs. She also joined *Newsweek*'s television syndicate but quit when they assigned her to do "back of the book," low-impact stories. In 1980 she founded the Television Corporation of America to produce documentaries for PBS and other clients. These specials included *Nancy Dickerson, Special Assignment: The Middle East* (1980), *784 Days That Changed America—From Watergate to Resignation* (1982)—which won a Peabody award—and *Being with John F. Kennedy* (1983).

She divorced Wyatt Dickerson in 1983 and six years later married John C. Whitehead, former deputy secretary of state in Ronald Reagan's administration, acquiring four additional stepchildren. From 1986 to 1991 she served as a commentator on Fox News, and in 1992 she coanchored PBS's coverage of the presidential election returns, an appropriate swan song for a career so identified with covering presidential politics. She died five years later of complications from a stroke and is buried at Arlington National Cemetery in Washington, D.C.

Dickerson departed from network news just as a new breed of women broadcasters arrived. She resented those who benefited from affirmative action, whereas feminists tended to deride her devotion to stylishness and her cultivation of friendships with powerful men. Nevertheless, news broadcasters such as Jane Pauley, Leslie Stahl, Jessica Savitch, and Judy Woodruff all cited Dickerson as a role model, recalling her calm, self-possessed manner on the air and the way she commanded the attention of numerous political leaders during her nearly four-decade broadcasting career.

★

Dickerson's autobiography is *Among Those Present: A Reporter's View of Twenty-five Years in Washington* (1976). Her career is profiled in Barry Gottehrer, "Television's Princess of the Press Corps," *Saturday Evening Post* (31 Oct. 1964); Winzola McLendon and Scottie Smith, *Don't Quote Me! Washington Newswomen and the Power Society* (1970); Judith S. Gelfman, *Women in Television News* (1976); Marion Marzolf, *Up from the Footnote: A History of Women Journalists* (1977); and John Dickerson, "On Her Trail," *Time* (13 Nov. 2000). Obituaries are in the *New York Times* and *Washington Post* (both 19 Oct. 1997). She gave oral histories to the John F. Kennedy and Lyndon B. Johnson presidential libraries.

DONALD A. RITCHIE

DICKEY, James Lafayette (*b.* 2 February 1923 in Atlanta, Georgia; *d.* 19 January 1997 in Columbia, South Carolina), writer known for his National Book Award–winning poetry and his best-selling novel *Deliverance* (1970), which was made into a popular movie by the English director John Boorman.

Dickey was one of three children of an Atlanta lawyer, Eugene Dickey, who preferred cockfighting to legal work, and Maibelle Swift, who inherited a small fortune from her father's Atlanta-based tonic company, Swift's Southern

James Dickey, 1990. AP/WIDE WORLD PHOTOS

Specific. Dickey's older brother, Eugene, Jr., died of meningitis two years before Dickey was born. Dickey grew up among servants in a fashionable neighborhood on Atlanta's West Wesley Road and attended North Fulton High School, where he distinguished himself athletically—as a football player and hurdler on the track team—rather than academically. Dickey graduated from high school in 1941 and then spent an extra year at Darlington School in Rome, Georgia.

In 1942 Dickey entered Clemson Agriculture and Military College (now Clemson University) to study engineering. Near the end of his first semester he enlisted in the Army Air Corps. Although he consistently maintained that he had been a pilot who had flown one hundred combat missions in the Pacific during World War II, Dickey, in fact, washed out during flight training in Camden, South Carolina, and was reclassified as a radar observer. He joined the 418th Night Fighter Squadron in the Philippines early in 1945 and operated radar equipment on thirty-eight combat flights over the Philippines and Japan.

World War II transformed Dickey. When he enlisted, he was a mediocre student with little direction. During the war he discovered his true passion—literature. He devoted almost all his free time between missions to reading books and writing poetry. When he returned to the United States in 1946, he enrolled at Vanderbilt University in Nashville, Tennessee, which was known as a center of the southern literary renaissance. Famous writers such as John Crowe Ransom, Allen Tate, and Robert Penn Warren had either taught or studied there. The university had spawned the Agrarian and Fugitive movements, which were political and literary attempts to establish a southern culture in opposition to the progressive, capitalistic northern culture that had prevailed after the Civil War. Dickey excelled in this new environment. An English major known to be one of the most talented poets on campus, Dickey graduated magna cum laude with a B.A. degree in 1949. In order to get a teaching job, he stayed at the university for another year, earning an M.A. degree in English for his thesis on the poetry of Herman Melville.

In 1950 Dickey found a position in the English department of the Rice Institute (now Rice University) and moved with his wife, Maxine Syerson, whom he had married on 4 November 1948, to Houston. Because of the Korean War, he was recalled by the air force early in 1951. Despite his claims about flying combat missions over Korea, he actually never left the United States; he taught radar operation in planes on several bases in Alabama, Mississippi, and Texas.

On 31 August 1951 Dickey's first son, Christopher, was born in Nashville. Christopher, who resembled his father in many ways, became a successful writer as a journalist for the *Washington Post,* a bureau chief in various cities around the world for *Newsweek,* a book reviewer for the *New York Times,* and a novelist.

War was always a catalyst for Dickey's imagination. During the Korean conflict and the years following it, he filled notebooks with ideas for novels, short stories, poems, and plays. He spoke to air force friends about the novel that became *Deliverance* (1970) and took detailed notes for the ambitious, 682-page novel *Alnilam* (1987). Shortly after the war, he completed a short novel—*Entrance to the Honeycomb,* which focused on a young man's difficulties with his girlfriend and his father—but never published it. With numerous literary projects either planned or under way, Dickey began to resent the time he sacrificed to teaching. He returned to Rice in 1952, but in 1954 a *Sewanee Review* fellowship allowed him to leave academe, travel to Europe like the modernist writers he most admired—T. S. Eliot, Ezra Pound, Ernest Hemingway—and write full time.

His reluctance to teach notwithstanding, Dickey returned to a job in the English department at the University of Florida when his fellowship expired in 1955. Realizing that his contract would not be renewed after his first year because of offensive remarks he had made to some members of the National League of American Pen Women, in the middle of the 1956 spring semester he abruptly quit, began training at the McCann-Erickson advertising firm in New York City, and soon after worked on the Coca-Cola account in Atlanta.

Dickey held several advertising jobs in Atlanta until 1961. During that period, he also wrote some of his best poetry. His first book, *Into the Stone and Other Poems,* was published by Scribners in 1960. On the strength of these poems, he received a Guggenheim Fellowship and in 1962 took his family, which had grown with the arrival of another son, Kevin, on 18 August 1958, back to Europe. Dickey's year of traveling was one of his most productive. Wesleyan University Press published his second poetry book, *Drowning with Others,* in February 1962. While staying in Positano, Italy, he began writing *Deliverance,* continued to publish poems in the *New Yorker* and other prestigious journals, and wrote many of the poems for his third collection, *Helmets.*

When Dickey returned to the United States, he decided to give teaching another try. He taught at Reed College in Portland, Oregon, from 1963 to 1964, at San Fernando Valley State College from 1964 to 1965, and at the University of Wisconsin at Madison for a semester in 1966. During these nomadic years, Dickey published the poems and articles that established his reputation as one of America's premier poet-critics. In 1964 Wesleyan University Press published *Helmets,* and the next year it published *Buckdancer's Choice,* which won the National Book Award. To confirm his standing as a poet, the Library of Congress made Dickey its poetry consultant from 1966 to 1968. After Dickey's successful stint as America's main ambassador of poetry, the University of South Carolina hired him as poet-in-residence and professor of English, a position he began in 1969 and held until his death.

In between "barnstorming for poetry," as he called it, and moving from job to job in the 1960s, Dickey wrote *Deliverance,* which Houghton Mifflin published in the spring of 1970 to laudatory reviews. In 1971 the novel won the Prix de Médicis for the best foreign-language book in France. Dickey quickly produced a screenplay, worked closely—and often contentiously—with the director John Boorman on the final script, and even made a brief appearance as the sheriff at the end of the movie. Dickey was a large, burly man with craggy features, a florid complexion, and unruly hair—well suited to the role. *Deliverance* was nominated for an Academy Award for best picture, and the film brought fame and fortune to Dickey. Afterward, he received lucrative offers to write screenplays, coffee-table books, poetry books, and a new novel. The success of *Deliverance* also marked the beginning of Dickey's long alcoholic decline.

Like many of his best poems, *Deliverance* (which, in fact, began as a poem) was built around Joseph Campbell's ideas concerning rites of passage and myths of the heroic journey. Dickey borrowed Campbell's formula for the mythical journey—departure, initiation, return—to structure his plot. The Atlanta men in *Deliverance* leave the safety of their homes and jobs in the city, get initiated into violent savagery on their canoe trip in the mountains of North Georgia, and return home transformed by the lessons they have learned. One of these lessons is that they must lie about the horrors they witnessed in the hinterland in order to survive in civilization.

The idea of lying successfully was central to Dickey's life and writing. Like the Romantics and their heirs, Dickey believed that the imagination was godlike because it could create a reality that was a "virtual reality," a fiction more appealing and more believable than reality. His poetry and prose repeatedly celebrated the imagination's ability to redeem the world by re-creating it into a paradisiacal fantasy—what he called a "creative lie." In his own life, he gave free rein to his imagination, exaggerating his accomplishments until he had transformed himself into a Hemingwayesque hero who triumphed in all arenas.

As a result, for years many people thought Dickey had been a poor boy from North Georgia, a combat pilot during World War II, a state-champion hurdler and football player with National Football League (NFL) potential in college, a successful advertising executive, a professional guitar player, a rugged outdoorsman, a tournament-winning archer, a womanizer with as many conquests as Lord Byron, and so on. As Henry Hart stated in the biography *James Dickey: The World as a Lie,* "Dickey could be either a Southern gentlemanly Dr. Jekyll or a racist, sexist, redneck, drunken Mr. Hyde."

Most critics agree that the last twenty-seven years of Dickey's life were marked by ambitious projects that never lived up to their full potential. These years were also marked by many domestic crises. His wife Maxine died in October 1976 from alcohol-related ailments. Two months later Dickey married his beautiful, troubled student Deborah Dodson, who later became a heroin and cocaine addict. He started a second family—his daughter Bronwen was born on 17 May 1981—but his two sons turned against him. Disapproving of their stepmother, especially after learning of her arrest for cocaine possession, the criminals who were her friends, and her violent fights at home, they remained estranged from their father until he separated from Deborah and began divorce proceedings, about a year before his death.

Having suffered a nearly fatal bout of hepatitis and cirrhosis in 1994, Dickey soon contracted fibrosis of the lungs and died on 17 January 1997. At the time of his death he was at work on a novel about World War II (*Crux*) and was supervising the preliminary work on a film adaptation of his novel *To the White Sea*. He is buried in Pawley's Island, South Carolina.

Dickey's success as a writer arose from his powerful rhetoric and his ability to universalize his private experiences and fantasies by imposing on them the archetypal shapes of myths. When he abandoned his narrative "mythic method" for a more fragmentary style, his writing grew diffuse. Although *Alnilam* bears some resemblance to James Joyce's *Ulysses* in its mythic scope and stylistic experimentation, most critics found it opaque and long-winded. Dickey returned to a more straightforward narrative method in his last novel, *To the White Sea* (1993), but the main character's regressive machismo and gratuitous violence (he was partly based on the serial killer Ted Bundy) left many readers cold. Although critics tended to dismiss the poetry Dickey wrote after 1970, the influence of his early work on southern poets such as Dave Smith, David Bottoms, R. T. Smith, and Henry Taylor was significant. The fact that he continues to shape the direction of southern writing is a testament to his enduring importance.

★

The main collections of Dickey's papers are located at Emory University in Atlanta and at Washington University in St. Louis. His son Christopher Dickey wrote a memoir, *Summer of Deliverance* (1998), which details his difficulties and ultimate reconciliation with his father. Dickey's literary executor, Matthew Bruccoli, published a large collection of Dickey's letters in *Crux* (1999). Henry Hart's biography, *James Dickey: The World as a Lie* (2000), offers the most comprehensive portrait of Dickey's life and writing. Obituaries are in the *New York Times* and *Chicago Tribune* (both 21 Jan. 1997).

HENRY HART

DIGGS, Charles Coles, Jr. (*b.* 2 December 1922 in Detroit, Michigan; *d.* 25 August 1998 in Washington, D.C.), congressman, mortician, and broadcast journalist best known as organizer and founder of the Congressional Black Caucus.

Diggs was the only child born to Charles Cole Diggs, Sr., and Mamie Ethel Jones. The grandson of Baptist ministers on both sides of his family, he grew up in an affluent family. His father was a successful mortician and businessman and the first black Democratic state senator in Michigan. His mother served as official attendant and hostess for the funeral home business. In 1940 Diggs graduated from Miller High School in Detroit, where he excelled as a debater and was class president. He attended the University of Michigan at Ann Arbor from 1940 to 1942, where he became

Charles Diggs, Jr. FISK UNIVERSITY LIBRARY

oratorical champion in 1941. When World War II began, Diggs volunteered for the navy but was rejected because of "poor eyesight." In February 1943, however, he was drafted into the United States Army. Despite ever-present racism in the military, Diggs quickly rose to the rank of sergeant and was sent to Army Air Corps Officers' Candidate School in Miami. In 1942 he received his commission as second lieutenant and was assigned to the black Army Air Forces Base at Tuskegee, Alabama, where he served as a processing officer.

On 1 June 1945 Diggs was discharged from the military and returned home to begin his studies in mortuary science, which he completed at Detroit's Wayne College of Mortuary Science in June 1946. After graduation he became general manager of the family funeral business, House of Diggs, Inc. He also served as host on a gospel music radio show. Meanwhile, Diggs married Juanita Rosario in 1947. They had three children before they divorced in 1960. Diggs would later marry Anna Johnston in 1960, with whom he had one child. When they divorced in 1971, Diggs married Janet Elaine Hall and had another two children. He married his fourth wife, Darlene, in 1983.

In the fall of 1950 Diggs began night classes at the Detroit College of Law. His political career began while he was still a law student. In 1951 he was elected to the Michigan State Senate, representing the thirteenth district. He successfully sponsored Michigan's first Fair Employment Practice Law and the legalization of DNA (deoxyribonucleic acid) blood testing to determine paternity. Diggs served in the Michigan senate until 1954, when he was elected to the U.S. Congress.

In January 1955 Diggs became the youngest of three African-American members of Congress, as well as Michigan's first black member of the U.S. House of Representatives. He soon became known as a champion of black civil rights, serving on the Committee of Interior and Insular Affairs and the Committee of Veterans Affairs. He actively promoted equal treatment in the armed forces, traveling all over the world investigating the grievances of soldiers. Diggs proposed an amendment to the 1938 Fair Labor Standards Act to increase minimum wage in the wake of the Supreme Court's *Brown* v. *Board of Education* decision of 1954. He also submitted legislation to alleviate unemployment in economically depressed areas. Meanwhile, he supported the Civil Rights Act of 1957 and called for enforcement of Section Two of the Fourteenth Amendment as a sanction against states that disenfranchised black citizens. In December 1959 Diggs lobbied President Dwight D. Eisenhower to pay a conciliatory visit to the two newly integrated high schools of Little Rock, Arkansas, in order to ease racial tensions.

Diggs worked to establish the Peace Corps, and he represented the United States at Ghana's independence ceremonies in 1957. In 1959 he joined the Committee on Foreign Affairs and a decade later became chairman of its subcommittee on Africa. In 1971 Diggs was appointed by President Richard M. Nixon to the U.S. delegation to the United Nations. As a longtime opponent of apartheid, Diggs resigned from the United Nations later that year in protest of U.S. support of South Africa and Portuguese involvement in Africa. He then fought for U.S. aid to newly independent African nations and founded TransAfrica, a think tank on African affairs.

In the 1960s Diggs backed successful measures to lower the voting age to eighteen and to aid minority-owned businesses. Possibly the most important achievement of his political career came in 1969–1970, when he cofounded the Congressional Black Caucus to promote the interests of African-American citizens in government. In 1972 Diggs tried unsuccessfully to organize the National Black Political Convention. This initiative attempted to unify African Americans and form an alternative political party. In 1973 Diggs was named chair of the District of Columbia Committee, established to win home rule status for the nation's capital and enable residents to elect a mayor and city council for the first time since 1874. He remained in the post until 1978.

In October 1978 Diggs faced charges that he illegally diverted $60,000 of office operating funds to pay his own personal expenses. He was convicted of the charges and appealed this conviction, charging that he was being treated more harshly than his white colleagues who committed similar infractions. On 3 June 1980 the Supreme Court refused to hear Diggs's appeal. According to the Almanac of American Politics, Diggs's "financial difficulties were not from greed or venality but passivity." Diggs resigned after he was censured and stripped of his seat of the 96th Congress on 3 June 1980. He was then sent to prison in Alabama, serving seven months of a three-year term. He returned to Washington, D.C., to his profession as a mortician and opened a funeral home in suburban Maryland, setting up residence in Hillcrest, Maryland. With an interest still in political affairs, he served as liaison to the Congressional Black Caucus.

Diggs received honorary Doctor of Laws degrees from Wilberforce University, North Carolina Central University, and the University of the District of Columbia. He was a Mason, an Elk, and a member of the Cotillion Social Club, the American Legion, Veterans of Foreign Wars, and past president of the Metropolitan Funeral Association. He was the recipient of numerous awards and citations for his public service. At the age of seventy-five, he died suddenly from a heart attack in Washington, D.C., and is buried in his native Detroit. He was survived by his wife, Darlene, and six children.

During twenty-six years of public service, Diggs made numerous important political contributions, but the significance of his work has often gone unacknowledged. At the time of his death, the media only emphasized the negative points of his career. Diggs's minister, however, eulogized him as one who had "broken down, leaped over, crawled under, walked around, and backed down barriers." His son Douglass stated that his father was a "hands-on" public servant and that constituent service was his mission. He was also a strong voice for the creation and retainment of businesses in the African-American community.

★

Carolyn P. DuBose's biography, *The Untold Story of Charles Diggs* (1999), is a source for further study. Personal papers, files, and documents from his congressional years are part of the Moorland-Spingarn Collection of Howard University, Washington, D.C. Further biographical information can be found in *Contemporary Black Biography,* vol. 21 (1999), and Jessie Carney Smith, ed., *Notable Black American Men* (1998). An obituary is in *Time* (7 Sept. 1998).

JOHNNIEQUE B. LOVE

DiMAGGIO, Joseph Paul ("Joe") (*b.* 25 November 1914 in Martinez, California; *d.* 8 March 1999 in Hollywood, Florida), star of the New York Yankees in the 1930s and 1940s who in 1969 was hailed as the "Greatest Living All-Time Baseball Player" by the Baseball Writers Association. He became an icon in a time when baseball had no competition as the national pastime, a symbol of perfection on the diamond and princely dignity off the field.

DiMaggio was born in the fishing village of Martinez, California, the fourth son and eighth child of Giuseppe Paolo and Rosalie Mercurio. His father had arrived in America in 1897 from Sicily, having heard from his father-in-law that fishing was good in California waters. Shortly after Joe was born, the family moved to North Beach, an Italian section of San Francisco. In the tradition of his family, Paulo expected his sons to follow him into fishing. Fishing, though, was not for Joe: he said he hated the smell of fish.

DiMaggio's two eldest brothers had no choice but to become fisherman. Three of the others, however, became big-league baseball players—all of them outfielders. Vince, four years older than Joe, played in the National League with several teams, six times leading the league in strikeouts, and Dominic, nicknamed the "Little Professor" because he wore eyeglasses and stood only five feet, nine inches tall, starred for the Boston Red Sox. Joe was the best player of the three, although his interest in making the game his life's pursuit came only slowly. Still, in choose-up games as a boy, the other kids knew that if Joe was on their team they were likely to win.

After briefly playing with the Boys Club League, DiMaggio quit Galileo High School in order to play professional baseball. Years later, he allowed his entry in *Who's Who in America* to state that he had graduated from high school. In 1932 he joined Vince on the San Francisco Seals in the Pacific Coast League, a feeder league for the majors. DiMaggio was then only seventeen years old, but his hand-eye coordination was remarkable, and his speed afield and on the bases made him an instant standout. At the age of eighteen he hit in sixty-one consecutive games, an all-time baseball record still not equaled. Meanwhile, his dark good looks and gap-toothed smile combined with a graceful stride and penchant for stylish clothes made him a head-turner wherever he went.

In 1933, his first full year as a professional, he played in 187 games, hitting .340 and driving in 169 runs. He continued to hit with sensational authority in the next two years, batting .398 in 1935. If he had not damaged a knee, he might have come up to the big leagues sooner, although the Seals were reluctant to part with their best "draw" at the gate. His biggest obstacle, however, was that during the

Joe DiMaggio, 1941. AP/WIDE WORLD PHOTOS

depths of the Great Depression, major league owners were loath to gamble money on a player they regarded as damaged goods. The New York Yankees took a chance, though, and in 1935 purchased his contract from the Seals for $25,000 and five players. They did not bring him up until 1936, anticipating that in an extra year he would be fit again.

When he finally arrived at Yankee Stadium, he was heralded as the new Babe Ruth and assigned the number 5, following Ruth's 3 and Lou Gehrig's 4. That first season an injured foot prevented him from playing until May. But when he made his debut, he lived up to his advance billing. Playing with the same aplomb he had shown as a Seal, he batted .323, driving in 125 runs and getting 206 hits that included twenty-nine homers. He became the first rookie to start in an All-Star game.

The Yankees, which boasted such other stars as Gehrig, Bill Dickey, and an accomplished and experienced pitching staff, won the American League pennant, the first of four straight trips to the World Series for the Yankees. In the Series against the New York Giants that first year, DiMaggio had nine hits in six games. In fact, in his thirteen years in Yankee pinstripes, New York would go to the World Series ten times and win nine of them. DiMaggio was not solely responsible for forging those championships, but the fans saw him as the team's kingpin.

In 1937 DiMaggio batted .346 and struck a league-leading forty-six home runs. In his career he would hit 361 home runs, despite, as a right-handed hitter, driving most of his four-baggers to the stands in left and left center fields in Yankee stadium, which was a much greater distance than to right field, where the left-handed Ruth aimed his homers. DiMaggio knew his worth at the box office. Still, when he held out for a salary of $40,000 for 1938 and had to settle for $25,000, he never forgot the snub. His characteristic aloofness from teammates and quest for privacy thereafter became more marked. Indeed, his teammate Eddie Lopat described him as the loneliest man he ever knew: "He led the league in room service."

Nevertheless, on the field he was a team player. Trim and lithe (he stood six feet, two inches tall and weighed 192 pounds), he seemed to glide effortlessly across the grass as he covered his position like a tent. Joe McCarthy, the Yankees' manager in DiMaggio's halcyon days, said he never saw Joe make a mistake in running the bases. Blessed with a strong and accurate throwing arm (he threw right-handed), DiMaggio had 153 assists in his thirteen-year career. At bat, he had a wide, flat-footed stance and a fluid, controlled swing with a full follow-through that was a model for every aspiring youth who ever saw him at the plate.

After hitting .324 in 1938, DiMaggio lifted his average

to .381 in 1939, winning his first batting championship. During most of the season he had been hitting over .400. In the fall he was named the American League's Most Valuable Player (MVP)—the first of three MVP awards he would win. The following year he again led the league in hitting, this time with an average of .352.

The year 1941 may have been the finest that baseball has ever known. That season, Ted Williams, the twenty-two-year-old right fielder of the Red Sox, hit .406, the last time a big leaguer hit over .400 in a full season; Bob Feller, a twenty-two-year-old fireball pitcher for the Cleveland Indians, won 25 games; and Lefty Grove, the veteran southpaw hurler of the Philadelphia Athletics, won his 300th game. Nevertheless, to many people, 1941 will forever be recalled as the "Year of the Streak," when DiMaggio hit safely in fifty-six consecutive games.

The streak began on 15 May and ran until 17 July. In that span of sixty-three days, DiMaggio in 223 times at bat averaged .408, with ninety-one base hits, including fifteen home runs and fifty-five runs batted in. As it went on, it mesmerized the country in this last season before the Japanese attack on Pearl Harbor ended the ability of heroics on the diamond to be vital national business. Every evening people would ask anybody they thought might know, "How did Joe do today?" Radio programs were sometimes interrupted to report on DiMaggio's "at bats." In Congress a pageboy was assigned to bring reports of Joe's exploits to the floor. The streak ended before 65,000 people in Cleveland's Municipal Stadium only because Ken Keltner, the Indian's sterling third-baseman, made two gorgeous plays on DiMaggio that robbed him of base hits, and Lou Boudreau, the young shortstop and player-manager, made another. The following day DiMaggio started another streak, which ran for sixteen games. Despite strong rivals for the award, no one begrudged DiMaggio the second MVP award he won in the fall.

DiMaggio's name became a household word. In tribute, Mel Allen, the Yankees' broadcaster, called him the "Yankee Clipper." Les Brown and his orchestra immortalized him with the song "Joltin' Joe DiMaggio." In 1952, when DiMaggio's friend Ernest Hemingway had the hero in his best-selling novella *The Old Man and the Sea* speak of hoping to meet "the Great DiMaggio," every reader knew who he meant.

With the war on in 1942, DiMaggio hit .305 as the teams limped through the season. He enlisted in the Army Air Forces on 17 February 1943, and spent the war years teaching baseball to servicemen in Hawaii and playing in games across the United States. When he returned to the Yankees in 1946, he was thirty-two years old and had lost three years at the height of his career. His incomparable talent was somewhat diminished, but he still had a few years of greatness ahead. In 1947 he earned his third MVP award, and

once again helped lead the Yankees to victory in the World Series. During a game in the 1947 Series, Al Gionfriddo of the Brooklyn Dodgers miraculously caught one of DiMaggio's drives in left-center field, taking away a sure hit. When the ball landed improbably in Gionfriddo's glove, the fans saw DiMaggio kick the dirt in frustration as he approached second base. It was a rare public display of DiMaggio's uncommon zeal to be a winner.

DiMaggio had a preternatural ability to rise to grand occasions, even when he was hurt or ill. Bob Feller said, "He always seemed able to get that crucial hit in the late innings any time he wanted." By 1949, for example, DiMaggio's skills were already eroding and he suffered from a heel spur so painful that it had to be anaesthetized to allow him to play. He did not get into the lineup until June—in Boston. And yet in the three-game series at Fenway Park, he hit a single and a homer in the first game, two homers in the second, and a third in the last game. By the end of the season, the Yankees were a game out of first place and needed to win two games against Boston to capture the pennant. Before a sell-out crowd celebrating what had been billed as "Joe DiMaggio Day" at Yankee Stadium, DiMaggio was severely weakened by a viral infection. Yet he dragged himself to the plate, striking a single and a double before retiring.

By 1950 time was running out on DiMaggio's career. Although he led the league in slugging percentage with a .585 average and won the second game of the World Series in the tenth inning when he hit a home run off Robin Roberts of the Philadelphia Phillies, baseball was no longer fun for him. DiMaggio retired in 1951, after hitting a double against the New York Giants in the World Series in what would be his final time at bat.

In 1955, his first year of eligibility, he was elected to the Baseball Hall of Fame. Pee Wee Reese, the beloved shortstop of the Brooklyn Dodgers, said to his son in admiration of his old Yankee opponent: "Son, you have to understand. There are Hall of Famers. And then there is Joe DiMaggio." DiMaggio had gone to bat 6,821 times and collected 2,214 hits, driven in 1537 runs and had enjoyed an on-base percentage of almost 40 percent. His lifetime average was .325.

In an exquisite wedding at Saints Peter and Paul Church in San Francisco, DiMaggio and Dorothy Arnold, a pretty blonde actress on contract to Universal Studios, were married on 19 November 1939. Their son, Joe, Jr., was born in October 1941, but DiMaggio's taciturn nature and affinity for showgirls and nightlife—he was a regular at Toots Shor's club in New York City—alienated his wife. He was also unwilling to let his wife continue her career, and her tendency to dress flamboyantly irritated him. They were divorced in 1944.

Following his retirement, with seeming implausibility,

he began to court movie star Marilyn Monroe. They were married in a civil ceremony at San Francisco City Hall on 14 January 1954. The marriage foundered quickly. Monroe was bent on continuing her career as an actress and sex symbol, but DiMaggio was offended by his wife's incessant flaunting of her body. He was revolted when her appearance in the 1955 movie *The Seven Year Itch* required her to shoot a scene in which she stood above a vent that allowed her skirt to float upward revealingly. These two illustrious celebrities, unsuited to each other, were divorced before the year was out.

DiMaggio, nevertheless, continued to carry a torch for Monroe. When she came close to a nervous breakdown in 1961, he was at her side to help. When she died of an overdose of barbiturates on 4 August 1962, DiMaggio took charge of her funeral and became a self-appointed guardian of her memory. Ever afterward, he was driven into angry silence by anyone who dared to speak to him about her. He sent fresh roses to her grave every week for twenty years and always maintained that she had not died by her own hand but had been murdered.

As a retiree, DiMaggio continued his affluent lifestyle and zealously guarded his reputation as a national idol. His corporation, Yankee Clipper Enterprises, administered his advertising endorsements and booked his public appearances, including autograph signings at baseball-card shows. He served as pitchman for the "Mr. Coffee" coffee maker and New York City's Bowery Savings Bank. He had friends, some of them unsavory, who took care of him in various ways, even squirreling away money for him in return for his presence at their restaurants or nightclubs. He was a familiar figure at old-timer games, always appearing dapper, often in a blue jacket and gray slacks, and always, at his explicit insistence, introduced last and as "baseball's greatest living player." Usually unsmiling, he carried himself with somber dignity. If anything gave him pleasure, though, it was the Joe DiMaggio Children's Hospital at Memorial Regional Hospital in Hollywood, Florida, which he helped establish in 1953.

In 1977 he received the Presidential Medal of Freedom, and in 1990 Columbia University awarded him an honorary Doctor of Laws degree. He also received the Silver Helmet award from the American Veterans of World War II, Korea, and Vietnam (AMVETS) in 1974; the Jim Thorpe Pro Sports Awards lifetime achievement award in 1993; and the Sports Legend award from the American Sportscasters Association in 1998. New York City renamed a Midtown section of the Henry Hudson Parkway for him after his death.

DiMaggio owned a house in the upscale Marina District of San Francisco, a home he had originally purchased for his parents. For several years he shared it with Marie, his widowed sister, with whom he had good relations. Di-

Maggio's relationship with other relatives, however, was strained. He was estranged from his son and his brother Dom, although he was close to and fond of his granddaughters. In later years, San Francisco's wet weather and the arthritis in his back prompted DiMaggio to move to Hollywood, Florida, where he worked tirelessly for the children's hospital named after him.

DiMaggio, a lifelong smoker, died of lung cancer in Hollywood, Florida, on 8 March 1999, after months of suffering. His body was flown to San Francisco, where, at Saints Peter and Paul Church—the scene of his communion, confirmation, and first marriage—a private funeral was held. His son was a pallbearer, and Dom delivered a eulogy. He was interred in Holy Cross Cemetery in nearby Colina, California. In addition to his son, he was survived by two granddaughters, their husbands, and four great-grandchildren. He bequeathed the bulk of his estate in a trust to his son, who died of a drug overdose a few months later. He left $100,000 to another Joe, a nephew, the son of DiMaggio's brother Michael. Unlike his baseball-playing brothers, Mike had fulfilled their father's devout wish that he become a fisherman. His fate had been to fall off his boat and drown.

Joe DiMaggio remains in the national memory as a symbol of consistency in great performance. A son of immigrants, his magnificence on the ball field incarnated for millions the American Dream of rising from humble beginnings to glorious achievement. His enduring status as hero remains pristine.

★

Records and memorabilia of DiMaggio's career are in the Baseball Hall of Fame in Cooperstown, New York. DiMaggio claimed authorship of two books: *Lucky to Be a Yankee* (1946) and *Baseball for Everyone* (1948), the latter a potpourri of baseball lore that contained contributions from an advisory panel of baseball experts. He also provided an introduction and commentary for Richard Whittingham, ed., *The DiMaggio Albums: Selections from Public and Private Collections Celebrating the Baseball Career of Joe DiMaggio* (1989). The first appreciative biography was written by Gene Schorr, *The Thrilling Story of Joe DiMaggio* (1950), later expanded as *Joe DiMaggio: The Yankee Clipper* (1956). A sentimental account written during the Vietnam War is Maury Allen, *Where Have You Gone, Joe DiMaggio? The Story of America's Last Hero* (1975). The hagiography continued with two books from sportswriters who had covered DiMaggio for the *New York Times:* George DeGregorio, *Joe DiMaggio: An Informal Biography* (1981), and Joseph Durso, *Joe DiMaggio: The Last American Knight* (1995). Valuable overviews of DiMaggio's place in American culture are Jack B. Moore, *Joe DiMaggio: A Bio-Bibliography* (1986), and the same author's *Joe DiMaggio, Baseball's Yankee Clipper* (1987). Three detailed evocations of DiMaggio's most famous feat are Al Silverman, *Joe DiMaggio: The Golden Year, 1941* (1961);

Michael Seidel, *Streak: Joe DiMaggio and the Summer of '41* (1988); and Dom DiMaggio with Bill Gilbert, introduction by Ted Williams, *Real Grass, Real Heroes: Baseball's Historic 1941 Season* (1990). An illuminating and offbeat presentation of conversations with DiMaggio and others is Christopher Lehmann-Haupt, *Me and DiMaggio: A Baseball Fan Goes in Search of His Gods* (1986). DiMaggio's tortured relationship with Marilyn Monroe is covered in excruciating detail in Roger Kahn, *Joe and Marilyn: A Memory of Love* (1986). A searching and not-always-complimentary report on the writer's effort to uncover the man inside the icon is Richard Ben Cramer, *Joe DiMaggio: The Hero's Life* (2000). Sentimental recollections were rushed into print at the end of DiMaggio's life: Richard Gilliam, ed., *Joltin' Joe DiMaggio* (1999), and David Cataneo, ed., *I Remember Joe DiMaggio: Personal Memories of the Yankee Clipper by the People Who Knew Him Best* (2001). Elegant obituaries are in the *New York Times* (by Joseph Durso) and *Los Angeles Times* (by Roger Kahn) (both 9 Mar. 1999).

HENRY F. GRAFF

DIXON, Jeane Lydia   (*b.* 5 January 1918 in Medford, Wisconsin; *d.* 25 January 1997 in Washington, D.C.), author, real estate agent, and psychic who was known as the "Seeress of Washington" and who came to international fame for predicting the assassination of President John F. Kennedy.

Jeane Dixon, 1981. AP/WIDE WORLD PHOTOS

The youngest of seven children of German immigrants Frank Pinckert and Emma Von Grafee, Dixon grew up in an intensely Catholic household. Dixon's father was a wealthy businessman who had made a fortune in the lumber business and retired at age forty-five. He reared his family in the European tradition, complete with a nanny. As a child, Dixon often astonished family members with unusual predictions that subsequently came to pass. According to her own statements, Dixon's life path was shaped by an encounter with a Gypsy woman at age eight in California. This unnamed Gypsy took one look at Dixon's palms and predicted international fame and a career as a prophet. She also gave the child a crystal ball that she used for prophetic meditations.

In 1926 the Pinckert family moved to Santa Rosa, California, where Dixon went to high school and later studied drama. She also met and apparently developed a childhood crush on James ("Jimmy") Lamb Dixon, a businessman and early partner of the movie producer Hal Roach. Dixon, some twenty years older than Jeane, married and divorced another woman during Jeane's high school years. In 1939, however, the two met again and fell in love. In a whirlwind five-week courtship, Dixon overcame Jeane's religious scruples against marrying a divorced man. The two received special dispensation to marry and were wed in a Catholic ceremony in San Diego. Jimmy Dixon's business in the automotive parts industry took him and his wife to Detroit

in 1940. There, Jeane Dixon met an old man who introduced her to the industrialist Henry Ford, who she predicted would outlive his son Edsel. The prediction turned out to be correct.

In early 1942 the Dixons relocated to Washington, D.C., where Jimmy served the U.S. Defense Department as a "Dollar-a-Year" man—a civilian volunteer who donated his time to the defense effort for a contracted wage of one dollar per year. During the war he handled real estate acquisitions for warehouses and depots. Jeane also took part in the war effort by joining the Washington Home Hospitality Committee; she entertained servicemen by doing psychic readings for them. Her clientele soon spread to include legislators and diplomats. She also had secret meetings with President Franklin D. Roosevelt in 1944 and January 1945, which were verified by the president's son Elliot Roosevelt. She told the president that he didn't have much longer to finish his work.

A small, elegant woman with expensive taste in jewelry, Dixon became part of Washington's high society, present at prestigious parties and diplomatic functions and frequently in the public eye when she made her startling predictions. Although her advice was typically free to those who knew her, she eventually went on the lecture circuit and earned hundreds of thousands of dollars per year, most of which she donated to her foundation to help sick children, Children to Children, Inc. The Hearst syndicate also paid her handsomely for her weekly astrology column in *Star* magazine.

After the war, Dixon's husband established James L. Dixon and Co. Realtors. Jeane worked with him as secretary/treasurer and later as chief executive officer (CEO). She continued her psychic life with many predictions. Some that proved to be correct include the Communist takeover of China; the merger of the AFL and CIO labor unions; the partition of the Indian subcontinent; the assassination of Mahatma Gandhi; the death of John Foster Dulles; bloodshed in racial conflicts within the United States; and the assassinations of Robert F. Kennedy and Martin Luther King, Jr.

As early as 1952 Dixon predicted that a young Democrat would be elected president in 1960 and that he would die while in office. She tried to warn President John F. Kennedy against going to Dallas, but he would not listen to her. While having lunch with a friend on 22 November 1963, she proclaimed "The president has been shot," more than a half-hour before the actual shooting. Newswoman Ruth Montgomery began running annual lists of Dixon's predictions in her political column in 1952. After the death of Kennedy in November 1963, she put together what she knew about Dixon for an article in *Reader's Digest*, which she later expanded into the book *A Gift of Prophecy* (1965). The book sold three million copies. Suddenly famous, Dixon began receiving up to 3,000 letters per week and as many as 1,000 per day. She hired five secretaries to deal with the flood.

A second book, *Jeane Dixon: My Life and Prophecies* (1969), continued the legend of Dixon's uncanny ability to see the future. With all the publicity, she became the best-known American prophet since Edgar Cayce, and her second career as lecturer and columnist began to flourish. Her religion led her to perform good works, such as the founding of Children to Children, Inc. (1964), and she spoke about God. Dixon served as the organization's president until her death. In 1968 she was chair of the Christmas Seal campaign in Washington, D.C., and was named the first Anglo Honorary Navajo Princess. She became involved in the fight against cystic fibrosis and served as honorary chair and hostess of the Mystic Ball Cystic Fibrosis Foundation from 1990 to 1994. Her charitable activities brought her many awards and honors from civic organizations, such as the Unsung Heroines Award from the Ladies Auxiliary of the Veterans of Foreign Wars. She was also a member of the National League of American Pen Women, the International Platform Association, the International Club (Washington, D.C.), and the American Society of Composers, Authors, and Publishers. Her last book, *A Gift of Prayer* (1995), shows her deeply religious nature.

After her flurry of fame in the 1960s, Dixon resumed her life as real estate agent, lecturer, and author. She wrote an astrology column for *Star* magazine of the Hearst syndicate, managed her children's foundation, and performed charitable work. Politically conservative, she maintained friendships with people such as the FBI director J. Edgar Hoover, Senator Strom Thurmond, and the First Lady Nancy Reagan. Although President Ronald and Mrs. Reagan tried to conceal and downplay their superstitious natures and belief in astrology, Dixon's influence on them was well known in Washington, D.C., and in California, where Reagan first ran for governor.

Dixon apparently never studied the psychic sciences. Although she had a home library of more than 1,000 books, none dealt with psychic phenomena. She divided her predictions into three classes: first, visions that came directly from God; second, meditations using the crystal ball; and third, impressions that came from telepathy (these she claimed would never replace the telephone). Her predictions seemed to be mostly spontaneous. She rejected all offers to test her psychic ability scientifically.

Critics point out that many of Dixon's predictions were either vague or failed to happen. Notable failures among her predictions include the outbreak of World War III with China in 1958; that Walter Reuther would run for President in 1964; that the Russians would land the first man on the Moon; that a comet would strike Earth; and that religious warfare would break out all over the world in 1999. She also predicted that the Antichrist would be born somewhere in the Middle East on 5 February 1962. Her proponents, however, concentrate on those predictions she made that actually happened. The result is a controversy that has made Dixon's name synonymous with both "psychic" and "charlatan" in the United States. The practice of making so many predictions that some of them are bound to come true is now known as the "Jeane Dixon effect."

Dixon died of heart failure at age seventy-nine. The accuracy of Dixon's predictions was best during the 1940s, 1950s, and 1960s but declined during the 1970s, 1980s, and 1990s, when she made many unsuccessful, far-fetched religious prophecies. Over the years Dixon entertained, encouraged, and inspired millions with her astrology columns and her books about religion and prophecy. Her lifelong efforts on behalf of children, animals, and cystic fibrosis sufferers showed her to also be a humanitarian.

★

Dixon's autobiographies and other books include *Jeane Dixon: My Life and Prophecies* (1969); *The Call to Glory: Jeane Dixon Speaks of Jesus* (1971); *Yesterday, Today, and Forever* (1976); and *A Gift of Prayer* (1995). There is a biography by Ruth Montgomery, *A Gift of Prophecies: The Phenomenal Jeane Dixon* (1965). Information on Dixon's political influence is in Kitty Kelley, *Nancy Reagan: The Unauthorized Biography* (1991). Other books that either focus on Dixon or discuss her include James Bjornstad, *Twentieth Century Prophecy: Jeane Dixon, Edgar Cayce* (1969); Mary Bringle, *Jeane Dixon: Prophetess or Fraud* (1970); Denis Brian, *Jeane Dixon: The Witnesses* (1976); Alice Braemer, *Cultism to Charisma: My Seven Years with Jeane Dixon* (1977); Donald T. Regan, *For the Record: From Wall Street to Washington* (1988); and Peggy Noonan, *What I Saw at the Revolution* (1990). Articles on Dixon include Barbara Holland, "You Can't Keep a Good Prophet Down," *Smithsonian* (Apr. 1999), and a chapter in Kathleen Krull, *They Saw the Future: Oracles, Psychics, Scientists, Great Thinkers, and Pretty Good Guessers* (1999). An obituary is in the *Detroit News* (26 Jan. 1997).

KENNETH E. ST. ANDRE

DMYTRYK, Edward (*b.* 4 September 1908 in Grand Forks, British Columbia, Canada; *d.* 1 July 1999 in Encino, California), film director who helped define the film noir movement and was one of the Hollywood Ten blacklisted during the House Un-American Activities Committee hearings of the late 1940s.

Dmytryk was one of four sons born to Michael Dmytryk and Franceska Berebowski, Catholic Ukrainians who, to escape persecution by Austrian Serbs controlling the Ukraine, emigrated to British Columbia, just north of the U.S. border. His father farmed in the summer and worked in a copper smelter during the winter; his mother was a homemaker. When World War I erupted, Canada began interning all Austrian nationals, so the family slipped across the border to Northport, Washington, where Dmytryk's father found work as a lead smelter. Dmytryk's mother died in 1917 of a ruptured appendix, the family moved to San Francisco, and then in 1919 they moved to Sherman (now West Hollywood), California.

Dmytryk left home at age fourteen to escape his abusive father and went to work for $6 per week running errands at the Famous Players Lasky Studio (later Paramount). He attended Hollywood High School and enrolled at the California Institute of Technology in Pasadena in 1926 to study mathematics. A year later, he went to work full-time as a projectionist and film cutter at Paramount, where over the next twelve years he learned the craft of film production. He married Madeleine Robinson in 1932 and they had one son. The couple separated in 1944 and divorced in 1948.

Dmytryk directed his first film, a low-budget independent production entitled *The Hawk*, in 1935. That same year he helped form the Film Editor's Guild and served as its first secretary. He became a full-time director in 1939,

Edward Dmytryk, 1957. ASSOCIATED PRESS

when he joined both the Screen Director's Guild and Paramount's B film unit. That same year, he was naturalized as a U.S. citizen. He left Paramount in 1941 to direct B productions for Monogram and Columbia, including entries in the popular Boston Blackie and Lone Wolf mystery series. At RKO he gained attention for a pair of propaganda films that became hits, *Hitler's Children* and *Behind the Rising Sun,* both released in 1943. That same year, he moved to the A film ranks with *Tender Comrade,* which starred Ginger Rogers and portrayed women on the World War II homefront.

Dmytryk gained a reputation as an innovator, using bizarre camera angles, symbolic mise-en-scènes (a cinema term borrowed from theater, referring to the physical stage setting), and dramatic low-key lighting to create atmospheric suspense. Although critics would not put a name to this style until the 1950s, his earliest work became recognized as a major influence in the film noir movement, which broke away from the romanticism typical of the Hollywood studio films. *Murder My Sweet* (1944), based on the novel by Raymond Chandler, became a prime example of the style and won Dmytryk an Edgar Award from the Mystery Writers of America. In 1947 he completed *Crossfire,* which addressed anti-Semitism at a time when Hollywood deliberately ignored such questions of ethnic persecution, and gained Oscar nominations for best film and best director. Dmytryk's personal life improved as well; while working on *Till the End of Time* (1946), he met the actress Jean Porter. They married on 12 May 1948 and had three children together.

Dmytryk's professional life changed dramatically when he was subpoenaed to appear before the House Un-American Activities Committee (HUAC) on 23 September 1947. A strong supporter of the labor movement, Dmytryk had joined the Actor's Lab and taught filmmaking for the People's Educational Center in 1944, initiatives supported by the Communist Party of America. On 6 May 1944 Dmytryk paid fifty cents for initiation costs and joined the party as Michael Edwards, number 84961. His enrollment was brief; he paid the $2.00 dues in June and an additional $2.50 in July, the sum of his financial contributions to the party, and left one year later over a dispute concerning content control of his film *Cornered* (1945). In trying to uncover communist leanings in the film industry, HUAC subpoenaed nineteen leftists, including Dmytryk; nine were deemed friendly, but Dmytryk and the remaining nine refused to testify and became known as the Hollywood Ten. They were held in contempt and faced a $1,000 fine and up to a year in prison. The Hollywood Ten appealed the decision for three years, during which time Dmytryk was blacklisted in Hollywood and went to England to make films. On 10 April 1950 the U.S. Supreme Court refused their appeal and, on 18 July, Dmytryk was sent to a minimum security prison at Mill Point, West Virginia, for a six-month term. He was freed on 14 November 1950.

Dmytryk shocked Hollywood by reappearing before HUAC on 25 April 1951 to recant his former position, name names, and disassociate himself from the Communist Party. Dmytryk was the only one of the Hollywood Ten to recant. Even then, he found himself greylisted when the major studios refused him work because many of his former associates in the film industry did not want to work with him. However, his reputation revived when he signed a four-picture deal at $60,000 per film with Stanley Kramer at Columbia. The first three films failed at the box office, but the last picture in the deal was *The Caine Mutiny* (1954), which became a major success and was nominated by the Motion Picture Academy as best picture of the year.

The rest of Dmytryk's career found him directing major productions starring top Hollywood stars. These films included *Raintree Country* (1957), *The Young Lions* (1958), and *The Carpetbaggers* (1964). Even with these successes,

Dmytryk's political past kept him apart from the mainstream. When opportunities to direct disappeared in the mid-1970s, Dmytryk became an author and teacher. He was a professor of film theory and production at the University of Texas at Austin from 1978 to 1981, and held a chair in filmmaking at the University of Southern California until two years before his death in 1999. Dmytryk wrote about his experiences and filmmaking, notably in two autobiographies, *It's a Hell of a Life but Not a Bad Living* (1978) and *Odd Man Out* (1996); a series of how-to books on screen acting, directing, and writing (1984 to 1985); plus a comprehensive study, *Cinema: Concept and Practice* (1988). In 1998 the Editor's Guild presented him with a lifetime achievement gold card for his outstanding contribution to filmmaking. He died at home in Encino of heart and kidney failure and is buried in Forest Lawn Cemetery in Los Angeles.

Dmytryk understood that after the HUAC hearings, he would forever remain an outsider to the Hollywood establishment and accepted that as part of his life. While he continued to work in the film business, the accolades and rewards once assumed for his rising young talent disappeared and he finished his days as a figure of controversy. He was originally blacklisted for maintaining silence and then was shunned when he recanted, identifying people as communists, although he always insisted he gave only names already known to the committee. In one of his autobiographies, Dmytryk quipped that his headstone would eventually read, "member of the Hollywood Ten." Political events obscured the fact that Dmytryk was an imaginative and creative director who produced films reflecting the turmoil and social unrest of his time. Most critics feel he did his best work in his early years or in smaller-budgeted films like *The Sniper* (1952), which followed the HUAC hearings. Dmytryk's films were some of the best produced during the golden age of film noir, and only with the passing years and rising interest in film scholarship has much of his work been reexamined in this context.

★

There are two autobiographies by Dmytryk, *It's a Hell of a Life but Not a Bad Living* (1978), and *Odd Man Out: A Memoir of the Hollywood Ten* (1996). Both are informative, but the second text goes into greater depth about the HUAC hearings and reprints large sections of the first autobiography. Also valuable are entries from Ephraim Katz, *The Film Encyclopedia* (1979), and *Leonard Maltin's Movie Encyclopedia* (1994); both provide complete filmographies. There is also an excellent interview by Tim Rhys and Tom Allen for *MovieMaker Magazine* (Dec. 1995), which covers Dmytryk's later years in some detail. An obituary is in the *New York Times* (3 July 1999).

PATRICK A. TRIMBLE

DORRIS, Michael Anthony (*b.* 30 January 1945 in Louisville, Kentucky; *d.* 11 April 1997 in Concord, New Hampshire), Native American activist and novelist whose nonfiction work *The Broken Cord: A Family's Ongoing Struggle with Fetal Alcohol Syndrome* (1989) won a National Book Critics Circle Award and brought national attention to fetal alcohol syndrome.

Dorris was the only child of Jim Dorris, a career army officer who was part Modoc Indian, and Mary Besy Buckhardt, an Anglo-American homemaker. In 1947, when Dorris was only two, his father died in a truck accident in Germany. Dorris was then raised in Louisville by his mother, aunt, and grandmother. While Dorris's aunt supported the family by working for the city, Dorris's mother stayed at home to take care of him and his aged grandmother.

Following graduation from high school in 1963, Dorris matriculated at Georgetown University in Washington, D.C., from which he graduated with a B.A. degree in English in 1967. Dorris went on to study at Yale University in New Haven, Connecticut, where he earned a Ph.M.

Michael Dorris, 1989. AP/WIDE WORLD PHOTOS

degree in anthropology in 1970. Following brief teaching stints at Redlands University in California in 1970 and at Franconia College in New Hampshire in 1971, Dorris joined the faculty at Dartmouth College in Hanover, New Hampshire, in 1972. There he established the first Native American studies program in the United States, remaining as its chair until 1985. Dorris also became the first single male to adopt a child in the United States when he adopted a three-year-old Sioux boy in 1971. Dorris later adopted two additional Native American children, a boy and a girl. Dorris established himself as a leading Native American scholar during this time, publishing *Native Americans: Five Hundred Years After* (1977), with photographs by Joseph Farber, and *A Guide to Research on North American Indians* (1983), with Arlene B. Hirschfelder and Mary Gloyne Byler.

In 1981 Dorris married the novelist and poet Louise Erdrich, a mixed-blood Turtle Mountain Chippewa, whom he had met while she was a student at Dartmouth in the 1970s. Erdrich adopted Dorris's three children, and the couple also had three daughters together. The marriage marked one of the celebrated literary partnerships of the late twentieth century. Living in Cornish, New Hampshire, during the 1980s, Dorris and his wife were extraordinarily productive writers. Initially, Dorris served as Erdrich's editor and literary agent, helping to obtain a publisher for her critically acclaimed, best-selling novel *Love Medicine* (1984). Later, the couple turned to collaborative writing, using the joint pseudonym Milou North for their early stories. Although they usually published novels under either Erdrich's or Dorris's name, they claimed that each contributed equally to every text, regardless of whose name appeared on the book's title page.

During the 1980s, Dorris published several important works that contributed to the growing body of Native American literature. In 1987 he published his first novel, *A Yellow Raft in Blue Water,* which told the story of three generations of Native American women; it was well received. Dorris's next work, *The Broken Cord: A Family's Ongoing Struggle with Fetal Alcohol Syndrome,* was published in 1989. Based on the life of Dorris's first adopted son, who had been diagnosed with fetal alcohol syndrome in 1982, the text focused on the disease's impact on both a child and his or her family. The best-selling work was awarded the National Book Critics Circle Award for the year and was later adapted into a television movie for ABC.

Dorris continued to publish a number of books during the 1990s. He and Erdrich wrote *The Crown of Columbus* (1991), a novel for which they received an unprecedented $1.5 million advance from HarperCollins. They also cowrote *Route Two and Back* (1991), a travel narrative. During this time Dorris published several young-adult novels, including *Morning Girl* (1992) and *Guests* (1995); a collection of short stories, *Working Men* (1993); and two collections of essays, *Rooms in the House of Stone* (1993) and *Paper Trail* (1994).

Despite the couple's literary success, the 1990s were marred by family tragedy. In 1991 one of their sons died after being hit by a car. In 1993 their other son made threats against the couple. Concerned for the family's safety, Dorris and Erdrich secretly moved their family in 1993, first to Montana and then to Minnesota. These family tensions took their toll on the marriage, and Dorris and Erdrich quietly separated in late 1995.

Following the separation, Dorris continued to write. In 1997 his second novel, *Cloud Chamber,* was published to lukewarm reviews. Dorris also began work on a second book depicting his experiences with fetal alcohol syndrome. Entitled *Matter of Conscience* and focusing on the sufferings of his adopted children from fetal alcohol effect, a form of the syndrome that is difficult to diagnose, the book was never completed.

During 1997, formal divorce proceedings began between Dorris and Erdrich. At age fifty-two, Dorris committed suicide at a hotel in Concord, only days before the twenty-fifth anniversary of the founding of the Native American studies program at Dartmouth. After his death, reports surfaced that Dorris had recently been accused of child abuse and that he had been hospitalized following an unsuccessful suicide attempt earlier that year. His final work, *The Window,* a novel for young adults, was published posthumously in 1997.

Dorris's complicated personal life threatened to overshadow his considerable scholarly and literary achievements. As a scholar, he was instrumental in bringing new attention and credibility to the field of Native American studies. He was an outspoken activist for Native American social and political issues and worked to bring national attention to the poverty inherent on many reservations. His work on fetal alcohol syndrome resulted in new public awareness of the issue and led to congressional hearings on the disease. Dorris also was a talented novelist, whose fiction helped to shape the growing canon of Native American literature.

★

Ann Weil, *Michael Dorris* (1987), provides a chronicle of the author's life. Detailed information about Dorris's working relationship with Erdrich may be found in *Conversations with Louise Erdrich and Michael Dorris* (1994), a collection of interviews edited by Allan Chavkin and Nancy Feyl Chavkin. For a contextualization of Dorris's work in comparison with other Native American authors, see Louis Owens, "Act of Recovery: The American Indian Novel in the 1980s," *Western American Literature* (May 1987). Literary critics have tended to focus on how Dorris examines cultural hybridity in his writing. See, for example, David Cowart,

"'The Rhythm of Three Strands': Cultural Braiding in Dorris's *A Yellow Raft in Blue Water,*" *Studies in American Indian Literature* (spring 1996). An obituary is in the *New York Times* (16 Apr. 1997).

ELIZABETH J. WRIGHT

DOUGLAS, Marjory Stoneman (*b.* 7 April 1890 in Minneapolis, Minnesota; *d.* 14 May 1998 in Coconut Grove, Florida), writer and environmental activist who helped to found Everglades National Park, founded and was the first president of the Friends of the Everglades, and authored *The Everglades: River of Grass* (1947).

Douglas was the only child of Frank Bryant Stoneman, a judge, and Lillian Trefethen, a concert violinist. Douglas's parents separated when she was young, and the bitter estrangement caused her mother to suffer a series of nervous breakdowns. At age six, Douglas moved with her mother to Taunton, Massachusetts, to live with her maternal grandmother. Meanwhile, Douglas's father moved to Miami, where he founded and became the first editor of the *News Record,* which later became the *Miami Herald.* She did not see her father again until she was an adult.

Douglas received her primary and secondary education at Taunton public schools. In 1912 she graduated from

Marjory Stoneman Douglas, 1986. KATHY WILLENS/ASSOCIATED PRESS AP

Wellesley College in Massachusetts with an A.B. degree in English composition. She married the journalist and writer Kenneth Douglas, who was thirty years her senior, in April 1914. Douglas soon realized that the marriage would not work. Within a year she had moved to Miami, where she reunited with her father and became a reporter for his newspaper. Douglas was philosophical about her failed marriage and later claimed that her independent nature, along with her interest in controversial causes such as women's suffrage, civil rights, and environmentalism, did not make her an ideal candidate for marriage. Her divorce was finalized in 1917.

During World War I, Douglas served as a relief worker for the American Red Cross in Belgium, France, Italy, and the Balkans. In 1920 she returned to Miami and became an assistant editor at the *Miami Herald*. She wrote editorials and poems for her literary column and also authored a one-act play, *The Gallows Gate* (1928). Douglas soon tired of the pressures of the newspaper business and left to become a freelance short-story writer. Her writing, much of which focused on southern Florida, was published in prestigious journals, including the *Saturday Evening Post*. In 1926 she built a small, unpretentious cottage in Miami's Coconut Grove neighborhood that served as her home and office until her death. Her short story "Peculiar Treasure of a King" won second place in the O. Henry Prize competition in 1928. The *Saturday Evening Post*'s volume of its best short stories of 1937 included Douglas's "Story of a Homely Woman."

Douglas was an associate professor at the University of Miami from 1925 to 1929 and a lecturer at Pennsylvania State College in 1929. She also developed an interest in protecting the Florida Everglades during the 1920s. Her father had argued for the protection of the Everglades early in the twentieth century when most Florida residents believed that the area was worthless swampland and should be drained. Douglas herself had written editorials in defense of the Everglades. In 1927 she was invited to join a committee to promote the establishment of a national park, a reserve to protect the Everglades' unique and fragile ecosystem for future generations.

In 1941 an editor from Rinehart Publishing asked Douglas to write a natural history of the Miami River for their American river series. Douglas was skeptical. She joked that the river was only about an "inch long" and was not worth a whole book-length treatment. She did, however, realize that the river was connected to the larger ecosystem of the Everglades, and that the natural history of the Everglades was worth investigating. Douglas spent the next few years doing research and traveling through the saw grass and mangroves of southern Florida in canoes, rowboats, and on foot. The result of her efforts was her celebrated *The Everglades: River of Grass*, which documented both the natural and human histories of the Everglades. The book was released in 1947; by Christmas, all copies of the first printing were sold. Since the book's original publication, it has sold, on average, 10,000 copies per year.

After the Everglades National Park was founded in 1947, Douglas continued to be an advocate for the region. In 1969 she established the Friends of the Everglades, an environmental organization opposed to construction projects, especially a proposed jetport in the area. The jetport was never built. Meanwhile, Douglas was a constant and outspoken critic of real estate developers, sugarcane growers, the U.S. Army Corps of Engineers, and anyone else whose projects threatened her beloved swamp. She continually reminded the public that the Everglades were critical to southern Florida's water supply and were a refuge for birds (including ibis, wood storks, and roseate spoonbills), manatees, alligators, and the endangered Florida panther.

Douglas was the book review editor for the *Miami Herald* from 1942 to 1949. She published her first novel, *Road to the Sun*, in 1951. Her *Freedom River*, a youth-oriented tale set in Florida in 1845, was published in 1953. She also served as an editor for the University of Miami Press from 1960 to 1963, was a member of the Society of Women Geographers, and was actively involved in the Junior Museum of Miami, the Coconut Grove Slum Clearance Association, and the Fairchild Tropical Garden. She received an honorary Litt.D. from the University of Miami on 9 June 1952.

Douglas remained active in the last years of her life despite being legally blind and losing her hearing. A petite woman, she had a reputation for strength and feistiness, and for not mincing words. With John Rothchild, she wrote her autobiography, *Marjory Stoneman Douglas: Voice of the River* (1987). In 1991 Queen Elizabeth II of England visited Douglas, and in 1993 President Bill Clinton awarded her the Presidential Medal of Freedom. Several Florida parks and schools, a Key Biscayne nature center, and a state building were named in her honor. Douglas died in her sleep at her Coconut Grove home. She was 108 years old. Her ashes were scattered over a section of the Everglades named in her honor.

In March 2000 Douglas was inducted into the National Wildlife Federation Conservation Hall of Fame for her leadership and tireless efforts in protecting the Everglades. As the region's greatest champion, Douglas will always be linked to Everglades National Park. She was one of the most celebrated and influential nature writers of the twentieth century.

★

Douglas's writings also include *Hurricane* (1958) and *Florida: The Long Frontier* (1967). Some of Douglas's short stories are collected in Kevin M. McCarthy, ed., *Nine Florida Stories* (1990).

Dava Sobel interviewed Douglas for *Audubon* (July 1991). Mary Joy Breton included Douglas in *Women Pioneers for the Environment* (1998). She was profiled in *People Weekly* (1 June 1998) and *Current Biography* (1953 and 1998). Her induction into the Conservation Hall of Fame was featured in *National Wildlife* 38, no. 3 (2000). Tricia Andryszewski, *Marjory Stoneman Douglas: Friend of the Everglades* (1994), and Sandra Wallus Sammons, *Marjory Stoneman Douglas and the Florida Everglades* (1998), are youth-oriented biographies. An obituary is in the *New York Times* (15 May 1998).

KATHY S. MASON

DRURY, Allen Stuart (*b.* 2 September 1918 in Houston, Texas; *d.* 2 September 1998 in San Francisco, California), Washington, D.C., reporter turned novelist who drew upon his insider knowledge of Capitol Hill politics to write the 1960 Pulitzer Prize–winning novel *Advise and Consent* (1959), a thinly veiled fictional exposé of government intrigue and scandal.

Drury was one of two children of Alden Monteith Drury, the general manager for several citrus growers' associations, and Flora Allen, the legislative liaison for the California Parent-Teachers Association. He grew up in Porterville, California, and graduated from Porterville High School in 1935. Drury attended Stanford University, wrote for the *Stanford Daily,* and graduated with a B.A. degree in journalism in 1939. He served as the editor of the weekly *Tulare* (California) *Bee* from 1940 to 1941, and as the county editor of the *Bakersfield Californian* from 1941 to 1942. He enlisted in the U.S. Army in 1942 but was discharged the next year due to a preexisting back injury. He subsequently found a job in Washington, D.C., as a Senate reporter for the United Press (UP).

While covering the Senate from 1943 to 1945, Drury kept a personal journal of his impressions of the legislators and their clashes with President Franklin D. Roosevelt, recording memorable events, personalities, and dialogue. After the end of World War II, returning UP reporters reclaimed their jobs and Drury turned to freelancing. In 1947 he became the national editor for *Pathfinder,* a newsmagazine aimed at small-town America, and wrote a column, "Westerner in Washington," for the *Palo Alto* (California) *Times* and the *Waterloo* (Iowa) *Courier.* Around 1951 he started to write a novel based on his Senate journal but put it aside when he joined the national staff of the *Washington Evening Star* in 1953. The following year, James Reston recruited him to cover the Senate for the *New York Times.* Drury chafed under the newspaper's finicky copyediting and quietly resumed work on his novel in his spare time. During the interval, McCarthyism had darkened the atmosphere of Washington. A resolute anticommunist, Drury

initially regarded Senator Joseph McCarthy as a harmless politician out to make his mark on history. However, his view changed when McCarthy threatened to expose a homosexual scandal within the family of Lester Hunt, a senator from Wyoming. Hunt's suicide revealed to Drury how cruel politics could be.

In 1959 Drury published his first novel, *Advise and Consent,* a thick book that told the story of a Roosevelt-like president whose nominee for secretary of state, the equivocal Robert Leffingwell (who is hiding a youthful attraction to communism), touches off a furious confirmation battle in the Senate. In a riveting manner, the novel moved behind the scenes to reveal the way Washington worked. Fortuitously, it appeared just as the Senate was rejecting the actual cabinet nomination of Lewis Strauss to be the secretary of commerce. A photograph of an airport encounter between the two front-runners in the 1960 presidential elections, John F. Kennedy and Richard Nixon, caught them perusing the novel. Drury obtained their permission to run the photo in an advertisement, headlined "Everyone is reading *Advise and Consent.*" Selling phenomenally, *Advise and Consent* set a record of 102 weeks on the *New York*

Allen Drury, 1977. CORBIS CORPORATION (BELLEVUE)

Times best-seller list, was a Book-of-the-Month Club selection, and won the Pulitzer Prize in 1960.

Part of the pleasure of *Advise and Consent* came from guessing the identities of characters based on recognizable politicians. Its most sensitively drawn character was Brigham Anderson, a Utah senator who commits suicide when blackmailed over a past homosexual relationship. Drury objected whenever people identified the older, dumpy Lester Hunt with his young, strapping Brig Anderson. He explained that his fictional characters were substantially reshaped composites. But in a later novel, *Capable of Honor* (1966), Drury insisted, over the objections of his publisher's libel lawyers, on naming a pompous Washington columnist "Walter Dobious," to make clear the connection to Walter Lippmann. He also regretted not having continued his Senate journal longer so that he could continue "cannibalizing" his recorded experiences for other novels.

Advise and Consent had a short run as a Broadway play in 1961, and in the following year the director Otto Preminger released it as an all-star Hollywood film, using the Senate Office Building as his set and real senators, staff, and reporters as extras. Although some senators complained that the story cast the Senate in a poor light, Preminger regarded it as less critical of the political system than of the powerful officeholders who abused it. But to Drury's chagrin, the liberal Preminger altered his message by casting the actor Henry Fonda as a more sympathetic Leffingwell.

Ample royalties enabled Drury to quit daily reporting, leave Washington, and return to California. He moved to then-rural Tiburon, across the bay from San Francisco, and spent the rest of his life there in a small house with a spectacular view. He never married and lived alone. Meticulous in his research for his novels, he followed government affairs closely and maintained his contacts with politicians and journalists through periodic visits to Washington, regular attendance at the national political conventions, and membership in the exclusive and conservative men's club the Bohemian Grove. All told, he wrote twenty novels, among them five sequels to *Advise and Consent,* and five books of nonfiction that included his original *Senate Journal* (1963). Most sold well, but none matched the extraordinary success of his first novel. His books contained an underlying admiration for those who favored military strength over diplomatic negotiation when confronting world communism, a militant stance that grew less appealing during the domestic turmoil and disillusionment associated with the Vietnam War. His output also varied in quality over the years and reviewers lambasted his later efforts. Yet Drury's large fan base continued to buy his books long after he fell out of favor with literary critics.

In 1971 Drury and the photographer Fred Maroon produced a sympathetic portrait of Nixon's presidency, *Courage and Hesitation.* Drury had known Nixon for years and resented attacks on him by liberal politicians and the media. The president gave him carte-blanche access to the White House, but Drury had trouble with the highly protective staff and the book's title reflected his dimmer view of the administration's actual performance. Not long afterward, the Watergate scandal broke and many of the top officials he interviewed were exposed for machinations more devious than anything in his novels. Beyond his books set in Washington, Drury also examined South African apartheid, wrote two novels on ancient Egypt, and based a trilogy on his class at Stanford. In 1982 President Ronald Reagan named him to the National Council on the Arts, a membership that he retained until 1988. Drury died of cardiac arrest on his eightieth birthday. He is buried in Saint Helena, California.

The expression "an Allen Drury novel" became synonymous with Washington intrigue. Despite his focus on corruption and conspiracy, Drury held an unshakable conviction that the U.S. government remained fundamentally decent and true to its basic principles. *Advise and Consent* was assigned in civics classes and in 1995 Newt Gingrich, Speaker of the House, listed it as recommended reading for newly elected representatives. Drury's success also inspired other journalists to try their hand at writing Washington novels, efforts that inevitably were measured against *Advise and Consent.*

★

Drury's papers are at the Hoover Institution Library and Archives, Stanford University. References to Drury's work appear in Gordon Milne, The American Political Novel *(1966); Gay Talese,* The Kingdom and the Power *(1969); Otto Preminger,* Preminger: An Autobiography *(1977); Tom Kemme,* Political Fiction, the Spirit of the Age, and Allen Drury *(1987); and Margo Hammond, "When Scandal Was Novel,"* Capital Style *(Jan./Feb. 1998), to which Drury responded in the May 1998 issue. An interview with Drury appears in* Contemporary Authors, *vol. 18 (1986). Obituaries and tributes are in the* New York Times *(3 Sept. 1998) and* Washington Post *(4 Sept. 1998).*

DONALD A. RITCHIE

DUBUS, Andre Jules (*b.* 11 August 1936 in Lake Charles, Louisiana; *d.* 24 February 1999 in Haverhill, Massachusetts), novelist, short story writer, and essayist whose works reflected his Catholic beliefs and featured a fictional locale based on the Merrimack Valley in Massachusetts.

Dubus was one of three children of Andre Jules Dubus, district manager of the Gulf States Utilities Company, and Katherine Burke, a homemaker; he grew up in a pious Catholic household in the Cajun region of Louisiana. He

Andre Dubus. AP/WIDE WORLD PHOTOS

attended Lafayette's Cathedral School, run by the De La Salle Christian Brothers, from grade three until the end of his senior year of high school. His story "If They Knew Yvonne" and his novella *Voices from the Moon* are considered to embody the psychological and spiritual struggles that Dubus faced as an adolescent. From his earliest days, Dubus remained faithful in his belief in the sacramental efficacy of the Catholic Church, particularly in the sacraments of reconciliation and the Holy Eucharist, as explained in his essay "On Charon's Wharf."

While attending McNeese State College (now McNeese State University) in Lake Charles, Dubus spent parts of two summers in the U.S. Marine Corps' platoon leaders' class in Quantico, Virginia. Graduating in 1958 with a B.A. degree in English, Dubus joined the marines for a five-and-a-half year tour of duty. He spent the first year in artillery school at Quantico, then three years at Camp Pendleton, California, followed by nine months as a first lieutenant with a marine detachment aboard the USS *Ranger* in the waters off the coast of Japan. He transformed these experiences into his only novel, *The Lieutenant* (1967), written in the tradition of Herman Melville's *Billy Budd* and William Styron's *The Long March*. Approximately one year before he left the marines in 1964, Dubus returned home from the naval air station on Whidbey Island, Washington, to help care for his ailing father, who died at age fifty-nine

from colon cancer. Some have speculated that Dubus entered the marines to prove something about his manhood to his father, and once his father died, resigned his commission.

Motivated by a desire to develop his own talents, as evidenced by the appearance of his story "The Intruder" in the April–June 1963 issue of the *Sewanee Review*, Dubus left Camp Pendleton for Iowa with his growing family, which included his wife Patricia Lowe, whom he had married on 22 February 1958, and their four children (one of whom, Andre Jules III, also became a recognized writer). Dubus attended the University of Iowa Writers' Workshop from January 1964 to August 1966, completing an M.F.A. degree. The workshop faculty included esteemed writers such as Richard Yates, Kurt Vonnegut, R. V. Cassill, and Vance Bourjaily.

Later that summer Dubus and his family moved first to Plaistow, New Hampshire, for two years and then in 1968 moved to Country Pond, New Hampshire, where they lived until 1970 so that Dubus could teach at nearby Bradford College, on the outskirts of Haverhill, Massachusetts. After four years in New England, Dubus and his wife divorced, and he moved by himself to Haverhill, where he lived for the rest of his life. His wife and children moved to Merrimack, New Hampshire. Dubus discovered in the Merrimack Valley, a region dotted with empty factories and warehouses, people that he could transform into the protagonists of his own imaginative locale, what novelist Anne Tyler called his "sad, brave, gritty fictional world."

In June 1975 Dubus married Tommie Gail Thigpen Cotter, a widow with two young children whom he had previously known in Lake Charles. They subsequently divorced, and in December 1979 Dubus married again, this time to Peggy Rambach, one of his former students. They had two daughters together but divorced in 1989. Dubus taught modern fiction and creative writing at Bradford College from 1966 to 1984 and published ten volumes of short fiction and two collections of essays.

On 23 July 1986 Dubus suffered an accident on highway I-93 north of Boston, which resulted in the amputation of his left leg. He had stopped to assist two motorists who had driven over an abandoned motorcycle, when an oncoming car hit the motorists' car, pinning Dubus to the ground and fracturing his legs. Gradually, with the help of family and friends, including a group of student writers, Dubus overcame a bout of depression and started writing again.

During his lifetime Dubus received the PEN/Malamud Award, the Rea Award for excellence in short fiction, the Jean Stein Award from the American Academy of Arts and Letters, the *Boston Globe*'s first annual Lawrence L. Winship Award, as well as grants from the National Endowment for the Arts (1978 and 1985), two fellowships from the Guggenheim Foundation (1977 and 1986), and a grant from the MacArthur Foundation (1988 to 1993). He died of a heart attack in his home at age sixty-two and is buried in Haverhill.

In general, Dubus's works tend to portray families, especially couples, who experience conflict, including premarital and extramarital sex, abortion, teenage cocaine use, arson, child abuse, death from AIDS, and attempted and accidental murder. Typically, his characters refrain from making preemptive decisions about the morality of what is happening. The three Edith and Hank Allison/Terry and Jack Linhart stories in *We Don't Live Here Anymore*, for example, apparently based on situations at Bradford College, explore the types of complexities that so intrigued Dubus. In addition to his masterpiece, "A Father's Story,"
the stories "Falling in Love," "All the Time in the World," "The Timing of Sin," and "Out of the Snow" (all in *Dancing After Hours*) are detailed psychological portraits that contain some of Dubus's best writing. He is often considered one of the best American fiction writers of the twentieth century.

★

There is no full-scale biography or complete critical study of Dubus's works, although Thomas E. Kennedy, *Andre Dubus: A Study of the Short Fiction* (1988), is helpful. Obituaries are in the *New York Times, Boston Globe,* and *Chicago Tribune* (all 26 Feb. 1999) and *Time* (8 Mar. 1999).

PATRICK SAMWAY

E

EDEL, (Joseph) Leon (*b.* 9 September 1907 in Pittsburgh, Pennsylvania; *d.* 5 September 1997 in Honolulu, Hawaii), literary critic best known for his biographies, notably of Henry James.

Edel was one of two sons of Simon Edel, a tailor, and Fannie Malamud. His parents were Russian Jewish immigrants living in Pittsburgh. In 1910 the family moved to Saskatchewan, Canada. Edel's mother created a cosmopolitan environment for her two sons, giving them violin lessons and taking them on an extended trip to Russia from 1912 to 1913. When Leon graduated from Yorkton Collegiate Institute in 1923, the Edel family moved to Montreal so he could attend McGill University. While studying contemporary literature, Edel joined four friends in founding what proved to be a well-regarded journal, the *Fortnightly Review,* which nevertheless survived only until they graduated. Edel received a B.A. degree in 1927 and an M.A. degree in 1928, both in contemporary literature. With these diplomas and a Province of Quebec scholarship, he set off for Europe.

Edel's decision to go to Paris, where he would focus his studies on the American novelist and short story writer Henry James, Jr., was profoundly motivated. Six decades earlier the young James had gone to Paris with only a few letters of introduction to carve out an identity separate from his famous father and brother. For decades James struggled against a sense of being an outsider, thus offering a perfect

parallel to Edel. Even in Edel's later life his friend Lyall Powers called him an "alien unsure of his identity . . . lacking a place distinctively his own." Was he American or Canadian? Was he the rude son of a tailor or the self-assured editor of a literary journal? One thing is certain; after arriving in Paris, Edel set about erasing all traces of his roots. He assiduously covered any hint of a midwestern accent, he grew a small mustache in the manner of Adolphe Menjou, the Franco-American actor, and he dressed in English tweed suits.

Edel undertook his study of James at a propitious time. Some people still living in Europe had known the man behind the work, notably Theodora Bosanquet, James's secretary, and Burgess Noakes, his valet. In addition, Edel won influential sponsors, such as Edith Wharton, who endorsed him to her wide literary circle, and Harry James, who granted Edel exclusive rights to his uncle's unpublished papers, rights that later generated controversy. Edel's doctoral dissertation, "Henry James: The Dramatic Years," gained him a docteur es lettres from the University of Paris in 1932. He returned to Canada, where he briefly held a position at Sir George Williams University in Montreal. But the Great Depression ended his hopes of an academic appointment, and for the next decade Edel supported himself through freelance journalism, working for the *Montreal Herald,* the Havas news agency, the Canadian press, and *P.M.* magazine. He was so poor, however, that when he was offered a Guggenheim Fellowship in 1937, he had to

Leon Edel. CORBIS CORPORATION (BELLEVUE)

receive it in installments so he could also continue his free-lance reporting. This decade of poverty and insecurity that Edel endured from 1932 to 1942 may have contributed to his later defensiveness toward those who sought permission to publish some of James's letters. Edel married Bertha Cohen in 1935; they had no children.

During World War II, Edel began service in the U.S. Army in 1943 and rose to the rank of first lieutenant. He served in General George Patton's Third Army during the Normandy campaign, the liberation of Paris, and the cross-ing of the Rhine. Along the way he earned five battle stars and the Bronze Star. When he returned to civilian life in 1947, he was still unable to obtain a permanent academic position, although he received visiting appointments at New York University (NYU), Harvard University, and Princeton University between 1950 and 1953. To the clubby world of academia, Edel was still a journalist, a Jew, and a foreigner. Moreover, he lacked a Ph.D. from a prestigious American university. In 1950 Edel divorced his first wife in order to marry Roberta Roberts on 2 December of that year. They had no children and divorced in 1979.

Edel's experiences during the war had given him con-fidence, and three years of psychoanalysis, from 1947 to 1950, had given him a vocabulary. Combining his experi-ences and his psychoanalysis, he began a series of ground-breaking psychobiographical studies. The first, published in 1947, was *James Joyce: The Last Journey.* It was followed by *The Complete Plays of Henry James* (1949). Edel also began work on *The Life of Henry James,* his definitive bi-ography of James, published in five volumes (1953–1972).

After the first volume of his magisterial biography of James demonstrated that he was the world's foremost au-thority on the subject, the doors that had been closed to the journalist Edel, the docteur es lettres Edel, or the lieutenant Edel finally opened. NYU appointed him a tenured pro-fessor in 1953; he subsequently became the Henry James Professor of English and American Letters and retired in 1972 as professor emeritus. By then he was splitting the academic year between NYU and the University of Hawaii, where he first taught in 1955. The latter named him Citi-zens Professor of English in 1972, and he continued to teach there after his elevation to emeritus status in 1978. In addition, the University of Toronto invited him to give the Alexander Lectures from 1955 to 1956 and named him Vis-iting Centennial Professor in 1967. Despite these belated signs of recognition, the scars remained. Edel ultimately bequeathed his archives to McGill, his alma mater.

In addition to his writing *The Life of Henry James,* Edel edited *The Complete Tales of Henry James* in twelve volumes (1962–1965), and *Letters/Henry James* in four volumes (1974–1984). His other books include *Willa Cather: A Criti-cal Biography,* with E. K. Brown (1953); *Henry D. Thoreau* (1970); the papers of his colleague Edmund Wilson; *The Psychological Novel, 1900–1950* (1955); *Literary Biography* (1957); a psychological portrait of the Bloomsbury group, *Bloomsbury: A House of Lions* (1979); and a book about writing biographies, *Writing Lives* (1984).

Edel's awards include the Pulitzer Prize and the Na-tional Book Award for volumes two and three of *The Life of Henry James,* published together in 1962; the Gold Medal for Biography from the American Academy and Institute of Arts and Letters in 1976; the National Arts Club Gold Medal for Literature in 1981; and the National Book Critics Circle Award for Biography for his one-volume abridged biography, *Henry James: A Life* (1985), in 1985. In 1981 he was named a "Living Treasure of Hawaii."

In 1980 Edel married Marjorie Putnam Sinclair; they had no children. Edel died four days before his ninetieth birthday from complications of heart surgery and is buried in Honolulu.

Edel revolutionized the art of biography. He trans-formed it from a form dedicated to superficial data and impressionistic judgments to one concerned with the com-plex inner life of the subject. Biography became less the articulation of the biographer's perspective and more the explication of the subject's aspirations, motives, and rationalizations as revealed in diaries and notebooks, dreams and nightmares. In the hands of lesser talents this new form sometimes led to unrestrained speculation and rumor mongering, but in the hands of a master like Edel it allowed readers to finish a biography with the feeling that they understood not only a life but a person.

★

Edel's papers are archived at McGill University in Montreal. He granted extensive interviews to *Contemporary Authors, New Revision Series,* vol. 22 (1986), and for an article by Jeanne McCulloch, "Leon Edel: The Art of Biography," *Paris Review* (winter 1985). See Gloria G. Fromm, ed., *Essaying Biography: A Celebration for Leon Edel* (1987), and Lyall H. Powers, "Leon Edel: The Life of a Biographer," *American Scholar* (Sept. 1997). An obituary is in the *New York Times* (8 Sept. 1997).

HARTLEY S. SPATT

EHRLICHMAN, John Daniel (*b.* 20 March 1925 in Tacoma, Washington; *d.* 14 February 1999 in Sandy Springs, Georgia), chief domestic policy aide to President Richard M. Nixon who was forced to resign for, and later was convicted of, crimes relating to the Watergate scandal.

Ehrlichman was the only child of Rudolph I. Ehrlichman, a successful investor, and Lillian C. Danielson. Both parents were Christian Scientists and raised their son in that faith. As a boy, Ehrlichman moved with his parents first to suburban New Jersey, near Manhattan, and then to Santa Monica, California. He was active in the Boy Scouts, becoming an Eagle Scout, and enjoyed hiking and outdoor recreation. At Santa Monica High School he ran for student-body president, but when he lost to the football team captain he decided to stay behind the scenes in politics. He graduated in 1942.

That autumn Ehrlichman enrolled at the University of California at Los Angeles (UCLA), and after a year he joined the U.S. Army Air Corps. During World War II, he became the navigator of a B-24 bomber and flew twenty-six missions over Germany. He received the Distinguished Flying Cross and the Air Medal with clusters and rose to the rank of first lieutenant. Ehrlichman left the army in 1945 and returned to UCLA on the GI Bill. There he studied political science and took part in debating. He also befriended Harry Robbins "Bob" Haldeman, a fellow Christian Scientist and Republican, with whom he served on the Interfraternity Council.

Ehrlichman earned his B.A. degree in 1948 and entered Stanford University Law School in California. He married Jeanne Fisher on 21 August 1949. They had five children.

John Ehrlichman testifying before the Senate Watergate committee, July 1973. ASSOCIATED PRESS AP

After earning his LL.B. degree in 1951, Ehrlichman was admitted to the California bar. The next year he moved to Seattle, where he worked briefly as an attorney for the United Pacific Insurance Company before setting up his own law practice with Jack Hullin, a family friend. Ehrlichman remained a partner with Hullin, Ehrlichman, Roberts, and Hodge until 1968. He specialized in real estate law, dealing with questions of zoning and land use. In 1967 the University of Washington hired him as an instructor in law.

In the 1950s Ehrlichman came to admire Vice President Richard M. Nixon. In 1959 Haldeman, who had become an advertising executive and then joined Nixon's nascent 1960 presidential campaign, brought his college friend on board. Ehrlichman worked as an advance man, organizing the logistics of Nixon's campaign appearances. He also participated in some of the "dirty tricks" for which Nixon would become known, once infiltrating the campaign of Nixon's rival, New York Governor Nelson A. Rockefeller, to gather information. He also posed as a delegate to the Democratic National Convention in 1960 for similar purposes.

After Nixon's defeat in November 1960, Ehrlichman returned to his family and his law practice. In 1962 Haldeman again persuaded him to come work for Nixon, who was running for governor of California. Nixon lost, but

Ehrlichman kept working for him sporadically as a political aide. In 1964 he helped to arrange Nixon's part in the Republican National Convention. In 1966 he trained advance men for the 1968 presidential race. In June 1968 he returned full-time to Nixon's employ as the campaign's national tour director. Ehrlichman organized the candidate's schedule, helped to plan advertising, and assisted in running the Republican convention. He also arranged, at Nixon's behest, for local policemen to rough up hecklers during campaign stops, he later wrote.

Nixon valued Ehrlichman's loyalty and efficiency. After winning the 1968 election, Nixon included Ehrlichman among a small group of aides invited to Key Biscayne, Florida, to plan the presidential transition. According to Ehrlichman, Nixon offered him the jobs of attorney general, director of the Central Intelligence Agency, and head of the Republican National Committee. Ehrlichman declined them, believing himself not appropriately qualified. Instead he accepted the job of White House counsel, which he began on 20 January 1969, Nixon's first day as president. Although it was not part of his job description, Ehrlichman found himself mediating among Nixon's domestic policy advisers, whose recommendations often clashed. In particular, the conservative Arthur Burns and the liberal Daniel Patrick Moynihan offered conflicting advice to the president on how to reform the welfare system. Ehrlichman sided with Moynihan, helping convince the president to propose the so-called Family Assistance Plan, which would have imposed work requirements on welfare recipients and provided a guaranteed minimum income. After the plan met resistance in Congress, Nixon lost his enthusiasm for it.

In November 1969, recognizing the role Ehrlichman was playing, Nixon formally named him the assistant to the president for domestic affairs. As the domestic counterpart to the national security adviser Henry Kissinger, Ehrlichman oversaw all domestic policy. Called Nixon's "honest broker," he supervised the preparation of policy on matters such as the environment, urban issues, and energy. Most important, he served as the channel through which all ideas reached Nixon. Ideologically, Ehrlichman was a moderate conservative. But he was less concerned with imposing his philosophical imprint on policies than with arbitrating among competing interests and deciding which would best serve Nixon's interests.

Ehrlichman subscribed to Nixon's strategy of courting voters in Middle America, the middle-class citizens in the South and Midwest, who were wary of the social changes of the 1960s. Once, when questioned by a reporter on the wisdom of a particular policy, he said, "Don't worry. It'll play in Peoria." That line, which references a city in Illinois, was often quoted thereafter as an example of the administration's calculated cultivation of such voters. Ehrlichman and Haldeman, who was the president's chief of staff, together served as a palace guard for the isolated and reclusive Nixon. Because of their Germanic names and the tenacity with which they restricted access to the president, they were called the "Prussians" or the "Berlin Wall." White House aides and reporters considered Ehrlichman, with his arched eyebrow and dour face, intimidating. Yet despite his importance, Ehrlichman never felt personally close to Nixon, who, he noted bitterly, repeatedly misspelled his last name, even when inscribing a book.

Ehrlichman played an active role in the abuses of power that culminated in the Watergate scandal and Nixon's resignation in August 1974. After the former U.S. Defense Department official Daniel Ellsberg leaked to the *New York Times* the "Pentagon Papers," a top-secret study chronicling U.S. involvement in the Vietnam War, Nixon and Kissinger sought retaliation. Believing he had Nixon's direct approval, in September 1971 Ehrlichman authorized the White House "plumbers unit"—a secret team devoted to stopping leaks by means fair and foul—to dig up dirt on Ellsberg. The plumbers, led by G. Gordon Liddy and E. Howard Hunt, broke into the Los Angeles office of Lewis Fielding, Ellsberg's psychoanalyst. Ehrlichman denied that he had sanctioned a break-in, although he had initialed a memorandum by his aide Egil "Bud" Krogh proposing such a plan and added the phrase, "If done under your assurance that it is not traceable."

In June 1972 many of the same men were caught breaking into Democratic Party headquarters in the Watergate office complex in Washington, D.C. Their arrest began the disclosure of the Nixon administration's vast array of similar illegal activities. In early 1973, as the burglars went to trial and the Senate began hearings, a series of stunning revelations quickly emerged. Ehrlichman was found to have participated in the cover-up of the Watergate break-in. He had agreed, for example, to pay the burglars for their silence about the involvement of their superiors. He also had urged Nixon to jettison his troubled nominee for director of the Federal Bureau of Investigation (FBI), L. Patrick Gray, once Gray's involvement in the cover-up surfaced. Famously, Ehrlichman told Nixon they should leave Gray "twisting slowly, slowly in the wind."

Trying to contain the damage, Nixon asked Ehrlichman, Haldeman, and John W. Dean III, the White House counsel, to resign. Nixon announced their departures in a televised address on 30 April 1973, calling Haldeman and Ehrlichman "two of the finest public servants it has ever been my pleasure to know." Shortly before he resigned, however, Ehrlichman spoke with Matthew W. Byrne, the judge overseeing Ellsberg's trial, about becoming the director of the FBI. When Ellsberg's lawyers learned of the contact, they argued that Byrne was compromised and they moved to have the trial dismissed. On 11 May, Byrne declared a mistrial.

In July 1973 Americans watched on television as Ehrlichman testified before the Senate Watergate committee. Unlike some previous witnesses, Ehrlichman was stoutly defiant and unapologetic, justifying his actions as legitimate for reasons of national security. At his own trial in December 1974 Ehrlichman changed his position somewhat. Having learned what Nixon said in secretly recorded conversations with others, Ehrlichman concluded that the president had played both sides of the fence and deceived his aides. He also recounted an effort by Nixon to bribe him for his silence.

Ehrlichman was convicted on 1 January 1975 of conspiracy, obstruction of justice, and two counts of perjury. About the same time, he left his wife, whom he later divorced, and moved to Santa Fe, New Mexico. After pursuing and then abandoning an appeal, he began serving a thirty-month to five-year sentence in a low-security federal prison in Safford, Arizona, on 28 October 1976. Before entering prison he wrote *The Company* (1976), a novel about a President Monckton who closely resembled Ehrlichman's former boss. It became a best-seller. Ehrlichman went on to write several other novels in the same vein: *The Whole Truth* (1979), *The China Card* (1986), and *The Rigby Files* (1989), which he coauthored. His memoir, *Witness to Power: The Nixon Years,* was published in 1982. After his release from prison in April 1978, Ehrlichman earned a living delivering syndicated radio news commentaries and lectures. He then went to work for the Law Companies Group, an environmental law consulting firm.

On 3 November 1978 Ehrlichman married Christine Peacock McLaurine, an interior designer. They had one son and then divorced in 1991. Ehrlichman moved to Atlanta and met Karen Hilliard, a restaurateur and cookbook author, whom he married on 14 January 1995. He died at age seventy-three in Sandy Springs, Georgia, after suffering from diabetes.

Upon his death, some colleagues and historians emphasized Ehrlichman's role in forging the Nixon administration's relatively progressive policies on such matters as environmental protection and Native American rights. Most Americans, however, remembered him as Nixon's loyal and inflexible gatekeeper who went to prison for his participation in the crimes of Watergate.

★

Ehrlichman's memoir, *Witness to Power: The Nixon Years* (1982), is a valuable resource. A solid study of Nixon's aides that focuses on Haldeman and Ehrlichman is Dan Rather and Gary Paul Gates, *The Palace Guard* (1974). Among the most thorough and reliable overviews on Watergate are J. Anthony Lukas, *Nightmare: The Underside of the Nixon Years* (1976), and Stanley I. Kutler, *The Wars of Watergate* (1990). On the Ellsberg affair, see Tom Wells, *Wild Man: The Life and Times of Daniel Ellsberg*

(2001). Valuable profiles of Ehrlichman include Robert B. Semple, Jr., "The Middle American Who Edits Ideas for Nixon," *New York Times* (Aug. 1969); "Mr. Nixon's Honest Broker," *Newsweek* (19 Jan. 1970); Helen Dudar, "The Good Life of an Ex-Con," *Washington Post* (29 Apr. 1979); and Bette Harrison, "Awash in Redemption," *Atlanta Journal and Constitution* (28 Jan. 1996). An obituary is in the *New York Times* (16 Feb. 1999).

DAVID GREENBERG

ELION, Gertrude Belle ("Trudy") (*b.* 23 January 1918 in New York City; *d.* 21 February 1999 in Chapel Hill, North Carolina), biochemist best known as a cowinner of the 1988 Nobel Prize in physiology or medicine for her work involving important principles for drug treatment.

Elion was the first of two children and the only daughter of Robert Elion, a dentist, and Bertha Cohen, a seamstress. Her mother emigrated from Russia at age fourteen, and her father came from Lithuania at age twelve. When Elion was a child of about six or seven, her family moved from Manhattan to the Bronx, where she attended public school. An outstanding student, she was advanced two grades and graduated from high school at age sixteen in the midst of the Great Depression. Although Elion's father was unable to pay for her further education, she was able to attend Hunter College, one of several New York City schools that waived tuition for students with excellent grades. Just be-

Gertrude B. Elion, 1988. CORBIS CORPORATION (BELLEVUE)

fore Elion began her studies at Hunter in the summer of 1933, her grandfather died of stomach cancer. As a result, Elion vowed to become a cancer researcher; she majored in chemistry, rather than biology, because she did not want to harm animals in her research.

In 1937 Elion graduated Phi Beta Kappa with a B.A. degree from Hunter College. It was at this time that Elion met Leonard, the man she wished to marry. Leonard's sudden death from a heart infection, however, ended Elion's thoughts about marriage for the rest of her life. During this trying time, she also had difficulty obtaining a job in the chemistry field. All the laboratories she contacted told her they had never employed a woman. Discouraged, she enrolled in secretarial school. By the end of six weeks, however, Elion was teaching biochemistry to nurses at New York Hospital for a semester, until finally acquiring a non-paying job in a friend's laboratory to gain professional experience. She lived with her parents, continued to teach as a substitute instructor, and saved money to attend graduate school. In 1941, when Elion graduated summa cum laude from New York University with an M.S. degree in chemistry, she was the only female in her class.

In 1942 Elion became an analytical chemist in a food laboratory for the Quaker Maid Company. Eighteen months later, she finally was hired as a research chemist at Johnson and Johnson, only to have her division closed down within six months. Elion declined the offer of a replacement position that involved testing the strength of sutures.

With the entry of the United States into World War II and the resulting lack of men on the home front, Elion was hired by George Herbert Hitchings at the Wellcome Research Laboratories in Tuckahoe, New York. "It was only when men weren't available that women were invited into the lab," Elion told the *Washington Post*. The professional relationship between Elion and Hitchings began on Flag Day (14 June 1944) and lasted for the rest of their careers. Each time Hitchings was promoted, Elion filled his previous position, until she finally became head of Wellcome's department of experimental therapy in 1967, a position she held until her retirement in 1983.

After acquiring the job of her dreams, Elion knew it was time to earn her Ph.D. She enrolled at the Brooklyn Polytechnic Institute, or Polytechnic University, the only school offering chemistry classes at night. Two years into her studies, Elion was called into the dean's office and told she would have to go to school full-time. Unwilling to leave her hard-earned position at Wellcome, Elion relinquished her dream of pursuing a Ph.D. This difficult choice bothered her, at least until her lab developed the first successful drug against childhood leukemia, 6-mercaptopurine (6MP) or Purinethol, in 1951. The drug was approved by the Food and Drug Administration (FDA) two years later. Elion was

also instrumental in the development of another leukemia-fighting drug, thioguanine, in 1950, which was FDA approved in 1966.

Although the structure of deoxyribonucleic acid (DNA) was not discovered until 1953 by James Watson and Francis Crick, Elion and Hitchings became interested in the dissimilarities between the replication of DNA in normal versus abnormal (cancerous) cells. Elion's primary focus was with purines, and her first breakthrough came with the development of 6MP, which led to the discovery of azathioprine (Imuran) and allopurinol (Zyloprim). Elion and Hitchings also developed pyrimethamine (Daraprim and Fansidar) and trimethoprim (Bactrim and Septra). In addition, Elion influenced the processing and development of acyclovir (Zovirax). In 1984 researchers who were trained by Elion and Hitchings developed azidothymidine (AZT), or zidovudine (Retrovir), the first drug to treat acquired immunodeficiency syndrome (AIDS).

As a result of their extensive research on drugs that led to the treatment of incurable illnesses such as cancer, malaria, herpes, and AIDS, Elion and Hitchings, along with the British biochemist Sir James W. Black, were awarded the 1988 Nobel Prize for physiology or medicine.

Although most of Elion's career was spent at Wellcome laboratories, she held other positions concurrently. She became a research professor of experimental medicine and pharmacology at Duke University in Durham, North Carolina (1971–1983), and at the University of North Carolina in Chapel Hill (1973–1999). After Elion's official retirement in 1983, she remained at Wellcome as a scientist emeritus and kept an office there as a consultant. Each year she also continued to mentor a third-year medical student on a research project at Duke. Elion served as a member of the National Cancer Advisory Board (1984–1990); as an honorary staff member of the Arthur G. James Cancer Hospital and Research Institute of Ohio State University (1990); and on the board of directors of the Burroughs Wellcome Fund (1991–1999).

Elion received many accolades, including the Garvan Medal of the American Chemical Society (1968); President's Medal of Hunter College (1970); Judd Award of the Sloan-Kettering Institute (1983); Distinguished Chemist Award and Cain Memorial Award of the American Association for Cancer Research (both 1985); Ernst W. Bertner Memorial Award from the M.D. Anderson Cancer Center (1989); Medal of Honor of the American Cancer Society (1990); and National Medal of Science (1991).

Elion was a member of the National Academy of Sciences; American Chemical Society; New York Academy of Sciences; American Society of Biological Chemists; and Academy of Pharmaceutical Sciences (honorary member). She served as president of the American Association for

Cancer Research (1983–1984) and as a fellow of the American Academy of Pharmaceutical Scientists. She was the first woman to be inducted into the National Inventors' Hall of Fame (1991), and she was also named to the National Women's Hall of Fame (1991) and the Engineering and Science Hall of Fame (1992). Elion died at the University of North Carolina Hospital in Chapel Hill on 21 February 1999, at age eighty-one.

Elion will always be remembered as a dedicated, brilliant, enthusiastic, down-to-earth person. She held forty-five patents and more than twenty honorary degrees, and she enjoyed travel, photography, and opera. She encouraged young people to play a greater role in the sciences, always emphasizing the importance of research. Her one unquestionable goal, however, was to find a cure for cancer. While that wish was not granted during her lifetime, she made significant contributions to cancer research, particularly in the development of drugs for treating leukemia.

★

Elion wrote a brief autobiographical sketch for the Nobel Foundation shortly after winning the Nobel Prize; it can be found at "The Nobel Prize in Medicine, Laureates," <http://www.nobel.se/medicine/laureates>. The following books contain short biographies about Elion: Sharon Bertsch McGrayne, ed., *Nobel Prize Women in Science* (1993); Martha J. Bailey, *American Women in Science: A Biographical Dictionary* (1994); Benjamin F. and Barbara S. Shearer, eds., *Notable Women in the Physical Sciences: A Biographical Dictionary* (1997); Pamela Profitt, ed., *Notable Women Scientists* (1999); and Marilyn Ogilvie and Joy Harvey, eds., *The Biographical Dictionary of Women in Science* (2000). Obituaries are in the *New York Times, Washington Post, San Francisco Chronicle, Los Angeles Times,* and *Newsday* (all 23 Feb. 1999).

ADRIANA C. TOMASINO

ESPY, Willard Richard ("Wede") (*b.* 11 December 1910 in Olympia, Washington; *d.* 20 February 1999 in New York City), word-play expert, light-verse writer, publisher, and author of numerous books about playful aspects of the English language.

Espy was the sixth of seven children born to Harry Albert Espy, a state senator who made his fortune buying up land at $1 per acre in Oysterville, Washington, and its environs, and Helen Medora Richardson, a homemaker. His father's love of language inspired a similar response in Espy. In *Oysterville* (1977), Espy's autobiographical tribute to the small town he loved beyond all other towns, he provided a thoughtful description of his father as a skillful user of the King's English: "Papa's sentences were as elaborate as a championship chess game, full of subordinate clauses and

unspoken parentheses." But however far his father's verbal ramblings strayed from the original topic, they always came back to where they started and always were grammatical. This last point was a source of great fascination for the young Espy.

Although he was born in Olympia and lived most of his adult life in New York City, Espy was most closely associated with Oysterville and even was hailed as "the bard of Oysterville." It was in Oysterville that Espy acquired the nickname "Wede." When he was six or seven, he hero-worshipped a ten-year-old boy named Aquila (pronounced akwil'a). Espy wrote in the original introduction to his rhyming dictionary *Words to Rhyme With* (1986) that when Aquila announced that he wanted to be known as "Quede," Espy was given a name to match. The pair thus became known as "Quede and Wede." Espy was quick to point out that one of the meanings of his nickname was "to become mad."

From his earliest years, Espy envisioned himself as a poet. When he was nine years old he used to dream of becoming a great poet, and he imagined returning in triumph to Oysterville. However, instead of becoming the poet of his daydreams, he became a lover of word-play and one of the most elegant light-verse writers of his generation. After graduating with a B.A. degree from the University of Redlands in California in 1930, Espy traveled to France and studied for one year at the Sorbonne in Paris. He later admitted that his main pursuit at the Sorbonne was not philosophy, but women. After returning to the United States in 1932, he worked briefly as a newspaper reporter on two California dailies, the Tulare *Times* and the Brawley *News*. In 1933 he journeyed east to New York City to join *World Tomorrow*, where he eventually became an assistant editor. He later had a stint as a correspondent for *The Nation*.

In 1933 Espy married Ann Hathaway. He was always amused that the name of his first wife was the same as the name of Shakespeare's wife. He once confessed that the romance of the name lured him into matrimony. The marriage produced a son but ended in divorce in 1962. For a brief time, Espy worked for the American League Against War and Fascism and headed the North American Committee to Aid Spanish Democracy. On 17 October 1940 Espy married Hilda Cole; they had five children, but the marriage ended in divorce in 1962. Espy married a third time, to Louise Mannheim, on 10 July 1962.

From 1941 to 1957 Espy was a manager of promotions and public relations for *Reader's Digest,* where he interviewed public figures such as Albert Einstein and Winston Churchill, using the interview as the basis for short essays endorsing the magazine. After leaving *Reader's Digest,* Espy became the creative advertising director for the Famous

Artists Schools and afterward went into radio where, from 1952 to 1953, he interviewed such figures as Marilyn Monroe, Boris Karloff, Ogden Nash, and Basil Rathbone. His radio program was called *Personalities in Print,* and although short-lived, it did much to promote the sales of many popular books. From 1960 to 1967, as the president and publisher of Charter Books, Espy experimented with the idea of selling paperback books in vending machines. Unfortunately, he was unable to bring the project to fruition. He then turned to his own writing and in 1971 published *The Game of Words* and started his remarkable career as a word maven, collector of linguistic oddities, and light-verse writer.

Espy's various careers gave the astute verse writer a great deal of material for his satirical work. His sense of the appropriate detail and the telling bit of characterization were ingredients that found their way into much of his writing. He frequently fastened upon an odd fact, such as "the female praying mantis consumes her mate in the process of copulation," and meditated upon that subject in verse (see his "For a Praying Mantis Standing in Need of Prayer," reprinted in *The Random House Treasury of Light Verse*, 1996). In his final years Espy conducted a regular column on English grammar and usage for *Writer's Digest* and compiled an important rhyming dictionary. Espy died of cancer in New York City at age eighty-eight; his ashes are buried in Oysterville. The Willard Espy Literary Foundation, centered in Oysterville, was created after his death to support the literary arts and to provide residencies for writers.

In a career that ranged from light verse to almanacs, from radio interviews to book publishing and books about language, Espy made an important contribution to U.S. literary culture in the late twentieth century. His many books include *Bold New Program* (1951); *Omak Me Yours Tonight* (1974); *An Almanac of Words at Play* (1975); *The Life and Works of Mr. Anonymous* (1977); *O Thou Improper, Thou Uncommon Noun* (1978), a collection of etymologies of words derived from proper names; *Say It My Way* (1980); *Have a Word on Me* (1981); *The Garden of Eloquence: A Rhetorical Bestiary* (1983); and *The Best of an Almanac of Words at Play* (1999). He retained a lifelong fondness for Oysterville, and the state of Washington was intensely proud of its eloquent native son. Espy received the Governor's Award for his contribution to Washington cultural life (1973–1976) and the Captain Robert Gray Medal from the Washington Historical Society (1979).

★

There is no full-length biography of Espy, but he did write an autobiography, *Oysterville: Roads to Grandpa's Village* (1977). An obituary is in the *New York Times* (25 Feb. 1999).

LOUIS PHILLIPS

EVANS, Thomas Mellon (*b.* 8 September 1910 in Pittsburgh, Pennsylvania; *d.* 17 July 1997 in New York City), financier whose aggressive approach to corporate investing in the 1950s helped usher in the modern era of hostile takeovers that began in the 1960s and continued to the end of the century.

Evans was originally named James but his name was changed after his father, Thomas Mellon Evans, a banker in McKeesport, Pennsylvania, died suddenly in 1913. His mother, Martha Jarnagin, died eight years later, leaving Evans and his older sister Elinor to be raised by their aunt and uncle, Hugh and Mary Jarnagin Rodman of Oakmont, Pennsylvania. As a teenager at the Shady Side Academy in Pittsburgh, Evans was befriended by William Larimer Mellon, the founder of the Gulf Oil Corporation, to whom he was distantly related. After Evans graduated from Yale in 1931 with a bachelor's degree in economics, he went to work at Gulf, eventually becoming Mellon's confidential assistant. In 1937 Evans approached his mentor for a modest loan, which he parlayed into a war chest for his first corporate takeover.

Evans's first target was the H. K. Porter Company, a struggling locomotive manufacturer in Pittsburgh. Evans quietly bought up Porter's defaulted bonds; when the company filed for bankruptcy in 1939, its bonds were converted into stock, and Evans emerged as the largest single shareholder. Not yet twenty-nine, Evans took over as Porter's chief executive and quickly rebuilt the ailing company. Evans expanded his empire by buying the Mount Vernon Car Manufacturing Company in 1944, a transaction that was a forerunner of similar leveraged buyouts of the 1980s. The deal was the first of at least eighty acquisitions by Evans, who was one of a small band of opportunistic postwar investors who were scooping up companies that had grown fat on wartime profits but were undervalued in the stock market of the 1940s, which was not experiencing either high or low volumes of trading. These takeovers shocked the Wall Street establishment, which denounced Evans as a "corporate pirate." But Evans and his fellow raiders insisted they were simply defending the real owners of American businesses, the shareholders who had been largely forgotten by management.

Evans once said his ideal target was a "family company run by a third-generation Yale man who spends his afternoons drinking martinis at the club." Starting with the Jarecki Manufacturing Company in July 1949, Evans quietly gobbled up nearly a dozen companies in less than five years. In 1954 he overcame fierce management resistance to acquire the Laclede-Christy Company, a large industrial tile maker in St. Louis, one of four takeovers he made that year alone. By 1955 raiders like Evans were creating such alarm among corporate executives that the U.S. Senate held hearings to explore their activities. The hearings, which focused on the 1954 fight for the New York Central railroad and the 1955 battle over Montgomery Ward, pushed the federal government to toughen the rules governing takeover fights. But they did little to discourage the raiders themselves.

Evans enhanced the raiders' reputation for ruthlessness with his 1959 takeover of the Crane Company of Chicago. To its defenders, Crane was a company that valued consensus and rewarded loyalty. To Evans, it was a bloated behemoth that was shortchanging its shareholders. He was roundly criticized for his radical measures—which included deep staff cuts and the sale of entire divisions—but Crane began to prosper under his autocratic leadership.

By the 1960s Evans had effective control of two strong public companies, Crane and H. K. Porter, and a reputation as a merciless corporate raider. In 1968 he made an unsuccessful bid for the Westinghouse Air Brake Company, which merged with American Standard to escape him. Then in 1970 he acquired the CF&I Steel Corporation, formerly owned by the Rockefeller family. Again he imposed severe cuts on staff and expenses to wring a profit from the ailing steel company. By the mid-1970s, Evans was so feared by corporate executives that several large copper companies, including Anaconda Copper, sought more amiable merger partners the moment Evans started buying their shares. One target that did not get away was the Missouri Portland cement company of St. Louis, which Evans took over in 1976 after a protracted court battle.

Evans's last two boardroom battles pitted him against members of his own family. Evans had married Elizabeth Parker, a California-born beauty, on 26 June 1935, and they had three sons: Thomas Mellon Evans, Jr., born in 1938; Edward Parker Evans, called Ned, born in 1942; and Robert Sheldon Evans, called Shel, born in 1944. The Evans marriage split apart in 1953 in a vicious public divorce, one casualty of which was Evans's relationship with his eldest son. Months after the divorce on 7 August 1953, Evans married Josephine Schlotman Mitchell; in 1977, while estranged from Evans, she committed suicide. A few months later, Evans married Betty Barton Loomis on 4 November 1977.

Ned and Shel Evans both worked with their father, the former at Porter and the latter at Crane. In 1979 Ned Evans steered Porter into making a sizable investment in the Macmillan publishing company and used his muscle as a shareholder to become chief executive. But in 1982, as Ned Evans was rebuilding the ailing publishing house, his father abruptly decided to sell Porter's stake in Macmillan, forcing his son to buy him out to preserve his control of the company. Then in early 1984, Shel Evans led a boardroom mutiny against his father's plan to sell Crane to a private investment partnership. Forced into retirement, Evans devoted his final years to his racing stables and his

formidable art collection. He died of heart failure and is buried in the Round Hill Community Church cemetery in Greenwich, Connecticut.

While largely forgotten by the late 1980s, Evans had helped introduce a new generation of lawyers and investment bankers to the techniques of corporate warfare—lessons they would put to good use in that deal-dominated decade. Harsh as his methods were, Evans championed an early vision of shareholder rights that would ultimately become a central tenet of the stock market boom of the last two decades of the twentieth century.

★

The only existing work by Evans is "A New and Dynamic Concept for Growth: H. K. Porter Company Inc.," a 1955 speech he made to the Newcomen Society in North America. Evans is the central figure in Diana B. Henriques, *The White Sharks of Wall Street: Thomas Mellon Evans and the Original Corporate Raiders* (2000). His fight for Missouri Portland and the family spat over Macmillan is described in Lawrence Lederman, *Tombstones: A Lawyer's Tales from the Takeover Decades* (1992). An obituary is in the *New York Times* (18 July 1997).

DIANA B. HENRIQUES

EWBANK, Wilbur Charles ("Weeb") (*b.* 6 May 1907 in Richmond, Indiana; *d.* 17 November 1998 in Oxford, Ohio), Hall of Fame professional football coach who won championships with the Baltimore Colts and New York Jets.

One of four children of Charles Ewbank and Stella Mae Dickerson, Wilbur became "Weeb" because his younger brother mispronounced his first name. As a boy, Ewbank made deliveries by horse-drawn wagon for his parents, who owned two grocery stores in Richmond. After graduating from Morton High School, he rejected an opportunity to pursue professional baseball, instead entering Miami University in Oxford, Ohio, where he was a quarterback on the football team, was captain of the baseball team, and also played basketball.

Planning to take classes in business and teaching, Ewbank switched to the newly created coaching program, only the second such curriculum in the country. While at Miami, he also married his high school sweetheart, Lucy Keller Massey, and they had three daughters. After graduating in 1928 with a B.S. degree in athletic coaching and physical education, Ewbank became football coach and athletic director at Van Wert High School (Ohio) for two years, before returning to Miami University to serve as head football, baseball, and basketball coach at McGuffey High School, a demonstration school run by the university's education department. To supplement his income, he also played semiprofessional baseball under the name Carl "Shorty"

Baltimore Colts coach Weeb Ewbank with the team's quarterback, Johnny Unitas, 1959. ASSOCIATED PRESS

Thomas. During his thirteen years at McGuffey, Ewbank taught in Miami's coaching school as an assistant professor of physical education. Taking summer classes, he also earned an M.A. degree in health and physical education from Columbia University in 1932.

In 1943 Ewbank joined the navy and was commissioned a lieutenant junior grade. Assigned to the Great Lakes Naval Training Station in Waukegan, Illinois, he worked under his former college football teammate Paul Brown, coaching their football team's offensive backs. After his discharge in 1946, Ewbank spent two years at Brown University as backfield coach of the football team and head basketball coach, before becoming head football coach at Washington University in St. Louis. Ewbank was then hired in 1949 by Paul Brown to be tackle coach and director of scouting for the Cleveland Browns of the All-America Football Conference (AAFC). When the AAFC folded in 1950, the Browns were absorbed into the National Football League (NFL).

In 1954 Ewbank was hired by owner Carroll Rosenbloom as head coach of the Baltimore Colts. Starting from scratch, Ewbank relied on an extensive network of scouts and, as he had done at Cleveland, sent questionnaires to college players and coaches around the country. His uncanny knack for picking up quality players who had been discarded by other teams—the most famous example being quarterback Johnny Unitas—helped to certify his reputation as a superior judge of talent. Ewbank kept voluminous records and graded every player on every play, including practice sessions, leading Rosenbloom to refer to him as "my crew-cut IBM machine." When the Colts defeated the New York Giants for the NFL championship in December 1958, it came to be considered by many as the "Greatest Game Ever Played," for it was both the first overtime game and the first nationally televised football contest. Ewbank was honored as NFL Coach of the Year, and the Colts went on to win a second championship the next year. However, following three years of mediocre performance by the Colts, Ewbank was fired in 1962.

He was then hired in April 1963 to be coach and general manager of the New York Jets, of the rival American Football League (AFL), on the same day that the bankrupt team's name had been changed from "Titans." As with the Colts, Ewbank inherited an unsuccessful team and started from the bottom. A turning point in the franchise's history was in 1965, when Ewbank convinced team president David "Sonny" Werblin to sign quarterback Joe Namath from the University of Alabama.

Although Ewbank was a tough contract negotiator and a demanding coach who stressed preparation and fined players for infractions of team rules, he also treated them like men and gave them the freedom necessary to succeed, as long as they produced on the football field. Thus he was able to successfully coach both Johnny Unitas, whose flat-top crew-cut and high-top black cleats reflected the conservative Eisenhower era, and "Broadway Joe" Namath, whose long hair, Fu Manchu mustache, and white cleats represented the more liberal 1960s. Namath once called the short, roly-poly coach "you little butterball," but grew to respect Ewbank as "one of the best coaches that ever lived." Unlike Paul Brown, Ewbank also allowed his quarterbacks to call their own plays.

After the Jets defeated the Oakland Raiders for the AFL championship in December 1968, they faced the NFL champion Baltimore Colts as seventeen-point underdogs in the "Third World Championship Game" (Super Bowl III) in January 1969. The Jets' victory, considered by many to be the greatest upset in sports history, helped legitimize the AFL and ushered in the previously agreed upon 1970 NFL–AFL merger. The Jets could not repeat their success, however, and Ewbank retired as head coach after the 1973 season, staying on as vice president before retiring from football a year later.

During his long retirement in Ohio, Ewbank enjoyed fishing and assisted a local high school football coach by reviewing game films. Diagnosed with myasthenia gravis, which was controlled with medication, he also had two artificial hips implanted. In later years, he suffered from a faulty heart valve and was advised by doctors not to watch the Jets play on television. He died at home in Oxford of natural causes at age ninety-one. He is buried in Oxford Cemetery in Oxford.

Although his overall record in twenty years as a head coach was only 130–129–7, Ewbank was 4–1 in the post-season and was the only coach to win championships with two different football teams. He was elected to the Pro Football Hall of Fame in 1978, and was also inducted into the Miami University, Indiana Sports, and Washington University halls of fame. Among his numerous awards were an honorary Doctor of Athletic Arts from Miami University (1960), the Arthur Daley Award for "long and meritorious service" to pro football (1974), and the Walter Camp Football Foundation Award (1988). In 2000 the NFL Alumni established an award in his name.

A kind and loyal man, Ewbank declined to gloat after the Jets' Super Bowl victory, even though he had defeated the owner who had fired him and the coach who had replaced him (Don Shula). Many of his coaching practices, such as the grading of players, later became commonplace. Underrated and not always appreciated, he laughed when his name was frequently misspelled or even reversed ("Eub Weebank"). He won two of the most important games in football history and coached in several other notable ones, including the famous "Heidi" game. (On 17 November 1968, NBC switched from the final sixty-five seconds of the New York Jets and Oakland Raiders game to a broadcast of the movie *Heidi*. Thus viewers missed seeing Oakland score fourteen points in the final seconds to come back from a three-point deficit and win.) Ewbank also coached in the first Monday Night Football game on 21 September 1970.

★

Although there is no full-length biography of Ewbank, Paul Zimmerman, *The Last Season of Weeb Ewbank* (1974), chronicles his final year as head coach of the Jets and includes reminiscences of his younger days. Insights into his coaching philosophy and his relationships with players can be gleaned from Jack Fleischer, ed., *My Sunday Best* (1971); Ewbank, as told to Neil Roiter, *Goal to Go: The Greatest Football Games I Have Coached* (1972); and Ewbank, Jack Buck, and Bob Broeg, *Football Greats* (1977). There are articles on Ewbank in *Current Biography Yearbook 1969*; David L. Porter, ed., *Biographical Dictionary of American Sports: Football* (1987); Denis J. Harrington, *The Pro Football Hall of Fame: Players, Coaches, Team Owners and League Officials, 1963–1991* (1991); and Ralph Hickok, *A Who's Who of Sports Champions: Their Stories and Records* (1995). Other valuable sources are an early article by Al Silverman, "Can the Colts Do It Again?," *Saturday Evening Post* (10 Oct. 1959), and Dave Anderson, "His Championship Seasons: Ewbank Reflects," *New York Times* (18 Sept. 1994). The 1958 championship game is dissected in John F. Steadman, *The Greatest Football Game Ever Played* (1988), and Super Bowl III receives similar treatment in Stephen Hanks, *The Game That Changed Pro Football* (1989). Among the many tributes to Ewbank, the most notable are Bill Wallace, "Remembering Weeb," *Pro Football Weekly* (23 Nov. 1998), and two by Joe Gergen in *Newsday*, "Weeb Leaves Us Fond Memories" (18 Nov. 1998) and "Ewbank: One from the Heart" (21 Nov. 1998). Obituaries are in the *Baltimore Sun, Cincinnati Post, New York Times,* and *Newsday* (all 18 Nov. 1998).

JOHN A. DROBNICKI

EXNER, Judith Campbell (*b.* 11 January 1934 in New York City; *d.* 24 September 1999 in Duarte, California), homemaker who claimed to have had affairs with President John F. Kennedy, Frank Sinatra, and the Chicago crime boss Sam Giancana.

Exner was born Judith Eileen Katherine Immoor, one of five children of Frederick Immoor, an architect, and Katherine Shea, a homemaker. When Judith was one year old, Immoor moved his family to Los Angeles, and they eventually settled in Martel, California. Judith attended local Catholic schools and graduated from Immaculate Heart Academy in 1952. The affluent Immoor family often welcomed Hollywood celebrities, including Bert Lahr and Bob Hope, into their home. In her teens, Exner dated the actor Robert Wagner, who was a friend throughout her life. In 1950 he introduced Exner to William Campbell, a televi-

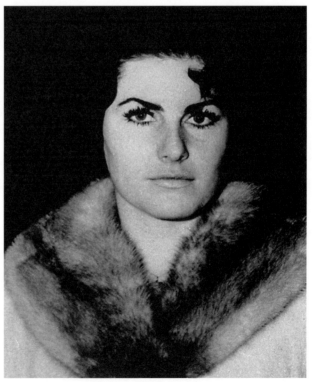

Judith Exner, 1960. ASSOCIATED PRESS AP

sion actor in his late twenties, setting her "on that bumpy road to romantic disaster." Although her parents tried to break up the courtship, the couple married in autumn 1952.

Exner stated that she could not recall the date of her first wedding because the entire marriage was "so distasteful." Except for sexual encounters, her husband either ignored her or treated her like a child. Campbell, whose career never developed, drank heavily and pursued sexual liaisons with other women. The marriage, however unhappy, allowed Exner to make contacts in the entertainment industry. Around 1957, she left Campbell and began a two-year affair with another actor, Tony Travis. She and Campbell divorced on 24 April 1959. Although Exner took extension courses at the University of California, Los Angeles (UCLA), she neither earned a degree nor sought steady employment. Instead, she relied upon alimony and family money to support herself, spending freely on clothing and grooming. (She also enjoyed singing and painting.) By the late 1950s, Exner had become a striking beauty, possessing thick, shoulder-length, jet-black hair, deep blue eyes, and a warm smile. She attracted attention from such actors as Richard Ney and Lloyd Bridges, and in November 1959 she began dating Frank Sinatra.

Sinatra opened a new world to Exner. She often traveled to Las Vegas, Nevada, or Palm Springs, California, to socialize with Sinatra's "Rat Pack," a clique that included such entertainers as Sammy Davis, Jr., Dean Martin, and Peter Lawford, a brother-in-law of John F. Kennedy. As a lover, Sinatra was "gentle, romantic, expressive, sensual, and very active," Exner remembered, but as a boyfriend he proved overbearing and selfish. They ended their romance but remained friends. In February 1960 Sinatra introduced Exner to Kennedy, who was seeking the Democratic nomination for president. Kennedy began telephoning her and on 7 March 1960, the eve of New Hampshire's presidential primary, they rendezvoused at the Plaza Hotel in New York City. Exner found her new lover to be less than dynamic. "His attitude was that he was there to be serviced," she lamented. "Partly this was due to his back problem, and partly I think he had been spoiled by women." Nevertheless, Kennedy's youthful good looks, "airy" personality, "marvelous" sense of humor, and ability to listen proved enticing. Exner continued to see him in New York City hotels, at his Georgetown home, and in the White House.

By late 1961, relations between Exner and Kennedy had settled into a routine. When she was in Washington, D.C., an official car would spirit Exner from her hotel to the White House at seven or eight in the evening. Either Kennedy or one of his aides would meet her in the entrance hallway, then escort her to the mansion's private quarters for dinner. According to Exner, she had fallen for the president but remained "skeptical" of Kennedy's professions of love "expressed in bed." She began questioning her importance, noting that "love was just another element in his life." Kennedy, for his part, wanted Exner to attend official functions. Although she declined his risky invitations, Exner telephoned the White House at least seventy times between 1961 and 1962.

A new man, Sam Giancana, entered Exner's life. She met the Chicago crime boss, a widower in his fifties, through Sinatra in 1960. A romance blossomed by 1962. "Love with Sam was not as exciting as it had been with Jack," she conceded, "but it was gentle and tender and emotionally fulfilling." Later on, Exner's love triangle seemed more than a coincidence. In 1988 she claimed to have arranged meetings between Kennedy and Giancana and to have shuttled messages and cash between the two men, perhaps in an effort to enlist mobsters in the Central Intelligence Agency's (CIA) plot to assassinate the Cuban leader Fidel Castro. Such claims lacked credibility because she earlier had pleaded ignorance of Giancana's business dealings. Moreover, Giancana's daughter denied that any meeting between her father and Kennedy had taken place. On 22 March 1962 the Federal Bureau of Investigation (FBI) director J. Edgar Hoover warned the president of Exner's ties to organized crime, leading Kennedy to end the affair. Interestingly, Exner's lovers both met violent ends; Kennedy was assassinated in Dallas in 1963, whereas Giancana was murdered in his suburban Chicago home in 1975.

During the 1960s and 1970s, Exner's life became turbulent. Under FBI surveillance and harassment, she learned that Giancana was more than a "Chicago businessman," and they parted in 1963. Exner fought an addiction to pain killers and gave birth to a son on 28 May 1965. She later married Daniel Exner, a professional golfer fourteen years her junior, on 20 May 1975. "All I ever wanted in life was love and peace of mind, to be *comfortable* with myself," she wrote. Then, in 1976, a Senate committee probing CIA activities exposed her affairs with Kennedy and Giancana, shattering her quiet life. Exner chose to give her version of events in a modestly titled memoir, *My Story* (1977).

My Story stirred controversy. Former Kennedy aides Evelyn Lincoln, Kenneth O'Donnell, and David Powers, who Exner claimed had helped her to see Kennedy, denied her account. Referring to Exner's earlier name, Powers joked that "the only Campbell I know is chunky vegetable soup." *Washington Post* critic William B. Furlong derided Exner's "banal prose and dreadful dialogue" from which Kennedy improbably "emerges as a bore." But Jeff Greenfield, writing in the *New York Times,* found *My Story* believable, noting that until the Senate committee had summoned her as a witness, Exner had "sought no publicity." White House logs and FBI documents corroborated many of her claims, leading several historians to conclude that Exner had been Kennedy's mistress.

Exner died at age sixty-five of breast cancer. She was cremated and her ashes were given to a family friend. Her "story" tarnishes the "Camelot" mystique associated with the Kennedy presidency. Dalliances with a mobster's girlfriend contradicted Kennedy's idealistic, public persona and underscored his reckless, seedy private life.

★

Exner's memoir (as told to Ovid Demaris) is *My Story* (1977). Insightful profiles include Sally Quinn, "Judith Campbell Exner," *Washington Post* (24 June 1977), and William Safire, "The Pres-ident's Friend," *New York Times* (4 Oct. 1999). Her romance with Kennedy receives mention in James N. Giglio, *The Presidency of John F. Kennedy* (1991); Michael R. Beschloss, *The Crisis Years: Kennedy and Khrushchev, 1960–1963* (1991); Thomas C. Reeves, *A Question of Character: A Life of John F. Kennedy* (1991); and Richard Reeves, *President Kennedy: Profile of Power* (1993). For J. Edgar Hoover's role in ending the affair, see Richard Gid Powers, *Secrecy and Power: The Life of J. Edgar Hoover* (1987), and Athan G. Theoharis and John Stuart Cox, *The Boss: J. Edgar Hoover and the Great American Inquisition* (1988). Obituaries are in the *Washington Post* (26 Sept. 1999) and *New York Times* (27 Sept. 1999).

DEAN J. KOTLOWSKI

F

FADIMAN, Clifton Paul   (*b.* 15 May 1904 in Brooklyn, New York; *d.* 20 June 1999 on Sanibel Island, Florida), writer, editor, literary critic, and radio and television personality noted for promoting literature to the general public.

Fadiman was the second of three sons born to the Russian immigrants Isidore Michael Fadiman, a pharmacist, and Grace Elizabeth Fadiman, a nurse. An intelligent child with an aptitude for reading, Fadiman read his first book at age four and was reading the classics by age ten. While a youth, he worked several jobs, including helping his older brother run a newspaper, the Forest Hill *Reporter*. Two years after graduating from Brooklyn Boys High School, he enrolled at Columbia University in New York City, financing his education not only with part-time jobs, including reading books to vision-impaired senior citizens, but also by writing book reviews for the *Nation* magazine, translating Friedrich Nietzsche's *Ecce Homo* and *The Birth of Tragedy* for Modern Library, and lecturing on French poetry for the People's Institute. Additionally, he edited the *Morningside,* Columbia's undergraduate magazine. He also worked full-time for a year in the stockroom for the Alfred A. Knopf Company before graduating Phi Beta Kappa with an A.B. degree from Columbia in 1925.

Beginning in 1925 Fadiman taught English at the Ethical Culture School in New York City for two years. He also lectured on the classics for the People's Institute until 1933. In 1927 Fadiman helped to translate Franz Werfel's

The Man Who Conquered Death and subsequently became an assistant editor for Simon and Schuster. Also in 1927 he married Pauline Elizabeth Rush, a writer. They had one child, a boy. In 1929 Fadiman became the editor in chief for Simon and Schuster, holding that position until 1935. Concurrently, he wrote book reviews for the *Nation, Harper's Bazaar, Stage,* and the *New Yorker* and served as the book-review editor for the *New Yorker* from 1933 to 1943. In 1934 he began presenting reviews over the radio.

In 1938 Fadiman became the moderator for *Information, Please!,* a radio show with a regular cast of experts who answered questions posed by listeners. The program became immensely popular, with 9 million listeners at its high point. Consequently, in 1940, the *Saturday Review of Literature* gave Fadiman and the show the magazine's first award for distinguished service to American literature for making "information about good literature palatable to the millions." Fadiman remained with *Information, Please!* until 1948. In the 1940s Fadiman also hosted the radio show *Keep 'em Rolling,* joined the board of editors of *Transatlantic,* worked with the Writers War Board, and operated a radio talent agency with his brother.

During these years, Fadiman undertook other literary activities. He edited anthologies, the most notable being the best-seller *Reading I've Liked* (1941), a collection of his favorite writings with an introduction explaining how he became enthralled by reading, especially in John Erskine's famous Honors course at Columbia, and with his views on

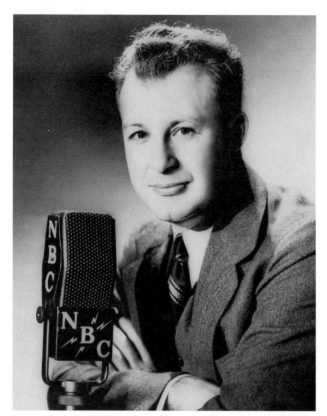

Clifton Fadiman, 1938. ASSOCIATED PRESS NBC

reviewing literature; each entry in the text was followed by Fadiman's commentary. In 1944 Fadiman joined the board of editors for the Book-of-the-Month Club and eventually served as the senior editor until a few months before his death. (When he became blind late in life, he continued to choose books for the club by listening to them on tape.) In 1949 Fadiman and Pauline divorced. The next year he married Annalee Whitmore Jacoby, a writer. They had two daughters.

In the 1950s Fadiman's professional endeavors expanded. In 1951 he began contributing monthly essays to *Holiday* magazine, which he did for ten years. He also moved into television, hosting *This Is Show Business* in 1952. He eventually hosted several radio and television shows, one of the most interesting being *Conversation,* a talk show with the Columbia history professor Jacques Barzun, which did not appeal to television viewers in 1954 but enjoyed success when it moved to radio. In 1955 he joined the board of editors for *Encyclopaedia Britannica,* and in 1963 he became the writer and general editor for *Britannica's* Humanities Film Series, remaining in that role until 1981. In 1992 he served as general editor for the *Treasury of the Encyclopedia Britannica,* a single volume of selected entries covering 200 years of the encyclopedia.

Fadiman also wrote and edited children's literature. He

contributed the entry on "Children's Literature" for the *Encyclopaedia Britannica,* which involved his learning to read Italian, Spanish, Swedish, and Dutch to complement his fluency in French, German, and English in order to do thorough research. His crowning achievement, however, was his three-volume *World Treasury of Children's Literature* (1984–1985). In 1986 he received the Dorothy C. McKenzie Award for distinguished contribution in the field of children's literature.

Fadiman continually promoted classic literature, and in 1960 he published his *Lifetime Reading Plan.* Offering a long, explicated list of noted literary works recommended by Fadiman, the book went into its fourth edition in 1997. In 1969 Fadiman received the American Library Association's Clarence Day Award for his promotion of books and reading. In 1979 he joined his good friend Mortimer J. Adler, a founder of *Britannica's* "Great Books" series, on the Paideia Council, a group promoting educational reform in elementary and secondary schools through Socratic discussion of great ideas. In the late 1980s he became the associate editor for three volumes in the "Great Books" series.

During his long career, Fadiman edited over thirty anthologies, wrote introductions to over sixty-five books, and composed numerous book reviews and essays. He also facilitated the publication of literary collections, including *World Poetry* (1998), which has been called "the greatest poetry anthology ever." Book-length publications of his own writings included collections of essays and commentaries on literature, reading, and writing, as well as two books about wine. In 1993 he received the National Book Award for Distinguished Contribution to American Literature. Fadiman died of pancreatic cancer at age ninety-five at his son's home on Sanibel Island, Florida.

Fadiman, who called himself an "amiable hack" and an "odd job man," once declared, "I haven't had an interesting life. I have only met interesting people." However, others held different appraisals of Fadiman. To some, he was the "high priest of middle-brow culture," merely a "literary popularizer." To at least one detractor, he was the "Lord High Executioner among critics." Yet a great many knew him as "America's consummate bookman, a tireless advocate for the pleasure of reading and the authors he loved." Described as wearing "his mantle of erudition with debonair flourish" and "popular for being brazenly smart," Fadiman gained recognition and celebrity by intertwining literature and show business and offering intellectual edification, education, and entertainment to millions.

★

No major or scholarly biographical study of Fadiman exists. However, his written work is widely available. Some autobiographical information is contained in his *Reading I've Liked*

(1941). Basic accounts of Fadiman and his professional life can be found in *Current Biography* (1941 and 1955); Stanley Kunitz and Howard Haycraft, eds., *Twentieth-Century Authors* (1942); and *Contemporary Authors, New Revision Series,* vol. 44 (1994). Obituaries are in the *New York Times* (21 June 1999) and *Time* and *U.S. News and World Report* (both 5 July 1999).

THOMAS BURNELL COLBERT

FARLEY, Chris(topher) Crosby (*b.* 15 February 1964 in Madison, Wisconsin; *d.* 18 December 1997 in Chicago, Illinois), popular, overweight comic actor known for his *Saturday Night Live* performances and starring roles in a number of comedy films.

Farley, raised Roman Catholic, was one of five children born to Thomas Farley, a road-paving contractor and oil company owner, and Mary Anne Farley, a homemaker. Farley's problems with obesity began by age ten, when other children snickered as he approached the swimming pool. Farley ignored them. His brother Tom proudly recalled, "he'd hit the water . . . and leave those kids in the dust."

Farley attended Madison's private Edgewood High School, played football, and made all-city defensive lineman. He dreamed of playing professional ball, but at five-feet, nine-inches tall, Farley realized he was not large enough. In 1986 he graduated with a degree in theater and communication from Marquette University in Milwaukee. During his sophomore year, he took a pratfall in a variety show and the audience roared. However, when he saw his father's reaction to John Belushi in *Animal House*, Farley knew his life's goal. "He wanted to follow in John's footsteps," said Joyce Sloan of Chicago's *Second City* comedy troup, Belushi's alma mater. Farley joined *Second City* in 1987 and was soon giving outstanding performances. He also began using drugs and alcohol to excess.

From 1990 to 1995 Farley gained national fame in the television series *Saturday Night Live* (*SNL*), portraying sweaty, intense characters. His alcohol and drug abuse was already a problem, however. In 1991 Lorne Michaels, producer of *SNL*, forced Farley into a drug rehabilitation program. After three months, Farley returned to *SNL* still addicted. In 1992 Farley entered a rehab center in Marina del Rey, California, and remained sober for three years. Although Farley controlled his substance abuse during those years, he binged on food and prostitutes. Aware of his obsessions, Farley admitted to "a tendency towards pleasures of the flesh," but he also struggled to control those tendencies so that he could continue to do comedy: "the two don't mix." His sobriety did not last, and he was in and out of rehabs until his death.

Chris Farley. KOBAL COLLECTION

During his four-year stint at *SNL*, Farley's talents as an actor and comedian were apparent in the roles he portrayed: motivational speaker Matt Foley, Cindy the Gap Girl, big-little Andrew Giuliani, Carne Phillips, General Schwarzkopf, a Chippendales dancer, and Relapse Man. Farley also satirized Newt Gingrich in 1995 at the House Republican Conference in Washington, D.C.

Farley's movie career began with supporting roles in *Wayne's World* (1992), *Wayne's World 2* (1993), *Coneheads* (1993), and *Airheads* (1994). *Tommy Boy* (1995), in which he costarred with fellow *SNL* comedian David Spade, gave him his first leading role. Farley feared the movie would bomb, but movie sales proved him wrong. *Billy Madison,* costarring another *SNL* comedian, Adam Sandler, was also released in 1995. Farley then left *SNL* to focus on making films. *Black Sheep* (1996), costarring Spade, and *Beverly Hills Ninja* (1997) were panned by critics, but the public loved them; Farley earned about $5 million a film. Inspired by John Candy's character in *JFK,* Farley considered trying a dramatic role and was scheduled to play Fatty Arbuckle in a serious film about Arbuckle's life.

Wealth and fame, however, did not cure Farley's loneliness. His friend Jeff Michalaski said that Farley never felt he fit in. He was driven by fear of not pleasing the public and not being loved in his personal life, yet his comedy had garnered him a host of fans. *SNL's* Michaels commented that Farley "knew how to get laughs, how to take hold of an audience and deliver everything," but that there was "a warm and generous part" of him as well. "Audiences could just see right through him, right through to his heart."

During the filming of *Almost Heroes,* a movie costarring Matthew Perry that was first titled *Edwards and Hunt* and released posthumously in 1998, Farley attended daily Alcoholics Anonymous meetings. He was placed on twenty-four-hour surveillance while recording a voice for the animated film *Shrek.* His friend, Jillian Seeley said, "The times he could stay sober were becoming limited." In the fall of 1997 Spade made a public appeal to his friend to pull himself together. Just months before his death, in a *Playboy* interview, Farley said, "I used to think that you could get to a level of success where the laws of the universe didn't apply. Once I thought that if I just had enough in the bank, that if I had enough fame, that it would be all right. But I'm a human being like everyone else. I'm not exempt." Farley's comedy often centered on his obesity, but it was his soul, nurtured by his upbringing and religious values, that made him real.

The last days of Farley's life were spent on exotic dancers, drugs, and alcohol. He had worn out his friends who had tried to help him. Farley knew he needed help, hoping to find it in ways he had found in the past. He attended Sunday evening mass at St. Michael's Catholic Church and then went to an Alcoholics Anonymous meeting. He had planned to be at Tuesday evening mass, but never made it. Addictions finally overtook the 296-pound comedian, and Farley's brother found him dead on the floor of his Chicago apartment in the John Hancock Tower from an accidental overdose of cocaine and morphine. The police found no sign of foul play or drugs on the premises. A similar combination of drugs killed Farley's idol John Belushi, who, ironically, was also thirty-three when he died in 1982. Farley is buried in Resurrection Cemetery in Madison.

Farley once said to Spade, "This notion of love is something that would be a wonderful thing. I don't think I've ever experienced it, other than the love of my family. At this point it's something beyond my grasp. But I can imagine it, and longing for it makes me sad." For years, Farley carried a copy of "A Clown's Prayer" in his wallet. It was printed on his funeral bulletin. Part of it read, "As I stumble through this life, help me create more laughter than tears, dispense more happiness than gloom, spread more cheer than despair."

★

Farley's relationships with members of the *Second City* are spotlighted in Sheldon Patinkin's *The Second City* (2000). His premature death limited biographical information. However, he is included in *Halliwell's Who's Who in the Movies* (1999) and Harris M. Lentz III, *Obituaries in the Performing Arts, 1997* (1997). There are informative tributes to Farley in several magazines and newspapers. The best are "Requiem for a Heavyweight," *Rolling Stone* (5 Feb. 1998); "Not a Guy Who Could Ever Blend In," *Rolling Stone* (5 Feb. 1998); "The Suffering of a Fool," *Time* (29 Dec. 1997–5 Jan. 1998); "'Saturday Night Live' Comedian Chris Farley Dies at 33," *Washington Post* (19 Dec. 1997); "Chris Farley: Tears for a Clown," *TV Guide* (17–23 Jan. 1998); and "Chris Farley," *Variety* (22 Dec. 1997–4 Jan. 1998). An obituary is in the *New York Times* (3 Jan. 1998).

SANDRA REDMOND PETERS

FARMER, Art(hur) Stewart (*b.* 21 August 1928 in Council Bluffs, Iowa; *d.* 4 October 1999 in New York City), jazz trumpeter, flügelhornist, and composer.

Farmer was four when his parents divorced and he moved with his mother, Hazel May Stewart, sister, and twin brother, Addison, to Phoenix, where he attended grammar school and high school. His father, James Arthur Farmer, a miner, died in a mining accident after the family had moved. Farmer began studying piano at age six and later studied violin and bass tuba. He started playing the trumpet and cornet at fourteen, and played bugle at flag-raising ceremonies and sousaphone in a marching band. As a teenager, he joined a dance band that covered arrangements by Count Basie, Duke Ellington, and Jimme Lunceford. While still in high school, he and Addison (a bassist) would invite members of touring swing bands to their house to jam.

In 1945 when the Farmer brothers were just sixteen, they spent a summer vacation in Los Angeles and then quit school to join the city's thriving Central Avenue jazz community. There they met great jazz innovators like Hampton Hawes, Sonny Criss, Eric Dolphy, Charlie Parker, and Dizzy Gillespie. Farmer recalled the Central Avenue scene as an open learning experience for young musicians and a period of experimentation. In 1945 he played with his brother at the Finale, alongside saxophonist Charlie Parker and trumpeter Miles Davis, and at Billy Berg's, until he was thrown out for being underage. Fulfilling a promise to his mother, Farmer graduated from Los Angeles's Jefferson High School, where he studied with the noted music teacher Samuel Browne. The young trumpeter found his first professional work with bands led by Horace Henderson, Floyd Ray, and Jimmy Mundy. He left school in his senior year, joining Johnny Otis and his group in New York City. From 1947 to 1948 Farmer freelanced in New York City and also worked as a porter in a theater while studying with Maurice Grupp.

Art Farmer, 1986. ASSOCIATED PRESS AP

In 1948 Farmer returned to Los Angeles and took various jobs with the bands of Eric Dolphy, Benny Carter, Roy Porter, Gerald Wilson, Dexter Gordon, and Jay McShann, with whom he first recorded. He played with the tenor saxophonist Wardell Gray from 1951 to 1952, and a historic session with Gray's sextet in 1952 yielded his signature piece "Farmer's Market" (*Central Avenue*), which showcased the clean, crisp articulation that became his trademark.

Farmer came of age in the 1950s as a trumpeter with big bands and then with bebop combos. Beginning in late 1952 he played with the Lionel Hampton Orchestra, which toured Europe from 1952 to 1953. In 1953 Farmer recorded tracks under his own name with the Hampton sidemen Clifford Brown, Quincy Jones, and Gigi Gryce. By 1953 Farmer had settled in New York City. (Addison followed in 1954; he died of a cerebral aneurysm in 1963, just after completing studies at the Juilliard School of Music.) Farmer worked with Teddy Charles in the group New Directions, with Charles Mingus and Ted Macero.

By the mid-1950s Farmer had become one of the more lyrical exponents of the school of jazz known as hard bop, his sparse melodic style reflective of the earlier Freddie Webster and sometimes compared to that of his contemporary Miles Davis. The Art Farmer–Gigi Gryce Quintet (1954–1956) recorded *When Farmer Met Gryce* (1954) and

Art Farmer Quintet, both on the Prestige label. Farmer then joined the pianist Horace Silver's bebop quintet (1956–1958; *Further Explorations; The Stylings of Silver*) and later worked with Gerry Mulligan's pianoless quartet (1956–1958). In 1954 Farmer played with Thelonius Monk, Charlie Parker, and Charles Mingus at New York City's Town Hall. He appeared at the Charles Mingus Jazz Workshop and with the Lester Young Quintet at the 1955 Newport Jazz Festival. During this time Farmer played with the biggest names in jazz, including Monk, Mingus, Coleman Hawkins, and Art Blakey, and pursued various avant-garde projects. *Modern Art,* a 1958 album by the Art Farmer Quintet, featured Bill Evans on piano. Farmer also played in various films, including *Last Night When We Were Young* (1957) and *The Subterraneans* (1960).

Farmer married Renée Amoretti on 10 June 1955, and the couple's only child was born in 1956. The couple divorced in 1958 but remained lifelong friends. He had no children with his second wife, Shirley Stewart, whom he married on 8 October 1961. In the late 1950s Farmer began a longtime collaboration with the tenor saxophonist Benny Golson. Their sextet, the Art Farmer–Benny Golson Jazztet (1959–1962), included McCoy Tyner on piano and Farmer's brother Addison on bass. The group's debut album, *Meet the Jazztet* (1960), included Farmer originals and sophisticated interpretations of jazz standards. In the early

1960s Farmer switched from trumpet to the warmer, richer flügelhorn. From 1962 to 1964 he led a quartet with the guitarist Jim Hall (and later, the pianist Steve Kuhn).

Farmer took solo tours of Europe in 1965 and 1966, then returned to the United States and led a combo with Jimmy Heath until 1968 when he immigrated to Austria after accepting an offer to join the Austrian Radio Orchestra in Vienna. Farmer settled in Vienna, where he married his third wife, Mechtilde Lawugger, on 2 August 1971; they had a son. Farmer continued to appear at festivals, clubs, and clinics throughout Europe, the United States, and Japan. In Europe he performed and recorded with the Kenny Clarke–Francy Boland and Peter Herbolzheimer bands and the band Österreichischer Rundfunk.

In 1972 Farmer toured Europe and Asia with Jimmy Smith. Farmer reformed the Jazztet with Benny Golson in 1982 and the band toured the United States for most of the 1980s. He also published a collection of nine transcriptions of flügelhorn solos, *Art Farmer Solos* (1984). In the 1980s and 1990s Farmer led groups in New York City at Sweet Basil (with Clifford Jordan) and later at the Village Vanguard (with Jerome Richardson and Ron Blake).

In 1991 Farmer began playing the flümpet, a hybrid instrument designed for him by David Monette. The flümpet combined the projection of the trumpet with the warmth of the flügelhorn. Farmer appeared with his own group at the Cork Jazz Festival in 1994. In June of that year he was awarded the Austrian Gold Medal of Merit (Das Goldene Verdienstzeichen des Landes Wien), and on 3 August 1994 Lincoln Center honored his lifetime musical achievement. His contemporaries Gerry Mulligan, Benny Golson, Slide Hampton, Ron Carter, Jim Hall, and Jerome Richardson joined him onstage. He later appeared as a special guest soloist at Lincoln Center for *Jeru: The Music of Gerry Mulligan* with the Lincoln Center Jazz Orchestra (1996).

In addition to his work with small combos, Farmer also performed with large orchestras in Europe and the United States as a featured soloist. He recorded J. S. Bach's Brandenburg Concerto with the New York Jazz Orchestra. In September 1994 he performed Haydn's First Trumpet Concerto with the Austrian-Hungarian Haydn Philharmonic Orchestra.

Farmer died of a heart attack at age seventy-one in New York City. Farmer was cremated and his ashes were taken to Phoenix and placed with the remains of his twin brother Addison.

Farmer's classic albums included *Early Art* (1954); *Sing Me Softly of the Blues* (1965); and *Farmer's Market* (1956), a collection of his early work with various groups, including those of Sonny Rollins and Horace Silver. Farmer's own favorite recording was *Portrait of Art Farmer* (1958). Farmer's discography as a sideman was exhaustive. The warmth of his playing, rich tone, and lyrical melodies blended into a distinctive style that let Farmer say more with less. Best remembered as a master ballad player and as a bebop trumpeter and flügelhorn player, whose careful lines and elegant solos were restrained and delicate, Farmer's legacy was his distinctive and penetrating lyricism.

★

An interview with Farmer is in *Cadence* (May 1984). For biographical information, see David H. Rosenthal, *Hard Bop: Jazz and Black Music, 1955–1965* (1992), and Leonard G. Feather, *The Biographical Encyclopedia of Jazz* (1999). The Oral History Program at the University of California also contains *Central Avenue Sounds Oral History Transcript, 1991: Art Farmer* (1995). An obituary is in the *New York Times* (6 Oct. 1999).

JONATHAN G. ARETAKIS

FARMER, James Leonard, Jr. (*b.* 12 January 1920 in Marshall, Texas; *d.* 9 July 1999 in Fredericksburg, Virginia), civil rights activist known for founding the pacifist Congress of Racial Equality (CORE) and as one of the "Big Four" African-American leaders of the 1960s, along with Martin Luther King, Jr., Roy Wilkins, and Whitney Young.

Farmer was the second of three children born to James Leonard Farmer, a minister and professor of philosophy and religion, and Pearl Marion Houston, a former teacher described by her son as a typical preacher's wife. The senior Farmer was the first African-American Ph.D. in Texas. As a young prodigy, Farmer lived an insulated life centered around the small African-American Methodist colleges in Texas and Mississippi where his father taught and served as chaplain. Farmer often recounted his first confrontation with racism at the age of three, when his mother explained that she could not buy him a drugstore soft drink on a long hot walk from town because he was black.

At the age of fourteen Farmer entered Wiley College in Marshall, Texas, on a full scholarship won through high school oratorical contests. He graduated in 1938 with a B.S. degree in chemistry and planned to pursue a medical career, but he decided on the ministry after realizing he became ill at the sight of blood. "It did not occur to me," he wrote in *Lay Bare the Heart: An Autobiography of the Civil Rights Movement* (1985), "that in the civil rights struggle I would see more blood than I ever would have seen in a doctor's office." Farmer entered Howard University School of Divinity in Washington, D.C., in 1938. Howard Thurman, one of Farmer's professors and mentors, introduced him to Mohandas Gandhi's ideas of nonviolent resistance. Another professor, V. F. Calverton, added the democratic socialist ideology of Eugene Debs and Norman Thomas.

Farmer secured a part-time job in Washington with the New York–based Fellowship of Reconciliation (FOR), a pacifist organization that advocated nonviolent social change. He was invited to join a White House discussion with other national youth leaders and President Franklin Roosevelt and Eleanor Roosevelt in 1941. Despite a heated debate with the president, Farmer was in awe of Mrs. Roosevelt, whom he regarded as one of his three heroes. (The other two were the social reformers Norman Thomas and A. Philip Randolph.) Farmer graduated from Howard with a B.D. degree in 1941, but, after completing a graduate thesis on the relationship between religion and racism, he refused Methodist ordination because of the church's segregation. His supportive father commented, "I know that whatever you do you'll do well, but what *are* you going to do?" The younger Farmer replied, "Destroy segregation."

During World War II, Farmer registered as a conscientious objector. In Chicago, while working as FOR's race relations secretary, he developed plans for a movement to bring about the destruction of racial discrimination in the United States utilizing Gandhian tactics of nonviolent civil disobedience. Farmer and his friends organized the first civil rights sit-in at a restaurant in his own Chicago neighborhood that had refused to serve him and a white friend. In his memoir *Freedom, When?* (1965), Farmer described the demonstration, in which twenty-five protesters forced the manager to reluctantly give up his policy of discrimination. The group of young activists formed the Committee (later Congress) of Racial Equality (CORE) in 1942 and implemented its new approach of nonviolent direct action. Farmer was elected to the unpaid position of national chairman in 1944. In 1945 he accepted a position as organizer for the Upholsterers International Union. Later he worked as a representative of the American Federation of State, County, and Municipal Employees Union.

After a long and stormy courtship, Farmer married Winnie Christie in 1945. They divorced in 1946. On 21 May 1949 he married Lula A. Peterson, a graduate student in economics at Northwestern University in Evanston, Illinois, who was a white member of CORE. Their relationship survived the pressures of a disapproving society, including later militant African-American separatists who argued that marriage to a white woman proved that Farmer was insufficiently "black." The couple had two daughters. Lula Peterson Farmer died in 1977 after a long battle with cancer.

In the early 1950s, a period of dormancy for the civil rights movement, Farmer worked for five years as student field secretary for the League for Industrial Democracy, a democratic socialist educational organization led by Norman Thomas. The civil rights movement revived explosively in 1956 with the Montgomery, Alabama, bus boycott. Since Farmer was known as the authority on such non-

James Farmer. PRINTS AND PHOTOGRAPHS DIVISION, LIBRARY OF CONGRESS

violent tactics, the National Association for the Advancement of Colored People (NAACP) asked him to join their staff in 1959 to develop direct action programs. However, bureaucratic infighting crippled his efforts.

When four African-American students began a sit-in at a Woolworth's lunch counter in Greensboro, North Carolina, the NAACP suggested they contact CORE for assistance. As civil disobedience demonstrations swept the South, CORE was at the forefront of the struggle. The white leadership of CORE felt it was vital to have an African-American spokesman; Farmer accepted the job of national director in 1961. He quickly began to organize the historic and dramatic Freedom Ride from Washington, D.C., south to Jackson, Mississippi. Farmer led an interracial group of thirteen who sat in the "wrong" sections of the buses and refused to move. Farmer was confident this tactic would force a showdown, but word of his father's death forced Farmer to leave the group before they entered Alabama. Soon after they arrived, a mob viciously attacked the riders and burned one of the Greyhound buses to the ground. The photograph of the burning bus made the front pages of newspapers throughout the world. Farmer directed his staff to superimpose that image on a photograph of the flame of the torch of the Statue of Liberty and use the composite as the symbol of the Freedom Ride. Hundreds of new volunteers joined the action, were trained in nonviolent resistance, and went south. Farmer rejoined the group as it headed to Mississippi. The activists were arrested, and Farmer served forty days in horrible conditions at Mississippi's Parchman State Penitentiary. In view of the escalating violence, U.S. Attorney General Robert Kennedy suggested postponing future Freedom Rides so everyone could "cool off." Farmer responded, "We have been cooling off for 350 years," and the rides continued. Public outrage at the violence directed at the riders built a momentum that brought legalized segregation in the South to an end.

Farmer frequently returned to the front lines of the struggle in the South, risking his own life. He liked to quote an Urban League official who said, "the NAACP is the Justice Department, the Urban League is the State Department, and we are the nonviolent Marines." Claude Sitton, who covered the civil rights struggle for the *New York Times,* commented, "CORE under Farmer often served as the razor's edge of the movement." In the summer of 1963 Farmer led a march of 200 people to jail in Plaquemine, Louisiana, as part of a CORE voter registration drive. When he was released, Louisiana state troopers armed with tear gas and cattle prods began a door-to-door search for him. "I was meant to die that night," Farmer later remarked. He was saved when a funeral home director hid him in the back of a hearse and drove him along back roads out of town. He was in jail when the famous March on Washington for Jobs and Freedom took place in August 1963 and refused to be bailed out ahead of others. Instead, a letter sent from Farmer was read at the Lincoln Memorial, proclaiming, "We are fighting not only to make our nation safe for the democracy it preaches, we are fighting also to give our whole world a fighting chance for survival. . . . We will not stop until the heavy weight of centuries of oppression is removed from our backs and like proud men everywhere we can stand tall together again."

Three young men Farmer had recruited for CORE's Mississippi Freedom Summer of 1964 were the organization's first fatalities. James Chaney, Andrew Goodman, and Michael Schwerner—an African American from Mississippi and two white Jews from New York—were murdered by the Ku Klux Klan. In later interviews Farmer was forthright about his fears during these years of struggle. "Anyone who said he wasn't afraid during the civil rights movement was either a liar or without imagination," he admitted in 1991. "I think we were all scared. I was scared all the time." Some militant African Americans considered his devotion to nonviolence a weakness. "When are you going to fight back?" they would ask. Farmer always replied, "We are fighting back, we're only using new weapons."

This split with the younger African-American separa-

tists led Farmer to resign as national director of CORE in 1966. He had gained the ear of President Lyndon B. Johnson, to whom he suggested the outlines of affirmative action, a key element of Johnson's Great Society program. He expected to head a new federally funded adult literacy program that had been his brainchild, but the president blocked funding as retaliation for Farmer's opposition to the Vietnam War. As a result, Farmer found himself unemployed and distanced from the movement he had helped create. He believed that his fiercely integrationist views cost him a place as a leading African-American spokesman. Despite this, he continued to hold those views. "I don't see any future for the nation without integration," he reiterated in a 1997 interview. "Our lives are intertwined, our work is intertwined, our education is intertwined."

After leaving CORE, Farmer taught at Lincoln University near Philadelphia, Pennsylvania, and at New York University in New York City. In 1968 he lost a race for the U.S. House of Representatives to Shirley Chisholm, giving him, as he noted wryly, "a most unique distinction: I was the first black man in U.S. history to be defeated by a black woman in a congressional race." He surprised civil rights activists in 1969 when he accepted President Richard M. Nixon's appointment as assistant secretary for administration in the Department of Health, Education, and Welfare. Although he did succeed in increasing the role of minorities in the agency and in strengthening Head Start programs in southern states, he resigned in 1970 in opposition to other administration policies.

In the 1970s he ran an educational think tank and then became executive director of an association of public employee unions. When this coalition dissolved in the early 1980s, Farmer moved to a farm near Fredericksburg, Virginia. There he completed *Lay Bare the Heart* (1985), which described his role in the integration battle and his personal struggles with increasing blindness. In a book review in the *New York Times,* Claude Sitton noted that "more than any other civil rights leader," Farmer had struggled against racism and had "attempted to hold the movement true to its purpose."

Farmer became a history professor at Mary Washington College in Fredericksburg in 1985. At one point his course drew 500 students a year. Despite declining health, he continued to teach until the spring of 1998. In that year President William J. Clinton awarded Farmer the nation's highest civilian award, the Presidential Medal of Freedom. Farmer said the award was a "vindication, an acknowledgment at long last." He also received twenty-two honorary degrees.

In his final years Farmer was confined to a wheelchair and often in need of an oxygen tent as he battled complications of diabetes, including blindness and leg amputations. He also underwent brain surgery in 1998 to remove a blood clot. He began to joke about his numerous close encounters with death, saying that he saw a tunnel at those moments, but at the end, instead of Saint Peter, he saw the devil, who said, "Oh my God, don't let him in! He'll organize a resistance movement and try to put out my fire." Farmer succumbed to his illnesses at age seventy-nine at the Mary Washington Hospital in Fredericksburg.

The moral foundation of Farmer's career was a belief in an integrated society where all races share ideals of justice and humanity. "James Farmer helped to make America a better nation," President Clinton said when he was informed of Farmer's death. "He is simply irreplaceable," added Kweisi Mfume, president of the NAACP. "James Farmer leaves this century as one of a few select men and women to be responsible for great change. His legacy begs that he not be forgotten."

★

James and Lula Farmer's personal papers are at the Center for American History at the University of Texas. Farmer authored two memoirs, *Freedom, When?* (1965), and the eloquent and candid *Lay Bare the Heart: An Autobiography of the Civil Rights Movement* (1985). No biography on Farmer has been published. His contributions to the civil rights movement are well covered in Taylor Branch, *Parting the Waters: America in the King Years, 1954–1963* (1988), which is critical of Farmer's role during this time; *Contemporary Black Biography,* vol. 2 (1992); *Notable Black American Men* (1998); *Encyclopedia of World Biography,* 2d ed. (1998); *Newsmakers 2000,* issue 1 (2000); and *Contemporary Heroes and Heroines, Book IV* (2000). Obituaries are in the *Washington Post, New York Times,* and *Los Angeles Times* (all 10 July 1999).

LOUISE A. MAYO

FASANELLA, Raphaele ("Ralph") (*b.* 2 September 1914 in New York City; *d.* 16 December 1997 in Yonkers, New York), union organizer and self-taught artist of the people known for his large, colorful, detailed paintings of U.S. working-class life and politics.

Fasanella was born on Labor Day, the fourth of six children of Giuseppe ("Joe") Fasanella, an iceman, and Ginevra Spagnoletti, a buttonhole maker, both emigrants from Apulia in southern Italy. Reared in a three-room Greenwich Village tenement, Fasanella delivered ice with his father each morning before school when he was about eight years old. Disagreements with his father over long work hours without pay sparked rebelliousness in the young Fasanella. At age ten, he was caught selling stolen goods and sent on the first of three trips to the New York Catholic Protectory, an East Bronx reformatory. By the middle of 1929 Fasanella had spent about twenty-nine months in the institution, smothered by what he called its "cold, calculating" and "oppressive" atmosphere.

Fasanella completed eighth grade between the three reformatory terms, marking the end of his formal schooling. However, his political education was just starting. He increasingly came under the influence of his mother, who had become active with the Amalgamated Clothing Workers' Union and was beginning to develop antifascist and socialist sentiments. Ginevra's outspokenness threatened her apolitical husband, resulting in the breakup of their marriage. Spurred on by his mother and the reality of the Great Depression, Fasanella joined the Workers' Alliance, a local Unemployed Council, and the Young Communist League. In 1937 he signed up for the Abraham Lincoln Brigade, traveling to Spain to fight for the loyalists in the Spanish Civil War.

Upon his return from Spain in 1938, Fasanella served a short stint in the U.S. Navy, before being medically discharged, followed by work at various unions. In 1942 he settled into a position with the United Electrical Workers and helped to organize Sperry Gyroscope, a Brooklyn-based industrial machine plant, and the Western Electric Plant in Manhattan. However, he quickly grew frustrated, sensing that organized labor was becoming disconnected from the working class. Fasanella married Matilda ("Tillie") Weiss in 1943; however, this union lasted only six months, ending in divorce the next year. In 1944, when a colleague suggested he take art classes to alleviate a developing pain in his hands, Fasanella balked. As a short, stocky man who spoke in a heavy New York accent often peppered with profanity and always full of enthusiasm, he envisioned himself as a worker and an organizer, not an artist. That view changed when, during a New Hampshire vacation in the summer of 1945, he took a friend's pad and pencil and began sketching. He drew a pair of shoes, a rowboat, and a cabin interior and exterior. He was "amazed" at the images and started drawing everything in sight.

Fasanella soon began to paint, his artistic vision born of his familiarity with working life. He painted what he knew best: working people, the immigrant experience, tenement life, labor strikes, street festivals, union meetings, the subways, and baseball games. He depicted events such as the funeral of his hero, the leftist East Harlem congressman Vito Marcantonio; the assassination of President John F. Kennedy; and the execution of Julius and Ethel Rosenberg. He also painted personal images such as his family at the supper table, the reformatory that claimed much of his childhood, and his father, crucified, with ice tongs in place of a crown of thorns.

In 1949 Fasanella ran for city council, joining Marcantonio's unsuccessful American Labor Party mayoral bid. With his political aspirations thwarted, he hoped to finance his painting by working as a machinist, but McCarthy-era blacklisting made it difficult for him to secure a job. He finally found work at the Morey Machine Shop in Queens,

Ralph Fasanella inspects his 1950 painting *Subway Riders* after it was installed in a New York City subway station in 1995. ED BAILEY/ASSOCIATED PRESS AP

but was laid off following the end of the Korean War in 1953. Fasanella married Eva Lazorek on 29 July 1950; they had two children. Eva provided a lifetime of support and encouragement for Fasanella and his art. Initially, her teacher's salary helped sustain his artistic endeavors, until he started a $30-per-week job at his brother Nick's gas station. Around 1959 Fasanella and two partners bought the Bronx gas station Happy and Bud's. For fourteen years he pumped gas from 4 to 11 P.M., painted all night, slept during the day, and even kept busy during the daily commute, sketching images of subway riders on *New York Times* classified advertisements.

Fasanella's first solo show at the Forty-fourth Street Gallery in 1946 was followed by two shows at the American Contemporary Art (ACA) Gallery in midtown Manhattan in 1947. Another exhibition in 1957 at the James Gallery in Greenwich Village elicited encouraging reviews. However, he struggled to make a living as an artist until 1972, when the folk-art critic Frederick Fried saw *Campaign Lucky Corner* (1968) at the Hudson River Museum. Impressed, Fried orchestrated a series of meetings that resulted in the 30 October 1972 *New York* magazine issue featuring Fasanella's paintings and life story, proclaiming on the cover, "This man pumps gas in the Bronx for a living. He may also be the best primitive painter since Grandma Moses." Around the same time, Fasanella's work was displayed at a show at Automation House, a Manhattan labor center, that attracted more than 10,000 people. In 1973 a glossy book on Fasanella's life and art was published.

While Fasanella's newfound celebrity allowed him to be a full-time artist, fame, coupled with his family's move to suburban Ardsley, New York, stifled his creativity. "I didn't paint my paintings to hang in some rich guy's living room," he once said. For nearly two years after the Automation House show, Fasanella had difficulty painting. To rekindle his artistic fire, he traveled in 1975 to Lawrence, Massachusetts, the home of the 1912 "bread and roses" textile strike. Staying at an $18-a-week YMCA room overlooking the Lawrence Common, he spent more than two years conducting research at libraries, mills, and museums, and by 1978 finished a series of canvases based on Lawrence and its surrounding areas, including *Lawrence 1912: The Bread and Roses Strike* (1977) and *The Great Strike* (1978).

In 1985 Eva conceived of "Urban Visions," the first large-scale retrospective of her husband's work. Around 1986, upset that virtually all of Fasanella's works were held by private collectors, the union organizer Ron Carver launched Public Domain, an initiative that raised money to place the artist's work in public places. In 1988 a Massachusetts civic group paid $100,000 for Fasanella's *Lawrence 1912: The Bread and Roses Strike,* hanging it in the Lawrence Heritage State Park Visitor's Center. From there, momentum grew and the artist's paintings were purchased and displayed in places such as the Ellis Island Immigration Museum, the subway station at Fifty-third Street and Fifth Avenue in Manhattan, and the Rayburn House Office Building on Capitol Hill in Washington, D.C. This last venue held *Lawrence 1912: The Great Strike* until Republicans removed it in 1995, when they regained majority control of the House of Representatives.

In his later years, Fasanella painted at his home in Ards-ley and spent his lunchtime talking with customers and sketching in a nearby Nathan's restaurant chain. Fasanella died of emphysema at age eighty-three. He is buried in Mount Hope Cemetery in Hastings-on-Hudson, New York. The final words of his epitaph read, "Change the World."

Fasanella knew from personal experience what was important to working people, and he painted with a style that fostered visual communication with them, filling canvasses with details familiar to their lives. His paintings illustrate a distinct working-class identity and culture, showing the value of struggle, hard work, sacrifice, and community. Critics largely viewed his work as primitive or as left-wing propaganda, misunderstanding his mission to give workers a sense of their heritage, an understanding of the forces, past and present, that shaped their lives, and a vision of the possibility of a truly democratic society. One visitor viewing the Lawrence series at the city's public library captured the essence of Fasanella's work perhaps better than any critic when he remarked, "This guy's painting our lives."

★

The most complete study of Fasanella's life and painting, including a comprehensive bibliography, is Paul D'Ambrosio, *Ralph Fasanella's America* (2001). An earlier and less scholarly attempt to chronicle Fasanella's art and its influences is Patrick Watson, *Fasanella's City* (1973). Alonzo Lansford, "Fasanella, Primitive," *Art Digest* (1 Dec. 1946), is a review of Fasanella's first solo show at the Forty-fourth Street Gallery. Nicholas Pileggi, "Portrait of the Artist as a Garage Attendant in the Bronx," *New York* (30 Oct. 1972), brought fame to Fasanella, serving as a turning point in his career. Peter Carroll, "Ralph Fasanella Limns the Story of the Workingman," *Smithsonian* (Aug. 1993), includes six of the artist's paintings and details the success of Public Domain. Tom Robbins, "Ralph Fasanella: Not for Some Rich Guy's Living Room," *Daily News* (14 Nov. 1999), is a succinct and lively account of the artist's life. Obituaries are in the *New York Times* and *Boston Globe* (both 18 Dec. 1997). The twenty-two-minute film *Fasanella* (1992), by Glen Pearcy, documents the Public Domain effort.

DANIEL MASSEY

FASCELL, Dante Bruno (*b.* 9 March 1917 in Bridge-hampton, New York; *d.* 28 November 1998 in Clearwater, Florida), politician who as a Democratic congressman played a leading role in shaping U.S. foreign policy from the 1960s to the 1990s.

Fascell was one of three children of Charles Angelo Fascell, a dairyman, and Mary Gullotti, both of whom were Italian. The family moved to Miami, Florida, in 1925, just in time to experience the Florida real estate bust a year later. Fascell attended Ponce de Leon High School in Coral Gables, graduating in 1933. He then earned a J.D. from the University of Miami School of Law in Coral Gables in 1938. That same year he was admitted to the Florida bar and began practicing law in Miami. He married Jeanne-Marie Pelot on 19 September 1941; they had three children, one of whom died in a car accident in 1984.

Fascell's wartime experience influenced his decision to become a public servant. When the United States entered World War II, Fascell was a private in the Florida National Guard, which he had joined in January 1941. Commissioned as a second lieutenant in May 1942, he commanded a truck company in the African, Sicilian, and Italian campaigns. He was discharged from the army with the rank of captain in January 1946. While experiencing the horrors of combat in North Africa, Fascell told a friend, "If American men are going to be sent to war, I want to know why and be part of the process that decides whether they should go." When he returned to the United States, Fascell entered politics, serving as a legal attaché to the legislative delegation representing Dade County (1947–1950) and as a legislator in the Florida House of Representatives (1950–1954). The state press twice recognized him as one of Florida's ten outstanding legislators.

Fascell won election to the U.S. House of Representatives in 1954 as a Democrat. He won nineteen consecutive elections (1954–1990), representing voters in Florida's Fourth (1955–1967), Twelfth (1967–1973), Fifteenth (1973–1983), and Nineteenth (1983–1993) Congressional Districts, which covered greater Miami and the Florida Keys. During his congressional career, Fascell served on several House committees, including Government Operations, Post Office and Civil Service, Foreign Affairs, and Narcotics Abuse and Control. He focused primarily on foreign affairs and environmental regulation. On the latter issue, Fascell drafted legislation directing federal funds to preserve Florida's Everglades and Biscayne Bay national parks, and to declare much of the area around the Florida Keys a national sanctuary. He also shaped legislation concerning consumer protection, drug policy, education, housing and urban development, energy, immigration reform, and promoting openness in government.

Fascell joined the House Foreign Affairs Committee in 1957 and served as its chair from 1984 to 1992. At various times, he presided over several subcommittees, including Inter-American Affairs; International Politics and Military Affairs; International Operations and Human Rights; International Organization; State Department Organization; and Arms Control, International Security, and Scientific Affairs. Fascell also served as vice chair of the House Select Committee to Investigate Covert Arms Transactions with Iran (1987). His major foreign policy achievements in-

Dante Fascell, 1986. ASSOCIATED PRESS

through the creation of the National Endowment for Democracy (1983) and through support for free trade policies, such as the North American Free Trade Agreement (1993). He advocated similar policies following the collapse of communism in Eastern Europe and the Soviet Union.

Fascell sought to enhance the role of his committee and the U.S. House of Representatives in foreign affairs by taking special interest in arms control. While he did not reject the use of force as an instrument of foreign policy (he supported President George H. W. Bush's military policies in Panama in 1989 and in the Persian Gulf War in 1991), Fascell opposed increases in defense spending and arms proliferation. His opposition to the development of the B-1 bomber, MX missile, Strategic Defense Initiative, and chemical weapons shaped the Intermediate-Range Nuclear Forces Treaty (1987) and the 1990 agreement between U.S. Secretary of State James Baker and the U.S.S.R.'s Eduard Shevardnadze to ban the use of chemical and biological weapons. Yet, every year after 1985, the House Foreign Affairs Committee failed to accomplish its chief legislative task of securing House approval of foreign aid bills directly out of committee, thus ruining Fascell's efforts to strengthen House input in U.S. foreign policy.

In not seeking reelection in 1992, Fascell chose not to challenge the anti-incumbent mood of U.S. voters when a court-ordered reapportionment of Florida's congressional districts took away three-quarters of his voting base in Dade County. Fascell's decision to leave Washington, D.C., that year may also have been influenced by his fear that the end of the cold war had made the House Foreign Affairs Committee's focus on foreign aid increasingly irrelevant.

Upon returning to Florida, in 1994 Fascell became a partner at the Miami law firm of Holland and Knight, where he practiced international law. He also championed the work of the North-South Center at the University of Miami that now bears his name. This institute studies trade, economic growth, drug policy, and refugee and immigration policy in an attempt to build social and economic bridges to promote prosperity and democracy in Latin America. Fascell received the Presidential Medal of Freedom in October 1998, one month before he died of colon cancer. He is buried at Sylvan Abbey Memorial Park in Clearwater.

Fierce, determined, and always well informed when promoting his positions, Fascell was often considered one of the leading legislative craftsmen in Congress. He could write legislation, explain it, and get it passed without crippling amendments. Yet Fascell's legislative skills and the strength of his convictions could not overcome traditional U.S. hostility toward foreign aid, thus demonstrating that without constitutional authority similar to the Senate's treaty-making power, the House would continue to lag behind the upper chamber in shaping U.S. foreign policy.

cluded drafting the War Powers Act (1973), an attempt to reassert Congress's constitutional authority to declare war in an effort to reduce the risk of U.S. involvement in future Vietnam-type conflicts. In addition, as chair of the Commission on Security and Cooperation in Europe (1976–1985), he championed human rights as an integral part of U.S. foreign policy. According to Fascell, this effort "helped lead to the disintegration of the entire Eastern empire."

As chair of the House Foreign Affairs Committee, Fascell often sought bipartisan support in guiding legislation through the committee and the U.S. House of Representatives. Unlike his predecessor Clement Zablocki, a Democrat from Wisconsin who allowed liberal Democratic subcommittee chairs to advocate dovish policies in the wake of the U.S. experience in Vietnam, Fascell moderated their views to mirror his own, particularly concerning U.S.–Latin American relations. Reflecting sentiments prevalent among the Hispanic refugees in his constituency, Fascell opposed any relaxation of the U.S. policy to ostracize Fidel Castro's regime in Cuba. He supported President Ronald Reagan's administration in its efforts to aid the Contra rebels in Nicaragua and to advance democracy in El Salvador. Fascell also tried to promote democracy in the Americas

★

Fascell's papers, which concentrate exclusively on his work in Congress, are located at the University of Miami School of Law. This collection is indispensable for studying Fascell's work on the House Foreign Affairs Committee, particularly during his tenure as committee chair. One should also consult committee reports, the *Congressional Record,* and *Congressional Almanac Quarterly* regarding Fascell's involvement in the Iran-Contra investigation and his efforts to promote human rights, free trade, the National Endowment for Democracy, arms control, and foreign aid. On Fascell's push to implement the Helsinki Accords on human rights, see Dante Fascell, "Did Human Rights Survive Belgrade?" *Foreign Policy* 31 (summer 1978): 104–118. Fascell's views on the War Powers Act are expressed in his "Additional View on War Power," *Foreign Policy* 8 (fall 1972): 37, a rebuttal to Thomas F. Eagleton, "Whose Power Is War Power?" *Foreign Policy* 8 (fall 1972): 23–32. Ann-Marie W. Scheidt, "The Origins and Enactment of the War Powers Resolution, 1970–1973" (Ph.D. diss., State University of New York at Stony Brook, 1989), covers Fascell's role in drafting the law. Regarding Fascell's involvement in the national debate on U.S.–Central American relations during the administrations of Presidents Jimmy Carter, Reagan, and Bush, see William M. LeoGrande, *Our Own Backyard: The United States in Central America, 1977–1992* (1998). An obituary is in the *New York Times* (30 Nov. 1998).

DEAN FAFOUTIS

FAYE, Alice (*b.* 5 May 1915 in New York City; *d.* 9 May 1998 in Rancho Mirage, California), actress and singer whose blonde beauty, engaging personality, and husky contralto made her one of the most popular film stars of the 1930s and 1940s.

Born Alice Jeanne Leppert in the Hell's Kitchen neighborhood of New York City, Faye was the daughter of the Irish-born Alice Moffat and Charles Leppert, a policeman. Along with her two older brothers, she attended Public School 84 at Sixth Avenue and Forty-fourth Street. At an early age, Leppert discovered that she loved to sing and dance, and when only thirteen, she auditioned for Earl Carroll's Vanities. She won the job, only to be rejected when she admitted how young she was. For three years, she toured the eastern vaudeville circuit with the Chester Hale dance group, once playing an extended engagement at the Capitol Theater in New York City. Around this time she changed her name to Alice Faye.

Eventually Faye landed a spot in the chorus of the popular musical revue, *George White's Scandals* (1931). The show's star, Rudy Vallee, heard Faye sing at a cast party and hired her for his radio program, where she became a popular featured attraction. When Vallee went to Holly-

Alice Faye. KOBAL COLLECTION

wood, he took Faye with him, and she made her film debut in *George White's Scandals* (1934), replacing actress Lilian Harvey in a starring role. Her rendition of the song "Oh, You Nasty Man" attracted critical attention, and she signed a contract with Twentieth Century–Fox Studios. When Vallee's wife sued him for divorce, she named Faye as a corespondent in the suit.

During Faye's first few years at Fox, in movies such as *Now I'll Tell* (1934), *Every Night at Eight* (1935), and *King of Burlesque* (1936), she was cast as a brassy blonde, with platinum hair and thinly penciled eyebrows that imitated those of the then-popular film star Jean Harlow. Faye also appeared in support of the studio's main attraction, the child star Shirley Temple, in two 1936 films, *Poor Little Rich Girl* and *Stowaway.* It was not until *Sing, Baby, Sing,* which was released in the same year, that the studio finally softened Faye's image, giving her a more natural, appealing look. *Sing, Baby, Sing* also featured a rising young singer named Tony Martin, whom Faye married on 6 September 1937. They divorced in March 1940.

By now Faye was one of Fox's most popular leading ladies, starring in a succession of lively, entertaining musicals such as *On the Avenue, Wake Up and Live,* and *You Can't Have Everything,* all released in 1937. The latter film marked her first appearance with a frequent costar, Don Ameche. Faye reached the peak of her popularity in 1938 with the release of *In Old Chicago* and *Alexander's Ragtime Band.* In *In Old Chicago,* she replaced the recently deceased Harlow to play a saloon singer caught up in the Great Chicago Fire of 1871. *Alexander's Ragtime Band,* Faye's personal favorite among her films, contained twenty songs by Irving Berlin and an over-the-years chronicle of a singer (Faye) and her romantic involvement with a bandleader (Tyrone Power).

Faye also starred in a series of period musicals set in the early years of the twentieth century, including *Rose of Washington Square* (1939), *Lillian Russell* (1940), *Tin Pan Alley* (1940), and *The Great American Broadcast* (1941). She also made *Hollywood Cavalcade* (1939), her first movie in Technicolor, in which she played an aspiring actress who becomes the queen of silent slapstick comedies. To bolster the heavily publicized U.S. Good Neighbor Policy with Latin America, Fox also starred Faye in several gaudy Technicolor "south-of-the-border" musicals, including *That Night in Rio* and *Weekend in Havana* (both 1941). During this period, on 12 May 1941, Faye married the bandleader Phil Harris.

After the birth of her first daughter in May 1942, Faye returned to films with another period musical, *Hello, Frisco, Hello* (1943), in which she sang one of her signature tunes, the Oscar-winning "You'll Never Know." The movie was popular, but after another musical film, *The Gang's All Here* (1943), it was clear that Faye's long association with Fox was nearing its end. Directed by Busby Berkeley, this lavish but mediocre musical gave Faye only one opportunity to shine, in a rendition of the wartime lament "No Love, No Nothing." Following the birth of a second daughter in April 1944, Faye was miscast in a straight dramatic role in Otto Preminger's film noir *Fallen Angel* (1945) as the small-town wife of a murder suspect (Dana Andrews). When her role in the film was severely cut, Faye exited the studio, merely waving good-bye at the front gate and leaving behind all her personal belongings. She returned to Fox only once, to play the mother of the Frake family in a poorly received remake of the musical *State Fair* (1962).

In September 1946 Faye and Harris began a Sunday-night radio program that dealt with the domestic tribulations of a married couple. The program broadcast until June 1954. From that time on, Faye appeared only occasionally as a guest star on radio and television programs. In December 1973 she began a nationwide tour with her former costar John Payne in a revival of the 1927 musical *Good News,* but Payne's role was played by Gene Nelson when the show opened on Broadway in December 1974. Faye made cameo film appearances in *Won Ton Ton, the Dog Who Saved Hollywood* (1976), *Every Girl Should Have One* (1978), and *The Magic of Lassie* (1978), in which she sang one tune as a waitress. She became a spokeswoman

for the pharmaceutical company Pfizer in 1984, encouraging "young elders" to live healthier lives.

Faye died of stomach cancer at the Eisenhower Medical Center in Rancho Mirage, California, at age eighty-three. She is buried in the Palm Springs Mausoleum in Palm Springs, California. Harris, her husband of fifty-four years, died in 1995.

Whether pouting prettily at Don Ameche or Tyrone Power, or singing her heart out in her inimitably husky voice, Faye's performances have retained a fond and enduring place in the top echelon of Hollywood's Golden Era.

★

Faye wrote *Growing Older, Staying Young* (1990), with Dick Kleiner, in which she discusses her secrets for youthfulness. For information on her life and career, see W. Franklyn Moshier, *The Alice Faye Movie Book* (1974). An interview with Faye by Michael Buckley appears in *Films in Review* (Nov. 1982). Obituaries are in the *New York Times* (10 May 1998) and *Variety* (18 May 1998).

TED SENNETT

FEHRENBACHER, Don Edward (*b.* 21 August 1920 in Sterling, Illinois; *d.* 13 December 1997 in Stanford, California), professor of history and American studies at Stanford University and a specialist in nineteenth-century U.S. history, the westward movement, the Civil War, American constitutional history, and California history.

Fehrenbacher was born in the small, northwestern Illinois industrial town of Sterling, the first of four children of Joseph Henry Fehrenbacher, a machinist and tool and die maker, and Mary Barton, who had their surname changed to Fehrenbach. Fehrenbacher's birth certificate showed the longer form, which the U.S. Army insisted on retaining.

None of Fehrenbacher's parents or grandparents attended high school but Fehrenbacher attended Central School in Sterling, Illinois, and then graduated from Sterling Township High School in 1938. The grounds of his grade school had a boulder designating the spot where Abraham Lincoln delivered a political address in 1856, but as a schoolboy he had no particular interest in either history or in Lincoln. Likewise, his maternal grandmother's reports of her father's death at the battle of Stones River, Tennessee, did not spark an interest in the Civil War.

As a boy Fehrenbacher loved movies and historical fiction, particularly the works of Joseph Altsheler, Walter Scott, Alexander Dumas, and Kenneth Roberts. He wrote that being an undisciplined but avid reader no doubt turned him toward the craft of history. He reminisced that when he got his adult library card the first book he checked out was Sax Rohmer's *The Case Book of Dr. Fu Manchu.* Over the years Fehrenbacher devoured *Tom Sawyer, Treasure Island, David Copperfield,* and his all-time favorite, *Pride and Prejudice,* along with the works of S. S. Van Dyne, Agatha Christie, P. G. Wodehouse, and Richard Halliburton. Reading literature of all sorts stimulated him to become a writer.

In high school, while working as a "stringer" reporting school news in the *Sterling Daily Gazette,* Fehrenbacher contributed a series of facetious stories to his school newspaper. His first job after high school was as a scaleman at the Northwestern Steel and Wire Company, where he weighed nails, wire, and other production items, and kept production record books.

Fehrenbacher entered Cornell College in Mount Vernon, Iowa, in September 1940, but his college studies were interrupted in February 1943 when he was drafted into the Army Air Corps, where he served for two years as a navigator of a "Flying Fortress" B-17 bomber. Flying thirty missions over Germany and occupied Europe, he was decorated with the Distinguished Flying Cross Air Medal with three clusters.

Following the war, he returned to college and graduated with an A.B. degree from Cornell in 1946 (listed with his class of 1944, according to a prerogative Cornell afforded veterans). His Cornell experiences convinced him that in addition to becoming a writer he would like to be a college teacher. While at Cornell, Fehrenbacher met fellow student Virginia Ellen Swaney, who graduated from there in 1944. They were married in Chicago, Illinois, on 9 February 1944. The couple had three children. Armed with the needed financial support of the GI Bill, Fehrenbacher enrolled at the University of Chicago in the fall of 1946 to pursue a Ph.D. His adviser, Avery Craven, led him into Civil War studies. He received an M.A. degree in history in 1948, and his dissertation "Illinois Political Attitudes" earned him a Ph.D. in 1951.

Fehrenbacher had a spectacular teaching career. Other than temporary appointments to teach at Roosevelt College in Chicago while he was a graduate student, Fehrenbacher's first college teaching experience was at Coe College in Cedar Rapids, Iowa, where he was an assistant professor from 1949 to 1953. Because of his close friendship with a dissident student leader, the college president informed him in the spring of 1952 that there was no future for him at the college. Fehrenbacher was vindicated in 1970 when Coe College conferred an honorary doctorate upon him.

In 1953 Fehrenbacher was given a one-year appointment to Stanford University, which ended up lasting until his retirement in 1984. There he taught the history of the American West, California history, the antebellum years, and the Civil War and Reconstruction.

Throughout his Stanford career, Fehrenbacher held concurrent positions teaching and lecturing in various institutions. He taught at Rutgers University in the summer of 1959, at Northwestern in 1964, and at Harvard in 1967. He held the Harmsworth Professorship of American History at Oxford University (1967–1968), was Harrison Professor of History at the College of William and Mary (1973–1974), was Commonwealth Fund Lecturer at the University College, London University (1978), served as the Walter Lynwood Fleming Lecturer at Louisiana State University (1978), taught at the University of British Columbia (1970), was Seagram Lecturer at the University of Toronto (1981), and delivered the Lamar Lectures at Mercer University (1987).

Fehrenbacher was a serious historian's historian, yet he took neither himself nor his craft too seriously. His mind searched for historical truth in a number of nonhistorical disciplines. His basic attitude toward his career in history was that it did not lead him to the truth and wisdom sought by Historicus. He wrote that after peering for a half century into what Marcus Aurelius called the "boundless abyss of the past," he was left uncertain about the net influence of historical knowledge on human intellect and behavior. Still, he was convinced that the practice of history could sharpen one's critical faculties and lend perspective to personal experience and enrich the life of the mind.

In pursuit of historical truth or reality, Fehrenbacher insisted that mere facts were not enough. A novel could have its facts "all mixed up" or rearranged and still capture in a holistic way the true character or the true personality of the individual. Fiction, he once said, is written about the real world, but there is even a fictional element in historical writing. With this in mind, he concluded that neither the historical nor the fictional Lincoln was the "real Lincoln."

Fehrenbacher was selected to be a Guggenheim fellow (1959–1960 and 1984–1985), a National Endowment for the Humanities Fellow (1975–1976), a member of the American Academy of Arts and Sciences (1980), and was elected to membership in the American Antiquarian Society (1976). He received a Diploma of Honor from the Lincoln Memorial University (1970), and was honored as a Huntington Library Fellow (1985–1986). In 1984 Fehrenbacher was elected President of the Pacific Coast Branch (PCB) of the American Historical Association (AHA). Gettysburg College awarded him its 1997 Lincoln Prize of $50,000.

Besides more than forty scholarly articles, Fehrenbacher's bibliography includes an array of outstanding and award-winning books in American history. The first, *Chicago Giant: A Biography of "Long John" Wentworth, Promi-*

nent Civil War Editor and Mayor of Chicago (1957), won the author the 1957 annual prize of the PCB of the AHA, and in 1958 the Award of Merit of the American Association for State and Local History.

Other early works by Fehrenbacher were *Prelude to Greatness: Lincoln in the 1850s* (1962), *Abraham Lincoln: A Documentary Portrait* (1964), *A Basic History of California* (1964), and *California: An Illustrated History,* with Norman E. Tutorow (1968). After 1968 Fehrenbacher focused more clearly on Lincoln and constitutional issues of the Civil War, with *The Changing Image of Lincoln in American Historiography* (1968), *The Era of Expansion, 1800–1848* (1969), *Manifest Destiny and the Coming of the Civil War, 1840–1861* (1970), *The Leadership of Abraham Lincoln* (1970), *Abraham Lincoln, A Documentary Portrait Through His Speeches and Writings* (1977), and *Tradition, Conflict, and Modernization* (1977).

Fehrenbacher's masterful 1978 work, *The Dred Scott Case; Its Significance in American Law and Politics,* was destined to become a milestone in American history. This comprehensive study of American political, legal, and constitutional history in the context of the 1857 Supreme Court decision on Dred Scott was the most thorough study ever made of a Supreme Court Decision. It won Fehrenbacher the Pulitzer Prize for history in 1979. Afterward, he wrote *The Minor Affair* (1979), *The South and Three Sectional Crises* (1980), *Slavery, Law, and Politics* (1981), *Lincoln in Text and Context* (1987), *Constitutions and Constitutionalism in the Slaveholding South* (1989), and *Recollected Words of Abraham Lincoln* (1996). Fehrenbacher and his wife Virginia spent twelve years collecting material for this collection of 1,900 quotations attributed to Lincoln by more than 500 of his contemporaries. At the time of his death Fehrenbacher was working on *The Slaveholding Republic* (2001). The book was completed and edited by Dr. Ward M. McAfee, one of Fehrenbacher's former graduate students. In addition to his own works, Fehrenbacher edited and wrote the final two chapters of David Potter's *The Impending Crisis, 1848–1861*, published in 1976 after Potter's death. Potter was awarded the 1977 Pulitzer Prize for this work.

Following a long illness, the seventy-seven-year-old Fehrenbacher died of heart failure at his Stanford campus home. He was survived by his wife, daughters, son, grandchildren, sister, and brothers.

★

Fehrenbacher's *Collected Words of Abraham Lincoln* is dedicated to his eight grandchildren. Five boxes of Fehrenbacher papers, mostly professional correspondence, are in the Special Collections of Stanford University Archives, SC 211. An obituary is in the *New York Times* (17 Dec. 1997).

NORMAN E. TUTOROW

FEININGER, Andreas Bernhard Lyonel (*b.* 27 December 1906 in Paris, France; *d.* 18 February 1999 in New York City), photographer for *Life* magazine whose work marks the intersection of modernist abstraction and American documentary traditions.

Feininger was the son of the American painter Lyonel Feininger and Julie Lilienfeld Berg. In 1908 the family moved from Paris to Zehlendorf-Mitte, Berlin, where two more sons were born: Laurence and Theodore Lux. In 1919 Lyonel accepted a post at the newly founded Bauhaus, and the family moved to Weimar, also in Germany. From 1922 to 1925 Andreas attended the Bauhaus, where he studied cabinetmaking with Walter Gropius and befriended architect Marcel Breuer and painter Joseph Albers. It was there that Feininger took his only photography course, a class taught by Walter Peterhans that he found too abstract in its approach. Feininger's first photograph, of crows against a winter sky, taken in 1925 with his mother's 6.5 × 9 cm Voightlander on a glass plate negative, exhibited what would become the artist's lifelong interest in the content of his art. As he explained in 1986, "my subject is the reason why I make a photograph, the spark that energizes my creative faculties."

Feininger's first experience with photography did not

Andreas Feininger, 1946. © BETTMANN/CORBIS

immediately influence his career. In 1925 he began architectural training at the Bauschule in Weimar, transferring to the Staatliche Bauschule in Zerbst when his family followed the Bauhaus to Dessau in 1926. He completed his architectural training in 1928 and was employed in workshops in Dessau and Hamburg until 1932. Feininger's work in Germany ended in 1932, when, denied a work visa due to his alien status, he emigrated to France. In Paris, with the help of Gropius, Feininger received his last architectural position as assistant in the studio of Le Corbusier. By the summer of 1933, Feininger was living in Sweden and working as a freelance photographer for local architects. On 30 August 1933 he married Gertrude Wysse Hägg; their only son, Tomas, was born two years later on 21 September 1935.

As Feininger began his photographic career, he also began writing, contributing technical essays to *Foto-Beabachter*, publishing a book-length photo-essay titled *Stockholm* (1936), and completing the instructional texts that became the basis for his first major volume, *New Paths in Photography* (1939). In 1939, as a response to the Soviet invasion of Finland, the Swedish government forbade the use of cars and cameras, effectively eliminating Feininger's livelihood. In 1940, on the penultimate voyage of the Norwegian liner *Oslofjord*, which was subsequently sunk by the Nazis, Feininger emigrated for the last time. He set up a home and studio in New York City.

Feininger's first year in America was spent documenting urban life for the Black Star Picture Agency, thus beginning his artistic relationship with New York City. Collected in four volumes, *New York* (1945), *The Face of New York* (1954), *New York* (1964), and *New York in the Forties* (1978), Feininger's images capture the metropolis from the Bowery in 1940 to Times Square in 1984. Feininger was retained by *Life* magazine as a freelance photographer in 1941 but soon thereafter took a job with the Office of War Information (OWI), for which he documented domestic wartime production. The OWI post lasted from 1941 to 1942, and the following year he was invited to join *Life* magazine as a staff photographer, a position he held until 1962.

Working for *Life* propelled Feininger into the upper echelon of American photography. He shared the pages with Margaret Bourke-White and Alfred Eisenstaedt, two of the artists who, like Feininger, shaped American photography at mid-century. Feininger completed 346 assignments for *Life*. His favorite work included self-initiated projects such as "Manmade Landscapes" (5 June 1948), on the desecration of the environment by commercial development, and "A Way of Life with Neighbors" (6 August 1951), on diverse housing in the United States. Such socially minded essays appeared along with other self-designed assignments that reveal the artist's interest in na-

ture. Feininger's favorites in this genre included "Insect Engineers" (29 August 1949) and "Pest Portraits" (20 March 1950). As subject matter sparked Feininger's creativity, it also inspired technical innovation. The urban landscape compelled Feininger to build four telephoto lenses, while the natural subjects encouraged him to experiment with macroscopic lenses. In the darkroom, Feininger enlisted a variety of effects, including solarization, reticulation, negative printing, and direct projection. While at *Life*, Feininger continued to produce books, including the first two of his volumes on New York City, *New York* (1945) and *The Face of New York* (1954), and a study of the female nude in sculpture, *Maids, Madonnas, and Witches* (1960), with accompanying text by Henry Miller.

After leaving *Life* in 1962, Feininger turned to independent book projects, further exploring his vision of urban life and nature. With his brother Theodore, Feininger published *Lyonel Feininger: City on the Edge of the World* on their father and the toys he created. Until the end of his life, Feininger published instructional texts and released new editions of his earlier manuals.

Feininger's work has been featured in numerous group exhibitions, including the historic *Film und Foto/Fifo* (1929), originating at the Deutscher Werkbund in Stuttgart, and *Family of Man* (1955) at the Museum of Modern Art. Solo exhibitions included *The Anatomy of Nature* (American Museum of Natural History, 1957), *The World Through My Eyes* (Smithsonian Institution, 1963), a retrospective at the International Center for Photography (1976), and *New York in the Forties* (New-York Historical Society, 1978). His awards included a Bronze Medal from the Fotografiska Föreningen, Stolkholm (1938 and 1939), the Gold Medal from the Art Directors Club of Metropolitan Washington, and the Robert Leavitt Award of the American Society of Magazine Photographers (1966).

Feininger died at the age of ninety-two at the New York University Medical Center in Manhattan. He is buried in Mount Hope Cemetery in Hastings on Hudson, New York.

Feininger's career marks the intersection of modernist photographic traditions born in the abstract experiments of the Bauhaus and modern architecture, and the documentary traditions of the depression-era United States. Like his peers at *Life* in the postwar years, Feininger often directed his camera at evidence of growth and prosperity in the American landscape. On his own, however, Feininger examined the underside of that development. He explained that "a good photograph must be more than simply an illustration, it must be an interpretation." Feininger's photographic interpretations started with an interest in the "relationship between form and function" and then gave this typically modernist concern a human and ethical dimension. Through his textbooks and photographic essays, Feininger taught thousands of people to make art with the camera and many more to see art in the world around them.

★

The most complete biographical information on Feininger is found in the autobiographical text and retrospective photo-essay *Andreas Feininger: Photographer* (1986). The Andreas Feininger archive is held at the Center for Creative Photography, Tucson, Arizona. Feininger's many books contain personal and instructional essays documenting his attitudes toward his particular subjects and photography itself. The artist's professional opinions can also be read in his columns for *Modern Photography Magazine*. Relevant biographical information and interviews can be found in Miriam Berkeley, "The Quiet Man," *American Photographer* 18 (Mar. 1987); Franklin Cameron, "Meet the Masters," *Petersens's Photographic Magazine* 15 (Mar. 1987); Franklin Cameron, "Relativity: Andreas Feininger Pays Homage to the Interrelationship of Function and Beauty in Natural Forms," *Petersens's Photographic Magazine* 17 (Oct. 1988); and Trevor Gett, "The Man from Manhattan," *British Journal of Photography,* no. 7187 (12 Aug. 1998). Feininger was featured as one of the six most significant living photographers in the British Broadcasting Corporation 1983 series *Master Photographers.* An obituary is in the *New York Times* (20 Feb. 1999).

PETER R. KALB

FLOOD, Curt(is) Charles (*b.* 18 January 1938 in Houston, Texas; *d.* 20 January 1997 in Los Angeles, California), talented outfielder for the St. Louis Cardinals remembered for challenging the operating procedures of baseball and opening the possibility of free agency, thus allowing players to pursue jobs with other teams and causing salaries to increase in spiraling proportions.

Flood, son of Herman Flood, Sr., a hospital attendant, and Laura Flood, a hospital worker, had five brothers and sisters and was raised in Oakland, California. Flood attended Oakland Tech High School and graduated in 1956 from McClymonds High School in Oakland, where he was an outstanding baseball player. He signed a contract in 1956 to play with the Cincinnati Reds organization. The only African American on the team, Flood faced discrimination regularly on the road. He played briefly for the Reds in both 1956 and 1957. His contract was then sold to the St. Louis Cardinals in 1958, and Flood became the regular center fielder there during his first year.

Between 1958 and 1969 Flood established himself as a strong defensive force, winning seven Gold Glove awards, making the National League All-Star team three times, and playing on three World Series teams for the Cardinals in the 1960s. During this period, he played 223 games with the Cardinals without an error, setting a major league rec-

Curt Flood. ARCHIVE PHOTOS, INC.

ord. On 19 August 1968 *Sports Illustrated* featured him in a cover story, "The Best Center Fielder in Baseball." He ended his career in 1971, after a brief stay with the Washington Senators, having appeared in over 1,750 games, with a .293 lifetime batting average During six seasons he had hit over .300. Flood married Beverly Collins in February 1959 and again in the mid-1960s. They had four children who remained with Collins after the second divorce. In 1978, he married Judy Pace.

By 1969 Flood, then thirty-one, had become a part of both the Cardinals organization and the St. Louis community. In addition to playing for the team, he operated a successful portrait business and had painted such individuals as the civil rights leader Martin Luther King, Jr. On the field Flood captained a multiethnic team, along with Bob Gibson, Mike Shannon, Lou Brock, Tim McCarver, Dal Maxville, Orlando Cepeda, Roger Maris, and Julian Javier. The group formed the core of a successful Cardinals organization that contended for the National League championship throughout the 1960s, winning three pennants and two World Series championships. These players had also overcome significant racial divisions in both the Cardinals organization and within the community to form a team that had a unity not usually seen in mid-twentieth-century America.

In October 1969 after a disappointing fourth-place finish, Cardinals management broke up the team, trading talented players with the Philadelphia Phillies. St. Louis sent Flood, McCarver, Byron Browne, and Joe Hoerner to Philadelphia for Richie Allen, Cookie Rojas, and Jerry Johnson. Flood and McCarver, along with Allen and Rojas, were the key players in the seven-player swap. Flood astounded the baseball world when he refused to accept the trade. On 24 December 1969 Flood wrote to Bowie Kuhn, commissioner of baseball, "I do not feel that I am a piece of property to be bought and sold irrespective of my wishes." On 29 December Flood announced that he intended to sue major league baseball. He filed suit on 16 January 1970 in federal court, contending that the reserve clause violated federal antitrust laws.

Although Flood was paid well for the time, earning $90,000 for the Cardinals and with a $100,000 offer from the Phillies, Flood believed that the reserve clause placed him and all other players in the position of servitude. He refused to report to the Phillies for spring training or for the 1970 season. As the case worked its way through the courts, Flood published a book, *The Way It Is* (1970), which became a best-seller and exposed to the public the private life of baseball players. Along with Jim Bouton's *Ball Four* (1970) and Jim Brosnan's *The Long Season* (1960), Flood's book exposed racial conflicts, sexual escapades, and a generally seamy side of life among big league players.

Flood's suit against baseball was heard in August 1970 before federal judge Irving Ben Cooper in New York, who upheld the legality of the reserve clause. Cooper, however, recommended that ownership and players should come to some common accord on this contentious issue, but that it should come from negotiations not court orders. In April 1971 a three-judge panel of the U.S. Court of Appeals affirmed the lower court's decision. Yet Flood had the support and backing of the Major League Player's Association and its dynamic executive director Marvin Miller. The association agreed to take the case to the Supreme Court, where former Supreme Court Justice Arthur Goldberg argued the case for Flood. *Flood* v. *Kuhn*, as the case came to be known, was heard in 1972, and the ruling came down on 18 June 1972. By a five to three margin the Supreme Court upheld the lower court rulings, thus upholding baseball's exemption from antitrust laws and the legitimacy of the reserve clause. The decision of the Court was narrowly construed, however, and allowed the reserve clause to be changed either by legislation or by collective bargaining.

While Flood lost his case and only returned to baseball for a brief stint with the Senators, player relations were never again the same. Flood, who was labeled as an ingrate, a destroyer, and a blasphemer of the game, was instrumental in opening the issue of free agency. By the end of 1972 the reserve clause was modified with the advent of salary arbitration, which was the owners' response to the possibility of collective bargaining. In 1975 an arbitrator, whose services had been included in the basic agreement in 1968 between players and owners, ruled that major league baseball had violated the contracts of two pitchers, Andy Messersmith and Dave McNally, and declared them to be free agents. From that point forward, baseball dealt with the issue of player contracts as a matter of the agreement between the players' union and management. What Flood had sought to achieve through his court case was accomplished through negotiations during the later years of the 1970s. In 1997 Congress approved what came to be known as the Curt Flood Act of 1997, placing baseball under the terms of antitrust law only for labor relations.

Following his baseball career, Flood spent five years painting and writing while running a café on the island of Majorca, off the coast of Spain. Flood also spent time in Sweden and Denmark. His personal life was less pristine than his professional life. His older brother Carl had been imprisoned early in life because of gang-related violence and crime on the streets of Oakland. Flood had developed an introspective, passionate attitude toward life, but he had trouble dealing with people close to him. He sporadically fought bouts with emotional crises, as well as alcohol and substance abuse.

In 1976, following his time in Europe, Flood moved back to his boyhood hometown of Oakland, living as a recluse in an apartment next to his mother. He remained unemployed until Charlie Finley, the maverick owner of the Oakland A's, hired him as a broadcaster for the 1978 season. The following year, Flood worked for Oakland Department of Sports and Aquatics as the commissioner of a sandlot baseball league. He subsequently moved to Los Angeles, where he lived in the Baldwin Hills section of Beverly Hills. In Los Angeles he managed a youth center and worked for a short period of time as a vice president for the abortive United Baseball League. He died at age fifty-nine in Los Angeles from throat cancer and is buried in Inglewood Park Cemetery, Inglewood, California.

Flood pinpointed civil rights as a primary motivating factor in his decisions. He considered himself to be a man of the 1960s who asked baseball to uphold traditional values of freedom and self-determination. He sensed his role as an excellent player diminished by his lack of ability to bargain his own contract and terms. The fact that the Cardinals had traded him without his consent and without consultation motivated Flood to fight for his own freedom and for the freedom of his fellow players.

★

The best source of information on Flood as a player and citizen is Flood's book, *The Way It Is* (1970). Articles regarding Flood's career and his influence on free agency include Dan Gordon,

"Flooding the Market: Are Today's Major-Leaguers Indebted to Curt Flood?" *Sport* (Jan. 1994); and "Curt Flood, Featured in *Ebony*'s Fiftieth Anniversary Issue, Battles Throat Cancer," *Jet* (13 Nov. 1995). An obituary is in the *New York Times* (21 Jan. 1997).

HARRY JEBSEN, JR.

FORREST, Helen (*b.* 12 April 1917 in Atlantic City, New Jersey; *d.* 11 July 1999 in Los Angeles, California), big band vocalist of the swing era.

Forrest was born Helen Fogel, the daughter of Louis Fogel and Rebecca Fogel, Jewish neighborhood grocery store owners. Forrest was deprived of a stable family life when her father died during the influenza epidemic of 1918. Her mother and three older brothers provided her with few childhood joys. A bout with scarlet fever damaged her hearing, which was not apparent until the mid-1940s, when she required medical treatment. In the late 1920s she moved to Brooklyn, New York, with her struggling mother, who married a part-time house painter. Forrest's stepfather proved to be a pimp and converted the family home into a daytime brothel. When he tried to rape Forrest, she fled to a neighborhood woman who took Forrest in and acted as

Helen Forrest. ARCHIVE PHOTOS, INC.

her surrogate mother. At age fourteen Forrest sang on weekends without pay in her brother Ed Fogel's band at Atlantic City dance marathons. She took piano lessons but never trained as a singer; her voice was natural. Forrest never graduated high school.

In 1934 Forrest changed her surname (but never legally) and turned professional, singing radio commercials anonymously as Bonnie Blue on WNEW in New York City. She joined Mark Warnow's orchestra on WCBS in New York City in 1935, then moved to the Madrillon supper club in Washington, D.C., late in 1936. Influenced initially by Ella Fitzgerald and Mildred Bailey, female vocalists of the Chick Webb and Red Norvo orchestras respectively, Forrest quickly developed her own warm, smooth style of interpreting a lyric, sensitively in romantic ballads or up-tempo in "swinging" arrangements. During the swing era the entire arrangement did not back up or highlight the vocalist. Instead, the big band singer had a function similar to an instrumental soloist, performing the melody with some individual interpretation.

One of Forrest's admiring fellow musicians, the trumpeter Ziggy Elman, recommended her to the rising band-leader Artie Shaw in 1938. Shaw hired Forrest that September, even though for a month she had to share the singing spotlight with the jazz great Billie Holiday, who had already given notice that she would be leaving. Forrest sang for network radio performances from hotel ballrooms, numerous appearances on the road, and forty-one recorded tunes with Shaw's band, and she became a major factor in its immense popularity. She also became one of the first big band singers to achieve star status. Among the many songs associated with Forrest are "All the Things You Are," "I Have Eyes," and "Day In, Day Out." While with the Shaw band she sang in three film shorts.

When Shaw suddenly quit the band business in November 1939, leaving Forrest unemployed, the "King of Swing," Benny Goodman, quickly hired her. From her first gig with the Goodman band on 11 December 1939 at the Waldorf Astoria Hotel in New York City, Forrest experienced success despite her dislike of its leader. Featured on no fewer than fifty-five sides, Forrest achieved her first "gold" record, *Taking a Chance on Love,* which sold more than a million copies. Other notable successes included the records *Bewitched* and *The Sky Fell Down.* In 1940 Forrest recorded two sides with pickup groups led by Lionel Hampton and including the Nat "King" Cole Trio, the first time a white female singer had recorded with a black leader. The initial disk was "I'd Be Lost Without You." The drummer on this side was Al Spieldock, whom Forrest had married in 1939 but saw so rarely that the marriage soon dissolved. Their divorce became final in 1944.

Forrest joined the bandleader Harry James in September 1941, when he agreed to build the arrangements of her tunes around her rather than around the band. This shift proved revolutionary for big bands generally and capitalized on the romantic appeal of James's trumpet and Forrest's perfect intonation in sentimental ballads. The combination resulted in two of Forrest's eighteen gold records, made before a musicians' union's strike halted recordings in August 1942. "I Don't Want to Walk Without You" and "I've Heard That Song Before" both reached number one in national music polls. Her other top sellers were "I Had the Craziest Dream" and "I Cried for You." Forrest also sang the songs in *Springtime in the Rockies* (1942) and *Bathing Beauty* (1944), two of five motion pictures in which she appeared with the James band. To enhance her appearance, she had cosmetic surgery on her nose.

Forrest's popularity, enhanced by public appearances of the James orchestra and its network radio broadcasts, led to *Downbeat* and *Metronome* magazine polls rating her the best female vocalist in the country in 1942 and 1943. Less successful was her torrid year-long love affair with James, who gave her an engagement ring she wore for the rest of her life. He abruptly married the actress Betty Grable instead, a crushing blow to Forrest, who left the band at the end of 1943 but never lost her affection for James. He retired her songs from his repertoire when her successors proved unable to match the key of her voice or her handling of them. James and Forrest reunited musically in 1955 on an album of old favorites that included four with her vocals.

A singing star in her own right by 1944, Forrest teamed up with Dick Haymes, who sang opposite her in the James band, for the popular weekly network *Autolite Radio Show* and several top-selling records (1944–1946). Simultaneously and afterward she cut more than seventy solo records, starting with the hit "Time Waits for No One" in 1944 and climaxing in 1956 with the album *Miss Helen Forrest: Voice of the Name Bands*. In 1947 she married the bit actor Paul Hogan; they divorced in 1956. In 1959 she married the businessman Charles Feinman; they had a son before they divorced in 1961.

Forrest's part in liberating female vocalists (for example, Peggy Lee, who followed her into the Benny Goodman band) from big band arrangements played a key role in the new ascendancy of singers in popular musical tastes. Forrest did not share in that success herself, however, mainly because her style was so well suited to the milieu of the big band. Throughout the remainder of her life Forrest continued to perform, singing in supper clubs, on the nostalgia circuit, on television, and at music festivals, in particular with Frank Sinatra, Jr., the Pied Pipers, and the reconstituted Tommy Dorsey Orchestra in the early 1960s. Her last recording was an album in 1983 on which she was uncharacteristically accompanied by a small combo. During retirement, Forrest lived in southern California. She died of congestive heart failure; her place of burial is unknown.

★

Forrest's autobiography, with Bill Libby, *I Had the Craziest Dream* (1982), includes a comprehensive discography. Additional perspectives are in D. Russell Connor, *Benny Goodman: Listen to His Legacy* (1988); and Peter J. Levinson, *Trumpet Blues: The Life of Harry James* (1999). Forrest's best work with Goodman is *Benny Goodman and Helen Forrest* (1992). A collection of radio air checks that includes her songs, some not recorded commercially, is *King of the Clarinet: Artie Shaw and His Orchestra 1938–1939* (1998). An obituary is in the *New York Times* (13 July 1999).

CLARK G. REYNOLDS

FRIENDLY, Fred W. (*b.* 30 October 1915 in New York City; *d.* 3 March 1998 in New York City), pioneering radio and television producer and influential media scholar.

Friendly was born Ferdinand Wachenheimer, the son of Samuel Wachenheimer, a jewelry maker, and Theresa Friendly; in 1938 he legally changed his surname to his mother's maiden name. He attended Nichols Junior College in Dudley, Massachusetts, but did not have the opportunity for further education. The child of Jewish immigrants, Friendly grew up with a passion for history and radio. His first opportunity to unite these interests came at

Fred W. Friendly, 1992. GABRIEL AMADEUS COONEY/ASSOCIATED PRESS/COLUMBIA UNIVERSITY

age twenty-two, when he was hired by a small radio station in Providence, Rhode Island, to write, produce, and narrate "Footprints in the Sands of Time," a series of five-minute biographies of historical figures. Friendly, like many young journalists during the Great Depression, overcame a lack of formal education in news reporting through hard work and natural talent. In a report during this period from a Massachusetts airport dedication ceremony, Friendly's flair for the dramatic was already evident in his use of the stentorian tone and cadence evocative of the newsreel narrator.

During World War II, Friendly served in the China-Burma-India Theater as a master sergeant with the Information and Education Service of the U.S. Army and was a correspondent for *CBI Roundup,* an army newspaper. He received the Soldier's Medal of Heroism for a rescue operation in Bombay, India, four battle stars, and the Legion of Merit. Friendly was also on hand for the liberation of the Nazi concentration camp in Mauthausen, Germany, in 1945, an experience that clearly had an impact on his iconoclastic approach to justice and ethics later in life.

Following the war, Friendly met Edward R. Murrow, a CBS war correspondent who became his professional partner and friend. Friendly's first idea for Murrow was to create an audio documentary of the years 1932 to 1945. The album, a potent combination of archival recordings and dramatic narration called *I Can Hear It Now* (1948) became the first successful talk album in America and a best-seller for Columbia Records. As a result of this success, CBS hired Friendly to develop more documentary projects with Murrow, which led to the creation of a one-hour radio series called *Hear It Now.*

In 1951 Friendly and Murrow took this documentary format to prime-time television, appropriately changing the program name to *See It Now.* Broadcasting from a windowless studio over New York Central railroad tracks in Grand Central Terminal, Friendly and Murrow helped shape television history by exploring critical sociopolitical themes in a unique visual style. Program topics ranged from a conversation with atomic-bomb physicist J. Robert Oppenheimer to a portrait of the poet Carl Sandburg. Their most notable broadcast, however, was a critical documentary about Senator Joseph McCarthy in 1954. In an unprecedented examination of a political figure on television, Friendly and Murrow created an audiovisual montage of McCarthy's speeches that was pivotal in changing the public's perception of the senator's anticommunist tactics. *See It Now* became an award-winning series that ran for seven years. It was also the first show to be broadcast live from coast to coast.

The format and content of Friendly-inspired programs reflected his view of television as "the greatest teaching tool since the printing press." Friendly wrote and produced programs on the principle that the role of television in a democratic society is to keep the public well informed. In 1959 Friendly became the executive producer of *CBS Reports,* an hourly documentary series. In line with his philosophy regarding television, he dedicated the next five years to educating viewers about difficult and troubling topics, creating such programs as *Harvest of Shame,* an exposé on the harsh conditions of migrant farm workers; *The Population Explosion; Abortion and the Law;* and *Ku Klux Klan: The Invisible Empire.*

In 1964 Friendly became president of CBS News. It soon became evident, however, that his views on journalism were at odds with the mandate of CBS management. While Friendly thought in terms of investing network time and money in quality reporting and extensive news coverage, network executives were becoming increasingly focused on entertainment value and corporate earnings. In February 1966 this conflict reached its head when CBS, over Friendly's objections, aired reruns of *I Love Lucy* instead of live coverage of the first Senate Foreign Relations Committee hearings on Vietnam War policy. In a decision that revealed the strength of his convictions, Friendly resigned from CBS.

In the years that followed Friendly turned his attention to writing, teaching, and public television. He had always been an admirer of the Constitution (in fact, he carried a copy with him at all times) and authored several books involving landmark Supreme Court decisions, including *The Good Guys, The Bad Guys and the First Amendment* (1976), *Minnesota Rag* (1981), and *The Constitution: That Delicate Balance* (1984). He also served as an adviser to the Ford Foundation, where he helped create the first live national educational television station, the Public Broadcast Laboratory (PBL). Although PBL lasted only two years, the programming service evolved into what is now known as the Public Broadcasting Service (PBS).

Perhaps Friendly's greatest contribution to the world of journalism came during his years as Edward R. Murrow Professor of Broadcast Journalism at the Columbia University journalism school. From 1966 to 1993, Friendly challenged the minds of young journalists by posing challenging ethical dilemmas in class. He required students to identify their principles early on, to know what they stood for before they were faced with a difficult decision. There would be no time to figure out what is "right" when working against a deadline, he explained to his students. It was during this time that Friendly became a self-taught expert on constitutional law, especially as it relates to civil liberties and journalists' rights. Armed with pocket-sized copies of the U.S. Constitution, Friendly traveled the country with the zeal of a preacher, distributing the document to anyone willing to engage him.

As an emeritus professor, Friendly created the Columbia University Media and Society Seminars, a television series that brought the classroom debates he loved to millions of PBS viewers. Inspired by the acrimonious relationship he believed existed between journalists and judges at the time, Friendly's seminars brought together U.S. presidents, journalists, government officials, and Supreme Court justices to discuss, in a Socratic format, various social, legal, and ethical issues. Topics included human rights, the Constitution, ethics in America, religion, and business and the media. Friendly opened each segment with a now famous definition of the seminars' purpose: "Our job is not to make up anyone's mind, but to open minds and to make the agony of decision-making so intense that you can escape only through thinking." Between 1973 and 1992, Friendly participated in over 600 seminars worldwide, eighty-three of which were broadcast on public television. They eventually became known as the *Fred Friendly Seminars*.

Friendly died at age eighty-two after suffering a series of strokes. He was survived by his wife of thirty years, Ruth Weiss Mark, a former schoolteacher who worked alongside her husband in his final years, his three children from a previous marriage, and three stepchildren. Friendly also had ten grandchildren. His first marriage to the former Dorothy Greene ended in divorce.

Friendly was buried with two copies of the Constitution in his inside coat pocket. One to keep, it was said at the time, the other to give away. Eulogists at his funeral included prominent journalists, Supreme Court Justice Antonin Scalia, and New York City Mayor Rudolph Giuliani, who referred to Friendly as an American version of Socrates. As a towering figure who became the conscience of television news, Friendly left an indelible mark on those who create and watch television journalism.

As a producer of CBS documentaries in the decade following World War II, Friendly helped create a dramatic television news style that inspired viewers as it enlightened them. As the producing partner to Edward R. Murrow and later, in the mid-1960s, as president of CBS News, Friendly developed a reputation as a perfectionist willing to fight to keep television journalism credible and free of corporate profit interests. When it appeared that he could no longer win his battles on behalf of television journalism, he left the profession to become a vocal critic of its ethical lapses and excesses. With a gift of gruff speech and unwavering principles, Friendly became more widely known as a professor and self-styled "dean of television journalism." In the 1980s and 1990s, Friendly emerged from behind the cameras to host a series of critically acclaimed roundtable discussions about law, journalism, politics, and ethics. By the time of his death in 1998, Friendly's career as an innovative producer and distinguished critic of broadcast news had spanned more than sixty years.

★

The *Fred Friendly Seminars* continues at Columbia University and PBS: <http://www.fredfriendly.org>. Tributes to Friendly include Nat Hentoff, "Fred Friendly's Faith in the Constitution," *Washington Post* (14 Mar. 1998), and "When TV Had Integrity," *Village Voice* (31 Mar. 1998); Eileen McNamara, "The Fred Friendly Impact," *Nieman Reports* 1 (spring 1998); Joan Konner, "Fred Friendly, 1915–1998," *Columbia Journalism Review* 37 (May/June 1998): 6; William F. Buckley, Jr., "The Testimony of Fred Friendly," *National Review* (1 June 1998). An obituary is in the *New York Times* (5 Mar. 1998).

MICHAEL M. EPSTEIN

FULLER, Samuel Michael (*b*. 12 August 1912 in Worcester, Massachusetts; *d*. 30 October 1997 in Hollywood, California), journalist, novelist, and filmmaker whose innovative and iconoclastic low-budget films made him one of the most influential of American directors.

Fuller was eleven when his father died and his mother moved her three children to New York City. Fuller sold newspapers on the streets, and this early contact with the newspaper business became a lifelong fascination. By the time he was thirteen, Fuller was a copy boy for the *New York Evening Journal*. By age fifteen Fuller had left formal schooling and worked his way up to being the personal

Samuel Fuller, 1980. THE KOBAL COLLECTION

copy boy for Arthur Brisbane, managing editor for the Hearst newspaper empire. At age seventeen he left the *Journal* to become a crime reporter and cartoonist for the *New York Evening Graphic,* a new tabloid practicing what Fuller called "creative exaggeration." Covering one of the toughest crime beats in the country, as the youngest reporter ever to do so, gave Fuller an early introduction to fast-paced narrative and sensational subject matter. His later novels and films would reflect this tabloid sensibility.

Fuller left New York in the early 1930s to pursue work on newspapers across the country, eventually covering the crime beat for the *San Diego Sun.* He published his first novel, *Burn, Baby, Burn!,* a tabloid-inspired retelling of the execution of a pregnant woman, in 1935. Two more dime-store novels based on true news accounts followed: *Test Tube Baby* (1936), about experiments with artificial insemination, and *Wake Up and Kiss* (1938), an examination of the power of cosmetic companies. It was also during this period that Fuller began to write for movies. He made a contact at Republic pictures and got the studio interested in a book he admired called *The Gangs of New York.* The film version of the book was released in 1937, and it was the first time Fuller's name appeared in the credits of a motion picture. Fuller's initial work in Hollywood was cut short when he was drafted into the U.S. Army in 1942. His best-known novel, *The Dark Page,* was published in 1944 while Fuller was serving with the First Infantry Division as it fought its way across France and Germany.

War, along with journalism, became a formative force in Fuller's life. As a member of the First Infantry Division, popularly known as "The Big Red One," Fuller saw combat in North Africa, Italy, and on blood-drenched Omaha Beach on D day. He was wounded twice and received the Bronze and Silver Stars. His unit liberated the Falkenau concentration camp in Czechoslovakia, and Fuller, armed with a sixteen-millimeter camera his mother had sent him, recorded much of what he saw. Along with his filming of events in the war, Fuller also kept extensive diaries of his experiences in combat that would later become the inspiration for his war films, including the largely autobiographical *The Big Red One* (1980).

After the war, Fuller met producer/director Howard Hawks, who bought the film rights to *The Dark Page.* Fuller also wrote screenplays for several films that never got made. In 1948 Fuller met independent producer Robert Libbert, who suggested they work together. Fuller jumped at the chance to have control over a film as writer and director, and the result was *I Shot Jesse James* (1948), a psychological Western made in ten days for slightly over $100,000. This first film is in many ways emblematic of Fuller's entire career: it was made quickly and cheaply; Fuller had sole control of its screenplay and direction; and it had a brash style that immediately announced a new

inventive take on narrative film. Another low-budget Western called *The Baron of Arizona,* starring Vincent Price, followed in 1949. However, it was Fuller's next film, *The Steel Helmet* (1950), that was his first great success and the first of his films to stir up controversy.

Made in ten days for $105,000, *The Steel Helmet* was one of the first films to depict the Korean War. In the film Gene Evans stars as Sergeant Zack, a hard-boiled World War II combat veteran who survives any way he can. The film was successful but immediately raised controversy. One editorial called it an "anti-American, pro-Communist" film because of its depiction of racism in the U.S. Army and its discussion of the internment of Japanese Americans during World War II. The success of *The Steel Helmet* caused the major studios to show interest in Fuller as a director, and he began a long relationship with Darryl Zanuck at Twentieth Century–Fox.

Under Zanuck's wing, Fuller was able to make a succession of idiosyncratic movies combining his brash storytelling with challenging critiques of politics, race, class, and gender in modern America. His first picture for Zanuck was *Fixed Bayonets* (1951), another Korean War film which was quickly followed by *Park Row* (1952), a film inspired by Fuller's love of journalism. Fuller personally financed *Park Row,* and when it failed at the box office he quickly countered with one of the classic film noirs, *Pick Up on South Street* (1953). A rapid succession of genre-bending films followed, including *House of Bamboo* (1955), the first American film shot in Japan; *China Gate* (1957), one of the first films about the political turmoil in Vietnam; *Forty Guns* (1957), an avant-garde Western; and *Underworld USA* (1961), a brutal crime drama.

Fuller entered the end of the studio era with two of his most famous and challenging films: *Shock Corridor* (1963), the story of a reporter who gets himself committed to an insane asylum to solve a murder; and *The Naked Kiss* (1964), a tabloid "yarn" about a prostitute who moves to a small town and takes on a new identity. Both films were shocking melodramas told in Fuller's jarring, iconoclastic style, but they were also provocative political statements. Unfortunately, both movies were received with apathy, and Fuller fell into a period of inactivity as the studio system changed and his style of filmmaking became hard to finance. Ironically, at the same time Fuller was having trouble getting films made, his place in critical circles altered radically under the scrutiny of the French film critics at the journal *Cahiers du Cinéma.* The French hailed him as an American auteur, whose experimental filmmaking inspired many of the figures in the French New Wave. As an homage to Fuller, French director Jean-Luc Godard had him appear in *Pierrot le Fou* (1965), where Fuller defines film: "A film is like a battleground—love . . . hate . . . action . . . violence . . . death . . . in one word—emotion!" More acting parts followed as Fuller was asked by the directors to appear in films such as Dennis Hopper's *The Last Movie* (1970) and Wim Wenders's *The American Friend* (1977) and *Hammett* (1983).

Fuller married the French actress Christa Lang in 1967; they had a daughter in 1974. Fuller's first European production, *Dead Pigeon on Beethoven Street,* appeared in 1972, but it was *The Big Red One* (1980) that marked Fuller's return to American filmmaking and the critical and commercial apex of his late career. A story of infantrymen moving through Africa and Europe during World War II, *The Big Red One* recounts Fuller's own war experience and documents the life of the foot soldier. Although Fuller's original version of the film was over four hours long, the studio edited it down to less than two hours. Fuller was satisfied with what was finally released, and the film was a great comeback. His next movie, *White Dog* (1982), the story of an animal trained to kill African Americans, was so shocking that Paramount Studios refused to support the film, and it was not released in the United States until 1991.

After the failure of *White Dog* to reach screens in the United States, Fuller moved to France where he made two more films, *Thieves After Dark* (1982) and *Street of No Return* (1989). He became a lionized figure in film circles and several major international film festivals were held in his honor. He died in his Hollywood Hills home after returning to the United States after suffering a stroke.

Fuller is unique in American cinema. One of the most influential and honored figures in Hollywood history, he was always an outsider whose films were often dismissed as "B" pictures at the same time they raised heated debate during the cold war. The filmmakers who have acknowledged his influence include Steven Spielberg, Francis Ford Coppola, Martin Scorsese, Jim Jarmusch, Wim Wenders, Jean-Luc Godard, and Quentin Tarantino. Jarmusch has called Fuller an "anti-totalitarian anarchist," and his twenty-three films embody this tough individuality and provide American cinema with one of its most powerful storytellers.

★

Among Fuller's eleven novels, *The Big Red One* (1980) can be read as his war autobiography as well as one of the most detailed accounts of combat in World War II. There is no full-length biography. The first two books written about Fuller, Nicholas Garnham, *Samuel Fuller* (1970), and Phil Hardy, *Sam Fuller* (1971), are still valuable for insights into his filmmaking. There are also several highly informative studies of his life and work. Two French studies, Jean Narboni and Noël Simsolo, *Il était une fois . . . Samuel Fuller* (1986), and Olivier Amiel, *Samuel Fuller* (1985), are informative appraisals of his career. See Lee Server, *Sam Fuller: Film Is a Battleground* (1994), for an excellent collection of interviews and commentary on the films. Obituaries are in the *Los Angeles Times* (31 Oct. 1997) and *New York Times* (1 Nov. 1997).

JOHN ROCCO

FUNT, Allen (*b.* 16 September 1914 in Brooklyn, New York; *d.* 5 September 1999 in Pebble Beach, California), creator, producer, and host of the *Candid Camera* television show.

Funt was the second child of Isodore Funt, a diamond importer, and Paula Saferstein, a homemaker, Eastern European Jews who passed through Ellis Island in 1913. He grew up in a working-class neighborhood on Brooklyn's Flatbush Avenue with his older sister and younger brother. Funt graduated from New Utrecht High School at age fifteen, then began studying at Cornell University in Ithaca, New York (1930–1934). At Cornell, Funt assisted in the pioneering experiments of Kurt Lewin, a refugee from Nazi Germany who became the founder of modern social psychology. In one experiment investigating the differences in eating patterns between babies who were fed by their mothers and those attended by nurses, Funt observed the sub-

Allen Funt. AP/WIDE WORLD PHOTOS

jects behind a two-way mirror and recorded the results. Eventually he would transform this preoccupation with catching people in "the act of being themselves" into his life's work.

Funt graduated from Cornell in 1934 and began working for an advertising agency in New York City, where he pitched ideas for radio shows. Funt also branched out into writing and producing. One of his most successful ventures was *The Funny Man,* in which listeners participated in pranks, such as paying ninety-nine cents for the shirt off someone's back. Funt was unhappy with what he called his "gimmick man" role, but he was drafted into the U.S. Army in 1941 before he could get his own production company off the ground. While serving in the Signal Corps during World War II, Funt acquired a German wire recorder and used his newfound recording skills to stage shows for army special services. In one show, *The Gripe Booth,* GIs were urged to vent their complaints about army life. The men, however, became tongue-tied when they went on the air and provided little entertaining material. In response, Funt decided to interview servicemen on the air without their knowledge. The candid commentary he elicited was much more provocative and provided the inspiration for Funt's subsequent career in commercial radio.

After Funt was discharged from the army in 1946, he obtained a grant from the Mutual Broadcasting System and began planting concealed microphones around New York City. The results, however, were not very funny. Then while bugging a dental office, a woman mistook Funt for a dentist, so he decided to play along and examined her teeth. When he revealed himself as an impostor, the woman was indignant, but Funt had found a formula for success— a scripted situation, coaxed along by a provocateur, was required to inject humor into his secretly taped scenarios. Mutual passed on this idea, but ABC picked up *Candid Microphone* in 1947, and the show quickly developed a cult following. Funt became so absorbed with the show that he barely had time to whisk his wife (the former Evelyn Kessler) to the hospital for the birth of their first child. The couple remained married from 1946 to 1964. In one popular stunt, Funt asked a tailor to design a zoot suit with pegged trousers for a kangaroo. The tailor agreed to give it a try and solemnly promised not to overcharge him. Although Funt was sued several times for candid scenarios aired on this show, most subjects were good sports and readily signed a release form in exchange for $50.

ABC launched a televised version of the show *Candid Mike* (1947–1949); it evolved into *Candid Camera,* which aired on NBC in 1949. In one memorable stunt, passersby were engaged in conversation by a talking mailbox. In this case the voice was supplied by one of Funt's assistants, but more often than not, the agent provocateur was Funt himself. Stocky, bald, with a flat, rasping voice, Funt was a chameleon who delighted in being recognized by his subjects when he revealed his real identity. He was equally pleased by the attention he and his programming won from prominent intellectuals. Funt was declared "the [second] most ingenious sociologist in America" by David Riesman in *The Lonely Crowd* (1950). In contrast, the *New Yorker*'s John Lardner called *Candid Camera* "coarse, nagging, suspicious, and misanthropic." (Many situations, in fact, relied on slapstick humor.) Funt defended his tactics in the book *Eavesdropper at Large* (1952), arguing that his stunts revealed Americans to be fundamentally "peaceful and gentle."

By the time *Candid Camera* went off the air in 1954, after its first five-year run, Funt was living comfortably on his 110-acre Croton-on-Hudson estate with his wife and three children (many of Funt's ideas for the show occurred to him on his commute to and from Manhattan). During a five-year sabbatical, Funt produced *Candid Camera* movie shorts, *Candid Microphone* records, and corporate training films (*Candid Research*).

Funt began producing ten-minute *Candid Camera* segments for CBS's *Garry Moore Show* in 1959. This led to his second, and most successful, run on network television. *Candid Camera* began airing again on network television in 1960 and quickly became a top ten hit. In one episode, a woman (singer Dorothy Collins) glided her car into a gas station and asked the attendant to look under the hood— to his surprise, it had no engine! In another, drivers began to turn their cars around when confronted by a highway sign, reading, "Delaware is closed." Funt was a taskmaster; the production crew (which now numbered around thirty) would spend forty hours filming in order to produce an episode's worth of stunts. In addition, Funt developed an on-camera interview show, *Tell It to the Camera* (1963–1964), but it was canceled after thirteen episodes. He also published his interviews with children as *Candid Kids* in 1964. In September of that same year, he was divorced and married Marilyn Laron. They moved to New York City where they raised their two children.

Funt's ambition was to create a more serious television show, but he was under continuous pressure by the network to make *Candid Camera* "broad" and "funny." When the show was canceled in 1967 because of low ratings, he reacted bitterly. Still, freed from the restrictions of television, in 1970 he produced his first full-length motion picture, *What Do You Say to a Naked Lady?,* a commentary on American attitudes toward nudity and sex. According to Funt, the picture contained "some of the funniest, thought-provoking, and poignant scenes of my career." The film was well received and became a certifiable hit; costing $570,000 to produce, it grossed $5 million despite an X rating. Having started the 1970s with a bang, Funt soon went bust in both his professional and personal life. His second film, *Money Talks,* died at the box office. His next project, a TV movie called *Smile When You Say You Do* (1973), was prophetic. By this time, Funt's second marriage was headed toward divorce. Meanwhile, Funt lost his life's savings in an embezzling scheme concocted by a trusted accountant, which forced him to sell his precious art collection.

Devastated, Funt left for California in 1975 and began rebuilding his life and career. A third version of the show, *The New Candid Camera,* was syndicated between 1974 and 1979. Funt also produced *Candid Camera* episodes for the Playboy Channel, and created *Candid Kids* for NBC in 1985. Funt enjoyed his greatest success doing fourteen specials on CBS beginning in 1987, with his eldest son, Peter, as cohost. With his newfound wealth, Funt established a fellowship at Syracuse University for graduate studies in radio and television and founded the Laughter Foundation to provide seriously ill patients with videocassettes. Funt owned three homes in California—one in Pebble Beach, another in Hollywood Hills, as well as a 1,100-acre ranch in Big Sur—and spent most of his free time with his companion, Anne Flynn. In 1989 he underwent successful coronary bypass surgery, but in 1993 he suffered a debilitating stroke, leaving Peter to manage the *Candid Camera* empire.

Funt died six years later as a result of complications from his stroke.

Funt parlayed a singular idea into a show business franchise that has influenced almost every reality-based program since. Although Funt claimed that *Candid Camera* made heroes out of ordinary people, the show's themes and methods, which could be exploitative and even cruel, were often controversial. But at its best, *Candid Camera* elicited humor from the subjects' attempts to maintain a sense of rationality, composure, and dignity when confronted with situations that defied conventional expectations. These observations of human nature led Philip G. Zimbardo to call Funt an "intuitive social psychologist." Funt, however, aimed to amuse as well as educate. His greatest satisfaction came from people saying, "Thanks, Allen. You made us smile."

★

Funt's autobiography, *Candidly, Allen Funt: A Million Smiles Later* (with Philip Reed) was published in 1994. He wrote two other books: *Candid Camera: Eavesdropper at Large* (1952), and *Candid Kids* (1964). Funt donated his records and films to Cornell University. Obituaries are in the *New York Times* (6 Sept. 1999) and *Los Angeles Times* (7 Sept. 1999).

RUBIL MORALES VÁZQUEZ

G

GADDIS, William (*b.* 29 December 1922 in New York City; *d.* 16 December 1998 in East Hampton, New York), modernist writer known for his complex satire and dark comedy, particularly in *The Recognitions* (1955) and *J R* (1975).

Gaddis's father, William Thomas Gaddis, worked on Wall Street and in politics, and his mother, Edith Gaddis, was an executive for the New York Steam Corporation. When Gaddis, an only child, was three, his parents separated, and he was raised by his mother in suburban Massapequa on Long Island. Gaddis's mother first sent him to a Congregationalist boarding school in Berlin, Connecticut. However, he completed grammar school on Long Island and then attended Farmingdale High School, graduating in 1941. A kidney disorder kept him out of World War II, during which time he studied English literature at Harvard College in Cambridge, Massachusetts (1941–1945). Found guilty of rowdiness, Gaddis was asked to leave the college in 1945, his senior year.

After leaving Harvard, Gaddis moved to New York City, where he worked as a fact checker for the *New Yorker*. He did not remain in the position for long, choosing to venture abroad. Gaddis recalled spending the next five years "in Central America and the Caribbean, Europe mainly Spain, and briefly North Africa before returning to complete the partially written novel [*The Recognitions*] finally published in 1955." At nearly 1,000 pages, *The Recognitions* was described by some critics as a novel in the league of Herman

Melville's *Moby-Dick* (1851) and James Joyce's *Ulysses* (1922). It was an encyclopedic work, centered around a group of artists and would-be artists living in Greenwich Village in the 1950s, the time when abstract expressionism was dominant. Episodes of the novel also took place in France, Central America, Spain, Italy, and North Africa. Gaddis created a large cast of characters with one, Wyatt Gwyon, who somewhat resembled a traditional protagonist. Gaddis portrayed Gwyon as a talented artist, working outside the prevailing abstractionist mode, who lacks the wherewithal to overcome the contemporary standard of aesthetic judgment. Gwyon makes a Faustian pact with the devil, embodied by the art dealer and businessman Recktall Brown, and begins painting expert forgeries of Flemish masterworks. By drawing contrasts between fifteenth-century Flanders and twentieth-century Europe and America, Gaddis used the novel to examine and question contemporary societal values.

Although *The Recognitions* later was considered one of the great American novels of the twentieth century, its initial reception from the critical community was one of bafflement and misunderstanding. The young Gaddis earned resentment for presuming that, at age thirty-three, he could write a fictional masterpiece in his first attempt. The most damning criticism came from the Marxist critic Granville Hicks, who, in the influential *New York Times Book Review,* wrote that Gaddis had "ostentatiously aimed at writing a masterpiece" but had produced a novel that was "no

William Gaddis. AP/WIDE WORLD PHOTOS

more than very talented or highly ingenious or, on another level, rather amusing." Gaddis described the critics' response to his novel as "a sobering experience." During this period, he married Pat Black, an actress from North Carolina, in 1955. They had two children and were divorced in the late 1960s. In 1968 he married Judith Thompson; the couple later divorced in 1978.

Unable to make a living from his writing, Gaddis supported his family by taking up corporate public relations work, assisting companies such as Pfizer, Kodak, and IBM. He turned these experiences to extraordinary advantage in his next novel, *J R* (1975). A 700-page work that was even more ambitious than *The Recognitions, J R* received the prestigious National Book Award in 1976. In his second book, Gaddis attempted to write a seamless narrative that was without chapters, sections, or even the introduction of speakers and involved scores of characters, most of whom existed as little more than overheard voices. Only the brilliantly rendered J R, a sixth grader, resembled a protagonist. J R, through a combination of sheer chutzpah and rank innocence, manages, while keeping his identity a secret, to build a corporate empire based upon junk bonds. Gaddis's satire anticipated America's later infatuation with junk-bond capitalism, while questioning the country's substitution of capitalism for a more sustaining cultural or spiritual telos.

In his next novel, *Carpenter's Gothic* (1985), Gaddis aspired to write a short narrative composed of the genre's understood maxims. He explained, "When I started I thought, 'I want 240 pages'—that was what I set out for. It preserved the unity: one place, one very small amount of time, very small group of characters, and then, in effect, there's a nicer word than 'cliché,' what is it? 'Staples.' That is, the staples of the marriage, which is on the rocks, the obligatory adultery, the locked room, the mysterious stranger, the older man and the younger woman, to try to take these and make them work." Gaddis achieved his literary aims by creating a bleak narrative that examined the tragicomic relationship between a woman down on her luck and her shadowy landlord. *Carpenter's Gothic* offered a biting critique of the U.S. military and corporate manipulations in the world's poorer countries, in contrast to Americans' general optimism in the late 1980s.

A Frolic of His Own (1994), which won the National Book Award in 1994, was the last novel that Gaddis published before his death. A send-up of the U.S. legal profession, it combined a wonderful sense of humor with a hankering for justice, centered around the hapless protagonist Oscar Crease. A community college professor, Crease pursues two lawsuits—one a negligence suit, the other a copyright infringement suit—through the courts, only to end up wishing that he had never left the quiet of his home. The novel provided a meditation upon justice, with Crease balanced by the character of Christina, his half sister and a woman possessed of a deeply caring and thoughtful nature.

In 1998 Gaddis died from prostate cancer at age seventy-five. He is buried in Oakwood Cemetery in Sag Harbor, New York. Shortly before his death, he completed work on a fifth, unpublished novel, *Agape Agape,* about "the secret history of the player piano," a subject important to the character Jack Gibbs in *J R.* Gaddis's novels place him in the company of such American practitioners as Nathaniel Hawthorne, Herman Melville, Henry James, William Faulkner, and Thomas Pynchon.

★

Gaddis discouraged interest in his private life, wishing readers to focus on his novels. For reviews of his works, see Steven Moore, *A Reader's Guide to William Gaddis's "The Recognitions"* (1982); *William Gaddis* (1989); John Johnston, *Carnival of Repetition: Gaddis's "The Recognitions" and Postmodern Theory* (1990); Gregory Comnes, *The Ethics of Indeterminacy in the Novels of William Gaddis* (1994); and Christopher J. Knight, *Hints and Guesses: William Gaddis's Fiction of Longing* (1997). The collection of essays edited by Steven Moore and John Kuehl, *In Recognition of William Gaddis* (1984), is also worthwhile. Obituaries are in the *New York Times* (17 Dec. 1998), *Newsday* (18 Dec. 1998), and *Economist* (2 Jan. 1999).

CHRISTOPHER J. KNIGHT

GARRITY, W(endell) Arthur, Jr. (*b.* 20 June 1920 in Worcester, Massachusetts; *d.* 16 September 1999 in Wellesley, Massachusetts), federal judge whose 1974 ruling ordering Boston to desegregate its schools ignited massive urban violence.

Garrity was the eldest of four children of Wendell Arthur Garrity, a prominent local lawyer, and Mary B. Kennedy, a former schoolteacher active in church and community affairs. Following in the footsteps of his Irish-American father, Garrity graduated in 1941 with an A.B. degree from the College of the Holy Cross and in 1946 with an LL.B. degree from Harvard Law School. His studies were interrupted in 1943 when he served as a sergeant in the army during World War II until 1945; he was awarded the Bronze Arrowhead for his participation in the Normandy invasion.

From 1946 to 1947 Garrity clerked for U.S. District Judge Francis J. W. Ford; he was an assistant U.S. attorney for the next three years. In 1950 Garrity entered private practice, becoming a partner in the law firm of Maguire, Roche, and Leen. He married Barbara ("Bambi") A. Mullins, an elementary schoolteacher, on 24 May 1952. The

W. Arthur Garrity, Jr., 1985. ASSOCIATED PRESS AP

couple had four children. Garrity worked for John F. Kennedy's successful 1952 and 1958 Senate campaigns. His efforts during Kennedy's 1960 run for the presidency were rewarded in 1961 when he was appointed U.S. attorney for the District Court of Massachusetts. His lengthy and controversial judicial career commenced in 1966, when, at the urging of Senator Edward Kennedy, he was nominated to the U.S. District Court of Massachusetts by President Lyndon B. Johnson.

The ruling that catapulted Garrity from relative obscurity to the media spotlight was rendered on 21 June 1974. Judge Garrity, assigned the case via lottery, ruled in *Morgan* v. *Hennigan* that the Boston School Committee had "knowingly carried out a systematic program of segregation affecting all of the city's students, teachers and school facilities and . . . intentionally brought about and maintained a dual school system." Evidence supporting these charges, including a policy that set the size and location of new school buildings so as to encourage segregation, was set forth in his 152-page opinion, which took fifteen months to prepare. Although Boston's schools were not, he wrote, formally segregated, they did demonstrate a pattern of de facto racial distribution that had to be corrected. Six months later the Court of Appeals upheld the ruling. The U.S. Supreme Court effectively concurred when it declined to hear the case.

Judge Garrity's remedy of choice was immediate, citywide busing. On 12 September 1974 the formerly benign, banal, banana-yellow school bus became the symbol and literal target of racial and class violence. Its sides were pelted with rocks and bottles, its underbelly was laced with Molotov cocktails and homemade bombs, and petrified passengers were bathed in taunts and curses. Images were on the news nightly and stories in the papers daily for the global community to see. Students of both races, ordinary people in the "wrong place at the wrong time," were stabbed and beaten, prompting calls to the National Guard. A city that Americans regard as the cradle of liberty and tolerance was birthing the mother of all urban riots. Hatred and resentment extended beyond the expected blacks against whites, however. Lower-class Irish in Charlestown and South Boston railed against the upper cadres of their own ethnic group—judges, journalists, law enforcement officers, and academics—whom they regarded as traitors, bleeding heart liberals, and duplicitous do-gooders.

Judge Garrity not only authored the tumultuous ruling but also managed its tortuous execution in every detail. He issued four hundred court orders exhibiting a nonjudicious "hands-on" approach regarded as extreme by supporters and out of control by critics. The first phase of his plan was followed eight months later by the second phase. On 10 May 1975 Garrity announced that he would double the number of children bused. The ferocious resistance to busing was aimed at the judge as well. Garrity received credible death threats; at least two attempts were made on his life. Demonstrators freely surrounded 40 Radcliff Road, his home in upscale Wellesley, harassing his family. In scenes reminiscent of pre-Revolutionary Boston, he was burned in effigy on city streets and squares. He remained under guard by U.S. Marshals every hour of every day from 1974 to 1978. Even so, the judge opined in a 1998 television interview, "I still think that given the circumstances that existed at the time, what I did was reasonable."

On 3 September 1985 Garrity withdrew from his overarching role in the case; the same year he took senior status on the bench. On 31 May 1989 he ruled that Boston could implement a "controlled choice" plan for students' school designations. The federal court's jurisdiction in the matter finally ended 31 May 1990. In the summer of 1999, with white children making up less than 20 percent of the school population (since September 1995), the Boston School Committee dropped race as a factor in pupil assignment. That September, just as another term was beginning, Garrity's life was coming to a quiet close. Twenty-five years after his famous directive, he succumbed to cancer at his Wellesley home at age seventy-nine. He is buried in Woodlawn Cemetery in Wellesley.

To this day the landmark ruling and the unyielding judge are subjects of hot debate. Opponents claim that Garrity destroyed the city by precipitating "white flight." Victims of busing label themselves the "lost generation" whose futures were severely compromised by the education they received, or rather the education they did not receive. During busing's early years, many "Southies" boycotted the schools and stayed home. Proponents counter that the tireless judge was a hero and defender of equal protection under the law. Commenting on his colleague, the district court's chief judge, William G. Young, declared that Garrity's ruling "was among the half-dozen most important decisions from this court in two hundred years."

★

Garrity's papers on the Boston busing decision are held in the Healey Library at the University of Massachusetts, Boston. The former *New York Times* correspondent J. Anthony Lukas won the Pulitzer Prize in 1986 for his book *Common Ground* (1985), in which he describes in graphic and jarring detail the Boston busing wars. This is the most complete and contextual source for researching the judge—his life, his persona, and his ruling. James S. Kunen wrote "The End of Integration," *Time* (29 Apr. 1996). Obituaries are in the *New York Times* and *Boston Globe* (both 18 Sept. 1999).

FRANCES PULLE

GATES, William ("Pop") (*b.* 30 August 1917 in Decatur, Alabama; *d.* 1 December 1999 in New York City), professional basketball player and coach who gained fame as a member of the New York Renaissance basketball team and who was elected to the Basketball Hall of Fame.

Gates was one of three children of Dan Gates and Lulu Gates. His family moved to New York City in 1920 and settled in Harlem. Young William was big for his age, so he often played in stickball games with older boys. Because of his size, his peers called him "Pop," a moniker that stayed with him for the rest of his life. Gates played basketball at the local 135th Street YMCA as well as for semi-professional teams, including the Harlem Yankees and the Passaic Crescents.

While attending Benjamin Franklin High School in Harlem from 1934 to 1938, Gates played on the varsity basketball team for four years, leading his team to the Public School Athletic League (PSAL) championship in 1938. He was named all-city center and was captain of his high school team for three years. Following graduation from high school, Gates enrolled at Clark College in Atlanta, Georgia, in the fall of 1938, but he left college a month

William "Pop" Gates at his induction into the National Basketball Hall of Fame, 1989. SUSAN WALSH/ASSOCIATED PRESS AP

later without ever playing for the basketball team. He then signed an agreement to play for the New York Renaissance (the Rens) in late November 1938, probably the best professional basketball team at that time.

In the decade before Gates joined the team, the Rens achieved an eighty-eight-game winning streak and regularly defeated all the top teams in the sport. Beginning in 1927, for fifteen years the Rens won at least 107 games each year and never lost more than 23 in a season. In 1939 the team won the World Pro Tournament. Gates was twenty-one years old and six feet, two (or three) inches tall when he became a member of this veteran team. The Rens were a top draw whenever they played out of town. In late December 1938, after a number of poorly attended games on the Rens's home court, the Renaissance Casino Ballroom, the team's owner, Bob Douglas, decided to play the rest of their games on the road. However, team members were subjected to Jim Crow laws in the South and similar discriminatory practices in parts of the Midwest. Gates and the other players often stayed in private homes and ate out of grocery bags while traveling because they were denied service at many hotels and restaurants.

Gates played with the Rens for the next six years, eventually becoming one of their starters. In 1943 he took a job with Grumman Aviation on Long Island, New York, but he continued to play basketball, including with three of the top black teams at the time: the Paterson Crescents, the Harlem Yankees, and the Washington Bears. He also played for the Grumman Flyers, a racially mixed team that took third in the 1942 World Pro Tournament. The next year Gates played for the Washington Bears when they became the world champions.

Gates was one of four black players, including "Dolly" King, Bill Farrow, and Willie King, who signed with the National Basketball League (NBL) in 1946. Although the four were not the first African Americans in the NBL—six black players had played for the Chicago Studebakers in 1942—the 1946 contingent was the first to play on more than one professional team, an achievement that helped to truly integrate the league. That same year, on 26 November, Gates married Cleo Pennington. Gates played for the Tri-City Blackhawks of Moline, Illinois, Rock Island, Illinois, and Davenport, Iowa. During his first season he was involved in what some have called a "nasty episode" with a white player from Syracuse. Asserting that the player threw him to the floor twice during a game, Gates challenged him to a fight. The subsequent encounter was quickly broken up, but the NBL, fearing more interracial incidents, decided to return to segregation in the league the next year.

In 1948 black players returned to the NBL but in an unusual manner. After the Detroit Vagabonds franchise withdrew from the league in December 1948, the entire Rens roster joined the league as the Dayton Rens playing out of Dayton, Ohio. They took on the Vagabonds' 2–17 record. Gates coached and played, averaging eleven points per game. However, a number of the great Rens players, including "Wee" Willie Smith, Dolly King, and John Isaacs, were past their prime and did not perform as well. The Rens went 14–26 and failed to return the next season. In his two seasons in the NBL, Gates averaged 7.6 and 11.2 points per game, respectively.

In the 1949 season Gates became the player-coach of the Harlem Globetrotters, a team that was both a traveling spectacle and a legitimate basketball squad. The previous year the Globetrotters had triumphed over the Minneapolis Lakers to win the World Pro Tournament held in Chicago Stadium and sponsored by the *Chicago American* newspaper. Gates was the only player who appeared in all ten pro basketball world tournaments from 1939 to 1948. In 1943 Gates and other former Rens had played for the Washington Bears, that year's tournament winner. Gates remained player-coach for the Globetrotters for five seasons until he left the game in 1955. He was also player-coach for the Scranton Miners in 1949–1950.

After he retired from basketball, Gates worked as a security supervisor for the New York City Department of Social Services from 1961 to 1968. He was elected a charter member of the New York City Basketball Hall of Fame in 1994. According to his wife, he was preparing to go to the hospital after a fall in their Harlem apartment when, at age seventy-two, he suffered a fatal heart attack. Gates is buried in New York City.

Although he was a center in high school, Gates primarily played forward during his professional career, and he became a guard near the end of his years with the Rens. He was a great ball handler with an excellent shot. At his induction into the Basketball Hall of Fame, Gates recalled that he "averaged 14 points a game when 14 were a lot of points," as stated in the *New York Times*. He is remembered as one of the first black basketball players who integrated the professional teams and the national league. Of course his basketball skills allowed him to achieve that breakthrough.

★

The James Naismith Memorial Basketball Hall of Fame in Springfield, Massachusetts, has a file on Gates. Little has been published on Gates or the Rens. Susan Rayl, "The New York Renaissance Professional Black Basketball Team, 1923–1950," Ph.D. diss., Pennsylvania State University, has excellent sources and commentary on Gates. An obituary is in the *New York Times* (5 Dec. 1999).

MURRY R. NELSON

GELLHORN, Martha Ellis (*b.* 8 November 1908 in St. Louis, Missouri; *d.* 15 February 1998 in London, England), novelist and war correspondent who covered many of the chief conflicts of the twentieth century.

Gellhorn was born into a prominent St. Louis family. Her father, George Gellhorn, was one of the city's leading physicians; her mother, Edna Fischel, was nationally known for her work on women's suffrage and other reforms. Martha had three brothers, all of whom achieved success in life. The Gellhorn family was liberal, sophisticated, and urbane. Their home was filled with music, books, and stimulating conversation. They traveled widely, and the children were encouraged to develop independent views and to express their opinions freely. Martha's first nine years of school were at Mary Institute, a private school for girls. She then enrolled in the new John Burroughs School, a progressive coeducational institution founded by a group that included her mother. Upon graduation in 1926, she enrolled in Bryn Mawr College in Baltimore, her mother's alma mater. Exhibiting the independence that characterized her adult life, she dropped out of college at the end of her junior year, much to her family's dismay.

From childhood Gellhorn knew she wanted to be a writer. While still a high school student, she published forty-two poems in the *John Burroughs Review.* She worked for a time as a reporter for the *Albany Tribune,* also writing

Martha Gellhorn, 1940. CORBIS CORPORATION (BELLEVUE)

book reviews in 1927 for the *New Republic* and articles for the *St. Louis Post-Dispatch.* Always seeking new experiences, she went to Paris, France, in 1930. She had little money, paying for her transatlantic passage and travels in Europe by writing articles for various magazines and newspapers in the United States.

While in Geneva, Switzerland, Gellhorn met Bertrand de Jouvenal, an aspiring journalist from a prominent French diplomatic family. The two traveled together for a few months and were married in 1933. Gellhorn soon grew tired of the marriage, which was marked by long separations, and obtained a divorce in 1935.

In 1934, during the Great Depression, Gellhorn returned to the United States and secured a job from Harry Hopkins, head of the Federal Emergency Relief Administration. Her task was to travel the country to observe conditions among the poor and report on the effectiveness of the relief effort. She was horrified by what she found and wrote Hopkins a series of scathing reports. They came to the attention of First Lady Eleanor Roosevelt, who greatly admired her work. Gellhorn became one of Roosevelt's close friends and was a frequent guest at the White House. She published her first novel, *What Mad Pursuit,* in 1934.

In 1936 she published her second book, *The Trouble I've Seen* (1936), about the effects of the Great Depression on ordinary people. That same year, while vacationing with her mother in Key West, she met the author Ernest Hemingway, whose writing she had long admired. Hemingway, in turn, was infatuated with the beautiful, well-dressed blonde. Gellhorn and Hemingway traveled together in Spain, where Gellhorn reported during 1937 and 1938 on the Spanish Civil War for *Collier's,* the first of many assignments from that magazine. In 1940, after living together in Cuba, traveling in Europe and the United States, and reporting on the war, Gellhorn and Hemingway were married. They traveled to China, where Gellhorn reported in 1940 and 1941 on the Sino-Japanese war. In addition to her work for *Collier's,* she also published the novels *A Stricken Field* (1940), *Heart of Another* (1941), and *Liana* (1944). The marriage lasted four tempestuous years. The complex personal and professional jealousies of their relationship and Hemingway's heavy drinking caused the relationship to end in a bitter separation in 1944. The couple divorced in 1945. Thereafter, Gellhorn resented being identified as "Hemingway's third wife."

Following her breakup with Hemingway, Gellhorn continued to report on the war in Europe. She went ashore at Normandy, France, on 7 June 1944, the day after the Allied invasion. Lacking proper credentials, she made the trip across the English Channel hidden in the bathroom of a hospital ship. Once ashore, she followed the war into Italy and across central Europe. She was at the Nazi concentration camp at Dachau on 7 May 1945, the day the Germans surrendered. Her European war reports, published in *Collier's,* brilliantly described the horrors of war.

After the war, hoping to find a permanent home, Gellhorn bought a house in London. She worked on a play with Virginia Cowles, *Love Goes to Press* (1946), which had a successful run. She covered the Nuremberg war crimes trials, the Paris peace talks, and the Dutch-Indonesian war. She then returned to the United States but soon became disillusioned with its complacent prosperity. After less than a year, she transferred her base to Quernavaca, Mexico. She spent approximately five happy, productive years there, publishing *The Wine of Astonishment* (1948) and *The Honeyed Peace* (1953). She also adopted a fifteen-month-old baby boy named Sandro, christened George Alexander Gellhorn but called "Sandy."

When Sandy reached school age, Gellhorn moved to Rome, Italy, where educational opportunities were better. She soon tired of living among the Italians and returned to London, which remained her home for the rest of her life. In 1954 she married Thomas Matthews, retired editor of *Time.* The marriage lasted a decade. Gellhorn's restless wanderlust could not accommodate itself to Matthews's desire for domestic tranquility. During the years of that marriage she published *Two by Two* (1958), *The Face of War* (1959), and *His Own Man* (1961). After her divorce, *Pretty Tales for Tired People* (1965) was published.

In 1966 Gellhorn was in Saigon reporting on the Vietnam War for the *Guardian.* Her dispatches were highly critical of the American effort. She published *Vietnam: A New Kind of War* in 1966. *Travels with Myself and Another,* originally published in 1978 and rereleased in 2001, is considered to be one of her most interesting books and recounts her extensive travels in the Far East, and in Europe with Hemingway. In her seventies Gellhorn covered conflicts in Nicaragua and El Salvador, and at age eighty-one the American invasion of Panama. When civil war erupted in Bosnia, she decided she was too old to go. She spent the last years of her life as a literary celebrity in her flat on Cadogan Square in London. She died of cancer at age eighty-nine; her ashes were spread in the Thames River.

Gellhorn thought of herself primarily as a novelist. Her novels received mixed reviews. None became a best-seller, although several were reprinted. A series of republications in the 1980s brought new attention to Gellhorn's novels. It is on her remarkable career as a pioneering war correspondent that Gellhorn's enduring reputation rests. She was, as Ward Just wrote in the *New York Times* after her death, "the premier war correspondent of the twentieth century."

★

Gellhorn's papers (closed until 2023) are in the department of special collections, Boston University. Karl Rollyson, *Nothing Ever Happens to the Brave: The Story of Martha Gellhorn* (1990), is the best, most available biography. Useful but less available is Jacqueline Elizabeth Orsagh, *A Critical Biography of Martha Gellhorn* (1977). Most biographies of Ernest Hemingway contain material on Gellhorn. See, especially, Carlos Baker, *Ernest Hemingway: A Life Story* (1969). Bernice Kert, *The Hemingway Women* (1983), provides an intimate account of the Gellhorn-Hemingway affair, marriage, and divorce. In the months following Gellhorn's death, there was a spate of articles about her. Among the best are Mary Blume, "Martha Gellhorn: A Life of Wit and Rage," *International Herald Tribune* (19 Feb. 1998); Martha Gellhorn, with an introduction by Bill Buford, "The Correspondent," *New Yorker* (22 and 29 June 1998); and Ward Just, "War: From Both Sides," *New York Times Magazine* (3 Jan. 1999). An obituary is in the *New York Times* (17 Feb. 1998).

JAMES C. OLSON

GENEEN, Harold Sydney (*b.* 22 January 1910 in Bournemouth, England; *d.* 21 November 1997 in New York City), innovative chief executive of International Telephone and Telegraph Corporation who through hundreds of acquisitions introduced the idea of the conglomerate.

Geneen was the son of Sydney Alexander Geneen, a Russian concert manager, and Aida DeCruciani, an English

Harold S. Geneen, 1974. ASSOCIATED PRESS/ITT CORP.

singer of light opera. The family immigrated to the United States when Geneen was one year old, and his parents later separated. He had one sister. In 1918 he became an American citizen. His high school years were spent at Suffield Academy, a boarding school in Suffield, Connecticut, from which he graduated in 1927. He enrolled in evening classes at New York University in 1930 and worked as a page for the New York Stock Exchange during the day.

After graduating with a B.S. degree in accounting and finance in 1934, Geneen began working at the Manhattan accounting firm of Lybrand, Ross Brothers and Montgomery. He left in 1942 to become chief accountant at the American Can Company. From 1946 to 1950 he served as controller at Bell and Howell Company in Chicago. Geneen's first marriage ended in 1946, and in December 1949 he married June Elizabeth Hjelm, his secretary at Bell and Howell; they had no children. The next year Geneen joined Jones and Laughlin Steel Corporation in Pittsburgh, Pennsylvania, where a colleague once observed him inspecting ledgers "like a bloodhound on the trail of a wasted dollar." While at Jones and Laughlin, he completed an advanced management program at Harvard Business School in Cambridge, Massachusetts, where he determined that he would make a change in employment.

In 1956 Geneen accepted the position of executive vice president of the then-ailing Raytheon Manufacturing Company, headquartered in Waltham, Massachusetts. His mandate from Raytheon's president, Charles Francis Adams, was to "make some money." Geneen complied by imposing strict measures to control costs, increasing working capital, and persuading banks to open new lines of credit. He insisted that Raytheon pay its bills promptly to receive standard discounts and dunned customers for debts outstanding.

At Raytheon, Geneen developed the basic system of management that he would perfect and become internationally renowned for in management circles. In an article in the *Christian Science Monitor* (19 May 1959), he described his management style. The company was divided into twelve semiautonomous divisions, with the head of each division responsible for all aspects of operation but under constant scrutiny by top management. Geneen focused especially on a comprehensive analysis of each division's five-year policies, plans, sales, and capital requirements.

Although Geneen increased Raytheon's earnings by 400 percent, he was never given absolute control and resigned in 1959 to assume the position of president and chief executive officer (CEO) of International Telephone and Telegraph Corporation (ITT). Founded by Colonel Sosthenes Behn in 1920, ITT manufactured telephone and telegraph equipment, operated telephone companies in Central America and the Caribbean, and built communications networks for the U.S. Department of Defense. After

ITT took a beating in World War II, Behn tried to find a new market in the postwar economy of the United States. By and large, this had proved futile, and Behn died in 1957, bitter and discouraged.

When Geneen came to the company, ITT was concentrated on the foreign telephone business and had sales of less than $800 million. Over the next two decades, Geneen transformed ITT into an international conglomerate by acquiring more than 350 companies, including such diversified firms as the Sheraton hotel chain, Avis Rent-A-Car, Continental Baking Company, and the Hartford Insurance Company. By 1970 ITT comprised more than 400 separate companies operating in 70 countries.

ITT's sweep of acquisitions stirred debate about the role of an individual in a corporation. He was a workaholic obsessed with detail. More than 100 managers furnished him with detailed weekly reports. In Europe, Geneen's system of control took the form of a monthly invasion. On the last Monday of each month, Geneen and sixty ITT executives flew from New York City to ITT's offices in Brussels, Belgium, for four days of meetings. While a large screen displayed endless statistics, Geneen would rock in his armchair in the center of the meeting room and watch the faces of those around him as they gazed at the screen. He knew every aspect of ITT's European and domestic operations and made certain that his employees did too.

Purchased for $1.4 billion in 1970, the Hartford Insurance Company was ITT's largest acquisition under Geneen's tenure. Following the takeover, the U.S. Justice Department filed an antitrust suit against ITT. An out-of-court settlement in 1971 allowed the company to retain the insurance company on the condition that it divest itself of several other holdings. In 1972 an ITT scandal emerged when a memo written by the company's Washington lobbyist, Dita Beard, appeared to link the settlement of the antitrust suit with a $400,000 contribution that ITT had pledged toward the 1972 Republican convention in San Diego. There were also allegations that ITT had conspired with the Central Intelligence Agency to sabotage the 1970 presidential bid of Socialist Party candidate Salvador Allende in Chile, who had promised to nationalize the ITT-owned Chilean Telephone Company. Geneen admitted to the accusation involving Allende but denied that ITT's contribution to the Republican convention was related to the Justice Department's antitrust suit.

When Geneen stepped down as head of ITT in 1977, the company was the eleventh largest industrial firm in the nation, with over 300,000 employees worldwide and sales of almost $17 billion. He stayed on as chairman until 1979 and as a member of the board of directors until 1983. After that point, Geneen continued to buy and sell companies from his office in the Waldorf-Astoria Hotel in New York City. Although work was an all-consuming passion, he fished, played golf, and enjoyed photography, Dixieland jazz, and banjo picking. Geneen died at age eighty-seven in New York Hospital after suffering a massive heart attack.

★

Geneen's correspondence and papers are housed in the Thomas F. Keller Center for M.B.A. Education at the Fuqua School of Business at Duke University in Durham, North Carolina. The Keller Center also houses the Harold S. Geneen Auditorium. Geneen gives a detailed description of his management style in his book with Alvin Moscow, *Managing* (1984). See also Geneen's *The Synergy Myth: And Other Ailments of Business Today* (1997), with Brent Bowers, and *Synergy and Other Lies: Downsizing, Bureaucracy, and Corporate Culture Debunked* (1998), also with Bowers. One biography of the corporate entrepreneur was written: Robert J. Schoenberg, *Geneen* (1985). Anthony Sampson, *The Sovereign State of ITT* (1973), includes coverage of the scandals that tarnished ITT's image in the early 1970s. Geneen appeared on the cover of *Time* (8 Sept. 1967) and was featured in the accompanying article, "Conglomerates: The New Business Giants." See also "The De-Geneening of ITT," *Fortune* (11 Jan. 1982). Obituaries are in the *New York Times* and *Washington Post* (both 23 Nov. 1997).

BETTY B. VINSON

GILL, Brendan (*b.* 4 October 1914 in Hartford, Connecticut; *d.* 27 December 1997 in New York City), prominent journalist and editor at the *New Yorker* who also wrote poems, short stories, novels, plays, reviews, and biographies.

Gill was the son of Michael Henry Richard Gill, a well-known Hartford physician and surgeon, and Elizabeth Pauline Duffy, a homemaker. Gill credited his father with helping him to develop a lifelong interest in reading. His father also bribed Gill and his five siblings to memorize long passages from the works of William Shakespeare, Sir Walter Scott, and William Cowper, the English preromantic poet, and paid them $1 per line. As a result, Gill not only made considerable amounts of money as a child—a sonnet would finance a weekend's pleasure in the 1920s—but also had thousands of lines of verse, especially passages from Shakespeare's plays, at hand for the rest of his life.

Gill also attributed the development of his literary proclivities to his mother's side of the family, the Bowens. Although he lost his mother when he was only seven years old, he remembered her reciting and singing from a vast repertoire of Irish tales and songs, which she had learned by heart from her Irish immigrant parents and grandparents, who came from County Leitrim. His mother's sister wrote many stories and a few novels, which were never published. Gill's aunt, however, gave him a strong sense of literary and cultural legacy that came down from eighteenth-century Ireland.

Brendan Gill. AP/WIDE WORLD PHOTOS

Gill attended grammar school and country-day school in Hartford, where he earned high grades, especially in literary studies. Even though he seriously entertained the notion of becoming a doctor like his father, or even a Catholic priest, he kept returning to writing. At age ten he began publishing poems in local newspapers. He sometimes signed them "By a Ten-Year-Old Boy" or "Brendan Gill, a Ten-Year-Old Boy." He claimed that this early success in publishing "infected" him with the lifelong disease of a writer's vocation.

By the time he was twelve years old, Gill had become the editor of his grammar school newspaper and literary magazine, the *Noah Webster Trumpeter.* He also became the editor of several publications at his high school, Hartford Day School, a prestigious preparatory school. Here, he won his first literary prize, for writing a long, narrative poem that contained echoes of his favorite poets: Walt Whitman, Edwin Arlington Robinson, Edgar Lee Masters, Robinson Jeffers, and Robert Frost. Gill attended Yale College in New Haven, Connecticut, and served as the editor of the *Yale Literary Magazine* during his four years there. At Yale, he became acquainted with Frost at one of the poet's readings; later Gill would interview Frost for a "Talk of the Town" piece in the *New Yorker,* but Gill became somewhat disillusioned with the poet as a person, and he

223

decided to scrap the project. Gill also became friendly with Wallace Stevens, a poet he held in high regard and who was his sister's neighbor. Gill's favorite poet, however, was William Butler Yeats.

While at Yale, Gill intended to become a lawyer, because most of his male relatives were either doctors or lawyers. At the same time his interest in architecture grew stronger. Gill's first love during his Yale years, however, was poetry, and he often claimed that poems were somatic manifestations for young men and women, that it was "a natural part of adolescence to become a poet." He published his first book, a collection of poems, at Yale and called it *Death in April and Other Poems* (1935), which won him his second literary prize. Gill received his B.A. degree in 1936. He married Anne Barnard on 20 June 1936; they had seven children.

Gill's short stories were first published in the *New Yorker*. He claimed that what got his stories noticed and then published was their subject matter. The WASP (White Anglo-Saxon Protestant) editors there were attracted to the novel Irish-Catholic backgrounds of Gill's protagonists. Gill asserted that the magazine's managing editor, Harold Ross, was actually terrified of priests and nuns. Once Gill used up his Irish-Catholic subject matter, he discovered another recurring theme emerging in his two novels and several of his more important short stories: fear of abandonment, a predictable theme given the early loss of his mother.

As a regular contributor to the *New Yorker* from 1936 until 1997, Gill occupied several editorial positions during those years. He was the film critic (1960–1967), drama critic (1968–1987), and author of the architecture column "The Sky Line" (1987–1997). Throughout his time at the *New Yorker* he wrote articles for "Reports at Large" and wrote hundreds of "Profiles" and "Talk of the Town" essays. During all of this activity, he continued to publish novels, short stories, plays, and biographies. He also edited books on Cole Porter's songs, a selection of Dorothy Parker poems and stories, Philip Barry plays, and books of photographs.

Gill's first novel, *The Trouble of One House* (1950), examined the social repercussions of the death of an upper-middle-class, Irish-American, Catholic matriarch. His next novel, *The Day the Money Stopped* (1957), concerned the career of the renegade son of a recently deceased New England judge. *The Day the Money Stopped* generally was praised by critics for the author's sensitive ear for dialogue and lyrical prose style. His only collection of short stories was *Ways of Loving: Two Novellas and Eighteen Short Stories* (1974); most critics agreed that Gill's stories were his most enduring literary accomplishment.

Throughout the 1960s, Gill was primarily occupied as a film and drama critic for the *New Yorker*, but he continued to review books of all kinds, particularly those recommended by the managing editor William Shawn, whom Gill greatly respected. One of Gill's notable failures was his inability to interest U.S. readers in the works of Henry Green and Ivy Compton-Burnett, two of his and Shawn's favorite British writers. But Gill saw himself first as a poet, and then as a short-story writer, novelist, and reviewer. He always judged himself in light of his early literary heroes and influences from the nineteenth century: Walt Whitman, Ralph Waldo Emerson, and Henry James. The poets Stevens and Yeats ranked first in Gill's aesthetic pantheon for the twentieth century.

As Gill got older, his range of interests expanded considerably. He began writing biographical studies of celebrities of all kinds. *Tallulah* (1972) was his homage to the legendary actress Tallulah Bankhead. *Cole: A Book of Cole Porter Lyrics and Memorabilia* was published in 1971. However, his most serious biographical work was the critically acclaimed *Lindbergh Alone* (1977), which Gill preferred to call a meditation rather than a biography. Gill's most successful biography was *Many Masks: A Life of Frank Lloyd Wright* (1987). Although Gill criticized Wright's penchant for self-promotion and prevarication, he treated him as a genuine visionary artist and analyzed the process by which Wright created his own heroic public persona.

The book that made Gill an authentic celebrity was his best-selling *Here at the New Yorker,* which was published in 1975 to coincide with the magazine's fiftieth anniversary. The book was primarily anecdotal—some called it high-class gossip—but also was autobiographical, showing Gill's involvement in the day-to-day routine of one of America's most prestigious and influential literary magazines. Gill worked with all four of the *New Yorker's* managing editors, and was particularly revealing on Ross's and Shawn's roles in maintaining the highest possible literary standards. *Here at the New Yorker* also recorded the editorial and creative careers of such writers as E. B. White, Katharine White, William Maxwell, James Thurber, John O'Hara, John Cheever, and John Updike. More than any other modern writers, O'Hara, Cheever, and Updike established their careers through the *New Yorker,* by publishing the bulk of their short stories in the magazine.

Gill also enriched exquisite gossip with stories of the adventures of the Algonquin Round Table, a group that included James Thurber, Dorothy Parker, Walcott Gibbs, Robert Benchley, and Sinclair Lewis, many of whom died at an early age because of their excessive drinking. *Here at the New Yorker* was both a critical and a financial success. It became a Book-of-the-Month selection and the *New York Times* critic John Leonard called it, "A splendid artichoke of anecdotes, in which not merely the heart and leaves but the thistles as well are edible. . . . [Gill's] tales of sudden death, inexplicable failure, impermissible misapprehension, even Nazism, are in this book just as graceful and charming as his tales of practical jokes, personal embarrassment, perfect occasions, surprising kindnesses." Throughout the 1970s and 1980s, Gill published several books about buildings, including *The New York Custom House on Bowling Green* (1976), *Summer Places* (1977), *Saint Patrick's Cathedral: A Centennial History* (1979), *The Dream Comes True: Great Houses of Los Angeles* (1980), *John F. Kennedy Center for the Performing Arts* (1982), and *A Fair Land to Build In: The Architecture of the Empire State* (1984).

Gill's last, and in many ways most controversial, book was *A New York Life: Of Friends and Others* (1990). Described by some as a collective biography, it concerned forty-seven friends and acquaintances Gill had known over a fifty-year period at the *New Yorker*. The book consisted of five- to ten-page biographical entries on such figures as Joseph Alsop, George Plimpton, Eleanor Roosevelt, Brendan Behan, Dorothy Parker, Georges Simenon, and Buster Keaton. Gill's damning portrait of Joseph Campbell, one of the twentieth century's most renowned scholars of mythology, drew thousands of letters of protest. Gill presented Campbell as an unapologetic anti-Semite who was racist, sexist, and a shoddy scholar. Campbell had become, due to his popular *Power of Myth* series on PBS, a modern-day spiritual guru, and Gill's mean-spirited deconstruction of Campbell's heroic status disturbed many of his devotees.

During the last decade of his life, Gill became an activist for all forms of historical preservation and was particularly strident when businessmen threatened to tear down the Grand Central Terminal. He served in many organizations with great enthusiasm: as a board member of the Irish Georgian Society; as vice president of the Victorian Society and the Lincoln Center Film Society; as board chairman of the New York Landmarks Conservancy and the New York Municipal Art Society; and as a member of the board of directors of the Whitney Museum of American Art, Pratt Institute, and MacDowell Colony. He also served as the president of the Institute for Art and Urban Resources. At age eighty-three, Gill died in New York City from a sudden heart attack.

Gill was famous in and around the offices of the *New Yorker* for his reliable and infectuous cheerfulness, his candid honesty, and his genuine gregariousness. He saw his primary role as a citizen and protector of the city of New York. He summarized his life and career at the *New Yorker* by explaining, "I started out at the place where I wanted most to be and with much pleasure and very little labor have remained here since." Few practicing journalists were also critically acclaimed short story writers, novelists, poets, and biographers, but none wrote with the ardor, verve, and urbanity of Brendan Gill.

★

There is no biography of Gill's life and accomplishments. There are short biographical entries and an obituary in *Contem-*

porary Authors, vols. 37, 73, 163 (1973, 1978, 1998). There is a long, informative interview with him by John Baker in Matthew J. Bruccoli, ed., *Conversations with Writers* (1977). Other biographical information can be gleaned from a close reading of *Here at the New Yorker* (1975), and *A New York Life: Of Friends and Others* (1990). An obituary is in the *New York Times* (29 Sept. 1997).

PATRICK MEANOR

GINSBERG, (Irwin) Allen (*b.* 3 June 1926 in Newark, New Jersey; *d.* 5 April 1997 in New York City), Beat Generation poet, teacher, and social activist whose protests against censorship, the criminalization of drug use, and the Vietnam War made him a 1960s cultural icon.

Ginsberg was the youngest of two children born to Louis Ginsberg, a poet and high school English teacher, and Naomi Levy (changed from Livergant), a Russian immigrant and ardent Marxist who was in and out of mental hospitals throughout Ginsberg's youth. Raised just outside of New York City in Paterson, New Jersey, Ginsberg grew up in a household saturated with literature and politics. From his father, Ginsberg inherited a love of poetry and a respect for

Allen Ginsberg. PRINTS AND PHOTOGRAPHS DIVISION, LIBRARY OF CONGRESS

artistic achievement. From his mother, he acquired a social conscience and an empathy for society's outcasts. Naomi's illness put a severe strain on the whole family, but Allen, much of whose early adolescence was spent caring for her, felt it most. To his family, Ginsberg seemed happy and well-adjusted. Troubled by homosexual desires during puberty, however, he himself felt lonely and out of place. Ginsberg graduated from East Side High School at age sixteen in June 1943, with high enough grades to be admitted to Columbia University.

At Columbia, Ginsberg majored in English, taking courses with Lionel Trilling, Mark Van Doren, and Raymond Weaver. His real education, however, took place at the West End Bar on Broadway and 113th Street, where he met and talked late into the night with Lucien Carr, Jack Kerouac, and William Burroughs. Influenced by Arthur Rimbaud, the group sought to create a "New Vision," adopting an artistic credo that stressed the value of self-expression and expanded consciousness. The budding literary movement suffered a severe set back in August 1944 after Carr was arrested for fatally stabbing David Kammerer, a homosexual who had stalked him for several years. Kerouac and Burroughs were held as material witnesses, but Ginsberg escaped any involvement.

In March 1945, after tracing obscenities on his grimy dormitory windows, Ginsberg was suspended from Columbia for one year and referred to a psychiatrist. (Ginsberg was feuding with the dormitory's housekeeper and his actions were designed specifically to get her to wash the windows.) He promptly joined Kerouac and his new bride Edie Parker, Burroughs and his future wife Joan Vollmer, and Hal Chase, a graduate student from Denver, in a large apartment at 419 W. 115th Street. To pay his share of the rent, he worked at various odd jobs, including a dishwasher at Bickford's and a spot welder in the Brooklyn Navy Yard.

While Ginsberg had supported America's entry into World War II, his homosexuality kept him out of the draft. In July, however, he enlisted in the merchant marine and began training at Sheepshead Bay in Brooklyn. After two short sea voyages, he returned to 115th Street, where Burroughs introduced him to Herbert Huncke, a merchant seaman, junkie, and petty thief who initiated the Beat writers into New York's underworld of drugs and crime. Ginsberg's stay at 115th Street was a liberating experience and a formative influence on his life and work. It ended abruptly, however, when Burroughs and Huncke were arrested on separate drug charges, and Vollmer was committed to Bellevue Hospital. Ginsberg took a room near Columbia and finished his coursework in December 1948. He was awarded his bachelor's degree in February 1949.

In the summer of 1948, Ginsberg experienced an auditory hallucination that was to obsess him for years to come. While reading William Blake's poems, he became con-

vinced that he heard Blake's voice chanting "Ah, Sunflower" and "The Sick Rose." Ginsberg later made an exhaustive study of Blake, setting many of his poems to music. His recordings appear on *Allen Ginsberg/William Blake: Songs of Innocence and Experience* (1970) and on a Thin Air video recording *Ginsberg Sings Blake: Songs of Innocence and Experience* (1995).

In February 1949 Huncke turned up at Ginsberg's apartment at 1401 York Avenue. Sick and exhausted, he asked Ginsberg to take him in. After recovering his health, he began a series of burglaries with two old friends, Jack Melody and Priscilla Arminger (also known as Vicki Russell). The thieves stored their loot in Ginsberg's place, making him an accessory to their crimes. Apprehended after a wild car chase on 21 April 1949, Melody led the police to Ginsberg's apartment, where everyone was arrested. A first-time offender with a history of psychological problems, Ginsberg avoided prison by accepting treatment at the New York State Psychiatric Institute of Columbia Presbyterian Hospital. There he met Carl Solomon, a dadaist poet, who became a lifelong friend, and to whom he dedicated his signal poem "Howl."

Released in February 1950, Ginsberg returned to Paterson to live with his father. Badly shaken by his brush with the law, he resolved to conform to society's expectations. He found a short-lived job in a ribbon mill and made friends with William Carlos Williams, who included some of Ginsberg's writing in his epic poem *Paterson* (1951), and who later wrote introductions for *Howl and Other Poems* (1956) and *Empty Mirror* (1961).

Moving to New York City in December 1951, Ginsberg held several jobs, remaining longest in a market research position. Over the next two years, he spent time with old friends, including Kerouac, Carr, and Solomon, and began a lifelong study of Buddhism at the New York Public Library. After traveling for several months through Florida, Cuba, and Mexico, Ginsberg arrived in San Francisco in June 1954. He visited briefly with former lover Neal Cassady, found a marketing research job with Towne-Oller and Associates, and began an affair with Sheila Williams, a young jazz singer. His conformist efforts ended when Robert LaVigne, a painter friend, introduced him to Peter Orlovsky. For Allen, it was love at first sight. After a breakthrough session with his analyst, Ginsberg accepted his homosexuality and moved into 1010 Montgomery Street with Orlovsky. In a promise that Ginsberg took as seriously as any wedding vow, the couple pledged themselves to each other. Although they were later separated for long periods, they remained committed to one another: Orlovsky was at Ginsberg's bedside when he died, and Ginsberg provided for him in his will.

Ginsberg abandoned market research and dedicated himself to becoming a poet. On 7 October 1955, with the help of Kenneth Rexroth, he organized a poetry reading at the Six Gallery, 3119 Fillmore. Several San Francisco poets read, including Gary Snyder, Michael McClure, and Philip Whalen, but it was Ginsberg's electrifying reading of "Howl" that launched the Beat Generation and changed the course of American poetry. Lawrence Ferlinghetti, the founder of City Lights Books, was in attendance. Alluding to Emerson's famous response to Walt Whitman's *Leaves of Grass,* he sent Ginsberg a telegram on 13 October: "I greet you at the beginning of a great career. When do I get the manuscript." Ferlinghetti's publication of *Howl and Other Poems* in 1956 led to his arrest on obscenity charges. The landmark censorship trial that followed turned "Howl" into a cause célèbre. After Judge Clayton Horn ruled that "Howl" was not obscene, sales skyrocketed. By the time of Ginsberg's death, there were over 800,000 copies in print.

During the furor over "Howl," Ginsberg was abroad. In March 1957 he joined Kerouac and Burroughs at the Hotel Muniria in Tangier, where they edited the manuscript of Burroughs's *Naked Lunch* (1958). He spent the summer touring the Mediterranean, before settling into 9 rue Git-le-Coeur, a cheap, Parisian rooming house that soon became known as "The Beat Hotel." While in Paris, he began "Kaddish," his moving tribute to his mother Naomi, who died only two weeks before he left San Francisco. (Kaddish is a Jewish prayer recited by mourners for the dead.)

Returning to New York at the end of July 1958, Ginsberg and Orlovsky moved into "The Croton," a tenement at 170 E. 2nd Street. There, Ginsberg finished "Kaddish" in two drug-fueled marathon writing sessions. His continued experimentation with mind-altering substances, including LSD with Timothy Leary, is reflected in poems like "Laughing Gas," "Mescaline," and "Lysergic Acid" in *Kaddish and Other Poems* (1961).

In March 1961 Ginsberg set out on an extended tour of Europe and the Far East. He met with Martin Buber in Israel and studied with holy men in India. His stay in India deepened his interest in Buddhism and prompted him to rely less on drugs and more on the practice of meditation. The spiritual awakening he experienced on this trip is recorded in "The Change: Kyoto-Tokyo Express" (1963).

Ginsberg returned to the United States in the fall of 1963, just after the publication of *Reality Sandwiches.* In October he participated in his first anti–Vietnam War rally in San Francisco, picketing Madame Nhu, the wife of the South Vietnamese chief of police and sister-in-law of President Diem. Back on Manhattan's Lower East Side, Ginsberg began a long association with singer-songwriter Bob Dylan before traveling to Cuba in 1965, where he was deported for criticizing Castro's policies on homosexuality. He went on to Prague and was crowned *Kral Majales* (King

of the May) by thousands of Czech students, only to be expelled from Czechoslovakia as well.

For the remainder of the 1960s, politics and Vietnam War protests dominated Ginsberg's life and work. In the fall of 1965, he drove across the country, reading at colleges and universities while composing the poems that appeared in *Planet News* (1968) and *The Fall of America* (1972), a collection that won him the National Book Award. In January 1967 he helped organize the Human Be-In in Golden Gate Park, where he is credited with coining the term "flower power." On 5 December 1967 he was arrested along with Dr. Benjamin Spock at an anti-draft rally in New York City. At the Chicago Democratic National Convention on 27 August 1968, Ginsberg chanted "Om" for over six hours in an effort to restore calm as police beat and tear-gassed demonstrators in Lincoln Park.

After Chicago, Ginsberg retreated to a farm he had recently purchased in Cherry Valley, New York, but he found little peace. He broke his hip in an automobile accident in November 1968, and in April 1969 he suffered an attack of Bell's palsy, which disfigured the left side of his face. The death of Jack Kerouac in October 1969 ended the decade on an ominous note.

In the 1970s, however, the bearded, long-haired poet and hippie leader found himself famous. His reading fees increased to over $1,000 and he was eagerly sought after by television talk-show hosts like Merv Griffin and Dick Cavett. A chance meeting with Chögyam Trungpa Rinpoche resulted in Ginsberg's founding, with Anne Waldman, of the Jack Kerouac School of Disembodied Poetics at the Naropa Institute (now University) in Boulder, Colorado, in 1974. That same year, Ginsberg was elected to the American Academy and Institute of Arts and Letters. In 1975 his longtime interest in reuniting poetry and song led to a tour with Bob Dylan's Rolling Thunder Review and to later collaborations with a wide range of musicians, including Philip Glass, Paul McCartney, and the Clash. *First Blues* (1975) reflected Ginsberg's growing interest in the blues as a uniquely American musical form. In February 1979 Ginsberg received the National Arts Club Gold Medal for lifetime achievement.

The 1980s establishment, which had grown out of the upheavals of the 1960s and 1970s, readily embraced the rebel poet who had played a major role in shaping its values. First hired in 1979 as a substitute for the poet John Ashbery, Ginsberg was named Distinguished Professor at Brooklyn College in 1986. Professor Ginsberg, who wore a jacket and tie and kept his beard neatly trimmed, signed a six-book deal with Harper and Row for $160,000 and sold his papers to Stanford University in 1994 for one million dollars. Critics accused him of selling out but Ginsberg remained controversial, even speaking out in support of the North American Man-Boy Love Association (NAMBLA):

"They have a right to talk about the age of consent," he told the *New York Times,* "I see it as a free speech issue."

The publication of Ginsberg's *Collected Poems* in 1984 was a career milestone. Despite the onset of diabetes and other ailments, he refused to slow down. While maintaining a grueling schedule of classes and readings at home and abroad, he managed to complete two major poetry collections, *White Shroud* (1986) and *Cosmopolitan Greetings* (1994). He also began to show his photographs, some of which were included in "Beat Culture and the New America: 1950–1965," an innovative exhibit sponsored by the Whitney Museum in 1995.

In September 1996 Ginsberg moved into a new loft apartment, bought with the proceeds from the sale of his archives in New York City. At the end of March 1997 he learned he had liver cancer, the same disease that killed his father. The doctors gave him six months to live but he died within a week, having just enough time to complete a few last poems, including "Death and Fame." A Buddhist funeral service was held at the Shambhala Meditation Center in New York City on 7 April. Ginsberg's remains were cremated and his ashes divided among the Rocky Mountain Shambhala Center in Colorado, the Jewel Heart Buddhist Center in Ann Arbor, Michigan, and the family plot at B'nai Israel Cemetery in Newark, New Jersey.

At the time of his death, Ginsberg was the most recognizable poet in America, having achieved a degree of fame usually reserved for rock stars. With the publication of *Howl and Other Poems* in 1956, Ginsberg became the spokesman for the Beat Generation, a role that, given his marketing background, uniquely suited him. Throughout his life, he tirelessly promoted the work of his friends, particularly that of Kerouac and Burroughs, turning the Beat Generation into one of world's most celebrated literary movements. The publication of *Kaddish and Other Poems* in 1961 would have assured Ginsberg's reputation as a major poet, but he went on to publish more than thirty-five books, including poetry, essays, letters, and journals. He also appeared in several films, including *Pull My Daisy* (1959), *Don't Look Back* (1967), and *Renaldo and Clara* (1978). Beyond his artistic achievements, Ginsberg will also be remembered for his antiwar activities, his advocacy of drugs, and his openly gay lifestyle. These earned him the enmity of conservative critics like Norman Podhoretz, who accused him of corrupting America's youth, and George Will, who found him symptomatic of a dysfunctional society. But these critics were in the minority. Most, like his friend William Burroughs, saw Ginsberg as "a pioneer of openness and a lifelong model of candor," who, for nearly half a century, had a greater influence on American literature and society than any other poet of his time.

★

Stanford University houses Ginsberg's extensive archive, including his library. Columbia University and the University of Texas at Austin also have significant holdings. Ginsberg's poems are full of autobiographical references, the main reason *Collected Poems* (1984) is organized chronologically. Other published autobiographical sources include the *Yage Letters,* with William S. Burroughs (1963), *Indian Journals* (1970), *To Eberhart from Ginsberg: A Letter About Howl* (1976), *As Ever: The Collected Correspondence of Allen Ginsberg and Neal Cassady* (1977), *Journals: Early Fifties-Early Sixties* (1977), *Straight Hearts' Delight: Love Poems, Selected Letters,* with Peter Orlovsky (1980), *Journals: Mid-Fifties* (1995), and *Family Business: Selected Letters Between a Father and Son* (2001). *Deliberate Prose: Selected Essays 1952–1995* (2000) contains a section devoted to "Autobiographical Fragments." There are five full-length biographies: Jane Kramer, *Allen Ginsberg in America* (1969), a sympathetic, if superficial portrait, born of a *New Yorker* profile (17 and 24 Aug. 1968); Barry Miles, *Ginsberg: A Biography* (1989, revised and expanded edition, 2000), a well-written and serviceable life; Michael Schumacher, *Dharma Lion: A Critical Biography of Allen Ginsberg* (1992), an exhaustively researched and richly detailed life of the poet; Graham Caveney, *Screaming with Joy: The Life of Allen Ginsberg* (1999), an illustrated biography, valuable primarily for its photographs; and Edward Sanders, *The Poetry and Life of Allen Ginsberg,* an epic poem, by a devoted friend, that highlights Ginsberg's political activism. *Spontaneous Mind: Selected Interviews 1958–1996* (2001) features some of Ginsberg's most important interviews, including those in *Paris Review* (spring 1966), *Playboy* (Apr. 1969), and *Gay Sunshine* (Jan./Feb. 1973). Ginsberg's unmistakable voice is preserved in numerous sound recordings, including *Holy Soul Jelly Roll: Poems and Songs 1949–1993* (1994) and *Ballad of the Skeletons* (1996); biographical film documentaries include *Allen Ginsberg: When the Muse Calls Answer* (1989), *The Life and Times of Allen Ginsberg* (1993), and *No More to Say . . . And Nothing to Weep For* (1997), a BBC production aired on cable television as a BRAVO profile in the United States. Obituaries are in the *New York Times* and *Washington Post* (both 6 Apr. 1997) and in the *Village Voice* (15 Apr. 1997).

WILLIAM M. GARGAN

GOIZUETA, Roberto Crispulo (*b.* 18 November 1931 in Havana, Cuba; *d.* 18 October 1997 in Atlanta, Georgia), chief executive officer of the Coca-Cola Company who oversaw the introduction of the highly successfully "Diet Coke" as well as the disastrous "New Coke," and who tripled the company's sales during his tenure.

Goizueta was the son of Crispulo Goizueta, a successful businessman with interests in both architecture and real estate and a significant position in one of the country's major sugar refineries. His mother, Aida Cantera, was heir

Roberto C. Goizueta. ARCHIVE PHOTOS, INC.

to a large sugar plantation. As a boy, Goizueta was heavily influenced by his maternal grandfather, Marcelo Cantera, who imbued the young Goizueta with a philosophy of self-reliance, independence, intellectual rigor, and single-mindedness that served him throughout his career. Goizueta was a shy, serious student who dressed and acted formally even outside of school. His only significant hobby was helping his father breed pedigreed bulldogs that were considered the finest in Cuba. Years later, in 1996, Goizueta and his daughter won a Best of Show award at the famed Westminster Kennel Club show in New York City with a Pembroke Welsh corgi named Fizz.

The young Goizueta attended grammar school at the prestigious Colegio de Belen, a Jesuit-run academy for the children of Cuba's government and business elite. Four years ahead of him was a student from the countryside named Fidel Castro. Goizueta attended Cheshire Academy preparatory school near New Haven, Connecticut, to improve his English, then studied chemistry as a diligent, if unremarkable, student at Yale University. He enjoyed singing American show tunes with his roommates, but was best known for studying hours on end without interruption. On 14 June 1953, a few weeks after Goizueta's graduation from Yale, he married Olguita Casteleiro, the daughter of a prominent Havana merchant. The ceremony was reported as a major social event in Havana's leading newspaper. The Goizuetas had three children, and in 1969 they became naturalized U.S. citizens.

The young Goizueta went to work for his father but quickly decided to buck Cuban tradition and leave the family business to pursue his own career. Answering a "Help Wanted" ad placed anonymously by the Coca-Cola Company, he went to work there on 4 July 1954. His father lent him money to buy 100 shares of Coca-Cola stock, which Goizueta never sold.

Goizueta soon was named production manager of the company's five Cuban bottling plants. After Castro seized power of the government in 1959 and began arresting and seizing assets of the intellectual and business elite, executives at Coca-Cola's headquarters advised Goizueta to leave the country while he could. He sent his children ahead of him to Miami, and he and his wife followed a few weeks later. Many Cuban refugees managed to get much of their wealth out of the country before they fled, but Goizueta always claimed he left with only $200 in his pocket and the 100 shares of Coke stock he had placed at an American bank.

He worked briefly in Miami and then was recruited to Coke's Atlanta headquarters by Paul Austin, then Coke's chief executive officer (CEO). Austin asked Goizueta to serve as a consultant as he introduced modern and professional management methods into the company. In 1966 Austin named Goizueta to oversee the company's research laboratories. This entitled Goizueta, in 1974, to become one of only two people at the company allowed to memorize the "secret formula" to make the syrup that is mixed with carbonated water to make the Coca-Cola soft drink. He also began developing new diet soft drink flavors and may have ordered early research on what eventually became New Coke.

During the next two decades, Goizueta earned the favor of Robert Woodruff, longtime Coke CEO who had built Coca-Cola into a major American consumer product recognized around the globe. When Austin fell ill from what was later diagnosed as Alzheimer's disease, Woodruff, one of the company's directors at the time, selected the forty-nine-year-old Goizueta to become president of the company in May 1980. Goizueta became CEO on 1 March 1981 and moved quickly to expand the company. One of his first acts was to introduce Diet Coke, a major success that was the first product ever to share the treasured Coke name.

Goizueta's next major product launch, however, was a disaster. The company introduced New Coke as a replacement for the original Coca-Cola soft drink on 23 April 1985, backed up by focus-group testing that showed that consumers preferred the taste of New Coke over both original Coca-Cola as well as archrival soft drink Pepsi-Cola. The introduction was an immediate failure, however, as consumers vehemently rejected the new formula. The unexpected severity of the backlash, a revolt from Coca-Cola bottlers worldwide, and a sharp drop in sales prompted Goizueta to reverse position, bringing back the original formula, which was renamed "Coca-Cola Classic," on 10 July.

In 1986 Goizueta announced a financial restructuring that was one of his most creative and important innovations. On the advice of a sharp young financial executive named Douglas Ivester, Goizueta in 1986 sold 51 percent of Coke's bottling operation to public investors. This raised $1.2 billion for Coke and enabled Goizueta to retain significant control through its 49 percent ownership stake. Goizueta's "49 percent solution" served Coke's investors well because it removed the costly bottling operations from Coke's financial reports.

International expansion and the rivalry with Pepsi soon consumed much of Goizueta's attention. He encouraged managers to "think global and act local." After the Berlin Wall fell in 1989, he invested aggressively, and Coca-Cola soon replaced Pepsi-Cola as the leading soft drink in Russia and most of Eastern Europe. In the early 1990s he moved aggressively into China and became one of the first American companies to operate profitably there. He launched an "anchor bottler" program in which Coke expanded at relatively little cost internationally by forming partnerships with major foreign companies.

Coca-Cola relies heavily on advertising, and Goizueta changed Coke's advertising dramatically. He criticized the famous late-1970s "mountaintop ad," with a multiethnic group of young people singing sweetly about love and Coke. He pushed instead for a harder sales pitch and universal themes. In 1992 he ended Coke's forty-year relationship with the McCann Erickson advertising agency. He turned over Coke's $600 million global advertising budget not to a traditional advertising firm but to Creative Artists Agency, a Hollywood talent agency. The firm developed hip and unusual ads with a new theme, "Always Coca-Cola," that was used in countries throughout the world.

Goizueta's backing of Atlanta's bid for the 1996 Summer Olympics fit the company's globalization strategy. Goizueta gave credibility to a group of local boosters by hosting an organizational meeting in his office; for him, this was a rare direct intervention into local issues. Goizueta's involvement and his personal friendship with Olympics chief Juan Antonio Samaranch led to charges that Coke, a major Olympics sponsor, had "bought" the Summer Olympics for his hometown. Just after the Olympics' closing ceremonies, Goizueta announced that Pepsi's longtime bottler in Venezuela would become half-owned by a Coca-Cola anchor bottler. The move was seen as a symbol of Coke's global lead over Pepsi, and soon led Pepsi to scale back its international ambitions.

Goizueta was richly compensated. In 1991 he received the largest compensation package of any U.S. executive, a then-record $86 million in cash and stock. Still, Goizueta lived frugally. While Castro's government turned his palatial boyhood estate into a government office building, Goizueta owned only two relatively modest Atlanta homes in his lifetime.

Coke's board of directors in 1996 indefinitely suspended the company's mandatory retirement age, allowing Goizueta to remain beyond age sixty-five. Goizueta was a chain smoker all his adult life, and in early September 1997 he was diagnosed with lung cancer. He succumbed quickly and at age sixty-five died at Emory University Hospital. He is buried at Arlington Cemetery near Atlanta.

Long before his death, Goizueta was recognized as one of history's most successful corporate executives, a leader among a new breed of financially sophisticated, globally focused corporate managers. During his sixteen years at the helm, Coke's stock-market value rose from $4 billion to $150 billion. Sales more than tripled, increasing from $6 billion to $19 billion. Emory University, which benefited because of the significant Coke holdings in its endowment, named its business school for him. Goizueta's singular mark was the way he expanded his company's fortunes by maximizing its financial resources, expanding abroad, and sharpening his company's focus on its single greatest asset—the Coca-Cola brand.

★

Information about Goizueta can be found in David Greising, *I'd Like the World to Buy a Coke: The Life and Leadership of Roberto Goizueta* (1998). Aspects of Goizueta's career are also covered in Thomas Oliver, *The Real Coke, The Real Story* (1987), and Frederick Allen, *Secret Formula: How Brilliant Marketing and Relentless Salesmanship Made Coca-Cola the Best Known Product in the World* (1994). An interview with Goizueta can be found in *Beverage Digest* (30 Sept. 1988). Obituaries are in the *Chicago Tribune* and *Washington Post* (both 19 Oct. 1997).

DAVID GREISING

GOLDENSON, Leonard Harry (*b*. 7 December 1905 in Scottdale, Pennsylvania; *d*. 27 December 1999 in Sarasota, Florida), head of American Broadcasting/Paramount Theaters and an influential force in merging film and television entertainment.

Goldenson was born in a small town about thirty miles southeast of Pittsburgh. His father, Lee Goldenson, was a partner in a men's clothing and family shoe store. His mother, Esther Broud, was born in Russia and came to the United States as a small girl. Goldenson's father had a one-seventh interest in Scottdale's two movie houses, giving

Leonard H. Goldenson, 1980. ASSOCIATED PRESS AP

young Goldenson experience in theater management and operation. Goldenson had two younger sisters who idolized their big brother.

During his teens, Goldenson worked at various summer jobs, which included spending steamy months on the production line of a U.S. Steel mill and less strenuous work at a local stock and bond firm. He played football in high school and, after graduation, began attending Harvard College in Cambridge, Massachusetts, in 1923. Goldenson graduated from Harvard in 1927 and entered Harvard Law School. Goldenson received an LL.D. degree from Harvard in 1930, during the Great Depression. It took nine months before he secured a position with a law firm, whose clients included Paramount Pictures Corporation. Paramount's stock had plummeted from $85 to $9, and the company was forced into bankruptcy court. Goldenson worked on selling off theaters and later was instrumental in the reorganization of Paramount Theaters.

Goldenson's success in the entertainment business was facilitated in part by a government antitrust action that resulted in the separation of two divisions of the Paramount Pictures Corporation. This decision made Paramount Theaters, the largest chain of movie houses in the country, independent from the Hollywood movie production arm. In 1938 Goldenson became head of Paramount's theater operations, which had some 1,700 movie houses and was more stable and profitable than its movie-making division.

In the 1940s the U.S. government also decreed that NBC, which boasted two radio networks, would have to divest itself of one of them. Sarnoff kept the stronger Red Network, while the weaker Blue Network was spun off and purchased in 1943 by Edward J. Noble, the head of the Life Savers Company. The Blue was renamed American Broadcasting Company (ABC). Because the network was losing money and needed funds to get into television, in 1953 Noble sold the company to United Paramount Theaters (UPT). The government approved the merger, and the combined company was named American Broadcasting/Paramount Theaters (AB-PT), with Goldenson as its chief executive officer.

In 1953, after UPT and ABC merged, friction developed between the men who came from the theaters and Robert E. Kintner, who headed ABC. The board backed Goldenson, who then fired Kintner. ABC at that time was the fourth network in what was regarded as a "two-and-one-half network industry." It was uncertain whether ABC or the DuMont network, which had been founded in 1946 (and would fail in 1955), would survive. ABC, in addition to its five owned stations, had a scant eight affiliates. Advertisers were reluctant to air programs on ABC, and the shows it did offer were undistinguished and low-rated.

To counter this lack of star power, Goldenson, now considered the "father of ABC," invested in some movie names, including Danny Thomas, Ray Bolger, and George Jessel. Previously, motion picture executives regarded television as an enemy whose growth would cause the death of the movie business. Goldenson had a different angle. He saw the small screen as a developing force that could help the silver screen. Because ABC was so far behind in its station lineup and audience, Goldenson needed to take chances. (The title of his 1991 autobiography, *Beating the Odds,* pays tribute to the gambling metaphor.) An opportunity came in 1954 with Walt Disney, who had plans for a theme park based on a projected television program called Disneyland. CBS and NBC had turned down the program and project, seeing the park "as just another Coney Island." Goldenson was eager to acquire a quality series and invested millions in Disneyland. Disney's hour-long ABC program quickly became the top-rated show in the Nielsens. And ABC's investment in the park proved highly profitable.

Goldenson developed another innovative series with Warner Brothers (WB). The concept was to create sixty-minute dramas, including westerns and action adventures, based on hit movies. In order to answer the Hollywood fear that television was stealing audiences from the cinema, ABC gave Warner Brothers one minute on each show to promote a film. The alliance worked well and did much to dispel the film colony's antagonism to the burgeoning television medium. In his personnel policies, Goldenson also departed from the Madison Avenue mode. He hired young executives of diverse backgrounds and gave them time and funds to innovate. An example was the hiring of Roone Arledge, first as the head of sports and later as the director of the news department. Among ABC's developments that set precedents were miniseries, such as *Roots* (1970), based on the African-American experience; *Monday Night Football* (begun in 1970), with its three commentators; Ted Koppel's late-night discussion program, *Nightline* (begun in 1979); prime-time cartoons, such as *The Flintstones;* children's shows, such as the *Mickey Mouse Club* (begun in 1955); and youth-oriented series, such as *American Bandstand*. In the late 1970s Goldenson also added original programs, such as *The Untouchables* and *77 Sunset Strip*, to the lineup. ABC was the only major network to cover in full the Congressional Army/McCarthy hearings of spring 1954. When cable television became a threat to on-air broadcasting, Goldenson gambled $185 million in 1979 on the entertainment and sports system ESPN. Some analysts called it "Goldenson's Folly," but after its success, they hailed Goldenson's vision.

Goldenson was less a program developer than an expert in corporate affairs. He was able to frustrate hostile takeover attempts by Harold Geneen, of Gulf + Western, and by the reclusive Howard Hughes. When the brothers Harold and Sidney Bass moved to take over ABC, Goldenson enlisted the help of a mutual friend to end the brothers' takeover attempt. In 1985, aware of his advanced age—he was seventy-nine—and his company's vulnerability, he arranged a friendly merger with a station group, Capital Cities Communications. At the time, his company was estimated to be worth $3.5 billion.

An informal, low-key person, Goldenson loved tennis and was an accomplished painter. He married Isabelle Weinstein on 10 October 1939. They had three daughters, the oldest of whom died of cerebral palsy. Goldenson founded the United Cerebral Palsy Association and supported other organizations conducting research and education in this field. In 1994 he and his wife contributed $60 million to Harvard Medical School for neurological research. Goldenson died at his home in Sarasota, Florida, at age ninety-four. A memorial service was held at Temple Emmanuel in New York City, where he is buried. His two surviving daughters, Loreen Arbus and Maxine Goldenson, are television producers.

Coming from a movie theater background, Goldenson was able to persuade some of those who feared that television would kill films to affect an alliance with the new industry. Moreover, he argued that working together could result in both industries becoming stronger. He brought Hollywood producers into television and aided the convergence of media and entertainment. Willing to gamble against his entrenched competitors, Goldenson took chances on people and programs "outside the mold" and added a leavening of diversity to television.

★

Goldenson's autobiography, with Marvin J. Wolf, *Beating the Odds: The Untold Story Behind the Rise of ABC: The Stars, Struggles, and Egos That Transformed Network Television by the Man Who Made It Happen* (1991), includes reminiscences from the company's alumni, associates in show business, and relatives. Ken Auletta, *Three Blind Mice: How the TV Networks Lost Their Way* (1991), is well researched and independent in its analysis. Sterling Quinlan, *Inside ABC: American Broadcasting Company's Rise to Power* (1979), written by a former ABC executive, lacks developments of the 1980s and 1990s. Huntington Williams, *Beyond Control: ABC and the Fate of the Networks* (1989), is by a former ABC speechwriter. An obituary is in the *New York Times* (29 Dec. 1999).

BERT R. BRILLER

GOLDWATER, Barry Morris (*b.* 1 January 1909 in Phoenix, Arizona; *d.* 29 May 1998 in Phoenix, Arizona), U.S. senator, Republican presidential candidate in 1964, and a leader of the U.S. conservative movement.

Born in Arizona when it was still only a territory, Goldwater was the grandson of an immigrant Jewish peddler. His parents were Baron Goldwater, who managed the family's Phoenix department store, and Josephine Williams, a nurse. Goldwater and his younger brother and sister were raised as Episcopalians and as members of the Phoenix elite. He attended public schools through the ninth grade, when poor grades and disciplinary problems led his parents to enroll him in Staunton Military Academy in Virginia. Goldwater graduated from Staunton in 1928. The academy reinforced his sense of patriotism and service; instilled a personal discipline and respect for authority; and fostered a devotion to military rituals, traditions, and needs. Although Goldwater sought appointment to West Point and a military career, his father's declining health persuaded him to enroll at the University of Arizona in 1928. His father's death the following year led Goldwater to leave college and enter the family business. On 22 September 1934 he married Peggy Johnson, an heir to the Borg-Warner automobile fortune; they had four children. She died in 1985, and he married Susan Wechsler on 9 February 1992.

During the Great Depression of the 1930s, Goldwater learned the family business and managed the Phoenix store with his brother. Meanwhile, he entered the U.S. Army reserves, built an extensive collection of Native American

Barry Goldwater. Prints and Photographs Division, Library of Congress

art, helped to establish the Arizona Historical Foundation, tinkered with his ham radio, and learned to fly an airplane. Flying became more than a leisure-time pursuit for Goldwater. During the severe winter of 1936 he helped to organize relief flights that dumped hay and feed to save stranded Navajo livestock. On other occasions he delivered medicines to Native American reservations and flew the sick to hospitals. He also developed his photographic skills, taking a wide montage of pictures that vividly contrasted Arizona's wide vistas with intimate portraits of native peoples. He published the first volume of his *Arizona Portraits* in 1940, with a second appearing in 1946.

Events at home and abroad during the 1930s and 1940s developed Goldwater's consciousness as a political and economic conservative. The legacy of his self-made immigrant grandfather in the harsh Arizona environment impressed on him the importance of self-reliance and an individual's power to succeed without government intervention. As a businessman, he chafed under President Franklin Roosevelt's New Deal and the expansion of government authority. Goldwater objected to federal efforts to prescribe prices, wages, and employees' hours. He believed that federal relief programs harmed the nation by inhibiting self-reliance and fostering dependency. Events overseas also drew his attention. The rise of Adolf Hitler and the Nazi campaign against the Jews stirred thoughts of his grandfather's exodus from Poland and his own Jewish roots. He saw in the German army's advances the lessons of military weakness and a lack of will before aggressors.

Goldwater was eager to do his part for the war effort and did not let his family responsibilities, age, bad knees, or astigmatism cause deferment. Even before the United States entered World War II in 1941, Goldwater was on active duty in the U.S. Army Air Corps. During the war Goldwater served as an aerial gunnery instructor, helped to train nationalist Chinese pilots, and ferried aircraft to the European front. In February 1944 he was assigned to "fly the Hump," airlifting war material along the hazardous 500-mile route from India over the Himalayas to Chinese airfields. He performed his duties with distinction and after six months was rotated stateside to a training unit in California. Goldwater mustered out of the service in November 1945.

Goldwater returned to Phoenix, but was no longer interested in merchandising. Instead he turned to politics, confident that his conservative message, pioneer's name, business credentials, and military service would appeal to voters. Handsome, athletic, and with a head of prematurely gray hair that gave him a look of maturity, Goldwater ran for the Phoenix city council, leading a reform ticket pledged to eliminate graft, cut waste, and lower taxes. The ticket's victory in November 1949 created the impetus for responsible and efficient management of city government. Goldwater worked hard on the council, and his fiscal conservatism and watchdogging of city administrators enhanced his reputation. True to his beliefs, he repeatedly insisted that government should not interfere in people's lives and consistently sought private solutions to community problems.

As the leading Republican officeholder in an overwhelmingly Democratic state, Goldwater was eager to reach for the next political rung. In 1952 he declared his candidacy for the U.S. Senate against the incumbent Ernest McFarland. At first glance, Goldwater's ambition appeared to exceed his grasp. McFarland, a two-term senator, an author of the GI Bill, and the Senate's Democratic majority leader, was a formidable opponent. But Goldwater had valuable assets. Twenty years of Democratic Party rule had intensified the pressure for change, exacerbated by scandals in President Harry Truman's administration, the Korean War, and fears of communist infiltration of the U.S. government. Gaining the support of the major Arizona newspapers, Goldwater crisscrossed the state in his airplane, hosted both Senator Joseph McCarthy and the Republican presidential candidate Dwight D. Eisenhower, and was able to ride the latter's coattails to a narrow victory in November.

In Washington, D.C., Senator Goldwater joined the conservative Republican bloc and sought to reduce federal spending; pare bureaucracy; control labor unions; and end Korean War–imposed wage, rent, and price controls. He championed President Eisenhower's emphasis on nuclear deterrence and "rolling back" communism to free captive nations. At the same time, Goldwater did not hesitate to oppose "modern" Republicanism, and he rejected efforts to preserve the welfare state and expand the federal role in social and economic affairs. Goldwater also rose to McCarthy's defense and voted against his censure by the U.S. Senate for his controversial investigations.

Goldwater's political rise accelerated with his appointment in 1955 as the chair of the Senate Republican Campaign Committee. In this position, he became a prime source for news reporters and the point man at the grass roots for rallying the faithful and raising money for Republican senatorial candidates. Those who listened to his speeches detected a greater mission than the election of Republicans to the U.S. Senate. He preached the cause of modern conservatism—individualism, the sanctity of private property, militant anticommunism, and the dangers of centralized power. During his tenure, which included additional terms in 1959 to 1960 and 1961 to 1962, he traveled hundreds of thousands of miles and visited nearly every state in the Union. This yeoman service laid the foundation for his political future, for he met, knew by name, and captured the loyalty of Republican partisans down to the district and county levels of the party organization. Charismatic and evoking the image of the western hero, the tanned, square-jawed Goldwater appealed to Americans as a man of action, a rugged individualist standing against all odds and refusing to compromise his beliefs or country. He was candid and quotable, ready to voice his convictions regardless of the consequences. The senator's staff nurtured the mystique by distributing publicity photographs of Goldwater clad in jeans and a cowboy hat, astride a horse or mounting the modern equivalent, a U.S. Air Force jet fighter.

His reelection to the U.S. Senate in 1958 and the defeat, at the same time, of more senior party conservatives gave Goldwater leadership of the Republican right wing. He cemented his position by publishing *The Conscience of a Conservative* (1960), which quickly became a best-seller and eventually sold 3.5 million copies. He followed this with *Why Not Victory?* (1962), a conservative primer on foreign affairs. His Senate voting record reflected his conservative ideology. He supported a strong military with heavy reliance on air power to counter the communist threat. He opposed the Nuclear Test Ban Treaty (1963) for fear that it would weaken U.S. defenses. He rejected President John F. Kennedy's New Frontier initiatives and the Great Society of President Lyndon Johnson. Thus, he voted against

aid to education and the Civil Rights Act of 1964 as unconstitutional extensions of federal power.

In the early 1960s a movement grew to draft an often-reluctant Goldwater for president. The focus was on capturing the party machinery for the 1964 Republican National Convention. The conservative strategy bypassed liberal organizations in the eastern industrial states to forge an alliance of white, middle-class voters in the South and West. This effort alone would assure the Arizona senator sufficient convention support to win a first-ballot victory. Looking forward to running against President Kennedy, Goldwater nearly left the race after his friend's assassination in November 1963. Believing he owed a debt to the conservative movement, he reconsidered and announced his bid in January 1964. He then entered primary contests against his opponents Henry Cabot Lodge and Nelson Rockefeller, the New York governor. Primaries in New Hampshire and Oregon stigmatized the Arizonan as a pawn of extremists, eager to trigger nuclear war, and a foe of social security. In June, Goldwater achieved a victory in the bitter California primary to clinch the nomination. Liberals and moderates refused to accept the power shift to conservatives, and balked at supporting him. Widening the breach, Goldwater made no overtures to his opponents and even provoked them by declaring in his acceptance speech, "Extremism in the defense of liberty is no vice. Moderation in the pursuit of justice is no virtue."

In the general election campaign, President Johnson boasted of peace and prosperity and raised the specter of Goldwater as a warmonger and extremist. Democrats exploited his gaffes to scare voters with the image of a politically inept and irresponsible candidate eager to destroy the world and social security. Goldwater countered by raising the "social issue," decrying pornography, racial quotas, busing, immorality, and urban violence. This had little effect, and Johnson slaughtered Goldwater at the polls in November, winning 61 percent of the 43 million votes cast. Only five states in the Deep South and Arizona fell into the conservative column. Yet the results masked crucial changes at the grass roots. Republicans had made significant inroads in the Democratic South, and Johnson received a clear majority of the white vote only in Texas. In northeastern cities, Irish and Italian voters continued to drift from the Democratic to the Republican Party. Most important, conservatives had taken hold of the Republican machinery.

Arizona voters returned Goldwater to the U.S. Senate in 1968. While supporting the policies of President Richard Nixon, he chafed at the administration's withdrawal from Vietnam and its diplomatic overtures to the People's Republic of China. The Watergate crisis found him an ardent defender of the president until August 1974, when White House tapes revealed the extent of Nixon's participation in the scandal. Part of a three-man delegation sent to the Oval Office, Goldwater informed the president that his support in the Senate had collapsed, and he pressed Nixon to resign.

Goldwater was easily reelected to the Senate in 1974 in what he believed would be his last campaign. Heart and hip surgeries confined him, but he still proved a strong critic of President Jimmy Carter's domestic and foreign policies. With his wife pleading for him to retire, he published his memoirs *With No Apologies* (1979), and began to settle his affairs in Washington, D.C. However, with the quickening momentum of the conservative movement and the surge toward Ronald Reagan, he reconsidered and launched another bid for the Senate in 1980. Long absent from Arizona, ailing, neglectful of constituent work, vulnerable because of his support of abortion rights, and facing a young and dynamic opponent, Goldwater faced an uphill battle and barely eked out a victory.

In his last Senate term Goldwater served on the Armed Services Committee and the Select Committee on Intelligence. He also authored the Department of Defense Reorganization Act (1986), his only significant legislative initiative. This measure clarified the chain of command and restructured the military establishment. In retirement after 1987, no longer constrained by political considerations, and consistent with his libertarian views, Goldwater championed gay rights, defended abortion, and assailed the religious right. He died in 1998 and his ashes were scattered over the Colorado River in the Grand Canyon.

Goldwater was a businessman, artist, historian, and philanthropist. In spite of his overwhelming defeat in the 1964 presidential election, the five-term U.S. senator from Arizona profoundly affected U.S. history. He led a conservative movement that captured control of the Republican Party, developing a campaign strategy that linked whites living in the South and West. Goldwater introduced the "social issue" to national politics, which became a staple of Republican campaigning. Goldwater's challenge to liberalism began the shift of the U.S. mainstream to the right.

★

Goldwater's papers are housed in the Arizona Historical Foundation, Arizona State University. Among his most important books are *The Conscience of a Conservative* (1960), *Why Not Victory?* (1962), *The Conscience of a Majority* (1970), and *The Coming Breakpoint* (1976). His autobiographies are *With No Apologies* (1979), and *Goldwater* (1988). Biographies include Robert Alan Goldberg, *Barry Goldwater* (1995); Lee Edwards, *Goldwater: The Man Who Made a Revolution* (1995); and Peter Iverson, *Barry Goldwater: Native Arizonan* (1997). See also Mary Brennan, *Turning Right in the Sixties: The Conservative Capture of the GOP* (1995). An obituary is in the *New York Times* (30 May 1998).

ROBERT ALAN GOLDBERG

GORE, Albert Arnold, Sr. (*b.* 26 December 1907 in Granville, Tennessee; *d.* 5 December 1998 in Carthage, Tennessee), Democratic member of the U.S. House of Representatives and Senate who broke with the conservative southern bloc in matters related to civil rights and who became an early and outspoken foe of the Vietnam War.

One of five children (two sons, three daughters) of Allen Gore, a farmer, and Margie Denny, a homemaker, Gore attended a one-room school in Possum Hollow, Tennessee, and graduated from high school in Gordonsville in 1924. After completing a brief teacher-training course, Gore worked his way through Middle Tennessee State Teachers College by teaching in rural, one-room schoolhouses; he graduated in 1932. In 1930 he ran unsuccessfully for the position of superintendent of schools in Smith County. When the victorious candidate died a year later, Gore was appointed to the remainder of the four-year term by the county court. With this new job security, Gore undertook nighttime legal studies at the YMCA Law School in Nashville, Tennessee, receiving his LL.B. degree in 1936. He married a fellow law student Pauline LaFon on 17 April 1937. Their marriage produced one daughter and one son, Albert, Jr., who later served as the vice president of the United States for eight years and who ran for president in 2000.

After Franklin D. Roosevelt's nomination for president in 1932, Gore became a political activist, organizing Young Democratic clubs across Tennessee. A strong backer of Roosevelt's New Deal, he launched his own political career in 1934, serving as the state campaign manager for Gordon Browning's unsuccessful run for a U.S. Senate seat from Tennessee. When Browning was elected governor two years later, he appointed Gore as the commissioner of labor. In this position, Gore won attention by setting up a model unemployment compensation program. In 1938, when the congressman from Tennessee's Fourth District retired, Gore declared for the post, even though he was opposed by the powerful Democratic machine run by the Memphis boss Edward Hull Crump and Senator Kenneth McKellar. In a campaign in which he entertained voters by playing the fiddle and delivering effective stump speeches, Gore easily won nomination and was then elected to the seat in his solidly Democratic district.

Reelected five successive times (including winning unopposed in his final race in 1950), Gore served in the House of Representatives from 1939 until his entrance into the U.S. Senate in 1953. While in the lower house of Congress, he served first on the Banking and Currency Committee and then for ten years on the Appropriations Committee. He was also a member of the Select Committee to Investigate Acts of Executive Agencies that Exceeded Their Au-

Former Senator Albert Gore, Sr., with his son, Vice President Al Gore, 1993. ASSOCIATED PRESS/THE WHITE HOUSE

thority. His term of service was broken briefly in 1945, when he resigned his seat to serve in the U.S. Army, but he was reelected upon his return from service the next year. As a congressman, he supported Roosevelt's and Harry Truman's administrations on most foreign-policy matters, making a strong internationalist record. He was less predictable on domestic issues. Although he supported New Deal agencies such as the Works Progress Administration and the Civilian Conservation Corps, he made his first mark in the House by opposing Roosevelt's federal housing bill. He exercised similar independence during Truman's presidency. In 1949 Gore voted to override the president's veto of the Taft-Hartley Act and led the successful conservative opposition to the Brannan Plan, a proposed income-maintenance program for farmers. He also backed the Mundt-Nixon anticommunist bill and opposed Truman's proposal for a new cabinet-level department for health, education, and security. Unlike many southerners, however, he voted consistently in favor of anti–poll tax measures, signaling his later break with conservatives on civil rights issues in the 1950s and 1960s.

In 1952 the octogenarian McKellar announced his intent to retire from the Senate, but shortly afterward recanted, choosing to run once more. In the meantime, Gore had declared his candidacy. In the ensuing primary—running on a liberal economic platform while largely avoiding race issues, and using the campaign slogan "Think Some More, Vote for Gore"—he defeated McKellar with 56.5 percent of the vote. In the general election, Gore swamped his Republican opponent, Hobart Atkins, winning with 74.2 percent of the vote even as the Republican presidential candidate Dwight D. Eisenhower narrowly won Tennessee.

In the Senate, Gore struck an increasingly populist stance and lined up more often with party liberals than with his fellow southerners. In most sessions, he supported the "conservative coalition" of Republicans and Southern Democrats less than one-third of the time. His liberal position on civil rights separated him from most southern politicians almost immediately after the Supreme Court's 1954 antisegregation decision in *Brown* v. *Board of Education of Topeka,* when he pointedly refused to sign the so-called Southern Manifesto in which nearly all southern senators declared their opposition to forced desegregation. He gained further national attention by opposing the proposed Dixon-Yates contract to take over certain functions of the Tennessee Valley Authority and by introducing the bill that became the Interstate Highway Act of 1956.

While still a freshman senator, Gore was considered a possibility for the Democratic vice presidential nomination in 1956. However, he withdrew his name at the convention in favor of his fellow Tennesseean Estes Kefauver, thereby ending John F. Kennedy's chance to secure second place on the Democratic ticket. Although attacked by a conservative challenger in the 1958 senatorial primary for his refusal to sign the Southern Manifesto and for his alleged connections with the eastern establishment, Gore won the Democratic Senate primary by more than 100,000 votes. He then defeated Atkins again, running 70,000 votes ahead of his party's segregationist candidate for governor.

After having briefly flirted with the idea of running for the Democratic presidential nomination in 1960, Gore worked smoothly with President Kennedy during his three years in the White House. Even though Gore participated in the hearings on the Bay of Pigs invasion and opposed the administration's tax-cut proposal, he generally supported the young president's New Frontier programs and served as an occasional confidant. Following Kennedy's assassination, the succession to the presidency of Gore's sometime-foe Lyndon Johnson marked the end of harmony between Gore and the White House. It did not help that in 1961 Gore had opposed a proposal that would have allowed then–Vice President Johnson to retain his leadership post in the Senate Democratic caucus after giving up his position as the Senate majority leader. Gore supported most of Johnson's Great Society legislation, but—having pushed as early as 1963 for the withdrawal of all U.S. advisors from Vietnam—became an early and outspoken critic of the administration's Vietnam policies and, like other Democratic foes of the war, was persona non grata in the Johnson White House.

As U.S. politics took an increasingly conservative turn in the mid-1960s, Gore's base of support in Tennessee began to erode. Although he easily disposed of his challenger in the 1964 Democratic primary, his margin of victory over the Republican Daniel Kuykendall in the general election was only 53.6 percent; he ran 65,000 votes behind Johnson at the top of the Democratic ticket. After the election of the Republican Howard H. Baker to Tennessee's other Senate seat in 1966 and Richard Nixon's razor-thin presidential victory in the state in 1968, Gore's political position crumbled further. Looking toward his 1970 reelection campaign, he was vulnerable not only because of his opposition to the war in Vietnam and support for gun control and civil rights legislation, but perhaps especially for his votes against the confirmation of Nixon's two southern U.S. Supreme Court nominees, Clement Haynsworth and Harrold Carswell. Targeted for defeat by the Nixon administration and the focus of especially venomous attacks by Vice President Spiro Agnew, Gore managed a narrow victory over Hudley Crockett, a television news broadcaster with no political experience in the Democratic primary. But he was soundly beaten by the conservative Republican congressman William Brock III in the general election. As well as losing normally Democratic west Tennessee, Gore lost the Republican east Tennessee by more than 80,000 votes.

Gore never ran again for political office, choosing to return to Carthage, where he stayed busy in retirement. In addition to running his cattle-breeding farm, he engaged in various business activities, including real estate. From 1972 to 1983, he served on the board of directors of Island Creek Coal Company and as executive vice president of Occidental Petroleum Company, and then continued to serve Occidental as senior director until the time of his death. Gore made occasional public appearances in his later years, especially in connection with his son's campaigns for national office in 1988 and 1992. He died of natural causes at his home in Carthage and is buried in Carthage's Smith County Memorial Gardens.

Gore was a handsome, well-built man with brown eyes and curly brown (later silver) hair. He was widely respected as a skillful debater during his years in Congress. A life-long Baptist, he combined dignified formality with fiddle-playing and folksiness on the Tennessee campaign trail. Like his fellow liberal Democrats J. William Fulbright and George McGovern, who also eventually lost their Senate seats by losing touch with their respective state constituencies, Gore remained a symbol of the rightward turn taken by U.S. politics during the 1970s and 1980s.

★

Gore's personal and political papers, through 1970, are housed at the Albert Gore Research Center at Middle Tennessee State University in Murfreesboro, Tennessee. He wrote two semiautobiographical books, both interlaced with political opinion and analysis, *The Eye of the Storm: A People's Politics for the Seventies* (1970), actually a campaign tract, and *Let the Glory Out: My South and Its Politics* (1972). An early biographical essay is in *Current Biography* (1952). Two interesting treatments of the decisive 1970 campaign are David Halberstam, "End of a Populist: Albert Gore," *Harper's* (Jan. 1971), and Richard E. Harris, "Annals of Politics: How the People Feel," *New Yorker* (10 July 1971). An obituary is in the *New York Times* (6 Dec. 1998).

GARY W. REICHARD

GOULD, Samuel Brookner (*b.* 11 October 1910 in New York City; *d.* 11 July 1997 in Sarasota, Florida), visionary leader in higher education who served as president and chancellor of several institutions, including the State University of New York system during its major expansion and development in the 1960s.

Gould, the only child of Nathaniel Gould and Lina Brookner, was raised in Connecticut, where his Lithuanian-born father operated wholesale grocery businesses in the towns of Shelton and Ansonia. He finished high school in an accelerated program at the age of sixteen and entered Bates College in Maine. The family's modest means required him to earn money to attend college, where, in spite of working and extensive extracurricular involvement, he earned a B.A. degree in 1930 at the age of nineteen. He participated on the debate team (at which he excelled), the track team, as a member of the theater group, and as a tutor in a private school. While at Bates he abandoned the Jewish faith of his parents and later became an active member of the Presbyterian Church.

After working briefly for a telephone company, Gould took a position in 1932 as teacher of English and speech at William Hall High School in West Hartford, Connecticut. He also worked part-time at a radio station, an activity that stimulated his interest in mass communications and foreshadowed one element of his vision for education. In 1934

Samuel B. Gould, 1965. AP/WIDE WORLD PHOTOS

he went to England to study literature at Cambridge University. In 1936 he completed an M.A. degree in English at New York University and in that same year, on 24 December 1936, he married Laura Johanna Ohman, a native of Finland. They met aboard a passenger liner during his sojourn to Cambridge University. They had one son and remained married until her death in 1989.

In 1938 Gould moved to Massachusetts to head the speech department at Brookline High School. He also engaged in doctoral work at Harvard University, though, after taking leave to serve in the U.S. Navy during World War II, he never completed the doctorate. He attained the rank of lieutenant commander and was honored for his service in the Pacific aboard the aircraft carrier USS *Yorktown* (CV-10). After military service he returned to teaching in Brookline, but accepted a job in 1946 to establish a communications department for Boston University. In addition to developing academic programs in speech, theater, film, radio, and television, he also established a student-run radio station, WBUR, the first FM station in Boston. In 1951 he became assistant to the new president of Boston University, thus providing his first insights into the administration of a complex institution.

Gould left Boston in 1953 to work for the management firm Cresap, McCormick and Paget, for which he consulted in the national higher education arena with the firm's clients. In 1954 he accepted the presidency of Antioch College in Yellow Springs, Ohio, an experimental and progressive institution that utilized a cooperative education model. Gould was popular there for his defense of the faculty during the McCarthy-era investigations into ties to Communist interests, a role analogous to his later defense of faculty in California against the John Birch Society.

Gould's reputation as an educator led to his appointment in 1959 as president of the University of California at Santa Barbara. The former teachers' college had been absorbed in 1954 into the University of California system. Gould built relations with the community, eliciting strong local support, and began creating a new academic image for the institution. The Santa Barbara campus grew rapidly during his three-year presidency and, following the Antioch tradition, he encouraged student involvement in university affairs. He expanded a study abroad program at Santa Barbara that became the site for administering study abroad for the entire University of California system.

He left Santa Barbara in 1962 to become president of the Educational Broadcasting System in New York City, where Channel 13 was a pioneer in public and educational television. Gould envisioned television as a means to utilize mass communication for education, but he felt constrained from the beginning in a position that compelled him to dedicate extensive time to fund raising and management issues.

In 1964 Gould was appointed by Governor Nelson Rockefeller to head the State University of New York (SUNY) system, at that time a loose federation of fifty-nine campuses bound together in 1948 by legislation. SUNY had not realized the aspirations of its founders as a true system of higher education. Under Gould's and Rockefeller's leadership, however, it rapidly expanded its enrollment, physical facilities, and academic programs. Gould worked ardently to realize for SUNY his vision of a unified system with quality education and research. In addition to fostering development of the four research university centers, as chancellor he oversaw the transformation of eleven state teachers' colleges into comprehensive colleges with liberal arts and sciences divisions. He constantly encouraged innovation, and under his leadership as chancellor SUNY founded—or planned—new campuses and refocused the missions of several others. Among the new campuses were two non-traditional institutions, the campus at Old Westbury and Empire State College; the latter opened after Gould left office.

Upon retiring from SUNY in 1970, Gould worked briefly as a director of McKinsey and Company. In 1971 he was appointed to chair the Carnegie Commission on Non-Traditional Study, a role consistent with his interest in innovation in education. During the 1970s he was a member of the Higher Education Commission of Florida and a trustee of Florida's public honors college, New College. He consulted on educational development with the Venezuelan Ministry of Education and served as interim chancellor for higher education in Connecticut during the 1976–1977 academic year. He was also a trustee of the Teachers Insurance and Annuity Association, a retirement fund for education and research personnel. His close friendship with Rockefeller continued, and during 1977 he accompanied Vice President Rockefeller on a tour of Latin America. Gould died of congestive heart failure at age eighty-six. His remains were cremated in Sarasota, Florida, where he lived at the time of his death.

Gould was a respected leader in higher education who understood student and faculty unrest as well as academic traditions. He resisted yielding to the radical philosophies of the day. Nevertheless, he felt it essential that tradition-bound colleges and universities change methodically through, for instance, development of interdisciplinary academic programs and research, adapting new electronic technology for instruction and information management, and expanding access to college education for a larger proportion of the public. His speeches of the late 1960s reveal a clarity about the impending impact of computers and information technology in higher education, and he staunchly advocated broadening access to college education. Many changes envisioned by Gould became integral to the fabric of higher education during the last decades of the twentieth century.

★

Gould's papers and books are in the Archives of Public Affairs and Policy of the Library at the State University of New York at Albany. The collection is replete with manuscripts of his speeches in which he regularly expounded his ideas. His books, *Knowledge Is Not Enough* (1959) and *Today's Academic Condition* (1970), are expositions of his vision for education. The book *Diversity by Design* (1973), for which he wrote an introductory chapter, resulted from work by the Carnegie Foundation's Commission on Non-Traditional Study, chaired by Gould. A biographical article on Gould, concentrating especially on his work as SUNY chancellor, appears in the *New Yorker* (18 Nov. 1967). Other magazine articles with substantial treatment of Gould and his role as an innovative university administrator appear in *Time* (12 Jan. 1968) and *Harper's* (Dec. 1966). An obituary is in the *New York Times* (16 July 1997).

W. HUBERT KEEN

GRAHAM, Virginia (*b.* 4 July 1912 in Chicago, Illinois; *d.* 22 December 1998 in New York City), talk-show personality and fund-raiser who won over female viewers with her bleach-blonde hair and vivacious personality.

Graham was born Virginia Komiss, one of two children of clothier David Komiss and Bessie Jane Feiges. Graham later boasted of winning a stint as a cub reporter for the *Chicago Tribune* in high school. After graduating from Chicago's Frances Parker High School in 1929, she spent a year being "finished" at the National Park Seminary in Maryland, where she purchased hair dye and traded in her brown locks for the blonde that would become her signature. She attended the University of Chicago from 1930 to 1931 and spent a semester at Northwestern University the following autumn. She worked in sales in Chicago and as a fashion reporter for WBBM radio, modeling occasionally as well.

On a visit to New York City in 1935, she met theatrical costumer Harry Guttenberg, whom she married on 2 May the same year. After the birth of a daughter in 1936, the outgoing Virginia Guttenberg went to work for WMCA radio in New York City, where she scripted commercials, ghostwrote an advice column, and even acted as an on-air cooking personality. Between 1940 and 1947 she threw herself into Red Cross volunteer work and in 1947 became involved in the battle against cerebral palsy, one of many charitable causes that occupied much of her life thereafter. In the late 1940s, she began showcasing her lively personality as mistress of ceremonies at fashion shows, using the name Virginia Graham. In 1950 she spent six months on New York daytime television as the sidekick for minor star Zeke Manners.

Virginia Graham, 1965. ASSOCIATED PRESS AP

Graham's show-business career was interrupted in 1951, when she was diagnosed with cervical cancer, an event she later called a turning point in her life; she would go on to raise money for that disease as well as many others. Other personal difficulties followed; shortly after her cancer operation, her husband was hospitalized with a nervous breakdown, and his New York business burned down. Graham kept busy while her husband and his firm recovered. In 1953 she participated in the first of hundreds of fund-raising telethons. During the 1950s, she returned to radio in a number of local venues and expanded her television work. From 1952 to 1957 she hosted *Food for Thought*, a daytime program for the DuMont network.

After her charity work was highlighted in February 1956 on the television program *This Is Your Life*, she worked for several months as cohost with Mike Wallace on NBC's daily radio program *Weekday*. "She was shrewd in a lovely way," Wallace later said of his colleague. She also guest hosted the *Today* show and appeared on Jack Paar's *Tonight Show*. In 1961 the Clairol company named Graham a goodwill ambassador for its hair-coloring products, and she traveled around the country talking about being a blonde.

In 1963 the starstruck Graham obtained the job she had always wanted and became the host of her own television show. The syndicated *Girl Talk*, on which Graham chatted with female guests in a living-room set, struck a chord with women all over the United States; its hostess garnered fans by being herself—loud and human. "Virginia Graham possesses every traditional fault developed by her sex," one reporter wrote. "She is an enthralling gossip, eager to give advice, constantly dieting but seldom succeeding." Another found her "shrewd, tart, warmhearted, interested." Graham treated the set like a home and reveled in mixing up guests, among them worldly actresses, dainty ingenues, and articulate authors. She adored stirring up a cat fight but projected homey niceness.

Graham was replaced on *Girl Talk* in 1969 but soon found another syndicated program, *The Virginia Graham Show,* which ran from 1970 to 1972, and on which she talked with both men and women. Her stock in trade was still her chatty, matronly personality. A *TV Guide* profile described its effect: "When John Cassavetes, Peter Falk and Ben Gazzara came on the show to plug a movie and became obstreperous in the process, she knew what to do. . . . After Falk said something insulting, she reached over and pushed the hair out of his eyes. 'So your mother can see how nice you look.' After that the trio was putty in her hands."

Graham managed during her television career to produce several books. Her first autobiography, *There Goes What's Her Name,* was published in 1965, followed by the beauty book *Don't Blame the Mirror* in 1967 and *If I Made It, So Can You* in 1978. Her husband's death in 1980 in-spired *Life After Harry: My Adventures in Widowhood* (1988). Although she never again had a program of her own, Graham periodically worked on game shows, talk shows, films, and daytime dramas, including *Texas* (1978), in which she played a gossip columnist, as well as in summer stock. In the time leading up to her death in December 1998 at age eighty-six from complications following a heart attack, she was a regular on the *Roseanne* talk show. She delivered gossip and proved a favorite of the loud-mouthed comedienne, who recalled, "She loved talking. She loved the camera. She was a trooper to the end."

Never glamorous although always neatly dressed, Graham presented a role model to Americans that departed from Hollywood stereotypes. She was everybody's sister or mother, one of the first female television personalities who achieved fame not because of talent or beauty but because of a shrewd focus on topics and guests that would interest her viewers. Graham shared and exploited the American fascination with show business, and she served as a model for future talk-show hosts. Entertainment historian James Robert Parish wrote, "Depending on whether one was pro- or anti-Virginia, she was outspoken or opinionated, boisterous or obnoxious, sincere or calculating, unabashed or naive. However, everyone agreed that this vivacious personality loved people, understood all types of women very well, and never, never was at a loss for words."

★

The most complete essay on Graham, aside from her own books, appears in James Robert Parish's *Let's Talk! America's Favorite Talk Show Hosts* (1993). Graham (as Virginia Guttenberg) is also profiled in *Current Biography* (1956); *McCall's* (Feb. 1962); *New York Times* (11 July 1965); and *Contemporary Authors* (1979). She was a favorite of *TV Guide*, where Edith Efron described her at the peak of her career in "She Often Gets the Last Word—And Most of the Others Too" (2 Apr. 1966), and Dwight Whitney and Dick Hobson published "The Glorious Metamorphosis of Virginia Graham" (8 Apr. 1972). Obituaries are in the *Detroit News* (24 Dec. 1998), *New York Times* (25 Dec. 1998), and *TV Guide* (30 Jan. 1999).

TINKY "DAKOTA" WEISBLAT

GREENFIELD, Mary Ellen ("Meg") (*b.* 27 December 1930 in Seattle, Washington; *d.* 13 May 1999 in Washington, D.C.), editorial page editor of the *Washington Post* and columnist for *Newsweek*.

Greenfield was the daughter of Lewis James Greenfield, a successful antiques dealer, and Lorraine Nathan, a homemaker. Greenfield's mother died when she was twelve, and her father's immersion in his business left Greenfield and her older brother Jimmy much to themselves. After gradu-

Meg Greenfield, 1978. BARRY THUMMA/ASSOCIATED PRESS STF

ating summa cum laude from Smith College in 1952, she spent a year studying at Cambridge University on a Fulbright scholarship. She subsequently lived in Rome and attempted to write fiction before moving to New York at age twenty-five.

Her first job was in the 1956 presidential campaign of Adlai Stevenson. This led to a research position at the *Reporter,* an influential, liberal opinion magazine published by Max Ascoli, a refugee from Fascist Italy, from whom Greenfield learned a great deal about political writing and editing. In 1960 she published her first article, a satiric piece entitled "The Prose of Richard M. Nixon." The article caused a sensation and launched her career. In 1961 she was promoted to staff writer at the *Reporter* and became Washington editor in 1965. Her tenure with the magazine ended with its demise in 1968.

Philip Geyelin, then editorial page editor of the *Washington Post,* lost no time in hiring Greenfield. In less than a year, she was named Geyelin's deputy at the suggestion of the paper's publisher, Katharine Graham, with whom Greenfield developed a close friendship. This promotion was unusual for a woman at that time and gave her entree to the paper's editorial staff, which guided the *Post* through the crises of the next two decades, including the publication of the Pentagon Papers; Watergate and the struggle with President Nixon; the protracted pressmen's strike of the mid-1970s; and the demise of the *Washington Star,* the *Post*'s chief rival in the metropolitan area.

As a reporter, editorialist, and influential opinion maker

for more than three decades, Greenfield provided insightful commentary about the administrations of presidents from Nixon to Clinton, as well as public policy debates on issues such as affirmative action, abortion rights, the Panama Canal treaties, and the Persian Gulf War. However, there was one avenue of public debate she avoided; she declined to become a "talking head" on the nation's television screens.

Greenfield succeeded Geyelin as editorial page editor in 1979, supervising and contributing to the editorial and op-ed pages until shortly before her death in 1999. In addition, in 1974 Greenfield began writing a biweekly column for *Newsweek,* thus introducing her to a national audience. In her opening column she noted, "I'll be writing about Washington life which, contrary to widespread belief, does not exclude everything human."

One adjective frequently applied to Greenfield was "tough." No doubt, toughness helped this small, attractive woman rise to the top of a male-dominated profession in a male-dominated political city. And nowhere was her toughness more evident than in the questions she posed to political figures, domestic and foreign, whose policies she perceived to be at odds with their public pronouncements. In 1988, while in Moscow, she enraged Mikhail Gorbachev by inquiring how he could promise glasnost and reform while continuing to jail dissidents and suppress the peoples of Eastern Europe.

One of her great strengths as an editor was the ability to spot talented newcomers. Among those she discovered or helped to promote were George F. Will, Charles Krauthammer, Michael Kinsley, Mary McGrory, Roger W. Wilkins, and David Remnick, later editor of the *New Yorker.*

Although Greenfield detailed her views on the issues of the day with great clarity, no one was ever able to pinpoint her position on the political spectrum. She opposed capital punishment, defended abortion rights and progressive taxation, and worked for a newspaper with a generally liberal reputation. However, she was a foreign policy hawk, a dedicated anticommunist, and a critic of identity politics. She scorned "political correctness" and those who perennially perceived themselves as victims. William Kristol, editor and publisher of the conservative *Weekly Standard,* commented, "Meg Greenfield contributed more than anyone realizes to modern American conservatism." However, Charles Krauthammer, a conservative columnist and a close friend of Greenfield, was quoted in the *New Yorker* as saying, "If she was [a conservative], she sure spent a hell of a lot of time hiding it from me."

Although Greenfield rose to the top of her profession during the flowering of the feminist movement, she never took an active role in the movement. Indeed, she viewed it with some skepticism, describing herself as a "wobbly spear-carrier in the feminist march." A reporter once asked why she never married and, after thinking for a moment, she replied, "Damned if I know. I think it was an awful mistake." When introduced at a speaking engagement as "a modern woman who elected not to marry," she remarked, "I don't recall voting in that election."

Greenfield guarded her privacy assiduously. If she had any romantic attachments, no one mentioned them, at least not in print. Invitations to her frequent dinner parties were coveted and, indeed, looked upon as a sign that one had "arrived." She was a passionate gardener at both her homes, one on R Street in Georgetown and one she acquired late in her life on Bainbridge Island in Washington's Puget Sound, where she often retreated during her final illness.

In 1978 Greenfield was awarded the Pulitzer Prize for commentary. She received honorary degrees from Smith College, Georgetown University, Wesleyan University, Williams College, and Princeton University. She died at her home in Washington, D.C., after a three-year struggle with lung cancer.

When she was already ill, Greenfield delivered a eulogy for Ann Devroy, a dear friend and highly regarded political reporter. Greenfield said of Devroy, "[Her] job was not her vehicle to anywhere. It was her joy and her obligation. She was a worker known for her tirelessness, for her sense of craft . . . she was impossible to fool or divert. . . . [Her work] was intense and honest and unembellished, yet another evidence of her particular virtues. I would sum up those values as excellence, unstinting effort, craft, loyalty and love." These words could apply as easily to Greenfield herself.

★

Greenfield's posthumously published *Washington* (2001) reveals little about the author, but the foreword by Katharine Graham and the afterword by Michael Beschloss are informative. Chalmers McGeagh Roberts's *In the Shadow of Power: The Story of the Washington Post,* revised and updated in 1989, gives an insightful picture of Greenfield's role at the newspaper. An assessment in Jude Wanniski, ed., *1987 MediaGuide,* and Naomi Schaefer's "Sisterhood Is Weak," *New Republic* (7 June 1999), provide somewhat critical assessments of her work. Hendrik Hertzberg's tribute, "Beltway Bluestocking," *New Yorker* (7 June 1999), fills in a number of blanks. Obituaries are in the *Washington Post* and *New York Times* (both 14 May 1999).

NATALIE B. JALENAK

GRIFFITH, Calvin Robertson (*b.* 1 December 1911 in Montreal, Canada; *d.* 20 October 1999 in Melbourne, Florida), baseball team owner who moved the Washington Senators franchise to Minnesota.

Griffith was one of seven children born to Jimmy and Jane Robertson. In 1922 Griffith's father died, and the children were entrusted into the care of his aunt, Addie Ann Rob-

Calvin Griffith *(left)* with the owner of the Baltimore Orioles, Clarence Miles *(center),* and the owner of the Senators, Clark Griffith, 1954. © BETTMANN/CORBIS

ertson, who was married to Clark Griffith. A former outstanding major league pitcher, Clark Griffith managed the Washington Senators baseball team and purchased a controlling share of the team in 1920, resigning as manager to become club president. He adopted Griffith and his sister Thelma Griffith Hayes. Having no children of his own, Clark Griffith began grooming the boy to inherit the family baseball business. Griffith described himself as a team mascot, and in 1924 he served as a bat boy when the Senators defeated the New York Giants in the World Series. However, Griffith would later express ambiguity regarding his adopted father, telling a reporter, "I did everything in the world to make that man happy. Everything. His eyes could pierce right through you. When he got mad at you, it was like they were coming out and pointing at you. Next to God, Clark Griffith was it."

Although not as athletically gifted as his adopted father, Griffith played baseball while attending Staunton Military Academy. From 1932 to 1935 Griffith was a student and baseball player at George Washington University. The senior Griffith allowed the reluctant scholar to devote his full attention to learning the baseball business, and in 1935 he was hired as team secretary of the Chattanooga, Tennessee, Lookouts, a farm club affiliated with the Washington Senators in the Southern Association. Griffith's minor league apprenticeship also included a brief stint as field manager and president of the Charlotte Hornets, the Senators' farm team in the Piedmont League. In 1942 Griffith returned to the major league level, serving as head of concessions for the Senators. As Clark Griffith's health deteriorated, Griffith assumed greater responsibility for team operations. In 1955 Clark Griffith died, leaving majority ownership of the team to Griffith and his sister Thelma. Griffith assumed his title as president of the Washington Senators.

Griffith inherited a baseball franchise with a losing tradition. The Senators' only World Series victory was in 1924, and the club's last American League pennant was won in 1933. Under Griffith's leadership there was little improvement. From 1955 to 1960 the Senators finished last four times, in seventh place once, and in fifth place once. The team never won as many games as it lost, and box-office receipts at Griffith Stadium languished, with season attendance often under a half million. Rumors abounded that Griffith would seek to move the franchise. In 1960 American League team owners approved Griffith's request to transfer the franchise to Minneapolis for the 1961 season. To lure Griffith, the city of Minneapolis promised increased attendance, full concession rights, and low stadium rental. Senators fans felt betrayed, and *Washington Post* sports columnist Shirley Povich proclaimed, "Washington supported the Griffith clan of baseball operations for the forty-nine years of 1912–1960 in an elegance unmerited by the quality of schlock baseball they gave Washington."

With the move to Minnesota, Griffith changed the team's name from Senators to Twins, in honor of the twin cities of Minneapolis and St. Paul. The franchise transfer worked well for Griffith during the 1960s, when the Twins led the American League in attendance, drawing over a million fans per season. In 1965 the Twins won the American League pennant but were defeated in the World Series by the Los Angeles Dodgers. In 1969 and 1970 the Twins were divisional champions. Team performance declined during the 1970s, but in 1979 Griffith sought to rebound by signing a thirty-year lease for the Twins to play in the Metrodome, a domed stadium to be constructed in the twin cities area at a cost of $55 million. However, the changing structure of major league baseball, in which free agency contributed to escalating player salaries, made it difficult for Griffith to compete during the 1970s and 1980s. Unlike many other baseball owners, Griffith earned his primary source of income from his sports franchise, and he insisted on running the team as a family enterprise, with sister Thelma Griffith Hayes, brothers Jimmy and Billy Robertson, and son Clark serving as club vice presidents. In addition to their son, Griffith and his wife, Belva Block, had two daughters.

In a 1978 speech before the Minneapolis Rotary Club, Griffith made remarks that were considered racist, saying "you've got some good hard-working white people here," although he insisted that his comments were taken out of context. Free agent Rod Carew left the Twins, asserting that he would no longer work on Griffith's "plantation." The Rotary Club speech and Griffith's reputation as a tight-fisted owner made it increasingly difficult for the Twins to succeed in the free agent market, and pressure

mounted for Griffith to relinquish ownership of the franchise. In 1984 Griffith sold his baseball club to Minnesota businessman Carl Pohlad for $36 million. Griffith was seventy-two.

After retiring Griffith divided his time between homes in Melbourne, Florida, and Edina, Minnesota. Suffering from heart ailments and a kidney infection, Griffith died at a rehabilitation center near his Melbourne home. He is buried in Fort Lincoln Cemetery in Washington, D.C.

Griffith, who brought major league baseball to the state of Minnesota, represented an older style of baseball team ownership—a style in which income was dependent primarily on the ownership of a sports franchise. However, the economic realities of ownership, with the advent of free agency in the late 1970s and early 1980s, made it increasingly difficult for a family enterprise to successfully operate in major league baseball. In addition, Griffith's paternalistic attitude irritated more assertive and independent athletes in the 1970s and 1980s. The reference to Griffith in an authorized biography as "baseball's last dinosaur" may be a proper epitaph.

★

A clipping file on Griffith is available from the Baseball Hall of Fame in Cooperstown, New York. Although shedding little light on his personal life, Griffith (with David Anderson), *Quotations from Chairman Calvin* (1985); and John Kerr, *Calvin: Baseball's Last Dinosaur—An Authorized Biography* (1990), document Griffith's baseball operation. For journalistic accounts of Griffith as a baseball owner, see Shirley Povich, "Cal Griffith Tries to Explain," *Baseball Digest* (Sept. 1951); Michael Lenehan, "Last of the Pure Baseball Men," *Atlantic* (Aug. 1981); and Gary Smith, "A Lingering Vestige of Yesterday," *Sports Illustrated* (4 Apr. 1983). Obituaries are in the *New York Times* and *Washington Post* (both 21 Oct. 1999).

RON BRILEY

GRIFFITH JOYNER, Florence Delorez ("Flo Jo") (*b.* 21 December 1959 in Los Angeles, California; *d.* 21 September 1998 in Mission Viejo, California), sprinter and three-time gold medalist at the 1988 Summer Olympics, remembered for her extraordinary speed and flamboyant fashion sense.

Griffith Joyner was one of eleven children of Robert Griffith, an electrical technician, and Florence Griffith, a seamstress and teacher. "Dee Dee," as she was called during childhood, grew up poor in the Jordan Downs housing project in the Watts section of Los Angeles. The family settled in the Mojave Desert, and when she was four her parents divorced.

At age seven, Griffith Joyner began attending the Sugar Ray Robinson Youth Foundation's sports days in the Los

Florence Griffith Joyner. AP/WIDE WORLD PHOTOS

Angeles projects. It was then that she began running faster than everyone—boys included. Yet, when meeting Robinson, she later recalled, "I was too shy to ever look him in the eye." But shyness never prevented Griffith Joyner, a natural eccentric, from being herself. While in high school she owned a pet boa constrictor named Brandy. Whenever Brandy shed, Griffith Joyner saved the skin and painted it different colors. Once, she was kicked out of a mall for having Brandy around her neck.

In 1978 Griffith Joyner graduated from Jordan High School, where she set school records as a sprinter and high jumper. That fall she attended California State University, Northridge, as a business major, with no intention of trying out for the track team. Instead, she worked as a bank teller to help support her family. In her freshman year Griffith Joyner had to drop out for lack of funds. Bobby Kersee, then the assistant track coach, got in touch with her, helped her apply for financial aid, and convinced her to join the team. Griffith Joyner could not compete until the following season, however, because of a strained lower hamstring.

Griffith Joyner began running for Cal State–Northridge in the 1980 season, but she didn't make the first rung of sprinters and had a difficult time getting out of the starting blocks. Eventually she learned to work within her own style. In that first season she placed eighth in the 100-meter event at the U.S. Olympic Trials in Eugene, Oregon, and finished fourth in the 200 meter, just missing making the team.

In the fall of 1980 Griffith Joyner followed Kersee to University of California, Los Angeles (UCLA), where he had accepted a coaching position. The transfer forced her to switch her major from business to psychology, since UCLA at the time did not offer an undergraduate major in business. The move to UCLA proved to be good for Griffith Joyner's track career. During her first season she competed on the European circuit, which ended at the World Cup in Rome, Italy. There, she ran the third leg on the U.S. 400-meter relay team, which broke the thirteen-year-old American record of 42.87 seconds with a time of 42.82. This experience helped Griffith Joyner establish herself as a sprinter and was a foretaste of her stellar achievements for the next season: she became the National Collegiate Athletic Association (NCAA) champion in the 200-meter event, defeating Jamaican Merlene Ottey of the University of Nebraska with a time of 22.39 seconds. She also ran the second leg on two more American record-setting relay teams. At the end of the 1982 season, *Track and Field News* ranked her number ten in the world in the 100-meter event and number seven in the 200 meter.

In 1983 Griffith Joyner graduated from UCLA with a degree in psychology. Briefly, she was engaged to UCLA star hurdler Greg Foster. She competed at the NCAA Championships that year, finishing first in the 400 meter and second in the 200 meter. At the U.S.A. Championships she placed third, qualifying for the World Championships in Helsinki, Finland. There, she placed fourth in the 200 meter. The following year Griffith Joyner finished second in the 200-meter event at the U.S. Olympic Trials, qualifying for the American team. At the Games, with her six-and-a-half inch nails painted red, white, and blue, Griffith Joyner won a silver medal in the 200-meter event with a time of 22.04 seconds. She lost to her longtime rival, Valerie Brisco, by less than a quarter of a second.

Discouraged, Griffith Joyner took time off from track in September 1986, accepting a full-time position at the Union Bank in Los Angeles. She also worked at night braiding women's hair and painting their fingernails. She returned to the track in April 1987, fifteen pounds overweight. Griffith Joyner asked Kersee to help her train for the 1988 Olympic trials, and after adhering to a rigorous training schedule and strict diet, her weight dropped to 130 pounds and her speed improved. Griffith Joyner's appearance was becoming more distinctive: "I was trying for a new idea and had cut one leg off some tights and happened to look in the mirror and said, 'That might work.'" This new look accentuated her long, muscular legs and contributed to her being labeled a track diva.

At the 1987 World Championship Games in Rome, Griffith Joyner won the silver medal in the 200 meter. She also ran the third leg on the gold-winning U.S. 400-meter relay team. Although Griffith Joyner broke no records in Rome that summer, she gained a lot of attention with her running suit, which was compared to that of a speed skater's from Pluto. Placing second in the 200 meter motivated Griffith Joyner. With much perseverance and Kersee's help, she undertook a demanding workout schedule involving running and weight training. By year's end Griffith Joyner was ranked first in the 200 meter.

Later that year she left Union Bank, taking a part-time job in the employee-relations department of Anheuser-Busch in Van Nuys, California, training vigorously, and designing clothes. On 10 October 1987 she married Al Joyner (the 1984 Olympic triple-jump champion) in Las Vegas, Nevada.

It was at the 1988 Olympic Trials in Indianapolis, Indiana, that Griffith Joyner was nicknamed "Flo Jo." On 16 July, wearing an apple-green one-legged body suit and orange, black, and white fingernails, Griffith Joyner won the first heat of the 100 meter with a record time of 10.60 seconds. But the wind gauge had recorded a tail wind that prevented her from claiming the record. In the second round, with no tail wind, Griffith Joyner ran an astonishing 10.49; this time she broke Evelyn Ashford's world record of 10.76. Later in the week Griffith Joyner won the semifinal in 10.70 and the final in 10.61. She also broke the 200-meter American record of 21.84 seconds with 21.77 and later won the final in the event.

After the trials Griffith Joyner replaced Kersee with her husband as her trainer, stating that Joyner could give her the full-time attention she needed. After her performance at the Olympic Trials, Griffith Joyner became one of the highest paid track and field athletes in history (pre-trials, she earned $1,500 a race; post-trials, $25,000).

At the 1988 Olympic Games in Seoul, South Korea, Griffith Joyner's performance was phenomenal. She broke the Olympic 100-meter record with a time of 10.62 seconds; in the finals she earned the gold medal with a time of 10.54. Four days later in the 200 meter, she broke the world record twice (21.56 seconds in the semifinals, 21.34 in the finals). On 1 October 1988 Griffith Joyner ran the third leg for the gold medal–winning American 400-meter relay team. Finally, she ran anchor in the 1600-meter relay as a late addition to the team, when U.S. coach Terry Crawford wanted to give her a chance to earn a fourth gold medal. Although they placed second to the U.S.S.R., so grateful

was she for the opportunity that Griffith Joyner claimed she valued that silver more than her golds.

In the course of the Olympics, controversy ensued over Griffith Joyner's possible drug use. Insinuations were made by Olympic champions Joaquim Cruz and Carl Lewis (both later apologized). Griffith Joyner passed every drug test administered by national and international federations. The following year former 400-meter runner Darrell Robinson told the German magazine *Stern* that he bought banned growth hormones for Griffith Joyner. She steadfastly denied these charges, calling Robinson a "compulsive, crazy, lying lunatic."

Meanwhile, on 7 October 1988 Griffith Joyner won the 100-meter event, in 10.91 seconds, at a race in Tokyo, Japan. This was her final race, though her official retirement did not come until 25 February 1989. Retirement, however, didn't prevent her from becoming a media sensation. She was bombarded with contracts (for appearances, modeling jobs, commercials, and so forth), leading to the advertising industry's nickname for her: "Cash Flo." Griffith Joyner also began plans to publish ten children's books she had written, as well as fictional and autobiographical accounts of her life. She also received a plethora of awards and honors, including the Amateur Athletic Union's James E. Sullivan Award; the Associated Press Female Athlete of the Year (1988); United Press International's Sportswoman of the Year; U.S.A. Track and Field's Jesse Owens Award; Tass Sports Personality of the Year; *Track and Field News* Female Athlete of the Year; and U.S. Olympic Committee Sportswoman of the Year (all 1989).

In time Griffith Joyner's life became less of a media frenzy, and she gave birth to a baby girl on 15 November 1990. In January 1992 she ran a 5-km road race in Miami, attempting a career in long-distance running. She finished in 20:30, prompting one observer to call her "Slo Jo." This was her only attempt at road racing. The following year Griffith Joyner was selected by President Clinton to be the first female chair of the President's Council on Physical Fitness. In 1994 she and her husband cofounded the Florence Griffith Joyner Youth Foundation for disadvantaged children. Griffith Joyner was inducted into the U.S.A. Track and Field Hall of Fame in 1995.

In February 1996 there was a rumor that Griffith Joyner would come out of retirement, but she did not. Then, two months later, she suffered a seizure. The family stated that it was stress related and that there were no other indications of bad health. In 1998 the thirty-eight-year-old Griffith Joyner died in her sleep from suffocation after an epileptic seizure. The autopsy cleared Griffith Joyner of any drug use and indicated that the seizure was caused by a congenital blood vessel abnormality.

During a public viewing on Friday, 25 September 1998, over one thousand mourners bid farewell to Griffith Joyner, who was wearing a silk top decorated with bright flowers and her long black hair arranged in ringlets. On the floor near her casket laid a small pile of flowers and cards addressed to her husband and daughter. Her funeral was held the next day at Saddleback Community Church in the Orange County community of Lake Forest. The sadness of the day was heightened when her seven-year-old daughter Mary, joined by another young girl, sang a song called "When the Wind Blew on Me." Before introducing Mary, Joyner told mourners of Griffith Joyner's desire for their daughter to sing.

In her eulogy for Griffith Joyner, fellow Olympic track and field star Gail Devers noted: "When you think of Florence Griffith Joyner, you think of beauty, style, long fingernails and speed. But she was so much more." As a child, Griffith Joyner, a poor black girl from Los Angeles, once told a teacher she wanted to be "everything." She lived her life chasing this dream, becoming, in a very brief lifetime, an Olympic athlete, a wife, a mother, a writer, and a humanitarian.

★

There is no biography on Griffith Joyner for an adult audience, although several have been written for children. These include Nathan Aaseng, *Florence Griffith Joyner: Dazzling Olympian* (1992); April Koral, *Florence Griffith Joyner: Track and Field Star* (1992); and Mark Stewart, *Florence Griffith Joyner* (1997). The one posthumous children's biography is Rob Kirkpatrick, *Florence Griffith Joyner: Olympic Runner* (2000). Many magazine articles were devoted to Griffith Joyner, both before and after her death. Among the best are Kenny Moore, "Very Fancy, Very Fast," *Sports Illustrated* (Sept. 1988), and "Go, Flo, Go," *Sports Illustrated* (Oct. 1988); Julie Cart, "From Shy Dee Dee to Flamboyant Flo Jo," *Sporting News* (Sept. 1998); and Merrell Noden, "Flo Jo Lived Her Life in Fast-Forward," *Sports Illustrated* (Sept. 1998). Also, a timeline of Griffith Joyner's life is offered by Pete Cava, "USATF Release on Florence Griffith Joyner's Life and Career," *U.S.A. Track and Field* (Sept. 1998). Obituaries are in the *Los Angeles Times* and *New York Times* (both 22 Sept. 1998).

CANDICE MANCINI KNIGHT

H

HALL, Theodore Alvin (*b.* 20 October 1925 in Far Rockaway, New York; *d.* 1 November 1999 in Cambridge, England), nuclear physicist and alleged Soviet spy during World War II who was later known as a pioneer of electron and X-ray microscopy and analysis.

Hall was the youngest of four children of Barnet Holtzberg, a furrier who had fled the Russian pograms, and Rose Moskowitz, a homemaker. When his father's fur business failed early in the depression, the family moved to a small apartment in Washington Heights, New York. After his bar mitzvah, he changed his surname from Holtzberg to Hall at his older brother's urging. He showed his brilliance for mathematics and science at an early age and by junior high school had skipped three grades. By age twelve or thirteen, Hall was following domestic and international events with keen interest. In 1940 he was admitted to Columbia University in New York City but then was turned away because of his young age. Hall enrolled at the city's Queens College in fall 1940 and transferred to Harvard College in Cambridge, Massachusetts, as a junior two years later.

In spring 1944, even before graduating from Harvard, Hall began working at the Los Alamos Nuclear Weapons Laboratory in New Mexico. At age eighteen, he was the youngest physicist assisting with the Manhattan Project, the U.S. government's program to develop an atomic bomb. Hall and other scientists working on the project worried that government officials viewed the emerging bomb primarily as a superior weapon they could use after the war for U.S. advantage, rather than as a global threat to all mankind that had to be controlled and neutralized. In October 1944 Hall returned home to Forest Hills, New York, on a two-week annual leave and contacted Saville Sax, his political soul mate and former Harvard roommate. Hall told Sax about his work at Los Alamos and of his deep anxieties "about the dangers of an American monopoly of atomic weapons if there should be a postwar depression."

An unalloyed idealist, Hall believed that if he could save the world from a nuclear war, he had a responsibility to do so. Sax devised a plan that led Hall to the headquarters of Amtorg, a Soviet trade company located at 238 West Twenty-eighth Street in New York City. Over the course of the next several years, guided by a Soviet handler, aided by Sax, and working with Lona Cohen as his courier, Hall passed on technical information that saved Igor Kurchatov, the physicist who directed the Soviet atomic bomb project, a year or two of development work. Hall's information confirmed and supplemented secrets the Soviets received from Klaus Fuchs, another Manhattan Project physicist and a German communist who had fled to England in the 1930s and was sent to Los Alamos as part of the British scientific team. Neither Hall nor Fuchs knew of the other's espionage activities.

After the war Hall left Los Alamos and began studying biology, finishing his doctorate at the University of Chicago's Institute for Radiobiology and Biophysics. He mar-

247

Theodore Hall, 1990. ASSOCIATED PRESS AP

absentia as a researcher who had made fundamental contributions to the advancement of science.

In mid-1995 Hall's wartime liaisons with Soviet agents became public knowledge when the U.S. National Security Agency released hundreds of intercepted messages that had been transmitted during World War II to Moscow from the Soviet embassy in Washington, D.C., and its consulate in New York City. Decrypted over the course of many years, these cables contained a message dated 12 November 1944 that implicated Hall, but he was never charged. Looking back fifty years later, Hall had second thoughts about his actions as a young scientist who was "immature, inexperienced, and far too sure of myself." If he had known about the horrors perpetrated by Joseph Stalin's Soviet government, Hall reflected, "I think my emotional revulsion against Stalin's terror would have stopped me in my tracks."

Hall died of inoperable kidney cancer at age seventy-four, and his body was cremated. After his death, one of his daughters told Alan Cowell of the *New York Times* that her father "did what he did out of a real motive to save people's lives. It was an obligation. He was a principled man of enormous integrity." Her statement applied both to Hall's wartime actions and his groundbreaking postwar research. In each of these phases of his life, the brilliant scientist was guided by an unswerving idealism grounded on principles of social justice and individual responsibility.

★

Information on Hall can be found in Joseph Albright and Marcia Kunstel, *Bombshell: The Secret Story of America's Unknown Atomic Spy Conspiracy* (1997), and in Joseph Albright and Marcia Kunstel, "The Boy Who Gave Away the Bomb," *New York Times* (14 Sept. 1997). An obituary is in the *New York Times* (10 Nov. 1999).

MARTIN J. SHERWIN

ried Joan Krakover on 25 June 1947; they had three daughters, one of whom was later killed in an accident. In the 1950s he accepted a research position in biophysics at Memorial Sloan-Kettering Cancer Center in New York City. After spending a year at the Cambridge University Cavendish Laboratory in England, Hall settled into a permanent position at Cambridge in 1962. There he worked with Ellis Cosslett in a group that pioneered techniques of electron and X-ray microscopy and analysis. Drawing upon his knowledge of particle physics, specifically the generation and focusing of particle beams and the detection of X rays and electrons, Hall developed a new process for clarifying the chemistry of biological samples. Among numerous other applications, the "Hall method" was the most effective means of assaying the level of calcium in the mineralized plaques that form in and degrade human arteries.

Hall's key contribution was "The Microprobe Assay of Chemical Elements," an article that established him as "one of the greatest pioneers of electron microanalysis," according to a colleague. Hall's work was of such fundamental importance to medical research that it became the subject of a panel at the scanning microscopy conference in Salt Lake City in 1989. Too ill with cancer of the kidney and Parkinson's disease to attend, Hall was honored in

HARRIMAN, Pamela Beryl Digby Churchill Hayward

(*b.* 20 March 1920 in Minterne Magna, Dorset, England; *d.* 7 February 1997 in Paris, France), Democratic fund-raiser, and U.S. ambassador to France.

Born Pamela Beryl Digby, Harriman was one of four children born to Edward Kenelm Digby, who became the family's eleventh baron, and Constance Pamela Alice Bruce. Harriman grew up in England in a fifty-room country mansion, surrounded by nannies and servants, but her family was not wealthy. Like many of the landed gentry, they had little income and were living on the only capital they possessed. Harriman's formal education ended at age sixteen. When the title to the estate passed to her only brother, Harriman inherited nothing because of her gender. Grow-

Pamela Harriman, 1993. Archive Photos, Inc.

ing up, she knew her task was to marry well. It was said that aristocratic mothers with sizable families told their daughters, "Never marry for money, love where money is."

Harriman was presented to court in 1938, but she did not immediately find a husband. The next year, the war with Germany began. Randolph Churchill, the son of the soon-to-be prime minister Winston Churchill, joined the British army and began frantically looking for a wife to preserve the Churchill bloodline, as he was about to be sent overseas. After a quick courtship, he married the nineteen-year-old Harriman on 4 October 1939. The union was both a tragedy and a triumph for her. The tragedy was that the younger Churchill, although brilliant, was an insolent alcoholic and a womanizer. The triumph was that the marriage elevated her into a politically important family with a prestigious lineage, and that it produced a son, Winston Spencer Churchill, who eventually became a member of Parliament. Harriman endeared herself to her father-in-law, the harried prime minister, who always had a warm spot in his heart for her. He vastly appreciated her support during World War II, when she played bezique with him for hours on end. And when he and his wife had to sleep

in the air-raid shelter under 10 Downing Street in London, Harriman joined them.

On her own in London while her husband served in the Middle East and North Africa, she became friends with several important Americans. She met John Hay "Jock" Whitney, worth $200 million, who was in England as an officer in the U.S. Army. She also was alleged to have fallen in love with the broadcaster Edward R. Murrow, who was momentarily estranged from his wife. She made the acquaintance, and soon a fast friendship, of the wealthy financier and diplomat W. Averell Harriman, who was in London expediting U.S. aid to Great Britain; his inheritance was perhaps $100 million. Although Averell Harriman had a wife in New York City, he conducted an open affair with the young Mrs. Randolph Churchill, paying for her London flat and other expenses. It is said that Winston Churchill not only knew about the relationship, but approved of it because it offered information about what the U.S. government, so essential to Britain's survival, might do to aid the war effort. Churchill's close friend Max Aitken, Lord Beaverbrook, a Canadian newspaper magnate, hired her as a reporter because of her powerful connections.

After the war, on 18 December 1945, she divorced Randolph Churchill and moved to Paris. Here, still supported by Averell Harriman and perhaps others, she dated Prince Ali Khan and met the scion of the Fiat automotive fortune, Gianni Agnelli. It was said that she converted to Catholicism to make herself acceptable to Agnelli, but that his family intervened and decided he should marry a more suitable Italian woman. She also had an affair with Elie de Rothschild, of the European banking family, that was the talk of Paris.

During this period Harriman not only enjoyed the pleasures of Paris, where her annual bill at the House of Dior was reportedly $125,000, but spent weeks and months in London and on occasion flew to New York City and Palm Beach, Florida. In New York City she attended a round of parties, and in Palm Beach she consorted with the Kennedy family. On 4 May 1960, after years of following the jet set between the three cities, Harriman married Leland Hayward, a successful Broadway producer. His hit show *The Sound of Music* (1959) had brought him a windfall and the couple lived on a grand scale. But eventually the box-office receipts dwindled, and the couple had to leave their large Manhattan apartment for an estate on Long Island. Hayward's ill health and alcoholism took their toll, and he died in 1971.

Within months of Hayward's death, his widow encountered Averell Harriman at a Washington, D.C., party. Their old relationship resumed at once, this time resulting in marriage on 27 September 1971. The new Mrs. Harriman also became a naturalized U.S. citizen that year. Observers predicted that, with this marriage, Harriman finally would settle down; she was in her early fifties and her latest husband was seventy-nine. As in her previous marriage to Hayward, no one could fault the manner in which Harriman looked after her new husband, doing her best to make his life interesting and satisfying in his declining years. At the beginning of the marriage, she was not socially active, which was unusual for her. In time, she grew tired of shuttling between the estate on Long Island where she had lived with Hayward and Harriman's Georgetown home, so she persuaded her husband to let her sell the Long Island property and purchase an estate in the horse country outside Washington, D.C. In 1977 the Harrimans moved to a new estate, which was close to Middleburg, Virginia. Harriman soon left her own personal stamp on the home and its grounds, changing things to suit her tastes. This included the estate's name, which she changed from "Journey's End" to "Willow Oaks."

When the Democratic Party came on lean times in the 1980s, with the triumph of the Republican Ronald Reagan in the presidential elections of 1980 and 1984, Harriman persuaded her husband to help refill the Democratic coffers by hosting soirees for wealthy contributors. At the Harrimans' Georgetown house, men and women of influence discussed the Democratic Party's future and contributed millions of dollars to support its candidates. In the course of establishing a political action committee, Harriman came to support William J. Clinton in his run for a second term as the governor of Arkansas. When Clinton was nominated as the Democratic candidate for president in 1992, Harriman raised $12 million for his campaign.

In May 1993 President Clinton appointed Harriman as the U.S. ambassador to France, a position she held until her death in 1997. She was viewed as a highly effective ambassador in her dealings with international trade, defense, and general diplomatic issues. In 1996 the French government made Harriman a Commander of the Legion of Honor's Order of Arts and Letters, and in 1997 she was awarded France's Grand Cross of the Legion of Honor.

Harriman died at the American Hospital in Neuilly, France, from a cerebral hemorrhage she suffered while swimming in the pool at the Ritz Paris hotel. Harriman's life was marked by the highest of living. The ability to be a man's woman undoubtedly lay at the center of her life. Not a classic beauty, she was pretty and knew how to use her looks. If not a wit, lacking humor, she possessed an often-observed ability to listen, which did much for her socially. By the last years of her life, she had become, with apparent satisfaction, a grande dame.

★

The first biography of Harriman is Christopher Ogden, *Life of the Party: The Biography of Pamela Digby Churchill Hayward Harriman* (1994). A masterful, clearly unauthorized biography is Sally Bedell Smith, *Reflected Glory: The Life of Pamela Churchill Harriman* (1996). Books by or about social figures who mingled with Harriman often pay tribute to her, but Harriman's stepdaughter Brooke Hayward wrote the critical *Haywire* (1977). Rudy Abramson, *Spanning the Century: The Life of W. Averell Harriman, 1891–1986* (1992), provides information about Harriman as seen through the eyes of her last husband. An obituary is in the *New York Times* (8 Feb. 1997).

ROBERT H. FERRELL

HARTMAN, Phil(ip) Edward (*b.* 24 September 1948 in Brantford, Ontario, Canada; *d.* 28 May 1998 in Encino, California), comedian and actor best known for portraying smarmy but likable characters on *Saturday Night Live* (1986–1994).

Hartman referred to himself as the Gene Hackman of comedians—always dependable but not a superstar. But it was hard to be a star in a family with eight children. His mother, Doris Wardell, was a homemaker who watched over Hartman and his seven siblings. His father, Rupert Hartmann, was a building-supplies salesman. (Hartman's last name was originally spelled like his father's, but he later dropped the last letter.) Although Hartman was born in Canada, he grew up in Connecticut and Los Angeles. His gift for comedy emerged when he was young. To get around the no-swearing rule in his house, he and a friend devised a secret code for cursing in the presence of adults.

Phil Hartman. AP/WIDE WORLD PHOTOS

From 1962 to 1966 Hartman attended Westchester High School in Los Angeles. Fittingly, he was voted Class Clown in his senior year. Hartman went to Santa Monica College from 1967 to 1968, and to California State University, Northridge, from 1972 to 1973, where he majored in graphic design. He married his first wife, Gretchen Lewis, in 1970. They later divorced.

Hartman parlayed his graphic-design background into a career. In the early 1970s he designed over forty album covers for rock bands, including America, Poco, and Crosby, Stills and Nash. He even designed the latter band's logo. In 1975 Hartman joined the Los Angeles comedy troupe The Groundlings, where he met fellow comedian Paul Reubens. He honed his comedic skills with the comedy troupe until 1980 and helped Reubens develop his Pee-Wee Herman persona. In 1979 Hartman made his voice-over debut on the *Scooby and Scrappy-Doo* animated television series. His first major film role was in *The Pee-Wee Herman Show* in 1981, where he portrayed Kap'n Karl, a character he created at The Groundlings. In 1982 he met and married his second wife, Lisa Strain. They later divorced.

Hartman cowrote and costarred in *Pee-Wee's Big Adventure* in 1985. After his work on this film, his career kicked into high gear. He was a regular on *Pee-Wee's Playhouse* for the 1986–1987 season and on *Saturday Night Live* from 1986 to 1994. While on *Saturday Night Live* he showed his true range as an impersonator, portraying President Bill Clinton, Phil Donahue, Jimmy Swaggart, Barbara Bush, Ed McMahon, and Frank Sinatra, among others. All told, Hartman played or imitated over seventy characters on *Saturday Night Live*. For being a mainstay of the company, he deservedly earned the nickname "The Glue," given to him by series creator Lorne Michaels.

In 1987 Hartman married Brynn Omdahl, a former model. They had their first child, Sean, in 1989 and their second child, Birgen, in 1992. They lived in mellow Encino, California, in a ranch house that Hartman dubbed "The Ponderosa." In 1990 Hartman became a U.S. citizen.

Hartman departed *Saturday Night Live* after eight seasons, citing burnout and the need to spend more time with his family as his reasons for leaving the popular show (which was taped in New York City). However, his television career continued to blossom. He had been doing voiceover work on the hit animated series *The Simpsons* since 1989. The characters he voiced included attorney Lionel Hutz and washed-up actor Troy McClure. In 1995 he joined the cast of *NewsRadio,* playing off-kilter news anchor Bill McNeal. The show was a critical darling but had a hard time finding an audience.

In the 1980s and 1990s Hartman appeared in several films. He mostly played offbeat yet loveable characters. His film credits include *Blind Date* (1987), *Fletch Lives* (1989),

So I Married an Axe Murderer (1993), *Houseguest* (1995), *Sgt. Bilko* (1996), and *Jingle All the Way* (1996). By 1998 Hartman was enjoying the fruits of his labor with a flourishing film and television career and a seemingly happy family life.

On the morning of 28 May 1998 police found Hartman dead in his home from two gunshots to his head and Brynn Hartman dead from a self-inflicted gunshot to her head. The timeline leading up to Hartman's death will forever remain sketchy and Brynn's motivation mysterious. She had been battling substance abuse and emotional problems. According to the Los Angeles Police Department, on the night of 27 May, Brynn had been out drinking with a female friend at a restaurant. At approximately 2 A.M. on 28 May, she shot Hartman while he slept at their Encino home. She then went to her friend Ron Douglas's house. She appeared intoxicated and spoke incoherently about murdering Hartman, then briefly fell asleep. Douglas confiscated a gun from Brynn's purse and accompanied her back to her home. When they arrived, Brynn barricaded herself in her room with a second gun, and Douglas called 911. As police arrived on the scene, Brynn shot herself. Douglas and the police removed the Hartman's sleeping children from the house at approximately the same time she shot herself. Hartman was dead at the age of forty-nine; Brynn at the age of forty.

Hartman's final film and television work were dealt with quietly. His last film, *Small Soldiers,* was released posthumously in the summer of 1998. His characters on *NewsRadio* and *The Simpsons* were written out of the scripts. His scenes on the season finale of *3rd Rock from the Sun* were reshot with another actor.

Per Hartman's instructions, he was cremated, and his ashes were scattered in Santa Catalina Island's Emerald Bay. Brynn's toxicology report indicated that she had a mixture of cocaine, the prescription drug Zoloft, and alcohol in her system on the night of the murder-suicide. Her family sued the makers of Zoloft after her death, blaming the drug for her erratic behavior. The Hartmans' children relocated to Wisconsin, where they live with Brynn's family.

Hartman's unnerving death threatened to overshadow his numerous career achievements. But Hartman positively altered the comedic landscape. He was a journeyman comedian who worked hard and often, leaving the world with a large body of work to laugh at and appreciate. Perhaps Mike Scully, executive producer of *The Simpsons,* said it best: "He was somebody who made you laugh the second he walked in the room. In the egomaniacal, back-stabbing world of comedy, Hartman was the anti-jerk."

★

There is no full-length biography or autobiography of Hartman. Valuable articles about Hartman include The Movie Guys,

"10 Questions Series," *Las Vegas Sun* (May 1998); Marcus Errico, "Drugs, Booze in Hartman Murder," *E! Online* (June 1998), <http://www.eonline.com>; and David Bianculli, "Jan Hooks Remembers Phil Hartman," *Saturday Night Live Online* (June 1998), <http://www.nbc.com/Saturday_Night_Live/>. Obituaries are in *People* and *Salon* (both 28 May 1998); *Variety* (1 June 1998); *Newsweek* and *Time* (both 8 June 1998); *Entertainment Weekly* (12 June 1998); and the *New York Times* (29 May 1998).

KRISTAN GINTHER

HELLER, Joseph   (*b*. 1 May 1923 in Brooklyn, New York; *d*. 12 December 1999 in Long Island, New York), novelist noted especially for *Catch-22* (1961) and other darkly comic tales of post–World War II American life.

Heller was the son of Isaac Heller and Lena Heller, Russian Jewish immigrants living in the Coney Island section of Brooklyn. His novel *Closing Time* (1994) includes vivid accounts of this primarily Jewish enclave that many critics feel was largely responsible for the street-smart, skeptical turn his writings later took. Whatever the mixture of autobiography and imagination, some facts about Heller's early years are indisputable. His father, a bakery-truck driver, died following a botched operation when Heller was five years old. To support the family Heller's mother worked as a seamstress and laundress, while his older step-brother Lee also contributed to the household. Heller, his mother,

and his older brother were forced to deal with the harsh economic realities that played out against the larger backdrop of Coney Island's carefree, carnival atmosphere. The conjunction could hardly have gone unnoticed by the young Heller.

Heller attended Coney Island's public schools. After graduating in 1941, he worked briefly in an insurance company (as did Robert Slocum, the protagonist of *Something Happened* [1974]) and as a blacksmith's helper in the Norfolk Navy Yard before enlisting in the U.S. Army Air Forces in October 1942. During World War II, Heller, a bombardier, flew sixty bombing missions and experienced a chilling, near-death episode that eventually took the form of Snowden's agonizing death in *Catch-22* (1961) and that solidified Heller's lifelong opposition to war.

Heller left the service with the rank of first lieutenant, and after his discharge in 1945 he married Shirley Held, also a Brooklyn native, on 3 September. They had two children. Their son Theodore eventually became a novelist himself. In 1945 Heller took advantage of the GI Bill and enrolled at the University of Southern California. Heller's California sojourn, however, was short-lived. In 1946 he transferred to New York University, where he majored in English. Elected to Phi Beta Kappa in 1948, he graduated with a B.A. degree the same year. Heller continued his education at Columbia University and received his M.A. degree in 1949. He was named a Fulbright scholar and spent the 1949–1950 academic year at Oxford University,

Joseph Heller. AP/WIDE WORLD PHOTOS

where he continued his studies in English literature and also wrote short stories.

Ultimately Heller's talents as a writer outstripped his considerable abilities as a student. He had published stories in such prestigious magazines as *Esquire* and the *Atlantic,* and it was just a matter of time until he became a full-time, professional writer. The decade between 1950 and 1960 represented the "just a matter of time" for Heller. He spent those years as an instructor at Pennsylvania State University (1950–1952), as an advertising copywriter for *Time* (1952–1956) and *Look* (1956–1958), and as a promotion manager at *McCall's* (1958–1961). He continued to write short fiction and movie scripts (under the pseudonym Max Orange), and the experiences he amassed in corporate America later resurfaced in *Something Happened,* a novel about the competition, anxiety, and domestic malaise of midlevel executives. Many critics regard this work as Heller's most significant novel, surpassing even *Catch-22* in its probe beneath the surface of life.

As Heller labored away at a variety of day jobs, he also worked on draft after draft of the novel that changed his life as well as the course of contemporary American fiction, *Catch-22.* He did occasional stints as a visiting writer at Yale University and the City University of New York, but always according to his terms. After the publication of *Catch-22* in 1961, Heller's days of teaching multiple sections of freshman composition were over, as were his years of grinding out advertising copy.

Catch-22, Heller's bitterly absurdist, antiwar protest novel about the waning days of World War II, added a significant phrase to the American national vocabulary. Contemporary literature's most enduring "catch" was originally called "catch-18." Heller's publisher forced the numerical change to avoid confusion with Leon Uris's *Mila 18* (1961), a novel that was forgotten in contrast to Heller's. Heller was surprised to find himself hailed as black humor's resident genius. Yet it is hardly surprising that Yossarian, the novel's edgy protagonist who is put upon by the small print of procedures and the small minds who administer the rules, quickly became an iconic figure for those who came of age in the countercultural 1960s, just as *Catch-22* became an extended trope for the war in Vietnam.

Heller's first novel gave gallows humor a brio it had not had before and in the process changed readers' minds about the form an antiwar novel could take. Rather than chronicling the painful initiations that lead sensitive protagonists to question the shibboleths of recruiting posters, Yossarian enters the fray all too aware of the central truth about war: people are out to kill him. That the European campaign is nearly at an end and its outcome certain only intensifies Yossarian's feeling that life on Pianosa (based on the Mediterranean island of Corsica, where Heller was stationed while in the U.S. Army Air Forces) boils down to long stretches of boredom interrupted by "milk runs," bombing missions uncontested by the enemy, during which an extraordinary number of aviators manage, nonetheless, to die absurd deaths.

Yossarian cannot see the logic in this situation, so he takes comic arms against it, feigning illness, moving bombing lines on the map, or perching naked in a tree during an official ceremony. It is a small wonder that he is written off as "crazy" or that he finds himself tilting against windmills and a wide assortment of loopy windbags. Yossarian is at once the quintessential outsider and a man dedicated to throwing comic monkey wrenches into the military machine.

With the notable exception of *Something Happened,* his second novel, Heller's subsequent work did not match the artistry of *Catch-22.* Critics tended to admire *Something Happened* more than general readers did. Those who had laughed out loud as Milo Minderbinder's empire became ever more comically entangled were unsure how to respond when Heller's portraits of suburban angst hit closer to home. Bob Slocum, the jittery protagonist of *Something Happened,* "gets the willies" whenever he sees a closed door, so fearful is he of what those behind the door might be saying about him or, worse, plotting against him. Slocum's defining characteristic is dread. The result was an achievement that for too long was hidden under the long shadow of *Catch-22.*

Heller's subsequent novels fared less favorably with critics and general readers alike. Tirades sometimes replaced plot lines, and Heller's wrath vented itself with increasing frequency in novels such as *Good as Gold* (1979); *God Knows* (1984); *Picture This* (1988); *Closing Time* (1994), the failed sequel to *Catch-22; Now and Then: From Coney Island to Here* (1998); and most acutely in the posthumously published *Portrait of an Artist as an Old Man* (2000). Not surprisingly the result pulls Heller's fictions in several competing directions. *Good as Gold,* for example, begins with the effort, probably ill advised, of its protagonist Bruce Gold to write a book about the Jewish experience in America. Gold's heart clearly is not in the project, and neither apparently is Heller's.

God Knows is if anything worse. Heller seemed incapable of writing a dull page or lackluster paragraph. Yet for all the novel's flashes of biblical knowledge and moments of stylistic dazzle, *God Knows* turns King David's complaints into a cheesy lounge act. At one point God insists that He never promised to make sense: "I'll give milk. I'll give honey. Not sense."

No Laughing Matter (1986), an account of Heller's scary bout with Guillain-Barré Syndrome (GBS), has the look of life imitating art. Heller suffered his first attack on 12 December 1981, when he was in the middle of writing *God Knows. No Laughing Matter* is a chronicle of and by a protagonist who is so weak he can hardly get out of bed. A similar condition travels to the book's author, not as an affliction of old age or as just punishment for a sinful life but unexpectedly, mysteriously, "existentially." To make matters worse, Heller was suffering through a nasty divorce, which provided him with ammunition to hurl against lawyers. Heller's illness brought him into contact with a nurse named Valerie Humphries, whom Heller married on 11 April 1987. *No Laughing Matter* is not a novel, nor is it a successful memoir. But its insider account of Heller's troubles—his extended bout with GBS as well as the saga of divorce lawyers out to pick him clean—and the recounts of visits by Mel Brooks, Dustin Hoffman, and Mario Puzo to his hospital bed create intriguing reading.

Unfortunately the same claim cannot be made with regard to *Picture This,* Heller's tedious exercise in deconstructing Rembrandt's *Aristotle Contemplating the Bust of Homer* (1653). Its ambiance can be described as an extended meditation on all manner of things, such as the life of Rembrandt and the death of Socrates, the rise of the Netherlands and the fall of Athens, what is real versus what is illusion, and, perhaps most of all, how money, then and now, talks. Heller was always partial to the oxymoronic as well as the possibilities that open up when one pushes an observation to its logical absurdity. In *Picture This* he writes about paintings that are "an authentic imitation of a Hellenic reproduction." But the fact remains that both Rembrandt's portrait and Heller's novel are effectively deconstructed in the process.

In 1994 Heller published *Closing Time,* his effort to reclaim the limelight that had been gradually slipping away since *Catch-22*. The book was simultaneously a brave and foolish effort—brave because *Closing Time* has sprawl and narrative energy, foolish because as a sequel to *Catch-22* it was destined to encourage comparisons and to lose. *Closing Time* reunites a handful of *Catch-22* survivors some fifty years later, as they deal with the body's decay and plots even wider and more insidious than those that energized the original novel. This time, however, Heller adds Jewish characters, including himself, who bring large dashes of growing up in Coney Island into the mix. Like *Good as Gold, Closing Time* is in effect several novels in one, each working against the grain of the other and none adding up to the power Heller unleashed in his first novels.

Heller died of heart failure at the age of seventy-six. When *Portrait of an Artist as an Old Man* was published posthumously in 2000, many critics, remembering Heller's more successful performances, argued that his reputation would have been better served if the manuscript had remained in his desk drawer.

Heller's *Catch-22,* however, is a classic. It changed how Americans think about war and also how Americans see the darkly comic entanglements that come with contem-

porary life. *Catch-22, Something Happened,* and sections of the other novels convey a sense of civilization's long decline and fall and the body's losing battle with entropy.

★

Many of Heller's manuscripts and papers are at Brandeis University in Waltham, Massachusetts. There is not a full-length biography of Heller, but critical studies include David Seed, *The Fiction of Joseph Heller* (1989); Sanford Pinsker, *Understanding Joseph Heller* (1991); Judith Ruderman, *Joseph Heller* (1991); and Brenda A. Keegan, *Joseph Heller: A Reference Guide* (1978). James L. McDonald, "I See Everything Twice: The Structure of Joseph Heller's *Catch-22,*" *University Review* 34 (1968): 175–180, and James Nagle, "*Catch-22* and Angry Humor: A Study of the Normative Values of Satire," *Studies in American Humor* 1 (1974): 99–106, are informative critical articles. A long, respectful obituary is in the *New York Times* (13 Dec. 1999), and Heller's death was duly noted on network television newscasts.

SANFORD PINSKER

HELMSLEY, Henry Brakmann ("Harry") (*b.* March 1909 in New York City; *d.* 4 January 1997 in Scottsdale, Arizona), real estate developer best known for his acquisition of the Empire State Building.

The son of a wholesale dry-goods buyer, Henry Helmsley, Sr., and Minnie Brakmann, Helmsley was born in the Inwood section of Manhattan but moved at an early age to the Bronx, New York. After graduating from Evander Childs High School in 1923, at the age of sixteen, he secured a $12 per week job at the real estate firm of Dwight, Voorhis, and Perry. Although he started out an errand boy, he was promoted to rent-collector for the company's holdings in the Hell's Kitchen section of New York City. Working through the boom years of the 1920s and into the Great Depression of the 1930s, Helmsley became adept at sizing up the value of buildings and finding potential buyers. He rose up in the firm to become secretary in 1936, vice president and partner in 1938, and eventually president in 1943.

All the while, Helmsley began amassing his own real estate empire. In 1936 he bought his first building, which he sold in 1946 for a net profit of $100,000. Two years later he began working with Lawrence A. Wien, a lawyer who matched Helmsley's skill at identifying potentially valuable buildings with a talent for securing outside capital. During the next two decades, the two joined forces with Alvin Schwartz and Irving Schneider to purchase dozens of properties. Although they started buying loft buildings in the garment district, by 1954 they bought the prestigious Lincoln Building on Forty-second Street across from Grand Central Terminal.

By then, Helmsley had proven himself one of the most

Harry Helmsley with his wife, Leona, 1989. ED BAILEY/ASSOCIATED PRESS AP

successful brokers and managers in New York City. He gained a reputation of being tough, honest, and true to his word. He also was quick to realize that his business practices should change with the economic climate of the times. In inflationary periods, he saw the benefits of securing long-term fixed mortgages, while in periods of falling interest rates, he recognized the need to buy with cash and reduce his debt. While these later became basic tenets in business school classes, Helmsey was one of the earliest developers to put these ideas into practice.

Helmsley's purchase of the Lincoln Building marked him as a major player in New York City, a fact emphasized one year later when he purchased Leon Spear's highly regarded real estate company and formed the partnership of Helmsley-Spear, Inc. More dramatic was Helmsley's successful bid in 1961 to purchase the Empire State Building for $65 million. Although a risky prospect at first, Helmsley cut operating costs in the building and increased rents, so that by 1986 his share of the profits stood at almost $4 million. In addition, he earned annual brokerage fees of between $2 and $3 million per year.

But the financial rewards from the Empire State Building deal in no way slowed Helmsley's appetite for real estate. Four years later, he added considerably to his holdings through the acquisition of two New York City brokerage houses, Charles F. Noyes Co. and Brown, Harris, Stevens, Inc. In 1969 he bought some thirty other buildings from the Morris Furman and Herman Wolfson real estate trust.

He also began to expand from being a broker and owner to being a developer. He erected among others the fifty-two-story Marine Midland Bank building in lower Manhattan, One Penn Plaza, the Pfizer building, and the Merchandise Mart in Los Angeles. By 1971 he owned office buildings all over Manhattan, as well as commercial and residential buildings in Philadelphia, Pennsylvania; Washington, D.C.; St. Louis; Chicago; Decatur, Illinois; Fort Wayne, Indiana; Houston; Los Angeles; and San Francisco. Eventually, he would establish 400 separate holding companies for these and other properties.

Helmsley shared his early success with wife Eve Ella Sherpick Green, a widow whom he met in the 1930s. They were married in 1938 and lived at first on Tiemann Place on the Upper West Side of Manhattan, before moving to 45 Gramercy Park North. But in 1972, after thirty-three years together, the couple divorced. By then Harry Helmsley had met a woman twelve years his junior, Leona Roberts (née Leona Mindy Rosenthal), who worked in sales for one of his subsidiaries, Brown Harris Stevens. In April of the following year the new couple married. With the new Mrs. Helmsley by his side, the man who had once been known as quiet and dedicated to his work became more outgoing.

Helmsley's new marriage also marked a new expansion of his career into hotel construction and operation. He had bought some as part of his earlier acquisitions, including the St. Moritz in 1961, but mostly they were investment opportunities. In 1971, however, at a time when most in the industry thought the luxury hotel market in New York was glutted, he opened the Park Lane hotel on Central Park South. The new hotel thrived and he quickly acquired others, including the Cleveland-based Harley chain. Before long Helmsley was running forty hotels, but none more impressive than the Palace hotel in New York City, which he built above the Villard Houses, previously owned by the Catholic Church.

The Palace hotel appeared to prove Helmsley's skills as a developer. He battled again landmark preservationists, the Catholic Church, and zoning ordinances, but eventually opened what many claimed was the most luxurious hotel in the city in 1980, the same year he named his wife president of Helmsley Hotels. The Palace, however, also became his undoing. Its construction costs soared above expectations, rising from $73 million to $110 million, and investors began legal proceedings to explore where the money was going. An arbitration panel eventually ruled for the investors, finding that Helmsley had hired his own subsidiaries to provide services, but at inflated prices, and that he had allowed Mrs. Helmsley to order costly changes during construction. He was forced to pay investors $757,616 and make changes in his accounting procedures.

The actions of investors spurred the state and federal government to begin investigating the Helmsleys for tax fraud. In April 1988 prosecutors announced charges on 188 counts of tax fraud, accusing the Helmsleys of paying personal expenditures with business funds, particularly on Dunnellen Hall, their home in Greenwich, Connecticut, and owing an additional $1.2 million in federal taxes. Helmsley faced a multi-million dollar penalty and up to 162 years in jail. The trial was delayed by various postponements, including a medical ruling that found Helmsley's memory was insufficient to assist in his own defense. In December 1988 he was removed from the trial. Mrs. Helmsley, however, was later found guilty and sentenced to a four-year jail term and fines of over $7 million. Helmsley died from pneumonia less than ten years after the trial at the age of eighty-seven, leaving an estate valued at nearly $1.7 billion to his wife. He is buried in Woodlawn Cemetery in the Bronx, New York.

★

The late 1980s placed Helmsley in the limelight, and several books came out about his life, including Michael Moss, *Palace Coup: The Inside Story of Harry and Leona Helmsley* (1989); Richard Hammer, *The Helmsleys: The Rise and Fall of Harry and Leona* (1990); Ransdell Pierson, *The Queen of Mean: The Unauthorized Biography of Leona Helmsley* (1989). All relied on interviews with key players and press coverage for information and all noted the difficulty in getting access to company documents and Mr. or Mrs. Helmsley for their own words. Sources for Helmsley and his accomplishments are hard to come by. For details on how Helms-

ley's empire has been dispersed since his death, see David Dunlap, "Dividing Harry Helmsely's Empire," *New York Times* (26 Nov. 2000). Obituaries are in the *New York Times* (6 Jan. 1997), *Daily News* (6 Jan. 1997), *People Weekly,* and *Time* (both 20 Jan. 1997).

THORIN TRITTER

HENRY, Aaron Edd Jackson (*b.* 2 July 1922 on the Flowers' Plantation in Coahoma County, Mississippi; *d.* 19 May 1997 in Clarksdale, Mississippi), state president of the National Association for the Advancement of Colored People (NAACP), politician, and champion of civil rights in Mississippi.

Henry was the youngest of four children born on a Delta plantation to Joseph Jackson and Elizabeth Henry. Following the death of his mother in 1925 and his father in 1927, he was adopted by his mother's brother, Edd Henry, a sharecropper and shoe cobbler, and Edd Henry's wife, Mattie Logan Henry, a beautician and real estate salesperson. The family moved to Webb, Mississippi, where they lived for a year before settling in Clarksdale, Mississippi, in 1928. Henry attended the segregated Myrtle Hall Elementary School and then went to Coahoma Agricultural High School, graduating in 1941. Henry was drafted into the U.S. Army in 1943.

Aaron Henry, 1977. AP/WIDE WORLD PHOTOS

Henry's lifelong commitment to the civil rights movement began during his service in the army from 1943 to 1946. While stationed in Hawaii, he participated in his first protest—a demand for integrated housing in the military. He later stated, "The army taught me that racial segregation and discrimination were not unique in Mississippi but confirmed my feeling that the situation was worse in my home state." When Henry returned to Clarksdale in 1946, he immediately sought to get blacks registered to vote and was the first African American in Coahoma County to vote in a Democratic primary. In the fall of 1946 he enrolled at Xavier University in New Orleans, where he served as president of his junior and senior classes and as president of the student body in his senior year. Upon graduating in 1950 with a degree in pharmacy, he returned to Clarksdale and opened Fourth Street Drug Store, which would become a hub for civil rights activists. On 11 June 1950 he married Noelle Celestine Michael, with whom he had one daughter.

In 1953 Henry organized and became president of the Coahoma County branch of the NAACP. He became state president of the NAACP in 1960 and served in that capacity until 1993. During the 1960s, Henry was involved in numerous civil rights activities. He was among those arrested in the Freedom Rides of May 1961, which were organized by the Congress of Racial Equality (CORE) to test the Supreme Court's 1960 ruling against segregated facilities for interstate travelers. Later in 1961 Henry was arrested for leading a boycott in Clarksdale to demand fair treatment of black employees and customers. In the fall of 1963 Henry was overwhelmingly elected governor of Mississippi in a mock election, designated the "Freedom Vote." Its purpose was to demonstrate to the nation that blacks were interested in politics and to show Mississippi blacks the potential power of their vote. About 80,000 blacks voted.

During Freedom Summer of 1964, Henry served as chairperson of the Council of Federated Organizations (COFO), an umbrella agency that attempted to coordinate the activities of the NAACP; the Student Nonviolent Coordinating Committee (SNCC); the Southern Christian Leadership Conference (SCLC); and CORE. He launched a number of voter registration drives during the 1960s, and he was often the target of abuse for his civil rights views. His house was firebombed twice, and he was arrested as many as thirty times. His pursuit for justice, however, continued. After the assassination of his close friend, the civil rights leader Medgar Evers, Henry is quoted as saying, "ever since Medgar Evers died, I have been making sure he didn't die in vain."

Henry cofounded and served as chairperson of the Mississippi Freedom Democratic Party (MFDP), a biracial coalition that challenged the exclusion of black members by the Democratic Party in Mississippi. The MFDP's principal goal was to have a delegation seated at the 1964 Democratic National Convention in Atlantic City, New Jersey. Although supported by delegates from other states, the MFDP delegation was denied seating and refused a compromise that offered only Henry and the Reverend Edwin King, a white MFDP member, seating as at-large, not Mississippi, delegates. Though it did not achieve its goal at the time, the MFDP opened the road for African-American delegates in Mississippi to represent their state at future Democratic conventions.

Henry was instrumental in securing congressional support for passage of the Economic Opportunity Act of 1964, an outgrowth of President Lyndon B. Johnson's "War on Poverty." He was a strong supporter of the Jobs Corps, a program the act established, and Project Head Start, a program for low-income preschool children established in 1965.

Henry left the MFDP in 1965 because he felt they had become too radical. He helped to form the Loyalist Democrats, a more moderate group composed of blacks, white liberals, and labor activists. He chaired their delegations to the 1968 and 1972 Democratic National Conventions. The regular democrats and the Loyalist democrats were unified for the 1976 National Convention. Henry was elected to the Mississippi House of Representatives in 1979 and held the seat until 1996. He used his seat in the House to fight for improved health care, housing for the poor, and educational reform. In 1980 Henry filed a lawsuit that led to the reapportionment of districts, allowing for the election of more representatives.

Henry's awards include the Distinguished Mississippian Award, the Rosa Parks Award, and the American Pharmaceutical Association Hubert H. Humphrey Award. He died at age seventy-four of congestive heart failure in the Northwest Regional Medical Center in Clarksdale and is buried in Jackson. In March 2000 the federal building in Clarksdale was renamed the Aaron E. Henry Federal Building and United States Courthouse.

As a leader in the NAACP, Henry participated in almost every aspect of Mississippi's struggle for equality. His entire life was committed to civil rights issues, although he was little known outside his home state of Mississippi. He refused to compromise with an unjust system that treated African Americans as second-class citizens, and he fought to lift poor Mississippi blacks and whites out of the grips of poverty. In his words, "the old Mississippi River has never had one ounce of racial prejudice. It will drown or wash away a white man just as quick as a Negro and never think twice about it. . . . The Mississippi gave both whites and blacks their water and food, and it accepted our waste—the giving and the taking were all on equal basis."

★

Henry's papers are archived at Tougaloo College in Tougaloo, Mississippi. Some materials, including correspondence with civil rights leaders, are contained in the *Citizens' Council/Civil Rights Collection* at the University of Southern Mississippi-McCain Library and Archives in Hattiesburg. Transcripts of Henry's oral history interviews are in the Ralph J. Bunche Oral History Collection at Howard University's Moorland-Spingarn Research Center in Washington, D.C., and in the University of Southern Mississippi-McCain Library and Archives in Hattiesburg. Henry's autobiography, *Aaron Henry: The Fire Ever Burning* (2000), ed. Constance Curry and with an introduction by John Dittmer, provides an excellent account of Henry's life and writings, including interviews from some of his friends and family. A short biography of Henry appears in George A. Sewell and Margaret L. Dwight, *Mississippi Black History Makers* (1984). Bill Minor, "The Life of Aaron Henry," *Madison County Journal* (31 May 2000), gives a sketch of Henry's life using *Aaron Henry: The Fire Ever Burning* as background. Obituaries are in the *New York Times* and *Clarksdale Press Register* (both 21 May 1997).

JOYCE K. THORNTON

HENSON, Paul Harry (*b.* 22 July 1925 near Bennet, Nebraska; *d.* 12 April 1997 in Rancho Mirage, California), pioneer in the telecommunications industry who took a high-risk gamble to create the first coast-to-coast fiber-optic network in the 1980s and, as the leader of what would become the Sprint Corporation, transformed a rural, independent telephone operation into an international telecommunications company.

Henson was the third of four children born to Harry Henson, a dairy farmer, and Mae Schoenthal, an occasional schoolteacher. The family ran a dairy herd on a 160-acre rented farm near Bennet, a small farming community southeast of Lincoln, Nebraska. It was a difficult existence. His father, gassed as a soldier during World War I, suffered health problems, and the Hensons, like many other dust bowl families, struggled during the Great Depression. His mother exposed the children to the cultural opportunities in nearby Lincoln, the state capital, and took them to the First Presbyterian Church—the beginning of Henson's lifelong religious commitment. Henson excelled in school, skipping a grade and graduating as the class valedictorian in 1942, at age sixteen, from Lincoln's College View High School. He also was the captain of the football team and an All-State quarterback.

Henson immediately took a job as a warehouseman for the Lincoln Telephone and Telegraph Company and enrolled in the University of Nebraska on a scholarship. In 1943, at age eighteen, he enlisted in the Army Air Forces and served for two years as a flight instructor, earning the rank of captain. When World War II ended, he returned to Lincoln Telephone and Telegraph as an engineer and district manager. On 2 August 1946 he married Betty Roeder, whom he had known since childhood; the couple had two daughters. Henson then resumed his undergraduate work at the University of Nebraska, earning a B.S. degree in 1948 and an M.S. degree in 1954; both degrees were in electrical engineering. He pursued postgraduate work exploring the new technology of transistors. Henson's technical background served him well, allowing him to see how technological innovations could change an emerging industry.

In 1955 Henson became the chief engineer for Lincoln Telephone and Telegraph, a position he held until 1959. Then he became the vice president of operations for United Utilities, a small independent telephone company that had recently moved from Abilene, Kansas, to Kansas City, Missouri. Henson advanced quickly at the company, becoming the executive vice president in 1960, president in 1964, and chief executive officer in 1966. He moved the company to suburban Westwood, Kansas, in 1966. Under Henson's leadership, United Utilities grew from a hodgepodge of small, mostly midwestern, rural phone companies into a national company with operations in twenty states. Henson guided the company through the major challenge of upgrading the rural phone systems from operator-assisted to direct-dial technology. By 1976 the company, now renamed United Telecommunications, had grown to 3.5 million local customers and $1 billion in revenues, but was nevertheless a Lilliputian concern compared to the industry giant American Telephone and Telegraph (AT&T).

In time, however, technological advances and freer competition resulting from judicial action led to a major restructuring of the telecommunications industry. The shift began in 1974 with the U.S. Justice Department's antitrust case against AT&T, and culminated a decade later in U.S. District Judge Harold Greene's landmark decision in January 1982 to break up AT&T into eight separate long-distance or local telephone companies. Prior to the decision, AT&T had held a near monopoly on the profitable long-distance business and, Judge Greene found, had used its dominance to compete unfairly against the independent telecommunications companies.

United Telecommunications moved quickly and boldly to take advantage of the new competitive opportunities. In 1984 it announced plans to build a coast-to-coast fiber-optic network—a major departure from the analog systems that transmitted information over twisted-pair cooper-wire lines, microwave radio, or satellite transmission. The analog system was slower and had less capacity, requiring separate lines for data and voice. The digital fiber-optic system, on the other hand, used bursts of light carried on glass fibers as thin as a human hair, and could simultaneously handle voice, data, and video signals traveling at the speed of light. It was an integrated telecommunications system and the nation's first digital highway.

Although this new technology had been proved to work, constructing a 23,000-mile fiber-optic network—a length nearly equal to the earth's circumference—was a daunting engineering challenge comparable, in some respects, to the challenges posed in building the transcontinental railroad a century earlier. The feat was completed in less than four years. It was a bet-the-farm move and well beyond the means of United Telecommunications. The network cost $2.5 billion to build, against corporate assets of $2 billion. The company incurred $785 million in losses and write-offs from 1982 to 1988. Besides promoting the new technology, Henson helped to form a partnership with GTE-Sprint, an industry competitor, to combine forces and fortunes to build the fiber-optic network. The successful partnership led to a 1992 buyout of GTE-Sprint and the merged parent company was renamed the Sprint Corporation.

In the early days of the project, the fiber-optic network's champion had been diagnosed with inoperable liver cancer; he suffered severe pain for the rest of his life. Henson resigned as the chief executive officer of United Telecommunications in 1984 but stayed on as the corporate chairman. By the time Henson retired in 1990, his twenty-four-year tenure as the chairman had seen the rural telephone operation grow from a $100 million operation to an international carrier with $8 billion in revenues. Henson soon became the nonexecutive chairman of Kansas City Southern Industries, a transportation and financial services company, and was scheduled to retire from that position in 1997, when he died of cancer while in California for medical treatment. He is buried in Overland Park, Kansas.

Throughout his career, Henson devoted extensive energy to leadership positions in several major Kansas City institutions, including the Children's Mercy Hospital, Kansas City Symphony, Greater Kansas City Community Foundation, and Midwest Research Institute. He was awarded honorary doctoral degrees by the University of Nebraska, Ottawa (Kansas) University, Bethany (Kansas) College, and University of Missouri-Kansas City. Henson was inducted into the National Business Hall of Fame in 1999. Henson's singular accomplishment was the construction of a coast-to-coast fiber-optic data system in the late 1980s. It was both a technological and engineering feat that made a major contribution to the development of the modern competitive telecommunications market. The digital network, built despite the ridicule of skeptics and financial analysts, was a vastly superior data transmission system; its completion was regarded as the first major artery of what later became popularly known as the information highway.

★

Henson's business career is well-documented in trade publications and newspaper profiles, which provide many details of his personal and business life. He published a few monographs, but there is no published biography, manuscript collection, or oral history. John Hoffman provides some insight into Henson's corporate and personal leadership in *That Was a Pin? The History of Sprint Corporation* (2000), whereas the technological achievement of the fiber-optic network is lauded in a corporate history of the project, *We've Got Light! Building the Nation's Coast-to-Coast Fiber-Optic Network* (1988). An obituary is in the *New York Times* (15 Apr. 1997).

BRENT SCHONDELMEYER

HERSHEY, Alfred Day   (*b.* 4 December 1908 in Owosso, Michigan; *d.* 22 May 1997 in Syosset, New York), biochemist and Nobel laureate best known for a series of experiments that used a blender to shake up the history of science.

Hershey, born to Robert Day Hershey, an employee of an auto manufacturer, and Alma Wilbur, was raised in Owosso and Lansing, Michigan. Hershey attended Lansing Central High School before earning both his B.S. degree in biology (1930) and his Ph.D. in chemistry (1934) from Michigan State College (now Michigan State University), where he developed an interest in the study of bacteria. His

Alfred D. Hershey, 1969. ARCHIVE PHOTOS, INC.

doctoral dissertation focused on the chemistry of Brucella, the causative agent of undulant fever. Also known as brucellosis, undulant fever is an illness characterized by fever, night sweats, extreme tiredness, weight loss, and headache.

After earning his Ph.D., Hershey took a position as a research assistant in the department of bacteriology at the Washington University School of Medicine in St. Louis. He spent the next sixteen years moving up the academic ladder at Washington, teaching and gradually shifting his research from bacteria to the viruses that infect them. These viruses, called bacteriophages (or phages), were beginning to be viewed as the biological tools that could offer researchers a window into life at the most basic level. Composed of a protein shell containing a core of nucleic acid, phages are too small to be seen with even the most powerful microscopes, yet they are capable of replicating and causing infection. Understanding phages, it was thought, could not only help scientists comprehend viruses in general and perhaps find new ways to fight the diseases they caused but might also open the door to understanding the nature of life itself.

Besides Hershey, by the 1940s phage studies had attracted some of the brightest minds in science, including the Italian virologist Salvador E. Luria and the German physicist Max Delbrück. In 1945 Luria and Hershey independently showed that phages and their bacterial hosts could spontaneously mutate, thus helping to explain the adaptability of viruses. The next year Hershey demonstrated that different strains of a phage infecting the same bacterial cell could combine or exchange genetic material (a finding also reached by Delbrück at about the same time). Although they worked in separate laboratories, Delbrück, Hershey, and Luria, through correspondence and conversation, created the beginnings of what would become the "phage group," an influential and important development in the history of molecular biology.

Hershey married Harriet Davidson, who had been his research assistant, on 15 November 1945. They had one son, Peter. In 1950 Hershey accepted a position as staff scientist in the department of genetics at the Carnegie Institute's Cold Spring Harbor Laboratory on Long Island, New York. It was there, in 1952, that he and his assistant, Martha Chase, performed the experiment that won Hershey a Nobel Prize.

While most geneticists of the day believed that traits were passed from one generation to the next via some molecule present in the chromosomes of cells, they were not certain what the molecule was. The two leading candidates were protein and nucleic acid, the primary chemical constituents of chromosomes. The evidence favored protein because of its complex structure and its presence everywhere in the body, forming the basic material of hair and horn, enzymes and hemoglobin. DNA (deoxyribonucleic acid,

the most common form of nucleic acid in advanced cells), which is made up of only four building blocks, appeared to exist in one basic form and was restricted mainly to the nuclei of cells. Compared with protein, DNA seemed a dumb molecule and was perhaps just a structural component that held protein in the correct shape in chromosomes.

There was, however, a smattering of evidence favoring DNA as the genetic material of cells, the most important of which was published in the mid-1940s by the American bacteriologist Oswald T. Avery. But Avery presented his results tentatively, and his work had little impact. What was needed was a definitive answer to the protein-or-DNA question, and Hershey provided it.

In a series of experiments in 1951 and 1952, Hershey and Chase devised a method for tracking the two alternatives separately in bacteria infected with a phage. By tagging the phage protein with radioactive sulfur and the phage DNA with radioactive phosphorus, they were able to pinpoint the location of phage DNA and protein as infection proceeded. They cleverly stopped the infection process at specific points by spinning the culture in a Waring blender to shake the phage particles loose from the bacteria. Hershey and Chase found that the phage protein remained outside the bacterial cells while the phage DNA entered the cells and was intimately involved in the replication process. Their results clearly showed that genetic information is carried by DNA.

The "Waring blender experiment," as it became known, was published in 1952, and Hershey amplified its effect by communicating the results in a number of letters before publication. The evidence moved DNA to center stage in the research of geneticists, chemists, biologists, and others interested in finding the molecular basis of life. The following year, James Dewey Watson, a former student of Luria's who was conducting postdoctoral research on viruses at the Cavendish Laboratory in England, and his lab mate, Francis Harry Compton Crick, published the molecular structure of DNA. Modern molecular biology was born.

Hershey's later research focused on the structure of phage DNA, which he discovered was single-stranded in some cases and circular in others, unlike the double-stranded DNA in humans. He was named director of the Genetics Research Unit at Cold Spring Harbor in 1962 and retired in 1974. A tall, quiet man, he enjoyed reading and sailing in his spare time, and his hobbies included working with wood and planting trees.

Hershey was elected to the National Academy of Sciences in 1958, receiving its Kimber Genetics Award in 1965. He shared the Nobel Prize in physiology or medicine in 1969 with Luria and Delbrück. The somewhat belated prize (Watson and Crick won theirs in 1962) prompted the *New York Times* to editorialize: "Delbrück, Hershey, and

Luria richly deserve their awards, but why did they have to wait so long for this recognition? Every person associated with molecular biology knows that these are the grand pioneers of the field, the giants on whom others—some of whom received the Nobel Prize years ago—depended for their own great achievements." This is certainly true of Hershey, whose simple, direct, and persuasive work set the stage for great advances in genetics, biochemistry, and medicine.

Hershey died of cardiopulmonary failure at his home in New York at age eighty-eight.

★

There is no book-length biography of Hershey. A collection of reminiscences by molecular biologists and six scientific articles by Hershey are gathered in Franklin W. Stahl, ed., *We Can Sleep Later: Alfred D. Hershey and the Origins of Molecular Biology* (2000). Significant sections on his contributions to molecular biology can be found in Horace Freeland Judson, *The Eighth Day of Creation: Makers of the Revolution in Biology* (1979), and Robert Olby, *The Path to the Double Helix: The Discovery of DNA* (1974; reprint, 1994). Obituaries are in the *New York Times* and *Washington Post* (both 24 May 1997) and *Guardian* (London) (27 May 1997).

THOMAS HAGER

HIGGINBOTHAM, A(loysius) Leon, Jr. (*b.* 25 February 1928 in Trenton, New Jersey; *d.* 14 December 1998 in Boston, Massachusetts), federal circuit court judge, legal scholar, and outspoken civil rights advocate.

Higginbotham was born to Aloysius Leon Higginbotham, a laborer, and Emma Lee Douglass, a homemaker. He went to a racially segregated elementary school in Trenton and was the first African American to attend Trenton Central High School. At age sixteen, Higginbotham enrolled at Purdue University in Indiana to study engineering, but he left after the school's president denied his request that he and the other African-American students be allowed to move from their cold, off-campus housing to the heated dormitory, telling Higginbotham that the school was not legally obligated to do so. Higginbotham transferred to Antioch College in Yellow Springs, Ohio, where he received a B.A. degree in sociology in 1949, and then went on to Yale Law School, earning an LL.B. degree in 1952. Higginbotham recalled bitterly in later years that despite having graduated with honors from Yale, he was turned down for a job at a top Philadelphia, Pennsylvania, law firm because of his race. When the interviewer saw that Higginbotham was an African American, he told him, "Of course, you know there's nothing I can do for you."

A. Leon Higginbotham, Jr.

Higginbotham began his professional life in 1952 as a law clerk to Justice Curtis Bok of the Philadelphia Court of Common Pleas, then served for a year as an assistant district attorney under Richardson Dilworth. In 1954 he helped form the African-American law firm of Norris, Green, Harris, and Higginbotham and remained in private practice until 1962. During that time, Higginbotham served as president of the Philadelphia chapter of the National Association for the Advancement of Colored People (NAACP). From 1960 to 1962 he was a special hearing officer for conscientious objectors for the U.S. Department of Justice.

President John F. Kennedy appointed Higginbotham to the Federal Trade Commission in 1962, making him the first African American to be named to a federal administrative agency. His seven-year term was cut short in 1964 when President Lyndon B. Johnson appointed him as U.S. District Court Judge for the Eastern District of Pennsylvania. At thirty-six, Higginbotham was the youngest person in thirty years to be named to the federal bench. President Jimmy Carter named Higginbotham to the U.S. Federal Court of Appeals for the Third Circuit in Philadelphia in 1977. He became chief judge of the Third Circuit in 1989.

While on the federal bench, Higginbotham authored more than 650 opinions. A staunch defender of abortion rights, he ruled in 1987 that local governments must pay for abortions for female prisoners when no other resources are available. His views as presiding judge in the appeal of a bankruptcy judgment were incorporated into the Bankruptcy Reform Act of 1994. Higginbotham's greatest contribution to American jurisprudence may have been his numerous articles, particularly those on civil rights and racial equality. He published two books in a planned four-book series on the history of race and law in the United States: *In the Matter of Color: Race and the American Legal Process: The Colonial Period* (1978) and *Shades of Freedom: Racial Politics and Presumptions of the American Legal Process* (1996). In these works, Higginbotham asserted that throughout its history, the United States had shown scant commitment to the ideal of racial equality, arguing that the founding fathers were guilty of hypocrisy in advancing the notion that all men are created equal while fostering slavery. In "West Virginia's Racial Heritage: Not Always Free," published in the *West Virginia Law Review* (fall 1983), Higginbotham argued that the creation of West Virginia only resulted in a milder form of racial bias. In Higginbotham's view, although West Virginia had separated from its "harsh legacy" of slaveholding Virginia, the separation of the western counties from the state—supposedly to prevent the evil of slavery—did not mean equality for African Americans for it initially forbade free colored persons to enter the state.

In the early 1980s Higginbotham visited South Africa, where he came face-to-face with apartheid. He later compared the intellectual arguments supporting that country's system of apartheid to the rationalizations supporting racial segregation in America. Higginbotham returned to South Africa in 1994 as a mediator in the country's first elections in which blacks were allowed to vote.

Higginbotham reacted to the 1991 appointment of the conservative judge Clarence Thomas to the U.S. Supreme Court by publishing an open letter to Thomas in the *University of Pennsylvania Law Review* chastising him for abandoning the gains African Americans had achieved since the Civil War. Higginbotham was criticized both publicly and privately for his attack on Thomas, while others applauded his candid remarks.

During his judicial career, Higginbotham taught sociology and law at the University of Pennsylvania and also taught at the law schools of the University of Michigan, Yale, New York University, and Stanford. Following his retirement from the federal bench in 1993, he taught at Harvard Law School and was named public service professor of jurisprudence at Harvard University's John F. Kennedy School of Government. Higginbotham continued to write and lecture and sat on several corporate boards. He also worked for the law firm of Paul, Weiss, Rifkind, Wharton, and Garrison in their New York City and Washington, D.C., offices. Higginbotham's first marriage on 21 August 1948 to Jeanne L. Foster ended in divorce in 1988; the couple had three children. He later married Evelyn Brooks, a professor of history and African-American studies

at Harvard, who had a daughter from her first marriage. Higginbotham adopted the daughter.

In September 1995 President William J. Clinton awarded Higginbotham the Presidential Medal of Freedom and in October 1995 appointed him commissioner of the U.S. Commission on Civil Rights. The NAACP awarded Higginbotham the Springarn Medal in 1996, and he held honorary degrees from more than sixty colleges and universities. Shortly before his death, Higginbotham appeared before the House Judiciary Committee to argue against the impeachment of President Clinton, stating that "the alleged perjurious statements denying a sexual relationship between the President . . . and another consenting adult do not rise to the level . . . that triggers the impeachment clause of Article II [of the Constitution]."

Higginbotham died at age seventy of a massive stroke at Massachusetts General Hospital. He is buried in Oak Bluffs Cemetery on Martha's Vineyard, Massachusetts. As both a mentor to his law students and an advocate for the disadvantaged, Higginbotham went out of his way "to let the rope drop back down," in the words of one of his friends. He would remember and address pleas for help years after he received them. At six feet, five inches tall and with a booming voice, Higginbotham's presence was a strong accompaniment to his passionate outspokenness on behalf of civil rights, affirmative action, and equality.

★

Higginbotham's judicial opinions while a federal district court judge appear randomly from 223 to 429 in the *Federal Supplement,* and those he issued as a Third Circuit court judge appear randomly from 560 to 983 in the *Federal Reporter.* Before he died, Higginbotham had begun to write his autobiography and had started to work on the third and fourth volumes of his series *Race and the American Legal Process.* His book *Shades of Freedom* (1996) contains an extensive listing of his published articles. For Higginbotham's views on the Anita Hill–Clarence Thomas controversy, see his essay "The Hill-Thomas Hearings—What Took Place and What Happened: White Male Domination, Black Male Domination, and the Denigration of Black Women" in *Race, Gender, and Power in America: The Legacy of the Hill-Thomas Hearings* (1995), ed. Anita Faye Hill and Emma Coleman Jordan. A tribute in the *Harvard Law Review* (June 1999) and Colin S. Diver's tribute in the *Pennsylvania Gazette* (Mar. 1999) are particularly informative. Obituaries are in the *New York Times* and *Philadelphia Inquirer* (both 15 Dec. 1998).

JOHN DAVID HEALY

HIRT, Alois Maxwell ("Al") (*b.* 7 November 1922 in New Orleans, Louisiana; *d.* 27 April 1999 in New Orleans, Louisiana), trumpeter, bandleader, and singer whose name became a household word in the 1960s.

Born to Alois Hirt, a policeman, and Linda Guepet, a homemaker, Hirt was given a pawn shop trumpet at age six by his father. One of four children, he took to the instrument at once and played in the Junior Police Band. After graduating from high school in 1940, Hirt won a scholarship to attend the Cincinnati Conservatory of Music (now a part of the University of Cincinnati) where he continued studying classical music. When Hirt saw his classmates earning money playing in dance bands, he decided to teach himself this style of music and carefully studied the recordings of Harry James and Roy Eldridge. Thus he began playing big band jazz and launched an amazing career in popular music.

After an early and unsuccessful marriage from 1940 to 1942, Hirt married Mary Patureau, also of New Orleans, on 13 August 1942. The couple had eight children. World War II ended Hirt's formal studies in October 1943 when he entered the U.S. Army. He played in an Army Air Forces Band and served overseas before his discharge in 1946.

Returning to civilian life, Hirt toured for several years with the big bands of Jimmy Dorsey, Tommy Dorsey, Ray McKinley, Tony Pastor, and others. In 1949 he won a Philip Morris Talent contest, appeared on Horace Heidt's

Al Hirt, 1991. BILL HABER/ASSOCIATED PRESS AP

radio program, and then toured both the United States and Europe with Heidt's orchestra. Weary of travel and missing his home and children, Hirt returned to New Orleans in the early 1950s and supported his growing family with various jobs. He was staff trumpeter for the local CBS radio station, played in the pit band of the St. Charles Theater, and entertained in various local nightclubs playing the Dixieland music so dear to the region. Classically trained and obviously gifted as a self-taught big band jazz musician, Hirt had almost no Dixieland experience whatsoever, and at first had to memorize his parts while everyone else in the band would improvise. Once again Hirt had to teach himself a new style of music.

Hirt formed his own Dixieland group which included his friend, the famous clarinetist Pete Fountain, in 1955. Although he played weekends with his group and recorded occasionally for the Verve and Southland labels, Hirt held down a day job at this time as a pest control salesman. Eventually, however, his band was heard in New Orleans by New York talent agent Gerard Purcell, who recognized Hirt's potential. After a November 1960 gig in Las Vegas, Nevada, arranged by Purcell, Hirt's career skyrocketed. The group played next in New York City, where Hirt was offered a recording contract by RCA. His first long-play recording for RCA, *The Greatest Horn in the World,* sold over 100,000 copies within a few months after its release in 1961.

The 1960s were lucrative for Hirt. He gave concerts with stars such as Ella Fitzgerald, and in 1962 he appeared in two Warner Brothers films, *Rome Adventure* and *World by Night.* After regular television appearances on the popular *Dinah Shore Show, Ed Sullivan Show, Andy Williams Show,* and others, Hirt had his own summer television program, *Fanfare,* in 1965 on CBS. In the same year, his RCA platinum album *Our Man in New Orleans* (1962), was beamed up to the two astronauts in the *Gemini 5* spacecraft orbiting Earth. Hirt continued to record, and many of the nearly three dozen albums he made during his long career are from the 1960s with RCA. He received over twenty Grammy nominations, and four of his albums sold more than two million copies each. His "Java" (one of the all-time best-selling instrumentals) won him the Grammy in 1964 for best non-jazz instrumental. In 1967 Hirt became part owner of the New Orleans Saints professional football team, but he sold his share at a loss soon after. Although musically gifted, Hirt was not successful when it came to finance and business.

During the 1970s Hirt's meteoric career leveled out, although he continued to record. During this decade he played mainly in New Orleans at his own nightclub on Bourbon Street, The Al Hirt Club, which closed in 1983.

Hirt divorced his wife of thirty-two years in 1974. In 1984 he married Zide B. Jahncke of New Orleans; this marriage was dissolved in 1987. At that time and on into the 1990s, Hirt toured the country, playing in settings as diverse as orchestra halls and state fairgrounds. Affectionately known as "Jumbo" to his friends, the six-foot-six performer weighed over 300 pounds at times, which affected his health. Hirt, however, was a generous and fun-loving performer who enjoyed wisecracking with both the audience and his sidemen. Ever the optimist, Hirt married Beverly Essel in 1991. Major health problems beset him in the mid-1990s, including a stroke and severe edema which kept him in a wheelchair during his last months. Hirt died of liver failure at his home and is buried at Lakelawn Cemetery in Metaire, a suburb of his beloved New Orleans.

Neither a pure jazz player nor an impressive improviser, Hirt was famous for his swing, or "roving," Dixieland style. Calling it "the Nashville sound," Hirt mixed pop, country, western and jazz music. His trumpet could growl one moment and abruptly soar into long, lyrical phrases the next. Hirt's facility for playing high, low, fast, or slow has been equaled by few and surpassed by none. Although some critics were uncomfortable with Hirt's popular, commercial style and felt he could have done more with his many talents, this never bothered the genial trumpeter. He once said simply, "I'm a pop commercial musician and I've got a successful format." During Hirt's career he played for six U.S. presidents, Princess Grace of Monaco, Pope John Paul II, and millions of fans worldwide. This was more than enough for a man who often called himself "a crowd pleaser" and who only wanted "to be remembered as a decent person and a good trumpet player."

★

Current Biography Yearbook (1967) provides an in-depth look at Hirt at the peak of his career. See also the Hirt article in Leonard Feather, *The Encyclopedia of Jazz in the Sixties* (1986). The interview "Big Man with a Trumpet," *New York Times* (4 July 1965), lets the trumpeter speak for himself. Obituaries are in the *Los Angeles Times, New York Times,* and *Washington Post* (all 28 Apr. 1999) and *New Orleans Times-Picayune* (29 Apr. 1999). The RCA recordings *The Greatest Horn in the World* (LSP 2366), *Horn a Plenty* (LSP 2446), and *Honey in the Horn* (LSP 2733) are among Hirt's best.

MICHAEL MECKNA

HITCHINGS, George Herbert, Jr. (*b.* 18 April 1905 in Hoquiam, Washington; *d.* 27 February 1998 in Chapel Hill, North Carolina), Nobel laureate best known for his research on the principles of drug action, which resulted in the development of new treatments for a variety of serious illnesses.

Hitchings was the son of a shipbuilder, George Herbert Hitchings, and his wife, Lillian Matthews. He had two older sisters. His father died of a prolonged illness when

George H. Hitchings with Gertrude Elion after they won the Nobel Prize in medicine, 1988. ASSOCIATED PRESS/BORROUGHS WELLCOME

he was only twelve years old, and Hitchings claimed that this event stimulated his interest in medicine. He entered the University of Washington as a premedical student in 1923, and graduated cum laude with a B.S. degree in chemistry in 1927. Hitchings remained at the University of Washington for a year to earn an M.S. degree in chemistry in 1928.

He then entered Harvard University to undertake further graduate work in chemistry. A year later Hitchings transferred to the department of biological chemistry in the Harvard Medical School, where he earned his Ph.D. in 1933 for a dissertation involving the development of analytical methods for purine bases. On 30 May 1933 he married Beverly Reimer, with whom he had two children.

Hitchings remained at Harvard as a research associate and instructor until 1939, when he moved to the Western Reserve University School of Medicine in Cleveland, where he did research on electrolytes. His career did not begin to blossom, however, until he became head of the biochemistry department at the Burroughs Wellcome Research Laboratories in suburban Tuckahoe, New York, in 1942. At first the sole member of the department, Hitchings soon assembled a small group of talented researchers. The most important addition to his staff was the chemist Gertrude

Elion, who was hired as a laboratory assistant in 1944 and began a career-long research collaboration with Hitchings that led to their winning the Nobel Prize.

Although working in the laboratory of a commercial pharmaceutical firm, Hitchings and his coworkers pursued basic research, which ultimately resulted in the discovery of a number of useful therapeutic agents. Hitchings and Elion initially investigated the synthesis of nucleotides, the building blocks of deoxyribonucleic acid (DNA). Hitchings was aware that sulfanilamide, an antibacterial drug that had been introduced in the 1930s, exerted its effect on bacteria because it was closely related chemically to a natural substance, para-aminobenzoic acid. Sulfanilamide replaced para-aminobenzoic acid in the metabolism of the cell, interfering with key biological processes. Substances such as sulfanilamide were known as antimetabolites because they blocked the action of enzymes involved in metabolism. Using the antimetabolite concept, Hitchings and Elion developed compounds that blocked the enzyme necessary for the production of DNA in the cell.

Their first therapeutic success was against leukemia, a form of cancer characterized by rapid production of white blood cells in the body. They found that the chemicals 6-mercaptopurine and thioguanine were effective in blocking the DNA synthesis involved in the formation of the white cells. Collaborating with the Sloan-Kettering Institute in the late 1940s and early 1950s, they showed that these drugs could bring about a remission of the disease without being too toxic to the other cells of the human host. The introduction of the concept of blocking DNA synthesis for therapeutic purposes was as important as the discovery of the specific substances used in the treatment of leukemia.

Hitchings and Elion continued their research on antimetabolites. In 1957 they synthesized azathioprine, which was shown by investigators at Tufts University to suppress the immune system's production of antibodies. The drug proved useful in organ transplantation, by helping to prevent the rejection of the implanted tissues by the body, and also in autoimmune diseases such as rheumatoid arthritis.

Another successful drug introduced by Hitchings and Elion was allopurinol, which inhibited the action of the enzyme xanthine oxidase, thereby interfering with the synthesis of uric acid. Allopurinol proved effective in the treatment of gout, which is caused by uric acid deposition in the joints.

By the 1960s Hitchings and Elion were investigating the use of antimetabolites against bacterial and viral diseases. Their research in this area resulted in the introduction of such drugs as pyrimethamine, effective against the microorganism responsible for malaria, and trimethoprim, used in the treatment of urinary and respiratory tract infections. In the 1970s the team developed the antiviral drug acyclovir for the treatment of herpes. Their work on antiviral drugs helped to lay the foundation for the development of drugs, such as azidothymidine (AZT), used against the HIV virus that causes AIDS.

In 1967 Hitchings became vice president in charge of research at Burroughs Wellcome Company, a position from which he retired in 1976 to become a scientist emeritus at the firm. He also became director of the company's nonprofit foundation, the Burroughs Wellcome Fund, in 1968, and then president of the fund in 1971. Hitchings moved to the firm's new site in Research Triangle Park, North Carolina, in 1971.

Hitchings shared the Nobel Prize in physiology or medicine for 1988 with Elion and British pharmacologist Sir James Black for their discoveries of important principles of drug treatment. Hitchings gave his share of the prize money to the Greater Triangle Community Foundation, which he founded in 1983. Other honors recognizing his work include election to the National Academy of Sciences in 1977 and honorary doctorates from thirteen universities. He was the author or coauthor of more than 300 published papers and was responsible for eighty-nine U.S. patents.

After fifty-two years of marriage, Hitching's wife, Beverly, died in 1985. On 9 February 1989 he married physician Joyce Shaver. He died at age ninety-two at his home in Chapel Hill from complications of Alzheimer's disease.

★

The best biographical articles on Hitchings are the entries by Marsha Meldrum in Daniel M. Fox, Marcia Meldrum, and Ira Rezak, eds., *Nobel Laureates in Medicine or Physiology: A Biographical Dictionary* (1990), and by Sanford S. Singer in Frank N. Magill, ed., *The Nobel Prize Winners, Physiology or Medicine,* vol. 3 (1991). Hitchings discusses his life and work in *Les Prix Nobel, The Nobel Prizes, 1988* (1989). Obituaries are in the *New York Times, Washington Post,* and *News and Observer* (Raleigh, N.C.) (all 1 Mar. 1998).

JOHN PARASCANDOLA

HOGAN, William Benjamin ("Ben") (*b.* 13 August 1912 in Stephensville, Texas; *d.* 25 July 1997 in Forth Worth, Texas), one of the twentieth century's most skillful and influential golfers.

Hogan was born to Chester Hogan, a blacksmith and mechanic, and Clara Hogan. Hogan's father committed suicide when Hogan was nine years old, and his mother raised him and his brother and sister in Forth Worth, Texas. Hogan's father's violent death probably contributed to the development of Hogan's difficult and reclusive personality. He attended school in Forth Worth but desperate economic circumstances forced him to leave high school without graduating. He then sold newspapers and within a year

Ben Hogan with his wife, Valerie, 1950.

was by far the best from tee to green that I've ever seen. He was a brilliant golfer, a wonderful strategist, a great general of the game." With his precise, repetitive swing ("like a machine stamping out bottle caps," one writer quipped), Hogan established a new standard for striking and controlling a golf ball; and with his penchant for unrelenting practice, he created a new professional work ethic. "There is not enough daylight in a day to practice all the shots you ought to be practicing," Hogan once lamented. What Hogan accomplished, how he achieved his success, and the mystique that surrounded him shaped golf in America in the second half of the twentieth century.

To his friend Byron Nelson, Hogan was "the man who could play for glory better than anyone I've ever seen." Ben Crenshaw, two-time Masters Champion and golf historian, noted, "Hogan has a special meaning to golfers everywhere. It's not just a following. He stands as a total inspiration." He was the "pro's pro," playing golf with total commitment and uncommon grace. All in all, it was Hogan who "led the PGA from its rowdy days into the modern era of professionalism," according to writer Charles McGrath.

Once Hogan began to win, after a decade of struggling to do so, he won or was in contention for winning practically every tournament that he entered. His PGA record lists sixty-three victories between his first individual win in 1940 (North and South Open) and his last (Colonial Invitational) in 1959. His majors included two Masters (1951 and 1953), four U.S. Opens (1948, 1950, 1951, 1953), the British Open (1953), and two PGA Championships (1946 and 1948). In 1953 he achieved the remarkable feat of winning the Masters, the U.S. Open, and the British Open in the same year. He was one of only five players to have won all four of the world's majors.

From 1946 to 1953, at the apogee of his career, Hogan won nine of the sixteen majors he entered, making him the most efficient winner of major championships in golf history. He won the Vardon Trophy for the lowest stroke average four times. He was the PGA player of the year four times and the leading money winner five times. He set the scoring record in the U.S. Open and the Masters. In fourteen consecutive U.S. Open Championships through 1960, and the same number of Masters to 1956, Hogan was always among the top ten. He was undefeated in Ryder Cup play (1947 and 1951).

With only a Masters championship eluding his grasp, Hogan was determined to win in 1949. He began the season by winning the Bing Crosby Invitational and Long Beach Open. But on 2 February while driving to El Paso, Hogan's Cadillac was struck head-on by a Greyhound bus. Just before impact, he threw himself across his wife to protect her. As a result, Valerie was relatively unharmed, but Hogan sustained serious multiple injuries. His left collarbone, ankle, and leg were badly broken; he sustained sev-

was also caddying at Glen Gardens Country Club. At five feet, eight inches tall and 130 pounds, Hogan first played golf as a left hander and was often beat. He had enough talent to turn professional in 1930 at age eighteen, however. Yet his long, loose swing produced drives that ended with an unpredictable snap hook, and his flawed swing was driving him deeper into poverty. As Byron Nelson, with whom Hogan learned to play while they caddied together, said, "Ben Hogan had more problems learning to play golf than any good player I ever saw."

On 14 April 1935 Hogan married Valerie Fox, whom he had known since childhood. The couple struggled financially until Hogan adjusted his swing in the late 1930s. Hogan won money in fifty-six consecutive tournaments between 1939 and 1941. He finished 1940 as the lead money winner with over $10,000 in earnings, and in 1942 he won the Hale America National Open, which replaced the PGA championship during World War II. His career was interrupted during World War II by two years of service in the Army Air Forces from 1943 to 1945.

After the war, Hogan emerged as the golfer against whom all professionals' play and careers henceforth would be measured. As golfing great Gene Sarazen noted: "He

eral broken ribs and a fractured pelvis. In the hospital he developed life-threatening blood clots that required tying off veins in his leg. His doctors worried whether he would walk again; no one—except Hogan himself—imagined that he would return to golf.

But eleven months later, in January 1950, Hogan was back. He entered the Los Angeles Open and battled Sam Snead to a playoff, which he lost. Five months later he was in contention at the U.S. Open at Merion. At the end of four rounds he was tied with Lloyd Mangrum and George Fazio. Few gave the limping, ailing Hogan much of a chance. But the following day, he extended an effort that is universally regarded as one of the most moving and heroic moments in sports history. With both legs bandaged from his ankles to his crotch, Hogan limped through the round, occasionally leaning on his caddie, achieving a stunning 69 victory over Mangrum's 73 and Fazio's 75. It was a superhuman effort but one that Hogan repeated annually for a decade until the pain became unbearable. "Golf was my business and pain shouldn't bother anybody," Hogan responded years later to a question about how he dealt with the agony. "My problem was the farther I [walked], the heavier my legs got." That year he also won the Greenbrier Pro-Am. Hollywood could not resist this heroic, emotional story. A movie based on Hogan's life, *Follow the Sun,* starring Glenn Ford as Hogan and Anne Baxter as his wife, screened in theaters across the United States in 1951.

Over the next three years, Hogan's achievements became the source of legend. Limited by his injuries to playing selected tournaments, Hogan nevertheless sustained an extraordinary record of victories. He won the World Championship in 1951. He then won the Masters and, for the third time, the U.S. Open, where he shot a final round 67—generally considered the best round of golf he ever played. His single victory in 1952 was the Colonial Invitational, a tournament that he won so frequently that locals dubbed it "Hogan's Alley."

Then came Hogan's *annus mirabilis,* 1953. First he won the Masters, with a record-breaking 274. Next he won the Pan-American Open and the Colonial before winning his fourth U.S. Open. Reluctantly, because travel was so uncomfortable for him, Hogan entered the British Open at Carnoustie in Scotland. Playing with the smaller British ball, on a totally different type of course, his scores improved daily (73–71–70–68), and he won by four strokes. It was a memorable exhibition of smart, controlled golf. With this win, Hogan reached the pinnacle of his sport as the sole player to win these three majors in a single season (the PGA conflicted with the British Open).

Hogan won the Canada (World) Cup in 1956, and he completed his career of tour victories in 1959 at the Colonial Invitational. But at the 1967 Masters Hogan had a victory of another sort. He shot a third-round 66, including a course record 30 on the back nine that brought fans and jaded writers alike to cheers and tears as he marched up the eighteenth fairway, tipping his trademark white hat. "I think I played the best nine holes of my life on those holes. I don't think I came close to missing a shot," Hogan said.

Hogan was a complex personality who was often bitingly cruel to anyone who violated his privacy. But his close friends talk about his warmth and generosity, his sentimentality, and his fairness. To U.S. Open Champion Ken Venturi, Hogan was "a very shy and a very humble man." He had a carefully concealed penchant for slapstick humor, which he exposed on *The Ed Sullivan Show,* imitating Ed driving a golf ball.

Short and slight of build, Hogan was known for his white hat, golf clothes in muted colors, and ever-present cigarette. He was called "the Hawk" during his career, a moniker that referred to his grim, steely-eyed style of play that mentally photographed every important aspect of a golf course and excluded everything else, including his fans and his playing partners. But in 1953, Cecil Timms, Hogan's caddy at the British Open, dubbed him "The Wee Ice Mon," which was a shrewder observation about the source of his extraordinary powers of concentration than of his countenance.

The two things that mattered to Hogan were his loving wife and golf. His terrible accident softened him, but it didn't change his general attitude toward life. It made him dig deep into his psyche to find the strength, courage, motivation, intelligence, and, as much as anything else, the "ice" he needed in his veins to win. "The man was so sick for so long, and fought it so successfully, that I think we have finally discovered the secret of [his] success. It was the strength of his mind." Hogan said that about Bobby Jones, but he was also commenting on his own life and character.

Hogan's wrote several instruction books, but his *Five Lessons: The Fundamentals of Golf* remains the golf-instruction classic. After retiring from tournament golf in 1971, Hogan spent his days in Fort Worth attending to business at the Ben Hogan Company (which he started in the 1950s), then lunch and practice at the Shady Oaks Club. Hogan was ill for several years before his death, suffering from Alzheimer's disease and undergoing surgery for colon cancer in 1995. He died following a stroke and is buried in Greenwood Cemetery in River Oaks, Texas.

★

Curt Sampson's biography *Hogan* (1996) is a critical look at the great golfer. Gene Gregston, *The Man Who Played for Glory* (1978), is an admiring biography that also surveys the changes in golf over Hogan's lifetime. Obituaries are in the *New York Times, London Times, Chicago Tribune,* and *Detroit Free Press* (all 26 July 1997).

MARTIN J. SHERWIN

HOLLOWAY, Bruce Keener (*b.* 1 September 1912 in Knoxville, Tennessee; *d.* 30 September 1999 in Orlando, Florida), four-star U.S. Air Force general and fighter ace who led the Strategic Air Command during the Vietnam War.

One of two children of Frank P. Holloway, a mill owner, and Elizabeth Keener, a homemaker, Holloway graduated from Knoxville High School in 1929. He studied engineering at the University of Tennessee for two years, then attended Marion Military Institute for two months before entering the United States Military Academy at West Point. He graduated from West Point in 1937 and received his pilot's wing in 1938 before joining the Eighteenth Pursuit Group, a fighter unit in Hawaii. Enrolled in a postgraduate course in aeronautical engineering at the California Institute of Technology in 1941, he left school when the United States entered World War II.

His next assignment was with the Fourteenth Fighter Group at Hamilton Field, California. He was promoted to major in February 1942 and in May went to Chongqing (Chungking), China. He was attached as an observer to the Flying Tigers, a unit of the American Volunteer Group (AVG), which, under contract to the government of Chiang Kai-shek, flew P-40s with distinctive tigershark-teeth markings in missions against the Japanese. Holloway began flying combat missions when the AVG disbanded on 4 July 1942 and became the Twenty-third Fighter Group of the U.S. Army Air Forces. His aerial combat during several strafing missions earned him the Silver Star. First as a squadron commander, and then as commander of the entire Twenty-third Fighter Group, Holloway, flying a propeller fighter, flew 106 missions, shot down thirteen Japanese planes, and gained recognition as one of the first fighter aces of World War II. Holloway also had the distinction of being one of only five American aces to fly the Zero 3372, a captured Japanese war plane, making him a member of the Zero Club, Twenty-third Fighter Group. Altogether he spent nineteen months in China, during which he led the Twenty-third Fighter Group through a period of distinguished growth and success. According to Holloway, "it was time well spent, and I learned much about warfare in a remote part of the world that you would never learn from a War College or Tactical School texts." Holloway returned to the United States in 1944. On 14 October 1944 he married Frances Purdy. They had three daughters.

When World War II ended, Holloway commanded the 412th Fighter Group. Equipped with the Lockheed P-80A Shooting Star, this was America's first jet-fighter outfit and it pioneered the new field of tactical jet air operations. Holloway graduated from the Air Command and Staff School at Maxwell Air Force Base, Alabama, in June 1947 and was assigned to Headquarters Air Defense Command (HQ ADC) as director of defense, and later as director of plans. After graduating from the National War College in 1951, he progressed through top-level assignments in operations and development. Receiving his first star and the rank of brigadier general in 1953, Holloway, as deputy director for requirements, helped establish Lincoln Laboratories, a facility in Massachusetts devoted to applied research in air defense, and played a major role in preparing and evaluating proposals for many of the aircraft and missiles used for the next fifty years. Beginning in 1955, he spent the next four years in Tactical Air Command as deputy commander of the Ninth and Twelfth Air Forces, successively. From 1959 to 1961 he served as director of operational requirements. In 1961 Holloway was named deputy commander of the U.S. Strike Command, headquartered at MacDill Air Force Base. Later in that assignment, he fulfilled additional duties as deputy commanding chief of the Middle East/Southern Asia and Africa South of the Sahara Commands.

In 1965 Holloway assumed command of the U.S. Air Force in Europe until his appointment as vice chief of staff of the U.S. Air Force in 1966. From 1968 to 1972 Holloway was commander in chief of the Strategic Air Command (SAC), the United States' long-range strike force comprised of a mixture of combat aircraft and intercontinental ballistic

General Bruce K. Holloway, 1966. AP/WIDE WORLD PHOTOS

missiles. In this position, Holloway oversaw more than 1,000 intercontinental ballistic missiles and 500 long-range giant jet bombers, which, by 1971, provided 85 percent of the American strategic nuclear strength. Holloway also headed a multiservice staff that provided the president with war plans by listing potential targets and suggesting what weapons might be used for each. Holloway was an active pilot until he retired on 1 May 1972 after thirty-five years of active service. He was the only four-star general to fly the highly secret SR-71, a long-range supersonic reconnaissance aircraft known as the Blackbird.

Holloway received many medals and honors, including the Army Distinguished Service Medal, the Air Force Distinguished Service Medal, the Silver Star, the Order of the Sacred Tripod (China), the Grand Cross of the Order of Merit of the Federal Republic of Germany, the French Legion of Honor-Order of Commander, and the Most Noble Order of the Crown of Thailand. After retirement, Holloway became a trustee for the New York Institute of Technology from 1972 to 1986 and for Nova University, Fort Lauderdale, Florida, from 1973 to 1982. On 30 September 1987 the Marion Military Institute named its Service Academy Preparation program the General K. Holloway School of Service Academy Preparation. The program's curriculum is designed to provide extraordinary preparation for students seeking appointments to the service academies. He often wrote articles for the *Vanguard* and the *Air Force Historian.*

Holloway died at age eighty-seven from heart failure at his home in Orlando, Florida. His body was cremated and the ashes were buried at the family plot in Knoxville, Tennessee.

A close friend, the actor Jimmy Stewart, said of Holloway, "he has never forgotten the difference between machines and people. You keep machines going with wrenches and hammers, but people with human understanding." His wife talked fondly of his love for the railroad and his interest in railroad mechanics, which he shared with Orlando school children who visited and rode a train run by Holloway's friend, John Cassidy. Holloway was referred to as the "gentleman general." His distinguished career was based not only on airborne exploits but also on effective leadership skills, particularly the sharing of information with those under his command, which he believed would increase their knowledge and understanding of the military.

★

Official papers and Holloway's unpublished diaries relating to his Air Force career are at the Air Force Historical Research Agency. Holloway was one of four authors of *Grand Strategy for the 1980s* (1978). Other career and biographical information is located in the Cullum File maintained by the Association of Graduates at West Point's Herbert Alumni Center. Carl Molesworth's *Sharks Over China: The 23rd Fighter Group in World War II* (1994) gives an excellent account of Holloway's aerial combat in China. Obituaries are in the *New York Times* (9 Oct. 1999) and *Tampa Tribune* (10 Oct. 1999).

JOYCE K. THORNTON

HOLZMAN, William ("Red") (*b.* 10 August 1920 in New York City; *d.* 13 November 1998 in New Hyde Park, New York), basketball player, scout, and Hall of Fame coach.

Holzman was born on the Lower East Side of New York City to Abraham Holzman, a tailor from Russia, and Sophie Holzman, a homemaker from Romania. The family moved from the Lower East Side to a tenement in Brooklyn when Holzman was four years old. The family, which included Holzman's older brother and sister, spoke Yiddish at home, and Holzman grew up with a love for the sound of the language.

Holzman attended Franklin K. Lane High School in Brooklyn (during his senior year, the school was relocated to Jamaica, New York, in the borough of Queens). He excelled in handball as well as in basketball and made

"Red" Holzman, 1968. © BETTMANN/CORBIS

Lane's All-Scholastic basketball team in 1938, his graduation year. At the same time he played for Lane, he also played basketball for the Workmen's Circle, a fraternal Jewish organization coached by Red Sarachek, who later became the coach at Yeshiva University. Through the Workmen's Circle, Holzman also met Selma Puretz, whom he wed on 12 November 1942; they had one daughter. Selma dubbed Holzman "Red" because of his fiery hair.

Holzman attended the University of Baltimore in Maryland from 1938 to 1939 and then transferred to the City College of New York, where he played basketball under Nat Holman and was selected for both the All-Metropolitan and All-American basketball teams (1940–1942). Following his graduation from City College in 1942, he enlisted in the U.S. Navy and was stationed in the morale unit at Virginia's Norfolk Naval Base. After completing his military service in 1945, Holzman, who was five feet, ten inches tall, played the guard position for the Rochester Royals in the old National Basketball League (NBL) until 1948. He then played with the Royals in the newly formed National Basketball Association (NBA) from 1948 to 1953.

During his years as a professional basketball player, Holzman was selected for the NBL All-Star First Team in 1946 and 1948 and for the NBL All-Star Second Team in 1947. Although he was never a prolific scorer (11.6 collegiate career scoring average, and 7.4 lifetime scoring average in the NBL and NBA), Holzman was chosen for the NBA All-Star team in the 1951 season, after the Royals won the NBA championship. Toward the end of his playing career, Holzman became a player and coach for the Milwaukee Hawks (1953–1954).

Holzman was one of only ten professional players to win championships as a player and coach. After his stint with the Hawks in 1954, Holzman coached the team full-time in 1955, and when they moved from Wisconsin to Missouri he became the head coach of the NBA St. Louis Hawks (1955–1957). In 1958 he became the assistant coach of the New York Knickerbockers, or Knicks, and in 1967 became the team's head coach until 1977, when he briefly stepped down. Holzman returned to coach the Knicks from 1978 until 1982, when he relinquished the job to Hubie Brown.

During his tenure as the Knicks coach, Holzman led the team to two championships (1970, 1973) and to the NBA finals (1972). Holzman's record with the Knicks was 613–384, and his overall regular season coaching record was 696–504 (.535). His play-off record was 58–48. In 1970, after the Knicks won the NBA championship, Holzman was selected as the NBA Coach of the Year. He coached the Eastern NBA All-Star team in 1970 and 1971, and in 1981 was voted the first recipient of the National Basketball Coaches Association Achievement Award.

As one of the NBA's premier coaches, Holzman was credited with nurturing the career of Bob Pettit, a future basketball Hall of Famer, whom he coached in Milwaukee and St. Louis. His greatest coaching fame, however, came from his time with the Knicks. Under Holzman's leadership, the Knicks personified a New York, street-smart style of basketball called the "city game," which was characterized by unselfish play and a pressing defense. During his champion years with the Knicks, Holzman coached five future Hall of Fame players: Willis Reed, Walt Frazier, Dave DeBusschere, Earl ("The Pearl") Monroe, and Bill Bradley, who later became a U.S. senator. His Knicks team also included Phil Jackson, who became the coach of the champion Chicago Bulls, led by Michael Jordan; later, Jackson coached the champion Los Angeles Lakers, led by Kobe Bryant and Shaquille O'Neal.

When Holzman retired from coaching in 1982 he was the most successful coach in the Knicks history and the second-winningest coach in NBA history (second only to Red Auerbach). He was soon hired by the Knicks as a team consultant, offering advice to the coaches Pat Riley and Jeff Van Gundy. In 1986 Holzman was inducted to the NBA Hall of Fame. During the 1996–1997 season the NBA recognized Holzman's achievements by naming him as one of the top-ten coaches in NBA History.

In January 1998 Holzman became ill and was diagnosed with leukemia. On 28 July 1998, after fifty-five years of marriage, his wife passed away at age seventy-five due to heart failure. Without his loving supporter, Holzman passed away in November of the same year at Long Island Jewish Hospital, due to complications resulting from leukemia. Both Holzman and his wife are buried in Beth Israel Cemetery in Woodbridge, New Jersey.

Holzman was known for his low-key coaching approach and for his ability to take players with diverse backgrounds and mold them into a team unit. Frazier, who played under Holzman, believed one of Holzman's greatest accomplishments as a coach was getting the Knicks to focus on winning game seven of the 1970 NBA finals against the Los Angeles Lakers, led by Wilt Chamberlain, instead of on the center Willis Reed's debilitating hip injury. In the *New York Times*, the columnist Ira Berkow remembered Holzman as "the molder, conductor, and architect of one of the most unusual, most thrilling, and, for the involved basketball fan, most gratifying teams ever assembled."

★

Anecdotes about Holzman's experiences in basketball can be found in his *Holzman on Hoops* (1989), coauthored with Harvey Frommer. His autobiography, also with Frommer, is *Red on Red* (1987). Holzman recounts his version of the 1970 Knicks championship season in *My Unforgettable Season, 1970* (1993), with Leonard Lewin. Holzman also authored *The Knicks* (1971), *Holz-*

man's Basketball: Winning Strategy and Tactics (1973), and *A View from the Bench* (1980). Obituaries are in the *New York Times, Washington Post*, and *Los Angeles Times* (all 15 Nov. 1998). Further remembrances are in the *New York Times* (27 Nov. 1998).

JACK R. FISCHEL

HORNBERGER, H(iester) Richard, Jr. (Richard Hooker) (*b.* 1 February 1924 in Trenton, New Jersey; *d.* 4 November 1997 in Portland, Maine), thoracic surgeon and author of *M*A*S*H* (1968).

Hornberger's father, Hiester Richard Hornberger, was a teacher at the Peddie School in Hightstown, New Jersey. His mother was a librarian. Hornberger grew up in Hightstown, where he attended public elementary school and then the Peddie School. As a child, Hornberger enjoyed summer vacations visiting his mother's family in Maine. After graduating from prep school, he earned an M.A. degree at Bowdoin College in Maine and an M.D. at Weill Medical College of Cornell University, where he specialized in surgery. Hornberger married Priscilla Storer in 1947; they had four children.

Hornberger was drafted into the U.S. Army in 1951 and served as a captain in the Army Medical Corps in Korea. As a surgeon in the 8055th Mobile Army Surgical Hospital (MASH), he often worked twelve-hour shifts trying to save the lives of the wounded. When the Korean War ended, Hornberger returned to Maine and bought a house on an inlet in Bremen, about sixty miles northeast of Portland. After working for two years at the Veterans Administration Hospital in Togus, he opened a surgical practice at Thayer Hospital in Waterville, where he remained until his retirement in 1988. Hornberger specialized in thoracic surgery but also operated on patients with morbid obesity. After performing his first gastric bypass in 1973, he was the second to publish his experience with the operation. His paper "Gastric Bypass" was published in the *American Journal of Surgery* in 1976. Hornberger was one of the founders of the American Society for Bariatric Surgery (ASBS) in 1983.

Wanting to record his experiences as an army surgeon in Korea, Hornberger began writing his first novel, *M*A*S*H,* after he returned from the war. It took him twelve years to write. He wove plots and characters during his daily commute through the Maine countryside to Thayer Hospital and admitted "writing the novel is tough when you have a bad patient hanging over your head." Writing under the pseudonym Richard Hooker (a reference to his golf game), Hornberger told the story of a group of drafted army surgeons working long, hard hours in makeshift operating rooms amid the horrors of battle casualties.

He modeled Benjamin Franklin ("Hawkeye") Pierce, the central character, after himself, a witty surgeon with a passion for Maine and golf. The book was rejected by a dozen publishers before William Morrow and Company, Inc., published it in 1968. *M*A*S*H* was a runaway best-seller. Hornberger's coworkers did not immediately discover that he was the book's author. "People in the hospital were whispering when he was passing, 'He is the man who wrote *M*A*S*H.*'" One of Hornberger's colleagues recalled that "one of his patients even insisted on postponing the operation so he could finish reading the novel."

The book attracted the attention of the director Robert Altman, who decided to make a movie based on it. With a screenplay by Ring Lardner, Jr., and starring Donald Sutherland, Elliott Gould, and Sally Kellerman, the film *M*A*S*H* was released in 1970 by Twentieth Century–Fox. The film was a hit among the youth culture because of the anti–Vietnam War sentiment in America and abroad at the time. Critics called it "one of the most irreducibly funny films ever made." William Johnson in *Film Quarterly* concluded that the film "is not really about army life or rebellion . . . it is about the human condition, and that's why it is such an exciting comedy." The film critic Pauline Kael described it as "a marvelous unstable comedy, a tough, funny, and sophisticated burlesque of military attitudes." The film earned Twentieth Century–Fox over $30 million within a year of its release. It received five Academy Award nominations, earning Ring Lardner, Jr., an Oscar for best adapted screenplay, and was awarded the best picture at the Cannes Film Festival.

William Self, the president of Twentieth Century–Fox, then turned the film into a television series. The first show aired on CBS in September 1972. The series ran for eleven years, becoming one of the most watched shows in television history. Hornberger felt that the portrayal of "Hawkeye" in the television series strayed too far from the book and movie character and was much more politically liberal than the protagonist he had created. He never liked the show and said in an interview, "I thought the movie was great, but the television thing isn't my kind of humor. It's someone else's idea of what medical humor is supposed to be."

Hornberger died of leukemia at age seventy-three at Maine Medical Center in Portland. He is buried in Breman, Maine. He was known as a publicity-shy, semireclusive man who applied his trade with utmost respectability. "The American Society for Bariatric Surgery has lost a leader in the development of obesity surgery," commented Edward E. Mason, M.D., a fellow ASBS member and professor emeritus of the University of Iowa College of Medicine, upon Hornberger's death. "He was an incredibly intellectually honest person. But just like the characters in *M*A*S*H,* he made his points with humor." Raymond

Carver, a longtime colleague and friend, spoke of Hornberger's dedication: "Before Medicaid, Dr. Hornberger would often treat patients for little or no fee. It would be very difficult to find any comparison to him today." But to millions of Americans, Hornberger is known and fondly remembered as the author of the book that spurred the film and television series that dealt with the confusion and turbulence of an era.

★

In the decade following the publication of his famous novel, Hornberger wrote fourteen sequels, all under the pseudonym Richard Hooker. Biographical and critical resources on Hornberger are in *New Republic* (31 Jan. 1970), *Today's Health* (Dec. 1970), *New York Times Book Review* (5 Mar. 1972), and *Saturday Review* (22 Apr. 1972). Obituaries are in the *Boston Globe* (6 Nov. 1997), *New York Times* (7 Nov. 1997), and *Los Angeles Times* and *Washington Post* (both 8 Nov. 1997).

YAN TOMA

HORST, Horst Paul (*b.* 14 August 1906 in Weissenfels-an-der-Saale, Germany; *d.* 18 November 1999 in Palm Beach Gardens, Florida), an internationally renowned fashion photographer for *Vogue, Harper's Bazaar,* and *House and Garden,* also well known for his travel photography, reportage, photographs of interiors, and for pioneering a new generation of photographic studies of nudes, especially male.

Horst, born Horst Paul Albert Bohrmann, was the second son of Max Bohrmann, a wealthy owner of a hardware business, and Klara Schonbrodt, both of whom were German. During Horst's childhood his mother was sent briefly to a sanitarium (1913). The following year, with the outbreak of World War I, Horst's father was called up for military duty; he did not return to the family until 1918. Horst's education included study at the School of Wisdom, founded in 1920 by the philosopher Count Hermann Keyserling. During his school years Horst met Rabindranath Tagore, the Indian poet championed by Ezra Pound, and Josephine Baker, the African-American dancer and entertainer. These relationships began the assembly of what was to become an enormous gallery of famous artistic and wealthy friends.

Throughout the 1920s Horst spent time in Weimar, Germany, at the home of an aunt, where he was introduced to another dancer, Eva Weidmann, who was a student at the Bauhaus. While he learned a great deal about currents in modern dance, theater, painting, and architecture during this period, Horst also spent a year in Switzerland for treatment of a lung ailment. Toward the end of the decade he took up study at the Hamburg Kunstgewerbeschule; however, his career path changed after he wrote to the architect Le Corbusier asking for a position as an apprentice in his Paris office. Horst began training with Le Corbusier in 1930.

Also in 1930 Horst met the photographer Baron George Hoyingen-Huene and began modeling for him. Soon Horst started taking his own photographs. While living with Hoyingen-Huene, Horst also worked as his assistant and occasional subject. Through his connection with

Horst P. Horst, 1989. PHOTOGRAPH BY DAVID FAHEY. COURTESY FAHEY/KLEIN GALLERY, LOS ANGELES.

Hoyingen-Huene, Horst began working for *Vogue* in 1931; his first published photograph appeared in the November issue. Their association lasted for decades, and many of Horst's most famous images of women in haute couture originally appeared in *Vogue*. In 1932 Horst was invited by *Condé Nast* to travel to the United States, where he photographed the actress Bette Davis, among others. His first exhibition, which was held in Paris at the Galerie La Plume d'Or, took place that same year. Horst's rapid rise to artistic prominence can be attributed to his unique photographic vision, one relying simultaneously on classical forms and an almost surrealist perception. In 1935, after Hoyingen-Huene moved from *Vogue* to *Harper's Bazaar,* Horst succeeded him as the head photographer for *Vogue*'s Paris photo studio. Horst traveled frequently to such places as England, the United States, Switzerland, Tunisia, and Austria during the mid-1930s. His peripatetic activities would only accelerate over the decades as he constantly increased his photographic range. In the 1930s he took portraits of such famous individuals as Katharine Hepburn, George Cukor, Cole Porter, Elsa Schiaparelli, and the model Lisa Fonssagrives, who was a frequent subject in Horst's more unconventional fashion shoots.

By 1937 Horst and Hoyingen-Huene had relocated to New York City, where they lived in Sutton Place. That year Horst also met the designer Coco Chanel, who became a lifelong friend. His first U.S. exhibition took place at Germain Seligman's Art Gallery in New York in 1938. After a few more years of international travel and meeting more famous people from all walks of life, Horst returned to the United States, where in 1940 he initiated the naturalization process. He adopted Horst P. Horst as his legal name when he was sworn in as a U.S. citizen on 21 October 1943, reportedly to avoid confusion with Nazi official Martin Bormann. During World War II, Horst served as a photographer for the U.S. Army. In 1944 he published his first book, *Photographs of a Decade,* which summarized his work of the 1930s. In 1945 he photographed Harry Truman, and at the war's end he traveled to Mexico on assignment and then returned to Paris, where he took several photographs of Gertrude Stein, another longtime friend.

In 1946 Horst again returned to New York City, this time to design and build a house in Oyster Bay on Long Island. That same year he met British diplomat Valentine Lawford, and the two began a personal and professional relationship that continued until Horst's death. Throughout the decade Horst worked sporadically on a second book, a collection of plant studies called *Patterns from Nature* (1946). During the 1950s Horst and Lawford traveled all over the world, including trips to Mexico, Lebanon, Iran, Europe, and the Caribbean. His work during these years included reportage, fashion shoots, and commissioned work for various advertisers. By the late 1950s Horst, who had spent several summers in the Tyrol region of Austria, bought as a summer retreat a mountain farm, which he renovated in 1960.

In 1961, after Diana Vreeland became editor in chief of American *Vogue,* Horst was encouraged to turn in a new direction by photographing the lifestyle of the international jet set. This new focus led to some of his most famous photographs of interiors. What followed throughout the 1960s was a staggering amount of travel and photographic activity, including a two-month trip in 1962 during which Horst traveled from California to Japan, Hong Kong, Thailand, India, Nepal, Egypt, and Rome. Nearly each year's activities included extensive travel. Hoyingen-Huene died in 1968, and Horst saw Coco Chanel for the last time in 1966, though she died in 1971. Horst's subjects during the 1960s included the duke and duchess of Windsor, the Rothschilds, Consuela Vanderbilt, Emilio Pucci, and Cy Twombley. *Vogue*'s *Book of Houses, Gardens, People* (1968) featured photos by Horst and text by Valentine Lawford.

Horst's pace barely slowed in the next decade, as extensive travel and photography continued to dominate his life. During the mid-1970s most of his time was devoted to photography for *House and Garden*. However, there were also several significant exhibitions, including one at the Sonnabend Gallery (1976) and one at the Andrew Crispo Gallery (1977), both in New York City. Horst's works were exhibited frequently throughout the rest of his life. Among his numerous exhibitions during the 1980s was the retrospective *Horst—Photography 1931–84,* held in the Fortuny Palace in Venice, Italy. In 1982 the Staley-Wise Gallery in New York City became his official representative. Horst remained active throughout the remainder of his life. In 1987 he appeared in a video that included a frank discussion of his personal and professional experiences. He died at his home in Palm Beach Gardens, Florida, at age ninety-three, following a bout with pneumonia.

Horst is known for the smoothness of his composition and for the shadow of disarray implied in many of his most famous images. This trait is accentuated by his exquisite control of lighting, which was both formal and innovative. Horst's use of light in his early fashion photography already set him apart from his contemporaries; from the outset his works were both elegant and detached. Horst was extremely influential in fashion photography, in black-and-white studies, and most particularly in the photography of interiors. *Horst: Interiors* (1993) features examples of Horst's photography of interiors, and another retrospective volume focussing on portraits, *Horst Portraits: 60 Years of Style*, was published in 2001.

★

Much of the available material on Horst is found in Valentine Lawford, *Horst: His Work and His World* (1984), and in introductory essays such as that by Martin Kazmaier in Richard J. Horst and Lothar Schirmer, eds., *Horst: Sixty Years of Photography* (1991). An obituary is in the *New York Times* (19 Nov. 1999).

JAMES J. SULLIVAN III

HRUSKA, Roman Lee (*b.* 16 August 1904 in David City, Nebraska; *d.* 25 April 1999 in Omaha, Nebraska), Nebraska Republican who served in the U.S. Congress from 1952 to 1954 and as U.S. senator from 1954 to 1976.

Hruska was one of eleven siblings born to Czech immigrants, Joseph C. Hruska and Caroline L. Dvorak. His father was a teacher and his mother a homemaker. Hruska attended the High School of Commerce in Omaha, Nebraska, from 1921 to 1925 and then entered the University of Omaha where he was a pre-law major. Following his graduation in 1925, Hruska attended the University of Chicago Law School for two years before receiving his J.D. (Juris Doctorate) from Creighton University College of Law in 1929. Hruska married Victoria E. Kuncl in 1930; the couple had three children.

Hruska's political career began when he was selected to fill a vacancy on the Douglas County Board of Commissioners in 1944. He became the chairman of the County Board in 1945 and held that position until 1952. He was

Roman Hruska, 1975. ASSOCIATED PRESS AP

proud of the fact that, during his seven-year tenure as chairman, taxes were reduced each year. When the incumbent Republican congressman from Omaha decided not to run for reelection in 1952, Hruska announced his candidacy and handily won the election. He served on the House Appropriations Committee, even though it was unusual for freshman members to be assigned to this important committee. In 1954 Hruska ran for the Senate seat vacated by the death of Senator Hugh Butler and won the first of four successful Senate races.

Hruska arrived in Washington just in time to vote with a minority of senators who opposed the resolution to censure Senator Joseph R. McCarthy of Wisconsin for the excesses of his anticommunist crusade. During his first two Senate terms, Hruska established himself as a solid conservative and firm anticommunist. He supported the war in Vietnam as well as cold war programs such as Radio Free Europe. Although Hruska voted for federal farm programs, he opposed nearly all the new domestic social legislation that emerged during the administrations of John F. Kennedy and Lyndon B. Johnson, including Medicare, federal housing programs, and urban aid. Hruska was also a relentless opponent of gun control; however, he did support the Civil Rights Act of 1964. By the late 1960s Hruska received a 100 percent rating from the conservative Americans for Constitutional Action.

During his years in the Senate, Hruska was a party loyalist, never publicly criticizing his fellow Republican Senate colleagues or Republican presidents. During Watergate, for example, he was publicly silent, although the scandal was clearly painful to him. He served on two of the Senate's most powerful committees, Appropriations and Judiciary. When Hruska retired in 1976, he was the ranking minority member of the Judiciary Committee.

Hruska's legislative accomplishments include leading roles in the enactment of the Criminal Justice Act, the Prisoners Rehabilitation Act, and the Bail Reform Act, all passed in 1965, as well as the Omnibus Crime and Safe Street Act of 1968. In 1974 he promoted the restoration of the death penalty for certain federal crimes and supported criminal penalties for the use of marijuana. Hruska was also a master of legislative obstruction. When a group affiliated with the consumer advocate Ralph Nader studied Congress and prepared biographies of every member of Congress in 1972, the profile on Hruska quoted an unnamed Senate colleague as saying, "He's holding up more legislation than anyone else I've ever seen. He's the most effective damn roadblock around here."

As ranking member of the Judiciary Committee during the Nixon administration, Hruska was expected to shepherd through the Senate presidential nominations that seemed to be in trouble. One such nomination was to gain him some uncomfortable notoriety. For many months in

1970, Hruska fought unsuccessfully for the Senate confirmation of Clement Haynsworth and G. Harrold Carswell, Nixon nominees to the Supreme Court. During the debate on the Carswell nomination, Hruska made a comment that would cloud his reputation for the rest of his Senate career. When liberal Democrats charged that Judge Carswell was too mediocre to deserve a seat on the Supreme Court, Senator Hruska stood before his Senate colleagues and argued "there are a lot of mediocre judges and people and lawyers. They are entitled to a little representation, aren't they, and a little chance? We can't have all Brandeises, Frankfurters, and Cardozos." The remark received national attention, and although Hruska would later admit that his remarks were ill-advised, he became the object of much ridicule. The Carswell nomination was defeated and the seat went to Harry S. Blackmun.

Hruska had been close to the late Senator Everett Dirksen of Illinois, the Republican leader of the Senate, and it was widely believed that Dirksen hoped that Hruska would succeed him as GOP leader. But Hruska decided against running for reelection in 1976 and spent his remaining years in Omaha practicing law. He died from complications resulting from a broken hip following a fall and is buried in Bohemian Cemetery in Omaha.

Hruska's career mirrored the conservative reaction to the social upheavals of the 1960s. An opponent of "big government," his political positions anticipated the conservative reaction of the Reagan years, and although he is chiefly remembered for his defense of a candidate deemed too mediocre to sit on the Supreme Court, Hruska's positions on gun control and media violence continue to resonate with a sizable portion of the American public.

★

There is no biography of Hruska. Readers wishing to learn more about him should consult Roman Hruska et al., "The Tasks of Penology: A Symposium on Prisons and Correctional Law," *Nebraska Law Review* (1966), and the profile of Hruska in the *Biographical Directory of the American Congress, 1774–1989* (1989). An obituary is in the *Omaha World Herald* (26 Apr. 1999).

JACK R. FISCHEL

HUGGINS, Charles Brenton (*b.* 22 September 1901 in Halifax, Nova Scotia; *d.* 12 January 1997 in Chicago, Illinois), physician who won the 1966 Nobel Prize for his groundbreaking work on the link between hormones and cancer of the prostate and breast.

Huggins was the eldest son of Charles Edward Huggins, a pharmacist, and Bessie Maria Spencer, a homemaker. From a very young age, Huggins was an astute, quick learner with an almost photographic memory. He attended the

Charles B. Huggins. PRINTS AND PHOTOGRAPHS DIVISION, LIBRARY OF CONGRESS

public schools in Halifax, then received a B.A. degree in just three years from Acadia University in Wolfville, Nova Scotia, in 1920. In 1924 he acquired both an M.A. degree and an M.D. from Harvard Medical School in Cambridge, Massachusetts.

From approximately 1924 to 1926 Huggins worked as an intern and resident in general surgery with Frederick A. Coller at the University of Michigan Hospital at Ann Arbor, where he met his future wife, a nurse named Margaret Wellman. Huggins then spent a year as the instructor in surgery at the University of Michigan before marrying Wellman on 29 July 1927. After they were married, Wellman became Huggins's collaborator and edited his scientific papers. The couple later had a son and a daughter.

In 1927 Huggins was awarded a research fellowship from the University of Chicago, where he also served as the instructor of surgery in 1928. Dallas Phemister, the founding chairman of surgery at the University of Chicago, requested that Huggins take over the urological surgery division. Although Huggins had no previous experience with medical research or urology, he quickly became an expert and memorized a urology textbook in just three weeks. He became an assistant professor in 1929 and an associate professor in 1933. In that same year, Huggins became a naturalized U.S. citizen. In 1936 he was promoted to full professor.

Huggins remained at the University of Chicago for his entire career; he held concurrent positions with other organizations. He was also a member of the National Advisory Cancer Council (1946–1948) and the founder and director of the Ben May Laboratory for Cancer Research. He won the Walker Prize from the Royal College of Surgeons; was a Mickle Fellow at the University of Toronto (1958); was the William B. Ogden Distinguished Service Professor at the University of Chicago (1962–1991); and was chancellor of Acadia University (1972–1979). Huggins reached the pinnacle of success with his extensive work linking hormones and the treatment of advanced cases of prostate and breast cancer when he became a corecipient of the 1966 Nobel Prize in physiology or medicine, with the virologist F. Peyton Rous.

Although Huggins was best known for cancer research, he was the first researcher to demonstrate the "competitive antagonism between male and female hormones," as well as the first to measure the concentration of elements that make up seminal fluid. He was influential in the development of the concept of chromogenic substrates, which allow the activity of certain enzymes to be measured, and he also helped found "a family of substances that induce bone formation," being investigated for use in orthopedic, reconstructive, and periodontal surgery. Huggins also wrote and published some 300 medical articles and scientific books during his career.

Huggins received honorary degrees from Acadia (1946), Yale (1947), Washington (1951), Leeds (1953), Torino (1957), and Aberdeen (1966). He also won the Gold Medal of the American Medical Association (1936 and 1940); the Gold Medal of the American Cancer Society (1953); the Comfort Crookshank Prize from the Middlesex Hospital, London (1957); the Cameron Prize of Edinburgh University (1958); the Valentine Prize of the New York Academy of Medicine (1962); the Laurea from the University of Bologna, Italy (1964); the Gold Medal of the Rudolf Virchow Medical Society (1964); the Gairdner Award (1966); the Gold Medal of the Worshipful Society, Apothecaries of London (1966); and the Bigelow Medal (1967). He was a fellow of the Royal College of Surgeons and the American College of Surgeons (1963).

Huggins belonged to many professional societies, including the National Academy of Sciences; American Physiological Society; American Association for Cancer Research (of which he served as president in 1948); Canadian Medical Association; and American Philosophical Society. In addition, he was a fellow of the American Academy of Arts and Sciences, and part of the Order "Pour le Mérite"

of the German Federal Republic. Huggins died at his Hyde Park home in Chicago at age ninety-five. Huggins and his wife had lived in the Hyde Park neighborhood since 1926; she had died in 1983.

As the last survivor of the original eight faculty members of the University of Chicago Medical School, and as a Nobel Laureate, Huggins will always be remembered as a medical pioneer. He dedicated his life to helping others, sometimes spending sixty to seventy hours per week in his laboratory, training and inspiring others to do the same. His alma mater, Acadia University, named a five-story building, the Huggins Science Hall, in his honor. Its purpose is to facilitate Huggins's motto, "Discovery is our business."

★

Acadia University possesses Huggins's medals and prizes, including his Nobel Prize. A biography of Huggins written for the Nobel Foundation can be found at <http://www.nobel.se/medicine/laureates>. See also Tyler Wasson, ed., *Nobel Prize Winners* (1987), and Emily J. McMurray, ed., *Notable Twentieth-Century Scientists* (1995). The University of Chicago Hospitals and Health System paid tribute to him in the article "Charles B. Huggins, MD, 1901–1997," at <http://www.uchospitals.edu>. Obituaries are in the *Los Angeles Times, Washington Post, Atlanta Journal, Tampa Tribune,* and *Newsday* (all 16 Jan. 1997).

ADRIANA C. TOMASINO

HUGHES, H(enry) Stuart (*b.* 7 May 1916 in New York City; *d.* 21 October 1999 in La Jolla, California), leading scholar of European intellectual history.

Hughes was the second of four children of Charles Evans Hughes, Jr., an attorney who became the U.S. solicitor general, and Marjory Bruce Stuart, a homemaker. He was the grandson of Charles Evans Hughes, a justice of the U.S. Supreme Court. Growing up in Morningside Heights and Riverdale in New York City, he attended the Horace Mann School and Riverdale Country School in New York, and the Saint Albans School in Washington, D.C. In 1931 he enrolled at the Deerfield Academy in Massachusetts, graduating in 1933. Hughes then attended Amherst College in Massachusetts, from which he graduated summa cum laude with a B.A. degree in 1937. As a graduate student at Harvard University in Cambridge, Massachusetts, he received his M.A. degree in 1938 and Ph.D. in 1940. His doctoral thesis was "The Crisis of the French Imperial Economy, 1810–1812."

In 1940 Hughes became an instructor at Brown University in Providence, Rhode Island. The next year he enlisted as a private in the 103rd Field Artillery of the Rhode Island National Guard. In December 1941 he was trans-

H. Stuart Hughes, 1962. AP/WIDE WORLD PHOTOS

ferred to the Office of Strategic Services (OSS), where he served as the chief of the research and analysis branch in the Mediterranean theater (1944–1945) and in Germany (1945–1946). When he left the army in January 1946, he held the rank of lieutenant colonel. From 1946 to 1948 he served as the chief of the division of research for Europe in the U.S. Department of State.

Hughes joined the Harvard faculty in 1948 as an assistant professor of history. In 1952 he became an associate professor at Stanford University in California, and in 1955 a full professor and the head of Stanford's history department. He returned to Harvard in 1957 as a full professor, where he directed the interdepartmental program in history and literature, and in 1967 became the department chair. In 1969 Harvard appointed him the Gurney Professor of History and Political Science.

Hughes's first major scholarly book was *Oswald Spengler: A Critical Estimate* (1952), an analysis of the twentieth-century German historian and his magnum opus, *The Decline of the West* (1918–1922). Another work, *The United States and Italy* (1953), offered Hughes's succinct introduction to Italian history and culture from the time of the risorgimento, the nineteenth-century period leading to Italy's political unification. A general survey, *Contemporary*

Europe: A History (1961), covered the period from World War I to the post–World War II era with both subtlety and sharpness. In the *History as Art and as Science: Twin Vistas on the Past* (1964), Hughes drew upon articles published in the *American Historical Review,* the *American Scholar,* and *Current Anthropology* to endorse neopositivism and plead for psychoanalytic approaches.

In the late 1950s Hughes began a major trilogy of European intellectual history with *Consciousness and Society: The Reorientation of European Social Thought, 1890–1930* (1958). As he covered such seminal figures as Emile Durkheim and Georges Sorel, he explored an intellectual universe increasingly divided between reason and emotion. The second volume, *The Obstructed Path: French Social Thought in the Years of Desperation, 1930–1960* (1968), focused on a generation of French thinkers who, in the wake of World War I and the Great Depression, turned from a national tradition that was morally and intellectually exhausted to fresher world views. The third work, *The Sea Change: The Migration of Social Thought, 1930–1965* (1975), was a psychological and social analysis of major intellectuals who migrated to Britain and the United States in the wake of fascism.

Hughes was politically active throughout the 1950s and 1960s. His first book, *An Essay for Our Times* (1950), admonished, "This whole civilization [might be] falling apart, or rather destroying itself, through systematic ignorance." He warned against dangerous misunderstandings on both sides of the cold war. In 1962 he published *An Approach to Peace and Other Essays,* which included articles that had appeared in *Dissent, Commentary, Partisan Review,* and *American Scholar.* Here he advocated unilateral initiatives toward disarmament, the theme of his abortive 1962 race as an independent for a Massachusetts U.S. Senate seat. Such activism led to his serving as the cochairman of SANE: A Citizen's Organization for a Sane World, from 1963 to 1967, and as the chairman from 1967 to 1970.

In 1975 Hughes left Harvard to join the faculty of the University of California at San Diego, where he taught until his retirement in 1986. Remaining productive in his later years, he wrote *Prisoners of Hope: The Silver Age of the Italian Jews, 1924–1974* (1983), a series of essays interpreting the experience of Italian Jews through novelists and other intellectuals. Then came *Sophisticated Rebels: The Political Culture of European Dissent, 1968–1987* (1988), a work showing Europe's dissenting intellectuals as archpragmatists, seeking political and cultural liberation in a piecemeal fashion.

Hughes held several visiting posts and received honors, including becoming a member of the Institute for Advanced Study in Princeton, New Jersey (1950), Guggenheim Fellow (1957 and 1958), fellow of the Center for Advanced Study in the Behavioral Sciences at Stanford (1957), and Bacon Exchange Professor at the University of Paris in France (1967). He was the president of the Society for Italian Historical Studies and founding chairman of the American Committee on the History of the Second World War. He received two decorations from the Italian government, was made a fellow of the American Academy of Arts and Sciences, and in 1997 was given the American Historical Association's Award for Scholarly Distinction.

On 28 December 1949 Hughes married Suzanne Rufenacht. They had a son and a daughter and were divorced in 1963. On 26 March 1964 he married Judith Markham, a graduate student at Harvard; they had one child. Hughes died at age eighty-three of pneumonia after suffering from Parkinson's disease.

Hughes was a thin man of average height, marked by horn-rimmed glasses, and extremely active in the disarmament movement. He was an elegant stylist, a superb synthesizer, and a pioneer in the study of European social thought. He combined intense involvement in learning with a strong activism rooted in the belief that intellectuals had an obligation to the wider world community.

★

The papers of H. Stuart Hughes are at Yale University in New Haven, Connecticut. His autobiography, *Gentleman Rebel: The Memoirs of H. Stuart Hughes* (1990), focuses far more on his personal odyssey than on his scholarship. For a scholarly treatment of Hughes, see Paul Robinson, "H. Stuart Hughes and Intellectual History: Reflections on the State of the Discipline," *Intellectual History Newsletter* no. 9 (1987): 29–35; Michael S. Roth, "Narrative as Enclosure: The Contextual Histories of H. Stuart Hughes," *Journal of the History of Ideas* 51 (July–Sept. 1990): 505–515; David M. Elston, "The Historiography of H. Stuart Hughes: The Historian as Intellectual," master's thesis, University of Vermont (1998); and Steven F. White, "Gentleman Rebel: H. Stuart Hughes, the OSS, and the Resistance," *Journal of Modern Italian Studies* 4 (1999): 64–67. For an interview with Hughes, see *The Center Magazine* 12 (1979): 52–59. For the influence of Hughes's OSS work upon his subsequent career, see Barry M. Katz, *Foreign Intelligence: Research and Analysis in the Office of Strategic Services, 1942–1945* (1989). An obituary is in the *New York Times* (24 Oct. 1999).

JUSTUS D. DOENECKE

HUNTER, James Augustus ("Catfish") (*b.* 8 April 1946 in Hertford, North Carolina; *d.* 9 September 1999 in Hertford, North Carolina), baseball player who starred as a pitcher with the Oakland Athletics and the New York Yankees and sparked major league baseball's first free-agent bidding war.

Hunter was the youngest of eight children of Abbott Hunter, a poor tenant farmer and logger, and Millie Hunter, a homemaker. As a youth, he played baseball in cow pastures, barns, and yards. He attended Perquimans High School from 1960 to 1964 in Hertford, North Carolina, where he exhibited little interest in academics but starred in football and baseball. At Perquimans he pitched several no-hitters and attracted the attention of numerous major league baseball scouts.

In November 1963 Hunter was accidentally shot by his brother while duck hunting. Thirty shotgun pellets were lodged in his foot and his little toe was shattered, injuries that threatened to end his pitching career. However, after doctors at the Mayo Clinic removed twenty-seven of the pellets, Hunter served as a batting-practice pitcher for the Kansas City Athletics (or A's). At the insistence of the scout Clyde Kluttz, in June 1964 the A's owner, Charles Finley, signed Hunter for a $50,000 "bonus" and paid for his Mayo Clinic visit. (The bonus rule required Finley to retain Hunter on the Kansas City roster or risk losing him.) Finley gave Hunter the nickname "Catfish." He wanted Hunter to tell the press that he had been missing one night and his parents found him in a stream with one catfish lying beside him and another on his pole. Hunter agreed to go along with the story.

At six feet and 195 pounds, the right-handed Hunter joined the Kansas City A's pitching in mid-May 1965. He earned his first major league victory in his second game against the Boston Red Sox that July, and he ended the season with an 8–8 record. Despite having appendicitis, Hunter made the American League All-Star team and compiled a 9–11 ledger in 1966. The following year, he finished 13–17 with a 2.80 earned run average (ERA) and, in the All-Star game, he hurled four shutout innings before surrendering the game-winning home run to Tony Perez in the fifteenth inning.

After the Kansas City A's moved to Oakland, California, in 1968 and became the Oakland Athletics, Hunter split twenty-six decisions that season. On 8 May he pitched the first regular-season perfect game in the American League since 1922. In a 4–0 game against the Minnesota Twins, he made 107 pitches and struck out eleven players. He followed with a 12–15 slate in 1969, surrendering thirty-four home runs. Hunter sharpened his control by determined concentration and learning to flex his knees. He earned marks of 18–14 with a 3.81 ERA in 1970; 21–11 with a 2.96 ERA in 1971; and 21–7 with a 2.04 ERA in 1972, the year he helped the Oakland A's capture a second West Division title. During the American League Championship Series in 1972, Hunter surrendered only two runs in nearly sixteen innings against the Detroit Tigers. That same year he helped Oakland twice defeat the Cincinnati Reds to win the team's first World Series.

In 1973 Hunter topped all of the American League pitchers with a 21–5 slate and 3.34 ERA. During the Amer-

Catfish Hunter, 1979. AP/WIDE WORLD PHOTOS

ican League Championship Series, he helped win the first and fifth games against the Baltimore Orioles, hurling a brilliant four-hit shutout in the clinching game. During the World Series, he twice bested pitcher Tom Seaver of the New York Mets. He also limited the Mets to just one run in 6⅓ innings in game six, which helped the Oakland A's take the world title.

In 1974 Hunter recorded career bests in victories (25), innings pitched (318), and complete games (23); won the American League Cy Young Award with a 25–12 record; and led the American League with a 2.49 ERA. He helped defeat the Baltimore Orioles 2–1 in the decisive game of the American League Championship Series. During the World Series, Hunter saved Game One and helped win game three against the Los Angeles Dodgers, and the Oakland A's prevailed in their third consecutive World Series.

In October 1974 Hunter sued Finley for breach of contract because the owner had failed to pay $50,000 of Hunter's $100,000 salary into a life insurance fund as agreed. Because Finley had reneged on this portion of the agreement, Hunter claimed that the entire contract, including the reserve clause, was void and that he was a free

agent. Although Finley personally handed Hunter a check for $50,000, the player rejected it. In December 1974 the arbitrator Peter Seitz ruled in Hunter's favor and voided his contract.

Hunter then became a free agent, triggering a precedent-setting, thirteen-day bidding war for his services. Fifteen major league clubs negotiated with Hunter's agent, the Cherry and Flythe law firm of Ahoskie, North Carolina. Six major league owners appeared in person. The New York Yankees, San Diego Padres, Kansas City Royals, and Cleveland Indians allegedly offered Hunter over $3 million apiece. On 1 January 1975 Hunter signed a five-year contract with the New York Yankees worth an estimated $3.75 million. The package included a $1 million signing bonus, a ten-year retirement plan, life-insurance policies, and a provision for legal fees. Hunter's action sparked a free-agency revolution in major league baseball.

Hunter pitched for the Yankees from 1975 to 1979. His best campaign for the team was in 1975, when he finished 23–14 for his fifth consecutive twenty-game victory season. Hunter helped the Yankees win American League pennants in 1976, 1977, and 1978, and split two decisions against the Kansas City Royals in the American League Championship Series in 1976. Although he was diagnosed with diabetes in March 1978, Hunter still recorded twelve victories and helped to win the decisive game six of the World Series against the Los Angeles Dodgers.

Hunter retired at age thirty-three allegedly because of arm problems but also because he wanted to spend more time with his family. Over the course of his career, he compiled 224 wins and 166 losses for a .574 winning percentage with 2,012 strikeouts in 3,449⅓ innings pitched and a 3.26 ERA. Hunter paced the American League twice in winning percentage (1972–1973) and victories (1974–1975), and once each in games started (1970), ERA (1974), complete games (1975), and innings pitched (1975). In addition to logging a 4–3 mark in six American League Championship Series games and a 5–3 mark in six World Series, he made the American League All-Star team in 1966, 1967, 1970, and 1972 through 1976.

Hunter and his wife Helen were married on 9 October 1966. The couple had three children. They resided on his 230-acre farm in Hertford, where, after retirement, he coached Little League Baseball and enjoyed hunting and fishing. In 1997 he discovered he could not lift his shotgun while duck hunting, and soon developed other alarming symptoms. Doctors diagnosed him with Lou Gehrig's disease (amyotrophic lateral scleroris), a rare muscular disorder, in September 1998. The incurable, paralyzing disease ended Hunter's life within a year. He is buried in his hometown of Hertford.

Hunter's importance far exceeded his baseball statistics. He changed the baseball establishment as the sport's first free agent and first $3 million player. In addition, he helped elevate the Oakland A's to world champions and return the New York Yankees to big winners. He was well liked by fans and the press, retaining his simple farm and family values and religious integrity. Hunter never complained about his diabetes and served as an inspiration to others with the disease. Carlton Cherry, his attorney, said, "He's lived in the country all his life. He's a good Christian young man. He doesn't dissipate. He doesn't carouse. He just sits home with his family." Hunter, who was popular with teammates, utilized a controlled, intelligent, but not overpowering pitching style. His repetitive motion brought superb control, but caused him to surrender 374 career home runs. He was elected to the National Baseball Hall of Fame in 1987.

★

The National Baseball Library in Cooperstown, New York, has a file of biographical material about Hunter. See also his autobiography, with Armen Keteyian, *Catfish: My Life in Baseball* (1988). Team histories portraying Hunter's role include Mark Gallagher, *The Yankee Encyclopedia,* vol. 3 (1997), and Bruce Markusen, *Baseball's Last Dynasty* (1988). Ronald A. Mayer, *Perfect* (1991), recounts Hunter's perfect game while the *New York Times* (1 Jan. 1975), and Paul Hemphill, "The Yankees Fish for a Pennant," *Sport* (Apr. 1975), examine his free-agent signing. An obituary is in the *New York Times* (10 Sept. 1999).

DAVID L. PORTER

HUTSON, Don(ald) Montgomery (*b.* 31 January 1913 in Pine Bluff, Arkansas; *d.* 26 June 1997 in Rancho Mirage, California), offensive end whose speed, agility, and pass-catching skills revolutionized the National Football League (NFL) passing game in the 1930s.

Hutson was one of four children born to Roy Basil Hutson, a Cotton Belt railroad conductor, and Mabel Agnes Clark, a homemaker. As a youngster, Hutson showed no remarkable athletic prowess; he was often overshadowed by his younger twin brothers, Ray and Robert (Robert was later a casualty of World War II). Hutson received more attention for his rattlesnake collection, which he put together to qualify for a Boy Scout merit badge, than for anything he did athletically; he eventually attained the Scout's highest rank as an Eagle Scout. Hutson also had a sister who died in infancy.

Hutson went out for the Pine Bluff High School football team after learning from neighbor and future teammate Bob Seawall that the team was going to a preseason camp in the Ozarks. Hutson was primarily interested in qualifying for the out-of-town trip. However, he proved to be more than just a happy camper. He developed into a fine

Don Hutson, 1951. ASSOCIATED PRESS AP

player, though not good enough for a depression-era college to commit to a scholarship. Seawall, who was an outstanding player coveted by several colleges, including the University of Alabama, insisted that Hutson become part of a "package deal" to play for Alabama's Crimson Tide.

At Alabama, Hutson developed into the South's leading receiver. He was also fast, running the 100-yard dash in 9.7 seconds and the 220 in 21.3, speeds only tenths-of-a-second greater than the National Collegiate Athletic Association (NCAA) records for these distances. However, football was Hutson's ticket to future fame. By his junior year at Alabama, he was a touchdown threat as a pass-grabbing end. Passer Millard "Dixie" Howell was able to connect often enough with Hutson that, as seniors in 1934, they both were consensus All-America choices. (Future coaching legend Paul "Bear" Bryant played the end opposite Hutson on those Crimson Tide teams.) In the 1935 Rose Bowl game, which at the time was arguably the most important college post-season game, Hutson increased his stock as a future professional player. Underdog Alabama upset heavily favored Stanford, 29–13. Hutson caught six passes thrown to him for 164 yards and two touchdowns.

Before the NFL draft of college players, each professional team was free to sign any collegian. Earl "Curly" Lambeau, coach of the Green Bay Packers, coveted Hutson. The Packers were about the only professional team that used the forward pass as something more than a desperation tactic. Lambeau said of Hutson that "He [Hutson] would glide downfield, leaning forward as if to steady himself close to the ground. Then, as suddenly as you gulp or blink an eye, he'd feint one way and go the other, reach up like a dancer, gracefully squeeze the ball, and leave the scene of the accident—the accident being the defensive backs who tangled their feet up and fell trying to cover him." Later, when Hutson got to the NFL, Eagles coach Earle "Greasy" Neale echoed Lambeau, saying, "Hutson is the only man I ever saw who could feint in three different directions at the same time."

Hutson who was six feet, one inch and 175 pounds, agreed to sign with the persuasive Lambeau for $175 a game, but said he wanted to notify NFL Brooklyn Dodgers player and part-owner John Simms "Shipwreck" Kelly, who was also courting Hutson, of his decision. When told, Kelly took a plane to Alabama and also got Hutson's signature on an NFL contract. Contracts were not valid until received and countersigned by league president Joe F. Carr. Both of Hutson's signed contracts arrived the same day at Carr's office in Columbus, Ohio. Carr used Solomon-like wisdom and declared the contract with the earliest postmark valid. The Packers' postmark read 8:30 A.M.; the Dodgers' 8:47 A.M. By a mere seventeen minutes, "The Alabama Antelope" became a Packer and professional football would undergo a change for the better.

Before reporting to the Green Bay training camp, Hutson was the starting left end for the College All-Stars in the *Chicago Tribune* Charities game versus the 1934 NFL champion Chicago Bears. The All-Stars (including future President Gerald R. Ford, then a fine center at the University of Michigan) lost to the Bears, 5-0, but Hutson almost led his team to a victory when his brilliant end-around play put the All-Stars in scoring position. Unfortunately, the drive stalled out at the Bears' five-yard line. Hutson married Julia Kathleen Richards on 14 December 1935; the couple had a daughter.

A pervasive myth sprang up, one still perpetuated by some unknowing reporters, that on Hutson's very first play from scrimmage as a Packer he scored on an eighty-three-yard touchdown reception against the Bears. This spectacular pass-and-run play did indeed occur against the Bears, and Hutson's touchdown was the margin of victory and the game's only score. However, Hutson actually made his NFL debut the previous week in a 7-6 loss to the Chicago Cardinals.

Hutson led the NFL in receiving in eight of the eleven years he played. His ninety-nine touchdown receptions stood as a record for decades, as did his 488 career recep-

tions, and his 7,991 receiving yards. He also held a long-standing record for at least one catch in ninety-five consecutive games between 1937 and 1945. An accomplished kicker, he scored 193 of his record 823 points on field goals and extra points. So dominant was Hutson that it was not unusual for him to have twice as many catches in a season as the next best receiver in the league.

From about midway through his career, the slightly built Hutson regularly threatened to play "just one more season." Required to play defensive end when the opposition had the ball, he often took a physical beating. In 1939 Lambeau, breaking from tradition, had rugged blocking quarterback Larry Craig play end on defense while Hutson played Craig's rather benign safety position. Hutson responded by leading the NFL in interceptions (six) in 1940. Consistent to the end, Hutson led the league in receptions (forty-seven) in his final season, 1945.

During and after his football career, Hutson, a wise businessman, owned a bowling alley and a Chevrolet-Cadillac agency in Racine, Wisconsin. He operated the agency until he sold it in 1984 and moved to Southern California. Hutson died at age eighty-four of natural causes and was cremated.

Voted to the NFL's All-50-Year and All-75-Year teams, Hutson is the one player from the sport's early days that football observers and historians agree could star in a modern, fast-paced game. Historian Bob Caroll said, "If you rated every pass catcher when Hutson was playing on a scale of 100, and you gave Hutson 100, the next highest guy would be about a 40. Jerry Rice [of the 49ers and Raiders] might, *might,* be a better receiver, but if you give Rice a 100 there are a lot of guys in the 90s." *Sports Illustrated*'s Paul "Dr. Z" Zimmerman said, "Hutson came to the game in 1935 like an emissary from another planet."

★

There is no biography of Hutson, but his life and career are discussed in Alexander Weyand, *Football Immortals* (1962); Chuck Johnson, *The Greatest Packers of Them All* (1968); Myron Cope, *The Game That Was: The Early Days of Pro Football* (1970); George Allen with Ben Olan, *Pro Football's 100 Greatest Players: Rating the Stars of Past and Present* (1982); Richard Whittingham, *What a Game They Played: Stories of the Early Days of Pro Football by Those Who Were There* (1984); and Brad Herzog, *The Sports 100: The One Hundred Most Important People in American Sports History* (1995). An obituary is in the *New York Times* (28 June 1997).

JIM CAMPBELL

J

JACKSON, Walter Milton ("Milt"; "Bags") (*b.* 1 January 1923 in Detroit, Michigan; *d.* 9 October 1999 in New York City), award-winning jazz vibraphonist and member of the Modern Jazz Quartet known for his improvisation from bebop to blues.

Jackson, the second of five boys, was born into a musical and religious family headed by his father, Manley Jackson, and his mother, Lillie Beaty. Active in the Detroit Church of God in Christ, Jackson was known as "the Reverend." His father played the guitar by ear, and all his brothers played instruments. Jackson sang tenor with the Evangelist Singers, a local gospel choir that traveled on Sundays to Windsor, Canada, for live radio broadcasts at Elder Morton's Church of God. Dizzy Gillespie claimed, "Where Bags really gets his rhythm is that his family's sanctified." When asked about his music, Jackson replied, "Why, that's where it all started."

Jackson's first instrument was guitar. When his mother hammered the dinner steak, young Jackson grabbed his father's guitar from the corner to strum the rhythm and pick out solos. At age seven, he played and sang gospel duets with his brother Alvin ("A.J.") on bass. Jackson also studied classical piano at ages eleven and twelve until his mother could no longer pay for lessons. He also played violin, timpani, xylophone, drums, and bass before he chose the vibraphone. Jackson took a full music curriculum at Detroit's Miller High School in order to play drums. During one semester, he finished the prescribed course in half the time, and his music teacher, Luis Cabrera, suggested

he take up the vibraphone to stay out of trouble. When he was sixteen, his father put a down payment on his first set of vibes and paid it off at five dollars a week.

Jackson's parents stressed stability, which included regular paychecks. After wartime service in the U.S. Army/Air Forces from 1942 to 1944, Jackson returned to Detroit and began playing professionally. He worked days in a restaurant and played vibes at the Twelve Horsemen Club for three dollars a night. Due to his work schedule and late-night sessions, he inherited the nickname "Bags," referring to those under his eyes.

In 1945 Dizzy Gillespie invited twenty-two-year-old Jackson to join his band in New York City. At first, Jackson's parents were uneasy about his decision. However, after he brought Ella Fitzgerald (a featured soloist) home for dinner, his mother bragged about her son. Jackson praised Gillespie. "Oh, man! I fell in love with everything that Dizzy did . . . there were so many things that he taught us." Jackson played in Gillespie's bop sextet from 1945 to 1946, his big band from 1946 to 1948, a new Gillespie sextet from 1950 to 1952, and with Howard McGhee, Thelonious Monk, Charlie Parker, and Woody Herman during seasonal breaks. He recorded several titles with Gillespie, including "A Night in Tunisia," before forming the Milt Jackson Quartet (the prototype for the Modern Jazz Quartet). Musicians in the quartet were members of Gillespie's rhythm section: pianist John Lewis, bassist Ray Brown, and drummer Kenny Clark.

In 1952 the group became the Modern Jazz Quartet

Milt Jackson, between 1946 and 1948. WILLIAM L. GOTTLIEB/WILLIAM L. GOTTLIEB COLLECTION/PRINTS AND PHOTOGRAPHS DIVISION, LIBRARY OF CONGRESS

(MJQ), creating a fusion of jazz and classical sound. That year, Jackson recorded "What's New?" Dressed in formal attire, the quartet sought precision over emotion, producing a cool jazz style, which music critics called "Third Stream." By the mid-1950s Percy Heath replaced Brown and Connie Kay replaced Clarke. During summer breaks from the MJQ, Jackson organized groups with Jimmy Heath in the 1960s and Ray Brown in the 1970s. The MJQ remained together until 1974, when Jackson left to freelance, due to economic frustration. Jackson rejoined the MJQ for a Japanese concert in 1981 and annual concert tours beginning in 1982. The quartet celebrated its fortieth anniversary in 1992 and final performance in 1995 (without Kay, who had died in 1994). Jackson was a member of the MJQ for a total of forty-four years.

In the 1940s Jackson had reduced the speed of the fans on his Deagan Imperial vibraphone to 3.3 revolutions per second, as opposed to Lionel Hampton's vibrato speed of about 10 per second. Jackson said, "I discovered that by using the speed control on the vibes, I could imitate the vibrato I used as a vocalist. Man, that fascinated me." By adjusting the oscillator, he produced warmer long notes and a more languid vibrato, which became his trademark.

Jackson's rhythmic variations ranged from spontaneous short notes (indicative of bop) to slow sustained phrases. His twelve-bar blues contributed an added dimension.

Jackson was his own stylist. "I was only inspired by Hamp[ton] in terms of taking up the instrument. But that stopped there." Jackson wrote well-known jazz pieces, such as "Bags' Groove," "Bluesology," "The Cylinder," and "Ralph's New Blues." In 1969 he won a Grammy for "That's the Way It Is." He was an annual winner of *Down Beat* readers' and critics' polls, was included in the *Playboy Jazz All Stars* recordings, received the National Music Award and the French Bicentennial Award, and was listed in the *Down Beat* Hall of Fame. Jackson performed with pianist Ray Charles and during the 1990s worked with Quincy Jones. In 1992 he formed a quartet with Mike Le Donne, Bob Cranshaw, and Mikey Roker. He was inducted into the Percussive Arts Society (PAS) Hall of Fame in 1996. Jackson collaborated with the bassist Ray Brown and the pianist Oscar Peterson on *The Very Tall Band*, released in 1999. Jackson's last record was *Explosive!* with the Clayton-Hamilton Jazz Orchestra.

Jackson married Sandra Kaye Whittington on 18 January 1959. They had one daughter. The couple resided in Teaneck, New Jersey, until Jackson's death at age seventy-six from liver cancer in a Manhattan hospital.

Jackson's musicianship was noted for "its uniquely personal voice." He was the first bebop jazz vibraphonist and, with a career spanning six decades, has been described as one of the greatest of all jazz musicians. Jackson enhanced the vibrato to make his vibes sing. A dedicated artist, Jackson said, "my music comes from the heart, and even if I never get to be a millionaire I got something that money couldn't buy no way. That's the bottom line."

★

Andre Hodeir, *Toward Jazz* (1962), provides informed commentary about Jackson's reputation in the jazz medium. Thomas Owens, "Improvisation Technique of the Modern Jazz Quartet," thesis, University of California–Los Angeles (1965), offers descriptive interpretation of the music and biographical information on members of the group. *The Harvard Biographical Dictionary of Music* (1996) gives Jackson's years with Gillespie. Ian Carr, Digby Fairweather, and Brian Priestley, *Jazz: The Rough Guide* (1995), provides information on Jackson's career and albums. Mark C. Gridley, *Jazz Styles* (1978), discusses bebop musicians, the percussive nature of vibraharps, and Jackson's groups through the 1970s. Leonard Feather and Ira Gitler, *The Biographical Encyclopedia of Jazz* (1999), includes factual dates of Jackson's early career. Many magazine articles cover Jackson's life and his role with the MJQ. Among the best are "Bags Groove," *Down Beat* (27 Nov. 1958); "Jackson of the MJQ," *Down Beat* (6 July 1961); "Open Bags: An Interview with Milt Jackson," *Down Beat* (30 April 1970); "Milt Jackson: Dollars and Sense," *Down Beat* (8 May

1975); "Milt Jackson: Vibes Original," *Jazz Times* (July 1984); "Bellwether of the Vibes," *Down Beat* (Jan. 1998); and "Lessons from Bags," *Down Beat* (Nov. 1999). Obituaries are in the *New York Times* (11 Oct. 1999) and *Variety* (18–24 Oct. 1999).

SANDRA REDMOND PETERS

JACOBS, Helen Hull (*b.* 6 August 1908 in Globe, Arizona; *d.* 2 June 1997 in East Hampton, New York), tennis champion who won nine Grand Slam titles including the U.S. Women's Singles Championships four years in a row (1932–1935), known for her fifteen-year rivalry with tennis great Helen Wills Moody.

Jacobs's parents were Roland Herbert Jacobs, a wealthy mining engineer, and Eula Hull, a descendent of Carter Braxton, a Virginia native who signed the Declaration of Independence. Jacobs was thirteen and living in San Francisco when she began to play tennis. At fifteen she won the 1923 California State Championships and came under the tutelage of William C. ("Pop") Fuller, the renowned junior coach at the Berkeley Tennis Club in Berkeley, California. Fuller was the coach of seventeen-year-old Moody, who won the U.S. National Singles Championships that year. Fuller recommended that the Jacobs family move to Berkeley and even found a house for them—the house vacated by Moody and her family. Jacobs idolized Moody and modeled her game after that of Moody.

Helen Hull Jacobs at Wimbledon, 1938. © UNDERWOOD & UNDERWOOD/CORBIS

Jacobs's game featured a forehand slice, a strong backhand, good footwork, and effective net play. In her midteens she won the National Junior Tennis Championships in 1924 and 1925. In 1926 she won the California and Pacific Coast titles, tournaments that Moody did not enter. When the two finally did meet in tournament competition, at the 1927 semifinals at Forest Hills, New York (site of the U.S. Championships), the seemingly invincible Moody won 6–0, 6–2. Between 1927 and 1933 Moody would not lose a single set against any player.

In 1932 Jacobs became a champion in her own right, winning the U.S. Singles Championships at Forest Hills. The following year Moody entered, and the two met in what has become an infamous match. Moody was playing with what was later determined to be a dislocated lumbar vertebra and was trailing Jacobs, 8–6, 3–6, 3–0, when she defaulted, leaving Jacobs with a hollow victory. During the next two years, while Moody was recovering from her back injury, Jacobs won the singles titles at Forest Hills. Moody returned to competition in 1935. In the Wimbledon finals that year, Moody and Jacobs clashed again, and many in the tennis world felt Jacobs could win. Jacobs played well and even held match point at 5–3 in the third set. However, she missed an easy shot, and Moody rallied for a 6–3, 3–6, 7–5 victory.

In 1936 Jacobs finally won the Wimbledon title after five appearances in the finals. Moody did not compete; Jacobs's final-round match was against Hilda Sperling of Germany. In 1938 Jacobs and Moody again met at Wimbledon. Jacobs had injured her Achilles tendon in an earlier match, and in the final match against Moody she came down hard on her injured leg. She lost the match. Jacobs played on her last Wightman Cup in 1939 and ended her career at Forest Hills in 1941. She had been ranked top ten in the world for twelve straight years starting in 1928. In the United States she had been in the top ten for thirteen years between 1927 and 1941. In 1933 the Associated Press named her Athlete of the Year, the first woman tennis player to be so chosen. In 1962 she was inducted into the International Tennis Hall of Fame.

In 1942 Jacobs enlisted in the U.S. Navy, completing her college credits at the College of William and Mary. She entered officer training school in 1943. She served as Commandant of Seaman, United States Naval Training School, and as a public relations officer and administrative assistant during World War II and the Korean War. She achieved the rank of commander while serving in naval intelligence during World War II, becoming one of only five women to achieve that rank. She retired as a commander in 1968.

Jacobs was the first woman to play in shorts at Wimbledon, a precedent that served her well in her next career as a designer of sports clothes for specialty department stores in New York and London after the war. Jacobs was also an accomplished writer. By nineteen she was writing for the McClure Syndicate, and later she became a senior editor at Grolier Council for Educational Research. She wrote numerous articles and books for adults and children, including *Beyond the Game: An Autobiography* (1936) and *Storm Against the Wind* (1944), a fictionalized account of her ancestor Carter Braxton.

Jacobs died at eighty-eight of heart failure on 2 June 1997. She was survived by her companion, Virginia Gurnee, sister Jean Jacobs Gross, a niece, and three great nieces.

★

Jacobs wrote her autobiography, *Beyond the Game: An Autobiography* (1936), under the pseudonym H. Braxton Hill. She described her life and careers in *Something About the Author: Facts and Pictures About Authors and Illustrators of Books for Young People*, vol. 12 (1977). A *Time* cover story (14 Sept. 1936) published at the height of Jacobs's career gives a personal account of Jacobs and her place in women's tennis. Her record and personal style are discussed in the *Official Encyclopedia of Tennis*, ed. Bill Shannon (1979). Larry Engelmann, *The Goddess and the American Girl* (1998), covers Jacobs's early training, tennis career, and life through the 1940s. An obituary is in the *New York Times* (4 June 1997).

JULIANNE CICARELLI

JAFFE, Leo (*b.* 23 April 1909 in New York City; *d.* 20 August 1997 in New York City), motion picture executive, philanthropist, and chairman of Columbia Pictures.

Jaffe was born and raised in New York City. After graduating from high school, he enrolled at New York University to study business administration. In the summer of 1930, he began working in the New York office of Columbia Pictures under the aegis of his brother-in-law, Abe Schneider, an accountant with the studio. At the time, Columbia was a family business founded by the legendary Hollywood mogul Harry Cohn and his brother Jack. Harry was in charge of production in Los Angeles, and Jack handled distribution from New York.

After a brief tryout as Schneider's assistant, Jaffe was offered a permanent position. He finished his business degree at night, graduating in 1931, and began working in the financial department. He would stay with Columbia for more than fifty years, during which his career shadowed Schneider's; when Schneider was promoted, Jaffe would frequently fill the position just vacated. Along the way, Jaffe earned a reputation as one of the brightest financial minds in the business.

When Jaffe joined the team, Columbia was just beginning to hit its stride as a studio. In 1932 a survey of motion picture exhibitors ranked Columbia sixth (of the "Big

Leo Jaffe, 1958. ASSOCIATED PRESS/COLUMBIA PICTURES

Eight" studios) in consistency of product. The arrival of the director Frank Capra in the late 1920s helped lift Columbia's fortunes. In 1934 the studio won seven Oscars: five for Capra's *It Happened One Night,* starring Clark Gable and Claudette Colbert, and two for *One Night of Love,* directed by Victor Schertzinger. Columbia truly arrived in the late 1930s with a string of Capra hits: *Lost Horizon* (1937), *You Can't Take It with You* (1938), and *Mr. Smith Goes to Washington* (1939). Throughout this era, when big stars had long-term contracts with a single studio, Columbia found success by employing freelance actors and promoting the film's director.

By the mid-1950s the Cohn brothers were facing serious health problems. Jack died in 1956 and Harry in 1958. Schneider assumed the presidency of Columbia Pictures in 1958 and promoted Jaffe to first vice president and treasurer. Together they transformed Columbia from a studio into a corporation. Their financial strategy was simple: diversification in television as well as real estate. They reversed Harry Cohn's ambitious expansion plans for the studio, dismissing 300 employees. Both Schneider and Jaffe took pay cuts.

In 1967 Jaffe became president of Columbia, and Schneider moved up to chairman. During the 1960s and

1970s, Schneider and Jaffe built Columbia into one of the strongest studios in the industry. But Jaffe had the more lasting impact. He aggressively cultivated friendships with some of Hollywood's most powerful directors and producers. His business approach was to recruit talented artists and leave the creative decision making to them. "I never wanted to get into production," he insisted.

According to the producer Ray Stark, Jaffe was responsible for Stark's long association with Columbia Pictures. Stark's Rastar Productions produced a number of hits for the studio, including *Funny Girl* (1968) and *The Way We Were* (1973). Stark recalled that Jaffe "very much wanted 'Funny Girl' for Columbia. He took the gamble with Barbra Streisand despite concerns from his executives who wanted an actress with a movie track record in the lead. When he felt he was right, he held to it . . . and he was right very often."

Jaffe became known as a filmmaker's executive and replaced Schneider as chairman of the board in 1973. During the next eight years, he was the main force in bringing talented producers and directors into the studio, including Stark and Sam Spiegel (*On the Waterfront* [1954] and *Lawrence of Arabia* [1962]), Otto Preminger (*Porgy and Bess* [1959] and *Anatomy of a Murder* [1959]), Stanley Kramer (*The Caine Mutiny* [1954] and *Guess Who's Coming to Dinner* [1967]), and Steven Spielberg (*Close Encounters of the Third Kind* [1977]).

At the same time, Jaffe felt isolated from Hollywood. Like Schneider and Jack Cohn before him, Jaffe was rooted in New York and his conservative upbringing. He devoted his energies to a number of philanthropic causes and in 1978 was awarded a special Oscar, the Jean Hersholt Humanitarian Award, by the Academy of Motion Picture Arts and Sciences. Jaffe never hesitated to decry the "carnal values" of Hollywood, as he phrased it in a 1972 "State of the Industry" speech to the Motion Picture Pioneers Foundation banquet.

Jaffe also applied morality to business decisions, as the screenwriter Gerald Ayres attested in revealing how Columbia lost the film rights to *Hair,* the 1968 Broadway musical that celebrated the 1960s counterculture. Jaffe was steadfast in his opposition to the project. "Leo looked at me and said, 'Gerry, I'm sorry, I can't help it. If Columbia Pictures ever produces a film which uses the word "fuck" while I'm still president, I'll jump out that window.' He was standing next to the eleventh floor window." It was little wonder that Jaffe became known as the "conscience of Columbia." Yet the pull between his conscience and his desire to liberate talented filmmakers was a difficult balance for him, and one that recurred throughout his entire career. Although Jaffe rejected *Hair,* Columbia produced perhaps the definitive counterculture film of the period—*Easy Rider*—in 1969.

Jaffe's leadership of the studio and his role as moral paragon were further tested during the 1970s, when Columbia was shaken by financial scandal. David Begelman, a studio president, was found to have misappropriated $40,000. In the wake of this revelation, which several Columbia executives tried to cover up, Jaffe was a sole voice of reason on the board of directors. In a dramatic plea, Begelman told the board that he was "cured" of the "aberrational behavior" that had led to his embezzling funds. Jaffe was unmoved. "There are certain things you can forgive a man for doing as a human being but that have no place in a publicly owned company." Begelman was dismissed, and Jaffe's stewardship helped Columbia regain its credibility and financial stability.

Jaffe stepped down as head of Columbia in 1981 and became chairman emeritus. Despite the purchase of Columbia by the Coca-Cola Company in 1982 and then by the Sony Corporation of Japan in 1989, Jaffe maintained a seat on the board and an office at the studio for the rest of his life. Jaffe also served as chairman of the motion picture and television division of the U.S. Information Agency under President Ronald Reagan, though this was largely an honorary post. As Herbert Allen, whose family controlled Columbia throughout much of Jaffe's tenure, said, "He was an old-fashioned company man." Jaffe turned Columbia into a haven for talented producers and directors and helped the studio weather one of Hollywood's worst scandals. At age eighty-eight, Jaffe died of pneumonia at his home in New York City. Twice widowed, he left behind his third wife, Anita, and six children.

★

Details of Jaffe's career are in a number of sources, including David McClintick, *Indecent Exposure: A True Story of Hollywood and Wall Street* (1982); Stephen Farber and Marc Green, *Hollywood Dynasties* (1984); and Bernard F. Dick, ed., *Columbia Pictures: Portrait of a Studio* (1991). Obituaries are in the *Los Angeles Times* and *New York Times* (both 21 Aug. 1997) as well as *Variety* (25–31 Aug. 1997) and *Time* (1 Sept. 1997).

TIMOTHY KRINGEN

JAMES, Dennis (*b.* 24 August 1917 in Jersey City, New Jersey; *d.* 3 June 1997 in Palm Springs, California), pioneer television personality who worked continuously as a commercial pitchman, game show host, wrestling commentator, actor, and producer for sixty years.

Born Demie James Sposa, James grew up in a working-class district of Jersey City, New Jersey, just across the Hudson River from the Manhattan financial district. He attended St. Peter's College in his hometown, and won admission to several medical schools upon his graduation

Dennis James, 1982. ASSOCIATED PRESS/CBS

in 1929. Against his family's wishes, however, he chose to forego a career as a physician and instead took acting courses at the Theater School of the Performing Arts at Carnegie Hall, where he earned a graduation certificate. He supported himself during much of the Great Depression with a variety of odd jobs, including a stint selling pet supplies at Abercrombie and Fitch, before finding work as an announcer at a New Jersey radio station.

Television was still in laboratory development in 1938, but that year James became one of the first performers to work in the new medium as the result of a family connection. His brother Frank recommended him to his employer, Allen B. DuMont, who was seeking on-air talent for experimental television broadcasts he was conducting at his Passaic, New Jersey, electronics factory. DuMont, the inventor of the cathode ray tube and other key components of television technology, hoped to become a dominant force in television distribution as well as manufacturing by launching his own national network.

Impressed by James's willingness to take on any assignment in front of the camera or behind it, DuMont signed him to a contract that doubled his radio salary. As a participant in these pioneering telecasts, James achieved several historic milestones, including the role of announcer in the first known television commercial. "It was a full half

hour given to Wedgwood china, about 1940 or 1941," he recalled. "Not a penny of cost. [DuMont] was anxious to get ads, so they gave the front time away." It is estimated that there were fewer than 1,500 television sets in the United States at the time.

Civilian television experimentation was suspended by government decree upon American entry into World War II, and James served in the army from 1942 to 1945. Upon discharge, he was offered a contract by the new DuMont Television Network, which began revenue telecasts in the fall of 1946.

Programming was sporadic that first season, with no more than one show aired each evening by DuMont. James emceed the Thursday-night program *Cash and Carry,* which gave him the distinction of being the first television game show host. He would become a familiar figure in that role, starring as host in more than a dozen such series over the next four decades, including *Chance of a Lifetime; Okay, Mother; High Finance;* and *Name That Tune.*

James's willingness to take on all kinds of roles and functions made him an ubiquitous figure on the home-screen. By 1953 he was appearing in thirteen different live weekly programs on all four networks (ABC, CBS, NBC, and DuMont, the latter going out of business in 1955) and earning approximately a half million dollars per year. Other notable credits include the announcer spot on *Ted Mack's Original Amateur Hour* from 1948 to 1960; a starring role on his own prime-time musical variety show, *The Dennis James Show,* from 1951 to 1952; and acting parts in live dramas, such as "Pardon My Prison" on *Kraft Television Playhouse* in 1954.

James was perhaps best known among first-generation television viewers as a wrestling announcer. Live coverage of professional wrestling was a major component of early prime-time programming. As chief blow-by-blow commentator for DuMont's Friday-night telecasts, he helped to popularize the "exhibition" sport by affecting a kind of innocent enthusiasm for the preposterous antics of Gorgeous George, Killer Kowalski, and other early wrestling stars. His penchant for yelling out "Okay, mother!" when the willing suspension of disbelief was being tested to its outer limits by a particularly stupefying event made that line one of the first "household" catchphrases of the television era. It was even used as a title for a James game show in 1948. James satirically reprised his role as a wrestling commentator in several feature films, including *Rocky III* (1982).

Another feature of early television pioneered by James was the charity telethon. It is believed that he raised as much as $700 million for research and patient care in the annual twenty-four-hour fund-raisers he hosted for the United Cerebral Palsy Foundation during the 1950s and 1960s. The *New York Times* estimated that this and his other philanthropic efforts on behalf of ChildHelp USA, the American Cancer Society, the American Heart Association, and other charities resulted in his raising more than one billion dollars for worthy causes during his lifetime. A tireless golfer, he took special delight in hosting celebrity golf tournaments, especially the one in Palm Springs bearing his name.

In 1962, following the drift of television production from New York to Los Angeles, James moved to the West Coast and established his own company. Dennis James Productions specialized in acquiring rights to cancelled prime-time game shows, including *The Price Is Right* and *Name That Tune,* and producing new versions for daytime syndication. James also enjoyed a lucrative career as a spokesperson for various products and services, including Old Gold Cigarettes and Kellogg's Cereals. Though paid a $350,000 yearly fee by Old Gold's parent, the Brown and Williamson Tobacco Company, he quit the relationship (as well as smoking) in 1967 after being convinced of the link between tobacco and lung cancer.

Although he never actually retired—he recorded a commercial for an insurance company shortly before his death—James moved to his Palm Springs vacation home in the early 1990s, where he played golf daily at the Mission Hills Country Club. He lived there with his second wife, Micki, whom he married in 1950. The couple had two sons. An earlier marriage, which ended in divorce, produced one son. James died of lung cancer at age seventy-nine. He is buried at Forest Lawn Memorial Park, Los Angeles.

James is a distinctive figure in American television history not only because of the milestones he achieved or the longevity of his career but also for the unassuming attitude that he was able to maintain in an industry notorious for swelling the heads of performers and then deflating them into obscurity. His willingness to work as a pitchman and bit-part player even after having had a taste of early stardom remains an unusual phenomenon in show business.

★

There are no biographies of James, nor have any collections of his papers or personal effects been catalogued. No major articles have been written about him, and he is often left out of major reference works concerning television. An obituary is in the *New York Times* (6 June 1997).

DAVID MARC

JOHNSON, Frank Minis, Jr. (*b.* 30 October 1918 in Haleyville, Alabama; *d.* 23 July 1999 in Montgomery, Alabama), federal jurist in many landmark racial discrimination cases and nonracial human rights cases.

The oldest of seven children of Frank Minis Johnson, a civil servant and probate judge, and Alabama Long, a

Frank M. Johnson, Jr. AP/WIDE WORLD PHOTOS

teacher, Johnson was raised in the hills of Winston County in northwest Alabama, a hotbed of unionist sentiment during the Civil War and a Republican stronghold thereafter. Several of Johnson's ancestors fought for the North in the war. His father was active in Grand Old Party (GOP) politics and at one time was the only Republican in the Alabama legislature.

Following graduation from Gulf Coast Military Academy in Gulfport, Mississippi, in 1935, Johnson was admitted to Birmingham-Southern College in Alabama on a football scholarship but found the experience unsatisfying and withdrew after a single term. He next graduated from Massey Business College and obtained a job as an accountant with a Birmingham firm. But when he married his childhood sweetheart, Ruth Jenkins, on 16 January 1938, he lost that position because his employer feared that a married employee who was poorly paid might be tempted to steal.

In 1939, after working a year and a half for the Works Projects Administration (WPA) in various towns and villages in northwest Alabama, he and Ruth entered the University of Alabama, from which he received an LL.B. degree in 1943. Following World War II service with General George S. Patton's Third Army in France, for which he received a Bronze Star and Purple Heart among other combat medals, he established a law practice in Jasper, Alabama, in 1946. Like his father, he also became active in Republican politics. His efforts on behalf of the 1952 Dwight Eisenhower presidential campaign led to his appointment in 1953 as U.S. attorney for the Northern District of Alabama. In 1955 he was named judge of the U.S. District Court for the Middle District of Alabama, in Montgomery, becoming at age thirty-seven the youngest member of the federal judiciary.

Johnson was to forge a significant record in civil rights litigation on the district court bench. But he had begun to develop that record even earlier. While a U.S. attorney, he secured indictments on peonage and slavery charges against members of a prominent Sumter County plantation family who regularly went to Mississippi jails and paid the fines of blacks being held on minor charges, then forced them to work on the family's farms. When one worker escaped, he was brought back to Sumter County and beaten to death. State officials attributed his death to natural causes, asserting that the horrendous bruises covering the victim's body were the result of skin deterioration following death. But Johnson pursued the case vigorously, winning convictions from an all-white jury against the two brothers just three days before the Supreme Court's historic 1954 school desegregation ruling in *Brown* v. *Board of Education*.

In 1956, within months of his elevation to the district court, Johnson confronted the first of many racial cases to reach his court—a challenge to segregation on Montgomery's buses following the arrest of Rosa Parks, which proved to be the inaugural battle of the modern civil rights movement. Although the Supreme Court had already declared segregated schooling "inherently unequal," the Court's 1896 *Plessy* v. *Ferguson* decision condoning segregated transportation had not yet been specifically overruled. One member of the three-judge panel convened to hear the Montgomery bus case urged his colleagues to follow *Plessy*, leaving to the Supreme Court any decision to reverse that precedent. Johnson and Judge Richard T. Rives of the U.S. Court of Appeals for the Fifth Circuit voted, however, to extend *Brown* and outlaw segregation on Montgomery's buses.

In the years that followed, Johnson gained a national reputation as an aggressive defender of civil rights. In voting cases, he enjoined discrimination by local registrars and became the first judge in the nation to order the names of qualified blacks added to county voter rolls. He also outlawed segregation in Alabama's bus and airline terminals, libraries, agricultural extension service, and political parties, as well as the Montgomery YMCA; wrote the first statewide school desegregation decree; and placed numerous state and local agencies under court order. Critics and admirers alike began referring to him increasingly as "the real governor of Alabama."

Johnson's civil rights rulings perplexed and angered white Alabamians, making him a convenient scapegoat for Governor George C. Wallace and other race-baiting politicians. Wallace and Johnson had been law school classmates and friends. But in 1959 Johnson ordered Wallace, then a state circuit judge, to turn over county voter records to the U.S. Civil Rights Commission. Following a late-night visit to Johnson's home, Wallace complied with the court order while proclaiming to the press that he was defying the federal government. When Johnson issued an opinion announcing Wallace's compliance, the future Alabama governor was incensed. In his first successful race for governor in 1962, Wallace lashed out at "lying, scalawagging, carpetbagging federal judges," leaving no doubt as to the target of his attacks. Court baiting would remain a familiar Wallace tactic for years, and on at least one occasion a Wallace aide urged Alabamians to ostracize federal judges, their wives, and their children. The state Ku Klux Klan, among others, scorned the judge as "the most hated man in Alabama."

Johnson was a pariah in his native state even before the Wallace era. After his decision in the Montgomery bus case, a dusk-to-dawn guard was placed at his home. It would remain there intermittently for eighteen years. His mother's house was bombed, crosses were burned on his lawn, and he was a regular target of hate mail. In 1975 the Johnsons' only child, an adopted son, committed suicide—the victim in part, some charged, of the harassment to which his family had been subjected.

One of Johnson's more controversial rulings authorized Martin Luther King, Jr., to lead a massive voting rights march from Selma, in Alabama's Black Belt, to Montgomery in March 1965, following the "Bloody Sunday" attack by local sheriff's deputies and thugs. In upholding the marchers, Johnson concluded that the scope of their First Amendment rights must be "commensurate with the enormity of the wrongs protested and petitioned against," particularly where "the usual, basic and constitutionally provided means of protesting in our American way—voting—have been deprived." In a number of prior cases involving civil rights demonstrations, the Supreme Court had balanced competing societal and First Amendment interests. But those rulings seemed a far cry from Johnson's apparent assumption that the scope of a group's freedom to protest its grievances depended on the virtue of its cause.

The vicious murder of Viola Liuzzo, a white Detroit homemaker transporting marchers back to Selma, also ended up in Johnson's court. After a state jury acquitted one of her assailants despite the testimony of a paid Federal Bureau of Investigation (FBI) informant present in the murder car, the three defendants, all members of the Ku Klux Klan, were tried on charges of violating the victim's civil rights. Shortly after the federal jurors began their deliberations, the jury foreman informed Johnson they were hopelessly deadlocked. But after a stern lecture from the bench on their responsibilities as jurors, they returned guilty verdicts against the accused. Each received a ten-year sentence.

In 1976 Johnson ordered massive reforms of Alabama's prisons, which prompted Governor Wallace to accuse his former friend of trying to create a "hotel atmosphere" for inmates and to announce that a vote for Wallace (in his latest, futile presidential bid) would assure "a barbed-wire enema" for federal judges. "The elimination of conditions that will permit maggots in a patient's wounds for over a month before his death," Johnson countered, "does not constitute the creation of a hotel atmosphere."

As black voter registration increased and racial politics subsided, white Alabamians' attitudes toward Johnson mellowed. But his landmark rulings requiring extensive improvements in the state's prisons and mental health system initiated attacks from other quarters. Critics contended that he and other "activist" judges were confusing personal preference with constitutional commands and encroaching on legislative and administrative domains. Johnson maintained that he was merely enforcing the clear commands of a "living Constitution" and decried the failure of state officials to fulfill their constitutional obligations.

Combined with his civil rights record, Johnson's mental health and prison rulings served largely to enhance rather than damage his judicial reputation. In 1977 President Jimmy Carter selected him to be director of the FBI. Although medical difficulties obliged him to have the nomination withdrawn, in 1979 Johnson accepted Carter's appointment to the U.S. Court of Appeals for the Fifth Circuit. When the Fifth Circuit was split into two jurisdictions in 1981, Johnson became a member of the new Court of Appeals for the Eleventh Circuit, with jurisdiction over Alabama, Florida, and Georgia.

As an appellate jurist, Johnson continued to give constitutional guarantees a broad reading. In one case, an Alabama district judge enjoined the further use of more than forty textbooks in the state's public schools, declaring that they propagated "secular humanist" religious values inappropriate for public education in the same manner that the Supreme Court had held state-directed school prayer to be. Speaking for a unanimous panel, Johnson reversed his fellow Alabamian. He spoke for a majority in upholding the right of consenting adult homosexuals to engage in sodomy, a decision later reversed by a five to four Supreme Court majority in *Bowers* v. *Hardwick* (1986). He vigorously dissented when a majority of the entire appeals court, rather than a three-judge panel, upheld Georgia's death penalty despite statistical evidence of gross racial disparities in its imposition.

Johnson retired from the bench in 1992. Much earlier, however, the state and nation had begun conferring honors on the judge and his record. In 1979 he was inducted into the Alabama Academy of Honor, a society recognizing outstanding contributions to the citizens of his native state. In 1993 the American Bar Association selected him for its first Thurgood Marshall Award. The same year, the federal courthouse in Montgomery was named in his honor. Alabama politicians who once vilified him now praised his record. Even George Wallace sought his forgiveness. In 1995 President Bill Clinton awarded Johnson the Presidential Medal of Freedom, the nation's highest civilian honor.

Johnson's health steadily declined in his last years. After a fall in the summer of 1999, he was hospitalized briefly, then returned to his Montgomery home where, at age eighty, he succumbed to pneumonia on 23 July. Following a memorial service in his courtroom, his body was taken to Haleyville for burial in the hills of his native Winston County.

During the memorial service, one of Johnson's clerks termed him "the embodiment of the Constitution in Alabama and the nation." In the wake of his expansive mental health and prison decrees, even some of his admirers had questioned whether he had overstepped the legitimate bounds of judicial authority. But few doubted the sincerity of his convictions, and none questioned the exceptional role he played in the modern struggle for human rights or the tremendous courage he displayed throughout that era.

★

Johnson's judicial papers are in the Manuscript Division of the Library of Congress. He is the subject of four biographies: Robert F. Kennedy, Jr., *Judge Frank M. Johnson, Jr.: A Biography* (1978); Tinsley E. Yarbrough, *Judge Frank Johnson and Human Rights in Alabama* (1981); Frank Sikora, *The Judge: The Life and Opinions of Alabama's Frank M. Johnson, Jr.* (1992); and Jack Bass, *Taming the Storm: The Life and Times of Judge Frank M. Johnson, Jr., and the South's Fight over Civil Rights* (1993). An obituary is in the *New York Times* (24 July 1999).

Tinsley E. Yarbrough

JOHNSON, Leon William (*b.* 13 September 1904 in Columbia, Missouri; *d.* 10 November 1997 in Fairfax, Virginia), U.S. Air Force general who was awarded the Medal of Honor for bravery during World War II for his role in a 1943 air raid against oil refineries in Ploesti, Rumania.

Johnson was the son of Francis Lusk Johnson, a banker, and Minnie Hayward. He grew up in Moline, Kansas, and in 1922 was admitted to the United States Military Acad-

General Leon Johnson, 1949. © HULTON-DEUTSCH COLLECTION/
CORBIS

emy at West Point, New York. He graduated in 1926 and was commissioned as a second lieutenant in the infantry. For the next three years he was a junior officer with the Seventeenth Infantry Regiment at Fort Crook, Nebraska. Eager for a more challenging assignment, Johnson transferred to the U.S. Army Air Corps in 1929 and, following completion of flight training in 1930, was assigned to the Fifth Observation Squadron. Johnson married Lucille Taylor in 1929; they had two daughters.

In 1932 Johnson, then a first lieutenant, went to the Philippines to serve with the Second Observation Squadron. He returned to the United States in 1935 and enrolled at the California Institute of Technology, where he earned an M.A. degree in meteorology in 1936. From 1936 to 1939 Johnson, who had been promoted to captain in 1936, was base operations officer at Barksdale Field, Louisiana, and then commander of the Third Weather Squadron. During the summer of 1939, Johnson was a student at the Air Corps

Tactical School at Maxwell Field, Alabama. There he was introduced to the doctrine of strategic air warfare, which centered upon the use of air power to win a conflict by destroying the enemy's ability and will to wage war. Over the next two years, Johnson served successively as commander of the headquarters of the Third Attack Group, as commander of the Ninetieth Attack Squadron, and as A-3, or operations officer, of the Air Support Command.

Shortly after the United States entered World War II in December 1941, Johnson, then a lieutenant colonel, was named A-3 for the Eighth Air Force, which went to England in the spring of 1942. There he oversaw the operations and training of the heavy bomber crews that were being sent to England for an air offensive against Hitler's Third Reich. In early 1943 Johnson, who was eager for a combat role, was given command of the Forty-fourth Bomb Group, one of the Eighth's first units outfitted with the B-24 Liberator. During the early months of 1943, Johnson led the Forty-fourth in many missions over France and Germany, suffering heavy losses while the pilots learned how to defeat Nazi air defenses and improve bombing accuracy.

In late June 1943 Johnson's bomb group was temporarily attached to the Ninth Air Force in the Mediterranean theater for a special mission against the oil refinery complex at Ploesti, Rumania, which was believed to supply some 60 percent of the oil requirements for Germany and its allies. Planners hoped that five groups of B-24s flying at low level from bases in Libya could catch the Germans and their Rumanian allies off guard and deliver a crippling blow against the enemy war effort.

The Ploesti mission was carried out on 1 August 1943. Johnson, copiloting the lead bomber in his group, was charged with hitting the Columbia Aquila and Creditul Minier refineries. Problems developed early in the mission. Navigation snafus and cloud coverage caused the groups to lose sight of each other, throwing off the time schedule and causing many planes to bomb the wrong targets. By the time Johnson arrived at the Columbia Aquila with two squadrons of B-24s, it was engulfed in flames as a result of being mistakenly bombed by another group. Despite the risk of being destroyed in the explosions of the delayed-action bombs already dropped on the target, Johnson flew ahead into the conflagration. Some of the group's planes crashed because of turbulence created by the flames; others were destroyed in bomb explosions. But Johnson's formation dropped its bombs on the refinery. Afterward he remained in the area to look for targets of opportunity before heading home. The Ploesti raid, one of the most daring air operations of the war, was only moderately successful in cutting German oil production, and then only at an exorbitant cost in planes and men. For his outstanding leadership and courage in leading the attack against the assigned target, Johnson won the Medal of Honor.

After the raid, Johnson went back to England to become commander of the Eighth Air Force's Fourteenth Combat Wing, where he assumed the rank of brigadier general. Consisting of two, and later four, bomb groups, the Fourteenth participated in every major bombing campaign in Europe through the end of the war there in May 1945.

Johnson returned to the United States in the summer of 1945 to serve as chief of personnel services in the headquarters of the Army Air Forces. In 1947 he was appointed commanding general of the Fifteenth Air Force and, the next year, with the rank of major general, was back in England as commander of the Third Air Division, later the Third Air Force. Beginning in 1952, Johnson, then a lieutenant general, was in charge of the Continental Air Command. A year later he was assigned to the Military Staff Committee of the United Nations. In 1958 Johnson became Air Deputy to the Supreme Commander, Europe. Six weeks after his retirement in 1961, Johnson was recalled to active duty to become director of the Net Evaluation Subcommittee Staff of the National Security Council, a post he occupied until retiring a second time in April 1965. He died at age ninety-three of a respiratory infection and is buried in Arlington National Cemetery.

A mustached, snub-nosed, and mild-mannered man, Johnson approached his assignments with a businesslike efficiency and was greatly admired by those who served under him for his courage and concern for their welfare. He stood out for his heroism during the Ploesti raid and as a leading practitioner of the strategic air war in Europe during World War II.

★

A collection of Johnson's papers covering the years 1948–1952, lectures, an oral history, and a film interview are located in the Air Force Historical Research Agency, Maxwell Air Force Base, Alabama. An overview of Johnson's career is provided in *Strategic Air Warfare: An Interview with Generals Curtis E. LeMay, Leon W. Johnson, David A. Burchinal, and Jack J. Catton* (1988). The best sources for the Ploesti raid are Leon Wolff, *Low Level Mission* (1957); James Dugan and Carroll Stewart, *Ploesti: The Great Ground-Air Battle of 1 August 1943* (1963); and Roger Freeman, *The Mighty Eighth: A History of the U.S. Eighth Air Force* (1970). Obituaries are in the *Washington Post* (13 Nov. 1997) and *New York Times* (15 Nov. 1997).

JOHN KENNEDY OHL

JOHNSON, Robert Samuel (*b.* 21 February 1920 in Lawton, Oklahoma; *d.* 27 December 1998 in Tulsa, Oklahoma), World War II hero and daring P-47 Thunderbolt ace who—in ninety-one missions in less than eleven months—destroyed twenty-seven German planes, the second-highest total for an American pilot in the European Theater and an unequaled kill rate in the history of the U.S. Army Air Forces in Europe.

Johnson was born to Lansing Burrows Johnson, a mechanic, and Irma Nixon Stephens, a homemaker. He had two older sisters. Johnson grew up at 1201 C Avenue in Lawton, where he enjoyed fishing, camping, hunting, and riding horses. At age eight Johnson attended an air show at Fort Sill and first saw airplanes, pursuit biplanes flown by an army air corps demonstration team. "Then and there I changed my goal from cowboy or railroad engineer to army aviator." Because of his small size, bullies harassed Johnson, so in ninth grade he learned to box. He eventually boxed for Lawton High School, from which he graduated in 1939. Johnson also played football—left guard at five feet, seven inches and 145 pounds—in high school and for Cameron State Agricultural College's 1939 National Junior College Champions. Johnson was also president of his Cameron freshman class and the student senate. He graduated from Cameron in 1941.

To achieve his army aviator goal, Johnson began flying lessons. At age thirteen he flew Wiley Post and Travelair biplanes. To pay for his lessons, Johnson worked at the Lawton Cabinet Shop. He soloed at age fourteen and obtained his student license on 20 February 1936. While Johnson was at Cameron, the dean loaned him the $50 fee for his Civilian Pilot Training Program. To repay this loan,

Captain Robert S. Johnson, 1944. © HULTON-DEUTSCH COLLECTION/ CORBIS

with interest, Johnson worked at a clothing store and the Lawton Fire Department. During this program, Duane Huscher instructed him in a Taylorcraft. On 11 November 1941 Johnson took the Army Air Forces cadet oath. The next day he left Lawton for Kelly Field in San Antonio, Texas. Around 20 December 1941 Johnson left Kelly for Sikeston, Missouri, to take primary flight training. At Sikeston, he flew a Fairchild PT-19A and a Stearman PT-18 under instructor Phil Zampini. During this training, Johnson learned of a new regulation allowing cadets to marry.

On 21 February 1942, his twenty-second birthday, Johnson married Barbara Ellen Morgan in Benton, Missouri. They remained married fifty-three years but never had children. The following day the newlyweds left Sikeston for Randolph Field in San Antonio, where Johnson took basic flight training. Barbara left Randolph on 26 February 1942 to return to Lawton. The next day Johnson began training in a North American BT-9 Yale under instructor M. R. Burgess. This training was followed by instrument training in a Link simulator. Johnson's second instructor at Randolph was T. M. Maloney, who, along with Zampini, was willing "to turn the fledgling into an eagle." After Maloney, F. B. Farnell taught Johnson how to fly in formation using a BT-9 Yale. "This was the beginning of my training in patience and air discipline."

Although he wanted to fly fighters, Johnson requested bomber training as better preparation for postwar commercial flying. So on 2 May 1942, back at Kelly Field, Johnson made his first flight as a bomber student pilot in a North American BC-1. Finally, on 3 July 1942, at Kelly Field, Johnson became an army aviator when he graduated from flight training, received his silver pilot's wings, and became a second lieutenant. Sixteen days later he reported to Bridgeport, Connecticut, to join the 61st Squadron of the Eighth Air Force's 56th Fighter Group—the famed Zemke's Wolfpack—to fly fighters. On 26 December 1942, Barbara left Bridgeport for home. Eleven days later the 56th boarded the *Queen Elizabeth* for England and arrived about a week later. From bases in England, Johnson eventually flew the rugged Republic P-47 Thunderbolt deep into the record books.

Initially, however, Johnson's success as a fighter pilot was not obvious or certain. Before a Sikeston training flight, he forgot to fasten his safety belt and would have fallen from his plane had he done a snap roll instead of a barrel roll. Before his first combat mission, he had not passed gunnery training or ever fired P-47 machine guns. Early in his combat tour, he was voted most likely to be shot down. Nevertheless, Johnson's keen eyesight, aggression, and determination to "even the score" made him a deadly opponent and the first European Theater pilot to surpass Eddie Rickenbacker's World War I mark of twenty-six kills. Johnson's twenty-seven kills—all in the air—were mostly Focke-Wulf Fw-190s and Messerschmitt Bf 109s and 110s that attacked B-17s on bombing missions into Germany. He made his first kill on 13 June 1943, another on 19 August, three in October, two in November, and three in December. In 1944 Johnson made four kills in January, two in February, six in March (four on 15 March), three in April (promoted to captain), and two on 8 May (promoted to major), his last mission. Although Johnson was never shot down, on 26 June 1943, 20mm cannon and over 100 machine-gun bullets riddled Johnson's plane. On 6 March 1944 he escorted B-17s on the first major daylight bombing of Berlin, Germany. His accomplishments earned him twenty-six medals, including nine Distinguished Flying Crosses, the Silver Star, and a Purple Heart.

Johnson returned to America in June 1944. President Franklin D. Roosevelt invited the famous fighter ace and his wife to the White House, and the U.S. Senate gave them a standing ovation. He helped sell war bonds and gave numerous speeches. In December 1945 the military discharged him. Afterward, Johnson worked for Republic Aviation, sold insurance, and participated in the Air Force Reserve. On 17 December 1983 he was inducted into the Oklahoma Aviation and Space Hall of Fame. He retired in 1991 and received Cameron's Distinguished Alumni Award in 1992. Barbara died in October 1995. On 20 March 2000 a combat picture of Johnson was dedicated in the Oklahoma senate chamber. Johnson died of heart failure in his sleep at Saint Francis Hospital in Tulsa, and is buried at River Hills Community Cemetery in Lake Wylie, South Carolina.

Johnson was friendly, humble, confident, and patriotic, and he saw flying as "bliss in the blue." He donated his military memorabilia to several museums, and his memoir inspired many people to aviation careers. Johnson participated in a "great adventure—that of establishing air superiority over Europe—which played a major role in the defeat of Germany." He described himself as "a fatalist, a strong believer that when your time is up you're gone, out of here."

★

All of the previous quotes are Johnson's and come from a variety of sources, one of which is *Thunderbolt!* (1958), his memoir written with Martin Caidin. Chapters twelve and sixteen of *Thunderbolt!* describe Johnson's 26 June 1943 and 6 March 1944 missions, respectively. Chapter eight describes Johnson's first flight in a P-47. The 6 March 1944 mission is also described in Edward H. Sims, *American Aces in Great Fighter Battles of World War II* (1958). Colin D. Heaton interviewed Johnson in *Military History* 13 (Aug. 1996): 26–32. The *Lawton* (Oklahoma) *Constitution* contains several articles about Johnson (7 Aug. 1955, 9 and 13 Feb. 1958, 23 and 26 Sept. 1958, 27 Oct. 1958, 21 Mar. 1961, 13 Aug. 1963, 31 Oct. 1976, 11 Nov. 1983, 4 Dec. 1983, and 17 July 1994).

Obituaries are in the *Lawton Constitution* (29 Dec. 1998), *New York Times* (1 Jan. 1999), *Lake Wylie* (South Carolina) *Magazine* (5 Jan. 1999), and *Air Power History* 46 (spring 1999). The movie *Fighter Squadron* (1948) is based partly on Johnson's exploits.

GARY MASON CHURCH

JOHNSTON, Alvin Melvin ("Tex") (*b.* 18 August 1914 in Admire, Kansas; *d.* 30 October 1998 in Mount Vernon, Washington), legendary test pilot who commanded the first flight of the B-52 bomber and performed the famous "barrel roll" of the Boeing 707 prototype.

Johnston was born on a farm in Admire, Kansas, to parents Alva Merril Johnston, a farmer, and Ella Viola Johnston, a homemaker. Johnston always sought speed, and used his earnings to buy a motorcycle and then a glider. In 1925 a barnstorming show came through Kansas, and the pilots offered free rides to anyone who was brave enough. Only eleven-year-old Johnston accepted. By the time he was fifteen he had completed his first solo flight. After graduating from high school, he went to work for the Inman Brothers Flying Circus, attended aeronautical school, and became a barnstormer himself.

Although Johnston loved flying, his real passion was engineering. He used the money he earned as a stunt pilot to pay for courses at a succession of small colleges, including Emporia State University, Spartan School of Aeronautics, and Kansas State University at Manhattan, where

Johnston sought to understand, rather than merely enjoy, aviation.

In 1939, short of his degree but in need of work, Johnston signed up as a civilian pilot-instructor with the Civilian Pilot Training Program of the U.S. Army Air Corps. Once America entered World War II, he transferred to service as a "ferry pilot" with the U.S. Army Air Corps Ferry Command, taking airplanes from factories in the Midwest to military airfields in Bakersfield, California; Valdosta, Georgia; and Winnipeg, Canada.

In December 1942 he began work as an engineering test pilot for Bell Aircraft. His first assignment was testing P-39s in Niagara Falls, New York. He also flight-tested the P-63 with an experimental V-tail design, the P-47, and the P-51. It was there that Johnston earned the nickname "Tex" when he arrived at the flight line in his trademark cowboy boots. (In later years he would have a new pair of boots custom-made to commemorate every new plane he flew.) In 1944 he was transferred to Muroc Flight Test Base in California, where he tested the X-59A, America's first jet aircraft, and assisted in the design of the X-1, America's first rocket plane. Johnston claimed credit for the X-1's ogive nose shape and its use of pressurized nitrogen propellants.

Johnston's work on the X-1 coincided with his effort to set a world speed record at the first postwar Thompson Trophy race in the fall of 1946. Flying a specially modified Bell P-39 Airacobra, Johnston set a world speed record of 374 miles per hour over a closed course (as opposed to the straight-line speed record that the X-1 would set the next

Tex Johnston (*left*) with William Allen, president of Boeing Airplane Co., 1955. © BETTMANN/CORBIS

year), but the victory was darkened by the crash of his training partner Jack Woolams.

Once the X-1 program had been turned over to the military, Johnston moved on to Bell Aircraft's next focus: helicopters. Named director of helicopter field operations and based in Houston, Johnston made the first sales of Bell helicopters for use in petroleum and uranium exploration, as well as for crop dusting. However, once he met the challenge of opening the market, he found himself bored and sought a return to test piloting. Since Bell was no longer developing fixed-wing aircraft, Johnston signed with Boeing Airplane Company in Seattle. He never regretted the move.

Johnston began with Boeing in July 1948 as project pilot on the XB-47 program and stayed with the company for twenty years. In 1951, with contract compliance testing on the B-47 completed, he became project pilot (and, later, chief of flight test) for Boeing's next bomber, the XB-52, which he flew on its first flight the next April. That same week in April 1952, Boeing's board of directors approved work on a four-engine jet transport plane that would change commercial aviation: the 367-80, prototype of the 707.

The Dash 80, as the plane was familiarly known, had its official rollout in May 1954 and its first flight in July. Demonstration flights for commercial customers began a year later, culminating in the famous barrel roll during Seattle's Seafair Week of July 1955. Although Johnston's mid-air rotation of the plane did not subject it to any additional stress—those inside the aircraft never experienced any G-forces—it appeared to onlookers a risky, even brazen maneuver. When Boeing's chairman asked him what he thought he was doing, Johnston calmly replied, "Selling your airplane." Two years later Johnston set another world speed record by flying from Seattle to Baltimore in three hours, forty-eight minutes—an average speed of 612 miles per hour—with fifty journalists on board. Johnston also established training programs for the commercial pilots who would fly the 707 and integrated Boeing's flight test and training programs.

In 1960 it was time to move on to the next phase of technological innovation: hypersonic flight. Johnston began overseeing the Dyna Soar program, which—although it was canceled after three years—would ultimately provide the design core of the Space Shuttle. Johnston then headed Boeing's Atlantic Test Center, preparing the lunar-landing module for its historic touchdown on the Moon in July 1969.

Johnston's later leadership roles included the presidency of Aero Spacelines, Inc., which built a famous cargo plane called the Guppy, and directorship of testing at Stanley Aviation Corporation. He was inducted into the National Aviation Hall of Fame in July 1993, the OX-5 (early en-gine) Hall of Fame in 1994, and earned the Elder Statesman Award from the National Aeronautic Association. During the early 1990s, Johnston developed Alzheimer's disease. He died from the disease in 1998 at age eighty-four.

Johnston and his wife, DeLores, whom he married in 1935, had three children. He was among the last of an old breed of test pilots who learned engineering by taking apart the family tractor, later translating such hands-on experience and knowledge into profound technical expertise and precise execution.

★

Johnston published his autobiography *Tex Johnston: Jet-Age Test Pilot* in 1991. Obituaries are in the *Seattle Times* (31 Oct. 1998) and the *New York Times* (14 Nov. 1998).

HARTLEY S. SPATT

JONES, Robert Reynolds, Jr. (*b.* 19 October 1911 in Montgomery, Alabama; *d.* 12 November 1997 in Greenville, South Carolina), evangelist and chancellor of Bob Jones University whose militant fundamentalist separatism and devotion to the fine arts earned him a reputation as one of the more paradoxical religious figures of the twentieth century.

Jones was the only child of Robert Reynolds Jones, a traveling evangelist whose contemporaries included revivalists such as Billy Sunday, and of Mary Gaston Stollenwerck, daughter of a prominent family in Uniontown, Alabama. Jones often accompanied his parents on the evangelistic circuit, meeting prominent revivalists of the day as well as observing firsthand the nascent fundamentalist movement of the early twentieth century. When not traveling with his parents, Jones was cared for by his maternal grandmother, Estelle Stollenwerck, who imbued the young Jones with a lifelong love of art and literature.

In 1923 Jones began high school at Starke Military Academy in Montgomery, Alabama, and in 1927 matriculated at the newly opened Bob Jones College in Panama City, Florida. Founded by Jones, Sr., in order to protect Christian young people from what he regarded as the ravages of secular, state-university education, as well as to combat the rising stereotype of fundamentalists as uncultured and anti-intellectual, Bob Jones College offered a liberal arts curriculum steeped in the mores of religious fundamentalism. Jones graduated in 1931 with a degree in history and earned an M.A. degree in history from the University of Pittsburgh in 1933. Jones took additional graduate work at the University of Chicago. In 1932 he returned to Bob Jones College, now located in Cleveland, Tennessee, to assume duties as the acting president of the college so that his father might return to the evangelistic circuit.

Bob Jones, Jr., 1959. AP/WIDE WORLD PHOTOS

Jones served as acting president from 1932 to 1947, presiding over a major expansion of the student body and of the school's academic program. Under Jones's leadership the college went from an enrollment of 300 to over 1,000, and the curriculum expanded to include graduate programs in religion and fine arts. Jones also served as chair of the history department and in the summers of 1934 and 1935, traveled to Stratford-upon-Avon, England, and studied with actors from the Royal Shakespeare Company. Jones created a one-man traveling show, "Curtain Calls," in which he portrayed and interpreted Shakespearean characters. "Curtain Calls" earned Jones offers to join a Shakespeare touring company as well as a 1937 screen test offer from Warner Brothers. He refused both offers in order to continue his work at the college. Jones married Fannie May Holmes, a student at Bob Jones College, on 1 June 1938. They had three children.

Bob Jones College relocated to Greenville, South Carolina, in 1946, a move which coincided with the school's transition to university status and the elevation of Jones from acting president to president. Shortly after the move to Greenville, Jones created a cinema division known as Unusual Films. Sending faculty members to Hollywood to study filmmaking techniques, Jones presided over a program that produced several feature length films, including *Wine of Morning,* a screen adaptation of a biblical play written by Jones that represented the United States at the Cannes Film Festival. Jones further strengthened the university's fine arts emphasis to include annual offerings ranging from the New York Metropolitan Opera to the Vienna Chamber Orchestra. Beginning in 1948, Jones worked with the art collector Carl Hamilton to amass a collection of European sacred art, including works by Rembrandt, Peter Paul Rubens, and Sir Anthony Van Dyke. The Gallery of Sacred Art also includes the Bowen Museum of Biblical Antiquities and is located on campus. It is acknowledged as one of the most important art collections in the southeastern United States.

During his presidency Jones embarked on a path of strident ecclesiastical separatism. Jones participated in the founding of the National Association of Evangelicals (NAE) in 1942 and in 1950 was elected as the vice president of the body. Jones left the NAE in June 1951 following the organization's refusal to hold its annual meeting at Bob Jones University, a decision precipitated in part by a faction in the NAE wishing to cultivate a more inclusive, moderate image. Jones lashed out at this "New Evangelical" movement, asserting that the moderates told "enemies" of the Christian faith, "we will call you 'Christian brothers' if you will call us 'doctor,' 'professor,' and 'scholar.'"

The tension of this period was exacerbated during the university's 1952–1953 academic year when a popular administrator, Theodore Mercer, was fired for allegedly attempting to foment a faculty revolt against Jones and for acting improperly with students. Mercer left along with a number of faculty in May 1953.

During his presidency Jones engaged in a series of battles with various evangelical leaders over the issue of ecclesiastical separatism. The most notable of these was his break with the evangelist Billy Graham in 1957. Graham, who attended Bob Jones for one semester in 1936, became a fixture in the nation's religious life with his 1949 crusade in Los Angeles, California. During his rise to prominence Graham became friendly with Jones, who periodically substituted for Graham at preaching engagements. By 1957 Graham was identified with the New Evangelical movement, and under the sponsorship of ministers in New York City, including liberal Protestants and Roman Catholic priests, Graham held one of the most successful crusades of his career. Thereafter, Graham continued to be inclusive in his theological associations, and Jones accused Graham of "building the church of Antichrist, masking the wickedness of popery, and providing a sheep's cloak of Christian recognition for the wolves of apostasy." Jones eventually broke fellowship with other evangelicals and evangelical organizations he deemed insufficiently separatist, including evangelist John R. Rice and the Moody Bible Institute. His hard-line stance on maintaining theological purity enabled

Jones to assume leadership positions in such organizations as the International Committee for the Propagation and Defense of Biblical Fundamentalism and the World Congress of Fundamentalists.

Jones became chancellor of the university in 1971 when his son Bob III assumed the presidency. Acknowledging that "what my duties are as chancellor neither I nor anyone else knows," Jones spent the rest of his career maintaining an arduous speaking schedule that took him from local Christian high school graduation ceremonies to international conferences, writing editorials in the university's *Faith for the Family* periodical, and offering public observations on a wide array of issues. In 1980 he labeled the Reverend Jerry Falwell as the "most dangerous man in America" for including Catholics and Mormons in his Moral Majority. In 1982 from the chapel pulpit of Bob Jones University, Jones prayed that God would "smite" then Secretary of State Alexander Haig and "destroy him utterly" for refusing to grant a travel visa to the militantly anti-Catholic Irish activist Ian Paisley. Jones also actively participated in the university's losing 1983 court battle, when the U.S. Supreme Court stripped Bob Jones University of its tax exempt status for practicing racial discrimination in its dating policies. Following the Court's decision, Jones remarked "we're in a bad fix when eight evil, old men and one vain, foolish woman can speak a verdict on American liberties. Our nation from this day forward is no better than Russia."

In addition to his wide travels and public pronouncements Jones also penned his memoirs, *Cornbread and Caviar,* in 1985. Jones was diagnosed with cancer on 27 September 1997 and succumbed to the disease in November. Like his father, Jones was buried on campus. The Bob Jones Jr. Memorial Seminary and Evangelism Center was dedicated on 23 March 2000.

The life of Bob Jones, Jr., was one of paradox. Raised in an environment of southern revivalism and camp meetings, Jones became a man who traveled Europe collecting Baroque art and whose onstage interpretations of Shakespeare won him regional acclaim and an offer of an acting career with Warner Brothers. He presided over a fundamentalist school that refused to allow its students to attend Hollywood films, but whose film division won international awards at the Cannes Film Festival. Jones refused to seek accreditation for his school because it might align him with "ungodly" secular educators, but his students regularly attended the finest graduate schools. Although he cultivated relationships with secular actors and artists, Jones also severed ties with fellow fundamentalists who associated with liberal Protestants and Catholics. Shortly before his death, Jones offered his own perspective on his life: "I have sought not only to be strong in defense of the Fundamental, biblical position but also . . . to combat the impression that those who were fundamentalists were red-necked, uncultured and out of touch."

★

Most sources of information about Jones include works by individuals connected directly to Bob Jones University. R. K. Johnson, former business manager of the school, wrote a firsthand account of the school's early years, *Miracle from the Beginning* (1971), which includes materials on Jones's presidency. Faculty member Dan Turner's history of Bob Jones University, *Standing Without Apology* (1997), is another in-house account with material on Jones from the university archives. The Fundamentalism File at Bob Jones University's J. S. Mack Library is a repository of newspaper and magazine articles on the fundamentalist movement with a substantial file on Jones. Mark Taylor Dalhouse, *An Island in the Lake of Fire* (1996), is the only history of Bob Jones University to date written by an outsider and contains archival information on Jones and his career. Jones penned his memoirs, *Cornbread and Caviar,* in 1985. While not written chronologically, it provides Jones's observations on the important people and events from his life. An obituary is in the *New York Times* (13 Nov. 1997).

MARK TAYLOR DALHOUSE

K

KAHN, Madeline Gail (*b.* 29 September 1942 in Boston, Massachusetts; *d.* 3 December 1999 in New York City), actress who lent her comedic talents to numerous film and stage projects.

Kahn was the only child of Bernard Wolfson, a garment manufacturer, and his wife, Paula, a homemaker. Her parents divorced when she was young, and Kahn moved to Manhattan's West Side with her mother, who occasionally worked as a nightclub singer and fashion model. Kahn's mother remarried, and the family adopted her stepfather's surname, Kahn. Although she was somewhat shy and withdrawn, Kahn showed an early interest in music and performing, which her mother strongly encouraged. She took piano, dance, and voice lessons and appeared as an amateur singer on a local radio talent show.

During her teenage years, Kahn lived with her parents and a half brother in the borough of Queens. After graduating from Martin Van Buren High School in 1960, she followed her mother's advice and enrolled at Hofstra University in Hempstead, Long Island, as a drama major. She was ambivalent about whether to pursue a performing career and considered becoming a teacher or speech therapist. However, after receiving a B.F.A. degree in 1964, she began auditioning for theater parts in New York City.

Kahn's big break came when she was cast in *New Faces of 1968,* a Broadway revue featuring young unknowns performing topical comedy sketches and songs. Her performance was praised by many critics and led to a role in the 1970 summer television series *Comedy Tonight*. She returned to Broadway that autumn and played a supporting role in the Richard Rodgers–Martin Charnin musical *Two by Two,* in which she had a flashy solo singing the operatic parody "The Golden Ram." In David Rabe's play, *Boom Boom Room* (1973), Kahn had the challenging lead of a dim-witted but tenacious go-go dancer who undergoes an identity crisis. Jack Kroll reviewed the play in *Newsweek,* noting "[Kahn] is extraordinary in the quality of her emotion, her evocation of a fighting vulnerability, her struggle to seize the sweetness of her humanity." Produced at Lincoln Center by the legendary Joseph Papp, *Boom Boom Room* earned her a Tony Award nomination for best actress in a play.

Kahn made her film debut in 1972 as Ryan O'Neal's jilted fiancée in the screwball farce *What's Up, Doc?* The film's director, Peter Bogdanovich, was so pleased with her work that he cast her in *Paper Moon* (1973) as the good-hearted prostitute Trixie Delight, for which she received an Oscar nomination for best supporting actress. Kahn worked for Bogdanovich again in his homage to the musicals of the 1930s, *At Long Last Love* (1975). The film was a critical and box-office flop and ended her relationship with the director, whom she said shortened her role in order to more prominently showcase Cybill Shepherd, his current girlfriend.

Kahn's roles in a trio of films directed by Mel Brooks

Madeline Kahn. KOBAL COLLECTION

are generally considered her greatest screen legacy. Her portrayal of a Marlene Dietrich–like saloon singer Lili Von Shtupp in Brooks's extremely popular 1974 Western parody, *Blazing Saddles,* garnered Kahn another Oscar nomination for best supporting actress. Later in 1974 she appeared in Brooks's takeoff on horror films, *Young Frankenstein,* and in 1977 starred in his Alfred Hitchcock spoof, *High Anxiety.* Kahn reflected, "I think I was good [in those kinds of movies] because I was a disparate element. Sort of like Margaret Dumont in the Marx Brothers' comedy." A petite redhead with large brown eyes, Kahn transformed her attractive appearance with subtle changes of facial expression and used her highly expressive voice to add humor to a characterization. George Hodgman, in *Entertainment Weekly* (1999), called her voice "a singular sensation. It could soar musically . . . and, in her non-singing roles, turn modern anxieties into arias that wavered, warbled, and quivered their way toward utter panic."

During the 1970s Kahn shored up her movie fame with frequent appearances on television talk shows. And although she had established herself as a screen personality, she never abandoned the theater. "In theater you get to [work] in one piece and you are in the moment and you get to explore yourself as an instrument," she noted. "You don't get to do that in film." In 1978 she costarred in the lavish Broadway musical *On the Twentieth Century,* receiv-

ing a Tony Award nomination for best actress in a musical. In *Born Yesterday* (1989) she took on the challenge of portraying Billie Dawn, the uneducated mistress of a shady businessman who learns the importance of informed citizenship. A revival of the long-running 1946 Garson Kanin comedy that starred Judy Holliday, the show received generally negative notices, but most reviewers had kind words for Kahn.

The opportunity to play a multidimensional, middle-aged woman similar to herself drew Kahn to Wendy Wasserstein's *The Sisters Rosensweig* (1992), a serious-sided comedy about three sisters coming to terms with their Jewish roots and with each other. Kahn played the role of the middle sister, Gorgeous Teitelbaum, a suburban homemaker who stayed closest to the familial model. In his 1992 review in the *New York Daily News,* Howard Kissel said Kahn's performance, for which she won a Tony Award, was both poignant and hilarious.

Kahn made several attempts at series television, including her own situation comedy, *Oh Madeline,* which aired in the 1983–1984 season. From 1996 until her death, she was a regular cast member on *Cosby.* Kahn, who resided on Manhattan's East Side, died at age fifty-seven of ovarian cancer in a New York City hospital. On 19 October 1999, two months before her death, she married John Hansbury, her longtime companion and an attorney. Kahn's distinctive personality made her among the most popular comedy actresses of her time.

★

Lengthy interviews with Kahn about the art of acting are in David Black, *The Magic of Theater* (1993), and Roy Harris, *Conversations in the Wings* (1994). Mervyn Rothstein, "Kahn's Way," *Theatre Week* (8 Mar. 1973), offers an in-depth interview with Kahn about her role in *The Sisters Rosensweig.* A sketch of her early life and career is in *Current Biography* (1977). An obituary is in the *New York Times* (4 Dec. 1999).

MARY KALFATOVIC

KALMAN, Tibor (*b.* 1949 in Budapest, Hungary; *d.* 2 May 1999 near San Juan, Puerto Rico), graphic designer, founder of M & Co., and editor of Benetton's *Colors* magazine whose iconoclastic creative aesthetic and social consciousness influenced contemporary graphic design.

Kalman was one of three children of George Kalman, an engineer, and Marianne Kalman. Kalman was seven years old when his family emigrated from Hungary to Poughkeepsie, New York, after the failed Hungarian uprising against the Soviet-sponsored government. He became an American citizen in 1956. Kalman attended public grammar schools and Our Lady of Lourdes High School, then entered New York University in 1967, where he studied journalism. He worked part-time at the Student Book Exchange (SBX), initially as a stock clerk and cashier, and later as a window display designer. This experience, Kalman's only training as a designer, would help with his visual merchandising career in later years.

In 1970, after becoming involved with the radical Students for a Democratic Society, he dropped out of college to join the Venceremos Brigade and traveled to Cuba to harvest sugarcane under the regime of Fidel Castro. He returned to the United States and to his old job in 1971. The SBX was owned at that time by Leonard Ruggio, who was developing a small chain of campus bookstores and eventually purchased the Barnes and Noble franchise. Ruggio hired Kalman as creative director, a position in which he was responsible for window displays, signs, advertisements, and store displays. Kalman designed the familiar Barnes and Noble trademark that is still used by the company.

In 1979 Kalman took a job as creative director at E. J. Korvette, where he was responsible for the discount department store's signs and displays. He soon became disenchanted with the lucrative, but boring, job and, in the same year, established his own design firm in his Greenwich Village apartment. He named it M & Co. The "M" referred to his partner, Maira Berman, a children's book author and illustrator. They married in 1981 and had two children. M & Co. quickly became successful by doing "design by the pound": producing store logos for a package manufacturer's customers and other clients. The business moved to offices on West Fifty-seventh Street, which featured a "goofy shaped conference room with a goofy triangular-shaped table." In the reception area, a hole smashed in the wall by a sledgehammer served as a window.

With the success of the studio solidified, Kalman began to stamp his creations with his personal vision of vernacular design. For Kalman, vernacular design received its inspiration from such common visuals as hand-lettered signs produced in neighborhood sign shops, coffee shop menus created by local printers, hamburger stands, glitzy motel signs, and quirky roadside shops. In this spirit Kalman designed business cards printed on cardboard stock for one client, and M & Co.'s own business cards adopted the look of an appliance repair service sticker. For an upscale restaurant he designed a menu with unmatched typefaces and deliberate misspellings and tucked the menu pages in plastic slip folders, as might be used on factory loading docks. "We tried to keep the design aggressively cheap, to keep the gloss off, to get it wrong just right," said Kalman. For another client, he hand-painted over set type in order to give it a less polished look.

Later, when M & Co.'s growth necessitated a move to a larger loft space, the new offices on Seventeenth Street off Sixth Avenue were "decorated" like an old factory. Kalman was reacting to the corporate International Style school of design, which emphasized the rectilinear, the undecorated, the asymmetrical, and was governed by the aphorism "less is more." Kalman bemoaned the new corporate logos that he felt looked worse than the old ones. He often cited as an example the Prudential Insurance logo, which had been redesigned from an evocative image of the rugged Rock of Gibraltar to an abstracted glyph.

Even though M & Co. was running against the current of contemporary design, the studio attracted a body of prestigious clients, including Subaru, The Limited, the Times Square Redevelopment Corporation, and other major real estate developers. Kalman often parodied the work of the design community: for the cover of *AIGA* (American Institute of Graphic Arts) magazine, he deliberately cropped the cover photo, a banana peel, off the page, and instead inserted a hand-scrawled warning "This is for AIGA Watch trim this page!" M & Co. also did product designs, such as watch faces. One of them, which displays only the numbers one, four, and ten, is now part of the permanent collection of the Museum of Modern Art.

Kalman was known for his radicalism and social consciousness. He was cochair of the 1989 AIGA conference "Dangerous Ideas," at which he urged designers to be "disobedient and insubordinate" and to "[subvert] what we've come to accept as the design process." He said, "If designers would approach clients with their own agendas, we might be able to have an impact on how companies do business, to make them smarter or more socially conscious." One Christmas, Kalman's corporate gift to each of his clients was a boxed lunch resembling those distributed to the homeless at city shelters. From 1987 to 1989, Kalman served as art director of *Artforum* magazine, and from 1989 to 1991 he served as creative director for *Interview* magazine. He frequently contributed to these and other magazines.

In 1991 Kalman was hired to act as editor in chief of Benetton's *Colors* magazine. The clothing company's house publication focused not just on fashion but on such issues as AIDS, racism, the environment, social justice, and global poverty. In one issue Kalman presented a series of racially transformed celebrities and international figures. For example, Queen Elizabeth and Arnold Schwarzenegger were black, the Pope was Asian, and Spike Lee was white. Kalman worked on the magazine out of his New York office until 1993, when he closed M & Co. and moved his family to Italy in order to give *Colors* a full-time commitment. Kalman returned to New York in 1997 when he was diagnosed with non-Hodgkins lymphoma. He reopened M & Co. and dedicated his time to producing and designing exhibits, videos, and books that had social relevance. In addition, he wrote several editorials for the *New York Times*.

Kalman died of non-Hodgkins lymphoma while in San Juan, Puerto Rico, and is buried in Ardsley, New York.

★

For comments from major designers who worked with Kalman, see Peter Hall and Michael Bierut, eds., *Tibor Kalman: Perverse Optimist* (1998). See also Liz Farrelly, *Tibor Kalman: Design and Undesign (Cutting Edge)* (1998). The archives of M & Co. are at the Cooper Hewitt Museum in New York. An obituary is in the *New York Times* (5 May 1999).

WILLIAM J. MALONEY

KANE, Robert ("Bob")   (*b*. 24 October 1915 in New York City; *d*. 3 November 1998 in Los Angeles, California), cartoonist and painter who was the original artist and cocreator of Batman, the comic book superhero.

Kane's parents were Herman Kane, an engraver for the *New York Daily News,* and Augusta Kane. Kane and his sister grew up in "a tough East Bronx neighborhood— Freeman Street and Westchester Avenue." By age twelve Kane had joined a youth gang, the Crusading Zorros. At fifteen a rival gang, the Vultures, broke his arm for the effeminate crime of playing the violin. The injury and subsequent physical therapy interrupted his drawing for months. Nevertheless, poverty motivated Kane to develop his "doodling" into a profession. His mother doubted that cartooning could be lucrative, but his father was more encouraging. An engraver for the *New York Daily News,* he knew that art could mean money if it reached the right audience. Kane's first income from art came at age fourteen, when bakeries bought his poster that read "Don't go by til you buy a pie." At fifteen Kane won a drawing contest and received original art from the comic strip *Just Kids,* a prize that started his lifelong collecting of original comic art.

Attending De Witt Clinton High School, Kane contributed cartoons to the school newspaper, as did fellow student Will Eisner, who later developed a comic-book crime fighter called The Spirit. Kane graduated at age seventeen and received a two-year scholarship to the Commercial Art Studio in the famous Flatiron Building in Manhattan. He began to sell one-panel cartoons and humorous strips, beginning in 1936 with *Wow What a Magazine!,* produced by Will Eisner and Jerry Iger. However, Iger paid only $5.00 per page, not much even then, and only one single-panel cartoon, bought by the *Journal American,* sold for more. Kane dropped out of art school after one year to work in the garment business for his uncle Sam. This job was his last outside of comics or art.

Kane joined the Fleisher Animated Film Studios in New York City in 1937, painting and filling in Betty Boop cartoons. Fortunately for Kane, when the work grew boring, he chose to pursue the then-new medium of comic books. Still mostly reprints of comic strips, comic books had begun to add new material, including the incredibly popular Superman stories by Jerry Siegel and Joe Schuster, which debuted in 1938. Kane's first adventure story, "The Case of the Missing Heir," appeared in the April 1937 issue of *Detective Picture Stories.* Kane continued with adventure stories influenced by Milton Caniff's work and with humor pieces influenced by the style of Walt Disney and by popular strips like *The Katzenjammer Kids.*

Given Superman's success, National Periodical Publications editor Vincent Sullivan suggested that Kane develop his own superhero. After a weekend of perusing old sketches, Kane invented "the Bat-Man," who appeared in "The Case of the Chemical Syndicate" in the May 1939 issue of *Detective Comics* (released in March). Kane was only eighteen years old, but the character Kane created eventually blossomed into its own massive industry, ranging from fine art to toys, T-shirts, and cereal. Batman has become a myth, known even to people who have somehow missed the decades of comic books and newspaper strips, the two 1940s film serials, the hugely popular television show starring Adam West, the five cartoon shows featuring Batman, and the six Batman movies (five live-action and one animated).

The Batman story features young Bruce Wayne, who, after witnessing a thief shoot his parents, vows to use his inherited wealth and considerable physical and intellectual abilities to fight crime. He dresses like a bat because criminals are "a superstitious and cowardly lot." Batman's costume and the foggy noir atmosphere of the comic were influenced by Leonardo da Vinci's drawing of an ornithopter and *The Mark of Zorro,* a 1920 film starring Douglas Fairbanks, Sr. Other influences include a 1931 movie, *The Bat Whispers*; *The Shadow* pulp novels and radio shows; and the foggy shadows of *Dracula* (1931), starring Bela Lugosi. A more important influence was fellow teen Bill Finger, who wrote many of the Batman stories. As a cocreator of Batman, Finger was never given due credit, which Kane himself later regretted, nor were Kane's many assistants, starting in 1939 with Jerry Robinson and George Roussos, or ghost artists, such as Dick Sprang in the 1940s. However, giving sole credit to one creator was then standard in comics and animation. Kane invented the character Robin in 1940, setting the style for young superhero sidekicks.

Aside from Batman, Kane's other projects included Courageous Cat and Minute Mouse, animated cartoons created in 1957; and *Cool McCool,* an animated spy-spoof series for NBC in 1967. From the 1960s on, Kane sold his original paintings and lithographs, primarily of Batman, with gallery showings on both coasts.

During much of his Batman work, Kane lived on the Grand Concourse—a better area of the Bronx—with his parents and his sister Doris. Kane married his first wife

Beverly in 1949; they divorced in 1957, and Kane valued the marriage primarily for having produced a daughter with whom he remained close. Kane moved to Hollywood during the divorce proceedings and throughout his life continued to periodically moved back and forth between the Los Angeles and New York City areas. When in New York City in 1980, Kane met actress Elizabeth Sanders; they married in 1987. Approximately thirty-five years younger than Kane, Sanders was both beautiful and a cheerful companion. After the couple moved back to California, Sanders played a bit part in *Batman Forever* (1995), and Kane appeared in a crowd scene in *Batman and Robin* (1997). Just before his death, Kane completed *The Silver Fox,* a screenplay about another superhero.

At age eighty-three, Kane had a heart attack in his Los Angeles home and was pronounced dead at Cedars-Sinai Medical Center. After a private funeral, he was buried at Forest Lawn Cemetery behind the grave of Stan Laurel, one of his comedy heroes. The Batman insignia decorates his tombstone.

President and editor in chief of DC Comics, Jenette Kahn, once said, "Bob Kane is a giant in the field of popular culture." Author Jules Feiffer pointed out that Kane's creation, Batman, was compelling as a superhero without superhuman abilities. Batman's traumatic origin also enabled troubled adolescents to identify with him. Another hallmark of Batman is, in Kane's own words, his ability to adapt to each era, as demonstrated in all media forms from the kitsch 1960s television show to Frank Miller's grim graphic novel *Batman: The Dark Knight Returns* (1986).

★

Batman and Me (1989), by Kane and Tom Andrae, combines autobiography with reprints of Kane's art and its inspirations. Key material appears in Jules Feiffer, *The Great Comic Book Heroes* (1965), and in Dwight Jon Zummerman, *Comics Interview Super Special* (1989). Roberta E. Pearson and William Uricchio, eds., *The Many Lives of the Batman: Critical Approaches to a Superhero and His Media* (1991), critically examines all Batman works, including Kane's. Many comic-reprint collections include informative introductions, including E. Nelson Bridwell, *Batman: From the 30s to the 70s* (1971), and Dick Giordano and Mike Gold, *The Greatest Batman Stories Ever Told* (1988). An obituary is in the *Washington Post* (7 Nov. 1998).

BERNADETTE LYNN BOSKY

KANIN, Garson (*b.* 24 November 1912 in Rochester, New York; *d.* 13 March 1999 in New York City), writer, director, and producer best known for his play *Born Yesterday* as well as the Tracy-Hepburn comedies *Adam's Rib* (1949) and *Pat and Mike* (1952).

Born Gershon Labe, Kanin was the one of three children of David M. Kanin and Sadie Levine. His father, a real

Garson Kanin. © ALEX GOTTFRYD/CORBIS

estate agent in Rochester, New York, owned a movie theater, and by the age of five Kanin was bitten by the acting bug. The family moved to New York City, where Kanin attended James Madison High School but dropped out in 1929 due to the depression. He played saxophone in his jazz band Garson Kay and the Red Peppers and studied at the American Academy of Dramatic Arts from 1932 to 1933. He appeared in a number of Broadway plays, such as *Little Ol' Boy* (1933), *Spring Song* and *Ladies' Money* (both 1934), *The Body Beautiful* (1935), and *Star Spangled* (1936). Kanin auditioned for the director George Abbott and soon found himself working as his assistant, casting and directing road companies of Abbott productions, including *Three Men on a Horse, Boy Meets Girl, Brother Rat* (all 1936), and *Room Service* (1937). During this period, he met and became a friend of the writer W. Somerset Maugham and of the playwright Thornton Wilder, who became Kanin's mentor and encouraged him to write.

Hollywood beckoned Kanin in 1937, when he was hired by studio chief Samuel Goldwyn. Kanin described himself as "a mildly successful minor New York actor, and the director of one Broadway failure." He was released by Goldwyn and made his first movie for RKO studios. *A Man to Remember,* his 1938 directorial debut, was a surprise hit, and Kanin found himself the toast of Hollywood at age twenty-five. *A Man to Remember* was followed by six more films: *The Great Man Votes* (1939), with John Barrymore; *Bachelor Mother* (1939), with Ginger Rogers; *My Favorite Wife* (1940), with Cary Grant and Irene Dunn; *They Knew What They Wanted* (1940), starring Carole Lombard and Charles Laughton; and *Tom, Dick, and Harry* (1941), featuring Ginger Rogers.

Kanin's career was interrupted by World War II. Drafted into the U.S. Army in 1941, he first served in the Signal Corps, but was later transferred to the Office of Strategic Services, where he produced and directed documentary shorts. His feature-length documentary about World War II, *The True Glory* (1945), which he codirected with Carol Reed, won an Academy Award for best documentary feature.

Toward the end of his military service Kanin turned to writing. He wanted to write a serious play about influence peddling in Washington, D.C., but the work turned into the comedy *Born Yesterday*, one of his best-known plays. Kanin both produced and directed the play, which ran on Broadway from 1946 to 1950. It starred Judy Holliday as the illiterate Billie Dawn, mistress of Harry Brock, a junk dealer looking to buy influence in Congress. Brock decides to educate Billie and hires Paul Verrall, a journalist, to tutor her. Through Verrall's tutoring, Billie realizes what kind of man Brock really is and is able to stop Brock's nefarious plans. The film version, directed by George Cukor, was released in 1950.

Kanin married actress/writer Ruth Gordon on 4 December 1942. The two met through director George Cukor in 1939. Though Gordon was sixteen years Kanin's senior, their marriage was successful and ended only upon her death in 1985. The two also successfully collaborated on four screenplays, *A Double Life* (1948), *Adam's Rib* (1949), *The Marrying Kind* (1951), and *Pat and Mike* (1952), all directed by Cukor. Both *Adam's Rib* and *Pat and Mike* starred close friends Spencer Tracy and Katharine Hepburn. Although all their scripts except *The Marrying Kind* were nominated for Academy Awards, Kanin and Gordon argued horrendously at work and decided not to collaborate again with the exception of a television script, *Hardhat and Legs* (1980). Kanin's next screenplay, *It Should Happen to You*, based on an idea he got while driving his wife around Columbus Circle, was filmed in 1954. However, Kanin soured on Hollywood when the ending was changed without his knowledge.

Kanin directed numerous plays on Broadway, including *Years Ago* (1946), *How I Wonder* (1947), and *The Leading Lady* (1948), as well as three plays he wrote, *The Smile of the World* and *The Rat Race* (both 1949) and *The Live Wire* (1950), none of which were successful. He did have great success with his Broadway production of the *Diary of Anne Frank* in 1955. Other directorial jobs included: *Small War on Murray Hill* (1957); *A Hole in the Head* (1957); his adaptation of *The Good Soup, Sunday in New York* (1961); his play *Come On Strong* (1962); his adaptation *A Gift of Time*, starring Henry Fonda (1962); the highly successful *Funny Girl* with Barbra Streisand (1964); *I Was Dancing* (1964); *A Very Rich Woman*, written by Ruth Gordon (1965); *We Have Always Lived in a Castle* (1966); and his adaptation of *Dryfus in Rehearsal* (1974). His adaptation of his play *The Rat Race* was filmed in 1960.

Kanin authored the screenplay *From This Day Forward* (1946) and coauthored *The More the Merrier* (1943). The versatile Kanin wrote a new libretto for *Die Fledermaus* which was performed in 1950 by the Metropolitan Opera in New York. He published his first novel, *Do Re Mi*, in 1955, adapting it for film as *The Girl Can't Help It* (1957), and later created a musical version that was produced on Broadway in 1960. Wilder had suggested that Kanin keep a personal journal, which later served as the basis for his 1966 biography *Remembering Mr. Maugham* and his 1971 biography *Tracy and Hepburn: An Intimate Memoir*. He wrote an autobiography, *Hollywood*, in 1974 with reminisces of the many actors, actresses, directors, and producers he had known. His other nonfiction works include *It Takes a Long Time to Become Young* (1978), a work of advocacy for the elderly, and *Together Again! The Stories of the Great Hollywood Teams* (1979).

Kanin's fictional works include *Blow Up a Storm* (1959), *Cast of Characters* (1969), *A Thousand Summers* (1973), *One Hell of an Actor* (1977), *Moviola* (1979), *Smash* (1980), and *Cordelia* (1982). In addition, Kanin continued to write screenplays, such as *Some Kind of Nut* and *Where It's At* (both 1969), and several television scripts, including *Hardhat and Legs* (with Ruth Gordon), *Mr. Broadway, An Eye on Emily, The He-She Chemistry, Something to Sing About*, and *Scandal*. The prolific Kanin also contributed articles and short stories to such diverse publications as the *Virginia Law Review, Playboy, Saturday Review, Modern Maturity, Newsweek, Paris-Match, Atlantic Monthly*, and *Theatre Arts*. His last published work was a play, *Peccadillo*, which came out in 1990. That year, on 19 June, he married longtime friend and Broadway actress Marian Seldes. After a long illness, Kanin died at his home in New York City.

The importance of Kanin's work lies in his presentation of the common person as a champion of the truth. This is particularly true of *Born Yesterday*, which is now a classic of the American theatre. In addition, *Adam's Rib* was an early representation of a marriage based on equality and remains relevant to audiences today. When one talks about the Tracy-Hepburn pictures, it is generally Kanin's scripts and story ideas (including his idea for *Woman of the Year*, which was written by his brother Michael) with their wit and verbal repartee that are remembered. Kanin's gifted dialog and phraseology distinguish all his works and are a trademark of the Kanin style.

★

Kanin's autobiography, *Hollywood: Stars and Starlets, Tycoons and Flesh-Peddlers, Moviemakers and Moneymakers, Frauds and Geniuses, Hopefuls and Has-Beens, Great Lovers and Sex Symbols* (1974), describes much of his involvement as a film writer and director. There is no full-scale biography, but biographical material on Kanin is in Patrick McGilligan, *A Double Life: George Cukor: A Biography of The Gentleman Director* (1991). Richard Corliss, *Talking Pictures: Screenwriters in the American Cinema 1927–1973* (1974), has an entry on Kanin as a writer. Both the *Dictionary of Literary Biography: Twentieth-Century American Dramatists*, ed. John MacNicholas (1980), and *Contemporary Authors, New Revision Series* (1999), contain extensive entries on Kanin. An obituary is in the *New York Times* (15 Mar. 1999).

ELKA TENNER SHLOMO

KAZIN, Alfred (*b.* 5 June 1915 in Brooklyn, New York; *d.* 5 June 1998 in New York City), literary critic and historian whose books, beginning with *On Native Grounds* (1942), inspired renewed interest in the history of American literature, and whose memoirs commemorated the experience of immigrant Jews in the twentieth century and the centrality of the city in American life.

Alfred Kazin. JERRY BAUER

At the heart of Kazin's writing was a love of language, ideas, and books, the very elements that had permitted him to escape the impoverished Jewish ghetto of Brooklyn's Brownsville neighborhood for Manhattan and the world beyond. He was the son of Charles Kazin, a house painter, and Gita Fagelman, a skilled seamstress who worked at home. Recent immigrants from Eastern Europe who spoke Yiddish, Kazin's parents were determined that their son and daughter would know a better life. Kazin's mother often sewed dresses into the early morning hours while Kazin and his sister slept on kitchen chairs grouped together to make beds in the cramped tenement kitchen. His father took Kazin and his sister on weekend excursions over the Brooklyn Bridge to the museums and Jewish theater in the city. He also provided Kazin with violin lessons and taught him the importance of education.

Educated in Brooklyn's public schools, driven by the need to excel, Kazin graduated from Franklin K. Lane High School in 1931, and in the autumn rode the subway to the College of the City of New York in Manhattan. The jewel in New York's public educational crown, City College in the 1930s was a hotbed of intellectuality, social radicalism, and political ferment where the gifted sons of immigrants gathered to argue, debate, and challenge the prevailing ideologies of the depression era. Emerging from the college as writers and academics of every stripe, a number of them went on to form the so-called *Partisan Review* crowd: the Jewish intellectual elite of post–World War II New York whose books and essays would have a profound impact on American culture in the second half of the twentieth century.

Kazin more than held his own in that highly competitive world, but, unlike many in his generation, he refused to embrace any core ideological system. Although he remained committed to political liberalism and the need for social revolution all his life, he was essentially detached from all ideologies save one. He believed wholeheartedly in the transforming power of literature and the capacity of a creative writer to effect change in the individual and in society. As he wrote later, he saw himself as a literary radical "indifferent to economics . . . Marxist solemnity and intellectual system building." His heroes lay among the "great wrestlers-with-God . . . the poets of unlimited spiritual freedom," such as William Blake, Ralph Waldo Emerson, Walt Whitman, Friedrich Nietzsche, and D. H. Lawrence. Kazin felt books were most powerful when they revealed a concern for the human experience, and he passionately believed that literature could make a difference in the way humanity lived.

Kazin graduated from City College in New York with a B.S.S. degree in 1935. Cobbling together a number of freelance jobs to pay his expenses—since early 1934, he had reviewed books for the *New York Times, New York Herald Tribune,* and *New Republic*—he entered Columbia University, where he earned an M.A. degree in English in 1938 with a thesis analyzing the literary criticism of the great English historian Edward Gibbon. That summer Kazin married Asya Dohn; the marriage was annulled in 1944. On 23 May 1947 he married Carol Bookman, who bore him a son; they divorced in 1950. Two years later, on 26 June 1952, he married Ann Birstein, with whom he had a daughter; they divorced in 1978. He married Judith Dunford, a writer, on 21 May 1983.

By the time of his first marriage in 1938 Kazin was already at work on a study of modern American literature, a topic suggested to him by Carl Van Doren, one of his graduate school teachers, who believed existing literary histories had scanted twentieth-century American writing. To support himself and his new wife, Kazin again took on a variety of jobs as a freelance book reviewer and essayist, a script writer for a small radio station in Brooklyn, and a teacher of English in evening classes at the New School, City College, and Queens College. For the next four years he spent every working day and weekends researching America's literary past in what he called his "church": the main reading room of the New York Public Library on Forty-second Street. It was a punishing existence—it would cost him his marriage—but in 1940 he received a Guggenheim fellowship that finally gave him the financial freedom to write full-time. The result, published in 1942 to critical acclaim, was *On Native Grounds: An Interpretation of Modern American Prose Literature,* Kazin's brilliant examination of recent American writers set against the grand sweep of nineteenth-century American social, intellectual, and literary history. The book was swiftly taken up by academic departments across the country and remained for the balance of the century the standard work on American literature from 1890 to 1940.

The success of his first book led directly to his appointment as literary editor of the *New Republic* in 1942. A contributing editor at that weekly from 1943 to 1945, Kazin was also an associate editor at *Fortune* from 1943 to 1944, hoping in vain that both publications might send him to Europe as a war correspondent. Continuing to write for the magazines, he taught in the 1944 fall term at the experimental Black Mountain College in North Carolina. A year later, after the war was over, he went to England (and subsequently Paris) to report on British educational programs for its lower ranks and trade unions for the Rockefeller Foundation and the Office of War Information.

Upon his return to America in 1946, Kazin set the pattern that would mark the rest of his career: short-term academic assignments coupled with freelance writing. For the next twenty-odd years Kazin was a professor or lecturer of English or American studies at the University of Minnesota (1946 and 1950), the Salzburg Seminar of American Studies (1947), Harvard University (fall 1952), Smith College (1953–1954), Amherst College (1955–1958), and New York University (1957). He then accepted two long-term appointments, first at the State University of New York at Stony Brook from 1963 to 1973, and finally a joint appointment at Hunter College and the Graduate School of the City University of New York from 1973 to 1985. Following his retirement, he continued as a guest lecturer at colleges and universities across the country. A passionate, caring teacher, by all accounts, he was highly respected by his academic colleagues. However, in many of his assignments he often felt like an outsider because he lacked a doctorate and because he had little use for the formalism and the literary theories that were often central to the academy. At times he felt that he was too much removed from the world of his intellectual peers in the city and that the pressures of teaching kept him from writing as much as he would have liked.

Still, his output was prolific. Even in the midst of his early teaching assignments he regularly contributed to a broad range of periodicals, including the *Reporter, New Yorker, Partisan Review, Commentary, Harper's, New Republic, American Scholar, American Heritage, New York Times Book Review,* and *New York Review of Books.* He delighted in the essay form that these publications required, both for the freedom the form offered and because the essay, in his view, was highly personal, an opportunity for the reader to see "the self thinking."

Kazin's reviews were notable for their vivid prose and for the clarity of his thought, his attention to the writer's style, and his grasp of a book's relevance and its place in the context of America's literary past. Most of all, his criticism—though he was writing about cultural matters of great complexity—was accessible to the common reader because it was devoid of jargon and unburdened by abstruse literary theory. He produced three books of collected essays: *The Inmost Leaf* (1955), *Contemporaries* (1962), and *Bright Book of Life: American Novelists and Storytellers from Hemingway to Mailer* (1973). In 1984 he wrote the monumental history *An American Procession,* which both extended and modified some of his earlier judgments in *On Native Grounds.* Kazin's *A Writer's America: Landscape in Literature* was published in 1988.

It was in his memoirs and journals that Kazin the literary artist appeared. Beginning with the semi-fictional *A Walker in the City* (1951), continuing with *Starting Out in the Thirties* (1965), and ending with the defiantly titled *New York Jew* (1978), Kazin recorded not only his own odyssey through the twentieth century but attempted to evoke the intellectual, social, and cultural forces at work at a particular time and place in American life. These were his most personal books, dealing with the immigrant experiences of his parents, the intellectual fervor of the 1930s, the drift and complacency of postwar America in the 1950s, and the growing tensions and divisions in the civil rights era. They focus especially on the outsider, on Kazin's growing awareness of his Jewishness and what that meant in the aftermath of the Holocaust. Each is also a celebration of the vibrancy and possibilities inherent in urban America, but especially in New York City. *Writing Was Everything* (1995) and *A Lifetime Burning in Every Moment: From the Journals of Alfred Kazin* (1996) offer insights into Kazin's belief in the transforming powers of literature. He returned to a celebration of the city in the lyrical text of personal reminiscences he composed to accompany photographs by David Finn in *Our New York* (1989).

Kazin edited a dozen texts beginning with *The Portable Blake* (1946), followed by *F. Scott Fitzgerald, The Man and His Work* (1951); *The Stature of Theodore Dreiser: A Critical Study of the Man and His Work,* with Charles Shapiro (1955); Herman Melville, *Moby Dick* (1956); *Ralph Waldo Emerson, A Modern Anthology,* with Daniel Aaron (1959); *The Works of Anne Frank,* with Ann Birstein (1959); Theodore Dreiser, *Sister Carrie* (1960) and *The Financier* (1961); *The Open Form: Essays for Our Time* (1961; rev., 1965); *Nathaniel Hawthorne, Selected Short Stories* (1966); *Writers at Work: The Paris Review Interviews: Third Series* (1967); and Henry James, *The Ambassadors* (1969).

His last book, *God and the American Writer,* was published in 1997. Kazin continued to write until just weeks before his death from cancer in Manhattan. Following a memorial ceremony under the Brooklyn Bridge, a box containing his ashes was launched into the East River.

By the time of his death, Kazin was generally regarded as the dean of American literary historians and critics. He had been widely influential in shaping the modern interpretation of the nation's literary past and in assessing the importance of contemporary writers to American life. A vigorous prose stylist, a passionate defender of his own literary judgments, he wore his scholarship lightly. Witty, judgmental, sometimes obtuse, he was never less than interesting and almost always provocative both in his essays and his books.

★

Kazin's papers are in the Berg Collection in the New York Public Library at Fifth Avenue and Forty-second Street. His memoirs, *Walker in the City* (1951), *Starting Out in the Thirties* (1965), and *New York Jew* (1978), are indispensable. Additional autobiographical material may be found in *Our New York* (1994), and *A Lifetime Burning in Every Moment: From the Journals of Alfred Kazin* (1996). There is no biography of Kazin. A mid-career

profile appears in *Current Biography* (1966). His widow, Judith Dunford, describes the placing of his ashes into the East River in "Crossing to the Great Beyond via the Brooklyn Bridge," *New York Times* (23 July 1999). See also Cathrael Kazin, "Memories of My Father, Alfred Kazin," *Paris Review* 40 (winter 1998): 232–235, and *American Scholar* 68 (winter 1999): 13–38, in which family members, friends, and former students offer brief reminiscences. The Oral History Research Office, Butler Library, Columbia University, has two taped interviews, "Reminiscences of Alfred Kazin," the first (1968) centering on his literary life, the second (1972) on his friendship with the historian Richard Hofstadter. An obituary is in the *New York Times* (6 June 1998).

ALLAN L. DAMON

KEMPTON, (James) Murray (*b.* 16 December 1917 in Baltimore, Maryland; *d.* 5 May 1997 in New York City), reporter and newspaper columnist whose elegant prose and wry commentary in a writing career that spanned fifty-five years earned him a Pulitzer Prize, a National Book Award, and an admiring audience of intellectuals and fellow reporters.

Kempton was the only child of James Branson Kempton, a stockbroker from an old Virginian family, and Sally Ambler, one of whose forebears had written the Fugitive Slave

Murray Kempton, 1985. AP/WIDE WORLD PHOTOS

Act of 1850. Another maternal relative was George Mason, whose political philosophy had helped to shape the United States Constitution. This heritage, given Kempton's antiestablishment and libertarian views, was a source of quiet amusement throughout Kempton's life. Kempton's father died in the influenza epidemic after World War I, leaving his family in genteel poverty.

Educated in the Baltimore public schools and the local library, Kempton was a lifelong reader who allegedly read a book a day when he was in college. He entered the Johns Hopkins University in 1935, where he studied government, history, and literature and edited the school paper. He spent his summers as a laborer in a variety of jobs, including a stint as a deck hand on a coastal freighter—an experience that led him to a period of radical political activity, including a brief flirtation with communism.

Graduating from college in 1939 with a B.A. degree in literature, Kempton worked first as a welfare investigator for the City of Baltimore, then in early 1940 as a paid organizer for the American Youth Congress in Manhattan. Later in the year Kempton was an organizer for the International Ladies Garment Workers Union in Peekskill, New York. He began his writing career in 1941 as publicity director of the American Labor Party and as a pamphleteer for both the Young People's Socialist League and the Workers Defense League. In the fall of 1942 Kempton was hired as a labor reporter by the *New York Post,* then a left-wing (some said radical) paper, whose political sympathies for the working class and the social outsider matched Kempton's own.

Kempton married Mina Bluethenthal on 11 June 1942; they had four children. The couple divorced in 1972, the same year in which Kempton married Beverly Gary, with whom he had one child. Gary died 29 October 1995, by which time Kempton had begun an association with Barbara Epstein, the coeditor of the *New York Review of Books,* a relationship that continued until Kempton's death.

Kempton entered the U.S. Army in late 1942, serving a combat tour in the South Pacific and the Philippines and mustering out as a corporal in late 1945. He spent the next year in North Carolina as a general reporter for the *Wilmington Star,* and in 1947 he returned to the *New York Post* as an assistant to the labor editor and columnist Victor Riesel, whom he replaced in 1949. Kempton's first columns for the *Post* (eventually there would be more than 8,000) centered on the labor movement in New York City and the associations of union leaders with city officials and organized crime. As time passed Kempton's hard-hitting, take-no-prisoners style led to the drying up of his sources, and he broadened his reporting to include the emerging civil rights movement in the 1950s, then both national and international politics. He interviewed major figures in the news, as well as peripheral characters who caught his fancy

and illustrated some part of the human condition he wanted to explore.

Kempton was moved by the same sense of outrage that had driven H. L. Mencken, America's leading literary gadfly and social critic in the 1920s, in his prime. He viewed established authority with suspicion and was especially drawn to the outsider and to those who operated on the margins of society or, as he put it, "had fallen from grace." Kempton was intrigued by the outlaw, in particular by those who violated ethical codes. "No great scoundrel," Kempton wrote, "is ever uninteresting," and so he was drawn to the principal figures in the scandals of his time.

Kempton always referred to himself as a reporter, considering the title "journalist" self-important and inflated and thus to be avoided. Just under six feet tall and of average build, sandy-haired and bespectacled, Kempton traveled the streets of New York City on a bicycle, dressed in a pin-striped suit, his trench coat flapping in the wind, a pipe held firmly between his teeth. In later years, Kempton wore a set of earphones so he could listen to his favorite jazz artists or baroque chorales as he sped to his job.

Kempton was a man in love with words, and he used them prolifically. His style, which matured in the 1950s, was instantly recognizable as a distinctive blend of convoluted sentences (often seventy-five to eighty words long) made up of a series of interlocking subordinate clauses and heavily freighted with irony and a cascade of literary, historical, or philosophical allusions. A single 800-word column might carry as many as a dozen such allusions, ranging from Sophocles or Pindar to Karl Marx or Thomas Carlyle to Groucho Marx or Paul Klee. Kempton's prose could be haunting, but also opaque; often warm and compassionate, it was also at times stiletto-sharp, though rarely cruel. At his best, Kempton was crystal clear; at his worst, he was mannered and unreadable.

Kempton left the *Post* in 1963 to write first for the *New Republic* (1963 and 1964) and then the New York *World-Telegram and Sun* (1964–1966). He returned to the *Post* for three more years, resigning in 1969 to work as a news commentator on *Spectrum,* a program on CBS Radio (1970–1977). Kempton did one more stint for the *Post,* from 1977 to 1981, before joining *Newsday,* a Long Island paper that hoped to break into the urban market with a New York City edition. Over the next decade and a half, Kempton wrote more than 2,500 columns for *Newsday.*

Kempton also wrote for a variety of national publications, including *Esquire,* the *Reporter, Commonweal, Atlantic, Harper's,* and *Playboy.* He published four books, three of which are compilations of his columns and essays: *Part of Our Time: Some Ruins and Monuments of the Thirties* (1955); *America Comes of Middle Age: Columns, 1950–1962* (1963); and *Rebellion, Perversities, and Main Events* (1994), a collection of seventy columns and essays from 1966 to

1991. Kempton won the National Book Award in 1974 for *The Briar Patch: The People of the State of New York Versus Lumumba Shakur, et al.* (1973), his account of the mismanaged 1970 trial of twenty-one Black Panthers accused of plotting to blow up several buildings in the Bronx. Kempton received numerous journalism prizes from, among others, the Newspaper Guild of New York and the American Society of Newspaper Editors, and received a Grammy Award in 1987 for record liner notes. He won the George Polk Memorial Award two times: for interpretative reporting in 1967, and for lifetime achievement in 1988; and received a Pulitzer Prize for commentary in 1985.

In his last years Kempton developed pancreatic cancer, and although he continued to write his newspaper column one day a week and longer pieces for the *New York Review of Books,* his output was sharply reduced. In the final weeks of his life he entered the Kateri Nursing Home in Manhattan, where he died at age seventy-nine of complications from a heart attack and stroke. He planned his own funeral at Saint Ignatius of Antioch Episcopal Church, near his home on Manhattan's West Side, where he was a regular worshiper. His burial was private and at an undisclosed place.

★

Kempton's personal papers, nearly 11,000 of his newspaper columns, and numerous magazine articles are in the Rare Book and Manuscript Library in Butler Library at Columbia University. For biographical information about Kempton, see *Current Biography* (1973); David Remnick, "Prince of the City," *New Yorker* (1 Mar. 1993); and Geoffrey C. Ward, "Unpackaged Goods," *American Heritage* 45 (Sept. 1994). Among the many tributes to Kempton following his death are the recollections of colleagues and friends in "Farewell, Murray Kempton," *Newsday* (8 May 1997); William F. Buckley, Jr., "Remembering Murray Kempton," *National Review* 49 (2 June 1997); Elizabeth Hardwick, "On Murray Kempton (1917–1997)," *New York Review of Books* (12 Jun. 1997); and Alfred Kazin, "Bookend: 'Missing Murray Kempton,'" *New York Times Book Review* (30 Nov. 1997). Kempton's hourlong television interview with Brian Lamb was broadcast on C-SPAN's "Booknotes" (3 July 1994). Obituaries are in the *New York Times* and *Newsday* (both 6 May 1997).

ALLAN L. DAMON

KENDALL, Henry Way   (*b.* 9 December 1926 in Boston, Massachusetts; *d.* 15 February 1999 in Wakulla Springs State Park, Florida), Nobel laureate in physics who confirmed experimentally that the basic components of the atomic nucleus, neutrons and protons, had a structure consisting of even more fundamental entities, which had been theoretically predicted earlier and designated as "quarks."

Kendall was the eldest of three children of Henry P. Kendall, a Boston businessman, and Evelyn Louise Way, originally from Canada. He grew up in Deerfield, a Boston suburb, where he attended grade school and subsequently Deerfield Academy, a college preparatory school. Although Kendall developed an active interest in projects involving chemistry, electricity, and mechanics, his high school grades were undistinguished. After graduating from Deerfield Academy in 1945, Kendall entered the United States Merchant Marine Academy in Kings Point, New York. He remained there for only one year and spent the winter of 1945 to 1946 on a troop transport in the North Atlantic. Kendall resigned from the Merchant Marine Academy in October 1946 and enrolled at Amherst College in Massachusetts. His academic pursuits encompassed physics, in which he wrote undergraduate research theses, as well as history, English, and biology. Kendall's wide range of interests would later become apparent as he became involved in social and political activities outside the realm of his scientific specialization. In addition, Kendall also spent considerable time during the summers, both while in college and afterward, in underwater photography, an activity that became a lifelong involvement.

After graduating with a B.A. degree from Amherst in 1950, and with the encouragement of Karl Compton, a family friend of the Kendalls and president of the Massa-

Henry W. Kendall, 1990, the year he won the Nobel Prize in physics. STEVEN SENNE/ASSOCIATED PRESS AP

chusetts Institute of Technology, Kendall began graduate studies in physics at MIT. The particular objective of his thesis research was an attempt to measure a difficult physical parameter of positronium, an atom having a positive electron (positron) for a nucleus and an electron in outer orbit, and having a radioactive half-life of less than ten-millionths of a second. Though he was unsuccessful, the investigation gave Kendall the necessary background for later scientific endeavors.

After obtaining his Ph.D. in nuclear physics in 1955, Kendall received a National Science Foundation postdoctoral fellowship for two years of study and research at MIT and Brookhaven National Laboratory in Upton, Long Island, New York, and at Stanford University in Palo Alto, California. At Stanford, Kendall met the research group studying the structure of the basic elementary particles in the nuclei of atoms: the positively charged proton and the neutron, a neutral particle having essentially the same mass as the proton. The group included Jerome Friedman and Richard Taylor, two scientists with whom Kendall was later to earn the Nobel Prize. Most importantly, the principal apparatus used in the experiments was at Stanford. This device was the two-mile-long accelerator known as SLAC (Stanford Linear Accelerator) and was used for bringing electrons—elementary atomic particles that are lighter than protons and neutrons and that are located in orbits outside the nucleus—to a velocity very close to the speed of light. This speed, 300,000 kilometers per second (about 186,000 miles per second), is one that cannot be exceeded in nature, and, in accordance with Albert Einstein's theory of relativity, as material particles such as electrons approach this velocity, they increase enormously in both mass and energy level.

In the group's experiments, these energetic electrons were used as projectiles to bombard targets consisting of atoms of ordinary hydrogen and deuterium. Hydrogen and deuterium atoms were used because of their simple structure: the nucleus of hydrogen has only one proton, whereas the deuterium nucleus consists of a single proton and a single neutron.

Between 1967 and 1973 Kendall and his associates conducted a series of experiments in which the energetic electrons were deflected or scattered from their original direction. Scattering was found to be inelastic, as distinct from elastic scattering, in which the momentum and energy of colliding particles are preserved and no new particles are produced. Inelastic scattering was evidence that the protons and neutrons had a structure in which internal constituents absorbed the electron bombardment energy.

Several years earlier in 1964, a theoretical physicist at the California Institute of Technology, Murray Gell-Mann, had hypothesized the existence of subatomic particles which made up neutrons and protons. Gell-Mann named these particles "quarks," a term he whimsically chose from an obscure phrase in James Joyce's novel *Finnegan's Wake*. Most physicists, including Gell-Mann, thought that proving the existence of such particles was improbable because of the difficulty of penetrating the inaccessible structures of protons and neutrons.

Kendall, Friedman, and Taylor shared the 1990 Nobel Prize in physics for demonstrating that quarks are real particles. Gell-Mann, who received the Nobel Prize in 1969 for, among other achievements, his quark hypothesis, summarized the work of Kendall and his colleagues: "Although quarks are trapped forever and cannot be detected in the laboratory, beautiful experiments have been performed that confirm their existence inside the proton." In addition, from their scattering experiments, the three scientists inferred the existence of other particles which are central to the contemporary scientific understanding of the structure of matter. These particles, designated as "gluons," are entities that have no charge but essentially bind quarks together in the neutron and proton.

Between 1956 and 1961 Kendall was in turn research associate, lecturer, and assistant professor at Stanford. He returned to MIT in 1961 and became a full professor in 1967. In 1991 Kendall was named MIT's J. A. Stratton Professor of Physics, a position he held for the remainder of his life. Kendall married Ann C. G. Pine in 1972. They were divorced in 1988 and had no children.

Kendall's specialized scientific pursuits were equaled by his concerns with the social impact of science and technology. In 1969 he was one of the founders of the Union of Concerned Scientists and became its chairman in 1974, which Kendall explained "presses for control of technologies that may be harmful or dangerous of a slowly growing interest among scientists to take more responsibility for helping society control the exceedingly powerful technologies that scientific research has spawned." Kendall was involved with the control of nuclear arms and the safety of nuclear power reactors. He opposed President Ronald W. Reagan's Strategic Defense Initiative ("Star Wars") in the 1980s, and advised President William J. Clinton of the hazards of global warming in 1997. That year he was one of the principal authors of a statement signed by 2,000 scientists in connection with the Kyoto Summit. This statement supported reducing the emission of dangerous greenhouse gases from the burning of fossil fuels—a process that contributed to global warming. In pursuit of what he regarded as important social objectives, Kendall served on the planning committees of the National Academy of Sciences and the American Physical Society and was a member of the executive board of Arms Control Association in 1979. As well as the Nobel Prize, Kendall received an honorary degree from Amherst College in 1975, a public service award from the Federation of American Scientists in 1976, the Leo Szilard Award in 1981, and the Wolfgang K. H. Panofsky Award from the American Physical Society in 1989. Kendall died at age seventy-two while on an underwater photography shoot with a team from *National Geographic* magazine in Wakulla Springs State Park, south of Tallahassee, Florida.

★

Among the books Kendall coauthored are *Energy Strategies— Toward a Solar Future* (1980) (with J. Nadis); *Fallacy of Star Wars* (1985) (with Richard L. Garwin, Kurt Gottfried, and John Tirman); and *Crisis Stability and Nuclear War* (1988). An accessible discussion of contemporary particle physics, including the role of quarks and gluons, as well as observations of Kendall and his work, may be found in Murray Gell-Mann, *The Quark and the Jaguar Adventures in the Simple and the Complex* (1994). An obituary is in the *New York Times* (17 Feb. 1999).

LEONARD R. SOLON

KENNEDY, John Fitzgerald, Jr. (*b.* 25 November 1960 in Washington, D.C.; *d.* 16 July 1999 off the coast of Martha's Vineyard, Massachusetts), lawyer and founder of the political magazine *George,* best known as the son of President John Fitzgerald Kennedy.

Kennedy was born on 25 November 1960 in Washington, D.C. His father, John Fitzgerald Kennedy, was the thirty-fifth president of the United States and the first Catholic to hold the office. Kennedy's mother, Jacqueline Bouvier, was a former photojournalist and later became a book editor. As children, Kennedy and his older sister Caroline often stole the attention of news reporters, enthralling the president and the U.S. public with their effervescent personalities, bringing a sense of youth and revitalization to the White House. Kennedy also had a younger brother, who died two days after birth in 1963. When Kennedy was approaching his third birthday in November 1963, his father was assassinated in Dallas, Texas. One of the most poignant moments in U.S. history occurred when Kennedy raised his hand to salute his father's coffin as it passed in front of St. Matthew's Cathedral in Washington, D.C.

After his father's assassination, Kennedy's mother moved the family to an apartment on Fifth Avenue in New York City, where she hoped to raise Kennedy and his sister more naturally, among their peers. Unable to escape the prying eyes of the public and the press, however, Kennedy's mother wed the Greek tycoon Aristotle Onassis in October 1968. Onassis's money and power ensured the security and privacy she so desperately desired for herself and her children. During his teenage years, Kennedy spent part of his time in Greece and part in New York City, establishing a grandfather-grandson type of relationship with his stepfather.

John F. Kennedy, Jr., 1999. MARTY LEDERHANDLER/ASSOCIATED PRESS AP

Despite their mother's new marriage, Kennedy and his sister remained close to their father's relatives. When Kennedy graduated from Phillips Academy Andover in Andover, Massachusetts, on 7 June 1979, his uncle, Senator Edward Kennedy, escorted his mother and sister to the graduation. When Kennedy graduated from Brown University in Providence, Rhode Island, on 5 June 1983 with a B.A. degree in history, the public eagerly watched and waited to see if he would live up to the legacy of his well-known father and uncles. As the son of an assassinated American president, many Americans looked to Kennedy as a potential leader who would uphold the democratic ideals his father and uncles worked to achieve.

After graduation, Kennedy worked as an actor, performing in *Winners* by Brian Friel for the Irish Arts Center in Manhattan. He also appeared in *A Matter of Degrees* (1991), and became a member of the board of Naked Angels, a nonprofit theater company for charities. Following his family's deep commitment to helping the underprivileged, Kennedy lent his name and support to a number of social service agencies. He volunteered to help earthquake victims in Rabinal, Guatemala in 1976, and in 1983 he helped to create the South African Group for Education in response to apartheid.

Kennedy then worked for the New York commissioner of business development (1984–1986) and the Forty-second Street Development Corporation (1986) before attending New York University (NYU) Law School. When he was not taking classes, Kennedy worked for the U.S. Department of Justice (1987), the NYU Juvenile Rights Clinic (1988), as a legal aide for juvenile defense in the Brooklyn Family Court (1988), and at the Mental Retardation and Developmental Disabilities Program (1988–1990). On 19 July 1988 Kennedy made his first major public appearance, taking center stage at the Democratic National Convention in Atlanta to introduce Senator Edward Kennedy. During this introduction, he noted, "I owe a special debt to the man his nephews and nieces call Teddy, not just because of what he means to me personally but because of the causes he has carried on. He has shown that an unwavering commitment to the poor, to the elderly, to those without hope, regardless of fashion or convention, is the greatest reward of public service." The younger Kennedy also came to exemplify this family creed.

In 1989 Kennedy joined his mother and sister in founding the John F. Kennedy Profiles in Courage Award at the John F. Kennedy School of Government at Harvard University in Cambridge, Massachusetts. That same year, Kennedy graduated from law school, and in 1990 he passed the New York State bar exam. He served briefly as an assistant U.S. district attorney in New York City, winning all six of his cases, before resigning in 1993. One year later, he braved the international press to tell the world that his mother, the beloved former First Lady, had died of lymphatic cancer.

In 1995 Kennedy joined with Michael Berman to create *George*, a political but nonpartisan glossy magazine named after President George Washington. He hoped it would "[illuminate] the points where politics converges with business, media, entertainment, fashion, art, and science." In *George,* Kennedy created a brilliant forum from which he was able to tackle many of the pressing political and social issues confronting Americans. While his father, uncles, and many of his cousins used politics to fight for a democratic ideology, Kennedy used *George* to support that ideology. This was particularly apparent in the October/November 1995 issue, in which Kennedy managed to obtain an admission from George Wallace, the former governor of Alabama and a strong opponent of the civil rights movement supported by Kennedy's father, that he no longer believed in segregation.

The most eligible bachelor in America, Kennedy finally made his way to the altar on 21 September 1996 to marry Carolyn Bessette, a publicist for Calvin Klein. They lived in a cooperative apartment in the Tribeca neighborhood of New York City. Although he was busy with his magazine, new wife, and many hobbies, Kennedy continued his charitable work for groups including Reaching Up, caregivers for the emotionally disabled; the South African Group for Education; and the Special Olympics.

On 17 July 1999 Americans awoke to the startling news that Kennedy and his wife were missing. Reminiscent of the Thanksgiving Day holiday of 1963, the American public collectively huddled, all weekend long, around their television sets to follow coverage of a tragic event in the lives of the Kennedy clan. After an exhaustive search of the Atlantic Ocean, it was determined that, at approximately 9 P.M. on 16 July, Kennedy, his wife, and her sister Lauren G. Bessette had died in a plane crash off the coast of Martha's Vineyard. Kennedy had been piloting a Piper Saratoga, en route to a cousin's wedding in Hyannis Port, Massachusetts, and apparently had lost his bearings. On 19 July 1999 Senator Edward Kennedy issued a statement in the *New York Times:* "John was a shining light in all our lives and in the lives of the nation and the world that first came to know him when he was a little boy. . . . We loved him deeply and his loss leaves an enormous void in all our lives." On 22 July 1999 a private naval commitment at sea was performed for Kennedy, his wife, and his wife's sister.

When President Kennedy was assassinated, the world seemed to stand still. The American people had to come to terms with the loss of their thirty-fifth president and his potential to make the world a better, safer place. With the death of his only surviving son, the nation had to face, once again, the loss of a potentially great leader. Following his family's tradition of using privilege, prestige, and power to help those who cannot help themselves, Kennedy contributed an enormous amount of philanthropic time and energy toward that goal.

★

Harrison Rainie and John Quinn wrote an early biography on the third generation of Kennedy children, *Growing Up Kennedy: The Third Wave Comes of Age* (1983). Another important biography is Peter and David Horowitz, *The Kennedys: An American Drama* (1984). A more recent but still somewhat dated biography is Wendy Leigh, *Prince Charming: The John F. Kennedy, Jr., Story* (1993). An obituary is in the *New York Times* (19 July 1999).

JANE FRANCES AMLER

KILEY, Richard Paul (*b.* 31 March 1922 in Chicago, Illinois; *d.* 5 March 1999 in Middletown, New York), actor and singer best remembered for his role as Don Quixote, the delusional but indomitable old "knight" in the musical *Man of La Mancha* (1965).

Born on the south side of Chicago, Kiley was the son of Leo Joseph Kiley, a railroad statistician, and Leonore Mc-

Kenna. After graduating from Mount Carmel High School in Chicago in 1939, he attended Loyola University for a year, then left to study acting at the Barnum Dramatic School in Chicago. After serving in the U.S. Navy as a gunnery instructor in World War II, he worked briefly as a radio actor and announcer. He made his professional stage debut in the 1946 season of summer stock in Michiana Shores, Michigan, then moved to New York City.

In 1947 Kiley made his first appearance on a New York stage as Poseidon in a production of *The Trojan Women* at the Equity Library Theater. In 1948 he became the understudy and eventual replacement for Anthony Quinn, who played Stanley Kowalski in the touring production of *A Streetcar Named Desire*. In that same year Kiley married Mary Bell Wood, whom he divorced in 1967.

In 1949 Kiley made his first Broadway appearance in a short-lived play called *The Sun and I*. Four years later, in 1953, he attracted attention in a revival of Bernard Shaw's *Misalliance*. In addition to appearing in dramas such as *Time Limit!* (1956) and *Advise and Consent* (1960), he won leading roles in musicals that took advantage of his robust singing voice. He played the Caliph in *Kismet* (1953), in which he sang the hit song "Stranger in Paradise," and a music-hall strongman in the musical murder mystery *Redhead* (1959), for which he won the Tony Award for Best Actor in a Musical. In *No Strings* (1962) he was a jaded expatriate novelist in love with a high-fashion model.

While acting regularly in the theater, Kiley played supporting roles in a number of films, including *The Sniper* (1952), *Pickup on South Street* (1953), *The Blackboard Jungle* (1955), and *The Phenix City Story* (1955). He was also active in television, starring in many original plays, weekly dramatic series, and virtually all of the major live dramatic showcases, including "Studio One," "Playhouse 90," and "Kraft Television Theatre." For thirty years he served as narrator for *National Geographic* television specials and documentaries.

Discouraged that his acting career had stalled ("I had fallen into the position of good old Kiley, the faithful leading man for the lady stars"), Kiley was elated when, in 1965, he was offered the dual role of the doddering but stalwart Don Quixote and his creator Miguel de Cervantes in a musical version of Cervantes's classic novel. Entitled *Man of La Mancha*, the musical had a book by Dale Wasserman (based on his play *I, Don Quixote*) and featured lyrics by Joe Darion and music by Mitch Leigh. After attracting attention at the Goodspeed Opera House in East Haddam, Connecticut, the production moved to the ANTA Washington Square Theatre in lower Manhattan, where it became a surprise hit. Eventually it moved to Broadway, where it ran for over six years, becoming the third longest running musical of the sixties.

For Kiley, the role of Don Quixote/Cervantes was both

Richard Kiley in *The Ceremony of Innocence*, 1972. KOBAL COLLECTION

challenging and taxing. Theatergoers were deeply stirred when he sang in praise of his beloved but imaginary "Dulcinea" or proclaimed his lofty credo in "The Quest," better known as "The Impossible Dream." At the end of its first season in 1966, *Man of La Mancha* won both the New York Drama Critics Circle Award and the Tony Award for Best Musical. Tony Awards were also given to Kiley, authors Leigh and Darion, director Albert Marre, and set designer Howard Bay. Kiley later relinquished his role to other actors but returned for a 1972 revival. He played the role again in 1977. In 1973, inspired by his abiding interest in the author of *Don Quixote,* he appeared in Norman Corwin's play *Cervantes.*

Kiley later appeared in Alan Ayckbourn's comedy *Absurd Person Singular* (1974), played Dr. Sloper in a 1976 revival of *The Heiress,* and starred in a 1987 revival of Arthur Miller's *All My Sons,* for which he received a Tony nomination. His film work also included *The Little Prince* (1974), *Looking for Mr. Goodbar* (1977), *Endless Love* (1981), and *Phenomenon* (1996).

In later years Kiley made more television appearances. He had roles in many dramatic plays, including *Murder Once Removed* (1971), *Friendly Persuasion* (1975), and *Golden Gate* (1981). In 1983 he appeared as Paddy Cleary, the brother of Australian sheep rancher Mary Carson (Barbara Stanwyck), in a ten-hour ABC production based on

Colleen McCullough's novel *The Thorn Birds,* winning both a Golden Globe Award for best supporting actor in television, and an Emmy Award for outstanding supporting actor in a limited series or special. In 1984 he played activist George Mason in a three-part, eight-hour CBS miniseries on the life of George Washington. He starred as the husband of Alzheimer's victim Joanne Woodward in the Emmy-winning drama *Do You Remember Love?* (1985). He also won an Emmy and a Golden Globe Award in 1988 for his performance in the dramatic series *A Year in the Life,* as well as an Emmy Award in 1994 for his guest-starring role in the drama series *Picket Fences.* In his last years, as he became ill, he gave up acting and instead narrated television documentaries. He was the voice of the tour guide in *Jurassic Park* (1993).

Kiley died weeks before his seventy-seventh birthday of a rare bone marrow disease and is buried in Warwick, New York. He was survived by his wife, Patricia Ferrier, a dancer he married in 1968, and the six children by his first marriage.

All actors hope for at least one signature role that will seal their record of achievement. An estimable actor and singer in many plays and films, Kiley found that role in *Man of La Mancha.* For most people, he will always be the embodiment of the brave, mad knight who never stopped tilting his sword at life's windmills.

★

A concise summary of Kiley's career appears in *Current Biography Yearbook* (1999). Obituaries are in the *New York Times* (6 Mar. 1999) and *Variety* (15 Mar. 1999).

TED SENNETT

KIRK, Grayson Louis (*b*. 12 October 1903 in Jeffersonville, Ohio; *d*. 21 November 1997 in Bronxville, New York), president of Columbia University from 1953 to 1968.

Kirk was the second of two sons of Traine C. Kirk, a farmer, and Nora Eichelberger, a schoolteacher. The Kirks were Scotch Presbyterians from Virginia. Kirk attended local schools and nearby Miami University in Oxford, Ohio. There he partook of fraternity life and edited the college newspaper. Despite a lifelong stutter, he was a top debater. He graduated with a B.A. degree Phi Beta Kappa in 1924. In 1924 Kirk went to Clark University in Worcester, Massachusetts, to study international relations. He earned an M.A. degree in 1925, then returned to Ohio to marry his college sweetheart, Marion Louise Sands, on 17 August 1925. After two years of college teaching in Texas, Kirk resumed graduate studies at the University of Wisconsin in Madison. From 1927 to 1928 he and his family (which by then included a son) lived in France, where he did research on the reintegration of Alsace Lorraine, a western Euro-

Grayson Kirk, 1966. ASSOCIATED PRESS/KARSH OF OTTAWA

pean frontier region located between France, Germany, Belgium, and Switzerland.

Kirk returned to Madison in 1928 to teach and complete his dissertation. An assistant professorship at Wisconsin followed on the completion of his Ph.D. in 1930. In 1935 a sabbatical leave allowed him to complete *Philippine Independence* (1936), a book about American attitudes on Philippine independence that brought with it an associate professorship. In the fall of 1938 Kirk went to Columbia University in New York City as a visiting associate professor. He accepted a permanent position a year later, swapping Madison, which he liked, for New York City, which he did not, because the latter was home to the Council of Foreign Relations. He was soon off to the State Department, where he held several wartime positions.

The leadership vacuum at Columbia after the retirement of President Nicholas Murray Butler in 1945 allowed Kirk to enter university administration. In 1948, upon Dwight D. Eisenhower's becoming Columbia's thirteenth president, Kirk became assistant to the provost. Within a year he was provost. When Eisenhower resigned in November 1952 to become president of the United States, Kirk became Columbia's fourteenth president. He was forty-nine years old. The Kirk presidency began auspiciously. Unlike Eisenhower, Kirk was a hands-on president; unlike

Butler, Kirk was not overly controlling. Deans who ran their respective schools during the interregnum continued to do so while faculty went about their business. Kirk resisted efforts to investigate his faculty's political leanings, however they clashed with his Republicanism. He welcomed federal support and solicited foundations for grants. He got along with trustees and donors by accommodating them.

The 1960s brought problems to Columbia: the university's finances deteriorated, faculty salaries lagged, and faculty were recruited away. Kirk's strategy was to hope that increases in government and foundation revenues would keep ahead of rising costs. In 1964 Columbia slipped into chronic deficit. Meanwhile, Columbia's undergraduates grew restive as the war in Vietnam accelerated and as racial tensions increased at home. Demonstrations in 1965 against the NROTC and military recruitment on campus soon broadened to include attacks on university real estate policies and classified research. A particularly rowdy demonstration led by Students for a Democratic Society (SDS) inside Low Library (the main administration building) in the spring of 1967 forced Kirk to ban indoor demonstrations. The fateful academic year of 1967–1968 began well enough. Divisions within SDS suggested that Kirk had outmaneuvered the radical students. Still, worsening finances, an administrative shake-up, and the personal embarrassment of endorsing a "revolutionary" cigarette filter that proved to be ineffective made life difficult enough that he planned to retire in 1969.

In February 1968 black undergraduates and Harlem political activists halted excavation for a long-planned college gymnasium in nearby Morningside Park. In late March, Kirk's chairmanship of the Institute for Defense Analysis (IDA), an academic advisory board to the military, occasioned a protest by 100 students in Low Library. Six SDS leaders were identified for disciplinary action. On 9 April, during a memorial service for Martin Luther King, Jr., the newly elected SDS leader Mark Rudd challenged the moral legitimacy of Kirk and his fellow administrators. Two weeks later, an open letter to "Uncle Grayson" included three demands: Columbia must pull out of IDA, abandon the gym, and take no disciplinary action against the Low Library demonstrators. Kirk rejected these demands. Privately, he acknowledged that the trustees were unwilling to stop the gym project, and he insisted on disciplinary action against disruptive students.

On Tuesday, 23 April, a noontime SDS rally drew the unexpected participation of the Society of African-American Students (SAS), which represented Columbia's black undergraduates. The rally also attracted students opposed to SDS's disruptive tactics. A confrontation was barely avoided when the radical students decided against trying to enter the locked Low Library and proceeded instead to the gym site. There they encountered a detachment of New York City police, who arrested one student. The crowd then returned to campus and entered Hamilton Hall, the seat of Columbia College. By late afternoon the indoor rally had evolved into a building occupation. Informed of the Hamilton Hall doings, which included the detaining of a dean, Kirk favored calling in the police. When his deans argued that they could persuade the students to leave, Kirk went along. That night, black students in Hamilton told white students to leave and "get your own building." Early the next morning they did. During the ensuing seven days, when five buildings were occupied by more than 1,000 students, Kirk remained convinced that only police action would end the occupations. He also knew that calling the police on campus would play into the hands of the radical students and destroy his credibility among faculty. It was faculty protestations that aborted a planned police action on the third night of the occupations.

Throughout the crisis Kirk received unsolicited advice from trustees and other university presidents that he not "cave in" to student demands. Meanwhile, through outside intermediaries, he tried to persuade the students in Hamilton that their separate demands would be favorably considered if they left the building. He also hinted about being open to changing disciplinary procedures, stopping the gym, and getting out of IDA—all to no avail. On 30 April 1,000 members of the New York Police Department cleared the five occupied buildings. The operation went smoothly until spectators on South Field were stampeded by police. Yet the fact that police physically removed 800 students from university buildings turned the community against the administration. "Kirk Must Go" signs appeared later that morning. Four months later Kirk submitted his resignation. He was then sixty-four years old. Grievances against two successors limited his subsequent campus visits. He lived for another thirty years, mostly in good health, in the Riverdale section of the Bronx. His oral history interviews in the late 1980s attest not only to his continued mental sharpness but also to his belief that he was a victim of the changing times more than of his own shortcomings. It is a credible judgment. Kirk died in his sleep at age ninety-four after suffering from congestive heart failure.

★

Information about Kirk is in *Oral History Interviews,* Columbia University, and *Proceedings of the American Philosophical Society* 143 (Dec. 1999). An obituary is in the *New York Times* (22 Nov. 1997).

ROBERT A. MCCAUGHEY

KIRKLAND, (Joseph) Lane (*b.* 12 March 1922 in Camden, South Carolina; *d.* 14 August 1999 in Washington, D.C.), president of the American Federation of Labor–Congress of Industrial Organizations (AFL-CIO) who unified the labor movement in a period of declining union membership.

Kirkland was one of five children of Randolph Withers Kirkland, a cotton buyer, and Louise Richardson, a homemaker and sometime vocalist and church organist. With roots in Camden going back to the American Revolution, Kirkland came from a line of cotton planters, one of whom signed the 1860 Ordinance of Secession that took South Carolina out of the union. When Kirkland was seven, his family moved to the textile-mill city of Newberry, South Carolina, where he and his siblings attended public schools. As a child, Kirkland became aware of the precariousness of mill workers and their families' existence and of the determination of the mill owners to retain advantage over employees and keep South Carolina the least unionized state in America. But foreign developments, not a local need for labor organizing, spurred the teenaged Kirkland to action. After the outbreak of World War II and before U.S. involvement, he twice tried unsuccessfully to enlist in the Canadian army. Kirkland returned to South Carolina in 1940 and entered Newberry College, but he left before the

Lane Kirkland. PRINTS AND PHOTOGRAPHS DIVISION, LIBRARY OF CONGRESS

end of the year to become a cadet aboard the merchant ship SS *Liberator*.

Appointed to the first class at the U.S. Merchant Marine Academy in 1941, Kirkland graduated in 1942 and served until 1946 as a deck officer on American merchant ships carrying war matériel to Allied forces in Europe and the Pacific. During these years—as a member of the International Organization of Masters, Mates and Pilots—he had his only experience as a rank-and-file union member. On 10 June 1944 he married Edith Draper Hollyday, with whom he had five children. In 1946 Kirkland settled with his family in Washington, D.C., where he drafted nautical maps for the U.S. Navy during the day and attended classes at Georgetown University's School of Foreign Service at night. Kirkland received a B.S. degree from Georgetown in 1948, but instead of joining the foreign service, he signed on as a staff researcher at the American Federation of Labor (AFL) headquarters in Washington.

As a researcher, Kirkland specialized in pension and social security matters; his first reports were so stylishly written that the AFL loaned him to the Democratic Party to write speeches for the 1948 vice-presidential candidate, Alben W. Barkley. Kirkland also later wrote speeches for the 1952 and 1956 Democratic presidential nominee, Adlai Stevenson. In 1955 the country's two major labor organizations merged as the American Federation of Labor–Congress of Industrial Organizations (AFL-CIO), under the leadership of AFL president George Meany. Organized labor then represented a record 34 percent of the U.S. workforce, though some important unions remained outside Meany's AFL-CIO. In 1960 Meany appointed Kirkland his executive assistant.

Kirkland was an effective troubleshooter for Meany and served as a liaison between the AFL-CIO and the administrations of Presidents John F. Kennedy and Lyndon B. Johnson. He not only lobbied Congress and the White House on labor's traditional bread-and-butter issues, but he also called for civil rights and fair-employment practices legislation. Kirkland's southern background enabled him to recognize, more readily than most union members, that race baiting and labor baiting were two sides of the same coin. Kirkland and Meany were strong supporters of Johnson's "War on Poverty" and the war in Vietnam. Kirkland kept a low profile until 1966, when he attracted national attention for helping to settle a transit strike that had tied up New York City. In 1969 the AFL-CIO executive council, at Meany's behest, elected Kirkland secretary-treasurer, the federation's second most important office.

Meany, a gruff, cigar-chomping plumber from the Bronx, and Kirkland, his heir apparent, an erudite southerner who chain-smoked cigarettes through a Franklin Roosevelt–style holder, differed in appearance but not on goals for the labor movement and a pragmatic approach to attaining them. When President Richard M. Nixon tried to stem inflation by imposing wage and price controls in 1971, Kirkland denounced the move with such vehemence that he won a place on the White House "enemies list." Nevertheless, the labor hierarchy supported Nixon on the Vietnam War and refused to endorse his 1972 Democratic opponent, George McGovern. Meany and Kirkland were staunch anti-Communists who deplored what they viewed as the cavalier attitude of many antiwar leaders toward American workers. They also feared the effects of McGovern's Democratic party reforms, designed to reduce the power within the party of traditional constituencies like the AFL-CIO.

Kirkland's marriage ended in divorce in 1972, and he married Irena Neumann on 19 January 1973. They had no children. Neumann, a Czech refugee from communism and a Jewish survivor of the Holocaust, gave her husband new insight into the underground labor movements of Soviet-dominated eastern Europe, which the AFL-CIO regularly supported in international forums. In 1976 the AFL-CIO enthusiastically backed the Democratic presidential nominee, Jimmy Carter. Carter did not return the favor; he made clear his disdain for the labor chiefs and other traditional Democratic power brokers and overloaded his administration with appointees from big business—for which he was roundly denounced by Meany and Kirkland.

On 19 November 1979 George Meany, at age eighty-five, stepped down as president of the AFL-CIO and was formally succeeded by Kirkland, then fifty-seven, duly elected without meaningful opposition at the federation's national convention. Kirkland took over at a time of declining power for American organized labor; since its peak in 1955, union membership as a percentage of the total workforce declined steadily. With foreign competition spurring productivity increases in basic industries, employment had leveled off in union-organized factories and mills, while new jobs added by the expanding economy were mostly in hard-to-organize service sectors. In the mid-1970s, as "stagflation" (economic stagnation accompanied by high inflation) set in, union membership began to decline absolutely as well as relatively. In 1979 organized labor only comprised 24 percent of the workforce and had only 13,600,000 members, not all of whom belonged to the AFL-CIO. In his inaugural address, the new AFL-CIO president announced his goal to bring the unaffiliated unions—principally the automobile workers, mine workers, and Teamsters—into the federation. An Episcopalian well versed in the scriptures, Kirkland declared that "all sinners belong in the church." He largely achieved his objective in 1987 when the Teamsters, the last of the major holdouts, signed up with the AFL-CIO. To accomplish this, Kirkland promised member unions more autonomy and their leaders more freedom of action than Meany had allowed, concessions that would weaken Kirkland's power and eventually lead to his downfall.

Of medium height and sturdy build, with a shock of wavy brown hair, Kirkland was said to have "an inexhaustible capacity for gin rummy." His wide-ranging interests included ancient and modern art, jazz, and gardening. He enjoyed socializing with union comrades and entertained them with his expert harmonica playing. Outwardly friendly, he was unfailingly polite to strangers and insisted that everyone address him as "Lane." In adversarial relationships, he could come across as stubborn and arrogant. He valued words and used them sparingly for maximum effect; he despised shallowness, a defect he found in the work of most journalists, who were frequently the target of his scathing wit. Kirkland did not get good press. His speech retained traces of his southern origins and was sometimes laced with powerful bursts of merchant-seaman profanity.

Under Kirkland's leadership, the AFL-CIO provided valuable aid to the Solidarity labor movement in Poland. Agents of the American federation smuggled $6 million worth of essential communications equipment into Poland in the early 1980s to aid the Solidarity underground. The peaceful revolution that began in Poland spread to the rest of Eastern Europe, putting an end to Soviet domination by the close of the decade. In the newly freed countries, leaders such as Lech Walesa of Poland and Vaclav Havel of the Czech Republic acknowledged their debt of gratitude to Kirkland and the AFL-CIO.

After President Ronald W. Reagan broke a nationwide strike by air traffic controllers in 1981, Kirkland organized a march on Washington by 250,000 union members and allied civil rights activists to protest Reagan's policies toward labor and minorities. The mobilization impressed the Democratic leadership in Congress, whose relations with the AFL-CIO had been weakened by the indifference of President Carter. Kirkland forged a close working relationship with the Democratic Speaker of the House of Representatives, Jim Wright, which produced some significant labor victories, including the override of Reagan's veto of a bill requiring a sixty-day notice for plant closings.

Kirkland demonstrated that labor was organized for political action and could turn out the vote in key districts and key states. In 1986 the AFL-CIO helped the Democrats regain control of the Senate. In 1992 the Democratic presidential nominee William J. Clinton, with Kirkland's enthusiastic support, captured the White House. The AFL-CIO helped formulate President Clinton's proposals for a comprehensive health-care system, which were overwhelmingly rejected in Congress. The AFL-CIO also lost on the North American Free Trade Agreement (NAFTA) of 1993, which Clinton favored. Kirkland, who said he favored free trade "in theory," fought NAFTA because he believed it would cost American jobs. Clinton gave Kirkland little, other than easy access to the White House and, in 1994, a Presidential Medal of Freedom. But Clinton listened and his appointments to the National Labor Relations Board were pro-labor.

Neither Clinton nor Kirkland anticipated the Republican sweep of Congress in the 1994 elections. For some labor leaders, this catastrophe, following on the heels of resounding defeats on health care and NAFTA, was too much to bear. They blamed Kirkland, saying he was too remote, too engrossed in foreign affairs, to attend to the needs of American workers. A campaign to oust Kirkland was begun by John J. Sweeney, president of the union representing service employees and the leaders of the recently affiliated Teamsters and mine workers unions. Kirkland fought back and refused an easy way out, Clinton's offer to appoint him as ambassador to Poland. By mid-1995 Kirkland realized that he lacked the votes to prevail at the national convention in October. He resigned in August in favor of his chosen successor, the secretary-treasurer Thomas R. Donahue, who then lost the election to Sweeney.

Kirkland kept a low profile in retirement. The long-term decline in union membership continued after his resignation, but he had shown his successors how to maximize labor's residual power through unified action and close association with the Democratic Party—which yielded good results in subsequent national and state elections. At age seventy-seven, Kirkland died of lung cancer at his home in Washington, D.C., and is buried in Arlington National Cemetery.

★

Papers relating to Kirkland's tenure as secretary-treasurer and president of the AFL-CIO (RG95–007, Lane Kirkland Papers, 1963–1998) are in the federation's George Meany Memorial Archives in Silver Spring, Maryland. The South Caroliniana Library of the University of South Carolina in Columbia is the repository for Kirkland family records, which include a collection of the labor leader's press clippings (*Lane Kirkland Vertical Files Collection, 1960–1999*). Kirkland's autobiographical remarks to the South Carolina Historical Society are published in Lane Kirkland, *My Journey from Camden to Warsaw* (1996). Kirkland has no full-length biography, but he appears prominently in most studies of the U.S. labor movement since World War II. See Taylor E. Dark, *The Unions and the Democrats: An Enduring Alliance* (1999). For a contrasting view, see Paul Buhle, *Taking Care of Business: Samuel Gompers, George Meany, Lane Kirkland, and the Tragedy of American Labor* (1999). See also Bruce Wetterau, *The Presidential Medal of Freedom: Winners and Their Achievements* (1996). Obituaries are in the *Washington Post* and *New York Times* (both 16 Aug. 1999) and *Economist* (28 Aug. 1999).

NEILL MACAULAY

KLUTZNICK, Philip M. (*b.* 9 July 1907 in Kansas City, Missouri; *d.* 14 August 1999 in Chicago, Illinois), secretary of commerce under President Jimmy Carter, housing and real estate developer, and leading American Jewish organizational figure.

Klutznick was one of four children born to Morris Klutznick and Minnie Spindler, who had emigrated from Eastern Europe with their young daughter in 1905. Klutznick's father, a cobbler, had a shoe store, later moved into the furniture business, and finally owned a grocery store, but the local Orthodox synagogue was the center of his life. Klutznick's mother, who never learned to read or write English, was the head of the family. Klutznick first lived above the shoe store, and eventually the family moved into a modest house.

Klutznick attended Woodland and Morse Grammar Schools. At Manual High School he was on the varsity debate team, and edited the *Manualite,* which was judged Missouri's best high school newspaper in his senior year. He graduated in 1924 with a gold medal in oratory. One of the first two Jews admitted to Manual's fraternities, Klutznick resigned when they refused admission to a third. He was elected as the vice president of the Hi-Y Boys Club of the Young Men's Christian Association (YMCA), but as a Jew he could not be the club's president. Klutznick chan-

Philip M. Klutznick. AP/WIDE WORLD PHOTOS

neled these crises into establishing the second chapter of Aleph Zadik Aleph (AZA), a Jewish youth organization. At the first AZA convention in Omaha, Nebraska, in July 1924, he met Ethel Riekes, his future wife, but she was not interested in him. Short and round-faced, Klutznick had a prominent birthmark on his forehead (later reduced by surgery) and weighed 212 pounds.

Klutznick enrolled in January 1925 in the nearby University of Kansas at Lawrence. Under the tutelage of James Naismith, the inventor of basketball, whose daughter had been his high-school teacher, Klutznick began a diet and exercise regime that he maintained throughout his life. Elected as the head of AZA in July 1925, Klutznick transferred to the University of Nebraska in Lincoln near AZA's Omaha headquarters and graduated in 1926. He entered Creighton University's law school in Omaha in January 1927. The next year Klutznick joined B'nai B'rith, becoming the president of the Omaha lodge at age twenty-three.

Klutznick obtained his J.D. in January 1930 and was admitted to the Nebraska bar. He earned $50 per month working for AZA and $75 per month at the law firm of Fradenberg, Stalmaster, and Beber, becoming a junior partner in 1934. Specializing in negotiations, appellate work, and public law, he argued constitutional cases before the Nebraska Supreme Court. Klutznick and Riekes married on 8 June 1930. In 1932 they had their first of six children (one stillborn).

Klutznick soon became involved in local reform politics. As the assistant corporation counsel, he brought federal housing to Omaha. He organized the citizens' committee on housing, was a special assistant to the U.S. attorney general for public lands (1935–1936), and served as the general counsel for the Omaha Housing Authority (1938–1941). After consulting for the defense housing coordinator Charles F. Palmer in Washington, D.C., Klutznick joined Palmer's staff in 1941 as an assistant administrator in charge of programming for housing during World War II. In 1944 President Franklin D. Roosevelt appointed him as the wartime commissioner of the Federal Public Housing Authority. Klutznick created "instant cities" for defense workers, including Oak Ridge, Tennessee, a secret atomic bomb facility. He planned for postwar housing problems. In 1947 he received the certificate of merit for "rapid-fire construction of half-a-million housing units."

Klutznick left Washington, D.C., for Chicago in July 1946. He rented an apartment at 199 East Lake Shore Drive and established a Chicago branch of his law firm. He formed the American Community Builders, whose first project was the new GI town of Park Forest, Illinois on the southern suburban edge of Chicago. Begun in September 1947, Park Forest ultimately housed 31,000 people. Klutznick was its first renter and stayed for thirteen years. A "model of intelligent planning," Park Forest was profiled in William H. Whyte's famous book *The Organization Man*. It won *Look* magazine's and the Municipal League's competition for the all-American city in 1953 and 1954. In 1948 Governor Adlai Stevenson appointed Klutznick vice chairman of the Illinois Housing Authority. He became one of Stevenson's confidants.

Klutznick served the Jewish community as the president of B'nai B'rith from 1953 to 1959, then as the first chairman of its International Council. One of his most pressing concerns was dealing with the fears of Jews in the South once B'nai B'rith officially supported the civil rights movement. He joined the board of the Conference on Jewish Material Claims Against Germany in 1953 and helped to establish the Conference of Presidents of Major American Jewish Organizations in 1954. In 1956 he went to Morocco to secure the release of 8,500 Moroccan Jews. He helped to plan the Israeli port city of Ashdod. In 1960 he was elected as the president of the United Jewish Appeal. He became, in the words of many, the leading Jewish American figure of the time. In tribute, the national B'nai B'rith museum in Washington, D.C., was named after him.

Klutznick served for three months on the U.S. delegation to the General Assembly of the United Nations (UN) in 1957. After his involvement in John F. Kennedy's presidential campaign, he came back in 1961 as the U.S. representative to the UN's Economic and Social Council. He resided at the old Park Lane Hotel in Manhattan. Klutznick had to withdraw from many Jewish organizational responsibilities. The U.S. State Department vetted his book *No Easy Answers* (1961) and insisted that two chapters on the Middle East be removed. He renewed his acquaintance with Eleanor Roosevelt and later chaired the Eleanor Roosevelt Memorial Foundation fund-raising committee. After two years he returned exhausted to Chicago, needing surgery for a benign tumor.

Klutznick formed KLC Ventures Limited, a partnership in development projects both urban and suburban, in 1964. He surveyed housing problems in Brazil for President Lyndon B. Johnson. In the 1960s and 1970s Klutznick chaired the Committee on Economic Development's research and policy committee. In 1968 KLC was dissolved, and the Urban Investment and Development Company (UIDC) was formed. UIDC created the "minitown" program, which anchored communities around shopping centers.

Aetna Life and Casualty Company acquired UIDC, and at age sixty-five Klutznick stepped down as the chairman and chief executive officer. He started work on Water Tower Place, a multi-use high-rise shopping center in Chicago. When the center opened in 1973 with 130 stores, a hotel, and 160 condominiums, it transformed the area and became a model for developments like Trump Towers in New York City. For years Water Tower Place drew more visitors annually than any other structure in Chicago.

Klutznick moved into one of its condominiums, joking that he once again was "living over the store." He also served as the president of the Chicago Bulls in 1973, having helped to organize the basketball team.

In autumn 1977 he was elected as the president of the World Jewish Congress. He met and began advising the Egyptian president Anwar Sadat on both Jewish and development issues. In November 1979 President Carter asked Klutznick to serve as the U.S. secretary of commerce, in which capacity he dealt with the embargo against the Soviet Union after the invasion of Afghanistan. He oversaw the 1980 U.S. census, established the Office for Productivity, Technology, and Innovation, and helped to revitalize the U.S. steel industry. He also campaigned tirelessly for Carter's reelection campaign before Jewish and business groups.

After Carter's defeat in 1980, Klutznick returned to Chicago. He joined a four-member fact-finding Middle East peace mission sponsored by the Seven Springs Center. Many Jews condemned the 1981 report, which was the centerpiece of hearings held by the House Committee on Foreign Affairs. Many Zionists labeled him a traitor when, on 30 June 1982, he issued the Paris Declaration with Pierre Mendès-France, the former prime minister of France, and Nahum Goldmann. The declaration called for Israel to cease hostilities in Lebanon and for Israel and the Palestinian Liberation Organization (PLO) to recognize each other. In 1987 Klutznick received the M. Justin Herman Memorial Award from the National Association of Housing and Redevelopment Officials for his "legendary" work as "the father of public housing."

Klutznick died at his home after suffering from Alzheimer's disease. Klutznick was a man of exceptional energy and drive. As a developer, he helped define suburban life and redefine urban life. A philanthropist and lifelong Democrat, he served under seven presidents and was a leading, and often controversial, international Jewish leader.

★

The best source for information on Klutznick's life is his autobiography, with Sidney Hyman, *Angles of Vision: A Memoir of My Lives* (1991). For Klutznick's insights on housing, see his article "Poverty and Politics: The Challenge of Public Housing," *Journal of Housing* (Jan./Feb. 1985). Klutznick's perspective on American Jewish life is described in his book *No Easy Answers* (1961). A lively portrait by Estelle Gilson appears in Murray Polner, *Jewish Profiles: Great Jewish Personalities and Institutions of the Twentieth Century* (1991). Obituaries are in the *Washington Post* and *Omaha World-Herald* (both 16 Aug. 1999), *New York Times* (17 Aug. 1999), and *Chicago Sun-Times* (18 Aug. 1999).

SHARONA A. LEVY

KRISTELLER, Paul Oskar (*b.* 22 May 1905 in Berlin, Germany; *d.* 7 June 1999 in New York City), internationally recognized authority on Renaissance thought whose numerous books and articles and extensive lecturing enriched and popularized Renaissance studies in the 1950s and 1960s.

Kristeller was born into a middle-class, German-Jewish family. His father died on the day of his son's birth. Kristeller was raised by his mother, Alice Magnus, and his stepfather, Heinrich Kristeller, the director of a small factory, who adopted him. Both parents later died in the Holocaust. Kristeller began a demanding course of classical education in 1914 at the Mommsen-Gymnasium in Berlin, supplementing his studies with a wide reading of Latin, Greek, German, and French literature. He began to collect books and became an accomplished piano player. His readings of Plato, Aristotle, and Kant impelled him to study philosophy and its history, a decision his family supported but did not applaud, as they had hoped he would enter the family business.

After graduating with honors in 1923, Kristeller entered the University of Heidelberg, where he studied under some of the leading German philosophers of the day, including Heinrich Rickert, Karl Jaspers, Richard Kroner, and Edmund Husserl, the founder of phenomenology, who, Kristeller said, "was not a good lecturer, but whose books I read with great profit." He went to the University of Marburg in 1926 to study with the noted German philosopher Martin Heidegger, but returned to Heidelberg to complete his thesis, on Plotinus, the founder of a system of thought that drew on and enlarged Plato's concept of the One. In addition to his work in philosophy, he had minors in mathematics and medieval history and explored many other fields, including art history, from which sprang a lifelong interest in Far Eastern art. Kristeller received his Ph.D. from the University of Heidelberg in 1928. His thesis, *Der Begriff der Seele in der Ethik des Plotin* (The concept of the soul in the ethics of Plotinus), was published in 1929. After three more years of study at the University of Berlin, he began work on his *Habilitationsschrift* (a postdoctoral dissertation that is required in order to teach in German universities) at the University of Freiburg. He completed his dissertation, on the fifteenth-century Italian philosopher Marsilio Ficino (a translator and commentator on Plato and founder of the Platonic Academy of Florence) in 1933, but the Nazi rise to power caused him to give up his academic career in Germany.

Kristeller went to Italy in 1934, and taught in Florence for a year as a lecturer in German at the Istituto Superiore di Magistero. With the help of the Italian philosopher Giovanni Gentile, he secured lectureships in German at Pisa's Scuola Normale Superiore and at the University of Pisa, positions he held from 1935 to 1938. His research during this period shaped his subsequent career and included Italian manuscript research on Ficino that resulted in a two-volume work, *Supplementum Ficinianum: Marsilii Ficini Philosophi Platonici Opuscula Inedita and Dispersa,* which the Scuola Normale published in 1937. He completed *Philosophy of Marsilio Ficino* in 1938, though it was not published until 1943. He and Gentile also collaborated on the publication of a series of previously unknown humanistic texts edited by students and graduates of the Scuola Normale—*Nuova Collezione di Testi Umanistici Inediti o Rari*—that is ongoing.

Kristeller lost his positions in Pisa because of the anti-Semitic laws instituted by Benito Mussolini. With the help of the Yale University historian Roland Bainton and others, he came to the United States in February 1939 and taught that spring at Yale in New Haven, Connecticut. In the fall of 1939 he accepted a one-year teaching assignment at Columbia University in New York City, where he remained for the rest of his career. He married Edith Lewinnek, a physician, on 26 June 1940, and in 1945 became a U.S. citizen. The couple had no children.

Kristeller moved very quickly to the front ranks of Renaissance scholars in the United States. Columbia University Press published his book *The Philosophy of Marsilio Ficino* in 1943, and he published a wide range of articles establishing himself as a major interpreter of the significance of Renaissance humanism and as a leading authority on Ficino, Pietro Pomponazzi (an Italian Aristotelian who taught at the University of Padua and the University of Bologna), Renaissance Platonism, and Aristotelianism. Kristeller collaborated with his Columbia colleagues John Herman Randall, Jr., and Ernst Cassirer on what would become a general best-seller, *The Renaissance Philosophy of Man: Selections in Translation* (1948), which has been a classroom staple since its release. His book *Eight Philosophers of the Italian Renaissance* (1964) was still a standard classroom text at the end of the twentieth century. His major scholarly achievement was the seven-volume work *Iter Italicum,* with the first volume published in 1963 and the last in 1996. It comprised a comprehensive list of the uncataloged and incompletely cataloged humanistic manuscripts and documents of the Renaissance in libraries around the world.

Kristeller lectured widely and received numerous awards for his scholarship, including the Serena Medal for Italian Studies from the British Academy (1958), the Premio Internazionale Galileo Galilei (1968), and a MacArthur Fellowship (1984). He was a member of the editorial board of the *Journal of the History of Ideas* and helped launch the *Journal of the History of Philosophy.* He served as president of both the Renaissance Society of America

(1957–1958) and the Medieval Academy of America (1975–1976). Columbia appointed him the Frederick J. E. Woodbridge Professor of Philosophy in 1968. He became professor emeritus in 1973, but continued as a special lecturer until 1976. He died at the age of ninety-four at his home in New York City.

Kristeller's accomplishments as a scholar and teacher were extraordinary in their wealth and reach, and his erudition and mastery of ancient texts secured his place as one of the world's foremost authorities on Renaissance thought and literature.

★

Kristeller's major works, as well as two autobiographical pieces describing his education and formation as a scholar, are housed at Columbia University's Butler Library. Kristeller spoke about his life's work in "A Life of Learning," an address he gave to the American Council of Learned Societies at its 1990 Charles Homer Haskins Lecture and which is published in Douglas Greenberg, Stanley N. Katz, and Candace Frede, eds., *The Life of Learning* (1994). Edward P. Mahoney, ed., *Philosophy and Humanism: Renaissance Essays in Honor of Paul Oskar Kristeller* (1976), includes an introductory essay by Mahoney that details Kristeller's development and achievements as a scholar. Obituaries are in the *Journal of the History of Ideas* 60, no. 4 (1999); *Renaissance News and Notes* 11, no. 2 (fall 1999); and the *New York Times* (10 June 1999).

ROBERT B. CAREY

KUBRICK, Stanley (*b.* 26 July 1928 in New York City; *d.* 7 March 1999 in Hertfordshire, England), director known for exercising total artistic control on films that reveal his obsessive attention to cinematic detail, meticulous and laborious production methods, and misanthropic worldview.

Kubrick was raised in the Bronx by his father, Jacob Leonard ("Jacques") Kubrick, a physician who taught his son chess and gave him his first camera, and his mother, Gertrude Perveler, a homemaker. After several moves in the Bronx, the family, which included a younger daughter, settled in a private home in a middle-class neighborhood, where Kubrick attended William Howard Taft High School. He graduated in 1945 as an academically below-average student.

As a high school senior Kubrick contributed photographs to *Look* and became the youngest photojournalist on the magazine's staff. He married his high school sweetheart, Toba Etta Metz, on 29 May 1948. In 1950, with no formal filmmaking training, he directed, edited, and photographed an independently produced short film, *Day of the Fight,* a documentary about the middleweight prizefighter Walter Cartier. The film, based on Kubrick's photojournalistic essay on the boxer in *Look,* was sold to RKO-Pathé and released in 1951. In that year, Kubrick made a second short also released by RKO, *Flying Padre,* about a priest who flies a plane across his New Mexico parish to serve his congregation.

Kubrick directed *The Seafarers,* an industrial commission from the Seafarers International Union, in 1953. Unlike many of his New York City contemporaries, who trained in the theater or in live television, Kubrick was self-taught, learning his craft through hands-on experience and quick technical lessons from equipment-rental salesmen in New York's Film Center building. Kubrick's first feature, *Fear and Desire* (1953), financed by an uncle, was a black-and-white, independently produced film about an unnamed war and its devastating psychological and moral effects on the men fighting it. Although clearly an amateur experiment by a young filmmaker, *Fear and Desire* showed early evidence of Kubrick's existential philosophy and misanthropic vision in its narrative, characters, and cinematic depiction of the surreal atmosphere of war.

Kubrick and Metz divorced in the early 1950s, and on 15 January 1955 he married Ruth Sobotka, a dancer with the New York City Ballet. She appeared in his second independent feature, *Killer's Kiss* (1955), a film noir about a down-and-out boxer whose struggle for self-identity and pursuit of a mysterious young woman lead him into the netherworld of crime. In the mid-1950s Kubrick and James B. Harris, an aspiring producer, formed Harris–Kubrick Pictures. Their first production, often considered the first true Kubrick film, was *The Killing* (1956), based on the Lionel White novel *Clean Break* (1955). Kubrick wrote the screenplay with the crime novelist Jim Thompson, whose ear for underworld dialogue and knowledge of the criminal mind gave the film authenticity. The book's time-shifting narrative allowed Kubrick his first major experiment with story structure, and his treatment influenced a future generation of filmmakers.

The success of *The Killing* brought Harris and Kubrick to the attention of Metro-Goldwyn-Mayer (MGM), which gave them the choice of any literary film project owned by the studio. Their selection, the antiwar novel *Paths of Glory* (1935) by Humphrey Cobb, was rejected by MGM for being too downbeat. They developed the project anyway, teaming with Kirk Douglas to produce *Paths of Glory* (1957), about three soldiers who were executed as a result of a maniacal general's ill-fated mission. The film was shot on location in Germany and Kubrick was exacting in his creation of a realistic World War I battlefield, where he dollied the camera in relentless tracking shots to capture Douglas asking his beaten-down soldiers to take on a hopeless mission.

Kubrick's marriage to Sobotka ended in 1957, and in 1958 he married Christiane Susanne Harlan, an actress and

Stanley Kubrick. ARCHIVE PHOTOS, INC.

painter. Harlan appeared in the emotional conclusion to *Paths of Glory* as a young German woman singing to the battle-weary French troops. Harlan had a daughter from a previous marriage, and she and Kubrick had two daughters together.

Kubrick's next project was the film epic *Spartacus* (1960), which Kirk Douglas enlisted him to direct after the original director, Anthony Mann, was fired. Kubrick was received with indifference and then hostility by the seasoned Hollywood crew, who complained about his systematic work process, excessive camera angles, and demands for numerous takes. Kubrick brought intelligence to the gladiator genre but vowed that he would never again work in Hollywood or as a hired hand. Subsequently, although his films were released by major Hollywood studios, he demanded having artistic and fiscal control over all of his films.

Kubrick and Harris worked together again in 1960 on an adaptation of the controversial Vladimir Nabokov novel *Lolita* (1955), about an older man's obsession with a young girl. For budgetary reasons, production of the film began in England, where Kubrick found the British crews civilized and competent. The screenplay was written by Nabokov but heavily doctored by Kubrick. Nabokov was, however, given full credit in the hope that his name would serve as a buffer in negotiating with the strict British and American production codes and the Roman Catholic Church's Legion of Decency. The result was a film filled with dark humor and sexual innuendos and references that, at the time, pushed the limits of acceptable adult content. Released in 1962, *Lolita* marked the amicable end of the collaboration between Harris, who wanted to direct, and Kubrick, who wished to exert even more control over his work by producing as well as directing.

Kubrick chose nuclear annihilation for the subject of his next film, adapting the 1958 dramatic novel *Red Alert* by Peter George. After extensive research for the project, he decided to make it a comedy. *Dr. Strangelove; or, How I Learned to Stop Worrying and Love the Bomb* (1964) embraced the innovative genius of the actor Peter Sellers, who played three roles, and the writer Terry Southern, who satirized the unthinkable notion that the United States and Russia could destroy the world with nuclear weapons. A benchmark in black comedy, the film brought Kubrick international acclaim as a director and producer, earning Academy Award nominations for best picture and best director.

In 1964 Kubrick asked the science fiction writer Arthur C. Clarke whether he would be interested in working on "a really good sci-fi movie." The result was the landmark *2001: A Space Odyssey* (1968). In production for four years, the film introduced a new special-effects technology and challenged the traditional three-act screenplay structure with a nonnarrative meditation on space, evolution, God, myth, and human purpose. Using little dialogue, Kubrick created a cinematic experience with images and sound that is arguably one of the most influential films ever made.

Kubrick moved his family to England in the late 1960s and spent the rest of his life working from his country estate in Hertfordshire, which was fully equipped with offices, production gear, and editing rooms and was within driving distance of several London soundstages. His 1971 adaptation of the Anthony Burgess novel *A Clockwork Orange* (1962) set off a firestorm with its depiction of rape, sex, and violence in a near future that predicted the punk movement and a nihilistic society. The film initially received an X rating, and when it was blamed for provoking copycat crimes in England, Kubrick pulled it from distribution in the United Kingdom. The director's ban on the showing of *A Clockwork Orange* in Britain lasted almost thirty years and finally was lifted after his death.

Kubrick's next film, based on William Makepeace Thackeray's *The Memoirs of Barry Lyndon, Esq.* (1844), was developed under a high level of secrecy. Because the property was in the public domain, Kubrick worried about other filmmakers using the story before his film was completed. He meticulously researched the period of the story and had a special high-speed lens mounted on his Panavision camera so that he could film scenes solely by candlelight. Embraced by Europe but largely ignored by American audiences, *Barry Lyndon* (1975) captured Thackeray's world in exacting detail and is often cited as one of the most beautifully rendered period films ever made.

The objective of Kubrick's next effort, released in 1980, was to make the scariest film ever attempted. After employing his legendary assiduous working method by examining the entire horror-genre library, he found a blueprint in Stephen King's *The Shining* (1977). He transformed the story of a hotel and a writer with troubled histories into an Oedipal drama about madness and reincarnation, engaging the actor Jack Nicholson to play the lead role. He built the Overlook Hotel, the story's setting, on a soundstage and explored time and space with a hypnotic use of the newly invented Steadicam, which allowed the camera to float, hover, and weave through the haunted rooms, corridors, and topiary garden.

Kubrick's obsession with humankind and war led him to *Full Metal Jacket* (1987), a disjointed, two-part film about young marines transformed into killing machines and confronted with godless immorality in the Vietnam War. Kubrick adapted the screenplay from Gustav Hasford's novel *The Short-Timers* (1979), which took place in the destroyed southern Vietnamese city of Hue, re-created by Kubrick on location in England. The contrast between the cartoon-like language, archetypical characters, and realistic battle environment created a disturbing portrait of America's military involvement in an unwinnable war.

Following *2001: A Space Odyssey,* the intervals between Kubrick's films had become longer, and he used the time to contemplate and research new ideas until he reached what he called "an obsessional state" that launched him into production. After *Full Metal Jacket,* Kubrick did not release another film until 1999. He started and then abandoned *Aryan Papers,* an adaptation of the Louis Begley novel *Wartime Lies* (1991), the harrowing story of a young boy and his aunt during the Nazi Holocaust, subject matter that would have allowed Kubrick to examine his Jewish roots. It was speculated that he stopped the project because of the international success of the director Steven Spielberg's *Schindler's List* (1993). Kubrick next developed "A.I.," a project that was inspired by a short story by the science fiction writer Brian Aldiss, about a boy robot. After exhaustive research and discussions with special-effects experts spanning some ten years, Kubrick concluded that the necessary technology to accomplish his vision was not yet available. Spielberg eventually took on the project as director of *A.I.: Artificial Intelligence,* released in 2001.

In the late 1990s Warner Brothers announced the production of Kubrick's *Eyes Wide Shut,* a tale of sexual obsession and jealousy starring the actors Tom Cruise and

Nicole Kidman. Kubrick kept this project, which was eventually revealed to be an adaptation of Arthur Schnitzler's *Traumnovelle* (1926), shrouded in secrecy until its release. *Eyes Wide Shut* (1999) updated Schnitzler's story, set in Vienna, to contemporary New York City. In English the book was known as *Rapture: A Dream Novel* or *Dream Story,* and Kubrick likened the act of watching a film to a dream state. *Eyes Wide Shut* evoked a vivid sense of the nocturnal subconscious and was the first film in which Kubrick examined the emotional state of a marital relationship. In 1997 Kubrick was honored by the Directors Guild of America, which presented him with the D. W. Griffith Award for lifetime achievement.

Kubrick died suddenly in his sleep on 7 March 1999 of natural causes at age seventy. He is buried at Childwickbury Manor, his estate in Hertfordshire, northwest of London. His legacy as a twentieth-century film director issues from his artistic integrity, consistent, thematic worldview, distinctive visual style, and a body of work that is diverse in both subject matter and narrative approach. Kubrick's dedication to the art of filmmaking has inspired moviemakers worldwide to create films that represent the voice and vision of the director, expressed through nontraditional narrative techniques and the inventive use of the cinematic crafts.

★

Kubrick's papers are in the possession of his family in England. Some materials concerning his films released by Warner Brothers are in the Warner Brothers Collection at the University of Southern California, Los Angeles. There are two full-scale biographies of Kubrick: Vincent LoBrutto, *Stanley Kubrick: A Biography* (1997), and John Baxter, *Stanley Kubrick: A Biography* (1997). Alexander Walker, Sybil Taylor, and Ulrich Ruchti, *Stanley Kubrick, Director: A Visual Analysis,* rev. ed. (1999); Norman Kagan, *The Cinema of Stanley Kubrick,* 3d ed. (2000); Michel Ciment, *Kubrick,* trans. Gilbert Adair (1983); Thomas Allen Nelson, *Kubrick: Inside a Film Artist's Maze,* rev. ed. (2000); and Mario Falsetto, *Stanley Kubrick: A Narrative and Stylistic Analysis* (1994), contain analytical and critical insights into Kubrick's films. Gene D. Phillips, the author of the excellent *Stanley Kubrick: A Film Odyssey* (1975), is also the editor of *Stanley Kubrick Interviews* (2001). Obituaries are in the *New York Times* and *Hollywood Reporter* (both 8 Mar. 1999).

VINCENT LoBRUTTO

KURALT, Charles Bishop (*b.* 10 September 1934 in Wilmington, North Carolina; *d.* 4 July 1997 in New York City), journalist best known for his "On the Road" reports that chronicled the lives of ordinary Americans in out-of-the-way places.

Kuralt was the eldest of three children of Wallace Hamilton Kuralt, a social worker, and Ina Bishop, a teacher and homemaker. After Kuralt's birth he and his parents lived on the tobacco farm of his maternal grandparents, but his father's career led the family on a number of moves throughout the South. In 1945 Wallace Kuralt was appointed Welfare Superintendent of Mecklenburg County, North Carolina, and the family settled in Charlotte.

Kuralt's interest in journalism surfaced early. He was only seven years old when he wrote, mimeographed, and sold the *Garden Gazette,* which carried news about his neighborhood, for two cents per copy. At age twelve Kuralt placed second in the annual sportswriting contest sponsored by the *Charlotte News.* In 1946 he entered Alexander Graham Junior High School, where he began formally studying journalism. He wrote for the school newspaper, the *Broadcaster,* and the following year introduced a column called "Kaleidoscope." Meanwhile, he drew inspiration and a love for language from the work of the great radio dramatist Norman Corwin. "They had a book of Corwin's plays in the school library in North Carolina," Kuralt once reflected. "I read it at thirteen and knew what I wanted to do with my life."

In the spring of 1947 Kuralt again entered the "My Favorite Hornet" sportswriting contest of the local paper and again placed second. But this time his prize included travel with the Charlotte Hornets, a minor league baseball team. Kuralt covered six games for the *Charlotte News.* A year later he participated in "I Speak for Democracy," a contest sponsored by the National Association of Broadcasters. Kuralt was among the four national winners and was invited to visit the White House, where he and his fellow winners met President Harry S. Truman. Edward R. Murrow read an excerpt of Kuralt's speech on a CBS Radio show.

Kuralt entered Central High School in 1948. He worked afternoons at a local radio station and was said to be the youngest radio announcer in the country. The rich, deep voice of Kuralt's adulthood was already in evidence. His on-air duties included color commentary for the Hornets' home games and occasional play-by-play duty. He also covered football for the Charlotte Clippers. In 1949 he won a scholarship to attend a summer writing program for high school students at Northwestern University in Evanston, Illinois. He considered attending college in Evanston but felt he belonged in North Carolina. Shortly before his high school graduation in 1951, Kuralt visited the University of North Carolina at Chapel Hill to hear Murrow speak. It was the beginning of a lifelong association with the institution.

At age sixteen Kuralt was voted most likely to succeed by his fellow Central High graduates. He entered the University of North Carolina at Chapel Hill in 1951 and

Charles Kuralt, 1988. TIM RUE/ASSOCIATED PRESS AP

worked at WUNC, the student radio station. He also became a staff writer for the *Daily Tar Heel* and eventually the editor. In 1953 he was hired at radio station WBT in Charlotte. Kuralt married his high school girlfriend, Sory Guthery, in August 1954, left college the next spring without completing graduation requirements, and took a job as a general assignment reporter for the *Charlotte News.*

Kuralt's exceptional writing eventually landed him at CBS News. He wrote a piece in 1956 about Charlotte's progress in the previous decade that was awarded the top prize for feature writing in 1957 by the North Carolina Press Association. Then he won the prestigious Ernie Pyle Award for the "People" columns he wrote for the *Charlotte News.* CBS news director John Day read about the Ernie Pyle Award and invited Kuralt to join the radio network in March 1957. Kuralt moved his family to Brooklyn. Later that year, Kuralt was promoted to writer for the television broadcast *CBS Evening News,* anchored by Douglas Edwards.

In March 1959, when he was only twenty-four years old, Kuralt became the youngest news correspondent in the history of CBS, and in 1960 he was chosen over Walter Cronkite to host the new public affairs series *Eyewitness to History.* Within four months, though, Cronkite replaced Kuralt, who returned to general assignment reporting. The amount of travel involved in his work put a strain on Kuralt's marriage. In 1960 he and Sory divorced, and she and their two daughters moved back to Charlotte.

Kuralt became chief of the CBS Latin American bureau, based in Brazil, in 1961. On 1 June 1962 he married Suzanna "Petie" Folsom Baird, an assistant to Douglas Edwards. After a brief stint as chief West Coast correspondent in 1963, he was transferred to New York City the next year to cover the Northeast. Changes in graduation requirements at the University of North Carolina allowed Kuralt to receive his B.A. degree in history in 1965. As a reporter of breaking stories, Kuralt covered conflicts in Africa, Europe, and Southeast Asia, including four tours of duty in Vietnam. But he also contributed to the documentary series *CBS Reports* and anchored several public affairs specials. In 1967 Kuralt was assigned to accompany a group of amateur explorers on an attempt to drive snowmobiles to the North Pole, an experience that inspired his first book, *To the Top of the World* (1968).

Weary from the grind of hard news, Kuralt convinced CBS executives to give him a three-month trial on a human-interest feature he called "On the Road." His first piece appeared as a closing segment on the *CBS Evening News* in October 1967. During the next twenty-five years Kuralt, along with his cameraman Izzy Bleckman and soundman Larry Gianneschi, logged more than one million miles in a motor home and produced some 500 "On the Road" features. Ideas for stories often came from viewers, and sometimes local chambers of commerce would recommend unusual citizens or unsung heroes in their communities. Kuralt kept a state-by-state clipping file and enjoyed total freedom in his search for the spirit of America. His avuncular appearance, chubby and bald, did not fit the traditional notion of a dashing, prime-time news anchorman. But Kuralt's looks were perfect for his endearing role as a roving chronicler of Americana.

Throughout the 1970s Kuralt served as a cohost and contributor to three short-lived series, *CBS News Adventure, Magazine,* and *Who's Who.* All the while, his journey on the back roads yielded periodic features on *CBS Evening News* and several prime-time specials. In 1979 Kuralt accepted the assignment as host of the new *CBS News Sunday Morning* on the condition that he could continue his "On the Road" reporting. The low-key tone and leisurely pace of the ninety-minute program suited its Sunday morning time slot. Each broadcast provided news headlines along with an in-depth cover story and special reports on music, education, law, the environment, and the arts. That same year Kuralt published his second book, *Dateline America.*

In October 1980 Kuralt suspended "On the Road" to become anchor for a daily program, *Morning with Charles Kuralt.* But the style that worked so well on Sunday mornings failed to attract weekday viewers. Eighteen months later Kuralt returned to the road. He received the George Polk Memorial Award for national television reporting in 1981. In July 1983 *Newsweek* magazine described Kuralt as "our beloved visiting uncle" and "de Toqueville in a motor home." *The American Parade,* another short-lived series that debuted in 1984, was structured around Kuralt's "On the Road" reports. Kuralt was named "Broadcaster of the Year" by the International Radio and Television Society in 1985. He published both *Southerners: Portrait of a People* and *North Carolina Is My Home* in 1986 and his autobiography, *A Life on the Road,* in 1990. Kuralt continued his *Sunday Morning* assignment into the 1990s.

As American journalism adopted tabloid values, Kuralt became a tough critic of his profession. "I am ashamed so many [anchorpersons] haven't any basis on which to make a news judgment, can't edit, can't write, and can't cover a story," he told *TV Guide* in 1994. Kuralt's retirement from CBS came with his last *Sunday Morning* broadcast on 3 April 1994. During his career Kuralt won a dozen Emmys and three George Foster Peabody awards.

Kuralt was hospitalized with chest pains in September 1995. The following month he underwent heart-bypass surgery but refused to give up smoking. "Smoking brings great pleasure to me," he said. "I don't want to concentrate on living to be a hundred, spending an hour a day on the treadmill and another hour eating a salt-free dinner. It's outside my philosophy." That same year Kuralt purchased radio station WELY in Ely, Minnesota, and the book *Charles Kuralt's America* was published. His unexpected death of complications from lupus on 4 July 1997 generated an outpouring of tributes memorializing Kuralt as a national treasure. He is buried in a 200-year-old cemetery on the campus of his alma mater.

After his death, revelations surfaced regarding Kuralt's private life when Patricia Shannon successfully sued his estate to claim ownership of a ninety-acre fishing retreat along the Big Hole River in Montana, where the two had spent time together. With surprise and fascination, the public learned that Kuralt and Shannon, unbeknownst to Suzanna Kuralt, had shared a close, personal relationship for twenty-nine years. He had provided financial support to Shannon and her children and essentially assumed the role of husband and father to his secret family. This was a distressing circumstance to many who believed that Kuralt's most valuable contribution was to provide gentle reminders to his viewers about the goodness and honesty at the heart of the American character. Others, though, acknowledged that his life was far more complex than his public image, and his body of work remains his legacy.

★

The Charles Kuralt Collection at the University of North Carolina at Chapel Hill contains more than 60,000 items, including scripts, letters, tapes, photographs, oral histories, and mementos of Kuralt's life and career. Autobiographical works by Kuralt include *North Carolina Is My Home* (1986) and *A Life on the Road* (1990). Magazine articles that deal with Kuralt include "Travels with Charlie and Bill," *Newsweek* (4 July 1983); "CBS Sunday Morning: Free To Be Smart," *Channels* (Oct. 1986); "Long Time on Less-Traveled Roads," *New York Times* (4 May 1994); and "Charles Kuralt Hits the Road," *TV Guide* (2 Apr. 1994). A detailed obituary, "Charles Kuralt, CBS' Poet of Small-Town America, Dies at 62," was posted on CNN's website. An obituary is in the *New York Times* (5 July 1997). News reports about the estate litigation were legion during the trial, which began in 2000.

Mary Ann Watson

L

LANCASTER, Kelvin John (*b.* 10 December 1924 in Sydney, Australia; *d.* 23 July 1999 in New York City), the John Bates Clark Professor of Economics at Columbia University and one of the leading economic theorists of the second half of the twentieth century.

Lancaster was the eldest child of John Kelvin ("Jack") Lancaster, an electrical engineer, and Margaret Gray, a homemaker. His parents divorced, and Lancaster lived with his mother and two sisters in Sydney, Australia, where he attended Sydney Boys' High School. He volunteered for the Royal Australian Air Force in 1943 and was training in Canada as a bombardier when World War II ended.

He went on to a brilliant career at Sydney University, receiving a B.Sc. degree in mathematics and geology in 1948 and a B.A. degree in English literature in 1949, graduating with first class honors and the University Medal award. He also obtained an M.A. degree in English literature in 1953. He was offered a teaching position in the English department at the university but decided instead to join an organization called Research Services of Australia. He worked in statistics and economics, both self-taught, on government projects. With his abstract cast of mind, the practical problems he dealt with on the job stimulated an interest in economic theory that led him to take the economics exam at the University of London in 1953. He obtained a First, which was very unusual for an external candidate, and was appointed assistant lecturer and later reader at the London School of Economics (LSE). He earned his Ph.D. in economics from the University of London in 1958.

The London School in the 1950s was enjoying one of its best periods, under the leadership of Lord Robbins. His legendary seminar was where the bright young faculty displayed their talents and Lancaster immediately established himself as the rising star of a very distinguished company. A rapid flow of incisive papers in the house journal *Economica,* on a wide variety of topics, bear witness to these very productive early years of his career. The paper that won him almost instant world renown in academic circles, however, was the "The General Theory of the Second Best" in the *Review of Economic Studies* (1956), written jointly with the Canadian economist Richard G. Lipsey, also on the LSE faculty at that time. Their paper addressed the work of the Italian economist Vilfredo Pareto (1848–1923), one of the founders of modern welfare economics.

Lancaster's first marriage, to Lorraine Cross, an anthropologist, ended in divorce, and he moved to the United States in 1961 with their young son and became a naturalized citizen. He was appointed professor of political economy at Johns Hopkins University in Baltimore, a position he held from 1962 to 1966. He married Deborah Grunfeld, an attorney and the widow of a young Israeli economist, Yehuda Grunfeld, on 10 June 1963. The family, including Grunfeld's son, left Baltimore for New York City in 1966, when Lancaster became professor of economics at Columbia University.

At Columbia he focused his research on the theory of consumer behavior and the blend of monopolistic and competitive forces in the structure of markets. A key innovation that he introduced was to view consumers as deriving satisfaction from the characteristics that goods embody rather than directly from the goods themselves. Lancaster's deceptively simple idea had far-reaching implications in the study of markets, industrial organization, international trade, and the measurement of product quality and consumer satisfaction.

Despite his prolific research, Lancaster never neglected administrative and teaching responsibilities. He was twice chair of the economics department (1970–1973) and served as director of graduate studies and as a member of the university senate. An undergraduate seminar on economics and philosophy that he taught with the philosopher Sidney Morgenbesser was a popular course that he particularly enjoyed. He was named the John Bates Clark Professor of Economics at Columbia in 1978 by the university. He was also a Fellow of the Econometric Society, a Distinguished Fellow of the American Economic Association, and a member of the American Academy of Arts and Sciences. He died of cancer at his home in New York City on 23 July 1999.

★

Lancaster's ideas about consumer marketing are developed in *Consumer Demand: A New Approach* (1971) and *Variety, Equity and Efficiency* (1979); the latter contains the fullest statement of his views on this and related questions. *Modern Consumer Theory* (1991) and *Trade, Markets and Welfare* (1996) are selections of his major published articles. An obituary is in the *New York Times* (28 July 1998).

RONALD E. FINDLAY

LANE, Burton (*b.* 2 February 1912 in New York City; *d.* 5 January 1997 in New York City), prolific composer for stage and screen who collaborated with many renowned lyricists.

Lane was born as Burton Levy, the younger of two sons of Lazarus Levy, a real estate agent, and Frances Fink, an amateur pianist. A child prodigy, Lane began studying piano at age eleven and played viola and cello in the music program at the High School of Commerce in Manhattan. While at Commerce, Lane composed two marches that were published by the Al Piantidosi Music Company. At the age of fourteen, Lane's writing impressed the music director Harold Stern, who arranged for him to audition for the music producer J. J. Schubert. Despite his young age, Lane was commissioned by Schubert to compose music for the upcoming edition of *Greenwich Village Follies* (1926). Although this show never made it to the theater, it was the beginning of what was to become an illustrious career.

Lane soon dropped out of high school to become a staff composer for J. H. Remick. During this time, he received help and encouragement from many of Tin Pan Alley's top composers, including George Gershwin. Lane's work was first heard onstage in *Artists and Models* (1930). In October of the same year, he and the lyricist Samuel Lerner had two songs accepted for the Broadway production of *Three's a Crowd*. In 1931 Lane began working with Harold Adamson as his lyricist, and had songs performed in *The Third Little Show*, *Earl Carroll's Vanities*, and *Singin' the Blues*. Adamson and Lane earned their first hit song with Gertrude Niesen's recording of "Tony's Wife," used in the MGM movie *Turn Back the Clock* (1933).

In 1933 Lane went to Hollywood under a contract with Irving Berlin, and worked there with a variety of lyricists including Adamson and Frank Loesser. He and Adamson wrote songs for the MGM musical *Dancing Lady*, which starred the young Joan Crawford. Released in 1934, this movie marked the debut of Fred Astaire. RKO's *Strictly Dynamite* was also released that year and featured "Swing It Sister," which became a huge hit for the Mills Brothers. Lane and Adamson's songs were used in at least seven films by four different studios that year. It was also in 1934 that Lane saw eleven-year-old Judy Garland perform at the Paramount. He arranged for her to audition for MGM and worked with her a few years later in the movie *Babes on Broadway* (1941). After collaborating in songs for five releases, Adamson and Lane dissolved their partnership in 1935.

On 28 June 1935 Lane married Marian Seaman, with whom he had a daughter. Toward the end of 1936, he signed a contract with Paramount and paired with the lyricist Ralph Freed. Lane remained with Paramount until 1941. *College Holiday* was their only film in 1936, but in the following year Lane and Freed had at least one song used in ten movies. Their songs from the Paramount years included "Swing High, Swing Low" and "(I Like New York in June) How About You." The latter, first sung by Garland and Mickey Rooney in *Babes on Broadway*, brought the songwriting team an Oscar nomination.

By 1940 Lane had become one of the leading songwriters in Hollywood and decided to return to Broadway. The 1940s saw his career continue to flourish with the Broadway scores for *Hold On to Your Hats*, with lyrics by E. Y. "Yip" Harburg, and *Laffing Room Only*, written for the vaudeville team of Olsen and Johnson. In 1947 Lane teamed up with Harburg again on *Finian's Rainbow*, for the biggest success of his career.

Finian's Rainbow combined satire with fantasy to deal with many contemporary U.S. social problems, including labor exploitation, racial prejudice, the right wing, and increasing greed. The show produced such classic songs as "Look to the Rainbow," "How Are Things in Glocca

Morra?" and "Old Devil Moon." *Finian's Rainbow* won the Donaldson Award as best musical of the season and ran for 725 performances. It would be eighteen years before Lane was on Broadway again.

In addition to writing for Broadway shows during the 1940s, Lane wrote songs for such movies as *Panama Hattie* (1942), *Ship Ahoy* (1942), *Du Barry Was a Lady* (1943), *Thousands Cheer* (1943), and *Hollywood Canteen* (1944). The 1950s saw the movie musical's popularity begin to dwindle. Despite this, *Royal Wedding* (1951), starring Astaire and Jane Powell, gave Lane his second Oscar nomination for "Too Late Now." Also in the movie was another Lerner-Lane composition with the unusually long title of "How Could You Believe Me When I Said I Love You When You Know I've Been a Liar All My Life?" The remainder of the decade saw Lane's work in such motion pictures as *Give a Girl a Break* (1953), starring Debbie Reynolds, *Jupiter's Darling* (1955), and *I Have a Dream* (1955). In 1958 Lane worked on the television special "Junior Miss," starring David Wayne and Don Ameche.

Lane's next Broadway score had an unusual beginning. After the death of Oscar Hammerstein, Richard Rodgers contacted Alan Jay Lerner to work on a play about a girl who possessed extrasensory perception. Creative differences over the play's direction resulted in Rodgers leaving the project. Now in complete control, Lerner brought in Lane as the composer. With the new title *On a Clear Day You Can See Forever,* the play opened at the Mark Hellinger Theater on 17 October 1965. A recording of the title song became a hit for Robert Goulet.

In 1961 Lane divorced Marian, and on 5 March of the same year he married Lynn Baroff Kaye, who had three daughters from a previous marriage. In 1968 *Finian's Rainbow* was made into a movie starring Astaire, and *On a Clear Day You Can See Forever* was filmed in 1970, with Barbra Streisand and Yves Montand. In 1979 Lane and Lerner teamed up again for *Carmelina*. Although the show included quality songs like "One More Walk Around the Garden," "Someone in April," and "I'm a Woman," it was a major flop. *Carmelina* was also Lane's final Broadway endeavor. His last complete score was *Heidi's Song,* written with Sammy Cahn in 1982.

Although he never achieved the public fame of some of his musical colleagues, Lane was held in high esteem in the world of theater and film music. From 1957 to 1966 he served as president of the American Guild of Authors and Composers, and he fought for greater copyright protection for songwriters. In 1966 Lane was presented with the Sigmund Romberg Award for "extraordinary achievements on behalf of composers and lyricists." He was elected into the Songwriters Hall of Fame in 1971. He was also a board member of the American Society of Composers, Authors, and Publishers from 1985 to 1996. At the age of eighty,

Lane was elected into the U.S. Theatre Hall of Fame. Lane died of a stroke at age eighty-four, in Manhattan.

Although not as well known as many of his contemporaries, Lane was one of the leading composers of twentieth-century American popular music. Working with the greatest lyricists of the time, many of Lane's songs have become standards. It was the landmark Broadway musical *Finian's Rainbow,* however, that proved to be Lane's greatest legacy. The play was one of the first to incorporate many of the social problems of the time, including race relations, into the plot. *Finian's Rainbow* had a lasting impact on the next generation of playwrights, allowing social commentary and more serious plots to become more acceptable.

★

There is no formal biography of Lane. Articles on Lane appear in David Ewen, *American Songwriters* (1987); Colin Larkin, ed., *The Encyclopedia of Popular Music* (1995); Stanley Sade, ed., *New Grove's Dictionary of Music and Musicians* (2001); and Nicolas Slonimsky, *Baker's Biographical Dictionary of Musicians* (2001). Obituaries are in the *New York Times* and *Washington Post* (both 7 Jan. 1997).

ROBERT PISPECKY

LAUGHLIN, James (*b.* 30 October 1914 in Pittsburgh, Pennsylvania; *d.* 12 November 1997 in Norfolk, Connecticut), publisher and founder of the New Directions publishing house, poet, and ski resort entrepreneur.

Laughlin was the youngest of two children born to H. Hughart Laughlin, of the Jones and Laughlin Steel Company of Pittsburgh, and Marjory Rea, also from a prominent Pittsburgh steel family. In 1927 Laughlin and his brother were sent to Le Rosey school on Lake Geneva in Switzerland, where the boys recited French poetry and in the afternoons were taken skiing in the mountains. Laughlin's schooling continued the next year at Eaglebrook in Massachusetts and, from 1929 to 1932, at Choate School in Wallingford, Connecticut. There he met the first of his important mentors, the classicist Dudley Fitts, who had his students read not only Catullus but also T. S. Eliot and Ezra Pound. Hating grimy Pittsburgh, Laughlin was practically adopted by his childless aunt, Leila Laughlin Carlisle, in Norfolk, Connecticut.

At Choate, Laughlin became editor of the yearbook and graduated at the top of his class. He entered Harvard University in September 1932 after being convinced by Fitts to attend. The following year, Laughlin sailed for Europe and met Gertrude Stein and, also encouraged by Fitts, visited Pound in Rapallo, Italy. Laughlin returned to Harvard in the fall, but in February 1934 he took a leave of absence to spend much of the year at the "Ezuversity," as Pound called his rambling tutorials. Pound pronounced Laughlin's poetry "hopeless" and advised him to "do something useful." Almost no one was bringing out avant-garde poetry in America, so Pound decided that Laughlin should become a publisher. Pound would tell his friends to send manuscripts.

In 1936 Laughlin launched his publishing company, New Directions, at Harvard. The first two volumes released by the company were the surrealist *Pianos of Sympathy* by Montagu O'Reilly, and the first *New Directions in Prose and Poetry* anthology, which included work by Elizabeth Bishop, Kay Boyle, Jean Cocteau, e. e. cummings, Henry Miller, Marianne Moore, Pound, Stein, Wallace Stevens, and William Carlos Williams. In all, fifty-five of these annuals would appear. The New Directions list of book titles would come to include work by hundreds of modernist and experimental writers, including Kenneth Rexroth, Dylan Thomas, Djuna Barnes, Delmore Schwartz, Vladimir Nabokov, Kenneth Patchen, Tennessee Williams, Jerome Rothenberg, David Antin, Michael McClure, Gary Snyder, and Thomas Merton. Important non-English writers such as Octavio Paz, Pablo Neruda, Céline, Yukio Mishima, Bei Dao, and Gottfried Benn became readily available to American audiences largely because of New Directions. Laughlin's guiding principles in publishing were simple yet revolutionary. Stein advised him that in choosing work for New Directions he must "hear the bell ring." New Directions would never publish a book simply to make a profit. And because Pound had said that it usually took twenty years for an avant-garde writer to find an audience, Laughlin kept books in print even when current sales did not warrant it. With only his annual stock dividends of $6,000 to keep himself and the company afloat, Laughlin had to operate with low overheads, pay small advances, and advertise hardly at all. It was nearly twenty-five years before New Directions showed a profit. Until then, Laughlin asked Aunt Leila to make up the annual deficits.

Retail booksellers scorned authors they had never heard of, so Laughlin set off cross-country in his Buick to sell to the stores. At six feet, six inches tall and dressed in an Austrian loden jacket, his dark hair waving over a high forehead, Laughlin strode into the bookstores of midwestern towns, consciously using his virile charm on the women who made up most of the book trade staff. When he graduated from Harvard in June 1939 and moved into a converted stable on his aunt's Norfolk estate, Laughlin was publishing about ten books a year.

Laughlin spent the 1940s traveling between Norfolk, Manhattan, and Alta, Utah. In 1941 he negotiated a free lease from the Forest Service on a ski slope in the Wasatch Mountains. Laughlin applied the same strict financial principles to his skiing business as he did to publishing. In 1942 he opened a New Directions office at 67 West Forty-fourth Street in Manhattan (later he moved to 333 Sixth Avenue and finally to Eighty-eighth Avenue), brought his publishing tally to twenty books a year, and married Margeret Keyser, from Salt Lake City on 13 March. The couple had two children and divorced in 1952.

In June 1950 Laughlin hired Robert MacGregor to manage New Directions, freeing himself to head up Intercultural Publications for the Ford Foundation in 1952. Laughlin published sixteen issues of the journal *Perspectives USA* in English, French, German, and Italian, in order to renew cultural contacts weakened by World War II. He spent months on Intercultural business in India, Burma, and Japan, as well as Europe. On 19 May 1956 Laughlin married Ann Clark Resor, and they had two sons, Robert and Henry.

Laughlin was reluctant to get into paperbacks, but in 1957 New Directions reissued Hesse's *Siddhartha* in this format, and the next year published Lawrence Ferlinghetti's *Coney Island of the Mind*. Each went on to sell a million copies. But as Robert grew from a difficult child into a troubled young man, Laughlin suffered from manic depression, an illness that had plagued both his grandfather and father. Despite this, Laughlin managed to lecture on Pound, William Carlos Williams, and other modernists at various universities throughout the 1970s and 1980s. In 1985 Robert committed suicide, and Ann died in 1989. On 5 December 1991 Laughlin married Gertrude Huston, whom he had known for forty years as the designer of many of the characteristic black and white New Directions book covers. Laughlin made careful plans for the continuation of New Directions after his death.

Despite Pound's condemnation of his poetry, Laughlin continued to write, developing what he called his "typewriter metric" in which each succeeding line varies no more than two spaces plus or minus from the length of the first line of the poem. The poet Hayden Carruth, Laughlin's mentor in poetry beginning in the late 1950s, praised his "wit, irony, fantasy, and breadth of allusion." Three small volumes contain most of Laughlin's poetic output from the period while he was creating New Directions, Alta, and Intercultural. But as he aged, Laughlin wrote at increasing speed, producing twenty-five books of poetry between 1978 and 1998.

Laughlin's altruistic service through the Ford Foundation advanced cultural contact between Western nations and Asia, and he set the tone for Alta, considered by many to offer the best skiing in the United States. Through New Directions, Laughlin was a key figure in the history of American literary modernism. His achievement is all the more outstanding when one realizes that Laughlin's judgment alone determined what New Directions would publish. Brendan Gill of the *New Yorker* summed up Laughlin's contribution when he declared him "the greatest publisher America ever had." As a poet, Laughlin is likely to earn a respectable place in the rank of American poets. While he does not have the epic range of Pound or the broad human vision of William Carlos Williams, he writes about remembered romance with tender wistfulness and real passion. Laughlin died from complications following a stroke. He is buried in Norfolk Cemetery.

★

Laughlin's correspondence and the New Directions archives are at the Houghton Library, Harvard. There are also important Laughlin collections at the John Hay Library at Brown University and the Beinecke Library at Yale University. Laughlin never completed a prose autobiography, but his *Random Essays* (1989), *Random Stories* (1990), and "The Emigration," give some information on his life. Much of his poetry is broadly autobiographical. Volumes of Laughlin's correspondence with Thomas Merton, Henry Miller, Ezra Pound, Kenneth Rexroth, Delmore Schwartz, and William Carlos Williams have appeared. Valuable material may be found in Bradford Morrow, ed., "A Festschrift in Honor of James Laughlin," *Conjunctions I* (winter 1981–1982); Laughlin with Richard Zeigfeld, "The Art of Publishing: James Laughlin," *Paris Review* 89, 90 (1983): 155–193, 112–151, respectively; Cynthia Zarin, "Jaz," *New Yorker* (23 Mar. 1992); and Hayden Carruth, *Beside the Shadblow Tree: A Memoir of James Laughlin* (1999). The most complete bibliographies are both by John A. Harrison, *Bibliography of New Directions Books* and *A Selective List of Published Writing, 1935–1998, By and About James Laughlin* and are published on the New Directions website. Obituaries are in the *New York Times* (14 Nov. 1997) and *Nation* (15 Dec. 1997).

IAN S. MacNIVEN

LEE, William Andrew (*b.* 12 November 1900 in Ward Hill, Massachusetts; *d.* 27 December 1998 in Fredericksburg, Virginia), the legendary "Ironman" of the U.S. Marines, whose dedication, courage, combat skills, and endurance were said to exemplify the Marine Corps ideal.

Lee was the oldest of five children of Benjamin Rufus Lee, a shoe-factory operating engineer, and Eda Petterson, a homemaker. He attended public schools in Ward Hill and Haverhill, Massachusetts. An adventurous youth more interested in sports than in academics, Lee left high school after completing his sophomore year in 1917. Sometime after his birthday in November 1917, Lee began trying to persuade his parents to sign for his enlistment in the marines because one had to have parental consent to enlist before the age of eighteen. In May 1918, at age seventeen, he enlisted in the U.S. Marine Corps.

Arriving in France with the 13th Marine Regiment in September 1918, late in World War I, Lee did not see the action he sought. The 5th and 6th Marines had won so much glory at the battle of Belleau Wood in June 1918 that resentful U.S. Army generals resolved never again to assign marine units to combat in Europe. The 13th Marines were held in reserve until the armistice went into effect on 11 November 1918, the day before Lee's eighteenth birthday. Returning to the United States a year later, Lee reenlisted in the marines and was assigned to sea duty aboard the USS *Arkansas.* Tall, lean, and muscular, Lee played fullback on the battleship's football team, pulled oars on a cockboat crew, and excelled as an intramural boxer. He was also a natural marksman, endowed with extraordinary powers of concentration, steady nerves, and superb eyesight. Soft-spoken and modest, Lee was promoted through the enlisted ranks to gunnery sergeant.

Lee was assigned in January 1927 to a battalion of marines that landed at Corinto, Nicaragua, to protect the railroad to Managua during a civil war between the Nicaraguan Conservatives and Liberals. Under U.S. pressure, the leaders of the warring parties agreed to cease fire, disarm, and turn over police power to the marines. However, one Liberal general, Augusto C. Sandino, rejected the peace agreement. In May 1927 Sandino ordered his forces to resist the "Yankees," launching a guerrilla war that would continue until the marines left Nicaragua on 1 January 1933. Lee served throughout the campaign against Sandino, first as a marine sergeant, then from 1930 to 1932 as a lieutenant of the Guardia Nacional, the Nicaraguan constabulary organized, trained, and, until the end of 1932, commanded by marine officers. Three times Lee was awarded the Navy Cross, a decoration second only to the Congressional Medal of Honor as a commendation for heroism in combat. Interrogation of enemy prisoners indicated that Lee was the marine the Sandinistas feared most.

Lee was second in command of the Guardia's "M" company, whose commander, Captain Lewis B. "Chesty" Puller, nicknamed him "Ironman." When Puller was on assignment in the United States for a year beginning August 1931, Lee led the company. Based in Jinotega, "M" company was the nemesis of Pedro "Pedrón" Altamirano, Sandino's ablest commander. The company relentlessly charged up and down hundreds of miles of jungle trails in pursuit of Pedrón, whose column just as determinedly countermarched along parallel trails attempting to ambush "M" company. Neither managed to wipe out the other, but Puller and Lee effectively won because they neutralized Pedrón.

Lee and the Sandinistas engaged in fierce psychological warfare. Sandino publicly advocated the mutilation and beheading of Nicaragua's enemies, and Pedrón was his most accomplished machete wielder, famous for his "vest cut"— beheading followed by the lopping off of both arms at the shoulder. Lee demonstrated his own prowess with knives in more benign ways, though some native "M" company enlisted men were photographed holding severed "bandit" heads.

Returning to the United States in 1933, Lee reverted to his marine rank of gunnery sergeant and was stationed at Quantico, Virginia. There he excelled in rifle and pistol competition and was the star of the marine shooting team led by Colonel Calvin A. Lloyd. He was promoted to warrant-officer rank on 1 May 1935 with the title "Marine Gunner." Lee married Colonel Lloyd's daughter, Helen Winefred Lloyd, on 19 May 1937; they had three daughters.

Lee was transferred from Quantico to China in September 1939 to serve with the 500-man U.S. Marine Legation Guard in Beijing. Although no government claiming sovereignty over China had resided in Beijing since 1928, the United States and Britain continued to exercise their rights under the Boxer Protocol of 1901 to maintain legations in the city and to station troops there to protect them. Japan, a signatory to the Boxer Protocol, already occupied Beijing and most of northern China when Lee arrived. He was assigned to the Horse Marines, a detachment of fifty marines mounted on Mongolian ponies and armed with pistols and sabers. The unit was disbanded when plans were made for the evacuation of the U.S. Legation Guard on the eve of war between the United States and Japan.

On the day of the Pearl Harbor attack (8 December 1941), Lee was in China with a detachment of twenty marines at the port of Qinhuangdao, preparing for the embarkation of U.S. personnel and equipment. Surrounded by hundreds of Japanese soldiers, Lee and the marines removed some machine guns from packing crates and prepared for action. Before any shots were fired they received orders not to resist, as the Legation Guard commander in Beijing believed the marines had diplomatic immunity and were entitled to repatriation. Lee and the rest of the Legation Guard accepted Japanese custody, expecting to return soon to the United States. At first the men were treated well, but in January 1942 the Japanese declared them prisoners of war. The marines were herded onto railroad boxcars and taken to Wusong, near Shanghai.

At Wusong, the Japanese soldiers first kicked out Lee's teeth. Then they shipped him to a prison camp at a coal mine near Sapporo, Japan, where they burned his ears with cigarettes and threatened to behead him. Lee and his fellow prisoners were starved, beaten, tortured, and subjected to unspeakable cruelties until one day in August 1945, when their tormentors vanished.

Lee headed home to his wife and children, arriving penniless in Washington, D.C. When the Marine Corps travel office there denied his request for transportation to Quantico, the Ironman threw his seabag over his shoulder and walked thirty miles down the railroad tracks to his home.

Lee was stationed at Quantico as a commissioned officer for the rest of his career. In 1946 he was promoted to lieu-

tenant colonel and appointed commander of the Rifle Range Detachment. His wife died in 1949. Lee retired with the rank of colonel in 1950 and married Anne Bradbury Lee in 1962; they had one child.

Lee remained active in Marine Corps affairs during his retirement and performed amazing feats of marksmanship into his nineties. A modernized rifle range at Quantico was named for him in 1992. Lee's straight-shooting image was enhanced by his candor. Reminiscing about his service in Nicaragua, he denounced the exploitation of the country by the American corporations he fought to defend. Lee died of cancer at the age of ninety-eight and is buried in Quantico National Cemetery in Triangle, Virginia.

★

There is no full-length biography of Lee, but most general histories of the Marine Corps refer to his activities in Nicaragua and China, including J. Robert Moskin, *The U.S. Marine Corps Story* (1987). Burke Davis's biography of Lee's partner in Nicaragua, *Marine! The Life of Lt. Gen. Lewis B. (Chesty) Puller, USMC* (1962), describes some of Lee's most famous exploits, which are further discussed in Neill Macaulay, *The Sandino Affair* (1967); Richard Millett, *Guardians of the Dynasty: A History of the U.S. Created Guardia Nacional de Nicaragua and the Somoza Family* (1977); and Lester D. Langley, *The Banana Wars: An Inner History of American Empire, 1900–1934* (1983). Obituaries are in the Fredericksburg, Virginia *Free Lance-Star* (29 Dec. 1998) and *New York Times* (2 Jan. 1999). Lee and Puller were interviewed jointly on audiotape in 1961 for the Marine Corps Oral History Collection; a transcript is available at the U.S. Marine Corps Historical Branch, Navy Yard in Washington, D.C.

NEILL MACAULAY

LEONARD, Sheldon (*b.* 22 February 1907 in New York City; *d.* 10 January 1997 in Beverly Hills, California), actor, writer, director, and producer who was a driving force behind several classic television shows in the 1950s and 1960s.

Leonard, born Leonard Bershad, was the older of two sons of Frank Bershad, a salesman, and his wife, Anna Levitt. Leonard's family lived in the Bronx during his early years, moved to suburban Belleville, New Jersey, when he was twelve, then moved back to New York City when he was fourteen. After his graduation from prestigious Stuyvesant High School in 1925, Leonard attended Syracuse University on an athletic scholarship and earned a B.A. degree in June 1929. He appeared in a number of plays in both high school and college. Leonard started a job as a stockbroker in October 1929 but lost it two weeks later in the aftermath of the stock market crash. As the Great Depression set in over the next few years, he held numerous jobs: millinery manufacturer, longshoreman, theater manager, and printing salesman, among many others.

Sheldon Leonard with Nancy McKeon on the set of *The Facts of Life*. KOBAL COLLECTION

Leonard married Frances Bober on 28 June 1931. They had two children. Helped by his wife's steady salary as a high school teacher, Leonard began to look for work as an actor. "I figured that as long as I couldn't make a living at anything else, I might as well not make a living at something I liked," he told the *New York Morning Telegram* in 1961. Leonard landed his first Broadway role in *Hotel Alimony*, which opened and quickly closed in 1934. But his next show, *Fly Away Home* (1935), had a long run. He played the lead role in the road company of *Three Men on a Horse* in early 1937, then scored major successes on Broadway as a lecherous millinery salesman in *Having Wonderful Time* (1937), and a lecherous producer in *Kiss the Boys Goodbye* (1938).

Leonard's first Hollywood movie role was as a psychopathic blackmailer in *Another Thin Man* (1939). He and his family moved to California in 1940, where Leonard pursued movie roles. Because of his imposing height, prominent eyebrows, hawk nose, and broad New York accent, he was frequently cast as a menacing underworld figure. Among Leonard's more than forty movie roles, he was the Mexican sheriff in *Tortilla Flat* (1942), the bartender who tossed out James Stewart in *It's a Wonderful Life* (1946), and Harry the Horse in *Guys and Dolls* (1955). In the 1940s he also worked steadily in radio. His most famous role was as the tout on *The Jack Benny Show*, but he was also was a regular on *Duffy's Tavern*, *The Judy Canova Show*, *Maisie*, and *The Phil Harris Show*.

Because Leonard's lucrative radio work never took more than two or three days a week, he had a good deal of spare time, which he spent writing scripts for radio anthology shows with meaty roles for himself. In the early 1950s he began rewriting his radio plays for television. "The minimum price in those days was $550 for a half-hour show," Leonard later said. "No respectable writer would sell for that, but I would." When Leonard was unhappy with the way one of his television plays was directed, he directed the next one himself, and a new career as a television director opened up.

In 1953 Leonard became the director of Danny Thomas's television series, *Make Room for Daddy* (1953–1965), which was later renamed *The Danny Thomas Show*. Leonard and Thomas proved to be an unusually strong combination, eventually becoming partners in T&L Productions, which produced most of the television series with which Leonard was involved. He became the producer as well as the director of Thomas's show in 1956. Leonard also directed the pilot and early episodes of *Lassie* in 1954, and *The Real McCoys* in 1957. Both shows went on to unusually long runs.

Leonard created and became the executive producer of *The Andy Griffith Show* (1960–1968) in 1960. The show, a low-key comedy about a small-town sheriff, was a runaway hit. The following year, Leonard was the executive producer of *The Dick Van Dyke Show* (1961–1966), a revamped version of a failed pilot about the home and work life of a

333

comedy show writer. The show had been conceived by the writer/performer Carl Reiner as a starring vehicle for himself. Leonard, convinced that the only problem with the pilot had been its casting, put Van Dyke in the Reiner role, and Reiner moved behind the cameras. *The Dick Van Dyke Show* was always a favorite with critics, while *The Andy Griffith Show* was often dismissed as corny and lightweight. However, both shows were recognized as television classics in subsequent years.

Leonard added another hit in 1964, with *Gomer Pyle, U.S.M.C.* (1964–1970), a spinoff from *The Andy Griffith Show*. Leonard's series tended to be character-driven comedies with accessible and engaging stars surrounded by sharply drawn, and frequently eccentric, supporting characters. Leonard also put a premium on quality scripts. He picked most of his producers from the ranks of his writers, and among the prominent television writer/producers who worked for him in the early years of their careers were Danny Arnold (*Barney Miller*) and Garry Marshall (*The Odd Couple, Happy Days*).

I Spy (1965–1968), about a tennis player (Robert Culp) and trainer (Bill Cosby) who were actually spies, was a departure for Leonard, who created, produced and frequently directed the series. An hour-long drama (albeit one with humorous overtones), it was not produced in partnership with Thomas, and it was the first television series to be filmed largely on location. *I Spy* was also the first television drama to star a black actor (Cosby) in a leading role. Complaints about stereotyping helped end the runs of *Beulah* (1950–1953) and *Amos 'n' Andy* (1951–1953), and sponsorship problems doomed *The Nat "King" Cole Show* (1956–1957). The success of *I Spy*, and of Cosby in it, broke television's color line.

Not all of Leonard's series were hits. Among those that did not last were *The Bill Dana Show* (1963–1965), *Good Morning, World* (1967–1968), and, most frustrating for Leonard, *My World and Welcome to It* (1969–1970), which won the Emmy Award for Best Comedy Series in 1970 but was canceled after one season. Leonard's final television series was the short-lived *Big Eddie* (1975), which he starred in but did not produce.

Leonard went into semiretirement in the late 1970s. However, he continued to do occasional television guest spots as an actor, served as secretary-treasurer of the Directors Guild of America from 1973 until his death, and wrote an autobiography, *And the Show Goes On: Broadway and Hollywood Legends* (1994). He was elected to Television's Hall of Fame in 1992. At the urging of Cosby, Leonard served as an executive producer one last time in the 1993 television movie *I Spy Returns*. Although Leonard was frustrated by network interference, which had grown exponentially since his heyday, he was happy overall with the television movie. Leonard died of complications from bac-

terial endocarditis and is buried at Hillside Memorial Park in Culver City, California.

Leonard was unusual because of the success he had in many aspects of show business. But his most lasting contribution was to the development of the television situation comedy. Many of the genre's conventions were developed by Leonard and Thomas in the early days of *The Danny Thomas Show*. And the influence that *The Danny Thomas Show*, *The Andy Griffith Show* and *The Dick Van Dyke Show* had on countless character-driven television comedies that followed cannot be quantified.

★

Both the Lincoln Center branch of The New York Public Library and the Margaret Herrick Library of the Academy of Motion Pictures Arts and Sciences in Beverly Hills, California, have clippings files on Sheldon Leonard. His autobiography, *And the Show Goes On: Broadway and Hollywood Adventures* (1994), is the most complete source on his life, but it is stronger on anecdotes than it is on biographical specifics. See also Danny Thomas with Bill Davidson, *Make Room for Danny* (1991). Valuable articles include Herb Stein, "Hollywood," *New York Morning Telegram* (20 and 21 Apr. 1961); Arnold Hano, "Sometimes Right, Sometimes Wrong, But Never in Doubt," *TV Guide* (15 Oct. 1964); Joan Barthel, "What a TV Producer Produces," *New York Times Magazine* (21 Nov. 1965); and Cheryl Lavin, "The Small Screen Became His Big Picture," *Chicago Tribune* (18 Oct. 1990). *Encyclopedia of Television* (1997) contains a detailed article on Leonard. An obituary is in the *New York Times* (13 Jan. 1997).

LYNN HOOGENBOOM

LEONARD, Walter Fenner ("Buck") (*b.* 8 September 1907 in Rocky Mount, North Carolina; *d.* 27 November 1997 in Rocky Mount, North Carolina), dependable, sweet-swinging first baseman who is considered among the greatest hitters in baseball's Negro Leagues and was one of the first African-American players admitted to the National Baseball Hall of Fame.

Leonard was born in Rocky Mount, a tobacco-farming town of 7,500 whose economy revolved around its status as a hub of the Atlantic Coast Railroad, a major southern line. Leonard was the third of six children born to John Leonard, a fireman on the railroad, and Emma Sesson, a homemaker who was a founding member of the Saint James Baptist Church. Leonard attended Lincoln Elementary School through his graduation at age fourteen. With no local high school available for African-American students, he was forced instead to go to work to help support his family. Like his father, who had died in the influenza epidemic of 1919, Leonard went to work on the railroad, making $3.92

Walter "Buck" Leonard receiving a plaque from baseball commissioner Bowie Kuhn at his induction into the Baseball Hall of Fame, 1972. ASSOCIATED PRESS AP

per day installing brake cylinders onto boxcars for the At-lantic Coast line. He soon joined the local semiprofessional baseball team, the Rocky Mount Elks. He played for them until 1933, when he lost his job with the railroad and left home to pursue a career as a professional baseball player.

Leonard served brief stints with the Portsmouth Fire-fighters and the Baltimore Stars before catching the eye of Dick Redding, the manager of the Brooklyn Royal Giants, a formidable independent team. Leonard went north with the Brooklyn team and finished the 1933 season with them. The next year, he received $125 per month after joining an even more impressive squad: the Homestead Grays of Pitts-burgh, a storied team for which he played first base for the next seventeen years. Leonard quickly became known as one of the greatest hitters in the game, with the ability to bat for both power and average. He terrorized pitchers with his smooth left-handed swing, and although statistical re-cords are inconclusive, he was said to have led the Negro National League in home runs and batting average several times each. In 1935 he was selected for the first time to the East-West Game, the annual Negro Leagues all-star con-test. He eventually made a record twelve appearances in the East-West Game, nine of them as the East's cleanup hitter (the fourth position in the team's batting order).

Leonard's even-tempered manner and consistency on the diamond made him one of the most respected players in the Negro Leagues and drew comparisons to Lou Geh-rig, the New York Yankees first baseman and the player

Leonard had modeled himself after as a teenager. Despite his modest size (five feet, ten inches tall and 185 pounds), Leonard was regarded as an outstanding defensive first baseman, with quick reflexes and a strong throwing arm. His quiet leadership led to his being named the team cap-tain of the Grays. In an era when ballplayers routinely in-dulged in excesses of drinking and womanizing, Leonard was a teetotaler and a devoted family man. He married Sarah Wroten of Hertford, North Carolina, on New Year's Eve 1937; their marriage lasted until her death in 1966. They had no children. The rival player Buck O'Neil re-called Leonard as "the most studious man in the Negro Leagues," calling him "a nice quiet man who would . . . sit in the hotel lobby working crossword puzzles rather than going to the night spots."

During Leonard's career the Grays were the most pow-erful team in African-American baseball, winning ten Ne-gro National League titles (nine of them consecutive) and three Negro League World Series titles. For eight years (1937–1939 and 1942–1946), Leonard and the powerful catcher Josh Gibson formed the best-hitting duo in African-American baseball. Like Gehrig, Leonard was soft-spoken, content to let Gibson have the spotlight as the team's big-gest star. They were so impressive that the Washington Senators owner Clark Griffith once met with Leonard and Gibson to ask if they were interested in joining the then all-white major leagues. They responded affirmatively, but Griffith never followed through with his offer, and Jackie

Robinson instead broke the major leagues color barrier in 1947. Robinson's success in integrated baseball soon brought hard times on the African-American leagues, and the Negro National League folded after the 1948 season. The Homestead club, with Leonard, survived another two years as an independent team before disbanding after the 1950 season.

At forty-three years old, Leonard had been making $1,000 per month in his final year with the Grays and was not ready for retirement, so he signed to play first base for the Torreón club in the Mexican League. Mexico was the fourth Latin American country Leonard called home, after previously playing winter seasons in Puerto Rico, Venezuela, and Cuba. In 1952 Bill Veeck, the iconoclastic owner of the St. Louis Browns, reportedly offered Leonard a major league contract, but Leonard turned it down because, he later said, "I was too old and I knew it." Instead he continued playing in Mexico, where, despite his advanced age, he posted an extraordinary on-base percentage of .477 over four seasons. "Down there we played three games a week," he said, "and I could still play like the devil for them three days, although I couldn't have played every day."

In 1955, at age forty-eight, Leonard retired from baseball after twenty-two professional seasons. He returned to his hometown of Rocky Mount, where he worked as a truant officer and physical education teacher for the local school system, a job he held for twelve years. Leonard completed the education he had missed as a youth, earning his diploma from the American Correspondence School in 1959. In 1962 he became one of the organizers of a minor league baseball team, the Rocky Mount Leafs, serving as a vice president. He opened his own real-estate company, Buck Leonard's Realty Agency, in 1966, and in his spare time taught Sunday school and served as a part-time scout for the Philadelphia Phillies. Following his wife's death, Leonard met Lugenia Fox in 1969 and, after nearly two decades of courtship, they were married on 7 July 1986.

During the 1970s, when the aftermath of the civil rights movement brought wider recognition to former Negro League stars, Leonard became one of Rocky Mount's best-known citizens. As one writer put it, he was "honored in the same town where he was once relegated to second-class citizenship." On 8 February 1972—a day he would forever after cite as the greatest in his life—Leonard received baseball's highest honor when he was elected to the National Baseball Hall of Fame in Cooperstown, New York. Six months later, on 7 August, he was officially inducted into that shrine along with Gibson, his late teammate. They were only the second and third Negro League stars so honored. Other accolades followed, as Leonard was inducted into the North Carolina Sports Hall of Fame in 1974 and the Washington Sports Hall of Fame in 1981. Leonard died at age ninety of complications from a stroke he had suffered in 1986. He is buried at Gardens of Gethsemane cemetery in Rocky Mount.

In a baseball world marked by turbulence and hard times, Leonard was a model of consistency and excellence. His seventeen-year term of service with one team is a record unsurpassed by any other Negro League player, and his exploits as a batter were rivaled by few. His life was also emblematic of the mythical American dream. Coming from a background of segregation and poverty, he used his remarkable talents and self-discipline to rise to the peak of his profession. Leonard's life endures as a monument to dignity and strength in the face of adversity.

★

Leonard's autobiography with Jim Riley, *Buck Leonard, the Black Lou Gehrig: The Hall of Famer's Story in His Own Words* (1995), is the foremost source for information about his life and career. The National Baseball Hall of Fame Library in Cooperstown, New York, has an extensive research file on Leonard containing clippings and correspondence. The definitive work of Negro Leagues oral history, John Holway, *Voices from the Great Black Baseball Leagues* (1975), contains a chapter on Leonard. Information about him can also be found in the biographies of two of his fellow Negro League players, William Brashler, *Josh Gibson: A Life In the Negro Leagues* (1978), and Buck O'Neil with Steve Wulf and David Conrads, *I Was Right On Time* (1994). Dick Clark and Larry Lester, eds., *The Negro Leagues Book* (1994), is the definitive source for statistical information on Negro League players. Obituaries are in the *New York Times* and *Washington Post* (both 30 Nov. 1997).

ERIC ENDERS

LEONTIEF, Wassily (*b.* 5 August 1906 in Saint Petersburg, Russia; *d.* 5 February 1999 in New York City), Nobel Prize–winning economist who originated the input-output technique, a method of analyzing economic production, and was also an educator and government adviser.

Leontief was the son of an economics professor, Wassily Leontief, and Eugenia Bekker. A schoolboy at the time of the Bolshevik revolution, he remembered the sound of bullets in his hometown as the war broke out. Leontief enrolled in the University of Leningrad at age fifteen, where he complained about constraints on intellectuals and was jailed for a time. He developed a growth that was thought cancerous and was allowed to leave the country in 1925 after qualifying as a "Learned Economist" (equivalent to an M.A. degree). Leontief enrolled in the University of Berlin and completed his doctorate after his parents joined him in Germany. After spending a year full-time at the Institut für Weltwirtschaf (Institute for World Economics), where he worked on deriving supply and demand curves, he left

Wassily Leontief *(right)*, winner of the 1973 Nobel Prize for economic science, is congratulated by Carl Cori, winner of the 1947 Nobel Prize for medicine; Mrs. Leontief is at center. © BETTMANN/CORBIS

for Nanking, China, as an economic adviser to the Chinese Ministry of Railroads.

Leontief arrived in the United States in 1931 and after a brief stint with the National Bureau of Economic Research moved later that year to Harvard University in Cambridge, Massachusetts, which agreed to help him publish his statistical research into the American economy. On 25 December 1932 he married Estelle Helena Marks, a writer. During the 1930s he began the work that would lead him later to found the International Input-Output Conference, which he attended for many years. Leontief's economics work was interrupted during World War II when he worked for the U.S. Office of Strategic Services. He quickly returned to Harvard after the war and established the Harvard Research Project on the structure of the American economy. With a staff of twenty and extensive use of IBM punch card sorting machines, he assembled a picture of the American economy. In 1956 *Business Week* noted that $240,000 from a Ford Foundation grant was not enough to keep Leontief's research going but that the economist believed that major advances in the understanding of the American economy would yield very large returns. Ironically, despite his championing of technology in his research, Leontief could not type well enough to use a personal computer.

Economists since Alfred Marshall and Leon Walras had described an economy as the sum of a number of inputs—land, labor, capital, and entrepreneurship—that became the output for specific industries. Leontief, aware of the theory and technique of what he was doing, took their work a step further by assembling a chart showing just how much

each industry's output became the input of another industry. The chart might say, for example, that 20 percent of the output of the rubber industry went into making parts for the automobile industry, but that 5 percent of the automobile industry output went into vehicles used in the rubber industry. Thus the magnitude of the ripple effect on a change in one sector of the economy on another sector could be easily quantified. As Leontief noted in the opening of *The Structure of American Economy* (1941), "This modest volume describes an attempt to apply the economic theory of general equilibrium . . . to an empirical study of the interrelations forming the different parts of a national economy as revealed through covariations of prices, outputs, investments and incomes."

Not satisfied with so significant an achievement, he took this concept further, but not without controversy. Leontief joined United Auto Workers union president Leonard Woodcock in calling for an Office of National Economic Planning, an idea that fell on increasingly deaf ears as economists turned to *laissez faire* and monetarist notions of economic strategy. In 1961 Leontief argued in an influential article in *Scientific American* written with Marvin Hoffenberg that input-output analysis could be applied to predict the effect on jobs from "the reallocation of the funds now expended for military purposes." At the time the Department of Defense consumed 10 percent of the gross national product. Leontief noted that private business probably could not absorb the entire loss of jobs but that "private and public spending could increase and foreign aid expenditures would require analysis outside" the closed economy model Leontief and Hoffenberg had employed. Leontief's arguments held weight as successive presidents made the military a smaller and smaller percentage of the national budget. In *Military Spending: Fact and Figures, Worldwide Implication and Future Outlook* (1983), Leontief and co-author Faye Duchin concluded, "The labor forces of all developed regions . . . seem to be used more efficiently in producing civilian than military goods and services." Still later, the input-output method was used in measurements of the effects of pollution on the production system.

Despite becoming Henry Lee Professor of Economics in 1948, Leontief became disenchanted with Harvard, ultimately joining a faculty group sympathetic to a student protest in 1969 and agreeing with a report highly critical of the school's economics department. In 1970 he became president of the American Economic Association. In 1973 he was awarded the Nobel Prize as "the sole and unchallenged creator of the input-output technique . . . an empirically useful method to highlight the general interdependence in the production system of a society." He left Harvard in 1975 for New York University, returning to the city that had been his first American home. There he specialized in developing input-output charts for foreign economies. One of his last projects was for the Chinese, who had rejected his work during the Mao Zedong period.

Another Leontief concept of note concerned the export of capital. The economist noted that the United States was relatively well supplied with capital. According to classical notions of international economics, the United States therefore should export capital-intensive goods. Leontief's studies, however, concluded that the United States was in fact exporting primarily labor-intensive products such as farm produce. This observation became known as the Leontief paradox.

Leontief died at New York University Medical Center at age ninety-three. He was very active in the last decade of his life. He had a wide network of contacts, including the French politician François Mitterand and the artist Franco Modigliani. Leontief himself had considerable skill as an artist, and his only child, Svetlana, became an art critic. In 1992 Leontief wrote a guest editorial in the *New York Times* bemoaning the rejection of a role for the government in economic planning. But despite this apparent rejection of his conclusions, Leontief's methods of modeling and analysis in economics have had a marked influence on the discipline.

★

The location of Leontief's papers is unknown. Biographical articles about Leontief include W. H. Miernyk, "Wassily Leontief," in *International Encyclopedia of Social Sciences* (1979), and R. Dorfman, "Wassilly Leontief's Contributions to Economics," in *Contemporary Economists in Perspective,* ed. H. W. Spiegel and W. J. Samuels (1984). The International Input Output Association devotes a portion of its website to Leontief, <www.iioa.org/leontief/memoriam.html>. An obituary is in the *New York Times* (7 Feb. 1999).

JOHN DAVID HEALY

LERNER, Nathan Bernard (*b.* 30 March 1913 in Chicago, Illinois; *d.* 8 February 1997 in Chicago, Illinois), photographer, designer, painter, and educator whose socially committed photographs and photographic light studies achieved renown, and whose simple, functional, and sometimes whimsical designs for consumer products became staples of everyday life.

Lerner was the second of three sons born to Louis Lerner, a tailor, and Ida Ripstein, a seamstress. Lerner's childhood friend Edmund Teske, later a well-known photographer in his own right, inspired Lerner's interest in photography. Many of Lerner's earliest photographic images reflected another of his interests, painting. After graduating from high school, he studied painting with Louis Ritman at the Art Institute of Chicago in 1933 and with Samuel Ostrowsky at the Jewish People's Institute in 1935 and 1936. Ritman and Ostrowsky were neoimpressionist painters, and Lerner's earliest paintings were similar to theirs.

From 1935 to 1937 Lerner made Maxwell Street, the heart of the colorful neighborhood in which he was born, the subject of many photographs. Not really documentary or journalistic in nature, these images captured juxtapositions that placed people or objects in unexpected contexts. Many of these photographs evoked the shared humanity of the variety of people who congregated on Maxwell Street, including African Americans, Gypsies, and recently arrived immigrants. In 1937 Lerner enrolled in the New Bauhaus in Chicago, directed by László Moholy-Nagy. Lerner's work there with György Kepes and Henry Holmes Smith engaged him in experimental photographic studies, such as making photograms (photographs made without a camera). A highlight of Lerner's student experiments was the light box, a method for studying light in a controlled environment. His photograph of an illuminated assemblage made with the aid of a light box was shown at the Museum of Modern Art in New York in 1938. Lerner continued his experimental and social-commentary photography throughout the 1940s.

At the School of Design in Chicago, organized in 1939 by Moholy-Nagy to replace the New Bauhaus, Lerner completed his studies while assisting with the photography classes. He graduated in 1942 and in that same year a touring exhibition that he cocurated with Moholy-Nagy and Kepes, *How to Make a Photogram,* was seen at New York's Museum of Modern Art. In his student work Lerner also showed his flair for design with a series of bent plywood chairs. None of these chairs was ever put into production, but they were very innovative, made from single sheets of three-eighths-inch plywood and bent with the aid of steam into curves.

From 1943 to 1945 Lerner worked as a civilian for the U.S. Naval Training Aids Center in New York City. In the autumn of 1945 he was appointed to initiate a curriculum in product design at the Institute of Design or I.D. (formerly the School of Design). Also in 1945 Lerner married Christine Sullivan. They had two children and later separated, finally divorcing in 1967.

Lerner left the I.D. in 1949 and formed Lerner-Bredendieck Design with his I.D. colleague Hin Bredendieck. They helped to spark the do-it-yourself movement of the postwar years through a number of carefully illustrated magazine articles in *Popular Home*, which was published by U.S. Gypsum and given away free in hardware and building supply stores and in retail lumberyards. The magazine reached millions of homes. Readers were guided step-by-step through tasks that ranged from making small pieces of furniture to partitioning a room to constructing a vacation cottage. Lerner and Bredendieck also designed a modular ceiling system made of a foam-core composite that was textured to add visual appeal.

The team also had the yo-yo tycoon Donald Duncan as a client. From 1950 to the mid-1960s Lerner designed numerous yo-yos with novel features, including one that lit up. Others made siren noises or stored their energy in flywheels. Lerner also designed toys for Tarco, originally the Sidney A. Tarrson Toy Company, during the 1950s and 1960s. These designs included a variety of coin banks, gumball machines, and pull toys.

After Bredendieck left the office in the early 1950s, it became Lerner Design Associates. Low-Cost Modern, an offshoot, was a popular but nonetheless short-lived experiment in the mid-1960s that featured simple and inexpensive products, including some attractive lamps that benefited from Lerner's extensive experience with controlling light. Gordon Barlow served as Lerner's design assistant for about three years, beginning in 1957.

From 1950 to about 1970 Lerner designed a range of products for the W. Braun Company of Chicago, suppliers of containers to many of America's best-known companies, such as Helen Curtis and Clorox. These designs ranged from the functionally sleek to the playful. Lerner created the practice he called "componetics," the use of stock container shapes with an assortment of stock caps, many of which he himself designed. Through changes in size and the use of differing plastic materials, componetics allowed for great variety, and many of Lerner's stock container and cap shapes still dominated retail shelves at the end of the twentieth century. Some of his work for Braun was more whimsical, such as a container in the shape of the cartoon

character Bugs Bunny, and a honey container in the shape of a bear.

Lerner closed his design office after the success of his first one-artist photographic exhibition in 1972, at Bradley University in Peoria, Illinois. *The Bauhaus Years, 1935–1945: Photographs by Nathan Lerner* was shown at a number of other venues, including the Museum of Science and Industry in Chicago and the Bauhaus-Archiv in Berlin. Lerner's photographs soon began to enter museum collections in Europe, the United States, and Japan.

In 1967 Lerner married the pianist Kiyoko Asai. They made numerous extended visits to Japan together, beginning in 1971. On these visits Lerner made color photographs that do not imitate the work of Japanese photographers, but nevertheless evoke a Japanese way of seeing. As a writer for a Tokyo newspaper noted concerning a 1975 exhibition, "Lerner's images recall, at times, the way ripples of blue dye become wave patterns in certain handmade Japanese papers." Nathan and Kiyoko Lerner also brought to light the work of outsider artist Henry Darger, who, posthumously, achieved international renown.

Lerner continued to paint throughout his later years, although he never exhibited these works. The best of his paintings showed a keen awareness of contemporary trends in the fine arts and provided a continuous link connecting his creative ideas. At the age of eighty-three, Lerner died of kidney failure. He was cremated and his ashes are stored in Matsuda Cemetery in Japan.

Lerner's legacy includes his role in inspiring the do-it-yourself movement in home improvement and his role in developing attractive and cost-effective containers that helped make self-service retailing a success. The strongly felt respect for humanity that guided his innovative approach to photography carried over into his work as a teacher and designer as he helped others share his vision of design as a humanistic discipline.

★

Lerner's writings consist of short pieces, including "Light, Creative Use of," coauthored with György Kepes, in Dagobert D. Runes and Harry G. Schrickel, eds., *Encyclopedia of the Arts* (1946); and "A Personal Recollection," in Stephen Prokopoff, *Henry Darger, the Unreality of Being* (1996). Archival collections documenting Lerner's work are in the Chicago Historical Society and the Bauhaus-Archiv in Berlin. Among museums holding his photographs are the Metropolitan Museum of Art; Museum of Modern Art, New York; George Eastman House, Rochester; Art Institute of Chicago; Milwaukee Museum of Art; St. Louis Museum of Art; University of Iowa Museum of Art, Iowa City; and San Francisco Museum of Modern Art. No single publication covers all of his life and career, but the best sources of information are Anita Feldman, "Art: People and Places," *Mainichi Daily News* (28 Apr. 1975); Nicholas Pavkovic, "Nathan Lerner and the New

Bauhaus," *Pulp Magazine* (winter 1989); Jo-Ann Conklin, *Nathan Lerner's Maxwell Street* (1993); and Astrid Böger and Robert Manley, eds., *Modernist Eye: The Art and Design of Nathan Lerner* (2000). An obituary is in the *New York Times* (15 Feb. 1997).

LLOYD C. ENGELBRECHT

LEVERTOV, Denise (*b.* 24 October 1923 in Ilford, Essex, England; *d.* 20 December 1997 in Seattle, Washington), poet and essayist whose work reflects her strong social and political convictions.

The daughter of Paul Philip Levertoff, a Russian Jewish immigrant who settled in England and became an Anglican priest, and Beatrice Adelaide Spooner-Jones, a teacher, Levertov was largely home-schooled. A self-described "child of the London Streets . . . of the Victoria and Albert Museum," frequently roaming "romantic and beautiful Wanstead and Valentines parks" near her home, yet anchored in a "house full of books . . . [where] everyone in the family engaged in some literary activity," Levertov early discovered a sense

Denise Levertov. AP/WIDE WORLD PHOTOS

of spiritual and natural wonder. Her father's background of religious scholarship and mysticism was a strong influence on her imagination, as was what she described as her mother's "Welsh intensity and lyric feeling for nature." During her childhood, her father's protests against the Italian dictator Benito Mussolini's invasion of Abyssinia and her mother's canvassing for the League of Nations set the stage for Levertov's humanitarian politics and her vocation as a writer. She began writing poems as a young girl.

During World War II, Levertov worked as a civilian nurse in London, writing many of the poems that would be published in her first book, *The Double Image* (1946). The American poet Kenneth Rexroth identified her work loosely with a group of English New Romantics whose poetry had a kind of "dreamy, nostalgic sorrow about it."

On 2 December 1947 Levertov married the American writer Mitchell Goodman, moving with him a year later to New York City, where in 1949 their son was born. Eased past her culture shock by new friendships and a lively exchange of ideas with American contemporaries, including the poets Robert Creeley and Robert Duncan, Levertov was able to discover the objects, rhythms, and voices of her new environment. In 1951 she began a fruitful literary correspondence with the poet William Carlos Williams, which blossomed into a warm creative friendship by 1953. She wrote that she was "deeply affected" by "Williams' interest in the ordinary, in the present . . . in the lives and speech of ordinary people; and his unsentimental compassion, which illumined the marvellous in the apparently banal."

Levertov became a naturalized American citizen in 1955, and in 1957 she published her first book in the United States, *Here and Now,* whose title suggests a Williams-like attention to things as they are. Other strong influences during this period were the poems of Wallace Stevens and the prose of Ezra Pound. Within a decade, Levertov published five more volumes of poetry, discovering in a blending of English roots and American places and experiences her own distinctive voice as a sensitive observer. Her books from the next decade include *The Jacob's Ladder* (1961) and *The Sorrow Dance* (1967).

"What the poet is called on to clarify is not answers but the existence and nature of questions," Levertov observed in a 1968 lecture at the University of Michigan. And in the steady stream of poems that she produced through the 1950s and 1960s, she raised pointed, often poignant, questions about the nature of human relationships, childbirth and childhood, family memory, the mystery of art, and, inevitably and increasingly, war and politics.

Levertov's exploratory poetry of the 1960s, which she came to call "organic poetry"—"organic form because it is not a form imposed but a form discovered in the relation of the events"—increasingly had as a goal "to awaken sleepers." What she described as her first political poem,

"During the Eichmann Trial" from *The Jacob's Ladder,* offers an unflinching portrait of human darkness, which concludes that, face to face with evil, we must still understand that "*Here is a mystery, / a person, an / other, an I.*" For the next three and a half decades, the poetry of politics, of human suffering, and of outrage and compassion would be central to Levertov's work.

By the fall of 1967 the United States was at war in Vietnam; already fully involved in the antiwar movement, Levertov was convinced that "it is not enough to write *or act,* we feel we must do both." In 1968 her husband was indicted with Dr. Benjamin Spock for conspiracy to oppose the military draft, and the poet's public protests and private life came together as a subject for her work. In *Relearning the Alphabet* (1970), Levertov produced a controversial poetry of political and social engagement. Her works of the 1970s confirmed her clarity of language, her exploration of the intricacies and wonders of the ordinary in human lives and places, and her commitment to worldwide peace and justice. Notable works from the period include *To Stay Alive* (1971), *The Freeing of the Dust* (1975), and *Life in the Forest* (1978). Levertov and Goodman divorced in 1974.

"Acknowledgement, and celebration, of mystery probably constitutes the most consistent theme of my poetry from its very beginnings," Levertov wrote in 1984, and in her works of the 1980s and 1990s her explorations of the mysteries of the human spirit were increasingly marked by Christian faith. Major works from this era include *Candles in Babylon* (1982), *Oblique Prayers* (1984), *Breathing the Water* (1987), *Evening Train* (1992), and *Sands of the Well* (1996).

A teacher as well as a sometime editor and an honored writer throughout her career, Levertov taught at a host of colleges and universities, including the University of California, Massachusetts Institute of Technology, Brandeis, Tufts, and Stanford. Poetry editor of *The Nation* in 1961 and again from 1963 to 1965, and of *Mother Jones* from 1976 to 1978, Levertov was the recipient of many awards, including the Lenore Marshall Poetry Prize (1975), the Elmer Holmes Bobst Award (1983), and the Lannan Award (1992).

Levertov once wrote that "the obligation of the writer is: *to take personal and active responsibility for his words.*" In her poems, in the classroom, and in support of social causes, she spent her life fulfilling that obligation. She died at age seventy-four from complications of lymphoma.

★

Levertov's papers are in the Department of Special Collections and University Archives, Stanford University. Christopher MacGowan, ed., *The Letters of Denise Levertov and William Carlos Williams* (1998), is valuable, as is *This Great Unknowing: Last Poems* (1999), which was published posthumously with a note on the text by Paul Lacey. Jewel Spears Brooker, ed., *Conversations with Denise Levertov* (1998), collects interviews with Levertov from 1963 to 1995. Useful critical books about Levertov's work include Linda W. Wagner, *Denise Levertov* (1967); Harry Marten, *Understanding Denise Levertov* (1988); Audrey T. Rogers, *Denise Levertov: The Poetry of Engagement* (1993); Albert Gelpi, ed., *Denise Levertov: Selected Criticism* (1993); Linda Kinnahan, *Poetics of the Feminine* (1994); and Anne Colclough Little and Susie Paul, eds., *Denise Levertov: New Perspectives* (2000). An obituary is in the *New York Times* (23 Dec. 1997).

HARRY MARTEN

LEWIS, Shari (*b.* 17 January 1933 in New York City; *d.* 2 August 1998 in Los Angeles, California), entertainer, puppeteer, musician, ventriloquist, and author, best known for her children's television shows featuring the sock puppet Lamb Chop.

Born Phyllis Hurwitz on Staten Island in New York City, Lewis was the elder of two daughters of Abraham B. Hurwitz and Ann Ritz. She grew up in the huge Parkchester housing complex of the Bronx. Her father, a professor at Yeshiva University in Manhattan, was also "Peter Pan the Magic Man," whom Mayor Fiorello LaGuardia named the official magician for the Parks Department of New York City. Her mother, the music coordinator for the Bronx Board of Education, began to teach her to play the piano at age two. Lewis studied music theory, orchestration, piano, and violin at the New York High School of Music and Art. She also studied dance at the School of American Ballet, acting at the Neighborhood Playhouse, with Sanford Meisner, and drama at Columbia University. Her father taught her magic and helped to develop her ventriloquism talents. At sixteen, sidelined by a dance injury, Lewis turned to puppetry. She changed her name to "Shari" after the Massachusetts Camp Shari (which means "head of"), where her parents were directors of the boys' and girls' camps.

In 1952 Lewis, a petite, dynamic redhead, was a winner on *Arthur Godfrey's Talent Scouts* television show. By 1953 she was hosting the New York City television show *Facts 'n' Fun* (WNBT-TV), followed by two more New York–based programs, *Shari and Her Friends* in 1954 (WPIX-TV) and *Shariland,* a one-hour Saturday morning show in 1957 (WRCA-TV). Also in 1957 she introduced Lamb Chop, her sock puppet with long mink eyelashes, on *Captain Kangaroo,* and was soon offered her own show. *Hi, Mom,* an hour-long program aimed at young children, was on NBC five mornings a week from 1957 to 1959. The well-reviewed show featured puppets, music, Lewis's dry humor, and magic tricks, as well as health and budget-stretching tips for mothers. *The Shari Lewis Show* ran Saturday mornings

Cast of the PBS television special "Shari's Passover Surprise": *(left to right)* Lamb Chop, puppeteer Shari Lewis, Hush Puppy, and Charlie Horse, 1997. DEB HALBERSTADT/ASSOCIATED PRESS KCET

on NBC from 1960 to 1963 and included the puppets Hush Puppy and Charlie Horse in addition to the popular Lamb Chop. By age twenty-five, Lewis had also published *The Shari Lewis Puppet Book* (1958).

Lewis's first marriage, to Stan Lewis (Stanley Lewis Lipschitz), whom she married in her late teens, ended in divorce after three years. On 15 March 1958 she married the book publisher Jeremy P. Tarcher, who encouraged her to write more books about puppet making and magic, as well as children's stories. Lewis legally changed her surname to Tarcher but continued to go by Lewis professionally. They moved to California, where their daughter, Mallory, was born in 1967. In 1969 Lewis and Tarcher cowrote an episode, "The Lights of Zetar," for the original *Star Trek* television series.

When animation became more popular than puppets and her live television show was replaced by cartoons, Lewis performed in Las Vegas. She also acted in summer stock and in Broadway musicals, including *Damn Yankees, Bye Bye Birdie, Funny Girl,* and her own Broadway musical, *Lamb Chop on Broadway* (December 1994). The syndicated *Shari Show* ran on television for one year in 1975. She had her own Sunday-night show, *Shari at Six,* on BBC-1 in England from 1968 to 1976, but was unhappy about the need to leave the United States to continue her creative children's programming.

In addition to her innumerable television appearances on game shows, dramas, and variety and talk shows, Lewis performed four times at Buckingham Palace; at White House Christmas parties during the administrations of Presidents Jimmy Carter, Ronald Reagan, and George Bush; and at the White House Easter celebration during the administration of President Bill Clinton. In 1977 she conducted the Dallas Symphony Orchestra and eventually conducted more than 100 orchestras worldwide. She wrote more than thirty children's books, including fifteen "one-minute stories" for children about Greek myths, Christmas, Bible stories, fairy tales, and animals.

In 1992 Lewis returned to television with *Lamb Chop's Play-Along* on the Public Broadcasting Service (PBS), which ran until 1997. With its interactive format, Lewis called it her "anti-couch-potato show." Lewis and Lamb Chop testified before Congress in 1993 about the Children's Television Act. In 1995 she produced her first interactive CD-ROM, *Lamb Chop Loves Music,* which won a ROM-MIE award. She also created twenty-four videos for children, seven of which went gold and one platinum. Lewis wrote "Lamb Chop's Special Chanukah" (1995) and "Shari's Passover Surprise" (1997) for PBS, to include Jewish children who were previously left out of religious television programming.

Lewis's list of awards is prodigious. In 1960 she won the

Peabody Award for outstanding children's television programs. Between 1993 and 2000, she received sixteen Emmy nominations and won eight awards, seven as outstanding performer in a children's series, and one for writing, including a 1993 award she shared with her daughter, who worked closely with Lewis as a writer, supervisor, and producer. In 1993 she won the ASCAP-Deems Taylor Broadcast Award for excellence for *Charlie Horse Pizza*. Lewis received a Kennedy Center Award for excellence and creativity in 1983, seven *Parents Choice* (magazine) Awards, and was inducted into the *Parents Choice* Hall of Fame.

Lewis served on the national boards of the Girl Scouts of America, Boy Scouts International, and International Reading Foundation. She received an honorary doctorate in education from New York's Hofstra University in 1993. Although not an observant Jew, she was a life member of the Jewish women's Hadassah organization, and she received the Dor L'Dor award from B'nai Brith in 1996.

Lewis was diagnosed with uterine cancer in June 1998. After six weeks of chemotherapy, she developed pneumonia and died at Cedar Sinai Medical Center. Following a private ceremony, she was cremated. In 1999 a public memorial service was held at Riverside Cemetery in Saddlebrook, New Jersey, where her paternal relatives are buried. A memorial bench was placed there in her memory.

Lewis was a female ventriloquist at a time when most in the profession were male, and she was one of the first women conductors in the United States. She was a perfectionist dedicated to producing quality entertainment for children by not "playing down to them." She taught tolerance and sharing and sought to develop a love for music in children because she believed that learning to play an instrument could teach children to think and learn.

★

There are no full-length biographies on Lewis. There is a 1981 interview in the *Boston Globe* and a 1997 interview with Kira Albin originally published in *Grand Times* (Dec./Jan. 1998) and is still available at <http://www.grandtimes.com/lambchop.html>. Obituaries are in the *New York Times, Washington Post,* and *Los Angeles Times* (all 4 Aug. 1998), *Variety* (10 Aug. 1998), and *People Weekly* (17 Aug. 1998).

JANE BRODSKY FITZPATRICK

LIBERMAN, Alexander Semeonovitch (*b.* 4 September 1912 in Kiev, Ukraine; *d.* 19 November 1999 in Miami Beach, Florida), art and editorial director, painter, sculptor, photographer, and author, who was the primary creative force at Condé Nast and its fashion magazine *Vogue.*

Liberman was the only child of Semeon Isayevich Liberman, a timber expert, and Henriette Pascar, a theatrical dilettante. Liberman spent his first five years in luxurious surroundings. However, when his father moved the family from Kiev to Moscow to offer his expertise to the new Bolshevik government, Liberman became profoundly unhappy. His father received permission to take him to London, and they left Russia in September 1921. Liberman never returned, and eventually his parents emigrated as well.

Liberman attended three English boarding schools and developed an interest in photography. At the end of the 1925 school term he joined his mother in Paris, where in March 1926 he became the first Jewish student admitted to the elite Calvinist Ecole des Roches in Normady. Liberman received a double baccalaureate degree with honors in 1930. Despite his automatic qualification to one of the advanced institutes, he chose to study painting in the modernist André Lhote's atelier. He then studied architecture at the Ecole Spéciale d'Architecture followed by the Ecole des Beaux-Arts, before finding his true métier; he was hired in 1933 by the publisher Lucien Vogel as the assistant art editor for the photographic news journal *Vu,* and in 1936 he became the managing director. During his three years at *Vu,* he created innovative layouts reflecting the influence of constructivist designs he had seen at the 1925 Exposition des Arts Décoratifs in Paris.

On 25 August 1936 Liberman wed Hildegarde Sturm, a model and competitive skier. They were divorced soon after. Liberman served in the French Army in 1940. He left for the South of France two days before the German invasion of Paris and immigrated to the United States in January 1941. Accompanying him were Tatiana Iacovleva, comtesse du Plessix, and her daughter, whom he had met in 1938, shortly after the end of his brief marriage to Sturm. He and Tatiana married in the fall of 1942.

Within a few months of their arrival in the United States, Liberman filed for citizenship (granted in 1946) and found work with the magazine publisher Condé Nast in *Vogue*'s art department. He was quickly singled out when one of his designs—that of a model lying on her back, supporting a ball on her feet that provided the "o" in *Vogue*—was published as the cover of the 15 May 1941 issue. In September 1942, when Iva Patcévitch took over the company upon Nast's death, Liberman was promoted to art editor; he became the art director of *Vogue* in 1943, and also of *Home and Garden* and *Glamour* in 1944.

Liberman altered *Vogue*'s appearance with changes designed to appeal to a wider audience. He relied on photographs at the expense of fashion drawings, and sped up the visual rhythm of each issue. He sought an easier-to-read layout with a sans-serif typeface, even as he packed the pages with more information. He used catchwords—"energizing" for the layout and "vitality" for the typeface—to convey his vision. He also sought a new look with models,

Alexander Liberman in front of his sculpture *The Way,* in Laumeier International Sculpture Park, Sunset Hills, Missouri, 1980. © BETTMANN/CORBIS

replacing haughty-looking European women with models exuding an all-American appeal. He also brought in a new type of photographer to capture this American image, hiring Irving Penn and eventually Richard Avedon, who both revolutionized fashion photography. As Liberman recalled, "I wanted to involve women in the life of the moment, and the war furthered this by destroying fantasy."

Vogue's editor in chief Edna Chase resisted Liberman's vision, and her successor, Jessica Daves, shared this attitude, although Daves did welcome Liberman's infusion of art and art criticism. For his part, Liberman developed a useful contempt for his job. "In a curious way," he recalled, "I felt myself superior . . . because I felt that I was an artist." In 1946 he returned to painting. He later described his pattern: he gave his days to Condé Nast, his evenings to Tatiana, and his weekends to art.

Although Liberman worked as a painter throughout his life, enjoying solo exhibitions at the Betty Parsons Gallery from 1960 to 1973, the national recognition he achieved as an artist came from his sculpture. His work evolved during the 1960s from welded scrap-metal pieces to monumental sculptures made from industrial pipes and disks. The architect Philip Johnson invited Liberman to create a relief sculpture for the 1964 New York World's Fair. In 1966 the Jewish Museum held his first solo museum exhibition, and in 1967 the André Emmerich Gallery gave him his first one-person sculpture show, with nearly annual exhibitions thereafter. In 1970 he received the first of many public commissions for his monumental sculpture. Yet Liberman's first retrospective, held at the Corcoran Gallery of Art that year, received virtually no critical attention. The art world

remained suspicious, because, as the critic Lawrence Alloway observed, "You weren't supposed to have both Condé Nast and Betty Parsons."

In 1958 the newspaper mogul Samuel L. Newhouse purchased Condé Nast and quickly developed a strong personal and professional friendship with Liberman, as did his son Si, who took over the company in 1975. Liberman was named as editorial director for all Condé Nast publications in 1962 and had authority over all magazine editors, including the legendary Diana Vreeland, who became *Vogue*'s editor in chief in 1963. She pinpointed radical changes in fashion and moved *Vogue* into a position of complete dominance in the industry. In 1971, when fashion consumerism leaned toward naturalness and comfort, Liberman chose Grace Mirabella to take over the helm. Sensing a shift in American sensibilities toward greater femininity, he appointed Anna Wintour in 1988. Liberman also oversaw the successful revival of *Vanity Fair* (which had closed in 1936) in the 1980s.

In April 1991 Tatiana died. Liberman married Melinda Pechangco in December 1992, and they lived in both Manhattan and Miami Beach. Liberman never retired from Condé Nast, but his attention to the details of the magazines gradually declined. In 1994 he stepped down as editorial director, remaining with the company as deputy editorial chairman. His energy did not flag; he prepared photographs taken over the course of a lifetime for publication. In addition to his well-known *The Artist in His Studio* (1960, reissued 1988), which stemmed from his 1959 solo photography exhibition at the Museum of Modern Art, and *Greece, Gods, and Art* (1968), Liberman authored *Mar-*

lene: An Intimate Photographic Record (1992), *Campidoglio* (1994), *Then: Photographs, 1925–1995* (1995), and *Prayers in Stone* (1997). He also continued to paint. Liberman died of natural causes in 1999 at age eighty-seven in Miami Beach.

Known as the "silver fox" for his dapper appearance and political manueverings, Liberman enjoyed enormous influence at Condé Nast. He had a style, identified by Calvin Tomkins as "protean and infinitely renewable," that adapted to an evolving audience, moving fashion publications from high-toned journals for the wealthy to magazines that captured the changing attitudes of society. Liberman described his approach as "anti-design." He posed the question, "What is design? It's making the use of the material—the way it's used—more important than the material itself."

★

The most important study of Liberman's life is the biography by Calvin Tomkins and Dodie Kazanjian, *Alex: The Life of Alexander Liberman* (1993), written with his full cooperation. His art is documented in Barbara Rose's monograph *Alexander Liberman* (1981) and James Pilgrim's exhibition catalogue for the Corcoran Gallery of Art, *Alexander Liberman: Painting and Sculpture, 1950–1970* (1970). Also notable is Liberman's introduction to Polly Devlin, *Vogue: Book of Fashion Photography, 1919–1979* (1979). Obituaries are in the *New York Times* (20 Nov. 1999), the business section of the *New York Post* (20 Nov. 1999), and Calvin Tomkins, "Balancing Act," *New Yorker* (6 Dec. 1999).

LEIGH BULLARD WEISBLAT

LICHTENSTEIN, Roy (*b.* 27 October 1923 in New York City; *d.* 29 September 1997 in New York City), painter and sculptor who was one of the foremost artists of the pop art movement.

Lichtenstein was the eldest of two children of Milton Lichtenstein, a realtor, and Beatrice Werner, a homemaker. As a boy, he designed model airplanes and listened to radio shows, among them "Flash Gordon" and "Mandrake the Magician." After attending Public School 9 in Manhattan, he studied at a private school, the Benjamin Franklin High School for Boys, graduating in June 1940. While at Franklin, he went to the jazz clubs around Fifty-second Street and made portraits of musicians. He took Saturday morning classes at the Parson School of Design, and in the summer of 1940 attended art classes at the Art Students League in New York, where Reginald Marsh was his instructor.

From the fall of 1940 until he was drafted by the U.S. Army in February 1943, Lichtenstein attended the School of Fine Arts at Ohio State University, where he was influenced by Professor Hoyt L. Sherman's theory of perception.

Sherman projected lantern-slide images briefly, then had the students draw what they had seen. Stationed in Europe with the Sixty-ninth Infantry Division, Lichtenstein drew landscapes and made portraits of soldiers. From October through November 1945 he attended history and French language classes at the Cité Universitaire in Paris, but returned to the United States upon the serious illness of his father. Reentering Ohio State in 1946, Lichtenstein received his B.F.A. degree in June 1946, his M.F.A. degree in June 1949, and taught there as an instructor until 1951, when he was denied tenure.

On 12 June 1949 he married Isabel Wilson, whom he met in Cleveland, where she was codirector of the Ten-Thirty Gallery. They had two sons, then divorced in 1965. On 1 November 1968 he married Dorothy Herzka. From 1951 to 1957 Lichtenstein worked in Cleveland as a graphic draftsman, a window designer, and a sheet-metal designer. In 1957 he made his first proto-pop work, a lithograph entitled *The Ten Dollar Bill*. From 1957 through 1960, while teaching as an assistant professor at the State University of New York at Oswego, he made renderings of the cartoon characters Mickey Mouse, Donald Duck, and others. From 1960 to 1964 he was an assistant professor at Douglass College of Rutgers University in New Brunswick, New Jersey, and while there he attended Allen Kaprow's "happenings."

In 1960 Lichtenstein's painting *Look, Mickey. I've Hooked a Big One!* was his first work taken directly from the panel of a comic strip, a picture of Donald Duck tugging at a fishing pole with its hook caught in his jacket. The next year he began using cartoon images regularly and also joined the prominent Leo Castelli Gallery in New York. In 1962 he was given his first solo exhibition at the Castelli Gallery. In 1963 he moved to Twenty-sixth Street in New York. That year he was one of ten artists commissioned by architect Philip Johnson to make twenty-foot-square works for his circular theater in New York's World Fair, and he was given a solo exhibition at the Galerie Ileana Sonnabend in Paris. Thereafter he was recognized as a major American artist.

In April 1967 Lichtenstein was given his first museum retrospective at the Pasadena Art Museum in California, and his first New York retrospective was held at the Guggenheim Museum in September 1969. In 1970 he moved to Southampton, Long Island, and that year was elected to the American Institute of Arts and Letters. On 11 November 1989 his *Torpedo . . . Los!* sold at Christie's for $5.5 million, making him only one of three living American artists (the others being Willem de Kooning and Jasper Johns) to sell at such a price.

By 1960 abstract expressionism, with its loose, painterly, rapidly executed improvisational style, was supplanted as the leading avant-garde aesthetic by new approaches,

Roy Lichtenstein. AP/WIDE WORLD PHOTOS

whether representational or nonobjective, that were cooler, tighter in execution, smoother in surface, conceptual in origin. Pop art, dealing in subject matter with mass-produced, commonplace, instantly recognizable objects, was one of these new approaches.

In his comic strip paintings, which he reproduced in a different medium and on a much larger scale, Lichtenstein used as his source a single panel of an actual comic-strip narrative, making certain modifications to get a leaner and more pared down image. He argued, "what I do is form, whereas the comic strip is not formed in the sense I'm using the word; the comics have shapes but there has been no effort to make them intensely unified." At the same time, so that the source could not be missed, Lichtenstein used for his paintings the benday dotted texture of the paper on which the comics were printed. He chose only emotionally-laden imagery dealing with war and romance. An example was *Whaam!* (1963), which depicted a dogfight between an American plane and its adversary, shown exploding after taking a direct hit. Some observers might have missed the distancing of war suggested by Lichtenstein in his "copy" of a copy (the comic book) of a representation (a painting or photograph of war) of the "original," which was the air battle itself. But the artist explained, "I want my work to look programmed or impersonal but I don't believe I'm being impersonal while I do it." And he ventured provocatively, "the closer my work is to the original, the more threatening and critical its content." There was a good deal of fastidiousness and skill that went into the making of each painting, but most crucial was the overriding concept.

Lichtenstein also made paintings based on paintings or parts of paintings by Paul Cézanne, Pablo Picasso, Henri Matisse, Piet Mondrian, and Claude Monet. His *Haystacks* (1968) and *Rouen Cathedral* series of 1969 were facsimiles of famous works by Monet dating to the 1890s. Lichtenstein gave them the look not of Monet's paintings, but of the cheap, garish posters often found in travel agents' offices, which themselves were reproductions of Monet's originals. Thus Lichtenstein's art dealt with the cheapening of experience, with vicariousness, with the coarsening of values endemic in society at large. Even sophisticated viewers could not be entirely clear as to how to take this art, whether as clever humor or as social commentary. That it can engender both responses simultaneously is part of its intriguing power.

One of Lichtenstein's most clever challenges to abstract expressionism was his rendering of brushstrokes as a subject in themselves, rather than using them, as the previous generation had, as the "building blocks" toward some sublime end. These broad swatches were at first set forth on canvases so large—the *Big Painting VI* (1965), for example, measured seven feet, eight and one-half inches by ten feet, nine inches—that the viewer was not sure what he or she was seeing. Discrepancies in size, as with the huge comic strip paintings (*Whaam!* was over thirteen feet in length), was an expressive device the artist commonly used to great effect. Sculpture of the brushstrokes came later. In 1977 Lichtenstein began making painted bronze sculpture. He made large, standing, open-air sculpture of the brushstrokes of painted aluminum, as a version of 1987 in which the swatches were set forth as a kind of frame. Sculpture in various media was an abiding interest. In 1979, through a grant from the National Endowment for the Arts, he received a sculpture commission and made a ten-foot-high *Mermaid* of steel and concrete for the Theater of the Performing Arts in Miami Beach, Florida.

In his comic strip paintings, in his works based on paintings of earlier modern masters, and in his series of *Brushstrokes,* Lichtenstein set forth an iconography of pop art as enduring as the most familiar works of Andy Warhol, James Rosenquist, and Robert Indiana. Lichtenstein died of pneumonia. He was survived by his second wife, Dorothy Herzka.

★

Diane Waldman's *Roy Lichtenstein* (1993) is the densest and most complete and scholarly book on the artist. See also Jack Cowart, *Lichtenstein 1970–1980* (1981), which has good illustrations, including some of colored pencil sketches and aluminum and bronze pieces; and Lawrence Alloway, *Roy Lichtenstein* (1983), by the noted critic who coined the term "pop art." See also Bernice Rose, *The Drawings of Roy Lichtenstein* (1987). An obituary is in the *New York Times* (30 Sept. 1997).

ABRAHAM A. DAVIDSON

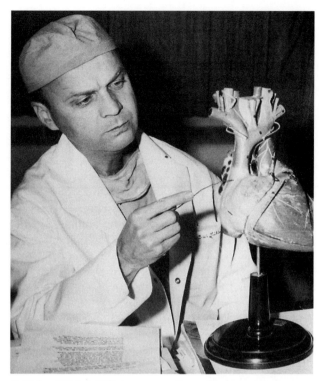

C. Walton Lillehei, 1957. ASSOCIATED PRESS AP

LILLEHEI, C(larence) Walton ("Walt") (*b.* 23 October 1918 in Minneapolis, Minnesota; *d.* 5 July 1999 in Saint Paul, Minnesota), physician who is considered the father of open-heart surgery.

Lillehei (pronounced LIL-la-high) was the eldest of the three children of Clarence Ingewald Lillehei, a dentist, and Elizabeth Lillian Walton, a professional piano player. He graduated from West High School in Minneapolis in 1935 and enrolled at the University of Minnesota in Minneapolis that autumn. He was drawn to medicine even though his high school chemistry teacher had predicted that he would not last six weeks in medical school. Despite this prognostication, Lillehei was awarded a B.S. degree in 1939 and an M.B. degree in 1941. He went on to earn an M.D. in 1942 and an M.S. degree in physiology and Ph.D. in surgery in 1951, all from the University of Minnesota.

Lillehei joined the U.S. Army in June 1942. He eventually commanded an army mobile surgical unit in North Africa and participated in the Allied landing at Anzio, Italy, for which he won a Bronze Star. He was discharged in February 1946. After he left the army, Lillehei joined the surgery department at the University of Minnesota Medical School in Minneapolis. He served as a research assistant to Dr. Owen H. Wangensteen, a renowned cancer specialist and the chief of surgery at the medical school, from October

1946 to December 1947, and as an assistant to Dr. Maurice B. Visscher, chairman of the Department of Physiology, from October 1948 to September 1949. Lillehei became a resident at the medical school in the autumn of 1947 and chief resident two years later.

In 1950 Lillehei developed lymphosarcoma, a cancer of the lymph system that often spreads to other parts of the body. Wangensteen performed radical surgery and prescribed radiation therapy, a grueling course of treatment that saved Lillehei's life. After a long and difficult recovery, he was able to resume his medical career.

In the years that followed, Lillehei developed techniques that made open-heart surgery possible. Until the 1950s, major heart defects could not be corrected surgically because there was no way to circulate or oxygenate the patient's blood during the operation. On 26 March 1954 Lillehei repaired a ventricular septal defect (VSD) on a thirteen-month-old infant by connecting the patient's bloodstream to that of his father, a technique called "cross-circulation." The operation was successful, although the boy died from pneumonia several days later. Despite the significant risk to the donor imposed by cross-circulation, Lillehei used the method to pioneer other open-heart surgical techniques, including the first repair of an atrioventricular canal, a heart defect considered more serious than VSD.

Lillehei and Richard A. DeWall developed a heart-lung machine, known as a helix reservoir bubble oxygenator, in

347

1955. The machine pumped oxygen through the blood during a heart operation, significantly reducing surgical risks posed by cross-circulation and increasing the survival rate of patients. In 1958 Lillehei pioneered a method to correct heart block, a condition that can occur during and after surgery when accidental injury prevents the body from producing the small electrical signals that regulate the heartbeat. Improving on an earlier design by Dr. Paul M. Zoll of the Harvard Medical School, Lillehei and his colleagues hooked wires directly to a living heart, supplying the missing electrical signals from outside the chest. The signals were generated by a battery-powered electronic device worn under the clothing—a pacemaker—that provided the electrical pulses for a steady heartbeat. An article in the *Saturday Evening Post* in 1961 showed Lillehei examining a boy named David Williams, who was holding the pacemaker that was keeping him alive. The device weighed eight to ten ounces and cost $385. At that time, only about 100 people in the world had pacemakers.

Lillehei left the University of Minnesota in 1967, after being passed over for the position of chairman of the department of surgery when Wangensteen retired. In November he became the chairman of the department of surgery at the Cornell Medical Center–New York Hospital, bringing along seventeen members of his Minnesota team. Two years later, Lillehei supervised the institution's first transplant of a heart and both lungs, during which the organs of a fifty-year-old woman were given to a forty-three-year-old man suffering from chronic emphysema. This was only the second such operation, and the patient survived for one week. In February 1968 Lillehei directed the team of surgeons who carried out the world's largest multiple-transplant operation and the first interhospital transplant. During this operation, the kidneys and corneas of a single person were donated to four people, and the heart and liver transplanted to two others.

By the end of the 1960s, Lillehei was widely known as the father of open-heart surgery. He had also developed artificial replacement heart valves, as well as a device that functioned like a booster pump. Lillehei belonged to forty-five scientific societies and served as the president of the American College of Cardiology from 1965 to 1967. He had trained 139 heart surgeons at Minnesota and 28 at Cornell. Twenty-three of his trainees became directors of cardiac surgery programs. Dr. Christiaan N. Barnard, the South African surgeon who performed the first heart transplant in 1967, was one of Lillehei's students at Minnesota, and Dr. Norman E. Shumway, who devised the techniques that made transplantation possible, was another. Lillehei also helped establish Minnesota's biotechnology industry, Medical Alley, a consortium of some 500 medical companies.

But Lillehei's reputation as a man who liked fast cars and the high life was also firmly entrenched. He was known to be arrogant and outspoken, often disregarding the advice of other physicians and defying medical conventions. His chronic habits of procrastination and inattention to paperwork caught up with him when was convicted on five counts of tax evasion between 1964 and 1968. Although he was facing twenty-five years in prison, Lillehei was fined $50,000 and sentenced to six months of community service. The American College of Surgeons suspended his license indefinitely, as did the state of Minnesota, temporarily.

Lillehei returned to Minnesota in 1975, where he became a professor of surgery at the University of Minnesota Medical Center and the Variety Club Heart Hospital. He also served as director of medical affairs at Saint Jude Medical, a manufacturer of surgical equipment in Saint Paul. During his career, Lillehei wrote over 700 hundred papers and articles, including 54 in 1969, his most prolific year. When presented with one of his many honors, he quoted the comedian Jack Benny: "I don't deserve this award. But I've got arthritis and I don't deserve that, either."

Lillehei met Katherine (Kaye) Ruth Lindberg in 1946 at Minneapolis General Hospital, where she was a nursing student; they married on New Year's Eve of that year. The couple were married for fifty-two years, and during that time contributed millions to charities through the C. Walton and Katherine R. Lillehei Foundation. When Lillehei succumbed to cancer in 1999, he was survived by his wife and three of their four children, two of whom were also surgeons. He is buried in Fort Snelling National Cemetery, Minneapolis.

In the year Lillehei died, more than 125,000 open-heart operations, approximately 600,000 coronary-bypass procedures, and over 2,200 heart transplantations were performed in the United States. None could have been performed without Lillehei's pioneering surgical work.

★

Lillehei's papers, mostly patient records, are deposited in the University of Minnesota archives. G. Wayne Miller has written a sympathetic and moving biography, *King of Hearts: The True Story of the Maverick Who Pioneered Open Heart Surgery* (2000). See also Leonard G. Wilson, *Medical Revolution in Minnesota: A History of the University of Minnesota Medical School* (1989); Stephen M. Spencer, "Making a Heartbeat Behave," *Saturday Evening Post* (4 Mar. 1961); and *Current Biography* (May 1969). Obituaries are in the *Minneapolis Star Tribune* (8 July 1999), *New York Times* (9 July 1999), and *Minnesota Medicine* (Dec. 1999).

JOHN L. SCHERER

LIMAN, Arthur Lawrence (*b.* 5 November 1932 in New York City; *d.* 17 July 1997 in New York City), trial and corporate lawyer who rose to fame as chief counsel in the congressional investigation of the Iran-Contra scandal, also chief investigator in Attica prison riot probe.

Arthur Liman, 1987. CORBIS CORPORATION (NEW YORK)

Liman, the younger of two children, was born to Harry K. and Celia Feldman. Celia taught Latin in the New York City public schools, while Harry manufactured dresses. Liman grew up in Lawrence, Long Island, New York, in the 1930s and 1940s amidst anti-Semitism and restricted communities. Liman thereby gained a respect for tolerance, due process, and civil liberties. He graduated from Lawrence High School in 1950. Majoring in government at Harvard, he was a member of Phi Beta Kappa and graduated in 1954. Outraged by the McCarthy hearings against suspected communists in Boston, he wrote his senior thesis on the constitutional limits of congressional investigations and decided to become a lawyer. In 1957 Liman graduated first in his class from Yale Law School. In November he turned down a teaching job there to join Paul, Weiss, Rifkind, Wharton and Garrison in Manhattan as a tax lawyer. As a young liberal democrat, Liman was thrilled when one of his first cases after switching to litigation was a May 1958 appeal with Adlai E. Stevenson, the two-time Democratic Party nominee for president.

Liman married Ellen Fogelson, a painter and designer, on 20 September 1959. The first of their three children was born in 1961. Taking a leave from the firm that year to help form the new Stock Fraud Unit to battle securities fraud under U.S. District Attorney Robert M. Morgenthau, Liman took a pay cut from $8,500 to $6,000. Morgenthau considered Liman "so brilliant he could take the socks off a witness without untying his shoes." Here he honed a courtroom style described as "plain, simple, orderly, and

sincere." In November 1963 Liman returned to Paul, Weiss to specialize in securities and white-collar litigation. Made partner in January 1966, Liman represented many high-profile corporate clients, including Herb Siegel (Cris-Craft Industries), William Paley (CBS), Steve Ross (Time Warner), and Felix Rohatyn (Lazard Frère). His business advice became as highly prized as his legal ability. By 1976 he became a leader of the firm, commanding fees of $450 an hour in 1991.

But Liman believed in combining private practice with public service. He took leave from Paul, Weiss a second time to serve as chief counsel to the New York State Special Commission on Attica (known as the McKay Commission), set up to investigate the country's worst prison riot. The Attica Prison riot, which occurred between 9 and 13 September 1971, left forty-three dead and more than eighty injured. The key to success in this year-long investigation was Liman's insistence, against the wishes of the authorities, on eating Christmas dinner with 500 maximum security inmates in order to win their trust. The resulting 470-page report, highly critical of Governor Nelson Rockefeller and the New York State prison authorities, was issued in book form on the riot's anniversary, 13 September 1972. Its thoroughness and eloquence won it a National Book Award nomination and helped start the prison rights movement in America. "Attica is every prison," the introduction explained, "and every prison is Attica." Liman was changed by this "searing, unsettling, and unforgettable" experience.

Liman returned to Paul, Weiss but continued his involvement in public service. In 1975 he helped found the Legal Action Center, which uses class action suits to fight discrimination in public employment. In 1976 he served as prosecutor in Richard Nixon's New York State disbarment proceedings. From 1983 to 1985 he served as president of the New York City Legal Aid Society, the largest criminal defense firm in the United States, at a time when morale was low, workload was high, and public support plummeting. He worked hard to rebuild the society and strengthen its civil division. In 1985 New York City Mayor Ed Koch asked Liman to head an investigation into the medical examiner's handling of the "unclassifiable" deaths of those who died in police custody. After a three month investigation, Liman reported that there was no cover-up, concluding that the medical examiner was merely "a terrible and terribly sloppy administrator."

In 1979 Liman brought suit against Rockwell Industries for providing New York City with 754 faulty R-46 subway cars. The jury awarded the city $72 million. It was one of his favorite cases. "We had shown the world that New York City, which had almost declared bankruptcy a few years earlier, was capable of fighting back," he explained, "I was able to give something back to the city that I love at a time of its greatest need." Other major public appointments were the Advisory Commission on the Administration of Justice (1981), the New York State Executive Advisory Committee on Sentencing Reform (1983–1985), and Chair, New York City Commission on Mayoral Appointments (1990).

Liman's most visible public appointment came between 5 May and 6 August 1987, when he served as chief counsel to the U.S. Senate Select Committee on Secret Military Assistance to Iran and the Nicaraguan Opposition, known as the Iran-Contra arms scandal. Chosen because of his experience in complex financial cases and his outsider status, he was nonetheless vilified as Americans watched the proceedings, a public relations disaster for Congress. The hate mail poured in, and for a time Liman received special police protection. Some felt Liman was sarcastic and combative when questioning Reagan administration figures like John M. Poindexter, Richard V. Secord, and Oliver North, while others thought him too accommodating. Liman later took responsibility for turning North into a national hero. Some blamed Liman for being too nonpartisan and treating this constitutional crisis as just another white-collar crime case. His defenders blamed political exigencies and Congress's timidity. Nonetheless, when the committee's report came out in November 1987, it, like the Attica report, was praised in the *New York Times* as "that rarest of species: a well-written, readable government report."

Liman again took the public stage when he defended Michael Milken against government accusations of securities fraud violations. Milken, the demonized "Junk Bond King," was portrayed by the media as embodying all the excesses and greed of Wall Street in the 1980s. Liman was devastated when Milken was sentenced in 1990 to ten years in prison, reduced on appeal to twenty-two months. Other famous clients in the 1980s included Robert Vesco and John Zaccaro.

Liman was a member of many corporate, educational, arts, and museum boards and foundations. He served on many legal commissions. In 1987 he was awarded the United Jewish Appeal's Judge Proskauer Award for Public Service. In 1996 Yale Law School established a professorship in his honor, as well as the Liman Fellowship and Fund for Public Service.

The Limans lived in elegance at 1060 Fifth Avenue in Manhattan, and had a waterside home in Westchester, New York. Their home was filled with the nineteenth-century board games that Liman collected. His other hobbies were tennis, deep-sea fishing on his boat, theater, and reading. Liman's manner outside the courtroom was distracted. At six feet three inches tall and 165 pounds, he was ungainly, rumpled, and notoriously absent-minded. His salt-and-pepper hair, which one late-night comedian called "baked ziti," lay across his forehead. But inside the courtroom he was focused and cold-blooded, especially talented at cross-examination. One writer described Liman, with his strong New York accent, as "Walter Matthau doing a Perry Mason impersonation," while another compared his "woeful countenance" at the Iran-Contra hearings to "a cross between Zero Mostel and Buster Keaton." A workaholic, he had a photographic memory for details. Liman believed that a trial is theater, with the lawyer not an actor but a director who needed a good story, a strong cast, and the right sets. From the very start, Liman decided that he would split his work between private practice and public service, and he excelled at both. He was one of the great lawyer-citizens.

Liman died in his home at age sixty-four after a long fight with bladder cancer. A memorial service was held at Lincoln Center.

★

Liman's autobiography, *Lawyer: A Life of Counsel and Controversy,* written with the assistance of Peter Israel, appeared posthumously in 1998. Many profiles of Liman appeared in the aftermath of Iran-Contra and the Milken trial. The best of these are *Current Biography* (1988); Tad Friend, "The Verdict on Arthur Liman," *Esquire* (Jan. 1989); and Jennet Conant, "The Trials of Arthur Liman," *Vanity Fair* (June 1991). Liman was also profiled in Donald E. Vinson, *America's Top Trial Lawyers: Who They Are and Why They Win* (1994). An obituary is in the *New York Times* (18 July 1997).

SHARONA A. LEVY

LINK, Arthur Stanley (*b*. 8 August 1920 in New Market, Virginia; *d*. 26 March 1998 in Advance, North Carolina), historian and editor best known for his biography of Woodrow Wilson and as the editor of the comprehensive printed edition of Wilson's papers.

Link was one of four children of John William Link, a Lutheran minister, and Helen Elizabeth Link (her maiden name was Link also), a homemaker. Arthur Link grew up and attended elementary and high schools in Mount Pleasant, North Carolina. He studied at the University of North Carolina at Chapel Hill from 1937 to 1941, receiving an A.B. degree with highest honors in 1941. He attempted to enlist for military service during World War II but was rejected because of the first of a long series of back ailments that would plague him throughout his adult life. Instead, he did graduate work in history at the University of North Carolina, receiving an A.M. degree in 1942 and a Ph.D. in 1945. During his graduate studies, he became interested in the life and political career of Woodrow Wilson, president of the United States from 1913 to 1921. The extensive collections of President Wilson's personal and public papers

Arthur S. Link. ARCHIVE PHOTOS, INC.

at the Library of Congress and the National Archives in Washington, D.C., were just becoming available for research. Link's doctoral dissertation was a study of the political campaigns in the American South from 1910 to 1912. He was already becoming known as a prodigious researcher and writer. He married Margaret McDowell Douglas on 2 June 1945; they had four children.

In 1945 Link began his teaching career as an instructor in history at Princeton University, where Woodrow Wilson had been an undergraduate, faculty member, and president. He was promoted to assistant professor in 1948. In 1947 he published *Wilson: The Road to the White House*, the first volume of his biography. In 1949 he became an associate professor of history at Northwestern University in Evanston, Illinois. He was promoted to professor in 1954 and remained at Northwestern until 1960. During these years he wrote *Woodrow Wilson and the Progressive Era, 1910–1917* (1954), the first published volume in the New American Nation Series; *American Epoch: A History of the United States Since the 1890s* (1955), which in that and later editions became a highly successful college textbook; *Wilson the Diplomatist: A Look at His Major Foreign Policies* (1957); and *Wilson: The New Freedom* (1956) and *Wilson: The Struggle for Neutrality, 1914–1915* (1960), the second and third volumes of his biography, both of which were awarded the Bancroft Prize for the best book in American history for their respective years of publication. From 1958 to 1959, he served as the Harmsworth Professor of American History at Oxford University.

In 1958 the Woodrow Wilson Foundation, a philanthropic agency established during Wilson's lifetime to perpetuate his ideals, decided to devote all of its financial resources to the publication of a comprehensive edition of Wilson's papers. A search committee chose Link as editor of the project. The editorial work was to be done at Princeton University, and the Princeton University Press would publish the volumes. Link returned to Princeton University as a professor of history in 1960 and for some years maintained a full teaching schedule. He served on the executive committee of the Organization of American Historians from 1959 to 1962 and was a fellow of the Society of American Historians. He became the Edwards Professor of American History in 1965 and the George Henry Davis Professor of American History in 1976. He also served as vice president and president of the Southern Historical Association.

Link produced two more volumes of his biography: *Wilson: Confusions and Crises, 1915–1916* (1964) and *Wilson: Campaigns for Progressivism and Peace, 1916–1917* (1965), which told the story from Wilson's reelection to the presidency in 1916 to the U.S. declaration of war against Germany and Austria-Hungary in April 1917. He also wrote several high school and college textbooks in American history as well as numerous shorter works. However, *The Papers of Woodrow Wilson* took up an increasing amount of his time, and he realized he would never be able to complete both the biography and the editorial project. Link assembled a small, highly competent staff, several members of which remained through virtually the entire life of the project. The first volume of the *Papers* was published in 1966, and the last volume, the sixty-ninth, appeared in 1994. There were sixty-four volumes of documents, each volume averaging 600 pages in length, and five index volumes. Link and his staff did not print every Wilson document. Rather, they attempted to print every significant document *by* Wilson himself; all documents *to* Wilson, such as letters, memoranda, and reports that had a genuine impact on him; and many third-party records, such as diary entries and reports of foreign diplomats to their governments that reported conversations with Wilson. The editors made every effort to recover the text of Wilson's speeches, many of which were to be found only in newspapers or in shorthand reports. The edition also includes Wilson's more important books and articles. All of this work was done without the use of computers, largely because Link and his associates were well along in their task before computers began to be used in historical editing in the 1980s and saw no reason to change their methods.

Link completed his editorial work on the *Papers* in 1992, a year after his official retirement from Princeton University. He and his wife then moved to Advance, near Greensboro, North Carolina. He died of lung cancer at the age of seventy-seven, and his body was cremated.

Link and Woodrow Wilson had in common a strong religious faith: both were active lay members of the governing bodies of the Presbyterian Church during their adult lives. Link, in fact, felt that he had a divine mission to edit Wilson's papers. As he told an interviewer, Terry Teachout, "I believe God created me to do this. . . . Not many people in this day and age would think there was such a thing as a divine call, but I do, and I had it." Link's admiration for Wilson could border on the idolatrous. Again speaking to Teachout, he remarked, "I've read a lot of history in my life, and I think that aside from Saint Paul, Jesus, and the great religious prophets, Woodrow Wilson was the most admirable character I've ever encountered in history, and the most wonderful person." Whatever one may think of sentiments such as these, they reveal the driving force in Link that enabled him to persevere and complete a vast editorial project in the face of often excruciating back pain and other physical problems that would have put an end to the careers of most people. He did not allow his admiration for Wilson to hinder the objective presentation of his papers. *The Papers of Woodrow Wilson,* as edited by Link and his associates, will stand as a basic resource for the study of Wilson and his era for generations to come.

★

A collection of Link's papers is in the Mudd Library at Princeton University. There is no biography or autobiography. Marcia G. Synnott, "Arthur S. Link," in Clyde N. Wilson, ed., *Twentieth-Century American Historians* (1983), and John Milton Cooper, Jr., "Arthur S. Link," in Robert Allen Rutland, ed., *Clio's Favorites: Leading Historians of the United States, 1945–2000* (2000), provide thoughtful evaluations of Link and his work. Jim Schlosser, "Historian Comes Full Circle After Pursuing Woodrow Wilson for a Half-Century, Arthur Link Has Come Back to North Carolina," *Greensboro News and Record* (30 May 1993); Terry Teachout, "35 Years with Woodrow Wilson: The Journey of a Long-Distance Editor," *New York Times Book Review* (31 Oct. 1993); and James Robert Carroll, *The Real Woodrow Wilson: An Interview with Arthur S. Link, Editor of the Wilson Papers* (2001), all provide useful biographical material and quotations. Obituaries are in the *Raleigh News and Observer* (27 Mar. 1998) and *New York Times* (29 Mar. 1998).

JOHN E. LITTLE

LOWE, Stewart Alexander ("Alex") (*b.* 24 December 1958 in Missoula, Montana; *d.* 5 October 1999 on Shishapangma, Tibet), expert mountaineer who set numerous international climbing records, earning acclaim as the world's best climber according to *Outside* magazine.

Lowe was the second of three sons born to James Lowe, an entomology professor at the University of Montana, and Dorothea "Dottie" Lowe, a schoolteacher. Lowe, who had enjoyed the outdoors since childhood, took up climbing at the age of sixteen when Marvin McDonald, a University of Montana student, taught him the fundamentals. Climbing quickly became Lowe's passion. Lowe graduated from high school in 1976. He was a gifted student of mathematics and received a chemical engineering scholarship to Montana State University in Bozeman. He dropped out of college after his sophomore year, however, to pursue climbing full time. He spent the next few years traveling and climbing in Europe, Canada, and the United States. In the winter, he worked in Montana's oil fields to finance his climbing trips. In 1981 Lowe and his future wife, Jennifer Leigh, began working with a seismic exploration crew, setting up equipment for geophysicists in Montana, Colorado, and Utah. After three months, the pair traveled around Europe, climbing in the Alps and other locales. They were married in 1982.

In order to start a career that could support a family, Lowe returned to Montana State University and earned a degree in applied mathematics. He started work on a graduate degree in mechanical engineering in 1988 but left school to work as an engineer at Schlumberger Oilfield Services. Jennifer gave up mountain climbing and began a

Alex Lowe. AP/WIDE WORLD PHOTOS

career as an artist. In 1990 Lowe left his job to help lead the first guided tour up Mount Everest. After this trip, his income was dependent upon temporary jobs and work as a climbing guide.

Lowe cemented his reputation as a world-class climber in 1993, when he became one of the first Westerners to compete in the Khan-Tengri International Speed Climbing Competition, an annual race to the summit of Kyrgyzstan's 22,950-foot-tall Khan-Tengri mountain and back to the base camp. Lowe not only won the competition but also broke the race record by more than four hours. In 1995 Lowe joined The North Face's "Dream Team" of world class mountaineers who tested equipment and served as spokespeople for The North Face, an outdoor equipment company. With The North Face providing a salary and financing his trips, Lowe could at last make a living from mountain climbing.

Lowe was regarded as one of the world's greatest mountaineers because of his versatility with rock and ice climbing and ski descents. A lank and muscular man, Lowe also set records and was willing to take on unique challenges. He made the first one-day ascent of the Andromeda Strain in the Canadian Rockies in 1983; solo-climbed the Root Canal in the Grand Tetons, Wyoming, in 1993; and made the first winter ascents of the South Buttress Right, South Buttress Direct, and Laughing Lion Falls of Mount Moran,

Grand Tetons, with his friend Jack Tackle between 1984 and 1986. He solo-climbed the North Face of Grand Teton in a record eighteen hours in the winter of 1991 and then beat his own record by three hours in 1993. Lowe made the first ski descents of the northwest couloir of Middle Teton in 1992 and Enclosure Couloir of Grand Teton in 1994. In 1991 he made the first winter ascent of the Northwest Chimney on the Grand Teton, and set the record time of eight hours, fifteen minutes for the Tetons's Grand Traverse. He made the first ascent of Prophet on a Stick in Provo Canyon, Utah, in 1992.

Lowe reached the summit of Mount Everest for a second time in 1993. In 1996 he pioneered five of the most difficult mixed-route climbs in North America. He made the first ascent of the smooth granite surface of Rakekniven in Queen Maud Land, a bitterly cold, unexplored climbing area in Antarctica in 1997, and climbed the remote Great Sail Peak on Baffin Island in 1998. His climbs included the Matterhorn in the Alps, Annapurna in the Himalayas, K2 in Kashmir, Anconcogua in Argentina, and Kusum Kanguru in Tibet. He also climbed El Capitan in Yosemite National Park in ten hours. Lowe distinguished himself in 1995 when he saved the lives of other climbers on Mount McKinley. In a storm, Lowe carried a Spanish climber, suffering from the last stages of hypothermia, uphill and over treacherous terrain to 19,500 feet and a waiting rescue helicopter. Later, he helped lead two lost Taiwanese climbers to safety.

Although he had had reconstructive knee surgery a few months earlier, in July 1999, Lowe made what he considered to be his most rewarding climb—an ascent of Grand Teton with his oldest son, Max, age ten. He also made the first ascent of Pakistan's Great Trango Tower's northwest vertical rock face that summer. His last expedition was to Tibet. He planned to become one of the first climbers to ski down Shishapangma, the fourteenth highest peak in the world. The adventure was being filmed for NBC. Although not the most hazardous trip that he had ever undertaken, Lowe and twenty-nine-year-old cameraman David Bridges were swept away by a sudden avalanche. Another climber, Lowe's friend Conrad Anker, barely escaped with his life. The bodies of Lowe and Bridges were not recovered.

In the months before his death, Lowe was hailed as "the world's best climber" by *Outside* magazine. Lowe modestly downplayed such accolades. Among climbers, he had earned the nicknames "Lung(s) with Legs," "The Mutant," "The Secret Weapon," and "The White Knight," and was celebrated for his strength and stamina. He maintained supreme physical conditioning at an age when most other climbers curtail their activities. Nonetheless, Lowe was devoted to his wife and three young boys and worked to strike a balance between fatherhood and mountaineering. Friends and fellow climbers remember Lowe for his humility, charisma, and boyish charm.

★

Lowe and his family are profiled in "The Mutant and the Boy Scout Battle at 20,000 Feet," *Outside* (Mar. 1999). Tributes to Lowe were published after his death in *Sports Illustrated* and *U.S. News and World Report* (both 18 Oct. 1999) and *People Weekly* (25 Oct. 1999). Obituaries are in the *Seattle Times* (6 Oct. 1999), and *New York Times* and *Oregonian* (both 7 Oct. 1999).

KATHY S. MASON

LUCKMAN, Sid(ney) (*b.* 21 November 1916 in Brooklyn, New York; *d.* 5 July 1998 in North Miami Beach, Florida), Hall of Fame football quarterback who pioneered the modern T-formation.

Luckman was the son of Meyer Luckman, a truck driver, and Ethel Drukman. He grew up in the Williamsburg area of Brooklyn and attended grammar school at P.S. 118. At age eight, Luckman got his first football and began playing in pickup games. "We used to wait for the cars to pass, then we'd start playing," he later recalled. An elusive run-

Sid Luckman, 1943. ASSOCIATED PRESS AP

ner and skillful defender, he led Brooklyn's Erasmus Hall High School to the city championship. Indeed, according to *Life* magazine, Luckman became "the greatest scholastic player the city has ever seen."

Although offered athletic scholarships by many colleges, Luckman selected Columbia University, where he paid his way by working as a painter, chauffeur, and babysitter. Luckman chose Columbia because he wanted an Ivy League education and also because he admired its legendary coach, Lou Little. "The first time I saw him, he had class all over him," Little said of his star recruit. Columbia opened the 1936 season against Maine, and the sophomore Luckman, making his first start at tailback, ran forty yards for a touchdown and threw for two more scores. Under Little's direction Luckman developed into a triple-threat back. He was an outstanding punter and place-kicker, a superb passer, and a breakaway runner.

In Luckman's three years at Columbia, the Lions lost more games than they won. "Even though we fought with all our hearts, we were always up against opponents who were bigger and stronger," he recalled. But Luckman was practically a one-man team. In his senior year, he led Columbia to a 20–18 upset over Army. He completed eighteen passes, including two for touchdowns, and returned a kick-off for an eighty-five yard touchdown. "He's the perfect football player," said Army Coach Gar Davidson.

Following the Army game, Luckman made the cover of *Life* magazine, which called him "the most talked-of football player in the U.S." and suggested that he might be the best passer of all-time. Luckman finished third in the balloting for the Heisman trophy and made the 1938 All-American team at tailback. Luckman graduated from Columbia in 1939. That same year he married Estelle Morglan; they had three children.

George Halas, the owner and coach of the Chicago Bears in the National Football League (NFL), had followed Luckman's career since high school and traded for his draft rights. "I have no intention of playing professional football," Luckman informed Halas. "In fact, I have been advised against it. My plans are to enter the trucking business." But Halas got Luckman to change his mind and signed him for $6,000 in 1939.

Halas and his coaching associate Clark Shaugnessy were in the process of inventing the modern T-formation with a man in motion. By adding the new position of flanker and putting a halfback in motion, Halas hoped to open up the game by giving the quarterback multiple options. "I'd been a single-wing tailback. You're set deep, the ball comes to you, and you either pass, run or spin," Luckman said in a 1998 interview with *Sports Illustrated*. "When I came to the Bears, we worked for hours on my spinning, on hiding the ball, only this time it was as a T quarterback. We spent endless time just going over my footwork, faking, spinning, setting up as fast as I could, running to my left and throwing right."

In his rookie season, Luckman played behind quarterback Bernie Masterson. The Bears were still using a single-wing offense. On 22 October 1939 the New York Giants were leading the Bears 16–0 in the fourth quarter at the Polo Grounds, when Luckman took over the offense. Striking for two quick touchdowns, he sparked a comeback that fell short but excited his teammates. Two weeks later he threw the winning touchdown pass for the Bears in a 30–27 victory over the Green Bay Packers, who went on to win the 1939 NFL championship. The Bears finished second with a record of 8–3.

Using the T-formation, Luckman, as starting quarterback, changed the game in 1940 as he led the Bears to the NFL title with a 73–0 blowout over the Washington Redskins. The *New York Times* observed: "No field general ever called plays more artistically. He was letter perfect." Luckman directed the Bears to five division titles and four NFL championships in seven years. During the 1941–1942 season, the Bears won eighteen straight games, including two playoff victories. They successfully defended their championship in 1941 but were upset in 1942. The offense that Luckman introduced in 1940 has remained the basic formation in professional football for more than sixty years.

"I don't think I can ever recall a game where Sid called the wrong play," Halas said. "Having this fellow at quarterback was the equivalent of having another coach on the field. He was the greatest play director I have ever seen."

The 1943 season was Luckman's greatest year. On 14 November he set a league record that has never been broken, throwing seven touchdown passes against the Giants. In the championship game that year, he threw five touchdowns against the Redskins. Luckman, who connected for twenty-eight touchdowns, was voted the NFL's Most Valuable Player in 1943.

During World War II Luckman served as an ensign in the U.S. Merchant Marine and did stints in the Atlantic on tankers and transport ships. On his return to the Bears, he led Chicago to the 1946 NFL title by running and passing for touchdowns against the New York Giants in a 24–14 victory. When the rival All-America Football Conference was founded in 1946, the Chicago Rockets offered Luckman a $125,000, five-year contract, which would have made him the highest paid player in the history of the game. Luckman declined the offer. "The Bears and Coach Halas meant too much to me," he told the *Chicago Sun-Times* in 1996. "How could I quit a club that had done so much for me?" Luckman ended his career in 1950 with 14,686 passing yards, 137 touchdown passes, and completion rate of 52 percent. A member of the All NFL team in five of his twelve seasons, Luckman was elected to the Pro Football Hall of Fame in 1965.

From 1940 until 1995 Luckman was part owner and sales executive for Cellu-Craft, Inc., a firm manufacturing packaging materials for food products. Luckman made shrewd investments and became a multimillionaire. He remained in the Chicago area and also had a home in Florida. He died of a heart attack and is buried in Memorial Park Cemetery in Skokie, Illinois.

★

Luckman is profiled in Murray Olderman, *The Pro Quarterback* (1966); George Sullivan, *The Gamemakers: Pro Football's Great Quarterbacks from Baugh to Namath* (1971); Lud Duroska, *Great Pro Quarterbacks* (1974); Beau Riffenburgh and David Boss, *Great Ones: NFL Quarterbacks from Baugh to Montana* (1989); Richard Whittingham, *The Bears: A 75-Year Celebration* (1994); and Ron Smith, *The Sporting News Selects Football's 100 Greatest Players* (1999). An interview with Luckman is included in Richard Whittingham, *What A Game They Played* (1984). "Legend of the Fall," a portrait of Luckman, is in the *Chicago Sun-Times* (15 Dec. 1996). Paul Zimmerman, "Revolutionaries," which cites Luckman as one of the six quarterbacks who had the most impact on professional football, is in *Sports Illustrated* (17 Aug. 1998). An obituary is in the *Chicago Sun-Times* (6 July 1998).

STEVE NEAL

LUKAS, J(ay) Anthony (*b.* 25 April 1933 in New York City; *d.* 5 June 1997 in New York City), journalist and author best known for using his craft to promote social justice and for winning two Pulitzer Prizes—one for newspaper journalism and the other for the book *Common Ground,* an in-depth investigation of the Boston busing crisis.

One of two sons born to civil rights lawyer Edwin Jay Lukas and actress Elizabeth Schamberg, Lukas grew up in New York City. His mother committed suicide when he was eight years old. After graduating from the Putney School in Vermont, Lukas attended Harvard College, where he worked as a reporter and assistant managing editor for the *Harvard Crimson.* His stories for the *Crimson* on the perils of McCarthyism gave the first hint of his later career as a keen analyst of American social and political tensions. Lukas graduated from Harvard with a B.A. degree magna cum laude in 1955, and pursued graduate studies at the Free University of Berlin from 1955 to 1956.

Following service in the army, Lukas began his journalism career in earnest. He worked first for the *Baltimore Sun* from 1958 to 1962, where he covered race relations in Maryland and chronicled the treatment of Filipino stewards at the Naval Academy in Annapolis, Maryland, whom he described as living in a "caste system of slavery." He left the *Sun* to join the *New York Times,* where he covered the 1964 uprising in the Congo and the 1965 war between India

J. Anthony Lukas, 1968. AP/WIDE WORLD PHOTOS

and Pakistan. Lukas proved his mettle as a combat reporter in the Congo when he reported that government troops in the capital of Kisingani (formerly known as Stanleyville) were guilty of killing rebel sympathizers.

Lukas's primary area of interest, however, remained the tensions within American society in the 1960s, and he returned to New York City in 1967 to begin his rise to prominence as one of the nation's keenest social observers. His first Pulitzer Prize was awarded in 1968 for "The Two Worlds of Linda Fitzpatrick," a detailed investigative report about a Connecticut teenager from a wealthy family who had moved to Manhattan ostensibly to begin a career as an artist, but was later found murdered with her "hippie" boyfriend in the East Village. In fact, Fitzpatrick had, without her parents' knowledge, led a life so alien to her upbringing that her family could scarcely come to terms with it. Lukas uncovered a startling second life in which Fitzpatrick's East Village friends described her as fully enmeshed in the neighborhood's counterculture. She regularly used LSD

and speed, smoked marijuana, panhandled in Washington Square Park, lived in a dingy hotel, traveled to San Francisco, and believed in her own supernatural abilities. Ultimately, this secret life challenged the assumptions of her traditional one. But it also resulted in her death, or so Lukas implied. In this way, Lukas bridged the sensibilities of his mainstream readers to this new world, a counterculture that was increasingly attractive to younger people. In his portrayal of the two realms as representative of the divisions plaguing American society at the time, Lukas acted as an interpreter for mainstream America, a reporter adventurous enough to brave this new world. He later expanded on the Fitzpatrick story with profiles of ten other young people in a book, *Don't Shoot—We Are Your Children!* (1971).

Following a year as a Nieman Fellow at Harvard, Lukas continued his examination of the social and political forces dividing the United States at the time. He covered the trial of the Chicago Seven, antiwar activists who were indicted for crossing state lines to incite a riot at the 1968 Democratic National Convention. In his trial reporting, Lukas grew frustrated with the editors at the *Times* who insisted that he substitute "barnyard epithet" for the word "bullshit" (which the defendants frequently shouted during the proceedings). After completing a book, *The Barnyard Epithet and Other Obscenities: Notes on the Chicago Conspiracy Trial* (1970), Lukas left the *Times* to do freelance work and to found his own monthly magazine, a journalism review called *MORE*. In 1973 and 1974 he covered the Watergate scandal for the *New York Times Magazine,* and he eventually produced one of the more highly regarded books on the subject, *Nightmare: The Underside of the Nixon Years* (1975).

Lukas then virtually disappeared for almost ten years as he worked on his masterpiece, *Common Ground: A Turbulent Decade in the Lives of Three American Families* (1985). In the course of investigating the Boston busing crisis from the perspective of three families who lived through it—one poor African-American, one working-class Irish, one Yankee professional—Lukas established his reputation as an obsessively thorough researcher. He conducted several hundred interviews and combed a variety of other sources. At one point, four years into the project, Lukas dropped one family for another because, he said, it "was not working dramatically." In addition, he traveled to Nova Scotia to visit the cemetery where the ancestors of one family were buried and flew to Ireland to trace the history of another. Friends said he agonized over how much context was needed and how to weave the family stories together. He found emotional support in Linda Healey, an editor at Pantheon Books, whom he married in September 1982.

Although the premise of *Common Ground* most obviously addressed Boston's strained race relations in the wake of Judge W. Arthur Garrity's federal court order to bus children from black neighborhoods to schools in white neighborhoods, Lukas uncovered a larger subtext rooted in class issues. The final product, a narrative that attends to not only the personal stories of the three families, but also to the public role of some of Boston's most important political figures, ends with the Yankee liberal (who worked for the mayor) suggesting that "only by providing jobs and other economic opportunities for the deprived—black and white alike—could the city reduce the deep sense of grievance harbored by both communities, alleviate some of the antisocial behavior grounded in such resentments, and begin to close the terrible gap between the rich and the poor, the suburb and the city, the hopeful and the hopeless." Such parting thoughts were typical of Lukas, who always sought to place his subjects in a larger context. After the book's publication, Lukas remarked that he devoted so much time and energy to the project because he believed "that what happened in Boston was not a random series of events but the acting out of the burden of American history."

In addition to winning the Pulitzer Prize, *Common Ground* won the National Book Award and the National Book Critics Circle Award, and later was made into a docudrama on network television. *Common Ground* proved a difficult act to follow. Lukas continued to write book reviews and freelance articles, but he soon embarked on another massive project that resulted in his final book, *Big Trouble: A Murder in a Small Western Town Sets Off a Struggle for the Soul of America* (1997). Acutely concerned with class issues and aware of his own era as one in which, as he noted in the book's introduction, "the gap between our richest and poorest citizens grows ever wider," Lukas for the first time began investigating a topic that did not take place in his lifetime: the 1905 bombing assassination of Frank Steunenberg, the former governor of Idaho. Steunenberg's murder was one act in a turn-of-the-century class war that pitted workers against bosses. The authorities immediately suspected labor agitators had killed Steunenberg

as revenge for his use of troops while governor in putting down labor unrest in the silver and lead mines of the Coeur D'Alene region of northern Idaho. The case took on national significance when the accused assassin implicated several leaders of the Western Federation of Miners (including Big Bill Haywood, also the leader of the radical Industrial Workers of the World), who then hired America's most famous defense attorney, Clarence Darrow, to defend them. Ultimately, only the assassin was convicted while the three union leaders were acquitted.

In *Big Trouble,* Lukas succeeded in recreating a world in which class warfare was readily apparent and in which the labor movement demonstrated its vitality and allure through its constant struggle with corporate and government forces. Lukas did not solve the crime for the reader (whether or not Haywood and the other leaders were involved) and, instead, went to great lengths to demonstrate the power of the forces arrayed against labor in that period. But Lukas's work on the book left him despondent and depressed. His notorious perfectionism led to doubt and dissatisfaction, and on 5 June 1997, after working on revisions for the book with his editor, Lukas committed suicide. Simon and Schuster published *Big Trouble* three months later.

Lukas devoted his career to exploring the divisions that plagued American society in the twentieth century. In all of his work he demonstrated a commitment to social justice and equality, and he used his writing to advance those causes. As one obituary writer commented, among his peers, no author was more revered than Lukas.

★

Although no biography of Lukas has been published, an interesting article by Joan Diver, one of Lukas's subjects in *Common Ground,* appears in *Media Studies Journal* (spring 1998), and a thoughtful appreciation piece by Anne Bernays appears in *Nieman Reports* (fall 1997). An obituary is in the *New York Times* (7 June 1997).

MICHAEL S. FOLEY

M

McCARTNEY, Linda Louise Eastman   (*b*. 24 September 1941 in New York City; *d*. 17 April 1998 near Tucson, Arizona), photographer, especially of 1960s rock stars; vocalist with Wings; activist for vegetarianism and animal rights; and wife of the former Beatle Paul McCartney.

One of four children of Lee Vail Eastman (born Leopold Epstein) and Louise Lindner, McCartney grew up in the New York City area. Her father was a lawyer who represented artists such as Willem de Kooning and Hoagy Carmichael. Her mother, a homemaker, died in a plane crash when McCartney was nineteen. After graduating from Scarsdale High School in 1960, McCartney attended the University of Arizona, where she left after two semesters without earning a degree. In June 1962 she married John Melvyn See, with whom she had a daughter. While in Arizona she studied photography with Hazel Archer at a local arts center. McCartney and See separated in 1964 and divorced in June 1965.

In early 1966 she and her daughter moved to New York City, where McCartney worked in the offices of *Town and Country* magazine. That year she photographed the Rolling Stones for two teen magazines, and these pictures gave her an entrée to shoot documentary photos of Jimi Hendrix, the Animals, and the Who. During the next five years she also photographed Janis Joplin, the Doors, the Mamas and the Papas, Bob Dylan, Frank Zappa, the Beach Boys, and the Grateful Dead. McCartney's photographs appeared in the first issue of *Rolling Stone* (1967).

Her photographs were also appearing in *Life* and *Mademoiselle* in 1967, and she photographed the Beatles when *Sergeant Pepper's Lonely Hearts Club Band* was released that year. Between May 1967 and May 1968 the Beatle Paul McCartney telephoned her four times, and in late June 1968 the superstar invited her to meet him in Los Angeles; they soon became inseparable. Leaving her five-year-old daughter with grandparents in August 1968, McCartney moved in with Paul in London. In October the couple returned to New York City to get Linda's daughter and bring her to England. On 12 March 1969 they married, to the dismay of many of Paul's female fans. McCartney's father and brother became Paul's lawyers.

Paul adopted McCartney's daughter from her first marriage, and the couple had three more children, two girls and a boy. The family lived primarily in their small farmhouse in West Sussex, England. The McCartneys tried to raise the children in a lifestyle as normal as possible, including educating them in the local, state-sponsored schools.

In 1971 they launched the rock group Wings, with McCartney on backup vocals and keyboard. This was not her strongest area, as critics frequently commented. However, Paul wanted her and the family with him, so she continued to sing and tour with him, always taking along the children and, during the school year, a tutor. McCartney wrote a few songs, including "Seaside Woman," which was released as a single in 1977.

Always an animal-rights activist, McCartney became an

Linda McCartney, 1995. ASSOCIATED PRESS AP

books depicting nature, animals, and still lifes included *Linda's Pictures* (1976), *Sun Prints* (1989), *Roadworks* (1996), and the posthumous *Wide Open: Photographs* (1999). In 1987 Women in Photography recognized her as their photographer of the year.

Her photographs also were exhibited internationally at the Royal Photographic Society in Bath, England, the Victoria and Albert Museum in London, the International Center of Photography in New York, and more than fifty galleries around the world. London's National Portrait Gallery put her photographs of John Lennon and Paul McCartney on permanent display. In 1993 in the *Washington Post,* the critic Lee Fleming noted, "In a contest between work like that of Annie Leibovitz, which manipulates and plays on public perception of her subjects, and McCartney's low-key revelations, the latter's pictures win hands down."

In 1995 a routine scan revealed that McCartney had a malignant breast lump, which was removed. Two years of chemotherapy and radiation treatment could not prevent the cancer from spreading to her liver. McCartney died at the family ranch, and she was cremated in Arizona. Two days later Paul and the children flew to London, where a memorial service was held in Saint Martin-in-the-Fields, the first reunion of the three surviving ex-Beatles. McCartney's ashes were scattered near the family's land in England and at the ranch near Tucson.

Friends remembered McCartney for her warmth and optimism and for her focus on her family. Paul once said, "Every love song I write is for Linda." After her death, Paul composed "Nova" and combined it with works by Ralph Vaughan Williams, John Rutter, David Matthews, and others in *A Garland for Linda: A Commemoration of the Life of Linda McCartney* (2000), which was sold to raise funds for breast-cancer research. Several exhibits of McCartney's photographs opened and toured posthumously, including the "Wide Open" show in New York City, which received widespread acclaim, and "Linda McCartney's Sixties," traveling to fifteen cities in the United States and Canada between 1999 and 2002, and first seen at the Rock and Roll Hall of Fame and Museum in Cleveland.

Although she was most frequently recognized as the wife of a former Beatle, McCartney's involvement in photography, vegetarianism, and animal rights "brought her message," as Yoko Ono wrote, "to a wider audience than that of rock and roll. But her most important contributions were all made in private."

★

The only full-length biography of McCartney is by her friend Danny Fields, *Linda McCartney: A Portrait* (2000). Other biographical material can be found in Bonni Benrubi, "Introduction," *Wide Open* (1998); Yoko Ono, "Linda McCartney Remembered," *Rolling Stone* (11 June 1998); and articles in the *New York*

outspoken member of Lynx (a British antifur group) and People for the Ethical Treatment of Animals (PETA). A vegetarian after the early 1980s, she repeatedly said, "Never eat anything with a face." McCartney published three popular vegetarian cookbooks, *Linda McCartney's Home Cooking* (1989), *Linda's Kitchen* (1995), and *Linda McCartney on Tour: Over 200 Meat-Free Dishes from Around the World* (1998). In 1990 she conceived and developed a line of prepared frozen meatless entrées, manufactured by United Biscuits and introduced in England in 1991. Several years later these McVege meals accounted for nearly 25 percent of the frozen meat-free meals sold in Britain, making McCartney a millionaire in her own right.

She continued to photograph a variety of subjects. Her best-known book was *Linda McCartney's Sixties: Portrait of an Era* (1992), a mixture of black-and-white and color photos, all taken with natural light on fast film. The subjects included rock musicians and fashion models for *Mademoiselle.* McCartney said she was able to get such intimate photos of the rock stars because she blended into their environment. She noted, "I became like a band member whose chosen instrument was the camera." Her other

Times (9 June, 11 June, and 23 June 1998). Other relevant articles include Lee Fleming, "Galleries Capturing the Outer Reaches," *Washington Post* (9 Oct. 1993), and "Wings Arose to Span a Time After the Beatles," *USA Today* (11 May 2001). Obituaries are in the *New York Times* (20 Apr. 1998; corrected 21 Apr. 1998); Barry Bortnick, "McCartney Did Not Die in California," *Santa Barbara News-Press* (24 Apr. 1998); *Newsweek* (4 May 1998); and *Rolling Stone* (28 May 1998). Also useful are the BBC documentary, a Nicholas Claxton production, "Linda McCartney: Behind the Lens" (1993), and Diane Sawyer, "A Conversation with Paul McCartney," *ABC Nightline* (27 Jan. 1999).

DESSA CRAWFORD

McCARTY, Oseola ("Kelli")   (*b.* 7 March 1908 in Shubata, Mississippi; *d.* 26 September 1999 in Hattiesburg, Mississippi), laundress who set an example for all Americans when she quietly established a major scholarship for the University of Southern Mississippi with her life savings.

McCarty was the daughter and only child of Lucy McCarty Zimerman. Her mother, grandmother, and aunt were the preeminent individuals in her life. McCarty's family moved to Hattiesburg, Mississippi, when she was young, around the time of the death of her mother's husband Willy Zimerman. Her mother was employed as a cook for the Forrest County Mississippi circuit clerk and sold candy at the local elementary school to supplement this income. McCarty started washing clothes at age eight to further assist with family finances, and quite early on she established a savings account at the First Mississippi National Bank in Hattiesburg. She claimed she became serious about saving money when she started making $10 for a bundle of laundry, but most who knew her said her frugality started earlier. She worked consistently as a laundress for almost eighty years until December 1994, when her arthritis became too painful for her to continue.

McCarty attended Eureka Elementary School in Hattiesburg until the sixth grade, when she left school to care for her aunt, who was unable to care for herself. McCarty was baptized in 1921 at age thirteen, and she remembered the details of that day vividly throughout her life. Her grandmother died in 1944, and in 1947 her uncle gave her the frame home that she had lived in to keep for the rest of her life. Her mother died in 1964, followed by her aunt in 1967. McCarty credited her faith for getting her through the lonely years that followed these losses. She said, "After my aunt died, leaving me alone, I hardly slept for three months. I had always been the littlest thing in the house, but the time came for me to grow up. I did." McCarty never married or had children.

Employees at the local bank helped McCarty to invest her growing savings in certificates of deposit and conservative mutual funds. In the later years of her life, financial advisers from Trustmark Bank helped her to manage her savings and to establish a plan for her money, after ensuring that her financial needs would be met for her lifetime. The Trustmark vice president and trust officer Paul Laughlin used ten dimes to help McCarty lay out a plan for dividing her life savings, allocating one dime (10 percent) for her church, one for each of three cousins (30 percent), and the other six (60 percent) for the University of Southern Mississippi (USM). McCarty had lived within three miles of USM for virtually her entire life but had never been on the campus until she gave the university $150,000 on 26 July 1995.

Although McCarty never expected praise for her generosity, the establishment of the Oseola McCarty Scholarship Fund generated a huge media fanfare, as did the announcement that the first $1,000 scholarship recipient would be Stephanie Bullock, from Hattiesburg High School, in 1995. The scholarship was the largest gift ever given to USM by an African American, and "primary consideration [was] given to those deserving African-American students enrolling at the University of Southern Mississippi who clearly demonstrate financial need." The businesspeople of Hattiesburg were so moved by McCarty's gesture

Oseola McCarty, 1996. ARCHIVE PHOTOS, INC.

that they matched her donation, bringing the total amount of money in the Oseola McCarty Scholarship Fund to $300,000. By mid-September 1995 more than $65,000 in matching gifts had been raised from local businesses, and donors worldwide had generated $200,000 one year later.

In the year following her gift, McCarty received a flood of attention and awards. She flew for the first time on an airplane on her way to a ceremony at the White House, at which she was honored with the Presidential Citizen's Medal. Other awards included an honorary doctoral degree from Harvard University, the National Urban League Community Heroes Award, and UNESCO's Avicenna Award, which was presented in Hattiesburg when McCarty refused to fly to Paris. She also received the Premier Black Woman of Courage Award from the National Federation of Black Women Business Owners, was profiled as one of the ten most fascinating people of 1995 on a CBS television special, and was an Olympic torchbearer. She was deluged with mail and personal gifts.

The impact of McCarty's unassuming, genuine presence was powerful. A collection of her quotes and personal photographs, *Oseola McCarty's Simple Wisdom for Rich Living,* was published in 1996. In 1998 *The Riches of Oseola McCarty* (1997), a children's biography by Evelyn Coleman, was named as a notable book for children by Scholastic. McCarty's personal travel and appearances were drastically curtailed after her surgery for colon cancer in 1998, and she was diagnosed with liver cancer on 7 September 1999. She died at age ninety-one. After a public visitation at the USM campus in celebration of her life, she was buried at Highland Cemetery in Hattiesburg, Mississippi.

McCarty never expected that her gift would generate the attention that it did. Humble and private, she was appreciative of the praise she received but was also persistent in not changing her daily life. McCarty's own words clearly state her message and the ultimate power of her gift: "We are responsible for the way we use of [sic] time on this earth, so I try to be a good steward. I start each day on my knees, saying the Lord's Prayer. Then I get busy about my work. I get to cleaning or washing. I find that my life and my work are increasing all the time. I am blessed beyond what I hoped."

★

Oseola McCarty, *Oseola McCarty's Simple Wisdom for Rich Living* (1996), and Evelyn Coleman, *The Riches of Oseola McCarty* (1998), provide excellent material about McCarty's life and beliefs. The Oseola McCarty homepage, housed at the University of Southern Mississippi website, <http://www.pr.usm.edu/>, maintains an extensive collection of biographical information, news releases, and interviews. An obituary is in the *New York Times* (28 Sept. 1999).

Martha E. Nelson

McCORMICK, Kenneth Dale (*b.* 25 February 1906 in Madison, New Jersey; *d.* 27 June 1997 in New York City), publisher and longtime editor in chief at Doubleday and Company who edited the works of former presidents and literary figures.

McCormick was the only son of John Dale McCormick, a Methodist minister, and Ida Pearl Wegner. The family remained in Madison for six months so that McCormick's father could complete an advanced degree at Drew University. The family then moved to southern Minnesota, where McCormick's father had his pastorates and McCormick spent his childhood. In 1919 the family moved to Salem, Oregon, where McCormick attended high school. He graduated with an A.B. degree from Willamette University in 1928.

After college, McCormick hitchhiked across the country to New York City. His first jobs in the book business were as a night librarian at the Twenty-third Street YMCA and then as a sales clerk at the Colony Bookshop. In 1930 McCormick became a night clerk at the Doubleday Bookstore in Penn Station. He would remain with Doubleday, in one role or another, for the rest of his career.

In 1932 McCormick was made a manager of a Doubleday bookstore in Philadelphia. He would later comment that, although he disliked the job, the experience proved to be invaluable. Between 1931 and 1934 he wrote several articles for *Publishers Weekly* on various aspects of bookselling, including special orders, book promotions, travel books, and Christmas sales. His articles caught the attention of his superiors at Doubleday, and in 1934 he was promoted to assistant promotions manager for Doubleday in New York. He quickly moved through the editorial ranks, first as a manuscript reader, then as associate editor, chief associate editor, and finally, in 1937, as assistant editor, coordinating the editorial departments. The first manuscript he purchased was Jimmy Collins's *Test Pilot* (1935). He traveled widely, recruiting and visiting authors. In 1937 McCormick married Elizabeth Tibbets; they had three children and divorced in 1950. In 1939 he edited his first best-seller, Oscar Levant's *A Smattering of Ignorance.*

In 1942, while on the road, he was promoted to editor in chief, at the behest of British author Somerset Maugham, thus becoming the youngest person to hold that position in a major New York publishing house. He would not enjoy it for long, however. With the outbreak of World War II, McCormick enlisted in the U.S. Army Air Forces. He was stationed in Winston-Salem, North Carolina, where he edited instructional books for pilots. In 1945 McCormick returned to Doubleday, and LeBaron Barker, who had been the interim editor in chief, stepped down so McCormick could return to his former position. In 1948

McCormick was named vice president of Doubleday, and in 1949 he was elected to the board of directors.

On 8 March 1948 McCormick delivered the annual Richard Rogers Bowker Memorial Lecture at the New York Public Library, outlining his philosophy and practice of editing and publishing. Entitled "Editors Today," the lecture ranged over topics as diverse as plagiarism, censorship, book manufacturing, and the social responsibility of an editor. However, what unified these diverse topics was the idea of an editor's threefold responsibility: to the author, to the public, and to the press. McCormick believed it was necessary for editors to pay attention to each author and to tailor their editorial efforts to the author's unique needs and motivations. The editor must never underestimate the intelligence of the reading public, he said, and must publish socially important works, no matter how difficult they might seem. Yet, he declared, the editor must also balance the cost of important works with profits from more popular titles.

McCormick's own editorial practice matched this philosophy. Not only did he edit the works of several political figures, he edited many best-sellers as well. Among the political books were Dwight D. Eisenhower's *Crusade in Europe* (1948) and *Waging Peace: White House Years* (1963–1965), Harry Truman's *Memoirs* (1955–1956), and Richard Nixon's *Six Crises* (1962). McCormick edited the works of numerous literary figures, including Somerset Maugham, Noël Coward, Daphne du Maurier, Nelson Algren, Irving Stone, and Robert Graves. Yet McCormick was always in touch with the popular literature of the time. In fact, when he stepped down as editor in chief of Doubleday in 1972, after almost twenty-five years, the top three best-selling novels had all been edited by him.

Even into retirement, McCormick was actively involved with Doubleday and the larger publishing world. He remained at Doubleday as a consulting editor until 1987. Along with Louise Thomas, a former publicity director, he edited the Doubleday papers for the Library of Congress, sifting through and annotating the publishing house's correspondence from its inception in 1897 through the mid-1980s. In 1990 McCormick coedited the book *Images of War: The Artist's Vision of World War II*. In retirement, he continued to work against censorship, a lifelong passion of his. Throughout his career, he served on many panels and committees devoted to this cause, including the Defend Your Freedom to Read Committee, the International Freedom to Publish Committee, and John F. Kennedy's Government Advisory Committee on Publishing and Reading. In 1984 he was awarded the Benjamin Award for his lifelong contribution to publishing.

In 1990 McCormick began to lose his eyesight. He died from complications of a stroke while at the Kateri Residence, a nursing home in Manhattan. He was survived by his wife, Anne Hutchens, whom he married in 1968, and three children.

During his tenure at Doubleday, the epicenter of English-language publishing moved from London to New York, and McCormick was a representative publisher of his time. He respected not only the quality of American culture, but its uniquely classless nature. He felt it was the editor's duty to keep the intellectual and the public in contact. McCormick was an egalitarian publisher, not an aristocratic one. He did not seek to elevate the stature of American letters, but to improve them. His authors appreciated his intensely personal approach and the attention he gave each book. Garry Wills called him "the editor every author dreams of," one who "gave the impression that nothing was more important to him [than my book]." Although not particularly open to experimentation, McCormick's publishing practice and commitment to fighting censorship, both legally and practically, represented a high point in the history of American publishing.

★

McCormick's letters have been collected, along with those of many other Doubleday employees, as part of the Kenneth McCormick Collection at the Library of Congress. While there is no full-length biography of McCormick, his wife wrote a useful biographic article in the *Dictionary of Literary Biography Yearbook: 1997* (1998). His Bowker lecture has been published in *Bowker Lectures on Book Publishing* (1957). Obituaries are in the *New York Times* (29 June 1997) and *Publishers Weekly* (7 July 1997).

MATTHEW L. MCALPIN

McDOWALL, Roderick Andrew Anthony Jude ("Roddy") (*b.* 17 September 1928 in Herne Hill, London, England; *d.* 3 October 1998 in Studio City, California), child actor and versatile, award-winning adult actor who appeared in films, on television, and onstage.

McDowall was the son of Thomas Andrew McDowall, an officer in the merchant marines, and Winifriede Corcoran, a stage mother; he had one sister. McDowall's career began early. He worked as an infant model and began elocution lessons at age five. His mother, who had wanted to act in films, provided the push. At age nine McDowall, a student at Saint Joseph's School in London, was acting in his first films, *Scruffy* (1938) and *Murder in the Family* (1938). As a child, McDowall appeared in more than seventeen movies. Because he was under fourteen, the age limit set by the child labor laws, he had to be smuggled into film studios, hiding on the floor of a car. McDowall's last British film was *This England* (1941).

On 24 September 1940 McDowall, his mother, and his older sister escaped the World War II bombing in London

Roddy McDowall, 1992. Nick Ut/Associated Press AP

and sailed from Liverpool, England, to live with friends in White Plains, New York. Shortly thereafter McDowall took a screen test and relocated to Hollywood. His first U.S. film was Fritz Lang's classic spy thriller *Man Hunt* (1941), in which he helped Walter Pidgeon escape the Nazis. McDowall's next film, also with Pidgeon, was John Ford's *How Green Was My Valley* (1941), in which he played the shy, sensitive Huw. The film won an Academy Award for best picture and McDowall became a highly sought-after child star.

McDowall played several film heroes as a child: he was the young Tyrone Power in *Son of Fury* (1942); the young Gregory Peck in *The Keys of the Kingdom* (1944); and the young Peter Lawford in *The White Cliffs of Dover* (1944). However, it was his roles with animals that are best remembered: *Lassie Come Home* (1943); *My Friend Flicka* (1943); and its sequel *Thunderhead, Son of Flicka* (1945). In an interview McDowall stated, "I loved Pal, the dog who played Lassie. He was a lot smarter than some of the people I know." But he hated the main horse that played Flicka. The filming of *Lassie* started a lifetime friendship with Elizabeth Taylor, who played Priscilla, a supporting role.

McDowall attended the Twentieth Century–Fox school for child actors in Hollywood, graduated in 1946, and completed one year of high school. McDowall became a U.S. citizen on 17 September 1949. In the 1940s, after filming *Molly and Me* (1945) with Gracie Field, McDowall was released from his Fox contract. He explained, "At seventeen my childhood career was over. My agent told me I would never work again, because I'd grown up." But McDowall found other parts. As he told *Coronet* magazine in March 1958, "I was playing fourteen-year-old parts until I was twenty-three, simply because I'm bedeviled by looking younger than I really am."

In 1946 McDowall made his stage debut in summer theater, playing the title role in *Young Woodley* in Westport, Connecticut. The following summer he played Malcolm in Orson Welles's production of *Macbeth* in Salt Lake City, Utah. He had other roles, including Lachie in *The Hasty Heart* (1948), in a number of small venues. In 1951, looking for more opportunities, he left Hollywood and relocated to New York City. There he studied acting with Mira Rostova and David Craig. McDowall made his New York City debut as Bentley Summerhays in a production of George Bernard Shaw's *Misalliance* on 18 February 1953. More theatrical roles followed. He performed in the inaugural season of the American Shakespeare Festival in 1955 as Octavius in *Julius Caesar* and as Ariel, one of his favorite roles, in *The Tempest*. His major roles in the late 1950s were as Ben Whitledge, the unhappy draftee in *No Time for Sergeants* (1955) and as Artie Straus, a character modeled on Richard Loeb, in *Compulsion* (1957), based on the Leopold and Loeb murder case.

In Hollywood, McDowall played a beatnik poet in *The Subterraneans* (1960) and a nasty Englishman in *Midnight Lace* (1960). Back on Broadway, he won an Antoinette Perry Award (Tony) for best supporting actor of the 1959–1960 season for his portrayal of Tarquin in Jean Anouilh's *The Fighting Cock*. In December 1960 he played the part of Mordred, his first singing role, in Alan Jay Lerner's and Frederick Loewe's *Camelot*. Both he and Richard Burton left the cast in September 1961 to film *Cleopatra* (1963), in which McDowall played the evil Octavian. Other films included *The Loved One* (1965) and *Lord Love a Duck* (1966). A major film series began with *Planet of the Apes* (1968), with McDowall playing Cornelius. He was also in *Escape from the Planet of the Apes* (1971), *Conquest of the Planet of the Apes* (1972), and *Battle for the Planet of the Apes* (1973). His later films include *Fright Night* (1985), *Overboard* (1987), and the 1988 sequel to *Fright Night*.

Television was another venue for McDowall's acting. His first television role was in 1951 on *Robert Montgomery Presents*. For McDowall, television provided a chance "to fail and grow." He remarked, "Working in television, you could be in two or three stage flops a year and not starve." He acted in television series, playing the Bookworm in *Batman* (1966–1968) and Galen in *The Planet of the Apes* (1974), and in television miniseries, including *The Rhinemann Exchange* (1977) and *The Martian Chronicles* (1980). He made numerous guest appearances. As an actor in movies made for television, McDowall appeared in a variety of films, ranging from *A Taste of Evil* (1971), *The Thief of Baghdad* (1978), and *Alice in Wonderland* (1985) to *Dead Man's Island* (1996).

He appeared in many television specials, including *Ah! Wilderness* (1951), *The Tempest* (1960), in which he recreated his role of Ariel, and *Not Without Honor* (1960), playing the role of Philip, the son of Alexander Hamilton; for this latter performance he won an Emmy. Other specials included *The Power and the Glory* (1961), *Saint Joan* (1967), *An All-Star Tribute to Elizabeth Taylor* (1977), and *Stars and Stripes: Hollywood and World War II* (1991).

McDowall was also an accomplished portrait photographer. Since childhood, he had enjoyed photography. The actress Gladys Cooper persuaded him to develop his avocation into a career. McDowall began shooting pictures on the set of *Cleopatra* and later sold these portraits to *Look, Life, Harper's Bazaar,* and *Architectural Digest*. McDowall published four books of his portraits. *Double Exposure* (1966) got its title from his black-and-white photographs of famous people in the arts and the commentary by other famous people. For example, the book included a series of five pictures of Jack Benny playing the violin, with commentary drawn as a Peanuts cartoon by Charles Schulz. *Double Exposure Take Two* (1989) included the inscription, "A Gallery of the Celebrated with Commentary by the Equally Celebrated." *Double Exposure Take Three* (1992) and *Double Exposure Take Four* (1993) followed the same successful format. McDowall donated the royalties from his books to the Motion Picture and Television Fund, which supported retired entertainment-industry workers.

Although McDowall loved acting, perhaps his greatest accomplishment was as a friend. Noted for his ability to respect a confidence and keep a secret, he made friends throughout his life, and his simple house was a sanctuary to many. McDowall never married. In August 1998 he learned that he was dying of cancer. McDowall died at his Studio City home on 3 October 1998. He was cremated and his ashes were scattered in the Pacific Ocean.

Depending on the audience, McDowall is best remembered for his depiction of the fresh-faced Huw; others see McDowall as Cornelius, picturing him as the personified chimpanzee. Throughout his career McDowall touched a varied audience as he took chances to appear in widely different roles.

★

A collection of manuscripts and correspondence by and about McDowall is at the Mugar Library at Boston University. Books that include sections on McDowall as a child star include Marc Best, *Those Endearing Young Charms* (1971); Dick Moore's study of child actors, *Twinkle, Twinkle, Little Star: But Don't Have Sex and Take the Car* (1984); and Thomas G. Aylesworth, *Hollywood Kids: Child Stars of the Silver Screen from 1903 to the Present* (1987).

Periodical articles on McDowall include "Living for Today," *Newsweek* (29 Nov. 1965); Michael Buckley, "Roddy McDowall," *Films in Review* (Aug./Sept. 1988); and Michael Buckley, "Roddy McDowall, Part II," *Films in Review* (Oct. 1988), which includes a list of McDowall's films and the parts he played in them. Tributes include Richard Natale, "Roddy McDowall," *Variety* (12 Oct. 1998); "Best Buddy," *People Weekly* (19 Oct. 1998); and Dominick Dunn, "The Company He Kept," *Vanity Fair* (Dec. 1998). Obituaries are in the *Los Angeles Times* and *New York Times* (both 4 Oct. 1998).

MARCIA B. DINNEEN

McGILL, William James (*b.* 27 February 1922 in New York City; *d.* 19 October 1997 in La Jolla, California), cognitive psychologist and president of Columbia University in the tumultuous 1970s.

McGill was born in Manhattan's East Harlem. His father was an Irish immigrant who was a musician and, during the Great Depression, a labor organizer. McGill's mother, Mary Rankin, a homemaker, was born in New York City

William J. McGill, 1970. ASSOCIATED PRESS AP

and was also of Irish ancestry. McGill had two younger sisters. He grew up in the Bronx and attended Catholic parochial schools and then earned a scholarship to the archdiocesan Cathedral Boys High School in Manhattan. The first in his family to attend college, McGill went to the nearby Fordham University in 1939. He graduated with an A.B. degree in 1943 and spent the next four years working in California. He was physically exempted from the draft during World War II.

In 1947 McGill returned to Fordham to pursue a graduate degree in psychology. In 1948 he married Ann Rowe, a nurse; they had two children. Discovering he had what his Jesuit professors called a "good mathematical mind," he transferred the following year to Harvard University in Cambridge, Massachusetts, to work in the new field of cognitive psychology. At Harvard and at the neighboring Massachusetts Institute of Technology (MIT), he studied with the field's founders and had as classmates Jerome Brunner and Richard Solomon, who became the next generation's leading cognitive scientists. In 1953 he completed his Ph.D. in communications theory and took his first regular job in the MIT economics department.

In 1956 McGill went to Columbia University in New York City as an assistant professor of psychology. Two years later he was tenured, and in 1960 he was made a full professor and the chair of the department. Meanwhile, he had become part of the larger community of Columbia quantifiers linked to the Bureau of Applied Social Research and its director, Paul Lazarsfeld. McGill was unhappy with the state of the psychology department at Columbia and with living in New York. He regarded both the department and the city as having seen their best days. In 1963 he went to Stanford University in California on a research fellowship and while there accepted an offer to head up a new department of psychology at the University of California, San Diego.

Once at San Diego, McGill became involved in campus politics. The mass student protests at the University of California, Berkeley, in 1964 had sent ripples throughout the state system, which had few administrators prepared to operate within the new confrontational environment. McGill so identified himself when he was elected to the statewide university senate in 1966 and a year later when he became the acting chancellor of the university's San Diego campus. In 1968 he became the chancellor, just as the San Diego campus experienced a student strike led by the African-American Marxist graduate Angela Davis and abetted by the visiting professor and Marxist philosopher Herbert Marcuse. McGill also had to contend with the California governor Ronald Reagan. Although McGill was never as feisty as he appeared, he proved to be a tough and imaginative administrator throughout the events on the San Di-

ego campus, which he later described in *The Year of the Monkey* (1983).

McGill's growing reputation as a crisis manager brought him to the notice of Columbia, which in the spring of 1968 had suffered through a week of building occupations and a police bust that soon led to the resignation of its president, Grayson Kirk. Relations between Columbia University and its neighbors were also volatile. The acting president Andrew Cordier and a group of senior faculty held Columbia together in the face of continuing student unrest and faculty defections. When approached in late 1969 about returning to Columbia as its president, McGill expressed interest in the position, and the trustee-faculty search committee took up his candidacy in earnest. His credentials as a New Yorker and one-time member of the university's faculty counted in his favor, while his Catholicism, which earlier would have excluded him from consideration, was conveniently ignored. What really won him the job was the perception that he was a street fighter equal to the task of standing up to all those who seemed to threaten Columbia.

McGill began his presidency in September 1970, at which time the trustees revealed an operating deficit of $15 million for the following year. It represented the university's fourth straight deficit budget. McGill was directed to bring Columbia back to financial stability as quickly as possible. He produced a plan to do so over five years, although in fact it took nearly ten. The measures taken to squeeze excess expenditures to increase income were often brutal and could not be effected without hardship and recriminations. Faculty ranks were thinned, programs were eliminated, and maintenance was deferred. Meanwhile, radical students reckoned with a president who was ready to take them on. By the mid-1970s student protests had become an occasional irritant rather than a chronic presence. Similarly, faculty defections slowed, in part because of a sluggish academic market, and slumping departmental rankings had stabilized. Rising enrollments in the university's professional schools offset declines in the arts and sciences. McGill opposed efforts to make the all-male Columbia College coeducational because of the likely negative impact on enrollments at the all-female Barnard College.

In 1979 McGill announced his intention to resign the following year. He simultaneously appointed Michael Sovern, the dean of the law school, as the provost, thus effectively identifying his successor. The change in leadership occurred on 30 June 1980. The timing was right, as most of what McGill had set out to do had been accomplished and a more positive, outgoing presidency that Sovern represented was now needed. McGill left New York City for his adopted home in La Jolla, California, where he served in several academic advisory capacities throughout the 1980s. He died of heart failure and is buried in La Jolla. Considering the difficult state of Columbia upon his arrival as the president and its stabilized condition at his retirement, McGill ranked as one of the most successful presidents since the university's founding in 1754.

★

Information about McGill can be found in Columbia University, *Oral History Interviews* (1979 and 1997); "William J. McGill, 1922–1997," *Current Biography Yearbook* (1996); and Richard Atkinson, "William J. McGill (1922–1997)," *American Psychologist* 55 (2000). An obituary is in the *New York Times* (21 Oct. 1997).

ROBERT A. MCCAUGHEY

MANN, Jonathan Max (*b.* 30 July 1947 in Boston, Massachusetts; *d.* 2 September 1998 near Nova Scotia, Canada), founder and first director of the World Health Organization Global Program on AIDS who was a pioneer in international AIDS awareness and linking human rights with health care.

Mann was the son of James Mann, a psychiatrist, and Ida Laskow, a social worker. He was the second of four children and grew up in the upper-middle-class suburb of Newton, Massachusetts. Mann graduated magna cum

Jonathan Mann, 1998. ASSOCIATED PRESS/KEYSTONE

laude in 1969 from Harvard College with a B.A. degree in history. In 1967 he attended the Institute d'Etudes Politiques in Paris, France, and earned a Certificat d'Etudes Politiques. He attended Harvard as a special student from 1969 to 1970, taking science classes for medical school, and received his M.D. from Washington University School of Medicine in St. Louis, Missouri, in 1974, when he was elected to Alpha Omega Alpha, the medical honor society. He also earned an M.P.H. degree from the Harvard School of Public Health in 1980. On 30 January 1970 he married Marie-Paule Bondat, whom he had met in Paris in 1967. They had twin daughters and a son and were divorced in September 1995.

After his internship at the Beth Israel Hospital in Boston in 1974, Mann served as an epidemic intelligence service officer for the Centers for Disease Control in Atlanta, Georgia (1975–1977). He was the state epidemiologist and chief medical officer for New Mexico's health services division from 1977 to 1984, when he went to Kinshasa, Zaire, to work on Projet SIDA (the French name for Project AIDS). He cofounded an innovative and successful program that became a center for research on acquired immunodeficiency syndrome (AIDS).

In June 1986 Mann became the first director of the United Nations (UN) World Health Organization (WHO) Global Program on AIDS. Starting with one assistant, it became the largest WHO program by 1990, with a staff of 280 and a $109 million budget. Mann developed a global AIDS strategy that was adopted by WHO and the UN General Assembly; the program included support to over 160 countries. He helped to develop global research and information exchanges, focusing on programs linking human rights, women's issues, and other social issues, and worked with other UN and nongovernmental organizations. Mann resigned on 16 March 1990 in a conflict with the WHO director-general Hiroshi Nakajima over the program's autonomy.

After leaving his position with the UN, Mann became a professor of epidemiology and international health at Harvard. In 1993 he became the director of the Francois-Xavier Bagnoud Center for Health and Human Rights at Harvard's School of Public Health (HSPH), and was the first endowed Francois-Xavier Bagnoud Professor of Health and Human Rights, staying in this role until 1998. He also directed the International AIDS Program at the Harvard AIDS Institute. Mann taught undergraduate, graduate, and postgraduate courses and oversaw AIDS research.

In 1990 Mann founded the U.S. affiliate of Doctors of the World. In 1991 he founded and was the director of the Global AIDS Policy Coalition, an independent research advocacy group. He chaired the Eighth International Conference on AIDS in 1992, which he moved to Amsterdam to protest the U.S. policy of excluding individuals infected with the human immunodeficiency virus (HIV) from entering the United States. In 1994 he founded and edited the *Health and Human Rights Journal,* a peer-reviewed international journal. A 1998 issue of the journal was dedicated both to Mann and the fiftieth anniversary of the UN Declaration of Human Rights. Mann developed the idea of presenting a copy of this declaration to each HSPH graduate along with their diplomas.

In 1994 Mann received the Frank A. Calderone Lectureship and Prize from the Columbia University School of Public Health, for "individuals who have made significant contributions to the field of public health and public health research." That same year, he organized the First International Conference on Health and Human Rights at Harvard and chaired the second conference in 1996. On 21 December 1996 he married Mary Lou Clements, a vaccine scientist and tenured professor at the Johns Hopkins University in Baltimore.

In January 1998 Mann became the first dean of the new School of Public Health at Allegheny University of the Health Sciences in Philadelphia, Pennsylvania. He took the new position so that his wife would not have to relocate from their home in Columbia, Maryland. Allegheny University had severe financial troubles, and Mann decided to explore new opportunities. On a trip to Geneva, Switzerland, his first since giving his WHO resignation speech there in 1990, Mann and his wife were killed when Swissair Flight 111 crashed off the coast of Nova Scotia. They are buried in Longview, Texas.

During his medical career, Mann wrote 169 articles for scientific journals including *JAMA: The Journal of the American Medical Association, New England Journal of Medicine, American Journal of Public Health,* and *Lancet.* He coedited two essay collections, *AIDS in the World: A Global Report* (1992), and *AIDS in the World II* (1996). He was also the editor in chief of *Current Issues in Public Health,* beginning in 1993. The last book Mann coedited, *Health and Human Rights: A Reader* (1999), was dedicated to him. The *Lancet* called the book "a powerful tribute to the memory and spirit of Jonathan Mann's exemplary work in the field." It was chosen as number two of the top humanitarian books of the world by the *Humanitarian Times,* whose June 1999 conference was dedicated to Mann and his wife.

Recognized by his signature bow tie, Mann was a charismatic, passionate, and sometimes controversial advocate for human rights. He spoke fluent French and Italian, and some Hebrew and Spanish. An avid reader and wine enthusiast, Mann also liked to draw and sculpt human hands. The esteem in which Mann was held by the medical, scientific, and human rights communities is exemplified by the many scholarships and awards he received, and by those established in his memory, including the annual Jonathan

Mann Award for Global Health and Human Rights. Mann believed the world could and should change based on the Universal Declaration of Human Rights and the irrevocable link between human dignity and human health.

★

There is no complete biography on Mann. Substantial obituaries are in the *New York Times* (4 Sept. 1998); *JAMA* 23/30 (Sept. 1998); *Hospital Practice* (15 Oct. 1998); *Harvard Public Health Review* (fall 1998); *American Journal of Public Health* (Nov. 1998); and *Social Science and Medicine* 48, no. 5 (1999).

JANE BRODSKY FITZPATRICK

MARS, Forrest Edward, Sr. (*b.* 21 March 1904 in St. Paul, Minnesota; *d.* 1 July 1999 in Miami, Florida), entrepreneur primarily known for building the Mars, Inc. global empire.

Born to candy manufacturer Frank Mars and Ethel G. Kissack, Mars was separated from his parents at age six when they divorced. He was raised by his maternal grandparents in North Brattleford, Canada, while his mother stayed in Minneapolis, working as a salesclerk. Frank Mars remarried, and in 1922 he established in Minneapolis the Mar-O-Bar Company, whose Victorian butter cream candies brought success the following year. He made no attempt to find his son or to support him.

After graduating from Lethbridge High School in Alberta (1919–1922) with a partial scholarship, Mars enrolled at the University of California, Berkeley, intending to become a mining engineer in Canada. While working as a salesman for Camel cigarettes during a summer vacation, he put up Camel posters on all the major buildings on State Street, the main street of Chicago. His arrest for doing this made newspaper headlines that were seen by his father, who came to Chicago to post bail.

At a time when Hershey was the only candy manufacturer distributing nationwide, Mars proposed that his father do the same and hire him as a salesman. He also maintained that an off-the-cuff idea he shared with his father of covering a chocolate malted filling with a hard chocolate coating resulted in the creation of the Milky Way, a nougat-centered candy to which Frank had added caramel. In 1924, the first year the bar was marketed, its sales reached $800,000.

Mars returned to Berkeley in September 1924, changing his major to metallurgy. He enrolled in Yale's Sheffield Scientific School to study industrial engineering in 1925. After graduating from Yale in 1928, Mars went to work for his father in Chicago, having persuaded him in 1927 to build a new plant on the city's West Side to take advantage of lower freight rates. The company, renamed Mars Candies, was established on a property north of Oak Park at a cost of $500,000. In 1929 the plant was producing twenty million Milky Way bars annually. Frank invented the Snickers bar in 1930 and Three Musketeers in 1932. By 1933 sales were at $25 million and Mars Candies ranked number two in the candy business after Hershey, its supplier of chocolate. Hershey scientists even developed different types of chocolate for each Mars candy. Dreaming of a global enterprise, Mars wanted his father to expand into Canada, but Frank Mars refused to heed his son's suggestion. Frank Mars fired his son in 1932, but gave him $50,000 and foreign rights to the Milky Way bar. Mars moved to Paris with his wife, Audrey, and their newborn son. Frank Mars died of kidney failure a year later at age fifty.

Mars's first independent business, the manufacture of shoe-trees, failed because he could not communicate in French. Early in 1933 he went to work for Tobler, manufacturer of Toblerone, and later Nestlé, intent on closely observing the manufacturing process of chocolate. Later that same year, he started his own candy manufacturing operation, called Mars, Ltd., in a small kitchen in Slough, England, thirty miles north of London, developing the anglicized sweeter version of the Milky Way, which was renamed the Mars Bar. Audrey returned to live with her parents until the couple's material conditions improved. Mars bought a British company, Chappel Brothers, which canned meat by-products for dogs, in 1934. He renamed the company Petfoods, Ltd., and within five years its sales increased five-fold. Not all was gain, however; in 1937 Mars lost money gambling on cocoa commodities.

By 1939 Mars, Ltd. ranked third after Cadbury and Rowntree and Co. in British candy manufacturing. Mars also opened a factory in Brussels. When tax changes for foreign residents caused him to leave his business in the hands of his manager, he returned to the United States in 1939. Meanwhile, Frank Mars had left his Chicago plant to his second wife Ethel (both wives were named Ethel) and daughter, with a provision in his will that Mars would receive half of Ethel's shares upon her death.

Intent on starting his own company in the United States, Mars made a deal with William Murrie, the president of Hershey, in August 1939. Murrie's son Bruce would put up 20 percent of the capital (to Mars's 80 percent) to manufacture candies that would be called M&Ms, for the initials of Mars and Murrie. Mars maintained that he had conceived the idea based on the chocolate-covered lentils he had seen in Spain. He already had a warehouse in Newark, New Jersey, with ten panning drums to candy-coat the chocolates and needed a partner to purchase more equipment, sugar, and chocolate. William Murrie was impressed by a chocolate that would not melt if held in a pocket for any length of time. Bruce Murrie saw this as an opportunity to have ownership in a business and hold the title of ex-

ecutive vice president. M&M, Ltd. was launched in the spring of 1940.

The U.S. government wanted to shut down the candy industry in 1942 by eliminating the importation of sugar and cocoa beans as unessential to the war effort, but Hershey, in conjunction with the National Confectioners Association, claimed that chocolate had nutritional value and should be included in troop rations. Hershey continued to supply chocolate to M&M, Ltd. even when the quantity to other manufacturers was reduced. Bruce Murrie, using his military connections, even secured contracts for M&Ms from the army.

In 1941 Mars sighted a notice in a trade journal that a small rice-processing plant just south of Houston, Texas, had discovered a parboiling method of making rice which yielded a more nutritious product that cooked faster and was fluffier than traditional rice. Mars bought the mill in 1942 and selected a nearby farm that grew a sweet long-grain variety. The farmer's first name was Ben and thus the brand name, Uncle Ben's Rice. Heeding the suggestion of adman Leo Burnett to use a strong, simple image in the product's advertising, Mars asked a black waiter with a friendly face to pose for a portrait. He paid the man $50 for the portrait and reserved all rights to himself. Uncle Ben's went on the market in January 1944. By the late 1990s production of 200,000 tons of rice annually would bring the company $400 million in sales. Mars understood the importance of dominating a market in order to guarantee the best shelf space, which, in turn, increased profits. Bruce Murrie, seeing no future ownership of M&Ms., Ltd. despite Mars's initial promises, resigned from the company in 1949. Mars bought out Murrie's stake for $1 million.

After a post–World War II sales decline for the Mars companies, brand recognition became all important. The jingle "The candy that makes you smile" succeeded in increasing sales of M&Ms. In 1950 Mars hired Chicago advertisers Ted Bates and Co. to produce a market analysis, a first in the candy industry, of M&M sales. Rosser Reeves, head of that advertising agency, originated the line "Melts in your mouth, not in your hands" and in 1954 added the cartoon characters Mr. Plain and Mr. Peanut, after the peanut version of M&Ms was introduced. With help from the advertising campaign, including commercials on popular children's television shows, the company's sales reached $40 million in 1956.

Mars's combined worldwide assets exceeded those of Mars Candies in Chicago, but Mars thought that he was the rightful heir of that business and persisted in his offer to acquire it. Ethel and her daughter Patricia initially refused to sell their shares, but after Ethel died in 1945, Mars got half her shares under the terms of his father's will. He then sued Ethel's half-brother William "Slip" Kruppenbacher, who had become president, for breach of fiduciary trust. He acquired three seats on the board of Mars Candies by 1950 and with that leverage persuaded it to spend $4 million to upgrade the plant in Chicago.

Mars announced a mechanized process for making candy bars in thirty-five minutes rather than sixteen hours in 1953. By 1959 the new 400,000-square-foot factory was fully automated. Air-conditioning and other technical improvements helped transform the company into the largest manufacturer of chocolate-covered bars. Kruppenbacher retired in December 1959 and Mars became chairman of the board, but James Fleming, Patricia's third husband, was designated president and chief executive officer.

While Mars was absorbed by the Chicago operation, in 1960 he gave his son Forrest, Jr., his first assignment at the firm, the supervision of the move of company headquarters to McLean, Virginia. Mars wanted to be nearer his home in The Plains, Virginia, where he enjoyed fox hunting, and to take advantage of McLean's airport.

As a result of the feud between Mars and Kruppenbacher, the Chicago plant had lost $8 million in sales by 1963. Patricia, fearing bankruptcy and ill with a brain tumor, sold her shares to Mars with the conditions that her husband be kept on the payroll and the name of Mars's umbrella organization be changed from Food Manufacturers, Inc. to Mars, Inc. By December 1964, Mars had bought out the remainder of the board's shares, and now held three titles: chairman of the board, president, and chief executive officer.

Mars was reclusive, temperamental, verbally abusive, and obsessively private, refusing to divulge any information either about his family or the corporation. Nevertheless, he allowed each manager full autonomy. He was regarded as a strategist by long-term associates (every employee was an associate), and he set targets that managers had to meet or resign instead. Employees knew exactly what to expect, because all criteria for performance and salaries were printed in a thirty-page booklet that was distributed to all.

Mars's policy at all his units was not to provide luxurious offices or perquisites, but to give higher salaries than those of the competition. Salaries were tied to profits based on return of all assets, with a 10 percent bonus for punctuality, as indicated by time cards that everyone had to use, including top executives and Mars himself. In contrast to all other major confectioners, Mars had no affiliation with the National Confectioners Association or any other trade group, and he refused to lobby against excise taxes on chocolate or to promote its nutritional value.

In 1963 Charles Kaufman, corporate vice president of research and development, enabled Mars, Inc. to make its own chocolate and end its dependency on Hershey through total automation, from mixing of the ingredients to boxing of the bars. He reduced twenty manufacturing operations to five high-speed ones able to produce 2,500 Snickers bars

a minute and he brought in the only self-loading wrappers in the candy business. Mars began phasing out its chocolate purchases in 1965. Although it would take ten years for Mars, Inc. to recoup its investment, Mars knew that only the total control of all a product's ingredients guaranteed quality control. The total automation at the Chicago plant effected a more hygienic handling of raw ingredients, as well as their even distribution, and made possible the imprinting of the letter *M* on each M&M. The policy of not incurring any debt and of reinvesting all profits in its operations enabled Mars, Inc. to sustain state-of-the-art equipment.

Hershey sold $150 million of chocolate in 1966; Mars, Inc. sold $90 million. By 1969 the companies were tied. From 1970 to 1973 Mars edged out Hershey as the number one confectioner in the United States. Even though inflation, oil embargoes, and the price controls put into effect in 1972 led to a rise in the cost of ingredients, Mars, Inc. was less affected than Hershey because the ingredients used in its products were less costly than those in Hershey's. Furthermore, Mars, Inc. continued to advertise; Hershey slashed its promotional budget in 1973.

Mars retired in 1973 and transferred ownership of Mars, Inc. to his sons, Forrest, Jr., and John, who would be co-presidents, and his daughter, Jacqueline, who later became executive vice president. However, Mars came out of retirement in 1980. He enlisted the help of a former associate, Dean Musser, to head up a firm in Las Vegas called Ethel M, which made chocolate liqueurs. The firm had seventy stores in the West, which garnered annual sales of $150 million. *Fortune* magazine, in recognition of Mars's entrepreneurial acumen, named him to its Business Hall of Fame in 1984.

When Mars, Inc. was losing ground to Hershey and other competitors in 1992, Mars intervened for the first time, meeting to discuss a possible merger between Mars, Inc. and Nestlé without consulting his sons. They rejected the proposal, insisting on retaining the company as a family business. In spite of Mars's concerns, the company that was worth $800 million when he left in 1973 grew to a $20 billion business a generation later, with plants on six continents.

Mars died of natural causes at his home in Miami, Florida. He was survived by his children and ten grandchildren.

★

Joël Glenn Brenner, *The Emperors of Chocolate* (1999), is the only full-length work that includes biographical information about Mars and his companies; a synopsis of the book is in *Readers Digest* (Feb. 1999). Thomas Lippman's two-part series in the *Washington Post* (6 and 7 Dec. 1981) was the first lengthy analysis of the Mars business. An obituary is in the *New York Times* (3 July 1999). Mars, Inc. has a policy against releasing information to the public, making an exception only in 1989, when Brenner began her research for her book. When the *New York Times* published its obituary, it stated that no information was made available by the Mars, Inc. spokesperson. This is still the policy.

BARBARA L. GERBER

MARSHALL, E(dda) G(unnar)   (*b.* 18 June 1910 [1914?] in Owatonna, Minnesota; *d.* 24 August 1998 in Bedford, New York), character actor on television, film, and stage who won Emmy Awards in 1962 and 1963 for portraying Lawrence Preston in the television series *The Defenders.*

Marshall was the son of Charles G. Marshall, a telephone-company employee, and Hazel Irene Cobb. (Records vary in reporting Marshall's birth year as 1910 or 1914.) His parents named him Edda Gunnar for a Norse king and the book of legends from which the character originated, but after years of childhood teasing, Marshall went by the initials "E. G." as an adult. After he graduated from high school, he attended Carleton College in Northfield, Minnesota, but then transferred to the University of Minnesota where he majored in English literature. He had intended to become a clergyman but began to pursue a career as an

E. G. Marshall, 1962. ASSOCIATED PRESS/CBS

actor following a brief musical performance on a Saint Paul, Minnesota, radio station in 1932.

In 1933 Marshall traveled around the country with a Shakespearean troupe called the Oxford Players, playing Guildenstern in *Hamlet,* as well as parts in other classics such as *Romeo and Juliet* and *Doctor Faustus.* By 1938 he was performing for the Federal Theater Project, first in Chicago and then in New York City. He studied acting with Robert Lewis, following Konstantin Stanislavsky's techniques at the Actors Studio in 1940. In the 1930s and 1940s he played a number of comedic small parts in plays such as Henry Onstoll's *Prologue to Glory,* Theodore Pratt's *The Big Blow,* Robert E. Sherwood's *The Petrified Forest,* and Thornton Wilder's *The Skin of Our Teeth.*

Marshall also began acting on film, with a small part in the thriller *The House on Ninety-second Street* (1945). In 1946 he landed the role of Willie Oban in the original cast of Eugene O'Neill's *The Iceman Cometh*; this role proved pivotal for the struggling young actor. He then acted in plays at the Philco Television Playhouse, Armstrong Circle Theater, Studio One, and Kraft Television Theater, among others. His early successes were shared with Helen Wolf, whom he married on 26 April 1939. They had two children, a girl and a boy. They divorced in 1953 and he married Judith Coy, with whom he had three children.

During the 1950s Marshall appeared in the television dramas *Valley Forge, Rip Van Winkle,* and *Macbeth.* On Broadway he appeared in Finlay Decker's *The Survivors,* Ugo Betti's *The Gambler,* and Sean O'Casey's *Red Roses for Me.* A more important role came for him in 1953 when he played the Reverend John Hale in the original cast of *The Crucible* by Arthur Miller; within six months Marshall was playing the lead role of John Proctor. In 1956 he played the part of Vladimir in Samuel Beckett's *Waiting for Godot,* where his talents were honed by acting alongside the legendary Bert Lahr, who played Estragon.

Just as busy in the movie industry as he was on Broadway, Marshall played a major role in *The Caine Mutiny* (1954). In 1954 he also played parts in the films *Pushover, Broken Lance,* and *The Silver Chalice,* but his more memorable role was as Juror Number Four in the Academy Award–winning *Twelve Angry Men* (1957). This riveting drama starring Henry Fonda examined the process that jurors experience in the deliberation of a murder trial.

From 1961 to 1965 the television network NBC produced the Emmy Award–winning series *The Defenders,* starring Marshall as the seasoned defense attorney Lawrence Preston. Robert Reed played his son Kenneth, a young law partner. The television critic Mark Alvey described the show as "perhaps the most socially conscious series the medium has ever seen." Grappling with explosive political issues such as capital punishment, abortion, black-listing, civil rights, censorship, and euthanasia, *The De-*

fenders took a liberal position, examining the fragility of the legal system while upholding a firm belief in the process itself. For his role in this groundbreaking series, Marshall won Emmy Awards in 1962 and 1963 and was honored by the Maryland State Bar Association.

Marshall returned to Broadway in 1967, playing Oscar Hubbard in Lillian Hellman's *The Little Foxes;* in 1968 he starred in Neil Simon's *Plaza Suite.* In between starring roles on Broadway, Marshall returned to NBC in 1969, this time as the physician David Craig in *The New Doctors,* part of a series called *The Bold Ones,* which again grappled with ethical and moral issues that previous television dramas had ignored. In the 1970s Marshall hosted CBS's *Radio Mystery Theater.*

Although he starred in D. L. Coburn's *The Gin Game* in 1978 and A. R. Gurney's play *Love Letters* in 1990, Marshall turned more toward film during the latter part of his career, starring in Woody Allen's *Interiors* (1978), in *Superman II* (1981), and in *Absolute Power* (1997), adapted from David Baldacci's novel. He was also a television host in the 1990s for specials such as *A Capitol Fourth, 1992,* and *This Was America, 1963.* Marshall died from lung cancer.

Throughout his career, Marshall was never afraid to tackle the most pressing social issues of his time. Through his acting roles he was able to awaken the collective American conscience to a deeper sense of the important moral and ethical questions of the twentieth century.

★

Magill's Survey of Cinema (1980) provides insight into Marshall's sensibilities as an actor in reviews of the following films: *Broken Lance* (1954), Lillian Hellman's adapted screenplay of Horton Foote's *The Chase* (1966), Woody Allen's *Interiors* (1978), and *Superman II* (1981). Mark Alvey, "The Defenders: U.S. Legal Drama," in *Magill's Survey of Cinema,* also provides an excellent review of one of Marshall's major television roles. Marshall is included in *Current Biography Yearbook* (1986). Anne Hodges's review of *The Defenders* in the *Houston Chronicle* (10 Oct. 1997) offers an excellent comparison of a revival of the show and the original 1960s television production, both of which starred Marshall. Obituaries are in the *Los Angeles Times, Washington Post,* and *New York Times* (all 26 Aug. 1998), as well as in the *Guardian* (27 Aug. 1998) and *People Weekly* (7 Sept. 1998).

JANE FRANCES AMLER

MARSTON, Robert Quarles (*b.* 12 February 1923 in Toano, Virginia; *d.* 14 March 1999 in Gainesville, Florida), leading medical educator and researcher who fought the separation of science and politics while directing the National Institutes of Health.

Marston was the son of Warren Marston and Helen Smith, a homemaker. He received a B.S. degree in 1943 from the

Robert Q. Marston, 1968. AP/WIDE WORLD PHOTOS

Virginia Military Institute in Lexington and then enrolled at the Medical College of Virginia in Richmond, where he received an M.D. in 1947. Marston married Ann Carter Garnett on 21 December 1946; the couple had three children. In 1947 he was given a Rhodes Scholarship to study at Oxford University in England. There he worked with key members of the research team that developed penicillin and earned a B.Sc. degree in 1949. After returning from Oxford, Marston completed his medical training with an internship at the Johns Hopkins Hospital in Baltimore (1949–1950) and a residency at Vanderbilt University Hospital in Nashville, Tennessee (1950–1951).

Marston was stationed at the National Institutes of Health from 1951 to 1953 as a member of the Armed Forces Special Weapons Project. During that time he conducted research on the role of infection after whole-body irradiation. He completed his residency at and accepted an appointment to the Medical College of Virginia, where he served on the faculty for three years. In 1958 Marston joined the faculty of the University of Minnesota in Minneapolis as assistant professor in the department of bacteriology and immunology. In 1959 he returned to the Medical College of Virginia as associate professor of medicine and assistant dean for student affairs. In 1961 he started his full-time administrative career by becoming dean of the University of Mississippi's School of Medicine and director of the University of Mississippi Medical Center in Jackson. He was appointed vice chancellor in 1965. Under his leadership, the first African Americans were admitted to Mississippi's medical college, and new standards were set for the integration of academic health centers.

Marston is perhaps best known for his meteoric rise and abrupt fall in the federal government's medical hierarchy. In 1966 the National Institutes of Health named him director of the newly created division of regional medical programs on heart disease, cancer, and stroke. In April 1968 he became administrator of the Health Services and Mental Health Administration, and he was full director of the National Institutes of Health by September 1968. His tenure was colored by conflict between scientific researchers and political opponents in Congress and the executive branch, who were unwilling to finance basic scientific investigation rather than research that would pay off quickly. As director, he helped implement the National Institutes of Health's legislation to work with universities to increase the nation's supply of health professionals. Disagreements over allocations and priorities resulted in President Richard M. Nixon firing him from the National Institutes of Health in 1973. Marston then accepted a temporary position as scholar in residence at the University of Virginia in Charlottesville (1973–1974). He also was named the first distinguished fellow of the Institute of Medicine of the National Academy of Sciences.

In 1974 Marston was named president of the University of Florida in Gainesville, a position he held for ten years. During his years at the helm, Marston showed his commitment to strengthening the university's academic programs and cultural life. He oversaw a sizable growth in endowment, enrollment, and campus building at the university and laid the groundwork for the university's entry into the Association of American Universities in 1985. After he retired as president in 1984, Marston became an eminent scholar at the Virginia Military Institute, where he later served on the school's governing board. In 1985 he returned to full-time academic work in microbiology and conducted research and presented papers for the departments of fisheries and aquaculture at the University of Florida. That year he also chaired the Symposium on the Medical Implications of Nuclear War. He died of cancer at the Hospice of North Central Florida in Gainesville. He is buried in Tappahannock, Virginia.

During his career Marston wrote more than fifty scholarly publications and coedited *Medical Implications of Nuclear War* (1986) and *Medical Education in Transition* (1992). He held various academic and administrative posts, among them president of the National Association of State Universities and Land-Grant Colleges, distinguished service member of the Association of American Medical Colleges, and two-term member of the governing board of the

Institute of Medicine of the National Academy of Sciences. Marston was an effective administrator who did not shy away from controversy and who fought for civil rights and the good of the general population in all his positions.

★

Information on the life and career of Marston can be found in *Leaders in Education*, 5th ed. (1974). Obituaries are in the *New York Times* (16 Mar. 1999) and *National Institutes of Health Record* (20 Apr. 1999).

MARÍA PACHECO

MARTIN, William McChesney, Jr. (*b.* 17 December 1906 in St. Louis, Missouri; *d.* 27 July 1998 in Washington, D.C.), president of the New York Stock Exchange and chairman of the Federal Reserve Board who played a critical role in the development of American finance during the 1950s and 1960s.

Born to a prominent St. Louis banker who eventually became president of that city's Federal Reserve Bank, Martin earned a B.A. degree from Yale in 1928 and joined the brokerage firm A. G. Edwards in 1929. He became a partner in the company in 1931 when he moved to New York City to represent it on the New York Stock Exchange (NYSE).

In 1938, at the age of thirty-one, Martin became president of the NYSE. His appointment to that post came at a critical time. During the 1930s Congress had, at the urging of the Roosevelt administration, enacted a series of measures to regulate financial markets. The NYSE, led by President Richard Whitney, had stubbornly resisted these developments. In 1937, however, the exchange learned that Whitney had been stealing from his clients. Badly discredited, the NYSE turned to Martin, attracted to him because of his integrity, intelligence, and focus, and because he was an outsider. Martin became the exchange's first full-time, salaried president. Over the next three years he worked with federal officials to implement a system of regulation that preserved the central role of the NYSE in securities markets, while abolishing a wide variety of abuses.

Drafted into the U.S. Army in 1941, Martin served in various mobilization agencies during World War II, eventually rising to the rank of colonel. In 1942 he married Cynthia Davis (daughter of Dwight Davis, founder of the Davis Cup tennis competition), beginning a happy union that produced three children and lasted until his death. In 1946 Martin became head of the Export-Import Bank, and in 1949 assistant secretary of the U.S. Treasury. From these positions he played a significant, if secondary, role in rebuilding the international economy after the war.

The most important moment in Martin's career came in 1951. During World War II, the Federal Reserve and the

William McChesney Martin, Jr. PRINTS AND PHOTOGRAPHS DIVISION, LIBRARY OF CONGRESS

U.S. Treasury agreed to "peg" the rate of federal government securities at 2.5 percent and decided to purchase as many bonds as necessary to keep interest rates from going above this level. This policy allowed Washington to finance the staggering expense of war cheaply, but after 1945 it became controversial. The "peg" committed the Federal Reserve to expand the money supply whenever the demand for credit threatened to force the cost of money over 2.5 percent, a policy that might well lead the central bank to reinforce rather than resist an inflationary boom. Cheap money, however, remained popular, particularly among government officials concerned with financing the huge federal debt. The matter came to a head with the outbreak of the Korean War, which sparked a sharp increase in prices. Martin brokered a new arrangement between the Federal Reserve and the Treasury that allowed the central bank to set interest rates at its own discretion. As his reward, he received appointment as chairman of the Federal Reserve Board. Subsequently, the Federal Reserve raised interest rates, a policy that, along with the imposition of wage-price controls, checked inflation. The Federal Reserve's new policy received further vindication when President Dwight D. Eisenhower was able to remove wage-price controls in 1953 without a significant jump in prices.

Martin remained at the Federal Reserve for nineteen years, reappointed every four years by Presidents Eisenhower, John F. Kennedy, and Lyndon B. Johnson. He tenaciously defended the independence of the central bank and the value of the dollar. Martin blamed recessions on booms that got out of control and sparked speculation and inflation. He considered it the duty of the central bank to resist overrapid economic growth—in Martin's words, "to take away the punch bowl just when the party gets going." This stance was not always popular. In particular, Martin faced relentless criticism from U.S. Representative Wright Patman, a monomaniacal champion of cheap money.

Although Martin's handling of monetary policy generally earned high marks, he received criticism in two important instances. In the wake of the 1957–1958 recession, the Federal Reserve kept interest rates relatively high, in all likelihood slowing recovery and contributing to the 1960 recession. Martin was concerned with restraining inflation and protecting the international value of the dollar, but in retrospect neither of these problems seemed pressing. In 1966 the Federal Reserve orchestrated a sharp increase in interest rates to check accelerating inflation, only to back down in the face of intense political pressure from President Johnson. In light of the problems created by rising prices in the 1970s, this failure to follow through was unfortunate. Nevertheless, the 1950s and 1960s were two of the most prosperous decades in American history, and Martin's stewardship of the Federal Reserve deserves at least some credit.

Ineligible for reappointment, Martin retired from the Federal Reserve in early 1970. Subsequently, he served on the boards of International Business Machines (IBM), American Express, and the National Geographic Society, and on advisory committees for the NYSE. An avid tennis player who, while chairman of the Federal Reserve, had a tennis court installed behind the Federal Reserve building, Martin also served as president of the National Tennis Hall of Fame. He died in his home at age ninety-one.

During Martin's long and productive career, he contributed substantially to the development of a system of regulating securities exchanges that endured into the twenty-first century and made American financial markets arguably the world's most efficient. He created and defended the independence of the Federal Reserve, which insulated monetary policy from day-to-day political pressures and made the central bank one of the government's most powerful bureaus.

Martin belonged to a small but influential group of

Americans, such as J. P. Morgan and Paul Warburg, who saw finance as a moral as well as an economic calling. In an earlier generation he would have worked at Morgan's bank. In the middle of the twentieth century, however, he gravitated to government service. There he did not earn the sort of fortune enjoyed by the Morgans and the Warburgs, but he wielded perhaps even more influence.

★

No single collection of Martin's papers exists, but papers remain at the New York Stock Exchange and the government bureaus in which he served. Robert Sobel's *N.Y.S.E.: A History of the New York Stock Exchange, 1935–1975* (1975), and Joel Seligman's *The Transformation of Wall Street: A History of the Securities and Exchange Commission and Modern Corporate Finance* (1982), devote considerable space to Martin's labors at the NYSE. Martin's leadership of the Federal Reserve is chronicled in Sherman Maisel's *Managing the Dollar* (1973); John T. Wooley's *Monetary Politics: The Federal Reserve and the Politics of Monetary Policy* (1984); and Donald Kettl's *Leadership at the Fed* (1986). Robert Solomon's *The International Monetary System, 1945–1981* (1982) covers international finance during Martin's tenure at the Federal Reserve. An obituary is in the *New York Times* (29 July 1998).

WYATT WELLS

MAS CANOSA, Jorge (*b.* 21 September 1939 in Santiago, Cuba; *d.* 23 November 1997 in Miami, Florida), self-made millionaire in the construction industry and leader of the anti-Castro Cuban American National Foundation.

Mas Canosa was the third of six children of Ramón Mas, a Cuban army veterinarian, and his wife, a homemaker. After attending school in Santiago, Mas Canosa, aged fourteen, attacked Cuban dictator Fulgencio Batista in a radio broadcast; as a result, his father, whose reputation for strictness he is said to have inherited, sent Mas Canosa to Presbyterian Junior College in Maxton, North Carolina, even though the family was devoutly Catholic. After receiving an associate in arts degree in 1959, Mas Canosa returned to Santiago to attend the University of Oriente, where he studied law. In the following year, he married Irma Santos, a childhood sweetheart; they had three children.

At first Mas Canosa supported Fidel Castro, but in 1960 he was jailed for criticizing the new dictator (some of his opponents deny that he was jailed). After serving a short sentence, he immigrated to Miami. For a few months he worked as a stevedore, washed dishes, sold shoes, and delivered milk. In 1961 he joined Brigade 2506, a group of exiles trained by the Central Intelligence Agency for the Bay of Pigs invasion, but did not actually fight. He then enlisted in the U.S. Army, becoming a second lieutenant.

Jorge Mas Canosa, 1964. CORBIS CORPORATION (BELLEVUE)

After his discharge he rose from employee to partner at Iglesia y Torres, a small Miami construction firm and subcontractor of telephone services. By 1969 Mas Canosa, borrowing from a bank, bought the company, anglicizing its name to Church and Tower. By the mid-1970s the firm had 400 employees and a gross income of $20 million per year. He also became chairman of Mastec, Inc., a publicly traded engineering contracting firm with more than 7,000 employees and a net worth of more than $1 billion at the time of his death, and Neff Machinery, a distributor of construction equipment. These business activities, involving contracting for Dade County and Southern Bell, brought Mas Canosa a fortune estimated at more than $9 million, enabling him to become a major power in Cuban exile and conservative politics. (At the time of his death, his net worth had grown to an estimated $100 million.) In 1980, two years before he acquired American citizenship, Mas Canosa, together with other Cuban-American businessmen, founded the Cuban American National Foundation. Its initial aim was to support Ronald Reagan's presidential candidacy, but it soon broadened to become the leading anti-Castro organization in the United States, with more than 50,000 members. Supporters within the exile community characterized Mas Canosa, who chaired the board of the foundation until his death, as an idealist fighting to restore Cuban democracy. Opponents, many of whom wrote for the politically liberal *Miami Herald* or its Spanish-language edition *El Nuevo Herald,* felt he wanted to substitute his own right-wing dictatorship in Cuba for Castro's left-wing one. Mas Canosa's forceful personality and explosive temper made many enemies: he once challenged a Miami politician to a duel (the politician suggested water pistols as weapons), and he lost a $1 million libel judgment in a suit brought by his brother. He successfully sued the *New Republic,* which had called him a mobster.

On 20 May 1985 Radio Marti, broadcasting to Cuba over Castro's vociferous objections, which extended to interfering with the signals of U.S. domestic stations, went on the air with American government assistance after ten years of campaigning by Mas Canosa. By 1990 TV Marti began operating. Mas Canosa was appointed chairman of the Presidential Advisory Board on broadcasting to Cuba, but in 1995 a federal investigation found that he had meddled in the stations' daily operations. Mas Canosa's supporters were quick to accuse the U.S. Information Agency's inspector general's office of partisan politics in the service of the Clinton administration, and an earlier investigation by the State Department's inspector general had cleared Mas Canosa of many of the charges.

Mas Canosa was largely responsible for Congress passing the 1992 Cuban Democracy Act, also known as the Torricelli Bill, named after the Democratic U.S. senator from New Jersey whose constituents included the second-largest Cuban exile community. The act tightened the U.S. trade embargo against Cuba. Mas Canosa was also a major influence in the passing of the 1996 Helms-Burton Act, which allowed Cuban Americans to sue foreign companies doing business with properties illegally confiscated under the Castro regime. According to Wayne Smith, who headed the United States Interests Section in Havana during the Carter administration, Mas Canosa almost single-handedly blocked the establishment of normal relations between the United States and Cuba.

In 1996 Mas Canosa debated the head of Cuba's parliament, Ricardo Alarcon, on international television. Two years earlier he had engaged in secret negotiations on the Cuban refugee influx with President William J. Clinton. Toward the end of his life Mas Canosa was active in initiatives for a post-Castro Cuba, including Misión Marti, an intensive education program for those planning to work in post-Castro Cuba. He was also active in pro-Israel causes.

By the beginning of 1997 Mas Canosa's health was beginning to deteriorate due to lung cancer and Paget's disease. He died at his home in Miami at age fifty-eight.

Thousands, including numerous members of both houses of Congress, attended his funeral. He is buried at Woodland Memorial Park in Miami.

★

There is no biography of Mas Canosa. Material on him, mostly critical, appears in Charles W. Kegley, Jr., and Eugene R. Wittkopf, *American Foreign Policy, Pattern and Process* (1992), and James S. and Judith E. Olson, *Cuban Americans: From Trauma to Triumph* (1995). Obituaries are in the *New York Times, Miami Herald,* and *El Nuevo Herald* (all 24 Nov. 1997) and *Exito* (28 Nov. 1997). See also Charles Cotayo and Pablo Alfonso, "Un año sin Jorge Mas Canosa," *El Nuevo Herald* (22 Nov. 1998).

STEPHEN A. STERTZ

MASON, (William) Birny J., Jr. (*b.* 27 February 1909 in Brownsville, Pennsylvania; *d.* 5 January 1997 in Rye, New York), chairman and chief executive officer (CEO) of the chemicals and consumer products company Union Carbide.

Mason was one of four children born to William Birny Mason, a railroad worker, and Mary Carmack. Like his father, he dropped his first name. After attending local public schools in Brownsville, he enrolled in the Hill preparatory school in Pottstown, Pennsylvania. Forsaking a youthful dream of a career in medicine, Mason followed the advice of a family friend and studied chemical engineering, receiving a B.S. degree from Cornell University in Ithaca, New York, in 1931. The following year he obtained a position with the Union Carbide Corporation, a producer of chemicals, metallurgical products, and carbon. Mason spent his entire career with the company, working initially in production and research at the Union Carbide Chemicals Company, a corporate subsidiary.

Mason married Elizabeth Brownson Smith on 22 March 1935; they had one son. Early in Mason's career, the family lived in South Charleston, West Virginia, before moving to Louisville, Kentucky, back to South Charleston, and then to Larchmont, New York, where Mason joined Union Carbide's management team. As a manager of industrial relations, beginning in 1952, Mason developed "infinite patience, receptiveness, [and] imagination, as well as strong convictions of his own," according to an associate. During a five-year period, he was rapidly promoted through a series of management positions: secretary of the Union Carbide Corporation (1955), president of the Union Carbide Development Company (1956), vice president and member of the appropriations committee (1957), director and executive vice president (1958), and president (1960). In 1963 he became CEO.

During his time at the helm of Union Carbide, Mason completed the restructuring of the company into a cohesive whole, rather than a series of semiautonomous subsidiaries with independent boards. Initiated by his predecessor and mentor Morse G. Dial in 1949, this process was completed during the first few months of Mason's term as CEO. He then turned his attention to cost cutting and a major new initiative in the consumer products area, a thrust that he described as "an evolutionary change . . . a natural extension of a strong position in basic bulk chemicals and research." Since the company already was producing Prestone antifreeze and Eveready batteries, Union Carbide was well known for consumer products, but under Mason, it manufactured and marketed such new items as battery-powered lawn mowers, baby baths, car seats, and Glad Bags and Glad Wrap for food storage. In 1964 the corporation underscored its emphasis on consumer products by acquiring Englander Mattress Company.

As Union Carbide continued its move into consumer products, Mason undertook further company restructuring. The three operating divisions that had been created in the early 1960s, domestic, international, and administration and finance, were replaced in 1964 by four groups administered by operating committees. Within two years of this restructuring, Mason's successful leadership of the corporation was recognized by the company's board of directors, who named him the chairman in 1966.

That same year Mason was elected to a three-year term as a public governor of the New York Stock Exchange. On the eve of his appointment, an associate described Mason's diligence and thoroughness to the *New York Times,* saying, "Before Birny Mason, Jr., took up golf in 1956 he studied a number of books on the subject. Like everything else he does in life, he took his new hobby seriously. Today he shoots in the eighties." Mason was also an avid sailor who did meticulous research before purchasing various boats. In the mid- to late 1960s, however, his time available for leisure pursuits was limited because in addition to his business responsibilities Mason served on the Economic Development Council (1966–1968) and was the vice chairman of President Lyndon Johnson's Business Council (1966–1969). In 1966 Mason also assumed the chairmanship of Mayor John V. Lindsay's Management Advisory Council, a group of six business leaders appointed to devise strategies for making New York City's government more efficient.

As daunting as this challenge was, it paled in comparison to the problem Mason faced in 1970 when residents of Anmoore, West Virginia, began a petition drive to persuade Union Carbide to implement air pollution abatement measures at a Carbide plant in their town. Assisted by the consumer advocate and activist Ralph Nader, the people of Anmoore demanded access to documents Union Carbide had submitted to West Virginia's Air Pollution Control Commission. They informed Mason, then a member of President Richard Nixon's National Industrial Pollution

Control Council, that his "failure to respond promptly and satisfactorily will be understood by us to mean that Union Carbide's long-standing policy of arrogance and indifference to the welfare of its neighbors remains unchanged." Within weeks, the company and the West Virginia Air Pollution Control Commission reached an agreement for a three-year, phased-in reduction in emissions from the Anmoore plant, and a four-year program for a Union Carbide plant in Alloy, West Virginia. A month later, however, the company was given six weeks by the federal government to submit a plan for curtailing pollution at a plant in Ohio, which, because of prevailing winds, was polluting the air in West Virginia. The company responded with a proposal to cut sulfur dioxide emissions by 12.5 percent instead of the 40 percent stipulated by the government. In January 1971 Union Carbide indicated that compliance could be achieved by a partial plant closure resulting in worker layoffs, something Nader termed an "act of economic and environmental blackmail."

Similar views were expressed at the corporation's annual meeting in 1971. Unlike the previous year, when an activist had disrupted the meeting by shouting "Carbide produces pollutants," the 1971 meeting was orderly. When one of Nader's associates asked whether company data on plant pollution was publicly available, Mason replied, "Only to those with legitimate interests, interests that run counter to yours." While contending that the limitations of current technology made full abatement an unattainable goal, corporate officials informed the shareholders about the company's expenditures for pollution control, and the Union Carbide president F. Perry Wilson presented details of the corporation's efforts at its plants in Ohio and West Virginia.

Following the meeting, Mason relinquished the position of chairman to Wilson. In retirement, Mason remained on the board of Union Carbide and was active in the business and civic life of New York City. In 1972 he played a pivotal role in a reorganization designed to make the board of the New York Stock Exchange more broadly representative of the public. He also served on the boards of New York's Presbyterian Hospital, the United Hospital in Port Chester, Cornell University, the National Safety Council, and the John A. Hartford Foundation. He held corporate directorships with the Metropolitan Life Insurance Company, Manufacturers Hanover Trust Company, Fidelity and Casualty Corporation, North American Philips Corporation, Bradford National Corporation, and the Consolidation Coal Company. He received the National Brotherhood Award from the National Conference of Christians and Jews in 1969. Mason died at his New York residence at age eighty-seven, following a long battle with cancer.

In the course of his long career, Mason, who in 1970 told the editor of *Nation's Business* that the greatest satisfaction in his career was "the resolution of difficult problems," witnessed the extraordinary transformation of the company where he spent his entire working life. He saw Union Carbide evolve from a holding company with semi-autonomous subsidiaries into a unified corporation producing an eclectic array of consumer goods. As the principal architect of the company's successful forays into foreign markets, he had a thorough grasp of globalization, as evidenced by his assertion at a New York Stock Exchange symposium in 1967 that the rewards of corporate expansion overseas "will become much clearer as underdeveloped nations of the world advance economically. As their standards of living begin to rise and their purchasing power increases, these nations will represent a huge growth market."

Just as he realized the potential for overseas expansion, Mason comprehended the problems inherent in conducting business, whether at home or abroad. In a 1962 speech criticizing government attacks on big business, Mason urged the government to "find an equitable balance between the rights of labor and the rights of business, between the farmer and the consumer, and between state and federal powers." He also noted that from 1900 to 1960, two-thirds of the one hundred biggest companies in 1900 had disappeared. In his opinion, there was no assurance that any business, large or small, would necessarily survive. Yet, during his tenure as CEO, Union Carbide was a thriving global corporation and Mason was highly respected in the business community.

★

Biographical data on Mason appears in *Who's Who in Finance and Industry: 1974–1975* (1974). His business career is discussed in the *New York Times* (2 Mar. 1956, 21 Nov. 1958, 29 July 1960, and 1 May 1963), and in "Birny Mason of Union Carbide," *Nation's Business* (Sept. 1970). Excerpts from his speech criticizing government attacks on big business appear in *U.S. News and World Report* (3 Dec. 1962). The pollution controversy is covered in the *New York Times* (15 Oct. 1970, 22 Oct. 1970, 29 Oct. 1970, 30 Oct. 1970, 14 Nov. 1970, 20 Dec. 1970, 24 Dec. 1970, 21 Jan. 1971, and 22 Apr. 1971). Obituaries are in *Newsday* and the *Pittsburgh Post-Gazette* (both 8 Jan. 1997), the *New York Times* (9 Jan. 1997), and *Chemical Week* (15 Jan. 1997).

MARILYN E. WEIGOLD

MATURE, Victor John (*b.* 29 January 1913 in Louisville, Kentucky; *d.* 4 August 1999 in Rancho Santa Fe, California), movie star who appeared in fifty-nine films, including biblical epics such as *Samson and Delilah* (1949), *The Robe* (1953), and *Demetrius and the Gladiators* (1954).

Mature was the son of the Italian immigrant Marcellus Gelindo Mature, a scissors grinder who became a business

Victor Mature in *The Bandit of Zhobe,* 1959. ASSOCIATED PRESS/CO-LUMBIA PICTURES

executive, and Clara Ackley, a physician's daughter and homemaker. He had two siblings, a sister who died in infancy and a brother who died at eleven years of age. Always an indifferent student, Mature first attended the George H. Tingley School in Louisville but was sent home on the first day because he bit one of the teachers. Later, he attended three Catholic schools and the Kentucky Military Academy, from which he was thrown out. He quit school altogether at age fifteen.

After leaving school, Mature sold magazines. He also became an elevator operator at Louisville's Brown Hotel but was fired for dancing on the roof garden while on duty. After turning to candy sales, Mature saved enough money to buy a Louisville restaurant. But he sold it in 1935 after a friend told him that his good looks and powerful physique (he was six feet, two inches tall, and had a weightlifter's body) could make him a Hollywood star.

After arriving in California, Mature worked at the Pasadena Community Playhouse, where he studied under Gilmor Brown and appeared in more than sixty plays. He made his movie debut in 1939, appearing briefly in Hal Roach's *The Housekeeper's Daughter.* In 1940 he starred as a Tarzan-like hero in *One Million B.C.,* another movie by Roach, who was impressed with Mature's leading-man potential. The same year, he also starred in the comedy *No, No, Nanette.* In 1941 he attracted yet more attention in the

Broadway musical *Lady in the Dark*. Known by now as a handsome hunk, Mature returned to Hollywood where he signed with Twentieth Century–Fox. He made several more movies in the early 1940s, before joining the coast guard after the United States entered World War II. He became a chief boatswain's mate and saw convoy duty in the North Atlantic, Mediterranean, Caribbean, and South Pacific.

After leaving the coast guard in 1945, Mature won widespread acclaim for playing the consumption-ridden Doc Holliday in *My Darling Clementine* (1946), a John Ford film that also starred Henry Fonda as Wyatt Earp. The next year he made *Kiss of Death* (1947), which was widely regarded as one of his best movies. Mature made his signature movie in 1949 when he starred in Cecil B. DeMille's biblical epic *Samson and Delilah*. In an unforgettable portrayal, Mature played a remarkably human, and therefore fallible, Samson to Heddy Lamar's Delilah. Yet Mature's Samson never lost faith in his God. After *Samson and Delilah* received much praise from reviewers, Groucho Marx said, "I don't want to see any movie where the guy's breasts are bigger than the girl's." Marx's good-natured joke probably influenced many people to see the movie.

Work in other biblical epics followed, including *The Robe* (1953), in which Mature shared star billing with Richard Burton. Mature played the part of Demetrius, the faithful slave who witnessed the death of Jesus and converted to Christianity. Mature appeared in several more films in the 1950s, including *Demetrius and the Gladiators* (1954), a sequel to *The Robe,* and the popular *Egyptian* (1954). He also starred in *Hannibal* (1959), an epic that centered on Hannibal of Carthage and his failed attempt to conquer the Roman Empire.

After filming *Hannibal,* Mature turned his back on Hollywood and went into retirement. He made a reported $18 million during his acting career and invested wisely in restaurants, retail stores, electronics, and real estate. In addition, his parents had left him a considerable inheritance. He was thus able to retire and live the good life in Rancho Santa Fe, San Diego County, California, where he pursued the hobbies of golfing, hunting, sailing, and swimming. One of Mature's most famous quotes comes from this time, "I'm no actor, and I've got sixty-four pictures to prove it." He also became a world traveler who loved to experience new places and meet new people.

Although he was successful in the movie industry and in his business ventures, Mature had a stormy domestic life. He was married five times. He met his first wife, Frances Charles, while both worked at the Pasadena Community Playhouse. They married in 1938 but the marriage was annulled in 1940. He then married Martha Stephenson Kemp on 18 June 1941; they divorced in 1943. He married his fourth wife, Dorothy Stanford Beny, on 27 September 1959; they later divorced. On 4 August 1974 Mature wed for the last time, to Lorey Sabena, a former opera singer, with whom he had his only child, a girl born in 1975. At various stages of his career, rumors also linked him romantically to several Hollywood stars, including Betty Grable, Lana Turner, Rita Hayworth, and Elizabeth Taylor.

Lured out of retirement in 1966, Mature staged a comeback by spoofing his own screen image. Playing a vain former movie star in Blake Edwards's *After the Fox,* a comedy that starred Peter Sellers, he charmed audiences with his ability to laugh at himself. Six years later he again spurned retirement long enough to make *Every Little Crook and Nanny,* a comedy. He played the Mafia boss Carmine Ganucci and received some of the best reviews of his career. In the 1970s he appeared in two more movies before making his television debut in 1984, playing Samson's father in a television version of *Samson and Delilah.* Mature died in his home at Rancho Santa Fe after a three-year bout with leukemia. His body was returned to his hometown of Louisville and was interred there at Saint Michael's Cemetery.

Mature was a true screen legend. Despite his early retirement from show business, he won lasting fame for his good looks and the epics in which he starred.

★

For more on Mature's career and personal life, see Don Freeman, "Brawny Vic Mature Was Indeed a Nice Guy," *San Diego Union-Tribune* (13 Aug. 1999); see also "Victor Mature: A Screen Star Renowned for Beefcake Roles in Biblical Epics, His Image Concealed a Solid Stage Actor," *Guardian* (11 Aug. 1999). Mature's best friend, actor Jim Backus, devoted a chapter of his autobiography—*Forgive Us Our Digressions* (1988)—to Mature. A briefer glimpse of Mature is found in Scott and Barbara Siegel, *Encyclopedia of Hollywood* (1990). Obituaries are in the *Louisville Courier-Journal* and *New York Times* (both 10 Aug. 1999), *Current Biography Yearbook* (1999), and *Film Comment* (Nov./Dec. 1999).

JAMES M. SMALLWOOD

MAYFIELD, Curtis Lee (*b.* 3 June 1942 in Chicago, Illinois; *d.* 26 December 1999 in Roswell, Georgia), singer, guitarist, songwriter, music publisher, and record company executive who was one of the first pop stars to incorporate civil rights themes into his music during the 1960s.

Mayfield was the first of five children and was raised primarily by his mother, Marion Pauline Washington, a postal worker, and his grandmother, the Reverend A. B. Mayfield (a preacher with the Traveling Souls Spiritualist Church and music director of the local gospel group the Northern Jubilee Gospel Singers). Mayfield was exposed to the rich musical milieu of postwar Chicago. The fertile combination of blues (Muddy Waters, Little Walter), spirituals from

Curtis Mayfield, 1990. JACK VARTOOGIAN

the Pentecostal church tradition, and rhythm and blues and doo-wop (the Dells, the Platters) reflected the huge northern migration of southern blacks during the early part of the twentieth century.

Mayfield taught himself to play guitar by age nine. The guitar was in an unusual F-sharp tuning, which he claims came from tinkling only the black keys on a piano. He sang with the Alphatones before meeting the Mississippi-born Jerry Butler at age twelve. After he moved to the Cabrini-Green federal housing project at fourteen, Mayfield was recruited by Butler to join the Roosters, a doo-wop group from Chattanooga, Tennessee, in 1956. He quit Chicago's Wells High School in tenth grade to pursue music full time.

The Roosters changed names and released their first single as Jerry Butler and the Impressions. "For Your Precious Love" (1958) became a hit, reaching number one on the charts. Rifts caused by Butler's top billing and by clashing egos forced the lead baritone to depart for a solo career. The Impressions replaced Butler with Fred Cash, but Mayfield continued to pen songs for and play guitar with Butler, whose next hit was "He Will Break Your Heart" (1961). Meanwhile, the Impressions's self-titled debut LP released

on ABC-Paramount catapulted the group to national fame in 1963.

The Mayfield-led Impressions devised a unique style that would often be imitated. Employing a switch-off technique, common in gospel music, Mayfield (tenor, falsetto), Sam Gooden (deep bass), and Fred Cash (tenor) would alternate singing lead and then provide backup harmony for each other. Mayfield also fused church and gospel music with secular lyrics, creating a new style: the so-called Chicago sound. In 1961 Mayfield and manager Eddie Thomas organized Curtom Music Publishing, the first black-owned music publishing company in the United States. The Impressions created a newer, distinct style when their unique vocals were used in the brassy arrangements of Johnny Pate, a veteran of the big bands and jazz.

In 1961 the Impressions's first single, the flamenco-inflected "Gypsy Woman," hit number twenty on the Billboard chart. Mayfield credits the then-popular western movie as influencing his lyrics. Pate's blaring horns and percussive rhythms made "It's All Right" (1963) the number-one rhythm and blues, and number-four pop, hit. The Impressions took off as a major national act as their inspirational anthem soothed a nation grieving for the slain President John F. Kennedy.

A noticeable stylistic and thematic change occurred with the gospel-sounding "Keep On Pushing" (1964), arguably the first rhythm and blues hit to rally black America behind the civil rights struggle. In what became the unofficial theme song for the movement led by the Reverend Martin Luther King, Jr., Mayfield preached perseverance, hard work, and faith as the keys to equality.

Mayfield continued to write for, record, and produce other Chicago soul acts, including Major Lance ("Monkey Time") and Gene Chandler ("Just Be True"). The Impressions' 1965 hit album *People Get Ready* featured the inspirational title song with a gospel arrangement, bluesy guitar riffs, lush strings, and the fusing of spirituals with civil rights themes. The result, one of Mayfield's masterpieces, was known as King's favorite song. By employing metaphors of the civil rights movement to address contemporary issues, "We're a Winner" (1968) was a success in spite of resistance by black radio programmers who feared the repercussions of playing a song with such a political message.

Mayfield left the Impressions in 1970 and released several successful solo albums: *Curtis* (1970), *Curtis Live* (1971), and *Roots* (1971). His best-known album was the score for the classic blaxploitation film *Superfly* (1972), which presented a negative view of the drug underworld. The story of Youngblood Priest, a Harlem drug dealer trying to go straight, was a critical success. The soundtrack, a pioneering funk classic, foreshadowed the hip-hop revolution to come and was the number-one album in the nation for four weeks. The score won four Grammy nominations, and its hit single "Freddie's Dead" (1975) dramatically blended Latin percussion and wah-wah–enhanced guitar riffs with Mayfield's trademark high falsetto tenor.

The 1970s was a busy decade for Mayfield, who toured Europe and Asia often and scored many black-oriented films. He wrote the scores for the Staple Singers' *Let's Do It Again* (1973), a Bill Cosby–Sidney Poitier action/comedy; Gladys Knight and the Pips for *Claudine* (1974), the Diahann Carroll–James Earl Jones film that Mayfield also acted in; and the song "Do Do Wop Is Big in Here" for the critically acclaimed adaptation of the Miguel Pinero prison drama *Short Eyes* (1977). Aretha Franklin said, "Curtis Mayfield is to soul music what Bach was to classics and Gershwin and Irving Berlin were to pop music."

The more conservative, less political Motown label adapted its sound after Mayfield's successes demonstrated that audiences demanded music and other art forms be relevant to the sociopolitical situation of people's lives. Motown's Tom Moon, writing in the *Philadelphia Inquirer*, stated that "without Mayfield there's no Marvin Gaye singing 'What's Going On,' no Stevie Wonder talking about living for the city." The popular funk acts Sly and the Family Stone and Earth, Wind, and Fire owed Mayfield a debt. And Parliament-Funkadelic founder George Clinton recalled, "Curtis is one of my favorite songwriters . . . you hear a lot of Curtis in Jimi Hendrix. In the sixties every guitar player wanted to play like Curtis."

As the granddaddy of the hip hop and rap sound that emerged in the inner city 1980s, his lyrics stressing black empowerment and protest struck a chord. Chuck D. of Public Enemy, a leading rapper claimed the modern-day griot "has influenced legions of rap artists, including myself, with his sound, inspirational lyrics, and commitment." In the 1990s his early hits were covered by the hip hop artists Dr. Dre, Coolio, and R. Kelly.

In 1990, while mounting the stage at New York's Wingate Field, Mayfield suffered a crippling freak accident as a gust of wind dislodged lighting rigs, which tumbled down on him. He suffered three broken vertebrae, massive spinal cord damage, and paralysis from the neck down. He was confined to a wheelchair, and his complications included diabetes and amputations.

His final album, the critically acclaimed *New World Order* (1996), was used as the theme for the Spike Lee film *Get on the Bus,* a dramatization inspired by the Million Man March. In 1996 Mayfield released a book of poetry, *Poetic License: In Poem and Song.* He was lauded with several tribute albums and won two Grammy Awards (Legend, 1994; Lifetime Achievement, 1995). He was inducted into the Rock and Roll Hall of Fame, once in 1991 as a member of the Impressions and once in 1999 as a solo act. Mayfield died from complications from his paralysis at North Fulton Regional Hospital. He was fifty-seven and had made his home since 1982 in Atlanta, where he is buried. Mayfield was survived by his mother Pauline Washington, his wife Altheida, eleven children and seven grandchildren. In a huge memorial service, former bandmates from the Impressions, Jerry Butler, Fred Cash, and Sam Gooden, honored this musical giant with an emotional rendition of their inspirational classic "Amen."

★

For an in-depth study of Mayfield and his contemporaries, see Robert Pruter, *Chicago Soul* (1991), a comprehensive and highly readable account. Irwin Stambler's article in *The Encyclopedia of Pop, Rock, and Soul* (1989) is an excellent source for information on his early years, and *The New Rolling Stone Encyclopedia of Rock and Roll* (1995) updates his career. For an interesting anecdotal and musicological analysis of more than a dozen Mayfield-penned or Mayfield-performed tunes, see critic Dave Marsh, *The Heart of Rock and Soul: The 1001 Greatest Singles Ever Made* (1989). An extended essay by Robert Pruter, the rhythm and blues editor of *Goldmine,* is in the 2 April 1993 issue—it is especially good on the early years of the Impressions. A highly technical analysis of Mayfield's unique guitar style is by Andy Widders-Ellis in *Guitar Player* (Aug. 1991), and for an in-depth essay on Mayfield's solo career, see Craig Werner, "A Deeper Shade of Soul," a fifteen-page article in *Goldmine* (4 July 1997). Clayton Riley's review of *Superfly* is in the *New York Times* (26 Nov. 1972). Obituaries are in the *New York Times* and *Philadelphia Inquirer* (both 27 Dec. 1999).

JEFFREY S. ROSEN

MEISNER, Sanford (*b.* 31 August 1905 in Brooklyn, New York; *d.* 2 February 1997 in Sherman Oaks, California), actor and director who was one of the most influential acting teachers in twentieth-century America.

Meisner was the oldest of four children of Hermann Meisner, a furrier, and Bertha Knoepfler. Soon after his birth his parents moved to the Bronx, where Meisner spent his childhood. At three, Meisner's frail health led his parents to take him and baby brother Jacob to a farm where Jacob contracted bovine tuberculosis from unpasteurized milk. He died two years later. Although the family, including a new daughter, moved back to Brooklyn and a third son was eventually born, the tragedy of Jacob's death had a profound effect on Meisner's life because his parents blamed him for the fatal move to the farm. The guilt-ridden boy withdrew into books, daydreams, and fantasy, a solitary existence that he relieved by playing the family piano. During World War I, the pleasure Meisner derived from browbeating cousins and friends into executing "little pageants" based on battlefront newsreels awoke in him a desire to be an actor.

Meisner graduated from Erasmus Hall High School in 1923, after showing "no ability" for acting in student productions. Turning to the piano, he attended the Damrosch Institute (the now-famous Juilliard School), leaving after a year. Hearing that the Theatre Guild wanted young actors, Meisner auditioned and was cast as an extra in Sidney Howard's Broadway drama, *They Knew What They Wanted* (1924), starring Pauline Lord, whose "genius, pure and simple" inspired Meisner's further pursuit of acting. Harold Clurman, whom Meisner met through composer Aaron Copland, recommended that Meisner enroll in Lee Strasberg's acting workshop at the Chrystie Street settlement house. "Strasberg's oldest professional student," as Meisner later called himself, found Strasberg "a great, uplifting influence" on many aspects of his life.

Meisner, Clurman, and Strasberg all worked on the Theatre Guild's *Garrick Gaieties of 1925,* a Rodgers and Hart revue. After small parts in six Theatre Guild productions, Meisner was invited to join the Group Theatre, a repertory company founded by Clurman, Strasberg, and Cheryl Crawford that was modeled on the influential Moscow Art Theatre. The twenty-eight handpicked actors of the Group (including Morris Carnovsky, Stella Adler, Robert Lewis, John Garfield, and Franchot Tone) spent the summer of 1931 at a Connecticut farmhouse training and rehearsing under Strasberg's direction, using his controversial version of Stanislavsky's acting exercises, later labeled "the Method."

Critics praised the Group's ensemble playing in their first Broadway production, Paul Green's *The House of Connelly* (September 1931), in which Meisner had a bit part. For three years, Meisner "carried a spear" in many Group productions, finally performing his "first full-fledged characterization" as Guy Button, Jr., in Melvin Levy's *Gold Eagle Guy* (1934). His best parts were written for him by his friend Clifford Odets, the Group's resident playwright. Meisner was critically acclaimed as Sam Feinschreiber in Odets's *Awake and Sing* (1935) and as Julie in *Paradise Lost* (1936). He codirected (with Odets) and acted in *Waiting for Lefty* (March 1935), succeeded Elia Kazan as the gangster Eddie Fuselli in *Golden Boy* (17 January 1937), and played Willie Wax in Odets's *Rocket to the Moon* (November 1938).

Meisner began teaching at the Neighborhood Playhouse School of the Theater in the fall of 1935, and he headed its acting department from 1936 until 1959. Resigning after a dispute with the administration, he moved briefly to Los Angeles in 1958 to teach acting and direct the new talent division at Twentieth Century–Fox studios. Meisner's personal life suffered during this period. His 1940 marriage to Peggy Meyer ended in divorce in June 1947. He married

Sanford Meisner, 1980. AP/WIDE WORLD PHOTOS

Betty Gooch six months later; the couple divorced in 1958.

In California, Meisner made his film acting debut as the prosecutor in *The Story on Page One* (1959), written and directed by Odets, and played the psychiatrist in *Tender Is the Night* (1962). Feeling betrayed when a studio executive warned young actors that his classes would "destroy their personalities," Meisner finished his contract and returned to New York City. He headed the drama department of the newly founded American Musical Theatre Academy (1962–1964), then returned to the Neighborhood Playhouse, heading the acting department there until his 1994 retirement.

Meisner continued to perform on stage, screen, and television but became uncomfortable with the "childish" qualities acting brought out in him, despite critical praise for his role in the 1955 revival of *The Time of Your Life*. He also felt unsuited to directing established professional actors, although he did so in several Broadway productions during the 1940s and 1950s. Meisner discovered that "the only time I'm free and enjoying myself is when I'm teaching. . . . I feel alive and related." The realization led him to devote his time increasingly to his students.

Meisner's teaching differed from that of Adler and Strasberg, the more highly publicized antagonists in the acrimonious "method" disputes of the 1940s and 1950s. When Adler returned from five weeks of intensive study with Stanislavsky in 1934 and reported to the Group, Meisner agreed with Adler that Strasberg's frequently painful "affective memory" exercises (involving recall and use of actors' deeply emotional personal experiences) could be harmful. He once told Strasberg, "You introvert the already introverted" by making conscious what should remain instinctive. Meisner called Adler "more a lecturer on plays" and commented "I am a technician, in the sense that the way you learn to act is the way you learn to play the piano—through exercises."

Meisner's frequent use of musical analogies to explain his technique revealed his early musical training as a crucial source for the genesis of his teaching method. In the first year of his curriculum, Meisner ruthlessly "weeded out false behavior" while students practiced what he called "scales and fingering," beginning with simple exercises in listening and observation, followed by Meisner's famous "word repetitions" that stressed the core of his teaching: the development of each student's "living connection" to his scene partner. In the second year, through improvisations and scene work, students learned to use their "instruments" (themselves) instinctively to play the "emotional music" demanded by the script, which Meisner likened to the libretto of an opera.

In his seventies Meisner was plagued by a series of health disasters. A 1974 operation for cancer of the larynx left him without a voice; he learned to speak by gulping air into his esophagus. He was struck by an out-of-control truck when he was seventy-eight, an accident that smashed his left femur and hip, both of which had to be rebuilt. Despite everything, Meisner's "unquenchable impulse to teach" kept him working for more than five decades, inspiring several generations of America's finest actors, directors, and writers, including Gregory Peck, Robert Duvall, Diane Keaton, Maureen Stapleton, Peter Falk, Joel Grey, Tony Randall, Joanne Woodward, Lee Grant, Eli Wallach, Sidney Lumet, Sidney Pollack, Bob Fosse, David Mamet, and John Frankenheimer.

In 1985 Meisner and longtime companion James Carville cofounded the Meisner/Carville School of Acting on the Caribbean island of Bequia, expanding it to North Hollywood in 1985 with Martin Barter as director. In 1995, with Barter and Carville, Meisner opened the Sanford Meisner Center for the Arts in North Hollywood. Even after his retirement, the wheelchair-bound Meisner continued to attend meetings and performances at the school.

The least controversial and perhaps most utilitarian in approach among the triumvirate of method teachers, Meisner was honored by Presidents Reagan, Bush, and Clinton. His well-known aversion to publicity was reflected in Sidney Pollack's "The Theater's Best-Kept Secret," a documentary film about Meisner that was broadcast on the PBS *American Masters* series on 27 August 1990, four days before Meisner's eighty-fifth birthday. Meisner gave his last performance at age eighty-nine as a patient on the NBC series

ER; this performance led Stephen Spielberg to write, "It is a pleasure to see that after so many years of teaching acting, the teacher finally gets to show the students that he's the best."

Meisner died on 2 February 1997 at his home in Sherman Oaks. He was survived by his longtime companion Carville and an adopted son, Julian Martin. Memorial services were held at Meisner's theater and acting school in California. His cremated remains are buried on Bequia, where he and Carville had a home.

★

Sanford Meisner on Acting (1987), by Meisner and Dennis Longwell, has an autobiographical first chapter and many personal references within its text, which consists of edited transcriptions of Meisner's classes and is arranged to take the reader through the two-year course. Detailed listings of Meisner's resume as actor and director appear in *Notable Names in the American Theatre* (1976). A portrait of the man and his artistic life is offered in Stephen Harvey, "Another Man's Method," *American Film* 8, no. 7 (1983). Clippings and photographs of Meisner throughout his acting career are on file at the New York Public Library for the Performing Arts at Lincoln Center. A tribute by former student Marian Seldes, "The Theater Was His Life and His Life a Legend," is in the *New York Times* (16 Feb. 1997). A clear picture of Meisner's classroom methods is vividly revealed in Sydney Pollack's 1985 documentary, "Sanford Meisner: The Theater's Best-Kept Secret," available as a videotape of the PBS *American Masters* broadcast (27 August 1990). In this documentary, class sessions recorded over a two-year period are interspersed with comments by famous students about their experiences with Meisner. An obituary is in the *New York Times* (4 Feb. 1997).

DANIEL S. KREMPEL

MELLON, Paul (*b.* 11 June 1907 in Pittsburgh, Pennsylvania; *d.* 1 February 1999 in Upperville, Virginia), billionaire philanthropist and art collector whose gifts led to the establishment of the National Gallery of Art and the Yale Center for British Art.

Mellon was born to Andrew Mellon, the son of a wealthy banker who made his fortune from investment banking, and Nora Mary McMullen, of Hertford, England. The couple settled in Pittsburgh, where their two children, Alisa and Paul, were born. Despite enormous wealth and the needs of a young family, Mellon's parents separated when Paul was two and divorced three years later. He and his sister endured the breakup of their parent's marriage at a time when divorce was rare and social stigma severe. As children they were shuttled between households in England and the United States and subjected to the strain of their mother's emotionalism and their father's reserve and

Paul Mellon, 1932. © BETTMANN/CORBIS

loneliness. Despite these difficulties, Mellon emerged a re-silient and elegant man, who throughout his life maxi-mized opportunities to pursue his own interests and plea-sures while ensuring to posterity a large public benefit.

Mellon attended the Shadyside Academy for elementary schooling and at age twelve began to board at Choate. He credited his mother for giving him an "instinctive feeling for beauty and natural things" and a love of everything English. Although he originally intended to attend Prince-ton in 1925, the arrival of a strict Princeton freshman hand-book and his growing interest in Yale's English and history departments convinced him to switch just two weeks before the term began. After graduating from Yale in 1929, Mellon spent two years pursuing postgraduate studies in English history at Clare College, Cambridge University in England.

During his first year at Cambridge, Mellon was intro-duced to foxhunting and remained devoted to it and to trail riding throughout his life. What attracted him was the horse, the mastery of skills necessary to handle it, and the thrill of the hunt. Similar elements drew him to racing, although it exhibited more aesthetic qualities. For Mellon, the well-trained horse was an art object. He bought his first racehorse, Drinmore Lad, in 1933 and went on to build racing and breeding operations on his farm in Virginia.

Two of his horses won the Belmont Stakes, beginning with Quadrangle in 1964, and followed by Arts and Letters in 1969. Mellon was especially proud that he bred and owned the great classic racehorse Mill Reef, which won both the Epsom Derby and the Prix de l'Arc de Triomphe in the 1971 season. His horse Sea Hero won the Kentucky Derby in 1992. Mellon combined his love of horses with his in-terest in sporting art as a trustee of the National Museum of Racing in Saratoga Springs, New York.

Mellon attributed his "good judgement and sound nat-ural sense and the sense of the importance of the outside world, a respect for logic and order and money" to his father. These qualities served him well in his charitable activities. After graduating from Yale, Mellon found himself "in an unusual situation. I wanted to do something useful with my life but knew there would never be compelling financial reasons for me to have to take a regular job." His scholarly inclinations and love of literature and history led him briefly to consider college teaching. After short stints in the financial world, Mellon recognized he did not have the interest or desire to follow his father into banking. At a poignant meeting on 29 November 1936, nine months before his father's death, he was relieved when the senior Mellon revealed he understood his son's concerns; his fa-ther had made changes late in his own life as his focus shifted from business to government service and art pa-tronage.

It was through public-spirited philanthropy that Mellon would follow his father's example. Mellon fulfilled his fa-ther's dream of a National Gallery of Art by overseeing its design, construction, and presentation to the country, along with his father's art collection, in 1941. President Franklin D. Roosevelt noted how the giver had chosen not to memorialize his name with this gift but instead made a monument to art and America. Not interested in self-aggrandizement and greatly valuing his privacy, Mellon's self-effacement encouraged other donors to contribute to the gallery's holdings. This modest giving style marked his work as a philanthropist.

Some of Mellon's early charitable efforts were jointly pursued with his first wife, Mary Elizabeth Conover Brown. Married on 2 February 1935, they had two children. In 1945 the Mellons established the Bollingen Foundation to promote translation and publication of foreign language works in English, and to publish new editions of classics benefiting a range of fields such as archaeology, anthro-pology, and comparative religion. The foundation also pro-vided fellowships and grants to scholars from diverse sci-entific and humanistic fields, and awarded prizes for poetry and translation. Mellon's Old Dominion Foundation, es-tablished during the early years of World War II, became a useful funding mechanism for general education and uni-versity programs, especially in the classics. Programs based on the idea of a liberal education, such as those at Saint John's College in Annapolis, Maryland, and the Center for Hellenic Studies located in Washington, D.C., under the auspices of Harvard University, have benefited from Mellon's generosity.

Mellon volunteered to serve in the U.S. Army in the spring of 1941. He attended basic training at the Cavalry Replacement Training Center at Fort Riley, Kansas, where he became an officer candidate and later served as an instructor in horsemanship. Mellon spent most of the war in England, France, and Belgium, working for the Office of Strategic Services, where he was promoted to the rank of captain. At the war's end Mellon resumed many of his earlier responsibilities, including a trusteeship at the National Gallery of Art. His wife, Mary, who suffered from asthma attacks severe enough to strain her heart, died unexpectedly during an attack on 6 October 1946.

Traumatized by this loss and left with young children to raise, Mellon sought solace from old friends, especially Rachel Lambert Lloyd, nicknamed "Bunny." They married on 1 May 1948, and the newly constituted family included her two children. Bunny's interests in gardening, architecture, decorating, and collecting influenced and enhanced their long life together. They maintained homes in Washington, Manhattan, Paris, Antigua, Cape Cod, and Virginia.

In selecting works of art, Mellon described himself as possessing a keen visual sense and making decisions based on intuition and association with things that he liked. He had a strong interest in French nineteenth-century painting and American works, but his passion was British paintings, drawings, books, and prints of the eighteenth and nineteenth centuries. His collecting of British art began in earnest in 1959, when art historian Basil Taylor started to advise him. Mellon initiated his collecting when the market for such items was subdued and not well represented in major British museum collections. He collected works by British artists such as George Stubbs, William Blake, John Constable, and J. M. W. Turner. Mellon was also an avid collector of sporting art, and he acquired works by artists such as Ben Marshall, James Ward, and John Ferneley.

Mellon also saw himself as a "collector of collections" because he felt it almost a duty to prevent the dispersal of existing important collections. He often bought collections with a possible repository in mind, such as the surviving portion of John Locke's library for Oxford's Bodleian Library. Through his philanthropy Mellon sought to share with others the pleasure he had derived from collecting while perpetuating interest in what he loved. His two greatest philanthropic and collecting enterprises, whose collections he ensured would always be free to the public, were the National Gallery of Art and the Yale Center for British Art.

Mellon served the National Gallery as a trustee for forty-one years, and as president for the year 1938 and again from 1963 to 1979. The architect I. M. Pei was commissioned to design an addition to the National Gallery in the 1970s. The building itself became a work of art. The new East Building opened in 1978 at a cost of just over $94 million. It housed not only exhibition space but also administrative offices, the library, and the Center for Advanced Study in the Visual Arts. Mellon's many bequests to the National Gallery included works of French impressionists such as Claude Monet, Paul Cézanne, and Edgar Degas, and American and British Art.

Mellon viewed Yale as the most important educational institution in the United States for British studies. That made it the best place for his collection and the study of British art. He spent over $249 million in founding and nurturing the Yale Center for British Art, which opened in April 1977. He eventually gave it 1,600 paintings, over 130 sculptures, 18,000 drawings and watercolors, 21,000 prints, and 27,000 books. He made it the leading location for British art outside London. Its London subsidiary is the Paul Mellon Center for Studies in British Art. Mellon was also associated with the Virginia Museum of Fine Arts, contributing to the construction of its north and west wings and developing its collections. Additionally, he extended support to many other museums, galleries, and educational and charitable institutions in the United States and Britain.

While Mellon's collecting reflected and defined his taste and connoisseurship, he also exemplified the critical role of the art patron for the field of art history by making art objects available to scholars and endowing the means to support their study. One measure of his impact is the 1986 volume of essays written and published in his honor as collector and benefactor of the National Gallery of Art. The book's entries illustrate the extent of his influence on scholars and the scope of their work in English, French, and American art.

In addition to this work on behalf of art history and the humanities, Mellon's philanthropy reflected his myriad experiences and diverse interests. He supported the sciences and medical research in areas that had touched his life. He was drawn to the work of C. G. Jung as he sought a cure for his first wife's worsening asthma and sorted out his father's influence on himself. His interest in psychiatry led to support for the Anna Freud Foundation and the Menniger Foundation. He contributed to the Grayson-Jockey Club Research Foundation, the National Academy of Sciences, the Virginia Polytechnic Institute and State University, the Royal Veterinary College of the University of London, and the Mellon Institute. Under his leadership, the latter merged with the Carnegie Institute of Technology to form the Carnegie Mellon University in 1967. At his death he gave $20 million to establish the Mellon Prostate Cancer

Research Institute at the University of Virginia School of Medicine.

Mellon was committed to the conservation and preservation of both natural and man-made treasures. He saved for the nation the Cape Hatteras National Seashore in North Carolina, the Great Beach of Cape Cod, Cumberland Island off the coast of Georgia, and Sky Meadows State Park in Virginia. He helped restore Lafayette Park across from the White House, Thomas Jefferson's Monticello, and various British monuments. He also assembled a large collection of Americana consisting of rare books, maps, manuscripts, and drawings relating to the history of the Americas and with a special focus on Virginia.

In recognition of his lifetime of munificence he received many awards and honorary memberships that included the rank of Honorary Knight Commander of the Order of the British Empire. He held honorary doctorates from Oxford, Cambridge, Yale, the Carnegie Institute of Technology, and the Royal Veterinary College of London. In assessing Mellon's art collecting, his friend and adviser John Baskett wrote, "There can be little doubt that Paul Mellon was the greatest collector of the second half of the twentieth century and, in the whole field of British paintings, drawings, books and prints, he may well have been the greatest collector of all time." In all of his educational and charitable giving, Mellon transformed his passions as art collector and patron, gentleman scholar and knowledge builder, thoroughbred racing and breeding enthusiast, conservationist and environmentalist, and Anglophile into a great public legacy of preservation, learning, and culture. Through creating and supporting museums and study centers, providing objects for study, and funding scholarships, Mellon became an extraordinary example of a wealthy art patron who contributed to the institutionalization of art history. During his lifetime, Mellon's beneficence exceeded $600 million, while his bequests brought this figure to well over a billion dollars. In his final years he was afflicted with cancer and died in his home at age ninety-two. He is buried in Trinity Church Cemetery in Upperville, Virginia.

★

The most important source for information on Mellon is his *Reflections in a Silver Spoon: A Memoir,* with John Baskett (1992). The National Gallery of Art archives contain material relating to his art collecting. His Festschrift, published to coincide with the opening of new galleries in the west building of the National Gallery of Art, is edited by the art historian John Wilmerding and entitled *Essays in Honor of Paul Mellon Collector and Benefactor* (1986). The Yale Center for British Art held an exhibition to commemorate Mellon's final gifts and published a catalogue by Malcolm Warner, *The Paul Mellon Bequest Treasures of a Lifetime* (2001). For early Mellon family history, see Thomas Mellon, *Thomas Mellon and His Times* (1994), which includes a preface

to the second edition by Paul Mellon. On the Mellons and the National Gallery of Art, see Philip Kopper, *America's National Gallery of Art: A Gift to the Nation* (1991). An obituary is in the *New York Times* (3 Feb. 1999).

MARIA T. IACULLO

MENUHIN, Yehudi (*b.* 22 April 1916 in Bronx, New York; *d.* 12 March 1999 in Berlin, Germany), renowned violinist and conductor who was also active in humanitarian causes around the world.

Menuhin (later Baron Menuhin of Stoke d'Abernon) was the eldest child of Moshe Mnuchin and Marutha Sher, Russian Jewish immigrants who met in Palestine and married in New York City in 1914. They were inspired to name their son Yehudi, which means Jew, after the landlord of an apartment in which they were interested told them that its best advantage was that there were no Jews living in the building. Menuhin's father, a Hebrew teacher, changed the family surname to Menuhin in 1919, at the suggestion of the judge who officiated at his U.S. citizenship ceremony. The family moved from the Bronx to Elizabeth, New Jersey, in 1917. However, Menuhin's parents were not happy with the East Coast climate or lifestyle, and in 1918 they

Yehudi Menuhin. CORBIS-BETTMANN

moved to San Francisco. His two sisters were born there in 1920 and 1921.

Menuhin's musical prowess became evident when he was around two years old. His parents, both of whom were musical, noticed that he could sing on pitch and seemed quite enchanted with the orchestral performances he attended with them on Sunday afternoons. He was given a toy violin on his fourth birthday and a real half-sized instrument soon after. That same year, his parents made the decision to educate Menuhin at home themselves, after he had a disagreeable experience on his first day in kindergarten. Both of his sisters also were schooled at home. In 1921 Menuhin began formal violin lessons with Sigmund Anker, a local violinist who taught many young children. Two years later he began studying with Louis Persinger, the concertmaster of the San Francisco Symphony Orchestra and an active chamber musician. Persinger himself had studied with the great Belgian violinist Eugène Ysaÿe.

Menuhin presented his first full-length solo recital in San Francisco's Scottish Rite Auditorium on 30 March 1925. Accompanied at the piano by Persinger, he performed Mendelssohn's Violin Concerto and Paganini's *Moto perpetuo*. It was an extraordinary achievement for an eight-year-old musician, and his performance received accolades from the press and the public. Later that same year the family returned to New York City, where Persinger had taken up residence to focus on his own chamber music work. Menuhin was enrolled briefly in the Institute of Musical Art (Juilliard's predecessor institution) from November 1925 to January 1926, studying music theory. On 17 January 1926 he presented his New York recital debut at the Manhattan Opera House. On 12 March he presented his first performance with a full orchestra, playing Lalo's *Symphonie espagnole* with the San Francisco Symphony Orchestra conducted by Persinger in San Francisco's Curran Theatre.

Thus began Menuhin's increasingly active concert career. Although his parents claimed to be protective of his youth and expressed a desire to shield him from too much attention or publicity, in fact his father craftily managed his performing career for most of his youth. Moshe even falsified his son's birth date for the first twenty years of Menuhin's life, stating that he was born nine months later (on 11 January 1917), thus making his already prodigious musical accomplishments those of a child a year younger.

In December 1926 the entire family traveled to Europe so Menuhin could pursue studies in Brussels with Ysaÿe, Persinger's teacher. Menuhin had just one lesson with Ysaÿe, who was ailing, before moving on to Paris for studies with Georges Enesco, the Romanian composer and violinist. Menuhin presented his Paris debut in February 1927, performing Lalo's *Symphonie espagnole* and Tchaikovsky's Violin Concerto. In November of that year he presented

his New York orchestral debut, performing Beethoven's Violin Concerto in Carnegie Hall with the New York Symphony Orchestra conducted by Fritz Busch. In 1928 he made his first recordings for the RCA Victor label. For his 1929 Berlin debut he performed Bach, Beethoven, and Brahms violin concerti on one program, with the Berlin Philharmonic conducted by Bruno Walter. Albert Einstein was present at this performance and apparently told Menuhin afterward that "his playing was proof of the existence of God."

During the summers of 1929 and 1930 the Menuhin family resided in Basel, Switzerland, where Menuhin studied with Adolf Busch. He presented his London debut in November 1929 and began a long and productive recording career with HMV Records. In 1931 the family made their home at Ville d'Avray, outside of Paris, and Menuhin resumed his studies with Enesco. In 1932 he made a landmark recording of Elgar's Violin Concerto with the composer conducting. It was the first recording of this work, and the composer was extremely pleased with the sixteen-year-old's performance.

Both of Menuhin's sisters were accomplished pianists. In 1933 he made his first recording with his sister Hephzibah for HMV, playing Mozart's Sonata K. 526; it won France's Candide Prize for the best new chamber music recording of the year upon its release. Hephzibah was his frequent recital partner over the years. Menuhin later said, "Ours was a special kind of collaboration. We needed few words. We played almost automatically, as if we were one person."

In 1933 Menuhin joined a group of prominent Jewish musicians who refused an invitation from the conductor Wilhelm Furtwängler to perform in Nazi Germany. His father organized his first world tour in 1935, with performances throughout Europe, Australia, New Zealand, and South Africa. Menuhin was supporting his entire family with the income from his performances and recordings. His father and his managers were thus concerned when he expressed interest in taking some time off from performing to immerse himself in closer study of musical literature. In April 1936 the family returned to California to live in their newly built estate in Los Gatos. Menuhin made few public appearances until the summer of 1937.

On 26 May 1938 he married Nola Ruby Nicholas, an Australian woman whom he had met in London two months earlier. Later that summer his sister Hephzibah married Nola's brother Lindsay, and his sixteen-year-old sister Yaltah married William Stix, a young lawyer. All of these marriages eventually ended in divorce. Menuhin's and Nola's daughter was born in 1939, followed by a son in 1940. The couple divorced in 1947.

Menuhin's career was transformed when the United States entered World War II. He presented more than 500 concerts for U.S. and Allied troops, sometimes under dangerous conditions. He performed in Antwerp, Brussels, and Paris in October 1944, shortly after the Allies liberated these cities from Nazi occupation. A month earlier he had met Diana Rosamond Gould, a British dancer and actress, while on a visit to London. They married three years later on 19 October 1947 and had two sons.

Menuhin presented the premiere performance of Béla Bartók's Sonata for Solo Violin, which he had commissioned, in New York's Carnegie Hall in November 1944. He also edited the published score of this important work. In April 1945 Menuhin was invited to perform for the delegates to the first United Nations (UN) conference in San Francisco. That July he and the composer Benjamin Britten performed for survivors of the Belsen, Germany, concentration camp. In 1947 he performed in Berlin with Furtwängler; he was the first Jewish musician to appear with the Berlin Philharmonic after the war. He was loudly criticized by other Jewish musicians for his support of and collaborations with Furtwängler, who chose to remain in Germany during the war and was considered by many to be too close to the Nazi cause. Among their numerous recordings was a highly acclaimed HMV recording of Beethoven's Violin Concerto, which was made in 1947.

During a 1951 tour to New Zealand, Menuhin came across a book about yoga while sitting in a doctor's waiting room. He was fascinated by the subject and sought out prospective yoga teachers during his 1952 tour to India. He was introduced to B. K. S. Iyengar, who eventually became his guru. He also met the sitar player Ravi Shankar at this time and developed a keen interest in Indian music.

In 1956 the Menuhin family left their California home and took up permanent residence in Europe, primarily in London and Gstaad, Switzerland, where they had been vacationing since 1954. Menuhin established an annual festival in Gstaad in 1957. In 1959 he took up the directorship of the Bath Festival in England and increased his conducting activities, working with the Bath Festival Orchestra (later called the Menuhin Festival Orchestra), with which he made numerous recordings. His conducting career actually had begun in 1947, when he conducted the Dallas Symphony Orchestra under the tutelage of his friend Antal Dorati. He stepped down from the directorship of the Bath Festival in 1968.

In 1963 he established the international Yehudi Menuhin School in London for training gifted musicians, aged seven to eighteen. The school moved to Stoke d'Abernon, England, one year later. Recognizing how much his own early training lacked in terms of technical instruction, Menuhin became increasingly concerned with pedagogy and the establishment of proper technique early in a student's musical development.

Menuhin continued to perform, conduct, and work on behalf of a wide range of humanitarian causes during the last decades of his life. In 1969 he was named the president of the International Music Council of the United Nations Educational, Scientific, and Cultural Organization, a position he held until 1975. In 1971 he began collaborating with the French jazz violinist Stephane Grappelli, with whom he made several recordings. In 1977 he founded the Menuhin Academy in Gstaad, as well as the organization Live Music Now!, which coordinated performances by young musicians in hospitals, nursing homes, and prisons around the world. In 1978 and 1979 he worked with the Canadian Broadcasting Corporation on the television series *Music of Man,* which explored musical cultures in different regions of the world. In 1983 he established the Yehudi Menuhin International Competition for Young Violinists. He was named the lifetime president of the Royal Philharmonic Orchestra in 1982 and in 1985 served as its principal conductor during a U.S. tour.

By the early 1990s Menuhin had curtailed his violin performances and was appearing primarily as a conductor. In 1996 he presented his last public performance as a violinist at the fortieth annual Gstaad Festival. He died at age eighty-two after suffering a heart attack while on tour with an orchestra in Berlin. He is buried at the Yehudi Menuhin International School in Stoke d'Abernon, under a tree he planted there.

Menuhin recorded most of the standard repertory throughout his long career, both as a violinist and conductor. In addition to commissioning the Bartók Sonata for Solo Violin, he commissioned works by numerous other composers, including William Walton (his Sonata for Violin and Piano), Lennox Berkeley, Ernest Bloch, Lukas Foss, Frank Martin, and Malcolm Williamson. Menuhin became a British citizen in 1985 and was knighted that same year. In 1993 Queen Elizabeth made him a life peer, with the title of Baron Menuhin of Stoke d'Abernon. He received numerous honors and awards from other countries, as well as honorary doctorates and fellowships from universities. In 1986 he was one of the recipients of the U.S. Kennedy Center Honors.

It was said that Menuhin maintained some of his childlike innocence and sense of wonder throughout his life. He was an extraordinarily talented musician who was able to transform himself from a sheltered child prodigy into a true citizen of the world.

★

Menuhin's archives are maintained by his family. He published two autobiographical works, *Theme and Variations* (1972) and *Unfinished Journey* (1977), as well as the technique books *Violin: Six Lessons with Yehudi Menuhin* (1971) and *The Compleat Violinist: Thoughts, Exercises, Reflections of an Itinerant Violinist* (1986). Two interview collections, Robin Daniels, *Conversations* with *Menuhin* (1980), and David Dubal, *Conversations with Menuhin* (1992), provide firsthand insights into his philosophy and musical ideas. Robert Magidoff, *Yehudi Menuhin: The Story of the Man and the Musician* (1955), contains some factual errors and misrepresentations, as does Tony Palmer, *Menuhin: A Family Portrait* (1991), which was based on Palmer's controversial television film. Family memoirs include Moshe Menuhin, *The Menuhin Saga* (1984), Diana Menuhin, *Fiddler's Moll: Life with Yehudi* (1984), and Diana Menuhin, *A Glimpse of Olympus* (1996). The most reliable biography is Humphrey Burton, *Yehudi Menuhin: A Life* (2001). Burton knew Menuhin and had access to the family archives. He corrects many errors found in other sources. The April 1996 issue of *The Strad* includes tributes to Menuhin on his eightieth birthday. An obituary is in the *New York Times* (13 Mar. 1999).

JANE GOTTLIEB

MEREDITH, (Oliver) Burgess (*b.* 16 November 1908 [some sources say 1907 or 1909] in Lakewood, Ohio; *d.* 9 September 1997 in Malibu, California), versatile and diversely talented actor, director, producer, and writer who won acclaim for numerous theater, film, radio, and television roles over his long career, including the Penguin character in the *Batman* television series and Mickey, the cantankerous boxing manager in the *Rocky* films.

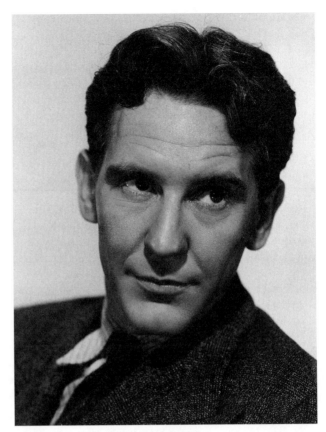

Burgess Meredith, 1938. KOBAL COLLECTION

Meredith was the youngest of three children born to physician William George Meredith and Ida Burgess, daughter of a Methodist revivalist, who had a brief career in the theater; he had one sister and one brother. In his memoirs, Meredith remembered his childhood as "dark, poor, and fearful"; his alcoholic father frequently abused his mother and eventually abandoned her after Meredith, a talented boy soprano, went to the choir school of New York City's Cathedral of St. John the Divine at age ten. From childhood through the first years of his theatrical career, his older sister, Virginia, "raised me, fed me, encouraged me," Meredith wrote. In 1923, when his voice changed, he was sent to Hoosac Preparatory School in Hoosick Falls, New York. In 1927 Meredith attended Amherst College in Massachusetts. On a scholarship but virtually penniless, he tried unsuccessfully to combine work, study, and (though poor grades forbade it) extracurricular dramatics. Expelled in 1928, he worked and quickly failed at a series of sales jobs and as a merchant seaman. Amherst College would eventually award Meredith an honorary M.A. degree in 1938.

In December 1929, living with his married sister in New Jersey, Meredith became an unpaid apprentice in Eva Le Gallienne's Civic Repertory Company, along with John Garfield, Robert Lewis, and Howard Da Silva. Meredith eventually moved to Greenwich Village and supported

himself by washing dishes, scrubbing floors, and delivering groceries. His first New York City speaking part was Peter in the Civic Repertory's *Romeo and Juliet* (1930). He subsequently played the Dormouse, Tweedledee, and a duck in their memorable production of *Alice in Wonderland* (1932); a revival was among the first plays recorded on 78 rpm records. In 1932, between shows at a summer stock theater, Meredith married divorcée Helen Berrien Derby, daughter of the president of American Cyanamide. Their often-violent union ended in divorce in September 1935.

Meredith's first leading role on Broadway, a nine-day run as a reform school inmate in *Little Ol' Boy* (1933), drew rave reviews, one calling him "the most thrilling actor of his day." The lucrative and "hilarious" part of Buzz Jones in the hit musical *She Loves Me Not* (1934) established Meredith's comedic reputation. Simultaneously playing the lead in the live radio series *Red Davis*, Meredith commuted from theater to studio by ambulance until a too-late arrival caused the cancellation of the series.

The greatest successes of Meredith's early career came with director Guthrie McClintic and McClintic's wife, Katherine Cornell. In 1935 Meredith had a small role opposite Cornell in *The Barretts of Wimpole Street*, followed by a larger role in *Flowers of the Forest*. McClintic directed

Meredith in his first starring role, Mio in *Winterset* (1935), a part that had been written for him by Maxwell Anderson, who became a close friend and father figure for Meredith. The 1936 film version of *Winterset* began Meredith's lengthy film career. In 1937 McClintic again directed Meredith, this time opposite Peggy Ashcroft in Anderson's *High Tor;* Richard Watts, Jr., said of Meredith, "There isn't a better American actor of any age."

In 1938, while starring with Lillian Gish in Anderson's *The Star Wagon* and directed once again by McClintic, Meredith became acting president of the Actor's Equity Association and chaired both the Federal Theater's National Advisory Council and the Arts Union Conference, during which he lobbied the National Endowment for the Arts. Meredith resigned after eight stressful months. At the same time, his two-and-a-half-year second marriage to Margaret Perry (daughter of producer Antoinette "Tony" Perry), which had begun on 10 January 1936, ended in July 1938. Years later, while undergoing psychiatric analysis, Meredith's hyperactivity and domestic problems were attributed to bipolar disorder, the cause of unpredictable mood swings during which he veered between euphoria and depression.

In 1939 Meredith appeared in the films *Idiot's Delight* and *Of Mice and Men*. In the same year, he appeared onstage as Prince Hal and Henry V to Orson Welles's Falstaff in *Five Kings,* Welles's compilation of Shakespeare's history plays. John Houseman found Meredith had "a warmth and energy I have never seen equaled in the part, even by Laurence Olivier." Despite such praise, the show closed in Boston, a financial disaster. In 1940 Meredith drew critical praise in the Broadway revival of *Liliom,* in which he played the title role opposite Ingrid Bergman.

In his memoir *So Far, So Good* (1994), Meredith, who had played Hamlet in a 1937 radio production, looked back fondly on his radio career, especially his work with Norman Corwin and others who wrote radio drama when it was a respected new art form. One of his major assignments in the 1940s was as master of ceremonies and actor in the CBS radio series *The Free Company,* which had been commissioned by Attorney General Francis Biddle to "make propaganda on behalf of Liberty and Free Speech."

Drafted the same day as Hollywood housemate James Stewart, Meredith began his World War II army career in February 1942. After three months, he was given leave to play Marchbanks opposite Katherine Cornell in *Candida,* produced to benefit Army Navy Relief. After six weeks in New York City and two in Washington, D.C., Meredith went "back to cleaning latrines."

Serving in Britain as a captain in the U.S. Air Corps, Meredith was assigned to make films that introduced American troops to Allied cultures. In 1944 he codirected *Welcome to Britain* and *Salute to France,* directed *Rear Gunner,* and narrated *Tunisian Victory.* In that same year he

also married again, this time to actress Paulette Goddard; they divorced in 1948. In 1945 Meredith was returned to Hollywood after legendary war correspondent Ernie Pyle personally requested that Meredith be cast to play him in *The Story of G.I. Joe* (1945). President Franklin D. Roosevelt discharged Meredith on 25 October 1944 to make the film.

After the war, Meredith resumed his busy and highly productive career. In 1946 he appeared with Paulette Goddard in Jean Renoir's *Diary of a Chambermaid,* for which Meredith wrote the screenplay and served as coproducer. That same year he also played President James Madison in *Magnificent Doll,* narrated the documentary *Hymn of Nations,* and played the title role in a Broadway revival of *Playboy of the Western World.* In 1947 he codirected and narrated the film *A Yank Came Back* and played Mio in the Dublin production of *Winterset.* In 1949 he directed and acted in the film *Man on the Eiffel Tower.* In 1950 Meredith was the first American actor ever invited to join London's Old Vic Theatre Company. He refused, preferring to continue as "a man moved by the rhythms of his time." From 1950 to 1953 he was involved in eight productions—staging, acting, or both—including three on Broadway.

Meredith's liberal politics, however, attracted the ire of Senator Joseph McCarthy and a "listing" in *Red Channels: The Report of Communist Influence in Radio and Television,* a pamphlet published in 1950 that named 151 writers, directors, and performers who were thought to be Communists or "fellow travellers." Blacklisted from films in the late 1950s as a result, Meredith worked at community, university, and summer theaters. He appeared in Charles Laughton's Broadway revival of *Major Barbara* (1956) and was part of the controversial *Four-Faced Hamlet* (1957), directed by Laughton and Paul Baker at Baylor University, in which Meredith and three supporting actors simultaneously portrayed different aspects of Hamlet's personality. Meredith also conceived and directed *Ulysses in Nighttown* (1958), an off-Broadway play starring Zero Mostel as Leopold Bloom and based on James Joyce's 1922 novel *Ulysses,* a book still officially banned in the United States at that time. In 1961 Meredith and Mostel did a special television presentation of *Waiting for Godot.* Challenging the blacklist, Otto Preminger revived Meredith's film career by casting him in *Advise and Consent* (1962), *The Cardinal* (1963), and three other films.

In 1966 Meredith gained a teenage audience as the Penguin in the *Batman* television series. It was "the first time my kids wanted to watch me," Meredith stated. Thrice-divorced, in 1952 Meredith married nineteen-year-old ballerina Kaja Sunsten. They had two children and lived happily together until 1976, after which they amicably maintained separate homes.

Meredith had a "splendid revenge" on the "McCarthy

gang" by winning an Emmy for his portrayal of Joseph Welch in the television film *Tail Gunner Joe* (1977), a reenactment of the McCarthy hearings. The most famous screen character of Meredith's later years was Mickey, the cantankerous manager in the *Rocky* films. His last major appearance was as Grandpa Gustafson in the film *Grumpier Old Men* (1995).

Meredith died at his home in Malibu of Alzheimer's disease and melanoma. He was survived by his fourth wife, a son, daughter, and granddaughter. Although he jokingly defined his career as going "from a duck to a penguin," the range of his work, from peanut butter commercial voice-overs to Shakespeare, vividly epitomizes the drastic changes that entertainment technologies imposed on the twentieth century's finest actors.

★

Meredith's refreshingly frank *So Far, So Good: A Memoir* (1994) richly evokes the Broadway and Hollywood social milieus from the 1920s through the 1950s, and includes affectionate, sometimes mischievous, portraits of friends, mentors, and the women in his life. His early life and career are summarized in an article in *Current Biography* (1940). Later interviews and articles include: *Ciné Revue* (2 July 1981 and 12 Jan. 1984); J. A. Henderson, "Burgess Meredith," *Film Dope*, (Oct. 1989); "Talking with . . . Burgess Meredith: The Old Men and the Sea," *People Weekly* (13 June 1994), and *Interview* (Jan. 1996). An obituary is in the *New York Times* (11 Sept. 1997).

DANIEL S. KREMPEL

MICHENER, James Albert (*b.* 3 February 1907 in New York City [?]; *d.* 16 October 1997 in Austin, Texas), prolific author of best-selling fiction and nonfiction who won a Pulitzer Prize for his first published book and whose epic novels provided a popular mix of entertaining narrative and informative documentary.

Left as a foundling, with no knowledge of his real parents or date of birth, Michener was raised from infancy in a Quaker household in Doylestown, Pennsylvania. His adoptive mother, Mabel Haddock Michener, a widow, made a scanty living as a laundress and by taking in other abandoned children. Nevertheless, she found the time to read stories to him, thereby encouraging his love of literature. Exhibiting the adventurous spirit and thirst for knowledge that marked his life, the teenage Michener hitchhiked and rode freight trains, exploring much of the United States while still in high school. In addition to supporting himself by working a series of odd jobs, he began to write professionally at age fifteen, doing a sports column for a local newspaper.

Following his graduation from Doylestown High

James A. Michener, 1989. AP/WIDE WORLD PHOTOS

School in 1925, Michener attended Swarthmore College in Pennsylvania on an athletic scholarship. He received his A.B. degree in English and history, summa cum laude, in 1929; he was also the class valedictorian and was elected to Phi Beta Kappa. Between 1929 and 1931 Michener taught at the prestigious Hill School in Pottstown, Pennsylvania. In 1931 Swarthmore awarded him a Lippincott travel grant, allowing him to visit and study abroad. Michener collected Hebridean folk songs, traveled to Spain on a Scottish freighter, and studied art in England and Italy. As he once wrote, it was thus he became "both an academic bum and a confirmed traveler."

On his return to the United States, Michener taught from 1933 to 1936 at the George School in Newtown, Pennsylvania. On 27 July 1935 he married his first wife, Patti Koon; they were divorced in 1948. He then went to Greeley, Colorado, to study at the Colorado State College of Education (now the University of Northern Colorado), from which he received an A.M. degree in 1937 and which, thirty-six years later, named its library in his honor. Between 1936 and 1939 he was an associate professor at Colorado State; between 1940 and 1941 he was a visiting professor at the Harvard University School of Education in Cambridge, Massachusetts.

Switching fields slightly, Michener moved to New York City in 1941 and worked as an associate textbook editor at the Macmillan Company. Despite his Quaker principles, he enlisted in 1942 in the U.S. Naval Reserve, serving throughout World War II as a naval historian in the South Pacific and eventually rising to the rank of lieutenant commander. After his discharge in 1946 he returned to Macmillan, working there until 1949. In the meantime, he submitted to Macmillan a series of eighteen loosely linked fictional sketches, written during his hours off naval duty and based on his wartime experiences. *Tales of the South Pacific* was published in 1947 and received the Pulitzer Prize for fiction in 1948. On 2 September that same year he married his second wife, Vange Nord. The couple adopted two children and were divorced in 1955. In 1949 Michener's tales of U.S. servicepeople and island natives were adapted by Richard Rodgers and Oscar Hammerstein II into the legendary Broadway musical *South Pacific*. Made into a motion picture in 1958, *South Pacific* was the first of several of Michener's works to be screened or televised.

His second book, *The Fires of Spring* (1949), was a full-length novel and, like many first novels, autobiographical. Its hero is a poor young Quaker struggling to become a writer in New York City. As with many second books, it was not a success. *Return to Paradise,* a series of essays and related stories about Pacific life, followed in 1951 and likewise did not fare well, although it was later screened. This book was issued by Random House, from then on Michener's chief publisher.

After the war, as an historian and political and social observer, Michener traveled to trouble spots in Japan, India, and other parts of the Far East. *The Voice of Asia* (1951), based on interviews with the people he met, combined their voices with his own comments on their situations, in what one reviewer praised as a work of "creative journalism." The Korean War provided a realistic backdrop for Michener's return to fiction with *The Bridges at Toko-ri,* a novella that ran first in *Life* (6 July 1953), and *Sayonara* (1954), the story of the ill-fated love of a U.S. Air Force officer and a Japanese woman. Both works were later made into movies.

In 1949 Michener moved to Hawaii, where he wrote the first of the books most generally associated with him—massive "place" novels, with one-word, self-descriptive titles. Stories of different generations of people living in these places unfolded against accounts of the geography and history of the places themselves. These multidimensional sagas were made accessible by Michener's clear, narrative style. As he admitted, "My intellectual life has been a long vacillation between English literature and the social sciences." *Hawaii* (1959), which Michener worked on for seven years, traced the development of modern Hawaii from its pre-Polynesian roots and intercultural minglings to the mid-twentieth century. Readers devoured the novel's

937 pages; it was a Book-of-the-Month Club selection and a *Reader's Digest* Condensed Book Club offering, and also was made into a star-studded movie. Maxwell Geismar, reviewing *Hawaii* in the *New York Times*, praised the book's combination of scholarship, literary imagination, and storytelling skill, but noted a thinness of feeling and the hortatory tone in its plea for interracial understanding. Geismar concluded that it was "a superior popular novel," if not a great one. In 1960 Michener and his third wife, Mari Yoriko Sabusawa, a Japanese-American editor whom he married on 23 October 1955, left the islands to live in northeastern Pennsylvania.

As with *Hawaii,* all of Michener's subsequent writing was based on his own extensive, conscientious research. Denying reports that he employed a staff of research assistants, he maintained in his *Writer's Handbook* (1992), a step-by-step account of how one of his manuscripts was developed, that he had only one such helper, who was mainly engaged in searching for and providing him with library materials and photocopies. Even after Michener suffered a serious heart attack in 1964, he continued to seek firsthand knowledge of the settings for his books. For *The Source* (1965), a novel that traced the 12,000-year history of a settlement in present-day Israel, the author lived in the country for two years. *Centennial* (1974), which was adapted for television (1978–1979), concerned the settlement of the U.S. West. It was based on Michener's own experiences in Colorado and his reflections on the state's contemporary social and environmental problems. While gathering material for *Chesapeake* (1978), he lived for a time in Maryland. In 1981 he accepted an invitation from the governor of Texas to come to Austin to live and write a novel about the state. The resulting book, *Texas* (1985), weighed in at 1,096 pages and had the largest first printing in Random House's history.

Michener preserved his rugged athletic physique as he grew older, managing to keep fit and active. Immediately after the publication of *Texas,* he and his wife set off on a trip to Sitka to gather facts for *Alaska,* which came out three years later. Several of Michener's works recounted the experiences of Americans living and working in far-flung parts of the world. These novels included *Caravans* (1963), set in 1946 Afghanistan, *Poland* (1983), *Caribbean* (1989), and *Mexico* (1992). His earlier work *Iberia* (1968) was purely nonfiction, but, according to some reviewers, it was enlivened with the author's affectionate recollections of Spanish life. Other critics claimed that the book reflected the shallow, apolitical ruminations of a bourgeois tourist.

But political and social issues were indeed of concern to a writer of Quaker background. In 1960 Michener campaigned for the presidential election of John F. Kennedy, and in 1962 he himself ran (unsuccessfully) for Congress as a Democratic representative from Pennsylvania. Between

1967 and 1968 he served as secretary of his state's Constitutional Convention and a year later wrote *Presidential Lottery,* on the issue of electoral reform. *Kent State: What Happened and Why* (1971) was his perceptive report on the killing of four university students in Ohio during a 1970 Vietnam War protest. A decade later his novel *The Covenant* (1980) dealt with the history of South Africa and the issue of apartheid. Michener served on the advisory council of the National Aeronautics and Space Administration (NASA) from 1979 until 1983. Based on his experiences at NASA he wrote the novel *Space,* which was published in 1982 and shown as a television miniseries in 1985. The book provided an earnest defense of continued scientific investigation in space, and employed a large cast of real and fictional characters who were engaged in the struggle to maintain the U.S. space program. A review in the *Nation* found it "less a historical novel than a tract," while the *Times Literary Supplement* termed it "an information-clogged docunovel," designed for the self-improvement of middlebrow readers.

Three of Michener's books attested to his longtime fascination with Japanese art: *The Floating World* (1954), a lively, erudite history of Japanese prints; *Japanese Prints: From the Early Masters to the Modern* (1959), illustrated with examples from Michener's own collection and telling the story of its formation; and an edition of the *Hokusai Sketchbooks* (1958). After Michener's death, his collection of more than 1,500 Japanese prints was given to the University of Hawaii. In 1968 he had donated his extensive group of contemporary U.S. paintings to the University of Texas at Austin.

Michener's last book, *This Noble Land: My Vision of America* (1996), made a series of anecdotal statements about some of the nation's problems—racism, the gap between the rich and poor, and health care—and offered suggestions for their solution. In all, he wrote more than fifty books, which were translated into as many languages. As he reflected in his *Writer's Handbook,* at any one time he always had ideas for eight or nine more possible writing projects. His long, active career brought him much public recognition during his lifetime, including thirty honorary academic degrees, inclusion in the press party accompanying President Richard Nixon on his 1972 trip to China, and receipt of the Presidential Medal of Freedom in 1977. Michener once admitted that he would rather "be remembered by that row of . . . books that rest on library shelves throughout the world." He died in his home in Austin at age ninety after deciding to discontinue dialysis treatments for kidney disease. He is buried in Austin Memorial Park, Austin.

The born storyteller, dedicated educator, and man of liberal humanist principles merge in Michener's writings. Always modest about his abilities, he remained committed to what a school administrator had told him in his teaching days, that he must always tell his young students what their world was all about. That may have led to Michener's zeal for facts, which sometimes marred his development of plots and characters and brought charges that his work was aimed at middlebrow audiences. But as an editorial in the *New York Times* (18 Oct. 1997) put it, he could not be labeled either highbrow or lowbrow, "he was simply brow." Although he poured forth millions of words and made millions of dollars by them, he gave millions of readers great pleasure. Generous outpourings of stories and information were matched by Michener's generous bequests, totaling more than $100 million, to the arts and education, including to his alma mater Swarthmore, the Writers' Workshop at the University of Iowa, and the Authors League; and more than $37 million alone to the University of Texas at Austin, the largest single donation made to the institution up to that time.

★

A major collection of Michener's manuscripts, notes, and personal papers—60,000 items in all—was bequeathed to the University of Northern Colorado. The Library of Congress also has holdings of his papers, and the libraries of Swarthmore College and the University of Hawaii have collections of his books and manuscripts. Michener's autobiography, *The World Is My Home* (1992), is an informal, anecdotal memoir of his career, atypical in that it begins with his later years and proceeds backward in time. Other biographical information can be found in Lawrence Grobel, *Talking with Michener* (1999), which records lengthy conversations with the author from 1994 to 1997 about his career and his opinions on a variety of subjects and ideas. Marilyn S. Severson, *James A. Michener: A Critical Companion* (1996), devotes individual sections to analyses of several of his works, supplemented by a general discussion of his style and method of writing and an overview of his life. See also F. X. Roberts and C. D. Rhine, *James A. Michener: A Checklist of His Works, with a Selected, Annotated Bibliography* (1995). Obituaries are in the *New York Times* (17 Oct. 1997), and *Time* and *U.S. News and World Report* (both 27 Oct. 1997).

ELEANOR F. WEDGE

MIDDLECOFF, (Emmett) Cary ("Doc") (*b.* 6 January 1921 in Halls, Tennessee; *d.* 1 September 1998 in Memphis, Tennessee), dentist who left his practice to play professional golf and who won several major championships.

Born in Halls and raised in Memphis, Tennessee, Middlecoff was the son of Herman Middlecoff, a dentist and an accomplished golfer who introduced his son to the game when he was seven. Middlecoff played frequently as a youngster, but it wasn't until high school that he began to play the game with determination and purpose. In 1937 he

Cary Middlecoff is congratulated by his wife, Edith, on winning the National Open Golf trophy, 1949. © BETTMANN/CORBIS

naments. He did most of his commuting by car. "Fifty thousand miles a year, mostly on Sunday nights and Monday," he said. "It was not like a vacation."

Middlecoff competed on the PGA tour from 1947 to 1967, an era crowded with legends of the game. Nevertheless, in the decade and a half following World War II, he was the biggest money winner in American golf. Between 1949 and 1956 he was consistently among the top ten, finishing second in 1949, 1951, 1952, and 1955. His forty victories have to date been exceeded by only six golfers—Sam Snead (eighty-one), Jack Nicklaus (seventy), Ben Hogan (sixty-three), Arnold Palmer (sixty), Byron Nelson (fifty-two), and Billy Casper (fifty-one)—and tied by one, Walter Hagen. He won three PGA major tournaments: the 1949 and 1956 United States Opens and the 1955 Masters, in which he beat runner-up Hogan by seven strokes.

Middlecoff was a "streak" golfer who was capable of stringing together several tournament victories in a row. In 1949 he had six wins and a tie for first with Lloyd Mangrum in the Motor City Open. Early in 1950 he followed his victory at Houston with four first place finishes in five tournaments. In 1951 he won six tournaments, four in his last ten starts. Between 1952 and 1954 he won eight tournaments. But 1955 was Middlecoff's most successful year. He won the Masters, the Bing Crosby tournament, the Cavalcade of Golf, and the St. Petersburg, Miller, and Western Opens. At the PGA Championship he was runner-up to Doug Ford. His tour earnings for the year ranked second to Julius Boros. In 1961 he won his last tournament, the Memphis Open.

On 16 April 1955 Middlecoff, the newly crowned Masters Champion, was invited to Augusta National—the course on which the Masters is played—to play with President Dwight D. Eisenhower. A year later Middlecoff took a remunerative position at the Diplomat Golf Club in Hollywood, Florida, a commitment that limited the number of tournaments he played: fourteen in 1957 and 1958, and thirteen in 1959. In 1957, in a strong bid for a third U.S. Open victory, he tied Dick Mayer but lost the eighteen-hole playoff. He won the 1958 Miller Open and the 1959 St. Petersburg Open, and finished second in the 1959 Masters. Inspired by his play in 1960 at the age of thirty-nine, he returned full-time to the tour. "I have the desire, which was something I didn't have for a while," he said.

A talented and graceful ball striker, Middlecoff had "the best hands of any postwar golfer," fellow golfer Gene Sarazen opined. He was an excellent putter and he swung his driver and long-irons in a sweeping arc (with a distinct pause at the top) that bent his six-foot, two-inch, 188-pound frame into a severe reverse "C." This picturesque swing gave him great distance and marvelous control, and probably contributed to the ruptured disc (L-5) that had to be surgically removed in 1963. His bad back and failing

won the Tennessee High School Golf Championship. He also won the Memphis City Amateur Championship in 1938 and 1939. In 1940 he won the Tennessee Amateur Championship and the West Kentucky Open, a feat that he repeated in 1941, adding as well the Southeastern Intercollegiate Championship. In 1942 and 1943 he again won the Tennessee Amateur Championship.

Despite his golfing prowess, Middlecoff was expected to follow the path to dentistry that his father and two uncles had taken. He attended the University of Mississippi, where he was a star golfer. He then attended the University of Tennessee, Memphis College of Dentistry, from which he graduated in 1944. Shortly thereafter he was inducted into the Army Dental Corps. While still in the army he managed to play in and win the 1945 North and South Open at Pinehurst, North Carolina. He was the tournament's first amateur champion.

Middlecoff was discharged from the army in 1946 and returned home to join his father's dental practice. However, after working with his father for a year, he quit to join the Professional Golfers' Association (PGA) tour. "When I got out of the army I didn't want to see any more teeth," he recalled. "I just wanted to play some golf." In 1947 he married Edith Buck, who often accompanied him to tour-

vision in his left eye (caused by a flying chard of carborundum during an army dental procedure) forced him to abandon professional competition in 1967.

Middlecoff was the embodiment of many an amateur golfer's fantasy: he left a prestigious profession to play golf, and he succeeded brilliantly. For all his skill and accomplishments, Middlecoff was a nervous, slow, and fidgety player. He would tug at various articles of his clothing, glance repeatedly at the target, and generally make his supporters as nervous for him as he appeared to be about the shot at hand. His slow play aggravated fellow players, stimulated the press to analysis, and held his fans in agonizing suspense during close matches.

Following his retirement from the tour, Middlecoff began an eighteen-year career as a golf commentator for television and a golf columnist whose articles, for the most part, were ghost written. He also wrote a number of books on golf. He plugged Viceroy cigarettes and Wheaties and was a well-paid member of the advisory staff of the Wilson Sporting Goods Company. Middlecoff's awards include the 1956 Vardon Trophy for lowest stroke average (a 70.35 average in sixty-six rounds) and induction into the Golf Hall of Fame in Pinehurst (1987). He was a member of the 1953, 1955, and 1959 Ryder Cup teams. From 1953 to 1954 he was chairman of the U.S. Professional Golfers' Association tournament committee.

Middlecoff died of congestive heart failure at age seventy-seven at the Allen Morgan Health Center in Memphis. He had been ill for five years after suffering a severe head injury in a fall. He was survived by his wife, Edith. They had no children.

★

There is no full-length biography of Middlecoff, but an interview with him is in Bill Fields, "'Doc' Will See You Now," *Golf Digest* 47, no. 11 (Nov. 1996). Tributes are in Jerry Tarde, "Farewell to Doc," *Golf Digest* 49, no. 11 (Nov. 1998); and Mike Purkey, "Seen and Heard," *Golf Magazine* 40, no. 11 (Nov. 1998). Obituaries are in the *Chicago Tribune* and *Los Angeles Times* (both 2 Sept. 1998) and *New York Times* (3 Sept. 1998).

MARTIN J. SHERWIN

MITCHUM, Robert Charles Durman (*b.* 6 August 1917 in Bridgeport, Connecticut; *d.* 1 July 1997 in Santa Barbara, California), motion picture actor for fifty years who cultivated the screen image of iconoclast and outcast, becoming a seminal cinematic tough guy and rebel.

Mitchum was the second child and first son born to James Thomas Mitchum, a half Blackfoot Indian, half Scotch-Irish railroad worker from Lane, South Carolina, and Ann Harriet Gunderson, a Norwegian immigrant who was the

Robert Mitchum.

daughter of a merchant seaman. His mother was seven months' pregnant with a third child when his father, a brakeman, was killed in a freight yard accident in Charleston, South Carolina. The family moved back to Bridgeport, Connecticut, to live with Mrs. Mitchum's parents. A month later, Mitchum's brother was born.

Mitchum's lifelong courtship with loneliness began in early childhood. At seven he ran away from home, getting as far as New Haven, Connecticut, before he was sent home and punished. His mother was bright and resourceful but received little help. She worked at the *Bridgeport Post-Telegram* as a photographer's assistant and married the reporter Bill Clancy in 1923, but they divorced within a year. When he was eight, Mitchum wrote poetry to humor and console her. When she was promoted to linotype operator, she had some of Mitchum's poetry published, much to his embarrassment. She married the paper's editor, Hugh Morris, in 1927 and they had a daughter. Mitchum resented his stepfather, skipped school, and finally was expelled. He then lived on his grandparents' farm in Woodside, Delaware, quit school at age eleven, and hit the hobo road. Juvenile authorities found him in Connecticut. A year later he was expelled from Felton High School for a childish prank involving the girls' shower.

Mitchum went to live with his sister, who was working

as a showgirl in New York City. There he fought his way through Hell's Kitchen, a tough neighborhood teeming with crime and corruption, and intermittently attended Haaren High School. In the summer of 1933 Mitchum hopped a freight car and was arrested in Savannah, Georgia, for vagrancy. He was sentenced to work on a Chatham County, Georgia, chain gang. The shackle wore a wound in his leg and led to blood poisoning. That fall he met Dorothy Spence, his future wife, at a swimming hole near Camden, Delaware. He was sixteen and she was fourteen. Over the next four years he rode the rails, working as a punch-press operator in Toledo, Ohio; a longshoreman in Long Beach, California; a bum fighter in Sparks, Nevada; and a coal miner in Libertyville, Pennsylvania. Mitchum also worked as a heavyweight boxer, quitting after twenty-seven professional fights. He shared the company of "blue-jawed characters with wanted stamped all over them" and suffered bouts of intense loneliness and occasional pellagra from poor nutrition.

In 1937 Mitchum moved in with his sister in Long Beach, where she worked in community theater. That summer he had a small part in a play called *Rebound*. Writing interested him more. The Long Beach Players Guild produced two of his children's plays. His oratorio *Refugees* was performed at the Hollywood Bowl in 1939. In the summer of that year he became the pitch man and publicist for the astrologer Carroll Righter. Mitchum used the money he made to marry Spence in Dover, Delaware, on 16 March 1940. On 8 May 1941 their first son was born. Mitchum supported his family by working at Lockheed Aircraft and by selling shoes.

Mitchum registered with Central Casting and came to the attention of Harry Sherman, the producer of the low-budget, but highly popular Hopalong Cassidy westerns at United Artists. To get a job, he said he had been a cow-puncher in Laredo, Texas. Mitchum "fell off horses" and played the heavy in seven films in the series released in 1943, beginning with *Hoppy Serves a Writ*. He was a natural who never seemed to be acting. Taking acting lessons, he observed, "was like going to school to learn to be tall." By the time his second son was born on 16 October 1943, Mitchum was a veteran of nineteen films made at six Hollywood studios. In *Thirty Seconds over Tokyo* (1944), he ably supported Spencer Tracy and Van Johnson in an Metro-Goldwyn-Mayer (MGM) blockbuster. Two Zane Grey westerns at RKO, *Nevada* (1944) and *West of the Pecos* (1945), gave Mitchum his first starring roles. His performance as Captain Bill Walker in *The Story of GI Joe* (1945) was widely praised and won him an Academy Award nomination in a supporting role. James Agee spoke for many critics in predicting stardom following the actor's grim portrayal of a soldier appalled by the war's sacrifice and suffering.

Mitchum's seven-month stint in the U.S. Army during World War II never took him beyond Fort MacArthur in San Pedro, California. When he was discharged in October 1945 he settled in as one of RKO's leading contract players. Second leads in *Till the End of Time* (1946) and *The Locket* (1946) led to loan out at MGM, where he costarred with Katharine Hepburn in *Undercurrent* (1946) and Greer Garson in *Desire Me* (1947). *Pursued* (1947) was a warmly received psychological western directed by Raoul Walsh for Warner Brothers; *Crossfire* (1947) marked an early attack by RKO executive Dore Schary on anti-Semitism; and *Out of the Past* (1947), with its touches of dread and nihilism, quickly became a film noir classic. Mitchum was developing a screen persona as a vaguely embittered, reluctantly vulnerable antihero, whose implacable calm worked well with postwar critics and audiences. A ruggedly handsome, vaguely dangerous-looking tough guy, Mitchum had come along at a time of more conventionally handsome actors, such as Burt Lancaster, Montgomery Clift, and Kirk Douglas.

Mitchum's arrest on 31 August 1948 for possession of marijuana deepened his developing reputation as a cinematic cynic. After serving his two-month sentence, Mitchum told reporters jail was "just like Palm Springs, but without the riffraff." Backed by the studio head Howard Hughes, Mitchum's popularity grew. Leading roles in *Rachel and the Stranger* (1948), *Blood on the Moon* (1948), and *The Big Steal* (1949) solidified Mitchum's standing as RKO's major star. Mitchum enjoyed the easy, family atmosphere at the small studio. His lack of pretentiousness and team play were warmly regarded on the set. He deplored the egotism of Hollywood and moved his family in the summer of 1949 to a farmhouse in the semirural Mandeville Canyon in southern California. His daughter was born there on 3 March 1952.

Mitchum's successful teaming with lifelong friend Jane Russell in *His Kind of Woman* (1951) and *Macao* (1952) and his critically acclaimed *The Lusty Men* (1952), which he coscripted, encouraged him to become a free agent. *River of No Return* (1954) and *Not as a Stranger* (1955) showed the self-confident underplaying of a mature actor. His role as a menacing and murderous minister in Charles Laughton's moody *The Night of the Hunter* (1955) was a revelation. Critics called Mitchum's preacher Harry Powell "a metaphor of malevolence." Top directors brought out the best in Mitchum. This was apparent in John Huston's *Heaven Knows, Mr. Allison* (1957), Mitchum's personal favorite, and in Vincente Minnelli's *Home from the Hill* (1960) and Fred Zinnemann's *The Sundowners* (1960), films that won him the best actor award from the National Board of Review. *Thunder Road* (1958), which he cowrote and produced, became a cult classic at drive-ins. Mitchum formed his own company, DRM Productions, to produce several of his films.

Mitchum bred quarter horses at his 300-acre farm on Maryland's Eastern Shore in the 1960s and visited the troops in Vietnam to boost morale. *The Longest Day* (1962), *Cape Fear* (1962), *El Dorado* (1967), *Ryan's Daughter* (1970), *The Friends of Eddie Coyle* (1973), *The Yakuza* (1975), and *Farewell, My Lovely* (1975) were his best work from this period. Critics charged he sometimes slipped into self-parody in playing the least of his sullen, sleepy-eyed roles. Mitchum remarked that in Hollywood, "You don't get to do better, you just get to do more." He turned down *Patton* (1970) because it would be a long shoot away from home and *Dirty Harry* (1972) because of its violence. In 1978 he moved his family to Montecito in Santa Barbara County, where the aging actor transitioned into television with the epic miniseries *The Winds of War* (1983) and *War and Remembrance* (1988–1989), where much of his immense authority was still on display. At age seventy-nine, Mitchum died of emphysema and lung cancer in Santa Barbara. He was cremated, and his ashes were scattered at sea.

By 1989 the American Film Institute had named Mitchum as one of the twenty-five greatest actors in the movies' first hundred years, someone capable of provoking an audience by his very presence. Although Mitchum made over 125 films, he never won an Academy Award. In 1992, however, he received a Golden Globe Lifetime Achievement Award. Mitchum characteristically viewed the adulation ironically. "I've got the same attitude I had when I started. I haven't changed anything but my underwear." His acting ease and unswerving self-deprecation had won the respect of colleagues and made him an existential hero to postmodernists, who considered him an icon of cool and celebrated his ineffable ability to always be himself.

★

The closest Mitchum came to an autobiography was a compilation of his extensive interviews in Charles Champlin, ed., *Mitchum: In His Own Words* (2000). A summary of press coverage of Mitchum's career appears in Jerry Roberts, *Robert Mitchum: A Bio-Bibliography* (1992). An affectionate account by his brother of their early days together can be found in John Mitchum, *Them Ornery Mitchum Boys: The Adventures of Robert and John Mitchum* (1989). Mitchum discussed his life and career in two broadcast interviews. One is in the *Reflections on the Silver Screen* series of the Library of Congress, telecast in 1991 by American Movie Classics; the other is a "Private Screenings" interview with Turner Classic Movies, telecast in 1996. Biographies include Mike Tomkies, *The Robert Mitchum Story: "It Sure Beats Working"* (1972); John Belton, *Robert Mitchum* (1976); David Downing, *Robert Mitchum* (1985); George Eells, *Robert Mitchum: A Biography* (1985); and Lee Server, *Robert Mitchum: "Baby, I Don't Care"* (2001).

Alvin H. Marrill chronicles the actor's screen credits in *Robert Mitchum on the Screen* (1978) and *The Films of Robert Mitchum* (1995). A filmography, interview, and biographical sketch are also included in Gene Ringgold, "Robert Mitchum Has Proven That a Juvenile Delinquent Can Make Good," *Films in Review* (May 1964). An obituary is in the *New York Times* (2 July 1997).

BRUCE J. EVENSEN

MONROE, Rose Leigh Will (*b.* 12 March 1920 in Somerset, Kentucky; *d.* 31 May 1997 in Clarksville, Indiana), "Rosie the Riveter," the symbol of the American women who worked in the defense industries during World War II.

Monroe was the third youngest of nine children. Her mother, Minnie Alice Calder, was a homemaker on the family's farm, and her father, Walter Green Leigh, was a bricklayer and builder. The household was warm and friendly, a place where neighborhood children would gather. As Monroe was growing up, she became familiar with the building trade. Her youngest daughter would later remark, "She was the one who was a tomboy who could use tools. She could do everything."

Rose Will Monroe, mid-1940s. ASSOCIATED PRESS/FAMILY PHOTO

Monroe received an eighth-grade education, which was typical for the times, and married Clarence Abbott in 1936 at the age of sixteen; they had two children. Around 1942, Rose and her husband separated, and Monroe moved with the children to Michigan in search of a job. She wanted to be a ferry pilot but was turned down because she was a single mother. Monroe began work as a riveter on B-24 and B-29 bombers at Ford's Willow Run plant in Ypsilanti, Michigan. Organized by the United Automobile Workers (UAW), the Willow Run plant built over 8,000 B-24 "Liberator" planes. The average building time was fifty-nine minutes. Overall, the standard workweek for the female workers, or "Rosies," was forty-eight hours, with only Sundays off. Many foremen liked women workers better than men because, in the words of one manager, "they are more conscientious than men . . . they take orders easily, have patience, and are more frank than men."

With food rationed during the war, life was tough. Monroe's children, who lived with their grandparents in Kentucky, visited her only on the weekends in her tiny Quonset hut. Men in the factories often treated women poorly. A typical prank played on female workers, including Monroe, was being asked for a left-handed wrench. Monroe, however, having grown up in a family of builders, knew that such a tool didn't exist.

Short of workers for the war effort, the federal War Manpower Commission (WMC) and the Office of War Information (OWI) started their first campaign in the spring of 1943, recruiting for "Women in Necessary Service" to fill civilian jobs, such as bank tellers or store clerks. The second national campaign, in the spring of 1944, launched by the WMC, OWI, and the U.S. War Department, started the "Women in War" campaign, which focused on housewives who had not yet joined the work force. War jobs were presented as similar to housework. Typical poster slogans read "I'm proud . . . my husband wants me to do my part," "I've found the job where I fit best," and "The more women at work, the sooner we win!" Both propaganda campaigns included short advertisement films, newspaper articles, posters, and celebrity endorsements. Women were recruited into the labor force as men went into the military.

Various accounts of the origin of "Rosie the Riveter" have appeared. A popular 1942 tune, "Rosie the Riveter," by bandleader Kay Kyser, includes the following lines: "Working for Victory / Rosie the Riveter / Keeps a sharp lookout for sabotage / Sitting up there on the fuselage / That little girl will do more than a male will do." Norman Rockwell painted a cover for the *Saturday Evening Post* in 1943 of a muscular Rosie, dressed in overalls, with her foot on a copy of Adolf Hitler's book *Mein Kampf*. In this environment J. Howard Miller's famous poster was born. Captioned "We can do it," it illustrated a beauty flexing her muscle. The woman portrayed was a fictitious char-

acter, but despite a superficial resemblance, and contrary to popular opinion, it was not Monroe, who was recruited after the poster was created.

Monroe's public role in the war effort began in 1944. Walter Pidgeon, a movie actor and director, was in the factory when he found out that there was an actual Rosie the Riveter working there. The opportunity was too good to pass up, and Monroe was recruited for a government film promoting war bonds. "Mom happened to be in the right place at the right time," said her youngest daughter, who added, "She never capitalized on her fame." The film was shown between features in movie theaters.

By the end of the war around six million Rosies had replaced men who had gone into the military. They accounted for almost 35 percent of all the women in the United States. Many women rose from lower paying to higher paying jobs in the defense industry, and they worked in every role, from light to heavy laborer. Another, lesser-known war effort character was "Rosie the Rubber Worker," who portrayed difficult work.

In the winter of 1944 the WMC asked the OWI to end the campaign to recruit women war workers. The national campaign had been a patriotic call to work, but the message was clear: employment for women was temporary. After the war women were laid off in large numbers so that returning men could replace them. Many women did not want to leave. Before the war women and men from minority groups had been subjected to significant discrimination, including low pay and job segregation. Now they enjoyed higher wages and better opportunities. Even so, some women, who had never expected to work for pay in their lives, returned to work in the home willingly. The budding television industry developed programming to support homemaking as the preferred role for women.

Near the end of the war, Monroe moved to Indiana. She reconciled with her first husband, but two weeks before they were to be remarried in 1944, Clarence Abbott was killed in a car accident. After the war Monroe drove a taxi, operated a beauty shop, and started a construction firm called Rose Builders, specializing in high-quality custom homes. She was determined never to take government assistance. Around 1947 she married Calvin Will; they had a daughter in 1954 and divorced in 1972. In 1979 she married Clifford Monroe, a marriage that continued until his death in 1996.

Monroe's adventurous spirit continued to show when she was in her fifties as she earned the pilot's license she had dreamed of for years. She enjoyed flying, but in 1978, the small plane she was piloting stalled on takeoff and crashed. In the wreck, Monroe lost a kidney and vision in her left eye. Almost twenty years later, her remaining kidney failed, leading to her death at age seventy-seven. In 1999 the Kentucky Aviation Hall of Fame honored Monroe with the Distinguished Service Award. Monroe is buried in New Albany, Indiana.

In 2000 Congress passed a bill that authorized a memorial park, the Rosie the Riveter/World War II Home Front National Historic Park, to be located in Richmond, California. Representative George Miller from California stated, "The 'Rosie the Riveter' National Park would [will] salute the role of the home front during World War II, particularly recognizing the significant changes in the lives of women and minorities that occurred during that era." The park and center are scheduled to open in 2003. Richmond was chosen because its four shipyards employed 90,000 people and produced 747 ships. In addition, the Rosie Monroe Society was formed to raise private funds for the World War II Memorial Foundation.

★

Major books about the "Rosie the Riveter" phenomenon include Sheila Tobias and Lisa Anderson, *What Really Happened to Rosie the Riveter? Demobilization and the Female Labor Force, 1944–1947* (1974); Leila J. Rupp, *Mobilizing Women for War: German and American Propaganda, 1939–1945* (1978); Miriam Frank, Marilyn Ziebarth, and Connie Field, *The Life and Times of Rosie the Riveter* (1982); Maureen Honey, *Creating Rosie the Riveter: Class, Gender, and Propaganda During World War II* (1984); Sherna Berger Gluck, *Rosie the Riveter Revisited: Women, the War, and Social Change* (1987); and Penny Colman, *Rosie the Riveter: Women Working on the Home Front in World War II* (1995). Monroe was featured in the National Public Radio show *All Things Considered* on 2 June 1997. An obituary is in the *New York Times* (2 June 1997).

GWYNETH H. CROWLEY

MONTAGU, Ashley (*b.* 28 June 1905 in London, England; *d.* 26 November 1999 in Princeton, New Jersey), anthropologist and popular writer, lecturer, and television personality who deconstructed the myths supporting racial inequality and brought anthropology to a broad segment of the American public.

Montagu was born Israel Ehrenberg in London's East End, the only child of Charles Ehrenberg, a tailor from Poland, and Mary Plotnick, a homemaker from Russia. He was educated in public primary schools and Hebrew afterschool programs, although much of his formative early education was self-taught. In childhood he began reading the works of John Stuart Mill, Thomas Henry Huxley, and Friedrich Nietzsche, collected from used bookstalls that were abundant in the London of his youth. By age ten he was observing the differences in language usage and accent between his cockney neighbors and the educated university students sometimes taken in as lodgers by his parents. Thus

Ashley Montagu, 1970. ASSOCIATED PRESS AP

began his lifelong interest in the influence of the environment upon the individual, a theme that resonated throughout his writings on human behavior.

In 1922, at the age of seventeen, Montagu went to University College London as a student of anthropology and psychology, studying with Grafton Elliot Smith as well as Charles Spearman and Karl Pearson, the founders of the British eugenics movement. During this period he served in the Welsh Guard and also enjoyed some success as a champion welterweight boxer. Montagu graduated from University College London in 1925 but did not earn a degree. By his early twenties, he was attending seminars at the London School of Economics under Bronislaw Malinowski, a charismatic formulator of British social anthropology and a formative influence on Montagu's thinking.

After the crushing of the 1926 General Strike in England, Montagu determined that the United States was a place likely to be more congenial to social justice, as well as to the career of a young anthropologist. At about this time he formalized his name change, in no small part as a response to the anti-Semitism present in many elite academic circles on both sides of the Atlantic. Crossing the Atlantic by ocean liner in the early 1930s, Montagu met a young American, Marjorie Peakes, with whom he shared a long, eventful, and sustaining partnership. He and Peakes were married on 18 September 1931; they had three children.

In the United States, Montagu continued his professional association with the foundational figures of early-twentieth-century anthropology, studying at Columbia University in New York City with Franz Boas and Ruth Benedict. Attracted to the culture and personality school, in part by Margaret Mead's radio presentations, he enrolled in Columbia's graduate program in 1934. He completed his doctorate on the issue of paternity knowledge among Australian Aborigines and published *Coming into Being Among the Australian Aborigines* (1937).

Montagu held a number of teaching positions at U.S. colleges and universities, including an associate professorship at New York University (1931–1938) and a post at Hahnemann Medical College in Philadelphia, Pennsylvania (1938–1949). In 1940 Montagu became a naturalized U.S. citizen. In the late 1940s and early 1950s he developed the anthropology program at Rutgers, in New Brunswick, and served as its first chair.

Because Montagu was an outspoken antiracist and peace activist, some powerful people considered his views "un-American" (the Federal Bureau of Investigation kept an active file on Montagu during the McCarthy period and the Vietnam War years). At the same time, university administrators often perceived him as arrogant and difficult to work with, which may have compounded his difficulties. He left Rutgers under pressure from the administration in the early 1950s and never again held a regular academic position, often remarking that true scholarship and the academic life were incommensurate pursuits.

Montagu wrote prodigiously for a popular audience, including a regular column for *Ladies' Home Journal*. He educated the U.S. public about the devastating consequences of social deprivation and stress on the development of children, the importance of a nurturing environment, the desirability of breast feeding, and the immense creative capacities of the young. In 1953 he wrote the early feminist classic *The Natural Superiority of Women*, which argued for complete equality of the sexes during a period in which this was a controversial topic. He was an accomplished belletrist and wrote *The Elephant Man* (1971), the first modern account of the life of Joseph Merrick who, like Montagu, had grown up in London's East End. His book *Touching: The Human Significance of the Skin* (1971) was the first to point out to a popular audience the importance of the skin as a sensory and social organ in human communication.

Montagu's greatest contribution was his demystification of race. The mistake of viewing races as typological, bounded categories, both within popular culture and academe, was a focus of his work as early as 1926, when he

published "Intelligence Tests and the Negro in America" in the *Journal of the West African Student Union of Great Britain*. By the late 1930s and early 1940s, as the dangers of Nazi racist doctrines became increasingly apparent, Montagu engaged in a highly public and often controversial debunking of the myth of biological races. In 1942 he wrote his most influential book, *Man's Most Dangerous Myth: The Fallacy of Race*, which called race into question as a biological category. This was a prescient move, as the book was published several decades before genetic data were available to support this thesis. In 1950 he was asked to become the lead writer of the United Nations Educational, Scientific, and Cultural Organization's first *Statement on Race*. The 1951 publication was controversial for its time, in the degree to which it asserted the social constructionist perspective on race. *Man's Most Dangerous Myth* was published in six editions between 1942 and 1996.

Montagu had a lighter side, and he wrote a number of humorous books and articles, including a tome on the history of swearing, *The Anatomy of Swearing* (1967). He appeared frequently on television programs, with a regular guest spot on *The Tonight Show with Johnny Carson*, as well as on *What's My Line?* and *The $64,000 Question*. As a result, Montagu was sometimes erroneously belittled as a mere popularizer of anthropology. Although his writing was witty and accessible, rigorous scientific research and scholarship always informed his books.

Montagu continued to work until the end of his life, revising two of his best-known books for publication as new editions in the late 1990s. A humanist and idealist, he was a friend to many famous people, including the philosopher Bertrand Russell, the birth-control pioneer Margaret Sanger, and the poet and novelist May Sarton. In the 1960s he joined with the pediatrician Benjamin Spock and others to protest the Vietnam War, and he wrote a number of articles and books decrying the increasing anonymity and automation of postindustrial life. Montagu suffered from heart disease and was hospitalized in March 1999 while working on his memoirs. He died at the age of ninety-four and was cremated. Up to the end of his life, he asserted that aggression and hatred were not innate human characteristics but products of the human social environment and thus capable of alteration through learning.

Montagu's extraordinary career influenced many disciplines, including biological and sociocultural anthropology, the history of science, and developmental psychology. His publications reflected an extraordinary erudition. Formal honors came to him late in life, in the 1990s, and included the American Anthropological Association's Distinguished Achievement Award, Society of American Physical Anthropologists' Darwin Award, and American Humanist Association's Humanist of the Year Award. An individual of complexity and extraordinary breadth, he may well have been the last anthropological scholar to master the cultural and biological realms of his discipline.

★

There are a number of insightful biographical pieces on Montagu. These include Stevan Harnad's 1980 essay in the *International Encyclopedia of the Social Sciences* 18 (1980); Andrew Lyons, "The Neotenic Career of M. F. Ashley Montagu," in *Race and Other Misadventures: Essays in Honor of Ashley Montagu in His Ninetieth Year,* ed. Leonard Lieberman and Larry T. Reynolds (1986); and Jonathan Marks, "Obituary Essay," *Evolutionary Anthropology* 9, no. 3 (1999): 111–112. The Ashley Montagu Institute, directed by Rod Gorney, also provides useful material on Montagu's life and work. Obituaries are in the *Los Angeles Times* and *Washington Post* (both 28 Nov. 1999) and *New York Times* (29 Nov. 1999).

SUSAN SPERLING

MOORE, Archie (*b.* 13 December 1913 in Benoit, Mississippi [sources vary]; *d.* 9 December 1998 in San Diego, California), boxer, actor, and author known for his diverse talents, his philosophical nature, and his fight record.

Moore was born Archibald Lee Wright and was the son of Thomas Wright, a farm laborer, and Lorena Wright. His father deserted the family when he was an infant. Raised by an uncle and aunt, Cleveland and Willie Pearl Moore, in St. Louis, he took their surname. At age eight, Moore decided to become a boxer after watching a boxing match. His uncle was accidentally killed, and Moore took to petty thievery. He sold a pair of oil lamps stolen from his aunt and used the money to buy a pair of boxing gloves. He was sent to reform school in Booneville, Missouri, for attempting to rob a streetcar fare box. He was freed in 1934, after twenty-two months for good behavior, and got a job in the forestry division of the Civilian Conservation Corps in rural Missouri. Determined to become a boxer, he would stand in truck beds on the way to work, dodging oncoming branches.

After a few Golden Gloves amateur bouts, Moore began a professional career as a middleweight in the mid-1930s. He knocked out "Piano Mover Jones" in 1935 and dispatched "The Poco Kid" in 1936. Moore fought about once a month, knocking out obscure boxers in backwoods towns. He lost his first major fight to Johnny Romero in 1938 but knocked Romero out in a rematch later that year. He married Mattie Chapman in Los Angeles before touring Australia in 1940 and beating its heavyweight champion, Ron Richards. His absence and itinerant boxing career caused tension in his marriage, and he and Mattie soon divorced.

Archie Moore after defeating Harold Johnson at Madison Square Garden, 12 August 1954. ASSOCIATED PRESS AP

In 1940 he purchased a house in San Diego, which became his permanent home.

In 1941 a perforated ulcer nearly killed Moore, but after recovering, Moore was a top middleweight contender throughout the 1940s, beating champions and ranked boxers but never getting a title bout. After 1945 he moved up to light heavyweight status. Racist policies, his inability to break into the New York City circuit, and the tendency of champions to avoid him relegated Moore's career to an endless series of obscure fights.

Moore wrote innumerable letters to key New York City sportswriters, demanding a title shot. Not until 1952, at age thirty-nine and after much publicity from Red Smith, A. J. Liebling, John Lardner, and other boxing reporters, did Moore secure a championship fight against Joey Maxim. Even though Moore decisioned Maxim in fifteen rounds, he earned only $800, having been charged a small fee in order to secure the match. Loquacious and clever, he became a favorite of journalists, who loved to tease him about his age.

The advent of television publicized boxing, and Moore benefited from the national exposure. In 1954 and 1955

Life, Look, Time, Newsweek, the *New Yorker,* and other top magazines did feature stories on him. Moore could turn even his loss to Rocky Marciano on 21 September 1955 for the heavyweight title into a personal triumph. Moore knocked Marciano down in the second round, but the champ, nine years younger than the forty-one-year-old challenger, won by knockout in the ninth round. Moore told enchanted reporters that boxing Marciano was like "fighting an airplane propeller.... The blades keep whirling past your ear and over your head." Moore acknowledged defeat by telling his listeners that "sometimes the matador gets caught," which *Life* used as the title of its feature article.

In 1955 Moore married Joan Hardy, a sister-in-law of the actor Sidney Poitier. They had five children and stayed married the rest of Moore's life. Moore pursued the heavyweight crown again in November 1956; Floyd Patterson knocked him out in five rounds. Moore's televised defense of his light heavyweight title against Yvon Durelle in 1958 thrilled the nation. Durelle knocked Moore down three times in the first round, but the champ put out Durelle in the eleventh round. The victory was Moore's 137th knockout, which is still a record. A month later Moore appeared in an exhibition against the writer George Plimpton. He surrendered his light heavyweight crown in 1962, and his nine-year reign was the longest on record. On 15 November 1962 he lost to Cassius Clay, who later changed his name to Muhammad Ali.

Moore retired from boxing in 1963 with a record of 194–28–8 (sources vary). His film debut as Jim in the movie *The Adventures of Huckleberry Finn* (1959) was favorably received; he also appeared in *The Carpetbaggers* (1964), *The Fortune Cookie* (1966), and *Breakheart Pass* (1976). He trained George Foreman for "The Rumble in the Jungle" championship fight against Ali in 1976. In addition, in 1965 he founded Any Boy Can Clubs, Inc., which used boxing instruction and counseling to combat drugs among young men in San Diego and Los Angeles.

Moore died in a hospice in San Diego after having undergone heart surgery in the 1990s. He is buried in Cypress View Memorial Gardens in San Diego.

★

The basic source for information on Moore's life is his autobiography, *The Archie Moore Story* (1960), augmented by Marilyn Green Douroux, *Archie Moore, the Ole Mongoose: The Authorized Biography of Archie Moore, the Undefeated Light Heavyweight Champion of the World* (1991). The best article on Moore is Frank Deford, "The Ageless Warrior," *Sports Illustrated* (8 May 1989). George Plimpton's chapter on fighting Moore is in his book *Shadow Box* (1977) and reveals the distinct lifestyle of professional boxers. An obituary is in the *New York Times* (10 Dec. 1998).

GRAHAM RUSSELL HODGES

MOORE, Jack Carlton ("Clayton") (*b.* 14 September 1914 in Chicago, Illinois; *d.* 28 December 1999 in West Hills, California), actor best known for playing the Lone Ranger on television.

Moore was born into affluence on Chicago's north side. His father, Sprague C. Moore, was a real estate developer; his mother, Theresa Violet Fisher, was a homemaker. The youngest of three sons, Moore attended Chicago public schools, graduating from Senn High School in 1932. The family lived in the predominantly Catholic precinct of Edgewater. As a child, Moore spent Saturdays watching cowboy movies featuring the likes of William S. Hart, Buck Jones, George O'Brien, and Tom Mix. He dreamed of becoming a policeman or a cowboy. Summers found the Moore family basking in the sunlight of Loon Lake in Canada, where the children raced speedboats, fished, and learned to use firearms.

Although athletic, Moore did not compete in high school team sports, choosing instead to join the Illinois Athletic Club (IAC) in downtown Chicago. There he lifted weights, swam competitively, and practiced gymnastics. He won the IAC championship in the 100-yard dash in swimming and teamed with the Flying Behrs, a trapeze act that performed during the 1934 Chicago World's Fair. Rather

Clayton Moore as the Lone Ranger *(right)* with Jay Silverheels as Tonto *(left)* and Silver *(center)*. AP/WIDE WORLD PHOTOS

than attend college, he struggled as a model while working for the Powers Modeling Agency in New York City during 1935.

In 1937, determined to work as a cowboy movie star, Moore headed for Hollywood, California. With the help of the acting coach Doc Fleishman, Moore signed a movie contract with Warner Brothers and in 1938 played minor roles in both *When Were You Born?* and *The Cowboy from Brooklyn.* Moore adopted "Clayton" as his first name when a movie producer suggested he change his name to promote his career. In 1942 he was featured in *The Black Dragons,* the first World War II film ever made and Moore's last movie before serving stateside in the U.S. Army Air Forces for three years. Moore married the actress Sally Allen in 1943, and the couple adopted a daughter in 1958.

Postwar prosperity created a demand for movies, enabling Moore to play opposite Roy Rogers in *The Far Frontier* (1949) and Gene Autry in *The Cowboy and the Indians* (1949). Matinee serials remained popular with children throughout the 1940s, and Moore got top billing as an action-adventure hero in the Republic Pictures serials *The Perils of Nyoka* (1942), *Jesse James Rides Again* (1947), and the cliffhanger *G-Men Never Forget* (1947). In eleven years Moore acted in more than seventy films and serials for MGM, Columbia, and Republic, playing a variety of roles. A movie serial in 1949 required him to wear a black mask as part of his costume for the first time; *The Ghost of Zorro* provided Moore with a new role and a ticket to stardom. So great a bond developed between the actor and this role that the man and persona of the character Moore portrayed became one, both in his personal life and in the public consciousness.

After evaluating the actor on film as Zorro, and on the recommendation of the talent agent Autrim Short, the entertainment mogul George W. Trendle, who had created the popular radio broadcast *The Lone Ranger,* hired Moore to bring the character to television. The growing popularity of television coincided with a robust U.S. economy and the beginnings of the baby boom generation. Even before the creation of nickelodeon westerns and *The Squaw Man* (1914), the first full-length western movie, the mystique and aura of the Old West had been part of U.S. culture and the nation's psyche. Through the medium of television, *The Lone Ranger* provided middle-class families with wholesome, home entertainment and became a memorable part of many baby boomers' childhood years.

The Lone Ranger retold the saga of John Reid and his command of five Texas Rangers who were bushwhacked by outlaws and presumed dead. Reid, the lone survivor, was discovered by Tonto, a Native American, who dressed his wounds, saved his life, and became his lifelong companion. After digging graves for his five dead companions and a sixth grave to make it appear as if he too had been killed,

Reid, wearing a black mask cut from the leather vest of his dead brother, swore to avenge his brother's murder by bringing law and order to the western frontier. In the fictional Wild Horse Canyon, the duo captured and tamed a wild white stallion that Reid called Silver. Reid and his "faithful companion" Tonto, riding the pinto Scout, made a formidable team crusading for justice throughout the West. Trendle and the writer Fran Striker cast Jay Silverheels, a Mohawk Indian, in the role of Tonto.

Moore, a skilled equestrian, opened every show riding Silver at a full gallop to a rock outcropping and rearing the horse high into the air, always to the shrill trumpet fanfare of the *William Tell* Overture. *The Lone Ranger* premiered on 15 September 1949, the first western series made for television. Although not apparent in the black-and-white format of early television, Moore's costume consisted of a light-blue jumpsuit with black-laced placket, accentuated by black leather gloves, boots, and silver-studded black holster used to carry his two Colt-45 revolvers. Always disguised by the famous mask, his blue eyes were set in a round face with rugged features and a square jaw; he always projected a contained expression of sincerity, honesty, and earnestness that, along with the white Stetson he wore, enhanced his image as a crime fighter and doer of good deeds.

The Lone Ranger character lived by an unspoken moral code of ethics, always used proper English, and avoided tobacco, alcohol, and situations that would compromise his secret identity. Although fistfights were common throughout the television series, and the masked man was heavily armed, he never used deadly force in gunfights. His marksmanship was so accurate that he often disarmed villains by shooting the weapons from their hands, leaving their fate to local sheriffs and a fair trial. The stories were dominated by chase scenes filmed on location instead of on a set and featured the horsemanship of Moore and Silverheels. Moore left the series in 1952 after a contract dispute and was replaced by John Hart, but he returned to the series two years later. The final episode aired on 6 June 1957 on ABC. Two movie spin-offs featured both original actors: *The Lone Ranger* premiered in 1956, followed by *The Lone Ranger and the Lost City of Gold* in 1958.

To promote the character, Moore made numerous public appearances, always wearing the mask and costume. In 1979, after purchasing the rights to *The Lone Ranger,* the Wrather Corporation obtained a restraining order prohibiting Moore from ever wearing the mask in public. The company planned to film *The Legend of the Lone Ranger,* starring a younger actor. Distraught, Moore appealed to public opinion through the media and filed a lawsuit claiming the restraining order deprived him of his livelihood, although he continued to make public appearances as the Lone Ranger, substituting wraparound sunglasses for his trademark mask. Only after the box-office failure of the new movie and after years of litigation did the Wrather Corporation lift the court order, allowing Moore to wear the mask once again on 20 September 1984. Moore has the only star on the Hollywood Walk of Fame to feature both the actor's name and that of his most popular character. In 1999 he accepted an honorary appointment to the Texas Ranger Hall of Fame and Museum and the Cowboy Hall of Fame (now the National Cowboy Western Heritage Museum) in Oklahoma City, Oklahoma.

Moore's first wife died in 1986 after a lengthy illness. On 18 January 1992 he married Clarita Petrone and, after the bitter litigation surrounding the mask, lived a reclusive existence in Calabasas, California, where he died at a nearby hospital after a heart attack. Moore is buried at Forest Lawn in Glendale, California.

The role of the Lone Ranger that Moore played on television defined the moral absolutes for an entire generation of young American viewers, who, coming of age during the civil rights, antiwar, and environmental movements of the mid-twentieth century, sought symbols for their idealism. In an Associated Press interview in 1986, Moore identified his portrayal of the masked man with patriotic idealism: "The Lone Ranger is a great character, a great American. Playing him made me a better person. I never want to take off this white hat."

★

Moore's autobiography, written with Frank Thompson, *I Was That Masked Man* (1996), contains an accurate chronology of his films and the popular television series, along with a bibliography. Obituaries are in the *New York Times, Chicago Tribune,* and *Los Angeles Times* (all 29 Dec. 1999).

JEAN W. GRIFFITH

MORRIS, William Weaks ("Willie") (*b.* 29 November 1934 in Jackson, Mississippi; *d.* 2 August 1999 in Jackson, Mississippi), writer and editor best known for his autobiography *North Toward Home* (1967) and other works on the American South.

Morris was the only child of Henry Rae Morris, a gas station owner, and Marion Weaks, a homemaker. When Morris was six the family moved to Yazoo City, Mississippi, where he attended public schools and displayed an early penchant for words as editor of his high school paper and as a part-time sportswriter for *The Yazoo Herald*.

After graduating from high school in 1952, Morris attended the University of Texas. After two years of fraternity frivolity with, by his own admission, no awareness that "there were ideas, much less ideas to arouse one from oneself," he finally discovered that books could be "as subver-

Willie Morris, 1971. ASSOCIATED PRESS AP

sive as Socrates." Morris edited and wrote for the student newspaper, the *Daily Texan*. Willing to take on controversial themes, he was forced out as editor after the paper accused powerful political figures in the state of being too friendly with the Texas oil and gas industry. After receiving his B.A. degree in 1956, Morris spent the next four years studying modern history at New College, Oxford University, as the winner of a Rhodes scholarship. There, he earned a second B.A. degree in 1959 and an M.A. degree in 1960. Morris married Celia Ann Buchan on 30 August 1958. Together they had one child before divorcing in 1969. On 14 September 1991 Morris married JoAnne Prichard.

Upon Morris's return to the United States in 1960, Ronnie Dugger, publisher of the *Texas Observer,* hired him as editor. The Austin-based weekly was a legendary source of exposés of corrupt Texas politics, and it provided a heady experience for the young Morris. But the frenetic pace and lack of adequate staff led him to resign in 1962.

After briefly attending graduate school at Stanford University, Morris moved to New York City and in 1963 joined *Harper's* magazine, where in four years he rose from associate editor to the magazine's youngest-ever editor in chief. With the Vietnam War and the civil rights movement in full swing, Morris had ample opportunity to highlight the works of some of the era's leading American writers, including an excerpt of William Styron's *The Confessions of*

Nat Turner; David Halberstam's reporting from Vietnam; a long essay by Norman Mailer, "Steps of the Pentagon," on a protest march against the war; and articles by Robert Penn Warren, Arthur Miller, Marshall Frady, and Ralph Ellison. Despite lifting *Harper's* circulation and renown, Morris resigned in 1971 after a long dispute over finances and editorial philosophy with the new owner, taking most of his staff with him.

Morris spent the next nine years as an independent writer living in New York. While at *Harper's* he had begun publishing works of his own. He edited *The South Today: 100 Years After Appomattox* (1965), essays reprinted from *Harper's* appraising the state of the modern South. *North Toward Home* (1967), his most notable book, is an autobiographical account of his years in Mississippi, Texas, and New York, and a masterful work of social history. He wove his own experiences into the larger tapestry of America in the 1940s, 1950s, and 1960s—small-town Mississippi, Texas politics, and Manhattan publishing. The first part, chronicling his youth amid the strains of desegregation in a bastion of the Old South, is at once replete with the humor of boyhood pranks, illustrative of a rapidly disappearing way of life, and optimistic about a future country of blacks and whites sharing a common history and system of values. The *Sunday Times* (London) called it "the finest evocation of an American boyhood since Mark Twain."

Yazoo: Integration in a Deep Southern Town (1971) explored the court-ordered desegregation of the schools in his hometown. After years of dodging the 1954 *Brown* v. *Board of Education* decision mandating public school integration, "[a]n immense façade was beginning to crack" in Mississippi, Morris wrote, and his book was a celebration of the peaceful transition his hometown underwent. *Good Old Boy: A Delta Boyhood* (1971) is a memoir for his son David in which Morris reminisces about growing up in the South. A rare foray into fiction, *The Last of the Southern Girls* (1973), received mixed reviews. It is the story of young Carol Hollywell from Arkansas, her romance with a congressman, and how she is ultimately swallowed up in the sordid political and social mayhem of Washington.

Some critics consider *James Jones: A Friendship* (1978) Morris's best work. It is an admiring memoir of his ten-year friendship with his Long Island neighbor. Jones, author of *From Here to Eternity, The Thin Red Line,* and other notable fiction of World War II, was an intensely private man with few close friends who had exiled himself in Paris for years. Morris succeeded as few others had in penetrating Jones's character.

In 1980 Morris accepted a position as writer in residence at the University of Mississippi. On moving to Oxford, Mississippi, he explained to a college audience, "Truman Capote told me once that all Southerners go home sooner or later . . . even if it's in a box. Well, I didn't want to wait

that long." There, his prodigious literary output continued. *The Courting of Marcus Dupree* (1983) describes the frenzy surrounding the college recruitment of a southern black high school football star. Morris wrote five books of essays and stories: *The Ghosts of Old Miss and Other Essays* and *Terrains of the Heart, and Other Essays on Home* (both 1981); *Always Stand in Against the Curve and Other Sports Stories* (1983); *Homecomings* (1989); and *After All, It's Only a Game* (1992). A second autobiography, *New York Days* (1993), recounted his time at *Harper's.*

As writer in residence, Morris was in a position to help the careers of other writers, whom he invited to Oxford to showcase their work. When a local lawyer named John Grisham sat in on some of Morris's classes, Morris gave him generous advice on his first novel, *A Time to Kill* (1989), helping to launch Grisham's career.

Morris served as a consultant on the 1996 motion picture *The Ghosts of Mississippi,* about the 1963 assassination of civil rights leader Medgar Evers and the conviction of Byron De La Beckwith for the crime. *The Ghosts of Medgar Evers* (1998) describes his work on the movie. Two of Morris's own books were made into movies: *Good Old Boy* (1971) and *My Dog Skip* (1995). Deemed "the ultimate dog book" by one reviewer, the latter is a loving memoir of his beloved pet with anecdotes about growing up in the South in the 1940s. Morris's fondness and indeed his obsession for his home state are reflected in such works as *Faulkner's Mississippi* (1990), based on a *National Geographic* cover story (March 1989) and, posthumously, *My Mississippi* (2000), an homage to his boyhood state featuring photographs taken by his son David.

Morris loved bourbon, cigarettes, socializing, and long late-night conversations. This lifestyle eventually caught up with him, and he died at age sixty-four of heart failure. He was the only Mississippi writer ever to lie in state in the rotunda of the Mississippi capitol building, and he is buried in Yazoo City. His only other novel, *Taps* (2001), was published posthumously. It is a coming-of-age tale of young Swayze Barksdale, who plays taps at the funerals of Korean War GIs from his Mississippi Delta hometown. (Morris himself had played taps at American Legion funerals as a young man.)

"I am an American writer who happens to have come from the South. I've tried to put the South into the larger American perspective," Morris said in 1997. This was undoubtedly his most enduring achievement, exemplified in *North Toward Home* and most of his other works. He both located the southern experience in the larger American scene and explained to his fellow countrymen—many of whom were rootless by the late twentieth century—what it was like to have an attachment to a region of the nation that had maintained its distinctiveness and sense of place. As he explained in *Yazoo,* "I go back to the South, physically and in my memories, to remind myself who I am, for the South keeps me going; it is an organizing principle, a feeling in the blood which pervades my awareness of my country and my civilization."

★

Morris's papers are in the special collections division of the University of Mississippi library. *North Toward Home, New York Days,* and *Good Old Boy* are the best sources about his early life. Joan Bobbitt, "Willie Morris," in *Dictionary of Literary Biography Yearbook 1980* (1981), provides a full discussion of his life and writings until 1980. *Contemporary Authors,* vol. 13 (1984), gives a good analysis of *North Toward Home* and *Yazoo,* and *World Authors 1975–80* (1985) is also useful. An obituary is in the *New York Times* (3 Aug. 1999).

WILLIAM F. MUGLESTON

MOTLEY, Marion (*b.* 5 June 1920 in Leesburg, Georgia; *d.* 27 June 1999 in Cleveland, Ohio), professional football player and pioneer in the racial integration of professional sports in the United States.

Motley was one of three children of Shakeful Motley, an iron and steel molder, and Blanche Jones, a homemaker. When he was two years old his family moved from Georgia to Canton, Ohio. Motley began his athletic career at Canton's McKinley High School. He played basketball but

Marion Motley. AP/WIDE WORLD PHOTOS

achieved stardom on the school's football team. During Motley's three years on the varsity team, McKinley only lost three games, all to legendary Massillon High School teams coached by Paul Brown.

After graduating from McKinley in 1939, Motley accepted a football scholarship to South Carolina State University. Unused to the Jim Crow South, with its strict segregation and requirements that African Americans continually show deference to whites, he was unhappy, and before the end of his first semester transferred to the University of Nevada at Reno. African-American players were still a rarity in Rocky Mountain college football. Motley occasionally faced taunting and late hits. In one game against the University of Idaho, the opposing coach objected to Motley playing at all. As a compromise he only played the second half. When given the chance, though, Motley excelled as a fullback and linebacker, and was considered to be the best player on an average team.

During the 1942 season Motley suffered the first of several knee injuries. He left school, returned to Canton, and began working for Republic Steel. The following year he married Eula Coleman. They had three sons. In 1944 Motley was drafted into the United States Navy and assigned to Great Lakes Naval Training Center in Great Lakes, Illinois. During World War II, Great Lakes, like other military bases, had a camp football team that played against college competition. The coach at Great Lakes was Brown. Remembering Motley from their high school games, Brown had Motley assigned to the team for the 1945 season. Motley's best game came in a 39–7 victory over Notre Dame, when he scored on a forty-four yard touchdown run. More important, Motley had impressed his coach.

Brown already knew in 1945 that the next year he would be coaching the Cleveland Browns in a new professional football league, the All-America Football Conference (AAFC). African-American participation in professional football had a mixed history. There were a number of black players on National Football League (NFL) rosters from the league's founding in 1920 until 1933. One, Fritz Pollard, even served as a player coach. Following the 1933 season, however, the NFL's team owners apparently entered into a gentlemen's agreement to segregate the game. The African-American players disappeared. Motley hoped that with a new league, and Brown's history of coaching integrated teams, he would be given a chance. Brown, at first, was noncommittal. A few days after training camp opened, though, he invited Motley to attend. Motley always believed he had been allowed to join the team because another African American, Bill Willis, had already been signed and Brown wanted someone for him to room with on road trips. Brown, however, maintained that he had always intended to have an integrated team and only brought Motley in late to avoid the media scrutiny that accompanied the opening of camp. Motley, Willis, Kenny Washington, and Woody Strode of the NFL's Los Angeles Rams broke professional football's color barrier in 1946, a year before Jackie Robinson integrated major league baseball.

The Cleveland Browns team that Motley joined was unique for its time. Unlike most offenses, the Browns' main weapon was the precision passing of quarterback Otto Graham. Motley's main duties were to protect the quarterback. He was sometimes called "Otto Graham's bodyguard" for his ferocious blocking. To keep the defense honest, the Browns often called the "trap" play, known today as the "draw" play. In this play Graham dropped back as if to pass and Motley pretended to block. Graham then simply handed Motley the ball. Often the pass rushers would be out of position, giving Motley a clear lane in which to run. At six feet, one inch and 238 pounds, Motley was as big as most linemen of the day. If he broke into the open field, smaller linebackers and defensive backs found it difficult to bring him down. For two years Motley started as both a fullback on offense and a linebacker on defense. Beginning in his third season he concentrated on fullback and only played defense in goal-line situations.

During the 1946 season Motley ran for 601 yards, averaging an astonishing 8.2 yards per carry. The Browns won the AAFC championship. Ironically, the Browns' very success doomed the league. Between 1946 and 1949 the Browns won forty-seven games and lost only four. They won the championship each year. The lack of competition led to fewer fans and, at the end of the 1949 season, the AAFC ceased independent operations. The Browns, San Francisco 49ers, and Baltimore Colts were absorbed into the older NFL. During the four AAFC seasons Motley rushed for 3,024 yards, more than any other back.

Most people expected the Browns would be unable to duplicate their success in the NFL. Before their first game, Philadelphia Eagles coach Earle "Greasy" Neale compared the Browns to a high school team. The Browns won 35–10. In 1950 the Browns won the NFL championship, beating the Los Angeles Rams 30–28 on a dramatic, last second field goal. Motley led the league in rushing, gaining 810 yards.

In 1951 Motley again injured his knee. He continued to play but less effectively than in the past. Prior to the 1954 season another knee injury forced Motley to sit out for a year. He tried to make a comeback in 1955 with the Pittsburgh Steelers, but at age thirty-five, still hampered by his bad knees, he only lasted a few games before retiring. Overall, Motley rushed for 4,720 yards during his career and scored thirty-one touchdowns on the ground. During his eight seasons with the Browns, the team played in eight championship games, winning four in the AAFC and two in the NFL.

Following his playing career Motley hoped to get into coaching, but he found few opportunities. He worked part-time as a scout for the Washington Redskins when his friend Otto Graham was the head coach and was briefly affiliated with a women's professional football league. Otherwise he worked at a number of non-sports jobs. Motley operated a tavern, was safety director for a construction company, worked for the post office, was supervisor of the Ohio State Lottery, and worked for the Ohio Department of Youth Services. The last job was probably his favorite. Motley believed his notoriety as a former professional football player helped him counsel troubled youth.

Motley was inducted into the Pro Football Hall of Fame in 1968. He died of prostate cancer in Cleveland. Funeral services were held at Mount Sinai Baptist Church in Cleveland. Motley is buried in the church's cemetery.

As one of four African Americans to integrate professional football, Motley handled a difficult situation with grace and dignity. His immense personal talents won him respect on the field. Paul Zimmerman, in his book *A Thinking Man's Guide to Pro Football* (1971), calls Motley the greatest player who ever lived. His willingness to sacrifice for the good of the team made him a favorite among his fellow Browns. Paul Brown once said, "Nothing devastates a football team like a selfish player. It's a cancer. The greatest back I ever had was Marion Motley. You know why? The only statistic he ever knew was whether we won or lost. The man was completely unselfish."

★

Memorabilia and newspaper clippings are in the Pro Football Hall of Fame in Canton, Ohio. Interviews are printed in Myron Cope, *The Game That Was: The Early Days of Pro Football* (1970), and Stuart Leuther, *Iron Men: Bronko, Crazylegs, and the Boys Recall the Golden Days of Professional Football* (1988). For Motley's role in the integration of pro football, see Robert W. Peterson, *Pigskin: The Early Days of Pro Football* (1997). Obituaries are in the *Cleveland Plain Dealer* and *New York Times* (both 28 June 1999).

HAROLD W. AURAND, JR.

MURPHY, Joseph Samson (*b.* 15 November 1933 in Newark, New Jersey; *d.* 17 January 1998 near Bishoftu, Ethiopia), government official and unconventional college president.

Murphy was the elder of two sons born to Joseph Murphy, an Irish immigrant and trade-union organizer on the East Coast waterfront, and Doris Milgrom, a left-wing Jewish homemaker and political activist. Murphy retained in his later life much of his parents' passion for social justice. His academic career began conventionally, graduating in 1951 from Weequahic High School in Newark, then studying at the University of Colorado from 1951 to 1953; he received a B.A. degree from Olivet College in Michigan in 1955. Murphy then won a Woodrow Wilson graduate fellowship to the University of North Carolina. After a year he transferred to Brandeis University, where he studied political theory with Norton E. Long and Herbert Marcuse. He earned an M.A. degree from Brandeis in 1959 and a Ph.D. in 1961 and taught there from 1957 to 1965. Murphy's learned but dry doctoral thesis examined the theory of universal concepts held by David Hume and other British empiricists. In his later governmental and administrative career, Murphy relied to an extraordinary degree on the tenets of classical political philosophy in addressing value conflicts, racism, diversity, and other multicultural issues.

The charming, sociable, and intelligent young Brandeis professor soon came to the attention of the Boston-area New Frontiersmen, supporters of President John F. Kennedy's philosophy of volunteerism combined with his idea and practice of vigorous global activism. For a while Murphy served as a part-time assistant to the Peace Corps director Sargent Shriver, and he began to consider government service as an attractive alternative to an academic career. This opportunity came in 1965, when he was offered a position as the director of the Peace Corps training center on Saint Croix in the U.S. Virgin Islands.

This job allowed Murphy to combine his previous professorial experience with a newly discovered interest in handling administrative matters. At the Saint Croix center, he taught courses and traveled to other training sites (mostly on college campuses), meeting and negotiating with college presidents. He then moved through a quick succession of other positions in the federal government, as John W. Gardner's assistant in the U.S. Department of Health, Education, and Welfare (1966–1967) and as the associate director of the Job Corps in the Office of Economic Opportunity (1967–1968).

In 1968 Murphy published *Political Theory: A Conceptual Analysis*. He also became the director of the Peace Corps program in Ethiopia, the largest in all of Africa. Rapidly learning Amharic, he threw himself enthusiastically into this new work. Most U.S. Peace Corps volunteers in Ethiopia were involved in training secondary-school teachers, and Murphy quickly became familiar with the country's educational system. Many students and teachers opposed the archaic and increasingly authoritarian regime of the emperor Haile Sellassie, and Murphy could not avoid the fray. He engaged the disaffected Ethiopians in earnest debate, arguing that the Peace Corps was not a prop for their unpopular government or a front for the U.S. Central Intelligence Agency (CIA). However, Murphy agreed with many of the criticisms made of the Ethiopian government and soon ran afoul of the U.S. ambassador, who opposed

Joseph S. Murphy. AP/WIDE WORLD PHOTOS

Murphy's insistence on equality of pay and status for Ethiopian Peace Corps employees.

What finally prompted Murphy's resignation was the emperor's 1969 decision to dispatch the Imperial Guard to the campus of Addis Ababa University to brutally suppress protests about the murder of a student leader. Murphy released a resignation letter in February 1970, stating that he could no longer work under a regime that responded to its problems by "shooting and beating [its] young people." Although Murphy did not return to Ethiopia until Sellassie had been deposed and the subsequent seventeen-year military regime had ended, he always regarded his two years there as among the happiest and most fulfilling of his life.

With his career as a federal government employee at an end, Murphy returned to New Jersey, where he worked from 1970 to 1971 as the state's vice chancellor for higher education. In 1971 he accepted the presidency of Queens College, where his predecessor had been unable to handle student protests against the Vietnam War and the firing of a popular radical instructor. Murphy, by contrast, displayed sympathy for the student and faculty antiwar protestors, refused to bring police to the college, and sometimes brought $100 bills as bail when protestors were arrested at off-campus demonstrations. These actions won him the admiration of much of the Queens College faculty, which stood him in good stead when New York City's mid-1970s fiscal crisis hit the City University of New York (CUNY) campuses.

Despite severe financial constraints, Murphy established a law school, began programs in workers' education, brought greater ethnic diversity (including students and faculty from Ethiopia) to the college, initiated campus day-care facilities, and turned over the previously deficit- and scandal-plagued cafeteria and bookstore to student control. He handled the difficult task of budget cutting by trimming administrative and nonessential teaching positions and services rather than weakening the college's overall educational level. As the fiscal crisis deepened, so did Murphy's radicalism. He came to perceive New York's financial, political, and business elites as undermining CUNY's ability to fulfill its historical role as an educational ladder of upward mobility for the city's poor. After seven years at Queens College, Murphy accepted a very different academic position, the presidency of Bennington College in Vermont.

Murphy arrived on the Bennington campus in 1977, just in time to handle a student protest with his characteristic disarming aplomb. During the six years of his presidency at the affluent, artsy New England college, he devoted himself to raising both academic standards and faculty salaries, and he gained the reputation of caring little about the college's buildings and their maintenance. But he seemed to feel the lack of an opportunity to advance his primary goal as an educator: to provide a first-rate college education for impoverished students. So, when Murphy was offered the position in 1982 as the chancellor of CUNY, managing a vast multicampus institution of more than twenty colleges and a graduate school, he accepted.

During his eight years as the CUNY chancellor, Murphy demonstrated his commitment to academic freedom by consulting the university system's many constituencies and by pursuing controversial policies that he thought right, especially greater access for disadvantaged students. As the chancellor, Murphy also taught at CUNY, first at the graduate school and then at the various CUNY workers' colleges he had set up in the 1970s. He also extended the day-care policies he had established at Queens College to other campuses. His most difficult task was the struggle to fund, retain, and expand educational opportunity despite growing national hostility toward such measures in the 1980s.

Murphy married Margaret Herrick in December 1954, with whom he had three children, but they later divorced. On 18 May 1984 he married Susan Crile.

Approaching age sixty in the early 1990s, Murphy was drawn back to Ethiopia. After his retirement from CUNY in 1990, he lived in Ethiopia for part of each year. He died at age sixty-four from an automobile accident. His ashes were scattered in an Ethiopian tributary of the Blue Nile and in Maryland's and Virginia's Chesapeake Bay, one of the bodies of water in which he loved to sail.

★

Murphy's correspondence, personal papers, speeches, and writings (covering not only the Queens College and CUNY years but also Ethiopia, the Peace Corps, and his post-CUNY career) are at the CUNY Archives, LaGuardia Community College, Long Island City, New York. The CUNY Archives also contain an unfinished manuscript of Murphy's that is a combination memoir and ethnography of Ethiopia. An obituary is in the *New York Times* (21 Jan. 1998).

MARVIN E. GETTLEMAN

MURRAY, James Patrick ("Jim") (*b.* 29 December 1919 in Hartford, Connecticut; *d.* 17 August 1998 in Los Angeles, California), one of the most widely read sports columnists in the United States and winner of a Pulitzer Prize for journalism.

Murray was the only child of James Murray, a businessman, and Molly O'Connell, a homemaker. He grew up in Hartford during the Great Depression and attended parochial schools. As a child, Murray's father took him to baseball games at Yankee Stadium, and he learned math by computing earned run averages, batting averages, and league statistics. While at Trinity College in Hartford, he demonstrated promise as a writer and served as the campus correspondent for the local community newspaper the *Hartford Times*. In 1943 Murray received a B.A. degree in English from Trinity. He married Geraldine Norma Brown on 20 October 1945; they had four children.

Murray began his professional writing career in 1943 as a staff writer for the *New Haven Register*, covering the police beat. His next position was in California, where he served as a general assignment writer and rewrite man for the *Los Angeles Examiner* (1944–1948). In 1948 Murray became the West Coast cinema correspondent for Time, Inc. (1948–1961), and during the 1950s he hobnobbed with some of Hollywood's top stars, including Humphrey Bogart, John Wayne, and Marilyn Monroe. He assisted in founding *Sport Magazine*, which became *Sports Illustrated* in 1961; Murray was its premier writer and served as its West Coast editor from 1959 to 1961. When he gave up the glamour of national exposure in 1961 to bang out a daily sports column for the *Los Angeles Times,* sportswriters thought there might be some merit to what they did for a living.

Murray was a sports columnist for the *Los Angeles Times* for thirty-seven years (1961–1998). He won the Pulitzer Prize for his columns in 1990. Murray penned the following on that occasion: "This is going to make it a little easier on the guy who writes my obit." According to fellow sports-

Jim Murray *(left)* with fellow sportswriter Peter Vecsey, 1996. JACK DEMSEY/ASSOCIATED PRESS AP

writers, Murray used to sit at the Rose Bowl football game and pray somebody would run the wrong way so he would have a story. He had a self-effacing sense of humor. Murray revered the golfer Ben Hogan. At one major tournament, Murray was standing near a sand trap watching Arnold Palmer surveying his buried ball. Palmer looked up and asked, "What would your boy Ben Hogan do down here?" Murray replied, "He wouldn't be down there." Like his rejoinder, his writing was simple and straightforward.

Murray never talked about himself. When he wrote *Jim Murray: An Autobiography*, the publisher rejected the manuscript, telling him, "This is supposed to be about you and you're not in here." He had written about the people he had met in his life and wouldn't change it. The book was published in 1993 as Murray wrote it.

Murray transcended sportswriting, carving out phrases of description artfully and vividly. On the occasion of being inducted into the writers wing of the Baseball Hall of Fame in 1987, he commented, "Somebody had to sit on the curb and watch the parade go by." His response to a television interviewer's request that he describe his job was, "I try not to bore people, basically." In his autobiography, he likened his column to "a raging master. It consumes you. It is insatiable. It becomes more than you. You are not a person; you are a publicly owned facility. Available on demand." The book also included this self-reflection, "I suppose I never grew up. That's all right with me. That's the nice thing about sports. You can be Peter Pan."

Among his other awards, Murray was named as America's best sportswriter by the National Association of Sports-

casters and Sportswriters fourteen times, including twelve years in a row; was a recipient of the Associated Press Sports Editors Association Award for best column writing; won a Red Smith Award for extended meritorious labor in sportswriting; and was the first sportswriter to win the coveted Victor Award. During his career at the *Los Angeles Times,* he wrote about many sports greats, including Arnold Palmer, Mark McGwire, Joe Montana, Don Drysdale, and Wayne Gretzky. He continued writing his twice-weekly columns even after being declared legally blind in 1979.

Murray's first wife died of cancer in 1984. He married his second wife, Linda McCoy, on 3 March 1997. Linda founded the Jim Murray Foundation, a nonprofit organization designed to give scholarships to first-year college journalism students. Murray died of a heart attack at age seventy-eight and is buried in Los Angeles.

Murray was considered by many to be the Babe Ruth of sportswriting. His untouchable wit and an unmatched frankness in his writing distinguished him as one of the century's best sports columnists. He created a distinctive style that always gave the impression he was writing about the ballet from the usher's perspective. Murray was one of only four sportswriters to win the Pulitzer Prize for general commentary.

★

There is no full-scale biography of Murray. *Jim Murray: An Autobiography* (1993) is a compilation of his observations about sports heroes that he encountered in his work as a journalist. Other works are collections of past columns published in the *Los*

Angeles Times and *Sports Illustrated*. These include *The Best of Jim Murray* (1965), *The Sporting World of Jim Murray* (1968), *The Jim Murray Collection* (1988), *Jim Murray: The Last of the Best* (1998), and *Jim Murray: The Great Ones* (1999). Obituaries are in *Sports Illustrated* (24 Aug. 1998) and *Time* (31 Aug. 1998).

REED B. MARKHAM

MURRAY, Kathryn Hazel (*b.* 15 September 1906 in Jersey City, New Jersey; *d.* 6 August 1999 in Honolulu, Hawaii), dance instructor, businesswoman, and host of the popular 1950s television show *The Arthur Murray Party*.

Murray was the only child of Abraham Lincoln Kohnfelder and Lenore Simon, a homemaker and teacher at an orphanage. Murray was a sallow, tiny child, always the smallest in any group, and always the homeliest. Her father, a business manager for the local daily newspaper, the *Hudson Observer*, contributed to her childhood feelings of unhappiness and lack of self-confidence, calling her a "homely little jigger." To become popular, the young girl practiced dancing by herself for hours, gaining the self-confidence and enthusiasm that became her signature trademarks in later years.

Murray graduated from high school at age fifteen, then attended the State Normal School in Newark, New Jersey,

Kathryn Murray with Arthur Murray. AP/WIDE WORLD PHOTOS

from which she earned a teaching certificate in the early 1920s. In 1924 the eighteen-year-old fledgling teacher went to meet a friend at a radio show in Newark where the host, Arthur Murray, gave dance instructions over the air, often inviting members of the audience to help demonstrate the dance steps. He called Murray onstage and later asked her for a date. Three months later, on 24 April 1925, the couple married, by which time Arthur's mail-order dance business, the Arthur Murray Correspondence School of Dancing, was netting more than $35,000 per year.

In 1926 the couple had twin girls. One of their daughters later became the wife of Henry J. Heimlich, the originator of the Heimlich maneuver, a technique for aiding people choking on food. After moving to Mount Vernon, New York, Murray had difficulty settling into the life of a suburban homemaker. She was bored and longed for a romantic, exciting life.

On a September evening in 1930, after drinking a little wine with some dinner guests, Murray went to the bathroom of her third-floor apartment and jumped out the window, breaking her back. She later admitted this had been a suicide attempt caused by severe bouts of depression, which she had kept hidden from her husband. The doctors at first feared she would never dance again, but after a successful fusion of her vertebrae, she recovered in a year's time. The family then lived in several New York and California locations before settling on Park Avenue in Manhattan in 1938.

In 1935 the first Arthur Murray franchised studio opened in Minneapolis. In 1943 the Murrays incorporated, and by then there were franchised studios in forty-seven cities. As a remedy for depression, Murray became the vice president of her husband's dance-studio empire. She wrote the training manuals for teachers in the franchises, as well as tips to instructors on how to keep students coming back for more. While the Great Depression had brought an end to their mail-order business, the franchise business flourished. By 1946 the couple's businesses were grossing $12 million per year, with branch schools in all of the major U.S. cities.

In 1947 severe competition emerged from the Fred Astaire Dance Studios. In response, Arthur bought five, fifteen-minute television segments on CBS in July 1950 and asked Murray to emcee a show where the couple would teach dancing. Americans loved *The Arthur Murray Party* so much that the program was soon expanded into an hour-long series on Sunday nights. It included a dance lesson, an amateur dance contest, celebrity appearances, and performances by the Arthur Murray dance professionals. Due to her elegance, enthusiasm, and self-deprecating humor, Murray became an instant star, the Queen of Ballroom Dancing, whose signature at the close of each show, "To put a little fun in your life, try dancing" became a popular phrase. The show, which ran for eleven years, was a pioneering infomercial and helped to increase the number of Murray dance-studio franchises to 500.

In 1952 the couple sold most of their franchises for $5 million, but stayed on as managers of the chain until the 1960s, when the Federal Trade Commission investigated the company's high-pressure sales tactics and bogus contests and promotions. In 1964 Arthur resigned as the president, and the following year the couple moved to Hawaii, where they lived comfortably off the proceeds from their stock portfolios. They spent most of their time entertaining friends at dinner parties in their penthouse overlooking Waikiki Beach. The Murrays surfaced again in the 1980s as judges on Merv Griffin's disco-era television show *Dance Fever*. Arthur died on 3 March 1991 from pneumonia at age ninety-five. Murray died of natural causes eight years later at age ninety-two. She is buried in Honolulu.

Murray exemplified the class of the ballroom dancer. She exuded confidence, grace, and charm both on the television screen and at home while entertaining friends. She combined the skill of performing with a sharp sense of business acumen, which helped her husband to expand his dance-studio empire. Above all, she made her family the top priority, shielding her twin daughters from unwanted celebrity publicity and displaying public as well as private affection for her husband throughout their sixty-six years of marriage.

★

Murray wrote a biography of her husband with Betty Hannah Hoffman, *My Husband: Arthur Murray* (1960), which is filled with personal anecdotes about the couple, as well as early stories of her own family life, and made personal revelations on the home page of the Arthur Murray Dance Studios, <http://www.arthurmurray.co.za/aboutus/kathrynmurray.asp>. Murray and her husband authored *How to Become a Good Dancer, with Dance Secrets* (1959). She also wrote *Family Laugh Lines* (1966), a collection of anecdotes about celebrity friends. Obituaries are in the *New York Times* (8 Aug. 1999), *Washington Post* (13 Aug. 1999), and *Economist* (14 Aug. 1999).

JOHN J. BYRNE

N

NABRIT, James Madison, Jr. (*b*. 4 September 1900 in Atlanta, Georgia; *d*. 27 December 1997 in Washington, D.C.), noted civil rights lawyer and United Nations diplomat who became the president of Howard University.

Nabrit was the eldest of eight children of the Reverend James Madison Nabrit, Sr., a theological seminary president and prominent Baptist minister, and Augusta Gertrude West, a homemaker. Nabrit's parents were one generation removed from slavery. His father, a Morehouse College graduate, moved the young family around frequently as he took the leadership of various local churches. Nabrit's primary education took place at the segregated Walker Baptist Institute in Augusta, Georgia. His father wanted him to enter the ministry and his mother wanted him to become a dentist, but at age ten, after witnessing an angry white mob lynch and burn an African-American man, Nabrit chose the field of law. Public high schools were not open to African Americans in Georgia, so in 1915 Nabrit moved to Atlanta on his own to attend the private high school academy at Morehouse College. He graduated in 1919.

In the fall, Nabrit enrolled in Morehouse as a college student and was an avid athlete there. He played on the college football team and was a shortstop on the baseball team. He was also an undefeated debater on the Morehouse debate team and joined the Omega Psi Phi fraternity. To pay for his education Nabrit worked in a steel mill in Pitts-

burgh and a hotel in Brooklyn, New York. While in college, he was arrested for exiting from the front (whites-only) section of an Atlanta streetcar.

Nabrit graduated with honors from Morehouse College with an A.B. degree in 1923 and then entered Northwestern University Law School in Chicago. Nabrit found Northwestern to be a racially hostile environment, and he was often ignored by professors and heckled by white students. Nabrit persevered, however, and became the editor of the university's *Law Review* and was elected to the Order of the Coif. To pay his way through law school he labored as a red cap at the Chicago train station. He also took a year off from 1925 to 1926 to teach English and to coach a college football team at Leland University, a small African-American college in Baker, Louisiana. On 30 December 1924 Nabrit and his high school sweetheart, Norma Clarke Walton, eloped in Aiken, South Carolina. He returned to Chicago in 1926 and graduated first in his law school class with a J.D. in 1927.

After graduation from Northwestern Law School, Nabrit found it difficult, because of his race, to enter the field of law, so in 1928 he returned to Leland as an instructor. He eventually moved to Pine Bluff, Arkansas, where he became the dean of the Arkansas State College for Negroes. In 1930 Nabrit moved to Houston and opened a law office with two other African-American attorneys, specializing in property rights, criminal, and early civil rights cases. In 1932 Nabrit and his wife had their only child, James Madison Nabrit III, who became a civil rights attorney like his father.

In 1936 Nabrit joined the law faculty of Howard University in Washington, D.C., during the presidency of Mordecai W. Johnson, the first African American to lead the institution. Nabrit played a significant role in litigating many of the major civil rights cases affecting African Americans in the United States. He argued several notable cases before the U.S. Supreme Court, including *Lane* v. *Wilson* (1939), an Oklahoma voter-registration procedures case; *Terry* v. *Adams* (1953), a voting-rights case in Texas; and *Bolling* v. *Sharpe* (1954), which argued against segregation in the District of Columbia's public schools.

In 1938 Nabrit designed and taught the first course in civil rights at a U.S. law school. Nabrit and other Howard Law School faculty members worked closely with the Legal Defense and Educational Fund of the National Association for the Advancement of Colored People (NAACP) in successfully ending legal racial segregation in the United States. Many of the legal theories used in the landmark civil rights cases before the U.S. Supreme Court were developed by Nabrit and his law students at Howard.

From 1958 to 1960 Nabrit served as the dean of Howard Law School. He also served concurrently as the secretary of the board of trustees of the university and as the director of public relations until 1960, when he was appointed as the president of Howard University, only the second African American to head Howard since its founding in 1867. Turbulent student protests marked his presidency (1960–1965, 1968–1969). Under his administration the number of foreign students increased, and the College of Fine Arts (1961) and the College of Nursing (1968) were established. Nabrit took a leave of absence from Howard from 1965 to 1967 to serve as the U.S. Permanent Deputy Representative to the United Nations (UN), where he helped to shape U.S. relations with developing nations. He retired from the presidency of Howard in 1969. Nabrit was appointed to numerous federal presidential commissions and corporate and regulatory boards throughout his career, including the International Labor Organization, the board of directors of the NAACP Legal Defense and Education Fund, and First National Bank of Washington, D.C.

Nabrit died from aspiration pneumonia after years of declining health. He is buried at the Lincoln Memorial Cemetery in Prince George's County, Maryland. His legal premise that racial segregation itself was unconstitutional was ground breaking in U.S. law. He argued that the rights of citizenship could not be limited by racial statutes. Nabrit's contributions as a civil rights lawyer, professor, UN diplomat, and university president significantly impacted the legal and social fabric of the United States in the second half of the twentieth century.

*

Nabrit's papers and official records are located at the Moorland-Spingarn Research Center at Howard University, Washington, D.C. His life story and critical legal work can be found in Richard Kluger, *Simple Justice: The History of Brown v. Board of Education and Black America's Struggle for Equality* (1976). J. Reuben Sheeler, "The Nabrit Family," *Negro History Bulletin* (Oct. 1956), has an exhaustive chronicling of his distinguished family. For a complete transcript of Nabrit's oral arguments before the U.S. Supreme Court, see *Argument: The Oral Argument Before the Supreme Court in Brown v. Board of Education of Topeka, Kansas* (1969). See also Michael R. Winston, "Building the Legacy," *The Jurist–Howard Law School News Journal* (1994). An obituary is in the *Baltimore Morning Sun* (29 Dec. 1997).

F. ROMALL SMALLS

NATHANS, Daniel   (*b.* 30 October 1928 in Wilmington, Delaware; *d.* 16 November 1999 in Baltimore, Maryland), pioneer in the use of restriction enzymes in the fields of virology and genetics, Nobel laureate, and the father of modern biotechnology.

Nathans was the youngest of nine children of Samuel Nathans, a small business owner, and Sarah Levitan, who were Russian Jewish immigrants. He was educated in the public schools of Wilmington and received a B.S. degree

Daniel Nathans. CORBIS CORPORATION (BELLEVUE)

in chemistry in 1950 (summa cum laude) from the University of Delaware and an M.D. from Washington University in St. Louis in 1954. Nathans then did a one-year medical internship at Columbia-Presbyterian Medical Center in New York City, followed by two years as clinical associate at the National Cancer Institute in Bethesda, Maryland (1955–1957). During his stay at the National Cancer Institute, he cared for patients and carried out research on the synthesis of immunoglobulin (a kind of protein) by myeloma tumors. On 4 March 1952 he married Joanne Gomberg; they had three children.

Returning to Columbia-Presbyterian Medical Center for two more years as medical resident, Nathans realized that his calling lay in medical research, not patient care. In 1959 he began basic research under the auspices of a U.S. Public Health Service grant at Rockefeller University in New York City, where he started studying the mechanism of protein synthesis in myeloma cells and then concentrated his efforts on the *Escherichia coli* bacterium. His first major research contribution was the development of a bacterial cell-free system that supported protein synthesis. Nathans then showed that the RNA of the virus could support the synthesis of a viral coat protein in a cell-free system. This was the first example of a purified messenger RNA that directed the synthesis of a specific protein. His discovery led to a number of fundamental insights into the mechanism of protein synthesis and was an example of the rigor and clarity that characterized his work.

Recruited in 1962 by the Johns Hopkins University, Nathans continued his work on bacteriophage and protein synthesis and carried out important studies on the regulation of bacteriophage "translation" by the viral coat protein, that is, the way in which the genetic code carried by messenger RNA directs the synthesis of proteins. He worked for thirty-seven years at Johns Hopkins, first as professor in the department of microbiology (1962–1972), then as chair of the department of microbiology and genetics (1972), and then as director of the department of molecular biology (1972–1982). He was named university professor of molecular biology and genetics at the School of Medicine in 1982 and served in that capacity until his death. In the late 1960s Nathans saw parallels between bacteriophages and viruses and realized that the study of simple animal viruses would provide important insights into carcinogenesis and the biology of animal cells. During that period of time, he decided to redirect his research efforts to the analysis of animal viruses, specifically SV40, a virus capable of inducing cancer in monkeys and rats.

During the next decade Nathans's work provided the tools that allowed detailed molecular genetic analysis of mammalian viruses and cells. In 1969 he took a sabbatical at the Weizmann Institute of Science in Rehovot, Israel. While he was there, he received information from Hamil-

ton Smith, a colleague at Johns Hopkins, about an enzyme that cut, or cleaved, DNA at specific nucleotide segments, or sequences. Nathans thought that it was possible to use these so-called restriction enzymes to dissect the genome of a small virus—all of its genetic material—and learn something about its mechanism of action and replication. He continued his work on the tumor-causing SV40 virus and by 1971 was able to show that it could be cleaved into eleven separate and specific segments. His results were published that year in the *Proceedings of the National Academy of Sciences* in a paper that ushered in the modem era of genetics. In 1972 he was able to determine the order of the segments in relation to one another and constructed the first cleavage map of a viral genome.

In the following years Nathans devised a series of approaches to exploit the specific cleavage of DNA by restriction enzymes to dissect the genome of SV40. He and his research group developed more sophisticated methods of site-directed deletion, leading to the precise localization of the DNA replication origin, and followed the genetic changes that occurred during virus evolution. In 1978 he received the Nobel Prize for physiology or medicine with Hamilton Smith and Werner Arber, who had theorized the existence of restriction enzymes. The award recognized the role their work played in the birth of modern genetics and the genetic revolution under way today. Upon being awarded the Nobel Prize, Nathans published the article "Restriction Endonucleases, Simian Virus 40, and the New Genetics" in *Science* (1978), which is a valuable source of information on his work.

Nathans took the position of senior investigator of the Howard Hughes Medical Institute in 1982. He also served for one year (June 1995 to August 1996) as interim president of the Johns Hopkins University. During his tenure he led the university through a challenging time that saw the successful redefinition of the relationship between the School of Medicine and Johns Hopkins Hospital. The later part of his life was dedicated to studies of the cellular response to growth signals. Nathans isolated and characterized some of the first cellular genes whose expression is regulated by growth factor treatment. During his lifetime Nathans received numerous honorary degrees as well as the National Medal of Science in 1993. He was a member of the National Academy of Sciences, the American Philosophical Society, and the Presidential Council of Advisors on Science and Technology. Nathans died of leukemia at his home in Baltimore.

Nathans and his research group pioneered the use of restriction enzymes to analyze DNA and changed the way we view viruses and genes. His application of restriction enzymes to separate DNA into its component parts has resulted in such breakthroughs as synthetic insulin and growth hormone and has permitted the mapping of the human genome. It also has helped in the understanding, prevention, and treatment of birth defects, hereditary diseases, and cancer. The use of restriction enzymes to assemble genes in new combinations has given rise to the entire field of genetic engineering.

★

Brief biographical entries on Nathans are in *Who's Who,* vol. 142 (1990) and *American Men and Women of Science,* 20th ed. (1998). An obituary is in the *New York Times* (18 Nov. 1999).

MARÍA PACHECO

NEWHOUSER, Harold ("Prince Hal") (*b.* 20 May 1921 in Detroit, Michigan; *d.* 10 November 1998 in Southfield, Michigan), baseball's most dominant pitcher during World War II who was the only pitcher to win consecutive Most Valuable Player awards (1944 and 1945).

Newhouser was the son of Theodore Newhouser, a wood patternmaker for the automobile industry and part-time gymnasium instructor, and Emily Macha, a homemaker. Both Newhouser and his older brother Richard, who later played minor league baseball, developed a love for sports at an early age, playing baseball as youngsters and developing strong, wiry physiques through exercise at the German *turnverein* where their Austrian-born father was oc-

Hal Newhouser sizing up a batter, 1940. ASSOCIATED PRESS AP

casionally employed. Newhouser's remarkable ability gained attention in a Detroit Baseball Federation competition when he was fifteen. In 1937 and 1938 he compiled a formidable record as a pitcher for the Roose-Vanker American Legion team in Detroit, with winning streaks of fifteen and nineteen games, five no-hitters, and sixty-five consecutive scoreless innings pitched. A part-time scout for the Detroit Tigers brought Newhouser's impressive record to the attention of Aloysius J. "Wish" Egan, the team's leading scout. Egan observed Newhouser carefully, befriending him and meeting his parents. Partly through Egan's intercession, and due to a difference of opinion with the baseball coach at Wilbur Wright Trade School (from which Newhouser graduated in 1940), Newhouser abstained from high school baseball to compete in the American Legion Baseball League, the country's first national amateur youth baseball organization. After his final American Legion game in August 1938, Newhouser signed a contract to play in the Detroit organization for $500 plus $150 a month, a decision influenced by his family's modest means. Moments after he signed with Detroit, representatives from the Cleveland Indians offered Newhouser a $15,000 bonus and a new car for his father, a deal he was forced to reject.

Newhouser spent the 1939 season with Alexandria (Evangeline League) and Beaumont (Texas League) and was called up by Detroit in September, pitching in one game. Although widely considered one of the most promising young pitchers in baseball, his first four years with the Tigers were mediocre at best. From 1940 through 1943 he won thirty-four games and lost fifty-one. A fiery competitor who, by his own admission, was "born stubborn," Newhouser developed a reputation as an immature young man, unable to control his pitches, his temper, or his displeasure when teammates erred behind him. He was a loner without close friends whose unpleasant, irritable behavior extended off the field and into the clubhouse. Described by sportswriter Red Smith as "impatient" and "bitterly ambitious," Newhouser received no pitching instruction from Detroit management during this time, their thinking being that he needed to resolve problems by his own efforts.

On 20 December 1941 Newhouser married Berle Margaret Steele, with whom he had two daughters. Newhouser would later cite his marriage and the birth of his first child as the stabilizing factors that helped transform him from a troubled but talented malcontent to a winning, polished, professional pitcher. Fellow player Paul Richards and Detroit Tiger's manager Steve O'Neill also assisted in Newhouser's metamorphosis. A veteran catcher and minor league manager, Richards joined the Tigers in 1943 and worked with Newhouser during spring training in 1944, helping him to make technical adjustments in his delivery, perfect his change-up and slider, and improve control of his pitches. Richards also advised Newhouser to control his emotions, to treat his teammates with respect, and to praise them for their efforts on the field. Newhouser had requested a trade during the winter of 1943–1944 after hearing rumors that he would be sent to Cleveland. He relented after an off-season conversation with Detroit manager O'Neill, who promised to pitch him every fourth day in 1944.

In 1944 Newhouser finally achieved greatness, compiling a record of 29–9 for the second-place Tigers, leading the American League in wins and strikeouts, and combining with teammate Paul "Dizzy" Trout for fifty-six of the team's eighty-eight victories. The following year, Newhouser had a 25–9 mark, leading the league in wins, winning percentage (.735), earned run average (1.81), innings pitched (313.1), strikeouts (212), shutouts (8), games started (36) and complete games (29). He started three games in the 1945 World Series, winning games five and seven and setting a record (since broken) for the most strikeouts in a seven-game World Series. He received the Most Valuable Player award in 1944 and 1945, the only pitcher ever to win the award in consecutive years.

The absence of many of baseball's best players during World War II prevented Newhouser from receiving due recognition for his achievements in 1944–1945. During the war, he had volunteered for duty in the U.S. Army Air Corps, but was declared 4F due to a heart ailment. In 1946 he continued to pitch at the highest level, winning twenty-six games with a league best 1.94 earned run average. In December 1946 Newhouser created Hal's Pals, a nonprofit organization that sponsored youth clubs, emphasizing sportsmanship, tolerance, community service, and charitable work.

Shoulder, back, and arm problems would hinder Newhouser's effectiveness for the remainder of his career, but he won seventy-one games from 1947 through 1950, and his 170 wins led all major league pitchers in the 1940s. During the winter of 1947–1948, Newhouser spent seven hours per day for three months writing *Pitching to Win*, a book on the technical aspects of pitching that was published the following summer.

After several years of physical problems and declining results, Newhouser was released by Detroit in July 1953. Signed by Cleveland the following spring, he won seven games for the pennant-winning Indians. His pitching career ended the following May. In seventeen major league seasons, Newhouser had 207 wins and 150 losses, thirty-three shutouts, and an earned run average of 3.06. He was named to six All-Star teams.

A left-handed pitcher at six feet, two inches tall and 190 pounds, Newhouser had an easy, fluid pitching motion; he was once described by Ted Williams as "a beautiful pitcher" with an "effortless style." He had an excellent fastball, a curveball he threw at three different speeds, and a deceptive change-up delivered off the same motion as his other pitches.

After his playing career ended, Newhouser scouted for the Baltimore Orioles and Cleveland Indians from 1955 to 1964. In October 1964 he accepted a position as customer service representative for the Community National Bank in Pontiac, Michigan. After twenty years, he retired as a bank vice president, having been involved in business development, public relations, and community affairs. Newhouser then became the Detroit-area scout for the Houston Astros from 1985 to 1993.

In 1992, after waiting thirty-one years, Newhouser was finally elected to the Baseball Hall of Fame. He died of emphysema and heart disease at age seventy-seven after a long illness and is buried at Oakland Hills Memorial Gardens in Novi, Michigan. He was survived by his wife, brother, two daughters, and a grandson.

A proud, emotional, and serious man who avoided publicity, Newhouser labored under the dual handicaps of achieving his greatest success during a period often maligned by baseball writers for the questionable caliber of major league competition, and for his reputation (established early in his career) as a surly hothead, one of the most disliked players in the game. Others saw in Newhouser a perfectionist with enormous capacity for work and self-improvement, a thoroughly focused, superbly conditioned athlete who studied films of his pitching motion to detect possible flaws, and one of the finest pitchers of his time. Newhouser was also a principled family man who, without fanfare, devoted much time and energy to working with youngsters and achieved success in a career outside the game of baseball.

★

David M. Jordan, *A Tiger in His Time: Hal Newhouser and the Burden of Wartime Ball* (1990) is a workmanlike account of Newhouser's life and baseball career in which the author promotes Newhouser's candidacy for the Hall of Fame. The following books also contain useful material: William Mead, *Even the Browns: The Zany, True Story of Baseball in the Early Forties* (1978); Frederick Turner, *When the Boys Came Back: Baseball and 1946* (1996); William Marshall, *Baseball's Pivotal Era: 1945–1951* (1999). Short but informative biographical sketches can be found in Tom Meany, *Baseball's Greatest Pitchers* (1951), Robert E. Shoemaker, *The Best in Baseball* (1954), and David L. Porter, ed., *The Biographical Dictionary of American Sports: Baseball* (2000). Newhouser's career record is found in *Total Baseball: The Official Encyclopedia of Major League Baseball*, 7th ed. (2001). Throughout his career, Newhouser was the subject of extensive magazine coverage. The most balanced and insightful piece is Milton Gross, "The Truth About Newhouser," *Sport* 5 (Aug. 1948). Also useful are Red Smith, "Doghouse to Let: Apply Newhouser and Trout," *Saturday Evening Post* (31 Mar. 1945); Kyle Crichton, "The Newhouser Nuisance," *Collier's* (19 July 1947); Larry Amman, "Newhouser and Trout in 1944: 56 Wins and a Near Miss," *Baseball Research Journal* 12 (1983); Paul Gaba, "Hal Newhouser Still Waiting for Hall of Fame Call," *Baseball Digest* 49 (June 1990); and Russell Schneider, "Hal Newhouser Looks Back on His Hall of Fame Career," *Baseball Digest* 54 (June 1995). An obituary is in the *New York Times* (11 Nov. 1998).

EDWARD J. TASSINARI

NITSCHKE, Ray(mond) Ernest (*b.* 26 December 1936 in Elmwood Park, Illinois; *d.* 8 March 1998 in Venice, Florida), football player who defined the marquee position of middle linebacker and was the defensive anchor and signal caller for the Vince Lombardi–coached Green Bay Packer dynasty in the 1960s.

Born of German-Danish parentage at the height of the Great Depression, in Elmwood Park, a working-class suburb of Chicago, Nitschke overcame incredible personal adversity as a youth. His father, Robert, who was a transit worker for Chicago's Surface Lines, was killed in a trolley wreck in 1939, and ten years later his mother, Anna Petersen, died from a blood clot (mentioned in some sources as

Ray Nitschke, 1963. ASSOCIATED PRESS AP

a heart attack). The thirteen-year-old orphan was raised by his two elder brothers and seethed at the cards life had dealt him. The attitude that emerged is discussed in his thoughtful autobiography *Mean on Sunday*: "Without a father I got much less discipline . . . now that my mother was dead . . . I had to let that anger find an outlet so I took it out on the other kids." The young bully found football to be a suitable avenue to vent his hostility: "What I like about this game is the contact, the man to man . . . the getting it out of your system." He would develop a reputation as one of the hardest hitters and most dominant defenders in the history of the game.

Under the tutelage of Coach Andy Pulpis (former All-America quarterback at Notre Dame) at Proviso East High School in Maywood, Illinois, quarterback Nitschke excelled on the gridiron. A multisport star in high school (he turned down a signing bonus to pitch for the St. Louis Browns), he accepted a football scholarship from the University of Illinois at Urbana-Champaign, where his speed and his six-foot, three-inch, 235-pound physique attracted professional recruiters. As a two-way starter, switched to fullback and linebacker by coach Ray Eliot, Nitschke performed with distinction for the Fighting Illini in the competitive Big Ten (1953–1957). At Urbana-Champaign, where he majored in physical education, he earned a reputation as a hellion: after a few drinks he would erupt into violent rages, wrecking furniture in bars and brawling with the patrons.

In 1958 Nitschke was drafted by the previously hapless Green Bay Packers in the third round (he was thirty-sixth overall) along with two key building blocks for the future Packer dynasty, fullback Jim Taylor and lineman Jerry Kramer. In 1959, after suffering through a dismal 1–11–1 rookie season, the Wisconsin-based Packers brought in strict disciplinarian Vince Lombardi as head coach. During his first year under Lombardi, Nitschke came close to being cut for violating team rules regarding drinking in hotel bars, and in 1960 an accident almost killed him. Longtime teammate Ken Bowman remembered that "Lombardi used to have this big tower that he'd climb up and watch practice from . . . one day the wind came up, the damn thing toppling and it came over and hit Ray right on top of the helmet . . . driving one of the bolts right through the plastic [and] knocking him to the ground." After Nitschke was flattened by the one-ton structure, Lombardi shouted, "Who got hit?" "Nitschke," the quarterback Bart Starr said. The new head coach was relieved, "Oh him, he'll be all right. Everybody else back to practice." The steel piping created a half-inch hole in Nitschke's helmet and barely missed his skull. Nitschke walked away dazed but unhurt.

The young linebacker was rarely allowed to play during the second season. However, Lombardi understood that if he could assist Nitschke in harnessing and redirecting his rage he would have a great player. According to Nitschke, the coach's constant needling helped "turn me around as a person . . . the guy never let up . . . he wanted me to be not only a good player, but a good guy. I needed that. Before I got married I was kind of runnin' them streets." Nitschke finally stopped drinking and in 1962 married Jean Forschette. They would adopt two sons and a daughter.

During the next few seasons, Nitschke began to channel his aggression. Star running back Paul Hornung recalled that Nitschke "hits harder than anyone I've seen. He likes it. He loves to hit." The 1962 Packers, still considered one of the all-time dominant National Football League (NFL) clubs, led the league with a 13–1 record, outscoring opponents 415–148. The season's highlight was defeating the formidable New York Giants 16–7 in the championship game. Nitschke anchored a smothering defense; he intercepted the ball near the Packer end zone and recovered two fumbles. He was named the Most Valuable Player in the contest, and the Packers won a second consecutive NFL title.

Nitschke made an appearance on the popular television show *What's My Line?* in 1983. His bald head and horn-rimmed glasses gave him a professorial demeanor. Only Bennett Cerf (the noted publishing executive), who had been a spectator at Yankee Stadium for the previous season's finale, recognized Nitschke. However, Humorist George Plimpton, in a *New York Times* profile, described the fear Nitschke instilled in his opponents on the football field. He wrote that Nitschke "had huge shoulders and oddly slim legs that moved him across the field in a crab-like scuttle. In training camp he developed a cut where the front rim of his helmet jammed down on his nose. It stayed there throughout the season—so opposing QBs looked across the line at a face caked with blood and dirt, lime from the yard lines . . . an unpleasant reminder that they could look the same if their blocking broke down and Nitschke got to them."

In football defenses, the middle linebacker position was crucial. Linebackers such as Dick Butkus, Joe Schmidt, Sam Huff, and Tommy Nobis displayed a take-no-prisoners attitude. But it was not simply brawn or attitude that allowed Nitschke to dominate the center of the field. He was known to watch as much film as quarterback Bart Starr, and his leadership on the field reflected intelligence and study. Longtime Packer trainer Dominic Gentile recalled that Nitschke drove "Lombardi crazy . . . because he was able to call out all the offensive plays before the snap, running around screaming 'Watch the pass! Watch out for the draw.' " Nitschke's determination to excel is best demonstrated by his unyielding attitude regarding ballcarriers. "I don't intend that he'll make an inch, let alone a touchdown . . . I want him to remember Ray Nitschke, even in his dreams." In Superbowl II Nitschke was voted the game's Most Valuable Player (MVP).

During Nitschke's celebrated fifteen-year career (1958–1972), the Packers boasted a 7–1 record in championship games, winning five NFL titles and the first two Superbowls (15 January 1967 and 14 January 1968, respectively); Nitschke's intimidating defense allowed only a 13-point average in those games, and he was the leading tackler. Selected All-Pro three times (1964–1966), he played 190 NFL games, and displayed outstanding pass coverage skills (with twenty-five career interceptions) and catlike quickness (with twenty career fumble recoveries). Longtime coach, television analyst, and former Chicago Bear tight end Mike Ditka opined, "He'd lay the wood on me all the time. No one hit harder, not even close."

Nitschke was inducted into the Canton, Ohio, Football Hall of Fame in 1978, the first defensive player in what has become known as the Lombardi wing of the Hall; eventually eleven teammates from the Packer's dynasty were enshrined. Nitschke's legendary number sixty-six jersey was retired by the Packers, and he was twice voted on to all-time NFL teams (the fiftieth and seventy-fifth anniversary squads).

After Nitschke hung up his cleats in 1972, he continued to make his home in Green Bay, Wisconsin. He chaired the local cerebral palsy telethon for twenty-two years, hosted charity golf tournaments, worked with recovering alcoholics, wrote and published the *Ray Nitschke Packer Report,* and remained a presence around the Packers camp. Sportswriter Dave Anderson wrote, "If he saw strangers approaching him he would introduce himself first. 'Hey man,' he would say in his gravelly voice. 'Ray Nitschke, man.' He never big-timed anybody. His home number was in the Green Bay phone book." His gruff exterior and soft heart proved an irresistible combination for Madison Avenue. He made a second career as a celebrity pitchman, doing "I want my Maypo" and a series of Miller Lite television commercials. He hawked Oldsmobiles alongside fellow Chicagoan Dick Butkus and made forays into Hollywood.

In *Head* (1968), a movie starring the pop band the Monkees and written and produced by Jack Nicholson, Nitschke assumed the farcical role of Private One, chanting in unison with Private Peter Tork (one of the Monkee characters) "we're number one" in a foxhole. In the critically acclaimed dark comedy *The Longest Yard* (1974), his tough-guy looks and scowl were immortalized on screen when he played the sadistic prison guard Bogdanski, whose team battles Burt Reynolds's inmate squad.

A champion lobby sitter in his retirement, Nitschke loved to revel in the Packer glory years and regale listeners with his football tales. His wife died of cancer in 1996, and two years later, while wintering in Florida, Nitschke suffered a fatal heart attack. His death and burial in Green Bay brought an enormous outpouring of grief. Thousands of fans attended his funeral along with legions of NFL alumni.

★

Nitschke's autobiography *Mean on Sunday* (1973, with Robert Wells), is alternately hard-hitting and sensitive. For an in-depth account of the Packer's heyday and an especially insightful look at the Lombardi-Nitschke relationship, see David Maraniss, *When Pride Still Mattered: A Life of Vince Lombardi* (1999). A football classic is fellow Packer great Jerry Kramer, *Instant Replay: The Green Bay Diary of Jerry Kramer* (1968), which is full of inside-the-locker-room detail. For a short profile of Nitschke, see Dennis Harrington, *The Pro-Football Hall of Fame: Players, Coaches, Team Owner and Game Officials 1963–1991* (1991). Obituaries are in the *Chicago Tribune* and *New York Times* (both 9 Mar. 1998) and again in the *New York Times* (15 Mar. 1998).

JEFFREY S. ROSEN

NORVO, Joseph Kenneth ("Red") (*b.* 31 March 1908 in Beardstown, Illinois; *d.* 6 April 1999 in Santa Monica, California), jazz xylophonist, vibraphonist, and bandleader.

Born Joseph Kenneth Norville, Jr., and nicknamed Red for his orange-reddish hair, Norvo was the youngest of four children born to piano-playing railroad dispatcher Joseph Norville, Sr., and trumpet-player-turned-homemaker Estelle Smith. A childhood infection weakened Norvo's hearing in one ear, but he did not require treatment and hearing aids until the mid-1960s. He took a few abortive piano lessons at age six and heard jazz bands on Illinois River excursion boats near his home. But he was not attracted to music until 1921 when the family moved to Rolla, Missouri, where he heard and befriended a marimba player at a local theater. With money earned from a summer job and the sale of his pony, Norvo purchased a xylophone and quickly taught himself to play it.

Following high school graduation in 1925, Norvo, playing the marimba, joined an all-mallet combo, the Collegians, who played on the Chautauqua circuit. Norvo then dropped out of the University of Illinois after only two months to play a vaudeville tour of the Pacific Northwest. Both the marimba and the higher-pitched xylophone were immensely popular in vaudeville acts, but Norvo was taken with the jazz recordings of Bix Beiderbecke and Frank Trumbauer. On the tour he taught himself to read music and began to play using jazz rhythms and improvisations. In 1926 Norvo was booked into Chicago as a solo vaudeville act which included a tap-dance routine. Bandleader-emcee Paul Ash consistently mispronounced his name, introducing him one night as "Norvo," a mistake that *Variety* magazine printed and Norvo decided to keep.

Red Norvo, 1947. WILLIAM L. GOTTLIEB/WILLIAM L. GOTTLIEB COLLECTION/PRINTS AND PHOTOGRAPHS DIVISION, LIBRARY OF CONGRESS

Norvo injected his gentle, optimistic disposition into his music. "Jazz should be fun," he said. He projected these moods through his facial expressions as he played. His booker also taught him another important principle of vaudeville entertainment that became a Norvo trademark: when performing always look at the audience and not at the mallets ("people listen with their eyes"). Norvo's greatest accomplishment, however, was melding the quiet mallet instruments into the boisterous medium of jazz. He pioneered a unique, understated, and exquisitely tasteful fluid style in innovative solos and in concert with fellow band members.

In 1928 Norvo invented slap hammers—hide-covered mallets that produced a muffled sound on the rosewood bars. Norvo taught himself to play the piano as well, accompanying singers and playing as part of a dance band he led with Charlie Barnet in the mid-1930s. In the mid-1940s he traded the wooden xylophone for the vibraharp, also known as the vibraphone or vibes, an electronic instrument that has aluminum bars and a lower range than the marimba. He had first played one in 1928.

Norvo led his first dance band in Milwaukee, Wisconsin, in 1929, then enrolled briefly at the University of Detroit that fall, playing nightly for dancers until orchestra leader Isham Jones bought the entire band from him. He then became a staff musician at a Minneapolis radio station and led another dance band by night, introducing jazz numbers like his brilliant interpretation of Beiderbecke's "In a Mist." Norvo was equally adept as composer, leader, and soloist. By 1930 his advanced harmonic and melodic ideas had earned him two orchestra jobs in Chicago on alternate days. He worked with Victor Young on NBC radio and with Ben Bernie at Hotel Sherman's College Inn, where bandleader Paul Whiteman, the self-styled "King of Jazz," heard him play. Whiteman hired Norvo to play all three mallet instruments with Whiteman's spin-off orchestras and lead a band that accompanied Whiteman's popular singer Mildred Bailey. Norvo and Bailey were married in May 1931 and toured with the Whiteman orchestra for a year.

Freelancing in New York City, Norvo made a series of small band jazz recordings from 1933 to 1935 that were revolutionary for their instrumentation, style, and subtle swing. The group's arranger, Eddie Sauter, who was strongly influenced by Norvo's ideas, further enhanced the music. With Norvo playing a marimba-xylophone using four mallets (two in each hand) and Benny Goodman on bass clarinet, Norvo recorded "In a Mist" along with his own very advanced but nonjazz "Dance of the Octopus." Norvo's music was not the only thing that was revolutionary. His band was a racially integrated combo that included white trumpeter Bunny Berigan, white clarinetist Artie Shaw, black pianist Teddy Wilson, and black saxophonist Leon "Chu" Berry. The group demonstrated Norvo's masterful touch with "Blues in E-Flat."

Using Sauter's arrangements, Norvo formed a sensational sextet at New York City's Famous Door on Fifty-second Street ("Swing Street") in the fall of 1935. Although lacking the customary drums and piano, the combo played a uniquely sensitive and blended, yet exciting, style that came to be known as "chamber jazz." Norvo continued to record with small pickup groups, notably the eloquent blues tune "Just a Mood" with Wilson and trumpeter Harry James in 1937.

Bowing to public preference for a bigger sound, Norvo doubled his sextet into a full swing orchestra in 1936 for an engagement at New York City's Commodore Hotel. Despite the band's bigger size, the music still had the same subtle style and effect, as reflected in the classic Sauter arrangement of "Remember," which contains a lyrical xylophone solo by Norvo. Joined by Bailey during a long stay at Chicago's Blackhawk Restaurant in early 1937, the couple was featured so much in public, radio, and recordings that they came to be known as "Mr. and Mrs. Swing." Sauter and the Norvos combined their talents on such

numbers as "A Porter's Love Song to a Chambermaid," but Bailey's volatile personality created such tensions that Norvo was forced to disband the group in 1939. The Norvos divorced in 1943, but continued to record together until Bailey's death in 1951.

Success eluded Norvo in his three subsequent big bands, prompting him to gather a superb septet of then-unknowns, average age nineteen, among them trumpeter Shorty Rogers and trombonist Eddie Bert, that dazzled Fifty-second Street. In spite of a union recording ban, their 1945 concert at New York City's Town Hall was preserved and released as *The Commodore Years* in 1948.

Given the hard-swinging jazz of the World War II years, Norvo switched permanently to vibes in 1943, the year before he joined the Benny Goodman sextet (1944 to 1945). The group performed in *The Seven Lively Arts* Broadway revue and made several recordings, including "Gotta Be This or That" with the full band. Alert to the bebop trend in jazz during these years, Norvo also organized epic recordings of swing players with Dizzy Gillespie and Charlie Parker (1944).

At the end of 1945 Woody Herman hired Norvo as associate leader of his First Herd orchestra and as leader-organizer of its Woodchoppers combo, performing classically influenced Norvo-Rogers arrangements. Norvo married Shorty Roger's sister Eve in 1946; the couple had a son and daughter. A late 1947 recording session using xylophone with woodwinds demonstrated Norvo's diversity, which culminated in another influential jazz combo, the Red Norvo Trio (1949–1956), a cohesive unit that combined the old gentility with swinging creativity, especially when Tal Farlow was on guitar and Charlie Mingus on string bass (1950–1951).

Norvo continued to be active through the 1950s under the auspices of Frank Sinatra, who featured him in trios or quartets, on a tour to Australia, and in recordings. Norvo also appeared in "Kings Go Forth," a 1958 film starring Sinatra for which Norvo wrote the music. (During his life Norvo made several movies, either playing himself or appearing in uncredited roles.) Benny Goodman included Norvo in a European tour in 1959 and several television shows from 1961 to 1985. In those years Norvo made several albums and played jazz concerts and clubs in southern California until a stroke ended his career in 1986. He died in Santa Monica at age ninety-one.

Norvo was a true original—one of the major jazz figures of the twentieth century who not only redefined the xylophone and vibraphone as solo instruments but also transformed American music.

★

The only biography on Norvo is the booklet by Don De-Micheal [*sic*] that accompanies the boxed *Time-Life* "Giants of

Jazz" LP set *Red Norvo* (STL-J14; 1980). Major discussions are in Richard M. Sudhalter, *Lost Chords: White Musicians and Their Contribution to Jazz 1915–1945* (1999); Gunther Schuller, *The Swing Era* (1989); and George T. Simon, *The Big Bands* (1967). An important LP is *The Commodore Years: Town Hall Jazz Concert 1945* (Atlantic SD 2–310). The 1944 sessions with Dizzy Gillespie and Charlie Parker are on the CD *Charlie Parker: The Street Beat* (Definitive DRCD 11107). An obituary is in the *New York Times* (8 Apr. 1999).

CLARK G. REYNOLDS

NOTORIOUS B.I.G. ("Biggie Smalls")   (*b.* 21 May 1972 in Brooklyn, New York; *d.* 9 March 1997 in Los Angeles, California), rap emcee and producer best known for his multiplatinum albums *Ready to Die* (1994) and *Life After Death* (1997).

Notorious B.I.G. was born Christopher George Latore Wallace, the only child of Voletta Wallace, a preschool teacher, and George Latore, a businessman and politician. His parents, both immigrants from Jamaica, divorced before their son turned two. He had virtually no contact with his father after the divorce and was raised solely by his mother. Growing up in the tough Bedford-Stuyvesant neighborhood of Brooklyn, Wallace attended local Catholic elementary and middle schools (St. Peter's Claver and Queen of All Saints, respectively) and Brooklyn's Boys and Girls High School. Although a promising student in his early years, Wallace dropped out of high school in 1989 during his junior year.

By this time Wallace had become a small-time, neighborhood drug dealer, and his involvement in selling drugs grew once he left school. Later he admitted, "I can't say I'm proud of dealing drugs. My mom sure didn't like it when she found out, but you do what you can to survive in the 'hood. Live in the real bad part of the 'hood for a while and you'll see how desperate it can make you." Hustling drugs led to run-ins with the law. He was arrested in 1989 for possession of a gun, a year later for violating his parole, and in 1991 for selling cocaine while visiting friends in North Carolina.

Wallace, however, was involved in far more than dealing drugs. His passion was writing, reciting, and recording rhymes, which he pursued vigorously in his late teenage years with a neighborhood friend. Using a back room in his friend's apartment as a studio, Wallace recorded several demonstration tapes, one of which landed in the hands of the prominent local disc jockey Mister Cee in 1992. Impressed, Cee passed the tape on to America's best-selling rap publication, *The Source*, which featured Wallace in its "Unsigned Hype" column in March 1992. This endorsement attracted the attention of the young Uptown Records executive Sean "Puffy" Combs, who signed Wallace to a recording deal in 1993. That same year Wallace made his recording debut with a guest appearance on the rhythm-and-blues singer Mary J. Blige's *What's the 411* remix; he

Rapper Notorious B.I.G. (Chris Wallace), c. 1997. COLIN HAWKINS/© S.I.N./CORBIS

also released his first solo recording, "Party and Bullshit," which appeared on the *Who's the Man?* soundtrack.

The breakthrough year in Wallace's rap career was 1994, when his first album, *Ready to Die,* was released. With hit singles like "One More Chance," "Big Poppa," and "Juicy," the album quickly went platinum, selling some 2 million copies. *Rolling Stone* called the album the best rap debut since Ice Cube's *Amerikkka's Most Wanted* (1990), and Wallace received numerous honors at the year-end *Billboard* and *Source* music awards in 1995, including awards for best rap album of the year and best rap lyrics for *Ready to Die.* In the wake of this success, Wallace made guest appearances on several albums, including Michael Jackson's *HIStory—Past, Present, and Future Book 1* (1995), and he helped other rap acts from his Brooklyn neighborhood, especially his girlfriend Lil' Kim and the Junior M.A.F.I.A., break into the music industry with albums of their own. Wallace's single "One More Chance" opened at number five on the pop singles chart in June 1995, tying with Jackson's "Scream/Childhood" as the highest-debuting pop single ever released. On 8 September 1995 Wallace married the rhythm-and-blues singer Faith Evans shortly after their first meeting. In late 1996 Evans gave birth to the couple's only child, Christopher Jr.

Despite his growing prominence in America's rap and pop music scenes, Wallace continued to have problems with the law. Between late 1994 and September 1996 Wallace was accused (though later acquitted) of beating and robbing a music promoter in Camden, New Jersey. He pleaded guilty to criminal mischief and fourth-degree harassment after a fracas with autograph seekers outside the Palladium nightclub in New York City. Wallace was also charged with possession of drugs and several weapons after the police searched his Teaneck, New Jersey, home. During these years, Wallace's marriage to Evans fell apart and they separated.

On 13 September 1996 Wallace was in a serious car accident, forcing him to spend several months in the hospital. This time appears to have been a turning point in Wallace's life. Wallace later noted that it "gave me a lot of time to think about my life and where it was headed. I said to myself, 'B.I.G., you're moving too fast.'" By early 1997 Wallace was speaking publicly about the changes he had made in his life. "I want people to look at B.I.G. like, 'He grew. He's a businessman now. He's a father now.'" Further exemplifying these changes was his new double album, set for release in late March 1997. Wallace explained, "I call the album *Life After Death* because . . . on *Ready to Die* I was dead. . . . There was nothing but anger coming out, about everything. But now, I can't do that no more."

Two weeks before the release of his new album, Wallace was on the West Coast attending the Soul Train Music Awards. Leaving an after-party for the event in the early morning of 9 March 1997, Wallace and friends were seated in a Chevrolet Suburban stopped at a red light at the intersection of Wilshire Boulevard and Fairfax Avenue in West Los Angeles. At approximately 12:50 A.M. another car pulled alongside the Suburban, and the driver pulled out a gun and fired more than a half-dozen shots at Wallace. Although he was rushed to Cedars-Sinai Medical Center, Wallace was pronounced dead on arrival at 1:15 A.M. Only twenty-four years old at the time of his death, Wallace was mourned by his family and rap music's elite at a private funeral service held in New York City on 18 March 1997. Following the service, a funeral cortege drove through Brooklyn's Bedford-Stuyvesant neighborhood, where thousands of people watched the procession. Wallace's remains were later cremated.

Police made little headway and no arrests in the Wallace murder case. Theories abounded, however, as to the killer and his motives. The two most prominent were that a Los Angeles gang member, whom Wallace allegedly hired as a security guard, shot Wallace over a financial dispute, or that Wallace's murder was part of an intensifying East Coast–West Coast rap feud and was retribution for the killing of the Oakland-based rapper Tupac Shakur six months earlier.

Wallace's double album *Life After Death*, released two weeks after his murder, was an immediate commercial success. In its first week in stores, the album sold almost 700,000 copies; by 2000 it had sold over 10 million. In 1997 *Spin* magazine named Wallace its artist of the year. In 1999 Wallace's producer and friend Sean "Puffy" Combs released a posthumous B.I.G. album, *Born Again*, containing Wallace's unreleased material and featuring guest appearances from numerous rap artists, such as Ice Cube, Snoop Dogg, and Eminem. The album sold more than 2 million copies.

Wallace, whose stage name was "Notorious B.I.G." and street name was "Biggie Smalls" (in part because he was six feet, four inches tall and weighed nearly 400 pounds), was a complex person. Those who knew him well spoke of his kindness, generosity, loyalty, intelligence, and sense of humor. In his music and in his life, however, he showed signs of a more tormented, angry, and sometimes violent personality. Appreciating this complexity, Wallace himself admitted, "I'm basically different things to different people." To most rap fans, however, Wallace was an exceptionally gifted artist, who, through captivating narratives and clever rhymes, chronicled the challenges of ghetto life with nuance and honesty, attitude and heart.

★

Only one book exists devoted solely to Wallace: Cathy Scott, *The Murder of Biggie Smalls* (2000). It provides information on Wallace's childhood, family life, and the events surrounding his murder. For the richest analysis of Wallace and his music, one must consult magazine articles and websites. For the former, see especially Bonz Malone, "The Thrill Is Gone," *Vibe* 5 (1997); Chairman Mao, "Forever the Illest," *The Source* 92 (1997); Selwyn Seyfu Hinds, "The Assassination of Christopher Wallace," *The Source* 92 (1997); Mimi Valdes, "Portrait of a Man," *The Source* 92 (1997); Charles Aaron, "The Year in Music: Artist of the Year: Notorious B.I.G.," *Spin* 14 (1998); and Sia Michel, "Heroes and Antiheroes: The Notorious B.I.G.," *Spin* 16 (2000). For informative websites with links to Wallace's interviews, songs, videos, biographical information, and photos, see especially <http://www.notoriousonline.com> and <http://www.badboyonline.com>.

THOMAS A. GUGLIELMO

O'DWYER, (Peter) Paul (*b.* 29 June 1907 in Bohola, County Mayo, Ireland; *d.* 23 June 1998 in Goshen, New York), lawyer who played a major role in New York City and New York State politics for nearly fifty years and took an active part in the civil rights and antiwar movements.

O'Dwyer's life embodied the classic American immigrant story: the poor but talented young man from abroad overcoming odds to rise to wealth, power, and prestige through determination, self-discipline, and hard work. The youngest of eleven children, he was the sixth son of Patrick O'Dwyer and Bridget McNicholas, both of whom were schoolteachers in the parish of Bohola in Ireland. Patrick O'Dwyer, who died when his son was thirteen, had a powerful influence on his son's later involvement in radical or liberal causes. The local firebrand, he worked closely with Irish nationalists to gain independence from Great Britain and organized the county chapter of the National Teachers Union—an act that almost cost him his job and generated an enduring anticlericalism in an otherwise faithful Roman Catholic family.

The O'Dwyers were part of what the Irish called "the shabby genteel"; they were better educated than most of their neighbors and were the owners of four acres of land and a small house, which was later enlarged and equipped with indoor plumbing. Although living on the edge of poverty, the family managed to provide for their children's education, the older children supporting the younger ones

through school. O'Dwyer completed his secondary schooling at Saint Nathy's College in County Mayo in 1924 and entered the National University of Ireland, Dublin, in the fall term of that year, but after six months he left for America, where his brothers lived.

O'Dwyer arrived in New York City on 21 April 1925, reportedly with nothing but $25 in his pocket, a single suit of clothes, and a straight razor. He met for the first time his eldest brother, William, a city policeman who had emigrated before O'Dwyer was born and who would become mayor of New York City (1946–1950). Changing his name from Peter Paul to just Paul, O'Dwyer settled into a rooming house on the Upper West Side of Manhattan and, while working days in a silk mill, took night classes at Fordham University. His social life centered on the activities of the Mayomen's Association, which he joined in 1926, the same year he enrolled in the evening division of Saint John's Law School in Brooklyn. Stubbornly refusing his brothers' offers of help O'Dwyer supported himself by working during the day as a checker on the docks of Brooklyn's waterfront and joined the longshoremen's union. In summers he went to sea as a deckhand on coastal freighters. Living then in Brooklyn, he joined the Kings County Young Democrats ("35 Jewish classmates and me," he wrote) and began a long education in clubhouse politics.

As he completed his legal studies, graduating from Saint John's with an LL.B. degree in 1929, O'Dwyer had in place the central concerns of his adult life: a mission to help the

Paul O'Dwyer, 1988. Susan Ragan/Associated Press

Much of his work in the 1940s centered on representing labor unions and defending the rights of immigrants. In the postwar years O'Dwyer worked for the creation of the state of Israel, raising funds in New York City and in Europe for the militant opponents of British rule. In the 1950s he defended victims of McCarthyism, and in the same period he added a number of Broadway and show-business celebrities to his client list.

In time, O'Dwyer became a millionaire, a circumstance that permitted him to buy an apartment on Central Park West in Manhattan and, with the encouragement of his law partner, to engage in a number of high-profile civil rights cases (often pro bono), including one of the first challenges to housing discrimination in New York City (1947) and a successful appeal to the U.S. Supreme Court to permit Puerto Rican citizens to take voting literacy tests in Spanish (1966). He was among the first Northern lawyers to volunteer in the defense of civil rights workers in the Southern integration struggles of the 1960s. In the same decade he directed the defense of eight miners in Kentucky who were indicted on federal charges of attempting to blow up a bridge during a bitter coal strike (1965–1966).

From 1960 to 1980 O'Dwyer took an active role in the political campaigns of black candidates for public office in both New York and the Deep South. He defended draft resisters during the Vietnam War and was himself both an unsuccessful antiwar candidate for the U.S. Senate in 1968 and a key leader in the movement against the war. As an active supporter of the movement to merge Northern Ireland with the Republic in the south, he was a registered agent in the United States for the Irish Republican Army (IRA) and other Irish organizations. O'Dwyer ran for public office twelve times, winning only twice, both times in races for the New York City Council. He served from 1963 to 1965 and again from 1973 to 1977, when he served as the council's president. He retired from active politics in 1977.

At five feet, eight inches tall and 170 pounds, speaking with a soft Irish brogue, O'Dwyer was instantly recognizable on the platforms and streets of New York; his white mane, black eyebrows, and ruddy complexion set him apart from those around him. A robust man for most of his life, he never recovered from the effects of a stroke that confined him to a wheelchair and left him in failing health through his last year. He died in his sleep of natural causes at his thirty-acre farm in upstate New York. His ashes were scattered on the grounds of the old family homestead in Bohola, now the site of a hospice for the handicapped, which is supported by funds he supplied.

O'Dwyer was the quintessential gadfly of New York City politics, a civil libertarian bound not by political affiliation but by a set of ideals that committed him to challenge authority gone awry in order to seek justice for the under-

impoverished, the laboring classes, and the trade unions; a deep commitment to the Irish-American community; a hatred of anti-Semitism; and the conviction that the liberal agenda of the Democratic Party could bring about real change in American society. Most of all, he believed that the American political and legal system, if properly used, was the avenue by which ethnic and religious minorities could secure their rights.

O'Dwyer was admitted to the bar in 1931, the same year he was naturalized, and began his legal career as a clerk in the financial district law office of Oscar Bernstein, who drew his clients from among the immigrant Jewish families in the Lower East Side and the Irish in Brooklyn. By 1935 he was a senior partner in the renamed firm of O'Dwyer and Bernstien. He married Kathleen Rohan on 19 August 1935; they had four children. Following her death in 1980, he married Patricia Hanrahan in a private ceremony in Mexico in late September 1984.

By the eve of World War II, O'Dwyer's law practice was flourishing, representing members of the city's large Irish-American community (then 25 percent of New York's population) in a broad range of civil and criminal cases.

dogs and the outsiders, as the *New York Times* once put it, and to see the political system as "the only machinery around by which you can really straighten things out." He was to the end an unabashed liberal, long after the liberals themselves had abandoned the agenda he championed for more than six decades.

★

O'Dwyer's papers are divided among three repositories. The principal collection, covering 1933 to 1977, is in the Municipal Archives at the New York City Department of Records and Information Services, Chambers Street Room 101, New York City. His papers from 1955 to 1983 related to Irish-American affairs, including his legal work on behalf of suspected IRA gun-runners, are at Saint John's University in Jamaica, New York. His correspondence and other materials related to his participation in groups urging the creation of the state of Israel are in the Library of the Jewish Theological Seminary of America in New York. O'Dwyer's autobiography, *Counsel for the Defense* (1979), should be supplemented by chapters and notes he added to his brother William's memoir, *Beyond the Golden Door* (1987). He wrote the foreword to Ronald H. Bayor and Timothy J. Meagher, eds., *The New York Irish* (1995). An early profile is in *Current Biography* (1969). An obituary is in the *New York Times* (25 June 1998). See also "Reminiscences of Paul O'Dwyer" (1962), Oral History Research Office, Butler Library, Columbia University, New York City.

ALLAN L. DAMON

David Ogilvy. PRINTS AND PHOTOGRAPHS DIVISION, LIBRARY OF CONGRESS

OGILVY, David Mackenzie (*b.* 23 June 1911 in West Horsley, Surrey, England; *d.* 21 July 1999 in Poitou, France), founder and driving force behind Ogilvy and Mather, one of the world's top advertising firms, who was best known for his advertising acumen and advice, especially in his *Confessions of an Advertising Man* (1963).

Ogilvy was the youngest of five children of John and Dorothy Ogilvy. His father was a stockbroker, weakened by years of financial hardship. His mother, an aloof woman, had ended her medical studies to marry and raise a family. Most of Ogilvy's early memories were of his father's kindness, his mother's abstract advice, and his grandfather's stern, patriarchal presence in the household.

Ogilvy was educated at British boarding schools, first at St. Cyprian's in London (1920–1924) and then at Fettes in Edinburgh (1924–1929). He received financial scholarships to attend both schools and then won a history scholarship to attend Christ Church College at the University of Oxford, where he spent several years (1929–1931) but did not receive a degree. Ogilvy's time at Christ Church was, as he termed it, "the real failure of my life. . . . I was supposed to be a star at Oxford. And instead of that, I was thrown

out. I couldn't pass the exams." This apparent setback, however, proved to be a blessing, as it rerouted Ogilvy's career path from that of a history don to, eventually, that of a successful advertising executive.

In 1931 Ogilvy went directly from Oxford to Paris and began working as a chef at the Hotel Majestic under Monsieur Pitard, who permanently impressed upon Ogilvy the necessity of understanding management and hiring meticulous people. After a year in Paris, Ogilvy returned to England to work as a door-to-door salesman for Aga, the English stove manufacturer. He sold so many stoves during his three-year tenure with Aga that the company commissioned him to write a sales manual. Years later, the business magazine *Fortune* called Ogilvy's guide "probably the best sales manual ever written."

Ogilvy grew tired of traveling the country selling stoves and, with his brother's assistance, secured work in 1935 at Mather and Crowther, a London advertising firm. He described his three years there as a "frivolous" time of dining with clients, attending concerts, and exploring London. He immigrated to the United States in 1938 with the idea of researching American advertising tactics for Mather and Crowther, but instead he accepted a job working for George

Gallup's polling organization in Princeton, New Jersey. Although the position didn't pay well, Ogilvy loved his work and felt he "had drawn a first-class ticket in the lottery of life." Ogilvy credited his time with Gallup, particularly the company's training in research methods, with providing the foundation he needed to understand the U.S. consumer. He worked with Gallup from 1939 until 1942, when he joined the war effort.

During World War II, Ogilvy worked for British intelligence in the United States (1942–1944) and served as second secretary at the British Embassy (1944–1945). The latter position taught Ogilvy two things: good writing skills are essential and the political world is dull and poisonous. Rather than enter the political realm after the war, he commenced life as a tobacco farmer among the Amish in Lancaster County, Pennsylvania. From 1946 until 1948 Ogilvy enjoyed this simple, hardworking lifestyle, but at age thirty-eight, realizing that he would never have the husbandry skills necessary to be a successful farmer, he moved to New York City with the intention of becoming an advertising man.

In 1948 Ogilvy founded Hewitt, Ogilvy, Benson and Mather (later known as Ogilvy and Mather) with a staff of two, no clients, and only $6,000. Ogilvy's approach to advertising soon altered the field's landscape. Perhaps his most widely quoted maxim was, "The consumer is not a moron. She is your wife. Try not to insult her intelligence." Ogilvy helped to transform advertising into a business where intelligence mattered; droning, repetitive, simplistic ads were replaced by witty, interesting ones that caught the consumer's attention. The new ads also caught the attention of clients. Within ten years of founding his firm, Ogilvy had single-handedly landed the accounts of major corporations like Shell, Rolls-Royce, Sears Roebuck, Schweppes, Steuben Glass, Dove Soap, Mercedes-Benz, and Guinness. In 1965 Ogilvy and Mather had the distinction of being one of the first U.S. advertising firms to open offices internationally; a year later, the company went public. By the end of the twentieth century, the firm had grown to a worldwide enterprise with more than 300 offices.

Ogilvy is perhaps best known for turning a brand into a byword. For example, his Schweppes campaign featured an actual Schweppes board member, who appeared in the ads as Colonel Whitehead and described the product as having "Schweppervesence." The ad was so popular that it ran for eighteen years. Ogilvy also is credited with inventing perhaps the most famous automobile advertisement of all time with his slogan for Rolls-Royce: "At sixty miles an hour, the loudest noise in this new Rolls-Royce comes from the electric clock." Ogilvy shared the secrets of his successful campaigns in *Confessions of an Advertising Man* (1963), which quickly became a best-seller and the most widely read book about advertising ever written, selling

more than 600,000 copies in eleven languages. Allen Rosenshine, the chairman and CEO of BBDO Worldwide, referred to Ogilvy's writings as "a bible of what constitutes good and bad advertising."

Ogilvy retired as chairman of the board of Ogilvy and Mather in 1975. He came out of retirement briefly in 1980 to serve as chairman of the firm's offices in India, and then acted as temporary chairman of the German division for a year. In 1989 Ogilvy and Mather was purchased by WWP, a British holding company that owned several other large advertising agencies, and Ogilvy was asked to serve as the company's nonexecutive chairman, which he did for three years. Most of Ogilvy's retirement years, however, were spent at Château de Touffou, his fourteenth-century castle in France, where he gardened, restored the castle, and kept in touch with his offices around the world. His correspondence was so prolific that the local post office had to be expanded.

Ogilvy was married three times. His first two marriages, to Melinda Street and to Ann Cabot, ended in divorce. Ogilvy and Street had one son. He then married Herta Lans in 1973. Late in life, Ogilvy said his only regrets were that he had not received a knighthood and had not had ten children. Never a man for understatement, Ogilvy was proud of his business achievements and, when describing his early years in advertising, said, "I doubt whether any copywriter has ever produced so many winners in such a short period."

Ogilvy also spent many years doing charitable work. He was on the board of directors of the New York Philharmonic (1957–1960), chairman of the Public Participation Committee for the Lincoln Center (1958–1960), a trustee of Colby College (1963–1969), chairman of the United Negro College Fund (1968), and a member of the executive council of the World Wildlife Fund (1975–1999).

Ogilvy was named Commander of the British Empire by Queen Elizabeth II (1967), elected to the U.S. Advertising Hall of Fame (1977), awarded an honorary doctor of letters by Adelphi University (1977), and elected to France's Order of Arts and Letters (1990). Ogilvy died at age eighty-eight at his château in Poitou, after a year of declining health, and he is buried on its grounds.

Ogilvy was a giant in the advertising world. For his epitaph, he requested a telling quote that is attributed to Horace, the Roman poet and satirist: "Happy the man, and happy he alone, He, who can call today his own: He who, secure within, can say, To-morrow do thy worse, for I have lived today."

★

Ogilvy's papers (1935–1966) are housed in the Library of Congress. In addition to writing *Confessions of an Advertising Man* (1963), Ogilvy authored the more personal *Blood, Brains, and Beer:*

The Autobiography of David Ogilvy (1978), which covers his early years through his retirement in France. The revised edition, *An Autobiography* (1997), fills in some of the gaps from his 1978 book and includes much more advice about business and interpersonal work relationships. As a retirement gift, Ogilvy's colleagues presented him with *The Unpublished David Ogilvy* (1986), a collection of memos, letters, and conversations culled from his lifetime. Ogilvy also wrote *Ogilvy on Advertising* (1983), delineating his ideas for success and leadership. Denis Higgins included his interview with Ogilvy in *The Art of Advertising: Conversations with Masters of the Craft* (1995). An obituary is in the *New York Times* (22 July 1999).

SHARON L. DECKER

O'SULLIVAN, Maureen   (*b.* 17 May 1911 in Boyle, County Roscommon, Ireland; *d.* 22 June 1998 in Scottsdale, Arizona), actress best known as Tarzan's mate, "Jane," in the Johnny Weismuller "Tarzan" films during the 1930s and as the mother of the actress Mia Farrow.

O'Sullivan was born to Major Charles Joseph O'Sullivan, an officer of the Connaught Rangers in the British Army, and Mary Lovett Fraser, a homemaker. She had one

Maureen O'Sullivan. © CORBIS

brother and three sisters. The O'Sullivans frequently moved around in course of the major's commissions, but after he was wounded in World War I, the family settled in Saintbury, County Dublin.

In 1923, at age twelve, O'Sullivan entered the Convent of the Sacred Heart at Roehampton in London. There she became friends with Vivien Leigh, who would later become famous for her portrayal of Scarlett O'Hara in the film *Gone with the Wind* (1939). O'Sullivan was voted second most beautiful student, runner-up to Leigh. In 1926 O'Sullivan attended a convent in Boxmoor and in 1928 her parents sent her to study in France for a year. Returning to Dublin, O'Sullivan spent her time raising poultry and watching American films. One day while dancing at the Plaza restaurant in Dublin, O'Sullivan was approached by well-known director Frank Borzage, who was in Ireland to shoot exterior scenes for a Twentieth Century–Fox feature. He asked her to take a screen test. After initial opposition from her father, O'Sullivan was finally allowed to take the test for a small role in *Song O' My Heart*.

O'Sullivan traveled to Hollywood with her mother to shoot the film, which was released to favorable reviews in 1930. O'Sullivan played the young daughter of tenor John McCormack's true love. As a result of her impressive film debut, O'Sullivan was signed to a contract with Twentieth Century–Fox. In *So This Is London*, also released in 1930, O'Sullivan played a young British girl with whom the son of Will Rogers's character falls in love. *Just Imagine* and *The Princess and the Plumber* followed the same year. At this point O'Sullivan became more important to Fox as a bargaining tool in their dispute with actress Janet Gaynor than she was as an actress in her own right, and after two more films for the studio in 1931, O'Sullivan was dropped. Metro-Goldwyn-Mayer (MGM) offered her a contract almost immediately. She also appeared in *The Big Shot* (1931) for RKO and *The Silver Lining* (1932) for Patrician Studios (United Artists).

O'Sullivan's first role for MGM, and the one that made her famous, was as Jane Parker in *Tarzan, the Apeman* (1932). Olympic champion swimmer Johnny Weismuller played Tarzan, and O'Sullivan as Jane brought to her role "an intriguing blend of innocence and sophistication, fine breeding with sensuousness, and fragile femininity with rugged tenacity," according to Rudy Behlman in *American Cinematographer* (January 1987). The chemistry between the two actors, and the overall charm of their story, were enthusiastically greeted not only by audiences but also by the original author of *Tarzan*, Edgar Rice Burroughs. O'Sullivan next starred in *Skyscraper Souls* (1932), based upon Faith Baldwin's popular novel, and in Eugene O'Neill's *Strange Interlude* (1932), as Madeleine.

In 1934 O'Sullivan again played Jane in the sequel *Tarzan and His Mate*. This film was even better received, largely because of the tender romance between the two principals. But the Catholic Legion of Decency objected to their skimpy jungle attire. In later films the costumes were rather more modest. O'Sullivan was busy beyond *Tarzan,* appearing in *The Thin Man* and *The Barretts of Wimpole Street* in 1934. In the following year she gave a notable performance as a dying girl in George Cukor's *David Copperfield.*

On 12 September 1936 O'Sullivan married director-producer John Neville Villiers Farrow in Santa Monica, California. She expanded into radio in the Lux Radio Theatre *Captain Applejack* broadcast on 19 October 1936. *Tarzan Escapes* was also released in late 1936. To the delight of their many fans, this film emphasized the tender relationship between Weismuller's Tarzan and O'Sullivan's Jane. O'Sullivan appeared in *Between Two Women* (1937), *A Yank at Oxford* (1938), and *Let Us Live* (1939). That year she also reprised her role as Jane in a film that began shooting as *Tarzan in Exile.* It was in this film that Johnny Sheffield was introduced as "Boy," and Jane was supposed to die. Jane's death was protested by audiences and the ending was changed, as well as the film's title. It eventually opened as *Tarzan Finds a Son!* During filming O'Sullivan was pregnant with the first of the seven children she was to have with Farrow.

In 1940 O'Sullivan appeared as Jane Bennett in *Pride and Prejudice,* and in 1941 she played Abby Rawlston in *Maisie Was a Lady,* the same year that she starred in *Tarzan's Secret Treasure. Tarzan's New York Adventure* was released in 1942 and was her last film for MGM. Wanting to attend to her children, O'Sullivan made no films between 1942 and 1948, but continued to work in radio until her husband persuaded her to appear in *The Big Clock* (1948). In 1950 she had a small part opposite Robert Mitchum in *Where Danger Lives,* another film produced and directed by Farrow.

Hosting *The Children's Hour* in 1951 was O'Sullivan's first exposure on the new medium of television, followed by *Irish Heritage* in 1954. O'Sullivan's dedication to raising her large family was acknowledged with the Mother of the Year award from the Benevolent Irish Society on 9 May 1954. Her eldest son, Michael, was killed in a plane crash in 1958, the same year that she received the Lateran Cross from the Vatican. The role of Nancy Fallon in *A Roomful of Roses* at the Drury Theatre in Chicago in November 1961 marked O'Sullivan's first appearance on the stage. In 1964

she was the "Today Girl" on television's *Today Show.* O'Sullivan's husband died in 1963, just as her theater career was taking off. She made her New York theater debut in 1962 as Edith Lambert in the comedy *Never Too Late,* a production that toured to England before returning to New York and a tour of the United States. In 1965 O'Sullivan repeated her role in the film version of the play.

In 1965 O'Sullivan received the Motion Pictures Exhibitors' award. She also starred in *Charley's Aunt* and *The Front Page.* The following year she appeared in *Butterflies Are Free* on stage and costarred with Douglas Fairbanks, Jr., in *Lonelyheart 555,* an ABC "Movie of the Week." In 1980 O'Sullivan starred as Esther Compton in *Morning's at Seven* on Broadway. On 28 November 1980 O'Sullivan was presented with the Hoey Award by the Roman Catholic Interracial Council for her work in combating racial and religious discrimination. The following year she received the Drama Critics' Award.

O'Sullivan received an Honorary Doctorate of Fine Arts from Sienna College on 22 May 1983. She married James E. Cushing, a construction company executive, on 22 August of that same year. She was praised for her role as Norma, playing the screen mother of her real-life daughter Mia Farrow in Woody Allen's 1986 film *Hannah and Her Sisters.* She also had a role in the popular Francis Coppola film *Peggy Sue Got Married* (1986), as Kathleen Turner's mother.

After a career of over sixty years on film, radio, television, and stage, O'Sullivan planned to write her autobiography, but the project was never completed. She died of a heart attack at age eighty-seven. In addition to being the quintessential "Jane" to Tarzan in the movies, O'Sullivan is also remembered as the mother of two actresses, Mia and Theresa ("Tisa") Farrow. O'Sullivan was a multitalented woman who was able to balance a successful career with a happy family life. She did so during an era when such accomplishment was unusual.

★

The most comprehensive and detailed coverage of O'Sullivan's life and career is found in Connie J. Billips, *Maureen O'Sullivan: A Bio-Bibliography* (1990). A lengthy entry is in *Contemporary Theatre, Film and Television,* vol. 20 (1999), which lists credits of all of O'Sullivan's appearances. An obituary is in the *New York Times* (24 June 1998).

THERESE DUZINKIEWICZ BAKER

P-Q

PAKULA, Alan Jay (*b.* 7 April 1928 in Bronx, New York; *d.* 19 November 1998 in Plainview, New York), director and/ or producer of more than two dozen films, including *The Parallax View* (1974), *All the President's Men* (1976), and *Sophie's Choice* (1982), which showed his trademark use of tension in both the story and visuals.

Pakula was one of two children born to Paul Pakula, the co-owner of a Manhattan printing business, and Jeannette Goldstein. When he was young, the family moved from the Bronx, New York, to Long Beach, on Long Island, where Pakula attended the public schools. He had an older sister, Felice. Although his passions were music and art, Pakula pursued his secondary education at the Bronx High School of Science. His senior year was at the private Hill School in Pottstown, Pennsylvania, from which Pakula graduated in December 1944.

Deferred from military service in World War II because of a collapsed lung, Pakula entered the Yale School of Drama in New Haven, Connecticut, in February 1945. Pakula's experiences during the two-month interval between high school and college changed his life. He answered a newspaper advertisement, gained employment as an office boy at the Leland Hayward Theatrical Agency, and became hooked on show business.

In 1948 Pakula completed a drama degree at Yale and departed for Hollywood, California, where he served as an assistant in the cartoon department at Warner Brothers.

Two years later, he became an apprentice to the writer-producer-director Don Hartman at Metro-Goldwyn-Mayer (MGM). In 1951 Pakula followed Hartman to Paramount Pictures as a production assistant. When Hartman left Paramount in 1956, Pakula remained at the studio and his filmmaking aspirations were encouraged by the production chief Dore Schary.

Pakula's career as a film producer was launched with *Fear Strikes Out* (1957), which starred Anthony Perkins as a baseball player struggling with mental illness. Following the modest success of this initial film, Pakula joined with the director of *Fear Strikes Out,* Robert Mulligan, to form a production company. The Pakula-Mulligan collaboration produced six films: *Love with the Proper Stranger* (1963), *To Kill a Mockingbird* (1962), *Baby, the Rain Must Fall* (1965), *Inside Daisy Clover* (1966), *Up the Down Staircase* (1967), and *The Stalking Moon* (1969). The most critically acclaimed and commercially successful of these productions was based on Harper Lee's Pulitzer Prize–winning 1960 novel, *To Kill a Mockingbird*. The film adaptation received five Academy Award nominations, including one for best picture, and won three Oscars.

Pakula served as the producer and made his directorial debut in 1969 with *The Sterile Cuckoo,* a comedy featuring Liza Minnelli. Two years later, Pakula produced and directed the crime thriller *Klute,* for which the actress Jane Fonda won an Academy Award. The filmmaker also produced and directed *Love and Pain and the Whole Damn*

Alan J. Pakula. KOBAL COLLECTION

Thing (1972), featuring Maggie Smith, and *The Parallax View* (1974), with Warren Beatty.

The Parallax View, a political thriller featuring a conspiracy theory, drew the attention of the actor Robert Redford, who had purchased the film rights to Bob Woodward's and Carl Bernstein's *All the President's Men* (1974). Pakula agreed to direct the film, which became the top-grossing picture of 1976, earning over $26 million in box-office receipts. *All the President's Men* was nominated for eight Academy Awards, including best director and best picture, and won four Oscars. Although he did not win the Academy Award for direction, Pakula's efforts with *All the President's Men* were recognized with best director awards from the National Board of Review and the New York Film Critics.

Pakula continued to make films for the next twenty-two years, although they failed to garner the critical and commercial heights achieved by *All the President's Men.* His later directorial efforts include *Comes a Horseman* (1978); *Starting Over* (1979), which he also coproduced; *Rollover* (1981); *Sophie's Choice* (1982), as screenwriter and coproducer; *Dream Lover* (1986), as coproducer; *Orphans* (1987), as producer; *See You in the Morning* (1989), as screenwriter and producer; *Presumed Innocent* (1990), as coscreenwriter;

Consenting Adults (1992), as producer; *The Pelican Brief* (1993), as screenwriter and producer; and *The Devil's Own* (1997). His screenplay for *Sophie's Choice* was nominated for an Academy Award.

In his personal life, Pakula kept homes in both Manhattan and East Hampton, New York. In 1963 he married the actress Hope Lange and assumed the role of stepfather to her two children. Pakula and Lange divorced in 1969, and on 17 February 1973 Pakula married the historian Hannah Colin Boorstin and became a stepfather to her three children. His stepson Robert Boorstin, who later achieved success as a reporter and government official, suffered from bouts of depression, which encouraged Pakula to take an active role in fund-raising for the National Alliance for the Mentally Ill.

In 1998 Pakula was working on a screenplay adaptation of *No Ordinary Time* (1994), Doris Kearns Goodwin's book about Franklin and Eleanor Roosevelt. Before Pakula was able to complete this assignment, he died in a car accident on the Long Island Expressway near Melville, New York. Pakula lost control of his car when a metal pipe on the road was struck by another car and sent hurtling through the filmmaker's Volvo, causing him to crash into a fence. He was pronounced dead at the North Shore Hospital in Plainview at age seventy. He is buried at Green River Cemetery in East Hampton, New York.

Pakula left a rich legacy of films that continue to entertain and provoke thought. As a director, he was best known for evoking outstanding performances from his actors. In a 1977 interview with the *New York Times,* Pakula explained, "The reason I became a director was that I've always loved actors." A reciprocal admiration was voiced by many of the performers who appeared in Pakula's productions. Harrison Ford, who starred in Pakula's last completed film, *The Devil's Own* (1997), asserted that the director was a "natural guide to inner realms." Candice Bergen, who was featured in Pakula's 1979 comedy *Starting Over,* remembered, "He made it safe for me to make a fool of myself."

Pakula's skills as a director elicited Academy Award–winning performances from Gregory Peck in *To Kill a Mockingbird,* Jane Fonda in *Klute,* Jason Robards in *All the President's Men,* and Meryl Streep in *Sophie's Choice.* His ability to create tension, suspense, and ominous moods—often making sophisticated use of surveillance and recorded conversations, in films such as *Klute, The Parallax View,* and *All the President's Men*—successfully evoked the political paranoia and instability of the 1960s and 1970s.

★

Pakula's assessment of his filmmaking may be found in several printed interviews: "Making a Film About Two Reporters," *American Cinematographer* (July 1976); "Dialogue on Film: Alan J. Pakula," *American Film* (Dec./Jan. 1978/1979); and "A Walk with

Good and Evil," *Cinema Papers* (Dec. 1990). For critical commentary on Pakula's films, see R. T. Jameson, "Pakula Parallax," *Film Comment* (Sept./Oct. 1976); Neil Sinyard, "Pakula's Choice: Some Thoughts on Alan J. Pakula," *Cinema Papers* (July 1984); Janet Maslin, "Finding Depth in Society's Shallow End," *New York Times* (23 Nov. 1998); and R. Seidenberg, "Presumed Innocent," *American Film* (Aug. 1999). Obituaries are in the *New York Times* and *Los Angeles Times* (both 20 Nov. 1998).

RON BRILEY

PAREDES, Américo   (*b.* 3 September 1915 in Brownsville, Texas; *d.* 5 May 1999 in Austin, Texas), prominent Latino scholar and one of the founders of the Chicano studies movement.

Paredes was one of two children of Justo Paredes, a rancher, and Clotilde Manzano-Vidal, a homemaker. Early in life Paredes was interested in music and poetry. He attended Brownsville High School and later Brownsville Junior College, graduating from the latter in 1936. By this time Paredes had published some of his early poems in *Los Lunes literarios* (Literary Mondays), a literary section of *La Prensa* of San Antonio, and in the *Brownsville Herald*. Before

Américo Paredes. RALPH BARRERA

World War II he worked as a reporter for the *Brownsville Herald*. He married Consuelo Silva, a singer, on 13 August 1939, but the couple divorced shortly thereafter.

Paredes enlisted in the army in 1941 (some sources state 1944), was sent overseas, and worked as a reporter on the *Stars and Stripes* in Japan. After the war he stayed in Asia to cover the Japanese war trials and to work as a public relations consultant for the American Red Cross in Japan. There, he met his second wife, Amelia Sidzu Nagamine, the daughter of a Japanese diplomat and the diplomat's Uruguayan wife. Amelia was fluent in Spanish, Japanese, and English. They were married in 1948 and had four children: three sons and one daughter.

Returning to Texas in 1950, Paredes went back to school, earning his B.A. degree summa cum laude in English and philosophy from the University of Texas at Austin, followed by an M.A. degree in 1953. In 1956 he earned his Ph.D. in English with a specialization in folklore and Spanish, joining the English faculty of the University of Texas at Austin in 1957, where he taught until his retirement in 1984.

The adaptation of Paredes's doctoral dissertation was published in 1958 as *With His Pistol in His Hand: A Border Ballad and Its Hero,* which later inspired a movie adaptation. In this book Paredes explored the story of Gregorio Cortez, a Mexican farmer who shot an Anglo sheriff in self-defense and became a folk hero for Mexican Americans. Paredes produced a pioneering study on Mexican-American folklore, focused on the prevailing cultural and sociopolitical conflict between Hispanic Americans and Anglos. Both the legend of Cortez and the ballad emphasized that the Anglo-Americans were able to capture him only because he decided to give himself up in order to spare his people any further suffering.

Paredes contributed to the development of Chicano studies in his research of Texas-Mexican folklore and music and in cofounding the Mexican-American Studies Center at the University of Texas at Austin in 1970. He served as its first director from 1970 to 1972. Paredes brought forth the idea that Chicano culture is unique, integrating both Mexican and American elements to create a new discourse. Combining ethnography, literature, and folklore, he studied the border folk song and its depiction of Mexican-American culture in Texas. He focused particularly on the often violent clashes between Mexicans and Mexican Americans with Texas Rangers and other Anglo authorities. In *Folktales of Mexico* (1970), a collection of folktales edited and translated by Paredes, he also presented his thoughts on researching folkloric traditions and introducing them to the public: for Paredes it was important that the researcher present background and source information to attest to the validity of the story as a folkloric tale.

In *Folklore and Culture on the Texas-Mexican Border*

(1993), Paredes examines the negotiation of identity by Mexican Americans and how that is translated into the different folktales of the region. Moreover, in this and other writings, he was one of the first to point out the bias inherent in many ethnographic reports, indicating how anthropologists without a full grasp of the language might have misinterpreted colloquial expressions. He demonstrated the need for the ethnographer to exercise a rigorous methodology when examining minority groups living in the same society as the ethnographers.

Paredes made contributions to fiction and poetry as well. His best known work of fiction is perhaps *George Washington Gómez: A Mexicotexan Novel*. Set in the Great Depression, it depicts the hardships faced by the Chicanos in southern Texas and placed Mexican Americans in opposition to Texans and Texas Rangers in particular. Paredes also wrote poetry, including *Between Two Worlds*, published in 1991 but containing poems in English and in Spanish dating from 1934 to 1970. Most of these poems ponder human nature and the internal tensions brought about by being a Mexican American.

In 1962 he won a Guggenheim Fellowship. The Américo Paredes Distinguished Lecture Series was established by the Mexican-American Studies Center in 1987. Paredes became the Dickson, Allen, and Anderson Centennial Professor of Anthropology and English at the University of Texas at Austin. In November 1988 Paredes received a lifetime achievement award at the state capitol during opening ceremonies for the Texas Book Festival. He received the Charles Frankel Prize from the National Endowment for the Humanities in 1989. In 1990 President Carlos Salinas de Gortari of Mexico awarded him the highest honor given to scholars from other countries, the Order of the Aztec Eagle (Aguila Azteca), in Mexico City. In 1997 he received the University of Texas Presidential Citation. He also received an award from the American Folklore Society's section on Latino, Latin American, and Caribbean Folklore, recognizing him as "the most important and influential American Folklorist in the field of Mexican-American and Borderlands folklore." On 27 April 1998 officials at the Austin Independent School District celebrated the Américo Paredes Middle School. Paredes died of pneumonia at Specialty Hospital of Austin.

★

Paredes's papers, including manuscripts, correspondence, songbooks, and more, are at the Nettie Lee Benson Latin American Collection at the University of Texas at Austin. Some of it can be seen at <http://www.lib.utexas.edu>. Included in this collection is the biography of Paredes that appeared in *Dictionary of Literary Biography*, vol. 209: *Chicano Writers, Third Series* (1999). Also see Stanley Rome, "A Border *Cancionero* and a Regional View of Folksong," in Ricardo Romo and Raymund Paredes, eds., *New Directions in Chicano Scholarship* (1978); José Eduardo Limón, *The Return of the Mexican Ballad: Américo Paredes and His Anthropological Text as Persuasive Political Performance* (1986); Luis Leal, "Américo Paredes and Modern Mexican-American Scholarship," *Ethnic Affairs* 1 (1987): 1–11; and Ramón Saldívar, "The Folk Base of Chicano Narrative: Américo Paredes's *With His Pistol in His Hand* and the Corrido Tradition," *Chicano Narrative: The Dialectics of Difference* (1990): 26–42. An obituary by Manuel Peña and Richard Bauman is in the *Journal of American Folklore* 113 (2000): 195–198, and another is in the *New York Times* (7 May 1999).

MICAELA WALDMAN

PARKER, Thomas Andrew ("Colonel") (*b.* 26 June 1909 in Breda, Netherlands; *d.* 21 January 1997 in Las Vegas, Nevada), controversial manager of the legendary singer and film star Elvis Presley.

Parker was born Andreas Cornelius van Kuijk, the fifth of nine children of Adam van Kuijk, a liveryman for a freight-hauling firm, and Maria Ponsie, a homemaker. He left home in his late teens, probably stowing away on a ship to the United States. After learning just enough English to get by, Parker enlisted in the U.S. Army in 1929, a time when such details as the nationality of able-bodied men willing to enlist where not questioned very closely. His commanding officer was named Thomas Andrew Parker and van Kuijk adopted the name as his own. After completing his military service, Parker found work as an advance man for a succession of carnivals. The hustle and slickness of carnival life became permanent features of his managerial style. In 1935 Parker married Marie Mott, a divorcée with a ten-year-old son. They had no children of their own.

Soon after his marriage, Parker left carnival life and settled in Tampa, Florida. In 1939 he briefly became the booking agent for Gene Austin, a fading country singer. Next Parker became the field agent for the Tampa Humane Society, but he continued to moonlight in show business, promoting country-and-western concerts in Tampa. Parker met a rising star of the Grand Ole Opry, Eddie Arnold, during a 1943 road show. Parker convinced Arnold into letting him become his manager. Arnold's career blossomed under Parker's management, and in 1948 Parker moved to Nashville, Tennessee, the country music hub. The same year, the Louisiana governor Jimmie Davis presented Parker with a citation proclaiming him an "honorary colonel." From that time on, Parker insisted that everyone address him as "Colonel."

Parker made valuable contacts while working for Arnold, notably with RCA Records, the music publishing firm Hill and Range, and the William Morris Agency. These

"Colonel" Tom Parker assisting Elvis Presley on location for *Love Me Tender,* 1957. ASSOCIATED PRESS AP

contacts earned Arnold a fortune, but in 1953 he fired Parker, saying only that the two men had "conflicting personalities."

The following year Parker went into partnership with Hank Snow, a successful country singer. While booking tours for Snow, Parker heard about a "sensational" young singer named Elvis Presley. After a brief meeting in 1954, Parker booked the singer on a road tour. Soon after, he negotiated a contract with Presley, naming himself as Presley's sole representative, thus cutting Snow completely out of the deal. Then Parker sold Presley's services to his contacts at RCA, Hill and Range, and William Morris.

Parker felt the need to control Presley by isolating him from the influence of others. Although this undoubtedly hampered Presley's growth as an artist, it also kept him under Parker's thumb. In return for Presley's docility, Parker promised to make him a movie star. In the spring of 1956 Parker and Presley signed contracts with both Hal B. Wallis, a Hollywood producer, and Twentieth Century–Fox. Four films were rapidly produced, with more attention paid to economy than quality. They were enormously successful.

Parker, always uncomfortable with the wild, raw energy of Presley's public performances, sought to tone down his client's public image. He found an ideal ally in the U.S. Army, into which Presley was inducted on 4 March 1958. He served for two years, mostly in the Third Armored Division in Friedberg, Germany. There was a risk that Presley would be forgotten after his years in the military, but Parker

managed to keep Presley's name before the public. And Presley also recorded some new material before shipping out to Germany. During Presley's military service, Parker was unable to visit him because he never became a U.S. citizen and feared that authorities would prevent him from reentering the United States after an overseas trip.

In March 1960 Presley completed his military service and returned home with a beautiful fourteen-year-old girl, Priscilla Beaulieu, in tow. Oddly, Parker paid scant attention, and the girl was installed at Graceland, Presley's home in Memphis, Tennessee, with few public repercussions. After a single television appearance, three live concerts, and the production of one record album, Presley stopped performing concerts for nearly a decade. Parker had decided that Presley would be a movie star. During the early 1960s, Presley made three movies per year until the public grew weary and profits began to plummet. Then in 1971 Parker put Presley back on the road. During this period, Parker was clearly not functioning in Presley's best interests. He refused to book foreign tours because of his own reluctance to leave the country. And the songs in Presley's films were of poor quality because Parker refused to use songwriters unless they worked for Hill and Range, a company that gave their writers such little creative leeway that the more talented writers had left to find greater profits elsewhere.

By the early 1970s it was evident that Presley's health was deteriorating. His weight had ballooned, he was exhausted from a grueling concert schedule, and his erratic behavior lent credence to the rumors of drug abuse. Parker was aware that Presley's days as a top performer were numbered. While doing nothing to help Presley come to grips with his problems, Parker made sure his own nest would be comfortably feathered if anything were to happen to his client. To this end, he made an arrangement with RCA to sell the masters of all the songs Presley had recorded before March 1973—more than 700 works—for a single lump sum and to relinquish all future royalties. The selling price was $5.4 million, a small fraction of what Presley would have received in royalties. Parker received $2.6 million. As a result of a number of side deals related to the buyout, Parker made more money from the arrangement than Presley.

Next Parker formed a company called Boxcar Enterprises, to which all of Presley's merchandising interests were transferred. Parker arranged to collect 40 percent of the profits from the sale of souvenirs and posters, while Presley and a number of Parker's hangers-on each collected 15 percent. Presley signed all of the contracts willingly, but apparently had little understanding of their contents.

When Presley was found dead from a drug overdose on 16 August 1977, Parker announced, "This won't change anything." Indeed, nothing changed for several years. But after the death of Presley's father, a probate judge in Memphis was puzzled by Parker's enormous commissions and decided to investigate. When the dust settled, Parker and RCA were found guilty of "collusion, conspiracy, [and] fraud." In June 1983 Parker settled with Presley's estate, emerging more comfortably than many thought he deserved.

After the death of his wife in 1980, Parker remarried in 1981. His second wife, Loanne Miller, cared for him during a long decline in his health. He died of complications from a stroke and is buried in Palm Cemetery in Las Vegas.

It is unlikely that Elvis Presley would have emerged from obscurity to become a show business icon without the inspired marketing strategies of Parker. It can also be argued that Parker was responsible for squandering Presley's talents and ultimately destroying him.

★

Dirk Vellenga, with Mick Farren, *Elvis and the Colonel* (1988), unearthed the facts of Parker's early life but presents an unremittingly negative view of Parker. Albert Goldman, *Elvis* (1981), provides impressive detail of the Memphis music scene but is equally negative. Peter Guralnick's two-volume biography of Presley, *Last Train to Memphis: The Rise of Elvis Presley* (1994), and *Careless Love: The Unmaking of Elvis Presley* (1999), paints a more balanced portrait. An interview with Blanchard Tual, the guardian for Presley's daughter during the 1980 litigation between the Presley estate and Parker, gave additional insights into Parker's personality. An obituary is in the *New York Times* (22 Jan. 1997).

NATALIE B. JALENAK

PATTERSON, Louise Alone Thompson (*b.* 9 September 1901 in Chicago, Illinois; *d.* 27 August 1999 in New York City), advocate of leftist causes and cultural critic who was a key participant in the intellectual and artistic ferment of the Harlem Renaissance, and a close associate of the poet Langston Hughes.

Patterson was the only child of William Poles and Lula Brown. Her parents divorced when she was a child, and her mother remarried. Her stepfather, Thompson, was a "jack of all trades" who constantly sought greater opportunity. Consequently, the family moved around the Midwest and West for several years, mostly living in conservative white communities where they encountered racist attitudes.

The family eventually moved to Oakland, California, in 1919, and Patterson enrolled at the University of California at Berkeley. There she heard W. E. B. DuBois give a compelling lecture on racism. Patterson graduated cum laude with a B.A. degree in economics in 1923. One of the first few African Americans to graduate from Berkeley, she found opportunities to be limited by her race and gender. Patterson moved briefly to Chicago to pursue graduate education but reconsidered and moved to Arkansas in 1925 for a teaching position. She moved to Virginia in 1926 to accept a faculty position at the Hampton Institute. In 1927 she collided with the white administration when she took the side of striking students. Patterson then headed off to New York City on an Urban League Scholarship to study at the New School for Social Research.

Patterson thrived in the cultural excitement of New York City in the late 1920s, but by 1930 she had become disenchanted with social work methods, believing that they fostered dependence. She abandoned her studies, shifting her focus to New York's Congregational Educational Society (CES); she admired its liberal approach to the relationship between race relations and labor problems. As Patterson became more involved in the CES, she also became part of the Harlem Renaissance artistic and literary flowering. Offering her large apartment as a meeting place for artists and intellectuals, she served as an editorial secretary for the writers Langston Hughes and Zora Neale Hurston. Patterson was briefly married to the writer and intellectual Wallace Thurman; the couple separated after six months of marriage.

During the 1930s Patterson became increasingly drawn to Communism as a political ideology. In the spring of 1931, nine African-American boys were arrested for raping two white teenage girls on a Memphis-bound train. The "Scottsboro Boys" were jailed in Alabama and found guilty of rape at the conclusion of a speedy and unjust trial. Eight were sentenced to death and the ninth, only thirteen years old, to life in prison. Writers publicized the event, and the

Communist Party played a critical role in seeking justice for the Scottsboro Boys. After several trials, the last prisoner was finally released in 1950. The case gave the Communist Party visibility as an advocate for victims of racism, contributing to its stronger presence and respectability in Harlem. The Vanguard, a social club Patterson founded with sculptor and community leader Augusta Savage, gave its members the opportunity to discuss Marxist theory and the party's position on the "Negro Question," and from these discussions developed a branch of the Friends of the Soviet Union (FOSU).

Patterson's instrumental role in FOSU, her keen intelligence, and her literary and political connections positioned her to organize a group of twenty-two artists, journalists, writers, and scholars to travel to the Soviet Union in June 1932 to make *Black and White*, a film about racism in the United States. The Americans, including Langston Hughes, were treated like celebrities. "For all of us who experienced discrimination based on color in our own land, it was strange to find our color a badge of honor," wrote Patterson as she reflected upon the treatment they received. Their experiences in the Soviet Union affirmed the young intellectuals' belief that there was international support for black Americans' struggle to secure rights and self-respect. *Black and White*, however, was an ill-conceived project hampered by a director who could not speak English or Russian, actors without any performance experience, and an implausible plot. The film project was canceled, and the Americans split into two groups. One camp believed the Soviets abandoned the film to win diplomatic recognition from the United States, but Patterson's group argued that the project collapsed despite the Soviets' good intentions. Her defense and trust earned her the nickname "Madame Moscow." Patterson returned to New York City in the fall of 1932 to care for her ailing mother, but she continued to praise the Soviet Union and communism, and in subsequent years returned for several visits.

Patterson worked for the National Committee for the Defense of Political Prisoners (NCDPP) in 1933, and through this affiliation, she formally joined the Communist Party. Patterson took a position in 1934 in the International Worker's Order (IWO) and worked on behalf of Communist causes nationally. For example, she was jailed in Birmingham, Alabama, for one night in 1934 while organizing a campaign for Angelo Herndon, a young man accused of insurrection. Patterson's connections with the literary community also continued, and she often served as a liaison between the Communist Party and the black cultural community. In 1938 Patterson and Langston Hughes organized the Harlem Suitcase Theatre, which was sponsored by the IWO and showcased black playwrights. Hughes's *Don't You Want To Be Free?* was the theatre's debut performance. Patterson's close, longstanding relationship with Hughes was revealed when he dedicated a 1942 collection of poems (*Shakespeare in Harlem*) to her.

Patterson married her longtime friend William L. Patterson, a lawyer and key figure in the Communist Party, in 1940. Their alliance was personally and politically powerful, and together they moved to Chicago and continued their work. They had a daughter in 1943, but motherhood did not undermine Patterson's commitment and passion for her causes, especially IWO work. (She also established a black community center on the south side of Chicago.) After World War II Patterson was a pioneer in the Civil Rights Congress (CRC). The anticommunist hysteria of the McCarthy era was the backdrop to the couple's testimony to the House Un-American Activities Committee (HUAC) in the 1950s (Patterson invoked her Fifth Amendment rights). When the actor and singer Paul Robeson was prohibited from leaving the United States, Patterson organized tours for him. Patterson and her husband were involved in many civil liberties cases, such as the Trenton Six, in which six black men were found guilty of murder in 1948 of a white elderly shopkeeper. Declared guilty by an all white jury in New Jersey, their conviction was based on flimsy evidence and their sentences galvanized a coalition of activists who intervened to secure them a new trial. The resulting 1951 trial freed four of the six accused. In the 1960s Patterson led the Free Angela Davis Committee in New York. After her husband died in 1980, Patterson served as an important source of information for scholars studying the Harlem Renaissance. She died of viral pneumonia at age ninety-seven and was cremated. Her remains are in Chicago with those of her husband.

Patterson demonstrated an unflagging commitment to social justice and was not afraid to consider political and cultural alternatives in a land that systematically denied its black citizens their rights and dignity. During the cultural explosion of the Harlem Renaissance, Patterson was acutely aware of the opportunity for the development of African-American identity. She facilitated it with her work and by serving as a liaison between art and politics, but also by opening her home, her kitchen, and her heart to people from all walks of life. Many benefited from the human, intellectual, and cultural exchanges that took place in her presence. In Patterson's later years, many scholars who were studying the past did so with the help of Patterson's precise memory, sharp wit, and commitment to communicating the rich history in which she played a formative role. Patterson was an exceedingly intelligent and unusually courageous woman who did not consider her race and gender as limitations but as opportunities.

★

The autobiography of William L. Patterson, *The Man Who Cried Genocide: An Autobiography* (1971), provides biographical material on Patterson. There is no full-length biography of Patterson, but several books consider her role, especially Mark Naison, *Communists in Harlem During the Depression* (1983); Arnold Rampersad, *The Life of Langston Hughes: I, Too, Sing America, Volume I: 1902–1941* (1986); and Gerald Horne, *Communist Front? The Civil Rights Congress, 1946–1956* (1988). Darlene Clark Hine, *Black Women in America: An Historical Encyclopedia* (1993), has an entry on Patterson. There is an interview with Patterson by Ruth Prago, *Oral History of the American Left*, at the Taminent Institute at New York University (1981). An obituary is in the *New York Times* (2 Sept. 1999).

LIANN E. TSOUKAS

PAYTON, Walter Jerry (*b.* 25 July 1954 in Columbia, Mississippi; *d.* 1 November 1999 in Barrington, Illinois), Hall of Fame running back of the Chicago Bears who retired in 1987 as the all-time leading rusher in the history of the National Football League (NFL) and, to many, its greatest all-around player.

Payton was one of three children of Peter Edward Payton, a parachute factory custodian who drove a truck and did odd jobs, and his wife, Alyne, who worked evenings at the factory. The Paytons lived in a segregated city in a house without indoor plumbing. Much of the family's food came

Walter Payton, 1984. FRED JEWELL/ASSOCIATED PRESS AP

from a four-acre garden that the children helped cultivate. Payton's dad "expected 100 percent out of us," and at an early age Payton learned to "work hard and stay with something even though the project seemed overwhelming."

Payton was a loner throughout his life. As a boy he liked playing war by himself. He took that mentality to the football field. Football was a war in which he would strike the enemy before being struck. In pickup games he learned to "shed tackles, dodge guys," or better yet, "go right over them." At age sixteen he was playing semipro baseball with the Columbia Jets after church on Sundays, competing with his older brother Eddie for the spotlight.

Payton played drums for the John J. Jefferson High School marching band, while Eddie starred at running back on the football team. When Eddie took a scholarship to Jackson State University, the way was open for Payton. As a junior at Jefferson High, he ran sixty-five yards on his first play from scrimmage in football, and he set school records in other sports. He long-jumped twenty-two feet, eleven-and-a-quarter inches and averaged eighteen points a game for the basketball team. The following year at newly integrated Columbia High School, he won over white fans when his balance, speed, and toughness assured the team's success and made him an All-State selection. Payton waited for a college scholarship while running in old army boots along the soft mud of the Pearl River in the quiet of the Mississippi woods. The predominantly white University of Kansas offered one, but Payton decided instead to follow Eddie to Jackson State in 1971.

The Payton brothers were paired as Jackson State's starting backfield in 1971 during Eddie's senior year with the team. They thrived under legendary coach Bob Hill, who emphasized "playing the game and not drawing attention to yourself." Payton would become the Tigers leading rusher by following Hill's advice to "never die easy." He "took great pride in neutralizing the attack of attackers" by "exploding into them." He fought for every yard and refused to run out of bounds. He learned how to block and how to catch the ball—in short, how to be a complete football player. Payton became a Division II All-American at Jackson State, rushing for 3,563 yards at 6.1 yards per carry and scoring 65 touchdowns in his career there. He led the nation in scoring as a junior in 1973 with 160 points. He ran and kicked extra points and field goals for the Tigers, graduating in 1975 after scoring 464 points, a National Collegiate Athletic Association (NCAA) record.

In Payton's third year at Jackson State, Hill introduced him to Connie Norwood, a family friend and high school senior living in New Orleans. She focused on dance during her freshman year at Jackson State, while Payton's moves on the football field helped him finish fourth in the Heisman Trophy voting. Skeptics discounted his Division II records and said he was too small to make it in the National

Football League (NFL). But Chicago Bears general manager Jim Finks made the five-foot, ten-and-a-half-inch, 202-pound twenty-year-old the fourth selection of the NFL's 1975 college draft.

The Chicago Bears had a proud history as the winningest franchise in league history, but by the mid-1970s the team was a perennial loser. Payton initially seemed no savior, gaining no yards in eight carries in his first game against Baltimore. He was so distraught that he cried openly after the game. Three weeks later Detroit stopped him again for no yards in ten carries. He was so nervous, he had headaches and experienced dizziness. The next week against Pittsburgh, he was held out of a game for the only time in his thirteen-year career. Payton was lonely and felt discouraged. The Bears were bad, finishing the season 4–10, but Payton gained 134 yards in their final game at New Orleans.

Payton and Connie married on 7 July 1976, one day before the opening of training camp for Payton's second season. He was voted All-Pro that year after rushing for 1,390 yards, nearly twice the total of his rookie season, including thirteen touchdowns. The 1977 year was even more extraordinary. He gained 1,852 yards on 5.5 yards a carry, even though he lacked classic sprinter's speed. He set an NFL record with 275 yards rushing on 20 November 1977 against Minnesota while suffering from the flu. The Bears barely won, 10–7.

One of Payton's greatest runs occurred the week before in a game against Kansas City that the Bears had to win if they hoped to make the playoffs. Payton took a handoff at the Chiefs' twenty-six yard line, evading a lineman who appeared to have him trapped in the Bears' backfield. He then ran right and spun away from a Chiefs defender who pinned him against the sideline, while simultaneously pivoting from a lineman who had a pursuit angle from the inside. He ran through a linebacker's arm tackle at the twenty-five, shifted around a linebacker at the twenty-four, and evaded a defensive end with a limp leg at the twenty-three. Head down, he crashed into and ran over a lineman at the twenty-one and went head to head with a halfback at the eighteen, sliding over the defender's back and landing on his feet, and kept running before being tackled from behind at the four. In those eight seconds Payton displayed creativity, strength, speed, and power rarely matched in the game's history. His brother Eddie joked that Payton was "the reincarnation of a great white shark. If he stops moving forward, he will die." Payton's passion carried the Bears into the playoffs in 1977, and he was voted at age twenty-three the youngest Most Valuable Player (MVP) in NFL history.

The unassuming player was nicknamed "Sweetness" by teammates for his elusiveness on the field and gentle leadership off it. They daily gathered near his northwest-side

suburban home in the off-season to train on "Payton's Hill." He led them up the steeply vertical incline throughout the summer, preparing them "to be ready to be the best." Payton ran for 1,395 yards in 1978 and caught fifty passes for an additional 480 yards that season. But the season ended tragically. His father died in a Hattiesburg, Mississippi, jail cell in December 1978 after his arrest following a minor traffic accident. Authorities charged Edward Payton with drunk driving, but he had actually suffered a brain hemorrhage. Black activists urged the NFL's biggest star to charge racism, but Payton told the media that he and his family blamed no one and had his father quietly buried.

Between 1975 and 1983 Payton established himself as the NFL's premier running back, gaining more than 1,000 yards in six consecutive seasons, but the Bears were 58–71. Opposing teams focused on stopping the Bears' only weapon, and each week his body took a beating. Payton considered retiring after the strike-shortened 1982 season, but the hiring of Mike Ditka as Bears coach infused the franchise with new optimism and a "no-nonsense, hard-nosed, ask no quarter, give no quarter mentality." Payton rushed for 1,684 yards in 1984, and on 7 October 1984, in a game at Chicago's Soldier Field against New Orleans, he surpassed Jim Brown's all-time rushing record of 12,312 yards. Brown observed that Payton's "heart is as big as anyone who ever played the game." The Bears advanced through the playoffs before losing the conference championship to San Francisco. Payton combined for more than 2,000 yards rushing and receiving in 1984, and Ditka hailed him as "the greatest football player I ever saw." Fred O'Connor, the Bears' backfield coach, spoke for many when he said, "When God said I want to make a halfback, he chiseled Walter Payton."

The following year Payton's relentless broken field fury and acrobatic end zone leaps energized the Bears' ball control offense and dominating defense. A season highlight was the 13 October 1985 rematch against Joe Montana and the 49ers in San Francisco. Payton rushed twelve times in a decisive fourteen-play fourth-quarter drive that included a ten-yard touchdown run over All-Pro safety Ronnie Lott. The emotional win catapulted the Bears to an 18–1 season that ended with their 46–10 rout of New England in Super Bowl XX, touching off a tumultuous civic celebration in Chicago.

When he retired from the game after the 1987 season, Payton held twenty-six Bears and eight NFL records, including 16,726 rushing yards, 21,803 all-purpose yards, 125 touchdowns, seventy-seven 100-yard rushing games, and ten 1,000-yard rushing seasons. He was perhaps proudest of never having missed a game through injury. Payton had carried the ball 3,838 times and caught 492 passes. It was estimated that he had been buried under 2,165,000 pounds during his thirteen-year pro career. Teammates liked to remember how his off-the-field teasing had kept the locker room loose.

Payton was intensely competitive and found life after football particularly difficult. He became a member of the Bears board of directors and in 1993 was inducted into the NFL Hall of Fame, with his twelve-year-old son, Jarrett, presenting him to a crowd that included his wife, Connie, and eight-year-old daughter, Brittney. Payton tried unsuccessfully to land an expansion franchise in St. Louis and later owned a team in the Arena Football League. He became a partner in several nightclubs and restaurants and had holdings in real estate, travel agencies, and nursing homes. He raced cars for two years on the Sports 2000 circuit and another year in the GT-3 series before becoming a Championship Auto Racing Teams (CART) owner. He provided commentary on Bears exhibition games and had a weekly radio call-in show. His great love, however, was raising money through the Walter Payton Foundation for underprivileged children. His Gifts for Christmas campaign would annually start the holiday season in Chicago by channeling $3 million in presents to needy kids.

In the summer of 1998 Payton began losing weight and having stomach pains and was generally fatigued. On 2 February 1999 he told a stunned city that he had been diagnosed with primary sclerosing cholangitis, a rare liver disease that would require a liver transplant. He received tens of thousands of get-well cards, and some fans offered Payton their own livers, perhaps thinking they had two. He appeared on national television to raise public awareness about organ donation.

On 10 May 1999 exploratory surgery showed that Payton had bile duct cancer that had spread to the lymph nodes. He was no longer a candidate for a transplant but continued to raise public awareness through the organ donor program. Donations nationally surged 5 percent and in Illinois reached record levels. Payton died on 1 November 1999, and a civic celebration of his life was held at Soldier Field on 6 November. Eddie Payton thought his brother's legacy had been that he competed "with pride, with dignity and respect for the game." His Hall of Fame teammate Mike Singletary saw Payton as the quintessential fourth-quarter player whose last great run had been what he had done for others.

★

Payton's autobiography *Never Die Easy*, which he coauthored with Don Yaeger, was published posthumously in 2000. An earlier autobiography, *Sweetness* (1978), was cowritten with Jerry B. Jenkins. Major biographical collections are kept at the National Football League Hall of Fame in Canton, Ohio, and the offices of the Chicago Bears in Lake Forest, Illinois. Biographical treatments of his life include Mark Sufrin, *Payton* (1988), and Mike Towle, *I Remember Walter Payton: Personal Memories of Football's*

"Sweetest" Superstar by the People Who Knew Him Best (2000). His contributions to the history of professional football are particularly emphasized in Cooper Rollow, *Cooper Rollow's Bears Football Book* (1985), and Richard Whittingham, *The Bears: A Seventy-five-Year Celebration* (1994). An obituary is in the *New York Times* (2 Nov. 1999), and a series of articles describing his life and career are in the *Chicago Tribune* (2 Nov., 4 Nov., and 7 Nov. 1999).

BRUCE J. EVENSEN

PEABODY, Endicott ("Chub") (*b.* 15 February 1920 in Lawrence, Massachusetts; *d.* 2 December 1997 in Hollis, New Hampshire), lawyer and politician who first gained notoriety as an All-America football player at Harvard College, served as the governor of Massachusetts from 1963 to 1965, and ran a quixotic campaign for the U.S. vice presidency in 1972.

Peabody was the second of five children of Malcolm Endicott Peabody and Mary Elizabeth Parkman, both of whom came from established New England families. A direct descendant of John Endecott, a founder of the Massachusetts Bay Colony, Peabody was related to the pioneering U.S. philanthropist George Peabody, the nineteenth-century historian Francis Parkman, and William C. Endicott, who served as the secretary of war in President Grover Cleveland's administration. His paternal grandfather, Endicott Peabody, was an Episcopal minister who founded the prestigious Groton School in Massachusetts in 1884 and was its headmaster for fifty-six years. His father, also a minister, was the Episcopal bishop of central New York from 1942 to 1964. His mother, a homemaker and community volunteer, made headlines when she was jailed during civil rights demonstrations in St. Augustine, Florida, in 1964. His sister Mary Endicott ("Marietta") Tree represented the United States on the United Nations Trusteeship Council with the rank of ambassador from 1965 to 1966.

Peabody spent his early years in Lawrence, Massachusetts, and Chestnut Hill, Pennsylvania, where his father served as the rector of Episcopal churches. A shy, introverted child, he was often picked on by schoolmates at the private academies he attended. However, after he demonstrated his proficiency at tackle football at the William Penn Charter School in Philadelphia, Peabody grew more confident and forceful. Moving on to Groton, he was elected as a class officer and captain of the football team before graduating in 1938. He also embraced the political liberalism of Richard Irons, his history and government teacher at Groton, and acquired the sobriquet "Chub," which another faculty member had given his father some thirty years earlier. Although Malcolm Peabody had successfully resisted the nickname, it stayed with his athletic son.

At Harvard College in Cambridge, Massachusetts, Pea-

Endicott Peabody, 1977. ASSOCIATED PRESS AP

body majored in history, served on the student council, and achieved national fame on the football field. After being relegated to reserve status on the freshman team, the six-foot, one-inch tall, 165-pound guard followed a rigorous exercise regimen, substantially increased his weight (to 190 pounds) and strength, and became the dominant player around whom the legendary coach Dick Harlow built his complex offenses and defenses. Called the "most savage blocker and tackler in the Ivy League," Peabody led Harvard to winning seasons in his junior and senior years. He was the only player in the country named to all twenty All-America teams in 1941 and was also awarded the Knute Rockne Trophy as the outstanding college lineman of the year. Peabody was elected to the College Football Hall of Fame in 1973.

Immediately after receiving his B.A. degree in June 1942, Peabody was commissioned as an ensign in the U.S. Navy. After spending two years on an obsolete World War I–era R-boat in the Caribbean, he was installed as a gunnery and fire-control officer on the USS *Tirante,* a newly built submarine sent to the Pacific to disrupt Japanese ship-

ping. Peabody led daring raids aboard enemy supply ships disguised as junks in the East China and Yellow Seas, and participated in a successful July 1945 assault on the Japanese-held harbor of Quelpart Island off the coast of Korea. For this last effort, the crew of the *Tirante* received the Presidential Unit Citation and Peabody was awarded the Silver Star. On 24 June 1944 he married Barbara Welch ("Toni") Gibbons, whom he had met during an eight-month assignment in Bermuda. They had three children.

Upon discharge in 1945 Peabody entered Harvard Law School. He also involved himself in politics, supporting the successful campaign of the Republican Robert F. Bradford for governor of Massachusetts in 1946. Subsequently repelled by the conservatism of Republican leaders in the Eightieth Congress, he became a Democrat.

In 1948 Peabody received his LL.B. degree from Harvard, passed the Massachusetts bar, and joined the elite Boston law firm of Goodwin, Procter, and Hoar. Residing in Cambridge, he remained politically active, serving as the legislative agent and chairman of the Bay State chapter of the progressive American Veterans Committee (AVC). In the former role, he led a successful drive to desegregate the Massachusetts National Guard, and in the latter capacity he fought off attempts by communists to gain control of the AVC. Peabody briefly left the private practice of law for government service during the Korean War. After serving as the assistant regional counsel for the Office of Price Stabilization in 1951 and as the regional counsel for the Small Defense Plants Administration in 1952, he and two law school classmates formed a new legal partnership, Peabody, Koufman, and Brewer, in Boston.

Peabody, who had worked for Harry Truman and Adlai Stevenson in the presidential campaigns of 1948 and 1952, decided to enter the political fray himself in 1954 as a candidate for the Executive (or Governor's) Council, which had the power to approve gubernatorial appointments, certain state expenditures, and paroles. An earnest and indefatigable campaigner, Peabody defeated the Republican incumbent by 2,765 votes to become the first Democrat ever to represent his district. But over the next two years he grew frustrated at his inability to exert any influence on a body dominated by Republicans.

Peabody ran for the Democratic nomination for state attorney general in 1956 and 1958, and for governor in 1960. As a Yankee Protestant whose main support came from reformist amateurs from Boston's suburbs, he fought decidedly uphill battles in a party controlled by Irish-Catholic leaders. Although he lost all three races, respectable second-place finishes in the 1958 and 1960 primary contests encouraged him to continue his political quest.

With the Democrats reeling from a succession of damaging scandals involving party officeholders and the loss of the governorship in 1960, Peabody finally was able to break through and become the nominee for governor in 1962. In the ensuing campaign, he charged that Republican John A. Volpe's failure to deliver on campaign promises to reform state government had left Massachusetts in the "mire of corruption." Peabody, who had worked for John F. Kennedy in West Virginia and other primary states in 1960, often invoked the president's name on the stump. He was elected by a margin of 5,431 votes (out of 2.1 million cast) in the closest Massachusetts gubernatorial election of the twentieth century.

Peabody began his term as governor by opposing the reelection of John F. Thompson, the powerful Democratic Speaker of the Massachusetts House of Representatives, whom he regarded as the principal enemy of change. After Thompson dispatched all challengers, however, the affable governor was able to make peace with the Speaker and win his support and that of the state senate president John E. Powers for an agenda that included the reorganization of state departments plagued by corruption and inefficiency; constitutional amendments to extend the term of the governor and other constitutional officers to four years and to reduce the powers of the Executive Council; increased aid to higher education; and the creation of the Commonwealth Service Corps, a state version of President Kennedy's Peace Corps.

Despite achieving important goals, Peabody was not a popular governor. His proposals for an income-tax increase to finance education for cities and towns and for the abolition of capital punishment provoked public outcries and were defeated in the legislature. Particularly impolitic was his effort to do away with the death penalty at the time of highly publicized shootings of police officers and the murders of women attributed to the "Boston Strangler." Peabody also proved to be an ineffective spokesman for his own initiatives. Although intelligent and personally charming, he handled press conferences clumsily and proved awkward and uncomfortable in front of a television camera. Portrayed by the media as a bumbler, Peabody was upset in the 1964 Democratic primary by Lieutenant Governor Francis X. Bellotti, who then was defeated by John Volpe.

The resilient Peabody bounced back to defeat Boston mayor John F. Collins in the race for the Democratic nomination for U.S. senator in 1966, but the general election went to the popular Republican attorney general Edward W. Brooke, who became the first African American in the Senate since Reconstruction. A strong supporter of President Lyndon B. Johnson's handling of the war in Vietnam, Peabody was named as the assistant director of the Office of Emergency Planning by Johnson in 1967. He left the post after a year to take part in the presidential campaign of Vice President Hubert Humphrey. Following Humphrey's defeat, Peabody became a founding partner of the law firm Peabody, Rivlin, Gore, Cladouhos, and Lambert (later Peabody, Rivlin, Lambert, and Meyers) in Washington, D.C.

In 1972 Peabody became a candidate for the Democratic nomination for vice president. Believing that the choice of the second-highest elected official ought to be made by the people in open primaries and conventions rather than by presidential nominees and their advisers behind closed doors, he stumped in New Hampshire and other states seeking delegate support. Although he received a few favorable newspaper editorials and a smattering of votes at the Democratic National Convention, Peabody's crusade was largely ignored.

Homesick for New England, Peabody left Washington, D.C., in 1982. He purchased an early-nineteenth-century parsonage in Hollis, New Hampshire, and became a country lawyer, working out of a one-man office in the nearby city of Nashua. He reentered politics as a delegate to the New Hampshire Constitutional Convention in 1984, and was the sacrificial Democratic nominee for the U.S. Senate against the Republican incumbent Warren Rudman in 1986. Peabody spent his last years campaigning for the preservation of the United Nations as an instrument of world peace and against land mines, which he regarded as "the most inhumane type" of weaponry because they killed civilians. He died of leukemia and is buried in the town cemetery in Groton, Massachusetts.

Peabody was one of the best football players of his college generation, a highly decorated naval officer in World War II, and a well-respected trial lawyer. Despite his best efforts, however, he never achieved the same kind of success in elective politics. But his political career cannot be considered a total failure. In addition to making anticorruption efforts bipartisan in Massachusetts in the early 1960s, he helped to bring needed structural changes to the state's government, and his nomination and election as governor paved the way for other reform candidates, including the future presidential nominee Michael Dukakis, in the following decade. At his death, Peabody was given a fitting epitaph by his youngest son, Robert, "He lost more campaigns than he won, but he never lost the passion."

★

Collections of Peabody's papers are in four repositories in Boston: the John F. Kennedy Library, the Massachusetts Historical Society, the Massachusetts State Archives, and the State Library of Massachusetts. A clipping file on Peabody is in the Harvard University Archives. Autobiographical notes on his life and career can be found in the periodic reports of the Harvard Class of 1942 (1952, 1957, 1962, 1967, 1972, 1977, 1982, 1987, 1992, 1997). The official record of his governorship is Lester S. Hyman, comp., *Addresses and Messages to the General Court, Public Speeches, and Other Papers of General Interest of His Excellency Governor Endicott Peabody for the Years 1963 and 1964* (1971). A biography up to

1964 is James L. Collier, *The Chub Peabody Story* (1964). A shorter summary of his first forty-four years is in *Current Biography 1964* (1965). Peabody's football heroics are covered in Allison Danzig, *The History of American Football: Its Great Teams, Players, and Coaches* (1956), and Geoffrey H. Movius, ed., *The Second H Book of Harvard Athletics, 1923–1963* (1964). For his political odyssey in Massachusetts, see Murray B. Levin with George Blackwood, *The Compleat Politician: Political Strategy in Massachusetts* (1962); Edgar Litt, *The Political Cultures of Massachusetts* (1965); and Alec Barbrook, *God Save the Commonwealth: An Electoral History of Massachusetts* (1973). See also Gloria Negri, "Ex-Governor Makes a Comeback," *Boston Globe* (5 Oct. 1997). Obituaries are in the *Boston Globe* (3 Dec. 1997) and *New York Times* (4 Dec. 1997).

RICHARD H. GENTILE

PERKINS, Carl Lee (*b*. 9 April 1932 in Tiptonville, Tennessee; *d*. 19 January 1998 in Jackson, Tennessee), singer, songwriter, and guitarist who was one of the founding fathers of rock and roll and who enjoyed a career that stretched across five decades, beginning with his first and biggest hit, "Blue Suede Shoes."

Carl Perkins. KEN SETTLE

Perkins, the second of three sons of Buck Perkins and Louise Brantley, was born into the third generation of a Tennessee sharecropping family. His older brother, James Buck "Jay" Perkins, was born in 1930, and his younger brother, Lloyd Clayton Perkins (known as Clayton), followed in 1935. At age six Perkins began attending the Lake County grade school and started picking cotton in the fields with his family. Early on, he displayed an interest in the music he heard on the radio, and he asked his father for a guitar. When he got one, he learned how to play it from an African American named John Westbrook

In January 1946 the family moved to Bemis, Tennessee, in search of work. Perkins stopped attending school after the eighth grade, and he made a transition from picking cotton to working in a dairy. But he already had aspirations to become a professional musician, and he wrote his first song at fourteen. By the end of 1946 he and his brother Jay were performing in local honky-tonks as the Perkins Brothers; Carl played lead guitar and Jay played rhythm guitar.

In the late 1940s Perkins persuaded his brother Clayton to take up the bass and join the group, now called the Perkins Brothers Band. Carl began appearing on local radio in Jackson, first on his own and then with his brothers. He also began sending demonstration tapes to record companies. On 24 January 1953 he married Valda Crider, an employee at a utilities service company; they had four children. Around the same time, he turned to music full time. Late in 1953 W. S. "Fluke" Holland joined the Perkins Brothers Band as a percussionist.

In the honky-tonks, Perkins and his band developed a hybrid style of popular music that employed elements of country and R & B. In 1954 Perkins heard something similar in the initial recordings of Elvis Presley made for Sun Records in Memphis. That October, he took his band to Sun and auditioned for its owner, Sam Phillips, who agreed to record Perkins billed as a solo act, though he retained his group as a backup band. Perkins's first single, "Movie Magg"/"Turn Around," was issued in February 1955, followed in September 1955 by "Let the Jukebox Keep on Playing"/"Gone Gone Gone." But it was his third single, "Blue Suede Shoes"/"Honey Don't," that made him a star. He had gotten the idea for the A-side when he overheard a fashion-conscious man on the dance floor warning his date not to "step on my blue suede shoes." In Perkins's hands, the refrain came to represent the aspirations of rural people to style and sophistication, and his music was an ideal representation of the raucous new style of rockabilly.

"Blue Suede Shoes" was released by Sun on 1 January 1956. It entered all three of *Billboard* magazine's popularity charts, eventually rising to number two on the pop and R & B charts, and number one on the country chart. During that ascent, Perkins was scheduled to make his national television debut on the *Perry Como Show*, but he and his band were involved in an automobile accident in Dover, Delaware, en route to the performance. Perkins suffered a broken collarbone, and though he recovered quickly, he missed crucial weeks of promotion and exposure as his breakthrough hit was reaching its peak. In contrast, Presley, also enjoying his first national recognition at the time, went on to a string of television appearances that consolidated his success.

By late April, Perkins was back on the road. His follow-up singles, "Boppin' the Blues" and "Dixie Fried," reached the country top ten but did not become pop hits. He left Sun for Columbia Records at the start of 1958, but as rock and roll declined in the late 1950s, he was unable to repeat his early success. In the early 1960s he continued to perform, notably in Las Vegas, Nevada, and he turned to writing songs for others, signing to Nashville-based Cedarwood Publishing. Over time, he wrote a number of country hits that included "So Wrong" (Patsy Cline, 1962), "Daddy Sang Bass" (Johnny Cash, 1968), "Let Me Tell You About Love" (The Judds, 1989), and "Silver and Gold" (Dolly Parton, 1991). But despite a series of record contracts, he never again scored a hit of his own.

In 1964 Perkins toured England, where he met the Beatles, who were greatly influenced by his Sun recordings. The group recorded three of his songs, "Honey Don't," "Everybody's Trying to Be My Baby," and "Matchbox." In 1966 he joined Johnny Cash's touring show as its opening act and, eventually, the guitarist in Cash's backup band, remaining with the troupe until 1975, when he formed the C. P. Express with his sons Stan and Greg. He regained the rights to his Sun compositions in a legal battle in 1977, and with his financial position secure he spent more of his time on charity work, founding the Exchange Club Carl Perkins Center for the Prevention of Child Abuse in Jackson, and supporting it with an annual telethon. He was inducted into the Rock and Roll Hall of Fame in 1987. In 1991 he overcame throat cancer and returned to performing. He died of a stroke at age sixty-five in Jackson, and is buried there in Ridgecrest Cemetery.

It could be argued that Carl Perkins was the most successful one-hit wonder in popular music history, able to turn a single chart-topping song into a forty-year career. But it could as easily be argued that only misfortune kept him from becoming as big a star as his friend and rival Elvis Presley. True, as a big, rawboned man with a rapidly receding hairline, he did not have Presley's matinee idol looks, but he had developed the same sort of kinetic style through his years in the honky-tonks, and he was a superior musician who, unlike Presley, wrote his own songs. That turned out to be his salvation after his own recordings ceased to be hits, and he remained one of the handful of true progenitors of rock and roll.

★

The definitive source for information about Perkins is *Go, Cat, Go!: The Life and Times of Carl Perkins, the King of Rockabilly*

(1996). Author David McGee cocredited Perkins for the book while acknowledging that his subject never actually put pen to paper, on the grounds that it is based almost entirely on extensive interviews with him. Michael Lydon, "Dirty Blue Suede Shoes," *Rolling Stone* (7 Dec. 1968), is a revealing portrait. It was reprinted in Dylan Jones, ed., *Meaty Beaty Big and Bouncy!* (1996). An obituary is in the *New York Times* (20 Jan. 1998).

WILLIAM J. RUHLMANN

PERKINS, James Alfred (*b.* 11 October 1911 in Philadelphia, Pennsylvania; *d.* 19 August 1998 in Burlington, Vermont), seventh president of Cornell University, leading theoretician of higher education, and founder and chairman of the International Council for Educational Development.

Perkins was born to H. Norman Perkins, a banker, and Emily Cramp Taylor, a social activist. Perkins had one sister. Although Perkins's parents were not Quakers, he was sent to a Quaker school, the Germantown Friends School in Philadelphia. Perkins's moral values were set by his experience at the school, his mother's social conscience, and the middle-class respectability provided by his father. These values were destined to be instrumental in guiding Perkins's actions during his time as president of Cornell University.

James A. Perkins, 1963. AP/WIDE WORLD PHOTOS

Perkins received a B.A. degree, graduating with high honors, from Swarthmore College in 1934. During his time at the college he joined the Religious Society of Friends (Quakers). Perkins received a Ph.D. in political science from Princeton University in 1937. He remained at Princeton until 1941, first as an instructor and assistant professor, then as assistant director of Princeton's School of Public and International Affairs. On 20 June 1938 he married Jean E. Bredin. They had five children.

During World War II Perkins served in the United States Office of Price Administration and the Foreign Economic Administration. After the war he returned to Swarthmore and served as vice president from 1945 to 1950. Perkins joined the Carnegie Corporation, a prominent educational foundation, as an executive associate in 1950. From 1951 to 1963 he served as vice president of the Carnegie Corporation of New York and the Carnegie Foundation for the Advancement of Teaching. From 1951 to 1952 he took a leave from the Carnegie Corporation to serve as deputy chairman of the Research and Development Board of the Department of Defense. He also served as a chairman of President John F. Kennedy's Advisory Panel on the National Academy of Foreign Affairs in 1963.

Perkins became the seventh president of Cornell University in 1963 and served until 1969, leading the university through its most tumultuous years of social change. Without doubt, the Cornell presidency was the jewel in Perkins's crown. Utilizing the connections he had cultivated with influential leaders and organizations, he seized the opportunity to influence social change. Academic innovations were a hallmark of his administration. By the late 1960s he was widely regarded as one of the leading theoreticians of higher education. During Perkins's six-year tenure as president, many new programs and academic organizations were initiated, twenty-three professorships were endowed, and the campus physical plant was significantly enlarged.

Perkins was committed to excellence in undergraduate education, especially encouraging diversity in the student body. He significantly increased the numbers of African-American and other minority students at Cornell. In 1964 the Committee on Special Educational Projects (COSEP) was established with the specific intent of providing educational opportunities for minority students. During Perkins's presidency, the number of African-American students on campus increased from fewer than 10 to more than 250.

The last year of Perkins's administration was preoccupied with the rising level of student political protest and activism. The activism culminated with the takeover of Willard Straight Hall, the Cornell Student Union, by armed black militant students. The takeover, subsequent presidential public humiliations, and lack of faculty support led directly to Perkins's resignation on 31 May 1969. Perkins's first wife died in 1970, and on 30 January 1971 Perkins married Ruth Bergengren Aall.

A continuing active involvement in national government and educational affairs marked Perkins's career. In 1970 Perkins founded and led the International Council for Educational Development. He became chairman emeritus in 1990. As CEO for twenty years, Perkins engaged the organization in identifying and analyzing key problems facing education around the world. He was also a member of the General Advisory Committee of the United States Committee for the United Nations Educational, Scientific, and Cultural Organization (UNESCO) and served on the board of trustees of the Rand Corporation. Perkins held board memberships on several educational and civil rights organizations, including the chairmanship of the board of trustees of the United Negro College Fund. He headed a Rockefeller Brothers Fund Committee that produced "The Power of the Democratic Idea," a report well known in the educational field.

In 1965 Perkins was elected to membership in the American Academy of Arts and Sciences and was a recipient of the gold medal of the National Institute of Social Sciences. He chaired the New York Advisory Committee on Educational Leadership from 1963 to 1967, the Presidential General Advisory Committee on Foreign Assistance from 1965 to 1969, and the board of trustees of the Educational Testing Service from 1967 to 1968. President Lyndon B. Johnson named him cochair of the International Conference on the World Crisis in Education in 1967. Perkins was the recipient of thirty-five honorary degrees. Perkins died from complications due to a fall while vacationing in the Adirondacks. He is buried in Princeton, New Jersey.

Perkins departed from Cornell as a tragic figure, but his legacy fared better. Cornell's Black Studies Program and the Africana Studies and Research Center were founded in 1969. Early in 1992 the James A. Perkins Professorship of Environmental Studies was established, and in June 1992 Perkins was also appointed President Emeritus by the Cornell Board of Trustees. In an almost bizarre turnaround, Tom Jones, a leader of the militant students involved in the famous takeover, was appointed as a Cornell Trustee in 1993. Having achieved considerable success in the financial sector, Jones established a fund at Cornell in 1994 that created the James A. Perkins Prize for Interracial Understanding and Harmony. The prize was an effort to promote the healing of wounds and bitterness after the events of 1969, which still reverberated on the Cornell campus.

★

The events of 1969, including the circumstances resulting in Perkins's resignation, are documented by Donald Downs, *Cornell*

'69: *Liberalism and the Crisis of the American University* (2000). Perkins wrote *The University in Transition* (1966) and edited *The University as an Organization* (1973). The former work was based on the Stafford Little Lectures Perkins delivered at Princeton in 1965. An obituary is in the Cornell News Service (21 Aug. 1998).

RICHARD E. RIPPLE

PETERSON, Esther (*b.* 9 December 1906 in Provo, Utah; *d.* 20 December 1997 in Washington, D.C.), a key advocate for consumer rights and truth in labeling and an activist in the movements for women's and workers' rights.

Peterson was the fifth of six children born to a Danish-American family. She received a traditional Mormon upbringing and attended the local public schools, where her father, Lars Eggertsen, was superintendent. Her mother, Annie Nielsen, was one of the first women to attend Brigham Young University in Provo; she kept boarders at home to supplement the family income. In 1918, at age twelve, Peterson witnessed a strike by railway workers in Provo, an experience that opened her eyes to the poor conditions for industrial workers.

Peterson earned a B.A. degree in physical education from Brigham Young University in 1927 and then taught for two years at Branch Agricultural College in Cedar City, Utah. Subsequently, she attended Teachers' College of Columbia University in New York City, where she received an M.A. degree in 1930. There, she met her future husband,

Esther Peterson, 1979. ASSOCIATED PRESS AP

Oliver A. Peterson, an activist in the labor movement. They attended many rallies and public gatherings together and shared many interests; they were married on 28 May 1932.

From 1930 to 1936 Esther worked as a teacher and department head at the Winsor School in Boston. In addition, she taught at the Bryn Mawr Summer School for Women Workers in Industry in Bryn Mawr, Pennsylvania, from 1932 to 1939. She also worked as an organizer for the American Federation of Teachers (1938), as the assistant director of education for the Amalgamated Clothing Workers of America (ACWA) in New York City (1939–1944), and then as the ACWA's Washington legislative representative (1945–1948). During this same period, she also served on the District of Columbia's minimum wage board as the representative for the laundry industry.

When Oliver, a foreign service officer, was appointed to a post in Sweden, she moved to Stockholm with him and the family, which now included four children. While in Sweden from 1948 to 1952, Peterson studied women's employment and worked with women's and labor groups. Later, living in Belgium from 1952 to 1957, she worked with women's organizations and set up a training course for the International Confederation of Free Trade Unions. Also, at La Brevière, near Paris, she taught at the First International School for Working Women.

Back in Washington, D.C., in 1958, Peterson worked as a legislative representative for the industrial union department of the American Federation of Labor–Congress of Industrial Organizations (AFL-CIO). In 1961 President John F. Kennedy asked her to head the Women's Bureau in the U.S. Department of Labor and, later the same year, to serve as assistant secretary of labor for labor standards. In addition, she was appointed executive vice chairman of the first President's Commission on the Status of Women (1961–1963), which was chaired by Eleanor Roosevelt until her death in 1962. Peterson also helped to found the National Committee on Household Employment (1964–1965), an organization that brought together voluntary groups and government agencies under the auspices of the Women's Bureau to improve the working conditions of household workers, develop training programs, and change public attitudes about household employees.

President Lyndon B. Johnson asked Peterson to remain as Women's Bureau director and named her to the newly created post of special assistant to the president for consumer affairs, a position she held until 1967. Until her reappointment to this post by President Jimmy Carter in 1977, she worked again as the legislative representative to the ACWA (1969–1970). From 1970 to 1977 Peterson was employed as a consumer adviser by the Giant Food Corporation in the Washington, D.C., metropolitan area, helping the company to develop an enlightened marketing policy to promote consumer education.

Peterson had already served as an adviser to three presidents (Kennedy, Johnson, and Carter) when President William J. Clinton appointed her in 1993 to the U.S. delegation to the United Nations (UN), to work with its Educational, Scientific, and Cultural Organization (UNESCO). Peterson also chaired the Consumer Affairs Council and served on the board of the United Seniors Health Cooperative. In her late seventies she persuaded the International Organization of Consumers Unions at the UN to pass the Consumer Protection Guidelines, which stimulated the passage of new consumer laws on three continents. She also persuaded the UN General Assembly to approve the creation of a list of banned or restricted products to alert nations to the international trafficking in such dangerous items.

Peterson was widely recognized for helping to organize garment workers and teachers. She was instrumental in bringing about legislative victories for the minimum wage, amendments to the Fair Labor Standards Act, the Equal Pay Act, and the Occupational Safety and Health Act, as well as legislation guaranteeing truth in packaging, truth in lending, unit pricing, and product labeling of ingredients. She worked actively to promote the rights of women, minorities, workers, consumers, and household employees; campaigned extensively for Democratic candidates; served as a visiting professor at the University of Illinois in Urbana-Champaign (1982); and traveled and lectured widely.

Peterson was awarded the Presidential Medal of Freedom in 1981 by President Carter. At her ninetieth birthday party, Senator Edward Kennedy, the well-known Democrat from Massachusetts, remarked that she was one of his heroes: "What extraordinary artists are to the arts, Esther Peterson is to consumers, working families, and children." Peterson herself observed, "Industry hated me, but you've got to say what you've got to say."

According to the National Council on Aging, she was unsurpassed as a model for vital aging. In *Restless: The Memoirs of Labor and Consumer Activist Esther Peterson* (1995), with Winifred Conkling, Peterson wrote, "I am an old lady in my ninth decade of life. . . . [But] you don't have to stop contributing when your hair turns white." Elsewhere in her memoirs she wrote, "I want people to believe. I want them to care. . . . I want them to look at injustice and ask, 'What can I do about that?' I want them to know that they certainly can make a difference." Peterson died of a stroke at age ninety-one. She was cremated and her ashes were scattered at her farm in Townshend, Vermont, where her husband's ashes were scattered after his death in 1979. The farm was their rural retreat from the hectic pace of political life in Washington, D.C. Peterson's memorial service was held on 23 January 1998 at Saint Columba's Episcopal Church in northwest Washington,

D.C. Among the hundreds of guests was President Carter. Peterson's family requested that contributions in her name be sent to the Eleanor Roosevelt Center at Val-Kill (ERVK), designated for the Girls' Leadership Program there.

On learning of Peterson's death, President Clinton described her as "the mother of the modern movement for consumer rights." The consumer activist Ralph Nader wrote, "Few if any individuals made so many significant contributions for so long on behalf of workers, consumers, and women in so many diverse areas, including government, civic, and business. . . . This complete public servant and public citizen did it all, raising four children, taking loving care of her husband who was stricken by cancer for years, and elevating the standards of living and justice by her work, her inspiring example, and the institutions that survive her."

★

Peterson's papers are housed at the Schlesinger Library, Radcliffe Institute, Harvard University, in Cambridge, Massachusetts. Additional papers can be found in the presidential libraries of John F. Kennedy, Lyndon B. Johnson, and Jimmy Carter, and in the archives of the National Consumers' League. Peterson wrote an autobiography with Winifred Conkling, *Restless: The Memoirs of Labor and Consumer Activist Esther Peterson* (1995). There is a profile by Marian Burros, "At 90, an Advocate Retains a Velvet Touch," *New York Times* (18 Dec. 1996). See also Ralph Nader, "In Memoriam: In Appreciation of Esther Peterson, Restless Activist," *Multinational Monitor* 18, no. 12 (Dec. 1997). Obituaries are in the *Washington Post* (21 Dec. 1997) and *New York Times* (22 Dec. 1997).

VERNE MOBERG

PETRY, Ann Lane (*b.* 12 October 1908 in Old Saybrook, Connecticut; *d.* 28 April 1997 in Old Saybrook, Connecticut), writer whose first novel, *The Street* (1946), about the hardships African Americans endured in Harlem, was the first best-seller by an African-American woman.

Petry was the younger daughter of Peter Clark Lane, Jr., a pharmacist, and Bertha James, a chiropodist, hairdresser, and entrepreneur. Despite growing up in the mostly white seaside resort town of Old Saybrook, Petry enjoyed a happy childhood in and around the town pharmacy. A precocious student, she enrolled in first grade at age four to keep her six-year-old sister company. Petry's early talent as a writer did not go unnoticed. Many years later, she gratefully recalled the encouragement she received from a stern English teacher: "The seed was sown by the praise of Caesar." However, following in the footsteps of her father and a beloved aunt, Petry earned a Ph.G. degree in 1931 from

Ann Petry, 1946. AP/WIDE WORLD PHOTOS

the Connecticut College of Pharmacy in New Haven. Her family's drugstores in Old Saybrook and nearby Old Lyme provided her with ready employment, but she was not destined to be a small-town pharmacist all of her life. On 22 February 1938 she married George Petry, an aspiring writer from New Iberia, Louisiana, and moved to New York City.

Although no stranger to the debilitating effects of prejudice, Petry did not comprehend the full reach of racism until she arrived in Harlem. Working for African-American newspapers, first as an advertising representative and reporter for the *Amsterdam News* (1938–1941), and then as a reporter, women's page editor, and columnist for the *People's Voice* (1941–1943), she became intimately familiar with the pain and hardship that poor African Americans experienced. A sympathetic outsider rather than a fellow sufferer, Petry helped found Negro Women, Inc., a consumer-protection organization, and worked in an after-school program at a local YMCA. In the mid-1940s she also performed with the American Negro Theatre and studied creative writing at Columbia University. Shortly thereafter Petry began to publish her writing. Her first story in print was "Marie of the Cabin Club," which the *Baltimore Afro-American* published in 1939 under the pseudonym Arnold Petri.

Petry's 1943 story "On Saturday the Siren Sounds at Noon" in the *Crisis,* the paper of the National Association for the Advancement of Colored People (NAACP) attracted

the attention of a Houghton Mifflin editor. Living on her husband's military allotment check and money she earned writing copy for a wig catalog, Petry began to write full time. Houghton Mifflin liked her work well enough to award her a $2,400 literary fellowship in 1945 that enabled her to complete a novel. *The Street* appeared to great fanfare in 1946. Eventually selling over a million and a half copies, it became the first best-seller by an African-American woman.

The Street revolves around Lutie Johnson, an upstanding young African-American woman trying to make a life for herself and her young son in Harlem. It is also the story of an entire community in quiet turmoil and contains memorable portraits of Lutie's fellow tenement dwellers. With *The Street,* Petry announced herself as a formidable chronicler of American life, the equal in African-American letters of Richard Wright, the acclaimed author of *Native Son.*

After World War II and a decade in the city, Petry chose the familiarity of her hometown over the hubbub of New York City. Petry and her husband returned to Old Saybrook in 1947 and bought an eighteenth-century home there. She wanted to be a writer, not a celebrity, and Old Saybrook afforded her the peace and quiet that she craved.

As Petry had in *The Street,* she drew on her surroundings in later books. Her second novel, *Country Place* (1947), tells the story of a community—much like Old Saybrook—adjusting, with difficulty, to postwar life. The novel employs a white male narrator, and all the primary characters are white, demonstrating Petry's versatility and creative range. Her third novel, *The Narrows* (1953), concerns an interracial love affair in a city similar to Hartford, Connecticut, where open minds are in remarkably short supply. Petry's last book expressly for adults was *Miss Muriel and Other Stories* (1971), a collection of thirteen stories she had written over three decades. It was one of the first volumes of short fiction published by an African-American woman.

Many readers know Petry as an author of forthright, engaging books for children and young adults. In 1949, the year that her daughter was born, Petry published *The Drugstore Cat.* She went on to publish two books for young adults, *Harriet Tubman, Conductor on the Underground Railroad* (1955), and *Tituba of Salem Village* (1964); she also published a nonfiction book for children, *Legends of the Saints* (1970).

Old Saybrook remained Petry's home for the rest of her days. She took a position as a visiting teacher at the University of Hawaii from 1974 to 1975, a surprising move for one so devoted to her hometown. She corresponded with scholars but granted interviews only when the spirit moved her, frequently changing her phone number to keep interlocutors at bay. A renewed interest in her books, especially *The Street,* nevertheless brought Petry back into the limelight in her later years. Young scholars embraced her as a major American author and role model. Her books began to be taught in college classrooms, and she received honorary doctorates from Suffolk University, the University of Connecticut, and Mount Holyoke College.

Though plump and robust in her youth, Petry grew small and delicate in old age. She wore her white hair piled on her head in an elegant bun and looked at her latest generation of admirers with a calm, discerning gaze. Like the actress Katharine Hepburn, another resident of Old Saybrook, Petry was a New England aristocrat who preferred to let her work speak for itself. She died of respiratory complications at a convalescent center near her hometown and is buried in Old Saybrook.

Petry remains an important figure in American literature because she wrote so clearly and movingly of African-American life at the middle of the twentieth century. Realistically portraying the all-too-timeless plight of poor African Americans struggling to survive in a blighted world, *The Street* provides both a companion and an antidote to Wright's male-centered, grotesquely deterministic *Native Son.* Much more than a writer of protest fiction, Petry understood that individuals, no matter what their race or gender, both define and are defined by the society in which they live.

★

The Ann Petry Collection at Boston University's Mugar Memorial Library contains many of Petry's personal papers and correspondence. Collections of her papers are also available at Shaw University, Yale University, Atlanta University, and Howard University. Petry's autobiographical essay, "Ann Petry" in *Contemporary Authors Autobiography Series* 6 (1988), is an excellent account of the author's life and influences. Hazel Arnett Ervin, *Ann Petry: A Bio-Bibliography* (1993), contains biographical material, including interviews with Petry, and an annotated bibliography. For biographical information and a critical analysis of Petry's books for adults, see Hilary Holladay, *Ann Petry* (1996). Marilyn Sanders Mobley, "Ann Petry," in *African American Writers* (1991), provides a helpful overview of Petry's life and publications. Two essays about *The Street* stand out: Keith S. Clark, "A Distaff Dream Deferred? Ann Petry and the Art of Subversion," *African American Review* 26, no. 3 (1992): 495–505; and Carol Henderson, "The 'Walking Wounded': Rethinking Black Women's Identity in Ann Petry's *The Street*," *Modern Fiction Studies* 46, no. 4 (winter 2000): 849–867. An obituary is in the *New York Times* (30 Apr. 1997).

HILARY HOLLADAY

POSTEL, Jonathan Bruce (*b.* 6 August 1943 in Altadena, California; *d.* 16 October 1998 in Santa Monica, California), computer scientist who was known as the "Father of the Internet."

Postel grew up in the San Fernando Valley in Southern California. Along with his two brothers and one sister he attended Van Nuys High School. When he then went on to Los Angeles Valley College as a general science major, there was nothing to distinguish him from hundreds of his peers. But in 1963 he saw a fellow student writing a computer program and became interested in those room-size behemoths used by banks, insurance companies, and the military to store and calculate millions of records. He transferred to the University of California, Los Angeles (UCLA), where he obtained a B.S. degree in engineering in 1966 and an M.S. degree in the same field two years later. He then applied for the graduate program in computer science, and was awarded a graduate fellowship at UCLA's Network Management Center.

During his first year at the Network Management Center, Postel made three critical contributions to the birth of the modern Internet. At that time the Defense Department's Advanced Research Projects Agency (ARPA) was developing a method of exchanging information between computers thousands of miles apart, an early computer network called ARPANet. Postel helped develop the software that enabled the exchange of "packets" of information, installing the ARPANet's first packet switch in October 1969; this moment has since been called the initiation of the Internet. Then, to keep track of the computers using the network, Postel began jotting down their file transfer protocol numbers in his notebook; this scrap of paper was the beginning of the Internet Assigned Numbers Authority (IANA), which ensured that the assignment of domain names and country codes would continue without obstacle throughout the Internet's explosive growth during the next thirty years. Finally, Postel began publishing a series of technical notes exchanged by scientists working on network development, called Requests for Comment, or RFCs.

These RFCs, compiled and stored in basic ASCII text, constituted a technical database of definitions and standards accessible to computer users anywhere in the world, using any computer language. Among the most basic of these working papers are Postel's formal definition of the File Transfer Protocol (FTP), first sketched out in 1971 but not codified until 1980 (RFC 765); the Transmission Control Protocol and the Internet Protocol, better known to contemporary computer users as TCP/IP (RFC 760–1, 1980); the Mail Transfer Protocol, one of the building blocks of e-mail (RFC 821, 1982); and TELNET (1983). Not content with such solemn activities, Postel also initiated what would become a tradition of April Fool's Day RFCs.

One of Postel's most prominent character traits was that of a hacker. That is, he derived immense pleasure from using his knowledge of the inner working of computer systems to access those system, legally or illegally. It was almost inevitable that someone capable of writing access codes for defense department computers would want to use those codes upon occasion. In one well-known 1980 episode, Postel used his hacking ability to solve a particularly knotty problem involving the transmission of e-mail between computer systems that did not share a common language. Ultimately, the covert hack became an accepted system: InterMail.

Postel was also known for his neglect of the usual trappings of authority. An ardent backpacker, he would often return to the institute directly after hiking near Yosemite; government officials expecting to see a stereotypical computer scientist, complete with short-sleeve shirt and narrow tie, were caught off guard by this symbol of the intelligent counterculture. Indeed, the U.S. Air Force once informed Postel that he was *required* to wear shoes while on the job.

Upon receipt of his Ph.D. in computer science in 1974, Postel worked briefly for the Mitre Corporation and for the Stanford Research Institute (SRI), one of the early leaders in software development, in their Augmentation Research Center. In 1977, however, he returned to academia, joining the Information Sciences Institute at the University of Southern California. As director of its computer networks division, Postel worked on such topics as electronic commerce, multimedia conferencing, and the theory of very large networks. He remained in this position until his death.

When the Internet Society was founded in 1992, he made sure he was enrolled as member number one, and was elected to its board of trustees in 1996. Shortly after his death, the society awarded Postel the newly created Jonathan B. Postel Service Award. When the Internet Architecture Board was conceived in 1983, he was a founding member. He was a member of the Association for Computing Machinery, and a recipient of its ACM Special Interest Group on Computer Communication (SIGCOMM) Award in 1987. He also received the Silver Medal from the International Telecommunications Union in 1997, an award usually reserved for heads of state.

Postel underwent heart surgery to replace a faulty valve in 1991. He recovered, but when that replacement valve began to leak in 1998, he had to undergo emergency surgery a second time, and died of postoperative complications at Saint John's Hospital in Santa Monica. His body was cremated, and both private and public memorial services were later held. Postel was survived by his partner Susann Gould, with whom he lived for many years, his mother, two brothers, and a sister.

Postel was not merely a creator of computer code; he was willing to accept responsibility for the monster he had created. As such, he carried on his work at IANA, and as RFC editor, against pressure from corporations and governments on the one side, and from anarchic computer users and hackers on the other—all in the service of the free interchange of information. If he was the "Father of the Internet," he was also its most devoted servant.

★

Postel's most cherished publications were his RFCs, listed at his home page: <http://Postel@isi.edu>. A memorial website can be found at <http://www.iana.org>. Memorial tributes were collected at the website of the Internet Society, <http://www.isoc.org/postel/index.shtml>. A tribute by Katie Hafner, "A Net Builder Who Loved Invention, Not Profit," appeared in the *New York Times* (22 Oct. 1998). A history of the Internet was published by Hafner and Matthew Lyon, *Where Wizards Stay Up Late* (1998). Obituaries are in the *New York Times* and *Washington Post* (both 18 Oct. 1998).

HARTLEY S. SPATT

POVICH, Shirley Lewis (*b.* 15 July 1905 in Bar Harbor, Maine; *d.* 4 June 1998 in Washington, D.C.), sportswriter and editor for the *Washington Post* whose career spanned eight decades, bridging the eras of Babe Ruth and Mark McGwire.

One of nine children born to Nathan Povich, who sold furniture, and Rosa Orlovich, a homemaker, Povich got his

Shirley Povich, 1965. AP/WIDE WORLD PHOTOS

name, common among Maine boys in those days, from a loose translation into Yiddish of the name of his grandmother Sarah. His parents were Orthodox Jewish immigrants from Lithuania who had settled in Bar Harbor, where many of America's wealthiest citizens spent their summers.

As a teenager, Povich worked as a caddy at the Kebo Valley Golf Club, where he was taken under the wing of Edward B. McLean, then the publisher of the *Washington Post*. For three summers, beginning in 1920, Povich was McLean's personal caddy. Povich graduated from high school in 1922; at the end of that summer, McLean told his seventeen-year-old protégé that he wanted Povich to return to Washington, D.C., with him. There, McLean said, Povich could work as his caddy and as a copy boy at the *Post*, while attending classes at Georgetown University.

On his first morning in the capital, Povich found himself caddying for McLean and the publisher's good friend President Warren G. Harding. Meanwhile, at the *Post*, Povich rose from copy boy to police reporter and night rewrite man before being lured to the sports department in 1924 by a $5-a-week raise. His first byline appeared that August over a story on the Washington Senators, who were on their way to a World Series title.

Povich was just twenty-one when McLean made him sports editor of the *Post* in 1926, the youngest man to head the sports section of a major U.S. newspaper. Shortly thereafter, he began writing a column, "This Morning, with Shirley Povich." Although Povich stepped down as sports editor after seven years, he continued to write the daily column. Povich wrote "This Morning" for more than seventy years, filing his final column the day before he died.

Povich was present when Babe Ruth clubbed his famous and much-disputed "called shot" home run in the World Series against the Cubs in 1932. Povich later said Ruth did not predict his home run, but rather was pointing at Cubs pitcher Charlie Root because Root's previous pitch had come before Ruth was ready. Povich was also in Yankee Stadium for Don Larsen's perfect game in the 1956 World Series, which generated one of his most famous leads: "The million-to-one shot came in. Hell froze over. A month of Sundays hit the calendar. Don Larsen today pitched a no-hit, no-run, no-man-reach-first game in a World Series."

Always sharply dressed, Povich, a dapper little man of about five feet, six inches was a near-perfect gentleman in the often rough-and-tumble world of sports. His longest-running feud was with George Preston Marshall, the owner who moved the National Football League (NFL) Redskins from Boston to Washington in 1937, and who earned Povich's enmity with his bullying, racist ways. When Marshall stood on the sidelines during a game, pacing nearer and nearer to the field of play as he made substitutions, Povich wrote, "If Marshall takes one more step, the Redskins will be penalized for having eleven and a half men on the field."

In 1943, after Povich wrote columns criticizing the Redskins for taking too big a cut from a wartime charity exhibition that was supposed to benefit the widows and children of servicemen, Marshall unsuccessfully sued Povich and his paper for $100,000.

Later, when the Redskins were the last NFL team with no black players on their roster, Povich wrote, after a clobbering by the Cleveland Browns on 31 October 1960, "Jim Brown, born ineligible to play for the Redskins, integrated their end zone three times yesterday."

During World War II, Povich was dispatched by the *Post* to cover the U.S. Navy's campaign to retake the Pacific from the Japanese. He covered the Iwo Jima and Okinawa campaigns before fracturing two vertebrae and returning home.

Povich achieved notoriety outside the world of sports in 1959 when he was included in the first edition of *Who's Who of American Women*. The mistake provoked newspaper stories, a *Time* magazine photo of Povich wielding an enormous cigar, and a telegram from Povich's friend Walter Cronkite: "Miss Povich, will you marry me?"

As Cronkite knew, Povich was already taken, having married Ethyl Friedman in 1932, two years after they met on a blind date at a Baltimore sorority dance. The couple had two sons and a daughter: David, who became a Washington lawyer; Maury, a broadcast journalist and television talk show host; and Lynn, a journalist and magazine editor.

Even after Povich officially "retired" from the *Post* in 1974, he continued filing regular columns—more than 15,000 in his career, according to a posthumous calculation. Povich covered heavyweight title fights, football championships, horse races, even the occasional basketball game, though he disliked the latter sport's aerial evolution, complaining, "They don't shoot baskets anymore, they stuff them, like taxidermists."

Baseball was Povich's favorite sport, and he covered most of the game's greatest names, from Babe Ruth, Lou Gehrig, and Walter Johnson early in his career; through Ted Williams, Joe DiMaggio, and Mickey Mantle; down to Cal Ripken and Mark McGwire in the 1980s and 1990s.

Along with DiMaggio, Povich was one of only two people present for both the end of Gehrig's streak of 2,130 consecutive games played and for the 1995 game in which Ripken surpassed that record. In his final column, published the morning after his death, Povich compared the feats of Babe Ruth with those of Mark McGwire, who months later would break the record for home runs in a season, a record that had been held most famously by Ruth. Not surprisingly, Povich came down in favor of Ruth's superiority, much as he maintained that no latter-day boxer—not Joe Louis, Rocky Marciano, or Muhammad Ali—could have matched Jack Dempsey in his prime.

Povich received numerous journalistic awards during his long career and served as president of the Baseball Writers Association of America. In 1976 he was elected to the writers' division of the Baseball Hall of Fame in Cooperstown, New York.

Povich died of a heart attack at his home in Washington, D.C., and is buried in Elevesgrad Cemetery in Washington. The child of immigrants, Povich lived a classic "made in America" success story, seizing the opportunity offered by Edward McLean and turning it into one of sports journalism's most remarkable careers. As Povich once wrote of his good fortune in being transferred off a World War II hospital ship just before it was attacked by the Japanese, "I was leading a charmed life, for reasons unknown to anyone before or since."

★

In 1969, five years before his official "retirement" from the *Washington Post*, Povich wrote a memoir, *All These Mornings*. Also see Ira Berkow, "Shirley Povich Dies at 92," *New York Times* (7 June 1998), and Jerome Holtzman, "Sportswriting Loses a Giant in Povich," *Chicago Tribune* (10 June 1998). Tributes to Povich and excerpts from some of his columns are in the *Washington Post*, including Thomas Boswell, "He Wrote from the Soul" (5 June 1998); Tony Kornheiser, "A Gentleman's Gentleman, A Pro's Prose" (6 June 1998); and Michael Wilbon, "An Immeasurable Resource, Typing Away in the Century's Press Box" (7 June 1998). An obituary is in the *Washington Post* (8 June 1998).

TIM WHITMIRE

Lewis Powell, Jr., 1972. ARCHIVE PHOTOS, INC.

POWELL, Lewis Franklin, Jr. (*b.* 19 September 1907 in Suffolk, Virginia; *d.* 25 August 1998 in Richmond, Virginia), associate justice of the Supreme Court of the United States known for his centrist views and his ability to compromise and build consensus among the Court.

Powell descended from a long line of Virginia settlers. The first Powell was one of the original Jamestown colonists in 1607. Powell's father, Lewis Powell, was a successful businessman who ran a small firm, and his mother, Mary Gwathmey, was a homemaker. Powell was the oldest of four children. He attended private schools, graduated from McGuire's University School in Richmond in 1925, and then entered Washington and Lee University in Lexington, Virginia. There he excelled, becoming president of the student government, playing football, finishing first in his class, earning induction into Phi Beta Kappa, and graduating magna cum laude. Upon his graduation in 1929, Powell chose to stay on and attend Washington and Lee's law school, from which he graduated in just two years and then passed the bar examination. Instead of going immediately into the practice of law, however, he decided instead to pursue an LL.M. (masters degree in law) from Harvard

University, which he received after one year of study. While there, he studied under Dean Roscoe Pound as well as future U.S. Supreme Court Justice Felix Frankfurter, under whom Powell wrote his thesis on administrative law.

In 1932 Powell joined the Richmond law firm of Christian, Barton, and Parker at the salary of $50 a month. In 1935 he moved to the firm of Hunton, Williams, Anderson, Gay, and Moore (later just Hunton and Williams), where he specialized in corporate law, did litigation, and counseled business clients. He became a senior partner and worked there until he joined the U.S. Supreme Court. He was also an instructor of economics at the Evening School of Business, University of Richmond, from 1938 to 1941.

On 2 May 1936 Powell married Josephine Pierce Rucker, whose father was a well-known physician. They had three daughters and one son. When World War II started, Powell enlisted in the Army Air Corps intelligence unit, where he rose to the rank of full colonel with the Twelfth Air Force. He was chief of operational intelligence for the U.S. Strategic Air Forces in Europe and was part of a team that deciphered German military communications: the ULTRA project. He was awarded the Legion of Merit and the Bronze Star for his service.

When he rejoined the law firm after the war, Powell not only practiced law but also served on boards of directors of several major companies. He became involved with clubs and civic activities, and from 1947 to 1948 he was a member of the Richmond City Manager Charter Reform Commission, which introduced the manager form of government to Richmond. This remarkable period of involvement included a stint as chair of the Richmond School Board from 1952 to 1961. During that time, the Supreme Court handed down the *Brown* v. *Board of Education* decision calling for the desegregation of public schools. Many in the South urged massive resistance, but Powell did not, and the schools stayed open, although they were not integrated. In 1961 Powell became a member of the Virginia State Board of Education and was president of that group during the 1968–1969 term. Accordingly, Virginia's schools were integrated disturbance free in 1969. Powell denounced the doctrine of interposition, wherein the state could interpose itself between the federal government and the people if the state felt that something the federal government mandated was unconstitutional.

In addition to his education activities, Powell was involved in other civic duties as well. For example, he headed the Richmond Family Services Society, the Richmond Citizens Association, the Colonial Williamsburg Foundation (where he served as general counsel from 1957 to 1971 and became chairman emeritus), and the Virginia State Library Board. He was also a member of the Virginia Constitutional Revision Commission from 1967 to 1968 (Virginia adopted a new constitution in 1970).

In the legal profession, Powell was elected president of the American Bar Association for the 1964–1965 term, and he pushed to create the legal services program of the Office of Economic Opportunity pursuant to the 1964 Economic Opportunity Act. He then became a member of the National Advisory Committee on Legal Services to the Poor, and vice president of the National Legal Aid and Defender Society. He also pushed for uniform standards in the criminal justice area, which led him to be appointed to President Johnson's National Commission on Law Enforcement and Administration of Justice from 1965 to 1967. While serving on this commission, he joined in a minority statement criticizing Supreme Court decisions upholding the right of suspects to remain silent. From 1969 to 1971 Powell was president of the American Bar Foundation, and he was an honorary "bencher" at Lincoln's Inn in London. Powell was appointed by President Nixon to serve on a blue ribbon defense panel to study the Department of Defense from 1969 to 1970.

In 1969 Nixon also asked Powell to join another group, the U.S. Supreme Court. Nixon had said during the 1968 presidential campaign that he wanted to put a Southerner on the Court, a move that he hoped would lead the Court toward a more strict interpretation of the Constitution, in contrast to many of the decisions of the Warren Court. Powell, however, turned down Nixon's appointment, and the Senate turned down Nixon's two Southerners, causing Nixon to temporarily abandon that tactic. However, in 1971 the long-serving justice Hugo L. Black, from Alabama, retired from the Supreme Court, and Nixon once again asked Powell to serve. At the urging of family and friends, and with his engrained sense of civic duty, Powell agreed, even though he was sixty-four years of age, making him one of the oldest persons nominated to the Court. The nomination was announced on 21 October 1971, and the American Bar Association's Committee on the Judiciary called him the best person available. He was endorsed by the Virginia NAACP and was unanimously recommended as qualified by the Senate Judiciary Committee. The Senate confirmed Powell by an eighty-nine-to-one vote in December 1971, and he took the oath of office on 7 January 1972, becoming the second oldest person to begin service on the Court and the first Virginian to be appointed to the Court since before the Civil War.

Once on the Court, Powell became a moderate, or centrist, who tried not to let his personal point of view overshadow legal principles. Even though the Court began to adopt a more conservative approach to the cases before it, Powell often cast the crucial fifth vote and was not as predictable as the more doctrinaire justices. Therefore, his vote was courted by lawyers arguing cases, as his vote often tilted the case in one direction or the other.

Abortion was a controversial issue during Powell's years on the Court. In three decisions he held that a state need not pay out of Medicaid for nontherapeutic abortions, even if it pays out of Medicaid for childbirth. He struck down a state law requiring that an unmarried minor have the consent of both parents for an abortion or, absent that, a state judge could permit it for good cause. He also struck down a number of city requirements imposed on women seeking abortions. For Powell, the woman's right to privacy was the key factor in all abortion cases.

Powell generally supported the First Amendment in cases involving restrictions placed upon those rights. He allowed a lawyer, whom a right-wing publication had falsely accused of being communist, to win a libel judgment, holding that truth or falsity was all that mattered—private persons, unlike public persons or officials, need not prove actual malice in order to win their cases. In a five-to-four decision, he struck down a state law that banned banks and businesses from trying to influence the outcomes of political referenda. He felt it an abridgment of free speech. Similarly, he struck down the refusal of a state university to allow student organizations to hold religious meetings in its facilities. Since other student organizations could use the rooms, Powell held that the refusal was an abridgment of free speech. He prohibited a state from requiring a power company to include in its billing envelope a message with which the company did not agree. He found the requirement once again to be a free speech violation.

In the area of criminal justice, Powell had already established a reputation due to his criticism of decisions concerning a suspect's right to remain silent. Powell's tendency toward moderation proved dominant in these cases. For example, Powell held that the government could not use unauthorized electronic surveillance in domestic matters if it considered the general focus of the investigation to involve national security. A federal law called for the government to get the authorization of a judge beforehand, and Powell said the government must adhere to the law, otherwise, it violated the Fourth Amendment's sanction against illegal searches and seizures. Powell also found unconstitutional holding suspects in jail for a substantial period of time when no arrest warrant was issued. Powell felt that due process of law required a judicial determination of probable cause by a magistrate as a prerequisite to extended restraint of liberty following arrest.

Powell also wrote two five-to-four opinions involving capital punishment. The issue in the first was whether the death penalty had been imposed unfairly due to race. A black defendant showed that in Georgia black defendants were more likely than others to get the death sentence, particularly if the person killed was white (the defendant in this case killed a white police officer during a robbery). While not disputing the statistics, Powell upheld the sentence, saying that racial discrimination was not proven in this particular case nor in the state's sentencing process. Upon retirement, however, Powell felt that he had erred in this decision. In the second, Powell struck down a state law requiring any statements made by the victim's family to be read to the jury before sentencing. He felt that sentencing is the punishment for what a defendant did to a victim and not for the impact that the crime might have had on the victim's family (the Court subsequently reversed this holding).

Powell also had a great impact in the area of equal protection of the law for minorities. Powell wrote a five-to-four opinion that upheld the financing of school systems by way of property taxes, even though it meant that schools in poor neighborhoods would be underfunded in comparison to those in more affluent neighborhoods. He felt that education was not one of the rights given explicit protection in the Constitution and that the means employed by the state were substantially related to an important governmental objective. Another five-to-four decision, which might have been his most famous, involved affirmative action. Powell said that a quota system in higher education was unconstitutional as an equal protection violation, yet race can be taken into account in admissions as long as it is simply one element to be weighed fairly against other elements. The split among the justices mirrored the split in American society on this difficult subject. Powell upheld an amendment to a state constitution that forbade state courts from ordering busing for desegregation purposes unless the federal courts gave such an order. Powell also held that race cannot be used by a prosecutor in the selection of a jury by use of peremptory challenges. In this case there was a black defendant and the prosecutor had struck all four black persons who were eligible for the jury. In addition, Powell struck down a voluntary affirmative-action plan between a school board and a union under which blacks in their probationary period would get preference over tenured whites when layoffs took place in order to maintain a black quota.

On 26 June 1987 Powell retired from the Court due to age and ill health, although he later said he wished that he had not retired so soon. Because he was such a consensus builder on the Court, approving a replacement for him was not easy. The first nominee, Robert Bork, was rejected by the Senate. The second, Douglas Ginsburg, withdrew his name, and finally the third, Anthony Kennedy, was approved. Powell continued to visit his chambers at the Court after retirement and stayed active by hearing cases until 1997 at the Fourth Circuit Court of Appeals in Richmond and keeping an office at the courthouse. He also taught at the law schools of both Washington and Lee and the University of Virginia. His wife Josephine died in 1996, and Powell died of pneumonia at his Richmond home two years later. He is buried in Richmond.

Powell will always have a place of honor among members of the Supreme Court. He conducted himself with dignity, his opinions were well crafted and largely devoid of any type of personal philosophy, and he was respected by his peers. Had he not served on the Supreme Court, however, Powell would surely be remembered in Richmond and in the entire state of Virginia for the many civic duties he performed, and nationally by the legal profession for the services he rendered. Nevertheless, it is his fifteen years on the Supreme Court that etched Powell's name into American history and is his legacy.

★

Powell's papers are at the Powell Archives in the Law Library of the School of Law of Washington and Lee University. J. Harvie Wilkinson discussed Powell in *Serving Justice: A Supreme Court Clerk's View* (1974). Jacob W. Landynski wrote "Justice Lewis F. Powell, Jr., Balance Wheel of the Court," in *The Burger Court: Political and Judicial Profiles* (1987). William J. Stuntz's *The Supreme Court Justices Illustrated Biographies, 1789–1993* (1993) includes a piece on Powell.

Magazine and journal articles about Powell include James Q. Wilson, "The Flamboyant Mr. Powell," *Commentary* 41 (Jan. 1966); A. E. Dick Howard, "Mr. Justice Powell and the Emerging Nixon Majority," *Michigan Law Review* 70 (Jan. 1972): 445; Gerald Gunther, "In Search of Judicial Quality on a Changing Court: The Case of Justice Powell," *Stanford Law Review* 24 (June 1972): 1001–1035; Suzannah Lessard, "Rehnquist, Powell, and the Cult of the Pro," *Washington Monthly* 3 (Dec. 1972); Larry W. Yackle, "Thoughts on Rodriguez: Mr. Justice Powell and the Demise of Equal Protection Analysis in the Supreme Court," *University of Richmond Law Review* 9 (winter 1975); Randolph C. Duvall et al., "Balanced Justice: Mr. Justice Powell and the Constitution," Gary C. Leeder, "Mr. Justice Powell's Standing," and J. Harvie Wilkinson, "Honorable Lewis F. Powell: Five Years on the Supreme Court," all in a symposium on Powell in *University of Richmond Law Review* 11 (winter 1977); Earl M. Maltz, "Portrait of a Man in the Middle: Mr. Justice Powell, Equal Protection, and the Pure Classification Problem," *Ohio State Law Journal* 40 (1979): 941–964; Melvin J. Urofsky, "Mr. Justice Powell and Education: The Balance of Competing Values," *Journal of Law and Education* 13 (1984): 581; and Paul W. Kahn, "The Court, the Community, and the Judicial Balance: The Jurisprudence of Justice Powell," *Yale Law Journal* 97 (Nov. 1987): 1–60.

Tributes to Powell include "Tribute to Justice Lewis F. Powell, Jr.," *Virginia Law Review* 68 (Feb. 1982): 161–332, and "A Tribute to Lewis F. Powell, Jr.," *Harvard Law Review* 101 (Dec. 1987): 395–420. Obituaries are in the *New York Times* and *Washington Post* (both 26 Aug. 1998).

ROBERT W. LANGRAN

J. F. Powers, 1963. AP/WIDE WORLD PHOTOS

POWERS, J(ames) F(arl) (*b.* 8 July 1917 in Jacksonville, Illinois; *d.* 12 June 1999 in Collegeville, Minnesota), short story writer and novelist best known for his portrayal of the conflict between the sacred and profane in worldly priests.

Powers was one of three children of James Ansbury Powers, a dairy and poultry manager for Swift and Company (and a talented pianist), and Zella Routzong, a homemaker who enjoyed painting. In Jacksonville, a predominantly Protestant town, the family's Catholicism was something of a problem. Powers never forgot his experiences there. In his novel *Morte d'Urban* (1962), the protagonist, Father Harvey Roche, says of his hometown, "Protestants were very sure of themselves there. If you were a Catholic boy you felt that it was their country, handed down to them by the Pilgrims."

When Powers was seven, the family moved to Rockford, Illinois, and in 1931 they moved to Quincy, Illinois, where Powers was enrolled in Quincy Academy, a Roman Catholic school run by Franciscans. Powers was athletically inclined and did particularly well in basketball. He also was

captivated by the work of Sinclair Lewis and Washington Irving. Although some speculate that he aspired to the priesthood, as did several of his classmates, Powers maintained that he did not. In 1935, after Powers graduated from high school, the family moved to Chicago. He worked at a variety of jobs, including selling men's shirts, clerking for an insurance company, and working in a bookstore, where he met Richard Wright and Nelson Algren. Like them, he was interested in and sympathetic toward the dispossessed, a theme that recurs in some of his short stories, particularly as it is exemplified in the tribulations of African Americans in northern American cities. In 1937 he was employed as a chauffeur by a man traveling through the South looking for investments. In 1938 he began work as an editor for the Illinois Historical Records Survey and attended the Chicago branch of Northwestern University at night. When the survey ended in 1940, Powers left Northwestern.

Chicago was a dynamic and exciting city, and Powers used many of his experiences there in his later fiction. In 1943 he published his first stories: "He Don't Plant Cotton" (*Accent,* winter); "Lions, Harts, Leaping Does" (*Accent,* autumn); and "A Night in the County Jail," "A Day in the County Jail," and "A Saint in the Air," (*Catholic Worker,* May, July, and December, respectively). A conscientious objector during World War II, Powers was imprisoned in a federal facility in Sandstone, Minnesota, for thirteen months and was released in 1944. He then worked as a hospital orderly in Saint Paul, Minnesota. He married Elizabeth Alice Wahl on 22 April 1946. They were introduced by a nun, engaged within a week, and married in six months. They had five children. Wahl also was a writer who published a novel, *Rafferty and Co.* (1969), and whose stories appeared in the *New Yorker* and elsewhere. In 1947 and 1949 Powers was in residence at the Yaddo writer's center in Saratoga Springs, New York, where he became friends with Robert Lowell, Theodore Roethke, and Bucklin Moon. In 1946 he published his first book, *Prince of Darkness,* a collection of short stories of which the title story is acclaimed along with three others: "Lions, Harts, Leaping Does" (reprinted from *Accent*), "The Valiant Woman" (winner of the 1947 O. Henry Award), and "The Forks."

In 1956 Powers published his second collection of short stories, *The Presence of Grace.* His first novel, *Morte d'Urban,* won the National Book Award in 1963, and it continues the main theme of his short story collections: the conflict between the sacred and profane in modern society, particularly as they are embodied in a worldly priest like Father Urban. Indeed, Powers is perhaps the best commentator on the priestly life in all its complexity in American literature.

He continued his trenchant examination of this theme in his third collection of short stories, *Look How the Fish Live* (1975). By then Powers had long been recognized as an extremely talented writer. In 1948 he received a National Institute of Arts and Letters grant and a Guggenheim Fellowship in creative writing. These were followed by Rockefeller fellowships in 1954, 1957, and 1967. In 1948 he taught at Saint John's University in Collegeville, and from 1949 to 1950 at Marquette University in Milwaukee, Wisconsin. From 1951 to 1952 the family lived in Greystones, Ireland, and from 1952 to 1956 in Saint Cloud, Minnesota. In 1956 Powers taught at the University of Michigan, and from 1957 to 1958 the family again lived in Ireland, in Dalkey. They returned to Saint Cloud and eventually to Greystones. From 1965 to 1966 Powers was writer-in-residence at Smith College in Northampton, Massachusetts.

From 1966 to 1975 the family again lived in Greystones, where Powers wrote in a room above a real estate office. There, with his pet spider, he lunched on Guinness and cookies, looked out the window and watched the goings-on behind a butcher shop, listened to his radio, read the *Irish Times* and two English papers daily, followed the horses, and wrote letters. In 1975 he was named Regents' Professor of English at Saint John's University in Collegeville, where he taught until 1993. His second and last novel,

Wheat That Springeth Green (1988), was well received and was nominated for a National Book Award and a National Book Critics Circle Award. In that same year his wife died, an event that threw him into doubt about all the verities he had so ardently believed and written about. He never left the faith, however, because for him the concept of God was the only idea that made sense out of human existence. This belief was the basis for his witty and sometimes caustic portrayal of Catholic priests.

He spent his last years in Collegeville, something of a recluse in his rented house, attending Sunday Mass in the balcony away from the crowd. He visited the graves of his wife and daughter Mary (who died in 1992) daily, tending them with loving care. Puttering around in his cluttered living room, he read and reread his favorite authors: James Joyce, Sean O'Faolain, Frank O'Connor, Katherine Anne Porter, Ernest Hemingway, F. Scott Fitzgerald, and Flannery O'Connor, the latter two his choices for greatest American writers. Of English writers, Evelyn Waugh was his favorite, and although he corresponded with Waugh, many of the letters cannot be found. Powers died unexpectedly at home shortly before his eighty-second birthday. He is buried in Collegeville.

For a writer of such talent, Powers's output was small: two novels and three collections of short stories. He ascribed this to laziness, but others suggest that he felt his work wasn't as well received as he had hoped, and indeed by the end of his life he felt that he might have lost his readers.

Nonetheless, these five books are so carefully written—he hated verbosity—and so searingly felt—his mundane clerics embodied his concept of the failure of human beings in a tough job—that he belongs in the top echelon of twentieth-century American writers. His daughter Katherine wrote in 1999 about her father and Evelyn Waugh, "They were fellow Tridentine Catholics who saw in the state of modern society, in its ruthless mediocrity, more compelling an argument for our having here no lasting home than could be found in any work of eschatology." Powers was a member of the American Academy of Arts and Letters and was awarded the French Chevalier de l'Ordre des Arts et des Lettres.

★

John V. Hagopian, *J. F. Powers* (1968), is a book-length biographical-critical study of Powers. Julia B. Boken, "J. F. Powers," *Dictionary of Literary Biography,* vol. 130 (1993), is useful. Katherine A. Powers, "Reflections on J. F. Powers—Author, Father, Clear-eyed Observer," *Boston Globe* (18 July 1999), and John Derbyshire, "Sub Species Aeteritatis: J. F. Powers, 1917–1999," *New Criterion* (18 Sept. 1999), are interesting and valuable articles. An obituary is in the *New York Times* (17 June 1999).

MARVIN J. LaHOOD

PRITZKER, Jay Arthur (*b.* 26 August 1922 in Chicago, Illinois; *d.* 23 January 1999 in Chicago, Illinois), highly successful businessman and billionaire, whose acquisitions ranged from real estate and hotels to business jets, known for creating the Hyatt Corporation and for funding the prestigious Pritzker Architecture Prize.

Pritzker was the eldest of three sons born to Abram Nicholas Pritzker, a lawyer, and Fanny Doppelt, a homemaker. The Pritzkers were an immigrant success story. His grandparents Nicholas and Annie Pritzker emigrated from Russia to Chicago in 1881, and Nicholas eventually went to law school and founded a firm that was later known as Pritzker and Pritzker. Pritzker's father studied law at Harvard University and joined the family firm but later left to form his own firm with his brother Jack. The brothers invested in real estate and small companies and made a large fortune.

Pritzker graduated from Francis W. Parker School and was also educated by his father, who at suppertime gave the Pritzker brothers mathematical problems to solve. Pritzker graduated high school at age fourteen and attended Northwestern University in Evanston, Illinois,

Jay Pritzker, 1968. AP/WIDE WORLD PHOTOS

where he received a B.Sc. degree in accounting in 1941; he also obtained a law degree from Northwestern in 1947. Between degrees, he served as a naval aviator during World War II, from 1942 to 1946. After becoming a partner in the family law firm in 1947, Pritzker married Marian ("Cindy") Friend in 1948. They had five children together.

At age twenty-nine Pritzker began to purchase businesses such as timber mills and a metal-goods company. Although he bought many more companies during his impressive career, his most famous acquisition was the first Hyatt hotel. Awaiting a flight at Los Angeles International Airport in 1957, Pritzker noticed the restaurant Fat Eddie's was very busy, and that the hotel in which it was housed had no vacancies. The hotel, which was named after its owner, Hyatt von Dehn, was for sale. Lacking his checkbook, Pritzker wrote his $2.2 million offer on a napkin.

Pritzker guessed that business travelers would appreciate having a quality hotel near large U.S. and international airports. The second Hyatt hotel was in Burlingame, California, near San Francisco International Airport, and Pritzker subsequently built Hyatt hotels in Seattle, Los Angeles, and a host of other major cities around the world. In 1967 Pritzker bought a half-finished Atlanta hotel that had a large atrium and turned it into a Hyatt Regency hotel. Skeptics thought it was a white elephant, but it became a success, and atria became standard in many hotels. At the end of the twentieth century, there were more than 200 Hyatt hotels worldwide.

Pritzker made other, more philanthropic gestures in the fields of building and architecture. In 1979 he funded a new annual award known as the Pritzker Architecture Prize. It soon became recognized as architecture's equivalent of the Nobel Prize. Winners of the $100,000 award included Philip Johnson, I. M. Pei, Hans Hollein, Frank O. Gehry, Fumihiko Maki, Jose Rafael Moneo, James Stirling, and Renzo Piano.

During the 1980s, when relaxed lending rules and an economically depressed real estate market led to the U.S. savings-and-loan scandal, regulators made agreements with Pritzker and other business leaders in which they allowed lenders to merge with stronger companies or to find new capital. Congress later criticized these agreements, and in 1996 the Supreme Court ruled that the government had shortchanged investors when they altered the rules at the apex of the savings-and-loan disaster. In 1998 Pritzker was one of the investors who filed civil lawsuits to recover billions of dollars from the government, claiming that it had unfairly altered the deal's criteria by eliminating an accounting practice that was favorable to their businesses.

In addition to the savings-and-loan situation, other facets of controversy entered the Pritzker family story. In 1986, when Pritzker's father died, his successors claimed that no estate taxes were owed to the government. For years, Abram

Pritzker had been transferring his assets into trusts in the Bahamas on behalf of his heirs. They claimed that when he died, he did not earn enough to owe taxes. The Internal Revenue Service (IRS) claimed that the trusts were a scheme and sent a bill for $53.2 million, although in 1994 the IRS settled with the family for $9.5 million plus interest.

Despite being publicity shy, Pritzker was a man with strong social skills, and he clinched business deals often with a handshake. He had a strong desire to win, and he chose firms that were well managed, delegating much of the responsibility for running the companies to subordinates who had more autonomy than was usual at other franchise operations.

In addition to his work as the Hyatt Corporation's chief executive officer (CEO) and eventually as the chairman of the board of directors, in 1967 Pritzker became the CEO of the Marmon Group, a privately owned holding company that managed the vast array of businesses owned by the Pritzker family. Pritzker also served as the CEO of the Amarillo Gear Company, a director of the Royal Caribbean Cruise Lines, and a partner in the Chicago Mill and Lumber Company. Pritzker was also a noted philanthropist. Recipients of his largesse included the University of Chicago, where he was a life trustee, Chicago Public Library Foundation, Chicago Symphony Orchestra, Northwestern University School of Law, and Stanford University. The Pritzker family foundation donated funds to more than 250 organizations.

Pritzker had a history of heart disease and succumbed to cardiac arrest at Northwestern Memorial Hospital in Chicago, the city in which he is buried. Pritzker's pioneering work in the establishment of good hotels at airports, as well as the inclusion of atria in Hyatt hotels in major cities, was sufficient to ensure his legacy. His other notable accomplishments included the establishment of the Pritzker Architecture Prize; the creation of an endowed chair at Stanford University in psychiatry and behavioral sciences in memory of his daughter Nancy Friend Pritzker; and the funding of the Pritzker Center at Northwestern University School of Law.

★

For some interesting insights into Pritzker's life, see Marilyn Much, "Financier Jay Pritzker," *Investor's Business Daily* (11 June 1999). There is a brief biographical entry in *Who's Who in Finance and Industry* (2000–2001). Information on the Pritzker Architecture Prize can be found in Martha Thorne, ed., *The Pritzker Architecture Prize: The First Twenty Years* (1999), and Martin Filler, "Eyes on the Prize," *New Republic* (26 Apr. 1999–3 May 1999). Obituaries are in the *New York Times* (25 Jan. 1999), *Economist* (30 Jan. 1999), *Crain's Chicago Business* (1 Feb. 1999), and *Architecture* (Mar. 1999).

JENNIFER THOMPSON-FEUERHERD

PURCELL, Edward Mills (*b.* 30 August 1912 in Taylorville, Illinois; *d.* 7 March 1997 in Cambridge, Massachusetts), experimental physicist and educator who shared the Nobel Prize in physics in 1952 with Felix Bloch (1905–1983) for, independently of each other, establishing a method, known as nuclear magnetic resonance (NMR), to detect and measure the very weak magnetic fields of atomic nuclei.

Purcell was one of two sons of Edward A. Purcell and Mary Elizabeth Mills. Both parents were natives of Illinois. His father was a general manager of a regional telephone company. Purcell attended the public schools of Taylorville and Mattoon, Illinois, and upon graduation from high school in 1929 entered Purdue University in West Lafayette, Indiana. Although he graduated with a B.S. degree in electrical engineering in 1933, he was already becoming interested in pure physics. One of his Purdue professors, Karl Lark-Horovitz, an expert in electron diffraction methods, permitted Purcell to participate in his research. After obtaining his degree, Purcell spent one year as an exchange student of the Institute of International Education at the Technische Hochschule in Karlsruhe, Germany.

Edward M. Purcell. PRINTS AND PHOTOGRAPHS DIVISION, LIBRARY OF CONGRESS

Upon returning to the United States in 1934, Purcell entered Harvard University, where he secured an A.M. degree in 1936 and a Ph.D. in physics in 1938. On 22 January 1937 Purcell married Beth C. Busser; they later had two sons. After receiving his doctorate, Purcell remained at Harvard as an instructor for two more years until 1940. With the advent of World War II, Purcell took a leave of absence from Harvard and joined a large and talented group at the Massachusetts Institute of Technology (MIT) in Cambridge, known as the Fundamental Studies Group, which was developing microwave radar, at least equal in importance to the better known Manhattan Project that developed the atomic bomb.

Among the scientific contacts the young Purcell made at the MIT Radiation Laboratory was the great Columbia University physicist I. I. Rabi (Nobel Prize in physics, 1944). In Purcell's capacity as supervisor of the Fundamental Studies Group between 1941 and 1945, he focused on securing new techniques for the production and detection of high-frequency radiation in the microwave region of the electromagnetic spectrum. Rabi, in his prior experimental investigations at Columbia, had considerable experience with exploring atomic and molecular properties with different wavelengths of the electromagnetic spectrum, including longwavelength radio frequency as well as shorterwavelength microwave radiation. Purcell made effective use of Rabi's specialized knowledge in both the Radiation Laboratory and his later work at Harvard after the war.

As early as the 1920s with the development of quantum physics, scientists knew that the nucleus of an atom has a spin (analogous to the rotation of a top) and acts as an extremely tiny magnet. To understand the performance of the nuclei, exact knowledge of the magnetic strengths (technically designated the magnetic moment) of different nuclei had to be known as well as the magnetic moment of a single proton, one of the components of every nucleus. In the 1930s Rabi developed a method for measuring magnetic moments using radio waves, but the method was destructive, requiring vaporization of the sample being studied.

Having returned to Harvard in 1946 as an associate professor, Purcell concentrated on developing a technique that would not involve destruction of the material being studied and would be more accurate than Rabi's early measurements. Purcell's method measured the precession—or behavior of a spinning object when the rotation of the axis is tilted—of an atomic nucleus in a magnetic field. The precession frequency of a nucleus acted upon by a magnetic field depends upon two parameters: the strength of the magnetic field and the magnetic moment of the particular atomic nucleus. In 1946 Purcell's method involved placing the material under study between the poles of a small mag-

net that was turned on by radio signals. The field of the magnet was turned on and off in accord with the frequency of the activating radio signals. The small magnet was then placed in the stronger field of another magnet, which caused the nuclei in the material sample to precess at an unknown frequency. When the frequency of the weak field precisely matched the previously unknown precession frequency, the spin orientation of the nuclei would suddenly reverse—a readily detectable effect designated as nuclear magnetic resonance (NMR). The reversal permitted the precession to be known exactly; it was the same as the radio frequency being used when the resonance occurred. Once the precession frequency of the nuclei in the material studied was known, the magnetic moment of the nucleus could be calculated with precision.

By employing this nuclear magnetic resonance method, widely different areas of scientific investigation were enormously enlarged. One early application was to study molecular structure, and NMR became an important tool of analytic chemistry. In 1951 Purcell used NMR to discover that hydrogen atoms of outer space emit electromagnetic radiation corresponding to a wavelength of twenty-one centimeters. This resulted in a remarkable new specialized tool for astronomical observation, namely a device to detect this twenty-one centimeter wavelength from the vast amount of hydrogen encountered in the universe and not accessible for viewing by optical telescopes. Applying the NMR method, Purcell and one of his graduate students, Harold I. Ewen, built the first radio telescope.

In terms of practical consumer interest, the most commonly encountered examples of nuclear magnetic resonance are the magnetic resonance imaging (MRI) machines used in medical diagnostics. The MRI designation was a semantic substitute for NMR because the "nuclear" in nuclear magnetic resonance was regarded as unacceptable to consumers in marketing the devices. Yet, unlike with X-ray machines, individuals are not exposed to external radiation when images are taken by nuclear magnetic resonance.

In 1952 Purcell at Harvard and Felix Bloch of Stanford University in Palo Alto, California, who had worked independently of each other but whose research accomplishments were nearly identical, were jointly awarded the Nobel Prize in physics "for their development of new methods for nuclear magnetic precision measurements and discoveries in connection therewith." In 1958 Purcell was named Donner Professor of Science at Harvard, and in 1960 he became the Gerhard Gade University Professor, a position he held until his retirement. Purcell also served as the scientific adviser in the administrations of Presidents Dwight D. Eisenhower, John F. Kennedy, and Lyndon B. Johnson.

In addition to the Nobel Prize, Purcell, who always referred to himself as a physics *educator* rather than a *physicist,* received the Oersted Medal of the American Association of Physics Teachers in 1967. The award reflected his important contributions to physics education at the high school and college levels, including service on a national study committee to improve the physics curriculum for American high schools. Purcell also wrote a text that was regarded as a model for college-level undergraduate teaching, *Electricity and Magnetism* (1965). He received the National Medal of Science in 1979 and the Harvard Medal in 1986. In 1970 he was elected president of the American Physical Society, the largest and most important organization of professional physicists in the United States.

In 1985 Purcell was among those scientists who took a strong public position against the continued efforts by President Ronald Reagan's administration to develop a unilateral American defense against long-range intercontinental ballistic missiles, popularly characterized as the "Star Wars" system. Purcell opposed the system based on what he regarded as its scientific inadequacies and its potential for escalating the nuclear-arms race between the United States and other nuclear powers.

Purcell died in Cambridge of respiratory failure at age eighty-four. He was survived by his wife and two sons.

In his Nobel acceptance lecture, Purcell made a particularly eloquent reference to the central concept in the nuclear magnetic resonance discovery: "I have not yet lost a feeling of wonder, and of delight, that this delicate motion (nuclear precision) should reside in all the ordinary things around us. . . . I remember in the winter of our first experiments . . . looking on the snow with new eyes. There the snow lay around my doorstep—great heaps of protons quietly precessing in the earth's magnetic field. To see the world for a moment as something rich and strange is the private reward of many a discovery."

★

Purcell was a contributing author to the extensive multivolume MIT Radiation Laboratory series published in 1949, which addressed, along with other topics, Purcell's activities as a group leader during the World War II years. Purcell's widely published papers included treatments of nuclear magnetism, astrophysics, radio astronomy, and biophysics. No full-length biography of Purcell exists, but biographical essays appear in *Modern Scientists and Engineers* (1980); *Pioneers of Science: Nobel Prize Winners in Physics* (1980); and *Notable Twentieth-Century Scientists Supplement* (1998). The closely parallel work of Felix Bloch is discussed in a biographical essay in the *Scribner Encyclopedia of American Lives,* vol. 1: *1981–1985* (1998). Obituaries are in the *Boston Globe* and *Washington Post* (both 9 Mar. 1997) and *New York Times* (10 Mar. 1997).

LEONARD R. SOLON

PUZO, Mario (*b.* 15 October 1920 in New York City; *d.* 2 July 1999 in Bay Shore, New York), novelist, screenwriter, essayist, short story and nonfiction writer who is best known for his successful novel and popular movie saga *The Godfather*.

A native of New York City, Puzo was born and raised in Hell's Kitchen, an impoverished and predominantly Italian and Irish neighborhood on Manhattan's West Side. His family had emigrated from the countryside of Avelino near Naples, Italy. His father, Antonio Puzo, was a railroad trackman who abandoned the family when Puzo was twelve. The seven children were left in the care of their mother, Maria LeConti, who ran the home in an autocratic fashion. Puzo later recalled, "She was a wonderful, handsome woman, but a fairly ruthless person." Puzo attended Commerce High School in New York City, where his teachers told him that his compositions were so good they could be published. As a teenager, Puzo dreamed of becoming a writer and was inspired by the novels of Fyodor Dostoyevsky.

During World War II, Puzo served in the Fourth Armored Division and won five battlefield stars for coming under fire, although he never fired a shot. Puzo also was

Mario Puzo. JERRY BAUER

stationed in Germany, where he met Erika Lina Broske, who became his wife in 1946. The couple had five children. Upon returning from the war, Puzo worked various odd jobs, including government clerk for the U.S. civil service in New York City. During the late 1940s and 1950s, he used his GI Bill to attend the New School for Social Research in New York City, where he won a literary prize. He then enrolled at Columbia University.

Puzo began writing pulp fiction stories for men's magazines, but his literary goals were much higher. He wanted to write an autobiographical story that explored the hardships and allure of cultural assimilation in America. His first novel, *The Dark Arena* (1955), based on his World War II experiences, told the story of a U.S. soldier and his companion in Europe. The novel was critically acclaimed but generally overlooked by the reading public.

In 1960 Puzo left his civil service position with the army reserves for employment with a group of men's magazines, where he became an assistant editor and contributor of adventure stories, book reviews, and short pieces. In 1964, after nine years of writing and rewriting, he published *The Fortunate Pilgrim*. Often cited as Puzo's best literary work, this second novel was widely praised for its authentic depiction of an ethnic community struggling for survival during the Great Depression. Puzo created a fictionalized version of his mother in *The Fortunate Pilgrim*, making it clear that without her ability to negotiate a bicultural world with savvy and wisdom, their family would not have survived.

In 1965 *Time* offered Puzo the idea of writing a book about the Mafia. Tired of being a poor artist, struggling to support his family, Puzo was determined to write a bestseller. On the basis of a plot outline, Putnam Publishers gave him a $5,000 advance. According to Puzo's longtime attorney and friend of twenty-five years, Bert Fields, "He was now going to write a commercial novel, and he was no longer ashamed of it."

In 1969 Puzo published *The Godfather,* which presented a Mafia family, the Corleones, "in a morally sympathetic light, as basically good and decent people who have had to turn to crime in order to survive and prosper in a corrupt and unjust society." The characters' appeal crossed all cultural lines, and *The Godfather* was read around the world. It became the best-selling novel of the 1970s, with over 21 million copies sold before the film version appeared. Puzo's book stayed at the top of the best-seller list for sixty-seven weeks, and many publishers believed the novel's success changed the dynamics of their industry. The films that were spawned from the book became American cinematic classics, and phrases were quoted in *Bartlett's Familiar Quotations.*

The Godfather became a seminal work in the literature of U.S. pop culture and formed the basis for three film classics; *The Godfather* (1972) and *The Godfather, Part II* (1974) both won Academy Awards for best picture, as well as the Oscars for best screenplay (shared by Puzo and director Francis Ford Coppola), best actor, and supporting actor. *The Godfather, Part III* (1990) was less successful, but did pick up an Oscar nomination for best picture. The first two films, made for a combined $21 million, grossed more than $300 million, including box-office receipts, television rights, and video sales. The actors Marlon Brando, Al Pacino, and Robert DeNiro brought Puzo's fictional characters to life. Robert Evans said that being one of the many involved in bringing *The Godfather* to the screen remained among the professional highlights of his life.

In 1972 chronic diabetes and a heart attack forced Puzo to curtail his cherished gambling trips to Las Vegas, Nevada. In 1978 he published his fourth book, *Fools Die,* an examination of the gambling scene in Las Vegas and its influence on the U.S. economy and society during the 1950s and 1960s. Also in 1978, Puzo's wife, Erika, died of breast cancer. He never remarried, but Carol Gino, formerly Erika's nurse, became Puzo's companion for the next twenty years.

In addition to creating successful novels, Puzo also wrote several screenplays that became major motion pictures, including *Earthquake* (1972), *Superman* (1972), *Superman II* (1981), *Cotton Club* (1984), and *Christopher Columbus: The Discovery* (1992). He continued to write novels that chronicled organized crime families, including *The Sicilian* (1984), *The Fourth K* (1991), and *The Last Don* (1996), which was made into a hit CBS television miniseries in 1997 and 1998. *The Fortunate Pilgrim,* his second novel, was rereleased in 1997.

Puzo's literary success allowed him to enjoy what he called the "bourgeois life." He had never lived in a house until 1968, but, with his earnings from *The Godfather* books and movies, he was able to purchase homes in both Los Angeles and Long Island, New York. After writing *The Fourth K* (1991), Puzo suffered a heart attack and underwent quadruple bypass surgery. As his health declined, Puzo relied solely on family members for professional and personal support; his home became his bastion. For the last three years of his life, he worked on the novel *Omerta* (the Mafia's code of silence). He completed the novel before his death, and it was published in July 2001. Puzo died of heart failure at his home in Bay Shore on Long Island.

In his first television interview about *The Godfather* on CNN's Larry King show in 1996, Puzo told King that Don Corleone, the book's main character, was, in fact, his mother. "Whenever the Godfather opened his mouth, in my own mind I heard my mother's voice," he said. "I heard her wisdom, her ruthlessness, and her unconquerable love for her family and for life itself." In using this voice, Puzo accomplished his goal of depicting the immigrant's struggle in the New World. Critics continue to debate Puzo's status in American literature. While his first two novels showed great literary promise, Puzo is more likely to be remembered for the commercial success of his sensational novels about the Mafia.

★

An extensive biography of Puzo can be found in *Contemporary Authors,* vol. 65 (1981). Literary criticisms can be found in *Contemporary Literary Criticism* (1986). An interview with Puzo by Camille Paglia can be found in the *New York Times Biographical Services* 28, no. 5 (May 1997). Obituaries are in the *New York Times* and *Detroit News* (both 3 July 1999).

JOHNNIEQUE B. LOVE

QUESTEL, Mae (*b.* 13 September 1908 in New York City; *d.* 4 January 1998 in New York City), vaudeville performer and actress who gained fame as the squeaky voice of the animated characters Betty Boop and Olive Oyl.

Questel, daughter of Simon Questel and Frieda Glauberman, was born and raised in the borough of the Bronx in New York City. Little is known about her youth except that she had a remarkable talent for mimicry. When she was seventeen, she captured the attention of a vaudeville agent with her performance in a neighborhood talent contest. The contest was mounted to find a girl who most resembled actress Helen Kane, "the boop-oop-a-doop queen." Questel won the competition and was thus propelled onto such vaudeville stages as the renowned Palace Theatre on Broadway. She appeared in ensemble acts as well as on her own, imitating stars of the era such as Maurice Chevalier, Marlene Dietrich, and Rudy Vallee.

Max Fleischer, producer of animated motion pictures, heard Questel's dead-on imitation of Helen Kane and hired her to be the voice of the character "Betty Boop," a coy Jazz Age cutie with marcelled hair, seductive garters, and a strapless dress. Although several other actresses had earlier provided the voice, once Questel was given the role, she was the voice of every Betty Boop short subject until the series ended in 1939—nearly 200 cartoons later. Saucy and witty, the Betty Boop series was a far cry from the gentle children's stories often thought to be typical of the art of animation. Cab Calloway sang the title tune for a 1932 Betty Boop short, "Minnie the Moocher," in which a "lowdown Hoochie-Coocher" is taken to Chinatown by a pimp named Smokey and is soon enveloped in a netherworld of opium dens. Betty Boop's seductive image, although popular with the moviegoing public, violated the conservative Hollywood Production Code enforced by the Motion Picture Producers and Distributors Association of America (MPPDA). In 1935 the agency insisted that producers address what the censors considered morally alarming images by lengthening the character's flapper skirt

Mae Questel, 1978. AP/WIDE WORLD PHOTOS

and tethering her adventures to the character of a watchful grandfather.

A popular feature of each animated short was a song performed by Questel as the Betty Boop persona. Questel's recording of Sidney Clare and Richard Whiting's 1934 composition "On the Good Ship Lollipop"—sung in Betty Boop's voice—was a hit during the depression, selling more than two million copies.

Specializing in piercing, comic vocalizations, Questel was also the voice of Olive Oyl, the scrawny love interest of Popeye the Sailor Man, beginning in 1933. Warbling "Oh, Popeye," Questel, who based her characterization on the voice of actress Zasu Pitts, was paired first with William Costello and then Joe Mercer as the spinach-gobbling hero. Mercer and Questel made nearly 300 "Popeye" animated films together. Questel's vocal range was extraordinary, ranging from the lovesick—and unmistakably adult— Olive Oyl to juvenile voices. She even performed the role of L'il Swee'pea, the orphan baby whom Popeye adopts. Questel also provided the voices for television cartoon characters "L'il Audrey" and "Winky Dink" in the 1950s. She commented later in life that pitching her voice to create Betty Boop and Olive Oyl had permanently altered the timbre of her day-to-day speech.

Questel's flexible vocal chords were not limited to providing behind-the-scenes voices for pen-and-ink characters. She appeared on Broadway in a variety of plays, including *Dr. Social* in 1948 and *Enter Laughing* in 1963. In 1970 she had the recurring role of Miriam Biskin in the NBC soap opera *Somerset*. Questel became a popular "pitchman" in television advertising in the 1970s. From 1971 to 1978 she appeared as grandmotherly Aunt Bluebell in a series of ads for paper towels for Scott Paper Company. She also sold products for Playtex from 1970 to 1972 and Speidel Watchbands in 1980.

Quintessential New York filmmaker Woody Allen used Questel's unique voice and association with classic animation in his 1983 film *Zelig*. Her Betty Boop performance of the song "Chameleon Days" was part of the soundtrack for his tribute to the early days of cinema. Questel worked with Allen again in 1989 in *New York Stories*. She appeared in the "Oedipus Wrecks" segment of the film as a nagging Jewish mother, haranguing her son (played by Allen) while suspended omnisciently over his world like a Cheshire Cat, coming down to earth only when he has found a suitable bride.

Her final appearance as cartoon flapper Betty Boop was in 1988, in the motion picture *Who Framed Roger Rabbit?*, a groundbreaking film directed by Robert Zemeckis that combined live action and animation. The Betty Boop character was rendered in traditional black and white, and Questel performed her unmistakable and ageless "boop-oop-a-doop."

Questel was a member of Hadassah, the women's Zionist organization of America, as well as a member of the Screen Actors' Guild, the Actor's Equity Association, American Federation of Television and Radio Artists, and Troupers. She received a variety of awards and honors for her stage and screen work, including the Annie Award in 1979 from the Animated Film Society, and a Troupers Award for Outstanding Contributions to Entertainment that same year. The New York University School of Social Work named her a Living Legend in 1979.

Questel married Leo Balkin on 22 December 1930 and was the mother of two sons. She married Jack E. Shelby on 19 November 1970. The Betty Boop image, licensed by King Features Syndicate, enjoys over 500 domestic and international licensees nearly sixty years after it was first introduced. It recouped $400 million dollars in sales in 1998—coincidentally, the year of Questel's death.

Questel died of complications from Alzheimer's disease in New York at age eighty-nine. She is buried at New Montefiore Cemetery in Farmingdale, New York. In 1963 the actress was asked about her philosophy for survival. "Don't make a megillah [Yiddish for "long story"] out of every little thing," she responded.

Although the name Mae Questel doesn't necessarily turn heads, mention the characters Olive Oyl or Betty Boop and smiles fill the room. Questel's unique comic talents indelibly stamped the early days of motion-picture animation and the memories of millions.

★

A cultural history of the Olive Oyl character is provided in Bud Sagendorf, *Popeye: The First Fifty Years* (1979). The motion pictures *New York Stories* and *Who Framed Roger Rabbit?* are available on home video. A complete filmography for Questel as both Betty Boop and Olive Oyl is available online from the Internet Movie Database at <http://www.IMDb.com>. *The Variety Music Cavalcade* (1962) provides composer information for "On the Good Ship Lollipop." An appreciation of Questel's career is in Britain's *Daily Telegraph* (25 Jan. 1998). An obituary is in the *New York Times* (3 Jan. 1999).

JESSICA HANDLER

QUINTERO, José Benjamin (*b.* 15 October 1924 in Panama City, Panama; *d.* 26 February 1999 in New York City), theatrical director who was recognized for reviving interest in Eugene O'Neill's plays and was cofounder and artistic director of the off-Broadway Circle in the Square Theatre.

Quintero was the son of Carlos Rivira Quintero, a farmer and politician, and Consuelo Palmorala, a homemaker. One of four children, Quintero grew up in a strict Catholic home. His youth in Panama and later in Los Angeles is subject to conflicting accounts, but apparently he attended a local boarding school where he enjoyed writing poetry and plays and acting in local church productions. He served as an acolyte and worked on his father's farm. In 1938 his parents separated, and Quintero, his brother Ernesto, and his sister Carmen accompanied their mother to Los Angeles, where Quintero attended high school. After unsuccessful stints at the University of Southern California and Los Angeles City College, Quintero entered the Goodman Theatre School in Chicago in the fall of 1944. But unable to find work in the United States, Quintero returned to Panama, where he worked as a ticket agent for Panamanian Airways, then as an English teacher, and finally as an assistant to the vice president of the Chesterfield Cigarette Company.

In 1948 Quintero convinced his father to allow him to return to the United States, and he journeyed to Woodstock, New York, in 1949 to act in a summer stock troupe. Though this group disbanded, Quintero remained in Woodstock and supported himself by tutoring wealthy residents. Quintero then moved with some friends to New York City, where they founded the Loft Players. In the summer of 1950 Quintero and the Loft Players staged seven

José Quintero. AP/WIDE WORLD PHOTOS

plays, six under Quintero's direction, including Tennessee Williams's *The Glass Menagerie,* John Millington Synge's *Riders to the Sea,* and Quintero's own "A Ribbon of Smoke," which has since been lost.

At Woodstock, Quintero met Theodore Mann, with whom he cofounded in 1950 the Sheridan Square Cabaret, at the former Old Greenwich Village Inn on Sheridan Square, where performances would be presented in the round. On 21 February 1951 the cabaret, which became known as the Circle in the Square Theatre, opened with a presentation—under Quintero's direction—of *Dark of the Moon* by Howard Richardson and William Berney. After several moderately successful productions at the Circle in the Square, Quintero directed a revival of Tennessee Williams's *Summer and Smoke* on 24 April 1952, which ran for an unprecedented year. Critics raved about Williams's play, Quintero's direction, and the first true off-Broadway star, Geraldine Page. With his success at the Circle in the Square, Quintero began receiving offers to direct on Broadway, and in December 1953 he directed his first Broadway play, Jane Bowles's *In the Summer House.*

Between 1951 and 1963 Quintero directed twenty productions at the Circle in the Square. None were more lauded than his revival of Eugene O'Neill's *The Iceman Cometh* (May 1956) and the American premiere of *Long Day's Journey into Night* (November 1956). Running for 565 performances, *The Iceman Cometh* launched the career of Jason Robards, and Quintero received the Vernon Rice Award and an Obie for his direction. During *The Iceman Cometh*'s run, Carlotta O'Neill, Eugene O'Neill's widow, offered Quintero the coveted rights to stage *Long Day's Journey into Night.*

While continuing to direct at the Circle in the Square, Quintero directed the opera *Lost in the Stars* (1958), which critics applauded. In June 1958 Quintero directed O'Neill's *A Moon for the Misbegotten* at the Festival of Two Worlds in Spoleto, Italy, after which he vacationed for the remainder of the summer in Europe. In the summer of 1959 Quintero directed his first play by Shakespeare, *Macbeth,* at the Boston Arts Center, and in 1961 he directed his first film, *The Roman Spring of Mrs. Stone,* based on Tennessee Williams's novel. During this time Quintero met Nick Tsacrios, who remained his companion until Quintero's death. In December 1962, citing differences with Mann, Quintero resigned as artistic director at the Circle in the Square.

Having become one of the foremost stage directors in New York City, Quintero became fearful of failure and began to drink heavily. During the middle and late 1960s and early 1970s, his excessive drinking led to addiction and depression. Finally, after consulting with several psychiatrists and trying various cures, in 1972 he consulted Vincent Tracy, who helped cure Quintero's addiction. At this time Quintero wrote his memoir, *If You Don't Dance They Beat You* (1974). In 1973, after some modest successes, Quintero directed the Tony Award–winning Broadway premiere of O'Neill's *A Moon for the Misbegotten,* starring Jason Robards and Colleen Dewhurst. In 1974 Quintero published his own play, *Gabrielle,* which was staged at the Studio Arena in Buffalo, New York, and in Washington, D.C. Between 1975 and 1982 Quintero worked in Washington, D.C.; New York City; Oslo, Norway; Chicago; and West Palm Beach, Florida.

Throughout the 1980s and 1990s Quintero served as an artist-in-residence, a part-time lecturer, and a distinguished artist for California State University at Fullerton, Florida State University, and the University of Houston. In 1987 doctors at Cedars of Lebanon Hospital in Los Angeles discovered throat cancer and removed his larynx, leaving him without his voice for a year. Quintero recovered and, speaking with the aid of a vibration-amplifying device, continued teaching. During the summer of 1996 he directed the Provincetown Repertory Theatre in Provincetown, Massachusetts, where Eugene O'Neill's career began. Quintero taught and directed until shortly before his death at age seventy-four. He died of cancer at Memorial Sloan-Kettering Hospital in New York City, whereupon his remains were cremated.

In addition to reviving Eugene O'Neill's dramatic works and reputation, Quintero found failed Broadway productions of plays written by leading writers and transformed them. In the process, off Broadway exploded in popularity during his thirteen-year tenure at the Circle in the Square. The *New York Times* reported, "The American theater expanded some forty blocks. Critics realized they would not fall into the Atlantic if they ventured south of Times Square." During his fifty-year career, Quintero directed seventeen productions of O'Neill's plays, more than seventy off-Broadway and Broadway plays, several operas, and play adaptations for television and radio. Having never taken a course in directing, Quintero achieved success through his innate ability to understand people and effectively cast roles. Rather than demanding that actors fulfill his vision, Quintero built mutual trust, often using stories from his difficult childhood to inspire new and seasoned actors.

★

Quintero's personal papers, correspondence, and theater memorabilia are in the special collections of the University of Houston. His memoir, *If You Don't Dance They Beat You* (1974), is a rambling account of the founding and development of the Circle in the Square Theatre. Though significant misinformation and a lack of information mar sources about Quintero's youth, some helpful resources include "The Passion of Quintero," *Los Angeles Times* (27 Apr. 1986), and David B. Cook's Ph.D. dissertation, "José Quintero: The Circle in the Square Years, 1950–1963, University of Kansas" (1981). Obituaries are in the *New York Times* and *Los Angeles Times* (both 27 Feb. 1999).

JONATHAN A. GATES

R

RANDOLPH, Jennings (*b.* 8 March 1902 in Salem, West Virginia; *d.* 8 May 1998 in St. Louis, Missouri), journalist, educator, and legislator. As a United States senator, he was responsible for initiating the constitutional amendment granting the right to vote to eighteen-year-olds.

Randolph, the son of Ernest Randolph and Idell Bingham, was named after William Jennings Bryan, the famous Democratic orator and presidential candidate who his father idolized. Randolph's father and mother both served as mayor of Salem. After attending the city's public schools, he graduated from the Salem Academy in 1920. In 1924 he earned an A.B. degree from Salem College.

Following graduation, Randolph began work as a newsman in nearby Clarksburg, West Virginia, on the editorial staff of the *Clarksburg Daily Telegram*. The following year, he became an associate editor of the *West Virginia Review* in Charleston, West Virginia. In 1926 he joined the faculty of Davis and Elkins College in Elkins, West Virginia, where he chaired the department of public speaking and journalism and served as athletic director.

Randolph made his first political bid in 1930 while still teaching at Davis and Elkins, running unsuccessfully as a Democratic candidate for the House of Representatives. He ran again two years later and, as part of President Franklin Roosevelt's landslide victory, was elected to the House as a member of the Seventy-third Congress by West Virginia's

Second District. A staunch supporter of the president's New Deal (Franklin Roosevelt's proposal for "relief, recovery, reform" to end the Great Depression and to prevent its recurrence), he won reelection for an additional six terms. During his last four terms, Randolph served as chairman of the Committee on the District of Columbia; during his last term, he also served on the Committee on Civil Service. In 1946 Randolph lost his bid for an eighth term.

Immediately after his arrival in Washington, D.C., as a new member of the House of Representatives, Randolph married Mary Katherine Babb on 18 February 1933. They subsequently became the parents of two sons. In 1935 Randolph joined the faculty of Southeastern University as a part-time professor of public speaking. He held this position until 1953, when he became dean of the school of business administration, a post he held until 1958. When Randolph failed in his bid for reelection in 1946, he became assistant to the president of Capital Airlines, then a major carrier, which had its headquarters in the nation's capital.

Although no longer a congressman, Randolph continued to perform public service. After learning to fly at the age of forty-three, he became an advocate for the burgeoning postwar commercial aviation industry. For five years he was chair of the West Virginia Planning Board of the Aviation Commission. From 1947 to 1949 he served on the Washington, D.C., Aviation Planning Commission. He co-authored (with James A. Bell) *Mr. Chairman, Ladies and*

Jennings Randolph. ASSOCIATED PRESS

Gentlemen: *A Practical Guide to Successful Speaking* (1951). In 1958, when Senator Matthew M. Neeley of West Virginia died, Randolph was elected to complete his term as senator. In 1960 Randolph ran successfully for a full term in the Senate; he also won three subsequent bids for reelection.

In the Senate, Randolph continued to promote projects that he had advanced during his time in the House. As a West Virginian, he was a firm supporter of the coal industry, but also expressed concern for the environment. Later he became an advocate for stricter mine safety laws. As early as 1943 he called attention through his speeches and his committee work to the problem of U.S. dependence on foreign oil.

During World War II, Randolph concluded that if young men were old enough to fight and die for their country, they were old enough to select their political leaders. In 1942 he introduced a bill to lower the nation's voting age from twenty-one to eighteen. As a senator, he continued this quest; the amendment finally passed on his eleventh attempt, 30 June 1971, and was ratified the next year.

In 1976 Randolph became chairman of the Public Works Committee (later the Committee on Environment and Public Works); when Republicans gained control of the Senate in 1980, he remained on the committee as rank-

ing minority member. He also served on the Committee on Labor and Natural Resources and the Committee on Veterans' Affairs. He was a member of both the steel caucus and the coal caucus. His long interest in aviation was capped by his successful introduction of the bill that created the National Air and Space Museum as part of the Smithsonian Institution.

In 1964 he cosponsored the bill that created the Appalachian Regional Commission, a federal agency that poured millions of dollars into the region in an attempt to eliminate its intractable "pockets of poverty." During Lyndon B. Johnson's administration, Randolph supported both the Civil Rights Act and the Voting Rights Act, and cosponsored the unsuccessful Equal Rights Amendment.

After serving as a delegate to the Interparliamentary Union meeting in Rome, Italy, in 1962, Randolph served on many international committees. He made four visits to Mexico for parliamentary meetings, and represented the United States at similar meetings in such disparate locations as Bermuda, Ankara, Turkey, and Prague, Czechoslovakia. From 1981 to 1984 he headed the American delegation to the Agri-Energy Roundtable in Geneva, Switzerland.

A consummate politician, Randolph was a member of numerous organizations. He was very active in the Baptist Church. Interested in education, he served on the boards of Salem and Davis and Elkins Colleges and Southeastern University. A frequent commencement speaker, he accumulated almost two dozen honorary degrees.

In 1984 Randolph chose not to seek reelection to the Senate. A few years later, his health deteriorated. Because his wife had already died, he moved to St. Louis to be near his son. After a decade at Saint John's Mercy Skilled Nursing Home, he died there at age ninety-six. He is buried in the Seventh-Day Baptist Cemetery in Salem.

Randolph considered himself a "mountaineer" until the end of his life. He once said: "I essentially am a West Virginia senator. I'm not what you would call a national senator or international senator." Yet his most lasting legacy, the amendment that lowered the voting age, had far-reaching impact.

★

The Randolph papers are at Salem-Teikyo International University in Salem, West Virginia. Jennings coauthored *Mr. Chairman, Ladies and Gentlemen: A Practical Guide to Successful Speaking* (1951) with James A. Bell. *Tribute to the Honorable Jennings Randolph of West Virginia in the United States Senate,* U.S. Congress, 98th Cong., 2d sess. (1984) is a record of the compliments bestowed upon him by his colleagues at the time of his retirement. Obituaries are in the *Washington Post* and *New York Times* (both 9 May 1998).

ART BARBEAU

RAY, James Earl (*b.* 10 March 1928 in Alton, Illinois; *d.* 23 April 1998 in Nashville, Tennessee), assassin of the Reverend Martin Luther King, Jr., who, after confessing to the crime, recanted his plea and claimed for thirty years that conspirators had orchestrated the murder.

James Earl Ray, the first child of nineteen-year old Lucille Maher and George "Speedy" Ray, was raised in abject poverty. His father held odd jobs, such as demolition and hauling work, while Ray's mother sometimes borrowed from relatives to manage a meager subsistence. The family moved to Bowling Green, Missouri, in 1929 and settled in rural Ewing, Missouri, in 1935. Ray ultimately had eight younger siblings, born between 1930 and 1952. He disliked school, where he was teased and fought often. Routinely absent, Ray finally quit during eighth grade. His upbringing was grim: the family inhabited a decrepit shack; his father and uncle were repeatedly jailed for offenses ranging from robbery to rape; his sister Marjorie accidentally burned herself to death in 1937; his mother suffered depression and deepening alcoholism; and Ray himself began dabbling in crime—petty theft and solicitation of prostitutes—as a teenager.

At age sixteen, Ray returned to Alton to live with his maternal grandmother and work at a shoe tannery. He learned the dyeing trade and saved nearly $1,200, more money than his parents had ever had. Laid off in 1945, Ray enlisted in the U.S. Army in February 1946. He served in Germany but was discharged in December 1948, following court-martial for drunkenness and dereliction of duty.

Upon his return, Ray worked briefly in Chicago before drifting to Los Angeles, where, within a week, he was arrested on 11 October 1949 for burglarizing a cafeteria. He served ninety days. His first night out, Ray robbed a restaurant and fled town. He returned to Chicago, taking factory work and briefly enrolling in the Academy for Young Adults, seeking, but not obtaining, a high school diploma. On 6 May 1952, Ray robbed a cab driver and, while fleeing, was shot by police and arrested. He served twenty-two months in prison and was released in March 1954.

Ray's family had by now collapsed. Two younger brothers were jailed for robbery, coincidentally at the same penitentiary housing their uncle, the other siblings had become wards of the state, and Ray's father had left his mother for another woman. Although Ray dated briefly in Chicago, his main relationships were with prostitutes, and he remained shy around women his entire life. Standing slightly under six feet, with a plain face and average build, he spoke softly, in broken grammar, and often avoided eye contact.

Ray spent several months in Alton and was arrested on 28 August 1954 after burglarizing a dry cleaner. He skipped bail but was recaptured on 23 March 1955, following a two-week spending spree across seven states, funded with forged

James Earl Ray, 1991. AP/WIDE WORLD PHOTOS

postal money orders. The crime sent Ray to Leavenworth Federal Penitentiary in Leavenworth, Kansas. Paroled in April 1958, he moved to St. Louis, where his mother and several siblings lived. Although biographers later focused upon Ray's recidivism as evidence of bungling, in fact, he became a skilled thief whose crimes far outweighed his convictions. Over the next year, he committed armed robbery at several supermarkets and bars, using the proceeds to travel as far afield as Mexico and Canada. His run ended on 10 October 1959, when he and an accomplice were arrested after robbing a St. Louis supermarket. Having undertaken a smattering of legal reading while in prison, Ray directed his own trial; he was sentenced to twenty years at the Missouri State Penitentiary.

Ray worked at the prison laundry and bakery and also sold illegal drugs, obtained from his brothers. He made two failed escape attempts, in 1961 and 1966, and was punished with solitary confinement. He made a third attempt on 23 April 1967, hiding inside a crate of bread marked for delivery from the bakery to an outlying building. Trucked past prison checkpoints, Ray climbed from the crate, changed clothes, and jumped to the road. After six days of walking and hiding in rural Missouri, he rode a freight train to St. Louis, then traveled to Chicago, where he worked as a dishwasher under the alias "John L. Rayns." Although Ray feared that authorities had launched a manhunt, they made few efforts to locate him beyond issuing standard wanted posters offering a $50 reward.

Ray quit work after a month and briefly joined his brothers in the St. Louis area, where it is believed they robbed an Alton bank of nearly $30,000. He purchased a used car and drove to Montreal, Canada, arriving on 17 July 1967 and leasing a room under the name "Eric S. Galt." He hoped to obtain a Canadian passport but, finding this difficult, left on 21 August and traveled to Birmingham, Alabama, where he remained for six weeks. Ray purchased another car, a white 1966 Mustang, and succeeded under Alabama's lax regulations in registering it and getting a license as "Eric Starvo Galt."

Fearful of discovery, Ray left in early October and journeyed to Nuevo Laredo, Mexico. He spent a few days smuggling goods across the border, then rented a room in Puerto Vallarta, Mexico. He claimed to be a vacationing writer and spent most days drinking and visiting whorehouses. He resumed drifting after five weeks, this time settling, on 19 November 1967, in Los Angeles. Ray attended "self-hypnosis" sessions, took dance lessons, and enrolled in locksmithing classes and a bartending course. He sought work briefly but, lacking social security identification, he feared appearing suspicious. In February 1968 he underwent cosmetic surgery to reshape his nose.

At some point early in 1968, Ray formed a plan to murder the Reverend Martin Luther King, Jr., who over the past decade had galvanized America's civil rights movement. Ray's motive appears to have been a mix of lifelong racism, political fervor (he was an enthusiastic supporter of Governor George Wallace's presidential campaign), desire for notoriety, and, most important, hope of receiving the $50,000 to $100,000 bounties offered by the Ku Klux Klan and other rabid segregationists. Ray had discussed the bounties with his brothers and fellow inmates, but he apparently never contacted these groups to share his plan or arrange payment. In mid-March Ray drove from Los Angeles to Selma, Alabama, arriving on 22 March, the same day as a publicized visit by King. The next day, Ray drove to Atlanta, King's hometown, and rented a room, where police later found a map marking King's former home, his father's church, and the headquarters of the Southern Christian Leadership Conference, the civil rights organization headed by King. Quickly returning to Alabama, Ray purchased a Remington .30-06-caliber scoped rifle from a Birmingham gun dealer on 29 March 1968, giving his name as "Harvey Lowmeyer."

On 1 April, King announced plans to attend a sanitation workers' rally four days later in Memphis, Tennessee. Ray drove to Memphis on 3 April, the same day King arrived. The next afternoon, using the alias "John Willard," Ray rented room 5-B at Bessie Brewer's Rooming House, the windows of which overlooked a street and the parking lot—slightly over 200 feet—of the Lorraine Motel, King's regular residence when visiting Memphis. Shortly before six o'clock that evening, King emerged onto a balcony, talking with friends for five to ten minutes. Ray had cleared furniture from his window and could see the Lorraine balcony, but a bathroom across the hall offered a better angle. Ray likely spotted King from his room and carried his rifle to the bathroom. Standing in the tub and braced against the wall and windowsill, Ray fired a single shot that struck King's jaw, tore through his neck and severed his spinal cord. King collapsed and died almost immediately.

Ray wrapped the rifle in a blanket and fled. Although his Mustang was parked less than a block away, he noticed police cars nearby and dumped the bundled weapon on the sidewalk. Police sealed the area and broadcast the Mustang's description within ten minutes, but Ray had escaped into Mississippi.

Ray reached Atlanta early on 5 April. He gathered his possessions and went by bus to Windsor, Ontario, Canada, then continued to Toronto and rented a room. Through a travel agent, he learned how to navigate the Canadian passport regulations and received a passport in the name of "Ramon George Sneyd." Although the Federal Bureau of Investigation (FBI) had unraveled Ray's prior aliases and widely published his photograph by 19 April, Ray kept to his room and avoided notice. Hoping to reach Rhodesia or South Africa, both segregated nations from which extradition would be difficult, he flew to London, England, arriving on 7 May. That evening, he continued to Lisbon, Portugal, where he sought passage to Africa by ship. Lacking a visa and low on money, Ray returned to London on 17 May. He inquired about enlistment in an African mercenary corps and robbed a bank. By this time the FBI had tracked Ray's fraudulent passport. He was seized on 8 June by Scotland Yard detectives, while boarding a flight to Belgium at London's Heathrow Airport.

Five weeks later Ray was extradited and returned to Memphis. On 10 March 1969, Ray's forty-first birthday, he pleaded guilty to first-degree murder, waived his right to trial, and received a ninety-nine year sentence to be served in the Tennessee State Penitentiary in Nashville. Had Ray been tried, he could have been executed. Although the plea specified that he acted alone, Ray had been floating conspiracy notions since his extradition and resumed doing so shortly after pleading guilty. His claims centered on a man called "Raoul," who allegedly directed Ray in the eight months prior to the murder. Ray claimed to have met Raoul in Montreal, smuggled goods for him at the Canadian and Mexican borders, rented rooms upon his instructions, purchased the murder weapon according to his specifications, and sat innocently in the Mustang while Raoul killed King from the boarding house. He proffered variations on the Raoul story for the rest of his life, arguing that he was the patsy in a sophisticated scheme.

Ray recanted his confession and petitioned for a trial within days of his plea. These efforts, continuing to his death, were repeatedly rebuffed in state and federal courts. His tenacity had an impact on the public, which widely entertained conspiracy suspicions in the King and Kennedy assassinations. Numerous conspiracy theorists wrote about the crime, usually arguing that operatives within the federal government had orchestrated it. In 1997, to bolster efforts for a trial, which they believed would shed new light on the crime, even King's family announced their belief in Ray's innocence. Yet the seeds of these conspiracy theories—the shifting details of the Raoul story—could never withstand close examination. Investigators assembled overwhelming proof of Ray's guilt, yet they found no hard evidence of Raoul's existence, much less his supposedly ubiquitous involvement. Although a trial never occurred, the U.S. House of Representatives Select Committee on Assassinations conducted an exhaustive investigation in 1977 and 1978. Although determining that circumstantial evidence supported "a likelihood" of a bounty-offer conspiracy, they found no government involvement and concluded that Ray alone murdered King.

Apart from five non-consecutive years in the Tennessee State Penitentiary, Ray served his sentence at Brushy Mountain State Penitentiary in Petros, Tennessee. He attempted two escapes in 1971 and a third in 1977, when he scaled the wall but was recaptured in three days. On trial for this offense, he met and, on 13 October 1978, married a courtroom artist named Anna Sandhu. She divorced him in November 1990. After two years of recurrent hospitalization, still petitioning for trial, Ray died at age seventy of liver disease, caused by chronic hepatitis, and kidney failure at a Nashville hospital.

★

The definitive examination of Ray's life, King's assassination, and the overwhelming evidence of Ray's solitary guilt is given by Gerald Posner, *Killing the Dream* (1998). A similarly engaging work, by a journalist who interviewed Ray extensively, is William Bradford Huie, *He Slew the Dreamer* (1968, 1997). Harold Weisberg, *Frame-Up* (1969, 1971), and William F. Pepper, *Orders to Kill* (1995), provide intricate conspiracy theories. Similar explanations are given in James Earl Ray, *Tennessee Waltz: The Making of a Political Prisoner* (1987), and James Earl Ray, *Who Killed Martin Luther King? The True Story by the Alleged Assassin* (1992). An obituary is in the *New York Times* (24 Apr. 1998).

DAVID DIAZ

REEDER, Russell Potter, Jr. ("Red") (*b.* 4 March 1902 in Fort Leavenworth, Kansas; *d.* 22 February 1998 in Alexandria, Virginia), educator, author, and army commander highly decorated for his pivotal role in the D day invasion of Normandy, France, during World War II.

Reeder was the oldest of the four children of an army colonel and Spanish-American War veteran, Russell P. Reeder, and Narcissa Martin. Russell, who was nicknamed "Red" because of the color of his hair, grew up on various military posts across the United States. At age eleven he received the U.S. Treasury Department's Silver Life-Saving Medal for rescuing a drowning six-year-old playmate. He graduated from Marbury High School in Marbury, Alabama, in 1919. Reeder briefly attended a preparatory school before becoming a student at the U.S. Military Academy at West Point in July 1920, where he earned six demerits in his first two hours. He failed math and was forced to leave the academy in mid-January 1921, reentering West Point as a plebe in July 1921. He lettered in football, baseball, and swimming, and was captain of the baseball team. According to the student newspaper, the *Howitzer,* Reeder was the

Red Reeder, 1962. AP/WIDE WORLD PHOTOS

most popular cadet at West Point during his six years there. He did not graduate until 1926, primarily because his studies were of secondary importance to his sports.

Reeder was commissioned a second lieutenant, and his first assignment in the U.S. Army was in the Thirty-fourth Infantry at Fort Eustis, Virginia. In the fall of 1926 he was assigned to the All-Army Football Squad at the U.S. Army Infantry School in Fort Benning, Georgia, as a player-coach. On a month's leave in 1928, Reeder tried out for the New York Giants baseball team and was offered a position as a pinch hitter, but he decided to remain in the army instead.

In 1928 Reeder was ordered to the Presidio in San Francisco for duty and to help coach the West Coast army football team. He also took on the seasonal assignment of helping to coach the football team at West Point. For several seasons, he flew from coast to coast on the transcontinental air transport because military planes were slower. Assigned to various posts in the United States, Reeder often performed two jobs: company officer and athletic coach. Reeder married Dorothea Darrah on 11 August 1934. They had four children.

Reeder was sent to Fort Clayton in the Panama Canal Zone in 1934. For the next seven years, he served two tours, one at Quarry Heights in the Canal Zone and one at Fort McClellan, Alabama. After completing a battalion commander course at the infantry school in Georgia in November 1941, Reeder was given one month's leave before he was due to report to Fort Ord in California. However, after learning about the bombing of Pearl Harbor in Hawaii on 7 December 1941, Reeder, now a major, reported to Fort Ord immediately to assume command of a reinforced battalion of the Thirty-second Infantry, Seventh Infantry Division. Reeder's Second Battalion headed for Camp San Luis Obispo, where the troops were responsible for observation and defense along the coast from the Point Lobos reserve to Pismo Beach, and where Reeder trained his command for desert warfare.

Promoted to lieutenant colonel in 1942, Reeder served for a short period as a regimental executive officer of the U.S. Army before General Dwight Eisenhower assigned him to the army's Operations Division of the War Department's general staff in Washington, D.C. In the fall of 1942 General George C. Marshall sent Reeder to the Pacific to analyze and report back on lessons the American troops learned fighting Japanese troops on Guadalcanal, an island in the West Pacific. Marshall was impressed by Reeder's recommendations, even though they were written in what Marshall called "out-of-line grammar" and slang. He wrote a foreword to the 1943 report, published as *Fighting on Guadalcanal* (1943), and had a million copies printed and issued to the troops as a training manual. The manual prompted changes in the army's training methods and

fighting practices and was also adopted by the British and Chinese armed forces. Reeder also played a pivotal role in the instigation of the Army Bronze Star for Valor, an Army combat award that Reeder suggested in a letter to General Leslie McNair be created to recognize outstanding ground soldiers.

On 1 April 1944, now a full colonel, Reeder reported to Tiverton, England, to assume command of the Twelfth Infantry Regiment of the Fourth Infantry Division under General Omar Bradley. His superlative ability to lead was shown when he turned a poorly trained regiment into a first-class fighting unit. On D day, 6 June 1944 (the first day of the Allied landing in Normandy, France), Colonel Reeder's 3,000-man regiment landed on Utah Beach, two miles south of their assigned post. While leading his men to link up with Brigadier General Theodore Roosevelt (the son of President Teddy Roosevelt), Reeder encountered heavy fighting and a flooded causeway, but made a quick decision to proceed and take the port city of Cherbourg. For six days, the Twelfth Infantry spearheaded the Normandy invasion.

The leadership and courage that Reeder inspired in his men earned him the Distinguished Service Cross (1944), the first to be awarded in Normandy. Some historians credit the success of D day to Reeder and other colonels who made quick and precise decisions. On 11 June 1944, an 88-millimeter round shattered Reeder's ankle, almost severing his left leg. After four months in the Walter Reed General Hospital in Washington, D.C., Reeder's leg was amputated. Reeder was awarded a Bronze Star and a Purple Heart while still in the hospital in 1944.

Reeder left military service in 1945, but was immediately recalled to active duty at the request of the superintendent of West Point, who asked him to create a leadership course for cadets. At the turn of the twenty-first century the course was still a part of the academy's curriculum. During the time between 1945 and 1947, Reeder sought refuge from his responsibilities as a regimental commander by dabbling in oil painting. After twenty-one years in the military, in 1948 Reeder joined the Army Athletic Association as assistant director and helped to coach the freshmen baseball team at West Point; he was an assistant coach for the varsity team. He retired from the Army Athletic Association in 1967.

Spurred on by the success of *Fighting on Guadalcanal,* Reeder embarked on his third career, writing. He ultimately wrote thirty-five books, mostly for young people. His sister Nardi Reeder Campion coauthored one of these, *West Point Story* (1956). Most of Reeder's books cover American military history and include biographies, histories, and historical fiction. His six novels about Clint Lane, a fictional cadet at West Point, inspired many cadets to enter the academy. *The MacKenzie Raid* was the basis for a television series broadcast from 1958 to 1959. In 1975 Reeder became bedridden with Guillain-Barré syndrome, a disease characterized by muscle weakness and paralysis. He and his wife moved to a military retirement community in Fairfax, Virginia, in 1989; his wife died in 1998.

As well as the Silver Star, the Bronze Star, the Distinguished Service Cross, the Purple Heart, and the Combat Infantryman Badge, Reeder was also awarded the Legion of Merit, the Croix de Guerre avec Palm, and the French Legion of Honor award. Other honors include the Freedom Foundation's National Recognition Award (1963), a citation from the Association of the United States Army (1968) for outstanding services to the U.S. Army, and the first Doubleday Society Distinguished Service Award (1991). The U.S. Military Academy at West Point presented Reeder with its Distinguished Graduate Award in May 1997, and the academy named its most valuable player award for football and a room in Washington Hall for Reeder. Reeder died of congestive heart failure at Inova Mount Vernon Hospital on 22 February 1998 and is buried at the West Point Cemetery.

In a *Saturday Evening Post* article, Wesley Price stated that, "Reeder was a colonel, a casualty, famous throughout the army as an unexampled leader of men." Reeder's gridiron will proved to be an asset on the battlefield. Resolute and fearless in battle, dauntless in the face of adversity, he earned the respect and admiration of those with whom he served. Reeder lived the biblical passage he loved, "Be not afraid. Only believe."

★

Reeder's autobiography, *Born at Reveille* (1966; rev. 1994), provides an excellent account of his life through 1948. Several histories of World War II and D day contain information on Reeder, including Richard Goldstein, *America at D-Day: A Book of Remembrance* (1994) and Stephen Ambrose, *D-Day, June 6, 1944: The Climactic Battle of World War II* (1994). Wesley Price, "The Factor X in Victory" in the *Saturday Evening Post* (18 Nov. 1944), provides information on Reeder's army career, with emphasis on the Normandy invasion. See also "Col. Red Reeder '26, a Lifetime of Achievement" in *Assembly* (July/Aug. 1997). Reeder's books are in the military history collections of many libraries. An obituary is in the *Washington Post* (27 Feb. 1998).

JOYCE K. THORNTON

REESE, Harold Henry ("Pee Wee") (*b.* 23 July 1918 in Ekron, Kentucky; *d.* 14 August 1999 in Louisville, Kentucky), star shortstop who helped the Brooklyn Dodgers win seven National League pennants between 1941 and 1956.

Reese was one of six children of Carl Reese, at different times a farmer, Ford Company worker, and Louisville and

Pee Wee Reese, 1941. ASSOCIATED PRESS AP

Nashville Railroad yard detective, and Emma Allen, a homemaker. He was born on a farm and moved to Louisville at age seven. He earned his nickname, "Pee Wee," when he used the "peewee" type of marble as his shooter to place runner-up in a national marble championship at age thirteen. Reese graduated in 1937 from DuPont Manual High School in Louisville; he did not try out for the baseball team until his senior year.

After high school, Reese worked for furniture and box companies, spliced cables for the Kentucky Telephone Company for $18 a week, and played shortstop on the weekends for the New Covenant Presbyterian Church. His professional baseball career began in 1938 when Captain Neal of the last-place Louisville Colonels signed him. In 1939 he paced Louisville to a pennant, leading the American League with eighteen triples and thirty-five stolen bases. Boston Red Sox owner Tom Yawkey was impressed and contemplated having the five-foot, ten-inch, 160-pound Reese replace thirty-four-year-old Joe Cronin as shortstop. When Cronin balked at relinquishing his job, the Red Sox sold Reese to the Brooklyn Dodgers for $75,000 in July 1939.

Reese, who batted and threw right-handed, replaced Leo Durocher as the Dodgers shortstop in 1940. In his first season he batted .272 until he broke a bone in his heel while sliding into second base that August. The Dodgers won their first National League pennant in twenty-one years in 1941, but Reese was still recovering: he hit just .229, although he managed to lead the National League shortstops with 346 putouts and 47 errors. He batted only .200 and made three errors when the New York Yankees defeated the Dodgers in the 1941 World Series. The next year was a better year, though: Reese made the National League All-Star team for the first of nine times and paced shortstops with 377 putouts and 482 assists. Reese married Dorothy Walton, a Louisville stenographer, on 29 March 1942; they had two children.

During World War II, Reese served in the U.S. Navy from 1943 to 1945. He played for the Norfolk, Virginia, Naval Air Station baseball team in 1943 and later served at the 14th Naval District in Hawaii. Upon returning to the Dodgers in 1946, he batted .284 and set a team shortstop record with a .966 fielding percentage. From 1947 to 1956 Reese helped the Dodgers average ninety-five wins a year and capture six pennants. In 1947 he hit .284 and shared the league lead with 104 walks.

Reese's calm leadership and example helped smooth the path when Jackie Robinson integrated major league baseball. Reese refused to sign a petition by six Dodgers saying they would not play if Robinson joined the team. Dixie Walker, who circulated the petition, was traded to the Pittsburgh Pirates. When opponents taunted Robinson, Reese walked over from shortstop and put his arm around Robinson's shoulder to show them that he, a white southerner from Louisville, considered the black rookie his teammate and friend. In fact, they formed a very effective double-play combination. In the notable book *The Boys of Summer*, author Roger Kahn called Reese a "catalyst of baseball integration" for his principled stand against racism.

In Brooklyn's 1947 World Series loss to the New York Yankees, Reese batted .304, drove in four runs, and stole three bases. He contributed a key single in game three and a double and two singles in game six. In 1949 Reese hit .279, paced the National League with 132 runs scored, and led shortstops with a .977 fielding percentage and 316 putouts. He batted .316 in the 1949 World Series, but the New York Yankees again prevailed. In 1950 Reese was elected team captain of the "Boys of Summer," as the Dodgers were known, a legendary team that featured Robinson, Roy Campanella, Duke Snider, Gil Hodges, and Don Newcombe. Reese, whose value far exceeded his statistics, held the star-filled team together. Teammates went to him for advice; he cooled hot tempers and soothed bruised egos.

Reese led the National League with thirty stolen bases in 1952. He batted .345 and made ten hits in another World Series loss to the New York Yankees. After the Dodgers won the 1955 National League pennant by thirteen and a half games, Reese batted .296 and scored five runs to spark their only World Series title over the New York Yankees. Besides driving in two runs in the second inning of game three, he led off the sixth inning with a single and scored to give Brooklyn a 2–0 lead in the decisive seventh game. In the bottom of the sixth, his relay throw to first base doubled off Gil McDougald after Sandy Amoros had made a sensational catch of a line drive by Yogi Berra into the left field corner. In 1957 Reese played most of his games at third base, and Charlie Neal moved to shortstop. Reese played fifty-nine games for the Dodgers in Los Angeles in 1958 and became coach for the team in 1959.

Reese finished among the top ten in the Most Valuable Player voting eight times during his career. A team leader on the field, he directed traffic, positioned outfielders, and cajoled pitchers. Defensively, the sure-handed fielder performed better than any other National League shortstop. Although not especially quick or strong, he led National League shortstops in fielding and assists once, double plays twice, total chances accepted three times, and putouts four times. A clutch hitter, Reese excelled as the number-two batter in the lineup and possessed outstanding bat control. He could bunt, hit and run, hit behind the runner, swing away, and supply power when necessary.

Reese compiled a .269 career batting average with 2,170 hits, 536 extra base hits, 1,338 runs scored, 885 RBI, and 232 stolen bases. He led all Brooklyn Dodgers in career stolen bases (231) and runs scored (1,317); ranked second in games played (2,107), hits (2,137), doubles (323), singles (1,612), and at bats (7,911); placed fifth in triples (78) and RBI (868); and stood eighth in home runs (122). He batted .272 in seven World Series.

After retirement from playing baseball, Reese did television commentary on NBC baseball's "Game of the Week" with Dizzy Dean, and he announced one year for the Cincinnati Reds. Upon returning to Louisville, he owned a storm-window business, a bowling alley, and part of a bank. His hobbies included golf and bowling. Reese also worked as a manufacturing representative for the Hillerich and Bradsby Corporation, maker of Louisville Slugger baseball bats. In 1984 he was elected to the National Baseball Hall of Fame and the Brooklyn Dodgers Hall of Fame. Reese, who later served on the Veterans Committee of the National Baseball Hall of Fame, underwent major surgery for lung cancer in 1997. He died of the disease at age eighty-one and is buried in Resthaven Memorial Park, Louisville. He was survived by his wife and two children.

A catalyst for baseball integration, Reese blended an intense drive to win with leadership, class, and civility. Roy Campanella observed, "He could do everything to beat you; running, fielding, throwing, stealing, and hitting."

★

Reese has a file at the National Baseball Library, Cooperstown, New York. For personal reminiscences, see Pee Wee Reese with Tim Cohane, "14 Years a Bum," *Look* (9 Mar. 1954). For general portraits of Reese, see Herbert Warren Wind, *The Gilded Age of Sport* (1961), and Roger Kahn, *The Boys of Summer* (1972). Milton Gross, "Pee Wee Reese Grows Up," *Sport* (June 1951), summarizes his early career. Team histories that discuss Reese's role include Tommy Holmes, *The Dodgers* (1975); Peter Golenbock, *Bums: An Oral History of the Brooklyn Dodgers* (1984); Richard Goldstein, *Superstars and Screwballs: 100 Years of Brooklyn Baseball* (1991); and Tot Holmes, *The Dodgers* (1997). Obituaries are in the *New York Times* and *Louisville Courier-Journal* (both 15 Aug. 1999).

DAVID L. PORTER

REINES, Frederick (*b.* 16 March 1918 in Paterson, New Jersey; *d.* 26 August 1998 in Orange, California), physicist and educator who received the Nobel Prize in physics in 1995 for having experimentally verified in 1956 the existence of the neutrino, an extremely difficult-to-detect fundamental nuclear particle, the existence of which had been theoretically postulated twenty-six years earlier.

Reines was one of four children of Israel Reines and Gussie Cohen, both immigrants from Russia. His father first worked as a weaver, then ran a silk mill, and finally operated a general store in Hillburn, New York. Reines was raised in Hillburn and graduated from Union Hill High School in New Jersey in 1935. He was educated at the Stevens Institute of Technology in Hoboken, New Jersey, where he received an M.E. (Master of Engineering) degree in 1939 and an M.S. degree in physics in 1941. Reines then entered New York University, where he received his Ph.D. in theoretical physics in 1944. He joined the scientific staff of Los Alamos National Laboratory in New Mexico, which was engaged in developing the atomic weapons later dropped on the cities of Hiroshima and Nagasaki in Japan in 1945 (also known as the Manhattan Project). In 1945 he was promoted to leader of a group in the theoretical division of the laboratory that was exploring the physics of atomic explosions. In this capacity he became the senior scientist in charge of Operation Greenhouse, the U.S. Atomic Energy Commission's extensive 1951 weapons test series in the Eniwetok atoll in the Pacific Ocean.

In the course of the fifteen-year Los Alamos period of his career, Reines met with fellow scientist Clyde Cowan,

Frederick Reines, 1995. ASSOCIATED PRESS HO

Jr. (1919–1974). Their subsequent collaboration led to one of the most important and fruitful experimental investigations of the twentieth century, the existence of the neutrino. Although the experiments were done between 1953 and 1956 while both Reines and Cowan were at the most important U.S. weapons laboratory, their investigation had little to do with the development of nuclear ordnance. The special resources in instrumentation, computer facilities, and technical personnel at Los Alamos, however, certainly contributed to their success. Their actual experiments were done elsewhere, but early plans of an experiment for detecting neutrinos contemplated the use of an atomic bomb as a possible large source of the hypothetical neutrinos.

The idea of hypothetical neutrino particles was first advanced by the Austrian physicist Wolfgang Pauli (1900–1958) in 1930. Earlier, scientists studying the radioactive decay of atomic nuclei confronted what appeared to be an insurmountable challenge to one of the fundamental laws of physics: the conservation of energy. In one important radioactive process, one particle at an atom's nuclear center, the electrically neutral neutron, is transferred into a proton—a particle of essentially the same size and mass but having a positive electric charge. The proton remained in the nucleus but emitted from the atom another elementary particle—the electron, having a mass much less than either the neutron or proton with the opposite, but equal in magnitude, electrical charge as the latter. In accord with the conservation of energy law, it was anticipated that the two particles, the proton and electron, should always yield the available energy of this radioactive process known as beta decay (the electron in this atomic event known as a beta particle) in the same way. On this basis, each electron from each individual radioactive decay should have the same energy.

However, numerous laboratories found that the electrons had a wide range of energies from essentially zero to some maximum energy. To explain this wholly unanticipated result, Pauli proposed that, along with the electron, another particle was emitted that had some unique properties. According to Pauli's theoretical conjectures, the particle had to be electrically neutral, have zero or very little mass, and spin about its axis like other fundamental atomic particles such as the electron or proton. Along with many other prominent scientists, the Italian physicist Enrico Fermi was initially skeptical of Pauli's daring hypothesis. Fermi was finally persuaded of its validity, and he incorporated Pauli's particle into his own theory of beta decay and gave Pauli's particle the designation "neutrino"—Italian for "little neutral one"—the name by which it became known.

Perhaps seeking diversion from their activities in nuclear weaponry, Cowan and Reines generated the idea in the 1950s of proving the existence of the phantom neutrino, which had been incorporated increasingly into the framework of theoretical atomic and nuclear physics. Scientists initially thought that an atomic bomb could supply a sufficient number of neutrinos from the decay of neutrons released in the nuclear fission process. This plan was diverted by the head of the physics division at Los Alamos, who suggested that Reines and Cowan look into using neutrinos from fission in a nuclear reactor rather than a fission bomb explosion.

After further study, the physicists fixed on a method equivalent to but slightly different from direct observation of a neutrino in beta decay. The process they chose is inverse beta decay, regarded as a conceptual mirror image of ordinary beta decay. In inverse beta decay a proton captures a neutrino (an antineutrino in more exact formulations), converting it to a neutron emitting a positron, a low-mass particle identical to an electron in atomic characteristics but having a positive rather than a negative electric charge. What results are two separate bursts of gamma rays—high-energy electromagnetic radiation—closely separated in time. One burst is from the instantaneous annihilation of the positively charged positron with an electron, and the

other gamma ray is from the capture of the neutron by a suitable material. The capturing substance chosen by the investigators was a solution of cadmium chloride because the element cadmium has a high affinity, or in physics terminology a large "cross section" for neutron absorption.

Reines and Cowan named their elaborate apparatus Poltergeist because of the ghostly elusive particle they sought. The principal structure after several modifications was a ten-ton detector comprising of three tanks of a liquid scintillator, which gave light pulses after absorbing the aforementioned gamma rays. Two smaller tanks with cadmium chloride solution were positioned between the scintillator tanks. The final detector system was constructed in 1955 at the Savannah River nuclear reactor in South Carolina. A preliminary experiment, conducted at the Hanford, Washington, nuclear reactor, yielded suggestive but inconclusive results. On 14 June 1956 the Poltergeist apparatus detected the gamma ray bursts unique to inverse beta decay and unambiguous detection of the long-sought neutrino. The scientists immediately sent the following telegram to Pauli, then in Zurich, Switzerland: "We are happy to inform you that we have definitely detected neutrinos from fission fragments by observing inverse beta decay of protons." Although Pauli drafted an immediate acknowledgement, for unclear reasons Reines did not receive a copy until many years after Pauli's death. Pauli's reply to Reines and Cowan read: "Thanks for the message. Everything comes to him who knows how to wait."

In 1995 Reines was rewarded for this experimental accomplishment with the Nobel Prize in physics, which he shared with Martin L. Perl of Stanford University for his discovery of a sub-atomic particle, the tau. Unfortunately, the equally responsible codiscover of the neutrino, Cowan, who certainly would have shared the prize with Reines, had died in 1974.

Reines remained at Los Alamos after the neutrino discovery until 1959, when he became professor and head of the physics department at the Case Institute of Technology (now Case Western Reserve University) in Cleveland, Ohio. In 1966 he joined the University of California, Irvine (UCI), as founding dean of the School of Physical Sciences. At UCI he served as dean until 1974, when he gave up administrative duties and resumed his primary interests in research and teaching. In 1987 he was named distinguished professor of physics and also joined the UCI College of Medicine faculty as professor of radiological sciences. Besides continuing investigation in the physics of neutrinos, Reines's career included research in nuclear fission, scintillation detectors, cosmic rays, and cosmology. In the latter sphere he is remembered for his pioneering development of observational neutrino astrophysics by the detection of neutrinos from a supernova outside Earth's galaxy. In 1988 he retired as professor emeritus but continued teaching through 1991.

In 1981 Reines was awarded the J. Robert Oppenheimer Memorial Prize from the University of Miami; in 1985 he received the National Medal of Science. The American Astronomical Society awarded him the Bruno Rossi Prize in 1989 for opening "a new window of the cosmos beyond the solar system" and providing "the first direct data on high energy processes occurring in the center of collapsed stars." Among honors referencing his outstanding investigations in neutrino physics were the Albert A. Michelson/Edward W. Morley Award by Case Western Reserve University in 1990, the American Physical Society W. K. H. Panofsky Prize in 1992, the Franklin Medal of the Franklin Institute the same year, and election to the Russian Academy of Sciences in 1994.

On 30 August 1940 Reines married Sylvia Samuels. They had two children. Besides his scientific endeavors, Reines had a deep lifelong involvement in choral music. He was an accomplished singer who trained with a voice coach at the Metropolitan Opera in New York City and was an active participant in the Cleveland Symphony Chorus between 1959 and 1962. His colleagues report that he could often be heard to sing Gilbert and Sullivan pieces at parties and while walking through the halls of the physics department at UCI. After a long battle with Parkinson's disease, Reines died at the UCI Medical Center in Orange, California.

Reines's innovative discoveries associated with experimentally demonstrating the existence of the elusive neutrino have led to contemporary physicists' view of the neutrino as the most common form of matter in the universe in terms of particle number. If the neutrino's still unestablished individual mass turns out to be non-zero, which appears to be likely, it is probably the largest quantity of material mass in the universe unless future cosmology reveals the presence of still undiscovered elementary particles.

★

A major collection of Reines's papers is in the special collections department at the library of the University of California, Irvine. Reines was a contributing author for the U.S. Atomic Energy Commission publication *Effects of Atomic Weapons* (1950). He wrote numerous articles for scientific journals, many of which have been gathered in W. Kropp et al., eds., *Neutrinos and Other Matters: The Selected Works of Frederick Reines* (1991). Accessible and excellent accounts of the physics involved and the detection apparatus used in Reines's experiments are given in George L. Trigg, "Reality of the Neutrino," in *Landmark Experiments in Twentieth Century Physics* (1975), and John Gribbin, *Q Is for Quantum* (1998). An autobiography is at the Nobel Prize website, <http://www.nobel.se/physics/laureates/1995/reines-autobio.

html>. Biographies are in *Notable Twentieth-Century Scientists* (1995); *World of Scientific Discovery*, 2d ed. (1999); and *UCI Journal* (winter 1999). An obituary is in the *New York Times* (28 Aug. 1998).

LEONARD R. SOLON

RIBICOFF, Abraham Alexander (*b.* 9 April 1910 in New Britain, Connecticut; *d.* 22 February 1998 in New York City), lawyer, state representative, judge, U.S. congressman, governor, cabinet secretary, and U.S. senator who played a major role in John F. Kennedy's rise to power, championed environmental causes, opposed the Vietnam War, and was one of the architects of the Camp David Accords.

Ribicoff was born in New Britain, Connecticut, the son of Sam Ribicoff and Rose Sablotsky, Jewish immigrants from Poland. Ribicoff's father was a factory worker and deliveryman who instilled a strong work ethic and religious devotion in his three children. Ribicoff's mother, an active volunteer and homemaker, nurtured their interest in social welfare causes. Ribicoff often noted his "special fortune" to have grown up in New Britain, an American melting pot

Abraham Ribicoff, 1966. ASSOCIATED PRESS AP

that seemed to him to be free of anti-Semitism and racism. "You took everyone as you found [them] and did not feel [like] an outsider."

Ribicoff worked as a newsboy and ditch digger before graduating from New Britain High School at age seventeen. After working for a year in a factory to earn money for college, he entered New York University in 1929. After a year, he accepted a job in Chicago, where he attended the University of Chicago at night. On 28 June 1931 he married Ruth Siegel. Admitted to the University of Chicago Law School without a college degree, he achieved outstanding academic honors and received a LL.B. degree cum laude in 1933. Following his graduation from law school, Ribicoff relocated to Hartford, Connecticut, passed the bar, and began a law practice with the judge Abraham Bordon, soon becoming a partner in the firm of Bordon and Ribicoff.

Despite his success in law, Ribicoff was destined for a career in politics. He immersed himself in Hartford's ward politics and befriended another lawyer with political aspirations, John Bailey. "Over corned-beef sandwiches," Ribicoff recalled, "we talked about what we would do if we controlled the Democratic Party." When turmoil fractured Hartford's Democratic Party machine in 1938, Ribicoff and Bailey took advantage of the split. They challenged the machine and won, sending Ribicoff to the state legislature and Bailey to party positions of rising importance.

Ribicoff thrived in Connecticut's state legislature—he was voted the "ablest legislator" by the press corps—but failed to gain renomination after two terms. He vowed to leave politics behind for the sake of his growing family, which now included a son and daughter, but even a successful stint as a police court judge in Hartford could not dim the allure of electoral politics. Again, Bailey played a major role, convincing Ribicoff to run for the U.S. Congress in 1948. "After saying, 'No, no,'" explained Ribicoff, "I succumbed to my love of politics, was nominated, and won."

In 1949 Ribicoff entered national politics for the first time. He served two terms in the U.S. House of Representatives, establishing a reputation for independence and integrity. When he blocked a multimillion-dollar appropriation earmarked for a Connecticut dam project, telling his constituents that national security took precedence over local needs, the subsequent publicity helped strengthen his reputation. The most significant result of his House career was not legislative action, however, but the strong political ties he formed during those years, particularly with John F. Kennedy. That alliance, combined with his own political ambitions, kept Ribicoff in public view for years, often in the role of kingmaker.

A 1952 vacancy in the U.S. Senate prompted Ribicoff to leave the House after two terms and seek a Senate seat. Running against the Republican Prescott Bush, Ribicoff lost his first statewide election. In 1954 he turned his attention to the Connecticut governorship. As Ribicoff later explained, his race against the incumbent governor, John David Lodge, "was the first and only campaign in ten where anti-Semitism reared its head." In the last weeks of the campaign, Ribicoff became the target of an anti-Semitic smear campaign, orchestrated not by Lodge but by another Democrat. In a televised speech just days before the election, Ribicoff asked Connecticut voters to rise above bigotry. "I threw away my script," he explained. "I just said what was in my heart." His television appearance won him the election, by a slim 3,200 votes, and caught the attention of the national Democratic Party.

As governor, Ribicoff honed his skills of compromise and learned the value of bipartisan action, relying upon colleagues to steer his agenda through the Republican-controlled legislature. In his first term, he promoted a strict highway safety program and guided the state to recovery following Hurricane Diane in 1955. The Democratic Party invited Governor Ribicoff to play a prominent role at its 1956 Chicago convention, where he nominated John F. Kennedy for vice president. Ironically, when Irish-Catholic politicians objected to Kennedy's nomination, fearing a Catholic would doom the ticket, Ribicoff rebelled. "I never thought I'd see the day," he scolded, "when a man of Jewish faith had to plead before a group of Irish Catholics about allowing another Irish Catholic to be nominated." Kennedy lost the nomination, but the convention propelled both men to national prominence, linking Ribicoff's career to Kennedy's for the next seven years. "Jack," Ribicoff told his friend at the close of the convention, "next time, we go all the way." Ribicoff easily won reelection in 1958, and the second-term governor, working again with Bailey, prepared for the 1960 presidential election. Ribicoff served as floor manager at the national convention in Los Angeles when Kennedy won the Democratic Party's nomination.

Kennedy's subsequent electoral victory in 1960 opened a new chapter in Ribicoff's career. He was given his pick of cabinet-level positions, including that of attorney general, and chose to be secretary of the Department of Health, Education, and Welfare (HEW). At HEW, he could deal "with, and for, people" to promote causes such as Medicare, youth fitness, and equal employment opportunity. Ribicoff often remarked on the excitement of being part of the Kennedy administration, but he just as frequently expressed frustration at no longer being the "number-one" man. So, in 1962, missing the power of elective office, he ran for and won a seat in the U.S. Senate, beginning the most rewarding phase of his political career.

Although he was a freshman member of the Senate in

1963, Ribicoff's high-profile service in the executive branch brought him considerable prestige. While some resented his position, others encouraged him to move ahead boldly. "You're not a freshman senator, Abe," Vice President Lyndon B. Johnson advised him. "Don't bother to act like one." Ribicoff's list of Senate achievements included a school integration policy, highway safety laws, and the creation of the Department of Education. He also made a mark as an environmentalist. He used his chairmanship of the Government Affairs Committee and the Executive Reorganization Subcommittee to explore a wide variety of issues, including pollution and pesticide control.

Senator Ribicoff achieved the peak of his fame at the tumultuous 1968 Democratic convention in Chicago, where antiwar demonstrations erupted into violence. Ribicoff broke with the party and many of his longtime allies, including Bailey, over the issue of U.S. involvement in the Vietnam War. He refused to back Hubert Humphrey, who supported the U.S. war effort. Instead, Ribicoff placed Senator George McGovern's name into nomination. "With George McGovern as president," Ribicoff told the audience in the hall and the television-viewing nation, who had seen footage of the violent confrontation between police and antiwar demonstrators, "we wouldn't have to have gestapo tactics in the streets of Chicago." Seated just a few feet away, the Chicago mayor Richard Daley and the Illinois delegation screamed racial epithets at Ribicoff, bringing the convention to near chaos. As the turbulent 1968 convention faded into memory, the image of a calm Ribicoff confronting the Daley machine became one of the event's defining moments. When McGovern gained the Democratic nomination four years later, he offered the vice presidency to his old ally. Ribicoff rejected the offer. "I had the experience of being the number-two man," he explained. "I didn't lust for that type of office . . . and I liked the Senate."

If Chicago 1968 was the most dramatic moment of Ribicoff's career, perhaps the defining legislative moment came a decade later. In 1978 President Jimmy Carter proposed selling U.S. warplanes to Egypt and Saudi Arabia, a plan criticized by the U.S. Jewish community. The independent Ribicoff supported Carter's proposal. "It was a tough position to take," he noted, and one that risked the support of his friends, colleagues, and constituents. Despite the opposition, Ribicoff led Carter's proposal to victory in the Senate and helped pave the way for the Camp David Accords and further Middle East peace talks.

Ribicoff easily won reelection to a third Senate term in 1974. Soon after, he decided it would be his last election. "There is a time to stay, and a time to go," he told the press. "I have admiration for the men who know how to go out at the top of their careers." When asked about holding future offices, Ribicoff said he would accept no offers.

"If I intended to stay in government, I'd remain in the United States Senate. It's the best job in government, and I've known 'em all."

Ribicoff entered retirement with a changed home life. His wife Ruth had died in 1972. After leaving Washington, Ribicoff and his second wife, Lois Mell Mathes, settled in Cornwall Bridge, Connecticut, and New York City. He returned to practicing law, becoming special counsel to the firm of Kaye, Scholer, Fierman, Hays, and Handler. Although he was diagnosed with Alzheimer's disease in 1992, Ribicoff continued to pursue legal and political interests for several more years. He died of heart failure on 22 February 1998, at the Hebrew Home for the Aged in New York City. Ribicoff is buried in Cornwall Cemetery in Cornwall, Connecticut.

From humble beginnings in New Britain, Ribicoff lived the American dream that he so often espoused, rising to the heights of political power. Known as an individualist in party politics, he became a guiding force in the Democratic Party. In a career that spanned four decades, he lost only one election and helped many others gain high office. He became the first Jewish governor of Connecticut and one of the most respected members of the U.S. Senate. As a lawyer, judge, and lawmaker, Ribicoff was known for his willingness to compromise. While some critics accused him of compromising too much, most political observers admired him for his ability to rise above partisan politics and for his courageous stand against the Daley machine in 1968.

★

Most of Ribicoff's papers are in the Manuscript Division of the Library of Congress. Papers from his service in the U.S. House of Representatives and as the secretary of HEW are archived in the Kennedy Presidential Library. Additional collections are housed in the American Jewish Archives in Cincinnati, Ohio, and the Connecticut State Library in Hartford. A 465-page oral history can be found in Columbia University's Oral History Project. Although he never wrote an autobiography, Ribicoff wrote a brief sketch of his life for *Connecticut Jewish History* (summer 1990). He was the author, with John O. Newman, of *Politics: The American Way* (1967), a primer on U.S. politics. His *America Can Make It!* (1972) is a summary of social problems facing the United States in the early 1970s. John F. Bibby and Roger H. Davidson, *On Capitol Hill: Studies in the Legislative Process* (1967), includes an interesting chapter on Ribicoff's time in the Senate. A collection of tributes from Senate colleagues upon Ribicoff's retirement are included in the U.S. Congress, Senate, *Tributes to the Honorable Abraham Ribicoff of Connecticut* (1980). Lengthy obituaries are in the *New York Times* and *Washington Post* (both 23 Feb. 1998).

BETTY K. KOED

RICHARDSON, Elliot Lee (*b.* 20 July 1920 in Boston, Massachusetts; *d.* 31 December 1999 in Boston, Massachusetts), moderate Republican politician whose decision to resign as U.S. attorney general, rather than obey an order to fire Watergate Special Prosecutor Archibald Cox, precipitated a chain of events known as the "Saturday Night Massacre," which presaged the end of Richard M. Nixon's presidency.

Richardson, the second son of Edward Pierson Richardson and Clara Shattuck, was raised in a First Period mansion where Susanna Boylston nursed her infant son, John Adams, in 1736, and Franklin Roosevelt came to holiday dinner while preparing for the presidency. The Richardsons and Shattucks, heirs to a fortune amassed in the China trade, produced generations of physicians affiliated with Harvard Medical School and Massachusetts General Hospital, where Richardson's father was the first chief of surgery. His mother died during childbirth when he was not yet two. He was brought up by a devoted but draconian "custodian," Marguerite Brown. He said she beat him often for not measuring up to family standards. His childhood became still more painful in 1931 when his father suffered a stroke, leaving him paralyzed and unable to speak.

Richardson's uncle, Henry Lee Shattuck, a member of the Boston City Council and the Massachusetts House of Representatives (also Harvard's treasurer and acting president), nurtured his nephew's passion for politics. Richardson, elected president of his school's Hoover Club, particularly admired the Republican secretary of state, Henry L. Stimson. He would adopt Stimson's maxim: "When in doubt, march toward the guns."

Roger Tory Peterson, the wildlife artist and author of *Field Guide To the Birds*, taught Richardson to paint and took him on intense bird-watching marathons. Richardson attributed his ability to concentrate and to endure pressure to those experiences. His custodian, who had traveled in summer stock, imparted to her ward a love of Shakespeare. As Falstaff in Henry IV, Part 1 in 1937, he basked in the applause of the audience and the praise of the famous Shakespeare authority, George Lyman Kittredge. It was the fondest memory of his youth, overshadowing his near-expulsion from Milton Academy for knocking out a boy who goaded him about finishing second in a track meet.

At Harvard Richardson studied Greek, philosophy, and political science, but concentrated on the *Lampoon*, Harvard's legendary humor magazine, where he was a prolific cartoonist. His best cartoon was a pair of flies rubbing forelegs over the caption, "In Boston, we lay the emphasis on breeding." (A 1999 award recognized him as one of the magazine's five finest satirists of the century.) Richardson was also quick to point out that his university middleweight boxing championship was earned in the most competitive

division. Richardson graduated cum laude from Harvard in 1941 with a degree in philosophy.

In 1942 Richardson enlisted in the army as a private, was commissioned, and served as the lieutenant in charge of a platoon of medics. He assigned himself the duty of rescuing a soldier whose foot had been blown off in the minefield beyond the dune at Utah Beach during the Normandy invasion of World War II. In battles across France, Richardson earned the nicknames "Lucky," "Cannonball," and "Fearless Fosdick." Twice his jeep ran over a land mine detonated by the vehicle following him, killing the occupants. A third time, he survived an explosion, which launched him to a branch ten feet up. He was awarded a Bronze Star and Purple Heart in 1945.

Returning to law school in 1946, Richardson was named president of the Harvard Law Review. He graduated in 1947 with an LL.B. degree and won a clerkship with Learned Hand, generally recognized as the greatest American jurist of his time, followed by a term with Supreme Court Justice Felix Frankfurter. Frankfurter secured a position for him with Secretary of State Dean Acheson, but Richardson questioned whether a Washington job would be a good start for a political career. His law professor, Archibald Cox, told Richardson that he "had always found it helpful to have been *from* somewhere." Swayed by Cox,

Elliot Richardson. CORBIS CORPORATION (NEW YORK)

Richardson went home to join the elite law firm of Ropes and Gray.

Richardson married Anne Francis Hazard on 2 August 1952. From a Rhode Island family whose estate dated to 1653, Hazard shared Richardson's New England values as well as his irreverent wit. She was her husband's intellectual equal and closest political adviser. The couple had three children.

As legislative assistant to Massachusetts' senior U.S. Senator Leverett Saltonstall, Richardson received an education in hard-edged, sometimes bipartisan politics. Tapped to be Assistant Secretary of Health, Education, and Welfare (HEW) in the Eisenhower administration in 1957, Richardson impressed the president and Attorney General William Rogers with his ideas for post-Sputnik science and mathematics initiatives. Ironically, it was Richard Nixon who secured Eisenhower's approval of controversial legislative proposals authored by Richardson, saving him from having to carry out his threat to resign if the president would not endorse them.

As U.S. attorney for Massachusetts in 1961, Richardson developed a reputation as a crusader against corruption. His inquiry into misconduct of Boston Democrats impelled the new administration of President John F. Kennedy and U.S. Attorney General Robert Kennedy to replace him immediately. Richardson acidly remembered "the time I was fired by Bobby Kennedy."

Richardson was elected lieutenant governor of Massachusetts in 1964 on a ticket headed by John Volpe, serving in that position until 1967. He captured headlines leading a Massachusetts group in the 1965 civil rights march at Selma. Drafted to run for state attorney general in 1966 against Frances X. Bellotti, who was rumored to have organized crime connections, Richardson accused him of unethical conduct and narrowly won a bitter race. Nixon's aide, Charles (Chuck) Colson, another graduate of Saltonstall's staff, branded this race "the dirtiest campaign in Massachusetts history."

Had Richardson not taken on Bellotti, he would have automatically succeeded to the governorship when Nixon made Volpe the secretary of transportation in 1969. Instead, Richardson's first opportunity for national prominence came when Rogers, now in charge of the State Department, asked him to be his deputy in December 1968. Richardson and National Security Advisor Henry Kissinger worked closely in executing Nixon's foreign policy: the opening to China; détente with the Soviet Union, strategic arms reduction talks; mediation of Arab-Israeli conflicts; and defense of South Vietnam.

When he elevated Richardson to Secretary of Health, Education, and Welfare in June 1970, Nixon remarked: "Every cabinet should include a future president." Indeed, Richardson wanted to be president so much that he said he

might have declined a seat on the U.S. Supreme Court, not knowing Nixon had told his right-hand man, H. R. Haldeman, that Richardson "would be a towering, historic chief justice," and should be considered for the next vacancy.

Richardson's management of HEW's sprawling bureaucracy was widely acclaimed by Nixon and cabinet members. He also defended the Nixon administration's position against busing to achieve school desegregation, campaigned against George McGovern's "harebrained [welfare] schemes," and assailed the isolationism of the Democratic presidential candidate's proposals for withdrawal from Indochina. Nixon rewarded Richardson with the nomination to secretary of defense in December 1972, but it was less than three months before Nixon reassigned him to the Department of Justice, a job Richardson did not want. Senate Democrats led by Edward Kennedy refused to confirm Richardson without his pledge to choose a special prosecutor and guarantee his independence. Turned down by many prominent lawyers, Richardson selected Archibald Cox, not appreciating how Cox's ties to the Kennedy family would fuel Nixon's paranoia. While trying to maintain neutrality in Cox's subpoena for White House tape recordings, Richardson rebuffed his deputy, the former acting FBI director William Ruckelshaus, who tried to tell him of Nixon's involvement in the Watergate cover-up. "I have not yet concluded that *myself*," he snapped.

Richardson believed that Vice President Spiro T. Agnew's receipt of kickbacks from Maryland highway contractors warranted a jail term, but that the emerging prospect of "double impeachment" demanded an expeditious plea bargain in which Agnew would acknowledge his wrongdoing and leave office. Taking personal command of the probe (thereby removing himself from contention to be Agnew's successor), Richardson swiftly forced Agnew's resignation on 10 October 1973. Ten days later, Nixon told Richardson and Chief of Staff Alexander Haig: "Now that we have disposed of that matter, we can go ahead and fire Cox." In Haig's office, Richardson recounted his D day experience in the minefield. It was his way of saying he would resign if ordered to dishonor his pledge to the Senate. Nevertheless, Richardson became a proponent of a deal in which the special prosecutor would get transcripts authenticated by Senator John Stennis, who was respected but infirm and hard of hearing. He also teased a baffled Cox: "You know, Archie, it is a lot better to lose your job than to have your head cut off!" Cox had no idea whose head Richardson meant.

Richardson's role was not saintly; he hoped to save Nixon's job along with his own. But Nixon linked the Stennis compromise with a prohibition on all further discoveries of White House materials and ordered Richardson to discharge Cox for refusing to capitulate. Richardson called

Cox, also a Learned Hand clerk, to read him the Iliad fragment the judge had inscribed on his photograph in 1948: two warriors must die a glorious death together. Richardson then resigned, saying that his decision was easy because he had no honorable alternative.

President Gerald R. Ford appointed Richardson ambassador to the United Kingdom in 1975, and asked him to come home to be the secretary of commerce in 1976. Richardson hoped to be considered for the vice presidency that year, but he was unacceptable to Goldwater-Reagan conservatives. Their antipathy toward him increased when he served as President Jimmy Carter's special representative to negotiate the Law of the Sea Convention, which conservatives regarded as a United Nations' giveaway of Western wealth and technology.

Against his wife's advice, Richardson jumped at the opportunity to run for the U.S. Senate in 1984. Early polls showed him defeating all Democratic contenders for a seat critical to control of the Senate. Richardson's right-wing opponent branded him a liberal "carpetbagger" who had been in Washington too long and would not fully support President Reagan. Richardson lost badly after appearing on national television to denounce the Republican party platform against new taxes, abortion, and equal rights for women.

At the end of his career, Richardson was the special representative of President George Bush for Multilateral Assistance to the Philippines, and was a leader of election monitoring teams in Namibia and Nicaragua. Richardson was president of the United Nations Association of the United States, and he tirelessly promoted ratification of his Law of the Sea Convention, which the Clinton administration unsuccessfully submitted to the Senate in 1994. President Clinton awarded Richardson the Medal of Freedom in 1999. In his last act in public life, Richardson testified before the House Judiciary Committee on Clinton's impeachment; he irked many Republicans with his argument that the offense did not warrant removing a president from office.

Richardson died of a cerebral hemorrhage. He is buried in the family plot at Mount Saint Auburn's Cemetery.

★

Richardson's papers are in the Manuscript Division of the Library of Congress. He explained his eclectic political philosophy in *The Creative Balance* (1976) and *Reflections of a Radical Moderate* (1996). Articles about him include Stanley Karnow, "Dreaming of the Presidency," *The New Republic* (May 1975); William Shawcross, "Virtue Rewarded," *Sunday Times Magazine* (London) (23 Mar. 1975); and Tad Szulc, "The Smile on the Face of Elliot Richardson," *Esquire* (July 1974). Obituaries are in the *New York Times* and *Washington Post* (both 1 Jan. 2000).

Donald Alan Carr

ROBBINS, Harold (*b.* 21 May 1916 in New York City; *d.* 14 October 1997 in Palm Springs, California), author of bestselling novels read in more than forty countries.

Born Francis Kane, Robbins spent his early years in the Hell's Kitchen section of New York City, in a Roman Catholic orphanage and a series of foster homes. Although Robbins said he never knew his parents, his agent and lawyer, Paul Gitlin, told the writer Ian Parker that Robbins knew that his father was Jewish and his mother was not. After his father remarried, to a woman with children of her own, Robbins was placed in the orphanage. In 1927 he was adopted by a Manhattan pharmacist and assumed the name of Harold Rubin (some sources say Rubins). When he began to write novels, he changed his name, on the advice of his editor, to Harold Robbins.

Robbins attended George Washington High School in New York City but dropped out at age fifteen. Lying about his age, he joined the U.S. Navy. When he left the navy two years later, he returned to New York and worked in a series of jobs including bookies' runner, cook, cashier, errand boy, and grocery clerk. At age nineteen, he decided to use his knowledge of the grocery business to deal in crop futures. Borrowing $800, he bought crop options from farmers and sold those options to canning companies for

Harold Robbins. Corbis Corporation (Bellevue)

482

contracts he then sold to grocers. By 1937, when he married Lillian Machnivitz, Robbins had amassed a fortune. His wealth disappeared, however, in 1939 when food prices were frozen, and his heavy investment in sugar futures turned into significant losses.

In 1940 Robbins went to work as a shipping clerk in the New York warehouse of Universal Pictures. Adept at figures, he advanced quickly in the company, moved to Los Angeles, and by 1942 was the executive director of budget and planning. In this position, he saw many of the novels for which Universal had purchased film rights. Convinced he could write more interesting stories, Robbins produced his first novel, *Never Love a Stranger*, published by Alfred Knopf in 1948. This coming-of-age story about a New York orphan who grows up surrounded by hustlers and racketeers was dismissed by one reviewer as a "book of great promise shamefully ruined through undue emphasis on sex," and criticized by another who found the writing strong but the book lacking "because it slithers across anything that might turn out to be serious." Readers responded by turning it into a best-seller.

Robbins's next novel drew on his experiences in Hollywood. *The Dream Merchants* (1949) was the first of three novels to explore the glamour and greed of the Hollywood film industry. Comments from critics were more favorable than they would be for *The Carpetbaggers* (1961) and *The Inheritors* (1969), which completed the trilogy. Before leaving Universal in 1957, Robbins completed *A Stone for Danny Fisher* (1952), *Never Leave Me* (1953), and *79 Park Avenue* (1955). *A Stone for Danny Fisher*, the story of a young prizefighter corrupted by gangsters, won favorable but mixed reviews. Writing for the *New York Times*, James Kelly noted that the novel "draws its strength from vivid characterization, a feeling for individual scenes." However, he found the "total effect one of uneasy make-believe" that might have benefited from skillful editing. Later, writing for *Life* magazine, Thomas Thompson commented that had Robbins stopped writing after *A Stone for Danny Fisher*, this novel "would have reserved him a small place in literature."

In the late 1950s Robbins was in court fighting over custody of his three-year-old daughter. He moved to South America and went deeply into debt. After being extradited back to the United States in 1959, Robbins allowed Gitlin to arrange the creation of Trident Press, an imprint of Simon and Schuster, to publish hardcover editions of his future works. *Stiletto* (1960), Robbins's first novel after leaving Universal, continued his exploration of the world of crime. In the preface to a 1997 edition, Robbins claimed that, of the many novels written about the Mafia, his was "one of the most important forerunners." It remained one of his favorites.

In 1962 Robbins and his wife divorced. He then married Grace Palermo, with whom he had a second daughter. He and Palermo divorced in 1992. Robbins publicly acknowledged only three marriages; the third took place on 14 February 1992 to his former assistant Jann Stapp. In interviews he sometimes alluded to having been married many times. Some sources put the number at six, three of which may have been brief unions. Others, mentioning Robbins's tendency toward supplying misinformation, maintain there were only three. Financially, Robbins recovered his fortune, thanks to sizable advances on his novels and the sale of movie rights. Interviewers sometimes commented on the parallels between the lifestyle of the characters in his novels and his own. As he told Thompson, "Anyone who wants to know a hundred years from now what I'm like, all they'll have to do is read my books. What I am is a part of my world." He acquired houses in Acapulco, Beverly Hills, and the French Rivera, as well as a yacht and luxury cars. He hosted lavish parties, enjoyed gambling, collected art, and continued to turn out books that were best-sellers with readers and scorned or ignored by literary critics.

After *The Carpetbaggers* (1961) and *Where Love Has Gone* (1962) came *The Adventurers* (1966), based on Robbins's experiences living in South America, including three months spent in the mountains of Colombia with a group of bandits. He created the ABC television series *The Survivors* (1969–1970), starring Ralph Bellamy and Lana Turner. For his eager readers, the novels kept appearing: *The Inheritors* (1969), *The Betsy* (1971), *The Pirate* (1974), *The Lonely Lady* (1976), *Dreams Die First* (1977), *Memories of Another Day* (1979), *Goodbye, Janette* (1981), and *Spellbinder* (1982). But critics continued to be unenthusiastic. One summed up his writing as "steamy, sordid, and violent," while another decried Robbins's "unprincipled use of characters who deliberately resemble well-known men and women now dead." In responding to speculations about who his characters might be in real life, Robbins insisted that his characters were composites of people, not fictional portraits of actual individuals. As he told Thompson, "When you write about what seems to be a familiar world, people tend to put labels on the characters right away."

Film versions of several of Robbins's novels were made, including *Never Love a Stranger* (1957); *King Creole* (1958), based on *A Stone for Danny Fisher*; *The Carpetbaggers* and *Where Love Has Gone* (both 1964); *The Adventurers* and *Stiletto* (both 1970); *The Betsy* (1978); and *Dreams Die First* (1979). To handle Robbins's expanding business interests, a company was created to coproduce movies and television shows and to manage his interests in a music company set up with Quincy Jones and Ray Brown.

Following a stroke in 1982, Robbins suffered from a slight case of aphasia. But his writing soon resumed with *Descent from Zanadu* (1984). Then in February 1985 Robbins fell in the bathroom of his Beverly Hills home, shattering one hip and breaking the other. Gradually, after three operations and extensive therapy, he was able to walk with the aid of crutches. The pain, however, remained. Adapting to his physical limitations, he sold the yacht and houses in France, Mexico, and Beverly Hills, and he moved into a spacious, single-story home in Palm Springs. In spite of the pain, by the end of the year, Robbins was writing again, finishing the most autobiographical of his novels, *The Storyteller* (1985), working on ideas for television series, and writing *The Piranhas* (1991). Although the pace of his writing slowed, readers were delighted with his newest books, including *The Raiders* (1994), *The Stallion* (1996), and *Tycoon* (1997). Robbins died of pulmonary arrest in Palm Springs and is buried in the Palm Springs Mausoleum. Following his death, his estate authorized the publication of two additional novels, *The Predators* (1998) and *The Secret* (2000).

In his books, Robbins touched on many important contemporary issues. His early books chronicled the struggle of his protagonists during economically depressed periods and the allure of the criminal underworld. His later books centered on the battle for power and wealth in many business enterprises, ranging from the automotive industry and publishing to organized labor and religious evangelism. Rather than subject those issues to thoughtful analysis, Robbins used them merely as the springboard for a fast-paced narrative filled with the adventures and sexual exploits of the characters. Throughout his career, Robbins appeared more interested in writing for money than in writing for critics. As he said, "I won't achieve my place in literature, if I ever have a place, by arguing with the critics. My work will do it for me."

While critics usually dismissed his books, readers repeatedly made Robbins a best-selling author. During his lifetime, each of his novels sold at least 600,000 copies and, translated into most of the world's languages, they sold more than 50 million copies in some forty countries.

★

Biographical profiles of Robbins appear in *Current Biography 1970* and *Contemporary Authors, New Revision Series* (1997). Several articles make use of interviews with Robbins and his associates at various stages of his career. These include Thomas Thompson, "A Tour Through the Harold Robbins Industry," *Life* (8 Dec. 1967); "Company," *New Yorker* (29 Nov. 1969); G. Kroll, "Master Harold," *Advocate* (22 Aug. 1995); and Ian Parker, "Making Advances," *New Yorker* (1 Apr. 1996). Critical appraisals appear in James B. Lane, "Violence and Sex in the Postwar Popular Urban Novel," *Journal of Popular Culture* (fall 1974): 295–308, and in Tom Dardis, "The Myth That Won't Go Away," *Journal of Popular Film and Television* (winter 1984): 167–171. An obituary is in the *New York Times* (15 Oct. 1997).

LUCY A. LIGGETT

ROBBINS, Jerome (*b.* 11 October 1918 in New York City; *d.* 29 July 1998 in New York City), innovative, award-winning choreographer, director, and creator of ballets and musicals.

Robbins was born Jerome Wilson Rabinowitz, the younger of two children of Harry Rabinowitz, who came to America from Poland in 1904, and Lena Rips, a homemaker. His father, who owned a delicatessen on Manhattan's Upper East Side, sold the business and moved the family to Weehawken, New Jersey, where he established the Comfort Corset Company. The young Robbins, who showed an early aptitude for music, dancing, and theatrics, attended schools in Weehawken and graduated from Woodrow Wilson High School in 1935. Intending to study either chemistry or journalism, he matriculated at New York University in the autumn of 1935, but when the Great Depression took a turn for the worse in 1936, his family could no longer support his education. Unwilling to work in the corset factory, Robbins tried to find employment in show business.

Jerome Robbins. HULTON-DEUTSCH COLLECTION/CORBIS-BETTMANN

Through his sister, Sonia, who had already danced professionally with Irma Duncan and Senya Gluck-Sandor's Dance Center, he got an apprenticeship with Sandor's company.

Gluck-Sandor was a hybrid as a choreographer—trained in the ballet, dedicated to modern dance, and also a veteran of Broadway, burlesque, and vaudeville. His expressive, theatrical style attracted Robbins from the outset. The fledgling dancer, who took the surname "Robbins" for his work in the theater, also studied ballet with Ella Daganova. In 1937 Robbins appeared in the Yiddish Art Theater production of *The Brothers Ashkenazi,* for which Sandor did the choreography. In the summer of 1937 Robbins began dancing and choreographing at Tamiment, a progressive-movement resort in Pennsylvania's Pocono Mountains. The resort featured a resident singing-acting-dancing troupe and weekend revues starring emerging talents like Danny Kaye, Imogene Coca, and Carol Channing. Robbins's work from this period consisted mainly of burlesque blackout sketches or dramatic works with a strong social content, like *Death of a Loyalist* or *Strange Fruit;* some of his dances were performed under the auspices of the Theater Arts Committee at New York's Ninety-second Street Young Men's Hebrew Association (YMHA), and others as part of *The Straw Hat Revue,* which opened on Broadway in 1939.

Robbins spent three summers at Tamiment. By taking on one-shot roles in ballet performances at Jones Beach, the New York World's Fair, and elsewhere, he found work during the regular theater season in the Broadway choruses of *Great Lady* (1938), *Stars in Your Eyes* (1939), and *Keep Off the Grass* (1940), which was choreographed by George Balanchine. In the summer of 1940 he was accepted into the newly formed Ballet Theater. He soon advanced from the corps de ballet to solo roles that showed off the fluid, theatrical style he used to compensate for his lack of heroic classical technique. He appeared as the Young Man in Agnes de Mille's *Three Virgins and a Devil,* an apple-munching Hermes in *Helen of Troy,* and the tragic puppet in *Petroushka,* the role that made him famous.

Robbins's greatest desire was to choreograph a ballet for Ballet Theater, preferably one with an American theme, but all of his ideas were too grandiose for the perennially strapped company to consider. Encouraged to "think small," he came up with the idea for a ballet about three sailors on shore leave in New York City. He sought out the services of a young unknown composer named Leonard Bernstein to write the score, and Ballet Theater's Oliver Smith agreed to design the scenery. On 18 April 1944 *Fancy Free* premiered at the Metropolitan Opera House to a raucous two dozen curtain calls. In December of that year *On the Town,* a musical based on the ballet, arrived on Broadway with music by Bernstein, dances by Robbins, sets by Smith (who also produced), and book and lyrics by a pair of Bernstein's cabaret buddies, Betty Comden and Adolph Green. From that moment on, Robbins's primacy on Broadway and in ballet was assured. But he did more than reach the top in his two spheres of influence; he changed each of his worlds from the inside out.

On Broadway, Robbins quickly established himself as the choreographer of the moment in the late 1940s because musical comedies were evolving out of the song-and-dance anthologies (stylish but lacking in substance) that had showcased the talents of Ira and George Gershwin, Cole Porter, and Richard Rodgers and Lorenz Hart. When Robbins began to direct as well as to create ideas and dances, he made sure his shows always had a story, characters, and a point. His Roaring Twenties musical, *Billion Dollar Baby* (1946), revolved around a gold-digging bathing beauty who serially married for money. *High Button Shoes* (1947), his first collaboration with the composer Jule Styne, was a nostalgic romp set in New Jersey in 1913, featuring a Keystone Kops ballet. And *Look, Ma, I'm Dancin'* (1948), which he codirected with George Abbot, was the autobiographical backstage story of an ambitious dancer-choreographer's collision with the brewery heiress backing his ballet company. Robbins's changed character was mirrored in the two ballets he created for this 1948 show: the first a brash, overcomplicated expression of youthful hubris, and the second altogether subtler, more thoughtful, and human. *Look, Ma* was succeeded by one of Robbins's rare flops, a show called *That's the Ticket* (1948), which Robbins directed but did not choreograph. An overly whimsical mishmash, it closed in Philadelphia after ten days.

Robbins had maintained his relationship with Ballet Theater while working on Broadway, following *Fancy Free* with a series of dances that integrated the classic vocabulary with modern subject matter. These included the bebop ballet *Interplay* (1945) and *Facsimile* (1946), an angst-ridden exploration of a love triangle with a new score by Bernstein. In 1949 Robbins left Ballet Theater to join George Balanchine's newly formed New York City Ballet, where he was almost immediately named associate artistic director. He danced in numerous quasi-dramatic roles for Balanchine, *Prodigal Son, Tyl Eulenspiegel,* and as a principal opposite the glamorous Tanaquil Le Clercq in *Bourrée Fantasque,* before retiring from performance in the mid-1950s. But it was as a choreographer that Robbins made his mark. Ballets like *The Guests* (1949), scored by Marc Blitzstein, *Age of Anxiety* (1950), with Bernstein, and the terrifying fable *The Cage* (1951), with Igor Stravinsky, showcased his flair for drama, his all-American sass and energy, and his affinity for modern music. His association with Balanchine gave him a security and sense of kinship that nourished his genius.

Robbins continued to work on Broadway as the choreographer for two Irving Berlin shows, *Miss Liberty* (1949) and *Call Me Madam* (1950), as well as for Rodgers's and

Hammerstein's *The King and I* (1951) and *Two's Company* (1952), a revue starring Bette Davis. In 1953 he made a controversial decision to appear before the House Un-American Activities Committee, where he admitted to membership in the Communist Party during the 1930s and named eight individuals who he said had also been members. Robbins's testimony was denounced by many, including some of his family, for whom McCarthyism was only steps away from Nazism. Robbins refused to justify or explain himself beyond a public statement that he had "made a great mistake . . . in entering the Communist Party." His decision haunted him, however, and ultimately he placed it at the center of an autobiographical drama, *The Poppa Piece,* with which he experimented in workshops during the early 1990s.

Ironically, his career seemed to take on added luster in this troubled time. He staged the all-American Ford Fiftieth Anniversary Show (1953) for television with Ethel Merman and Mary Martin; codirected *The Pajama Game* (1954) on Broadway; conceived, directed, and choreographed *Peter Pan* (1954), starring Martin; directed Aaron Copland's opera *The Tender Land* (1954); directed and cochoreographed *Bells Are Ringing* (1956), starring Judy Holliday; and choreographed the film version of *The King and I* (1956). Meanwhile, at the New York City Ballet he created two masterpieces, the lyrical *Afternoon of a Faun* (1953) and the hilarious send-up, *The Concert* (1956), among other works.

In 1957 he teamed up once again with Bernstein on a musical he had been discussing with him and the playwright Arthur Laurents for some years. *West Side Story* was a retelling of William Shakespeare's *Romeo and Juliet,* set against a backdrop of gang warfare in a Puerto Rican ghetto of New York City. Directed by Robbins, with his electrifying street-smart choreography integrated into the action, *West Side Story* was arguably the first "concept musical." It broke the mold of the Broadway show and established Robbins's reputation as a perfectionistic, difficult taskmaster, a reputation that was one factor in his dismissal as the director of the 1961 film version. He won an Academy Award for his film direction nonetheless, sharing the Oscar with his codirector Robert Wise, and also won an award for choreography.

After *West Side Story* Robbins left the New York City Ballet and formed his own company, Ballets USA. They appeared at the Festival of Two Worlds in Spoleto, Italy, with his explosive *New York Export: Opus Jazz* (1958), a ballet without music called *Moves* (1959), and other works. The company toured extensively in Europe but, despite enthusiastic notices and even an appearance at the White House, it failed to find an ongoing U.S. audience and was disbanded in 1961. In the meantime, Robbins also directed the ultimate backstage musical, *Gypsy* (1959), with Mer-

man, and began to branch out into nonmusical theater. In 1962 he directed the American premiere of Arthur Kopit's mordant mother-son comedy *Oh, Dad, Poor Dad, Mama's Hung You in the Closet and I'm Feelin' So Sad,* and in 1963, a production of Bertolt Brecht's *Mother Courage and Her Children,* starring Anne Bancroft.

Two more Broadway hits followed, both shows he had originally agreed to direct, then withdrew from, and finally returned to when each seemed in danger of shipwreck during out-of-town tryouts. Even though the reviews for *A Funny Thing Happened on the Way To the Forum* (1962) did not mention his name, and the program for *Funny Girl* (1964) listed him only as the production supervisor, he reshaped both musicals radically. He got full credit, however, for choreographing and directing *Fiddler on the Roof* (1964), bringing Sholem Aleichem's stories and the lost world of the Russian shtetl to life as an organic, musical whole.

Robbins accomplished a similar feat with his mammoth staging of Stravinsky's *Les Noces* (1965) for American Ballet Theater. He then retreated from the pressures of huge collaborative productions. Broadway was moving in the direction of rock spectacles like *Hair* and *Jesus Christ, Superstar,* and Robbins didn't want to move with it. Using a 1966 grant from the National Endowment for the Humanities, he established the American Theater Lab to explore experimental music-theater techniques, from dance to Japanese Noh drama, with a small handpicked company in a workshop setting for a period of two years.

Seemingly recharged from this work, he reemerged at City Ballet with *Dances at a Gathering* (1969), a poignant and playful celebration of youth and love that was widely hailed as a masterpiece. There followed a fertile creative period in which Robbins made such vastly different works as the moonlit, expressive *In the Night* (1970); *The Goldberg Variations* (1971), which explored J. S. Bach's thematic geometry; and *Watermill* (1972), a Noh-like meditation on the passage of a man's life. He also collaborated with Balanchine, with whom he now shared the title of ballet master, on dances for the *Firebird* (1970) and *Pulcinella* (1972); collegiality and mutual respect continued to mark their relationship. As Balanchine once said to him, speaking of the legendary Russian ballet master Marius Petipa, "Very few people can do. Petipa, you, me—we can do."

Robbins never really left City Ballet again. The exceptions were a leave of absence in 1989 and forays into the theater for workshops of an adaptation of Brecht's *The Exception and the Rule* (1987) and of *The Poppa Piece* (1991), and the triumphant staging of his anthology show *Jerome Robbins's Broadway* (1989), for which he won his fifth Tony Award. His work seemed to move in an increasingly abstract direction, away from the character-driven dances of his youth, a process reflected in the changes he made in his last collaboration with Bernstein. Premiered as *Dybbuk* (1974) and based on the S. Anski play, it was first revised as *The Dybbuk Variations* (1974) and then as *A Suite of Dances* (1980), a ballet-in-progress that Robbins kept trying to reduce to its essence.

Essence did not mean homogeneity, however. Robbins's work was still as protean as ever, from the sensuous and jazzy lyricism of *In G Major* (1975) and the opera-house pyrotechnics of *Four Seasons* (1979) to the spiky *Opus 19: The Dreamer* (1979) and the elegiac *In Memory of . . .* (1985). He was still experimenting with contemporary music, with ballets to Philip Glass in *Glass Pieces* (1983) and to Steve Reich in *Octet* (1985). But it was Bach who spoke most clearly to him in his last decade, when he made the spare, poetic *A Suite of Dances* (1994) for Mikhail Baryshnikov to Bach's suites for unaccompanied cello; the deceptively simple *Two- and Three-Part Inventions* (1994) for the students of the School of American Ballet; and the exuberant *Brandenburg* (1997) for City Ballet.

By then Robbins was in fragile health, following a bicycling accident in 1990 and heart-valve surgery in 1994. In 1996 he began showing signs of a form of Parkinson's disease and his hearing was poor, yet he insisted on staging *Les Noces* for City Ballet in 1998. It was the last project he completed. Two months later he suffered a massive stroke, and died at his home in New York City.

In the more than sixty years in which he had been active in the theater, Robbins had won five Donaldson Awards, five Tony Awards, two Academy Awards, one Emmy Award, the Kennedy Center Honors, and numbers of other prizes, including the chevalier's rosette of the French Legion of Honor. More, he had transformed it because he never stopped asking questions. "Why can't we do ballets about our own subjects, meaning our life here in America?" he asked before making *Fancy Free*. And, speaking of the collaboration that made *West Side Story*, "Why couldn't we, in aspiration, try to bring our deepest talents together to the commercial theater?" His own work answered both questions in the affirmative.

★

Robbins's voluminous papers, including correspondence, diaries, memoirs, scenarios, notes, films, photographs, and miscellany, were left to the Jerome Robbins Dance Division of the New York Public Library for the Performing Arts; much of this material is closed to the public until 2013. A mildly scandalous biography by Greg Lawrence, *Dance with Demons* (2001), is limited by its reliance on oral and public sources. For a photographic book with biographical text and liberal quotations from Robbins's published interviews, see Christine Conrad, *Jerome Robbins: That Broadway Man, That Ballet Man* (2001). There is a full chronology of Robbins's choreographic work by Jody Sperling in Lynn Garafola with Eric Foner, *Dance for a City: Fifty Years of the New York City*

Ballet (1999). In addition, the *Journal for Stage Directors and Choreographers* 11, no. 2 (fall/winter 1998), devotes an entire issue to Robbins, including a biographical essay by Doris Hering and criticism and remembrances by Mindy Aloff, Grover Dale, Yuriko Kikuchi, Gerald Freedman, and others. Obituaries are in the *New York Times* (30 July 1998) and *Time* (10 Aug. 1998).

AMANDA VAILL

RODBELL, Martin (*b.* 1 December 1925 in Baltimore, Maryland; *d.* 7 December 1998 in Chapel Hill, North Carolina), biochemist, molecular endocrinologist, and winner of the Nobel Prize (shared with Alfred G. Gilman) in 1994 in physiology or medicine, whose theory of signal transduction and discovery of the "GTP effect" explained how cells communicate with each other and started a revolution in molecular biochemistry.

Rodbell was the son of Milton William Rodbell and Shirley Helen Abrams, who provided what he called "the wonderful childhood atmosphere . . . where my father's grocery store served as a focal point for contact between people in the area." He attended Baltimore City College, a public high school that prepared students to enter college as soph-

Martin Rodbell, 1994. AP/WIDE WORLD PHOTOS

omores. "I had acquired a great interest in chemistry," Rodbell recalled, "through a special boyhood friendship with two individuals [Angus MacDonald and Neil Zieler] from my neighborhood. . . . The three of us . . . were together from elementary school to Johns Hopkins."

Rodbell entered the Johns Hopkins University in Baltimore in 1943. The next year he was drafted into the U.S. Navy, where he was a radio operator attached to the marine corps until he contracted malaria in the jungles of the Philippines. After recovering, he served as a radioman on navy ships off China and Korea, later remarking, "All day I listened to Morse code. If that isn't preparation for looking at cell signaling, I don't know what is." In 1946, after the end of World War II, Rodbell returned to Johns Hopkins, where he studied French literature and biology. He especially enjoyed a biology class taught by James Ebert, and he graduated in 1949 with a degree in biology. On the advice of Bentley Glass, Rodbell entered the field of biochemistry, spending his first postgraduate year at Johns Hopkins studying chemistry. On 10 September 1950 Rodbell married Barbara Charlotte Ledermann, an actress, dancer, and photographer, who had lived in Amsterdam, Holland; they had four children.

In the autumn of 1950 Rodbell entered the Ph.D. program in biochemistry at the University of Washington in Seattle, while his wife worked as a secretary to support the family. Under Donald H. Hanahan and influenced by Edward Krebs, he completed his dissertation on "Some Aspects of Lecithin Metabolism in the Liver" (1954). Rodbell was a postdoctoral fellow at the University of Illinois at Urbana, where he worked with Herbert E. Carter. In 1956 Rodbell became a research biochemist in the laboratory of Christian Anfinsen, a Nobel laureate, at the National Heart Institute of the National Institutes of Health (NIH) in Bethesda, Maryland. Rodbell spent 1960 to 1961 at the University of Brussels in Belgium and at Leiden University in the Netherlands.

On his return to the United States, Rodbell worked as a research chemist under DeWitt Stetten in the Laboratory of Nutrition and Endocrinology of the National Institute of Arthritis and Metabolic Diseases (NIAMD) in Bethesda (1961–1967). The Nobel laureate Bernardo Houssay visited Rodbell's laboratory in 1963 and was enthralled by Rodbell's research on how hormones work on individual cells. In 1964 Rodbell published his often-cited "Metabolism of Isolated Fat Cells"; his technician was Ann Butler Jones. From 1967 to 1968 Rodbell was a professor at the Institute of Clinical Biochemistry of the University of Geneva, Switzerland. Lutz Birnbaumer joined his lab there in 1967 and, Rodbell said, "He proved to be a prime source for the next two years of the important information that led ultimately to the concept of transducers and the principles of signal transduction."

Returning to the United States from Geneva, Rodbell was joined by Michiel Krans and Stephen L. Pohl in his research at NIAMD. In 1969, after additional conversations with Oscar H. Hechter, Rodbell developed his theory of signal transduction or transmission, which explains how cells communicate. In 1970 Rodbell discovered the role of GTP (guanosine triphosphate), a small intracellular molecule, in the way cells get their directions. Another Nobel laureate, Earl Sutherland, had given a lecture at NIH on his second-messenger theory of hormone behavior. Rodbell explained that GTP stimulated what would later be called the G-protein (guanine nucleotide), which produced crucial effects in a cell. Rodbell identified the G-protein's activation as the second messenger. His theories were controversial at the time and defending them required great courage.

One reason for the productivity of Rodbell's lab may have been his ability to motivate people at every level. "It was his great gift," according to his daughter, "to share his exuberance with everyone, from the grocery clerk to the latest postdoctoral student. He was always expansive in his excitement, and people tended to respond in kind, suddenly feeling the stir of creative possibility within themselves." As his last postdoctoral student, Fernando A. P. Ribeiro-Neto, explained, "Marty was the same with the cleaning staff and the King of Sweden."

From 1968 to 1975 Rodbell was the chief of the section on membrane regulation at the NIAMD. He then served as the chief of the Laboratory of Nutrition and Endocrinology at the NIAMD (1975–1985), while working as a visiting professor in the department of clinical biochemistry at the University of Geneva (1981–1983). In 1985 Rodbell moved to North Carolina, where he was the scientific director of the National Institute of Environmental Health Sciences (1985–1989) and the chief of its section on signal transduction (1989–1994), at which time he became scientist emeritus. He worked in Research Triangle Park and lived in Chapel Hill, where he loved to attend classical music concerts at the University of North Carolina and Duke University. He also played the piano and tennis and loved to walk.

In October 1994 Rodbell was informed that he won the Nobel Prize for physiology or medicine for his trailblazing research and discovery of G-proteins, which are important regulators of hormones in the human body. At age seventy-three Rodbell died of cardiovascular problems at the University of North Carolina Hospitals where, his daughter recalled, even at the end of his life "he was questioning the young doctors' methodologies and lecturing them on the latest scientific theories behind hormone action, and they were lapping it up."

Rodbell's research on G-proteins and signal transduction opened up new possibilities in oncology, epidemiology, neuropharmacology, and gene therapy. Fernando Ribeiro-Neto was especially influenced by his new way of thinking about cell communication.

★

Rodbell's papers are at the National Library of Medicine, Bethesda, Maryland, where they are being digitized. A detailed account of Rodbell's work is available online from the library's Martin Rodbell Papers, including his inaugural NIEHS Rodbell Lecture, "Fifty Years in Science: Zigs and Zags with a Common Theme," and a biographical sketch, "The Autobiography of Martin Rodbell" (1994). The material is also available online from the Nobel Museum. PubMed has an online bibliography of Rodbell's articles, which include "Metabolism of Isolated Fat Cells II," *Journal of Biological Chemistry* 241 (1966); "The Beginnings of an Endocrinologist," *Endocrinology* 129 (1991); and "Nobel Lecture, Signal Transduction: Evolution of an Idea," *Bioscience Reports* 15 (1995). Excellent newspaper articles are "Hopkins Graduate Wins Nobel Prize," *Johns Hopkins Gazette* (17 Oct. 1994), and Suzanne Richardson, "The Death of Dr. Martin Rodbell, Nobel Laureate: A Daughter Accepts Her Father's Final Lesson," *Washington Post* (21 Nov. 2000). Obituaries are in the *New York Times* (11 Dec. 1998) and *NIH Record* (12 Dec. 1999).

RALPH KIRSHNER

Buddy Rogers. © UNDERWOOD & UNDERWOOD/CORBIS

ROGERS, Charles ("Buddy") (*b.* 13 August 1904 in Olathe, Kansas; *d.* 21 April 1999 in Rancho Mirage, California), actor, bandleader, and husband of the Hollywood movie star Mary Pickford.

Rogers grew up in Olathe, Kansas, the son of Bert Henry Rogers, a probate judge and newspaper publisher, and Maude Rogers. He delivered his father's newspaper as a child and fell in love with music, learning to play a variety of instruments. As a student at the University of Kansas in Lawrence in 1925, Rogers planned to be a bandleader until his father persuaded him to enter a Paramount Pictures talent contest. "I did it for Dad," he told *Films in Review* in 1987. "I didn't have any talent. I had no feeling for it." Nevertheless, Rogers's boyish good looks appealed to the studio, which signed him to a contract. He then studied at the Paramount School of Acting in New York City and was cast in his first picture as the son of W. C. Fields in *So's Your Old Man* (1926).

Soon Rogers went to Hollywood, where he starred in his best-known film, *Wings* (1927), which won the award for best picture at the first Academy Awards. In the film, Rogers and Richard Arlen play boyhood friends who enlist in the U.S. Army Air Corps and are sent to Europe to serve as pilots in World War I. Director William Wellman took full advantage of his leading man's naiveté, sending Rogers up in the air for combat scenes that terrified him and getting him drunk in order to shoot a scene in which his character had overindulged in champagne.

Rogers's second best-known film was also made in 1927. Rogers was picked as the male lead in *My Best Girl* playing opposite of superstar Mary Pickford, who was departing from her standard juvenile persona to play in a romantic comedy. Rogers portrayed the son of a department store owner who falls in love with Pickford, who played a clerk at the store. Pickford, who was twelve years older than Rogers, was still known as "America's Sweetheart." Rogers, who would soon be dubbed "America's Boyfriend," fell in love with her. At the time, Pickford was married to the athletic actor Douglas Fairbanks, one of the most famous marriages of that era.

Rogers never again hit the cinematic heights he achieved in 1927. Over the next few years he played a succession of unmemorable juveniles in minor Paramount pictures. He asked the studio to release him from his contract in 1931 so he could pursue his lifelong interest in music. He toured with a succession of bands during the 1930s, making frequent radio appearances and the occasional film. All the while he kept in touch with Pickford.

In the early years of the sound era of motion pictures, the careers of both Pickford and Fairbanks dwindled. At loose ends, Fairbanks began to stray, and Pickford turned to the ever loyal Rogers for comfort. In 1936 Pickford divorced Fairbanks, who was carrying on a public affair with the woman he later married, and wed Rogers on 26 June 1937. They began married life in Rogers's house, but Pickford hankered for Pickfair, the home Fairbanks had built for her in Beverly Hills, and the two moved there. Soon Rogers claimed, "Now I think I love Pickfair more than Mrs. Rogers does."

Pickford's star had waned by the mid-1930s, but she was still a prominent figure in Hollywood and one of the richest women in the world. Although some at first thought that Rogers married her for money, this seems unlikely; Pickford retained careful control over her finances. Even skeptics eventually paid tribute to Rogers's good-natured adoration of a woman who was often difficult and, increasingly, alcoholic. Rogers puttered at his career, making films from time to time and touring with his band until Pickford asked him to stay at home. The pair adopted a child in 1943 and a second in 1944. In parenting, as in other aspects of their marriage, Pickford was the dominant partner. When she tired of the children, they were ignored or sent away to school.

During World War II, Rogers volunteered as a flight instructor for the U.S. Navy, and during the Korean War he entertained troops. Increasingly, however, he stayed home, caring for a more and more reclusive Pickford. When he bungled a line during his short-lived tenure as host of *Cavalcade of Bands* on television in 1951, Pickford said, "Don't worry, dear, you don't have to work," and he seems to have taken her words to heart.

His final film project was the minor western *The Parson and the Outlaw* (1957), which he and Pickford produced. He occasionally appeared in television programs such as *The Lucy Show* during the 1960s. In the 1960s and 1970s, however, Rogers concentrated on tending to Pickford, playing golf, and administering his wife's charitable donations. He received the Jean Hersholt Humanitarian Award from the Academy of Motion Picture Arts and Sciences in 1986 for his charity work.

After Pickford died in 1979, Rogers built a smaller home on the grounds of Pickfair. The mansion itself and remaining property were sold to raise money for the Mary Pickford Foundation, which preserves Pickford's film legacy. Rogers married Beverly Ricono, a realtor, in 1981. Nevertheless, he continued to dedicate much of his time to Pickford's memory, working with the foundation and speaking publicly about their union.

He attended a 1987 Library of Congress screening of *Wings* and spoke to the press. With a tear in his eye, he said, "I'm only crying because I saw so many of my pals I'll never see again." Rogers died at age ninety-four of natural causes and is buried in the Palm Springs Mortuary and Mausoleum in Palm Springs, California.

After briefly conquering Hollywood with his boyish charm, Rogers had an undistinguished career in film, radio,

music, and television. His most challenging role was off-screen as the consort of one of the world's most famous women, and he played it as a nice, middle-American man with a pleasant smile. He is also credited with persuading Pickford to save the negatives of many of her films. More than any other quality, Rogers radiated likeability, on and off the screen and bandstand. A 1987 profile in *Films in Review* concluded, "In many ways, Buddy Rogers is very little changed from the Kansas boy who went to Hollywood in the roaring Twenties. . . . He still looks like America's boyfriend as he plays his piano and trombone."

★

The Academy of Motion Picture Arts and Sciences has a file of biographical materials on Rogers, and the New York Public Library holds a few of his letters. Most sources that contain biographical information on Rogers are books written about Pickford, including Scott Eyman, *Mary Pickford* (1990), Eileen Whitfield, *Pickford: The Woman Who Made Hollywood* (1997), and Robert Windeler, *Sweetheart* (1974). The actor was in the spotlight in a *Films in Review* profile, "Charles 'Buddy' Rogers: America's Boyfriend" (Dec. 1987), by Kevin Lewis. Aljean Harmetz, *Rolling Breaks and Other Movie Business* (1983) provides a brief glimpse into Rogers's final years with Pickford. Rogers's attendance of the showing of *Wings* in 1987 is chronicled in the *New York Times* (31 Oct. 1987), and obituaries are in the *New York Times* (23 Apr. 1999), *Variety* (26 Apr. 1999), and *People* (10 May 1999).

TINKY "DAKOTA" WEISBLAT

ROGERS, Roy (*b.* 5 November 1911 in Cincinnati, Ohio; *d.* 6 July 1998 in Apple Valley, California), star of Western motion pictures, television, radio, and recordings who was known as the "King of the Cowboys."

Born Leonard Frank Sly, Rogers was the only boy of four children born to Andrew E. Sly, a shoe factory worker and itinerant laborer, and Mattie Martha Womack. His youth was characterized by poverty, hard work, and a budding musical talent. In 1912 Rogers's father moved his family onto a houseboat and traveled up the Ohio River to Portsmouth, where they settled by the river bank until 1919, when he bought a little farm near Duck Run, Ohio (population 14). There the eight-year-old Rogers helped his father build their home, which had neither electricity nor indoor plumbing. Rogers worked the land and learned to ride his horse bareback to school and to the movie theater, where he watched cowboy hero Hoot Gibson.

In spite of their hardships, the family was close and happy. Rogers's parents taught him guitar, mandolin, and banjo, and he later learned clarinet. His three younger sisters could also sing and yodel, and at age twelve, Rogers, who already had a repertoire of cowboy songs, began calling

Roy Rogers. KOBAL COLLECTION

square dances. He won a race with his black mare and won prizes with his pigs at 4-H Club fairs. With his Winchester .22 carbine, a gift he received for his twelfth birthday, Rogers taught himself to be a marksman and hunter and developed a lifelong love of guns.

Rogers dropped out of McDermott High School in 1928, his sophomore year, to return to Cincinnati with his family and join his father working in a shoe factory. His earlier childhood ambition to be a physician or a dentist faded. Though he attended night school for a while, this premature end to his education helps to explain the unique simplicity in Rogers's character that remained throughout his life. In 1930 the Sly family piled their belongings and their dog into a 1923 Dodge and headed for California, where their daughter Mary and her husband lived. Rogers drove dump trucks, picked peaches, and played his guitar in the evening for his fellow workers. Step by step he moved from manual labor to making a living as a singer.

For a while Rogers teamed with a cousin as the Slye Brothers (adding an "e" to the name), then joined and toured with other groups during the early 1930s—Uncle Tom Murray's Hollywood Hillbillies, the Rocky Mountaineers, the International Cowboys, the O-Bar-O Cow-

boys, and finally the Sons of the Pioneers—often singing for little or no pay. In 1933, at age twenty-one, Rogers married nineteen-year-old Lucile Ascolese, from Long Beach, California, a beauty college student who had seen him sing. But Lucile, jealous and temperamental, did not adapt easily to life on the road. They decided to divorce in 1935, and Ascolese's name never appears in official biographies of Rogers. Then on 11 June 1936, three days after the divorce became final, Rogers married Grace Arline Wilkins, whom he had met in 1933 when she gave him a lemon pie in exchange for a performance of the song "Swiss Yodel." Rogers and Wilkins adopted a girl in 1941; their own daughter was born in 1943. Wilkins gave birth to Roy, Jr. (Dusty) in 1946, but she died of an embolism a few days later.

One band that Rogers toured with, the Sons of the Pioneers, was attracting attention. The group appeared on radio station KFWB and in several films, including some with Gene Autry, who was then the top singing cowboy in movies. Prompted by a contract dispute with Autry, Republic Studios started looking for a new face. Rogers sang "Tumbling Tumbleweeds" and yodeled his way into the job in 1937. Under a new name, Dick Weston, he made two more films. Finally, when Autry dropped out of his contract, the studio tapped "Weston" to star in *Under Western Stars* (1938). They changed his name to Roy Rogers, because Roy meant "king" and Rogers reminded audiences of the beloved western entertainer Will Rogers, who had recently died in a plane crash. The studio mounted Rogers on a six-year-old palomino horse named Golden Cloud (last seen carrying Olivia de Havilland in *Robin Hood*) and changed the horse's name to Trigger. Studio publicity then announced that Roy Rogers had grown up on a ranch in Cody, Wyoming, to associate him with Buffalo Bill. After Autry joined the U.S. Air Forces in 1943, Rogers's title as "king" was secure.

Between 1938 and 1951 Rogers starred in over eighty feature films for Republic. Each was a little longer than an hour and in black and white; from 1947 on, they were filmed in Trucolor. Compared to other B-Westerns, production values were high; plot lines concerned cattle rustlers, land grabbers, unpaid mortgages, horse thieves, and abandoned mines; and Rogers and his leading lady and the Sons of the Pioneers or, later, the Riders of the Purple Sage, usually sang six songs. The opening scene usually showed the cast riding across the desert singing; the final scene, riding away and singing the theme song again.

Articles on Rogers's films emphasize their relative nonviolence, yet director Quentin Tarrantino, in a 2000 *New York Times* article in which he discusses *The Golden Stallion* (1949), suggests that under the influence of director and scriptwriter William Witney, Rogers's films took on a darker tone, which teenage boys were quick to appreciate.

In *The Golden Stallion,* when Trigger is accused of killing one of the villains, and the sheriff is about to carry out a summary execution, Rogers confesses to the crime he did not commit and endures years on the chain gang in order to save his equine friend. Another film, *Bells of San Angelo* (1947), concerns silver smugglers on the Mexican border, a pretty Western novelist from the East (Dale Evans), and a foxhunting English solicitor, searching for the heir of an English lord's American estate. In one scene Rogers is brutally beaten by the silver smugglers. In a final shootout at the mine, about a dozen smugglers are shot dead. At the climax Rogers and several dogs chase two smugglers to the edge of a cliff, where the dogs force one man over the edge, and he plunges to his death.

Although the horse Trigger was the subject of three films, few fans realized that "Trigger" was a name applied to several, perhaps six, horses who often substituted for the "real" Trigger in personal appearances and in dangerous action shots in films. Rogers bought the original Trigger for $2,500, partly to keep the studio from using the horse with another actor. He had taught Trigger to rear, dance, untie knots, appear indoors without dropping manure, and sign a hotel register with a pen in his teeth. When Trigger died at thirty-three in 1965, Rogers kept his death secret for a year. He then had Trigger's hide stretched over a Plexiglas form and displayed rearing up in the Roy Rogers Museum.

In the middle of one of their 1947 rodeo appearances in Chicago, Rogers proposed to his costar, Dale Evans, with whom he had been friendly for several years. Rogers was at a high point in his career. He had started a radio show in 1944 which lasted until 1955. Under various publishers, his comic books appeared from 1944 to 1967. Rogers was receiving over 900,000 fan letters a year and was developing a new image that featured fancy pseudo-Western costumes with fringed and flowered shirts and jeweled saddles. He called his new ranch the Double R Bar, the same as his ranch in the films.

The "King of the Cowboys" married "The Queen of the West" on 31 December 1947. Dale Evans, born Lucille Wood Smith (a later document calls her Frances Octavia Smith), in Uvalde, Texas, in 1912, had been divorced three times and had a twenty-year-old son from her first marriage. Determined to be a good mother, and under the influence of her son, she became increasingly religious, and Rogers, who had not cared about religion, turned to God as well. When their own daughter Robin was born with Down's syndrome in 1950, Rogers and Evans were admonished to put her in an institution lest she detract from their perfect-family image; but they insisted on raising her at home until she died two years later. Evans wrote about Robin in one of her many inspirational books, *Angel Unaware.*

To deal with their sorrow over the loss of Robin, they adopted a son and daughter in 1953. They added a foster child from Scotland in 1955, and a Korean war orphan, In Ai Lee (Debbie), in 1956. Debbie died in a school bus accident when she was twelve while Rogers was in UCLA medical center in danger of death from an infection following a spinal cord operation. Their adopted son Sandy enlisted in the army at age seventeen; he died in Frankfurt, Germany, after a drinking accident in 1965.

Rogers's public "family" included Trigger, his golden palomino stallion, "The Smartest Horse in the Movies"; his wife and costar Dale Evans, "Queen of the West"; the singing group with whom he got his start, Bob Nolan and the Sons of the Pioneers; a succession of comic sidekicks, from George "Gabby" Hayes to Andy Devine to Pat Brady; and his German shepherd, Bullet, the "Wonder Dog."

Rogers ended his contract with Republic in 1951 in order to start a weekly half-hour TV series on the National Broadcasting Corporation (NBC), which ran from 1951 to 1957, followed by syndication and reruns until 1964. The show always ended with Rogers and Evans singing "Happy Trails," and the sign-off, "So long, and may the Good Lord take a likin' to you." Rogers and Trigger appeared in the 1952 Paramount color comedy, *Son of Paleface,* with Bob Hope and Jane Russell. That year Rogers and Evans returned to the Madison Square Garden Rodeo, breaking all attendance records. When the management told them they could not sing a religious song about Jesus Christ, Rogers replied that he would sing a hymn or he would not appear at all. They sang "Peace in the Valley," as they had planned.

Although Rogers counted both Democrats and Republicans among his friends, his political views were conservative. He supported Ronald Reagan's campaign for governor in 1966 and traveled to Vietnam during the war to entertain the troops. In Vietnam, a patrol of Viet Cong was captured when the soldiers came out of the jungle to hear Rogers sing.

The Roy Rogers–Dale Evans Museum in Victorville, California, opened in 1967. Rogers made one more picture, *Macintosh and T.J.,* about an old cowboy and a little boy, in 1975. At the time, an article in *Esquire* magazine by Mark Goodman, titled "The Singing Cowboy," which the family found offensive, depicted Rogers as out of touch with the reality of modern life, shocked to discover that the film *Midnight Cowboy* was not a Western but a "sick" portrayal of sex.

Both Rogers and Evans continued a heavy schedule of appearances, with the Billy Graham Crusade, openings of his restaurants, the Reagan Inaugural, the David Letterman Show, and raising money for children's hospitals. Rogers underwent heart bypass operations and battled pneumonia several times. In leisure moments he hunted, bowled, raised horses, joined celebrity golf and trapshooting tournaments, and enjoyed his fifteen grandchildren and thirty-three great grandchildren. The success of his 1991 audiocassette tape, "Roy Rogers Tribute," demonstrated that Rogers retained his yodeling skill and pleasant voice that had popularized a number of songs, including "Tumbling Tumbleweeds," "Blue Shadows on the Trail," "Along the Navajo Trail," and Cole Porter's "Don't Fence Me In." Rogers died of heart failure in Apple Valley, California, where he is buried.

In a profession that depends on illusion, Rogers shared both the triumph of his career and the tragedies of his family life with his fans and made his private life at least approximately close to his public persona. Although he initially drank and smoked and was not always religious, Rogers later avoided cigarettes and beer and turned to God in order to be a better role model for his young admirers. Nevertheless, "Roy Rogers" was a role he played, appearing as "himself" in his films and TV shows. Like many cinema heroes, Rogers was a commodity—an entrepreneur who put his name on hundreds of products, from lunch boxes to bed sheets, and a chain of fast-food restaurants.

Somehow, even late in life, Rogers still seemed young. Those who saw him in person or racing that splendid stallion across the screen, or who once saw him gallop out into the center ring of the Madison Square Garden World Champion Rodeo and rear up and wave his white hat in the golden spotlight, will remember that sight for the rest of their lives and for a moment feel forever young again.

Roy Rogers's place in American entertainment history is elusive, yet clear. No one element of his talent—like Gary Cooper's silent strength or Bing Crosby's mellow voice—defined his public persona. His youthful face exuded innocence and honesty, and he could sing, ride, fight, joke, and stand up for basic virtues in a way that convinced several generations that he was real; he mastered all the media—film, radio, recordings, personal appearances, rodeos, television—all the while presenting a dignified, even admirable, private life for sixty years.

★

The definitive book on Rogers is Robert W. Phillips, *Roy Rogers: A Biography, Radio History, Television Career Chronicle, Discography, Filmography, Comicography, Merchandising and Advertising History, Collectibles Description, Bibliography and Index* (1995). This encyclopedic study traces the lives of Rogers and Evans year-by-year, chronicling details like name changes and including marriages left out of authorized accounts. Phillips is an admirer, although a spokesperson for the Roy Rogers Museum described him as "not a friend of the family." Roy Rogers and Dale Evans with Jane and Michael Stern, *Happy Trails: Our Life Story* (1994), is told in Rogers's and Evans's alternate voices and

testifies to their religious faith. Mark Goodman, "The Singing Cowboy," *Esquire* (Dec. 1975) is condescending but balances mostly adulatory reports. An obituary is in the *New York Times* (6 July 1998).

RAYMOND A. SCHROTH

ROSE, Frederick Phineas (*b.* 16 November 1923 in New York City; *d.* 15 September 1999 in Rye, New York), builder, engineer, real estate developer, and philanthropist who contributed substantially to many of New York City's major cultural institutions.

Rose was the second of four sons born to Samuel B. Rose and Belle Bernstein. The boys grew up in the bustling borough of Brooklyn, and their parents instilled in them a love of art, music, and culture by surrounding them with books and frequently taking them to concerts and museums. Education, formal and informal, was sacrosanct in the Rose household; Rose's erudite father was largely self-educated and his mother would attend Manhattan's Hunter College in her eighties. After the couple's eldest son, Joseph, was hit and killed by a bus at age eleven, the family moved upstate in 1934 to Mount Vernon, a modest suburb north of New York City. Samuel Rose became partners in Rose Associates, Inc., the real estate company that his brother, David, had started in 1928.

In 1940 after graduating from Horace Mann, a prestigious New York City preparatory school, Rose visited Yale University as a prospective student and fell in love with it. He enrolled that fall and finished his coursework in three years, finding time for athletics and singing in the Yale Glee Club. He officially graduated with the class of 1944 with a B.A. degree in civil engineering. Rose put his degree and experience from summer construction jobs to work immediately by joining the Seabees (motto: "We build, we fight"), a U.S. Navy unit responsible for constructing bridges, roads, airstrips, and hospitals. He was stationed in the Pacific during World War II and became a lieutenant before he was discharged in 1945.

After completing the practical training provided by the Seabees, Rose embarked on a career at Rose Associates, where his younger brothers later joined him. Over the next seven decades of Rose's stewardship, the family business that had begun with the construction of one apartment building in the Bronx burgeoned. It grew into a large, highly successful real estate investment firm that develops, owns, and manages more than 30 million square feet of residential and commercial property in New York City and other cities. After Rose became chairman in 1980, two of the company's buildings were singled out for design awards: the Bankers Trust Building and a forty-story apartment house at 45 East Eighty-ninth Street. Rose, who loved to visit construction sites and held a deep respect for workmen, was known for meticulously overseeing the details of the company's projects.

Rose married Sandra Priest on 28 June 1948; they had four children. He was devoted to family and friends and an eclectic array of interests, including chess, tree identification, gardening, photography, origami, piano, travel, and foreign languages. Eschewing spectator sports, Rose hiked and skied instead, and played golf, squash, and tennis.

Rose was extraordinarily civic-minded and generous. He felt a duty to contribute his time, talents, and wealth to give back to the community a measure of what he had received from it. This feeling of obligation had been passed on from his parents, who were philanthropic within their means, but Rose believed it was also the legacy of Eastern European immigrants, whose Jewish tenets informed their sense of righteousness and giving. During his lifetime, Rose served on the boards of more than thirty-five institutions and, in partnership with his wife, gave away approximately $100 million dollars, mostly to major institutions in New York City.

Among the many trusteeships Rose held were those at cultural institutions (Lincoln Center for the Performing Arts, Metropolitan Museum of Art, American Museum of Natural History, Philharmonic-Symphony Society of New York); social service agencies (Federation of Jewish Philanthropies, Children's Aid Society, Mount Sinai Medical Center); business and government agencies (Consolidated Edison, New York Real Estate Board, Council on Foreign Relations, Citizens Budget Committee of New York City); and educational institutions (Rockefeller University, Yale University). Rose was a longtime member of the Century Association in New York City, serving three years as a trustee and overseeing the renovation of its landmark building.

To Rose, participation as a trustee was not simply a way to enhance his business or social standing. He believed the role of a board member was to guide and direct an institution, to aid it with more than just money, but with whatever talent or ability he possessed. Since his métier was building, he particularly enjoyed supporting construction or renovation projects. The most prominent of these include the restoration of the Rose Main Reading Room of the New York Public Library, the construction of the Samuel B. and David Rose Building at Lincoln Center, and, his last project, the erection of the Frederick Phineas Rose and Sandra Priest Rose Center for Earth and Space at the American Museum of Natural History, a grand and fitting coda to the couple's widespread generosity.

Rose's undergraduate years at Yale were the start of a lifelong relationship with the institution. His brothers, four

children, and many of his nieces and nephews were also graduates, and the university was the beneficiary of much of Rose's largesse. He supported or sponsored at least seventy-five university programs and causes, including professorships, scholarships, and construction. He helped establish the Association of Yale Alumni, was a member of the University Council, and a Fellow of the Yale Corporation. Awarded the Yale Medal for outstanding service and the Medal of Honor from the Science and Engineering Society, he was also delighted to receive an honorary L.H.D. in 1998.

Rose invested as much energy giving away his money as he had earning it. He condemned "deathbed philanthropy" and supported the estate tax because he believed that leaving the bulk of one's wealth to heirs robbed them of initiative. Despite the publicity surrounding his donations, Rose and his wife preferred to make their gifts anonymously, or frequently prohibited recipients from revealing their name until projects were near completion. In this way, Rose could participate as a hands-on adviser without wielding a donor's clout.

Rose died at age seventy-five at his home in suburban Rye, New York. Survived by his wife and three of his children, he is buried at Mount Eden Cemetery in Hawthorne, New York. At his funeral, Ellen V. Futter, president of the American Museum of Natural History, remarked that he had both a "generosity of spirit and a spirit of generosity." A lodestar in New York City philanthropy, Rose left behind an enormous legacy that has inspired others to reach for similar levels of altruism.

★

An article about Rose's extensive philanthropy is in the *New York Times* (13 Sept. 1997), where an obituary is also published (16 Sept. 1999). He was posthumously profiled by the *Yale Alumni Magazine* (Nov. 1999/Vol. LXIII) and the Yale Bulletin and Calendar (Vol. 28, No. 6). A videotaped interview of Rose, *Giving Your Money Away While Giving of Yourself*, is in the holdings of the National Film Archive of Philanthropy.

CARRIE C. MCBRIDE

ROSTEN, Leo Calvin (*b.* 11 April 1908 in Lodz, Poland; *d.* 19 February 1997 in New York City), writer and sociologist best known for *The Joys of Yiddish* (1968), a landmark study of the language.

Rosten was the older of two children born to Samuel C. Rosten and Ida Freundlich, Polish trade unionists. The family left Lodz when Rosten was two and settled in a Jewish neighborhood on the south side of Chicago, where they opened a knitting shop. Rosten and his sister grew up speaking English along with their parents' Yiddish. Early

Leo Rosten, 1974. TONY VACCARO/ASSOCIATED PRESS/McGRAW-HILL

on, Rosten showed a keen interest in language and writing. He began composing dramatic stories at age nine; he later wrote a tribute to the English teacher who taught him to diagram sentences at Crane Technical High School.

As an undergraduate at the University of Chicago, Rosten immersed himself in philosophy, literature, and politics. After receiving his B.A. degree in 1930, he taught English in the Chicago public schools, lectured throughout the Midwest on politics and international relations, and studied at the London School of Economics in 1937. Later in life, he wrote about how his "craze for omniscience" pushed him toward pursuing graduate studies in the social sciences at the University of Chicago.

The Great Depression forced Rosten to interrupt his studies and to support himself by, among other work, teaching English to new immigrants. In one of his night-school classes he met the man who became the inspiration for his literary character Hyman Kaplan, an overly confident butcherer of English who starred in Rosten's *The Education of H*Y*M*A*N K*A*P*L*A*N* (1937) and the book's two sequels, *The Return of H*Y*M*A*N K*A*P*L*A*N* (1959) and *O K*A*P*L*A*N! My K*A*P*L*A*N!* (1976). This series established Rosten as a humor writer.

At the University of Chicago, Rosten had met Priscilla Ann Mead, another graduate student. She and Rosten married on 30 March 1935. The previous year, Rosten had resumed his graduate studies full-time with a grant from the Social Science Research Council to conduct the first scientific study of the Washington, D.C., press corps. The

study, which became his doctoral dissertation and later a book acclaimed on the cover of the *New York Times Review of Books,* analyzed both the character of the correspondents and the quality of the information they provided to readers. Rosten took a break from his Washington studies one weekend to write the first Hyman Kaplan story, which earned him $125. He received his Ph.D. from the University of Chicago in 1937.

Later that year the Rostens moved to Los Angeles, where they had their three children and Rosten became a screenwriter. He worked on twelve films, including authoring *All Through the Night* (1942). Rosten next applied his skills as a social scientist to Hollywood, California, as the director of the Motion Picture Research Project from 1939 to 1941. On grants from the Carnegie Corporation and the Rockefeller Foundation, he shadowed the stars and convinced hundreds of actors and producers to fill out questionnaires that asked about everything from their salaries to their home lives. "I wanted to analyze the community that makes movies for the world the way [an] anthropologist might study the Maori," Rosten wrote. The study included the observation, from a mathematical tracking of gossip columns, that most romantic links between movie stars were self-serving publicity manufactured by the movie studios.

During World War II, Rosten worked for several government commissions and agencies, including the Office of Emergency Management and Office of Facts and Figures, where he was the chief of the motion picture section. In 1942 he was appointed the deputy director of the Office of War Information, where he remained until 1944. Among his contributions to the war effort were developing short studies of various national customs to help U.S. soldiers understand Europeans.

For a short time after the war, Rosten consulted with the Rand Corporation in Los Angeles. But a 1946 job offer from *Look* magazine took him to the East Coast. He settled his young family in North Stamford, Connecticut, and commuted to *Look*'s editorial offices in Manhattan. The magazine gave Rosten ample room to write about his wide-ranging interests and became his professional home for the next twenty-eight years. *Look* allowed him to write on lofty subjects for a general audience. His recurring column "They Made Our World" profiled fifty great thinkers, from Socrates to Voltaire, in 1,100-word essays. In "The Story Behind the Painting" Rosten wrote lively short histories and commentaries on his favorite works. In 1955 Rosten received the Freedom Foundation Award and the George Polk Memorial Award.

The Rostens moved to New York City in the 1950s, a time of wrenching change for the family; Rosten and his first wife divorced in 1957. On 5 January 1960 he married Gertrude Zimmerman, a woman with a strong sense of humor who shared his appetite for travel and art. Rosten and Zimmerman enjoyed New York City together: its architecture, art galleries, and the Sutton Place apartment where they lived and he wrote. Rosten read and traveled widely. He studied from books, but also from life and friends, collecting anecdotes and characters for his essays, lectures, and humor writing. Rosten founded the Chaos Club, a monthly luncheon of artistic and literary luminaries, including Irving Kristol. An interest in psychiatry made Rosten a regular visitor to the wards of Saint Elizabeth's Hospital in Washington, D.C. His *Captain Newman, M.D.* (1961), the funny and poignant stories of a wartime army psychiatrist assigned to a base in the U.S. Southwest, showed the author knew his main character's work well. His quipping dialogue in "Why Not Rent a Child?" and other humorous essays seemed to reflect the influence of his friend Groucho Marx.

Although the Hyman Kaplan books, *Captain Newman,* and his *Look* essays gave Rosten a national following as a young man, one of his later works endured as his international legacy. The best-selling *The Joys of Yiddish,* first published in 1968, was an ode to the richness of the language of his parents, a German dialect heavily influenced by Hebrew and Russian. Rosten provided pronunciations, derivations, and numerous and often humorous examples and anecdotes that offered glimpses into twentieth-century Jewish American culture.

In the preface, Rosten called *The Joys of Yiddish* a work more about English than Yiddish, in that it showed how Yiddish words, phrases, and idioms had come to influence English. Most of the book was a "lexicon of Yiddish-in-English"—entries for words such as "kvetch," "chutzpah," and "nudnick"—that explained nuances not easily expressed in English. Even more important than the "invasionary" force of Yiddish words into English, Rosten believed, was English speakers' adoption of Yiddish "linguistic devices." He offered, for example, "Blithe dismissal via repetition with an *sh* play-on-the-first sound: 'Fat-shmat, as long as she's happy.'" With *The Joys of Yiddish,* the book of which he was most proud, Rosten wrote the definitive work of a declining language and provided the groundwork for its revival in the late twentieth century. He also authored *Leo Rosten's Treasury of Jewish Quotations* (1972) and *The Joys of Yinglish* (1989).

Rosten died of natural causes at age ninety-seven in his New York City apartment a year after the death of his second wife and two years after his son died of lung cancer. Successful as both an academic and a popular writer, Rosten is remembered for the work that bridged the worlds of serious study and entertainment. *The Joys of Yiddish* endures as an astute linguistic study and hilarious social commentary.

★

For a complete listing of works by Rosten, see *Contemporary Authors* (2000). There are no full-length books devoted to Rosten's life, however many contemporary newspaper articles offer salient information, including the *New York Times* (29 Aug. 1937, 17 Dec. 1968, 25 Jan. 1969), *Saturday Review* (21 Aug. 1937, 26 Sept. 1959, 7 Dec. 1968), and *Chicago Tribune* (20 Sept. 1959). Obituaries are in the *New York Times* (20 Feb. 1997) and *Los Angeles Times* (21 Feb. 1997).

LAUREN MARKOE

ROTHWAX, Harold J(ay) (*b.* 28 August 1930 in Brooklyn, New York; *d.* 22 October 1997 in New York City), lawyer who started as an idealistic defense attorney and became a judge who gained fame by seeking to limit the rights of defendants.

Rothwax was the son of Louis Rothwax and Freda Matlin. As a child in Brooklyn, his idol was Clarence Darrow, the famous early-twentieth-century legal advocate for those who were accused unjustly. The source of this passion was Rothwax's mother, who was a strong and controlling woman. Nevertheless, he was part of a loving family. From his childhood experiences, Rothwax learned to challenge authority while at the same time respecting it.

Rothwax received a B.A. degree from the City College of the City University of New York in 1952. He then en-

Harold J. Rothwax. AP/WIDE WORLD PHOTOS

tered the U.S. Army and was discharged as a first lieutenant in 1955. Following his military service, Rothwax became a student at Columbia Law School in New York City, where he received his LL.B. degree in 1958. Admitted to practice in New York State in 1959, he began his career as a senior trial attorney of the Criminal Defense Division of the Legal Aid Society in New York City, where he served from 1959 to 1965. Rothwax married Yona Gutman, a school psychologist, on 22 December 1963. They had two children.

From 1965 to 1970 Rothwax was a director of the Mobilization for Youth Legal Services, an antipoverty group located on New York's Lower East Side. He was also a consultant to the Vera Foundation of New York City, a legal advocacy group (1963–1970); adviser on the President's Commission on Law Enforcement and Administration of Justice (1966–1967); lecturer of law at Columbia Law School (1971); lecturer in the trial advocacy program of Harvard Law School in Cambridge, Massachusetts (after 1983); member of the advisory board of the Criminal Justice Research Center of New York University School of Law in New York City (after 1983); and consultant to the Felony Case Processing Time Study at the Criminal Justice Center of John Jay College of Criminal Justice in New York City (1984–1986). Rothwax received a 1982 award from the New York State Bar Association for outstanding achievement in the field of criminal law education. In 1984 he was selected to be a Guggenheim fellow at Yale Law School in New Haven, Connecticut.

Rothwax achieved his lasting fame as a judge. His first position was on the Criminal Court of the City of New York, where he served from 1971 to 1986. Rothwax also served as an acting justice on the New York State Supreme Court in New York City from 1972 to 1997. Rothwax was noted for the efficiency of his courtroom. He managed to dispatch the mountains of paperwork that so intimidated other justices. Also, lawyers, court officers, and other functionaries were made to perform their jobs with thoroughness and speed.

Rothwax was a master at negotiating the plea bargain, a mainstay of modern criminal jurisprudence. However, the apparent arbitrary nature of his rulings and sentences so antagonized some attorneys that they nicknamed him "Yahweh," the Hebrew word for God, or, occasionally, "Prince of Darkness." Rothwax's most famous case was that of Joel B. Steinberg, who was accused of killing his adopted daughter. The trial was a newspaper sensation. Steinberg was found guilty of manslaughter and, on 24 March 1989, Rothwax sentenced him to the maximum time in prison, 8⅓ to 25 years.

Although Rothwax started his career as a defense attorney, he came to believe that the courtroom laws and rules favored the defendant too much. In his book *Guilty: The Collapse of Criminal Justice* (1996), Rothwax argued that the

criminal justice system should be reformed to such an extent that even the *Miranda* v. *Arizona* (1966) ruling, which requires an arresting officer to inform an alleged perpetrator of rights (particularly the one to remain silent), should be abolished. The book's recommendations caused a storm of controversy.

In *Guilty,* Rothwax put forth ten points for criminal court reform: simplify and clarify search and seizure laws; abandon the *Miranda* ruling; measure the time needed to bring a case to trial by reasonableness, not by speed; give defendants the right to an attorney only in the pretrial and trial stages of a case; instruct the jury to consider a defendant's failure to explain or deny evidence on the stand as an indication of the truth of such evidence; require defendants seeking pretrial discovery from the state to place their own version of events in a sealed envelope to prevent lying and manipulation; limit peremptory challenges to three or fewer to avoid juries biased toward one side of the case; replace unanimous juries with ten-to-two or eleven-to-one verdicts in criminal trials; allow judges to take more active roles in the courtroom; reevaluate fundamental philosophy and procedure to avoid having decisions reversed on technical and often irrational grounds.

Rothwax died at the age of sixty-seven at Mount Sinai Medical Center in New York City. The cause was complications from a stroke he suffered on 6 September 1997. During his long and distinguished career, Rothwax often was mocked and derided as a destroyer of the U.S. Constitution. In reality, his one firm goal was to see that, no matter how unpopular and seemingly harsh, justice was done.

★

A good summary of Rothwax's judicial career and the legal philosophy he drew from it is found in his own *Guilty: The Collapse of Criminal Justice* (1996). Paul Hoffman, *Courthouse* (1979), shows Rothwax, among other jurists, in action. A biographical sketch by Ami Walsh was featured in *Newsmakers, 1996* (1997). A courtroom portrait is found in Loudon Wainwright, "Making Things Happen: The Genius of Judge Harold Rothwax," *Saturday Review* (10 June 1978). Obituaries are in *Time* (3 Nov. 1997) and the *New York Times* (23 Oct. 1997).

JOHN MORAN

ROUNTREE, Martha (*b.* 23 October 1911 in Gainesville, Florida; *d.* 23 August 1999 in Washington, D.C.), radio and television producer who cocreated and moderated the weekly public affairs interview show *Meet the Press.*

Rountree was the second oldest of five children of Earle S. Rountree, a lawyer and banker, and Mary Jane Tennant, a homemaker. As a young child, Rountree moved with her

Martha Rountree with New York Governor Thomas E. Dewey on *Meet the Press,* 19 December 1952. ASSOCIATED PRESS AP

family to Columbia, South Carolina, where she attended public schools and developed an interest in writing. At age nine, she wrote her first short story, "This Crazy World." Anticipating a career in journalism, she enrolled in the University of South Carolina and, at the same time, wrote for the *Columbia Record,* a local newspaper. She left the university before graduation and returned to her native Florida to become a reporter for the Tampa *Tribune.* There she gained a variety of journalistic experiences including sportswriting. One of her sports columns attracted the attention of the manager of the CBS affiliate in Tampa, who introduced her to the field of radio programming.

In 1938 Rountree moved to New York City, where she freelanced as a journalist and wrote advertising copy for several magazines. She was soon joined by one of her siblings, Ann, and they founded Rountree Productions and Radio House, which produced radio programs and singing commercials. One of these productions, *Leave It to the Girls,* became a pioneering radio talk show. The format included a panel of five well-known women and a male guest who together answered questions sent in by listeners.

As a freelance journalist in New York, Rountree soon made the acquaintance of Lawrence E. Spivak, publisher and editor of the *American Mercury* (a magazine of social and political commentary) and sponsor of a radio program that dramatized articles from the magazine. After criticizing the program in a discussion with Spivak, Rountree worked with him to create a new format, similar to that of *Leave It To the Girls.* The resulting program, *Meet the Press,* was introduced in June 1945 on the Mutual Broadcasting

System radio network, with Rountree as moderator. On the show, Spivak was a permanent member of a panel of four noted reporters who questioned an important public figure.

During the eight years in which Rountree served as moderator, interviews on *Meet the Press* made headlines and had an important influence on national and international affairs. In 1948 Whittaker Chambers's accusation that Alger Hiss (a State Department official) had been a Communist was made on *Meet the Press* and eventually resulted in the trial and conviction of Hiss. In April 1949 millions of listeners first learned from this program that the Soviets were developing their own atomic bomb. In appearances on *Meet the Press,* Thomas E. Dewey took himself out of the 1952 presidential race, and Adlai E. Stevenson first revealed that he might run against Dwight D. Eisenhower, the ultimate victor.

On 6 November 1947 Rountree made her television debut when *Meet the Press* became a regular part of NBC's network programming. The show became the longest running program on American television, celebrating its fiftieth anniversary in 1997. It was the recipient of numerous honors, including three George Foster Peabody Awards for excellence in broadcasting. One of the Peabody Awards was earned in 1952 during Rountree's tenure with the show. Critics admired the unrehearsed nature of the program, as well as the careful preparation and consistent professionalism of the moderator. For Rountree, the program was a vital part of the democratic process: "I think it is important that the public should hear its elected officers speak out and take their stand in answer to direct questions without preparation or oratory." By the time she left the moderator's seat in 1953, virtually every major public figure in the United States and many foreign leaders had appeared on the program.

In addition to her work with *Meet the Press,* Rountree served as a roving reporter for the *American Mercury* and produced several other radio and television shows. In November 1953 she sold all her interest in *Meet the Press* to Spivak. Their agreement stipulated that she would not make a program similar to *Meet the Press* for at least two years after she left the program. On 4 July 1956, she unveiled a public affairs show called *Press Conference.* Three years later she launched *Capital Closeups,* a daily news show broadcast from her home.

Her television career made Rountree a popular lecturer, and in 1965 she founded Leadership, a Washington nonprofit political research foundation, and served as its president until 1988. She was a director of the Girls' Club of America and a leader of the Women's National Press Club. Having become acquainted with many of the capital's most prominent public figures, she served for many years as a popular Washington, D.C., hostess.

Rountree was married in 1941 to Albert N. Williams, Jr., a magazine and radio writer whom she divorced in 1948. Four years later she married Oliver Presbrey, an advertising agency executive, with whom she had two daughters. Presbrey died in 1988. Rountree had blond hair, was five feet, seven inches tall, and spoke with a pleasant South Carolina accent. After suffering from Alzheimer's disease, she died at age eighty-seven from a stomach aneurysm and is buried in Silver Springs, Maryland.

Rountree was a spirited proponent of the principle of press freedom, which she called "America's first line of defense." Her pioneering work on *Meet the Press* helped shape both television history and public affairs journalism. In addition to originating and producing the show, she was the only woman moderator in its history. *Meet the Press* became part of the American democratic process and set the standard for all subsequent public affairs interview shows.

★

There is a segment on Rountree in Rick Ball and Tim Russert, *Meet the Press: Fifty Years of History in the Making* (1998). She was the subject of several magazine articles during the time in which she produced *Meet the Press.* Obituaries are in the *New York Times* (25 Aug. 1999) and *Variety* (6 Sept. 1999).

KEVIN J. O'KEEFE

ROYKO, Mike (*b.* 19 September 1932 in Chicago, Illinois; *d.* 29 April 1997 in Chicago, Illinois), Pulitzer Prize–winning columnist renowned for his hard-hitting style and wry wit.

Royko was the son of Mike Royko (born Mikhail Rojko), Sr., a Ukrainian immigrant, and Helen Zak, a first-generation American of Polish and Russian descent. After working as a taxi driver and milk deliveryman, Royko's father opened a tavern on Chicago's northwest side and the family lived in an upstairs apartment. Royko attended the Hans Christian Anderson and Salmon P. Chase elementary schools. In 1940 his parents were divorced, and he remained with his mother. Partly because of his family's troubles, Royko became an indifferent student. In the fall of 1946 he enrolled at Morgan Park Military Academy, a boarding school on the city's far southwest side. He dropped out in his freshman year after flunking several courses. He next attended Tuley High School on the northwest side but quit attending classes after a month. He then went to live with his father, who was running a tavern on the south side.

Royko began tending bar in his father's saloon, serving shots and beers, taking bets on the horses, and "giving [a] monthly cash-stuffed envelope to [a] police bagman for assorted favors such as overlooking a fourteen-year-old bartender." When found by truant officers, Royko was escorted back to school, but he stayed at Harrison High School for less than a day. Splitting his time between his mother's

Mike Royko, 1984. CORBIS CORPORATION (NEW YORK)

apartment on the northwest side and his father's home on the south side, Royko worked as a pin boy at a bowling alley. Caught again by school officials, he was taken away to Montefiore, a reform school, where he stayed until he could legally drop out at age sixteen.

On quitting school, Royko worked as an usher at the Chicago Theater in the Loop and handled packages in the shipping room at Marshall Field and Company's department store on State Street. In 1949 he enrolled at the Central YMCA High School, where all of the students paid tuition and many of his classmates were returning veterans from World War II. He liked the school in part because students were allowed to smoke in the halls. Royko completed his four-year program in half that time, was elected president of his senior class, and graduated in 1951. He briefly attended Wright Junior College as a sociology major, but soon got bored and quit.

In the spring of 1952 Royko joined the U.S. Air Force, took basic training at Lackland Air Force Base in Texas, and then spent eight months of training as a radio technician in Mississippi. Royko was sent to Korea in January 1953 and saw limited combat. Following the Korean armistice in the summer of 1953, he was stationed for a year at Blaine, Washington. On 19 June 1954 he was promoted to airman first class. He married Carol Duckman, with whom he had grown up, in Seattle, Washington, on 6 November 1954. Two months later, he was transferred to the air force base at Chicago's O'Hare Field. On learning that the editor of the base newspaper was leaving, he volunteered for the job. "I told the personnel officer I was a former reporter for the *Chicago Daily News*. I just flat-out lied," he later recalled. "I guess after three years in the service they didn't check resumes."

Royko took a three-day leave, which he spent reading books about journalism in the Chicago Public Library. As the editor of the base newspaper, he began writing a column called "Mike's Views," which often stirred controversy. He criticized the American Legion for endorsing the wild excesses of Wisconsin's Red-hunting Senator Joseph R. McCarthy. Discharged with the rank of sergeant in March 1956, he sought to pursue a career in journalism.

Royko soon joined the *Lincoln Belmont-Booster,* a twice-weekly newspaper published by the Lerner chain. On the city's northwest side, he covered police, sports, and politics. In the fall of 1956 he applied to the City News Bureau, a wire service owned by Chicago's major daily newspapers that was also their farm club. "I think I can write. I've got a pair of strong legs, lots of energy, and I don't plan on being rich. And I can type," he wrote in his application. "What I lack in formal education, I've made up, to a certain point, in personal experience and a heck of a lot of reading. . . . Unfortunately, a recently acquired wife squelched my plans to get a college degree so I'm faced with doing it the hard way."

Hired by the news bureau, Royko was assigned to the police and court beats. From the start, he showed energy, a keen understanding of the criminal justice system, and a competitive drive. Within six months, he was assigned to the news desk as an editor. In 1957 he unsuccessfully applied to all four Chicago daily newspapers. During this period he worked part-time selling tombstones.

Finally, in May 1959, Royko landed a job at the *Chicago Daily News* and began working nights as a rewrite man. Eventually, he moved on to the police beat and in 1963 was assigned to cover Cook County government. Royko quickly made his reputation as a front-page reporter, shedding new light on insider deals and cronyism. As part of this beat, he wrote a weekly column that quickly attracted a wide following. Raymond R. Coffey, a *Daily News* colleague, said that Royko's humor and engaging style set him apart from other political columnists.

"I found that Chicago politics as it was being covered didn't really reflect reality," Royko said in a 1997 interview with the *Chicago Tribune*. "The beat reporters would clean up the language. They would make really idiotic people sound reasonably normal. And I wanted to write about them the way they really were. There was no shortage of investigative reporting. Trying to nail the bad guys. But there was something I thought was lacking; the color of it. The humor. The comic scene. That's the way I felt about pols. They were comedic material."

On 6 September 1963 he became the *Chicago Daily News* full-time metropolitan columnist. "It was a sad surprise to hop into a cab and find that the driver was a man we once knew as a neighborhood tavern keeper," Royko wrote in his first column, describing how city planners had destroyed a neighborhood saloon in the name of urban renewal. Over the next three decades Royko would write frequently about the arrogance of power and how governmental bureaucracies were unfair in their treatment of ordinary people. In the 1960s he wrote mostly about Chicago but traveled to Selma and Montgomery, Alabama, to write about civil rights marches there in 1966.

Royko took pride in his craft and sought to make his column accessible to a general audience. "I sweat out the closer more than I do the lead," he said in a 1993 interview with Chicago's public radio station. "I don't worry about the lead. Just get it started somehow, get people into it, and tell the story. My approach has always been to keep it fairly simple, not to use words that send people to the dictionary. Whatever word pops into my mind, if it does the job, that's it."

From 1963 until his death, he wrote more than 8,000 columns. During most of this time, his wrote five columns per week. Mayor Richard J. Daley and the Chicago Democratic organization were among his more frequent targets. He invented a colorful cast of characters who appeared regularly in his column: his alter ego, Slats Grobnik; the wacky psychiatrist I. M. Kookie; and a conservative friend, Grump. "Royko is like his city," the editorial cartoonist Bill Mauldin wrote in 1967. "He has sharp elbows, he thinks sulphur and soot are natural ingredients of the atmosphere, and he has an astonishing capacity for idealism and love devoid of goo. He has written about Chicago in a way that has never been matched."

In 1971 Royko's *Boss: Richard J. Daley of Chicago,* a critical portrait, became a national best-seller and greatly enhanced the author's reputation. "It is the best book ever written about a city of this country," Jimmy Breslin observed. "And perhaps it will stand as the best book ever written about the American condition at this time." A year later, Royko was awarded the Pulitzer Prize for commentary.

One of his more moving and powerful columns, "A Faceless Man's Plea," appeared in the *Chicago Daily News* on 10 December 1973. It was about the Vietnam veteran Leroy Bailey, who was denied medical benefits by the Veterans Administration (VA). "Until he was hit by a rocket, Bailey had teeth," Royko wrote. "Now he has none. He had eyes. Now he has none. He had a nose. Now he has none. People could look at him. Now most of them turn away." As a result of this column, President Richard M. Nixon ordered the VA to provide Bailey with full medical coverage.

After the *Chicago Daily News* closed in 1978, Royko moved to the *Chicago Sun-Times,* where he stayed until 1984, when he switched to the *Chicago Tribune,* where he spent the remainder of his career. His first wife, Carol, died in 1979. They had two children. He married Judy Arndt on 21 May 1985, and they later adopted two children. Royko's final column, about his beloved Chicago Cubs, appeared on 21 March 1997. At age sixty-four, Royko suffered a stroke in his Winnetka, Illinois, home. He died at Northwestern University Memorial Hospital in Chicago six days after undergoing brain surgery. Royko was cremated and his ashes are buried at Chicago's Acacia Cemetery.

At the height of Royko's career, his well-known column was syndicated in more than 600 newspapers. From 1987 through 1989, he was selected as the nation's best columnist in annual surveys by the *Washington Journalism Review.* "He was the soul of journalism," said James D. Squires, the editor of the *Chicago Tribune* from 1981 until 1989. "Royko was the one who inspired my generation and this generation to act and think on behalf of the interests of little people."

★

F. Richard Ciccone, *Royko: A Life in Print* (2001), is a briskly written and authoritative biography by the former managing editor of the *Chicago Tribune.* Doug Moe, *World of Mike Royko* (1999), is also a useful source, particularly about the columnist's family background. Royko's published anthologies include *Up Against It* (1967); *I May Be Wrong, But I Doubt It* (1968); *Slats Grobnik and Some Other Friends* (1973); *Sez Who? Sez Me* (1982); *Like I Was Sayin'* (1984); *Dr. Kookie, You're Right* (1989); *One More Time* (1999); and *For the Love of Mike* (2001). Obituaries are in the *New York Times, Chicago Sun-Times,* and *Chicago Tribune* (all 30 Apr. 1997).

STEVE NEAL

RUDOLPH, Paul Marvin (*b.* 23 October 1918 in Elkton, Kentucky; *d.* 8 August 1997 in New York City), architect and educator known for his innovative post–World War II houses in Florida, major public projects in North America and Southeast Asia, and his tenure as chair of the School of Architecture at Yale University.

Rudolph was born in southwestern Kentucky to Keener Lee Rudolph, a Methodist minister, and Eurie Stone. He had two sisters. In the itinerant tradition of the Methodist church, Rudolph's father moved the family to various congregations throughout the state. It was in this context that Rudolph was first exposed to the range of vernacular architecture of the American South. In 1935 he entered the architecture program at the Alabama Polytechnic Institute in Auburn, Alabama, where he received his B.A. degree in architecture in 1940. While studying at Alabama Polytechnic, he was introduced to Walter Burkhardt, a professor who had been part of the massive migration of German intellectuals and academics from Nazi Germany. Burkhardt's work for the Historical American Buildings Survey in Alabama documented adjustable shutter systems and organizational devices, such as dogtrots and porches, which had been developed over many decades to catch breezes and provide shade from the sun. These elements would all play an important part in Rudolph's early development as an architect.

After graduating from Alabama Polytechnic, Rudolph worked for the firm of E. B. Van Koeren in Birmingham, Alabama. It was in this office that Rudolph realized that architecture school had taught him very little about the technology of building construction. After a year of practical experience, a former classmate recommended that he contact Ralph Twitchell, an architect who was doing some progressive work in Sarasota, Florida. After a short time in Sarasota with Twitchell, Rudolph was accepted into the Graduate School of Design at Harvard University to study under Walter Gropius and his colleague from the Bauhaus, Marcel Breuer. While at Harvard, Rudolph was recognized for his remarkable design and drawing abilities. His Harvard classmate Philip Johnson attempted to sum up his

501

Paul Rudolph. PRINTS AND PHOTOGRAPHS DIVISION, LIBRARY OF CONGRESS

admiration in the quote: "Every one of us said, 'Well, Paul Rudolph is going to be the [Frank Lloyd] Wright of his time.'"

Rudolph's education was interrupted for three years of military service at the Brooklyn Naval Yard as a supervisor of ship construction, which brought another practical dimension to his education. Upon completion of his graduate degree study in 1947, Rudolph spent a year traveling abroad on a Wheelwright fellowship from Harvard, where he immersed himself in the architecture of European modernism and also began a lifelong fascination with traditional urban form. Rudolph returned to Sarasota, Florida, to work again with Ralph Twitchell, first as an associate and then as a full partner. Rudolph and Twitchell began articulating a distinctive regional ethic, modeled on a resolution between the natural landscape, local architectural precedent, and the exploitation of innovative construction materials. As Rudolph made the transition into independent practice in the early 1950s, these ideas were developed into a complex set of interrelationships that set the groundwork for much of

his later work in the northeastern United States and abroad. In the context of Florida, he designed more than sixty projects, including the Cocoon House (1950), Walker Guest House (1952–1953), Umbrella House (1953–1954), and the Milam House (1959–1961). From this experience, a distinct body of work emerged that came to represent the possibility of a modest, locally inspired American modernism.

The architect's early residential work in Florida, produced over a twenty-year period, provided him with the necessary testing ground for the development of his design methodology. Rudolph worked at an astonishing rate throughout the 1950s, introducing new spatial concepts that relied heavily on innovative structural concepts and emerging construction materials. He was creating a new kind of regional domesticity that was based on the integration of new building materials and the relation of the built environment to the natural landscape. Built before subtropical architecture was homogenized by the proliferation of air-conditioning, these structures were lauded for Rudolph's innovative use of mediating devices, such as screens and operable flaps, to modulate the spatial qualities of the design and foster a sense of integration with the adjacent landscape.

By the time that Rudolph was thirty-six years old, he was a significant force in the national architectural scene. In 1954 he received the Outstanding Young Architect Award in São Paulo, Brazil, based mainly on the reputation of his Florida houses. That same year, he was commissioned to design the installation for Edward Steichen's epic photography exhibition, the Family of Man, at the Museum of Modern Art in New York City, and he traveled to Jordan where he had been commissioned to design the United States Embassy. Out of this experience came the design and construction of his first large-scale public building, the Mary Cooper Jewett Arts Center at Wellesley College in Wellesley, Massachusetts, completed in 1958.

By 1958, when Rudolph accepted the chairmanship at the Yale University School of Architecture, his practice began the transition toward large-scale projects in the northeastern United States. In fact, most discussions of Paul Rudolph's work begin with his design of the Art and Architecture Building at Yale University (1958–1963), due to complex spatial juxtapositions of the interior and the way in which it aggressively relates to its local context. Attempts at generalizing this architecture are inevitably problematic because Rudolph always worked on multiple levels, but this intense exploration of spatial and visual attributes speaks to the visceral appeal of much of his later work. The thin folded planes of the Milam house set against the bright Florida sky would soon give way to the brooding rusticated surfaces of the Art and Architecture Building at Yale University, the Temple Street Parking Garage in New Haven, Connecticut, and the Mental Health Building and Health,

Welfare and Education Building at Government Center in Boston (1962). In each of these projects, Rudolph presented a built-in critique of the functionalism inherent in many of his earliest projects in favor of what came to be known as the "Brutalist" aesthetic of the 1960s.

In 1965 Rudolph set up his New York office to continue developing major public projects, such as the Boston Government Services Center (1962–1971) and the Southeastern Massachusetts Technological Institute in North Dartmouth, Massachusetts (1963–1972). From his New York studio, he continued to explore his fascination with urbanism by creating dense megastructures based on repetitive modules for projects such as the Graphic Arts Center at Colgate University in Hamilton, New York (1963) and a study for the Lower Manhattan Expressway (1969–1972).

In the 1980s Rudolph's unswerving belief in the basic tenants of modernism as a way to engage contemporary culture came into direct conflict with the dominant architecture culture, forcing his practice offshore. He increasingly focused his practice on projects in Southeast Asia, where his brand of modernism was still in favor. His designs there include major high-rise developments, such as the Collonade Condominiums in Singapore (1980–1987), the Bond Centre in Hong Kong (1984–1988), the Dhar-mala Sakti Building in Djakarta (1982–1988), and the Concourse Complex in Singapore (1981–1993). This later work was documented in an exhibition at the National Institute for Architecture Education in New York in 1993. This was the last major exhibition of Rudolph's work to be mounted before his death from asbestos-related cancer. Rudolph's remains were cremated.

★

Rudolph's archives are in the Architecture, Design and Engineering Collections at the Library of Congress in Washington, D.C. Major book-length publications about the architect include Sybil Moholoy Nagy and Gerhard Schwab, *The Architecture of Paul Rudolph* (1970); Rupert Spade, *Paul Rudolph* (1971); Yukio Futagawa, ed., *Paul Rudolph: Architectural Drawings* (1982); and Christopher Domin and Joseph King, *Paul Rudolph: The Florida Houses* (2001). "100 Works of Paul Rudolph" was published in a special issue of the Japanese periodical *Architecture and Urbanism* 80 (Jul. 1977), and *The Yale Art + Architecture Building* (1999), with an introduction by Philip Nobel, was part of the Building Blocks series of Princeton Architectural Press. Obituaries are in the *New York Times* (14 Aug. 1997) and *Architecture* 21 (1997).

CHRISTOPHER DOMIN

S

SANFORD, (James) Terry (*b*. 20 August 1917 in Laurinburg, North Carolina; *d*. 18 April 1998 in Durham, North Carolina), state governor, U.S. senator, and university president who is remembered for his contributions to education and the fight against racial discrimination.

Sanford was one of five children born to Cecil Sanford, a businessman who had been wiped out by the Great Depression, and Elizabeth Martin, a dedicated teacher. The product of a small town in eastern North Carolina, he grew up when and where segregation was a way of life. Growing up during the Great Depression, Sanford worked throughout his teen years raising pigs or chickens; delivering telegrams, prescriptions, or newspapers; selling vegetables or magazine subscriptions; and doing almost anything that would earn a few dollars. As an Eagle Scout, he qualified as a lifesaver swimmer. He spent the rest of his spare time playing the saxophone, even forming a small dance band. He graduated from Laurinburg High School in 1934 with dim prospects, but decided he could afford to attend Presbyterian Junior College seven miles away in Maxton. Sanford received his A.B. degree from the University of North Carolina at Chapel Hill in 1939, after working as a dishwasher to help pay his tuition. From 1941 to 1942 he served as a special agent with the Federal Bureau of Investigation (FBI). On 4 July 1942 he married Margaret Rose Knight; they had two children.

When the United States entered World War II, Sanford enlisted in the army. As a paratrooper, he was involved in five major European campaigns, including the Battle of the Bulge. He was awarded the Combat Infantryman's Badge, the Bronze Star, and the Purple Heart, and rose to the rank of first lieutenant. After earning his law degree from the University of North Carolina in 1946, Sanford practiced law in Fayetteville, North Carolina, and served a term in the state senate from 1953 to 1955.

Sanford followed in the tradition of leaders who believed that the role of government was to provide assistance for the disadvantaged, to educate children, and to create an environment for employment. He won the nomination for the governor of North Carolina by turning back the segregationist campaign of an opponent. Then, when he took office in 1961, he enrolled his children in an integrated public school and created a biracial Good Neighbor Council to help deal with the inequities of a system that relegated African Americans to second-class jobs and second-class lives. He also made his mark as an education governor, risking his political future on a tax increase to pay for an ambitious program for public schools. Sanford's list of accomplishments is uncommonly long, especially for a man who served only one four-year term as governor. In addition to statewide improvements in the public schools, he created the nation's first state-sponsored school of the arts to train future dancers, musicians, and artists. Sanford also convinced lawmakers to create the Governor's School, a racially integrated, eight-week program for 400 students

Terry Sanford, 1990. JOHN DURICKA/ASSOCIATED PRESS AP

with extraordinary talents in the arts and sciences. He mobilized legislative support for the creation of a system of community colleges to put post–high school training within easy reach of any who sought it.

As governor, Sanford found private money to establish the North Carolina Traffic Safety Council and set up a commission to develop new concepts in traffic law. Legislators approved the use of chemical tests on suspected drunk drivers and the requirement that seat belts be installed in all automobiles. He also established the North Carolina Commission on the Status of Women, one of the first of its kind in the nation, and asked the commission to study a wide range of women's issues, including discrimination in jobs and pay. Before the commission was established, Sanford had raised the visibility of women in government when he elevated Superior Court Judge Susie Sharp to the state supreme court, an appointment that caught the members of the all-male court by surprise.

Sanford created the North Carolina Fund, which used private money and government support to extend the reach of education to the disadvantaged. The fund helped create community organizations that became the center for programs that both improved and empowered low-income neighborhoods. The fund's North Carolina Volunteers recruited young people in the summer of 1964 to work with

community action programs and other local agencies. President Lyndon B. Johnson was so impressed with the North Carolina initiatives to encourage local solutions to poverty and housing that some of the state's programs became models for the War on Poverty. The North Carolina Volunteers, for example, was a forerunner to the federal government program VISTA (Volunteers In Service To America).

By the time Sanford left office in January 1965, he had brought a new day to North Carolina and inspired a generation. He returned to private law practice. In April 1965 the Ford and Carnegie Foundations announced that Sanford would lead a special $280,000 study of the American states from a base at Duke University. His book, *Storm Over the States*, was the product of that study. He also wrote *But What About the People?* (1966), an account of his experiences as governor. Sanford accepted the presidency of Duke in 1969 when antiwar demonstrations were creating problems for college administrators all around the country. He assumed office in April 1970 and dealt effectively with student protests that threatened to close the campus by talking and working with students to channel their energies into political change. Sanford had planned to remain at Duke until 1976 when he hoped to mount a campaign for the Democratic presidential nomination. Students short-circuited his schedule by urging him to run earlier, and he entered the race in 1972, with the endorsement of Duke's board of trustees. The campaign ended when he failed to win the North Carolina presidential primary against another southerner, George Wallace. He tried again in 1976, but withdrew early on after he developed health problems.

Sanford continued as president of Duke until 4 July 1985. He proved to be a very successful fund-raiser. During his presidency, two fund-raising campaigns raised a total of more than $435 million, alumni giving rose to nearly $6 million per year compared with $750,000 in 1970, and the endowment more than doubled to $200 million from $80 million. Sanford was responsible for the construction of forty new buildings, which cost more than $190 million total. Of the new structures, twenty-three were in the university's medical center; the most significant project was Duke Hospital North, completed in 1981 at a cost of approximately $95 million.

Sanford built Duke's Institute of Policy Sciences and Public Affairs into a major national program. He recruited the American Dance Festival to Duke each summer and established the Institute of the Arts, which sponsored visits by distinguished artists, and the Duke in New York Arts Program. He was awarded nineteen honorary degrees and was a member of several boards of trustees and boards of visitors at other colleges and universities.

In retirement, Sanford showed he had not lost his enthusiasm for politics. In early 1986 he joined the crowded field of candidates for the Democratic nomination for the

U.S. Senate. Not many observers believed he had much of a chance of winning, but he confounded doubters by campaigning hard and emphasizing the positive. That November, the sixty-nine-year-old Sanford joined an unusual group of thirteen freshmen in the Senate that included former Governor Bob Graham of Florida and Democratic Congresswoman Barbara Mikulski of Maryland. Sanford already knew most of the Democratic leaders in the Senate and quickly began to forge friendships and alliances with several, particularly New Jersey's Bill Bradley, Georgia's Sam Nunn, and Tennessee's Al Gore, Jr.

By his own admission, the Senate had never been Sanford's highest ambition, and Sanford served six years in relative obscurity. His biggest success came when he engineered the creation of a quasi-governmental, foundation-funded commission to help bring about peace in Latin America. The report, prepared by what came to be called the Sanford Commission, was endorsed by the governments of eight nations and helped set the stage for Central American peace, according to some observers. He also strongly opposed the Supreme Court nomination of Robert H. Bork and spoke against United States' participation in the Persian Gulf War.

After being defeated in his bid for reelection to the Senate in November 1992, Sanford again settled down to a private law practice and took up teaching at Duke. In late 1997 he was diagnosed with cancer of the esophagus and liver and died at age eighty. He was survived by his wife and two adult children.

Sanford's funeral four days later in Duke Chapel was attended by a host of dignitaries, including the North Carolina Council of State, governors, and former governors, and a large Senate delegation state. Governor Jim Hunt asked the huge crowd to "imagine what North Carolina would be like if we had not had Terry Sanford striving for us all these many years." Sanford's life was one of exemplary public service, and he never stopped trying to improve conditions for all citizens of his state.

★

For further information on Sanford, see Howard E. Covington, Jr., and Marion A. Ellis, *Terry Sanford: Politics, Progress, and Outrageous Ambitions* (1999). Sanford's own works includes *Outlive Your Enemies: Grow Old Gracefully* (1996). An obituary is in the *New York Times* (20 Apr. 1998).

MARION A. ELLIS
(WITH HOWARD E. COVINGTON, JR.)

SARAZEN, Gene (*b.* 27 February 1902 in Harrison, New York; *d.* 13 May 1999 in Naples, Florida), golfer who became the first player to win all four major professional golf championships.

Sarazen was born Eugenio Saraceni. He was one of two children born to Federico Saraceni, a carpenter, and Adela Saraceni, a homemaker. His father had studied for the priesthood in Italy before economic circumstances forced him to immigrate to the United States. Sarazen began life too poor even to continue in school past the sixth grade. "It was, all in all, a pretty grim childhood," he wrote in his autobiography, *Thirty Years of Championship Golf*. In 1910 the opportunity to earn a few cents as a caddie at the Larchmont Country Club in Larchmont, New York, introduced the eight year old to golf. Three years later, the former caddie Francis Ouimet's stunning victory at the U.S. Open against the British giants Harry Vardon and Ted Ray at the Country Club in Brookline, Massachusetts, inspired Sarazen to become a professional golfer. His father, who had no use for golf, was vehemently opposed, but Sarazen's strong will and determination, traits that helped him survive a near fatal bout with pneumonia in 1918, led him to persevere.

Indeed, this fierce will to win propelled Sarazen, who stood five feet, five inches tall, to thirty-eight victories on the Professional Golfer's Association (PGA) tour, eight of them in 1930. Sarazen's achievements, which led to his election in 1974 to the World Golf Hall of Fame and to

Gene Sarazen, 1973. ROBERT RIDER/ASSOCIATED PRESS AP

being honored in 1996 as the first recipient of the PGA Tour Lifetime Achievement Award, began in 1922. That year, at age twenty, he defeated Walter Hagen and Bobby Jones to win the U.S. Open with a final-round score of sixty-eight, thus making him the second-youngest winner of the tournament. Later in 1922 Sarazen went on to win the PGA championship at the Oakmont Country Club in Oakmont, Pennsylvania, and in 1923 he beat Hagen again to take his second PGA title. Sarazen was invited to play golf with President Warren G. Harding, and the Wilson Sporting Goods Company signed him to a contract in 1922 that was renewed continuously throughout his life. Sarazen was dubbed "the Squire" after he purchased a farm in Germantown, New York.

Sarazen's successes straddled the hickory-shafted and steel-shafted club eras. In all, he won three PGA championships (1922, 1923, and 1933), two U.S. Opens (1922 and 1932), the 1932 British Open, and the 1935 Augusta National Invitational Tournament (the Masters), becoming the first player to win all four major professional golf titles. (He was followed by Ben Hogan, Gary Player, Jack Nicklaus, and Tiger Woods.) Sarazen won the PGA Seniors Championship in 1954 and in 1963, at age sixty-one, he was the oldest player to make the thirty-six-hole cut at the Masters. He was a member of all six Ryder Cup teams in the decade that spanned 1927 to 1937 (1927, 1929, 1931, 1933, 1935, and 1937), compiling a record of 7–2–3.

Three of Sarazen's victories were especially memorable. In the 1923 PGA championship, he outplayed his longtime rival Hagen in a gripping battle over thirty-eight holes. At the U.S. Open in 1932 he charged from nine down, with twenty-eight holes to play, to triumph by three strokes over Phil Perkins and Bobby Cruickshank at Fresh Meadow Country Club in Lake Success, New York. Bobby Jones declared this performance the most "relentlessly spectacular" round of golf he had ever witnessed.

The most famous of Sarazen's victories—one of the most dramatic in the history of the PGA—occurred in 1935 at Augusta, on the course Bobby Jones had recently built. On the fifteenth hole of the fourth round, three strokes behind Craig Wood, Sarazen accepted his caddie's advice to go for the green. Toeing in his four-wood, he struck the "shot heard round the world," sending the ball 235 yards into the hole for a double eagle, the most famous golf shot made by Sarazen. Having tied Wood with that one incredible stroke, the next day Sarazen made twenty-four consecutive pars to beat Wood 144–149 in a thirty-six-hole playoff. In 1955 the Masters renamed the bridge at that fifteenth hole after Sarazen.

Sarazen was also one of golf's most imaginative player-innovators. He designed the weighted practice club, and in 1931 he invented the modern sand wedge, which was the key to his 1932 victory at the British Open. (Arnold Palmer

said that the club should have been called the Sarazen wedge.) After retiring from competition, Sarazen hosted *Shell's Wonderful World of Golf,* a 1961 television series that introduced millions of Americans to the game and its history. At age seventy-one, to commemorate the fiftieth anniversary of his British Open victory, he returned to Scotland and delighted British golf fans by driving a five-iron shot through the wind into the hole on Royal Troon's "Postage Stamp" 126-yard eighth hole. "When you discuss or research the history of golf," Jack Nicklaus observed, "the name Gene Sarazen is unavoidable. He was the cornerstone of the game we all enjoy today."

Sarazen, one of golf's great ambassadors, was also intellectually curious. During his career he traveled to every continent except Africa. "My tours," he wrote in his autobiography, "have not only provided me with some of my greatest pleasures, but also with a working background for understanding the peoples and the problems of the world we live in." He traveled throughout South America in 1934, playing exhibitions with the Australian trick-shot specialist Joe Kirkwood; in 1938 he toured the world. "Gene wasn't insular in his thinking," Gary Player noted. "He contributed worldwide."

Sarazen was both a pragmatist and a sharp critic. His ambitions as a young man led him to choose a new name that he considered more appropriate for a golfer, yet his background made him particularly sensitive to economic conditions. In 1936 during the Great Depression, when the purses for touring golf professionals were meager, Sarazen chose to highlight the plight of his colleagues in an interview with a United Press reporter. "I am the biggest money winner in the history of golf," he noted. But, he added, "if I had to depend upon my prize money . . . I would be sitting in the poorhouse." Thirty-two years later, when golf and corporate money were becoming synonymous, Sarazen publicly urged the PGA to clamp down on "permitting individual sponsorship of its newly-recruited tour pros [or], golf could be headed for a scandal [worse than] baseball's Black Sox fix case."

Sarazen married Mary Catherine Henry on 10 June 1924; they had two children. In his autobiography, he credits his wife with getting him to the 1932 British Open, his record-breaking tournament (283 strokes for 72 holes for a record 13 under par). She had secretly saved money and mortgaged their home to pay for the trip. Sarazen also gave his caddies full credit. He wrote that he owed his victory at the 1932 British Open to the competence and advice of his caddie, Skip Daniels. Likewise, he reported, it was the insistent urging of his 1935 Masters caddie, "Stovepipe," that led him to gamble on the shot that resulted in the double eagle. Sarazen's wife died in 1986. After her death, Sarazen retired to Marco Island, Florida, and died of complications from pneumonia in a hospital in Naples, Florida.

Sarazen's accomplishments and longevity led to his ranking among the most prominent golfers of the twentieth century. In the seventy-seven years from 1922, when he won his first of seven major tournaments, to April 1999, when, at age ninety-seven, he again participated with Byron Nelson and Sam Snead in the ceremonial opening drive at the Masters tournament, Sarazen was one of golf's great players and personalities. As a young man he dueled with Harry Vardon and James Braid, and beat Bobby Jones, Walter Hagen, and Sam Snead. In 1948 at age forty-six, Sarazen played even with Ben Hogan to the final green before losing by a stroke in the third-round match at the PGA championship. He had an efficient swing and exceptional ball control. According to Bobby Jones, "He could do just about anything he wanted to do with a golf ball."

★

Sarazen's autobiography, written with Herbert Warren Wind, is *Thirty Years of Championship Golf: The Life and Times of Gene Sarazen* (1950). Obituaries are in the *Chicago Tribune*, *Los Angeles Times*, and *New York Times* (all 14 May 1999).

MARTIN J. SHERWIN

SCHAWLOW, Arthur Leonard (*b.* 5 May 1921 in Mount Vernon, New York; *d.* 28 April 1999 in Palo Alto, California), physicist and educator who performed pioneering research in maser and laser development and shared the Nobel Prize in physics in 1982 for an important use of laser device application in spectroscopy.

Schawlow was one of two children of Arthur Schawlow, an immigrant from Riga, the capital of Latvia, then part of Czarist Russia, and Helen Mason, a Canadian. His father, who had left Riga in 1910 to study electrical engineering in Darmstadt, Germany, arrived too late for the beginning of the semester and elected to visit his brother in New York City. There Schawlow's father found employment as an insurance agent and met Mason, whom he married. They settled in suburban Mount Vernon. In 1924, when Schawlow was three years old, the family moved to Toronto, Canada, where Schawlow graduated from the Vaughan Road Collegiate Institute, a Toronto high school, in 1937.

Schawlow was an excellent student and at an early age demonstrated a broad interest in science, reading widely in astronomy, mechanics, and electricity. Though he originally intended to study radio engineering, severe economic conditions at the time prevented his father from paying his engineering school tuition at the University of Toronto. Scholarships were not available for engineering, but Schawlow was able to secure a scholarship for the study of physics at the university in 1937.

Schawlow graduated from the University of Toronto

Arthur L. Schawlow, 1996. PAUL SAKUMA/ASSOCIATED PRESS AP

with a B.A. degree in 1941 and an M.A. degree a year later. During World War II he taught classes at the University of Toronto to personnel in the Canadian armed forces and worked on microwave antenna development for a radar factory. After the war Schawlow earned his Ph.D. in 1949 with a dissertation in optical spectroscopy. He then received a Carbide and Carbon Chemicals Company fellowship for postdoctoral work at Columbia University in New York City.

At Columbia University, Schawlow met Charles Townes, who led Columbia's effort in microwave spectroscopy and who received the Nobel Prize in 1964 for research in this area, which included his development of the maser—an acronym for microwave amplification by stimulated emission of radiation. Schawlow worked under Townes's supervision before joining him as a full collaborator. Schawlow also married Townes's sister, Aurelia Keith Townes, on 19 May 1951. They had a son and two daughters.

In 1951 Schawlow left Columbia and joined Bell Telephone Laboratories in New Jersey, where the principal focus of his research was superconductivity, the decrease in electrical resistance of certain materials at extremely low temperatures. Schawlow's collaboration with Townes continued with the book *Microwave Spectroscopy* (1955). In addition, in 1957 and 1958, he and Townes collaborated on extending the principles of Townes's earlier maser work (to which Schawlow had also contributed) to shorter wavelengths in the electromagnetic spectrum, or the wavelength of light. Their objective was to achieve an optical maser or, as later designated, a laser—an acronym for light amplification by stimulated emission of radiation.

The laser and prior maser devices had their earliest genesis in the stimulated emission of radiation phenomenon predicted theoretically between 1916 and 1917 by Albert Einstein. Essentially, the picture of the atom derived from pioneering efforts of Einstein and other scientists was an atom consisting of electrons clustering around a heavy central nucleus, those electrons confined in motion to discrete orbits, with each orbit defining a unique energy. This atom, described later as the Bohr Model, after its principal investigator, was viewed as having its electrons changing its orbit or going from a lower to higher energy state by absorbing specific electromagnetic radiation (light, X rays, gamma-radiation, microwaves, radio waves). This radiation was in the form of energy bits designated quanta or photons. An electron that had been moved to a higher energy level soon fell back to an orbit of lower energy, with the energy change from higher to lower orbit being accompanied by a radiation photon corresponding to the energy difference between the orbits.

In 1951 Townes, with considerable assistance from Schawlow, experimentally confirmed the validity of the stimulated emission hypothesis in the microwave region of the electromagnetic spectrum. Using ammonia as the microwave target, they built the first maser. Because a small microwave signal produced a large output of microwaves of the same frequency, the ultimate result was amplification. For this discovery, Townes shared the Nobel Prize in physics in 1964 with Soviet physicists who had independently pursued maser development.

During 1957 and 1958 Schawlow and Townes focused their joint research on extending the maser concept to the optical region of the electromagnetic spectrum. Though the stimulated emission principle was still applicable, the actual experimental demonstration proved more formidable. In the December 1958 issue of *Physical Review,* they published an important paper, "Infrared and Optical Masers," outlining the parameters for achieving an optical maser, even though they did not have the support of an experimental demonstration.

Using as the principal guidance the published work of Schawlow and Townes, the first optical maser was demonstrated two years later on 16 May 1960 by Theodore H. Maiman of Hughes Aircraft Company in Malibu, California. The device used a ruby crystal as the target material, and the light radiation causing excitation was from neon lamps coiled around the crystal. Schawlow and Townes, along with others in different laboratories, succeeded in building working devices along the same lines the same

year. Ironically, when Schawlow and Townes first submitted the concept of an optical resonant cavity, an essential component of all lasers, to the Bell Laboratory patent office, it was initially rejected on the grounds that "optical waves had never been of importance to communication and hence the invention had little bearing on Bell System interests."

One regrettable aspect in the history of the invention of the laser was a protracted legal controversy including challenges of plagiarism among some of the principals. Schawlow and Townes were awarded the original patent for the laser in 1958. However, (Richard) Gordon Gould, a graduate student who studied under another prominent Columbia physicist, Polykarp Kusch (Nobel Prize for physics, 1955), after a lengthy court battle was judged in 1977 to be the valid patent holder of optically pumped lasers. Gould is reported to be the first to suggest the preferred name "laser" for optical maser, confining the designation maser, as originally intended, to microwave devices.

Schawlow returned to Columbia in 1960 as a visiting associate professor. In 1961 he became professor of physics at Stanford University in Palo Alto, California, where he influenced many young scientists. Schawlow continued his research, employing lasers to investigate atomic and molecular structure in the then-new field of laser spectroscopy. One of the principal devices developed by Schawlow for spectroscopic applications was the tunable laser, with which the intense coherent light was adjustable to desired single monochromatic frequencies, making it practical to secure precisely clear spectra with relatively few atoms or molecules. Among the significant results of Schawlow's work was the ability to obtain the value of certain fundamental parameters in optics with unprecedented accuracy. Of particular importance is the Rydberg constant, named after the Swedish physicist who presented a formula in 1889 that described atomic line spectra and contained the constant (later given his name).

Between 1966 and 1970 Schawlow was head of the department of physics at Stanford. He was named J. G. Jackson–C. J. Wood Professor of Physics in 1978, a position he held until his retirement as professor emeritus in 1991. He was well known for his sense of humor, his advice, and his words of wisdom. He once said, "To do successful research, you don't need to know everything, you just need to know of one thing that isn't known."

In 1981 Schawlow shared the Nobel Prize for physics with Nicholaas Bloembergen of Harvard and Kai M. Siegbahn of Uppsala University, Sweden, for their parallel but independent development of laser spectroscopy. The citation presentation noted that "These methods have made it possible to investigate the interior of atoms, molecules, and solids in greater detail than was previously possible."

Schawlow received numerous honorary degrees. In 1962 he was the recipient of the Ballantine Medal of the Franklin

Institute in Philadelphia, Pennsylvania. He received the National Science Foundation Medal of Science in 1982 and the Ronald H. Brown American Innovation Award of the U.S. Department of Commerce in 1996. Schawlow served as a director-at-large of the Optical Society of America between 1966 and 1968 and was elected president of the society in 1975.

In addition to his important scientific work, Schawlow was joined by his wife in support of organizations offering assistance to autistic children. Their son, Arthur Keith, was afflicted with autism. In May 1991 Schawlow's wife died from an auto accident that occurred while she was on her way to visit their son in Paradise, California. At the age of seventy-seven, Schawlow died in a Palo Alto hospital from congestive heart failure induced by leukemia.

★

For information on Schawlow, see George L. Trigg, "The Maser and the Laser," in *Landmark Experiments in Twentieth Century Physics* (1975), and Nick Taylor, *Laser: The Inventor, the Nobel Laureate, and the Thirty-Year Patent War* (2000). An obituary is in the *New York Times* (30 Apr. 1999).

LEONARD R. SOLON

SCHULTZ, Theodore William (*b.* 30 April 1902 near Arlington, South Dakota; *d.* 26 February 1998 in Evanston, Illinois), Nobel Prize–winning agricultural economist who made contributions to many aspects of economics, including analyses of education and human capital.

Schultz was one of nine children, eight of whom survived to adulthood, of Henry Edward Schultz, a farmer, and Anna Adeline Weiss, a homemaker and farm helper. Although he did not attend high school because he was needed on the farm, in 1921 he attended a short course at South Dakota State College, and in 1924 he was admitted as a regular student and received his B.S. degree in 1927. He attended graduate school at the University of Wisconsin, where he studied agricultural economics, receiving his Ph.D. in 1930. That same year he married Esther Florence Werth, and they had three children. That year he also accepted a position as assistant professor in the department of economics and sociology at Iowa State College of Agriculture and Mechanic Arts (now Iowa State University) in Ames, Iowa.

In 1935, at age thirty-two, Schultz became head of the department of economics and sociology and promoted to full professor. By a variety of means over the next several years, Schultz acquired the resources to attract several young economists who later were recognized as outstanding. Through personal persuasiveness and good use of limited resources, he built a department of the first rank. Of

Theodore Schultz, 1979. AP/WIDE WORLD PHOTOS

the economists that he attracted in a brief period of eight years, four became presidents of the American Economic Association, four were named members of the National Academy of Sciences, and one became a Nobel laureate.

In late 1943 Schultz left Iowa State because the president of the college, in reaction to a pressure group purported to speak for farmers, repudiated a publication authored by a member of the faculty. The pamphlet, "Putting Dairying on a Wartime Footing," part of a series titled *Wartime Farm and Food Policy,* argued that oleomargarine was nutritionally equivalent to butter and suggested that the war effort could be furthered by eliminating taxes and regulations restricting its production and consumption, since producing oleomargarine cost significantly less than producing butter. Although the college president did get the pamphlet withdrawn, Schultz aided in the publication of a revised version in 1944 that strengthened the case being made.

Schultz began teaching at the University of Chicago in 1943, where he had a distinguished career as a professor and was chairman of the department of economics from 1946 to 1961. In 1952 he earned the school's title of Charles L. Hutchinson Distinguished Service Professor of Economics, and he became president of the American Economic Association in 1960. He retired in the early 1970s but served as professor emeritus. In 1979, however, he received the Nobel Prize in economics, which he shared with W. Arthur Lewis, for his work on human capital and economic development, later published as "The Economics of Being Poor" in the *Journal of Political Economy* (1980). Ironically, Schultz happened to be at Iowa State University when he was informed of his award.

Schultz made major and lasting contributions to the understanding of the economics of agriculture in developed countries in three important books: *Agriculture in an Unstable Economy* (1945), *Production and Welfare of Agriculture* (1949), and *The Economic Organization of Agriculture* (1953), and in more than twenty articles in professional journals. Among his publications related to agriculture, he probably is best remembered for authoring *Transforming Traditional Agriculture* (1964), which transformed thinking and policy about the role of agriculture in economic development. Before its publication, the conclusion that the marginal product of labor in farming was zero, that labor could be withdrawn from agriculture without an adverse effect on farm output, and that farmers in developing countries did not respond to incentives and were guided by tradition or culture were widely accepted. Schultz proved that these views were erroneous, and the history of agriculture in developing countries since has fully substantiated his views. He argued that when farmers were provided with new and profitable methods of production and appropriate incentives, they would increase production; over the past four decades, where these conditions have prevailed, Schultz's theory has proved correct.

Schultz was among the earliest economists to emphasize investment in people—human investment or human capital. Economists had long studied investment in machinery and buildings but had given little attention to investment in people as a means of increasing production. Schultz published an early article, "Investment in Man: An Economist's View," in *Social Service Review* (1959), and he reiterated his views in his presidential address to the American Economic Association, "Investment in Human Capital," later published in *American Economic Review* (1961). At the time there were many who found the idea of investing in people repugnant and demeaning. But Schultz argued that "by investing in themselves, people can enlarge the range of choice available to them. It is one way free men can enhance their welfare."

In 1993 Schultz suffered a hip injury. He moved to a nursing home until his death by pneumonia at age ninety-five. He was survived by his three children and is buried in Arlington, South Dakota.

★

There are no full-length biographies on Schultz, but valuable details about his life can be found in Mark Blaug, *Great Economists*

Since Keynes (1985), and *Who's Who in America* (1998). He edited two volumes of research papers that had major impacts on the areas involved: *The Economics of the Family: Marriage, Children and Human Capital* (1973) and *Distortions of Agricultural Incentives* (1978). Obituaries are in the *Chicago Tribune* (28 Feb. 1998), *New York Times* (2 Mar. 1998), and *Washington Post* (3 Mar. 1998).

D. GALE JOHNSON

SCHWANN, William Joseph (*b.* 13 May 1913 in Salem, Illinois; *d.* 7 June 1998 in Burlington, Massachusetts), organist, musicologist, and compiler and publisher whose catalog of recordings became the prime reference source to American recorded music.

Schwann was the son of Henry W. Schwann, a minister, and Effie A. Garthwait. A native of Illinois who was raised in Kentucky, Schwann studied music at Louisville Conservatory of Music from 1930 to 1931, and he earned a B.A. degree in music from the University of Louisville in 1935. During these years he began his music career as an organist and choir director in Louisville churches. According to Schwann, he would have gone to the prestigious Curtis Institute of Music in Philadelphia, Pennsylvania, for graduate study if he had not "stepped on a nail" and been unable to audition for a scholarship there. Instead he went to Boston University, where he was offered a scholarship that did not require an audition. Schwann also undertook graduate studies at Harvard University (1938–1939), attending classes given by Arthur Tillman Merritt, Hugo Leichtentritt, George Wallace Woodworth, and Walter Piston. He studied organ privately with Edward Power Biggs and Raymond Robinson. Schwann performed recitals at local churches and gave music lessons from 1935 to 1950, and he wrote music criticism for the *Boston Transcript* and the *Boston Herald* from 1937 to 1941. In 1939 Schwann opened the Record Shop on Massachusetts Avenue in Cambridge, across the street from the Massachusetts Institute of Technology (MIT).

During World War II, Schwann served on the staff of the Radiation Laboratory of MIT from 1942 to 1945. He also helped organize an association of local record dealers that allowed stores to share resources and trade inventory. The association became Schwann's market base when he started his record catalog in 1949. In 1948 Columbia Records introduced the long-playing (LP) microgroove record that revolutionized the recording industry, and by 1949 the explosion in record repertory prompted the birth of the Schwann catalog. His initial idea was practical—to compile a comprehensive catalog of released recordings to facilitate his retail operations and to aid record purchasers. His first issue of classical recordings, *Long Playing Record*

Catalog, was released in October 1949. It contained twenty-six typewritten pages that listed 674 LP records by ninety-eight composers on eleven labels.

The catalog was so successful that 6,000 catalogs, at ten cents apiece, were purchased within the first week, and within a month the total printout of 11,000 copies was sold out. Meanwhile, the catalog became obsolete so quickly that Schwann had to revise it monthly. It expanded with the recording business and often offered thousands of listings. Business became so brisk that Schwann sold his record store in 1953 and devoted himself full-time to publishing. He hired a staff of eight and eventually installed information on a computer database. On 1 June 1959 Schwann married Aire-Maija Kutvonen, a linguist and native of Finland who later became an officer of the Schwann firm.

By the time Schwann sold his catalog to ABC's Leisure Publications in 1976, it had expanded to more than 300 pages with more than 40,000 listings. Schwann remained active in its operations as publisher and president until his retirement in 1985. He gradually enlarged the categories to include not only classical music but also popular music, jazz, musical shows, rock, folk, electronic music, ballet, opera, comedy, and children's music. Along with the development of new technologies, Schwann added listings for open-reel tapes, cassettes, eight-track tapes, three competing quadraphonic formats, and, finally, compact discs. After his retirement, Schwann lived in Lincoln, Massachusetts, with his wife and spent time traveling to Scandinavia, Europe, and South America.

The Schwann catalog was bought by *Stereophile* magazine in 1991 and was expanded to include reviews and feature articles by the magazine's staff. Finally, the catalog grew so large that it was divided into two volumes: *Schwann Opus,* for classical records, and *Schwann Spectrum,* for jazz and popular music. The catalog was taken over by Valley Media in 1996. At the time of Schwann's death in 1998, the quarterly catalog had more than 1,000 pages. Famous for its comprehensiveness and reliability, the Schwann catalog is used by record store owners, record buyers, librarians, critics, radio stations, and musicians from around the world, and is regarded as the most authoritative compilation of recorded music.

Because of his accomplishment and authority in the field, Schwann was twice commissioned, in 1973 and 1980, by the Recording Industry Association of America to create and compile *The White House Record Library Catalog.* His other publications included the *Schwann Artist Issue,* the *Schwann Children's and Christmas Record and Tape Guide,* the *Schwann Catalog of Country and Western Long Playing Records,* and the *Basic Record Library.*

Schwann received honorary doctorates from the University of Louisville (1969) and the New England Conservatory of Music (1982). Among his many awards were the Music Library Association's citation for distinguished services to music librarianship (1983), the George Peabody Medal for outstanding contributions to music in America from the Peabody Institute of the Johns Hopkins University (1984), the Honorary Gold Record Award for thirty-five years of service to the music industry and publishing from the Recording Industry Association of America (1984), the Silver Medal for distinguished public service to his profession from Boston University (1985), and the Arion Award from the Cambridge Society of Early Music (1991). Schwann served on the boards of the Marlboro School of Music, the Longy School of Music, the Greater Boston Youth Symphony Orchestra, the Cambridge Society for Early Music, the Boston Ballet, and the Handel and Haydn Society, the oldest continuing choral organization in the country.

Tall and distinguished, Schwann was friendly and soft-spoken, and he played several keyboard instruments, including two harpsichords. His two homes were in Lincoln, Massachusetts, and Center Harbor, New Hampshire. As a former church organist, Schwann loved Baroque music; his favorite composer was Johann Sebastian Bach. For decades he and his wife were regular patrons of the Friday afternoon concerts of the Boston Symphony Orchestra. Schwann was friendly with many composers and musicologists, such as Elliott Carter, Aaron Copland, and Nicolas Slominsky. In his leisure time and after retirement, Schwann enjoyed canoeing and mountain climbing. He had conquered most of the 4,000-foot peaks in New Hampshire's White Mountains and was an active supporter of environmental issues and organizations. Schwann died at age eighty-five in Lahey Hitchcock Medical Center in Burlington, Massachusetts. A memorial service was held on 28 June 1998 at Hancock United Church of Christ in Lexington, Massachusetts. Schwann is buried in the Lincoln Cemetery in Lincoln, Massachusetts.

Accuracy and completeness were always the hallmarks of the Schwann catalog. As a trained musicologist, Schwann was careful about facts and a stickler for exactness. As the record industry evolved, the amount of information Schwann encountered grew at a fast pace, but he was able to organize and maintain the catalog with clarity and efficiency through the consistency of formatting, presenting the highest quality to his readers.

★

There is no full-length biography of Schwann. Articles about Schwann include John M. Conly, "Boswell of LP," *Opera News* (20 Nov. 1965); Robert Lasson, "Call Me Schwann—As in Catalogue," *New York Times* (29 Apr. 1973); William Sonzski's piece in the *Boston Globe* (9 May 1979); and Ellen Pfeifer, "Classical Music: Death of Schwann's Founder Ends an Era," *Boston Herald* (19 June 1998). Obituaries are in the *Boston Globe* (10 June 1998),

New York Times (18 June 1998), and *Los Angeles Times* (19 June 1998).

DI SU

SCOTT, George Campbell (*b.* 18 October 1927 in Wise, Virginia; *d.* 22 September 1999 in Westlake Village, California), craggy-faced, raspy-voiced actor whose intense, vigorous performances on stage, screen, and television established him as one of the leading actors of his generation.

Scott was born in an Appalachian coal town to George D. and Helena Scott. Facing the depression, his father moved his family to Detroit, where he worked for the Buick Motor Company. Young Scott's mother died when he was eight, and he was largely raised by his older sister Helen. After graduating from Redford High School in 1945, Scott joined the U.S. Marine Corps, where he spent much of his four years burying the dead at Arlington National Cemetery. Following his discharge, he began to study journalism at the University of Missouri but was soon attracted to acting. He finally left college in 1950, without obtaining a degree.

For the next few years Scott traveled widely, acting in more than 125 parts in many stock productions and, between roles, supporting himself mostly with construction

George C. Scott. AP/WIDE WORLD PHOTOS

work. He married actress Carolyn Hughes in August 1951 (divorced, 1955). He then married singer Patricia Reed, with whom he had two daughters and a son before their marriage ended. Finally, after catching the attention of producer Joseph Papp, he began acting in productions of Papp's New York Shakespeare Festival. His fierce, bold performance in the title role of *Richard III* electrified critics in 1957, as did his role as Jacques in *As You Like It* (1958) and later as Shylock in *The Merchant of Venice* (1962). He also performed regularly in off-Broadway plays, and while appearing in the play *Children of Darkness* he met actress Colleen Dewhurst. Their stormy marriage began in 1960; they divorced in July 1965, remarried in July 1967, and divorced again in February 1972. Their marriages added two more sons to Scott's family, one of whom, Campbell, followed his father into acting.

Scott made his Broadway debut in November 1958 in the play *Comes a Day,* with Judith Anderson. For his role as Tydings Glen, he received his first Tony nomination. He was next seen as a prosecuting judge advocate in *The Andersonville Trial* (1959), for which he received another Tony nomination, and as a Jewish resistance leader in the Warsaw ghetto in *The Wall* (1960). By this time his strong acting style had attracted Hollywood producers, and he was soon appearing in major supporting roles.

In his first film, a Western entitled *The Hanging Tree* (1959), he played a loathsome zealot named Grubb, but it was his second movie, *Anatomy of a Murder* (1959), that established him as an important new character actor. As district attorney Claude Dancer, fiercely prosecuting a murder case, he made a vivid impression that earned him his first Oscar nomination for best supporting actor. In a gesture that would alert everyone to his lifelong distaste for awards, he asked that his nomination be withdrawn, but he was ignored. Buoyed by his success in *Anatomy of a Murder,* Scott became a well-employed film actor, bringing a vivid intensity to every role. As Bert Gordon, the malevolent promoter of pool shark Eddie Felsen (played by Paul Newman) in *The Hustler* (1961), he received another Oscar nomination, which he again rejected with a curt "No, thanks" in a note to the Academy of Motion Picture Arts and Sciences. He was equally effective as the fanatic, belligerent General Buck Turgidson in Stanley Kubrick's corrosive satire, *Dr. Strangelove or: How I Learned to Stop Worrying and Love the Bomb* (1964). His granite face and gravelly voice also dominated the screen as Abraham in *The Bible* (1966), as a smooth-talking con man in the depression years in *Flim-Flam Man* (1967), and as a weary surgeon entranced by oddball Julie Christie in *Petulia* (1968).

Scott's most celebrated film role came in 1970, when he appeared as General George Smith Patton in Franklin J. Schaffner's epic war drama *Patton.* As the World War II commander who loved the sting and excitement of battle and who despised anyone he perceived as cowardly, Scott gave a masterly performance that exposed many facets of this complex man. It won him the Academy Award as the year's best actor. In a move that stunned all, Scott rejected the award, asserting that he would not "march in a meat parade" and denouncing the awards as "offensive, barbarous, and morally corrupt." Despite his opposition, the academy proclaimed him the winner, yet years later Scott continued to insist that he had "never received it, never possessed it." He also won a Golden Globe Award and the New York Film Critics Award for the performance.

Though he was the first actor to reject the award, Scott's dismissal of the Oscars never jeopardized his position as a film star, and for the rest of his career he continued to be active on the screen. He won another Oscar nomination for his performance as a burned-out physician in the scathingly funny dark comedy *The Hospital* (1971). His steely presence and authoritative manner also dominated such films as *They Might Be Giants* (1971), *The Day of the Dolphin* (1973), *Islands in the Stream* (1977), and *Hardcore* (1979). On two occasions he served as both director and star: in *Rage* (1972), as a rancher who turns into a vengeful killer when his ranch is sprayed by nerve gas, and *The Savage Is Loose* (1974), for which he was also producer, and acted as a scientist stranded with his wife and son on a desert island for twenty years.

Over the years Scott managed to make many notable television appearances. As early as October 1959, he could be seen in a Hallmark Hall of Fame production of Maxwell Anderson's play *Winterset*. In 1967 he starred opposite Dewhurst in a television version of Arthur Miller's play *The Crucible*. In 1971 he received an Emmy for his performance in a television adaptation of Miller's play *The Price*; once again he refused the award. In 1976 he won an Emmy nomination for playing the Beast in the Hallmark presentation of *Beauty and the Beast*. He was especially active in television during the 1980s, starring as Fagin in *Oliver Twist* (1982), as Ebenezer Scrooge in a well-staged new version of *A Christmas Carol* (1984), as Benito Mussolini in the miniseries *Mussolini: The Untold Story* (1985), and, once again, as General Patton in *The Last Days of Patton* (1986). He even tried his hand at starring in his own television series, first in 1963 with *East Side, West Side* as a crusading social worker, for which he won yet another Emmy nomination; in 1987 in a situation comedy called *Mr. President*, with Scott as a fictional U.S. chief executive; and finally in 1984 as a police officer in *Traps*. As late as 1997 he won an Emmy for his performance in a new production of Reginald Rose's *Twelve Angry Men*.

Throughout his career Scott returned whenever possible to live theater, which he loved above all else. In 1967 he won strong reviews for his performance in a revival of Lillian Hellman's *The Little Foxes*, and in 1968 he enjoyed a long run playing three disparate roles in Neil Simon's three-part comedy *Plaza Suite*. He excelled as Astrov in a star-filled 1974 revival of *Uncle Vanya*. His performance as Willy Loman in a 1975 revival of Miller's play *Death of a Salesman* was acclaimed by the *New York Times* as "an unforgettable portrait." He also proved to be an excellent comic actor, romping through *Sly Fox* (1976), which transported Ben Johnson's *Volpone* to the Yukon.

In later years Scott could be seen in new productions of *Present Laughter* (1982), *On Borrowed Time* (1991), and *Inherit the Wind* (1996). While appearing in the latter play, he had to leave the cast early in the run when he suffered an aortic aneurysm. Four years later, in 1999, he made his final television appearance, repeating his role of Henry Drummond in a new staging of *Inherit the Wind*, with Jack Lemmon as his antagonist, Matthew Brady.

Apart from recurring health problems, Scott struggled with alcoholism over the years, and his often-belligerent nature sometimes involved him in brawls that broke his nose in several places. In 1996 Julie Wright, a former personal assistant, sued him for sexual harassment. He died in his home of a ruptured abdominal aortic aneurysm and was survived by his fourth wife, actress Trish Van Devere, whom he married on 14 September 1972. He is buried in Westwood Memorial Park in Los Angeles. Scott had a house in Beverly Hills, California, and an estate in Greenwich, Connecticut.

Scott once said: "There are only two kinds of actors: risk actors and safe actors. Safe actors hold back, experiment not, dare not, change nothing and have no artistic courage. I call them walkers. I stagger a little now and then, but I have never been accused of walking." Scott was, indisputably, one of the finest of risk actors, forever challenging himself and his audiences. His towering figure looms large in our collective memory.

★

An interview with Scott can be found in *Theater Week* (14–20 Oct. 1991), and a summary of his life and career appears in *People Weekly* (11 Oct. 1999). Obituaries are in the *New York Times, Chicago Tribune, Washington Post,* and *Variety* (all 24 Sept. 1999).

TED SENNETT

SEABORG, Glenn Theodore (*b.* 19 April 1912 in Ishpeming, Michigan; *d.* 25 February 1999 in Lafayette, California), Nobel Prize–winning nuclear chemist and educator who led the scientific team that created plutonium, the fissionable element in the atomic bomb that destroyed Nagasaki on 9 August 1945.

Seaborg was one of two children of Herman Theodore Seaborg, a machinist, and Selma Olivia Erickson, a home-

Glenn T. Seaborg. PRINTS AND PHOTOGRAPHS DIVISION, LIBRARY OF CONGRESS

maker. His father was the son of Swedish immigrants, and his mother came to the United States from Sweden in 1904 at age seventeen. Seaborg's parents were fluent in Swedish, and Seaborg learned this language at home before he learned English. He identified proudly with his Swedish heritage. Seaborg attended the public schools in Ishpeming until age ten. His father was a skilled machinist and steadily employed, but his mother wanted more opportunities so the family moved to Home Gardens, California, near Los Angeles (now a part of South Gate). Seaborg's father never again secured permanent employment as a machinist, and the family resources declined. In 1923 the Victoria Avenue Grammar School was established in Home Gardens. An excellent student, Seaborg skipped several grades at Victoria and obtained an eighth-grade diploma in 1925.

Seaborg was required to travel to the Watts district to attend David Atarr Jordan High School. He studied chemistry and physics and graduated as valedictorian in June 1929. The following summer he worked as a junior chemist at the Firestone Tire and Rubber Company's factory in South Gate and earned enough money to enroll at the University of California, Los Angeles (UCLA). He selected chemistry as his college major and also studied physics. Seaborg worked as a laboratory assistant in chemistry until

his graduation from UCLA with an A.B. degree in chemistry in 1934.

Seaborg was accepted for graduate study at the University of California, Berkeley, in August 1934. He secured a teaching assistantship in freshman chemistry and studied nuclear chemistry with Willard F. Libby, the Nobel Prize–winning discoverer of radioactive carbon dating. Seaborg also joined the Physics Journal Club, supervised by another Nobel Prize winner, Ernest Orlando Lawrence, who had built the first cyclotron. Seaborg's classmates included such future notable scientists as J. Robert Oppenheimer, who became the scientific director of the American atomic bomb project (1941–1945), and Edwin Mattison McMillan, who later shared the Nobel Prize with Seaborg. Seaborg completed his dissertation in inelastic neutron scattering and was granted a Ph.D. in 1937.

That summer Seaborg became a personal research assistant to the dean of Berkeley's College of Chemistry, Gilbert Newton Lewis. At the invitation of the physicist John Jacob ("Jack") Livingood, Seaborg collaborated for five years (beginning in 1936) in producing and chemically identifying radioactive isotopes using the most advanced twenty-seven-inch Berkeley cyclotron. Among the radioisotopes discovered by Seaborg, Livingood, and other members of the nuclear science staff were 53 iodine-131, 26 iron-59, and 27 cobalt-60. (For clarity, the atomic number has been placed before the designated element name. It is the number of protons in the element's atomic nucleus. A different isotope for each element is then defined by the difference in the atomic weight number 131 which is the number of protons plus neutrons in the nucleus. Thus 53 iodine-131 has 53 protons in the nucleus like all iodine isotopes and the particular radioactive iodine isotope cited has 131 minus 53 or 78 neutrons in the nucleus.) In collaboration with another investigator, Emilio Segrè (who was awarded the 1959 Nobel Prize in physics), Seaborg discovered 43 technetium-99m, which was to become important as a tracer to monitor a wide variety of physiological functions in the diagnosis of medical conditions.

This early work was preparation for the decisive part of Seaborg's scientific career—the discovery of transuranium elements. The heaviest element found in nature is uranium, a combination of two long-lived isotopes. Most abundant is 92 uranium-238; the second is the fissionable isotope 92 uranium-235. In 1934 a group led by Enrico Fermi at the University of Rome in Italy bombarded a natural uranium target with neutrons—fundamental nuclear particles discovered only two years earlier. Fermi thought that the resulting products he had discovered were transuranium elements. The evidence was sufficiently persuasive to his scientific peers that he received the Nobel Prize in physics in 1938 in part for this apparent discovery. In 1939, however, research in Germany, conducted by Otto

Hahn, Lise Meitner, and Fritz Strassman, showed conclusively that Fermi had observed not transuranium elements but fission products—lighter elements than uranium that resulted from the splitting, or "fission," of the uranium nucleus. Seaborg heard about the discovery at a physics department seminar in January 1939.

In 1940 Seaborg's more senior colleagues, McMillan and Philip Hauge Abelson, identified the first transuranium element by bombarding natural uranium with neutrons from the new 60-inch cyclotron at Berkeley. They named this element 93 neptunium-239. McMillan started a search for the next transuranium element, but in the fall of 1940 he left Berkeley to join the Radiation Laboratory at the Massachusetts Institute of Technology in Cambridge. Seaborg received McMillan's permission to continue this work; with the assistance of a graduate student, Arthur C. Wahl, and a fellow instructor in chemistry, Joseph W. Kennedy, he discovered in February 1941 what was to become the most important transuranium element, 94-plutonium. Identification of the element was made 23 February 1941 in room 307 of Gilman Hall in Berkeley. In 1966 the room was designated as a National Historic Landmark. The isotope first discovered was 94 plutonium-238. On 28 March 1941, the team led by Seaborg and Segrè produced the first sample of the fissionable plutonium isotope, 94 plutonium-239. This isotope was to be incorporated into the first atomic bomb test ("Trinity") at Los Alamos, New Mexico, on 16 July 1945, and on 9 August 1945 as the nuclear weapon used against Nagasaki, Japan.

To explore how the kilogram quantities of 94 plutonium-239 required for weapons could be achieved, Seaborg was granted a leave of absence from Berkeley to direct the basic research with the Manhattan Project at the University of Chicago in 1942. Seaborg and his colleagues synthesized and identified the next two transuranium elements, 95 americium and 96 curium. Later in 1944, Seaborg evolved the method for precisely positioning the transuranium elements in the classic periodic table, furnishing a key to finding other elements. In May 1946 Seaborg returned to Berkeley as full professor. Seaborg and his associates at Los Alamos and Argonne National Laboratory in Illinois continued their investigations and were successful in producing and identifying seven more elements, including the only element named after a living person, 106 seaborgium. Seaborg's achievements in both the experimental and theoretical aspects of the chemistry of transuranium elements earned him the Nobel Prize in chemistry in 1951.

Although Seaborg is best known for his scientific work, he had an exceptional career as a university administrator and as a high-level federal executive. He became chancellor of the University of California in 1958. During his stewardship between 1958 and 1961, important academic initiatives were undertaken, including the development of the Space Sciences Laboratory, the College of Environmental Design, and new research institutes. Seaborg also established the Townsend Center of the Humanities.

President Harry S. Truman appointed Seaborg to the first General Advisory Committee (GAC) for the U.S. Atomic Energy Commission (AEC). He served as a member of the AEC from January 1947 to August 1950. In January 1961 President John F. Kennedy designated Seaborg chairman of the AEC. He held that position for ten years, through the presidential terms of Kennedy and Lyndon B. Johnson and part of the term of Richard M. Nixon. His responsibilities included surveillance of nuclear weapons development, nuclear reactors for electric power plants, fundamental research in physical and biological science, and international cooperation in the peaceful application of nuclear materials.

Seaborg played an important role in helping formulate the 1963 Limited Nuclear Test Ban Treaty between the United States and the Soviet Union. The treaty provided for interdiction of nuclear bomb testing in the atmosphere or under water and was the initial step in management of the nuclear threat to humankind. He remained a decisive voice in advancing a treaty for the nonproliferation of nuclear weapons. Seaborg was not altogether immune from political self-interest. As one of nine members of the AEC's GAC, Seaborg wrote a letter early in October 1949 to Oppenheimer, then chairman of the GAC and director of the Institute for Advanced Study in Princeton, New Jersey. The letter was written in anticipation of a meeting of the GAC later that month (which Seaborg did not attend) and addressed the question of what the GAC should recommend to the AEC regarding the proposed development of the hydrogen bomb. This nuclear weapon could be thousands of times more powerful than atomic bombs. Development of such weapons was endorsed enthusiastically by the AEC commissioner, Lewis Strauss, and by Ernest Lawrence and Edward Teller, colleagues of Seaborg's at Berkeley. Their support for the SUPER, as the weapon was designated, was based on the concern that the Soviet Union, having just succeeded in achieving an atomic bomb explosion on 29 August 1949, would construct such a weapon and gain military superiority over the United States. Resistance to hydrogen bomb development was led by Oppenheimer, who successfully persuaded the majority of GAC members that the hydrogen bomb was superfluous to American military preparedness and would create an arms race. Seaborg wrote a paragraph in support of the hydrogen bomb project.

Oppenheimer conceded almost five years later, in 1954, during the controversial hearings that ended with his secret atomic energy clearance being revoked, that he did not recall reading Seaborg's letter to the other members of the GAC. Many witnesses, including the Nobel Prize winners Fermi, Isador I. Rabi, and Hans Bethe, testified at the hearing, not in support of Oppenheimer's position on the hydrogen bomb but in defense of his loyalty and his security trustworthiness. Seaborg opted not to testify but did have an opportunity to present his position at a meeting in December 1949. He elected not to express his view, saying years later that as the youngest member of the GAC (age thirty-seven) he was reluctant to disagree with the unanimous opinion of his eight older colleagues.

On 6 June 1942 Seaborg married Helen Lucille Griggs, who worked as Ernest Lawrence's secretary; the couple had six children. Seaborg experienced a stroke from a fall in August 1998 while attending a scientific meeting in Boston. He was paralyzed and died from his injuries the following February.

In addition to the Nobel Prize, Seaborg received numerous tributes, including the AEC Enrico Fermi Award (1959), the Franklin Medal of the Franklin Institute (1963), and the Great Swedish Heritage Award (1984). He also was named an Officer of the French Legion of Honor (1973). Fifty colleges and universities awarded him honorary doctorates. Seaborg was one of the nuclear statesmen of the twentieth century. His contributions to the application of nuclear chemistry and physics to medical science and other areas of improving human well-being was matched by his clear recognition of the hazards that required confronting both nuclear weapons testing and the growing nuclear bomb making capability by nation states. Seaborg was active until his death as University Professor of Chemistry at the University of California, Berkeley.

★

Seaborg's autobiography, written with Eric Seaborg, is *Adventures in the Atomic Age: From Watts to Washington* (2001). His findings in physics are discussed in "Transuranium Elements," in *The Encyclopedia of Physics,* 2d ed., ed. Robert M. Besancon (1974). For a personal view of his scientific work, see Ronald L. Kathren, Jerry B. Gough, and Gary T. Benefiel, eds., *The Plutonium Story: The Journals of Professor Glenn T. Seaborg 1939–1946* (1994). Philip M. Stern with Harold P. Green, *The Oppenheimer Case: Security on Trial* (1969), details the Oppenheimer controversy. An obituary is in the *New York Times* (27 Feb. 1999).

LEONARD R. SOLON

SEPKOSKI, J(oseph) John, Jr. (*b.* 26 July 1948 in Presque Isle, Maine; *d.* 1 May 1999 in Chicago, Illinois), paleontologist who documented and quantified patterns of biological diversity in the fossil record; his work with David Raup generated the controversial hypothesis that major extinctions occur in cycles approximately every 26 million years.

Sepkoski was the oldest of five children of Joseph John Sepkoski, Sr., an industrial chemist, and Sally Toyo

Feuchtwanger, a librarian. His interest in paleobiology emerged around age ten, when he started a collection of bones, fossils, and rocks that he retained through adulthood. He received a B.S. degree, magna cum laude, from the University of Notre Dame in 1970, then began studying for a Ph.D. in geological sciences under Stephen Jay Gould at Harvard University. His doctoral research focused on the geology and paleontology of the Black Hills of South Dakota. Sepkoski married Maureen Meter in 1971; they had one child.

In 1973 Gould charged Sepkoski with the tedious task of compiling origination and extinction dates for all fossil marine organisms he could find in the paleontological literature. Sepkoski accepted the assignment and carried it with him for the rest of his working career, which started with an instructorship at the University of Rochester in 1974. He received his Ph.D. from Harvard in 1977 and was soon promoted to assistant professor at the University of Rochester. He joined the Department of Geophysical Sciences at the University of Chicago in 1978. In the same year, Sepkoski published the first of a series of papers in the journal *Paleobiology* that drew on ecological biodiversity theories to derive a mathematical model of long-term taxonomic diversification. This work was the first to reveal that three sequential evolutionary faunas (categories of animals characteristic of specific regions, periods, or environments) had dominated marine ecosystems since the Cambrian period, suggesting that consistent, though incompletely understood, processes have driven large-scale evolutionary patterns.

Sepkoski became a research associate at Chicago's Field Museum of Natural History in 1980 and an associate professor at the University of Chicago in 1982. Also in 1982, the Milwaukee Public Museum published a tabulation of his relentless library work—stratigraphic ranges for approximately 3,500 marine families—as *A Compendium of Fossil Marine Families*. In recognition of his many accomplishments, in 1983 the Paleontological Society awarded Sepkoski the annual Charles Schuchert Award for outstanding young paleontologist.

Though Sepkoski's compendium was created in an attempt to understand biotic diversification, it also yielded striking insights into the nature of extinction. In collaboration with David Raup, Sepkoski showed that the past 600 million years have been characterized by intervals of low extinction risk punctuated by catastrophic extinction levels. Raup and Sepkoski also found that intervals between extinction events over the past 250 million years have been remarkably regular, with major extinctions occurring approximately every 26 million years. They suggested that periodic extraterrestrial phenomena might drive these extinction cycles. This controversial hypothesis contributed to newly emerging ideas like the nemesis theory, which envisions a companion star to the Sun with an orbit that generates comet storms at regular intervals; these storms may be related to catastrophic extinctions like the one that killed the dinosaurs.

Sepkoski coedited *Paleobiology* from 1983 to 1986 and was on the journal's editorial board from 1987 to 1989. In 1986 he advanced to the rank of professor at the University of Chicago and was a visiting professor at California Institute of Technology. In 1987 he was divorced from Maureen Meter. He lectured at the Polish Academy of Sciences and was a senior fellow at the University of California at Los Angles in 1988, and he was a visiting professor at Harvard University from 1990 to 1991. Sepkoski married Brown University paleontologist Christine M. Janis in 1991.

With another decade in the library behind him, in 1992 Sepkoski published a revised and expanded edition of his *A Compendium of Fossil Marine Animal Families,* with entries for about 35,000 fossil genera (a category of biological classification between the family and the species). In 1994 he established the Paleontological Society International Research Program (PalSIRP) to provide small grants for paleontologists from the former Soviet Union and Eastern Europe, where research funds were scarce. He served as president of the Paleontological Society from 1995 to 1996 and was honored in 1997 with the Medal of the University of Helsinki and election to the Polish Academy of Sciences.

During the 1990s Sepkoski continued to investigate the evolution of biodiversity, and he occasionally managed to escape from the library and head into the field, where he studied Cambrian stratigraphy and the effects of ancient burrowing animals on sedimentation patterns. Sepkoski also continued as a dedicated teacher at the University of Chicago, where he was particularly popular as a graduate adviser. At the end of his life, he was collaborating on the construction of an enormous fossil database at the National Center for Ecological Analysis and Synthesis, which was ongoing in 2001. Sepkoski died in his home in Chicago's Hyde Park neighborhood of sudden heart failure related to high blood pressure. His ashes were scattered on the beach of the Warwick, Rhode Island, home Sepkoski had shared with his wife.

Stephen Jay Gould considered his former student "one of the leading lights of the profession." Sepkoski's most tangible legacy is his fossil compendium and his extensive list of publications, which scientists continue to mine for insights into the history, and hopefully the future, of biodiversity. Sepkoski is also remembered for pioneering the rigorously quantitative methodology that drove the so-called Chicago school (to adversarial colleagues, the "Chicago Mafia") of paleontological research. In memory of his generosity in founding the PalSIRP program, the organization's grants were renamed the Sepkoski Grants. The gravity of the accolades heaped upon Sepkoski after his

death, however, belie the quirkier pursuits for which friends and family remembered him. These include his affection for loud punk music, his miniature plastic dinosaurs, and, perhaps most curiously, his collection of memorabilia relating to Elizabeth, the Queen Mother of England. In telling homage to his personality, the site on which Sepkoski's ashes were scattered features a replica of Stonehenge built to the ludicrously small proportions specified in Rob Reiner's film comedy *This Is Spinal Tap* (1984).

★

Sepkoski presents an autobiographical history of his work on the fossil compendium in "What I Did with My Research Career: Or, How Research on Biodiversity Yielded Data on Extinction," in William Glen, ed., *The Mass-Extinction Debates: How Science Works in a Crisis* (1994). Michael Ruse devotes a chapter to Sepkoski's influence on evolutionary biology in *Mystery of Mysteries: Is Evolution a Social Construction?* (1999). A tribute by David Raup in *Paleobiology* 25 (1999) provides a list of Sepkoski's scientific publications, including several that were in the works at the time of his death. An obituary is in the *New York Times* (6 May 1999).

CHRISTINE A. ANDREWS

SHABAZZ, Betty Jean (*b.* 28 May 1936 in Detroit, Michigan; *d.* 23 June 1997 in New York City), educator and civil rights advocate who devoted much of her professional life to perpetuating the legacy of her assassinated husband, Malcolm X.

Shabazz was the adopted only child of Lorenzo and Helen Malloy, who together operated a shoe repair business in Detroit. Although little is known about her biological mother, Shabazz chose to keep her name, Sanders, rather than taking that of her adoptive Methodist parents. Shabazz attended Northern High School in Detroit, graduating in 1952. She went on to study elementary education at Tuskegee Institute in Alabama but transferred two years later to the Brooklyn State Hospital of Nursing, where she graduated as a registered nurse (RN) in 1958. Shabazz met Malcolm X (Malik Shabazz) while she was enrolled in nursing school and converted to Islam before marrying him on 14 January 1958. The couple had six daughters.

On 21 February 1965 Shabazz, pregnant with twins, was sitting with her four daughters in the Audubon Ballroom on 165th Street when gunmen shot down her husband as he was speaking on stage. Malcolm X, who was thirty-nine when he was assassinated, had broken with the Nation of Islam after making a pilgrimage to Mecca. A week earlier, the family's home had been firebombed while they were inside. Three men connected with the Nation of Islam were convicted of the assassination, but speculation continued for many years that Louis Farrakhan, who had branded

Betty Shabazz, 1997. AP/WIDE WORLD PHOTOS

Malcolm X a traitor for criticizing Nation of Islam leader Elijah Muhammad, was behind the murder.

Following Malcolm X's death, Shabazz raised her children while simultaneously pursuing advanced college degrees. In the year following her husband's assassination in 1965, Shabazz graduated from Jersey City State College with both B.A. and M.A. degrees in public health administration. She then went on to receive a Ph.D. in education administration from the University of Massachusetts at Amherst in 1975. In January 1976 Shabazz joined the faculty of Medgar Evers College in New York, where she was named director of institutional advancement (1980) and then director of communication and public relations (1984), a position she held until her death in 1997. Unlike Coretta King, who after Dr. Martin Luther King's assassination was immediately embraced by rich and powerful members of both the white and African-American communities, Shabazz received little financial help. Nevertheless, she provided for her family, first from the proceeds of royalties from *The Autobiography of Malcolm X,* published in 1965, and later from fees for consulting work for Malcolm X College in Chicago. Shabazz provided a good education for her children. But in spite of the growing popularity of her late husband among young African Americans, Shabazz appears to have received little recognition from middle- and upper-class African Americans.

In her professional life, Shabazz promoted the legacy of her husband and was a popular speaker at high school and university commencements, African-American history conferences, and college campuses. She also made frequent appearances on television. Shabazz denied that her husband had preached the language of violence when he said that African-American determination should be attained by "any means necessary." "Malcolm X's agenda was human rights and self-determination," she said in a 1992 interview with the *Atlanta Journal and Constitution.* "Free people have a right to self-determination, self-defense. Now a lot of people say, 'Self-defense? Oh, my God, that's violence.' If people think 'by any means necessary' means violence, what that says is that individual is violent and hostile. But not my husband." In addition to maintaining a high profile on matters pertaining to civil rights, Shabazz was also active in speaking on behalf of health and education for disadvantaged children.

Shabbaz, long estranged from the Nation of Islam, charged publicly in 1994 that Farrakhan had played a role in Malcolm X's assassination. "Nobody kept it a secret," she told a television reporter. "It was a badge of honor." In 1995 Shabbaz's daughter Qubilah was accused of hiring an old friend to kill Farrakhan because she believed that he had a role in her father's death and was a threat to her mother. The old friend turned out to be a government informer, and friends and family insisted Qubilah had been framed. In the aftermath of Qubilah's arrest, Shabazz reconciled with Farrakhan, shaking his hand on the stage of Harlem's Apollo Theater as 1,400 people cheered at a fundraiser for Qubilah's defense. Later that year in October, Shabazz spoke at Farrakhan's Million Man March. The charges against Qubilah were eventually dropped after she agreed to complete treatment for chemical dependency and psychiatric problems.

When Qubilah developed drug problems in the early 1990s, Shabazz agreed to help raise her daughter's son Malcolm. In 1997, Malcolm, age twelve, apparently angry over his mother's absence and his long stay with Shabazz at her home in Yonkers, New York, set a fire in the house. Shabazz received severe burns over 80 percent of her body; she remained in critical condition for more than twenty days and never recovered. Shabazz is buried in Ferncliff Cemetery in Hartsdale, New York.

Ironically, at the time of her death, Shabazz had finally attained the respect and praise of African Americans that had been denied her throughout much of her life. Among the reasons for her newfound popularity were a widespread receptiveness to Malcolm X's message that African Americans should establish economic self-sufficiency and rebuild self-esteem; Spike Lee's biographical movie, *Malcolm X* (1992), which concluded with a tribute by Nelson Mandela; and Shabazz's 1995 decision to publicly make her peace with Louis Farrakhan. Shabazz's popularity soared along with her dead husband's legacy as his message entered into the mainstream of both African-American and white America.

★

Shabazz is prominently mentioned in *The Autobiography of Malcolm X* (1965). See also Amy Alexander, "Betty Shabazz: Keeping Faith Amid Tragedy," in *Fifty Black Women Who Changed America* (1999); and Betty Shabazz, *Gifts of Speech: Remembering Malcolm X* (1996). Magazine and newspaper articles about Shabazz include Joy Cain, "Dr. Betty Shabazz: Twenty Years After Malcolm X's Death, His Widow Speaks Out," *Essence* (Feb. 1985); and Herb Boyd, "Dr. Betty Shabazz Expresses Views on Spike Lee's Film About Her Husband," *Amsterdam News* (17 Aug. 1991). An obituary is in the *New York Times* (24 June 1997).

JACK R. FISCHEL

SHANKER, Albert (*b.* 14 September 1928 in New York City; *d.* 22 February 1997 in New York City), "educational statesman" and president of the American Federation of Teachers who transformed the union into a powerful defender of the public school system.

Albert Shanker was born into a family of Russian immigrants on New York's Lower East Side. His parents, Morris and Mamie Shanker, were ardent socialists and trade unionists. His father, a newspaper deliveryman, worked so many hours that he was rarely at home; his mother, a garment worker and active member of the Amalgamated Clothing Workers Union (now part of UNITE), also

worked long hours. The effects of their grueling working conditions were not lost on their son.

Shanker's family moved to an Irish-Catholic neighborhood in the borough of Queens, where the "radio priest," Father Coughlin, and his anti-Semitic preaching were popular. Shanker was continuously bullied. "At the age of twelve," he recalled, "I was six foot three and 110 pounds. I was Jewish and living in an Irish-Catholic neighborhood, so everybody took turns beating up the biggest kid." He turned to books and his studies and excelled as a student. Shanker's skills as an organizer and leader found early expression in the Boy Scouts. When his scout leader was drafted during World War II, Shanker took charge of his troop and increased its membership.

Shanker attended Stuyvesant High School, one of the most academically challenging public schools in the United States, and then went to the University of Illinois at Urbana-Champaign. After receiving his B.A. degree in 1949, he began a Ph.D. program in philosophy at Columbia University. In 1952, for lack of funds, he took a leave of absence from his doctoral studies at Columbia and began teaching elementary school for a salary of $38 a week. Shanker never completed his dissertation, nor did he receive a Ph.D. Meanwhile, he left the elementary school to teach at a junior high school in Queens. After first teaching gifted students, he was reassigned to teaching lesser-prepared students as punishment for a run-in with the school principal.

Shanker soon became dismayed with the poor treatment of teachers, their low pay, and the near-dictatorial powers

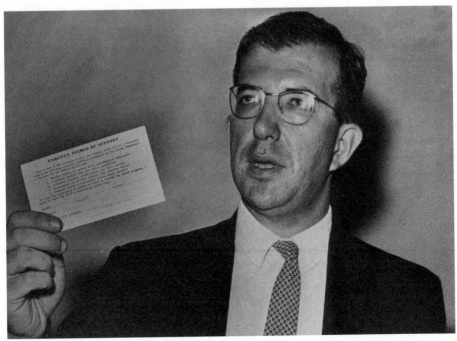

Albert Shanker. PRINTS AND PHOTOGRAPHS DIVISION, LIBRARY OF CONGRESS

of principals, and he looked to the teachers' union for support. But in the 1950s teachers' unions were weak, disunited, and wholly ineffective. In New York City, the issue of communism divided the teachers' union movement into two camps, and there were more than 100 teacher unions. Shanker, a staunch anticommunist, joined the Teachers Guild and became editor of its newspaper. In 1959 Shanker left his position as a junior high math teacher and became a full-time union organizer. Within a short time he had visited 75 percent of the city's schools. In 1960 a merged and unified teachers union, the United Federation of Teachers (UFT), won the right to collectively bargain for all city teachers. Shanker was the UFT's first secretary and was elected its second president in 1964.

By 1972 Shanker also became head of the American Federation of Teachers (AFT), the national teachers' union. He gained control of the "Unity Caucus" in the UFT and the "Progressive Caucus" in the AFT, and through these caucuses controlled key votes on appointments, policy, and activity. Shanker also had tremendous influence within the ranks of unionized labor through his involvement with the Social Democrats-USA. The party's leader, Max Shachtman, was a socialist, but as the cold war developed, Shachtman and his followers within the AFT drifted toward the right as anticommunism become more important to them than socialism. They, including Shanker, voiced concern that labor was becoming too militant and weakening liberal capitalism. Shanker and his followers supported a strong vibrant social democracy, even if it meant supporting conservative Republicans—something he opposed in his early years—and he slowly began to attack the social movements of the time.

In the late 1960s, as the idea of "community empowerment" gained ground, New York mayor John Lindsay, New York governor Nelson Rockefeller, and Ford Foundation president McGeorge Bundy advocated giving minority neighborhoods control over their schools. This put the UFT in an awkward position. Shanker, a longtime and vocal civil rights advocate, found himself opposing the minority community when it challenged union work rules over the hiring, transferring, and firing of teachers. The Ford Foundation funded three experimental school districts, the most famous of which was Ocean-Hill Brownsville in Brooklyn. In an effort to gain control over their schools, the local school districts promptly fired many of the mostly Jewish teaching staff.

By the fall of 1968, with union contract work rules being continuously violated and anti-Semitic incidents on the rise, Shanker called a citywide strike. He quickly found himself and his union targets of his former friends when the New Left supported the community over the union. Once the darling of the left, Shanker became a symbol of the "old" union and undemocratic leadership in the 1970s. In Woody Allen's 1973 movie *Sleeper,* the main character awakes in the year 2173 only be told that the world as he knew it had come to an end when a man named Albert Shanker got hold of a nuclear weapon. Shanker also became a spokesperson for traditional values in education, and he lashed out at what he called educational fads, including ebonics (African-American vernacular English), racial quotas, and race-based standards. Although his ideals were often controversial, Shanker repeatedly demanded that there be no shortcuts to a decent education.

Shanker found himself isolated politically by the end of his life. A longtime Democrat, he watched as the party drifted from what he saw as its core values. He also watched as his union, the AFT, was outpaced by the National Education Association (NEA). In the 1990s, as new leaders took control of the AFL-CIO, Shanker saw his influence within labor diminish. In 1994, however, he was unanimously elected for another two-year term as president of the AFT. Shanker continued to be a voice for better education, proposing strict discipline and standards in schools. In order to defend his ideas, for twenty-five years he kept the AFT's position in the public eye with "Where We Stand," his paid advertising column in the Sunday edition of the *New York Times.* Shanker died at Memorial Sloan-Kettering Cancer Center in New York after a long bout with cancer. He was survived by his second wife and four children.

Shanker transcended his union post to become a leading advocate of teachers and educational reform. He made the American Federation of Teachers an integral part of the transformation of education in the United States. He was also arguably the most famous and influential figure in American education, referred to by President William J. Clinton as "one the greatest educators of the twentieth century."

★

Shanker's life and political legacy are assessed in Dickson A. Mungazi, *Where He Stands: Albert Shanker of the American Federation of Teachers* (1995); Diane Ravitch, "Albert Shanker," *New Leader* 80 (24 Feb. 1997); Lois Weiner, "Albert Shanker's Legacy," *Contemporary Education* 69 (summer 1998); Sara Mosel, "Albert Shanker," *New Republic* 216 (17 Mar. 1997); Arch Puddington, "Albert Shanker," *Commentary* 104 (July 1997); Paul Buhle, "No Flowers," *New Politics* 6, no. 3 (1997); and Marjorie Murphy, *Blackboard Unions* (1990). An obituary is in the *New York Times* (24 Feb. 1997).

RICHARD GREENWALD

SHAW, Robert Lawson (*b.* 30 April 1916 in Red Bluff, California; *d.* 25 January 1999 in New Haven, Connecticut), preeminent choral director who founded the Collegiate Chorale and the Robert Shaw Chorale and who led the Atlanta Symphony; his rehearsal techniques promoting precision in rhythm, diction, and intonation were widely adopted by choral directors across the United States.

Robert Shaw was the eldest son of Shirley Richard Shaw, a Protestant minister, and Nelle Mae Lawson, a singer and choir director. After graduation from high school in Ontario, California, he enrolled at Pomona College in 1934, planning to follow his father into the ministry. This interest in theology was to surface later as he approached the preparation of sacred choral music with religious fervor. He joined the Pomona College Men's Glee Club and soon became the student conductor of the group. When the director, Ralph ("Prof") Lyman, was given a year's sabbatical in 1936, Shaw was hired to direct the club for that season.

In 1937 Fred Waring and the Pennsylvanians visited the Pomona campus to film *Varsity Show,* in which the glee club appeared briefly. When Waring saw Shaw in action, he offered him a job in New York City to recruit and train a new group called the Fred Waring Glee Club. Shaw's enthusiasm, charisma, and instinctive know-how turned his singers into a highly professional organization. In 1939 Waring lent Shaw to Billy Rose to assemble a vocal group to sing at the Aquacade amphitheater at the New York World's Fair. On 15 October of that year Shaw married Maxine Farley, a Macy's employee; they had three children and were divorced in 1973. On 19 December 1973 he married Caroline Saulas Hitz, with whom he had one son.

Shaw's next move, in 1941, led him to the Marble Collegiate Church in New York City, whose pulpit was then occupied by Norman Vincent Peale preaching his message of "positive thinking." Shaw named his sixty-voice choir the Collegiate Chorale, which eventually broke off from the church. This chorus became Shaw's first major choral "laboratory," with which he could experiment with his unique ideas about pitch, rhythm, intonation, and blend. His rehearsal techniques involving "count singing" (in which the singers intone the numbers of the beats instead of the words) to establish impeccable rhythm and gradually raising a pitch by a half-step over sixteen beats to instill perfect intonation are used by many choral conductors today. He developed his conducting style in the service of many kinds of music, stressing major choral masterpieces such as Bach's *Christmas Oratorio* and Beethoven's Ninth Symphony.

In the early 1940s Shaw studied at the Berkshire Music Center (now Tanglewood), where Serge Koussevitzky was conductor of the Boston Symphony Orchestra and Leonard Bernstein and Lukas Foss were fellow students. Aaron Copland was the head of the composition faculty at the time. After collaborating with Shaw in 1942 in preparing Beethoven's Ninth Symphony, the great conductor Arturo Toscanini said that in Robert Shaw "I have at last found the maestro I have been looking for."

In 1945 Shaw commissioned Paul Hindemith to compose *When Lilacs Last in the Dooryard Bloom'd (A Requiem for Those We Love)* for the Collegiate Chorale. The text was derived from Walt Whitman, commemorating the death of Abraham Lincoln. Hindemith, who was then teaching at the Yale School of Music, dedicated his work to Franklin Delano Roosevelt and to those who died in World War II. Shaw considered Hindemith the most important composer and music teacher of the twentieth century.

While conducting the Collegiate Chorale, Shaw directed the choral program at the Juilliard School, where Julius Herford became his mentor, providing the knowledge of musicology and music literature that the young conductor still lacked during his rapid, somewhat self-taught rise to celebrity. In 1948 he founded the Robert Shaw Chorale, which became widely known and respected. In 1960 he stepped down from the Collegiate Chorale.

Shaw traveled internationally and made many recordings. One of his most remarkable achievements with the Robert Shaw Chorale was a six-week, thirty-six-concert tour of the United States performing the Bach B Minor Mass. The recording made at the end of this tour (RCA-Victor, 1960) still stands as a landmark in choral perfection.

The manager of the Robert Shaw Chorale was Thomas Pyle; his wife, Alice Parker, became Shaw's collaborator in arranging folksongs and hymns for the Robert Shaw Choral Series, published by the newly created Lawson-Gould Company. (The name of the company was derived from Shaw's middle name and Walter Gould's last name. Gould was Shaw's personal manager and the brother of the composer Morton Gould.) The Shaw-Parker arrangements have become a staple in the repertoire of choruses through-

Robert Shaw, 1983. JOE HOLLOWAY, JR./ASSOCIATED PRESS AP

out the world, and most of them were first recorded by the Robert Shaw Chorale.

In 1952 Shaw returned to California to take on the directorship of the San Diego Symphony, another step in his musical development that would show his abilities as an orchestral conductor. In the late 1950s George Szell invited Shaw to serve as associate conductor and director of choruses of the distinguished Cleveland Symphony Orchestra. The Cleveland Orchestra Chorus quickly became "the first chorus of the land," as one critic put it. He also continued traveling with the Robert Shaw Chorale until 1965.

From Cleveland, Shaw moved in 1967 to take over the Atlanta Symphony and form another extraordinary chorus, with which he made many other recordings for the Telarc label. He held this, his final post, until 1988. During this period Shaw engaged in many choral workshops and was guest conductor of college choruses throughout the country. He also initiated a yearly Carnegie Hall workshop leading to performances with experienced singers and teachers from all over the world. In the summers he conducted the Robert Shaw Festival Chorus at various locations in southern France and made yearly recordings in cathedrals throughout the region.

His wife, Caroline, died in 1995, and his son Tom came as a freshman to Yale College, from which he graduated in 1999. Shaw was visiting his son and watching a play Tom was directing when he suffered a fatal stroke. He died at the Yale–New Haven Hospital and is buried in Westview Cemetery in Atlanta. Yale had played an important part in Shaw's life. He conducted the Yale Glee Club with orchestra on five occasions: in Charles Ives's Second Symphony, in Hindemith's *When Lilacs Last in the Dooryard Bloom'd* twice, in the Berlioz Requiem, and in the Britten *War Requiem.* He received an honorary Doctor of Music degree from Yale at commencement one year before he died.

Among Shaw's many awards were sixteen Grammys, twenty-five honorary degrees, a Guggenheim fellowship, the 1992 National Medal of Arts, and the Kennedy Center Medal. His distinguished career made him a mentor to choral conductors everywhere, and the legend of his enormous contributions lives on through them. Shaw's greatest gift was in bringing to choral music the same professional standards of excellence that had previously been associated only with orchestral performance.

Shaw's devotion to the spiritual values of music can be observed in the following paragraph from the book *Dear People* by Joseph Mussulman. It describes rehearsals of Beethoven's *Missa Solemnis,* during which Shaw said:

> I am amazed, again and again, how the mastery of successive minute technical details releases floods of spiritual understanding. At every instance wherein we achieve this ex-

act balance, or that unequivocal intonation, or, yea, rhythmic meshing, or an absolute precision of enunciation or an unassailable property of vocal color the miracle happens—the Flesh is made Word—and dwells among us. We put in muscle and blood and brains and breath—and out comes a holy spirit.

★

Shaw's letters and other papers are to be deposited in the Yale University Library. Joseph A. Mussulman, *Dear People . . . Robert Shaw: A Biography* (1979), offers a treatment of his life and career. At least one other biography is in preparation at this writing. An obituary is in the *New York Times* (26 Jan. 1999).

FENNO HEATH

SHEPARD, Alan Bartlett, Jr. (*b.* 18 November 1923 in East Derry, New Hampshire; *d.* 21 July 1998 in Monterey, California), astronaut in the Mercury program who was the first American in space and the fifth man to walk on the Moon.

Shepard was the son of Alan Bartlett Shepard, a retired army colonel and Renza Emerson, a homemaker. He grew up on a farm, was educated in the East Derry public schools, and then spent a year at the Admiral Farragut Academy in New Jersey preparing for entrance to the

Alan B. Shepard, Jr. ARCHIVE PHOTOS, INC.

United States Naval Academy at Annapolis, Maryland. Shepard received a B.S. degree from the Naval Academy in 1944, graduating 462nd out of a class of 913. He married Louise Brewer on 3 March 1945, and they had two children.

During World War II, Shepard served on a destroyer in the Pacific and then underwent naval flight training at Corpus Christi, Texas, and Pensacola, Florida, receiving his certification as a naval aviator in 1947, with tours of duty on aircraft carriers in the Mediterranean. In 1950 Shepard was selected for the Navy Test Pilot School at Patuxent River, Maryland. He then served in the Pacific as operations officer of a night fighter unit on the carrier USS *Oriskany*. Returning to Patuxent River, he flight-tested the F3H Demon, F8U Crusader, the F4D Skyray, the F11F Tigercat, and the F5D Skylancer, finally serving as an instructor in the test pilot school. After graduating from the Naval War College in Newport, Rhode Island, in 1958, he joined the staff of the commander in chief of the Atlantic fleet.

In 1959 Shepard was named one of the original seven Mercury astronauts, along with John Glenn, Scott Carpenter, L. Gordon Cooper, Walter Schirra, Deke Slayton, and Gus Grissom. The country hailed them as national heroes—and regarded them with almost morbid fascination, since, considering the explosive results of America's early attempts at rocketry, theirs seemed to be a suicide mission.

On 5 May 1961 Shepard lay crammed into a tiny Mercury space capsule, Freedom 7, on top of a Redstone rocket at Cape Canaveral, Florida. Twenty-three days earlier Soviet cosmonaut Yuri Gagarin had become the first human being in space after a one-orbit flight. Ever since 4 October 1957, when the Soviet Union had shot Sputnik, the first earth satellite, into orbit, the United States space program had endured one humiliating failure after another in a race that had become a symbol of the competition—political, military, and scientific—between the two cold war superpowers. Shepard's flight had been delayed from 2 May, and now delay was piling on delay, four hours in all, until Shepard, his space suit soaked with urine, sensing that indecision was setting in among the technicians at launch control, barked over his intercom, "I'm cooler than you are. Why don't you fix your little problem, and light this candle." The technicians quickly decided that the fuel pressure that had concerned them was within tolerances, and resumed the countdown. Just before ignition, Shepard said to himself, "Don't screw up, Shepard. Don't screw up. Your ass is hauling what's left of your country's man-in-space program."

Fifteen minutes later, and 302 miles down the Atlantic Missile Range, after a flight 115 miles above the earth, Shepard splashed down, and America had sent its first man into space. Three weeks later, elated by the success of Shepard's Mercury mission, President John F. Kennedy went before Congress to say, "I believe this nation should commit itself to achieving the goal, before the decade is out, of landing a man on the Moon and returning him safely to the Earth." And on 19 July 1969 Neil Armstrong did achieve that goal. Before the end of the Apollo program in 1972, twelve Americans had set foot on the Moon, and Shepard, the first American in space, became one of them when he stepped out of Apollo 14 on 5 February 1971, the only one of the original seven Mercury astronauts to make a moon landing. At the end of Shepard's final moon walk, his scientific and exploration tasks completed, he fitted together a six-iron he had smuggled aboard, and smacked two golf balls "for miles and miles," although more specific calculations figured that one traveled 40 yards, the other 200.

After Shepard's Mercury flight (he was presented with the Distinguished Service Medal by President Kennedy and honored with a parade in Washington, D.C., seen by a quarter of a million people), he was eager to return to space. But just after his selection as commander of the first Gemini mission (Mercury's successor), he was grounded because of a disorder of the inner ear called Meuniere's syndrome, which cost him his medical clearance as a pilot and an astronaut. He remembered that as the worst moment of his life: "I couldn't fly solo. Can you imagine the world's greatest test pilot has to have some young guy in the back flying along with you? I mean, talk about embarrassing situations!"

From 1965 to 1974 Shepard served as head of the astronaut office in the Flight Crew Operations Directorate led by fellow Mercury astronaut Deke Slayton, who had lost *his* medical clearance due to a heart murmur. In the summer of 1968 Shepard underwent experimental surgery to correct his ear problem, and by the next spring regained his medical clearance. He quickly asserted his seniority in the crew rotation and was appointed by Slayton to command Apollo 13, with crewmates Stuart A. Roosa as pilot of the command module (*Kitty Hawk*) and Edgar D. Mitchell as pilot of the lunar module (*Antares*). Their assignment to Apollo 13 was overruled by NASA, which required the crew to undergo more training because of Shepard's long layoff. They were bumped to Apollo 14, while Apollo 13 endured a harrowing trip around the Moon and returned to Earth without achieving a lunar landing.

Shepard's Apollo 14 mission launched from Cape Kennedy, Florida, on 31 January 1971. The command module's escape rocket alone was more powerful than the Redstone that had launched Shepard on his Mercury flight; the Saturn rocket that powered Apollo was (and still is) the single most powerful engine ever built. The flight to the Moon was marked by several potentially serious problems, all overcome by the crew and mission control. But after Shepard and Mitchell had separated from *Kitty Hawk* and begun their descent to the lunar surface, the landing radar malfunctioned. It did not respond properly until *Antares* was uncomfortably close to the mandatory abort altitude of 10,000 feet. When they had landed (on 5 February, within fifty meters of the target touchdown area in the Fra Mauro highlands), Mitchell asked Shepard whether he would have piloted the craft to the surface manually if the radar had not come back to life. Shepard replied, "You'll never know." He afterward confessed, "I would have gone down. . . . I'd come that far. It was my job to land. And I'd done hundreds of these things. I knew that if I could see the surface, man, I could get down, maybe not exactly where we were supposed to, but I could get down close to it." As he explained, "As a Navy pilot, as a carrier pilot . . . believe me, it's a lot harder to land a jet on an aircraft carrier than it is to land a LM on the Moon. That's a piece of cake, that Moon deal!"

Five hours after touchdown, Shepard stepped out onto the lunar surface. Speaking for himself and for the rest of the human race, he said, "It's been a long way, but we're here." He and Mitchell raised an American flag, set up apparatus for scientific experiments, and readied their modularized equipment transporter for the next day's journey of exploration. After a night of fitful sleep, Shepard and Mitchell emerged again. Their mission was to explore the region between their spaceship and the rim of the Cone crater, gathering rock samples along the way, with special emphasis on impact debris from the crater rim. Their journey lasted four hours and twenty minutes and covered three kilometers. They returned with forty-five kilograms of samples. Their experience taught NASA several valuable lessons: the difficulty of navigating from maps and photos on the deceptive surface of the Moon (Shepard and Mitchell were not able to locate the rim of the crater, and turned back some sixty-five feet from their objective), and the need for thorough scientific, especially geological, training of the astronauts to realize the full potential of lunar exploration, since Shepard and Mitchell's documentation of the samples' original locations was not sufficient for scientists on Earth to make a complete analysis of the samples.

After Shepard's golf shot heard round the world, *Antares* lifted off on 6 February after thirty-three hours on the Moon. Shepard and Mitchell docked with *Kitty Hawk,* transferred into it, separated, and then rode *Kitty Hawk* back to a Pacific Ocean splashdown on 9 February, about one kilometer from their target.

After his Apollo 14 flight Shepard returned to his duties as chief of the astronaut office. He retired on 1 August 1974 with the rank of rear admiral. He became chairman of the Marathon Construction Corporation in Houston, and later started his own company, Seven Fourteen Enterprises, named after Freedom 7 and Apollo 14. He died at age seventy-four in Monterey after a long battle with leukemia. His body was cremated and his ashes scattered in the Pacific Ocean, along with those of his wife, Louise, who died in August 1998.

Shepard stands with Wilbur and Orville Wright, Charles Lindbergh, Chuck Yeager, Yuri Gagarin, John Glenn, and Neil Armstrong as one the great pilots and explorers in aviation history. He was the very personification of what the writer Tom Wolfe, in his saga of the Mercury astronauts, called the "right stuff"—the highest level of technical expertise, natural talent for flying, uncompromising attention to procedural detail, absolute self-confidence, relentless competitiveness, and, above all, the ability to rationally, quickly, and creatively solve complex, unprecedented problems in the face of extreme danger. When the Mercury program chose Shepard to make the first American space flight, it signaled to the aviation world that he had emerged as the very best of the great pilots of his era, which was, moreover, the greatest age in the history of stick-and-rudder flying. "That was competition at its best," he recalled. "Not because of the fame or the recognition that went with it, but because of the fact that America's best pilots went through this selection process down to seven guys, and of those seven, I was the one to go. That will always be the most satisfying thing to me."

For his accomplishments, Shepard received nearly every award given in the field of aerospace, including the Langley Medal and the Collier Trophy. He and the other Mercury astronauts (and Betty Grissom, the widow of Gus Grissom) founded the Mercury Seven Foundation, later the Astronaut Scholarship Foundation, which raises money for science and engineering scholarships for college students. Shepard was also the founder of the Astronaut Hall of Fame, a museum in Titusville, Florida. When Mercury astronaut Wally Schirra unveiled the statue of Shepard at the hall, he testified that it captured Shepard perfectly: "It's got a lot of brass."

★

For information about Shepard's life and career, see Tom Wolfe, *The Right Stuff* (1979); for information on the history of the American manned space flight program, see Alan Shepard and Deke Slayton, *Moon Shot: The Inside Story of America's Race to the Moon* (1994); NASA Manned Spacecraft Center, *Apollo 14 Preliminary Science Report,* NASA SP272 (1971); and Andrew Chaikin, *A Man on the Moon* (1994). Obituaries are in the *Los Angeles Times* and *Washington Post* (both 23 July 1998).

RICHARD GID POWERS

SHERWOOD, Roberta (*b.* 1 July 1913 in St. Louis, Missouri; *d.* 5 July 1999 in Sherman Oaks, California), torch singer and entertainer who performed with Mickey Rooney, Don Rickles, Joey Bishop, and Milton Berle, proving that a star can be born after the age of forty.

The daughters of Robert Sherwood, the director of an old-time minstrel show, and Marjorie Ashley Sherwood, a performer, Sherwood and her younger sister Anne were brought up by their father. Her mother left the family when Sherwood was seven and her sister was three, and the children traveled with their father to county and state fairs all over the country. Sherwood did not see her mother again until she was fourteen.

Although Sherwood later told the *Fort Lauderdale News & Sun-Sentinel* (8 September 1974) that she had been a vaudeville performer since the age of four, it was in her early teens that she and Anne left school and began to work in earnest at fairs as a song and dance team. One fall, they left their father at his touring minstrel show's winter quarters in Alabama to take a job at the Princess Theater in Youngstown, Ohio. When they arrived they discovered they had been booked into a burlesque show, and Sherwood made her sister stay in the dressing room during the strip act. Other jobs followed, and the sisters honed their routine to become a vaudeville and nightclub act.

The Sherwood sisters appeared in a 1932 revue under the direction of Don Lanning at Miami's Silver Slipper nightclub. Lanning, a Broadway veteran who had played musical comedy juvenile roles for the Shubert Brothers in the early 1920s, was eighteen years older than Sherwood. He took her in hand and taught her the stagecraft she used throughout her career. Sherwood sang in movie theater stage shows and in small nightclubs for the next seven years, but the stardom everyone predicted never came. In an interview for *Life* magazine (15 October 1956), Sherwood remarked, "The closest I got to Broadway was Newark." Lanning opened a restaurant and lounge bar on Biscayne Boulevard in Miami and persuaded Sherwood to quit show business and marry him. They married in 1938 and had three sons. For the next fifteen years Sherwood performed at the lounge bar; following the birth of each son, she took breaks between songs to breast-feed. She remembered her childhood and did not want to put career before family.

Lanning lost the lease on his restaurant in 1949 and took over the lounge bar concession at the Robert Richter Hotel on Miami Beach, with Sherwood as the singer. When Lanning had surgery for lung cancer in 1953, the owners of the hotel assumed the operation of the concession, leaving both husband and wife jobless. With Lanning dying of cancer, Sherwood had to find work. All she knew was singing, but trying to resurrect a singing career at age forty-one was difficult. She went from one audition to another, but no one wanted her. Desperate, Sherwood took jobs at local functions for $15 or $25 a night. One night in September 1955, returning home from the Miami Civic Entertainment Center where she had done a show for $15, Sherwood stopped at Murray Franklin's small, late-hour lounge next

Roberta Sherwood holding the Dinah Award for outstanding artistry in the field of nightclub entertaining, 7 March 1957. ASSOCIATED PRESS/ SIMMONS ASSOCIATES

to Miami Beach's Roney Plaza to ask for work. Franklin called her several days later and asked her to audition. The lounge pianist Ernie DeLorenzo balked at accompanying Sherwood for the audition; he had never played for a singer before, and here was some housewife asking him to play "It Had To Be You" in the key of C.

After watching Sherwood perform, Franklin offered her a job at $150 a week. To Sherwood, it seemed like a fortune. For the first four months, she sang five times a night. During the day, she was a homemaker and caretaker of her sick husband; at night she worked as a torch singer. In January "The Names" started to stop into Franklin's place. Comedian Red Buttons liked Sherwood and brought in columnist Walter Winchell. After Winchell heard her, he praised her in his column and on his radio broadcasts, telling millions of Americans to get down to Miami to hear Sherwood, that "they owed it to themselves." Soon everyone rushed to see this singer, an older woman wearing a cardigan and glasses banging on a battered cymbal while she sang. The sweater was a defense against the air conditioning in the lounge. And glasses were a necessity since Sherwood made her entrance from the audience, greeting people as she progressed toward the microphone. In a 1956 interview in *Life* magazine, Sherwood explained that she wore glasses because she "didn't want to walk into somebody's shrimp cocktail." Because Franklin did not have a drummer, the cymbal provided the strong beat Sherwood needed for the swinging rhythm of her music. The cymbal, glasses, and sweater became part of her act. Sherwood's style was described in the same 1956 *Life* magazine interview as "flashy, richly sentimental, . . . and as unpretentious as her $49.50 dress." Sherwood's repertory included songs such as "You Don't Have to Be a Baby to Cry," "Gee, But I Hate to Go Home Alone," and "Love Is a Many-Splendored Thing," sung in her warm, husky voice.

Other offers came in. The Eden Roc Hotel in Miami Beach hired Sherwood for $1,700 a week to do two shows a night before her late stint at Franklin's. Decca signed her to do an album, *Introducing Roberta Sherwood* (1956). Jackie Gleason put her on his *Stage Show* television revue with the Dorsey Brothers (1956). Sherwood was booked into the Copacabana in New York City in July 1956, and in August performed for four weeks, at $2,500 a week, at the New Frontier Hotel in Las Vegas with Mickey Rooney. She also worked at the Riverside in Reno, and the Mocambo in Hollywood. When Sherwood opened at the Mocambo in October 1956, she received, according to Louella Parsons, "as great a reception as I have ever seen anyone get in this town." Sherwood was now paid $5,000 a week.

Sherwood became a favorite guest on television shows such as *The Ed Sullivan Show, The Steve Allen Show, The Garry Moore Show,* and *The Joey Bishop Show,* and also appeared on *Person to Person* with Edward R. Murrow. Her appearance in April 1958 with Tennessee Ernie Ford on his television show has been described as a television classic. Sherwood recorded nine albums for Decca. Her dozens of hit recordings included "You're Nobody 'Til Somebody Loves You" and "Up a Lazy River." After her husband's death in 1960, Sherwood moved the family to California, where she played the role of Mrs. Livingston in the film *The Courtship of Eddie's Father* (1963). In the 1980s she joined Anna Maria Alberghetti, Cyd Charisse, and others to tour the country in a variety show. Sherwood continued singing into her late seventies. She won the Film Welfare League's Lifetime Achievement Award in 1985.

Sherwood died of complications of Alzheimer's disease at her home and is buried at Forest Lawn Cemetery in Hollywood Hills, California.

Although Sherwood had been in show business all her life, she never achieved fame as a singer until she was past the age of forty. Forced to sing for her family's supper, the matronly Sherwood, clad in her off-the-rack dresses, finally became a star.

★

Periodical articles about Sherwood include Joe McCarthy, "Matron with a Torch Song," *Life* (15 Oct. 1956); "Middle-Aged Siren," *Time* (18 Mar. 1957); and Joan Brazer, "Granny Sherwood Still Belts 'Em Out," *Fort Lauderdale News and Sun-Sentinel* (8 Sept. 1974). Obituaries are in the *Los Angeles Times* and *New York Times* (both 9 July 1999).

MARCIA B. DINNEEN

SIDNEY, Sylvia (*b.* 8 August 1910 in New York City; *d.* 1 July 1999 in New York City), actress best remembered for her roles as vulnerable, victimized, yet tenacious heroines in movies of the 1930s.

Born Sophia Kosow, Sidney was the daughter of Romanian-born Victor Kosow, a clothing salesman, and Russian-born Rebecca Saperstein. Her parents divorced when she was nine and her mother married Sigmund Sidney, a dentist. As a teenager, Sidney left Washington Irving High School to study acting at the Theatre Guild School in Manhattan. Determined to become an actress, she adopted her stepfather's surname and changed her first name to Sylvia. Talent scouts discovered her at a school production held at a Broadway theater. At age sixteen, she made her Broadway debut in *The Squall* (1926). She continued to win roles in such stage productions as *Crime* (1927), *Gods of the Lightning* (1928), and *Bad Girl* (1930). For a brief period she went to Hollywood, where she ap-

Sylvia Sidney. AP/WIDE WORLD PHOTOS

peared unbilled in the film *Broadway Nights* (1927), and then played a featured role in *Thru Different Eyes* (1929). Hollywood soon took notice of her heart-shaped face, large, expressive eyes, and low, tremulous voice.

While appearing onstage in *Bad Girl,* Sidney impressed the Paramount producer B. P. Schulberg, who offered her a leading role in the 1931 film version of Theodore Dreiser's novel *An American Tragedy.* When the film was postponed, she replaced Clara Bow in the director Rouben Mamoulian's crime drama *City Streets* (1931), where her sensitive performance as a mobster's daughter was duly noted by the critics. When *An American Tragedy* was finally made in 1931, under the direction of Josef von Sternberg, it proved to be a disappointment, although Sidney's performance as Phillips Holmes's ill-fated girlfriend won admiring notices. She also excelled as a city girl caught up in domestic tragedy in King Vidor's adaptation of Elmer Rice's play *Street Scene* (1931) and as a troubled wife in Alfred Hitchcock's *Sabotage* (1936).

Now under contract to Paramount, Sidney was cast in starring roles that often had her playing the victim of deceitful men or a heedless society: *Madame Butterfly* (1932), *Jennie Gerhardt* (1933), *Good Dame* (1934), and *Mary Burns, Fugitive* (1936). Occasionally, she was given the chance to play comedy, such as in *Thirty Day Princess* (1934) and *Accent on Youth* (1935). But on the whole, the studio decreed (to Sidney's dismay) that her plaintive demeanor was not conducive to laughter. Her fragile beauty also lent itself well to Technicolor in her role as a Kentucky backwoods girl in *The Trail of the Lonesome Pine* (1936), the first three-color-process movie to be filmed outdoors.

It was away from the Paramount lot, however, that Sidney starred in her best films. In 1936, on loan to Metro-Goldwyn-Mayer (MGM), she appeared opposite Spencer Tracy in *Fury,* a powerful indictment of mob violence, under the direction of the authoritarian Fritz Lang. Sidney's close-ups were harrowing as she watched her lover apparently burn to death in his prison cell. Lang also directed her in *You Only Live Once* (1937) as the wife of the wrongly convicted Henry Fonda. She had one of her best roles in a well-made adaptation of Sidney Kingsley's play *Dead End* (1937). Under the direction of William Wyler, she played Trina, the spunky slum girl whose younger brother (Billy Halop) gets into trouble with the law. During this active period of moviemaking, Sidney was married twice, first in October 1935 to the publisher Bennett Cerf, whom she divorced in 1936, and then in 1938 to the actor Luther Adler, whom she divorced in 1947. With Adler, she had a son, who died in 1987 of amyotrophic lateral sclerosis, better known as Lou Gehrig's disease.

Unhappy with her roles as a contractual player, Sidney returned to the Broadway stage in the late 1930s, starring in Ben Hecht's short-lived drama *To Quito and Back*

(1937), and in the Group Theater's production of *The Gentle People* (1939), by Irwin Shaw. She also toured in Bernard Shaw's *Pygmalion* and in Noël Coward's *Tonight at 8:30.* During the 1941–1942 Broadway season, she won good notices as a replacement for Judith Evelyn in Patrick Hamilton's thriller *Angel Street.* Throughout the 1940s Sidney made only a handful of films, but the roles were far removed from her earlier, hapless heroines. She played a Eurasian double agent in *Blood on the Sun* (1945), an idealistic journalist in *The Searching Wind* (1946), and the unsuspecting wife of a killer in *Love from a Stranger* (1947). In 1947 Sidney married her third husband, the publicity agent Carlton Alsop, divorcing him in 1950.

For the rest of her career, Sidney remained busy, alternating between films, the stage, and television. As she grew older, she began to play a variety of character roles in films, ranging from the ill-fated Fantine in a remake of *Les Misérables* (1952), to the sharp-tongued mother of Joanne Woodward in *Summer Wishes, Winter Dreams* (1973), a role for which she won an Academy Award nomination as best supporting actress. She had featured parts in such films as *Damien: Omen II* (1978), *Beetlejuice* (1988), *Used People* (1992), and *Mars Attacks!* (1996). Over the years, she retained her devotion to the theater, acting on Broadway in *Enter Laughing* (1963) and touring in productions of such plays as *Joan of Lorraine, Anne of the Thousand Days,* and *The Madwoman of Chaillot.* She had numerous roles in television dramas, notably as a cancer-ridden patient in *The Shadow Box* (1980) and as the compassionate grandmother of an AIDS victim in *An Early Frost* (1985). She received a Golden Globe Award for the latter performance. In November 1990 she was honored by the film society of New York's Lincoln Center.

In her last years, Sidney was invariably cranky and outspoken in interviews. Asked how she managed to live as long as she had, she replied, with a characteristic cackle, "Cigarettes, vodka, and the will not to move unless I have to." She died of throat cancer at Lenox Hill Hospital in Manhattan.

Despite misgivings about her early roles ("They always had me ironing somebody's shirt"), Sidney left behind indelible images of a waiflike woman, battered but seldom defeated by society's malevolent forces. A dedicated actress for sixty years, she was versatile and aggressively sought work. As she said in an interview, "I'm an actress and I have to work. I wouldn't know what to do with myself if I retired."

★

Apart from her acting, Sidney's main avocation was needlework and her designs were sold as kits. She wrote two popular instruction books, *Sylvia Sidney's Needlepoint Book* (1968) and *The Sylvia Sidney Question-and-Answer Book on Needlepoint* (1975).

There is an informative interview with Sidney by Gregory J. M. Catsos, *Interview* (Nov. 1990). Obituaries are in the *New York Times* (2 July 1999) and *Variety* (12 July 1999).

TED SENNETT

SILVERSTEIN, Shel(don) Allan   (*b*. 25 September 1930 in Chicago, Illinois; *d*. 10 May 1999 in Key West, Florida), cartoonist, songwriter, playwright, and author best known for his poetry for children.

Silverstein was one of two children of Helen Balkany, a homemaker, and Nathan Silverstein, a bakery owner. He grew up in the lower-middle-class Palmer Square neighborhood of Chicago, and graduated from Roosevelt High School. He said that he began to draw when he was twelve or fourteen years old, because "I couldn't play ball, I couldn't dance . . . so I started to draw and to write. . . . I would much rather have been a good baseball player or a hit with the girls." After he was thrown out of the University of Illinois at Chicago, he "really learned to draw" at the Chicago Academy of Fine Arts. He studied English at Roosevelt University in Chicago for three years but never graduated, and later described the experience as a waste of

Shel Silverstein. SHEL SILVERSTEIN

time. Drafted into the U.S. army in 1953, he served as private first class in Japan and Korea until 1955. Silverstein drew satirical cartoons about army life for "Take Ten" in the *Pacific Stars and Stripes,* a military newspaper. Often in trouble for his irreverent cartoons, he described himself as "the worst soldier in the regiment."

In August 1956 Silverstein began drawing cartoons and writing stories and poems for Hugh Hefner's new magazine, *Playboy*. He became friendly with Hefner, even living in the *Playboy* mansions in Chicago and Los Angeles, and he continued to contribute cartoons and stories to *Playboy* until 1998. In 1960 Silverstein's first prose book, *Now Here's My Plan: A Book of Futilities,* was published. In 1961 Silverstein published the cartoon alphabet *Uncle Shelby's ABZ Books: A Primer for Tender Minds,* followed by *A Playboy's Teevee Jeebies* in 1963.

Silverstein wrote his first children's book, *Uncle Shelby's Story of Lafacadio, the Lion Who Shot Back,* in 1963. Silverstein had not intended to become a children's writer, but was "dragged kicking and screaming," he said, by friend Tomi Ungerer to Harper and Row editor Ursula Nordstrom. His next book, *The Giving Tree* (1964), was not successful at first, but after churches began to use the book as a parable, it became a best-seller. Silverstein refused to discuss the lessons that people drew from the story about a little boy who is nurtured by a tree that gives everything to the boy as he grows up. The tree ends up as a stump, happy to have sacrificed all to the boy into his adulthood. In later years, the self-sacrifice of the female tree was criticized by feminists.

Where the Sidewalk Ends, dedicated to Ursula Nordstrom, is a book of irreverent and silly poems published in 1974 and selected as a *New York Times* Outstanding Book that year. It has been translated into over twenty languages, and in 1984 Silverstein won a Grammy Award for a recorded album of the book. In 1981 his next book of poetry, *A Light in the Attic,* was published. It stayed on the bestseller list for 181 weeks, including several weeks as number one on the adult nonfiction list, and received a *School Library Journal* Best Books Award. In 1982 *The Missing Piece Meets the Big O* received the International Reading Association's Children's Choice Award. Silverstein's final book of poetry, *Falling Up,* was published to positive reviews in 1996.

Silverstein was also a lyricist and playwright. He appeared in the 1971 film *Who Is Harry Kellerman and Why Is He Saying Those Terrible Things About Me?,* for which he wrote the soundtrack. He penned songs such as "A Boy Named Sue," made famous by Johnny Cash in 1969; "The Unicorn," recorded by the Irish Rovers; and Dr. Hook's "Cover of the Rolling Stone." Silverstein's songs were recorded by Mel Tillis, Marianne Faithful, Kris Kristofferson, Judy Collins, Loretta Lynn, Burl Ives, and many more. He also recorded over seven albums himself, the best known being the 1980 country-western album *The Great Conch Train Robbery.* "I'm Checking Out," from the film *Postcards from the Edge,* was nominated for both an Academy Award and a Golden Globe for best original song in 1990.

In the early 1980s Silverstein turned to playwriting with *The Lady or the Tiger Show* (1981) and *Remember Crazy Zelda?* (1984), both produced in New York City. In 1988 Silverstein collaborated with playwright David Mamet on the film *Things Change.* His one-act play *The Devil and Billy Markham* ran at Lincoln Center in New York in 1989 to generally positive reviews.

The five-foot, ten-inch Silverstein was a burly figure, with a bald head, full beard, and raspy voice. He practiced yoga and walked for excercise. Silverstein was a private person, having declared in 1975 that he would no longer give interviews, and telling his publicist not to give out any biographical information. In a 1973 interview Silverstein mentioned a two-year-old daughter (who died in 1982, according to some sources), and said he had never been married. At the time of his death, obituary notices also mentioned a fifteen-year-old son, Matthew.

Silverstein died from a heart attack at age sixty-eight. His body was discovered by two cleaning women at his Key West home, where he had lived since 1978. He also had residences in Martha's Vineyard, Massachusetts, and in New York City, and he had a houseboat in Sausalito, California. He briefly lived in San Francisco's Haight-Ashbury section in the late 1960s. He is buried in his family's plot at Westlawn Cemetery in Chicago.

Silverstein's poetry succeeded because he did not talk down to children or write the typical sweet rhymes normally addressed to children. Silverstein was compared favorably to Dr. Seuss and Edward Lear. His black-and-white line drawings are simple yet moving, in the same style as his cartoons. He wrote honestly about the darker side of life but with a humor that appeals to children as well as adults. Eighteen million copies of his children's books sold in hardcover during his lifetime.

★

No biographies have been written about Silverstein. Ruth K. MacDonald, *Shel Silverstein* (1997), is a critical assessment of Silverstein's work and includes some biographical information. Jean F. Mercier interviewed Silverstein for *Publisher's Weekly* (24 Feb. 1975). Other biographical details can be found in Lynn Van Matre's interview in the *Chicago Tribune* (4 Mar. 1973); Richard R. Lingeman, "The Third Mr. Silverstein," *New York Times Book Review* (30 Apr. 1978); and Allan R. Andrews, "Light in the Attic First Shone in the Pacific," *American Reporter* (14 May 1999). Obituaries are in the *New York Times, Washington Post, Boston Globe,* and *Miami Herald* (all 11 May 1999).

JANE BRODSKY FITZPATRICK

SIMPSON, Alan (*b.* 23 July 1912 in Gateshead, England; *d.* 5 May 1998 in Lake Forest, Illinois), historian and president of Vassar College who led its pioneering change from educating women only to coeducation.

Simpson was one of eight children of George Hardwick Simpson and Isabella Graham; two siblings died in infancy, three sisters and two brothers reached adulthood. The family moved to Newcastle-upon-Tyne, where his father managed circulation for the daily newspapers. Simpson attended Dame Allan's School there, then earned a B.A. degree with first class honors in history from Worcester College, Oxford University, in 1933. He received his M.A. degree from Merton College in 1935, spent a year at Harvard University as a commonwealth fellow, and then completed his D.Phil. at Oxford in 1940. From 1941 to 1946 he served as a Royal Artillery officer.

In 1938 he married Mary McEldowney, an American graduate student at Oxford; they would have three children. In 1946 the Simpsons moved to the University of Chicago, where he became the Thomas E. Donnelly Professor of History and she became associate editor of the *Bulletin of Atomic Scientists.* He received American citizenship in 1954.

Alan Simpson, 1965. AP/WIDE WORLD PHOTOS

Simpson published a prize-winning interpretation, *Puritanism in Old and New England* (1955), and a case study, *The Wealth of the Gentry, 1540–1660* (1961). He won the University of Chicago's award for excellence in undergraduate teaching in 1952.

In 1959 the university appointed Simpson as dean of the University College to further the transition, already underway, from Robert Maynard Hutchins's vision of undergraduate education, which had abolished all usual course requirements and replaced them with comprehensive examinations in fourteen areas of general study. The curricular reorganization that Simpson led helped bring Chicago back toward the mainstream of American higher education. In a typically pungent, controversial aside, Simpson wondered aloud "if beauty and brawn do not deserve a place on our campus as well as brains."

Turbulence had not yet come to many campuses when Simpson accepted the presidency of Vassar College in Poughkeepsie, New York, in 1964, although student discontent with academic and social regulations was growing. During his first two years the new president sought "to strengthen the old Vassar," conserving its tradition as a distinguished college for women through fund-raising, physical planning, faculty development, and curricular reform. Simpson said that his Chicago experience had taught him that a "coed campus is a male-dominated campus."

By 1966, however, his Vassar experience suggested that a fundamental rethinking of the college's future was needed. Reports of student unhappiness with Vassar's geographic isolation from comparable colleges for men and with its social and curricular regulations (restrictive social regulations and highly structured curricular requirements) helped prompt his creation of a "committee on new dimensions" to consider possible changes, including graduate studies and coeducation. This investigation was overshadowed in November by an invitation from Yale University to study a possible affiliation between the two schools, with Vassar moving to New Haven, Connecticut, a proposal that excited Simpson.

Opposition to the move from many alumnae led to a parallel study of alternatives if Vassar remained in Poughkeepsie. Simpson wanted further study of affiliation with Yale, but in November 1967 the divided trustees chose not to move, decreeing instead that the Vassar student body would begin to include men, become more diverse, and be given more opportunities for independent study, field work, and study abroad. The trustees' ambitious agenda also included the possibility of graduate institutes, an adjacent state university center, and cooperative programs with other educational institutions. Simpson changed direction, enthusiastically announcing "full steam ahead in Poughkeepsie." Within a few years, after some failed starts, the ambitious agenda dwindled to improvements that could be made in the undergraduate college. Simpson especially regretted the defeat of an institute of technology, planned in cooperation with IBM, by bitter opposition from some faculty and students.

In 1968 Vassar chose to become coeducational by admitting men rather than by creating a coordinate college, having concluded that coordinations elsewhere had proved difficult. Revamping Vassar to include men posed one challenge after another in the next two years. The student government voted to end all parietal and curfew regulations, opposing any double standard whereby women were subjected to rules not applied to men. Simpson refused to veto the change, despite parental protests, a controversial abolition of in loco parentis that was eventually adopted by most other major academic institutions. A new curriculum with minimum requirements gave students the primary responsibility for their academic programs. At the same time, Simpson implemented his earlier desire to strengthen the Vassar faculty by making scholarship part of the formal criteria for tenure, fixing the time of tenure decisions, and creating a system of frequent automatic leaves for research.

Compounding Simpson's challenges as he launched coeducation were new kinds of student protests that brought turbulence to higher education generally. In 1969 African-American students at Vassar demanded speedier achievement of racial and curricular diversity, staging a much-publicized sit-in that resulted in an expanded black studies program. The larger issue of "student power" led Simpson to create a series of retreat conferences in 1968 and 1969 that brought together students, faculty, administrators, and trustees to devise ways to include students in college governance.

Simpson had served on a presidential task force on women's rights and responsibilities in 1969, but he did not face a strong resurgence of feminism at Vassar itself until coeducation had begun. Simpson accommodated, but did not lead, the demand for women's studies. The last years of his presidency saw a growing preoccupation with issues of equality between the sexes in all aspects of college life, a preoccupation that competed with administrative efforts to attract male applicants.

Throughout the contentious process of creating a new Vassar, Simpson faced fractious audiences with good grace and flashes of wit. In 1977 he retired to his beloved farm in Little Compton, Rhode Island. He remained a trustee of Colonial Williamsburg, and he and his wife collaborated on several scholarly publications, including editing a classic diary of King Philip's War (1975) and a selection of Jane Carlyle's letters (1977). He died of pneumonia at age seventy-five, and his ashes were scattered at the farm. He was survived by his wife, Mary, two daughters, and two grandchildren.

To Simpson, the educated person combined intelligence

with style; he brought both to his presidency of Vassar, along with civility, infectious buoyancy, and optimism. His legacy is the successful transformation of a college dedicated to increasing women's opportunities to a college educating both sexes in an environment that continues to emphasize their equality.

★

Current Biography (Feb. 1964) describes Simpson's career before Vassar. He provides his own perspective on the changes he initiated in "The New Vassar; Report of the President, 1964–1970" (1971). For a fuller account, see Elizabeth Daniels and Clyde Griffen, *Full Steam Ahead in Poughkeepsie: The Story of Coeducation at Vassar, 1966–1974* (2000). An obituary is in the *New York Times* (8 May 1988).

CLYDE GRIFFEN

SINATRA, Francis Albert ("Frank") (*b*. 12 December 1915 in Hoboken, New Jersey; *d*. 14 May 1998 in Los Angeles, California), singer and actor who became a universally admired interpreter of the twentieth-century American popular song during a professional career that spanned seven decades.

Sinatra was the only child of Anthony Martin ("Marty") Sinatra, a prizefighter, saloon-keeper, and fire captain, and Natalie Catherine ("Dolly") Garavente, a midwife and Democratic party committeewoman. Sinatra's parents emigrated from Italy as young children. In 1945 Sinatra's birth certificate was amended to record his name officially as Francis Albert Sinatra instead of the family's original name, Sinestro.

Sinatra's parents moved the family from a tenement at 415 Monroe Street in Hoboken's "Little Italy" section to an apartment on Park Avenue, and by 1932, to a house on Garden Street. Sinatra attended A. J. Demarest High School but was more interested in clowning with or impressing his classmates than in scholarly achievement. During his senior year at Demarest, he was expelled for "general rowdiness."

As a youngster, Sinatra was a member of the school choir at St. Francis Church, and he occasionally performed with the school band at Demarest. It soon became clear that he would not be the first member of his family, as his parents had hoped, to pursue an education beyond high school. Sinatra found work at a shipyard in Hoboken and on a loading dock in New York but performed at any opportunity, often singing on New York radio stations in return for transportation expenses. He had his own portable sound system as well as a supply of music arrangements, and he persuaded local bands to let him work with them at nightclubs, political functions, and social clubs.

In the summer of 1934, nineteen-year-old Sinatra met seventeen-year-old Nancy Rose Barbato while vacationing at the shore in Long Branch, New Jersey, and he began courting her. The following summer, Nancy accompanied Frank to a Bing Crosby performance at Loew's Journal Square in Jersey City. Upon seeing the popular vocalist in a live performance, Sinatra's ambition crystallized. His first break came in the fall of 1935, when he and a local trio named the Three Flashes appeared together on the radio program *Major Bowes's Original Amateur Hour* as the Hoboken Four. The group was signed to tour with Bowes's amateur companies for the winter of 1935 to 1936. Sinatra, however, found life on the road to be tedious and left the company before the end of the year in late 1935.

Returning to Hoboken, Sinatra continued to seek out singing jobs, aided by the publicity his mother had encouraged in the local press. He worked on his craft, performing wherever he could and taking voice lessons. Sinatra won a spot as a singing waiter and emcee at a roadhouse in Englewood, New Jersey, in 1938. With the swing era in vogue, Sinatra had the opportunity to perform with a professional band, which aired live remote broadcasts every Saturday on WNEW radio in New York. On 4 February 1939 he married Nancy Barbato. The couple had three children: Nancy Sandra (born 8 June 1940), who also became a singer; Franklin Wayne (born 10 January 1944), who became known as Frank Sinatra, Jr., and was also a

Frank Sinatra, 1963. AP/WIDE WORLD PHOTOS

singer; and Christine ("Tina") (born 20 June 1948), a television producer and an employee of several of the Sinatra enterprises.

In 1939 the trumpeter Harry James signed Sinatra at a salary of $75 per week, and Sinatra appeared with James's band for the first time in Baltimore on 30 June 1939. Although he toured with James for only six months and recorded just ten songs, Sinatra credited this association as the start of his professional career. In January 1940 Sinatra received an offer to join the nationally popular Tommy Dorsey Orchestra at a salary of $100 per week, and Harry James tore up their contract to allow Sinatra to play with Dorsey. Being a featured vocalist with Dorsey represented the pinnacle of achievement for a singer. Sinatra made the first of his eighty-three RCA recordings with the Dorsey band and played to his largest audiences yet at the Paramount Theatre in New York. He recorded "I'll Never Smile Again" with Dorsey and the Pied Pipers, his first number-one hit.

During June 1940 Dorsey's band began an extended stay in New York City, performing live and on radio broadcasts. They returned to Hollywood in October to film Sinatra's first feature length movie, *Las Vegas Nights,* with Paramount (1941). The years Sinatra spent with Tommy Dorsey were marked by a second film, *Ship Ahoy,* with MGM (1942), sold-out performances, recording sessions for RCA, and numerous radio broadcasts. Not only did this national exposure earn Sinatra the designation of "top male vocalist" in *Billboard* magazine in May 1941, but Dorsey taught him valuable musical lessons, particularly about phrasing and breathing techniques. By adapting a breathing method he learned from Dorsey, Sinatra developed his technique of long, flowing vocal lines.

Sinatra was exempt from military service because of a punctured eardrum. He continued to perform and record with Dorsey after the Japanese attack on Pearl Harbor, but he was anxious to receive the solo recognition he believed he deserved. Dorsey was not as gracious as Harry James had been about letting Sinatra out of his contract, but the contract was finally terminated in August 1942. Not yet twenty-seven years old, Sinatra became his own boss.

Sinatra was booked to perform at the Paramount in New York at the end of 1942. When he came onstage for his first performance on 30 December, the audience of teenage girls erupted in screams. A new popular music phenomenon had surfaced, and the ensuing adulation of the "bobby-soxer" fans sustained Sinatra's career for several years of concerts, radio appearances, recordings, and films. Between 1943 and 1945 he was a regular on the popular radio program "Your Hit Parade." He signed with Columbia records in 1943, and a rerelease of "All or Nothing at All" became a hit and was one of more than 280 songs released by the label between 1943 and 1952. Teenagers

flocked to see him. On Columbus Day 1944, crowds of youngsters rioted in Times Square when they could not gain entry to the Paramount for a holiday concert.

Sinatra moved his family to California in late 1944 to continue his motion picture career, making musicals such as *Higher and Higher* with RKO (1943) and *Anchors Aweigh* with MGM (1945). Sinatra earned a special Academy Award for *The House I Live In* with RKO (1945). In 1949 two more MGM musicals were released, *On the Town* and *Take Me Out to the Ball Game.*

Outwardly, Sinatra appeared to be a dedicated family man. But the late 1940s marked the beginning of a difficult time in the singer's life. His espousal of "liberal" causes raised the ire of conservative columnists such as Hedda Hopper, Louella Parsons, and Lee Mortimer. Sinatra's purported association with known mobsters further tarnished his image in the press, and he acquired the reputation as a hot-tempered, free-spending bad boy. In 1947 a confrontation between Sinatra and Mortimer in a Hollywood nightclub ended with Sinatra's arrest for assault. Furthermore, although the Sinatras had a third child in June 1948, Sinatra had become conspicuously indiscreet in his flirtations with Hollywood beauties. An affair with Ava Gardner proved to be such a public scandal that Nancy filed for legal separation in 1950, and Sinatra divorced her the following year. He married Gardner in Philadelphia on 7 November 1951, but their tumultuous relationship could not survive their strong personalities and career conflicts, and they divorced in 1954.

Most significant, however, was Sinatra's declining fortune as a singer. The bobby-soxers had outgrown their fixation on him, and he was having creative differences with Columbia Records. Between August 1946 and 1954 not one of Sinatra's records reached the top five positions on *Billboard* magazine's charts, and in 1952 and 1953 he had no hits at all. Sinatra's relentless schedule of performances and recording dates, combined with the excesses in his personal life, began to take a toll on his voice. Dropped by his publicist, his movie studio, and his record company by 1952, Sinatra seemed to be at the end of his career.

Perhaps the most remarkable accomplishment of Sinatra's professional life was his personal reinvention and the revival of his career in the years following 1952. With the help of friends, Sinatra secured a recording contract with Capitol Records. He recorded more than 300 songs for Capitol between 1953 and 1962, including some of his finest work. Sinatra's voice now had a deeper, more adult sound that reflected his life experiences, and his music swaggered with the confidence of an artist at the top of his craft in recordings such as "I've Got the World on a String" (1953). Sinatra defined the "concept album" by including songs with similar themes and tempos, such as the ballad-oriented *[Frank Sinatra Sings for] Only the Lonely* (1958), and the up-tempo *Come Dance with Me!* (1959). The latter album won Grammy awards as album of the year, best male vocal performance, and best arrangement, and it remained on the *Billboard* charts for 140 weeks.

During the reinvention phase of the 1950s, Sinatra's movie career was transformed. He won the part of Maggio in *From Here to Eternity,* made at Columbia Studios, and earned an Academy Award for best supporting actor (1953) for his performance. In *The Man with the Golden Arm*, made for United Artists (1955), Sinatra played the lead role of a heroin-addicted car mechanic and was nominated for the Academy's best actor award.

Sinatra established his own record company, Reprise, in 1960 and released *Ring-a-Ding-Ding* (1961) on the new label. He recorded more than 450 songs for Reprise through 1988, collaborating with Neal Hefti, Count Basie, Quincy Jones, Duke Ellington, and Antonio Carlos Jobim, as well as with old friends such as Nelson Riddle and Billy May. Sinatra was able to compete effectively for an audience when American popular music charts were dominated by baby boomers and rock and roll. In the summer of 1966, the fifty-year-old singer's single "Strangers in the Night" reached the top of the *Billboard* chart, displacing the Beatles; the song swept Grammy Awards for record of the year, best vocal performance by a male, best arrangement, and best engineered record. His album of personal recollections and songs, *Sinatra: A Man and His Music* (1966) won album of the year.

In the 1960s Sinatra owned a share of the Sands Hotel, a Las Vegas nightclub that became a playground for Sinatra and his "Rat Pack," which included Dean Martin, Sammy Davis, Jr., Joey Bishop, and Peter Lawford. The Rat Pack made films together, including *Ocean's Eleven* for Warner Brothers (1960), set in Las Vegas, but their films would be overshadowed by *The Manchurian Candidate* (1962), regarded as one of Sinatra's best dramatic performances. Sinatra and the Rat Pack often convened at the Sands for performances they nicknamed "the Summit" as they partied on and offstage. In 1963, in trouble with the Nevada gaming commission, Sinatra divested himself of interests in casino properties. He made tabloid headlines again when he married Mia Farrow, a nineteen-year-old actress, on 19 July 1966; the marriage ended in divorce in 1968.

Following the defeat of Hubert Humphrey in the 1968 presidential election and the subsequent fragmentation of the Democratic Party, Sinatra became friendly with Richard Nixon and prominent Republicans, performing at the White House in 1970. On 13 June 1971, Sinatra at fifty-five made what he declared was his final performance at a Los Angeles benefit for the Motion Picture and Television Relief Fund. He retreated to Palm Springs and the company of family and friends but did not disappear entirely from the public eye, attending charity and political events.

By April 1973 Sinatra had come out of retirement to perform at the White House in honor of Italian President Giulio Andreotti. On 18 November his concert *Ol' Blue Eyes Is Back* aired on NBC television; an album by the same name had reached number thirteen on the *Billboard* charts earlier that year. Sinatra began to perform to massive audiences in arenas and stadiums worldwide.

Sinatra married Barbara Marx on 11 July 1976; their union lasted until his death. From 1977 until 1994 Sinatra continued a busy schedule of concerts and recording dates. His last concert performance was an appearance in Japan in December 1994. Although his final years were spent in relative seclusion, Sinatra was honored with a Legend Award for lifetime achievement at the Grammy ceremonies in March 1994. Sinatra died of a heart attack in Los Angeles and is buried in Desert Memorial Park, Cathedral City, California.

As an icon of American popular culture, Sinatra both reflected and influenced the time in which he lived. His records provided a soundtrack for many of the memorable moments of his era, and his rich, often turbulent, personal life mirrored the dreams and fears of ordinary people. Always generous with his time, talent, and money, Sinatra was a philanthropist of the first order, although much of the press he received during his lifetime was negative. His friends included entertainment luminaries, politicians, ordinary folk, and people of dubious reputation. Sinatra's masterful rendition of the American popular songbook and his careful articulation of lyrics have been admired by his fans as well as by the composers, lyricists, and arrangers of his music. With more than sixty films, two Oscars, and an Academy Award nomination for best actor to his credit, Sinatra was also among the most successful actors of his time. Sinatra became an enduring and universally recognized symbol of America in the twentieth century.

★

Only two authorized biographies of Sinatra have been published, both written by his daughter Nancy with Sinatra's cooperation: *Frank Sinatra: My Father* (1985) and *Frank Sinatra: An American Legend* (1995). Tina Sinatra, *My Father's Daughter: A Memoir* (2000), was published after the singer's death. Kitty Kelley, *His Way: The Unauthorized Biography of Frank Sinatra* (1986), offers a sensationalized and often unflattering point of view; whereas Donald Clarke, *All or Nothing at All: A Life of Frank Sinatra* (1997), presents a more balanced perspective on Sinatra's life and cultural significance. Leonard Mustazza, *Sinatra: An Annotated Bibliography, 1939–1998* (1999), is an exhaustive descriptive listing of print resources. Noteworthy articles are reprinted in Steven Petkov and Leonard Mustazza, *The Frank Sinatra Reader* (1995), and in Ethlie Ann Vare, *Legend: Frank Sinatra and the American Dream* (1995). Will Friedwald, *Sinatra! The Song Is You: A Singer's Art* (1995), and Charles Granata, *Sessions with Sinatra:*

Frank Sinatra and the Art of Recordings (1999), provide thorough analyses of Sinatra's musical legacy. Books documenting Sinatra's importance to American culture include John Lahr, *Sinatra: The Artist and the Man* (1997); Bill Zehme, *The Way You Wear Your Hat: Frank Sinatra and the Lost Art of Livin'* (1997); and Pete Hamill, *Why Sinatra Matters* (1998). For many, Sinatra's recordings comprise the most significant archive, and virtually all his recordings on RCA, Columbia, Capitol, and Reprise have been released on compact disc. Video recordings of many films and television shows are also available. Complete discographies are found in Leonard Mustazza, *Ol' Blue Eyes: A Frank Sinatra Encyclopedia* (1998), and Luis Carlos do Nascimento Silva, *Put Your Dreams Away: A Frank Sinatra Discography* (2000). Obituaries are in the *Los Angeles Times* and *New York Times* (both 15 May 1998).

JAMES F. SMITH

SISKEL, Eugene Kal ("Gene") (*b.* 26 January 1946 in Chicago, Illinois; *d.* 20 February 1999 in Evanston, Illinois), film critic famous for his television partnership with Roger Ebert.

Siskel was the youngest of three children of Nathan William Siskel and Ida Kalis. He spent his early years in Chicago with his family, but by age ten, Siskel had lost both parents. Unable to remember the death of his father, he felt the loss of his mother more profoundly. When he learned of her death, he "couldn't handle it" and "thought she was alive for a significant time after she was dead." Suddenly orphans, Siskel and his two older siblings moved to Glen-

Gene Siskel. AP/WIDE WORLD PHOTOS

coe, a suburb of Chicago, to live with an aunt and uncle, Mae and Joseph Gray, who raised them alongside their own three children. During this time, he attended the Culver Military Academy in Indiana, graduating in 1963.

Siskel then attended Yale College in New Haven, Connecticut, where he majored in philosophy and planned to become a trial lawyer. He earned a B.A. degree in 1967. The next year, he won a Coro Fellowship in public affairs and worked on a political campaign in California. When he joined the U.S. Army Reserves later in 1968, he was assigned to write press releases for the U.S. Department of Defense Information School. These postgraduate experiences diverted him from law and opened his eyes to a new career as a journalist.

In January 1969, armed with a recommendation from the Yale professor and author John Hersey, Siskel found a job as a neighborhood news reporter with the *Chicago Tribune*. Within seven months, he had written his first movie review (for the Disney film *Rascal*, released in 1969) and had earned a promotion to film critic. The story behind this promotion became legendary. After the film critic Cliff Terry left the *Chicago Tribune* in 1969 for a Nieman Fellowship, the newspaper decided to use several reporters in rotation to fill his spot until he returned. The young and ambitious Siskel convinced them to do otherwise. In a memo to the Sunday editor, he explained that the *Tribune*, to stay competitive, should promote only one movie reviewer. The editor followed his advice and gave him the job. In a 1984 interview, Siskel speculated that the paper promoted him in part to dethrone Roger Ebert, his rival film critic at the *Chicago Sun-Times*.

During their early rivalry, Siskel and Ebert successfully sustained an atmosphere of intense and constant competition. In 1970 Siskel issued his first set of Academy Award predictions for the *Tribune*. The next year, he challenged his readers to outdo him, inaugurating the annual "Beat Siskel" contest. By 1998 "Beat Siskel" had become the largest annual Oscar-predicting contest in the world, drawing 34,904 entries from eighty-nine countries. In this case, Siskel did best Ebert. It took the *Sun-Times* nearly ten years to launch a similar contest.

In 1974 Siskel made his first appearance as a television film critic. The local CBS affiliate, WBBM, hired him to provide reviews during its newscasts. Then in 1975 Siskel forged the partnership that would make him famous. A producer from the local PBS station, WTTW, proposed that Siskel and Ebert cohost a television show about movies. Although neither critic was thrilled with the idea, they both finally agreed to try the new program. As Ebert later reported, he suspected they only consented "because we didn't want the other guy to do it first."

The program, called *Opening Soon at a Theater Near You*, did not succeed initially. It quickly went off the air and then reappeared in 1976 as *Sneak Previews*. The show established a familiar format: one critic would introduce and review a film; then the other would offer his comments, often leading to heated arguments. The unpredictable and acerbic nature of these arguments fueled the popularity of the show. When it went national in 1978, *Sneak Previews* became the highest-rated PBS series in history at the time.

A movie fanatic, Siskel loved the film *Saturday Night Fever*, seeing it seventeen times during its initial release in 1977. At a celebrity auction in the early 1980s, he outbid the actress Jane Fonda for the white suit worn by John Travolta in the film, paying $2,000 for it. Remarkably, he kept the suit in his closet until 1995, when it sold for $145,000 at a Christie's auction in New York City.

In 1982, after their PBS contract for *Sneak Previews* expired, Siskel and Ebert moved their show to commercial television. Signing with Tribune Entertainment, they renamed their program *At the Movies* and forever changed the nature of film criticism. Hollywood executives came to fear their negative reviews while embracing their positive comments. For example, in 1981 Siskel and Ebert turned the obscure film *My Dinner with Andre* into a hit. Other films, weighed down by their criticism, did not fare as well. As the comedian Eddie Murphy once admitted at a press conference, their reviews could "definitely kill a movie."

The pair changed venues once again in 1986. They signed with Buena Vista Television, which began distributing their show as *Siskel and Ebert at the Movies* (later, simply *Siskel and Ebert*). In this incarnation the duo premiered their famous thumb critiques, spurring numerous advertising campaigns to acknowledge their "two-thumbs-up" pronouncements for films approved by both reviewers. Also in the mid-1980s, the *Tribune* removed Siskel as their movie critic and made him a movie columnist instead because of the increasing external demands on his time. In this new role, he continued to contribute weekly columns, capsule reviews, and occasional features but no longer wrote full-length reviews.

Throughout Siskel and Ebert's syndicated history, they reached from three million to eleven million viewers weekly, and their programs often appeared among the top-ten weekly shows in syndication. Not surprisingly, the pair used this popularity and fame to their advantage. They championed independent films, foreign films, and documentaries. They advocated black-and-white photography and wide-screen video releases while decrying teen sex comedies, violent horror films, and colorization of old movies. Most significant, they led the campaign for a new adult movie rating to replace the much maligned "X." Their efforts ultimately resulted in the creation of the "NC-17" rating.

In 1980 Siskel married Marlene Iglitzen, a producer for the WBBM newscasts on which he appeared. They had three children; the family lived in the Lincoln Park area of Chicago, where they developed a famously strong bond. Ebert once remarked of Siskel, "As a husband and a father, his love knew no bounds." Siskel also loved his hometown and its championship basketball team, the Chicago Bulls. He attended their home games religiously, cheering passionately from his courtside seat.

In May 1998 Siskel underwent surgery to remove a growth in his brain. He immediately returned to work, phoning in his part on *Siskel and Ebert* from his hospital bed. Before long, he was filming the show once again and returning to his four other jobs contributing to the *Chicago Tribune, TV Guide,* WBBM News, and *CBS This Morning*. Friends and viewers alike noticed differences in his speech and appearance. Nine months after his surgery, in early 1999, Siskel took a leave from the show, announcing that he was "in a hurry to get well because I don't want Roger to get more screen time than I." His health continued to deteriorate, and he was eventually admitted to Evanston Hospital, just north of Chicago. He died there at age fifty-three from complications related to his brain surgery. He is buried in Westlawn Cemetery in Chicago.

Siskel, in partnership with Ebert, made film criticism powerful and mainstream. Their influence was worldwide, and their reviews often affected box-office receipts. For their efforts, Siskel and Ebert were nominated for seven Emmy Awards, inducted into the National Association of Television Program Executives Hall of Fame in 1984, and honored by the Hollywood Radio and Television Society as men of the year in 1993. As a further honor, the Art Institute of Chicago renamed its film center in Siskel's memory in 1999.

★

Although he was a prolific writer, Siskel authored only one book, *The Future of Movies: Interviews with Martin Scorsese, Steven Spielberg, and George Lucas* (1991), cowritten with Ebert. The book presents fascinating interviews but contains no biographical information on Siskel. Additionally, no full-length biography exists about him. Scott Smith, *The Film 100: A Ranking of the Most Influential People in the History of Movies* (1998), ranks Siskel and Ebert as the seventy-fourth most influential people and provides a concise history of their careers and influence. *Contemporary Authors: A Bio-Bibliographical Guide to Current Writers in Fiction, General Nonfiction, Poetry, Journalism, Drama, Motion Pictures, Television, and Other Fields*, vol. 113 (1985), contains a brief but informative biography, one of the few on Siskel alone. Numerous magazines have published articles on Siskel and Ebert, but very few delve into their personal lives. Some of the more interesting and informative articles include Charles Leerhsen with Donna Foote, "The Odd Couple's Oscars," *Newsweek* (11 Apr. 1983); Bill Zehme, "Twenty Questions with Siskel and Ebert," *Playboy* (June 1984); and Richard Zoglin, "'It Stinks!' 'You're Crazy!'"

Time (25 May 1987). Obituaries are in the *Chicago Tribune* (20 Feb. 1999), *Los Angeles Times* (21 Feb. 1999), and *New York Times* (22 Feb. 1999).

BRIAN DANIEL QUIGLEY

SKELTON, Richard Bernard ("Red") (*b.* 18 July 1913 in Vincennes, Indiana; *d.* 18 September 1997 in Rancho Mirage, California), "cornball" gag-line and physical comedian, star of vaudeville, radio, cinema, and especially television, where his weekly comedy show aired for two decades as one of the most popular prime-time series; in his later years a famous painter of circus clown portraits.

As is the case with many comedians, Skelton had a less than idyllic childhood. The son of Joseph Skelton, an alcoholic ex–circus clown who died two months before Skelton's birth, and Ida Mae Skelton, who was left penniless with four sons, the comedian began his life in show business as a young child performing card tricks for tips in small-town pool rooms. He got his first formal job at age ten, making summer tours of the lower Mississippi Valley as a blackface "mammy singer" in Doc R. E. Lewis's Medicine Show. But a summer job was not sufficient to make ends meet. He was forced to drop out of school and look for full-time work at age twelve because, as he told an interviewer years later, "the family was hungry."

Skelton spent his youth learning the ropes as an actor, singer, dancer, and all-purpose entertainer in a remarkable succession of dying grassroots American show business venues. He performed in blackface with Clarence Stout's Minstrels, joked and juggled for passengers along the Ohio River on Captain Happy's Cotton Blossom Showboat, and played dramatic roles in tent productions with the John Lawrence Stock Company. A relentless mugger specializing in goofy faces, the young performer was, in all he did, a funnyman. His penchant for getting laughs in noncomic dramas cost him his job with the Lawrence Company. At age fourteen, like his father before him, he signed on as a clown with the Hagenbeck and Wallace Circus, but abruptly quit after witnessing the mauling of the famous lion tamer Clyde Beatty.

Not yet sixteen, Skelton used his six-foot, two-inch frame and a copy of his oldest brother's birth certificate to break into burlesque as a runway comic, a kind of master of ceremonies whose main job was to make wisecracks about the dancing girls as they paraded by. During these years competition from motion pictures was pushing burlesque into more overtly sexual material, something that made Skelton increasingly uncomfortable. He made a point of avoiding "blue" material for the rest of his life. "I don't think anybody should have to pay money at the box office to hear what they can read on restroom walls," he told his biographer.

In 1930 he met Edna Marie Sitwell, a twenty-four-year-old usher at the Gaiety Theatre in Kansas City, Missouri. The couple married within a year. Despite the fact that Sitwell had virtually no show business background, she became her husband's chief writer and business manager, and even served as onstage second banana. Appalled by Skelton's lack of education, she hired a tutor for him and goaded him toward a high school equivalency diploma, which he received in 1938. Even after the couple's 1943 divorce, she remained his manager. In 1945 Skelton married Georgia Maurine Davis, a model with whom he had two children. The younger child, a son, died of leukemia at age nine. That marriage ended in divorce in 1973. A third marriage, to Lothian Toland, took place that same year.

"The Skeltons," as the act was called at first, graduated from burlesque to big-time vaudeville in the 1930s, in large part due to Sitwell's material and her handling of the act's business affairs. The act consisted of one-liners, pantomimes, and snappy patter sketches. The verbal humor was decidedly homespun ("Webster wouldn't have written his dictionary if it wasn't for his wife. She was always saying, 'What's that supposed to mean?' "). But even critics who found Skelton's jokes and pratfalls a bit too familiar had

Red Skelton. KOBAL COLLECTION

praise for his pantomime artistry. Two of his silent routines became fan favorites: "Guzzler's Gin," which was one of many in which he portrayed an inebriated character; and "Donut Dunking," which could last as long as thirty minutes, even in theaters where pieces of that length were routinely cut shorter by heckling.

Skelton broke through as a bona fide vaudeville star in 1936 when he was held over for almost six months at Loew's Montreal Theater. This led to engagements in New York City, Chicago, and other cities at the top of the circuit. Though it might be said that so physical a comedian was "made" for the stage, it was also true that vaudeville could no longer hold its own stars by the mid-1930s. Like many other headliners, Skelton quickly abandoned it when more lucrative opportunities arose in broadcasting and the movies.

Skelton made his national radio debut on the *Rudy Vallee Program* in 1937. Other invitations followed, and he was soon a sought-after guest for popular network variety shows. In 1941 he was afforded his own prime-time series on NBC, *Red Skelton's Scrapbook of Satire*. It was on radio that the comedian developed many of the stock characters he would later use on television. *Scrapbook* was consistently among the highest-rated shows on American radio, catapulting the comedian into the company of such stars as Bob Hope and Jack Benny.

Skelton, with the benefit of Sitwell's management, developed his film career, appearing in dozens of Hollywood films between 1938 and 1957. Following false starts with RKO and Warner Brothers, he signed with MGM, where he worked with one of his lifelong idols, Buster Keaton. Keaton coached him through a series of talkie remakes of his own silent classics, including *I Dood It* (1943 after *Spite Marriage*) and *Watch the Birdie* (1951 after *The Cameraman*).

Skelton starred in three films as Wally "The Fox" Benton, a radio detective who gets caught up in real-life murder mysteries: *Whistling in the Dark* (1941), *Whistling in Dixie* (1942), and *Whistling in Brooklyn* (1943). Similarly, in *The Fuller Brush Man* (1948) and *The Yellow Cab Man* (1950), he played a good-hearted, if not terribly bright, working-class Joe who stumbles into foul play while just trying to do his job. Musicals such as *Lady Be Good* (1941), *Ziegfeld Follies* (1946), and *Three Little Words* (1950) allowed Skelton to show off the talents he had developed in his boyhood. His one attempt at a dramatic lead was *The Clown* (1953), a remake of the silent classic *The Champ* (1931). In it, Skelton played the role of a broken-down entertainer who is nonetheless idolized by his young son. Over the years he appeared on screen with such stars as Ginger Rogers (*Having a Wonderful Time*, 1938), Lucille Ball (*DuBarry Was a Lady*, 1943), and Esther Williams (*Bathing Beauty*, 1944).

The Screen Actors Guild awarded Skelton its Lifetime Achievement Award in 1987.

During the first part of World War II, Skelton did volunteer work entertaining servicemen at the Hollywood Canteen and elsewhere. In 1944, however, he was drafted into the U.S. Army as a private in the field artillery and served in the Italian campaign. In the final months of the war he suffered what the army described as a "nervous breakdown" and was reassigned to an entertainment unit. Skelton was burdened with personal despair and suffered from numerous bouts of depression throughout his life.

According to critic Leonard Maltin, "Skelton's film career started to peter out" following the end of the war. Like many other vaudeville comedy veterans, including Milton Berle, Jack Benny, and the team of George Burns and Gracie Allen, Skelton found himself at a peculiar crossroads of media history. Very much identified with "the old Hollywood" of the pre-war era, his film career had reached a plateau. At the same time, his radio popularity, which had never flagged, was gradually losing its marketability as the medium turned away from variety entertainment toward recorded music and talk. Television, and specifically the comedy-variety show genre (or "vaudeo," as it was sometimes called), lifted Skelton out of this dilemma to new heights of popularity and wealth.

The Red Skelton Show premiered on NBC in 1951 and was an immediate hit, finishing fourth in the Nielsen ratings and winning the first of its three Emmy Awards. During this period CBS was aggressively raiding stars from it competitors, and in 1953 CBS founder William S. Paley successfully courted Skeleton away from NBC, ending an eleven-year relationship dating back to the radio era. *The Red Skelton Show* (doubled in length to *The Red Skelton Hour*) became a fixture on CBS for the next seventeen seasons.

The show was a television adaptation of its star's vaudeville act. Following the credits sequence, the star came out in front of a theater curtain to greet the audience from what appeared to be the lip of a proscenium stage. His monologue typically consisted of a half-dozen one-liners ("I bought Oral Roberts' Christmas record album but I couldn't play it. The hole healed up"). He enjoyed doing improvisations with a single prop, often a hat.

After the first commercial, the program was given to one or several long sketches featuring Skelton's signature characters: Klem Kadiddlehopper, a slow-witted rube; the Mean Whiddle Kid, a mischievous man-boy played with no suggestion of innocence; San Fernando Red, a ruthless con man; George Appleby, an insufferable prig; and Sheriff Deadeye, one of several of the comedian's drunks. Freddie the Freeloader, a tramp, was played entirely in pantomime. Movie stars were often featured as guests on the show, and Skelton took particular delight in breaking them up during the middle of sketches. At the end of each show, in a brief coda following the final commercial, the star would appear one last time, half in costume, to bid the audience, "Good night and God bless."

Skelton took a kind of auteur credit for the show and harbored a particular animus for writers. Sherwood Schwartz, who later created such hits as *Gilligan's Island* and *The Brady Bunch,* was his head writer from 1954 to 1962. Schwartz found Skelton so personally abrasive that he stayed on after 1955 under the written condition that he could send his scripts by messenger each week and would not have to meet face-to-face with Skelton. He recounted this incident in which the star dressed down a writer after a slip in his ratings: "Red always had firearms around. He said, 'Maybe this will make you write funnier,' and he took out a gun and shot at Artie Standard's feet, yelling 'Write! Write!' He always bad-mouthed writers. He has insulted them to their face and shot at their feet. I didn't need that."

Yet despite all this, Schwartz did not deny Skelton's genius. "Red Skelton," he told an interviewer, "can't get eight words out of his mouth in the right order. But nobody is better at pantomime. Nobody! I include Marcel Marceau, because I wrote shows for the two of them together, and he'd put Marcel Marceau away." In 1970, despite a seventh-place finish in the national Nielsen ratings, *The Red Skelton Hour* was cancelled by CBS because of what it believed to be the aging demographics of the show's audience. NBC gave Skelton a brief reprieve, scaling the show back to its original half-hour format, but failed to renew it at the end of its first year. Though "heartbroken," as he put it, the veteran performer refused to retire. He found bookings at several top Las Vegas nightclubs and played college campuses as well. His continuing popularity led to three annual HBO comedy specials beginning in 1982.

In 1986 Red Skelton was inducted into the Academy of Television Arts and Sciences' Hall of Fame. He also received the Governors' Award, a special Television Academy honor he accepted on the annual Emmy Awards national telecast. Responding at the end of a long standing ovation from his peers, he looked into the camera and said, "Thank you for sitting down. I thought you were going to pull a CBS and walk out on me."

The comedian had several hobbies and avocations that he took up at mid-life, including model railroading, musical composing, and oil painting. After the cancellation of his weekly television show, however, he turned his love of painting into a new career. Sticking to a single subject— portraits of clowns—he earned millions of dollars for his artwork, with some going for as much as $80,000. An active philanthropist, he donated generously to children's charities, especially the Pacific Lodge, an orphanage, and the Red Skelton Needy Children's Fund.

Few comedians today can claim Red Skelton's legacy.

The forms he worked in, from medicine shows to TV comedy-variety, are show business dinosaurs. Of more contemporary interest is his treatment of subject matter. Characters such as Klem Kadiddlehopper, Cauliflower McPugg (a punch-drunk boxer), and Rupert the Stupert (a moronic European aristocrat) test the borders of "low comedy" with shameless mockeries of the mentally deficient. Similarly, Willie Lump Lump and Sheriff Redeye push traditional comic portraiture of drunkenness over the line of ridicule. The Mean Whiddle Kid got laughs by holding a cat by its tail and explaining, "I'm just holding it. The cat's doing the pulling."

In an age where these traditional subjects of slapstick humor are often thought of as learning disabilities, alcoholism, animal cruelty, and child sadism, it becomes difficult to take them as laughing matters. Yet there was such an utter lack of self-consciousness in Skelton's treatment of these latter-day taboos that at his best he was capable of bringing a viewer full circle by evoking a childlike innocence of any transgression.

★

Skelton wrote two books, *A Red Skelton in Your Closet: Ghost Stories Gay and Grim* (1965) and *Red Skelton's Gertrude and Heathcliff* (1971), the latter a collection of jokes from his television monologues in which he plays a pair of cross-eyed seagulls. Arthur Marx, *Red Skelton* (1979), is probably the authoritative work on the comedian. Most reference works on relevant subjects contain biographical entries. Suggested are Robert Lemieux in Horace Newcomb, ed., *The Encyclopedia of Television* (1997), and the chapter on Skelton in Karen Adir, *The Great Clowns of Television* (1988). Also see "I'm Nuts and I Know It," *Saturday Evening Post* (17 June 1967). An interview with Sherwood Schwartz, revealing the darker side of the comedian, is held in the Steven H. Scheuer Collection in Television History at the Syracuse University Library. An obituary by Richard Severo is in the *New York Times* (18 Sept. 1997).

DAVID MARC

SMITH, Ralph Corbett (*b.* 27 November 1893 in Omaha, Nebraska; *d.* 21 January 1998 in Palo Alto, California), decorated soldier who fought in both World Wars and was the oldest general in the United States when he died.

Ralph Corbett Smith was the son of Miles Carl Smith and May Corbett. After growing up in Omaha, Nebraska, he attended but did not graduate from Colorado State College. He also joined the Colorado National Guard. By 1916 Smith had decided to pursue a military career and was a second lieutenant in the regular army. His first action came that year when he campaigned against the Mexican bandit-revolutionary Pancho Villa with American forces under the

General Ralph C. Smith, 1943. AP/Wide World Photos

his flying instructor was none other than aviation pioneer Orville Wright. Upon completion of his training, Smith received pilot license number 13, appropriately signed by the famous aviator who had taught him to fly. Afterward Smith sailed for France, where he studied French at the Sorbonne in Paris and eventually became fluent in the language.

While serving in France, Smith married Madeleine Fereyre on 1 March 1924; the couple had two children. Between the World Wars, Smith taught French at West Point (1920–1923), attended Army Infantry School (1924–1927), and first attended and then taught at the Army Command and General Staff School in Fort Leavenworth, Kansas (1930–1934). He went to the Army War College before becoming an observer with the French army and enrolling in Ecole Superieure de Guerre in France. He also worked in the military intelligence division of the United States War Department.

When the Japanese bombed Pearl Harbor on 7 December 1941, Smith held the rank of brevet colonel and—despite his knowledge of Europe—was ordered to the Pacific theater. By early 1942, his superiors had promoted him to major general and given him command of the Twenty-seventh Infantry Division. Notably, Smith's division fought with distinction in November 1943 at Makin Atoll in the Gilbert Islands. With Smith wading through water to lead his men ashore and taking part at the beginning of the fight, the atoll became the first Central Pacific island to be conquered by U.S. forces, and Smith received much praise for planning and leading the assault. After winning the island, Smith's first short two-word report to his superiors made military history: "Makin Taken." The two words became a rallying cry for the American counteroffensive against Japan, as the "island hopping" campaign against America's adversary began in 1944.

Despite his excellent record, the 1944 battle for Saipan ended in disaster for Smith. Lieutenant General Holland M. "Howling Mad" Smith, commanding the U.S. Marine Amphibious Corps V, relieved Smith of command for failing to "attack on time." Lieutenant General Smith also publicly condemned the entire Twenty-seventh Division because the men "would not fight." He added that Smith "could not make them." With such assertions, "Howling Mad" Smith started a national controversy that reached the highest levels of command in Washington, D.C.

The controversy also stirred two national publishing empires into action. The Hearst interests, headed by William Randolph Hearst, backed the army and said that the marines incurred too many unnecessary casualties. The Henry R. Luce interests took the side of the navy and the marines, holding that the marine general's criticism of the army was valid. A military board of inquiry later cleared Smith of all charges, "exonerating" him completely. More-

command of General John J. "Black Jack" Pershing. Smith was also part of the World War I American Expeditionary Force, commanded by Pershing, that went to rescue French forces from German soldiers who had broken out of their trenches and were moving toward Paris. He participated in the famous Meuse-Argonne offensive of 1918 that hastened the end of the war. Smith was wounded twice in the fighting but fought on, winning battlefield promotions to major in 1918. Subsequently, the army awarded him the Silver Star with Oak Leaf Cluster for two instances of uncommon valor during the campaign. He also won the Purple Heart and the French Croix de Guerre with Palme in 1919.

After the war, Smith returned to Colorado State College, where he received his B.S. degree in 1919. Smith wanted to become an aviator, perhaps because he saw how effective the Army Air Forces had been during World War I, and

over, casualty figures and other objective data proved that the Twenty-seventh Infantry had done its part in conquering Saipan. Of 3,119 Americans killed in action at Saipan, 1,052 were from the Twenty-seventh. The fighting unit was also credited with causing about 35 percent of the 17,801 enemy losses. However, Smith never returned to combat, and as a result of the controversy, another marine general did not command a large number of troops until the Persian Gulf War in 1991.

Smith finished his World War II service as a military attaché at the United States Embassy in Paris, France, and also served as attaché to General Charles de Gaulle's government. He was also chief of mission in France for the voluntary organization Co-Operative for American Remittances to Europe (CARE). In this post, in addition to his duties in France, he supervised CARE's operations in other West European countries. Before Smith retired from the armed services in 1948, he was decorated by the governments of France, England, and Belgium. After his retirement, Smith became a fellow of the Hoover Institute on War, Revolution, and Peace at Stanford University.

Smith's first wife died in 1975. After living alone for almost five years, he married Hildy Jarman in 1980, who died in 1995. Smith lived long enough to become the army's oldest general before he died of a long-standing lung ailment at his home in Palo Alto, California. He outlived his children, but his survivors included three grandchildren and six great-grandchildren. Smith will be remembered for his exploits in both world wars as well as for his dramatic, rallying signature words: "Makin Taken."

★

Smith left no personal papers, but various brief accounts of his life, most focusing on his career during World War II, include "Ralph C. Smith, 104, Oldest General Officer in Army," *Cleveland Plain Dealer* (26 Jan. 1998), and "Major General Ralph C. Smith, 1894–1998," *Army Magazine* 48 (Mar. 1998). Other accounts of Smith's experiences in World War II can be found in Edmund G. Love, *The 27th Division in World War II* (1949), and *The Capture of Makin* (American Forces in Action Series, 1946). Obituaries are in the *Los Angeles Times* (24 Jan. 1998), *New York Times* (26 Jan. 1998), *Washington Post* (27 Jan. 1998), and *Economist* (31 Jan. 1998).

JAMES M. SMALLWOOD

SMITH, Robert Emil ("Buffalo Bob") (*b.* 27 November 1917 in Buffalo, New York; *d.* 30 July 1998 in Hendersonville, North Carolina), radio and television personality who was among the first stars of children's television as host and master of ceremonies of *The Howdy Doody Show,* which aired on NBC from 1947 to 1960.

Little in the family background of Smith, born Robert Emil Schmidt, might have predicted his career in children's television. Emil Henry Schmidt, an Illinois coal miner, was persuaded by his wife, Emma Kuehn, to take up carpentry following his narrow escape from a cave-in. The couple followed a job opportunity to Buffalo, New York, where they started a family. This, rather than a youth spent on the western prairies, is the origin of Smith's television stage name. The boy showed musical talent, and his mother saw to it that he received private lessons in piano, guitar, and voice. While attending public high school during the Great Depression, he formed a singing trio, the Hi-Hatters, which included the future comedian Foster Brooks. The group performed at dances and social functions and made live appearances on Buffalo radio stations.

A personal break came for Smith in 1934, when the singer Kate Smith (no relation), who was playing a Buffalo vaudeville theater, asked him to substitute for her regular piano player and master of ceremonies. Impressed by his performance, she invited him to New York City to perform on her nationally broadcast NBC radio program. Billing himself as "Smith" rather than "Schmidt," he returned to his hometown as something of a prodigal son and em-

Buffalo Bob Smith and Howdy Doody, 1952. ARCHIVE PHOTOS, INC.

barked on a career as a radio personality in upstate New York. He married Mildred Caroline Metz on 21 November 1940; the couple had three sons.

In 1947 WEAF, the flagship station of the NBC radio network, summoned Smith to New York City to become host of its morning wake-up show. Not used to being in the media spotlight of the nation's largest market, Smith became involved in a bit of mischief that under other circumstances could have cost him his career. In 1949, more than a decade after the "War of the Worlds" incident, during which the actor Orson Welles frightened listeners with a realistic-sounding radio broadcast reporting a Martian invasion of New Jersey, Smith announced in the tones of a newswire story that a space ship had landed in rural Virginia and that an army of tiny aliens was disembarking from it. Although the station received a stern warning from the Federal Communications Commission, Smith's ratings protected him from being sacked.

His first foray into children's entertainment also came at WEAF. In addition to his full-time weekday duties, he was made host of *Triple B Ranch,* a Saturday morning radio quiz show. School-age contestants on the show were asked questions by various fantasy characters created by Smith and his writers. One of them, a hayseed named Elmer, who sounded like Edgar Bergen's famous radio dummy Mortimer Snerd, greeted the audience by saying, "Howdy doody, everybody." Elmer was the prototype for the marionette that would bring Smith stardom. *The Howdy Doody Show* was born in 1947 in the midst of Bob Smith's breakneck radio schedule. As if his daily and weekly programs were not enough, NBC assigned Smith to host an afternoon children's show, *Puppet Playhouse,* on its recently launched New York City television station. The show did so well that NBC upgraded it to a network broadcast the following season, renaming the series for its most popular character.

Dressed in the fringed leather outfit of a frontier hunter, Buffalo Bob Smith was as familiar a figure to early television viewers as the comedians Milton Berle and Lucille Ball. He opened more than 2,300 live afternoon telecasts with the famous question "Hey, kids! What time is it?" "It's *Howdy Doody* time!" shot back an onstage bleacher section of children, known as the Peanut Gallery. At the peak of its popularity the show's daily audience was more than 15 million viewers.

The deepness of *Howdy Doody*'s penetration into the psyche of America's children provides an etiologic example of television at its most effective. Bob Smith, renamed Buffalo Bob by the writer Edward Kean, became an interlocutor between the everyday world of demanding adults and a place where "kid think" ruled. With his big ears and forty-eight freckles ("That's one for each state, kids!"), Howdy, though a nerd and even a "sissy" according to

Kean, just wanted to have fun. The Native American characters, who lived on a reservation in the green world just outside Doodyville, had no problem with that. Laconic Chief Thunderthud had little to say besides "Kowabunga!" (Bart Simpson, or his writers, no doubt borrowed the phrase from Chief Thunderthud.) Princess Summerfall Winterspring began the series as a puppet but reappeared, Pygmalion-like, in 1953 as a fully fleshed woman. According to the *New York Times,* "Buffalo Bob wanted something beautiful and life-sized for girls to identify with."

Doodyville itself was run by the evil (though strictly nonviolent) Mayor Phineas T. Bluster. He presided with the assistance of his two brothers, Don Jose, a hot-blooded Latin, and Hector Hamhock, a cold-blooded Anglo. The corrupt civic officials, for all their bluster, were no real threat to either Buffalo Bob or Howdy. Conflict, when there was any, more often came from the seltzer bottle of Clarabell, a humanoid clown who spritzed Bob at will and then hid behind his back as the kids in the Peanut Gallery went bananas trying to clue Bob in on what was happening. "He's right behind you, you idiot," at least one child could not help but yell. Among other highlights were the antics of Flub-a-Dub, a mutant wild animal who ate only meatballs. There were also sessions at the Super Talkascope, where Buffalo Bob and Howdy could look at anything that was happening anywhere in the world at any time, and sing-a-longs featuring such songs as "Iggly Wiggly Spaghetti" and "Ooga Booga Rocka Shmooga." Giddiness was *Howdy Doody*'s gift to children at the end of the rigors of the school day.

In 1954 Buffalo Bob suffered a heart attack. While he was still in the hospital, NBC constructed a studio in the basement of his home in suburban Westchester County, New York, so that the show could continue. Live remote broadcasts allowed viewers to follow Bob on a "secret mission" while Howdy and the gang held forth at Rockefeller Center in New York City. Smith returned to full-time work in less than a year and forged ahead for six more seasons. By the time of the show's cancellation at the end of the 1959–1960 season, the show had become a national institution, with the product tie-ins to prove it. Satisfied to have made "a pile of money," Smith told the press that he had enjoyed "a good run" and had no regrets. He moved back to Buffalo, once again a local hero, and bought three radio stations in Maine and a liquor store in Florida, his favorite spots, respectively, for summer and winter vacations.

Smith remained frozen in time as Buffalo Bob for the rest of his show business career. He first realized that he had become a kind of totem for a generation in 1970, when he received an unexpected invitation from a University of Pennsylvania student organization. Appearing in public in his Buffalo Bob outfit for the first time in ten years, he sold out the Ivy League gathering. Over the next five years

Smith rode a powerful wave of pop culture nostalgia. Referring to his fans as "alumni," he conducted a national Howdy Doody revival tour of college campuses, followed by some fifty shows for the United Service Organizations (USO), playing to American troops in Germany. The theory that recreational drug use among the Doodyphiles had a role in *Howdy Doody* chic is supported by some of Buffalo Bob's bookings. At New York's Fillmore East, he brought down the house with a medley of period commercial jingles from such sponsors as Colgate toothpaste, Sealtest ice cream, and Texaco gasoline. In 1975 Buffalo Bob made it to prime time when he appeared on an episode of the top-rated sitcom *Happy Days,* which was set in the 1950s.

The limits of wistfulness were reached soon after. In 1976 the graying Smith returned to daily television as host of *The New Howdy Doody Show.* The syndicated program, however, was cancelled in a matter of months. Some industry analysts believed that local programmers had inadvertently sabotaged the show by placing it on their afternoon children's schedules. Kids had become more interested in animated superheroes. A better strategy might have been to place the show in a time slot that did not conflict with baby-boomer work schedules. Buffalo Bob had a last hurrah in 1987 when he hosted a two-hour TV tribute on Howdy's fortieth birthday. In 1991, hoping to expand his golf season, Smith left his beloved Buffalo for Flat Rock, North Carolina. He died in Hendersonville, North Carolina, of cancer.

★

An autobiography, *Howdy and Me: Buffalo Bob's Own Story* (1990), was written with Donna McCrohan. Stephen Davis examines Smith's impact in *Say Kids! What Time Is It?* (1987) and "It's Howdy Doody Time," *Television Quarterly* (summer 1988). An obituary is in the *New York Times* (31 July 1998).

DAVID MARC

SMUCKER, Paul Highnam (*b.* 21 April 1917 in Orrville, Ohio; *d.* 17 December 1998 in Orrville, Ohio), president and chief executive officer of the J. M. Smucker Company who led his family's regional jam and jelly business to national prominence.

Smucker, the only son of Willard Smucker and Letha Highnam, who also had a daughter, followed his father and grandfather, Jerome Monroe Smucker, into the family's jam and jelly business centered in Orrville, Ohio. In 1897 Jerome Smucker, an inventive and practical farmer and businessman, added a small Orrville cider mill to his farms, creamery, and penmanship school. The grandson of Swiss Mennonites who had emigrated to eastern Pennsylvania in 1752, Jerome Smucker used the apple pulp from his cider presses to make custom apple butter for the farmers who supplied his mill. Aware that there was a market for commercially produced apple butter, he began to buy apples directly from local farmers. As a guarantee of the product's quality, he boldly signed his name to the paper cap on the apple butter's stoneware crock. In 1906 Jerome Smucker's sixteen-year-old son, Willard, joined him and helped with the cider and apple butter business, working in the mill and driving a wagon door to door to deliver the crocks of apple butter. By 1915 the revenue from the Smucker businesses was nearly $60,000 and in 1923, two years after the J. M. Smucker Company was incorporated, father and son began to produce preserves, jams, and jellies as well.

For Paul H. Smucker, the founder's grandson, life in Orrville and his connection to the family business seemed seamless. He attended local schools, played football in high school, and worked in the Orrville plant. One of his jobs at Smucker's was as an assistant cook; another was to unload hundred-pound bags of sugar. Smucker also did cement work during the construction of a processing facility in Wenatchee, Washington, when in 1935 the company expanded to the Pacific Northwest to capitalize on that region's rich supply of premium fruits and berries. As a student at Miami University in Oxford, Ohio, he earned a B.S. degree in business and worked summers in the family company. He joined the Smucker Company full time in 1939 as a cost accountant. The members of the board of directors were his aunts and uncles.

On 23 June 1940 Smucker married Lorraine Evangeline Smith. The couple had a daughter and two sons. The sons, like their father and grandfather, made the family business and its connection to the people of Orrville the focus of their careers. In 1943 Smucker was called to serve in World War II. He trained as an ensign at Fort Schuyler in New York City. As an officer aboard the destroyer *Cassin Young,* Smucker saw action in the Pacific theater against the Japanese. When his ship was brought to Boston Harbor and berthed next to "Old Ironsides" as part of the naval museum, Smucker actively collected World War II memorabilia for the exhibit. After his service, he returned to manage a Smucker's plant in Salem, Ohio, in 1945. The plant, intended to produce applesauce and dehydrate potatoes for potato flour, supplied Berlin during the 1947 Berlin airlift.

During the late 1940s and early 1950s, the Smucker family concentrated on growth and expansion beyond the Midwest. As the country shifted from small grocery stores to supermarkets, they shifted their business in two significant ways. In order to intensify flavor and improve their product, the Smuckers developed a system of capturing and reducing the volatiles, or essences, otherwise lost from fruits during cooking the jams. By restoring distilled, concentrated essences to jams, preserves, and jellies, Smucker was able to make his products more intensely flavorful and attractive to consumers. Secondly, the family began to address the national consumer directly by making Smucker responsible for directing sales. His efforts led to the introduction of products that would appeal to homemakers and to producing the individual portions of jam, jelly, and syrup demanded by fast-food restaurants and airlines. In 1958, as executive vice-president of the company, Smucker extended the business to capitalize on the Western market by building a Smucker's manufacturing plant in Salinas, California. In 1959 he helped persuade the board to allow the company—then the nation's largest independent producer of apple butter, jams, and jellies—to go public to raise funds for taxes and further expansion.

Although the Smucker Company had never supported a budget for national advertising, in 1962 Smucker persuaded them to accept the Wyse Advertising campaign that made light of their name. "With a name like Smucker's, it has to be good" gave Smucker's jams and jellies almost instant national prominence and reminded consumers of the connection between the product and the family's promise of wholesome quality. Smucker's good humor, his attention to his father and grandfather's established values of excellence and economy, and his concern for the people and products connected to his business made the joke pay off. In 1962 Smucker, president since 1961, listed the company on the New York Stock Exchange. For the fiscal year 1963–1964, Smucker's made a dramatic sales increase of 38 percent, creating a net income gain of 32 percent against steadily rising sugar costs.

Smucker oversaw the introduction of new products— some failures, like the pickle initiative, and others successes, like the collaboration with Kellogg's in the manufacture of Pop-Tarts. In 1970 he added peanut butter to the jelly products. Smucker supervised new manufacturing and processing plants across the country and encouraged the innovation of new products. Under his leadership, the company captured the market in the Midwest, followed by the West Coast and major cities in the East. Although he led the company to national prominence, the J. M. Smucker Company retained the personal, ethical values of fairness and integrity lived by its manager. In 1970, after the death of his father, Smucker became chairman and chief executive officer. In 1981 he was succeeded by one of his sons, Timothy, as president and in 1987, ninety years after his grandfather began producing cider and apple butter, he retired, with Timothy moving into the position of chairman and CEO and Smucker's other son, Richard, stepping up as president.

Miami University awarded Smucker an honorary doctor of law degree, as did the College of Wooster in 1988. Through Smucker's intervention, Akron University opened an extension site, Wayne College, in Orrville, where he served as president of the Orrville Campus Foundation. Smucker also served as a director of the Grocery Manufacturers' Association, the Kellogg's Company, the First National Bank of Orrville, and the W. W. Kellogg Foundation. Active in his church, Smucker received the Charles E. Wilson Award from Religion in American Life.

Managing his family's company with easy grace and deep commitment to quality and integrity, Smucker took a local, family-run business to national prominence, steady growth, and persistent success. His evenhandedness, quiet philanthropy, and concern for his employees led to management innovations that created a fierce loyalty to him and his company, which was listed three times by *Fortune* as one of the hundred best places to work in America. Smucker's leadership provided a framework for flextime, personal support, and respect for individuals. He died of pneumonia after a short illness, at age eighty-one. A lifelong member of the Christian Science Church in Wooster, Ohio, Smucker is buried with his ancestors and relatives in Orrville.

★

The J. M. Smucker Company website, <http://www.smucker. com>, and its public relations office have press releases on Smucker's career, retirement, and death. Articles about Smucker's influence on his family's business are available in many news and business magazines and newspapers. Particularly helpful are Everett Groseclose, "Paul Smucker Takes Great Pains to Preserve His Products' Quality," *Wall Street Journal* (3 Feb. 1975); Andrew Malcolm, "Of Jams and a Family," *New York Times Magazine* (15 Nov. 1983); Sandra Clark, "Living Up to Its Name: Smucker's Delivers on Its Promise," *Plain Dealer* (1 Nov. 1992); and Candace Goforth, "Key Ingredient for Happy Workers: Smucker's Says It's Respect," *San Diego Union-Tribune* (1 May 2000). William Donohue Ellis wrote *With a Name Like . . .* (1987) for the J. M. Smucker Company at the time of Smucker's retirement. Obituaries are in the *Press Release Newswire* (18 Dec. 1998), *Akron Beacon Journal* (19 Dec. 1998), *New York Times* (23 Dec. 1998), *Cleveland Plain Dealer* (24 Dec. 1998), and *Washington Post* (27 Dec. 1998).

WENDY HALL MALONEY

SNOW, Clarence Eugene ("Hank") (*b.* 9 May 1914 in Brooklyn, Nova Scotia, Canada; *d.* 20 December 1999 in Madison, Tennessee), country music singer, guitarist, and songwriter known as "the Singing Ranger" who was inducted into the Country Music Hall of Fame in 1979.

Snow was the fifth of six children born to George Lewis Snow, an itinerant sawmill foreman, and Marie Alice Boutlier, a former pianist in a silent movie theater who later took up Hawaiian slide guitar. Snow's two eldest siblings, a brother and sister, both died in infancy. Snow spent his

Hank Snow. AP/WIDE WORLD PHOTOS

Brakeman," and he set the standard for country trouba-dours to follow. Snow made his public debut in 1931, appearing in blackface makeup and singing one song as part of a minstrel show held at Bridgewater, Nova Scotia. Snow set his sights on performing live on radio station CHNS, in the province's capital city of Halifax. In what would become standard practice for Snow, when his written request to be heard was rejected, he traveled to the station unannounced and proceeded to seal the deal in person. Following a successful on-air audition in the summer of 1933, Snow was given his own weekly show. When the show proved to be a success, the CHNS station director suggested that Snow adopt the name Hank. About the same time, Snow changed his sobriquet from "the Cowboy Blue Yodeler" to "the Yodeling Ranger." When yodeling went out of fashion in country music in the mid-1940s, he changed it to "the Singing Ranger."

Snow married Minnie ("Min") Blanche Aalders on 2 September 1935. Over the years she proved to be his biggest fan, working to support him as he struggled to establish himself as a viable country music star, first in Canada and then in the United States. They had one son, Jimmie Rodgers Snow. The couple endured a restless, nomadic existence, as Snow frequently moved to towns where he felt he had a chance of advancing his career. Sometimes his instincts proved correct; on other occasions, the family was forced to beat a hasty retreat back to southeastern Nova Scotia, chased by bill collectors. During the mid- to late 1930s, Snow gave guitar lessons to augment his income from various odd jobs.

Snow made his recording debut on 29 October 1936 in Montreal for Canadian RCA Victor. He made further recordings in 1937 and 1939. Two songs he wrote and recorded in 1939, "The Blue Velvet Band" and "Wandering On," became Canadian country hits. Snow then formed a band and toured Nova Scotia and Prince Edward Island, playing in small theaters and community halls. By 1944 country music fans in the United States had begun to catch on to Snow, and he set his sights on radio station, WWVA in Wheeling, West Virginia. Within a year he had moved his family to Wheeling, had two shows daily on the station, and was a star of the Saturday Jamboree, which also featured Big Slim, the Lone Cowboy, a local country star.

Perhaps because of his impoverished childhood, Snow developed a lifetime obsession with keeping up appearances. As his fame outstripped his income, he wore flamboyant, custom-tailored Western-style suits on stage and drove late-model, expensive cars (including his canary yellow 1947 Cadillac convertible, now enshrined in the Hank Snow Country Music Centre in Liverpool, Nova Scotia). He continued to live in this style, even when his bank balance said that he could not afford it. Snow took a gamble in 1945 when he spent his $2,000 savings to obtain a trained

early years in Brooklyn, a tiny fishing village on Nova Scotia's southeastern shore. Snow's parents divorced in 1922, and Snow was sent to live with his grandmother, with whom he did not get along. After several months, Snow returned to live with his mother in Liverpool, about two miles from Brooklyn. Later Snow lived with his mother and her second husband in Stonehurst, near Lunenburg. Unfortunately, his stepfather was an abusive alcoholic who delighted in beating young Jack, as Snow was called at this stage of his life.

At age twelve, Snow left school in Brooklyn and got a job as a flunky aboard a fishing schooner (similar to the famous Bluenose depicted on the Canadian dime). Having already taught himself to sing and play using his mother's Hawaiian guitar, Snow entertained fishermen on their voyages from Lunenburg to the fishing grounds off the coast of Newfoundland. He spent his free time listening to country music on the shipboard radio. After nearly losing his life in a 1930 storm, Snow returned to live with relatives near the tourist village of Bluerocks.

Snow modeled his singing and playing style on his hero, Jimmie Rodgers. A former railroad worker from Mississippi, Rodgers was "America's Blue Yodeler, the Singing

horse that he named Shawnee. He supplemented his musical performances with trick riding and comic skits with Shawnee, and his popularity grew. Snow conceived an idea for a traveling show costarring Big Slim and went into debt to buy a custom-built truck for Shawnee as well as a portable corral, grandstand, public-address system, and large truck to haul everything on tour. Just before launching his ambitious 1946 Canadian tour, Snow traveled with Shawnee to Hollywood, where he was unsuccessful at persuading producers that he and the horse were Canada's answer to the popular American cowboy actor Roy Rogers and his horse Trigger.

Snow accepted an invitation in 1948 to travel to radio station KRLD in Dallas, Texas, which had been playing his Canadian records to enthusiastic response. He became a regular performer on a weekly show called the Big D Jamboree and met and played with such country music greats as Hank Thompson, Floyd Tillman, and "the Texas Troubadour," Ernest Tubb. Snow became close friends with Tubb, who later booked Snow into country music's most prestigious venue, Nashville's Grand Ole Opry; he took the Opry stage for the first time on 7 January 1950. Snow used his popular success in Dallas to persuade the legendary RCA producer Steve Sholes to record him in Chicago in the spring of 1949. Snow recorded four songs for Sholes and then returned to Canada, where he continued to perform sporadically with Shawnee (his ambitious outdoor show having been forced to fold after Big Slim left and the portable grandstand collapsed, injuring several spectators).

On 28 March 1950, while living in Nashville and performing as a regular on the Opry, Snow recorded four more songs for Steve Sholes and RCA. These songs included one written by him that became the number one country song of the year, as well as Snow's ticket to riches and his immortal calling card: a rhythmic tale of leaving on a train to escape a failed love affair called "I'm Movin' On." The 1950s were Snow's golden years. His second U.S. release, "The Golden Rocket" (1950), another original train song, also zoomed to number one. Snow scored numerous top-ten hits that decade and three more number one singles: "Rhumba Boogie" (1951), "I Don't Hurt Anymore" (1954), and "Let Me Go, Lover" (1954). "The 1950s were the heyday of good down-to-earth country music," Snow later wrote in his autobiography. "My timing was perfect."

Snow also performed country duets with Anita Carter of the Carter Sisters; in 1951, the duo had a number four hit with "Bluebird Island." Snow hit the top of the charts in 1962 with "I've Been Everywhere," which he did not write and which was his last number one song until the 1974 surprise hit "Hello Love." Snow and his family became U.S. citizens in 1958. He recorded some 800 songs for RCA and remained under contract from 1936 to 1981,

when his deal was terminated unceremoniously. He is one of the few country artists to have had songs on the charts in five consecutive decades. In addition to being a skilled singer-songwriter and an exciting "breakout" guitarist (as lead guitarists are known in country music), Snow was also an excellent scout of songwriting talent. In the basement office of his home in Nashville, he made it a point to listen to every demo tape he was sent, just in case one of them contained a potential hit.

In 1955 Snow helped persuade Sholes and RCA to lure an unorthodox young country and rockabilly performer named Elvis Presley away from Sam Phillips's Sun Records. (Earlier that year Snow had introduced Presley in his first appearance on the Grand Ole Opry stage.) Until his death, Snow maintained that he and Colonel Tom Parker had an agreement to co-represent Presley in the deal with RCA, but that Parker double-crossed him to keep Presley as his exclusive client. Although Snow enjoyed drinking vodka after his performances, he was a demanding showman who insisted that his band, the Rainbow Ranch Boys, not touch alcohol before a show. He had a strict policy against performing songs that glorified drinking or drug use or were sexually suggestive. Snow gave up drinking in 1970 and cigarettes, which he had chain-smoked for years, in the 1980s.

Snow built a recording studio in his home in Madison (a suburb of Nashville), which he called Rainbow Ranch. He also owned a music store in downtown Nashville and two radio stations. Among his close companions were such other members of the country music aristocracy as Ernest Tubb, Lloyd "Cowboy" Copas, and Red Foley. Snow entertained U.S. troops overseas in both the Korean and Vietnam wars. Having never fully outgrown the scars of his abusive childhood, Snow formed the Hank Snow Foundation for the Prevention of Child Abuse and Neglect, International in 1976; after operating for several years, the foundation was subsumed by a larger charitable organization. Snow's final recording was an album of duets with Willie Nelson in 1984. His son, Jimmie Rodgers Snow, a popular country music performer in his own right, became a gospel preacher in Nashville. Snow died at age eighty-five of heart failure at Rainbow Ranch and is buried at Spring Hill Cemetery in Nashville.

Snow was one of the classic country music performers from the genre's golden era. He influenced many leading singer-songwriters who came after him, including Bob Dylan and Willie Nelson, and his incisive flat-picking, nasally vocal tone and plainspoken lyrics continue to reach new generations of country music fans.

★

Snow's exhaustively detailed autobiography, *The Hank Snow Story,* was published in 1995. He is also covered in Patrick Carr, ed., *The Illustrated History of Country Music* (1979); and Bill Malone, *Classic Country Music* (1990). An obituary is in the *New York Times* (21 Dec. 1999).

GREGORY K. ROBINSON

SOLTI, Georg (*b.* 21 October 1912 in Budapest, Hungary; *d.* 5 September 1997 in Antibes, France), renowned conductor who brought the Chicago Symphony Orchestra worldwide acclaim during his twenty-two-year tenure as its music director.

Solti, born György Stern, was the second child of Móricz Stern and Teréz Rosenbaum, assimilated Hungarian Jews who had settled in Budapest. His father worked at various times as a flour merchant, insurance salesman, and real estate broker but was not successful as a businessman. The family relocated temporarily to Veszprém when World War I broke out in 1914, returning to Budapest in 1918 when Solti was six. It was at this time that his mother, who was quite musical, noticed that her younger child had a good ear and engaged a piano teacher for him. His older sister Lilly, who was born in 1904, studied voice and eventually had a minor career as a singer. Móricz Stern changed his

Georg Solti, 1993. ASSOCIATED PRESS AP

children's last name to Solti (the name of a small Hungarian town) during the upsurge in Hungarian nationalism that followed World War I. He thought it would help their careers.

At age ten Solti was admitted to the Ernö Fodor School of Music in Budapest, where he studied piano and theory with Miklós Laurisin. Two years later he entered the city's prestigious Franz Liszt Academy of Music, where he remained for six years, studying with Arnold Székely, Zoltán Kodály, Leó Weiner, Ernö Dohnányi, and, briefly, Béla Bartók. Solti later wrote that he considered his years at the Liszt Academy to be the most significant part of his formal musical education. He received a diploma in piano in 1930 and a diploma in composition in 1931.

Solti's decision to pursue a career as a conductor came at the age of fourteen, when he heard Erich Kleiber conduct Beethoven's Symphony no. 5. Upon graduation from the Liszt Academy he was engaged as a répétiteur, or coach, at the Budapest Opera House, which was an appropriate apprenticeship for a prospective opera conductor. Although he gained significant knowledge of the operatic repertoire in this position, he knew that as a Jew he would not be allowed to conduct the Budapest Opera. In October 1932 he obtained a position as assistant to Josef Krips, who was music director of the opera house in Karlsruhe, Germany. However, Solti returned to Budapest after a few months because of the anti-Semitism he encountered in Germany. During the summer of 1936, he attended the Salzburg Festival in Austria and returned the following year to work under the Italian conductor Arturo Toscanini.

Solti presented his operatic conducting debut with the Budapest State Opera (becoming the first unconverted Jew to conduct the opera since the independence of Hungary) in a performance of Wolfgang Amadeus Mozart's *Le nozze di Figaro* (*The Marriage of Figaro*) on 11 March 1938, the night that Nazi troops marched into Austria. He knew that he would have to leave Hungary to pursue his musical career and departed for Switzerland on 15 August 1939, two weeks before the border was closed. He spent the war years in Switzerland, supporting himself primarily through teaching piano and accompanying, since there were few conducting opportunities open to him. Solti was a prodigious pianist and won first prize in Geneva's Concours International Piano Competition in 1942.

In 1946 Solti was invited by the U.S. Army to conduct performances of Beethoven's *Fidelio* in Stuttgart and Munich, Germany. These performances led to his appointment that year as music director of the Bavarian State Opera in Munich. During Solti's six-year tenure, he successfully rebuilt the company from its postwar ruins and established his own reputation as an opera conductor. While in Munich he met Richard Strauss and conducted a performance of *Der Rosenkavalier* in the composer's presence. Solti made his home in Frankfurt, Germany, from 1952 to 1961, where he held the position of music director of the Frankfurt Opera. He presented his first non-European performance when he traveled to Buenos Aires, Argentina, to conduct the Buenos Aires Philharmonic in 1952. He made his U.S. debut in 1953 with the San Francisco Opera conducting Strauss's *Elektra* and returned the following year to conduct the San Francisco Symphony. Appearances at the Edinburgh Festival in Scotland (1952) and the Salzburg Festival (1956), and with the Chicago Symphony Orchestra (1954) and the New York Philharmonic (1957) helped establish his international reputation.

Another important development at this time was Solti's engagement by Decca Recording Company to record Richard Wagner's complete *Ring* cycle, with John Culshaw as producer. (Solti's association with Decca began in 1947 and lasted until his death.) The four operas of Wagner's *Der Ring des Nibelungen—Das Rheingold, Die Walküre, Siegried,* and *Gotterdämmung*—had never been recorded as a complete set. This was a monumental project, and Decca and Culshaw took a chance in engaging the young Solti, who had not yet established his reputation as a Wagner interpreter. The project, begun in 1958, was pioneering in its use of stereo sound, which had been developed recently for the commercial recording market. The entire cycle was finally completed in 1965; it remains one of the most successful *Ring* cycle recordings.

Solti made his Covent Garden debut in London in 1959 with a performance of Strauss's *Der Rosenkavalier.* This led to his 1961 appointment as music director of the Royal Opera at Covent Garden, a position he held until 1971. In his enormously successful ten-year tenure, the company presented works by Ludwig von Beethoven, Georges Bizet, Benjamin Britten, Christoph Willibald Gluck, Mozart, Jacques Offenbach, Giacomo Puccini, Maurice Ravel, Arnold Schoenberg, Strauss, Pyotr Tchaikovsky, Giuseppi Verdi, and Wagner. In 1972 Solti became a British subject and was knighted by Queen Elizabeth II in recognition of his extraordinary work at Covent Garden.

While living in Zurich during the war, Solti had met Hedwig (Hedi) Oechsli; they married on 29 October 1946. The couple separated during Solti's third season at Covent Garden and eventually divorced in 1966. On 11 November 1967 he married Anne Valerie Pitts, a London journalist; they had two daughters. Solti assumed the position of music director of the Chicago Symphony Orchestra in 1969, while fulfilling the last two years of his contract with Covent Garden. His twenty-two-year tenure with the orchestra brought it to international prominence. He organized the orchestra's first European tour and eventually led it on five trips to Europe, three to Japan, and one to Australia, as well as on numerous trips to other cities throughout the United States. Solti worked with civic leaders and the or-

chestra's management to increase its subscription sales and its local support and to improve the salaries and benefits for the players. He raised the orchestra's musical standards to new heights and recorded most of the standard classical and romantic repertory with them. He ended his tenure as musical director in April 1991 with performances of Verdi's *Otello* in Chicago and New York City.

Solti maintained his primary residence in Europe during his years with the Chicago Symphony. He concurrently served as music director of the Orchestre de Paris (1970–1975), music adviser of the Paris Opéra (1971–1973), and principal conductor of the London Philharmonic (1979–1981). Solti conducted Wagner's *Ring* at the Bayreuth Festival in Germany in 1983 on the occasion of the centenary of the composer's death. Following his retirement from the Chicago Symphony, Solti appeared as guest conductor with numerous ensembles throughout the world. On 5 December 1991, the 250th anniversary of Mozart's death, he conducted a commemorative performance of the composer's *Requiem* at Saint Stephen's Church in Vienna. On the fiftieth anniversary of Bartók's death in 1995, Solti conducted performances of *Bluebeard's Castle* in Paris and Lille, France. He was committed to working with young musicians and presented master classes and conducting workshops in New York City and Chicago. Solti died at age eighty-four of a heart attack while vacationing with his wife and daughter in Antibes, France. He is buried in Farkasreti Cemetery in Budapest, next to Béla Bartók. At the time of his death, Solti was preparing for a London Proms concert performance of Verdi's *Requiem.*

Solti left a substantial recorded legacy. He made more than 250 recordings for the London/Decca label (including forty-five complete operas) and received thirty-two Grammy awards (one of them a lifetime achievement award)—more than any other performer. He received numerous other honors and awards in his lifetime, including the National Medal of Arts, which was bestowed on him by President William J. Clinton in 1993. Solti was known as an energetic and forceful conductor. He specialized primarily in the German classical and romantic repertory, although he conducted notable performances of works by numerous twentieth-century composers, including Samuel Barber, Alban Berg, Benjamin Britten, Elliott Carter, John Corigliano, David Del Tredici, Hans Werner Henze, George Rochberg, Arnold Schoenberg, Roger Sessions, and Ellen Taaffe Zwilich. Although some critics disagreed with Solti's style or approach, he was recognized as a superb musician who could bring orchestras to new heights of music making.

★

Archival materials relating to Solti's years with the Chicago Symphony Orchestra are housed in the orchestra's Rosenthal Archives. His *Memoirs* (1997), which were written with the assistance of Harvey Sachs, includes a complete chronicle of his life and career. Paul Robinson, *Solti* (1979), focuses on his musical activities and includes a discography (through Feb. 1979) compiled by Bruce Surtees. Solti's years with the Chicago Symphony Orchestra are documented in William Barry Furlong, *Season with Solti: A Year in the Life of the Chicago Symphony Orchestra* (1974). The making of his 1958–1965 *Ring* cycle recording is described in John Culshaw, *Ring Resounding* (1967); it also was documented in the 1965 British Broadcasting Corporation (BBC) film *The Golden Ring: The Making of Solti's Ring,* which was released on video in 1992. Peter Maniura produced a film biography, *Georg Solti: The Making of a Maestro,* for the BBC in 1997; it is also available on video. Obituaries are in the *Chicago Tribune, New York Times,* and *Los Angeles Times* (all 6 Sept. 1997).

JANE GOTTLIEB

SPOCK, Benjamin McLane ("Dr. Spock") (*b.* 2 May 1903 in New Haven, Connecticut; *d.* 15 March 1998 in La Jolla, California), pediatrician, author, and political activist best known for his *Common Sense Book of Baby and Child Care* (1946) and for his opposition to the Vietnam War.

As the oldest of six children born to Mildred Louise Stoughton, a homemaker, and Benjamin Ives Spock, a lawyer for the New Haven Railroad, Spock learned much about child care growing up in New Haven. "I had changed a lot of diapers and given a lot of bottles," he once reflected. Spock's parents, like so many in that era, were loving but not affectionate toward their children, and he later claimed that his progressive views on child rearing developed in part out of his mother's strict Victorian parenting.

After graduating in 1921 from Phillips Academy in Andover, Massachusetts, Spock matriculated at Yale College in New Haven, where he majored in English and rowed for the crew team. In 1924, following his junior year, he and his teammates in the heavyweight eight division set a world record and won the gold medal at the Paris Olympic Games.

Spock received a B.A. degree from Yale in 1925 and began his medical education at Yale University School of Medicine. In 1927 he married Jane Davenport Cheney and transferred to Columbia University's College of Physicians and Surgeons in New York City; he graduated at the head of his class with an M.D. in 1929. Spock interned at Presbyterian Hospital in New York City (1929–1931) and took two residencies—one in pediatrics at the New York Nursery and Child's Hospital and the other in psychiatry at New York Hospital. The combination of pediatrics and psychiatry was unusual, and Spock continued to pursue it after

he set up his own practice in 1933 by taking part-time training at the New York Psychoanalytic Institute until 1938. In the midst of these changes, Jane gave birth to their first son, Michael, in 1933.

During the Great Depression, Spock slowly built his pediatric practice in New York City. Some attributed the early success of his practice to his outgoing personality and ability to calm patients. "One of my faults as a pediatrician has always been that I whoop it up too much with children," he once said. But the pediatrics practice and concurrent study of psychiatry proved important in shaping a philosophy of parenting and child care that would later make him famous.

In 1943 Spock began writing a comprehensive book for parents on child rearing. He was interrupted by his wartime service as a navy psychiatrist (and by the birth of his second son, John), but by the end of the war he had clarified most of his ideas for the *Common Sense Book of Baby and Child Care.* It sold 750,000 copies in the year after its publication in 1946, and by the time Spock died in 1998, the book had sold 50 million copies worldwide and had been translated into forty-two languages. After the Bible, it is the biggest-selling book in history.

Baby and Child Care's publication coincided with the baby boom and the suburbanization of the United States.

Benjamin Spock. PRINTS AND PHOTOGRAPHS DIVISION, LIBRARY OF CONGRESS

Young suburban couples counted on Spock to assume a role that in earlier times may have been filled by nearby family and friends. It was one of few books of its kind available to parents at the time.

Most important, Spock's application of Freudian psychiatry to pediatrics resulted in an approach that completely overturned prevailing ideas on child rearing. Until 1946 the most commonly used book on the subject had been John B. Watson's *Psychological Care of Infant and Child* (1928), which included advice that parents should never kiss their children, hold them in their laps, or rock their carriages. Spock, in contrast, espoused a more practical approach, central to which were constant expressions of nurturing and warmth. And he conveyed the lessons in a comforting, reassuring manner. Spock's book opens with the now famous lines, "Trust yourself. You know more than you think you do." As Thomas Maier noted in a 1998 article, Spock also helped parents to understand the complicated emotions arising from breast-feeding, toilet training, spanking, the Oedipus complex, and penis envy, but "without using any of [Sigmund] Freud's exact terms." The ultimate result empowered parents, encouraging them to think for themselves and to rely on their own instincts and common sense.

A year after the publication of *Baby and Child Care,* Spock became the first consultant on child psychiatry at the Mayo Clinic in Rochester, Minnesota (1947–1951). Later, he held positions as professor of child development at the University of Pittsburgh (1951–1955) and at Western Reserve University in Cleveland (1955–1967).

In the 1950s and 1960s, while the baby boom generation grew up, Spock became a national icon. More significant, the heightened tensions of the cold war moved Spock to increasingly use his notoriety to speak out on political issues. He served as cochair of the National Committee for a Sane Nuclear Policy (SANE) from 1962 to 1967. A widely circulated 1962 SANE newspaper advertisement criticizing the increased number of nuclear tests featured a photo of Spock standing behind a child, the slogan "Dr. Spock Is Worried," and Spock's own words describing his concern for the future of the world's children in a nuclear age.

Spock's political career blossomed after 1965, as the American war in Vietnam escalated. He had supported President Lyndon Johnson's election in 1964, in part because Johnson promised to pursue peace in Southeast Asia; a year later Spock, feeling betrayed, began to speak out stridently against the U.S. presence there. "There's no point in raising children if they're going to be burned alive," he said. Spock gradually became estranged from SANE, which he felt did not go far enough in its opposition to the war, and he soon resigned his post with the organization.

For his role as part of a delegation that returned 1,000 draft cards to the U.S. Department of Justice in October 1967, Spock was indicted with four others for conspiracy to aid and abet draft resisters. The indictment galvanized the antiwar movement in 1968, for it seemed the war protestors had finally attracted the U.S. administration's attention. The so-called Spock Trial was, until the Chicago Conspiracy Trial in 1969, *the* political trial of that tumultuous era. Spock was the most outspoken and unrepentant of the defendants and earned the respect of his prosecutor who, years later, admitted that he had been converted to oppose the war during the trial. The jury found Spock and three others guilty, and sentenced him to two years in prison. The following year, however, the verdict was overturned on appeal.

Spock's new political career gave rise to critics' charges that *Baby and Child Care* encouraged permissiveness, and that Spock had spawned a whole generation of children who did not respect authority. The Reverend Norman Vincent Peale blamed Spock for what he saw as a generation of spoiled children: "Feed 'em whenever they want, never let them cry, satisfy their every desire." Many mothers and fathers who supported the war returned their copies of the book to Spock with angry letters, and sales of the book plummeted. Spock defended himself by saying, "I didn't want to encourage permissiveness, but rather to reject rigidity," but the charge of permissiveness stayed with him for the rest of his life.

Supporters of Johnson's and Richard Nixon's war policies had reason to worry about Spock's influence: *Baby and Child Care* had sold 22 million copies by 1968. In spite of the criticism that seemed to suggest that a pediatrician had no place in the political arena, Spock pressed on. Just as his activism infuriated some, it inspired the young people he joined in marches and demonstrations. He also helped to sustain the movement financially by donating every speaking honorarium he received to movement organizations (he often traveled twenty-five days a month, giving speeches against the war).

In 1972 Spock ran for U.S. president on the People's Party ticket. (Opponents of the war had urged Spock and Martin Luther King, Jr., to run on the same ticket for vice president and president, respectively, in the 1968 campaign.) The party's platform included planks supporting universal health care, the decriminalization of abortion and marijuana, and the immediate withdrawal of U.S. troops from foreign soil. He made it onto the ballot in ten states and received nearly 80,000 votes.

In the 1970s Spock also took criticism from the women's movement for advancing sexist assumptions about gender roles. One paragraph of *Baby and Child Care* disapproved of women "acting more and more like men." In an embarrassing confrontation, the leading feminist Gloria Steinem told Spock, "I hope that you understand that you are considered a symbol of male oppression—just like Freud." Spock was contrite. In 1976 he revised the book to remove the "sexist biases" that "help to create and perpetuate discrimination against girls and women."

Spock's marriage, long strained, finally broke down in 1975. He married Mary Morgan, forty years his junior, the following year. Morgan, a writer and activist, joined Spock in his protests and assisted in writing his memoir, *Spock on Spock,* which was published in 1989. Spock stayed active in political issues primarily through antinuclear demonstrations in the 1980s (he was arrested in 1987 at Cape Canaveral Air Force Station at age eighty-four for trespassing to protest the launching of a Trident 2 missile). He also continued to write, often about his new interest in macrobiotic diets and alternative health care, into his nineties. After several bouts with illness, Spock died at age ninety-four of natural causes. His remains were cremated.

Spock wrote or cowrote thirteen books, including *A Baby's First Year,* with John Reinhart (1954); *Dr. Spock Talks with Mothers: Growth and Guidance* (1961); *Caring for Your Disabled Child,* with Marion O. Lerrigo (1965); *Dr. Spock on Vietnam,* with Mitchell Zimmerman (1968); *Decent and Indecent: Our Personal and Political Behavior* (1970); *Raising Children in a Difficult Time: A Philosophy of Parental Leadership and High Ideals* (1974); *Dr. Spock on Parenting: Sensible Advice from America's Most Trusted Child-Care Expert* (1988); and *A Better World for Our Children: Rebuilding American Family Values* (1994).

Spock's two careers in medicine and politics established him as one of the most significant figures in twentieth-century America. He taught millions of parents how to raise their children with compassion and respect, and extended those lessons through his political activism to many of those same children who, in adulthood, inherited a world that troubled Spock for the rest of his life. Although he was sometimes caricatured as a radical, in both careers Spock represented well-worn traditions of American individualism and dissent.

★

Spock's papers are deposited at the Bird Library at Syracuse University in Syracuse, New York. With Mary Morgan he authored *Spock on Spock: A Memoir of Growing Up with the Century* (1989). He is the subject of two full-length biographies: Lynn Z. Bloom, *Doctor Spock: Biography of a Conservative Radical* (1972), and Thomas Maier, *Dr. Spock: An American Life* (1998); see also Maier's "Everybody's Grandfather," *U.S. News and World Report* (30 Mar. 1998). For more on Spock's 1968 conspiracy trial, see Jessica Mitford, *The Trial of Dr. Spock, the Rev. William Sloane Coffin, Jr., Michael Ferber, Mitchell Goodman, and Marcus Raskin* (1969), and essays by Noam Chomsky et al., *Trials of the Resistance* (1970). An obituary is in the *New York Times* (17 Mar. 1998).

MICHAEL S. FOLEY

STANS, Maurice Hubert (*b.* 22 March 1908 in Shakopee, Minnesota; *d.* 14 April 1998 in Pasadena, California), financial consultant, U.S. government official, and Republican Party campaign fund-raiser during the 1960s and early 1970s.

Stans was one of two children of J. Hubert Stans, a house painter and musician, and Mathilda Nyssen, a homemaker. Stans's early life could have been written by Horatio Alger, one of his favorite authors. His parents were second-generation Belgian immigrants, and Stans grew up in a small town, working-class environment near Minneapolis. Stans attended St. Mark's, a Catholic elementary school, and Shakopee High School. A scrawny boy, ill at ease on the athletic field, Stans excelled scholastically and was valedictorian for his graduating class.

On the advice of a high school teacher, Stans moved to Chicago in 1925 to study accounting. He worked as a stenographer by day and studied business administration at Northwestern University at night. He later took courses at Columbia University. Although Stans never earned a college degree, he joined the Chicago-based public accounting

Maurice Stans testifying before the Senate Watergate Committee, 1973. ASSOCIATED PRESS

firm of Alexander Grant and Company. Between 1928 and 1931 he rose from office boy to junior accountant to partner. Stans married Kathleen Carmody on 7 September 1933; they adopted two sons and two daughters.

As Stans climbed the corporate ladder, he left forever the poverty of his youth. By 1935 was traveling with his wife, first to fishing spots, then to more exotic places such as Africa, where they went on safari. Following Alexander Grant's death in 1938, Stans became managing partner of his firm, which by 1955 would emerge as the tenth largest accounting agency in the United States. Stans also acquired holdings in several companies and became chairman of the board of the Moore Corporation, a stove manufacturer. He amassed a sizable fortune and in 1940 founded the Stans Foundation to fight heart disease and cancer, aliments that had claimed the lives of his parents.

Stans, a lifelong Republican, entered public service in 1953 when he became a consultant to the Appropriations Committee of the U.S. House of Representatives. He studied operations at the U.S. Post Office and recommended a reform of its practices at branch offices. Stans earned a reputation for fiscal discipline and administrative competence, and a succession of appointments followed. He served as deputy postmaster general (1955–1957), then deputy director (1957–1958) and director (1958–1961) of the Bureau of the Budget. As budget director, Stans rejected proposals to jump-start the economy with public works, derided "extravagant spending" by the Democrat-controlled Congress, and achieved a balanced budget for 1960. President Dwight D. Eisenhower later praised Stans as "one of the ablest and finest men I have known in government." Stans settled in Los Angeles in 1961 and became an investment banker.

Stans's association with Richard Nixon made him a national figure. Both men became acquainted during their service in the Eisenhower administration. In 1962, after Stans threw a fund-raising dinner for the Republican Party, Nixon tapped him to be the finance chairman of his California gubernatorial campaign. Stans also managed the Finance Committee of Nixon's 1968 presidential campaign and helped raise $34 million for the Republican ticket. "Nobody ever gets offended by being asked for too much," he said of his fund-raising prowess. Voters, Stans explained, "are flattered by being asked to give more than they can afford." Nixon named Stans secretary of commerce in 1969.

Stans was one of the most conservative and least effective members of Nixon's cabinet. An advocate of business interests, he resisted product safety legislation, no-fault auto insurance, and environmental protection. Elsewhere, his record was mixed. Stans's visit to Moscow in 1971 paved the way for Nixon's successful meeting with Soviet leader Leonid Brezhnev in Russia a year later. But his gaffes—insisting that Japan voluntarily restrict textile exports to the United States and praising Greece's military regime for welcoming U.S. investment—proved embarrassing. However, Stans oversaw Nixon's most original civil rights initiative, helping racial minorities form businesses. He established the Office of Minority Business Enterprise and worked hard to sell the program. But civil rights leaders expressed skepticism, and the policy only yielded results after the White House assumed control. Nixon deemed Stans an inadequate spokesman for the administration, and the commerce secretary never penetrated the president's inner circle.

Stans left the Department of Commerce in 1972 to become finance chairman of the Committee to Re-Elect the President. To bypass the new Federal Election Campaign Act, which mandated financial disclosures by candidates, Stans encouraged large contributors to donate money before the act went into effect on 7 April 1972. He also raised a staggering $60 million war chest for Nixon's reelection. On 10 May 1973 Stans and former Attorney General John N. Mitchell were indicted on ten counts of perjury and conspiracy regarding a $200,000 donation from the financier Robert Vesco. Stans allegedly advised Vesco on how much to contribute, illicitly accepted the cash in $100 bills on 10 April 1972, and kept it in his safe to fund the Nixon campaign's espionage activities. The evidence against Stans and Mitchell was not overwhelming, and a jury acquitted them in 1974. As the jury foreman read the verdict, Stans covered his eyes and wept. But in 1975 Stans pleaded guilty to five misdemeanor violations of campaign finance laws and accepted his sentence, a $5,000 fine. A year later, the American Institute of Certified Public Accountants found Stans not guilty of discrediting its profession.

Stans tried to distance himself from the Watergate scandal for the rest of his life. There is no evidence that he had prior knowledge of the break-in at the Democratic National Committee's headquarters at the Watergate Hotel; Stans asserted that it was his job to get money for the campaign and "someone else's" to spend it. He published two books, *The Terrors of Justice* (1978), a bitter memoir of his Watergate experience and trials, and *One of the President's Men* (1995), his autobiography. Yet Stans remained loyal to Nixon and raised funds for the Richard Nixon Library and Birthplace, explaining, "I felt an obligation." After his wife died in 1984, Stans remarried. He later died of heart failure at age ninety.

Although three years of investigations and trials cleared him of any knowing violation of any law, Stans remained linked to the worst scandal in U.S. political history. His fund-raising activities encouraged Congress to limit individual contributions to political campaigns.

★

Stans's papers are at the Minnesota Historical Society in St.

Paul. His two memoirs, cited above, cover most aspects of his public career. Insight on Stans's ties to Nixon can be found in John Ehrlichman, *Witness to Power: The Nixon Years* (1982), and H. R. Haldeman, *The Haldeman Diaries: Inside the Nixon White House* (1994). Stans's support for minority business enterprise is covered in Maurice H. Stans, "Richard Nixon and His Bridges to Human Dignity," *Presidential Studies Quarterly* 26 (winter 1996): 179–183; and Dean J. Kotlowski, "Black Power—Nixon Style: The Nixon Administration and Minority Business Enterprise," *Business History Review* 72 (autumn 1998): 409ff. Obituaries are in the *New York Times* and *Washington Post* (both 15 Apr. 1998).

DEAN J. KOTLOWSKI

STEEL, Dawn Leslie (*b.* 19 August 1946 in New York City; *d.* 20 December 1997 in Los Angeles, California), movie producer and first female head of a motion picture studio, known for her determination and for breaking new ground for women in Hollywood.

Steel was the only daughter of Nathan ("Nat") Speilberg and Lillian Tarlo. Her father was a salesman and a semi-professional weightlifter who changed his surname to "Steel," performing in athletic competitions as the "Man of Steel." Steel had one brother. She spent her early years in relative affluence, first in Manhattan and then in suburban Rockville Centre, New York, in a home she described as similar to the mansion Tara in the 1939 movie *Gone with the Wind.* In 1957 her father suffered a business setback and the family moved to Great Neck, Long Island, New York, where her mother supported the family as an accounts receivable supervisor and eventually rose to a management position in an electronics business.

Steel graduated from Great Neck South High School in 1964 and then enrolled in Boston University's College of Business Administration, leaving after a year. She returned to New York City, where she attended classes at the New York University (NYU) School of Commerce, working part-time as a bookkeeper. Anxious to begin a career, Steel left NYU before completing her degree. She first worked as a receptionist in the garment industry and then at the Stadia Publishing Company, a publisher of sports guides such as *Major League Baseball Digest.* Steel was hired as a receptionist and later was promoted to a researcher. Denied admission to the Yankee Stadium press box because of her gender, Steel reported on the games from an ancillary press box.

In 1969 Steel began working at the then-fledgling *Penthouse,* eventually becoming the head of merchandising. Because of the magazine's sexual content, Steel initially told her parents that she was employed by *Mademoiselle,* a women's publication. She traveled internationally, searching for suggestive products to brand and market for *Penthouse.* In 1972 Steel became romantically involved with Ronald Richard Rothstein, who became her business partner in Entrepreneuse Enterprises, which she ran in addition to her role at *Penthouse.* Her personal company's biggest success was the mail-order sale of amaryllis plants, which she marketed under the slogan "Grow Your Own Penis," a reference to the plant's phallic shape. Steel left *Penthouse* in 1975 and married Rothstein on New Year's Eve that same year.

Also in 1975 Steel and Rothstein launched the company Oh, Dawn, marketing toilet tissue printed with an image reminiscent of the Gucci logo of linked "Gs," which was hugely popular at the time. Oh, Dawn, named for people's reactions when Steel told them she was in the toilet-tissue business, was eventually sued by the Gucci family for copyright infringement. The case was settled out of court. Steel and Rothstein divorced in 1978.

That same year Steel became the vice president of merchandising at *Playboy* and at Paramount Pictures the following year. One of her first assignments involved securing corporate product tie-ins with the Coca-Cola Company and the McDonald's Corporation, defraying production costs related to *Star Trek: The Motion Picture* (1979). Steel's efforts were successful and launched her rapid rise at Paramount Pictures. She was named the president of production in 1985. Feature films produced under Steel's watch at Paramount included *Flashdance* (1983), *Top Gun* (1986), and *Fatal Attraction* (1987).

Steel married the producer Charles Roven in 1985 and gave birth to their daughter in 1987. That same year she left Paramount; some sources say she learned while in labor that she had been replaced. Steel was hired later in 1987 to head the Columbia TriStar Motion Picture Group, becoming the highest-ranking female studio executive in history. While at Columbia TriStar, Steel oversaw the production of films such as *When Harry Met Sally* (1989) and *Awakenings* (1990), and the restoration of David Lean's 1962 classic *Lawrence of Arabia,* released in 1989. In 1989 she received the Crystal Award for Women in Film for outstanding achievement in the film industry. Steel's leadership of Columbia TriStar, once struggling under the helm of David Puttnam, prepared it for sale to Sony Pictures Entertainment in 1991. She left the studio at that time, with a reported landmark settlement of over $6 million.

After leaving studio management, Steel became an independent producer, forming Steel Pictures and Atlas Entertainment. As an independent, her biggest success was *Cool Runnings,* a 1993 Disney hit that earned nearly $70 million in the U.S. release. An offbeat, true story about the trials and triumphs of the Jamaican bobsled team that competed in the 1988 Calgary Winter Olympics, the film reflected her belief in the popularity of movies about the underdog. During this time, she also wrote an autobiography,

They Can Kill You, But They Can't Eat You: Lessons from the Front (1993), which emphasized her support of mentorship and traced her professional and personal accomplishments and disappointments.

In March 1996 Steel was diagnosed with brain cancer. After keeping up a busy schedule for nearly two years, she died at Cedars-Sinai Hospital in Los Angeles. She is buried at Mount Sinai Memorial Park, Los Angeles.

Steel, a diminutive woman known for her thick red hair and determined demeanor, had her share of detractors. Sometimes called "Steelie Dawn" or the "Queen of Mean," she was included in a 1988 cover story in *California* about bad bosses. Although not the first woman to hold a position of power in the Hollywood film industry, she was widely recognized for advocating the hiring and promoting of women into senior positions. She was also an industry activist and one of the many Hollywood producers to support the presidential campaigns of William J. Clinton.

★

Steel's autobiography, *They Can Kill You, But They Can't Eat You: Lessons from the Front* (1993), is out of print but is available in media history and popular library collections. There is an interview with Steel in the *Los Angeles Times* (29 Aug. 1993), as well as a profile (23 Dec. 1997). Her death was widely chronicled in the entertainment and business press; feature-length obituaries are in the *New York Times* (22 Dec. 1997) and *Variety* (5–11 Jan. 1998).

JESSICA HANDLER

Herbert Stein, 1973. © BETTMANN/CORBIS

STEIN, Herbert (*b.* 27 August 1916 in Detroit, Michigan; *d.* 8 September 1999 in Washington, D.C.), economist best known for promoting a business-oriented Keynesianism and for his service on President Richard Nixon's Council of Economic Advisers.

Stein was one of two children of David Stein, a machinist and storekeeper, and Jessie Segal, a homemaker. His father was a Jewish immigrant from Russian-held Poland employed at a Ford Motor Company plant in Detroit. In 1929 the family moved to New York State and eventually settled in Schenectady, where Stein's father worked for General Electric. Academically gifted, Stein graduated early from Schenectady High School and, on a scholarship, attended Williams College in Williamstown, Massachusetts (1931–1935). At Williams, he excelled in debate and graduated with a B.A. degree, magna cum laude. Stein's senior thesis was later published as *Government Price Policy in the United States During the World War* (1938). Stein pursued graduate work in economics at the University of Chicago beginning in 1935, but did not complete his dissertation and receive his Ph.D. until 1958. On 12 June 1937 he married fellow graduate student Mildred Sylvia Fishman, with whom he had two children.

In 1938 Stein took a job with the Federal Deposit Insurance Corporation in Washington, D.C., and discovered that he was good at the kind of memorandum writing prized by government officials, and probably was more suited to doing economics in Washington than at a university. In 1940 he moved to the National Defense Advisory Commission and later, following the United States' entry into World War II, to the War Production Board's economic analysis section. In these positions Stein developed a strong distaste for the new price control apparatus. In 1944 he accepted a naval commission as ensign and was put to work on postwar planning projects. In the same year, he won the Pabst Brewing Company prize of $25,000 for the best essay on postwar employment problems. Foreshadowing later prescriptions, Stein urged that full employment be maintained through a mixture of tax revision, antitrust enforcement, stimulants to private expenditure, and limited doses of countercyclical government spending.

In 1945 Stein began a twenty-two-year association, as economist and research director, with the Committee for Economic Development (CED), an organization founded in 1942 by business leaders interested in reconversion planning. With Stein's assistance, the CED became the promoter of conservative macroeconomics (less favorably known as commercial Keynesianism), a philosophy that supported using fiscal policy to maintain aggregate demand through a system in which taxes and spending commitments remained relatively stable, and fluctuations in the economy automatically produced compensatory changes in revenue and social spending. Such thinking appeared in debates leading to the Employment Act of 1946 and, in the years that followed, Stein's work for the CED helped to win further business support for conservative macroeconomic policies. Stein believed this "taming" of Keynesianism enabled the completion of a fiscal revolution in the 1960s, which was symbolized by the Kennedy-Johnson tax cut of 1964. In *The Fiscal Revolution in America* (1969), Stein traced in detail how the revolution had come about, particularly discussing its forerunners, its progress during the depression and war years, and the postwar role of the CED.

In 1967 Stein became a senior fellow at the Brookings Institution in Washington, D.C., and a year later wrote "Unemployment, Inflation, and Economic Stability," an essay that received wide attention. In 1969 he began serving on President Richard Nixon's Council of Economic Advisers (CEA). Stein's economic prescriptions were in line with the Nixon administration's early efforts to check inflation through restraints pushing unemployment slightly above its natural rate. But when 1970 brought stagflation (further inflation despite rising unemployment), the administration turned, in August 1971, to a price freeze as a prelude to price and wage ceilings. As a longtime foe of such measures, Stein disliked the path being taken. In hopes of limiting the damage, he volunteered to head the task force preparing the new controls. Stein's elevation to the CEA chairmanship, which he held from 1 January 1972 to 31 August 1974, meant that he remained deeply involved in the revisions and eventual dismantling of the control system and in the collateral efforts to define "acceptable" deficits.

After leaving the government in 1974, Stein took up an endowed professorship at the University of Virginia in Charlottesville. He also served as a consultant to the Congressional Budget Office and other government agencies, became an active member of the *Wall Street Journal*'s board of contributors, and from 1974 to 1980 wrote a weekly newspaper column, "The Economy Today." In addition, he became a senior fellow at the American Enterprise Institute (AEI) in Washington, D.C., and from 1977 to 1988 edited its *AEI Economist*. In the 1980s Stein carried on running debates, both with the planning-oriented advocates of industrial policy and with the supply-siders of

Ronald Reagan's administration. In the 1990s he enjoyed writing for the online magazine *Slate,* contributing both an "It Seems to Me" column and a "Dear Prudence" advice column on "manners, morals, and macroeconomics." Stein also wrote an impressive string of books, the most notable being *Presidential Economics: The Making of Economic Policy from Roosevelt to Reagan and Beyond* (1984), *Governing the $5 Trillion Economy* (1989), and *An Illustrated Guide to the American Economy* (1992), which he coauthored with Murray Foss. In his 1989 book Stein called for a second fiscal revolution that would regularize the use of fiscal policy to further an agreed-upon allocation of the entire national output.

As a personality, Stein combined an owlish appearance and general aura of gravity with an impressive articulateness, a keen and subtle mind, and a wry sense of humor at its best in his delivery of deadpan witticisms. Typical of the latter was his coining of Stein's Law, which held, "If something cannot go on forever, it will stop." As an economist, he tended to be too liberal for conservatives and too conservative for liberals, and for some critics his openness to further argument and willingness to concede how little economists actually knew made him the master of the "don't know" school. Still, he left behind an impressive record of public service and economic and historical scholarship. Stein was more an implementer than a shaper of the Nixon administration's economic policies, but his earlier work, particularly as a CED salesman of conservative macroeconomics, left its mark on U.S. economic policy development. Following his death of heart failure at age eighty-three, the National Association for Business Economics in Washington, D.C., established the Herbert Stein Public Service Award.

★

Stein's papers are held by his family, although some are expected to go to the Richard Nixon Library in Yorba Linda, California. There is no biography, but some of Stein's writings contain substantial autobiographical components. In addition to the previously noted *Fiscal Revolution in America* and *Presidential Economics: The Making of Economic Policy from Roosevelt to Reagan and Beyond,* these include *Washington Bedtime Stories: The Politics of Money and Jobs* (1986), *On the Other Hand: Essays on Economics, Economists, and Politics* (1995), and *What I Think: Essays on Economics, Politics, and Life* (1998). Useful biographical sketches can be found in *Current Biography Yearbook* (1973), and Eleanora W. Schoenebaum, ed., *Political Profiles: The Nixon-Ford Years* (1979). Helpful as well are the contexts provided and the treatments of Stein in Leonard Silk, *Nixonomics*, 2d ed. (1973), and Robert M. Collins, *The Business Response to Keynes, 1929–1964* (1981). An obituary is in the *New York Times* (9 Sept. 1999).

ELLIS W. HAWLEY

STEINBERG, Saul (*b.* 15 June 1914 in Rîmnicu-Sărat, Romania; *d.* 12 May 1999 in New York City), artist and cartoonist whose satirical drawings primarily appeared in the *New Yorker.*

Steinberg was the son of Moritz (Maurice) Steinberg, a printer, bookmaker, and manufacturer of cardboard boxes, and Rosa Jacobson, a baker and homemaker. When he was six months old, he moved with his family to Bucharest. After elementary school, he entered the Licuel Matei Basarab, a tough, overcrowded school that focused on Latin. Steinberg and his sister spent their summers with their grandfather, a military tailor, in a town near Bucharest.

In 1932 Steinberg graduated from high school and entered the University of Bucharest. In 1933 he moved to Milan, Italy, and entered the Reggio Politecnico, an architecture school with a curriculum influenced by cubism. He began drawing cartoons in 1934, and in 1936 was published in the Italian biweekly *Bertoldo.* His cartoons appeared in other Italian magazines from 1936 to 1939. Steinberg received his doctorate in architecture in 1940. He practiced architecture in Milan from 1939 to 1941, but in the latter year his drawings were published in *Harper's Bazaar* and *Life,* solidifying his career shift toward art.

Saul Steinberg, 1978. FELICE QUINTO/ASSOCIATED PRESS AP

In 1941 Steinberg fled Italy in the midst of World War II, using a doctored passport. He was deported from Ellis Island in New York because the quota of Romanians was already filled and was sent to Ciudad Trujillo (later Santo Domingo), Dominican Republic. From there he sent the *New Yorker* some cartoons. They first used one of his cartoons on 25 October 1941 and supported his entry into the United States the following year.

Steinberg married Hedda Lindenberg Sterne, a painter, in 1943. They had no children. That same year he became a United States citizen and was immediately given a commission in the U.S. Navy teaching demolition techniques to Chinese guerrillas. During the war the *New Yorker* published his cartoons from Asia, North Africa, and Europe. His pictures from this period, which ranged from satiric drawings of the Nazis to United States soldiers' reactions to war, were published in a book in 1945 called *All in Line.* Steinberg was discharged from the navy in 1946. That same year he received his first major recognition as an artist when his work was exhibited at the Museum of Modern Art in New York City.

Though a nonobservant Jew, Steinberg had a sense of the Jewish people as wanderers. As an émigré, he was able to visualize and portray America with startling insight. Steinberg traveled the country and the world throughout the 1950s, gathering fodder for his art. His style became more abstract and philosophical, and he used many symbolic characters in his work: cats, crocodiles, horses, and knights. His favorite travels were by bus in the American heartland. In 1954 he spent the summer with the Milwaukee Braves baseball team, traveling throughout the Midwest and Northeast. According to Steinberg, "It is impossible to understand America without a thorough knowledge of baseball." According to fellow cartoonist Edward Koren, "He fixed on American life without being too close to it." Roger Angell of the *New Yorker,* in Steinberg's obituary, said "There was a strange combination of things in Saul. He was a famous person and a private person."

In the 1960s Steinberg's work encompassed geometrical shapes, letters of the alphabet, and especially the question mark. He served as artist-in-residence at the Smithsonian Institution in 1967. Steinberg drew biting, insightful pictures of New York street life in the late 1960s and 1970s. Most of these works appeared in the *New Yorker,* the most famous being a drawing of a provincial Manhattanite's view of the world from New York City. According to Adam Gopnik, Steinberg's colleague at the magazine, "he was a poet-reporter, and he grew as poet-reporters grow, by seeing new things and finding new ways of showing them. More than any other artist, high or low, he recorded the great change that overcame New York between 1950 and 1975."

Steinberg separated from his wife in the 1970s, though they never divorced. In the 1980s he became self-conscious about what he would publish. According to Gopnik, "He had drawn America that was safe and America scary, and he had no real response, no picture language, for an America that was neither all that safe or all that scary, but just rich and sloppy." Gopnik also wrote that "critics have missed the piece that he wrote about himself: the life's work of drawing that showed a man far sadder and wiser than the serene and epigrammatic talker. Although he had a reputation as an ironist, a theoretician, a meta-commentator, he was upset by the notion that his work was sly, or even subtle. He loved simplicity and straightforward statement more than anything else."

Steinberg's place in the art world was always in question. "I don't quite belong to the art, cartoon or magazine world, so the art world doesn't quite know where to place me," he observed. He ended up belonging to all three. He did eighty-five covers and more than six hundred drawings for the *New Yorker* and published several illustrated books, including *The Art of Living* (1949), *The Inspector* (1973), and *The Discovery of America* (1993).

In addition, Steinberg's work, which has been compared to that of Picasso, Klee, Beckett, Chaplin, and Joyce, has been exhibited at dozens of galleries and museums in the United States and abroad, including a retrospective at the Whitney Museum of American Art in 1978. Art critic Harold Rosenberg called Steinberg "a writer of pictures, an architect of speech and sounds, a draftsman of philosophical reflections." His work remains in the permanent collections of many museums, including the Smithsonian American Art Museum, the San Francisco Museum of Modern Art, the Dallas Museum of Art, and the Museum of Modern Art and Metropolitan Museum of Art in New York.

The genius of Steinberg was his ability to blend art, caricature, and illustration to create thought-provoking images. "What he did was sum up a century of art by making this graceful and seamless crossing over of categories but inventing something brand new," said Art Spiegelman, cartoonist and contributor to the *New Yorker*. "He was neither cartoonist nor painter. He was Steinberg." Steinberg died in Manhattan of cancer at age eighty-four.

★

There is no full-length biography of Steinberg. A critical analysis of Steinberg's art, in addition to a brief biography, can be found in Harold Rosenberg, *Saul Steinberg* (1978). Obituaries are in the *New York Times* (13 May 1999) and *Newsweek* and *Time* (both 24 May 1999). In addition, Adam Gopnik wrote a biographical feature about Steinberg for the *New Yorker* (13 Nov. 2000).

MOLLY JALENAK WEXLER

STEPHENS, Woodford Cefis ("Woody") (*b.* 1 September 1913 in Stanton, Kentucky; *d.* 22 August 1998 in Miami Lakes, Florida), Hall of Fame horse trainer and Eclipse Award trainer of the year who trained winners of the Kentucky Derby and the Preakness Stakes and five consecutive winners of the Belmont Stakes.

Stephens was the third of seven children of Lewis Stephens, a sharecropper, and Helen Stephens, a homemaker. Stephens's earliest years were consumed with working "dark to dark," scrabbling to raise tobacco. His only luxury was a pony, given to him by his grandfather when he was six years old. He attended local grammar schools, and in 1928 Stephens's father moved the family from Stanton to Midway, Kentucky, in the heart of the famed bluegrass and horse-breeding county. Stephens's life changed when J. M. Parrish, a banker and racehorse owner, saw how well Stephens had trained his pony. Parrish asked Stephens to work in his stable under the trainer Howard Rouse. Stephens's

Woody Stephens. AP/WIDE WORLD PHOTOS

work consisted of learning the rudiments of "breaking" a horse: putting on a bridle and saddle, adding the weight of a rider, and finally schooling the animal to learn to react to the reins. When Stephens was fifteen, the racehorse owner John Ward decided that Stephens would become a jockey, and in 1930 Stephens signed a three-year contract to be a "stable boy and jockey for $25 a month plus room and board and reasonable medical attention." Stephens never finished high school.

Stephens raced in Chicago and at Hialeah in Florida but did not earn his first win until January 1931, when he took a filly, Directly, at seventeen-to-one odds to the winner's circle. Stephens's own $20 bet on the horse earned him $357, almost a year's wages. In the third year of his contract, his weight hit 130 pounds, and the owner demoted him from jockey to groom. About two years later, Sherril Ward, the son of John Ward, allowed Woody to train Deliberator. During this period, Woody met Lucille Easley, whom he courted and married in September 1937; they had no children.

Stephens trained horses for a couple of years before eventually signing a contract in 1943 with Jule Fink, a horseplayer and owner, for $1,000 per month. Stephens moved to New York, where he trained and ran Fink's horses at tracks in New York and the Northeast, and in Florida during the winter months. Fink was in the practice of buying "claimers," horses that could be purchased after a race for the claiming price. Fink looked for horses who had potential far beyond their claiming price, and he concentrated on buying horses that had speed. The conventional wisdom of owners and trainers at the time paid almost exclusive attention to endurance and stamina. Fink's practice paid off, and in two and a half years, Stephens acquired 157 victories, including a stakes race victory in 1944. These results were so unexpected that in 1945 the powerful Jockey Club, which regulated racing at the time, suspected Fink and Stephens of cheating. They were locked out of racetracks, and Fink's license was lifted. (Fink took the club to court and years later won.) Once Stephens signed with another owner, he was permitted to again stable horses.

Between 1945 and 1954 Stephens contracted with a number of owners and enjoyed growing successes, which included a win in the Preakness Stakes, the second leg of horse racing's Triple Crown, in 1952 with Blue Man. In 1955 Captain Harry Guggenheim hired Stephens to train solely for the Cain Hoy Stable. The first couple years of losses gave way to a streak of winnings. By 1959 Stephens was able to boast that the farm was the biggest moneymaker in horse racing, with winnings over $742,081 for that year and a stable of horses like Bald Eagle and One-Eyed King,

which captured seven major stakes purses between them. Stephens was especially proud of Bald Eagle's back-to-back wins in the Washington, D.C., International in 1959 and 1960. In total during the Guggenheim years, Stephens saddled winners in twenty-nine of the most competitive horse races on the eastern circuit. Stephens left Cain Hoy Stable in 1965.

Stephens continued training and compiling impressive win records. His career highlights in the years following 1965 included winning the Kentucky Derby with Cannonade in 1974. In 1976 Stephens was elected to the racing Hall of Fame, and in 1983 he won the Eclipse Award for best trainer. But it was during the 1980s in New York that Stephens achieved his greatest successes, winning the Kentucky Derby with Swale in 1984 and winning the third leg of the Triple Crown—the Belmont Stakes—five years in a row. The string started in 1982 with Conquistador Cielo, followed by Caveat in 1983 and Swale in 1984. In 1985 Stephens's horses Crème Fraiche and Odyssey finished first and second in the Belmont Stakes, respectively. His fifth Belmont Stakes victory came with Danzig Connection in 1986.

Stephens was successful with horses of all types and age groups and at all racing lengths and conditions. Various horses he trained were voted Eclipse winners a total of eleven times, including winners six years in a row, between 1978 and 1983. Bald Eagle, Never Bend, and Bold Bidder were voted Champion Horse of the Year, a precursor to the Eclipse Award. His horses held speed records for several races.

Stephens developed emphysema and later endured long stays in hospitals, often directing his training operations from his bed. In fact, he watched Devils Bag win the Derby Trial in 1984 from a hospital bed. He curtailed his activities after 1985; heart problems, a broken hip, and pleurisy forced Stephens to slow down. He had to carry an oxygen tank with him to the barns during the last years of his career, officially retiring in 1997. He died of complications from chronic emphysema while in Miami Lakes, Florida. He is buried in Lexington, Kentucky.

Even without his five consecutive wins in the Belmont Stakes, Stephens was undeniably one of the great horse trainers of the twentieth century. But his string of Belmont Stakes victories, which has been compared to Joe DiMaggio's fifty-six-game hitting streak in baseball, put him in the class of superstars.

★

Stephens penned *Guess I'm Lucky: My Life in Horseracing* with James Brough in 1985. Besides career highlights, the book provides insights on training and racing. Andrew Beyer wrote a piece with personal anecdotes about Stephens in the *Daily Racing Form* (22 Aug. 1998). Obituaries are in the *Lexington Herald Leader* (22 Aug. 1998) and *New York Times* (23 Aug. 1998).

WILLIAM J. MALONEY

STEWART, James Maitland ("Jimmy") (*b.* 20 May 1908 in Indiana, Pennsylvania; *d.* 2 July 1997 in Beverly Hills, California), actor who remained a durable icon of American film for more than six decades. Despite an on-screen image that grew darker and more complex with time, he came to represent a uniquely American sense of decency and integrity.

Stewart was the oldest child of Alexander Maitland Stewart, who owned a popular hardware store in the town of Indiana, and Elizabeth Ruth ("Bessie") Jackson. His sister Mary Wilson ("Doddie") was born in 1912, and his sister Virginia ("Ginny") in 1914. Stewart was greatly influenced by his father, a strong-willed, deeply religious man who served as a captain in World War I.

Stewart received his elementary education at the Model School in Indiana. After completing the ninth grade, he enrolled in Mercersburg Academy in Mercersburg, Penn-

James Stewart. ARCHIVE PHOTOS, INC.

sylvania, a private boarding school steeped in Presbyterian ritual and tradition. Following his graduation from Mercersburg in June 1928, he enrolled in Princeton University, his father's alma mater, with the intention of becoming an electrical engineer. While there he joined the Triangle Club, Princeton's theater group, which was enormously popular for its productions combining music with irreverent humor.

After graduating from Princeton in 1932 with a B.S. degree in architecture, Stewart began to think seriously of acting as a career. Encouraged by a friend and fellow Princetonian, Joshua Logan, he joined the University Players, a theater group operating out of a movie house in West Falmouth on Cape Cod, Massachusetts. There Stewart was able to play a variety of roles, joining aspiring actors Henry Fonda and Margaret Sullavan. Eventually he came to Broadway in New York City in a short-lived play called *Carry Nation* (October 1932), then won a small role in the hit comedy *Goodbye Again*. Other fleeting appearances in unsuccessful plays led to a sizable role in Sidney Howard's play *Yellow Jack* (1934) and to a role in a play entitled *Divided by Three* (1934), in which he came to the attention of film scouts at Metro-Goldwyn-Mayer (MGM). Thin, lanky, and not especially handsome, he seemed an unlikely candidate for movie stardom, but after a screen test MGM offered him a seven-year contract.

It was clear from the start that the studio intended to use their new player in largely homespun roles. In his first feature film, *The Murder Man* (1935, with Spencer Tracy), he appeared as a reporter improbably named "Shorty," then was seen as Jeanette MacDonald's fugitive brother in *Rose Marie* (1936), as Jean Harlow's working-class boyfriend in *Wife vs. Secretary* (1936), and as a rustic character in *The Gorgeous Hussy* (1936). Occasionally he was given an unusual assignment: he sang (in his own voice) and danced in the Cole Porter musical *Born to Dance* (1936) and even got to play the villain in *After the Thin Man* (1936).

Gradually, as filmgoers responded to the gawky, drawling young actor, his roles became more prominent. In the drama *Of Human Hearts* (1938), he played a young frontiersman who becomes a doctor in the Civil War. Many of his MGM roles in the 1930s, however, were perfunctory; he fared best when he was loaned to other studios. At Universal, in *Next Time We Love* (1936), he played a roving journalist who marries a stage star, played by Margaret Sullavan. At RKO General, Inc. he revealed an agreeable sense of comedy as a naive college professor in *Vivacious Lady* (1938), and a warm appeal as a young husband burdened with life's problems in *Made for Each Other* (1939). He also appeared to advantage as the romantic lead in director Frank Capra's film version of the George S. Kaufman–Moss Hart stage comedy *You Can't Take It with You* (1938).

It was Capra who rewarded Stewart with a star-making

role in *Mr. Smith Goes to Washington* (1939). Casting the actor as Jefferson Smith, the naive young man who inherits a seat in the U.S. Senate and then is thrown to the Washington, D.C., wolf pack, Capra saw Stewart as the resolute American who triumphs over seemingly insurmountable odds with his innate strength and decency. Smith's climactic filibuster in the Senate chambers helped to win Stewart an Oscar nomination as well as the New York Film Critics Award as the year's best actor.

Stewart's subsequent movies saw his persona now fully in place: the earnest young man whose easygoing air concealed a backbone of steel. He excelled in *Destry Rides Again* (1939) as a pacifistic deputy sheriff in the Old West, and in *The Shop Around the Corner* (1940) as a love-struck sales clerk in a Budapest store. In *The Mortal Storm* (1940), he played a young German whose anti-Nazi sentiments in the early years of fascism result in tragedy for him and his "non-Aryan" sweetheart (Margaret Sullavan). To Stewart's own surprise (and almost everyone else's), he won an Oscar as best actor for his performance as a reporter who falls for haughty society girl Katharine Hepburn in *The Philadelphia Story* (1940).

In March 1941 Stewart became the first prominent Hollywood actor to be drafted into the U.S. Army. Five days after his induction, he was assigned to air force school, where he became a fully qualified B-17 bomber pilot. For a while he served as a flying instructor and squadron officer. Starting in November 1943 he participated in twenty-five missions over Germany, winning the Distinguished Flying Cross with oak leaf cluster and the Croix de Guerre with palm. He rose to the rank of full colonel, eventually becoming a brigadier general in the Air Force Reserve in 1959. He retired in 1968.

Returning to the United States after more than four years abroad, Stewart resumed his film career with Frank Capra's *It's a Wonderful Life* (1946). It was a warmly human parable about a man (Stewart) at the end of his tether who learns what would have happened to his town and his family if he had never been born. Although the film won several Oscar nominations (including one for Stewart as best actor), it was not well received by the critics. However, after repeated showings on television over the years, it became a holiday staple and an annual ritual for many viewers.

For a while Stewart's movies were either mediocre (*Magic Town*, 1947) or merely competent (*Call Northside 777*, 1948), and one, *Rope* (1948), was an anomaly in his career. Alfred Hitchcock's first film in color, it was the director's attempt at an experiment. A grisly tale of two young men who commit a murder only for "thrills," the movie was filmed in an unbroken time span of sustained, continuous action. Stewart was miscast as the killers' ex-teacher, who uncovers the crime.

By the 1950s the actor was in his forties and no longer able to sustain the image of the boyish, fumbling young man of earlier years. Also, he was no longer one of Hollywood's most eligible bachelors: on 9 August 1949 he married Gloria Hatrick McLean, a socialite with two sons from her previous marriage, and in 1951 they had twin daughters. As a mature actor he was ready and willing to take on roles that required greater depth. In *The Stratton Story* (1949), he played real-life baseball pitcher Monty Stratton, who lost his leg in a hunting accident. The following year he appeared in the film version of Mary Chase's play *Harvey* (1950) as the amiable alcoholic Elwood P. Dowd, whose constant companion is a tall, imaginary rabbit named Harvey. Stewart was nominated as best actor for his engaging performance.

In the 1950s, in addition to perfunctory appearances in such movies as *No Highway in the Sky* (1951) and *The Greatest Show on Earth* (1952), Stewart devoted much of his film career to westerns that projected a tougher, grittier image. There were now hints of anger, bitterness, and regret imbedded in the usual easygoing Stewart persona. Such movies as *The Naked Spur* (1953), *The Far Country* (1955), and *The Man from Laramie* (1955), all directed by Anthony Mann, revealed a more seasoned actor, with a face lined by life experiences. He could still play contemporary figures with conviction—the popular band leader Glenn Miller in *The Glenn Miller Story* (1954), the famed pilot Charles A. Lindbergh in *The Spirit of St. Louis* (1957), or a shrewd lawyer in *Anatomy of a Murder* (1958), a performance for which he won the New York Film Critics Award as best actor. Yet the echoes of Jefferson Smith and Tom Destry were largely gone forever.

This more mature actor emerged most fully in the trio of films he made in the 1950s with Alfred Hitchcock. In at least two of the three films, he played characters whose motives are suspect and whose actions have fatal or near fatal consequences. *Rear Window* (1954) cast him as a photographer, confined to a wheelchair because of a broken leg, whose spying on his neighbors leads to the uncovering of a murder and, incidentally, to the near killing of his fiancée (Grace Kelly). *The Man Who Knew Too Much* (1956), a remake of the director's 1934 movie, cast Stewart as a doctor trying desperately to rescue his kidnapped young son. In *Vertigo* (1958), Stewart gave one of his most intense performances as a man whose obsession with a dead woman ends in tragedy.

Still active in the 1960s, Stewart continued to make lighthearted (and sometimes light-headed) comedies such as *Take Her, She's Mine* (1963) and *Dear Brigitte* (1965), but many of his films during this period were westerns that were increasingly dark, gritty, and psychologically motivated. Stewart's characters were often far from heroic: in *Two Rode Together* (1961), he played a frankly mercenary sheriff assigned to bring in a group of people kidnapped years before by Indians, and in John Ford's gloomy *The Man Who Shot Liberty Valance* (1962), he was a man whose legendary fame in Western annals was built on a lie. Stewart's characters in *Firecreek* (1968) and *Bandolero!* (1968) also involved him with moral dilemmas that would have confounded his previous character Tom Destry. In November 1968 Stewart was honored by the Screen Actors Guild for "outstanding achievement in fostering the finest ideals of the acting profession."

Although he was no longer in great demand, Stewart continued to act into the 1970s. He appeared in such films as *The Cheyenne Social Club* (1970) and *Fools' Parade* (1971), and he took small but incisive roles in *The Shootist* (1976), *Airport '77* (1977), and *The Big Sleep* (1978). By the end of his career he had made eighty-one films. Stewart also tried his hand at television, first with *The Jimmy Stewart Show* (1971), as an absentminded professor, then with *Hawkins* (1973), as a private detective. Neither show was very successful. In February 1970 he returned to the stage to star in a new production of *Harvey,* opposite Helen Hayes as his sister. They repeated their roles for NBC's "Hallmark Hall of Fame" in March 1972, and in 1974 he again played Elwood P. Dowd in a London revival.

In the 1980s Stewart received many honors. In March 1980 he was presented with the Lifetime Achievement Award by the American Film Institute, and in December 1983 he became a Kennedy Center honoree. In March 1985 he received an honorary Oscar from the Academy of Motion Picture Arts and Sciences, and several months later he was given the Presidential Medal of Freedom, the nation's highest civilian award, by President Reagan. His final on-screen role was as the southern attorney Miles Colbert in the television miniseries *North and South: Book II* (1986), while his final part was as the voice of the famous gunfighter and hound dog Wylie Burp in the animated film *An American Tail: Fievel Goes West* (1991).

Stewart died of a blood clot on the lung on 2 July 1997 at the age of eighty-nine; his wife Gloria had died of lung cancer in February 1994. In 1987 Stewart said, "I'd like to be remembered as someone who worked hard for what happened, and who had certain values that he believed in. Love of family, love of community, love of country, love of God." Despite changing fashions and attitudes, he held fast to these values with dignity and pride.

★

The Jimmy Stewart Museum, displaying artifacts and memorabilia of the actor's life and career, opened in Indiana, Pennsylvania, in May 1995. A book of his poetry, *Jimmy Stewart and His Poems,* was published in 1989. Books on Stewart's life and career include Howard Thompson, *James Stewart* (1973); Jhan Robbins, *Everybody's Man: A Biography of James Stewart* (1985);

Jonathan Coe, *Jimmy Stewart: A Wonderful Life* (1994); Donald Dewey, *James Stewart* (1996); and Gary Fishgall, *Pieces of Time* (1997). Jeanine Basinger, ed., *The "It's a Wonderful Life" Book* (1990), provides complete information on that film. A documentary film on the actor, *James Stewart: A Wonderful Life,* was aired by PBS (Mar. 1987). Obituaries are in the *New York Times* (3 July 1997) and *Variety* (14 July 1997).

TED SENNETT

STEWART, (William) Payne (*b.* 30 January 1957 in Springfield, Missouri; *d.* 25 October 1999 en route from Orlando, Florida, to Dallas, Texas), a golfer whose early death curtailed a brilliant career.

Stewart was the son of William Stewart, a furniture salesman, and Bee Payne, a homemaker. He was introduced to golf at age four by his mother, who took her toddler with her to the Hickory Hills Country Club. But it was his father, a two-time Missouri state amateur golf champion, who was his first coach and lifelong mentor.

A natural athlete and a three-sport letterman in high school, Stewart easily learned to play golf. He became a professional golfer after graduating with a degree in business administration from Southern Methodist University in Dallas in 1979. Failing in his first attempt to earn his Professional Golfers' Association (PGA) tour card at qualifying school, he joined the Asian tour in 1980, where both professional success and marriage followed quickly. In 1981 Stewart met Tracey Ferguson, an Australian who became his wife on 13 December 1981, in Kuala Lumpur and won the Indian and Indonesian Opens. He then returned to the United States to play on the PGA tour that same year. He made five cuts in ten starts and earned $13,400 to finish 160th on the money list for the year. In 1982 Stewart won his first tour victory at the Quad Cities Open, and in 1983 he won the Walt Disney World Classic and finished twenty-fifth on the tour money list.

Stewart enjoyed a breakthrough year in 1989. He won his first major, the PGA Championship, at Kemper Lakes, with a blistering closing in which he made birdies on four of the last five holes to win by one stroke. He also captured the MCI Heritage Classic and the GTE Byron Nelson Classic, finishing third on the money list for the year. In 1990 he won twice again, and the next year he won the 1991 U.S. Open at Hazeltine in Chaska, Minnesota, in an eighteen-hole playoff against Scott Simpson.

But Stewart then entered a bad slump, athletically and psychologically, which reached its nadir in 1994 when he dropped to 123rd on the money list. The cause may have been the general pressures that often accompany dramatic success, the change of clubs that went with his change of representation from Wilson Sporting Goods to Spalding, or the attention deficit disorder that would later be diagnosed. However, a combination of marital support, a new spiritual commitment, will power, and excellent golf and psychological coaching brought Stewart back in 1995 with a victory at the Shell Houston Open. That year he jumped to twelfth on the money list.

By 1999 Stewart was at the top of his game again. He won the rain-shortened AT&T Pebble Beach National Pro-Am, and, more spectacularly, achieved a dramatic third major victory in the U.S. Open at Pinehurst, North Carolina, with a pressure par putt of at least fifteen feet, reportedly the longest putt ever to decide the Open on the final hole in its ninety-nine-year history. Stewart also was a member of the 1999 U.S. Ryder Cup team, which pulled off a dramatic comeback victory at The Country Club in Brookline, Massachusetts. On the last hole he conceded a long putt to Colin Montgomerie, in recognition of the terrible heckling the Scotsman had been subjected to by rude American fans. "My individual statistics don't mean anything in the Ryder Cup [the American team had clinched victory], and I wasn't going to put him through that," Stewart said in defense of the controversial decision that conceded another half point to the Europeans.

In his nineteen-year career Stewart won eighteen tournaments worldwide, including eleven PGA tour titles with three major championships, among them the 1989 PGA championship and the 1991 and 1999 U.S. Opens. He played on five Ryder Cup teams: 1987, 1989, 1991, 1993, and 1999, compiling a record of 8–9–2 overall, 2–3 singles. A self-conscious patriot, he held these international competitions among his most cherished moments in golf. In 1986 he set a single-season PGA tour record for most money won without a victory ($535,389). His career earnings on the tour totaled almost $12 million.

Stewart had two distinguishing characteristics on the golf course: his trademark, colorful, early-twentieth-century golf clothes and his rhythmic, graceful swing, both of which he credited to his father's influence. His often outlandishly colored golfing outfits included knickers (introduced to American golf in the 1920s by the great Walter Hagen), matching or contrasting cap and stockings, and exotic golf shoes. His swing was as eye-catching as his clothes. "It was the most beautiful, effortless motion. It was a thing to envy . . . or a thing to marvel," 1999 U.S. Ryder Cup captain Ben Crenshaw observed. Even Arnold Palmer admitted to envying Stewart's swing.

Stewart began his roller-coaster career as a self-confident and occasionally arrogant young man, but he grew into one of the game's most caring, respected, and generous personalities. Family, success, personal loss, and religion appear to be the influences that changed him from grade school class clown, college party animal, and insensitive young

golfer into an admirable professional. After winning the 1987 Bay Hill Classic, he donated his $108,000 winner's check to the Florida Hospital to help establish the William L. Stewart House for families of cancer patients, in memory of his father, who had died of bone cancer in 1985.

Some years later, he and his wife formed the Stewart Family Foundation to aid disadvantaged children. They donated $500,000 to the First Baptist Church of Orlando, where their children attended school. "Tracey and I and our kids have more than we deserve. That's just the way it is, so it's not hard to give something back," Stewart reflected.

With the birth of his daughter in 1985 and his son in 1989, Stewart's perspective on life broadened and deepened. "Golf isn't everything," he noted, discussing his commitment to his family in a television interview. "I'm going to a special place when I die, but I want to make sure that my life is special when I'm here. When I'm done here, then my time's done."

That time came earlier and more dramatically than anyone could have imagined. On 25 October 1999 Stewart boarded a Learjet 35 near his home in Orlando for a flight with several business associates to Dallas. Shortly after takeoff the plane experienced a devastating cabin pressure failure, which almost certainly killed everyone aboard nearly instantly. On automatic pilot, the jet then commenced an eerie four-hour, 1,600-mile flight, followed by air force interceptors, which ended when it ran out of fuel and crashed into a field in South Dakota.

Stewart's death traumatized the PGA world. By 1999 he had become one of the tour's most popular and respected players. Tom Lehman reflected the prevailing sentiments of his fellow players when he said, "There's a golf tournament missing a hero. When he died on Monday, a big part of us died, too." Stewart's friend and neighbor Tiger Woods added, "He was a super person with a huge heart."

★

The Golf Channel produced a ninety-minute documentary, *Payne Stewart* (June 2000). Books on Stuart's life include Tracey Stewart, with Ken Abraham, *Payne Stewart: The Authorized Biography* (2000); Michael Arkush, *I Remember Payne Stewart* (2000); and Larry Guest, *The Payne Stewart Story* (2000). Obituaries are in the *New York Times* and *Washington Post* (both 26 Oct. 1999).

MARTIN J. SHERWIN

STONE, Lawrence (*b.* 4 December 1919 in Epsom, England; *d.* 16 June 1999 in Princeton, New Jersey), pathbreaking social historian who became a leading figure in American academic life.

Stone was born to Lawrence Frederick Stone, a watercolor artist, and Mabel Reid. Stone's private school education was mostly supported by scholarships. From 1934 to 1938 he attended Charterhouse, an English prep school, where he trained in the classics. Despite his dislike for the classical curriculum with its emphasis on memorizing Latin, under the tutoring of gifted teachers he learned to love scholarship. Among these teachers was a new headmaster, Sir Robert Birley. After a year and a half of his coaching, Stone was awarded a history scholarship to Oxford. Birley also sent Stone to Paris in 1938 to attend the Sorbonne. He was introduced to French intellectual culture, which included the Annales School of historians such as Marc Bloch and Lucien Febvre, whom he both admired and criticized throughout his life. The Annales School rejected traditional political and narrative history and sought new ways of documenting and understanding the past. Stone was drawn to its approach of applying social science techniques to history.

John Prestwich, an Oxford medieval tutor, taught Stone the importance of "sheer factual information—erudition if you like—in the cut-throat struggle for survival in the life of learning." Stone "discovered that knowledge is power" and decided to become "an archive-based historian." R. H.

Lawrence Stone, 1987. PHOTOGRAPH BY ROBERT MATTHEWS. COURTESY OF PRINCETON UNIVERSITY.

Tawney, the Christian socialist, English labor leader, and distinguished historian of the 1540–1640 period, inspired Stone to study the sixteenth century and become an early modernist. Educator Sir Keith Hancock taught Stone to use an interdisciplinary and transcultural approach to history. Stone believed himself fortunate to have met these men early in his intellectual development and attributed to them his survival "as something of a dinosaur, the last of the Whigs, and in many ways still a child of the Enlightenment."

During World War II, Stone served for five years in the Royal Navy Volunteer Reserve. While working as a navigator on a destroyer in the South Atlantic, he wrote his first historical article on Elizabethan seamen and the Armada campaign of 1588. This was the first of many instances in which Stone's research was influenced by contemporary surroundings and events. Jeanne Caecilia Fawtier, daughter of the medievalist Robert Fawtier, became Stone's wife on 24 July 1943. They had two children. Throughout their long marriage Jeanne was a devoted companion who often worked with him on his research.

At the end of the war Stone returned to Oxford in time to graduate in June 1946 with both B.A. and M.A. degrees. He remained at Oxford as a Bryce Research Student in an era when pursuing a doctorate was viewed as being beneath the dignity of Oxford and Cambridge graduates, because it was something only foreigners did. Instead, he commenced scholarly research and writing and never enrolled in a doctoral program. Beginning in 1947, he served for three years as a lecturer at University and Corpus Christi Colleges, Oxford.

In 1946 Stone began work on a medieval English sculpture textbook in the *Pelican History of Art* series edited by Sir Nikolaus Pevsner. Although not trained as an art historian, Stone's passion for collecting and his receptivity to visual culture as the son of an artist led him as a youth to photograph English Romanesque sculpture and to participate in a national survey of Anglo-Saxon sculpture. Stone's *Sculpture in Britain: The Middle Ages* (1955), which quickly became a classic, analyzed artistic development in the context of political and social history and was extensively illustrated with many of Stone's own photographs.

Stone also studied economic history. Inspired by Tawney's seminal articles on the rise of the gentry in the hundred years before the English Civil War, Stone in 1948 published "The Anatomy of the Elizabethan Aristocracy" in the *Economic History Review*. Here, Stone's claim that the gentry had been near financial ruin launched his entrance into the intense scholarly debate that became known as the "Storm Over the Gentry." Facing harsh criticism, Stone did not falter but displayed traits that characterized his scholarly life—resilience, optimism, inquisitiveness, openness to new ideas, the ability to raise large questions and to delight in controversy. In 1956 he published a biography, *An Elizabethan: Sir Horatio Palavicino.*

The convergence of his own interdisciplinary interests and the influence of the Annales School excited Stone about the possibilities of what was called the New History with its emphasis on social history and put him in the forefront of its development. Launching an extensive study of the English nobility, Stone published *The Crisis of the Aristocracy, 1558–1641* (1965), in which he focused on the history of the ruling class and examined its decline. Stone made the case for his earlier position—that had so inflamed scholarly discourse—through a masterful display of learning, extensive factual evidence, and engaging prose. His discovery of Max Weber led Stone to consider distinctions between class and status and the relationship of ideas and ideology to social and political realities.

Beginning in 1950, Stone became a fellow of Wadham College in Oxford. In 1963 he left Oxford for Princeton, rejecting what he felt was a crushing tutorial teaching load, a curriculum stifling in its national insularity and limited view of history. Stone had been introduced to Princeton two years earlier while holding an appointment at the Institute for Advanced Study. There, he discovered a world of historical scholarship that extended beyond Europe and was introduced to a range of computerized, quantitative historical studies. At Princeton, Stone became Dodge Professor of History and served as chair of the department of history from 1967 to 1970. Despite this move, he retained a deep affection and connection to England throughout his life and maintained homes both in Princeton and Oxford. However, Stone committed himself to the United States and became a citizen in 1970.

During these years, Stone was instrumental in founding the Shelby Cullom Davis Center for Historical Studies. Stone served as its first director in 1968 and continued until he retired in 1990. The Center was designed to encourage innovations in teaching and writing history, and it established the Davis Research Seminar to draw scholars from America and abroad to work on a common problem or theme. Stone attracted as fellows and seminar participants leading European and American historians such as Carlo Ginsburg, Natalie Davis, and Emmanuel Le Roy Ladurie. Colleague Theodore Rabb described Stone as "a lightning bolt—tall, angular, vivid and direct—he flashed through the historiographic clouds, illuminating and transforming everything he touched." Under Stone's guidance, the Davis Center made the Princeton history department a leading source of new ideas in historical scholarship. Stone's leadership also extended to the wider university community. For example, he served as a faculty spokesperson during the period of student unrest in the late 1960s and early 1970s, and his willingness to have women as his doctoral students helped admit them to graduate study in the Princeton history department and to the university at large in the 1960s.

In conjunction with these responsibilities and interests, Stone continued as a productive and stimulating scholar. His synthesis and interpretation of *The Causes of the English Revolution, 1520–1642* appeared in 1972. Stone's *Family and Fortune: Studies in Aristocratic Finance in the Sixteenth and Seventeenth Centuries* (1973) expanded earlier themes of the fate of wealth and its connection to civil war, and stood on its own as a work of family history. He further advanced the field of family history and the history of sexual attitudes and behavior with his *The Family, Sex and Marriage in England 1500–1800* (1977), which showed his interest in anthropology and psychology. Stone was especially influenced by the anthropologist Clifford Geertz and the psychologists Erik Erikson and Jerome Kagan. Stone edited several anthologies in the 1970s that emerged from the Davis Center; among them was *The University in Society* (1974–1975), which contributed to the history and sociology of higher education. In 1984 Stone authored, with his wife, *An Open Elite? England 1540–1880*, which studied social mobility in the higher levels of English society. Stone also served on the editorial board of the British journal *Past and Present* and wrote articles advocating varied approaches to the study of history, especially social history. Stone aroused controversy through his trenchant criticism of what he viewed as the shortcomings of quantitative and analytic history and his embrace of traditional narrative history among some practitioners of the New History.

A prolific scholar committed to his students, Stone was a popular undergraduate lecturer and graduate adviser who did much to stimulate American interest in English history. At Princeton, he taught undergraduate courses that included "The First Road to Modernization: England, 1470–1690," and graduate seminars in "The Coming of the English Revolution, 1529–1641" and "England, 1660–1770." Stone achieved a legacy through his students and their works. In 1989 *The First Modern Society: Essays in English History in Honour of Lawrence Stone* marked Stone's retirement from Princeton. The volume was an affectionate tribute by his students who attempted to represent the breadth of his interests in English history from both sides of the Atlantic. Stone emerges from these essays as a fiercely competitive scholar and dedicated teacher. At tutorials and Davis Center seminars he was intense and aggressive, contentiously slashing through papers as well as discussions. He challenged the logic of arguments and demanded evidence to substantiate assertions and provoked students and colleagues to dispute ideas. His formidable traits—tempered by kindness, thoughtfulness, and humor—were reflected in the label "Lorenzo il Magnifico" bestowed on Stone by his early students. Stone's mentoring continued after his retirement.

Stone was awarded Princeton's first annual Howard T. Behrman Award for distinguished achievement in the humanities. He received honorary doctorates from universities such as Princeton, Oxford, University Illinois at Chicago, and the University of Edinburgh. He was a member of the American Philosophical Society and a fellow of both the American Academy of Arts and Sciences and the British Academy. He wrote and edited more than fifteen books and more than 200 articles and reviews. Stone also reached a wider audience by making available cheaper, abridged versions of his scholarly works and by reviewing books for publications such as the *New York Review of Books*. After his retirement to emeritus status at Princeton in the spring of 1990, Stone continued to pursue an active scholarly life by publishing a trilogy about marriage and divorce during the early 1990s. Stone, in his later years, suffered from Parkinson's disease. He died unexpectedly from cardiac arrest at his home in Princeton at age seventy-nine. Stone was cremated and his ashes were scattered.

In presenting his view of history, Stone argued that great events have important and multiple causes—what he called "a feedback model of mutually reinforcing trends, rather than a linearly ordered hierarchy of causal factors." Rejecting narrow specialization, Stone's work ranged chronologically from the Middle Ages to the nineteenth century. His energy and insatiable curiosity led him to write biography, art history, and economic, social, cultural, educational, and family history. Exhaustive research delivered in lucid prose and supported by statistical analysis characterized his work. Stone demonstrated that historians could analyze large amounts of data but humanize their work through descriptive, anecdotal narrative. Although he focused mostly on England and elites, Stone sought and used a diverse range of theories, concepts, and models to deepen his understanding of history. In so doing, he became a leading social historian of early modern England and pioneer in the history of the family. During a time of increasingly narrow specialization and categorization in historical scholarship, Stone illustrated both the possibilities and problems inherent in a larger view and greater breadth of vision and erudition. From such a vantage point, Stone became a giant in Anglo-American historical scholarship and was likely the most versatile, provocative, and influential social historian of his day in the English-speaking world. Fellow Princeton historian Robert Darnton stated in 1999 that "when Lawrence Stone arrived in Princeton and unpacked his intellectual baggage, he released a fresh set of ideas, which are still buzzing in the air, not merely here but everywhere in the country."

★

Stone's autobiographical essay, "Lawrence Stone—as Seen by Himself," is in his Festschrift by A. L. Beier, David Cannadine, and James M. Rosenheim, eds., *The First Society: Essays in English*

History in Honour of Lawrence Stone* (1989). For a history of the Davis Center and Stone's role in it, see the Shelby Cullom Davis Center for Historical Studies at Princeton University. Related works include Mark Silk, "The Hot History Department: Princeton's Influential Faculty," *New York Times Magazine* (19 Apr. 1987); see also the preface to Susan E. Whyman, *Sociability and Power in Late Stuart England: The Cultural Worlds of the Verneys, 1660–1720* (1999). Notable obituaries are in the *Princeton Packet* (18 June 1999), *New York Times* (19 June 1999), *Times* (London) (21 June 1999), and *History Today* (Sept. 1999).

MARIA T. IACULLO

STRASBERG, Susan Elizabeth (*b*. 22 May 1938 in New York City; *d*. 21 January 1999 in New York City), actress whose career reached its height at age seventeen with her radiant performance in *The Diary of Anne Frank* (1955), and who seemed better known for her legendary romances, friendships, and parents than for her own accomplishments.

Strasberg was the elder of two children of Lee Strasberg, the famed director of the Actors Studio, and Paula Miller, also renowned as a Method-acting coach. Strasberg was onstage before she was born when her pregnant mother appeared on Broadway. The producer eventually fired her mother, protesting, "But Paula, the audience just can't accept a prostitute who's seven months' pregnant." Strasberg's birth announcement proclaimed her "a four-star

Susan Strasberg with her father, Lee Strasberg, at the premier of *Coolhand Luke,* Hollywood, 1967. © BETTMANN/CORBIS

hit." As a child, she recalled crawling around "in and out of a lot of legs" of "famous and soon-to-be famous" guests. In her 1980 memoir, *Bittersweet,* Strasberg wrote about growing up in a home that was more like a theater workshop, with guests ranging from stars to starving actors and playwrights.

After a brief stint as a teenage model, Strasberg made her theatrical debut in 1952 in an off-Broadway play, *Maya.* She followed this performance with several television roles including a live production of *Romeo and Juliet* on the Kraft Television Theater. At age fifteen she was the youngest American actress to play the part of Juliet. To accommodate her working schedule, she enrolled in the High School of Performing Arts in New York City. In 1955 she appeared in two successful Hollywood films, *The Cobweb,* directed by Vincente Minnelli, and William Inge's *Picnic.* That same year, she was asked to read for the second time for the part of Anne Frank. She later recalled that she held the script tight, "like a security blanket," to keep her hands from trembling, and began to weep when she read the lines. There was silence in the room when she finished until Joseph Schildkraut, who was to play Otto Frank, Anne's father, said, "Hello, Anne."

Strasberg's performance in *The Diary of Anne Frank* (1955) stunned Broadway audiences and critics. Brooks Atkinson in the *New York Times* declared, "By some magic that cannot be explained, Miss Strasberg has caught the whole character of Anne in a flowing, spontaneous, radiant performance." Strasberg never had any formal acting training. According to her friend the actress Lee Grant, "She refused to take her [parents'] classes, or their advice. She did Anne Frank out of that instinctive talent of hers." Her father was amazed. "Through you," he told her, "I feel I touch the world." She later commented that she "shuddered with the burden of his admiration." The play was a great hit, winning the Pulitzer Prize, the Drama Desk Award, and the Tony Award for best drama and running for two years. With her immense talent and luminous dark-eyed beauty, she seemed destined for stardom. In a toast on opening night at the famous restaurant Sardi's, the actor Franchot Tone announced, "Little Susan, you have been launched on a long and glittering career."

In 1957 she starred in the Broadway play *Time Remembered* with Richard Burton, during which time she became romantically involved with Burton. Later she wrote, "I threw myself into my affair with Richard with total abandon and passion. I did not care about the consequences. Richard didn't seem to, either." When the show's run ended, Burton terminated the relationship, causing Strasberg considerable pain. She next appeared onstage in a revival of Sean O'Casey's *Shadow of a Gunman* (1958), followed by a reunion with Tone in a 1959 tour of *Caesar and Cleopatra.* Strasberg also continued to star in films, includ-

ing *Stage Struck* (1957), with Henry Fonda, *Kapo* (1960), and *Adventures of a Young Man* (1962). Within a few years, however, it was clear that her career had stalled. In the early 1960s she began using drugs, and her private life was chaotic. In 1963 she returned to Broadway in the title role of Franco Zeffirelli's production of *The Lady of the Camellias.* It closed in two weeks, dealing a major blow to her already fragile self-esteem.

In 1965 Strasberg married the actor Christopher Jones. The marriage rapidly descended into violence and abuse and was over within a year. The couple had one daughter, Jennifer, who was born with a congenital birth defect. Despite the lack of medical evidence linking her child's problems with her drug use, Strasberg blamed herself and devoted the following years to taking care of her daughter. She wrote her autobiography when her career seemed to have ground to a halt. "It became totally untenable to me," she wrote, "that after acting for 25 years—I've played Juliet, Cleopatra and Anne Frank—there I was, sitting in Hollywood, just waiting for somebody to want me."

Strasberg began to accept lesser roles, but ultimately appeared in more than thirty films, including *The Trip* (1967), *Rollercoaster* (1977), *In Praise of Older Women* (1978), *Manitou* (1978), *Sweet Sixteen* (1983), *Delta Force* (1986), and *Prime Suspect* (1988). She was also featured in more than two-dozen television programs and many plays, and toured nationally in a variety of productions in the late 1980s and early 1990s, including *Agnes of God* and *A Woman's Rites.*

Her turbulent relationship with her parents took a surprising turn in 1954 when they "adopted" the twenty-eight-year-old Marilyn Monroe, who had come to the Actors Studio in a desperate attempt to gain respect as a serious actress. Ultimately the two women became close friends, a relationship described in Strasberg's 1992 book, *Marilyn and Me: Sisters, Rivals, Friends.* Strasberg was shattered by Monroe's death in 1962. At a memorial service for Monroe in 1987, Strasberg read a eulogy. "I cannot say good-bye," she read, weeping, "Marilyn never liked good-byes."

Strasberg died at age sixty of breast cancer, which had seemed to be in remission. In some financial distress, a month before she died, she sold one of her most cherished possessions—a string of pearls Monroe had given to Strasberg's mother—for $100,000. She once told a reporter, "I wear these pearls whenever I need confidence or strength. I can feel Marilyn's and mother's energy, and I can know they are with me."

A friend once commented, "You know, Susan, your father loved three things: beautiful women, psychotics, and geniuses." Strasberg wrote, "I realized that I'd tried to be all three." Although she was never able to replicate her marvelous success as Anne Frank, those who experienced Strasberg's "beautiful spirit" in that role could not forget her.

★

Strasberg authored two well-written autobiographies, *Bittersweet* (1980) and *Marilyn and Me: Sisters, Rivals, Friends* (1992). Obituaries are in the *New York Times, Los Angeles Times,* and *Washington Post* (all 23 Jan. 1999), *Variety* (1 Feb. 1999), and *People Weekly* (8 Feb. 1999).

LOUISE A. MAYO

SWANSON, Robert Arthur (*b.* 29 November 1947 in Brooklyn, New York; *d.* 6 December 1999 in Hillsborough, California), venture capitalist and chemist who founded, with Dr. Herbert Boyer, Genentech Inc., the first research-based genetic engineering company.

Swanson was the only child of Arthur John Swanson, an electrical maintenance foreman at Eastern Airlines, and Arline Baker, a homemaker. Shortly after his birth, the Swanson family moved from New York to Miami Springs, Florida, close to the Eastern Airlines corporate headquarters. His father and mother taught Swanson the importance of setting goals, and it was a lesson that influenced the rest of his life. Swanson attended Hialeah High School in nearby

Robert A. Swanson, 1984. © ROGER RESSMEYER/CORBIS

Hialeah, Florida. While in school, Swanson became president of the National Honor Society and was a member of the Key Club. Swanson graduated tenth in his class of 1,200 in 1965 and earned a scholarship to the Massachusetts Institute of Technology (MIT). Although he had trouble during his first year, Swanson went on to earn a B.S. degree in chemistry and an M.S. degree in management from MIT's Sloan School of Management in 1970. Swanson also received an M.B.A. from the same school, becoming the first MIT graduate to earn a master's degree in his fourth year.

After graduation in 1970, Swanson began his career in New York at First National City Bank (now called Citibank) as an investment officer for Citicorp Venture Capital Limited. Three years later, he was transferred to California to open a branch office. In 1975 Swanson took a job offer from a client and became a partner at Kleiner and Perkins (now known as Kleiner, Perkins, Caufield, and Byers), an influential venture capital firm in the San Francisco Bay Area. While employed there, he interviewed Herbert W. Boyer, a biochemist at the University of California at San Francisco, who was studying recombinant gene therapy. Boyer believed that commercial applications for gene splicing were possible, but he was not sure they could succeed as a marketable commodity. What began as a ten-minute meeting moved to a local tavern and lasted three hours, and Swanson convinced Boyer that a commercial venture could work. In 1976 Swanson persuaded his employer, Thomas Perkins, to provide seed money so that he and Boyer could form their biopharmaceutical company.

Genentech Inc. (Genentech standing for "genetic engineering technology") is commonly thought to be the first biotechnology company ever formed. The company achieved many firsts. The synthesis of human insulin for the treatment of diabetes was achieved in 1978, and they licensed the rights to their invention to the Eli Lilly pharmaceutical company that same year. Genentech produced the first human protein by splicing a human gene into one bacterium, turning cells into protein factories. According to an 8 December 1999 *New York Times* article, "It was the first biotechnology company to sell a drug that it had developed on its own." It was also the first company of its kind to sell stock shares in an initial public offering, and "it demonstrated that a viable business could be founded on genetic engineering." According to Karl Thiel, "Swanson recruited young talent from the pharmaceutical industry to build his company." Other products developed by Genentech during Swanson's tenure include interferon, human growth hormone, and tissue plasminogen activator, a drug that helps restore blood flow after a heart attack. Swanson served as chief executive officer of the company from its founding in 1976 until 1990 and as its chairman from 1990 until his retirement in 1996.

Swanson was a deeply private man, preferring to remain out of the limelight. However, the same did not apply to his company. Both he and Boyer were famous for weekly parties, known as Ho-Hos. At the company's Halloween Ho-Ho this short, stocky, serious-looking man was known to don Hawaiian grass skirts and dress up as a bumblebee or as Tweedledee, a character from Lewis Carroll's *Through the Looking Glass*.

During Genentech's rise, Swanson met Judy Church. They were married on 2 September 1980 and later had two daughters. Despite his busy life, Swanson made time to coach both of his children's soccer teams. He had learned from his father that team sports were not just for play; they taught a person how to be a part of a team. Swanson wanted to instill this lesson in his daughters.

In addition to his work in the commercial applications of genetic engineering, Swanson engaged in numerous civic and academic activities. He served on various advisory councils at MIT; as trustee of the San Francisco Ballet, the San Francisco Museum of Modern Art, and the San Jose Tech Center; and as chairman of the board of the Neuva School. Swanson was a member of the American Chemical Society, the America Association for the Advancement of Science, the American Society for Microbiology, and the Royal Swedish Academy of Engineering Sciences. He was named Entrepreneur of the Year by the Chicago Research Directors Association in 1981 and Gold Medal Chief Executive for the Biotechnology Industry by the *Wall Street Transcript* in 1984. He was also a recipient of the National Medal of Technology in 1999.

Following retirement from Genentech, Swanson continued to be active in community service and business. He formed K and E Management, a private investment firm, and was chairman of two new biotechnology startup companies, Tularik Inc. and AGY Therapeutics Inc., both of which focused on creating and marketing therapeutic pharmaceutical drugs. Swanson also served on the board of overseers of the Memorial Sloan-Kettering Cancer Center in New York and was a member of the board of fellows for the Harvard Medical School until his death. Swanson was diagnosed with a cancerous brain tumor in 1998. He immediately sought treatment but learned that his tumor was inoperable. He died fourteen months after the diagnosis, at age fifty-two.

Swanson was hailed as the founder of the biotechnology industry and regarded by the Japanese press as the "Man Who Captured the Rainbow." He worked hard to establish his dream of using science and business acumen to create benefits for humankind. Those who knew him understood that, although he aggressively focused on the success of his business, he also was a dedicated community supporter and not afraid to share the limelight with his fellow employees at Genentech.

★

Michael Meyer, *The Alexander Complex: The Dreams That Drive the Great Businessmen* (1989), a series of biographical sketches of great businessmen of the late 1980s, includes detailed personal information on Swanson. Other biographical material is in *Esquire* (Dec. 1984); *Technology Review* (May/June 1985); *Fortune* (5 Jan. 1987); a special issue of *Business Week* (17 Apr. 1987); and *Who Was Who in America*, vol. 13 (1998/2000). Obituaries are in the *New York Times* (7 and 8 Dec. 1999).

BRIAN B. CARPENTER

T

TARTIKOFF, Brandon (*b.* 13 January 1949 in Freeport, Long Island, New York; *d.* 27 August 1997 in Los Angeles, California), broadcast executive and head of NBC programming who was responsible for a resurgence of quality television in the 1980s.

Tartikoff was one of two children born to Jordan Tartikoff, a clothing manufacturer, and Enid Shapiro, a marketing executive. At an early age, he displayed an interest in broadcasting, setting up his own public address system in the backyard of his home until neighbors complained about the nightly chatter. He attended prep school in Lawrenceville, New Jersey, and then enrolled at Yale College in New Haven, Connecticut, as an economics major, changing to English and graduating with high honors and a B.A. degree in 1970.

Tartikoff's first television effort came in 1970 when he pitched a soap-opera parody, *George and Martha,* to WTNH, an ABC affiliate in New Haven. The effort failed, and he went on to work as an ad agency copywriter, but in 1971 WTNH offered him a job with their promotion department. In 1973, already outgrowing the small-market station, Tartikoff approached ABC's offices in Los Angeles and San Francisco looking for work; they directed him to WLS, ABC's Chicago station, where he was named the executive for dramatic programming. In 1976 Tartikoff landed a low-level job as the manager of dramatic development for ABC in Los Angeles, working under Fred Sil-

verman. In August 1977 Dick Ebersol, the vice president of comedy and variety programming at NBC, called; two years earlier, Tartikoff had shown him a tape of comedy shows he had produced for WLS, as an audition to write for Ebersol's new show *Saturday Night Live.* Ebersol remembered Tartikoff's work and offered him the position of director for comedy programs at NBC's production studios in Burbank, California.

NBC, a broadcasting pioneer, had always been successful with variety shows, made-for-television movies, and long-form television dramas, but had only experienced minor success with situation comedies. During the 1970s they slid into third place in the ratings wars and, by the end of the decade, their annual profits were $100 million less than those of the second-place ABC. Also, their rivals had successfully stolen the NBC affiliates in places like San Diego, Minneapolis, and Jacksonville, Florida. NBC retaliated by luring Silverman, the ABC programming head and Tartikoff's former boss, away in 1978. One of Silverman's first acts was to promote Tartikoff, first to vice president of programs for the West Coast and then, in 1980, to president of programming. At thirty-one, Tartikoff was the youngest man ever to hold this presidency.

Tartikoff did not change NBC's fortunes overnight. The network continued to struggle, and when Grant Tinker replaced Silverman in 1981, only a vote of confidence from Tinker kept Tartikoff in his job. In 1982 Tartikoff's personal life became a roller coaster. He married Lilly Sa-

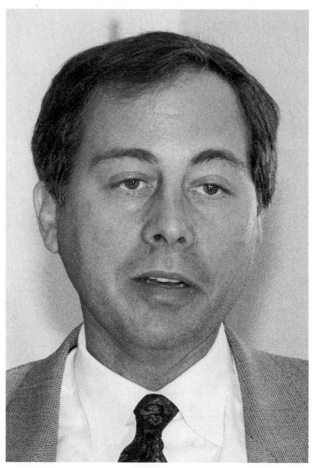

Brandon Tartikoff. AP/WIDE WORLD PHOTOS

gritty *St. Elsewhere,* a medical drama, on the air in October 1982. That same year, Tartikoff oversaw the development of *Cheers* and brought *Taxi* over from ABC. While NBC's ratings continued to struggle, the critics adored the new lineup, and in 1983 NBC garnered 133 Emmy nominations, winning for both outstanding comedy series (*Cheers*) and drama series (*Hill Street Blues*).

NBC's ratings changed dramatically in 1984. Tartikoff pitched the idea of an MTV-style cops show to *Hill Street Blues* writer Tony Yerkovich, and *Miami Vice* joined the network lineup. In his biggest success, Tartikoff talked the network and Bill Cosby into doing *The Cosby Show,* which started in September 1984. The series was developed in defiance of conventional industry wisdom that situation comedies were passé and that, aside from the success of *I Spy* in the 1960s, Cosby had a poor track record in television. *The Cosby Show* finished second in the ratings in its first season and was number one, often by large numbers, for the next four years.

Tartikoff drastically reduced the number of prime-time movies and miniseries to promote more comedies and hour-long dramas. His range of programming included *The A Team* (1983–1986), *Highway to Heaven* (1984–1988), *The Golden Girls* (1985–1992), and *L.A. Law* (1986–1994). His success was rewarded in 1989 with a promotion to chairman of the NBC Entertainment Group. Tartikoff continued to bring new talent to NBC, ensuring that his influence would be felt long after his retirement. Before he left NBC in 1991, Tartikoff signed the stand-up comedian Jerry Seinfeld as a possible replacement for the late-night talk-show host Johnny Carson, and then allowed him to develop *Seinfeld* as a summer replacement in May 1990. That same year, Tartikoff also signed the actor Will Smith and produced *The Fresh Prince of Bel Air.* The success of both new shows allowed NBC to dominate the ratings throughout the 1990s.

In April 1991 Paramount Communications hired Tartikoff as the head of Paramount Pictures, where he optioned into production such popular films as *Wayne's World* (1992) and *A Clear and Present Danger* (1994). Later that year, Tartikoff and his oldest daughter, then age eight, were seriously injured in an automobile accident. Although Tartikoff quickly recovered, his daughter required extensive treatment, and the family moved to New Orleans to facilitate her recovery. Tartikoff left Paramount in 1992 to spend more time with his family. In 1994 he formed his own production unit, H. Beale Productions, named after Howard Beale, the crazed anchorman in the film *Network* (1976), and began developing programming for New World Entertainment.

Tartikoff's lifetime service to the community was recognized with two awards: the American Jaycees named him one of ten outstanding young Americans (1981) and the

muels, a dancer with the New York City Ballet, with whom he had two daughters, but his health took a turn for the worse. In 1974 he had been diagnosed with Hodgkin's disease, but since the disease had been caught in stage one, it had not been considered life-threatening. After six months of radiation treatment and additional chemotherapy, doctors had pronounced him cured. But the disease resurfaced in 1982, and Tartikoff underwent a year-long treatment at the UCLA Medical Center.

By the time he entered a second phase of remission in 1983, Tartikoff had begun to turn around NBC's fortunes. In the face of new industry challenges—cable television, videocassette recorders, and the beginnings of the Fox Network and MTV—Tartikoff had updated NBC's program content. In 1981 Tartikoff talked Steven Bochco and Michael Kozoll into producing a new type of gritty television police show, *Hill Street Blues.* The program floundered in its first year, but Tartikoff allowed it to remain on the air when he discovered the show performed well in households with cable. *Hill Street Blues* won awards with its adult content and themes, and allowed Tartikoff to put the equally

Jewish National Foundation made him a recipient of the Tree of Life Award (1986). On 27 August 1997 Tartikoff died at the UCLA Medical Center, from complications of Hodgkin's disease. He is buried in Mount Sinai Cemetery in Los Angeles.

When Tartikoff left NBC in 1991, he had been the head of network programming for twelve years, longer than anyone before him. As a young man, Tartikoff had once worked as an usher in a movie theater and, according to his autobiography, he delighted in watching not the screen but the audience; knowing the audience became the key to his success. Tartikoff was one of the first programming executives to recognize fully the diversity and complexities of television viewers, putting to rest forever the myth of a singular, homogenized mass audience. He encouraged the development of creative talent and gave artists the freedom to work on their own projects. Tartikoff raised the quality of television programming by adding diversity and adult content to a medium most recognized for its sophomoric shows; he inspired a new generation of producers and viewers to want more meaningful television. Tartikoff was instrumental not just in rallying the failing fortunes of NBC, but also in showing the way for network broadcasters to create programming that could compete with the influx of cable in the 1980s and into the 1990s.

★

The best source on Tartikoff's life is his autobiography, *The Last Great Ride* (1992). There are also useful insights in Mark Christensen and Cameron Stauth, *The Sweeps: Behind the Scenes in Network TV* (1984). There are brief references to Tartikoff in Les Brown, *Encyclopedia of Television* (1982); Michael Winship, *Television* (1988); and Grant Tinker, *Tinker in Television* (1994). An obituary is in the *New York Times* (28 Aug. 1997).

PATRICK A. TRIMBLE

TAYLOR, Telford (*b.* 24 February 1908 in Schenectady, New York; *d.* 23 May 1998 in New York City), lawyer, scholar, and human rights activist most famous for his role as a principal U.S. prosecutor at the International Military Tribunal trials at Nuremberg in 1946.

Taylor was one of five children born to John Bellamy Taylor and Marcia Estabrook Jones. Telford's father was an electrical engineer and inventor with several patents in audio electronics. Taylor attended local schools in Schenectady, after which he enrolled in Williams College in Williamstown, Massachusetts, where he was known as an accomplished clarinetist. He graduated from Williams in 1928 and then attended Harvard Law School. A superior student, he qualified for the editorial board of the *Harvard Law Review* in his final year. Taylor became a protégé of

Telford Taylor. CORBIS CORPORATION (NEW YORK)

Professor Felix Frankfurter, who obtained a clerkship for him in 1932 with Augustus Hand in the Second Circuit Court of Appeals in New York City

In 1933, in the depths of the Great Depression, Taylor joined the many young Ivy League lawyers in the Roosevelt administration. Like many of his contemporaries, he moved from one Washington, D.C., agency to another. He began his federal career working as an assistant solicitor in the Department of the Interior (1933), then moved to the legal staff of the Agricultural Adjustment Administration (1934), and later to Senator Burton Wheeler's Senate Interstate Commerce Committee as associate counsel (1935 to 1939). Taylor married Mary Eleanor Walker, an attorney, on 2 July 1937; the couple had three children.

In 1939 and 1940 Taylor served on the legal staff in the claims division of the Department of Justice. This stint gave Telford his first of many appearances before the Supreme Court. It was here also that Taylor became associated with Robert Jackson and Francis Biddle, central figures in the U.S. legal team at Nuremberg, Germany.

In 1940 Taylor became general counsel to the Federal Communications Commission, where he pursued an aggressive agenda in licensing and antitrust areas. In 1942 he received a major's commission and went into army intelligence. Shortly thereafter he was chosen to lead an on-site

573

American team to work with the British at Bletchley Park, the center for England's Government Communications Headquarters (GCHQ) or Signals of Intelligence during World War II. His job was to assess the relevance of intelligence material to American units and oversee its proper distribution. In this position, he gained expertise on Germany that he later used at the military tribunal. He became military attaché in the United States embassy in London and was promoted to full colonel in 1944.

In 1946 Taylor became an assistant to the chief counsel, the former United States Attorney General Robert H. Jackson, the principal prosecutor of Nazi leaders accused of crimes against humanity. The Russians favored the execution of Nazis with little fanfare; British Prime Minister Winston Churchill was inclined to agree with that view. Jackson and Taylor were determined that the horrified reaction to what the Nazis had done not lead to actions that would diminish the principles for which the war had been fought. They were keenly aware of the precedent-setting nature of the Nuremberg Military Tribunal and were concerned especially that the trials be conducted in a manner clearly based on sound legal principles. The charges were carefully based on existing international treaties and customary law. Taylor saw the trials as essential to bringing closure to the war and in bringing to justice those most responsible.

Taylor was promoted to brigadier general in 1946. When Jackson returned to his duties in Washington, Taylor was named to succeed him. From the autumn of 1946 through the spring of 1949, Taylor took the lead in the American part of the trials. The initial indictment of twenty-two of the highest-ranking military and civilian leaders of the Third Reich resulted in nineteen convictions, of whom twelve were sentenced to death. As a follow-up to the International Military Tribunal, the United States planned a second round of trials of high-ranking Nazi officials. However, many British and French officials were not inclined toward further proceedings, while American officials were increasingly hostile to further legal cooperation with the Soviets.

Known as United States Military Tribunals and staffed by American judges, the proceedings included the trials of 185 persons. Of this number, 142 were found guilty. Twelve received a death sentence. Taylor won praise from every quarter, including the Russians, for his handling of these difficult and complex cases.

The trials were both historic and significant. Taylor's devastating prosecution of the defendants reinforced the principle of the accountability of individuals in international law. Narrowing the defense of superior orders and limiting personal liability for waging aggressive war to the most senior active participants can be traced directly to these trials. Other legal norms, such as the centrality of

disclosure and informed consent in human experimentation, can also be traced to the tribunals. Taylor was pleased that he was able to prove to often skeptical judges that massive and intentional violations of the law had occurred. By 1948 the beginning of the cold war shifted the political winds against the trials. Many believed that the undoing of Nuremberg was necessary to bring West Germany into an alliance dedicated to containing Communism. John J. McCloy, appointed the high commissioner for the American sector of Germany in 1949, promptly began a review of the Nuremberg cases and commuted many sentences, accelerated releases, and granted pardons. Taylor condemned the post-1949 commutations.

Taylor, now decorated by the United States and several foreign governments (including the receipt of the Order of the British Empire and the Legion of Honor from France), returned to New York City in 1949 to practice law. He served on the board of several universities, became active in New York reform politics, and returned briefly to Washington during the last year of the Truman administration. By the late 1940s and early 1950s several apologetic works for the Nazi period convinced many cold war observers that the Third Reich was in fact misunderstood. In his first book, *Sword and Swastika* (1952), Taylor challenged this revisionist history. It was a valuable contribution because it was written at a time when many of the archives were still closed, by an individual who had interrogated as well as prosecuted many of the new apologists.

In the 1950s no one was immune from suspicion of having Communist sympathies. The conservative press suggested that Taylor was a "pink general" who had shirked combat service and served Moscow's ends by pursuing good Germans. Taylor did not shrink from the accusations. He began to defend accused Communists. He was the first general officer to publicly speak out against McCarthyism. He said that Senator Joseph McCarthy's investigations did not hurt Communism but was "a vicious weapon of the extreme right against their political opponents." He criticized President Dwight Eisenhower for not standing up to the "shameful abuse of Congressional investigating power." Taylor's book *Grand Inquest: The Story of Congressional Investigations* (1955) used his own experience as an investigator and knowledge of constitutional history to point out McCarthy's shortcomings. Taylor's defense of personnel in the state and defense departments and at the United Nations did much to ease the suspicions of the American international law community in the 1950s.

From the late 1950s on, Taylor mostly taught at Columbia and Yale law schools and published his second and third volumes of German military history. He played, conducted, and composed music, and served on the boards of numerous legal groups. The war in Vietnam led him to write *Nuremberg and Vietnam: An American Tragedy* (1970).

In this book Taylor condemned the Vietnam War in very measured legal disputation and rejected more emotional legal critiques. He referred to the war as "the most costly and tragic national blunder in American history." Telford was alone among the senior law faculty at Columbia in sympathizing with students who took over campus buildings to protest the Vietnam conflict. He urged Congress to appoint a commission to investigate the origins and conduct of the war. Taylor was named Nash Professor of Law at Columbia in 1974. On 9 August 1974 Taylor married attorney Barbara "Toby" Golick.

Taylor campaigned for the release of Soviet Jews from prison and subsequently also joined the faculty of Cardozo School of Law in 1976. He wrote *Munich: The Price of Peace* (1980), which won the National Book Critics Circle Award for general nonfiction. He never lost his passion for ethical conduct of government and condemned Admiral John Poindexter and Colonel Oliver North for citing the Fifth Amendment and refusing to answer questions before the Senate Intelligence Committee. In reaction to evidence of genocide in Bosnia, Taylor said that such crimes against humanity should be the basis of criminal indictments.

Taylor died of a stroke at age ninety. He was survived by his wife, Golick, and eight grandchildren.

★

Taylor was interviewed in Linda Metzger and Deborah A. Straub, eds., *Contemporary Authors, New Revision Series*, vol. 16 (1986). The interview ranges over Taylor's perception of many of the most salient events in which he was involved during his career. See Telford Taylor, *The Anatomy of the Nuremberg Trials: A Personal Memoir* (1992), his account of Nuremberg. The best source for views about Telford Taylor is to be found in the *Columbia Journal of Transnational Law* 37 (1999). This issue is dedicated to Taylor and contains many tributes to his personal qualities. Richard Severo provided an excellent summary of Taylor's life and influence in his obituary in the *New York Times* (24 May 1998).

CHARLES L. COCHRAN

THOMPSON, Kay (*b.* 9 November 1902[?] in St. Louis, Missouri; *d.* 2 July 1998 in New York City), singer, author of the "Eloise" books for children, and composer whose stylish, confident public persona was immortalized in the 1957 film *Funny Face.*

Thompson was born Kitty Fink, one of three children of a St. Louis jeweler. Details of her early life—and indeed of much of her later life—are hard to pin down; she reinvented herself periodically and shed the skins of previous selves. She went to high school in St. Louis and attended Washington University there as well. She is said to have begun playing the piano at age four, and in 1928 she made

Kay Thompson with Eloise dolls, 1958. ASSOCIATED PRESS AP

her professional debut on that instrument with the St. Louis Symphony. She also sang with a dance band in her hometown. Nevertheless, she later told a reporter, "I was a stagestruck kid and I got out of St. Louis fast."

She went to Los Angeles in 1929 to become a diving instructor and ended up singing. She also straightened her nose and adopted the name she would use for the rest of her life. In the 1930s she sang on a variety of radio shows, including her own program on CBS in 1935, and worked as a vocal arranger for others. She also made nightclub appearances and had a minor role in the film *Manhattan Merry-Go-Round* in 1937. Nevertheless, her career did not congeal in this decade, which she spent partly in New York City and partly in Los Angeles. Her big break was slated to be the musical comedy *Hooray for What!* in 1937, but its producer, searching for a more traditionally sexy singer, fired the angular Thompson early in the show's run. According to biographer Marie Brenner, this debacle permanently soured Thompson on Broadway.

Thompson married musician Jack Jenney in the mid-1930s and divorced him in 1939 to marry radio producer Bill Spier, with whom she stayed until 1947. She later told critic Rex Reed, "I've lived with quite a few men and alone is better. That doesn't mean I'm a loner; I just don't like to ask permission."

In 1944, when the composer Hugh Martin left his position as vocal arranger at the Metro-Goldwyn-Mayer

(MGM) film studio to enter World War II, he suggested Thompson as his replacement. At MGM, where movie musicals were in their heyday, she made her mark on such films as *Ziegfeld Follies* (for which she composed as well as arranged, 1946), *The Harvey Girls* (1946), *Good News* (1947), and *The Pirate* (1948). Thompson also served as a coach to MGM's singers, influencing American music for decades to come. Lena Horne called her "the best vocal coach in the world." Thompson helped Judy Garland reinvent herself as an adult singer and forged a friendship that would last through Garland's life; Thompson was godmother to Garland's oldest child, Liza Minnelli.

MGM colleagues fondly recalled Thompson's performances at parties, for which she composed and arranged special numbers. These spectacles inspired Thompson's next career, as a cabaret performer. From 1947 into the 1950s, she toured in an act, frequently with the Williams brothers (crooner Andy and his siblings). The act moved from comedy to music to dance, showcasing Thompson's energy and rhythm.

Andy Williams later remembered, "It's hard to imagine there wasn't an act like us before, because there have been so many since. Up to that time, everyone just sang around a microphone, and when the song was over, the singers would raise their arms. . . . What Kay and [choreographer] Bob Alton put together was like a mini-musical revue." Williams added, "She taught me more about singing and show business than anyone in the world."

As a lark during cabaret rehearsals, Thompson invented an alternate persona, a precocious six-year-old named Eloise, in which to joke with her colleagues. In 1955 she collaborated with the illustrator Hilary Knight on a book, *Kay Thompson's Eloise*, regaling child and adult readers with the exploits of her heroine, a well-to-do brat who lives in New York City's Plaza Hotel. An immediate success, it was followed by *Eloise in Paris* (1957), *Eloise at Christmastime* (1958), and *Eloise in Moscow* (1959). Eloise inspired a range of products, from dolls to hotel kits. Eventually, the Plaza was named a literary landmark, complete with a portrait of Eloise by Knight in the lobby.

As Eloise's fame began to grow, Thompson performed less frequently but was finally lured in front of the motion-picture cameras again for the musical *Funny Face* (1957), in which she costarred with Fred Astaire and Audrey Hepburn. As the ultra-chic editor of a fashion magazine, she told American women to "Think Pink" and held her own with Astaire, singing and dancing an energetic version of "Clap Yo' Hands." Rex Reed would dub this persona "dazzling . . . like Coco Chanel cross-pollinated with Diana Vreeland."

In 1962, for reasons that baffled her friends, Thompson moved to Rome and cut back on performances and writing. She spent the rest of her life alternating between that city and New York City, where she still maintained roots, first at the Plaza and eventually at the home of her goddaughter. She put in a final film performance in Minnelli's 1970 film *Tell Me That You Love Me, Junie Moon*. After that, she puttered, keeping up with contemporary show business but no longer participating. She was living with Minnelli when she died in 1998, at the age of ninety-five or perhaps ninety-two. "She would have enjoyed the slight discrepancy," wrote columnist Liz Smith.

Thompson was a woman of many talents. "If artistically you are able to do one thing," she told a reporter for *McCall's* in the 1950s, "you are more than likely able to do them all." Although her most lasting legacies are the Eloise books and the fashionable whirlwind she played in *Funny Face*, colleagues remembered her most for her influential musical stylings at MGM and her striking cabaret appearances; columnist Walter Winchell dubbed her act the greatest in nightclub history. Above all, friends mourned her sleek, energetic personality. "She was a dynamo," actress Gloria DeHaven said of Thompson. "Wildly talented, wildly flamboyant, and wildly wild."

★

The most comprehensive profile of Thompson can be found in Marie Brenner, *Great Dames* (2000), a slightly expanded version of an essay Brenner originally wrote for *Vanity Fair*. Other helpful articles include Cynthia Lindsay, "McCall's Visits Kay Thompson," *McCall's* (Jan. 1957); Barbara Bannon, "Authors and Editors: Eloise Is Back," *Publishers Weekly* (12 May 1969); and Rex Reed, "You've Never Seen Anything Like Her," *Harper's Bazaar* (Nov. 1972). Obituaries and memorial pieces are in the *New York Times* (7 July 1998); Tom Vallance's obituary in the *London Independent* (8 July 1998); Liz Smith, "Celebrities in History," *Newsday* (8 July 1998); Rex Reed, "Oh, Kay! You're O.K. with Me," *New York Observer* (20 July 1998); and Jim Caruso, "Kay Thompson: 'Pure Heaven,'" *In Theater* (26 Apr. 1999). An Eloise website contains much material on Thompson; it may be found at <http://www.gti.net/iksrog/eloise>.

TINKY "DAKOTA" WEISBLAT

TILBERIS, Elizabeth Jane Kelly ("Liz") (*b.* 7 September 1947 in Alderley Edge, Cheshire, England; *d.* 21 April 1999 in New York City), editor in chief of British *Vogue* from 1987 to 1992 and *Harper's Bazaar* from 1992 to 1999 who also became a major fund-raiser for ovarian cancer research.

The oldest of three children, Elizabeth Jane Kelly was born to Thomas Stuart-Black Kelly, an eye surgeon, and Janet Stome, a cartographer, at her maternal grandmother's house in Alderley Edge outside Manchester, England. Her childhood was idyllic; she grew up in the English countryside near Bristol, Hereford, and Bath. Tilberis studied

Liz Tilberis, 1998. PATRICK DEMARCHELIER/ASSOCIATED PRESS/
HARPER'S BAZAAR

piano and ballet, went horseback riding, and, as early as age eight, loved to make costumes for her dolls and to draw girls in eighteenth-century dress. At age five she was enrolled in Margaret Allen Preparatory School in Hereford. Later she attended Malvern Girls' College, a boarding school in Worcestershire and her mother's alma mater, where she excelled in drama and drawing and was known for her aggressive play on the lacrosse field. She studied art and design at Leicester Polytechnic starting in 1965, transferred to Jacob Kramer Art College in Leeds, and finished her studies back at Leicester, graduating in 1970 with a B.A. degree in fashion design. While at Leicester Polytechnic she wrote a fashion page for the *Bath Evening Chronicle*.

Tilberis entered a British *Vogue* essay competition, judged by the actor Peter Sellers and the photographer Anthony Armstrong-Jones (Lord Snowdon), in 1969. She was a runner-up, but when the winner was unable to accept the prize, Tilberis won the honor. She received twenty-five English pounds as prize money and a chance to work in the magazine's fashion department. In 1970 she began as an intern, picking up pins and running errands, and then rose through the ranks to become an experimental stylist, fashion director, and, finally, editor in chief (1987) and director of Condé Nast Publications (1991). Her promotion to editor was prompted when she was offered a position with the American fashion designer Ralph Lauren for a rumored $250,000 to join his New York design team.

On 17 July 1971, while she was at *Vogue,* Tilberis married Andrew Tilberis, a photographer and her college tutor at Jacob Kramer College of Art. They adopted two boys after failing to conceive children of their own. As editor, her reputation for forward thinking was well known, and the magazine's circulation soared. She was the only editor in the world to succeed in persuading Diana, Princess of Wales, to pose as cover girl. Her major achievement, however, was to find a new connection between the eccentric photography and styling that was British *Vogue's* greatest strength and the more practical approach to clothes demanded by advertisers and readers. Tilberis's success at British *Vogue* made her a candidate for the editorship of the American magazine *Harper's Bazaar,* whose owners, Hearst Magazines, were looking for ways to revive its sophisticated style. Her submission of an eighteen-page proposal to "make *Harper's Bazaar* the most beautiful fashion magazine ever" convinced the owners that she was the person for the job.

She became editor in chief in 1992, the year the Hearst Magazines publication marked its 125th anniversary. She introduced more art features, uncluttered graphics, and high-quality fashion journalism. The September 1992 issue, the first under her direction, ran the cover line "Enter the Era of Elegance" and received international recognition. Tilberis's style and charm, aided by Hearst Magazines's checkbook, attracted a vast array of talent, including the photographers Patrick Demarchelier and Peter Lindbergh and the art director Fabien Baron. Within eighteen months Tilberis won two Ellies (the American magazine world's equivalent of the Oscar), National Magazine awards for photography and design, and the Society of Publication Designers' Gold Medal for overall redesign. Princess Diana presented her with a special award from the Council of Fashion Designers of America in 1994, and *Advertising Age* named her editor of the year. Tilberis had brought *Harper's Bazaar* to a new level of excellence with its highly stylized images. She was successful in sparking a 25 percent rise in newsstand sales, tripling advertising, and providing a significantly more chic and elegant format.

Shortly after Tilberis arrived in New York City, she was diagnosed with ovarian cancer, an illness that she believed was the result of treatment for infertility. Her cancer treatment included radical surgery, followed by intensive chemotherapy. She remarked that the illness changed her view of the world. In 1994 the cancer recurred and was diagnosed as stage III. (At stage IV, it usually is suggested that patients put their affairs in order.) She had a bone marrow transplant and continued to conduct editorial meetings from her hospital bed. In 1995 Tilberis received the Matrix Award from the Association for Women in Communications, presented to those who have distinguished themselves in their respective fields of communications. She remarked once to a *New York Times* reporter, "I think we made the niche we wanted to make, and I think we are the elegant fashion magazine I really wanted to create."

Tilberis became president of the Ovarian Cancer Research Fund in 1997 and was active in the New York charity social scene. She also served as chairwoman of benefits for such causes as pediatric AIDS, the New York City Ballet, and the Costume Institute of the Metropolitan Museum of Art. When she returned to work, she was determined to raise public awareness of ovarian cancer. That year her blood tests indicated the presence of cancer cells, and she underwent further chemotherapy treatment. She lost her six-year battle with cancer at the age of fifty-one at Mount Sinai Medical Center in Manhattan. A memorial service was held at Lincoln Center in New York, and the fashion designer Donatella Versace held a memorial party at Syon House in London. Versace and her co-host, Anthony Oppenheimer, used this party to aid the Ovarian Cancer Research Fund.

Tilberis's courage in the face of her illness and the debilitating treatments touched the hearts of the hardened fashion community and won their support and praise. The Humanitarian Award from the Council of Fashion Designers of America was given to her posthumously in June 1999. She was highly respected for her ability as an editor and renowned for her fashion sense. Her tireless efforts to increase awareness of various health causes made Tilberis a memorable and formidable crusader against ovarian cancer and other ills.

★

Tilberis wrote about her struggle with ovarian cancer in her book *No Time to Die,* coauthored with Aimee Lee Ball (1998). She is highlighted in *Newmakers 1994,* edited by Louise Mooney Collins. Many tributes have been written about Tilberis, including Julia Reed, "A Woman of Substance," *Newsweek* (3 May 1999), and Anne-Marie O'Neill, et al., "Ever in Fashion," *People Weekly* (10 May 1999). Obituaries are in the *New York Times, Washington Post,* and *Boston Globe* (all 22 Apr. 1999), *MediaWeek* (26 Apr. 1999), and *Obituaries in the Performing Arts, 1999* (2000).

CONNIE THORSEN

TOMBAUGH, Clyde William (*b.* 4 February 1906 near Streator, Illinois; *d.* 17 January 1997 in Las Cruces, New Mexico), astronomer who discovered the planet Pluto.

Tombaugh was born into a farming family, the eldest of six children of Muron D. Tombaugh and Adella Pearl Chritton, and became fascinated with the mechanics of farm machinery as a child. Noting the boy's technical aptitude, his uncle, Lee Tombaugh, loaned him a telescope and a book on astronomy. Tombaugh, then twelve, soon

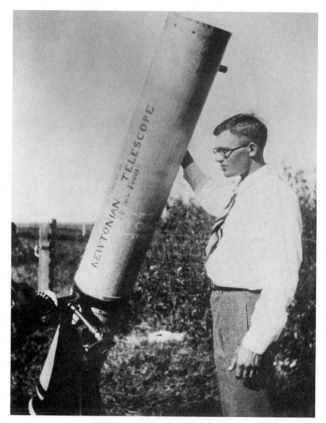

Clyde Tombaugh, 1928. © BETTMANN/CORBIS

had memorized statistical figures on the planets, the sun, and major stars.

In August 1922 Tombaugh's father moved the family from Illinois to big wheat country in southwest central Kansas. The preparation of their new farm near Burdett was time consuming, and Tombaugh had to drop out of high school for a year to help. When time permitted, Tombaugh turned his two-and-a-quarter-inch (fifty-seven millimeter) Sears Roebuck telescope to the Kansas firmament and parsed the heavens. The dry weather of the plains made for superb viewing, and Tombaugh spent his nights at the eyepiece or reading everything he could on astronomy by kerosene lamp (because the farm had no electricity). Tombaugh graduated from Burdett High School in 1925. Because he was needed on the farm, he had no prospects for college.

In 1926 Tombaugh built a telescope from pine boards, obsolete farm machinery, and a shaft from his father's 1910 Buick. He ground the mirror by hand. Over the next two years he built two more telescopes, improving on the design with each attempt. After a hailstorm on 20 June 1928 flattened the family's promising wheat crop, Tombaugh worked neighboring farms by day and pursued amateur astronomy by night. He began to sketch the markings he saw on Mars and Jupiter and mailed some of his drawings to the Lowell Observatory in Flagstaff, Arizona, for professional critique.

The precision of the renderings impressed the observatory's director, Dr. Vesto M. Slipher, who needed an assistant to help operate a new photographic telescope. After a brief correspondence, Slipher invited Tombaugh to Flagstaff to work for a few months on a trial basis. Tombaugh left Kansas by train on 14 January 1929. The Lowell Observatory did not then enjoy a sterling reputation among astronomers. It had been founded in the late nineteenth century by the eccentric Percival Lowell, who had become obsessed with the notion that markings he observed on the surface of Mars revealed an intricate network of canals created by an alien race trying to leverage the dwindling water supply on their arid planet. His comments excited the masses and brought ridicule from the scientific establishment.

Lowell was also obsessed with Planet X, a world he believed circled the sun beyond the orbit of Neptune. He began searching for the phantom in 1905, but it eluded him to the end of his days. He left it to the observatory to continue the hunt. The task—requiring time-exposure photography in the freezing Arizona night and painstaking star-by-star examination of the developed plates—was wearying and tedious. Veteran astronomers at Lowell had more important observations to pursue, and the job fell to the young farm boy from Kansas. Tombaugh would photograph identical slivers of the night sky a few days apart, then load the plates into a device called the Zeiss Blink-Microscope-Comparator. It would flash first one plate and then the other into an eyepiece. Tombaugh examined the images, containing between 50,000 and 900,000 stars, inch by inch, seeking the telltale jump in a point of light indicating the movement of a planet against the stationary background of stars.

On 18 February 1930 at about 4 P.M. MST, Tombaugh was examining two plates taken the previous month in the constellation Gemini. A pinprick of light hopped across the field in the rapidly alternating views. For the next forty-five minutes, Tombaugh checked and rechecked the faint object. Its parallactic shift indicated that it was in motion far beyond Neptune. He went down the hall to Slipher's office. "Trying to control myself, I stepped into his office as nonchalantly as possible," Tombaugh later recalled. Then he announced, "Dr. Slipher, I have found your Planet X." Slipher hurried to the device, examined the images, and concurred with Tombaugh's observation. Since more proof would be required, another plate needed to be taken, but clouds hung over Flagstaff that night.

Crestfallen, Tombaugh went to the movies to kill time, hoping the skies would clear. He saw *The Virginian,* starring Gary Cooper, but had a hard time keeping his mind on the show. He returned to find an overcast sky still in place between him and the tantalizing object. But the next night was clear, and he found the planet right where it should have been, drifting westward from the earlier observations. It was a needle in a cosmic haystack. The planet, subsequently named Pluto, is the ninth and farthest planet from the sun in the solar system. To the unaided eye, Pluto has the brightness of a candle at a distance of 300 miles. In the night sky, 15 million stars outshine Pluto. The announcement was made 13 March 1930 that a new planet had joined the sun's retinue, discovered by a twenty-four-year-old, self-taught astronomer without a college degree. The Associated Press quoted the suddenly world-famous Tombaugh: "How would you feel if you saw a new world giving you the high sign beyond the rim of the solar system?"

Tombaugh took a leave of absence from Lowell from 1932 to 1936 to attend the University of Kansas on scholarship, where he earned an A.B. degree in astronomy. There he met Patricia Irene Edson. They married on 7 June 1934 and eventually had two children. Tombaugh returned to the university in 1938 and was awarded an M.A. degree in astronomy the following spring. In the intervening years and until he left the observatory during World War II, he searched for a possible tenth planet but never found it. In 1943 he began teaching celestial navigation for the U.S. Navy at Arizona State College in Flagstaff. After World War II, he was stung when he learned that his position was no longer open at the Lowell Observatory, ostensibly for financial reasons, though he believed it was because of professional jealousy. His name, not the names of more prominent members of the staff, was tied to the discovery of Pluto.

In 1946 Tombaugh went to the White Sands Proving Grounds near Las Cruces, New Mexico, where captured German V-2 missiles were being tested, and became the chief of the Optical Measurements Branch in the Ballistics Research Laboratory. He developed optical tracking telescopes that were later applied to the nation's space program. In 1955 he joined New Mexico State University and founded the school's astronomy program. He taught there until retiring in 1973, after which he lectured widely. Few, if any, astronomers have seen as much of the sky as Tombaugh. In the course of his search for trans-Neptunian planets, he examined 35 million star images and discovered among them two comets, five open star clusters, a globular star cluster, a supercluster of galaxies, an exploding nova, and 775 asteroids.

He loved puns and wordplay and clung to his Midwestern modesty all his life. When the Smithsonian Institution in Washington, D.C., sought to add to its collection the telescope he built in 1928 and through which he made the sketches that impressed the Lowell staff, Tombaugh refused, explaining, "I'm still using it." Weakened by congestive heart failure and breathing problems, Tombaugh died at age ninety at his home in Las Cruces, New Mexico. He was cremated and his ashes were spread in southern New Mexico.

★

Tombaugh's personal papers are in New Mexico State University's Historical Collections. His autobiography *Out of the Darkness, the Planet Pluto* (1980), written with Patrick Moore, contains his recollections of the discovery of Pluto. Other important books include Alan Stern and Jacqueline Mitton, *Pluto and Charon: Ice Worlds on the Edge of the Solar System* (1998); David H. Levy, *Clyde Tombaugh: Discoverer of Planet Pluto* (1991); and William Graves Hoyt, *Planets X and Pluto* (1980). Books for children are Dennis B. Fradin, *The Planet Hunters: The Search for Other Worlds* (1997), and Margaret K. Wetterer, *Clyde Tombaugh and the Search for Planet X* (1996). The Lowell Observatory maintains a website about Pluto and its discovery at <http://www.lowell.edu/users/buie/pluto/pluto.html>. An obituary is in the *Los Angeles Times* (19 Jan. 1997).

MARK WASHBURN

TORMÉ, Mel(vin) Howard (*b.* 13 September 1925 in Chicago, Illinois; *d.* 5 June 1999 in Los Angeles, California), vocalist, composer, arranger, pianist, drummer, author, and actor, best known as the Velvet Fog for his luxurious, full-throated voice.

One of two children of William David Tormé, the owner of a dry goods store and a salesman for a clothing firm, and Betty Sopkin, a seamstress and a homemaker, Tormé came from a Russian Jewish background. His mother was born in the United States and his Russian father entered the country at New York's Ellis Island. An immigration official, unable to read the last letter of the family name Torma, changed the name to Torme. The accent mark on the last letter was probably added by his mother, who named her son for the actor Melvyn Douglas and her daughter for the actor Myrna Loy.

The Tormé and Sopkin families were musical, both as instrumentalists and singers. Tormé attributed his talents for vocal group arranging and performing to the family sing-alongs. He began to show musical ability at an early age, and in the 1920s he regularly listened to the famous Coon-Sanders Original Nighthawk Orchestra, broadcasting from the Blackhawk restaurant in Chicago's Loop district. As a special treat, Tormé's parents took him to dinner at the restaurant in 1929. When patrons noticed the boy's enthusiasm and pointed him out to the leader, Joe Sanders, he approached the lad's parents, and invited them to let the boy sing one of the band's numbers. Tormé gave such a professional performance that he was invited back to sing

Mel Tormé, 1957. ASSOCIATED PRESS/WILLIAM MORRIS AGENCY

regularly. Tormé spent six months with the Coon-Sanders orchestra and also performed with groups led by Louis Panico, Frankie Masters, and Buddy Rogers.

By 1933 Tormé was well known locally for singing, dancing, or playing an instrument in weekend musical productions, and it was evident that he wanted a career in show business. In 1934, the year following the opening of the Chicago World's Fair, Tormé won the Children's Division Cup in the Radio Auditions Finals. This accomplishment provided him with an entrance to the field of radio, which at that time was centered in Chicago. Within the next few years, Tormé was one of the major child actors in the business, performing on such programs as *Captain Midnight, Jack Armstrong: All-American Boy*, and *Little Orphan Annie*, as well as more adult serials. In addition to these activities, Tormé attended the Shakespeare Grammar School and played in its drum and bugle corps. He became increasingly interested in playing drums and began taking lessons at age seven. A major career move came in 1941, when Harry James and his band recorded Tormé's first song, "Lament to Love" and played it on *Your Hit Parade*.

From 1942 to 1943 Tormé played in the band led by the comedian Chico Marx, who appeared regularly in movies with his brothers. Tormé, still young enough to avoid the draft, left Chicago and met Marx in Los Angeles, where he was hired to sing, organize a vocal group within the band, write arrangements, and play drums if the regular drummer was drafted. Tormé was first assigned to arrange some numbers for a group of band members called the Revellis, after the movie name used by Marx. The experience the teenage Tormé gained was priceless, as he learned how to deal with both his audience and his fellow musicians.

While in Los Angeles, Tormé made his movie debut in *Higher and Higher* (1943), alongside another young artist, Frank Sinatra. Following this film he played in *Pardon My Rhythm* (1944), starring Gloria Jean, which featured the vocal group the Schoolkids. By 1944 he was old enough to be drafted into the U.S. Army. Before being inducted, however, he graduated from Los Angeles High School, concluding his formal education.

After World War II he reconnected with the Schoolkids for another film, *Let's Go Steady* (1945). This time, the group was renamed and Tormé received his first top billing with Mel Tormé and the Mel-Tones. Tormé had been working on writing lyrics for his songs, and began collaborating with another developing lyricist, Bob Wells. In 1945 the two composed "The Christmas Song," which was recorded that year by the Mel-Tones. The vocalist Nat "King" Cole made a recording of the number in 1946 and it became a runaway best-seller. The Mel-Tones had their own hit in 1946 with Cole Porter's "What Is This Thing Called Love?" At this time, Tormé also met the drummer Buddy Rich, who became a lifelong friend. Before Rich passed away on 2 April 1987, he asked Tormé to finish his already begun "warts-and-all" biography, which was subsequently published as *Traps, the Drum Wonder: The Life of Buddy Rich* (1991).

In February 1949 Tormé married the first of his four wives, Florence Ann Gertrude Tockstein, better known as "Candy Toxton." But Tormé's work schedule, together with his love for sports cars, flying with his private pilot's license, collecting antique guns, and his private social life, placed an impossible strain on the marriage. The couple divorced in 1955, after having two children. Tormé then married Arlene Miles in October 1956. They had a son and divorced in 1966. In May of the same year, he married Janette Scott; they had two children and divorced in 1976. Tormé met his fourth wife, Ali Severson, in 1976 and they married in May 1984. She had two children by a former marriage, a daughter and a son.

In addition to continuing his work in motion pictures, Tormé performed on radio. One of his programs was *The Mel Tormé Show*, a comedy with music by the Mel-Tones in a college-campus setting. Starting in 1949 Tormé also began working on a serious, album-length production called *California Suite*, which became Capitol Record's first long-playing album. *The Mel Tormé Show* was canceled in the spring of 1953, and he took a job on television costarring with Theresa Brewer. Following that, he headlined at New York City's Roxy Theater. Tormé's career advanced throughout the 1950s, as he became a popular solo entertainer and earned recognition as the Velvet Fog, a name originally given to him in 1946 by Fred Robbins, a New York City radio station disc jockey. While Tormé disliked the appellation, believing it did not best describe his vocal quality, it was eagerly adopted by his youthful fans.

Tormé continued to perform in movies and clubs while moving into the new medium of television. After substituting as a host on Perry Como's television show, he was offered his own daytime talk show on CBS in 1953. Later, he was nominated for an Emmy as best supporting actor for a role in the 1958 CBS television film *The Comedian*. During the television season from 1963 to 1964, he was the musical director for Judy Garland's television program, which provided the basis for his book *The Other Side of the Rainbow* (1970), chronicling Garland's fall into prescription-drug addiction. He was also the host and producer of the nostalgic series *It Was a Very Good Year* (1971) and appeared with Benny Goodman on a Monsanto-sponsored television special in 1974. After enduring a brief slump in the late 1970s, his fame was reignited in the early 1980s. This was due in part to help from the actor and Tormé aficionado Harry Anderson, whose character Judge Harry Stone on the television comedy *Night Court* was also an ardent fan. Tormé appeared as himself on the show several times.

The 1980s also saw Tormé at his peak as a musician. Recalling the early years of his life growing up in an African-American section of Chicago, where his baby-sitter was a pianist with a five-piece combo at the Savoy Ballroom, he had made a transition in the mid-1950s from emphasizing pop to more jazz-flavored music. In 1976 Tormé was recognized with an Edison Award (the Dutch equivalent of the Grammy) and a *Down Beat* magazine award as the best male jazz singer. But his real musical breakthroughs came in concert, in 1977 at Carnegie Hall with George Shearing and Gerry Mulligan, and in 1978 at the Newport Jazz Festival. After a history of bouncing from record company to record company, he began recording on the Concord jazz label in 1982, sometimes with the pianist George Shearing or with Cleo Laine or Marty Paich.

Paich was noted for his use of a musical group called a "dektette," which produced a light sound that blended well with Tormé's voice. He was able to sing scat perhaps better than anyone else with the possible exception of Ella Fitzgerald, who also had impeccable pitch and timing that enabled her to make up the words and nonsense syllables so necessary for that type of vocalization. Both of Tormé's first albums with Concord, *An Evening with George Shearing and Mel Tormé* (1982) and *Top Drawer* (1983), won him Grammys for the best male jazz vocal performance. In February 1999 he received a lifetime achievement award from the National Academy of Recording Arts and Sciences.

In 1996 Tormé suffered a stroke that effectively brought an end to his career. He died in the Medical Center of the University of California at Los Angeles from complications following the stroke. He was interred in the Westwood Memorial Park in Los Angeles.

★

The best source of information about Tormé's life is his autobiography, *It Wasn't All Velvet* (1988). Leslie Gourse, *Louis' Children: American Jazz Singers* (1984), contains one chapter about Tormé, "You Are My Goddam Sunshine." Other useful sources include George Hulme's *Mel Tormé: A Chronicle of His Recordings, Books, and Films* (2000); Kirk Silsbee's article, "A Voice Beyond Velvet," *Jazziz* (Oct. 1999); and Tormé's *My Singing Teachers* (1994). Leonard Feather and Ira Gitler, *The Biographical Encyclopedia of Jazz* (1999), contains basic biographical data, as does Ian Carr, Digby Fairweather, and Brian Priestly, *Jazz: The Rough Guide*, 2d ed. (2000). Roger D. Kinkle, *The Complete Encyclopedia of Popular Music and Jazz, 1900–1950* (1974), contains fairly complete biographical data through the 1970s with a discography. An excellent profile of Tormé is Whitney Balliett, "A Vast Majority," *New Yorker* (16 Mar. 1981). Obituaries are in the *Los Angeles Times* and *New York Times* (both 6 June 1999) and *Down Beat* (Aug. 1999).

BARRETT G. POTTER

TOURÉ, Kwame. *See* Carmichael, Stokely.

TRACY, Arthur (*b.* 25 June 1899 in Kamenetz-Podolsk, Moldavia; *d.* 5 October 1997 in New York City), Great Depression–era musical star known as the "Street Singer."

After the drowning of their eldest son by a gang of anti-Semitic youths, Morris Michael Tracovutsky and Fannie Bernstein left their home in Kamenetz-Podolsk on the Russian-Romanian border and immigrated to the United States in 1906. The family, which included five daughters and a son, Abba Avrom, arrived at Ellis Island, New York, where an immigration officer changed their name to "Tracy." The unforeseen result of this transformation was to allow the future singing star, his Jewish identity concealed, to pursue an international career during the most virulently anti-Semitic period in modern history. The Tracys moved to Philadelphia, Pennsylvania, where Fannie's mother and several of her siblings had settled years earlier. Abba became "Arthur" at an uncle's suggestion and eventually had an American-born brother. The Tracys' home was on Fifth Street and Fairmont Avenue. Tracy's father, a descendent of rabbis and cantors, was an educated man who had been a teacher of mathematics and languages in the old country, running his own school. In America he struggled to support his large family as a weaver on fifteen dollars a week. He recognized his son's musical talent,

Arthur Tracy, 1935. AP/WIDE WORLD PHOTOS

building a theater for him in their backyard and encouraging him to sing for friends who returned to the Tracy home after Sabbath services.

In 1918 Tracy graduated from Central High School, where he had produced and starred in class plays. He then studied architecture at the University of Pennsylvania but quit before graduating. Up to this point, Tracy had been a self-taught vocalist, inspired by the recordings of his boyhood idol, Enrico Caruso. A patroness of the arts who befriended Tracy introduced him to a vocal coach, who temporarily ruined the young man's voice. After a seven-month period of recuperation, Tracy, whose resolve to sing professionally never wavered, auditioned at the prestigious Curtis Institute of Music in Philadelphia and was accepted in 1919 as a scholarship student. There he received a thorough training in classical technique and repertoire. While at Curtis, Tracy began to earn a modest income as a singer working weekends at Atlantic City hotels and at clubs in Philadelphia. He also began singing tenor roles with the Philadelphia Operatic Society. Tracy, whose first language was Yiddish, had a parallel career in the Yiddish theater starting when he was a teenager. Throughout the 1920s Tracy worked for both Boris Thomashefsky and his brother Mike as juvenile lead in their productions *The Woman Cantor* and *The Bar Mitzvah* in Philadelphia, Los Angeles, and New York City.

In Philadelphia, Lawrence Shubert of the famous family of theatrical impresarios heard the handsome, tall young singer with blond wavy hair, icy-blue eyes, and a sturdy physique and engaged him for a touring production of Sigmund Romberg's operetta *Blossom Time* (1921). That led to his being offered a part in a touring Shubert production of *The Student Prince* (1924). Tracy also played vaudeville dates in small-town houses and entertained vacationers in Catskill Mountain hotels along the "borscht," or "Jewish vaudeville," circuit. Tracy moved to New York City in 1924 to establish himself in the show business mainstream. In 1931 one of his vaudeville cronies suggested that he try to break into prime-time radio, which was booming. Tracy arranged to audition for CBS; he was overheard by William Paley, head of the company, and was offered a fifteen-minute show five nights a week. To incorporate a gimmick in his show, Tracy billed himself as "the Street Singer," a name he found in a newspaper review of a Broadway play. An aura of mystery was added to the vibrant "baritenor" voice with a two-and-a-half octave range and a touch of anguish. His CBS radio debut on 13 July 1931 was an overnight success. A recording contract with Decca followed quickly, first with the American company and later with the British namesake, gaining him international stardom.

The next year he was contracted by Paramount Films to appear in the film *The Big Broadcast of 1932,* starring Bing Crosby. Tracy sang a duet with Crosby and introduced his new theme song, "Marta, Rambling Rose of Wildwood." The tune was indelibly associated with him from then on and eventually sold nineteen million recorded copies. He was at the pinnacle of his American career. In October 1932 Tracy married his first wife, Beatrice Weinfeld. (He later referred to this marriage as "half a marriage.") By 1934, the childless marriage had broken up in mutual accusations of cruelty. He rode the airwaves until 1935, earning $20,000 a week from theatrical, radio, screen, and recording work, but being on the losing side of a sensational divorce case took its toll. He lost his public appeal, his employers became squeamish, and his radio contracts were not renewed.

Tracy took refuge in a seven-week contract in London in 1935, not returning to the United States until 1940. By that time he had reestablished himself as one of the most successful popular singers of all time, having played the London Palladium and starred in four films—"Limelight" (1936), "Street Singer" (1937), "Command Performance" (1938), and "Follow Your Star" (1939). Nonetheless, he was unable to revive his American career. He had been away too long, and his formal singing style did not appeal to the young generation. Although he entertained troops during World War II, sang for innumerable charities, and

did occasional radio work, his life as a top entertainer was over.

Always an astute businessman, Tracy became a multimillionaire real estate agent. In 1937 he found a suitable investment for the fortune he had amassed when he and a brother-in-law became owners of a sixty-five-acre estate in Washington, D.C., later called Brentwood Village, on which they built housing for 2,000 families. They also built Oxford Heights Village in Philadelphia and acquired many other properties, including the Roosevelt Hotel in Washington, D.C. As senior vice president of the Nassau Management Company, Tracy was unwittingly involved in a stockholder swindle in 1958 and was investigated by New York State Attorney General Louis Lefkowitz. He was cleared by the courts of any guilt but lost several million dollars in the scandal. Although sources are unclear, some indicate that Tracy married a second wife, Valerie Rowell, in 1940. They divorced in 1950, and Tracy married his third wife, Blossom Stern, an artist, in 1958. The couple had no children and eventually divorced in 1967. Tracy continued to live in the swank nineteenth-floor apartment in the Parc Vendome at 350 West Fifty-seventh Street in Manhattan, where he surrounded himself with a veritable museum of memorabilia from his superstardom days. His love of performing never waned; even into his late nineties he was determined to express himself artistically.

After decades of relative inactivity, Tracy had a comeback. In 1981, the director Herbert Ross used Tracy's sorrowful 1937 recording of "Pennies from Heaven" in the eponymous movie starring Steve Martin. As a result of publicity from the film, Tracy was hired in 1982 for a gig at the Cookery in Manhattan; critics and audiences were charmed by his "spellbinding" performance. In 1986 he attracted 7,500 fans, who gave him a standing ovation at a concert in New Jersey's Garden State Arts Center. On his last visit to Britain in 1995, on the way to being interviewed on radio, he was met by crowds of fans requesting autographs. Tracy died at Mount Sinai Hospital in New York City at age ninety-eight. He is buried in a Jewish cemetery outside Atlantic City, New Jersey.

★

During Tracy's heyday as an entertainer, press releases cited much incorrect biographical information about him. Fanciful accounts of how his name became "Tracy" and how his singing career began were common. This misinformation was reprinted in many sources. The oral history Tracy gave in 1993 to the American Jewish Committee sets the record straight. It is housed, with a transcript, in the New York Public Library Dorot Jewish Division. Among the few resources to mention Tracy's immigrant origins or career in the Yiddish theater are John Simons, ed., *Who's Who in American Jewry,* vol. 3 (1937–1939); Richard F. Shepard and Vicki Gold Levi, *Live and Be Well: A Celebration of Yiddish*

Culture from the First Immigrants to the Second World War (1982); and Zalmen Zylbercweig, comp., *Lexicon of the Yiddish Theatre*, vol. 2 (1934), which includes a 1927 essay in Yiddish about Tracy. The clipping files in the Music Division and the Billy Rose Theatre Collection of the New York Public Library contain material about Tracy's domestic woes and his career as a real estate tycoon. An obituary is the *New York Times* (8 Oct. 1997).

HONORA RAPHAEL WEINSTEIN

TRUMP, Frederick Christ (*b.* 11 October 1905 in New York City; *d.* 25 June 1999 in New Hyde Park, New York), New York City real estate developer and founder of the Trump real estate empire.

Trump, the son of Friedrich Trump, a German immigrant barber who became a home builder, was born in the Bronx in New York City but grew up in the borough of Queens after his family moved there shortly before his third birthday. Five years after his father died in the influenza epidemic of 1918, Trump graduated from Richmond Hill

Frederick C. Trump, 1987. ASSOCIATED PRESS AP

High School. He was already certain he would become a builder. During high school he had taken night courses on plumbing, masonry, and carpentry. Upon graduation he secured a full-time job for a builder but continued to take courses at schools like the Pratt Institute in Brooklyn on engineering and estimating.

Within a short time he started his own construction company with his mother, Elizabeth Trump, called E. Trump and Son. Because he was only seventeen years of age, Trump relied on his mother to sign all legal documents. His first efforts were single-family homes built in Woodhaven, Queens Village, and Hollis, all in Queens. Using the sale of one house to pay for the construction of the next, Trump completed nineteen within his first three years out of high school. However, the building industry was hit hard by the stock market crash of 1929 and the ensuing Great Depression. As banks reduced their loans to buyers, Trump found it more difficult to sell his homes. He gave up housing construction and opened a food market. That, however, was a short-lived career diversion, for in 1934 the Federal Housing Administration (FHA) was created and empowered to insure private banks against losses on loans to home buyers. This dramatically increased the credit available to home builders and spurred the housing industry. Trump quickly returned to his true passion, taking advantage of readily available credit, his political connections, and his business savvy to start building on a larger scale.

Working with Charles O'Malley and Bill Hyman, Trump created the Trump Holding Company and secured one of the first FHA loans in New York City to build a 450-home project in East Flatbush, Brooklyn. By 1938 he had put up more than 500 buildings, and long rows of "Trump Homes" had sprouted on streets in central Brooklyn. They were known for being well built, with brick exteriors, fine interior detailing, and attached garages. Regardless of these expensive features, they sold at prices affordable to middle-class families, ranging from $3,000 to $6,250 per house. These reasonable prices were possible because Trump built on a large scale. In an industry previously dominated by small builders, Trump found a way to mass-produce homes and to benefit from economies of scale. By 1938 the *Brooklyn Eagle* could call him "the Henry Ford of the home-building industry." Three years later he was building over 300 homes at once and had expanded from Flatbush into Brighton Beach. Overall, between 1934 and 1942, he built 2,000 single-family homes, mostly in Brooklyn.

In 1941 most housing construction was brought to a halt as materials were directed to defense industries for World War II efforts, but the Office of Production Management (OPM) invited Trump to build workers' housing near the Brooklyn Navy Yard. After the bombing of Pearl Harbor, that project was postponed, but Trump was urged to build housing for military personnel stationed at the large naval base in Norfolk, Virginia. Working with James Rosati, a highway builder from Queens, Trump erected the 216-unit Oakdale Homes, his first apartment house and his first rental property. That was quickly followed by Talbot Park, with 500 more apartments. By 1944 he had put up a total of 1,360 units in Norfolk.

Trump's business success in these years was mirrored by a flowering family life. In January 1936 he married Mary Anne MacLeod, a Scottish immigrant. They had their first child one year later, a daughter named Maryanne, followed by Fred, Jr., in 1938, Elizabeth in 1942, Donald in 1946, and Robert in 1948.

After the end of World War II, Trump and his family returned north to New York City. In 1946 they moved into what became a twenty-three-room mansion in the upscale Queens neighborhood of Jamaica Estates. One year later Trump began planning Shore Haven, a massive 1,344-unit apartment complex of thirty-two six-story buildings on a fourteen-acre plot of Brighton Beach. In 1947, as construction progressed on that project, Trump began an even larger apartment complex, called Beach Haven, with 1,860 units. In these projects Trump showed mastery of both building and marketing. As biographer Gwenda Blair noted, Trump created essentially brand-name recognition in Brooklyn for his reliable housing.

However, Trump faced scrutiny as concerns spread about private building developers benefiting from federal programs meant to alleviate postwar housing shortages. In 1954 the Senate Banking and Currency Committee, chaired by Indiana Senator Homer Capeheart, launched an investigation into real estate practices and called Trump to testify. The *New York Times* listed him as one of thirty-five New York City area builders accused of milking the government for personal gain, and the *Brooklyn Eagle* claimed he had pocketed over $4 million through government programs. While the committee found Trump had done nothing illegal, his reputation was scarred.

However, Trump rebounded. In 1957, relying on loans provided through the newly formed New York State Housing Finance Agency (HFA), he began planning a 3,800-unit apartment complex on Coney Island named Trump Village. The project, completed in 1964, was one of the first in the city to comply with the 1961 zoning laws and included large sections of landscaped open space between buildings. While it reestablished Trump as a major builder in Brooklyn, it did not mean the end of criticism.

One year after the completion of Trump Village, Trump purchased Steeplechase Park, the last of Coney Island's entertainment pavilions. But Trump had no plans to refurbish the deteriorating rides. Instead, he saw its 12.5-acre site as prime real estate. While his plan may have made financial sense, he was bitterly attacked by local residents, who successfully blocked his efforts and eventually lobbied the city to buy back the property.

Trump's image was further tarnished in 1966 when the State Investigation Commission (SIC) launched a probe into the operations of Trump Village. The state, like the earlier Senate investigation, was interested in how Trump had earned large private profits using a government program designed to solve the city's housing shortage and promote low-cost rental apartments. SIC found Trump had benefited from overestimating construction costs and from subcontracting to his own companies. Yet they admitted that nothing Trump had done was illegal, and his only penalty was a requirement to lower rental charges slightly.

While Trump continued to expand his real estate holdings in the following years, his son Donald Trump took an increasing role in the family business. The onset of Alzheimer's disease reduced the elder Trump's involvement, although he continued to commute to his office on Avenue Z in Coney Island until his death in 1999. He left an estate valued at approximately $250 million. Trump is buried in the Lutheran All Faiths Cemetery in Middle Village, New York.

★

The only significant biography of Trump is Gwenda Blair, *The Trumps: Three Generations That Built an Empire* (2000). Other sources on Fred Trump include Marvin Schlegel, *Conscripted City: Norfolk in World War II* (1991); Irving Welfeld, *HUD Scandals: Howling Headlines and Silent Fiascoes* (1992); and Wayne Barrett, *Trump: The Deals and the Downfall* (1992). A profile that compares Trump with his son Donald was published in *New York Times Magazine* (2 Jan. 2000). Government sources include U.S. District Court, Eastern District of New York, archives relating to *in the matter of Julius Lehrenkrauss et al.* (1934); William F. McKenna, *Final Report on FHA Investigation* (13 Aug. 1954); and New York State's *Records of the New York State Commission of Investigation Concerning the Limited-Profit Housing Program* (Apr. 1966). Obituaries are in *New York Newsday* (26 June 1999) and the *Chicago Tribune* and *Washington Post* (both 28 June 1999).

THORIN TRITTER

TSONGAS, Paul Efthemios (*b.* 14 February 1941 in Lowell, Massachusetts; *d.* 18 January 1997 in Boston, Massachusetts), congressman and U.S. senator from Massachusetts who became an intellectual leader of the "neoliberal" faction of the Democratic Party in the 1980s and who made a spirited run for the presidency in 1992.

Tsongas was the son of Efthemios George Tsongas, a businessman who had immigrated to the United States from Greece at age four, and Katina Pappas, a homemaker who died of tuberculosis in 1948. He had a twin sister and a half sister from his father's second marriage. Tsongas grew up in Lowell, Massachusetts, an economically depressed old mill city forty miles northwest of Boston. His father had dropped out of Harvard in 1933 to take over the management of his family's dry cleaning shop; he later expanded it into a large dry cleaning plant. Tsongas worked for his father after school, first twisting wire into clothes hangers and then driving a delivery truck. He graduated from Lowell High School in 1958 and enrolled at Dartmouth College, where he majored in history and was a member of the swimming team.

After receiving his B.A. degree in 1962, Tsongas, who had never traveled farther than Annapolis, Maryland (with the Dartmouth swimming team), answered President John F. Kennedy's call for volunteers for the newly created Peace Corps. He was sent to the village of Wolisso, in Ethiopia, to teach school and live in a mud hut. The experience proved exhilarating. "I found I could think like an Ethiopian," he later recalled, "and it was the first time in my life that I had done something well, and I was enormously satisfied with that." His two-year Peace Corps stint left him with genuine affection for Africa and an enduring interest in the countries of the Third World.

Upon his return to the United States, Tsongas attended Yale University Law School from 1964 until 1967, when he received his LL.B. degree. He also received a political education during these years as a summer intern in the Washington, D.C., office of F. Bradford Morse, a liberal Republican who represented Lowell in Congress. Influenced by Morse, Tsongas registered to vote as a Republican and took part in the successful campaign of another Republican House member, John V. Lindsay, for mayor of New York City in 1965.

Following his graduation from Yale, Tsongas signed on for another hitch in the Peace Corps. Assigned to the Virgin Islands to serve as coordinator of training programs for the Caribbean countries, he spent much of his time thinking about politics back home and left after only a year. When he returned to Massachusetts in the spring of 1968, Tsongas strongly opposed the Vietnam War and was attracted to the antiwar presidential candidacy of Democratic Senator Robert F. Kennedy of New York. After Kennedy's assassination, however, Tsongas turned away from the national campaign and began to focus on his own political future. While working in low-level posts in state government (for a gubernatorial committee on law enforcement and as a deputy assistant attorney general), he aligned himself with the Democratic Party, with which he had become more philosophically compatible, and ran for the Lowell City Council. After a grueling, door-to-door campaign, Tsongas finished fifth among the nine successful at-large council candidates in the 1969 election. He was reelected to the city

Paul Tsongas with his wife, Niki, 1991. ELISE AMENDOLA/ASSOCIATED PRESS AP

council in 1971. Tsongas married Nicola "Niki" Sauvage, whom he had met when both were interns in Washington, on 21 December 1969. They had three daughters.

Tsongas expanded his political base by winning election as one of three county commissioners for Middlesex County, the largest county in Massachusetts, in 1972. As a city councillor and county commissioner, Tsongas built a solid reputation as a reformer, fighting for the appointment of a professional administrator as city manager in Lowell and attacking patronage abuses in county government. On both issues, the former Republican clashed with local Democratic leaders.

Tsongas ran for the congressional seat in the Fifth Massachusetts District in 1974. After easily defeating a party regular in the Democratic primary, he rode the wave of voter resentment against Republicans for the Watergate scandal and the pardon of former President Richard M. Nixon to victory over incumbent Paul Cronin by nearly 35,000 votes in the general election. The first Democrat to represent Lowell in the U.S. House since 1895, he won a second term in 1976.

A member of the staunchly liberal "Watergate Class" in the overwhelmingly Democratic House, Tsongas was strongly prolabor. He was especially interested in environmental issues, energy conservation, and human rights questions as they pertained to developing countries. He voted for the common situs (job site) picketing bill and the establishment of the Consumer Protection Agency, and opposed funding the B-1 bomber and deregulating natural gas prices. He also backed an arms embargo against the repressive military regime in Ethiopia. His most significant legislative achievement proved to be securing funding for the establishment of the Lowell National Historical Park to commemorate the birthplace of the industrial revolution in America in 1978. The success of this legislation in 1978 marked the beginning of Tsongas's long public effort to reverse the economic fortunes of his native city.

When Tsongas announced his candidacy for the U.S. Senate in 1978, party leaders and pundits thought the little-known congressman an unlikely prospect to unseat two-term liberal Republican incumbent Edward W. Brooke. However, Brooke, the first African American elected to the Senate since Reconstruction, was subsequently weakened by disclosures that he had misrepresented his finances during bitter divorce proceedings, and barely beat back a stiff conservative challenge in the Republican primary. Although Tsongas himself only narrowly won a hard-fought five-way Democratic contest, he went on to defeat Brooke by over 202,000 votes out of 1.9 million cast. Having declined to discuss Brooke's personal problems during a gentlemanly, issue-oriented campaign, Tsongas said of his opponent: "I tried to dislike him, but I couldn't."

It was generally expected that Tsongas would toil forever in the shadow of his senior colleague, the more nationally prominent Edward M. Kennedy, concentrating primarily on Massachusetts issues. He continued to channel federal grant money to Lowell and other depressed cities, and to assist political and business leaders in building public-private partnerships to foster urban economic development in his home state. At the same time, however, Tsongas involved himself heavily in national questions and showed considerable legislative skill and a willingness to take controversial stands. In 1979 Tsongas and conservative Republican Richard Lugar of Indiana, a fellow Banking Committee member, fashioned a $4 billion "bailout" package for the ailing Chrysler Corporation, including a three-year wage freeze for workers, which aided the automaker's recovery but antagonized organized labor. A year later, Tsongas substituted his own conservationist version of the Alaska Lands Bill and maneuvered it through the Energy Committee (past the opposition of chairman Henry Jackson of Washington) to final passage. The bill, which created 104.3 million acres of national parks, wildlife refuges, and other protected areas, was lauded by President Jimmy Carter as the most important conservation measure of the twentieth century.

With the election of President Ronald Reagan in 1980, Tsongas became a leading critic of Reagan's foreign and defense policies. On the Foreign Relations Committee, he cast one of only two votes against the confirmation of Secretary of State Alexander Haig in 1981 and vigorously fought the nomination of Kenneth Adelman as disarmament negotiator. Adelman, whom Tsongas and other opponents deemed insufficiently committed to arms control, lost a committee vote but won confirmation from the full Senate. Strongly opposed to the administration's aggressive effort to combat Soviet and Cuban influence in Third World countries, Tsongas helped block Reagan's attempt to repeal the Clark amendment, which prohibited American aid to antigovernment guerrillas in Angola in 1981, and denounced the 1982 invasion of Grenada. He was not averse to all anticommunist initiatives, however, as evidenced by his sponsorship of a 1982 resolution calling upon the president to provide material assistance to the Muslim forces resisting the Soviet occupation of Afghanistan.

Tsongas gained national attention for his frank keynote address to the convention of Americans for Democratic Action (ADA) in 1980. The recipient of a 100 percent ADA rating twice in his five years in Congress, Tsongas nonetheless told the keepers of the liberal flame that their philosophy had become outdated and in need of revision. Liberal Democrats, he said, would have to become less reliant upon the big government programs and corporation-bashing rhetoric of the 1960s in the more conservative 1980s, or their cause would be "reduced to an interesting topic for PhD-writing historians." Tsongas enlarged upon his pragmatic "neoliberal" themes in a well-received book, *The Road from Here: Liberalism and Realities in the 1980s* (1981). Although some prominent supporters of Edward Kennedy attacked Tsongas's speech and book as part of an effort to gain publicity by challenging the traditional liberalism that Kennedy represented, relations between the two Massachusetts senators remained cordial.

By the fall of 1983 Tsongas was organizing his reelection campaign and thinking about a possible bid for the presidency in 1988. But all future plans were shelved after a lump on his groin was diagnosed as non-Hodgkins lymphoma, a form of cancer of the lymph nodes. Tsongas announced he would eschew another Senate term to return home to fight the disease and be with his family. "I was no longer the senator from Massachusetts," he wrote in *Heading Home* (1984), an affecting personal account of the events that led to his decision not to seek reelection, "I was a frightened human being who loved his wife and children and desperately wanted to live." Over the next four years, chemotherapy and a painful, experimental bone-marrow transplant appeared to restore his health. Tsongas joined

587

the elite Boston law firm of Foley, Hoag and Eliot in 1985 and became a board member for a number of important corporations. Governor Michael Dukakis brought Tsongas back into government in 1989 as chair of the Massachusetts Board of Regents of Higher Education, which oversees the state college and university system.

Seemingly cancer-free and again active in public affairs, Tsongas was mentioned as a possible candidate for Massachusetts governor in 1990, but he declined to run. A year later, however, he launched a long-shot candidacy for the 1992 Democratic presidential nomination. Believing that neither Republican President George Bush nor prospective Democratic candidates were adequately addressing the problems of mounting deficits and a faltering economy, Tsongas saw an opportunity for himself running on a neoliberal platform calling for a balanced budget, the reform of Medicare and Social Security, and a cut in capital gains taxes to aid slumping businesses. Campaigning on a shoestring, he crisscrossed neighboring New Hampshire, widely distributed *A Call to Economic Arms* (1991), an eighty-three-page pamphlet he had written, and won the first-in-the-nation primary with 33 percent of the vote. Despite Tsongas's victory in the primary, Bill Clinton, the charismatic governor of Arkansas who ran second in New Hampshire (with 24 percent of the vote), remained the Democratic frontrunner in the eyes of party leaders and the national media. Although Tsongas went on to win primaries in Maryland, Utah, Massachusetts, and Rhode Island, and caucuses in Washington, Delaware, and Arizona, he lost crucial contests in the South and Midwest to the better financed and organized Clinton, and he had to suspend his campaign in late March. Tsongas endorsed the Arkansan prior to the Democratic National Convention and took some satisfaction in the fact that the November election was decided on the issue of the economy. He was also pleased that President Clinton ultimately supported the idea of deficit reduction and in 1995 declared an end to the "era of big government."

Following the 1992 campaign, Tsongas and another former senator, Republican Warren Rudman of New Hampshire, formed the Concord Coalition, a nonprofit group that lobbied for a balanced federal budget. Active in the civic affairs of Lowell throughout the 1990s, Tsongas was a key participant in the efforts to build a hockey arena and a baseball park and to attract minor league franchises to play in the city. He also published a third book, *Journey of Purpose: Reflections on the Presidency, Multiculturalism, and Third Parties* (1995).

In late 1992 Tsongas's health again began to deteriorate. A recurrence of his lymphoma was treated successfully with radiation. Three years later, however, he was diagnosed with a myelodysplasia, a blood disorder probably caused by earlier cancer treatments. It was cured by a transplant of bone marrow from his twin sister Thaleia, but Tsongas continued to weaken and died at age fifty-five of liver failure and pneumonia in Boston's Brigham and Women's Hospital. He is buried in Lowell Cemetery.

Of slight build and possessing a high-pitched voice and a preachy style that gave rise to the derogatory nickname "Saint Paul," Tsongas was, in many ways, an improbable political success. He won elections and presidential primaries because voters viewed him as honest and in firm command of the issues they deemed important. Even before his cancer diagnosis and decision to leave the Senate, Tsongas strenuously avoided the Washington social circuit to spend most of his time after work with his family. He also remained devoted to his native city of Lowell, working for its betterment for nearly all of his adult life. Though his political career was relatively short, Tsongas had an impressive list of accomplishments, including the national park in Lowell, the Chrysler bailout, and the landmark conservation legislation for Alaska (which he never visited). Although ended in defeat, his 1992 presidential campaign helped convince the Democratic Party to oppose budget deficits and to repair relations with business. President Clinton, who came to embrace much of Tsongas's platform, paid tribute to his former rival as a "great American" who "cared deeply about his beloved state of Massachusetts and about our country and its future. In a life dedicated to public service, he set an unparalleled example of integrity, candor, and commitment."

★

Tsongas's congressional papers and materials from his 1992 presidential campaign are housed in the Center for Lowell History at the University of Massachusetts in Lowell. His books, *The Road from Here, Heading Home,* and *Journey of Purpose,* contain considerable autobiographical information. E. J. Kahn III, "Paul Tsongas," *Boston Magazine* 73 (Feb. 1981) is a substantial interview. Short accounts of Tsongas's life and career are in *Current Biography 1981* (1982); Michael Barone et al., *The Almanac of American Politics* (1975, 1977, 1979, 1981, 1983); and Alan Ehrenhalt, ed., *Politics in America* (1981 and 1983). Tom Rosenstiel, *Strange Bedfellows: How Television and the Presidential Candidates Changed American Politics* (1992); Jack W. Germond and Jules Witcover, *Mad as Hell: Revolt at the Ballot Box, 1992* (1993); and Peter Goldman et al., *Quest for the Presidency, 1992* (1994) all cover the Tsongas presidential campaign in considerable detail. Useful articles include David Osborne, "The Other Senator from Massachusetts," *Mother Jones* 7 (July 1982); E. J. Kahn III, "Paul Tsongas Is Alive and Well and Living in Lowell," *Boston Magazine* 80 (Apr. 1988); Jon Keller, "Tsnooze," *New Republic* 205 (12 Aug. 1991); Gloria Borger, "The Democrats' Castor-Oil Candidate," *U.S. News & World Report* (24 Feb. 1992); Morton Kondracke, "Punch-Puller," *New Republic* 206 (16 Mar. 1992); and Sidney Blumenthal, "The Puritan," *New Republic* 206 (23 Mar.

1992). Obituaries are in the *Boston Globe, Boston Herald,* and *Lowell Sun* (all 19 Jan. 1997) and the *New York Times* (20 Jan. 1997).

RICHARD H. GENTILE

TURNER, Clyde Douglas ("Bulldog") (*b.* 10 March 1919 in Yoakum County, Texas; *d.* 30 October 1998 in Gatesville, Texas), professional football player who earned enshrinement in the Pro Football Hall of Fame as a two-way center/linebacker for the Chicago Bears.

Growing up on the windswept, sandblasted plains of west Texas, Turner was one of four children born to Willie Lloyd ("Bill") Turner, a cowboy, and Ada Fay Rushing, a schoolteacher. In his early years the family moved to Plains, Texas. He experienced a hardscrabble life even before the Great Depression hit. Turner's father was unable to provide many of the luxuries of life and began dealing in cattle. As a child, Turner went out into the cotton fields to work. Like nearly everyone else who ever picked cotton, he described the work as backbreaking. To make work easier, he said, he put rocks in the cotton sacks to make them weigh more. Even so, he earned only pennies a day.

Clyde "Bulldog" Turner, 1945. AP/WIDE WORLD PHOTOS

When Turner was a junior in high school, the family moved nearly 100 miles southeast to Sweetwater, Texas. At Newman High School, he noticed how the prettiest girls seemed to gravitate to the boys who wore letter sweaters and was determined to earn one. So, as a fifteen year old, the 155-pound Turner went out for the Newman High varsity football team. As he tells it, it was tough. "The first day was the roughest day I ever spent on a football field. I had cleat marks all over my shins. . . . We had a lousy team, . . . but I got . . . my sweater and I developed something I didn't anticipate. I found I loved to play football." He played four different positions in his only season of scholastic football—end, tackle, guard, and halfback. Oddly, he did not play center, the position at which he earned football immortality.

It turned out to be Turner's only year of high school football; he graduated at sixteen. School without football did not hold much interest for Turner, so he left home to try to earn a place on a college team. He sold one of the family cows to provide himself with new clothes and money to hitchhike around the area, looking for a school where he could play. They all turned him down. He spent the next summer buying and selling cattle and once again tried to obtain a football scholarship at a college. It was during a tryout at Hardin-Simmons, a small school in Abilene, Texas, that he acquired the nickname that stuck with him the rest of his life. According to Turner, he and another aspiring football player, A. J. Roy, decided to embellish their reputations by yelling to each other during the football drills. Turner said, "When ol' Roy did something, I'd holler, 'Way to go, Tiger, just like back home,' and when I'd do something, he'd yell 'That's the way, Bulldog, hit 'em like you did back home.'" The moniker stuck.

Turner briefly played end at Hardin-Simmons. One day the starting center suffered an injury, and a call went out for a replacement. Turner had never played center, but he said he could. His knack for assimilating "all things football" helped. He put into practice what he had observed and performed the intricate center's duties. Thanks to a publicity photo, which showed Turner in uniform running with a calf on his shoulders, he overcame the relative obscurity of Hardin-Simmons to gain national recognition. Turner played so well that he was contacted by the Detroit Lions of the National Football League (NFL), who planned to make him their first choice in the annual NFL college player draft. In one of those twists of fate that often affect an athletic career, the Lions instead chose a quarterback from the University of Southern California, who had performed off-the-bench late-game heroics in the most recent Rose Bowl. Turner was quickly snapped up by the Chicago Bears, whose scout Frank Korch also was impressed with him. When Dick Richards, the Lions owner, learned what had happened, he told Turner to tell the Bears that he was not interested in pro football. Richards's plan was to pay Turner for sitting out a year and then acquire him later. The president of the NFL heard of this tactic, fined the Lions, and officially awarded Turner to the Bears.

Turner's rookie season (1940) was the start of a long and storied career. In the championship game, the Bears won 73–0. It is still the highest point total garnered by one team in an NFL title game and the most lopsided game in NFL history. Turner supplanted the perennial choice Mel Hein as the All-NFL center and continued throughout his career as the NFL's top center. Turner entered the military in 1945, playing football for the Army Air Forces Super-bombers. He was discharged in early 1946 and married Gladys Webber on 4 July 1946; they had two daughters.

Turner's active career ended in 1952 with so many accolades, honors, and accomplishments that when the Pro Football Hall of Fame was founded he was quickly inducted. At the height of his playing career, he wrote an instructional book entitled *Playing the Line* (1948). After coaching as an assistant with the Bears, he became head coach of the New York Titans (forerunners to the New York Jets) of the American Football League in 1962. Without enough players of his ilk, he was only moderately successful in his lone season at the helm. After leaving the pro game, he retired to a ranch outside Gatesville, Texas, where he died of complications of lung cancer. He is buried in Greenbriar Cemetery in Gatesville.

Turner was the dominant center/linebacker in the NFL during his time. He was a heady player who seldom, if ever, missed an assignment. At six feet, two inches tall and 235 pounds, Turner fit coach George Halas's mold as a Chicago Bear when the team ruled the NFL as "the Monsters of the Midway."

★

There is no biography of Turner, but his life and career are discussed in George Sullivan, *Pro Football's All-Time Greats: The Immortals in Pro Football's Hall of Fame* (1968); Myron Cope, *The Game That Was: The Early Days of Pro Football* (1970); Murray Olderman, *The Defenders* (1973); and Don Smith, *Pro Football Hall of Fame All-Time Greats* (1988). An obituary is in the *New York Times* (2 Nov. 1998).

JIM CAMPBELL

TURNER, Francis Cutler ("Frank") (*b.* 28 December 1908 in Dallas, Texas; *d.* 2 October 1999 in Goldsboro, North Carolina), engineer and public servant who is recognized as the "Father of the Interstate Highway System."

Born and raised in Dallas, Turner was one of five children born to Linneaus (Linn) Cutler Turner, a railroad engineer, and Fannie Elizabeth Brewer, a homemaker. Study-

Frank C. Turner, 1967. AP/WIDE WORLD/TRANSCENDENTAL

ing soil science, Turner graduated from North Texas Agricultural College (NTAC) in 1927 and earned a B.S. degree in civil engineering from Texas A&M in 1929. He joined the Bureau of Public Roads (BPR) that year as a junior highway engineer. BPR first assigned Turner to the division of management. In keeping with the then-popular "time and motion studies," he evaluated highway construction techniques to improve the efficiency of road-building machinery such as steam shovels and trucks. Turner married Mable Marie Nanney on 18 December 1930 in Fort Worth, Texas; the couple had three children. In 1933 Turner was posted to the Bureau's Arkansas division office in Little Rock. There he first confronted many of the political issues relating to roads that he would encounter throughout his career.

The Federal Aid Road Act of 1916 required that all states establish road construction field offices in order to receive federal funds. The responsibility of these field offices included approving state plans and construction estimates while providing a liaison with state counterparts. These "front line" jobs were particularly important in Southern states and rural areas, where road construction had been historically subject to political influence. Arkansas officials had been resistant to the creation of field offices, leading the head of the BPR to suspend funding to the state. Turner's combination of technical and diplomatic expertise were well honed during his time in the Little Rock field office. During the 1930s he studied the connection between road maintenance and subgrade and soil base characteristics. BPR-funded research of soil mechanics was becoming a significant part of highway engineering, and Turner's academic background and interests proved valuable to the bureau.

Turner earned an M.S. degree in civil engineering from Texas A&M in 1940 and moved to the BPR's construction division at its Washington, D.C., headquarters. Although little road construction occurred during World War II, Bureau Chief Thomas H. MacDonald sent Turner to Alaska in 1943 to handle maintenance for the newly completed Alaskan Highway. Turner's success in keeping the highway open and passable earned him a reputation for leadership and reliability. He returned to Washington, D.C., in 1946 and was immediately sent to the Philippines, where he trained and developed an engineering organization to support that country's transportation network. By 1950 Turner was back in Washington, D.C., as the assistant to now Commissioner MacDonald. Turner was given responsibility and oversight for all BPR foreign aid programs related to highways. Working with MacDonald, Turner also began to contribute to the proposals for an immense highway project, the interstate highway program.

The idea for a U.S. interstate system was not new. BPR had made proposals to construct a national network of roads in the late 1930s, and a more detailed version would come from the National Interregional Highway Committee, appointed by President Franklin D. Roosevelt on 14 April 1941. Written by BPR Information Division Chief Herbert S. Fairbank, the committee's report was released on 14 January 1943. The Federal-Aid Highway Act of 1944 was accepted by Congress, and preliminary routes for some 40,000 miles of express roads were approved in 1947. Congress appropriated some money for the project in the early 1950s, though not nearly enough. Members of Congress became deadlocked over funding for the project, and most states simply could not match the road construction cost, yet the momentum for building a new vast system of roads had begun. Germany's high speed *Autobahns* had convinced President Dwight D. Eisenhower that America needed "broader ribbons across the land." Pressure from the automotive industry and suburban development galvanized the public debate. Turner was at the center of this debate, helping to draft legislation and push it through Congress.

When Francis V. DuPont succeeded Commissioner MacDonald as head of the BPR in April 1953, Turner was tapped once again to support the national highway effort. Working as the executive secretary of President Eisen-

hower's advisory committee on the national highway program, Turner served as the BPR "point man" on matters related to federal highway legislation. When Congress created the "National System of Interstate and Defense Highways" in 1956, Turner's expertise had been essential in winning congressional acceptance. Turner was appointed Deputy Commissioner and Chief Engineer for Public Roads in 1957. This job demanded the unprecedented responsibility of moving the multilane road system from the drawing boards to reality. Turner confronted tremendous problems, particularly in urban areas where property acquisition, road design, and creation of standards had to be addressed. Turner relied on highway planning survey data and innovative origin and destination studies to organize the technical components of the project. Philosophically, Turner argued that engineers and experts should guide the process in which roads became " . . . arteries of commerce, not tools for planning or land use determination."

By the 1960s, highway construction was underway. Turner, an "old school" engineer, drew the ire not only of environmentalists, but of others angered by the lack of relocation programs for those living in the paths of urban interstates. The "freeway revolt" led to raucous public hearings in cities throughout the United States, drawing varied constituencies to debate about aesthetics, divided neighborhoods, and historic preservation. Turner's background and outlook failed to prepare him for the public outcry. Appointed Director of Public Roads in 1967, he answered these concerns by holding more public hearings, conducting environmental impact studies, and adjusting his personal perspective.

Turner achieved the pinnacle of his career as a dedicated, informed public servant when he was appointed, with unanimous Congressional approval, as the Federal Highway Administrator in 1969. Until his retirement in 1972, Turner continued to build on his vision and mission of the "road builder." He understood the relationship between roads and social change and sought to adjust the perspective of the road-building community by considering the impact transportation had on the environment, lifestyle, employment, and social fabric of the United States. Never a fan of mass transit, Turner's commitment to road building led to significant demographic shifts, as Americans emptied the old urban neighborhoods and traveled to the suburbs or to the South and West.

After his retirement, Turner was recognized by colleagues at the Federal Highway Administration as the "Father of the U.S. Interstate Highway System" and remembered for the loyalty and respect he had always shown them. In 1983 Secretary of Transportation Elizabeth Dole dedicated the Francis C. Turner Building as part of the Turner-Fairbank Research Center in McLean, Virginia. When

American Heritage magazine reached its fortieth anniversary in 1994, the publication celebrated this milestone by naming ten people who, although completely unknown to the public, had changed the way Americans live during the past forty years. Frank Turner was one of these ten "agents of change." The Federal Highway Administration established the Frank Turner Medal in 1998 to recognize Turner's lifetime achievement in transportation. Texas A&M University selected Turner as the first inductee in the Texas A&M "Hall of Honor" in 2000. Turner remained active in the transportation community for many years after his retirement. He died of cancer at the age of ninety and is buried in National Memorial Park in Falls Church, Virginia.

★

Bruce E. Seely, *Building the America Highway System: Engineers as Policy Makers* (1994), is a good overview of the development of the interstate system. See also Seely, "Special Feature— Frank C. Turner, 'Father of the U.S. Interstate Highway System': An Historical Appreciation," *TR News* no. 213 (2001). D. C. Oliver, "In Footsteps of a Giant: Francis C. Turner and Management of the Interstate," *Transportation Quarterly* 48 (spring 1994), offers another retrospective. "The Superhighway Superman," *U.S. News and World Report* 127, no. 25 (27 Dec. 1999) describes Turner's career and contributions. Obituaries are in the *Washington Post* (5 Oct. 1999) and *New York Times* (6 Oct. 1999).

ELOISE F. MALONE

U-V

UDALL, Morris King (*b.* 15 June 1922 in St. Johns, Arizona; *d.* 12 December 1998 in Washington, D.C.), liberal Democratic congressman who was known as the conscience of the U.S. House of Representatives and as a presidential contender, reformer, and environmentalist.

A member of Arizona's most enduring political dynasty, Udall was the grandson of David King Udall, a Mormon pioneer; the son of Levi Stewart Udall, who served as a chief justice of the Arizona Supreme Court; and the brother of Stewart L. Udall, a future congressman and secretary of the U.S. Department of the Interior. His mother, Louise Lee Udall, was a political activist. One of seven children, Udall attended public schools in Saint Johns. At age six he lost his right eye after being accidentally cut with a knife while playing with another boy. An alcoholic physician provided such incompetent treatment that the other eye became infected, and Udall nearly lost his sight. Years later, Udall said that this incident shaped his lifelong commitment to social justice. At age nine, he nearly died from spinal meningitis.

As a student at Saint Johns High School from 1938 through 1940, Udall excelled in athletics and became interested in politics. Despite his eye injury, he played quarterback on the football team and was captain of the basketball team. He also edited the yearbook, played trumpet in the school band, served as the student-body president,

and graduated first in his class. In the fall of 1940 he entered the University of Arizona on a basketball scholarship.

After the United States entered World War II, Udall was determined to serve and maneuvered his way into the U.S. Army Air Corps, despite having only one eye. He was assigned to a limited service, noncombat unit in Fort Douglas, Utah, and then was transferred to Lake Charles, Louisiana, where he served for two years as the commander of an African-American squadron. "I fought their fights with them. We had some battles over local discrimination," he said years later. Udall unsuccessfully defended a black airman accused of killing a white guard while attempting to escape confinement. An all-white military tribunal sentenced the man to death. For the rest of Udall's life, this case haunted him. He later served in the South Pacific and was discharged in 1946 with the rank of captain.

Returning to the University of Arizona, Udall was elected as the student-body president. As an all-conference forward, he led the Wildcats to the basketball championship of the Border Conference (1947–1948). Udall, who was six feet, five inches tall, played professional basketball for the Denver Nuggets in 1948 and 1949. During this period, he took several courses at the University of Denver, which enabled him to graduate with an LL.B. degree with distinction from Arizona in 1949.

That same year, he and his brother Stewart formed the law firm of Udall and Udall in Tucson, Arizona. He be-

Morris K. Udall. ARCHIVE PHOTOS, INC.

came the chief deputy attorney of Pima County in 1950 and in 1952 was elected as the county attorney. In 1954 Udall resigned to make an unsuccessful race for superior court judge. He then taught labor law at the University of Arizona Law School in 1955 and 1956 and practiced law until 1961.

Udall's brother Stewart was elected to the U.S. House of Representatives in 1954 and resigned in 1961 to become the secretary of the interior in President John F. Kennedy's administration. Udall ran for his brother's open congressional seat in a 2 May 1961 special election and narrowly won. After spending a frustrating time learning the job during his freshman term, Udall wrote *The Job of a Congressman* (1966), so that other representatives would not have such a struggle; the book was still considered "a bible" for new members of Congress decades later.

As a freshman representative, Udall joined the Interior and Insular Affairs Committee to work on Arizona land and mining issues, as well as the Post Office Committee at the request of the Democratic leadership. He became the chairman of the Interior and Insular Affairs Committee in

1977 and held that position for fourteen years. The *Congressional Quarterly* observed in 1990, "Udall's legislative career is striking evidence that a member of Congress can find important work to do anywhere in the committee system. For twenty years, Udall never had anything resembling a major assignment."

Despite this observation, Udall was one of the more respected and productive national legislators of his time. He was the first influential Democrat to express opposition to the Vietnam War during President Lyndon B. Johnson's administration. He gained congressional approval of the Postal Reform Act in 1970, which made the U.S. Postal Service a semiprivate corporation. Because of Udall's sponsorship of the 1971 Campaign Reform Act, candidates for federal office were required to disclose contributions and expenditures. This law enabled the news media and the special prosecutor to follow the money in the Watergate scandal and thus contributed significantly to the breakdown of Richard Nixon's presidency. Udall also led a long struggle to tighten restrictions on strip mining. President Gerald Ford twice vetoed the strip-mining legislation, but in 1977 President Jimmy Carter signed the Surface Mining Control and Reclamation Act.

During President Ronald Reagan's administration, Udall fought efforts by James Watt, the secretary of the interior, to open up public lands for private development. Udall's most enduring legislative accomplishment was passage of the 1980 Alaska National Interest Lands Conservation Act, which protected more than ninety-seven million acres of wilderness, doubling the size of the National Park System and tripling the size of the National Wilderness System. He also secured approval of a bill designating more than eight million new acres of wilderness in twenty states, and added more than two million acres of Arizona desert to the federal wilderness system. However, Udall failed to win congressional approval to provide federal aid for state and local land-use planning. He was also frustrated in repeated efforts to pass legislation establishing public funding for congressional campaigns.

Early in his House career, Udall had leadership aspirations. His 1969 challenge to the aging Speaker John W. McCormack was more symbolic than real. But in 1971 Udall lost a bitterly contested race for majority leader to the conservative Hale Boggs of Louisiana. In 1976 he was a serious contender for the Democratic presidential nomination. His self-deprecating wit became his trademark. Udall often told a story about stopping in a New Hampshire barber shop and introducing himself as a presidential candidate. "Oh yes," the barber responded, "we were laughing about that in here this morning." Udall peaked in the early primaries as the leading contender among Democratic liberals. He would have won the New Hampshire, Wisconsin, and Michigan primaries if the former senator Fred Harris had dropped out. Udall finished a close second to Jimmy Carter in six primaries. He told the *Philadelphia Inquirer*, "The most poignant moment of the campaign was when I read in post-primary polls that one out of ten Carter voters preferred me but felt I had no chance to win."

The former Watergate special prosecutor Archibald Cox, who nominated Udall at the 1976 Democratic convention, summed up the importance of his campaign: "By the count of votes, he did come in second, but he succeeded in the larger aim. His defeat was a greater triumph than victory, for he proved that a public figure, even in a long and heated political contest, can exemplify the best of the American spirit, that honor need not yield to ambition, that open-mindedness and willingness to listen are not inconsistent with devotion to principle, that civility can accompany tenacity, and that humility should go hand and hand with power." In 1980 Udall delivered the keynote speech at the Democratic National Convention in New York. Throughout his career, Udall won sixteen consecutive terms and provided ongoing legislative and party leadership to the U.S. House of Representatives.

Udall married Patricia Emery in 1949; they had six children and divorced in 1966. In 1968 he married Ella Royston, who committed suicide in 1988. On 6 August 1989 he married Norma Gilbert. In 1980 Udall was diagnosed with Parkinson's disease and his health gradually declined; he resigned from Congress in May 1991 after a fall in his home in Arlington, Virginia. In November 1998 Udall's son Mark was elected to the U.S. House of Representatives from Colorado, and his nephew Tom Udall was elected to Congress from New Mexico. The following month, Udall died of complications from Parkinson's disease at the Veterans Affairs Medical Center in Washington, D.C.

In 1992 Congress passed the Morris K. Udall Scholarship and Excellence in National Environmental Policy Act, which provided $40 million for a foundation in Udall's name and also provided funding for the University of Arizona's Udall Center for Studies in Public Policy. After Udall's resignation from the House in 1991, David Broder wrote in the *Washington Post*, "The legacy he left there is imposing and enduring. . . . For a whole generation of congressmen, Udall became a mentor and a model—and they will miss him as much as the press galleries do." In 1996 President William J. Clinton presented Udall with the Presidential Medal of Freedom, saying, "Morris Udall represents everything a lawmaker should be. His work is a gift to all Americans."

★

Udall's papers are at the University of Arizona. His books include *Education of a Congressman: The Newsletters of Morris K. Udall* (1972) and *Too Funny To Be President* (1988). *Addresses and Special Orders for the Hon. Morris K. Udall* (1993) includes summaries of his political and legislative careers. He is profiled in *Politics in America* (1990) and *The Almanac of American Politics, 1990* (1989). Obituaries are in the *Washington Post* and *New York Times* (both 14 Dec. 1998).

STEVE NEAL

VERNON, Raymond (*b.* 1 September 1913 in New York City; *d.* 26 August 1999 in Cambridge, Massachusetts), economist and leading scholar in the study of multinational enterprises (MNEs) and their role in international trade, finance, and economic development; he has been called the father of globalization.

Vernon was one of four children of Hyman and Lillian Visotsky. His father, a Russian-Jewish immigrant, was a truck driver who delivered bottled water to bars and restaurants in the Bronx. As children, Vernon and his two brothers helped their father make deliveries. Vernon's eldest brother, Sidney, studied medicine and changed his surname to Vernon. The siblings (including a sister) followed suit; eventually, all earned doctorates and changed their names.

Vernon studied at City College (now City College of the City University of New York), graduating with an A.B. degree cum laude in 1933, and went on to earn a Ph.D. at Columbia University in 1941. In 1959 Vernon received an honorary M.A. degree from Harvard Univesity. He once described himself as "coming out of the slums in New York via the City College route," thus having "overcome the handicap of a slow start."

Vernon graduated from Columbia at the height of the Great Depression and found few job prospects. In 1935 he accepted a position at the Securities and Exchange Commission (SEC)—given the times, a rather moribund institution. Vernon found his way out of the SEC by moving to the Department of State in 1946 as assistant director of the Trading and Exchange Division. He spent the next eight years in various positions at the Department of State, working to promote European and Japanese economic recovery by helping to implement the Marshall Plan and formulating domestic international trade policy.

Vernon worked in the Mission on Japanese Combines, a post–World War II project directed at deconstructing the Japanese *zaibatsu*, or economic monopolies. In an oral history interview conducted in 1973, Vernon described the controversy surrounding post–World War II Japanese economic policy. Many, including Vernon, argued that the concentration of land held by the elite in Japan had and would continue to erode Japan's economic growth. To cure the *zaibatsu* problem, Japan's agricultural base had to be dismembered and replaced by family farms. Vernon later noted how the most dynamic Japanese enterprises—Sony, Matsushita, Toyota, and Nissan—were all non-*zaibatsu* enterprises.

Eventually, Vernon helped to negotiate Japan into the General Agreement on Tariffs and Trade (GATT) and secured nondiscriminatory treatment for Japanese exports. The Japanese government recognized Vernon's role in Japan's postwar recovery by awarding him the Order of the Rising Sun, Third Class, one of the highest honors bestowed on a foreigner by the Japanese government.

In the early 1950s Vernon served as a chief action officer for the Office of International Trade Policy, working on drafts of the International Trade Organization Charter. Gradually, he was assimilated into the larger activities of the office and finally to the work of GATT. Among the concerns Vernon addressed was how to reconcile GATT with European recovery. Vernon described his role in this activity as that of "peacekeeper and compromise-developer." As such, he served as a member of the U.S. delegation to GATT in Geneva in 1950 and in Torquay, England, in 1951. In 1952 he became vice chair of the U.S. delegation. In later years Vernon described his experience at the Department of State as the source of many subsequent scholarly ideas. In recognition for his contributions leading to the integration of Europe, Vernon received the Department of State Meritorious Service medal in 1952.

Because Vernon's outlook differed from that of the Eisenhower administration, he left the Department of State and joined Hawley and Hoops, a candy company located in Newark, New Jersey, in 1954. As director of planning and control, Vernon was committed to new product development. His lasting legacy, the peanut M&M, was first sold in 1954 and was an immediate hit. In the candy industry, Vernon is still known as the "man who put the crunch in M&M."

Though successful, Vernon disliked the business world and shifted his career again. This time he became director of the New York Metropolitan Region Plan Study, funded by the Ford Foundation and the Rockefeller Brothers Fund under the auspices of the Harvard Graduate School of Public Administration. This three-year project produced ten books that characterized the growth and development of the New York City region. The study influenced a generation of urban planners by predicting, sometimes accurately, the commercial and residential growth patterns of the region.

Vernon joined the Harvard faculty in 1959 and held various posts over the years of his affiliation. In 1965 he directed the Multinational Enterprise Project at the Harvard Business School. The project analyzed the operation of U.S. and foreign-based multinational enterprises (MNEs), particularly their financial base, organization, marketing strategies, and government relations. By 1976 Vernon's project had a database describing hundreds of corporations. This research laid the groundwork for his visionary research regarding the activities of multinational corporations.

Vernon predicted that MNEs, in seeking efficiency, would shift labor-intensive work on standardized products to less-developed countries. He pioneered a behavioral study of MNEs that recognized the complexity of their oligopolistic interaction, particularly with governments. Among his most significant contributions was the product life cycle theory (1966), which showed how new products eventually become involved in international trade. Vernon divided the product life cycle into three stages: the new product, the maturing product, and the standardized product. In the final stage the MNE shifts production to developing countries with lower labor costs.

Vernon wrote various books on the role of the MNE in globalization. As noted in the *Economist* (September 1999), their titles provide "a kind of synopsis of his study of the impact of globalisation over several decades." They include *Sovereignty at Bay* (1971), *Storm over the Multinationals* (1977), *Beyond Globalism* (1989), and *In the Hurricane's Eye* (1998). Among the important policy implications of Vernon's work was his stand on the creation of state-owned corporations, or privatization. Vernon argued that privatization was shortsighted. Though he sympathized with government officials who thought they were losing control of the economy, Vernon argued that governments would never compete effectively with the more flexible MNE.

Always athletic, Vernon rowed on the Charles River well into his eighties. His wife Josephine Stone Vernon, whom he had married in 1935, died in 1995. Vernon died of cancer at age eighty-five, survived by two daughters and four grandchildren.

Vernon was a pioneer in forecasting the rise of the MNE; his style was described as conditional and even-handed. Rarely prescriptive, he sought to educate his readers by clear yet nuanced analysis and reasoning. He distrusted grand theory and worried that empirical models failed to capture the complexity of the dynamic multinational enterprise. Described as a man of high energy and great decency, Vernon concluded his career at Harvard's John F. Kennedy School of Government, Center for Business and Management, where he was the Clarence Dillon Professor of International Affairs Emeritus. Vernon also served as the founding editor of the *Journal of Policy Analysis and Management*.

★

An informative oral history interview of Vernon conducted by Richard D. McKinzie in 1973 is included in "Foreign Service Officers and Department of State Officials Oral History Interviews, 1971–1988," in the Harry S. Truman Library in Independence, Missouri; the interview provides an interesting overview of Vernon's State Department career. Subramanian Rangan, *The Unending Embrace: Raymond Vernon, Multinational Enterprises and National Government* (2000), examines Vernon's contributions to economic theory. Other background pieces include Charles Wolf, "Remembering JPAM's First Editor, Raymond Vernon," *Journal of Policy Analysis and Management* 19, no. 2 (2000): 191–192. Obituaries are in the *New York Times* (28 Aug. 1999) and *Economist* (11 Sept. 1999).

ELOISE F. MALONE

W

WALD, George David (*b.* 18 November 1906 in New York City; *d.* 12 April 1997 in Cambridge, Massachusetts), biologist and winner of the Nobel Prize for discoveries of the biochemical basis of vision who also made important advances in biochemical evolution and became an outspoken critic on various social and political issues, especially in opposition to the Vietnam War and U.S. nuclear policy.

Wald was born on the Lower East Side of New York City to immigrant Jewish parents, Isaac Wald from Poland and Ernestine Rosenmann from near Munich, Germany. His parents worked in the garment industry, and he grew up in a working neighborhood in Brooklyn, where he showed early interest and ability in science and things mechanical. He attended the public Manual Training High School, later named Brooklyn Technical High School, whose mission was to educate students in mechanical subjects. He was also interested in performance and participated in vaudeville shows.

Upon entering Washington Square College of New York University, Wald intended to study pre-law, but he soon switched to pre-medicine and then by his senior year to science. After earning a B.S. degree in zoology in 1927, he entered Columbia University, where during his first year he took a genetics course with Selig Hecht and the great geneticist T. H. Morgan. Hecht, who became his mentor, was well known for his research on photosensory systems of simple animals and of humans, and Wald later acknowl-edged that Hecht had greatly influenced him. He earned a Ph.D. while working in Hecht's laboratory at Columbia in 1932.

Wald married Frances Kingsley in 1931. They had two sons before the marriage ended in divorce. He married Ruth Hubbard, a fellow biologist and research collaborator, in 1958. They had a son and a daughter and remained together until his death.

Wald's research on visual systems at Columbia set the direction of his life's work, and, importantly, it clarified hypotheses that, once tested, would yield far-reaching discoveries about light reception in the eye. Some of his most important work was performed between 1932 and 1934 on a National Research Council (NRC) fellowship. He worked in the laboratories of three European Nobel laureates, first with Otto Warburg in Berlin, where he identified vitamin A in the retina and predicted a link between it and the visual pigment rhodopsin. Wald then moved on to Zurich, Switzerland, and the laboratory of Paul Karrer, who had just identified the chemical structures of vitamin A and beta-carotene. There, Wald confirmed the link between vitamin A and beta-carotene before moving to the laboratory of Otto Meyerhof at the Kaiser Wilhelm Institute in Heidelberg, Germany. While in Heidelberg his research led to hypothesizing a system of interconversions between vitamin A and the derivatives of the protein pigment rhodopsin.

With Hitler's coming to power in January 1933, Ger-

George Wald. PRINTS AND PHOTOGRAPHS DIVISION, LIBRARY OF CONGRESS

many had become hostile to Jews, and the National Research Council directed Wald to return to the United States. He spent the second year of his fellowship at the University of Chicago before going to Harvard University in 1934 to assume his first academic position as tutor in biochemical sciences. He remained there for forty-three years, earning the rank of professor of biology in 1948. He was appointed Higgins Professor of Biology in 1968 and retired from the Harvard faculty in 1977.

While at Chicago and during his early years at Harvard, Wald expanded his research to various vertebrates, including frogs and marine fishes. The fishes were investigated during his many summers at the Marine Biological Laboratory at Woods Hole, Massachusetts, where he taught, along with other professors, a physiology course that enjoyed great renown among biologists. Comparative research on fresh and saltwater fishes, and on the aquatic and terrestrial stages of amphibians, stoked Wald's interest in evolution and the origin of life, topics on which he would write and lecture extensively.

During World War II Wald participated in research on human visual perception at low light levels, helping to advance the military's interest in infrared viewing devices for night surveillance. After the war he returned to research on the biochemical basis of vision.

Recognition of Wald's accomplishments came early and frequently during his career. He received the Eli Lilly Award from the American Chemical Society in 1939. This was followed by awards from many health and medical societies as well as societies focused on the basic sciences. In 1967 he was awarded the Nobel Prize for Physiology or Medicine jointly with Haldan Hartline and Ragnar Granit. He was elected to the prestigious National Academy of Sciences in 1950, and in 1967 he was honored, jointly with his wife Ruth Hubbard, with the Paul Karrer Medal by the University of Zurich, where he had conducted research during his NRC fellowship in 1932 and 1933. Wald also received numerous honorary doctorates from colleges and universities in the United States, Canada, and Europe.

According to John E. Dowling, a student of Wald's and later a Harvard University professor himself, Wald was one of Harvard's most outstanding teachers. He was admired by generations of students for his introductory biology course, "The Nature of Living Things," taught to both science and nonscience students. In 1966 *Time* magazine honored him as one of the nation's ten best teachers. His dedication to excellence in scholarship manifested itself in his own writing as well as in detailed critiques of the writing of others.

Motivated by an abiding social conscience and prompted at the time by his intense opposition to the Vietnam War, Wald became active during the late 1960s in political and social causes. Political and social activism constituted a major portion of his work thereafter, and he adamantly opposed the Vietnam War in many public forums. On 4 March 1969 he gave a speech, "A Generation in Search of a Future," at the Massachusetts Institute of Technology that propelled him nationally into the role of activist. In 1972 he campaigned in Senator George McGovern's unsuccessful bid for the U.S. presidency. He traveled to China and Vietnam, where he was allowed to visit U.S. prisoners of war, and in 1972 he was arrested and jailed in Washington, D.C., while protesting the Vietnam War.

Wald was also an outspoken opponent of nuclear energy and campaigned for nuclear arms reduction. His stature as a scientist carried much weight in the debate over the banning of recombinant DNA research in Cambridge, Massachusetts, out of concern that altered living material might contaminate the community. He worked on behalf of human rights, serving on commissions as an observer in Guatemala and other countries. His participation in the "Crimes Against Iran" conference in Tehran, Iran, in 1980 was highly controversial in light of the tense hostage situation wherein Americans were being held hostage by Iranian religious activists. He died of natural causes at the age of ninety.

Wald's talents led to great accomplishment and wide recognition in science as well as in public social and political advocacy. He earned the highest honors of his profession, culminating in the Nobel Prize for his discoveries of the biochemistry of visual systems. However, the breadth of his interests, including teaching undergraduate students and research on biochemical evolution, expanded Wald's reputation to make him one of the best known and most highly regarded biologists of the twentieth century. His accomplishments as scientist and teacher, in combination with his ability as a public speaker, increased his effectiveness as a public critic. His strong convictions compelled him to enter the public arena in his later years, when he became known—admired by many and detested by others—to a far larger audience than he would have had he restricted his life to science and education.

★

Wald's papers are housed in the Harvard University Archives. Biographical articles with emphasis on his scientific work appear in John E. Dowling, *Biographical Memoirs, Vol. 78* (2000), and Ruth Hubbard and Elijah Wald, *Rhodopsin and Phototransduction* (1999). His Nobel lecture, "The Molecular Basis of Visual Excitation," is in *Physiology or Medicine 1901–1995: Nobel Lectures* (1999). The speech, "A Generation in Search of a Future," that gained Wald national prominence as a political critic is published in the *New Yorker* (1969). Obituaries are in the *Washington Post* and *New York Times* (both 14 Apr. 1997).

W. HUBERT KEEN

WALKER, (Ewell) Doak, Jr. (*b.* 1 January 1927 in Dallas, Texas; *d.* 27 September 1998 in Steamboat Springs, Colorado), All-America football tailback at Southern Methodist University in Dallas, Texas; winner of the Heisman Trophy; and six-year star for the Detroit Lions of the National Football League (NFL) who led his team to two NFL championships.

Walker was the only child of Ewell Doak Walker and Emma Walker, both of whom were teachers. The day Walker was born, his father, who was a football coach, predicted that his son would become an All-America football player. Walker attended Highland Park High School, graduating in 1945, and starred on its football team while also playing basketball and baseball. After playing freshman football at Southern Methodist University (SMU) in Dallas in the 1945–1946 season, he served in the army as a private but returned to school in 1947. Considered a quadruple threat, Walker ran with the ball, threw it, caught it, and kicked it. He even returned kickoffs and punts. In part because of his versatility and in part because of simple talent and skill, he won All-America honors three times (1947–1949). He also won the Heisman Trophy as the outstanding football player in America in 1948, during his junior year, and he might have won again in his senior year but injuries and illness forced him to miss games.

Doak Walker, 1950. ASSOCIATED PRESS AP

At SMU Walker played tailback in an offense that used a single-wing and double-wing formation. In his college career, he averaged 4.2 yards per carry, completed more than 50 percent of his passes, and averaged 16.7 yards per catch while also returning punts for a 15-yard average and kickoffs for 29.1 yards. In just thirty regular season college games, Walker scored 303 points in 35 games. He was such a phenomenon at SMU that fan interest reached an all-time high. Ticket sales were so astounding that SMU began playing its home games in the Cotton Bowl, an arena that had to be enlarged twice while Walker played. The expanded Cotton Bowl became known as the "house that Doak built." Walker also played on SMU's basketball and baseball teams.

After his stellar college career, Walker was drafted by the Detroit Lions despite questions about his size (he stood only five feet, eleven inches tall and weighed just 173 pounds) and speed (some critics said he was too slow). In six seasons, Walker proved his critics wrong by being named All-Pro four times and leading the Lions to two NFL championships. In addition, in his first season, he was named Rookie of the Year and led the league in scoring. He was chosen to play in the Pro Bowl five times. At Detroit, he ran behind a good friend, the future Hall of

Fame quarterback Bobby Layne, with whom Walker had played at Highland Park High School. Reunited, the two men outclassed and outplayed the other excellent backs of the NFL, especially during their two championship seasons.

Over his pro career, Walker ran for 1,520 yards and had a 4.9-yard average per carry. He had 2,359 yards on 152 passes caught. He punted for a 39.1-yard average and also averaged 15.8 yards on punt returns and 25.5 yards on kick-off returns. He found the end zone often, scoring a total of 534 points (34 touchdowns, 49 field goals, and 183 extra points). When he retired, he was third on the list of all-time leading scorers in the NFL. In 1950 Walker married Norma Peterson, his college sweetheart and an SMU homecoming queen. The couple had four children.

Walker invested his money wisely and retired at the end of the 1955 season to become a public relations executive with George A. Fuller Co., a construction company. He moved to Denver, Colorado, and founded Walker Chemical Co. He also opened a sporting goods store. Walker later became vice president of Fischback and Moore, electrical contractors, after he sold his business. He was inducted into both the College Football Hall of Fame (1959) and the Pro Football Hall of Fame (1986). *Sports Illustrated* named him to the "team of the century." Immortalized by the Doak Walker Award, which is given annually to the nation's best collegiate running back, Walker once was asked if he ever regretted leaving the Lions after only six seasons. He said no, adding that he still had all his teeth, two good legs, and most of his good sense.

Peterson and Walker were divorced in 1965, and Walker was remarried in 1969 to Skeeter Werner, a one-time Olympic skier and New York model from Steamboat Springs, Colorado. In later life, the couple retired to Steamboat Springs, where they both enjoyed skiing and hiking. They also ran a ski shop. Tragically, on 31 January 1998, Walker was skiing when he sustained serious injuries. Speeding along into changing terrain, he lost his balance and was thrown high into the air before slamming back into the ground and tumbling seventy-five feet. The accident left him paralyzed and unable to talk. Through physical rehabilitation, he regained some of his ability to talk, but other complications from his massive injuries caused his death. Walker's body was cremated, and his family scattered his ashes at Long's Peak, Colorado, at Estes Park. A great football player, Walker ranks as one of the best and most versatile running backs in the history of the game.

★

Books on Walker include Whitt Canning's *Doak Walker: More Than a Hero* (1998) and Dorothy Kendall Bracken's *Doak Walker: Three-Time All-American* (as told by Doak Walker, 1950). Books and articles summarizing aspects of his sports career include John Devaney's *Winners of the Heisman Trophy* (1990); Denis J. Har-

rington's *The Pro Football Hall of Fame Players, Coaches, Team Owners, and League Officials, 1963–1991* (1991); and Jan Reid's "Legends of the Fall," in *Texas Monthly* 25 (Nov. 1997). For brief glimpses of Walker's football career, consult Robert M. Ours, *College Football Encyclopedia: The Authoritative Guide to 124 years of College Football* (1994), and David S. Neft, Richard M. Cohen, and Richard Korch, *Football Encyclopedia: The Complete History of Professional Football, from 1892 to the Present* (1994). For more on Walker's career and the injury that took his life, see Terry Frei, "Mountain of a Man Legend Faces Struggle After Accident," *Denver Post* (10 Feb. 1998). Obituaries are in the *New York Times, Dallas Morning News,* and *Fort Worth Star-Telegram* (all 28 Sept. 1998).

JAMES M. SMALLWOOD

WALLACE, Christopher George Latore. *See* Notorious B.I.G.

WALLACE, George Corley (*b.* 25 August 1919 in Clio, Alabama; *d.* 13 September 1998 in Montgomery, Alabama), influential national political figure who made his reputation as an enemy of civil rights for black Americans, served four terms as Alabama's governor, unsuccessfully sought the Democratic presidential nomination three times, and was the 1968 presidential candidate of the American Independent Party.

Born in the tiny hamlet of Clio in southeastern Alabama's Barbour County to George C. Wallace and Mozelle Smith, respectable but not wealthy farming people, young George was obsessed with politics from an early age. His only other interest was boxing, and he was the state Golden Gloves bantamweight champion in 1936 and 1937. After earning a law degree at the University of Alabama at Tuscaloosa in 1942, he enlisted in the Army Air Forces, served as a B-29 engineer in General Curtis LeMay's Twentieth Air Force, and was promoted to sergeant. While on leave from the army, he married a sixteen-year-old Tuscaloosa dime-store clerk named Lurleen Burns on 23 May 1943. The stress of flying numerous bombing missions left him with "battle fatigue," or severe anxiety, and he was hospitalized for this emotional condition, leading to his honorable discharge from the army. He later received a Veterans Administration check for a "ten percent" mental disability.

Returning home in late 1945, Wallace worked briefly (from 1946 to 1947) as an assistant state attorney general. In 1946 he opened a law practice in Barbour County and won election to the state legislature, where he became an ally of incoming governor James E. "Big Jim" Folsom, a reform-minded populist with liberal racial attitudes. Reelected to the legislature in 1950, Wallace was elected circuit court judge in 1952, and two years later was south Alabama campaign manager for Folsom when the former governor

George C. Wallace. PRINTS AND PHOTOGRAPHS DIVISION, LIBRARY OF CONGRESS

won a second term. His affiliation with the racially moderate and economically liberal wing of his state's Democratic party was short-lived, and only months after Folsom's second inauguration Wallace began a strategic retreat from "Big Jim." The 1954 Supreme Court decision declaring racial segregation in public schools unconstitutional led to great anger in Alabama, and when Folsom refused to support southern efforts to defy the court, Wallace alleged that his mentor had grown "soft on the nigger question" and declared his independence of the governor. In 1958 Wallace sought the governorship, garnering enough votes to force a Democratic primary runoff with State Attorney General John Patterson. In a contest dominated by the race issue, Wallace vowed to protect segregation, but Patterson projected an image of even greater militancy against race mixing and won the primary. Shortly after the election, Wallace stated that in future campaigns he would be the strongest segregationist, and would never be "out-niggered" again.

In 1959 Wallace proved his mettle as a segregationist when he refused to honor a subpoena for voting records in his judicial circuit from the U.S. Civil Rights Commission, which was investigating racial discrimination in voter registration. Wallace's refusal to release the records led federal Judge Frank M. Johnson, Jr., to threaten him with jail. After a surreptitious meeting with Johnson, a former university classmate and friend, Wallace agreed to give the records to a state grand jury, which then produced them for the commission. When he publicly claimed that he had successfully defied Johnson, the federal judge issued an opinion exposing Wallace's behind-the-scenes surrender. An infuriated

Wallace accused his old friend of lying and decided to make both Johnson and defiance of the federal government the leading issues in his next campaign.

To win the governorship in 1962, Wallace ran as the "fighting little judge" who had defied a federal court. Saying that he would "stand up" for Alabama by standing in the doorway of white schools to block black children from integrating them, he nevertheless insisted that his opposition to desegregation was based solely on his belief in the constitutional right of state and local governments to run their schools as they saw fit. At every campaign stop Wallace claimed that he had backed down "that federal judge," and that Frank Johnson was an "integratin', carpetbaggin', scallawaggin' liar" for saying otherwise. Wallace's strategy paid off, as a segregation-obsessed white Alabama electorate gave him a landslide victory.

Wallace began his governorship by inviting trouble in an inaugural address remembered for its racist rhetoric. "I draw the line in the dust and toss the gauntlet before the feet of tyranny," he shouted, and "I say, segregation now! Segregation tomorrow! Segregation forever!" Despite this clarion call for confrontation between Alabama and the federal government, there were notable achievements in Wallace's first term. The governor's administration raised teacher salaries, gave free textbooks to Alabama's school children (of all races), and created new and expensive junior colleges and trade schools. These programs were financed with a regressive sales tax that took a larger bite of revenue from the poor, the elderly, and others on fixed incomes than from the wealthy. Wallace never again matched these successes and never addressed the festering problem of Alabama's inadequate and unfair tax system, which left the state with little revenue and insufficient public services. Instead, Wallace put resistance to desegregation at the top of his agenda.

The governor dispatched Alabama state troopers to Birmingham, Alabama, in the spring of 1963 in an effort to halt civil rights demonstrations led by Martin Luther King, Jr. Interfering with efforts by local authorities to restore peace, troopers precipitated a confrontation with demonstrators that led to police violence. When a bomb blew up an African-American church in Birmingham and killed four young black girls, many people blamed Wallace for creating the kind of atmosphere that led to the tragic incident. The governor's efforts to force local authorities to join him in opposing racial integration led to a 1964 court order by Wallace's nemesis, Judge Frank Johnson, compelling the desegregation of the state's entire public school system, but such defeats did not deter Wallace. He grew ever more popular in Alabama, and in the summer of 1963 he performed a stunt that brought him national notoriety.

When federal courts ordered the desegregation of the University of Alabama at Tuscaloosa, Wallace conducted a charade that unfolded on national television. Standing in front of a university building where two black students were to register, Wallace stopped U.S. Justice Department officials sent to help the students enter school and made a lengthy speech attacking the power that the Kennedy administration was using to enforce desegregation. Claiming that he was "interposing" himself between the "central government" and Alabama's people, he thus invoked a legal doctrine held in disrepute since before the Civil War. After federal authorities ordered him to, the governor agreed to move out of the doorway to permit the historic integration of the university, but he had won the nationwide publicity he wanted. The "stand in the schoolhouse door" propelled Wallace into presidential politics.

In September 1963 Wallace tried to prevent integration of public schools in Mobile, Tuskegee, Birmingham, and Huntsville, Alabama, by using the state troopers to stop black students from enrolling. But after Wallace put the Alabama National Guard in their place, President Kennedy federalized them and ordered them to return to the armories, in effect, allowing the black students to enter the schools and enforcing the schools' integration.

In 1964, as a monumental civil rights bill was pending before Congress, Wallace decided to take his anti–federal government campaign into northern states. Aware that efforts by blacks to gain access to better housing, higher paying jobs, and private restaurants and hotels were resented in the North as well as the South, Wallace shrewdly decided to exploit a northern white backlash against civil rights. Running in Democratic presidential primaries in Indiana, Wisconsin, and Maryland, Wallace said that if he got 15 percent of the vote, it would "shake the eyeteeth" of federal bureaucrats. Winning 30 percent in Indiana, 34 percent in Wisconsin, and 43 percent in Maryland, he claimed victory and shocked commentators who had treated his candidacy as a joke. The campaign also revealed Wallace's exceptional ability as a public speaker and performer. Interviewed on national television by reporters who sought to ridicule him for his racial attitudes, Wallace deftly handled their questions, demonstrating that he was a force to be reckoned with. Carefully avoiding racial epithets or other direct references to race, he stuck to his theme of protecting Americans against a prying national government. Reveling in his growing image as a cocky, feisty little man unafraid to "stand up" for his beliefs anywhere in the nation, Wallace began to plan his next presidential campaign.

Problems at home, however, demanded Wallace's attention. In the spring of 1965, when black civil rights leaders held voting rights demonstrations in Selma, Alabama, Wallace dispatched state troopers to stop them from marching fifty miles to the state capitol in Montgomery. The nation watched with horror on television as troopers attacked demonstrators with tear gas and clubs at Selma's Edmund Pettus Bridge. Judge Frank Johnson then ordered the state to

protect the marchers, and several days later when they reached the state capitol, Wallace skulked inside, refusing to come outside and greet them. These incidents led to the passage of the 1965 Voting Rights Act and the empowerment of black voters in the South. Once again, Wallace's defiance and posturing for the benefit of segregationists led to successes by the civil rights movement, while his popularity among white Alabamians soared yet again.

Alabama's constitution prohibited Wallace from succeeding himself, and in the summer of 1965 a courageous group of legislators stopped the governor from pushing through a constitutional amendment that would have allowed him to run again in 1966. Taking a risky political gamble, Wallace asked his wife Lurleen to run "in his place," saying that he would serve as her "one dollar a year assistant." She accepted the challenge and won a landslide victory, becoming the first woman governor of Alabama. It was an incredible show of political clout by Wallace, and as he prepared for the 1968 presidential campaign, events at the national level also seemed to be playing into his hands.

Riots in the black ghettos of northern cities, a movement against the unpopular Vietnam War that led to unruly demonstrations, the rise of a youth counterculture that challenged the traditional religious and economic values of older generations, and skyrocketing crime rates that led many people to fear for their safety were all grist for Wallace's political mill. Believing he could best exploit these emotional issues by running as a third-party candidate, he helped create the American Independent Party, which nominated him for president in 1968. Wallace understood that he had little chance to win, but he hoped to gain enough votes to throw the election into the U.S. House of Representatives. The Wallace campaign suffered a major blow when on 7 May 1968 Governor Lurleen Wallace died after battling cancer for several months. Her husband barely paused from his campaign, and by early June was back on the hustings, claiming that it was what his wife had wanted him to do.

Running as the candidate of "law and order," Wallace asked for a get-tough policy against rioters and demonstrators, mocking young antiwar demonstrators in crude and vituperative language, saying that if one of them lay down in front of his car "it'll be the last one he lays down in front of." When he was elected, said Wallace, he would give the demonstrators a passport to the capital of Communist North Vietnam. Blaming the "liberals" and their "pseudo-intellectual" supporters for all of America's problems was central to all of Wallace's speeches. A liberal elite and a "bunch of briefcase toting bureaucrats" had taken control of the nation's government and were determined to undermine the white, patriotic, God-centered, hard-working, middle-class world. Wallace proposed to speak for "this barber and beautician, this truck driver and steel worker" and against social engineering schemes planned by the elite. Both political parties were to blame, he said, and there "wasn't a dime's worth of difference between them." Wallace's rhetoric caught hold outside the South, and by September national polls showed that he might win between 20 and 25 percent of the vote.

The 1968 Republican candidates, Richard Nixon and Spiro Agnew, took up Wallace's themes, hammering away on behalf of law and order, criticizing antiwar demonstrators, and promising to go slow on civil rights enforcement. They cut into Wallace's support, but the biggest blow to the third-party candidate was self-inflicted. Wallace selected as his running mate his World War II commander, General Curtis LeMay. At a news conference announcing LeMay's candidacy, the general suggested that he might favor the use of atomic weapons to end the Vietnam War and that the world could survive nuclear war. Wallace was stunned, and his standing in the polls deteriorated. When northern labor leaders pointed out that Wallace, the self-designated candidate of the working man, had supported policies in Alabama that damaged organized labor, he began to lose blue-collar support as well. On election day he took only 13 percent of the national vote and won only five southern states.

Wallace returned home to recapture the Alabama governorship in 1970, but incumbent Governor Albert Brewer was Wallace's opponent in the Democratic primary, and the entire nation watched with interest as Brewer put Wallace's presidential plans in jeopardy. President Nixon, who feared that Wallace might run as a third-party candidate again, directed his operatives to pour money into Brewer's campaign coffers. It nearly worked, as Brewer led the 1970 primary field, but he faced a runoff with Wallace, who ran one of the most blatantly racist campaigns in Alabama's history. He defeated Brewer, whom he accused of being the recipient of the "black block vote." On 4 January 1971, prior to his inauguration, Wallace remarried, this time to the former Cornelia Snively, a tall, attractive, and stylish young divorcée, and the niece of former governor Jim Folsom. She proved to be a great asset in the governor's upcoming 1972 presidential campaign.

Wallace surprised his political cronies in late 1971 when he suddenly decided not to run as a third-party presidential candidate. Close observers of his career believe the decision was a quid pro quo for a Nixon administration's decision not to indict Wallace's brother Gerald for income tax invasion and other corrupt activities. Nixon was frightened by the possibility that Wallace might take enough electoral votes from him to elect a Democrat. A trial of Gerald Wallace would have exposed wrongdoing inside the Wallace administrations that might have ended George Wallace's career. He deserted the American Independent party and entered the Democratic presidential primaries, which further fueled suspicions that Nixon had made a deal with Wallace.

New racial tensions in the North made Wallace a formidable candidate once again. Federal court decisions between 1969 and 1971 ordered that students be transported out of school districts in which they lived in order to end de facto racial segregation in other districts. This created an issue defined by Wallace and other conservatives as "busing to achieve a racial balance." Continued disorder in the streets over the Vietnam War, combined with the busing issue, allowed Wallace to win traditionally liberal Democratic but patriotic and culturally conservative blue-collar workers to his side in early primaries. He won a plurality of the Florida primary vote and ran a surprising second in Wisconsin, Pennsylvania, and Indiana. Then, while campaigning in Laurel, Maryland, on 15 May 1972, he was shot with a pistol five times at close range by a mentally unstable man named Arthur Bremer. Wallace miraculously survived, but he would never walk again or control his lower bodily functions, and he would be in constant pain. On the day after the assassination attempt the governor won both the Maryland and Michigan primaries, but his inability to campaign led to the inevitable victory of his leading opponent, Senator George McGovern.

The 1972 campaign was Wallace's last hurrah as a serious presidential candidate. Despite his reelection as governor of Alabama in 1974, he was badly beaten by Georgia Governor Jimmy Carter in several Democratic presidential primaries in the South in the early months of 1976. Wallace withdrew from the race, and his strong endorsement of Carter helped the Georgian win several southern states in the general election.

Wallace went through a messy and public divorce from Cornelia in 1978, and in September 1981 he married a thirty-three-year-old former country music singer named Lisa Taylor. Unable to walk and heavily medicated for the pain he constantly suffered as a result of his gunshot wounds, Wallace still made a political comeback in 1982 and won his fourth term as governor. During his last two terms as governor he sought forgiveness for his opposition to racial justice, appointed a number of blacks to high posts in his administration, renounced segregation, and won surprising black support in his 1982 campaign. Retiring from politics at the end of his last term in office in 1987, he held fund-raising jobs at two state universities, but Wallace loved the adulation and the roar of the crowd and was never really happy except on the campaign trail. His third marriage also ended in divorce in 1987, and during much of the last decade of his life he was bedridden, dependent upon the emotional support of his and Lurleen's four children and former aides. Wallace died of heart failure and is buried in Greenwood Cemetery in Montgomery.

Wallace's legacy in Alabama is chiefly negative. He badly neglected his duties as governor, failing to address many of the state's most pressing problems. These failures were underlined when Judge Frank Johnson, who always seemed to be around to point out the governor's negligence, issued numerous court orders forcing the state to do something about atrocious conditions in the state's mental health and prison systems. Indeed, commentators began to refer to Johnson as the "real governor of Alabama." Wallace's most lasting legacy to the nation was in the damage he did to liberalism. His attacks on the liberal wing of the national Democratic Party helped to take the South and many northern blue-collar workers out of the party, and his tactics heavily influenced the Republican Party to adopt a generally successful strategy of appealing solely to white voters, which pushed the GOP toward an increasingly more conservative stance.

★

The best primary sources for information on Wallace are the Montgomery *Advertiser* for the years 1962 to 1986 and the papers on Wallace's governorship at the Alabama Department of Archives and History. This essay leans heavily on such standard secondary sources as Marshall Frady's book-length journalistic essay, *Wallace* (1968); Jack Bass and Walter DeVries, *The Transformation of Southern Politics: Social Change and Political Consequences Since 1945* (1976); Jack Bass, *Taming the Storm: The Life and Times of Judge Frank M. Johnson, Jr., and the South's Fight over Civil Rights* (1993); and Dan T. Carter's comprehensive biography, *The Politics of Rage: George Wallace, the Origins of the New Conservatism, and the Transformation of American Politics* (1995). An obituary is in the *New York Times* (14 Sept. 1998).

SAMUEL L. WEBB

WALLIS, W(ilson) Allen (*b.* 5 November 1912 in Philadelphia, Pennsylvania; *d.* 12 October 1998 in Rochester, New York), statistician, economist, college professor, and adviser to four U.S. presidents, served as president then chancellor of the University of Rochester during the institution's transformation into a top national university.

Wallis was the son of Wilson Dallam Wallis, a distinguished anthropologist at the University of Minnesota, and Grace Stelle Allen, a homemaker. In 1932 he earned his bachelor's degree in psychology magna cum laude from the University of Minnesota, where he remained briefly to do graduate work in economics. In 1933 he entered the University of Chicago, where he formed lifelong friendships with future Nobel laureates Milton Friedman and George Stigler. He married Anne Armstrong on 5 October 1933; the couple had two children. In October 1994, after fifty-nine years of marriage, Anne Wallis passed away.

W. Allen Wallis, 1962. AP/WIDE WORLD PHOTOS

Wallis began his working career in 1935 as an economist and statistician on the National Resources Committee. He then taught at Yale, Columbia, and Stanford Universities before becoming in 1942 the director of research for the U.S. Office of Scientific Research's Statistical Research Group. As director, he recruited a group of young statisticians and mathematicians who contributed to the U.S. war effort by solving problems ranging from optimal patterns of submarine searches to efficient testing of naval artillery shells.

In 1946 Wallis began teaching in the Graduate School of Business at the University of Chicago; in 1956 he became dean of the school, after he had developed an international reputation as a free-market economist who often wore a tie decorated with the silhouette of Adam Smith (the father of modern market economics). In 1959 he served as a special assistant to President Dwight Eisenhower, collaborating with vice president Richard Nixon on the Cabinet Committee on Price Stability for Economic Growth, the first of eleven presidential commissions on which Wallis served. In 1962 Wallis became president of the University of Rochester, serving in that capacity until he was appointed chancellor and chief executive officer (CEO) in 1970, the only time in the twentieth century that the position of chancellor existed at Rochester.

Under Wallis's leadership, the University of Rochester initiated a successful capital campaign that raised nearly $50 million, increased the annual budget from $33 million to $200 million, doubled the number of graduate students, increased the size of the faculty by more than a third, and made extensive additions and improvements, including remodeling the Eastman School of Music and expanding the library and the medical center. The cumulative impact of these and other changes transformed the University of Rochester from a largely provincial institution into a national university. In 1975 Wallis relinquished the title of CEO to Robert L. Sproull, although he continued as chancellor until he retired from the university in 1982.

During the 1970s Wallis served in the Nixon and Ford administrations as a member of the National Council on Educational Research and the National Commission on Productivity. He was also chair of the President's Commission on Federal Statistics and of the Advisory Council on Social Security. He was chair of the Corporation for Public Broadcasting in 1977 and 1978 when he introduced a television producer to Milton Friedman, leading to the production of Friedman's acclaimed PBS series *Free to Choose.*

In 1982 Wallis was named undersecretary of state for economic affairs. At the State Department, Wallis coordinated U.S. economic programs and policies abroad and served as President Ronald Reagan's personal adviser for several major international economic summits. He left the State Department in 1989 but maintained numerous professional commitments, including directorships of Macmillan, Bausch and Lomb, Rochester Telephone, and Eastman Kodak.

As an economist, Wallis was noted for his strong beliefs in free markets and minimal government intervention. His 1976 book, *An Overgoverned Society,* a collection of essays and speeches written over three decades, described how bureaucratic rules and regulations were shackling the U.S. economy and individual freedoms. Wallis was an adviser to four Republican presidents but was not an extreme conservative. His philosophy of economic freedom was reflected in his championship of individual and academic freedoms. He advocated abolishing the military draft and was appointed to a presidential commission on the draft that recommended ending conscription, which occurred in 1973.

During the turbulent Vietnam War era, Wallis supported the controversial appointment of Eugene Genovese as a professor in the University of Rochester's history department. Genovese, a Marxist and Socialist, had left Rutgers University after President Richard Nixon attacked him for his views on the conflict in Vietnam. After examining Genovese's academic qualifications and scholarly activities, Wallis concluded that the professor's political beliefs had not colored his roles as a teacher and scholar, and he approved Genevose's appointment in 1969. At Rochester, Genovese earned national and international acclaim for his economic analysis of slavery.

In recognition of Wallis's dedication to the combined study of economics and politics, and in acknowledgment of his service to the country and higher education, the W. Allen Wallis Institute of Political Economy at the University of Rochester was named in honor of the former president and chancellor. The institute, which opened in December 1992, supports the study of how political institutions influence market forces. Wallis died of a stroke six years later at the age of eighty-five while in the city of Rochester for a university event.

★

The most readily available, detailed biography of Wallis can be found on the website of the W. Allen Wallis Institute of Political Economy, which is linked to the University of Rochester's website. Ann Crittenden's "Aide Reflects Shultz Style," *New York Times* (21 July 1982), describes the rationale for choosing Wallis as undersecretary of state for economic affairs and contains some biographical information. Obituaries are in the *New York Times* (14 Oct. 1998) and *Chicago Tribune* (13 Oct. 1998).

JAMES CICARELLI

WEAVER, Robert Clifton (*b.* 29 December 1907 in Washington, D.C.; *d.* 17 July 1997 in New York City), economist, educator, and public administrator who was the first African-American member of a presidential cabinet and who dedicated his life to fighting discrimination and improving race relations.

Weaver was the younger of two children born to Mortimer Grover, a postal clerk, and Florence Freeman, the daughter of the first African American to graduate from Harvard College with a dentistry degree. Weaver and his brother grew up in a comfortable, middle-class family in the segregated suburbs of Washington, D.C. A multitalented man, Weaver demonstrated his skills and capacity for hard work even before he graduated from Dunbar High School. By his senior year, Weaver was operating his own electrical business, but he was denied membership in the electrical union because of his race.

In 1925 Weaver entered Harvard College in Cambridge, Massachusetts, and majored in economics. He lived off-campus because Harvard did not offer on-campus housing for African Americans. A bright student, Weaver won the Pasteur Medal and the Boylston Speaking Prize during his first year at Harvard and earned a B.S. degree cum laude in 1929. He immediately entered graduate school at Harvard, completing an M.A. degree in 1931. That same year, he taught economics at the Agricultural and Technical Col-

Robert C. Weaver, 1942. PRINTS AND PHOTOGRAPHS DIVISION, LIBRARY OF CONGRESS

lege in Greensboro, North Carolina. In 1932 he returned to Harvard as an Austin Scholar and in 1934 completed a Ph.D. in economics. On 18 July 1935 Weaver married Ella V. Haith, who had earned a Ph.D. in speech from Northwestern University in Evanston, Illinois. They later adopted one son, Robert, Jr.

Weaver began his government career in 1933 as one of the young professionals drawn to Washington, D.C., by the New Deal administration of Franklin D. Roosevelt. He received a succession of assignments advising various agency administrators on minority problems, and he soon became an adviser to the secretary of the U.S. Department of the Interior. He earned respect as an expert on civil rights and race relations and became part of President Roosevelt's Black Cabinet. Weaver used his influence with the White House to lobby for greater minority rights, including access to more jobs and better educational opportunities. He left the Department of the Interior in 1938 to become a special assistant with the U.S. Housing Authority. From 1940 to 1941 Weaver served as an administrative assistant with the National Defense Advisory Commission. During World War II he held several offices concerned with mobilizing African-American labor and promoting the cause of integration. He left the federal government in 1944.

After the war Weaver served as executive director of the Mayor's Committee on Race Relations in Chicago. In 1946 he became a member of the United Nations Relief and Rehabilitation Administration mission in the Ukraine and served there in several official capacities, including acting deputy chief. Weaver soon returned to Chicago and became an officer of the American Council on Race Relations. He then commenced a new academic life as a lecturer at Northwestern University (1947–1948) and as a visiting professor in New York City at Columbia University Teachers College (1947–1949), New York University (1948–1951), and the New School for Social Research (1949). During this period he wrote *Negro Labor: A National Problem* (1946) and *The Negro Ghetto* (1948). Weaver focused his research and writing on segregation and bettering the conditions of blacks. His book, *The Negro Ghetto*, for example, was one of the first works to explore black segregation in the North.

In 1949 Weaver became the director of opportunity fellowships for the John Hay Whitney Foundation in New York City. At the same time, he was a member of the Fulbright fellowship national selection committee, the Julius Rosenwald Fund, and the United Negro College Fund fellowship committee (also chairman) and a consultant to the Ford Foundation. In 1955 he left the Whitney Foundation to become the deputy commissioner of housing for New York State. In December 1955 Weaver was promoted to rent control commissioner with cabinet rank, becoming the first African American to hold a cabinet position in New York State. He served as rent commissioner until 1959. In 1960 Weaver served as national chairman of the National Association for the Advancement of Colored People (NAACP). That same year, he called the student strikes against segregated lunch-counter service in the South.

In 1960 President John F. Kennedy appointed Weaver the administrator of the Housing and Home Finance Agency, making him the first African American to hold such a position at the national level. Kennedy tried to have the agency elevated to cabinet rank, but Congress blocked his plan. Five years later President Lyndon B. Johnson revived the idea and the agency was included in the president's cabinet. In 1966 Johnson appointed Weaver the secretary of the new U.S. Department of Housing and Urban Development (HUD), making him the first African-American presidential cabinet member in U.S. history. Weaver created federal housing programs that were still in existence decades later.

After leaving his cabinet position at the end of the Johnson administration, Weaver returned to New York City. In 1969 he became president of Bernard M. Baruch College of the City University of New York, where he stayed until 1970, when he accepted a post as distinguished professor of urban affairs at Hunter College. After eight years at Hunter, he retired as professor emeritus.

A Democrat and a Lutheran, Weaver was active in many service organizations, including the National Committee Against Discrimination in Housing, American Jewish Congress, Citizens' Committee for Children, and the New York Civil Liberties Union. Weaver was a member of the African-American Omega Psi Phi Fraternity and received more than thirty honorary doctorates, as well as many awards, including the NAACP Spingarn Medal; Russworm Award; Albert Einstein Commemorative Award; New York City Urban League's Frederick Douglass Award; and the M. Justin Herman Memorial Award of the National Association of Housing and Redevelopment Officials.

A prolific writer, Weaver authored several books and published about 175 articles. He died of lung cancer at age eighty-nine; he was predeceased by his son (1962) and his wife (1991). In July 2000 the HUD headquarters in Washington, D.C., which was formally opened by Weaver in 1968, was renamed the Robert C. Weaver Federal Building. Throughout his life Weaver served as a role model and an inspiration for many people. As reported in the *Negro Vanguard,* he was one of the "bold fighters, brilliant, high-minded, fearless, incorruptible, and self-assertive among all African Americans."

★

Weaver's papers are at the Schomburg Center for Research in Black Culture in New York City. There is no complete biography. Useful biographical information appears in *Current Biography Yearbook* (1961), *Contemporary Black Biography* (1994), *A Memorial Tribute to Robert Clifton Weaver, 1907–1997* (4 Sept. 1997), at the Schomburg Center, and James Haskins, *Distinguished African-American Political and Governmental Leaders* (1999). Weaver's career is discussed in Jessie Carney Smith, ed., *Notable Black American Men* (1999). Obituaries are in the *New York Times* (19 July 1997), *Washington Post* (20 July 1997), and *New York Times Biographical Service* (July 1997).

NJOKI-WA-KINYATTI

WEESE, Harry Mohr (*b.* 30 June 1915 in Evanston, Illinois; *d.* 29 October 1998 in Manteno, Illinois), architect of the Washington Metro rapid transit system and of several landmark buildings in Chicago.

Weese was the eldest of the three sons and two daughters of a Chicago banker, Harry Ernest Weese, and Marjorie Mohr, a homemaker. As a child, Weese spent so much time doodling that his father suggested architecture as a way to channel the urge into a respectable career. The son agreed, traveling east to attend Yale University before transferring to the Massachusetts Institute of Technology (MIT), where

he studied under Finnish architect Alvar Aalto before graduating with a degree in architecture in 1938. During a fellowship year in Michigan at the Cranbrook Academy, Weese absorbed the teachings of another Finn, Eliel Saarinen, whose emphasis on context and history set him apart from the Bauhaus modernists. He also found time to make lasting friendships with Saarinen's son Eero, Charles Eames, Benjamin Baldwin, and other classmates.

Weese's first job was with Skidmore, Owings, and Merrill (SOM) in Chicago. He left in 1941 to start a partnership with Baldwin, but World War II pulled him away to be chief engineer of a navy destroyer, in charge of eighty-five men. During a shore leave in 1945, Weese married Baldwin's sister, Kate ("Kitty"), with whom he eventually had three daughters. After mustering out of the service, he briefly returned to SOM and then in 1947 opened his own firm, Harry Weese and Associates, in the back room of Kitty's modernist interior design shop. For a time, his main client was his father, who commissioned a series of houses. J. Irwin Miller, chairman of the Cummins Engine Company, became another important early patron, commissioning thirteen buildings in Columbus, Indiana, including the First Baptist Church (1965), as well as a series of showrooms and industrial buildings for the company. In 1957 his brother Ben joined the firm. The third Weese brother, John, became a partner at SOM, marking the beginnings of a multigenerational Weese architectural dynasty.

Weese earned national fame with two projects designed in the late 1950s. In the redeveloped southwest section of Washington, D.C., he planned the Arena Stage (1961), a theater in the round, as an unpretentious, neighborly building for a largely residential part of the city. An ocean away, he showed the same concern for the local setting in his design for the U.S. embassy in Accra, Ghana (1958), which was later decommissioned. For this project, he combined a modernist outline with local materials and details, coming up with a flat, glass box, perched on stilts and clad in mahogany shutters. Professional recognition came with election to the American Institute of Architects' College of Fellows (1961) and the Arnold W. Brunner Memorial Prize in Architecture from the National Institute of Arts and Letters (1964).

In an unusual turn for an architect, Weese is perhaps most famous for work he did underground. In 1966 he won the commission to design the stations for a rapid transit system in Washington, D.C., later named Metro. After touring subways throughout Europe and Japan, Weese proposed building Washington's underground stations as long, spacious vaults, free of the columns that interrupt sightlines in older subway systems, such as those in New York City and Philadelphia. The project's engineers convinced Weese that rectangular, cross-sectioned "box" stations would be more appropriate for cut-and-cover stations downtown. But

Harry Weese. ARCHIVE PHOTOS, INC.

after repeated rejections of the box by the Commission of Fine Arts, Weese returned to his vault design, adding rectangular coffers that served structural functions while recalling the domes of the Pantheon and the U.S. Capitol. These concrete ceilings, complemented by monumental accents in bronze and granite, were repeated throughout the system's underground stations, providing a sense of unity to the 103-mile system. When the first stations opened in 1976, they were hailed by critics and patrons. Their acclaim gained the firm additional work on the Washington system and on transit systems in Singapore, as well as in Miami, Buffalo, Los Angeles, and several other cities, thereby greatly expanding its size.

By the late 1970s Weese had built projects all over the world, but he remained rooted in Chicago, where he built the Time-Life Building (1970), notable for its space-saving double-decker elevators, and the Metropolitan Correctional Center (1978), a jail elegant enough to ornament the city's chic downtown. His firm now employed more than 100 architects, but Weese continued to provide conceptual

sketches to be worked out by his staff. He never lost his habit of doodling, doing some of his most important work on airplanes or on vacation, and both his designs and his drawings remained playful. In 1978 Harry Weese and Associates won the American Institute of Architects' Firm of the Year Award, though Weese joked that so many of his architects—including his brother Ben—had moved on to partnerships elsewhere that he should have been given the "infirm award." As an architect at the top of his profession, he served on the jury for the Vietnam Veterans Memorial in Washington, drawing attention to the design by Maya Lin that eventually won the commission.

In addition to designing new buildings, Weese was a pioneer in restoring and reusing old buildings. His first restoration, begun in 1963, was Dankmar Adler and Louis Sullivan's 1889 Auditorium Theatre in Chicago, which had been left vacant and rotting. After returning the theater to its former glory, he went on to restore Washington, D.C.'s Union Station, Chicago's Field Museum of Natural History and Newberry Library, and Singapore's Raffles Hotel, among other projects. His preservation work extended beyond architecture—he revived the magazine *Inland Architect*. Weese finally retired in the early 1990s, spending his last years in a nursing home, weakened by a series of strokes and eventually unable to recognize visitors. He died of a final stroke at age eighty-three, and his remains were cremated.

Weese never developed a single style, preferring to experiment and work with the particulars of site and program. He rejected both the Bauhaus rigid dependence on boxes of glass and steel and postmodernism's pastiche. Combining modernism's emphasis on function with a concern for history, tradition, and context, he sought an architecture defined less by ideology than by a respect for people.

★

Weese's extensive professional papers, mostly organized by project, are held by the Chicago Historical Society. Kitty Baldwin Weese's seventieth birthday present to her husband, *Harry Weese Houses* (1987), presents some of the eighty-two houses designed by Weese in the course of his career. Walter McQuade, "Harry Weese: A Young Architect Recalls the Old Chicago School," *Architectural Forum* 116 (May 1962), and "Current Work of Harry Weese," *Architectural Record* 133 (May 1963), capture Weese's work during his rise to fame, whereas Andrea O. Dean, "Harry Weese of Chicago," *AIA Journal* (May 1978), profiles a mature, established Weese. Among Weese's obituaries, Stan Allan, "A Man of Many Words and Works," *Inland Architect* 116, no. 1 (1999), is particularly thorough and tender. Weese told his own story in a 1988 interview with Betty J. Blum for the Chicago Architects Oral History Project of the Art Institute of Chicago.

ZACHARY M. SCHRAG

WEIL, André (*b.* 6 May 1906 in Paris, France; *d.* 6 August 1998 in Princeton, New Jersey), mathematician and cofounder of Bourbaki, a group of French mathematicians who collectively published many important works.

Weil (pronounced "VAY") was the son of Jewish parents, physician Bernard Weil, whose family had moved from Alsace, France, to Paris, and Selma Reinherz, whose family immigrated to Paris from Russia via Belgium. During World War I, Weil's father served as a physician in various French army hospitals, and the family, including Weil's younger sister, Simone, traveled with him. (Simone later became a well-known social philosopher and mystic.) Weil was a child prodigy who began reading at age four; by age ten he was studying Latin and was addicted to mathematics. In 1919 he entered the scientifically oriented Lycée Saint-Louis. At fifteen, he met the great French mathematician Jacques Solomon Hadamard, who become his mentor. Weil was admitted to the prestigious École Normale Supérieure in 1922.

Weil earned his *Aggrégation* from the École Normale in 1925, after which he decided to travel to study with as many great mathematicians as he could. He first spent an academic year at the University of Rome (1925–1926), where he learned about the Italian advances in algebraic geometry. As in his subsequent travels, he also immersed himself in the art, architecture, music, and poetry of the country. In 1927 he was awarded a fellowship at the University of Göttingen, Germany, where he met Richard Courant, Amile Emmy Noether, and many other mathematical luminaries. During the break between the winter and summer semesters in Germany, he went to Sweden, where Magnus Gösta Mittag-Leffler promised to publish Weil's dissertation in his journal, *Acta Mathematica*. Weil completed his doctorate at the University of Paris in 1928, and his dissertation, which solved a problem posed by Jules-Henri Poincaré twenty-five years earlier, was published in *Acta* by Mittag-Leffler's successor.

Weil served in the French army from 1928 to 1929. He was then invited to teach mathematics at the Aligarh Muslim University in India, not far from Delhi, where he stayed just over two years, from 1930 to 1932. During this time he delved into the country's Sanskrit literature and other indigenous arts and continued his research into the theory of functions of several complex variables.

Upon his return to France in 1932, Weil taught at the University of Marseilles for one year, then at the University of Strasbourg from 1933 to 1939. At Strasbourg, he and his friend and fellow mathematician Henri Cartan often discussed how best to teach various topics in the calculus and bemoaned the inadequacy of the leading instructive texts. At Weil's suggestion, they contacted fellow mathematicians who had graduated from the École Normale and together formed a group they called "Bourbaki" (reportedly the last name of a highly unsuccessful French general). Their goal was to publish a series of mathematics texts that would provide a firm and logical foundation for all mathematics. The resulting texts, published over the next few decades under the collective pseudonym Nicolas Bourbaki, were extraordinarily influential in setting the standard for logic, rigor, and abstraction in mathematics.

On 30 October 1937 Weil married Eveline Gillet, who already had a son, Alain de Possel, from a previous marriage. Early in 1939 Weil and Eveline left for a vacation in Finland. Weil had decided that if war broke out, he would not serve in a French army run by incompetent officers and politicians, but instead would devote his life to mathematics by immigrating to the United States. But after Eveline returned to France (Weil stayed in Finland), Russia invaded Finland, making it impossible for Weil to go to the United States as planned. He was arrested under suspicion of spying (he had corresponded with Russian mathematicians) and was about to be executed when a Finnish mathematician suggested to the chief of police that he be deported instead. Weil became a prisoner in Sweden, England, and finally at Le Havre and Rouen in France. While awaiting trial in Rouen, he made major progress in his research, which later resulted in his extremely influential book, *Foundations of Algebraic Geometry* (1946). On 3 May 1940 Weil was tried and convicted, not of desertion but of failure to report for duty. When given the choice of five years in prison or service in the army, he chose the latter. While Weil was serving in Normandy, the German advance forced the French army there to evacuate to England.

Weil returned to Vichy, France, after its occupation by Germany, and in January 1941 he, Eveline, and Alain set sail for the United States. With support from the Rockefeller Foundation, Weil spent part of 1941 at the Institute for Advanced Study in Princeton, then obtained a non-salaried teaching position at Haverford College in Pennsylvania. His daughter Sylvie was born in September 1942. From 1942 to 1943 he taught at Lehigh University, and from 1945 to 1947 at the University of São Paulo in Brazil. His second daughter, Nicolette, was born in December of 1946.

Although Weil had established himself as the leading French mathematician of the time and a driving force behind the Bourbaki group, his reputation for being difficult contributed to his inability to obtain a teaching position at a first-rate American university. When Marshall Stone became chair of the mathematics department at the University of Chicago, he hired several outstanding mathematicians, including Weil, who taught there from 1947 to 1958. In 1948 Weil formulated the Weil Conjectures, which were key to advances in algebraic geometry.

From 1958 until he retired in 1975, Weil was a professor at the Institute for Advanced Study in Princeton. Beginning in 1976, he was professor emeritus, concentrating on historical studies in mathematics and on writing his autobiography, *The Apprenticeship of a Mathematician* (translated from the French, 1992), partly as a tribute to his wife, who died in 1986. Weil died suddenly from a heart attack at age ninety-two. His body was cremated and the ashes were buried in the Princeton Cemetery.

Although Weil worked in pure mathematics, his results were applied in elementary particle physics and in creating a secure method for transmitting data. He was one of the most influential mathematicians of the twentieth century and received many awards and honors during his lifetime, including the Wolf Prize in 1978, the prestigious Kyoto Prize in 1994, and the Barnard Medal from Columbia University in 1980.

★

Weil published fifteen books, including *Foundations of Algebraic Geometry* (1946; 2d ed., 1962), *Elliptic Functions According to Eisenstein and Kronecker* (1976), and *Number Theory: An Approach Through History from Hammurapi to Legendre* (1984). His mathematical correspondence is at the Académie des Sciences in Paris. The three-volume *André Weil Oeuvres Scientifiques Collected Papers* (1979) consists of writings from 1927 through 1978 in French, German, and English, with commentary by Weil in French. His autobiography, *The Apprenticeship of a Mathematician* (translated from the French, 1992), covers Weil's life in detail up to his arrival in the United States, with a brief epilogue about his life in the Americas. *The Notices of the American Mathematical Society* (Apr. 1999) is a special issue devoted to Weil, with articles by several mathematicians who knew him. Obituaries are in the *New York Times* (10 Aug. 1998) and *Washington Post* (12 Aug. 1998).

HOWARD ALLEN

WEST, Dorothy (*b.* 2 June 1907 in Boston, Massachusetts; *d.* 16 August 1998 in Boston, Massachusetts), writer who was the last surviving member of the Harlem Renaissance.

West was the only child of Isaac Christopher West and Rachel Pease Benson. Her blue-eyed father, born a slave in Virginia, was freed at age seven. By age ten, he had learned reading, writing, and arithmetic and had started his own business, an ice-cream parlor in Springfield, Massachusetts, where he met West's mother. By the time his daughter was born, Isaac, known as the "Black Banana King," was the only black produce wholesaler in Boston, and his business was so successful that it was listed with Dun and Bradstreet.

Dorothy West, 1995. AP/WIDE WORLD PHOTOS

West's mother, a generation younger than Isaac, was herself the daughter of South Carolina slaves. West grew up with many of Rachel's twenty-two siblings, nieces, and nephews in her family's upper-middle-class home in Boston.

West was tutored at age two, attended school by age four, and by age seven was writing short stories. She was admitted to the prestigious Girls' Latin School at age ten, where she was placed in the sixth grade with mostly twelve-year-olds. When she was fourteen, one of her stories won the weekly fiction contest sponsored by the *Boston Post.* She continued to compete in that contest and often won. She graduated from Girls' Latin in 1923 at age sixteen and attended Boston University and, later, Columbia University in New York City.

In 1926 West tied for second place with Zora Neale Hurston in a contest sponsored by the Urban League's *Opportunity, A Journal of Negro Life,* for her story "The Typewriter." She traveled to New York City for the awards presentation and, once there, decided to stay. Coming from the white suburb of Brookline, Massachusetts, she had never seen so many black people as she saw in Harlem. She was the youngest member—called "The Kid" by the poet Langston Hughes—of the Harlem Renaissance. "The Typewriter" was published in the *Best Stories of 1926,* and some of West's other stories were published in the *Saturday*

Evening Quill, a publication of the Quill Club (a group of African-American writers in Boston), which she had joined in 1925.

In 1929 West had a small part in a production of the play *Porgy* and traveled to London with the cast. British audiences had difficulty understanding the black dialect, and the troupe returned to New York City within three months. In 1932 West traveled to the Soviet Union with Langston Hughes and other black artists to make a film called *Black and White,* about race relations in the United States. The project, labeled by the journalist George Schuyler, among others, as Communist propaganda, never materialized. With Hughes, West stayed in the Soviet Union for about a year, only returning home when her father died.

Back in New York City, West founded the magazine *Challenge* (1934), which she hoped would rekindle the spirit of the Harlem Renaissance that had subsided when the Great Depression began in 1929. Though she published stories by well-known black authors, she was criticized for being politically moderate and for not publishing lesser known and more innovative writers. West was disappointed in the quality of submissions, and by 1937 *Challenge* had failed. She then chose Richard Wright as associate editor of *New Challenge,* but after only one issue, in 1937, it too failed, partly because West, firmly rooted in middle-class life and at odds with Wright's leftist ideology, felt she was being used to disperse Communist propaganda. Despite its problems, *New Challenge* succeeded in publishing early stories by writers who later became famous, including Frank Yerby, Arna Bontemps, and Ralph Ellison.

To survive the depression years, West took a job as a relief (welfare) investigator in New York City. (Her 1940 short story "Mammy" is based in part on that experience.) West also worked in the Federal Writers Project of the Works Progress Administration (WPA), and began to publish stories in the *New York Daily News,* to which she contributed fiction until about 1960. Because many magazines refused to publish her work on the grounds that they would lose white readers, she called herself "the best known unknown writer of the time."

West moved to the town of Oak Bluffs on Martha's Vineyard in Massachusetts in the mid-1940s. There, she lived alone in the cottage her father had purchased as a summer home for the family in 1908 and wrote her semiautobiographical novel *The Living Is Easy* (1948), a book based on her parents' marriage. The novel offered a unique look at the urban New England black middle class and explored social climbing and snobbery. Reviews in several publications, including the *New York Times, Commonweal,* and the *New Yorker,* were mostly positive. The novel was reprinted in 1969, in 1982, the year West was honored at Boston University during Black History Month, and in 1987.

In 1965 West was hired by the *Vineyard Gazette* as a billing clerk. To supplement her income, she also worked as a cashier in a local restaurant, the Harborside Inn. She began writing the "Highlands Water Boy" nature column for the paper, and then the "Cottagers' Corner" column, named for a philanthropic group of black women who summered on the island. By 1975 she was writing the "Oak Bluffs" column, about year-round residents, a column she continued to produce until 1993. In 1991 Boston's WGBH-TV (PBS) produced a documentary about her.

Rediscovered and encouraged by Vineyard resident and Doubleday editor Jacqueline Kennedy Onassis, West published her second novel, *The Wedding,* written decades earlier, in 1995. West dedicated the novel to Onassis, writing that "though there was never such a mismatched pair in appearances, we were perfect partners." In that same year a collection of her stories and essays, *The Richer, the Poorer: Stories, Sketches, and Reminiscences,* was also published. At her ninetieth birthday in 1997, at a celebrity-filled party attended by more than 600 guests, First Lady Hillary Rodham Clinton called West "a national treasure." Acting Massachusetts governor Paul Cellucci declared 29 August "Dorothy West Day," and on Martha's Vineyard a road was renamed in her honor. *The Wedding* was produced for television by Oprah Winfrey in 1998.

After being hospitalized in May 1998 for a stomach aneurysm, West broke her hip. She died at age ninety-one at the New England Medical Center in Boston. Never married, she was survived by many first and second cousins. Following her cremation, a memorial service was held at the Union Chapel in Oak Bluffs on 22 August 1998.

During her lifetime, West published approximately forty short stories in addition to the two novels. She wrote about race and class stereotypes and about elitism based on light versus dark skin color, in both her columns and her fiction. (West herself was dark skinned, and less than five feet tall.) Her writing concerned psychological, emotional, and social issues as well as class, which she considered to be more important than race. Her prose was ironic and humorous; critics generally praised her observations more than they did her plots. She cared deeply about social justice, and her newspaper columns spoke of war and peace, children, and poverty. Her fifty-year publishing hiatus was due at least partly to her fear that *The Wedding* would be neither understood nor accepted during the socially turbulent 1960s. By the early 1980s, however, the feminist movement had rekindled interest in West's work, and she found a ready audience.

★

West's manuscripts and correspondence are held at Mugar Memorial Library at Boston University, with some early writings in the James Weldon Johnson Collection at Yale University. The *Vineyard Gazette* has a clippings file. The introduction to the 1969 edition of *The Living Is Easy* contains a biographical and critical assessment by Robert A. Bone, as does the afterword by Adelaide Cromwell Gulliver in the 1982 and 1987 editions. *The Richer, the Poorer* (1995) contains many autobiographical essays as well as stories. A posthumous collection of West's newspaper columns, *The Dorothy West Martha's Vineyard: Stories, Essays, and Reminiscences by Dorothy West Writing in the "Vineyard Gazette,"* by James Robert Saunders and Renae Nadine Shackelford, was published in 2001. Obituaries are in the *New York Times* and *Washington Post* (both 19 Aug. 1998), *Los Angeles Times* (20 Aug. 1998), and *Vineyard Gazette* (18 Aug. 1998). The Schlesinger Library at Radcliffe College has an oral history transcript (Genii Guinier, 1978) in the *Black Women Oral History Project Interviews* (1991), as well as the video *As I Remember It: A Portrait of Dorothy West*.

JANE BRODSKY FITZPATRICK

WHITNEY, Betsey Maria Cushing (*b.* 18 May 1908 in Baltimore, Maryland; *d.* 25 March 1998 in Manhasset, New York), philanthropist, socialite, and patron of the arts who, with her husband, Jock Whitney, amassed one of the nation's great art collections and served on the boards of the Whitney Museum of American Art, the John Hay Whitney Foundation, and the Association for Homemakers Service and as benefactor for New York Hospital–Cornell Medical Center (now New York Weill Cornell Medical Center) in New York City and North Shore University Hospital in Manhasset, New York.

Named after her maternal grandmother, Betsey Maria Cushing was the third of five children of Harvey William Cushing, a prominent neurosurgeon at Johns Hopkins University Hospital in Baltimore and the first Sterling Professor of Neurology at Yale, and Katharine Stone Crowell, a homemaker and the daughter of a socially prominent family from Cleveland, Ohio. When Whitney's father returned to teach at his alma mater, Harvard Medical School, and became surgeon in chief at Peter Bent Brigham Hospital in Boston, the family settled in the suburb of Brookline in 1912. There Whitney, with her sister Minnie, attended Miss May's School, a private day school, through her junior year, leaving when her father went on to a professorship at Yale Medical School. The school was strict, and students spoke only French. Betsey then attended Westover, a finishing school in Middlebury, Connecticut. Her father encouraged her to take "constructive courses" so that she would know how to do something useful if she ever had to earn her own living. In all other aspects of her life Whitney's mother was in control and insisted that her daughters learn to sew, create menus, cook, and master the fine art of entertaining. Katharine Cushing once told a columnist that she expected her girls "to marry into the highest level of European nobility or into America's moneyed aristocracy." Of the three daughters, Whitney was considered the most like her mother, accepting her manners and aspirations. She was a slim brunette, known in her debutante days for her beauty and charm.

As a twenty-two-year-old debutante, Whitney met James Roosevelt, son of Franklin Delano Roosevelt, who was then governor of New York, and Eleanor Roosevelt. Almost immediately they fell in love and quickly announced their engagement. Both Eleanor Roosevelt and her mother-in-law, Sara Delano Roosevelt, tried to dissuade the young couple from marriage. On 5 June 1930, just two days

Betsey Cushing Whitney with her husband, John Hay Whitney, 1957. ASSOCIATED PRESS AP

after Roosevelt's graduation from Harvard, they were married at Saint Paul's Episcopal Church in Brookline. As newlyweds, the couple lived with the Cushings while Roosevelt studied law at Boston University Law School. They later purchased a home in Framingham, Massachusetts, when Roosevelt went into the insurance business in September 1930.

When Franklin Delano Roosevelt (FDR) became president of the United States in 1933, Whitney, a favorite of FDR's, became the unofficial hostess at the White House during Eleanor's frequent absences. The couple lived nearby in Georgetown while Whitney's husband served as his father's aide. Whitney did not get along with Eleanor Roosevelt; the two women were both too strong-willed and too different in personal style and social preferences to coexist comfortably.

In 1938 James Roosevelt left his appointment to the president and went to Hollywood to work as an aide to Samuel Goldwyn. Whitney followed him to California, but they soon separated and were divorced in 1940. The couple had two daughters. Two years later, on 1 March 1942, she married John Hay ("Jock") Whitney, heir to one of America's greatest fortunes. The wedding took place in the Manhattan drawing room of her mother's East Eighty-sixth Street apartment. The couple honeymooned at Greenwood Plantation in Thomasville, Georgia, one of Jock Whitney's family estates. They returned with her two daughters to Washington, D.C., where Jock Whitney served Nelson Rockefeller in the Office of Coordinator of Inter-American Affairs. FDR was one of the first visitors at the Whitney home and continued to visit during their stay in Washington. Whitney's fondness for the president kept her from allowing Whitney to adopt her two daughters until 1949, long after FDR's death.

In 1957 President Dwight D. Eisenhower appointed Jock Whitney ambassador to the Court of Saint James's in London. The family moved to Winfield House in Regent's Park, the ambassador's official residence, where Whitney renewed her acquaintance with Elizabeth, now the Queen Mother. Jock Whitney was renown for his knowledge and long involvement with horse breeding and racing; this cemented the friendship of the royal family, also known for their love all things equestrian. Upon leaving London in 1961, Whitney remarked that she would "miss everything about London, even the weather." As a parting gift, the Whitneys loaned their art collection to the Tate Gallery in London for six weeks. It was the first time the collection, consisting of works by Henri Matisse, Vincent van Gogh, and Pablo Picasso, had been shown in one place. After they returned from England, Whitney's life revolved around her family at their Greentree estate in Manhasset, New York (Jock also shared ownership of Greentree Stud, a horse farm in Kentucky with his sister, Joan), and her husband's

business ventures, including the *New York Herald Tribune*. She also took an active role on the board of the John Hay Whitney Foundation and was involved in charitable works for the Museum of Modern Art, Yale University, and New York Hospital–Cornell Medical Center. But she spent the largest portion of her time and energy at North Shore University Hospital in Manhasset.

When Jock Whitney died in 1982, the majority of his vast estate went to his wife. The estate included a bequest of $5 million; the 500-acre Greentree estate in Manhasset; an apartment in New York City; a house in Surrey, England; Greenwood Plantation in Georgia; a summer house in Fishers Island, Connecticut; and a racing cottage in Saratoga Springs, New York. In addition, Whitney received his art collection. Three trust funds provided her with an annuity of $500,000 per year. She donated $8 million to the Yale Medical School, the largest gift in the school's history, and bequeathed fifteen major works by Picasso, van Gogh, Matisse, Henri Toulouse-Lautrec, and other masters to the National Gallery of Art in Washington, D.C., and to the Museum of Modern Art in New York City. At the time, their value was estimated at $300 million. The Yale Art Gallery in New Haven, Connecticut, and the National Portrait Gallery in Washington, D.C., each received a painting after her death.

Whitney established the Greentree Foundation in 1983 to assist local community groups, serving as the foundation's president, and she was a benefactor of North Shore University Hospital. The hospital was built on fifteen acres donated by Jock Whitney and his sister in the early 1950s. In 1990 Whitney made art history by selling, through Sotheby's auction house, one of Pierre-Auguste Renoir's most famous paintings, *At the Moulin de la Galette*. It set a record auction price for Impressionist art of $78.1 million, the second-highest price paid for any artwork sold at the auction. Jock Whitney had purchased it for $165,000 in 1929. Whitney died at North Shore University Hospital of heart failure. A memorial service was held at Christ Church in Manhasset on 25 April 1998. Whitney is buried at Christ Church Cemetery.

Although Whitney was noted for her social sense of propriety and harmony and her ability to create a cozy, down-to-earth setting in any of the family's residences, her philanthropic contributions to the arts, patient care, medical research and education, and community service left a permanent contribution to society.

★

David Grafton's book *The Sisters: Babe Mortimer Paley, Betsey Roosevelt Whitney, Minnie Astor Fosburgh—The Lives and Times of the Fabulous Cushing Sisters* (1992) is a comprehensive biography of the Cushing family. Biographical information is also in Elisabeth Bumiller, "The Last Princess," *New York Times Mag-*

azine (3 Jan. 1999). Obituaries are in the *New York Times* and *New York Newsday* (both 26 Mar. 1998), *Boston Globe* (27 Mar. 1998), and *London Daily Telegraph* (3 Apr. 1998).

CONNIE THORSEN

WHITNEY, Ruth Reinke (*b.* 23 July 1928 in Oshkosh, Wisconsin; *d.* 4 June 1999 in Irvington, New York), editor in chief of *Glamour* magazine for thirty years.

Born to Leonard Reinke, a tombstone engraver, and Helen Diestler, a homemaker, Whitney was the youngest of three children. In 1945 she won a four-year, full-tuition scholarship to Northwestern University in Evanston, Illinois, where she received her B.A. degree in English, with honors, in June 1949. She married Daniel A. Whitney, whom she met at the university, on 19 November 1949. Shortly thereafter, the couple moved to Irvington, New York. They had one son, Philip, born in 1963.

At five feet, nine inches tall and slim and elegant in appearance, the dry-humored Whitney was admired for her fearless journalistic stances and efficient management. Despite her public advocacy of many controversial positions, her friends and coworkers regarded her as a private person. Whitney's first job was as a copywriter at Time, Inc., where she worked from 1949 to 1953. She became a copychief at *Better Living* magazine in 1954, and she was promoted to editor in chief in 1955. She left in 1956 to become associate editor of the monthly magazine *Seventeen*. In 1962 Whitney was promoted to executive editor, serving in that capacity until the latter part of 1967.

S. I. Newhouse, Jr., chairman of Condé Nast Publications, Inc., hired Whitney to be editor in chief of *Glamour* in 1967. Her name first appeared on the masthead in January 1968. When she took over, the advertisement revenues were $11.7 million per year, and thirty years later they totaled $137.3 million. The first issue under Whitney's leadership carried a guest editorial by Gloria Steinem stating, "Every value system needs to be questioned and reevaluated regularly." This questioning attitude was to mark Whitney's stewardship. Although Whitney never wrote editorial notes in the magazine, she invited well-known guest editors to address important social issues. She also read the 2,000 monthly letters from readers and authorized periodic surveys to ascertain reader response on controversial topics, such as contraceptives, the Vietnam War, and interracial dating.

Although most cover girls were blond and blue-eyed, in 1968 Whitney convinced Condé Nast to put a black woman, Kiti Kironde II, a college student from Newfoundland, on the cover of the August *Glamour,* making it the first mainstream American women's magazine to do so. Fearful that sales would dip, Whitney and Condé Nast were surprised when the issue earned the magazine its highest sales to date. Her response to the fear of offending some advertisers, who had now become the major source of revenue, or readers was, "If six months go by and you've offended neither readers nor your advertisers, you're not doing your job." Beverly Johnson, a black model, appeared on the October 1969 cover, and she and other black models were featured inside the magazine and on at least two covers per year thereafter. The magazine's higher circulation led to the placement of black models in its advertisements as early as 1971.

In recognition of the changing needs of college students and working women, in the 1970s *Glamour* introduced several how-to guides, written by specialists; for example, *How to Do Anything Better* and *How to Get More for Your Money,* which were aimed at "young women who have just begun to make and spend money." Whitney's awareness that the *Glamour* reader was on a modest budget brought about *The Penny Pincher's Guide to College—How to Cut Costs on Clothes, Textbooks, Health, and Beauty.* In addition to new columns about home economics, others were added regarding health, love, and sex.

In fact, change was the key focus of the magazine. A feminist and board member of the National Organization for Women (NOW) Legal Defense Fund, Whitney encouraged features on women as practitioners of careers that were less traditional at the time: lawyer, sportswriter, or engineer. The column called "18" changed to "The Breaking Away Years," and later to "On Your Own," reflecting an enlarged readership of women between ages eighteen and thirty-five. The "College" column, renamed "Education," expanded coverage "to meet the needs of all women—not just those who choose traditional four-year college programs." In contrast to other editors of women's magazines, Whitney objected to the use of unusually thin models, preferring instead models who looked more like the readers. When her staff wrote articles on sexiness, they related it to the notion of the "new woman" and the evolution of the "new man."

In the 1980s under Whitney's leadership, the magazine added "Washington Report," an update on legislation and new women in Congress, and "New Tech," a regular feature to help make women comfortable with computers. In January 1987 a five-year national survey regarding sex, money, work, and family became the basis for more columns and feature articles. For example, "The New Racism: Don't Deny, Ignore, or Accept It," in September 1987, addressed resurgent racism. *Glamour* was in the vanguard of the feminist movement and was an advocate of a social agenda—help for battered women, appointment of qualified women to key government positions, and more research on women's health issues—that would take more than twenty years to realize.

The 1990s yielded further changes in *Glamour,* with new columns that indicated Whitney's constant rethinking of the magazine format. The January 1990 issue devoted twenty-four pages to "Men and Romance," yet its lead article was "The Sexually Confident Woman," continuing *Glamour*'s tradition of balance in its points of view. Whitney also introduced a feature, the "Notable Women of the Year."

Despite the assurance of Steven Florio, the president of Condé Nast, in September 1997 that Whitney would retire when she felt ready, she was asked by S. I. Newhouse, Jr., the chairman of the company, to resign on 17 August 1998, when she was seventy years old. Her last day as editor in chief was 5 October 1998. Whitney was replaced by Bonnie Fuller, who had been for eighteen months the editor in chief of *Cosmopolitan,* one of *Glamour*'s chief competitors during Whitney's tenure. Whitney expressed misgivings about her successor, whom she did not consider a serious journalist. Fuller served less than three years at *Glamour* before she was asked to resign in May 2001. This brief tenure made Whitney's thirty-year direction all the more extraordinary.

Because of her impact on women's magazines, especially through her journalistic seriousness, Whitney was elected president of the American Society of Magazine Editors (ASME) from 1975 to 1977. She continued to serve on its executive committee from 1989 to 1992. Her success as an editor was confirmed by a Matrix Award from Women in Communication in 1980, and she garnered multiple awards from the ASME: two awards for *Glamour* for general excellence, in 1981 and 1991; one in the category of public interest in 1992; and another for her personal service in 1997. She received the Cosmetic Executive Women Achiever Award in 1993. When accepting the Magazine Publishers of America Henry Johnson Fisher Award in 1996, she said: "Let's all take more risks more often— editors and publishers alike." She was admitted to the ASME Hall of Fame in 1996.

A supporter of younger generations, Whitney accepted at least one intern to work at the magazine annually. She declined parties to celebrate her twentieth, twenty-fifth, and thirtieth anniversaries at *Glamour,* requesting instead that two scholarships be established in her name at the New-house School of Public Communications at Syracuse University. She was also a founding member of a "Council of 100 Women" at her alma mater, which mentors undergraduates. Northwestern University recognized her contributions with an alumni medal in 1995.

Whitney died in June 1999 of Lou Gehrig's disease, amyotrophic lateral sclerosis, at her home in Irvington. Her husband predeceased her in 1995. She was survived by her son.

★

No biography exists on Whitney. Cynthia White, *Women's Magazines, 1693–1968* (1970), provides information about *Seventeen* during Whitney's editorial tenure and about *Glamour* just prior to her appointment there. Condé Nast has the complete collection of *Glamour* in print. The best articles about Whitney are Robin Pogrebin, "The Long-Term Low Profile Behind the Buzz at Glamour," *New York Times* (8 Sept. 1997), which evaluated Whitney's career on the occasion of her thirtieth anniversary at *Glamour;* and E. Meer, "Glamour Queen," *People* (5 Oct. 1998), an evaluation of Whitney on her last day at *Glamour.* Richard Turner and Yahlin Chang, "Styles and Substance," *Newsweek* (24 Aug. 1998), and Ginia Bellafante, "A Rival Takes the Reins," *Time* (24 Aug. 1998), are about Bonnie Fuller's replacement of Whitney. An obituary is in the *New York Times* (5 June 1999).

BARBARA L. GERBER

WHYTE, William Hollingsworth, Jr. (*b.* 1 October 1917 in West Chester, Pennsylvania; *d.* 12 January 1999 in New York City), writer and social critic best known for his book *The Organization Man* (1956) and for many penetrating books and essays on mid-century American culture.

Whyte was the first of two children of William Hollingsworth Whyte, Sr., a railroad executive, and Louise Troth

William H. Whyte, Jr., 1979. AP/WIDE WORLD PHOTOS

Price. His parents divorced soon after the birth of his brother Richard, and his father soon married Margaret Parry. In his youth, Whyte was close to his family members, including his formidable "Grandmother Price," his stepmother, and stepbrother James Parry. Whyte was raised in the East End section of West Chester, and spent many summers at the bustling Price farm in Wellfleet, Massachusetts. He attended an Episcopalian boarding school, Saint Andrews School in Middletown, Delaware, from 1931 to 1935, where he was editor of the school newspaper. This led Whyte to major in English at Princeton University from 1935 to 1939, where he won an undergraduate playwriting contest, was an editor of *Nassau Lit,* and graduated cum laude. As World War II loomed, Whyte curtailed his unfulfilling first job as a trainee and sales manager for Vick Chemical Company in eastern Kentucky from 1939 to 1941. He volunteered for the U.S. Marine Corps in October 1941 "because it was the best, and I wanted to be part of it." Whyte later authored *A Time of War* (2000), a chronicle of his experiences with the First Marine Division in Guadalcanal, "the most exciting four months of my life." By the end of the war Whyte was a captain.

Following a Marine Corp sergeant's jibes at his first roll call on 28 October 1941, Whyte changed his name. Whyte recalled, "It was my first Marine Corps lesson: Keep it simple. From then on I was William H. Whyte, Jr." From boyhood, those close to Whyte knew him as "Holly," the same moniker as his father. He is not to be confused with several other prominent William Whytes, including the slightly older, similarly long-lived and prolific sociologist William Foote Whyte (*b.* 1914).

In June 1946 Whyte's wartime articles for the *Marine Corps Gazette* helped him join *Fortune* magazine, first as a staff writer, then as an associate editor in 1948, and later as assistant managing editor in 1953. He headed the *Fortune* study on communications from 1949 to 1951, which led to his first book, *Is Anybody Listening? How and Why U.S. Business Fumbles When It Talks with Human Beings* (1952), coauthored with the editors of *Fortune.* The book was a well-received critique of the failure of U.S. corporations to "sell" their free enterprise system to the U.S. public, and was excerpted in *Life* magazine (7 January 1952). Whyte won the Benjamin Franklin magazine writing award in 1953.

The second of Whyte's dozen books was his classic, *The Organization Man* (1956), a sweeping critique of U.S. corporate culture. It had emerged from a series of essays in *Fortune* in which Whyte compared postwar graduates unfavorably with his own prewar 1939 graduating class at Princeton; detailed the creation of a nomadic new breed of U.S. "Management Men" willing to relocate often to rise up the corporate ladder; decried the complacency of America's burgeoning middle-class suburbs; blasted the growing

use of preemployment selection tests; and faulted corporate programs in management training. The book's jacket described "the clash between the individualistic beliefs he is supposed to follow and the collective life he actually lives—and his search for a faith to bridge the gap." The tome's unblinking, on-target analysis stirred a national debate, sold over 2 million copies in a dozen languages, and was recognized by the American Library Association with its first Liberty and Justice Book Award (1957). Like Alexis de Tocqueville a century earlier, Whyte revered the American tradition of individualism as superior to the conformism, obedience, and collectivism he saw in America's battlefield foes—Germany, Italy, Japan, Russia—yet Whyte was saddened to see burgeoning postwar U.S. corporations eroding this American mettle from within.

For Whyte, the rapid postwar growth of huge new corporations and conglomerates offered such a safe haven and promise of advancement that they were molding a new breed of American manager. This organization man was a conformist who valued "team-playing" above individualism, was obedient to superiors, autocratic over subordinates, loyal to his firm, cautious in his decisions, security-conscious, traditional, and noncreative. Whyte rued this new "social ethic," which he saw eclipsing Max Weber's traditional "Protestant ethic" of self-reliance, ambition, and individualism. Through the end of the century, Whyte's *Organization Man* continued to be described as "the most compelling portrait of middle-class Americans at midcentury and the starting point for all subsequent investigations of their legacy" (Leinberger and Tucker, 1991).

Another series of six *Fortune* articles that ran from 1957 to 1958 led to a third book, *The Exploding Metropolis* (1958), critiquing the rapid and sprawling postwar growth of U.S. cities and suburbs. Hefty royalties permitted Whyte to leave his lucrative *Fortune* post in 1958, "to pursue my growing interest in the environment and open spaces." That year a chance encounter on Madison Avenue with Conrad Wirth, director of the National Park Service, led Whyte to a $35,000 grant. The first of several from the National Geographic Society's Committee for Research and Exploration, its purpose was to study urban and suburban life with an eye toward social policy. Whyte's one brush with academe was a one-year appointment as Distinguished Visiting Professor of Urban Sociology at Hunter College of the City University of New York from 1970 to 1971. From 1970 to 1986, with pen or camera in hand, Whyte directed the Street Life Project on Midtown Manhattan streets, with Laurance S. Rockefeller as his patron. Whyte published a series of treatises on how the suburbs or cities stifled American culture and what might be done about it: *Conservation Easements* (1959); *Open Space Action* (1962); *Cluster Development* (1964); *The Last Landscape* (1968); *Plan for the City of New York* (1969); *The Social Life of Small Urban Spaces*

(1980); *The City as Dwelling: Walking, Sitting, Shaping* (1980); and *City: Rediscovering the Center* (1988). For Whyte, U.S. suburbs were a bastion of mediocrity, complacency, and "gated communities" while the unregulated growth of cities also had its perils of congestion, crowding, crime, and disorganization. A lifelong lover of New York City, Whyte felt the ideal community was a well-planned city, "vibrant with a nice bustle of humanity." He was a champion of Midtown parks and zoning ordinances based on empirical research. Rather than letting builders choke cities by building to maximum densities, Whyte advocated "easements" to allow unusually tall buildings only in proportion to the size of adjacent street-level public-access space provided by these developers. He felt this would result in an optimal balance of cost-effective, high-density housing interspersed with the natural beauty of well-used public parks and, indirectly, lower crime rates, taxes, congestion, and transportation problems. In 1975 a front-page article in the *New York Times* hailed the city's adoption of Whyte's open-space zoning plan, laid forth in *Plan for the City of New York* (1969), as a model for other turnaround cities. His use of time-lapse photography and other sophisticated methods made him a frequent consultant for urban planning and the focus and narrator of a highly visual "Nova" documentary on city life (1980).

On a personal level, Whyte was a lifelong Episcopalian and a Democrat, with a strikingly cheerful, affable way about him. He had hazel eyes, brown hair, and 170 pounds on a five-foot, eleven-inch frame. At age forty-seven he wed fashion designer Jenny Bell Bechtel in October 1964, and they raised their only daughter in their Manhattan townhouse at 175 East Ninety-fourth Street.

Through the 1990s Whyte worked with his sedulous editor-turned-friend Albert LaFarge on his contracted memoirs, but failing health prevented completion, except for two volumes with Fordham University Press that appeared just after his death. One was *A Time of War* (2000), on his Marine Corps years, prepared with his wife and stepbrother James Parry, a writer for the *Wall Street Journal*. The other was a finely annotated reader compiled by LaFarge, *The Essential William H. Whyte* (2000). From these two volumes and his other writings, at least two ironies emerge about Whyte's long and prolific career. First, Whyte's deep disdain for the organizational life that he saw suppressing our individualism contrasted with his deep affection for the Marine Corps, where he was impressed by his sergeants' skills "at putting us lowly beginners down and then building us up, so that we can say we are Marines"—even to the point that he modified his own name. Second was Whyte's odd place within the behavioral sciences. Others have variously labeled Whyte a sociologist, pop psychologist, anthropologist, or urban planner, but his own proud self-description was a "layman" writing for

other laymen. Whyte's redoubtable skills in behavioral research were self-taught since he held no membership in behavioral science associations and no graduate degree. In fact, at *Fortune,* Whyte went so far as to use the fatuous pseudonym "Otis Binet Stanford" for his more vitriolic antipsychology articles like "The Fallacies of Personality Testing" (1954) or "The Case for the Universal Card" (1955). His contempt for testing and social engineering to match individual humans with the organizations they inhabit contrasted with Whyte's own later fame in learning and applying scientific methods to test how urban environments could be engineered to match the individual humans who inhabit them. It was these award-winning ergonomic research skills coupled with Whyte's passion for city life that made him such an effective champion of urban planning. When asked by Adam Smith in a 1990s television interview to name his three favorite U.S. cities, Whyte crisply replied, "New York, New York, New York." From the 1940s on, Whyte remained a proud New Yorker until his death at age eighty-one from complications following bypass surgery. He was interred at his family's plot in West Chester.

★

The best sources of information on Whyte are his own books, as well as an article he wrote, "Standing on Those Corners, Watching All the Folks Go By," *Smithsonian* (1 Feb. 1989). Secondary sources are Albert LaFarge, ed., *The Essential William H. Whyte* (2000), and Paul Leinberger and Bruce Tucker, *The New Individualists: The Generation After "The Organization Man"* (1991). Obituaries are in the *New York Times* (13 Jan. 1999) and *Washington Post* and *Los Angeles Times* (both 14 Jan. 1999).

HAROLD TAKOOSHIAN

WILLIAMS, Joe (*b.* 12 December 1918 in Cordele, Georgia; *d.* 29 March 1999 in Las Vegas, Nevada), eminent singer, known as the "Emperor of Jazz," who was able to deliver blues, ballads, and standards with heartfelt tone and impeccable timing.

Williams was born and christened Joseph Goreed, the only child of Willie Goreed, a farm laborer in the small lumbering community of Osilla, Georgia, and Anne Beatrice Gilbert, a cook and organist. There is no record of Williams's birth because the state of Georgia did not keep birth or death records until 1921. Shortly after he was born, his mother took Williams to live in the home of her parents. Determined that her son would not have to endure the barriers that she had faced as a black woman in the South, Gilbert decided to move to Chicago, leaving Williams behind to be cared for by her mother and sister. When Wil-

Joe Williams, 1996. JACK VARTOOGIAN

liams was four years old, his grandmother and aunt took him to Chicago to live with his mother. After settling in Chicago, Williams attended Carter Grammar School. Later he attended the predominantly white Austin Otis Grammar School up to eighth grade, where he finished in the top 10 percent of his class. Williams found joy in singing the spirituals he heard in the church where his mother played the organ and his aunt sang in the choir. His mother began to teach him to play piano, and he soon was able to finger songs on his own.

Williams listened to jazz and opera on the radio, particularly Ethel Waters, whose precise diction and deep emotion made a lasting impression on his style. At the early age of fourteen, Williams joined a gospel quartet, the Jubilee Temple Boys. His baritone voice led the group in numerous performances throughout Chicago. At age fifteen Williams was found to have tuberculosis; one lung was collapsed as treatment. Amazingly, his voice was not damaged. At age sixteen he was singing solo at formal events with local bands, earning as much as five dollars a night. He soon dropped out of high school to help support the family. In 1934 his family decided that he would have greater success if he adopted a stage name. In a family meeting it was decided that his name would be changed from Goreed to Williams. His first few solo engagements led to work with the bands of Joe Long and Erskine Tate.

Williams's first full-time job came at an all-white club called Kitty Davis's. Hired to clean the restrooms, he sang with the band in evening performances and kept his tips,

which would frequently total twenty dollars a night. His first major break came in 1938, when he sang with the clarinet and saxophone master Jimmie Noone on the CBS radio network. It was the big band era, and remote broadcasting brought the big band sound into homes. According to Leslie Grouse, "Williams found great satisfaction in the broadcast experience. It is where he educated himself about the audience's ear, the awareness of being heard once, and the importance of making a lingering impression." Williams toured the Midwest with the Les Hite band in 1939 and 1940 and between engagements with Noone. In 1941 Williams joined the saxophonist Coleman Hawkins's big band until it dissolved in 1942. For steady employment, Williams became the doorman and security guard at the Regal Theater in Chicago, where he met leading musicians of the jazz and rhythm and blues circuit, among them Lionel Hampton. In 1942 Williams joined Hampton in performances at the Tic Toc Club in Boston, working on the road with Dinah Washington, and touring for six weeks as a replacement for Big Joe Turner. Williams's work ended when Hampton's former singer returned. By that time Williams was in great demand.

Williams married Wilma Cole in 1942; they divorced in 1946. He then married Ann Kirksey in 1946 and was divorced in 1950. Williams experienced a nervous breakdown in 1947 and entered the Elgin State Hospital in Elgin, Illinois, where he stayed for a year. In 1950 he worked as a door-to-door salesman, selling Fuller Brush cosmetics. This gave him time to regain his strength and motivation, slowly rebuilding his reputation of electrifying audiences at the Club DeLisa; recording his first record with Red Saunders, *In the Evening;* and singing with George Shearing's quintet. In 1951 he married Lemma Reid; they had two children. Constant travel affected his family life. After several difficult years Williams and Lemma separated, and they divorced in 1964.

Williams's first opportunity to work with Count Basie came in the early 1950s, when disc jockey Daddy O-Daily secured an engagement for him to sing for the most powerful bandleader of that era. In 1954, when Basie established a new band and was performing in Chicago, Williams joined the Count Basie Orchestra on a regular basis and remained with the band until 1961. With Basie, Williams was able to introduce his own repertory, using his own soulful techniques and style. In 1955 Williams recorded what came to be known as his signature song, "Everyday (I Have the Blues)," arranged by Ernie Wilkins, which was the first major hit for Basie in fifteen years. Williams also won his first *Down Beat* magazine international critics poll award as best male band singer and *Down Beat's* New Star Award. He made his first television appearance that year on the CBS show *Music 55.* In 1957 the Count Basie Orchestra played at the Waldorf-Astoria's

Starlight Roof on same bill with Sarah Vaughan, the first performance by African-American artists at the Waldorf. In 1959 the Count Basie Orchestra toured Europe. While Williams was in England, he met an Englishwoman, Jillean Milne Hughes-D'Aeth; they married on 7 January 1964.

During the 1960s Williams's style was changing, and interest was waning in Basie's "blues" regimentation. Williams's compelling interest in ballads created a new musical venue to showcase his talent and skill as a singer. He decided to leave Basie's band. Without remorse, Basie agreed to let him go, giving him valuable advice and establishing engagements that would get him started in his solo career. In January 1961 Williams gave his last performance with the Count Basie Orchestra at the Apollo Theater in New York City.

In 1962 Williams retained John Levy as his manager. Levy was a longtime friend from Chicago who already was managing such artists as Nancy Wilson, George Shearing, and Julian ("Cannonball") Adderley. After Williams's marriage to Hughes-D'Aeth, Levy, along with Hughes-D'Aeth, formed a strong support system for him. They maintained his schedule, allowing him to concentrate on his singing and performances. While many jazz musicians struggled to find jobs, Williams was unaffected because his music appealed to a broader audience. He worked regularly and appeared as a frequent guest on several talk shows. In the mid-1980s he returned to television, playing Bill Cosby's father-in-law, Grandpa Al, on *The Cosby Show*. Although Williams kept busy forty weeks of the year on solo engagements, he never turned down an offer for reunions with Basie's band until Basie's death in 1984. At year earlier, his star was placed next to Basie's on the Walk of Fame in Hollywood. In 1984 he won a Grammy Award for his release of *Nothin' but the Blues*.

Williams received honorary doctorates of music from Berklee School of Music in Boston (1988) and Hamilton College of New York (1991). In 1997 he was inducted into the International Jazz Hall of Fame. He was an avid golfer and played until respiratory problems prevented him from playing. Williams died from a respiratory ailment in Las Vegas, Nevada.

It is often said that Joe Williams never had a bad or dull performance, nor did he ever miss an engagement. He was always in control and exciting to hear. Some say that he could sing better with a cold than other singers with their best voices. Leonard Feather in *Pros Folios* described Williams as "utterly lacking affectation and thoroughly versed in the ways of keeping an audience engrossed, entertained, and enthralled." Williams's wife, Hughes-D'Aeth, noted that Williams has never been appreciated fully as an artist. With his special sense of the audience, he knew what moved people. Live performances were his forte, making him one of the most exciting big band singers ever.

★

Williams wrote "Where I Stand" as guest columnist for the *Las Vegas Sun* (1 Aug. 1998). Leslie Gourse has written the only full-length biography of Williams's life, *Every Day: The Story of Joe Williams* (1985). Other good biographical sources include Devra Hall, *Pros Folios* (1986); *Contemporary Black Biography,* vol. 25 (2000); and *Contemporary Musicians,* vol. 11 (1994). Obituaries are in the *Las Vegas Review-Journal* (30 Mar. 1999) and the *Chicago Tribune* and *Las Vegas Sun* (both 31 Mar. 1999).

JOHNNIEQUE B. LOVE

WILLIAMS, Sherley Anne (*b.* 25 August 1944 in Bakersfield, California; *d.* 6 July 1999 in San Diego, California), poet, novelist, playwright, literary critic, and educator well known for her contribution to neoblack literature and her historical novel *Dessa Rose* (1986).

Williams was the third of four daughters of Jesse Winson Williams and Lena Lelia Marie Siler, both migrant farm laborers. From early childhood, Williams had to overcome the difficulties of growing up in a low-income housing project in Fresno, California. Her hardships intensified after her father died of tuberculosis when she was eight and her mother died when she was sixteen. Williams supported herself by picking cotton in the fields where her parents used to work for their livelihood. The challenges of her struggling childhood provided much of the impetus for Williams's writing in later years.

Of her three sisters, Williams was closest to Ruby (Birdson), who became her mentor and guardian after the death of her parents. She attended Edison Junior High School in Fresno, California. With inspiration from her sister and her chemistry teacher at school, Williams became interested in higher studies and devoted herself to reading about the black experience, and authors including Sterling Brown, Langston Hughes, and Eartha Kitt shaped the ideas she later developed in her own works. Williams received a B.A. degree in history from Fresno State College (now known as California State University, Fresno) in 1966. She started graduate work at Howard University but left the university in 1967. Between 1970 and 1972 she worked as a community educator at Federal City College, Washington, D.C. She also received an M.A. degree in American literature from Brown University in 1972.

Of medium height and build, Williams had dark brown eyes and a wonderful voice; whenever she was asked to speak, she was engaging and profound. In 1972 and 1973 Williams was associate professor of English at California State University, Fresno. She joined the department of English at the University of California, San Diego, in 1973 and continued to teach at the university until her death.

There she served as chair of the department of literature from 1976 to 1978. Williams was named Fulbright lecturer at the University of Ghana in 1984. She also served as visiting professor at Cornell University, Stanford University, Sweet Briar College (Virginia), and the University of Southern California. The alumni association of the University of California, San Diego, named Williams Distinguished Professor of the Year in 1987.

Williams's writing career began with "Tell Martha Not to Moan," a short story published in 1967. This was followed by *Give Birth to Brightness: A Thematic Study in Neo-Black Literature* (1972), a book of literary criticism that helped launch her career as an important neoblack writer. In this book, Williams explores how the black hero evolved in African American literature, specifically focusing on such authors as Amiri Baraka, James Baldwin, and Ernest Gaines. Her study of the black hero involves a poignant analysis of the fundamental difference between the African-American literary tradition and the western tradition and the way in which the hero is characterized in each. Williams underscores the importance in black literature of exploring "the indigenous currents of Black experiences."

Written in the blues tradition, *The Peacock Poems* was published in 1975. This autobiographical collection of poetry documented the poet's childhood and the life of her only child, John Malcolm. The volume was nominated for the Pulitzer Prize and National Book Award in 1976. Williams received an Emmy Award for a televised reading of poems from her second volume of poetry, *Some One Sweet Angel Chile* (1982), also written in the blues tradition. In both of her poetry collections, Williams foregrounds the struggle of working class people, including her own family, while paying tribute to their enduring spirit. In almost all her writings, Williams demonstrated that "Blues is a basis of historical continuity for black people. It is a ritualized way of talking," she said in an interview for *Black Women Writers at Work* (1983).

In Williams's historical novel, *Dessa Rose* (1986), the theme of slave rebellion is interwoven with the account of the relationship between a pregnant slave woman, Dessa, and a white woman named Rufel who helps Dessa escape and thus elude capture for crimes, including murder, against white men. Rufel is instrumental in ensuring Dessa's freedom, and she also suckles Dessa's newborn baby as her own, creating a bond beyond races. Williams also made contributions to the field of drama and children's literature. Her one-act play *Letters from a New England Negro* was performed at the National Black Theatre Festival in 1991 and at the Chicago International Theatre Festival in 1992. *Working Cotton* (1992), a children's tale, earned Williams an American Library Association Caldecott Medal and a Coretta Scott King Award.

Williams was an active member of the Christian Fellowship Congregational Church, United Church of Christ, and a driving force in creating an annual endowment fund event at the church to give support to six historic black colleges and universities in the southern part of the United States. During her tenure at the University of California, San Diego, she lived in the Emerald Hill section of San Diego at 5595 Fifty-sixth Place. Williams died at age fifty-four of cancer at the Kaiser Permanente Hospital and is buried at Greenwood Mausoleum in San Diego.

The *New York Times* noted that in her works Williams "fused her experiences in the dusty cotton fields and fruit orchards of the San Joaquin Valley with historical research to articulate the African American experience." The energy and vitality of her works draw from her passion for the blues tradition and the intimacy with which she shared the experiences of the working class people, especially lower-income black women, their pain and despair along with the triumphs in their daily lives. In Williams's writings, the blues theme, black history, and black dialect intersect and intermingle with her interest in exploring interpersonal relationships beyond races.

★

Claudia Tate, ed., *Black Women Writers at Work* (1983), includes an interview with Williams addressing the pivotal concerns of her works. Another important interview appears in Shirley M. Jordan, *Broken Silences: Interviews with Black and White Women Writers* (1993). Melissa Walker's chapter on Williams in *Down from the Mountaintop: Black Women's Novels in the Wake of the Civil Rights Movement, 1966–1989* (1991), is an interesting analysis of the interplay between historical issues and ahistorical themes in *Dessa Rose*. An obituary is in the *New York Times* (14 July 1999).

SAIYEDA KHATUN

WILLS, Helen Newington (*b.* 6 October 1905 in Centerville, California; *d.* 1 January 1998 in Carmel, California), one of the greatest women tennis players of all time; her poise and championship play raised women's tennis into a major sport internationally.

Wills was the only child of Clarence Wills, a surgeon, and Catherine Anderson, who had been trained as a teacher. Because Wills was not a robust child, her father encouraged her in a variety of physical activities to improve her health. When she was eight, he suggested tennis, playing with her every afternoon and teaching her the fundamentals of the game. By age fourteen, having beaten most of her opponents on the public courts, she was discovered by coach William C. "Pop" Fuller of the Berkeley Tennis Club. Fuller spoke of Wills's special gift: the rare ability to concentrate on the shot to be made, with everything else excluded.

Helen Wills. INTERNATIONAL TENNIS HALL OF FAME

Even at a young age, Wills displayed extraordinary co-ordination and stamina, along with mental alertness and self-control. Fuller arranged matches for her every day, and put her up against the best men players at the Berkeley Club. Dressed in her schoolgirl tennis outfits and signature white visor, pigtails flying, Wills was a formidable player, determined to defeat every opponent. She learned by watching the best players of the day. The game she developed depended on sheer power, and she controlled play simply by hitting the ball so hard, thus overpowering her opponents.

Wills won the California State Women's Championship in 1921 when she was fifteen. The next year, she surprised herself and others by reaching the singles final of the National Women's Championship at Forest Hills in New York City. She lost to eight-time winner Molla Mallory, but, with Marion Z. Jessup, captured the doubles championship. During the summer, she played against Mallory several times and later said her best lessons came from playing the champion. She learned the value of power and accuracy, a steady game, and endurance. By 1923 her play was awesome, and, at age seventeen, she defeated Mallory, winning the first of her seven U.S. singles titles at Forest

Hills (1923–1925, 1927–1929, 1931). In 1923 she was invited to play in the Wrightman Cup, the team championship between Great Britain and the United States. She played as a member of the team from 1923 to 1938, winning 18 singles matches for the United States.

With her 1923 national win, Wills began her fifteen-year dominance of women's tennis. She was ranked number one in the world from 1927 to 1934, and, in the 1924 Olympics, she won gold medals in both singles and doubles. Adored by fans all over the world, her fame reached far beyond tennis.

In 1926 Wills played in what was proclaimed by newspapers worldwide as the match of the century. Set on the French Riviera, this much ballyhooed extravaganza pitted the twenty-year-old Wills, christened the "American Girl," against the great French tennis star Suzanne Lenglen. At age twenty-six, Lenglen was acknowledged as the preeminent women's tennis player of her time, and was so beloved by the French that she was called a goddess. This historic match remains a testimony to the skill and the dogged determination of both players. The highly emotional Lenglen was a superb tactician who beat the less-experienced Wills in two sets. Yet the hard-fought win left Lenglen sobbing and devastated; the loser, Wills, was confident and encouraged.

Press coverage of that match, coming after the 1924 Olympics, engendered widespread interest in women's tennis and gave Wills international celebrity status. She had cut off her pigtails, and her bobbed hair and stylish beauty symbolized the new American woman. It was suddenly fashionable to be athletic. Like Lenglen before her, Wills adopted tennis clothes that suited her personality and is credited with helping reform what had been a restrictive dress code. She abandoned long-sleeved blouses, long-trailing skirts, and silk stockings, saying the long skirts were a mental and physical hazard. When she opted instead for a knee-length pleated white skirt, sleeveless white blouse, red sweater, and her signature white visor, women everywhere followed suit.

In 1927 Wills became the first American woman to win at Wimbledon since 1905. She would go on to win a record-breaking eight Wimbledon singles titles, an achievement that would stand until Martina Navratilova won a ninth championship in 1990. Wills's string of 180 consecutive singles wins—during which she did not lose a set—lasted from 1927 until 1933. This record was not broken in the twentieth century and may never be surpassed. On 23 December 1929, she married financier Frederick Moody, and henceforth played as Helen Wills Moody.

Because of her unsmiling demeanor and legendary concentration, Wills was called "Little Miss Poker Face." Although at times she played when injured or in pain, she never complained or made excuses. Because she was personally aloof, other players often thought her cold and un-friendly.

After Lenglen, whom she admired, her most noted rival was Helen Jacobs. In 1933 they met in the singles finals at Forest Hills, with Jacobs the defending champion. Although they played each other twenty times in their careers, Jacobs's only victory—won by default—was in this 1933 match. Undecided about playing because she had been bothered by back pain, Wills finally decided to enter the tournament. Against Jacobs, she lost the first set 8–6, but then won the second set 6–3. However, after falling behind 3–0 in the decisive third set, she informed the umpire that she was defaulting. Her withdrawal caused a public outcry, and later Wills said she would have rather passed out on the court than defaulted as she did. It was soon learned, however, that she had been playing with a dislocated lumbar vertebra. She spent time in the hospital and then took two years to recover sufficiently to return to competitive tennis. In 1933 she made her final appearance at Forest Hills, but she and Jacobs met again in 1935, this time at Wimbledon. In the match, Jacobs held match point in the third set but missed what appeared to be an easy shot. Wills went on to win the match and the championship. That year the Associated Press selected her the female athlete of the year.

In 1938 Wills and Jacobs again competed in the Wimbledon final, with many believing that Jacobs would win. But she was playing with a badly injured leg, and during the match she came down hard on it, tearing an already ailing Achilles tendon. By the end of the match, Jacobs was immobile, but though racked in pain, she did not forfeit. Wills won her eighth Wimbledon title, but it was considered a tainted victory. Wills then eased herself out of competitive tennis, although she continued to play well into her eighties. She was elected to the International Tennis Hall of Fame in 1959.

Outside tennis, Wills led a charmed life. She graduated from the University of California with Phi Beta Kappa honors in 1928, majoring in fine arts, and painted all her life. She traveled with the rich and famous. Charlie Chaplin said the most beautiful sight he had ever seen was Wills playing tennis. The muralist Diego Rivera chose her as the model of his two-story mural, *The Riches of California*, in the former San Francisco Stock Exchange. In those years, the tennis world frowned on the word "professional," but Wills managed to live in luxury, and she was well provided for by the tennis world. Newspapers and magazines paid her to write articles and bought her sketches of tennis scenes. She sold her art and published several books, including her memoir *Fifteen–Thirty* in 1937.

In 1937 Wills divorced Frederick Moody, and two years later she married Aidan Roark, a film writer and noted polo player. Their marriage ended in divorce in the early 1970s.

About the same time, Wills's parents, who had always been her closest companions, became invalids, and she dropped everything to care for them. Wills herself had no children.

In the summer of 1984, after an absence of sixty years, tennis returned to the Olympics. Wills, as the last surviving member of the 1924 American Olympic tennis team, wrote a special message to the players: "We are happy not to be remembered as 'the last team'—we now belong to the future." At the age of ninety-two and in failing health for several years, Wills died on 1 January 1998. Her record of eight Wimbledon singles championships stood for more than fifty years, and her 180-match winning streak from 1927 to 1933 remains unbroken.

★

For a thorough account of Wills's place in tennis history, see Larry Engelmann, *The Goddess and the American Girl* (1988), which gives a glorious account of Wills's life, the era in which she lived, her rivalries with Lenglen and Jacobs, and an accurate dating of her records. Wills's memoir, *Fifteen–Thirty* (1937), provides the reader with insight into her personality and her view of her default to Jacobs in 1933. For a description of what Bud Collins calls Wills's "transcendent" ability and tennis skills, see Collins and Zander Hollander, *Bud Collins's Modern Encyclopedia of Tennis* (1994). *The Official Encyclopedia of Tennis* (1979), edited by Bill Shannon, places Wills in an historical context. Janet Woolum, *Outstanding Women Athletes, Who They Are and How They Influenced Sports in America* (1998), addresses the contributions of Wills. An obituary is in the *New York Times* (3 Jan. 1998).

JULIANNE CICARELLI

WILSON, Carl Dean (*b.* 21 December 1946 in Hawthorne, California; *d.* 6 February 1998 in Los Angeles, California), singer, guitarist, songwriter, and record producer best known as a founding member of the Beach Boys, one of the most successful American rock bands, for which he served as musical director for more than thirty years.

Carl Wilson was the youngest of the three sons of Murry Gage Wilson, a foreman at AiResearch, the manufacturing subsidiary of Garrett Aeronautics Corporation, and an aspiring songwriter, and Audree Neva Korthof, a homemaker. He displayed an early interest in music when he became a fan of country-and-western fiddler Spade Cooley, who had a show on local television when Carl was a child. He asked his parents for a guitar at age twelve. When they bought him one, he took a few lessons, but soon began teaching himself to play early rock-and-roll songs.

Carl's enthusiasm for music was encouraged by his parents and more than matched by the enthusiasm of his oldest brother, Brian. In 1961, when Carl was fourteen, Brian organized a group that included the three brothers, their

Carl Wilson *(front right)* with the other Beach Boys *(back row, left to right)*, Brian Wilson, Al Jardine, and Dennis Wilson, and *(front left)* Mike Love, 1979. ASSOCIATED PRESS AP

first cousin Mike Love, and Alan Jardine, a friend of Brian's. At the suggestion of Dennis, the other Wilson brother, Brian Wilson and Love wrote and recorded "Surfin'," an ode to the local craze. When "Surfin'" was issued as a single credited to the Beach Boys (a name chosen by the small record company that released it), it reached the national charts in February 1962.

The Beach Boys were signed to Capitol Records, a major record label, and became enormously popular in the early 1960s, scoring major hits like "Surfin' U.S.A." and "Surfer Girl." Although Carl was the youngest member of the group, which was led by Brian, he was its lead guitarist, and starting with "Surf Jam" on the 1963 album *Surfin' U.S.A.* he began to contribute his own compositions to its repertoire. Meanwhile, his increasing celebrity made it difficult for him to continue at Hawthorne High School, and for his senior year he transferred to the Hollywood Professional School, graduating in 1964. That December, "Dance, Dance, Dance," which he cowrote with Brian, became a top ten hit.

The same month, Brian suffered a nervous breakdown on the way to a concert engagement and later announced to the group that he was going to retire from touring, although he would continue to work on the group's records. Carl became musical director for the band's live appear-

ances from then on. He also gradually increased his involvement on their records; he was awarded his first vocal lead in "Girl Don't Tell Me" on the 1965 album *Summer Days (And Summer Nights!!!)*. On 3 February 1966 the nineteen-year-old Carl Wilson married sixteen-year-old Annie Hinsche, sister of Billy Hinsche of the group Dino, Desi and Billy, who would later become a backup musician for the Beach Boys. The couple had two sons before they separated on 4 July 1978. Carl filed for divorce in 1979, but negotiations were not settled until October 1982.

Carl sang lead on "God Only Knows," the opening track on the album *Pet Sounds* (1966), which is widely considered to be the Beach Boys best album and is routinely ranked among the greatest rock albums ever made. He also sang the verses on "Good Vibrations," which topped the charts in December 1966. These recordings were the highwater mark of Brian's creative work with the Beach Boys. Brian failed to complete the band's intended next album, *Smile,* and increasingly withdrew from involvement with the group. Meanwhile, Carl was facing another crisis. On 3 January 1967, with the Vietnam War raging, he refused compulsory induction into the U.S. Army as a conscientious objector. This refusal initiated a court battle that lasted four years before a settlement allowed him to perform community service instead of serving in the military.

With Brian on the sidelines, Carl began playing more on records, and he sang lead vocals on Beach Boys hits such as "Wild Honey" (1967), "Darlin'" (1967), and "I Can Hear Music" (1969). He also became the group's primary producer on albums like *Carl and the Passions—So Tough* and *Holland* in the early 1970s. Although the band was declining in popularity, Carl's writing on songs like "Long Promised Road" and singing on songs like "This Whole World" was some of the band's best work of the period. The Beach Boys enjoyed a commercial comeback in the mid-1970s thanks to a greatest hits album, *Endless Summer* (1974), and a remake of Chuck Berry's "Rock and Roll Music" (1976). But by the end of the decade, Carl decried their musical stasis and left the band in 1980 for a solo career. As a solo artist, he recorded the album *Carl Wilson* (1981), and backed the album with a solo tour. Although this album did not sell, he recorded a second, *Young Blood* (1983), before returning to the Beach Boys in October 1982. His brother Dennis, who had been dismissed from the group, drowned on 28 December 1983.

Carl was heavily involved in the band's next album, *The Beach Boys* (1985), a critical and commercial success. Now living in Colorado, he married Gina Martin, daughter of singer and actor Dean Martin, on 8 November 1987. The Beach Boys scored a surprise number-one hit in 1988 with "Kokomo," which increased their profile and allowed them to tour successfully for another decade. In the 1990s Carl teamed with musicians from two other bands, Gerry Beckley of America and Robert Lamm of Chicago, for the album *Like a Brother*. This album had been recorded over a five-year span but was not released until two years after Carl died at age fifty-one of lung and brain cancer. He is buried in Westwood Memorial Park in Los Angeles.

A calming influence in an often rancorous organization, the pudgy, bearded youngest Wilson held the Beach Boys together for over thirty-five years. In contrast to his gifted but troubled brother Brian and his volatile brother Dennis, Carl was able to deal with the complexities of running a successful band over the long term, and he also managed to produce some worthy music of his own. No greater testimony of his accomplishment can be given than that, without him, the band fell apart, breaking down into warring and litigious factions within a year of his death.

★

There are no biographical sources devoted solely to Carl Wilson, but there are many sources for information about the Beach Boys. Their mid-1970s career resurgence led to the publication of a number of minor illustrated biographies, including Ken Barnes, *The Beach Boys: A Biography in Words and Pictures* (1976); Bruce Golden, *The Beach Boys: Southern California Pastoral* (1976; 2d rev. ed., 1991); and John Tobler, *The Beach Boys* (1978). By far the best book from this period is David Leaf, *The Beach Boys and the California Myth* (1978; enl. ed., 1985, as *The Beach Boys*), though Byron Preiss's authorized biography *The Beach Boys* (1979; rev. ed., 1983), is also useful. Later studies include John Milward, *The Beach Boys Silver Anniversary* (1985), and Mark Ribowsky and Bill Feinberg, *The Beach Boys* (1986). *Surf's Up! The Beach Boys on Record, 1961–1981* (1982), by Brad Elliott is a definitive discographical reference work up to the date of its publication. Steven Gaines, *Heroes and Villains: The True Story of the Beach Boys* (1986) is the inevitable tabloid-style tell-all. The best general book on the Beach Boys is the verbose, but exhaustively researched *The Nearest Faraway Place: Wilson Wilson, the Beach Boys, and the Southern California Experience* (1994), by Timothy White. An obituary is in the *New York Times* (9 Feb. 1998).

WILLIAM J. RUHLMANN

WILSON, Flip (*b.* 8 December 1933 in Jersey City, New Jersey; *d.* 25 November 1998 in Malibu, California), writer and television comedian.

Wilson was born Clerow Wilson, the tenth of twenty-four children of Clerow Wilson, a carpenter and handyman, and Cornelia Wilson. He was raised in foster homes after his mother abandoned the family when he was seven. Wilson ran away repeatedly to stay with his older siblings but was

Flip Wilson, 1985. AP/WIDE WORLD PHOTOS

regularly returned to foster care. He was eventually remanded to reform school and then returned to the care of his father at age thirteen. He attended P.S. 29 and P.S. 14, both in Jersey City. His interest in performance began in the third grade, when he took over the part of Nurse Clara Barton in a school play when the female lead fell ill. Ironically, drag roles later became critical to his comedic success.

Wilson quit school at age sixteen and lied about his age to join the U.S. Air Force in 1950. He worked on his English writing skills and found his niche by entertaining his comrades with impromptu skits and stories. His fellow enlistees commented that he "flipped out" during these performances, and the nickname "Flip" was born. Wilson was discharged in 1954 with the rank of airman first class and went to San Francisco, a popular place for stand-up comedy and one of the few where black comedians were welcome. He worked as a bellhop at the Manor Plaza Hotel in San Francisco and soon persuaded the manager to let him take the stage, where he portrayed a drunken bellhop during wardrobe changes of the main act. Wilson began to write his own material and develop a comedy routine. He then worked at small local clubs and bars and in the late 1950s hitchhiked across the country to get to his performances. In 1959, while playing at the Fontainebleu Hotel in Miami, he met a businessman who agreed to sponsor him, paying Wilson $50 per week for a year. Wilson later traveled from Miami to New York City, and in the mid-1960s he worked as an emcee and regular comic at the Apollo Theater in Harlem.

Wilson got his first big television break in 1965; the comedian Redd Foxx recommended that Wilson appear on Johnny Carson's *Tonight Show.* He was preempted from the show many times but finally appeared in August 1965. Hollywood had opened the door to black comics at this time, and Wilson's career blossomed. He appeared on *The Ed Sullivan Show* and *Rowan and Martin's Laugh-In* during the 1967–1968 television season, in addition to *The Joey Bishop* and *Merv Griffin* shows. NBC signed Wilson to a five-year contract in 1968, and he eventually substituted for vacationing Johnny Carson numerous times in 1969 as host of *The Tonight Show.*

After starring in his own NBC television special later that year, Wilson was offered an hour-long prime-time television variety show. *The Flip Wilson Show* debuted on 17 September 1970 and aired on Thursday nights at 8:00 P.M. It featured no regular supporting cast and took place on a circular stage with little scenery, surrounded by the audience. The show's formula for success was a combination of storytelling and stand-up comedy sketches. Unprecedented at the time, Wilson produced the show, wrote a third of the material, edited the work of the writers, and insisted upon a five-day workweek from both staff and guests to prepare for each one-hour broadcast. Guests included Lucille Ball, John Wayne, and Dean Martin, with musical performances by James Brown, Aretha Franklin, and the Temptations. A monologue generally opened each show. Wilson then performed sketches portraying such characters as Reverend Leroy of the Church of What's Happening Now, a character based on a preacher he had observed in his youth; Freddy the Playboy; Sonny the White House Janitor; and Flip's most popular character, Geraldine Jones. Geraldine allowed Flip to use drag humor and challenge the censorship guidelines of the 1970s. Her one-liners "The devil made me do it" and "What you see is what you get" became national slogans.

The Flip Wilson Show won two Emmy Awards and a Golden Globe Award in 1971. For two seasons, it was rated the second-best show nationally, behind *All in the Family.* Wilson also worked on stage in Las Vegas and in 1970 won a Grammy Award for his comedy album *The Devil Made Me Buy This Dress.* Although *The Flip Wilson Show* was still among the top ten, Wilson left the show to devote more time to his family. The show went off the air on 27 June 1974, defeated in the ratings by *The Waltons* on CBS, and falling victim to a change in televised comedy that began to embrace the edgier humor of Redd Foxx and Richard Pryor.

Wilson retreated from public performances and attended to his personal life. He had married the dancer Peaches Wilson in 1957, but they divorced within a year. He had a common-law marriage with Blonell Pitman from 1960 to 1970. Wilson adopted Pitman's daughter, and the couple had four more children before separating. Wilson gained custody of all the children in the mid-1970s. Wilson wed Cookie Mackenzie in 1979; they had no children and divorced in 1985.

Wilson's later work was limited to minor roles in films in 1974 and 1979. In 1984 he appeared as host of a short-lived game show, *People Are Funny,* and in 1985 he co-starred with the singer Gladys Knight in a CBS sitcom, *Charlie and Company,* which lasted for only a few episodes. In a 1993 interview with *Jet* magazine, Wilson said that he spent much of his time raising his family, riding motorcycles, hot-air ballooning, traveling the world, and studying the works of the Syrian poet and philosopher Kahlil Gibran, author of *The Prophet.* An astute businessman, Wilson had his own company, Clerow Productions, which owned the exclusive rights to his show. In 1997 Wilson sold these rights to the cable network TV Land for an estimated $10 million. Wilson underwent surgery for liver cancer in October 1998 and died in his sleep at his home in Malibu, California. He was cremated, and his ashes were given to his family.

★

James Albert Hudson wrote a biography aimed at young

adults, *Flip Wilson Close-Up* (1971). *On Stage, Flip Wilson* (1976), by Thomas Braun, also targets young readers. Further biographical information is in Laura S. Hightower and Terrie M. Rooney, eds., *Newsmakers* (1999), and *Current Biography Yearbook* (1969). Obituaries are in the *New York Times* and *Boston Globe* (both 26 Nov. 1998 and 27 Nov. 1998) and *Washington Post* (27 Nov. 1988).

ANTHONY TODMAN

WISDOM, John Minor (*b.* 17 May 1905 in New Orleans, Louisiana; *d.* 15 May 1999 in New Orleans, Louisiana), federal judge who authored over 1,500 decisions as a member of the U.S. Fifth Circuit Court of Appeals, including groundbreaking civil rights decisions that desegregated schools, juries, and voting rosters in the Deep South during the 1960s.

Wisdom was one of three sons of Mortimer Norton Wisdom, who was in the insurance business, and Adelaide Labatt, a member of a socially prominent New Orleans family that could trace its U.S. roots to the 1650s, when Wisdom's mother's forebears, the Minors, arrived from Holland. The Minors initially settled in Virginia. Over the next eight generations, they became wealthy and prominent members of the landed gentry, including John Barbee Minor, a noted school and law professor at the University of Virginia; Virginia Louisa Minor, founder of the women's suffrage move-

John Minor Wisdom, 1957. © BETTMANN/CORBIS

ment in Missouri; Henry Hyams, the first Jewish lieutenant governor in America; and various military officers, planters, lawyers, doctors, and a steamboat captain. The paternal branch of Wisdom's family tree immigrated to America from England in 1730 and eventually settled in New Orleans in the 1840s, where Wisdom's grandfather built a successful cotton and tobacco commission business.

Like many well-born New Orleanian males of his day, Wisdom, as his father before him, went to Lexington, Virginia, to do his undergraduate work at Washington and Lee University. While there, he concentrated his studies on history, geology, and English literature, the impact of which was reflected years later in a judicial career characterized by a lyrical blend of historical perspective, literary references, and legal analyses. After receiving his A.B. degree from Washington and Lee in 1925, Wisdom spent one year as a nondegree student at Harvard University with permission to audit any of Harvard's courses. Although he initially chose to attend literature classes, he soon abandoned his dream of becoming a literary critic after attending law school classes with his roommate and friends. He returned to New Orleans in September 1926 to enroll in law school at Tulane University, where his maternal grandfather, David Cohen Labatt, a leading Jewish lawyer in New Orleans and distant cousin of Confederacy-legend Judah P. Benjamin, had received the first law degree conferred by that school.

Wisdom graduated from Tulane Law School in 1929 at the top of his class, then opened a law firm with a law school classmate. During his twenty-eight years as a member of the bar, his most famous case culminated in a stunning victory before the U.S. Supreme Court. In *Schwegmann Brothers* v. *Calvert Distillers Corp.* (1951), the Supreme Court endorsed Wisdom's argument that federal antitrust law prohibited liquor manufacturers from requiring retailers to adhere to minimum price schedules for the resale of their products. But Wisdom's activities during this period were not limited to the legal arena. On 24 October 1931 he married Bonnie Stewart Mathews, the great-granddaughter of George Mathews, the second presiding judge of the Louisiana Supreme Court; they raised two daughters and one son.

In addition, Wisdom served in the intelligence division of the U.S. Army Air Forces from 1941 to 1946. He also became the driving force behind a revival of Louisiana's long dormant Republican Party and played a crucial role in securing the presidential nomination for General Dwight Eisenhower at the Republican Party's national convention in 1952. In 1957 President Eisenhower nominated Wisdom to fill a vacant seat on the U.S. Fifth Circuit Court of Appeals, the court with appellate jurisdiction over all federal trial courts in Texas, Louisiana, Mississippi, Alabama, Georgia, and Florida.

During the mid-1960s Wisdom became the moral force behind that court. He was the undisputed, though invariably self-deprecating, intellectual leader of "The Four," a coalition of progressive judges committed to enforcing the constitutional right to equal protection under the law. In judgments that dismantled historically segregated school districts, jury panels, and voting rosters throughout the Deep South, Wisdom's opinions became noted for their unpretentious eloquence; their comprehensive and scholarly reliance on history, philosophy, and literature; their farsighted vision; and their bedrock commitment to fairness.

Among the most notable and momentous of these opinions were decisions that compelled the then-segregated University of Mississippi to enroll an African American named James Meredith; overturned Orleans Parish's racially biased jury selection system; ordered all public parks and playgrounds in New Orleans to be made available to everyone without regard to race; set aside the State of Louisiana's racist voter-registration law; and authorized private employers to engage in a limited form of voluntary, racially based affirmative action to redress the effects of generations of racially discriminatory employment practices.

In Wisdom's view, the opinion he authored in *U.S.* v. *Jefferson* (1966) was his most significant contribution to American jurisprudence. Local school boards throughout the Deep South had attempted to circumvent the ruling issued by the Supreme Court in *Brown* v. *Board of Education*, which declared racially segregated school districts unconstitutional. This attempt by local school boards to frustrate the Court's mandate to desegregate public education was predicated on the theory that even though the Constitution prohibited discrimination, it did not affirmatively require integration. Wisdom vigorously denounced this theory in *U.S.* v. *Jefferson*, ruling that school boards had an affirmative duty to develop desegregation plans. In his characteristically blunt, pragmatic manner, Wisdom advised the local school boards that "the only school desegregation plan that meets constitutional standards is one that works."

In a 1993 ceremony at the White House, Wisdom was awarded the Presidential Medal of Freedom, the nation's highest civilian honor, capping the many honorable degrees and awards he had received in his lifetime. One year later, President William J. Clinton also signed into law a bill renaming the U.S. Fifth Circuit courthouse in New Orleans the John Minor Wisdom United States Court of Appeals. Wisdom died of natural causes two days short of his ninety-fourth birthday. He was survived by his wife and two daughters.

★

There are no full-length biographies of Wisdom, but Jack Bass,

Unlikely Heroes (1981), describes the Fifth Circuit Court's role in the civil rights movement. The sixty-ninth volume of the *Tulane Law Review* (June 1995) is a tribute to Wisdom. Obituaries are in the *New York Times* and *Charlotte Observer* (both 16 May 1999).

JOEL WM. FRIEDMAN

WOOD, Beatrice (*b.* 3 March 1893 in San Francisco, California; *d.* 12 March 1998 in Ojai, California), bohemian artist known for her wit, her acquaintances, her longevity, and the pottery and luster glazes that brought her acclaim in her later years.

One of two children born to Benjamin and Carrara Wood, Wood grew up on New York City's Upper East Side, at-

Beatrice Wood at her 100th birthday party, 1993. AP/WIDE WORLD PHOTOS

tending well-known private schools such as the Shipley School in Bryn Mawr, Pennsylvania, and Ely and Finch Schools in New York City, as well as a convent school in Paris, where she lived with her mother in the early 1900s. Her father made his money in real estate and the family lived comfortably, with governesses and servants. Her mother had every expectation that Wood would come out in society and marry into her class; she, however, had no intention of following this path.

Wood returned to France in 1912 to study art, both on her own in Giverny and at the Academie Julian in Paris, only returning to New York City in 1914 with the onset of World War I. Determined to become an actress, she joined the French Repertory Company in New York City, where she acted in more than sixty parts. While there, she met the French diplomat and art collector Henri-Pierre Roché, who became her first lover. In 1916, on a visit to the composer Edgar Varèse, who was laid up in a New York City hospital and unable to speak English, she met Marcel Duchamp, the dadaist who had achieved notoriety at the 1913 Armory Show with his *Nude Descending a Staircase, No. 2.* Through the influence of Roché and Duchamp, Wood became absorbed into the New York City Dada group—Europeans who were waiting out the war years in New York City. In this circle, she gained full exposure to modern art and became a close acquaintance of Walter and Louise Arensberg, collectors of modern art who held salons for artists and literati in their home. It was at this time that she established her friendships with Man Ray, Francis Picabia, Joseph Stella, Mina Loy, Vaslav Nijinski, Edna St. Vincent Millay, and Isadora Duncan.

This exciting milieu inspired Wood, and she began creating witty sketches that are now often displayed in museum shows as a sort of pictorial diary of the period. She also exhibited a controversial piece, *Un peu(t) d'eau dans du savon* (A little water in some soap), in the First Exhibition of the Society of Independent Artists in New York City in 1917; contributed to the first issue of *Blindman,* an irreverent Dada magazine, and copublished the second with Duchamp; and designed a poster for the Blindman's Ball. Her relations at this time with Roché and Duchamp, which became increasingly intertwined in a menage à trois, were later immortalized in Roché's novel *Jules et Jim,* the basis for François Truffaut's celebrated film of the same title.

In 1918 she joined the French Theatre in Montreal; eventually, in defiance of her mother, she married the theater's manager, a Belgian named Paul. He spent all her money, including an expected inheritance, by borrowing from the Arensbergs. This unconsummated marriage was annulled in 1922, after it was proven that he was a bigamist with a wife and children in Belgium. Meanwhile, Wood supported herself with her drawings, writing articles, and some acting jobs, all the while trying to pay off her hus-

band's debts. At this low point in her life, she looked for spiritual sustenance, finding it eventually in the Theosophical Society, which she joined in 1923. Through this society, she gained acquaintance with, and was influenced by, Dr. Annie Besant, the English theosophist, and Jiddu Krishnamurti, the Indian philosopher.

The Arensbergs had moved to California in 1921, and Wood visited them regularly. She met the British actor, stage director, and poet Reginald Pole on one of her visits and began spending summers with him in Los Angeles, finally moving there in 1928, where she continued her close friendship with the Arensbergs.

It was during a 1930 trip to Holland with a friend, the actress Helen Freeman, to hear a Krishnamurti lecture series that Wood purchased six lusterware plates at an antique shop. These plates became the inspirational spark for the rest of her artistic career, for after failing to find a matching teapot, she determined to make one herself. In 1933, on the advice of a friend, she attended a Hollywood High School adult education program in ceramics and at the age of forty embarked on a whole new artistic life. She quickly learned that she was not going to be able to make a teapot—at least not right away. Instead, she produced some tiles and charming small figurines, the production of which enabled her to support herself for the next few years. Realizing that she needed more training, she studied for several years with Glen Lukens at the University of Southern California in 1938, and then in 1940, briefly, with Gertrud and Otto Natzler, who had fled the Nazis and settled in Los Angeles. From Gertrud she learned to use the wheel and from Otto, to formulate glazes. Her first pottery exhibitions began in 1940, and from this point on she exhibited regularly.

She married for a second time in 1938—again, she claimed, not for love but for convenience—this time to Steve Hoag. They had shared a home in Los Angeles, which had been destroyed in a flood, and she was under the belief that they had to be married to receive aid. They remained married but lived mostly apart until his death in 1960. Wood always claimed that she had loved seven men she had not married, and married two she had never loved.

In 1948 she moved to her first Ojai, California, home, where she became involved with and taught in the Happy Valley School, an artistic, nonsectarian school founded in 1946 by Besant, Aldous Huxley, Krishnamurti, and Rosalind Rajagopal. Here, she perfected her now famous luster glaze technique. She studied under Viveka and Otto Heino intermittently from 1954 to 1979 and continued to be shown in increasingly more prestigious galleries and museums.

In 1961 and 1962 Wood was sent to India by the U.S. State Department at the request of the Indian government to exhibit her work and lecture on other American potters in a fourteen-city tour. She became entranced with India and for the rest of her life wore saris and copious amounts of silver jewelry. She later exhibited in Japan, returning in 1965 to India to photograph folk art. In 1972 she made a third visit to India and lectured in Israel, Nepal, and Afghanistan. When she moved in 1973 to a new home and studio at the Happy Valley Foundation, just outside Ojai, she was joined by Ram Pravesh Singh, her escort in India who continued to look after her for the rest of her life. In 1981 she began regularly exhibiting her works through her agent, Garth Clark, and at one point was so prolific that her works were shown simultaneously in his galleries in New York City, Kansas City, and Los Angeles. Upon her death in 1998 at the age of 105, her body was cremated and her ashes scattered upon Topatopa Mountain in Ojai, California, at her behest.

Wood received a Gold Medal from the American Craft Council in 1973 and the Living Legacy Award from the Women's International Center in 1989; in 1994 the Smithsonian Institution named her an Esteemed American Artist, and she was honored as a California Living Treasure by Governor Pete Wilson. "Beato," as she was called by her friends, maintained a regular work schedule until she was 103. Although she was also called the "Mama of Dada," she liked to say, "What is Dada? I know nothing about Dada. I was just in love with two men connected with it. That's all I can say."

★

Wood has drawings and pottery in many museums, including the Everson Museum of Art, the Smithsonian Institution, the Detroit Institute of Art, and the Metropolitan Museum of Art. She wrote seven books, including her autobiography, *I Shock Myself* (1985), which revolves largely around the men in her life and illuminates little more than she revealed in her many interviews; *The Angel Who Wore Black Tights* (1982); and *The Thirty-Third Wife of the Maharajah* (1992), an account of her travels in India. She is also the subject of a film by Tom Neff and Diandra Douglas, *Beatrice Wood: Mama of Dada* (1992), and was the inspiration for the character Rose in James Cameron's movie *The Titanic*, although she was not actually aboard the infamous ship. Obituaries are in the *New York Times* (14 Mar. 1998) and *Los Angeles Times* (15 Mar. 1998).

PAMELA ARMSTRONG LAKIN

WOODWARD, C(omer) Vann (*b.* 13 November 1908 in Vanndale, Arkansas; *d.* 17 December 1999 in Hamden, Connecticut), historian of the U.S. South and of race relations in the post–Civil War period.

Woodward grew up in small towns in Arkansas, in a genteel family of modest means, the son of Hugh Alison Woodward, a high school principal, and Bessie Vann, a music teacher. He had one sister. He attended Henderson-Brown College in Arkedelphia, Arkansas, for two years and then transferred to Emory University in Atlanta, where he studied literature and received his A.B. degree in 1930. After teaching English for a year at the Georgia Institute of Technology in Atlanta, he went to New York City for graduate school at Columbia University. By this early point in his life, he was captivated by the southern literary renaissance and already was a political activist, sympathetic to the "masses" as opposed to the "classes." After briefly studying sociology, he was so appalled at the pedestrian language and intellectually stultifying content of the field that he transferred to political science. Finding that little better, he spent most of his time in Manhattan sampling the forbidden delights of the artistic flowering then in full bloom in Harlem. He received a master's degree in political science from Columbia in 1932.

Back at Georgia Tech for another year of teaching, Woodward became involved in the defense of Angelo Herndon, an African-American member of the Communist Party who had been jailed for public protest activity. He also began a biography of Thomas E. Watson, the flamboyant leader of a biracial agrarian protest movement in the 1890s. While engaged in this effort, Woodward met by chance Howard W. Odum who, with Rupert B. Vance, was the major intellectual magnet at the University of North Carolina at Chapel Hill. Odum was impressed with the young writer and arranged a fellowship for him in history at Chapel Hill.

Woodward arrived at the University of North Carolina in 1933 with four chapters written and much of the research done on his biography of Watson. Four years later he submitted the typescript to the faculty as his dissertation and received his Ph.D. in history in 1937. That same year he married Glenn Boyd McLeod on 21 December; they had one son, Peter, born in 1943. Woodward also sent a copy of his dissertation to his publisher and it appeared in 1938 as *Tom Watson, Agrarian Rebel*. His adviser was Howard K. Beale, who, with the more celebrated Charles Beard, championed economic interpretation. Both Beale and Beard greatly influenced Woodward's early work.

On the strength of his first book, Woodward was invited to write a volume in the Louisiana State University series on the history of the South, an opportunity that led him to abandon a biography of Eugene Debs. He taught successively at the University of Florida in Gainesville (1937–1939), the University of Virginia in Charlottesville (1939–1940), and Scripps College in Claremont, California (1940–1943), all the while doing research on the post–Reconstruction South. The U.S. entry into World War II and Woodward's service as a lieutenant in the U.S. Naval Reserve interrupted that work. As soon as it was discovered

C. Vann Woodward. © Oscar White/Corbis

that Woodward had published a book, he was assigned to naval intelligence and spent 1943 to 1945 writing three accounts of naval battles, intended for quick distribution to the fleet for instruction and morale building. The third of those works was published as *The Battle for Leyte Gulf* (1947). Upon leaving the service at the end of the war, Woodward returned to the archives and also settled at the Johns Hopkins University in Baltimore in 1946. He remained there until moving to Yale University in New Haven, Connecticut, in 1961, where he held the position of Sterling Professor of History until his retirement.

Woodward announced his arrival as a major figure in historical studies with the publication of *Reunion and Reaction* (1950), an intricate story that revised the existing understanding of the Compromise of 1877 and the end of Reconstruction. Conventionally, the congressional compromise to resolve the presidential election of 1876 and end Union occupation of the South was seen as purely political. Woodward introduced into the history of the post–Reconstruction South the theme of economic self-interest. This was a radical departure from the view of most twentieth-century historians, who depicted the Southerners involved in ending Reconstruction as selfless regional patriots.

Woodward's version of the Compromise of 1877 was summarized in the first chapter of his masterpiece *Origins of the New South, 1877–1913* (1951), which recast the story of the South in the period from Reconstruction to World War I. In contrast to prevailing historical interpretations, Woodward portrayed the leaders of the New South as self-interested capitalists with few concerns for the economic or human rights of the region's poor whites and African Americans. In this narrative, it is clear that the author's sympathies lay with the poor whites and African Americans, the defeated classes, rather than with the New South leaders, who are pictured as an unattractive lot. Furthermore, Woodward successfully challenged two dominant attitudes among historians and American intellectuals more generally in the early 1950s. In *Origins,* the Civil War and Reconstruction are a decisive turning point, as Charles and Mary Beard had argued previously, so American history is not the uninterrupted and gradual working out of a divine plan for the "chosen people," as believers in American Exceptionalism would have it. Second, American history is driven by conflict—especially the clash of economic interests—rather than being an unproblematic story flowing smoothly within the confines of a broad consensus.

Woodward presented history as contingent upon the choices that humans make, with every present moment containing the potential for various futures. *Origins,* which won the 1951 Bancroft Prize, was his lament for paths not taken, a theme he pursued with regard to race relations in a series of lectures at the University of Virginia in 1954. The lectures were published in 1955 as *The Strange Career of Jim Crow.* Martin Luther King, Jr., called them the "Bible of the civil rights movement." It was by far the most popular and controversial book that Woodward wrote, going through five editions and three major revisions during his life. The implied message of *Strange Career* was clear: If segregation and disfranchisement were created by the law they could also be eliminated through the law, contrary to President Dwight D. Eisenhower's famous statement that "you can't legislate morality." Meanwhile, Woodward and his friend John Hope Franklin each contributed historical essays to Thurgood Marshall, as part of the National Association for the Advancement of Colored People's suit that resulted in the U.S. Supreme Court's landmark *Brown* v. *Board of Education of Topeka* decision in 1954. Woodward never wavered from his commitment to racial equality and civil rights; he marched from Selma to Montgomery, Alabama, in the civil rights protest of 1965, and then testified before Congress in the 1980s in favor of the extension of the Voting Rights Act.

Beginning with his presidential address to the Southern Historical Association in 1952, Woodward grappled repeatedly with the question of the Southern identity and its use and abuse in U.S. intellectual life. His essays on this theme were first brought together as *The Burden of Southern History* (1960). Woodward hoped that the humbling lessons of Southern history would save the United States from the arrogance of power. Alas, they did not, as the tragedy of the Vietnam War revealed. Throughout his career, Woodward was always seeking answers to historical questions that would inform current political debate. In the years after *Origins of the New South* appeared, many scholars modified Woodward's interpretations. In his own intellectual autobiography, *Thinking Back* (1986), he not only accepted many of the refinements and corrections, but admitted that he may have overstated his case in his zeal to displace the dominant hagiographic version of the South's history.

When the various social justice movements of the 1960s fragmented soon thereafter, Woodward became concerned about the radical fragments corrupting U.S. universities. Without altering his own political commitments, he spoke out against left-wing threats to academic freedom and free speech within the university setting. He also joined others in condemning "political correctness," a form of fashionable dogmatism that seemed to support the demands of oppressed groups no matter how outrageous those demands were. In 1973 Woodward and fourteen other historians were requested by the House Committee on the Judiciary to prepare a study to be used in the impeachment of President Richard Nixon. This study, edited and with an introduction by Woodward, was published in 1974 as *Responses of the Presidents to Charges of Misconduct*.

Woodward retired from teaching in 1977 during a particularly low point in his personal life. He lost his wife in 1982 and, having lost his son in 1969, became discouraged. Yet he remained active as an essayist and as a person of influence in the publishing world, and he was a respected presence at the meetings of three major historical associations, each of which he had served as president during his long career: American Historical Association, Organization of American History, and the Southern Historical Association. He received the Pulitzer Prize in 1982 for editing *Mary Chesnut's Civil War* (1981), a primary historical account written by the wife of an aide to Jefferson Davis. His work continued to be recognized; in 1986 he received the American Historical Society Life Work Award and in 1990 the Gold Medal for History from the American Academy of Arts and Letters. Woodward died of heart failure at his home in Hamden at age ninety-one. His body was cremated.

Woodward was at heart an essayist, a writer with a literary bent, a wry sense of humor, self-deprecating wit, and a taste for irony, rather than an analytical builder of interpretive systems. However, he placed the study of U.S. Southern history on a new and legitimate footing, created a new framework for understanding the period between Reconstruction and World War I, instructed the reading public in subtle ways on the great questions of the day, provided an admirable model of scholarly civility, and reigned as a supremely influential man of letters in the intellectual world of the last half of the twentieth century.

★

Woodward's papers are on deposit in the Yale University Library in New Haven, Connecticut. For an account of his life, a bibliography of his writing, and a collection of articles assessing Woodward's work, see John Herbert Roper, *C. Vann Woodward, Southerner* (1987), and Roper, ed., *C. Vann Woodward, A Historian and His Critics* (1997). See also the special memorial section in the *Journal of Southern History* (May 2000). Woodward's own account of his career is found in *Thinking Back: The Perils of Writing History* (1986). Obituaries are in the *New York Times* (19 Dec. 1999) and *New Republic* (10 Jan. 2000).

SHELDON HACKNEY

WU, Chien-Shiung [Jianshiung] (*b*. 29 May 1912 in Liuhe, near Shanghai, China; *d*. 16 February 1997 in New York City), experimental physicist regarded by many of her scientific contemporaries as the greatest woman physicist since Marie Curie and one of the outstanding nuclear scientists of the twentieth century.

Wu was one of three children of Zhongyi Wu, an engineer and a distinguished progressive educator who founded the first school for girls in China, and Fuhua Fan, an educator. Her given name in Chinese means "strong hero." Wu attended her father's elementary school and then entered the

Chien-Shiung Wu. AP/WIDE WORLD PHOTOS

Suzhou Girls' School. Her decision to become a physicist was made while she was attending high school in Suzhou, where she learned English. After graduating from high school as valedictorian in 1930, she entered the National Central University of Nanjing and, despite the disruptions created by the Japanese invasion of China, succeeded in securing a B.S. degree in 1936. That same year she went to the United States to do graduate work at the University of California at Berkeley. Her senior adviser was the prominent physicist Ernest O. Lawrence, who received the Nobel Prize in 1939 for the invention of the cyclotron. After receiving her Ph.D. in 1940, Wu became a lecturer in physics at Berkeley until 1942. There she met Luke Jialiu Yuan, also a physicist, whom she married in 1942; they had one child. That year she was appointed assistant professor at Smith College in Massachusetts, where she remained for a year. Between 1943 and 1944 she was an instructor in physics at Princeton University in New Jersey.

In 1944, during World War II, Wu joined the staff of the Division of War Research at Columbia University in New York City as a senior scientist on the Manhattan Project, the American program to develop an atomic bomb. The Columbia phase of the effort was directed toward techniques to separate the fissionable isotope uranium 235 employed in the nuclear weapon detonated over Hiroshima, Japan, on 6 August 1945 from the far more abundant but essentially non-fissionable isotope uranium 238 found in nature. Though the particular method addressed at Columbia was not the one finally employed in the separation process used for atomic bomb manufacture, Wu's work in radiation detection instrumentation found significant application in her later experimental work in fundamental particle physics.

Following the war, Wu remained at Columbia. She and her husband were both offered positions at the National Central University in China, but they hesitated to return to their homeland, which had fallen under the control of the Communists. Instead, they both became naturalized citizens of the United States in 1954. Wu was named associate professor of physics at Columbia in 1952 and full professor in 1958. She was honored as the first Pupin Professor of Physics in 1973, a position she held until she retired as professor emeritus in 1981. During most of her career, Wu addressed herself to investigating nuclear structure and forces, with particular focus on beta disintegration. Beta disintegration is the radioactive process by which a neutron, an electrically neutral particle in an atom's nucleus, is converted to a positively charged fundamental particle, or proton, with the emission of an electron. The electron is a particle of low mass but having a negative electric charge opposite and equal to the proton's positive charge. The electron is known as a beta particle, and thus the process is designated "radioactive beta decay."

In view of her specialized knowledge and experience with beta decay, the theoretical physicists Zongdao Lee, a colleague in the Columbia physics faculty, and Zhenning Yang of the Institute for Advanced Study at Princeton approached Wu to investigate and verify or reject a revolutionary hypothesis they had advanced in 1956. The thrust of Lee and Yang's theory was to challenge the conservation parity principle, which had been regarded as one of the foundations of atomic physics since the early development of quantum theory in the 1920s. In nuclear reactions, it was thought, nature does not distinguish between left and right. In terms of electrical charge, the conservation principle states that the total electrical charge would be the same on all particles before and after physical and chemical changes. Lee and Yang theorized that this principle does not apply to the so-called weak reaction (one of four basic forces of nature), and they outlined experiments that might test the theory. Accepting Lee and Yang's invitation, Wu led a group of scientists in conducting difficult parity experiments at the National Bureau of Standards in Washington, D.C.

Wu set about measuring what happened to cobalt 60 nuclei as they broke down during atomic interactions. Her experiment consisted of cryogenic cooling of the beta-emitting radioactive isotope cobalt 60 to about 459 degrees below zero Fahrenheit. This very cold temperature reduced heat-induced movement of cobalt 60 nuclei, permitting the measurement of beta disintegration without interference from background effects. Through these experiments Wu discovered that more particles flew off in the direction opposite the spin of the nuclei. If the beta particles (electrons) had been emitted in equal numbers in both directions along the spin axes of the cobalt 60 nuclei, the traditional understanding of the parity conservation law would have been found to be accurate. Instead, the electrons were emitted overwhelmingly in a strongly preferential direction opposite their nuclear spin, establishing that beta decay is not always symmetrical and that parity is indeed violated. In 1957 Yang and Lee received the Nobel Prize in physics for postulating what Wu had confirmed experimentally. That Wu was not selected to share the award must be regarded as an oversight by the Nobel committee.

Wu's contributions to science were in no way overlooked, however. Elected a member of the National Academy of Sciences in 1958, she received the Cyrus B. Comstock Award of that organization in 1964. She also received the Achievement Award of the American Association of University Women in 1960 and the Scientist of the Year Award from *Industrial Research Magazine* in 1974. In 1975 she became the first woman to head the American Physical Society, the most important professional organization of physicists in the United States, which conferred upon her the Tom W. Bonner Prize in 1975. That year she also received the National Medal of Science, the United States' highest science award, and later was the first recipient of Israel's Wolf Prize in Physics (1978). In addition, Wu received honorary doctorates from Princeton University, Smith College, Rutgers University, Yale University, and Harvard University, among others.

Emilio Segrè, who received the Nobel Prize in 1959 for the discovery of the anti-proton, first met Wu when she had enrolled as a graduate student at the University of California in Berkeley. He describes her in his 1993 autobiography: "she was very handsome, and very elegant in her Chinese dresses. When she walked on campus, she was often followed by a swarm of admirers, like a queen. She was a fiend for work, almost obsessed by physics, highly talented, and very shrewd as well as witty." Wu suffered a fatal stroke at age eighty-four.

Wu's scientific career has been summarized by many of her colleagues and other distinguished scientists. The Nobel laureate Zongdao Lee observed that "C. S. Wu was one of the giants of physics. In the field of beta decay she had no equal." William Havens, professor emeritus of applied physics and nuclear engineering at Columbia, commented that she was the world's most distinguished woman physicist of her time. Her book, *Beta Decay* (1966), written with S. A. Moszkowski, is a standard, frequently referenced text. Her confirmation of the invalidity of the law of conservation of parity deeply influenced nuclear physics research in the last decades of the twentieth century.

★

Reference to parity and Wu's experimental research in beta radioactivity and parity no-conservation can be found in almost all modern books on atomic and nuclear physics, whether for lay audiences or advanced study. Clearly written expositions include George L. Trigg, "Disproof of a Conversation Law," in *Landmark Experiments in Twentieth Century Physics* (1975); John Gribbin, *Q Is for Quantum* (1998); Abraham Pais, *Inward Bound: Of Matter and Forces in the Physical World* (1988); and Harrie S. W. Massey, *The New Age in Physics,* 2d ed. (1966). Biographical sketches can be found in Emily J. McMurray, *Notable Twentieth-Century Scientists* (1995), and Benjamin F. and Barbara S. Shearer, eds., *Notable Women in the Physical Sciences* (1997). An obituary is in the *New York Times* (18 Feb. 1997).

LEONARD R. SOLON

WYLIE, Chalmers Pangburn (*b.* 23 November 1920 in Norwich, Ohio; *d.* 14 August 1998 in Columbus, Ohio), attorney and politician who served thirteen terms in the U.S. House of Representatives (1967–1993) and who was the ranking minority member of the House Banking Committee at the time of his retirement.

Chalmers P. Wylie. ROSE BENNETT STUDIOS, INC.

Wylie was the only son of Chalmers Wylie, a railroad worker, and Margaret Pangburn, a housekeeper; he had three sisters. Raised in Pataskala, Ohio, Wylie graduated high school in 1939 as class valedictorian. Later that year, he attended Otterbein College, and from 1940 to 1943, he was enrolled at Ohio State University before enlisting in the U.S. Army in early 1943. Wylie arrived in France just days after the Normandy invasion and served in a battalion medical aid station with the 30th Infantry Division (Old Hickory) through five European campaigns. He attained the rank of first lieutenant. Wylie earned the Purple Heart for wounds received on 17 November 1944 and was presented the Bronze Star for meritorious achievement later that year. For gallantry in action on 23 March 1945, he was awarded the Silver Star: following Rhine River crossing operations and subjected to intense mortar fire, Wylie disregarded his personal safety to rescue wounded soldiers stranded in an enemy minefield. Later, as a member of the Army Reserve, Wylie rose to the rank of lieutenant colonel.

Following the war, Wylie attended Harvard Law School and earned his J.D. in 1948. Returning to central Ohio, he briefly served as an assistant state attorney general (1951–1954), then as assistant city attorney for Columbus, Ohio, under Mayor James Rhodes (1949–1950). From 1951 to 1954 Wylie again served as an assistant state attorney general. His first electoral victory occurred when he became city attorney (1953–1956), yet in 1956 he failed to gain the Republican nomination to run for state attorney general.

His selection as administrator of the Ohio Bureau of Workers' Compensation in 1957 was followed by an appointment as first assistant to Governor C. William O'Neill. Wylie was also elected president of the Ohio Municipal League in 1957. He returned to practicing law in 1959, then won a seat in the Ohio House of Representatives in 1961; he served three terms before being elected as a Republican to the Ninetieth Congress in 1966. Divorced from his first wife for several years, Wylie married Marjorie Ann Murnane, a widow, on 19 September 1964; together they raised her two children.

In Congress, Wylie's interests and abilities led to meaningful behind-the-scenes service in molding economic and fiscal policy. Wylie consistently pushed for a balanced federal budget and responsible government spending. He supported the International Monetary Fund for its stabilizing influence and sought a presidential line-item veto. In the late 1970s U.S. Congress passed legislation that allowed savings and loan operations to invest capital outside of home mortgages (their traditional investment). In response, many savings and loan operations invested capital in a wide array of areas, especially in real estate. With keen insight, Wylie early (1982) offered legislation to redress growing concerns over these operations. Although rebuffed in that effort, Wylie later received the thanks of the banking committee chairman for his efforts to prevent the subsequent savings-and-loan crisis. Throughout Wylie's tenure, his innate ability to gain cross-party consensus on divisive issues earned him the respect of many Washington power brokers.

Typically returned to Congress with landslide victories in his Republican stronghold district, Wylie proved a staunch supporter of a strong national defense. He also promoted expanded veterans' benefits. Yet because personal integrity formed the foundation for all his actions, Wylie refused to blindly follow party lines. He rejected President Ronald Reagan's efforts to provide aid for Contra rebels fighting the Nicaraguan government in November 1986. In the early 1970s, Wylie had harshly questioned President Richard Nixon's involvement in the Watergate cover-up.

Perhaps most important to the congressman were the needs of his 15th District constituents. Wylie championed many local initiatives that directly enhanced the quality of life in central Ohio, including the revitalization of downtown Columbus through the Columbus City Center mall project; the Franklinton floodwall to protect and spur development in an older neighborhood subjected to periodic flooding; the establishment of a major cancer research hospital on the Ohio State University campus; and a model urban recreation center that remained dear to Wylie's heart. In an era of chronic congressional pork barrel spending, Wylie's hometown initiatives rarely met with harsh criticism.

Wylie's decades of selfless public service, however, closed with personal embarrassment in April 1992 when the House Ethics Committee declared him among the worst offenders in the House banking fiasco, with more than 500 personal bank account overdrafts over three years. Wylie was not alone, however, as more than 350 House members were cited. Having previously announced that he would not run for reelection, Wylie insisted that he had "abided by the rules" and had only participated in a long-standing practice in which a House member's checks were automatically covered until the next payday, regardless of account balance. None of Wylie's checks "bounced"; Ethics Committee members found no willful wrongdoing on his part; and even a former Democratic House colleague from Ohio came to Wylie's defense.

Upon retirement from Capitol Hill in January 1993, Wylie received presidential thanks and widespread praise from organizations, such as those concerned with animal rights and affordable housing. Returning to Columbus, Wylie practiced law with the firm of Kegler, Brown, Hill and Ritter, was an adjunct law professor at Ohio State University, and served on the boards of Columbus Life Insurance Company and Western-Southern Life Insurance Company. He also donated $50,000 of unused campaign funds to Ohio State University to endow a graduate scholarship in public administration. Wylie suffered a massive heart attack at age seventy-seven while waiting for a routine eye examination at the Ohio State University Medical Center in Columbus. He is buried in Saint Joseph's Cemetery in southern Franklin County, Ohio. As a fitting Veterans Day tribute three months after Wylie's death, President William J. Clinton signed legislation renaming Columbus's Veteran's Affairs Outpatient Clinic for the decorated combat veteran.

Tall in stature and with a powerful baritone voice, Wylie presented an imposing figure in the halls of government. Yet he was known for his civility, and the gentleness and humility that he displayed in public were genuine and unabated. Serving in the House minority for his entire tenure, Wylie sought to remain above what he called "the acrimonious partisanship" of post–Watergate Congressional politics. Hence, he consistently promoted consensus in order to prevent legislative gridlock. That Wylie has largely been forgotten by the American public only enhances his legacy of selfless service to his 15th District constituents, his state, and his nation.

★

The Ohio Historical Society in Columbus has a collection of Wylie's papers. Many tributes to Wylie in the days immediately following his death and funeral appear in the *Columbus Dispatch*, including Alan Johnson and Catherine Candisky, "Wylie's Loyalty, Service Praised" (15 Aug. 1998); "Chalmers Wylie, Gentleman Lawmaker Served with Dignity" (16 Aug. 1998); and James Bradshaw, "Mourners Recall Wylie's Charm, Caring" (19 Aug.

1998). Obituaries are in the *New York Times* (15 Aug. 1998) and *Columbus Dispatch* (17 Aug. 1998).

WILLIAM E. FISCHER, JR.

WYNETTE, Tammy (*b.* 5 May 1942 in Itawamba County, Mississippi; *d.* 6 April 1998 in Nashville, Tennessee), the "First Lady of Country Music" and "Heroine of Heartbreak" who sold more than 30 million records and was known for her songs of women's romantic endurance, including the hits "Stand by Your Man" and "D-I-V-O-R-C-E."

Born Virginia Wynette Pugh near Tupelo, Mississippi, Wynette was the only child of William Hollice Pugh, a guitarist, and Mildred Faye Russell. Her father had been diagnosed with a brain tumor prior to her birth, and he died on 13 February 1943 when she was still a baby. Her mother moved to Memphis, Tennessee, temporarily to work in a defense plant, placing her daughter in the care of her parents, Chester and Flora Russell. "Wynette," as she was called, grew up in a socially restrictive and economically limited Southern Baptist household, and picked cotton along with her family on her maternal grandparents' farm. She inherited her father's love of music and performing, and she sang and played piano at the Providence Baptist Church and in the company of girlfriends. With her income from picking cotton, she was able to afford music lessons for five years, favoring the instruments her father

Tammy Wynette. AP/WIDE WORLD PHOTOS

had played: piano, mandolin, guitar, accordion, and bass fiddle.

Wynette attended a rural, three-room elementary school and later Tremont High School in Tremont, Mississippi. While in high school, she met a local boy several years her senior named Euple Byrd. They were wed in 1959 and she left high school in favor of marriage, never receiving her diploma. Byrd was an itinerant laborer and moved his young wife from town to town in Mississippi in search of employment. Early in their marriage, they lived in a cabin with no plumbing or electricity. Wynette's marriage to Byrd was stormy, and she was plagued by the poor health that would follow her throughout her life. She studied for her beautician's license and waitressed at a bar in Memphis, where she was encouraged to sing, reigniting her desire to perform. Wynette gave birth to two daughters, in 1961 and 1962, before she and Byrd separated.

Wynette and her daughters moved to Birmingham, Alabama, in 1963 to live with her paternal grandparents, Margaret and William Pugh. Byrd reappeared in her life sporadically, and they had a third daughter in 1965. Wynette garnered a spot as a singer on the early-morning television program *Country Boy Eddy* on WBRC-TV in 1964 and 1965, making the connection through an uncle who worked as an engineer at the station. She rose at dawn to perform each day on the program, then worked a full shift at a beauty salon, leaving her small daughters in day care.

Wynette attended the annual disc-jockey convention in Nashville in October 1965, performing impromptu on a flatbed truck to gain the attention of producers. She traveled from Birmingham to Nashville periodically in the hope of meeting producers and landing a recording contract. She divorced Byrd in 1965 and moved with her daughters to Nashville in January 1966. She tirelessly made the rounds of recording companies on the city's famed Music Row, sometimes singing songs while playing a borrowed guitar, leaving her children waiting in her car. She signed with the producer Billy Sherrill of Epic Records, releasing her first single, "Apartment Number Nine," in October 1966. Sherrill dubbed her "Tammy Wynette," saying that with her blonde ponytail, she resembled the character Tammy played by Debbie Reynolds in a series of 1960s teen films.

"Apartment Number Nine," penned by Johnny Paycheck and Bobby Austin, was the first of a series of hits for Wynette. "I Don't Wanna Play House," her first solo record to reach number one on the charts, won a Grammy in 1967 for best female country-and-western vocal performance. Hits such as "D-I-V-O-R-C-E" followed in 1968, then "Stand by Your Man," which brought her music to a wider audience as a crossover hit, reaching number one on the country-music charts and number nineteen on the pop-music charts in the same period. The lyrics to "Stand by

Your Man," in which the singer commiserates that "sometimes it's hard to be a woman," exhorted the listener to stand by her husband as he does things she "won't understand." The song title became cultural shorthand for the plight of an unliberated, oppressed woman. The album won her a second Grammy Award in 1969 and sold over 2 million copies. Nearly twenty-five years after this song first appeared, the future first lady and politician Hillary Rodham Clinton cited it disparagingly, although she later apologized. Conversely, Wynette said that the song was about triumph over adversity.

Wynette married the singer-songwriter Don Chapel in 1967. This marriage, too, was troubled. She had begun performing on a double bill with the established country singer George Jones, and a romance had developed between the two superstars. Wynette, her daughters, and Jones moved in together while she was married to Chapel. Wynette's marriage to Chapel was later annulled based on a technicality relating to her prior divorce from Byrd. Wynette, her children, and Jones then moved to Lakeland, Florida.

Although Wynette and Jones did not marry until 16 February 1969, they performed together as "Mr. and Mrs. Country Music," scoring a series of hits as a duo, including "We're Not the Jet Set" and "We're Going to Hold On" (1973). During this period, Jones and Wynette maintained a heavy performing schedule, including appearances at country music's traditional home, the Grand Ole Opry in Nashville. Wynette was named the Country Music Association Female Vocalist of the Year for 1968, 1969, and 1970. The Academy Award–nominated motion picture *Five Easy Pieces* (1970), directed by Bob Rafelson, showcased her music in the soundtrack and exposed her style to an even larger audience.

Wynette and Jones enjoyed a lavish lifestyle that reflected their success and popularity, and purchased an antebellum-style home on forty-three acres in Lakeland, which Jones had renovated and turned into a country-and-western theme park and performance center. Old Plantation Park attracted performers such as Conway Twitty, Porter Wagoner, and Dolly Parton, and was in operation from 1969 to 1973. Jones and Wynette had one daughter together in 1970, and Jones adopted Wynette's three daughters from her first marriage. Sadly, Jones's excessive drinking was legendary, and his alcohol-fueled exploits caused strife in their marriage. Wynette and Jones separated in 1974 and their divorce was finalized on 13 March 1975.

Wynette continued to perform as a solo artist. She moved back to Nashville and married the real estate businessman Michael Tomlin on 18 July 1976; they divorced within two months. She and Jones renewed their professional association in 1976, recording "Golden Ring." On 6 July 1978 Wynette married her fifth husband, her friend and business associate George Richey.

Wynette's health had declined after the birth of her

fourth daughter. Her personal life, already a source of fodder for tabloid newspapers, took a turn for the bizarre in the mid-1970s. Portions of her 17,000-square-foot Nashville home were burned to the ground by an unidentified arsonist in 1975. In October 1978 Wynette claimed to have been abducted at gunpoint from a Nashville shopping center, beaten, and released. She collapsed onstage in 1986, and spent several months at the Betty Ford Center in Rancho Mirage, California, in rehabilitation for an addiction to painkillers.

By the end of the 1980s Wynette had achieved twenty number-one singles, thirty-nine top-ten hits, and eleven number-one albums, and had sold over 30 million records. She then extended her appearances from the world of music into drama, appearing as the waitress Darlene Stankowski on the CBS daytime drama *Capitol* in 1986 and 1987. Wynette's musical career continued unabated as the decades rolled on. She enjoyed a pop dance hit in 1991, "Justified and Ancient," with the British band KLF, and released an album called *Honky Tonk Angels* with the country stars Loretta Lynn and Dolly Parton in 1993.

Wynette received numerous awards throughout her career. During her lifetime, she received the Music City News Country Award for most-promising female artist of the year (1967), Grammy Award for best female country vocal performance (1969), Academy of Country Music Award for top female vocalist (1969), and TNN/Music City News Living Legend Award (1991). Wynette was nominated for membership into the Country Music Hall of Fame a few weeks prior to her death in 1998, and was elected posthumously. She also received the Grammy Hall of Fame Award (1998) and Academy of Country Music Pioneer Award (2000).

Wynette died at age fifty-five while napping on her couch at First Lady Acres, her home in Nashville. The cause of death was originally identified as a blood clot. Wynette is buried at Nashville's Woodlawn Cemetery. A memorial service was televised live on 9 April 1998 from the Ryman Auditorium in Nashville and featured performances by her celebrity peers such as Wynonna Judd and Dolly Parton, who was overcome with emotion and had to leave the stage.

On 5 April 1999 three of Wynette's daughters filed a wrongful death suit against George Richey (who was later dropped from the suit) and Wynette's personal physician, James Wallis Marsh, seeking $50 million in damages. The suit claimed that Wynette's death was the result of improperly administered painkillers and careless medical supervision. Her body was exhumed and autopsied on 14 April 1999 with the intent of determining if she died of natural causes. The Nashville medical examiner Bruce Levy stated six days later that her death had been the natural result of heart failure.

Wynette's rags to riches road from crushing poverty to

stardom was the archetypal country-music success story. Her troubled marriages, heartbreak, and love for her children made her lyrics piercingly true to her listeners, who responded to her vital voice with its hint of a teardrop.

★

Wynette's autobiography, *Stand by Your Man* (1979), is an illustrative source for much of the story of her early life and later fame. The *Comprehensive Country Music Encyclopedia* (1994) and the *Country Music Hall of Fame's Encyclopedia of Country Music* (1998) are concise sources for the milestone events in Wynette's life and for career highlights. Also see the tribute in *Rolling Stone* (14 May 1998) for a peer review and commentary on her musical style. Wynette's death, and the subsequent lawsuit and exhumation, were widely covered in the international news media; see the *New York Times* (10 Apr. 1998), *USA Today* (12 Apr. 1999), and *Montreal Gazette* (10 May 1999). An extensive discography and a listing of industry awards are available on the Country Music Hall of Fame website at <http://www.country.com>.

JESSICA HANDLER

WYNN, Early, Jr. ("Gus") (*b.* 6 January 1920 in Hartford, Alabama; *d.* 4 April 1999 in Venice, Florida), Hall of Fame pitcher who combined his physical gifts with intimidation and determination to overcome early struggles and become one of the most dominant players of his era.

Wynn was the only child of Early Wynn, Sr., an auto mechanic and semiprofessional baseball player, and Blanche Phelps, who held a number of jobs. A natural athlete with a love of sports, Wynn gravitated toward baseball thanks to encouragement from his father. "Since the first time I saw my father play semipro ball in Alabama, it has been my greatest ambition and desire to be a big league ballplayer," Wynn once said. Working summers as a teenager at a cotton gin for ten cents an hour in his small southern hometown, Wynn, who claimed to be of Indian-Scotch-Irish descent, realized that this depression-era life was not for him. Wynn's athletic prowess first began to show at Hartford High School, when he soon realized that baseball might be a good career to pursue.

While a high school sophomore, Wynn was expected to become a star back for the football team. Just before the season began, his leg was broken while returning a punt. Wynn would later call it, "My best break ever. It sort of forced me into baseball." The spring after his football injury, Wynn left school to attend a baseball school in Sanford, Florida, where an aunt lived. Instead of returning to school, which he originally planned, he impressed Washington Senators scout Clyde Milan with his pitching speed and control and signed a minor league contract in 1937 for $100 a month.

Wynn's first professional stop was with Sanford of the

Early Wynn. AP/WIDE WORLD PHOTOS

Florida State League, where the seventeen year old finished the 1937 season with a 16–11 record. It was while playing with Sanford that teammate Ellis Clary gave Wynn the long-standing nickname of "Gus," claiming, "He looked like a Gus to me." The following year Wynn was assigned to Charlotte, North Carolina, in the Piedmont League, where he met his first wife, Mabel Allman. They married after the 1939 season and had a son two years later.

Wynn played for Sanford and Charlotte before he made his big league debut with three appearances with the Senators late in the 1939 season. After spending all of the 1940 season with Charlotte, Wynn began the 1941 campaign with Springfield, Massachusetts, in the Eastern League and ended it with five appearances with the Senators, where he went 3–1 with a 1.58 earned run average (ERA). During these early years with the Senators, Wynn began to gain a reputation for his meanness on the mound, exemplified by his willingness to knock down a batter if the occasion warranted. Among his famous quotes concerning this subject are, "A pitcher has to look at the hitter as his mortal enemy," "A pitcher will never be a big winner until he hates hitters," and "I've got a right to knock down anybody holding a bat."

Playing for a bad Senators team in 1942, Wynn finished his first full major league season with a 10–16 mark. Tragedy struck later that year when Wynn's twenty-three-year-old wife was fatally injured on 6 December 1942, when her car collided with a bus at a street intersection in Charlotte. Wynn recovered enough to win eighteen games and help the Senators to a second-place finish in 1943, but followed that up with a disappointing 8–17 mark and a last place finish in 1944. It was while he was serving a twenty-three-month tour in the army tank corps that Wynn met his second wife, Lorraine Follin. They were married on 12 September 1944. This marriage, which produced a daughter, ended with Lorraine's death in 1994.

Wynn spent all of the 1945 season in the army and returned for part of the 1946 season. His up and down career in the nation's capital continued for the next two seasons—winning seventeen games in 1947 but losing nineteen in 1948. After nine seasons with mediocre Washington teams, in which he had a 72–87 mark, Wynn and first baseman Mickey Vernon were traded to the Cleveland Indians on 14 December 1948 for pitchers Joe Haynes and Eddie Klieman and first baseman Eddie Robinson.

The move to Cleveland, where he teamed up with Bob Feller, Bob Lemon, and Mike Garcia to give the team one of baseball's greatest pitching rotations, proved fortuitous for Wynn in that he would meet up with pitching coach Mel Harder and resurrect his career at age twenty-nine. "He showed me how to improve my grip and delivery of the curveball and also encouraged me to throw a knuckleball," Wynn said. He won eleven games in 1949, his first season with the Indians, then broke out in 1950 by going 18–8 and leading the league with a 3.20 ERA. With Wynn winning a combined sixty games between 1951 and 1953, the Indians finished second behind the New York Yankees for three straight seasons.

In 1954 Wynn and teammate Lemon tied for the league lead with twenty-three wins each, and the Indians won the American League pennant with a record of 111–43. Wynn started game two of the World Series against the New York Giants, who went on to sweep the series in four games. He allowed four hits and three runs in seven innings in the 3–1 loss. Despite good teams, the Indians could not recapture the magic of the 1954 season. In 1955 Wynn won seventeen games, but the Indians finished three games behind the Yankees. Wynn won twenty games in 1956, but New York won its seventh pennant in eight years.

Although Wynn led the league in strikeouts in 1957, he posted a 14–17 record, and Cleveland finished in sixth place. On 4 December 1957 Wynn, who had compiled a 163–100 record for the Indians from 1949 to 1957, was traded to the Chicago White Sox with infielder-outfielder Al Smith for outfielder Minnie Minoso and infielder Fred Hatfield. Wynn's first year in Chicago produced a 14–16 record, a league-leading 179 strikeouts, and a win in the All-Star game. Things got even better in 1959 when at age thirty-nine, he led the league in wins (twenty-two) and innings pitched (255.2), started the first 1959 All-Star game,

was named the Cy Young Award winner, and pitched the White Sox to the 1959 pennant. Much like 1954, Wynn's 1959 postseason experience against the Los Angeles Dodgers would prove to be disappointing. Although he tossed an 11–0 shutout in the opener, he got a no-decision in his game four start and lost game six as the Dodgers won the world championship in six games.

After suffering from gout for a number of years, Wynn kept pitching and finished the 1962 season with 299 career wins. He was released by the White Sox on 20 November 1962 but was signed on 31 May 1963 by the Indians. The forty-three-year-old hurler posted his 300th win on 13 July 1963, when he left after five innings with a 5–4 lead against the Kansas City Athletics.

Wynn, who pitched in four different decades, finished his big-league pitching career with a record of 300–244, 2,334 strikeouts, and an ERA of 3.54. While 1963 would prove to be Wynn's last season as an active player, he later became a pitching coach with the Indians (1964–1966) and Minnesota Twins (1967–1969) and managed one season (1972) for the Twins' Orlando, Florida, farm team. After retiring from coaching, Wynn became a broadcaster for the Toronto Blue Jays (1977–1981) and the Chicago White Sox (1982–1983). He died of complications related to a stroke at age seventy-nine. His body was cremated, and in 2000 his family scattered his ashes on the pitcher's mound of Jacobs Field, home of his former team, the Indians.

A battling pitcher whose toughness on the mound was legendary, Wynn remained effective for longer than anyone would have expected. Though well past his prime, he was determined to reach the 300-win plateau and would eventually become the fourteenth hurler in major league history to achieve the milestone. He won at least twenty games in a season five times and was named an All-Star every season from 1955 to 1960. When he finally retired in 1963, he had pitched longer than anyone else in baseball history. In 1972 he was inducted into the National Baseball Hall of Fame.

★

There is no full-scale biography of Wynn, but he is included in *Famous American Athletes of Today* (1958), which gives a good overview of his life and career up to that point. Many magazine articles were written on Wynn, the most informative being "Early Wynn: The Story of a Hard Loser," *Sport* (Mar. 1956); "Early Wynn: More Than a Hall of Fame," *Grassroots South* (July/Aug. 1977); and "Leather-Tough Wynn . . . A Blue-Ribbon Battler," *Sporting News* (25 July 1981). The best source for material is housed at the National Baseball Hall of Fame Library in Cooperstown, New York, which has a number of clippings on Wynn that include newspaper and magazine stories from his lengthy baseball career. An obituary is in the *New York Times* (6 Apr. 1999).

BILL FRANCIS

Y

YORTY, Samuel William (*b.* 1 October 1909 in Lincoln, Nebraska; *d.* 5 June 1998 in Los Angeles, California), three-term mayor of Los Angeles who became a national figure for his contrary, outspoken ways and who was a nearly perennial candidate for one office or another, transforming himself from populist liberal to neoconservative foe of federal welfare programs.

Yorty was one of three children born to Frank Patrick Yorty, whose occupations included contract painter, truck driver, and restaurateur, and Johanna Egan. He attended public schools in Lincoln, Nebraska, and during his high school years excelled in track and worked for the Lincoln *Star,* handling newsstand sales and complaints. In 1927, shortly after graduation, he migrated to Los Angeles. While working in retail sales, he began studying law; he received his law degree from LaSalle Extension University in 1939. As was common at that time, Yorty skipped straight from high school to evening law classes at LaSalle, bypassing the traditional undergraduate college degree. On 1 December 1938 he married Elizabeth ("Betts") Hensel, with whom he had one son. After her death in 1984, he married Gloria Haig on 8 June 1986. Haig also passed away, and Yorty married his third wife, Valery King, who survived him.

Yorty launched his four-decade political career in 1933 as a campaign speaker and organizer for a successful Los Angeles city council candidate, which landed him a supervisor's job in the city's Department of Water and Power.

He won his first race—for California State Assembly—in 1936 and was reelected in 1938. In the assembly, he alienated his liberal supporters by sponsoring a bill to establish an Un-American Activities Committee, the first such committee at the state level. In 1940, on the improbable slogan "Stop Hitler Now," he ran a quixotic and unsuccessful campaign for nomination to the U.S. Senate (a year earlier, he had run unsuccessfully for the Los Angeles City Council). He was again nominated for the state assembly in 1942 but chose to enlist in the U.S. Army Air Corps. During the war, he served as an intelligence officer in the South Pacific.

Upon his return in 1945 Yorty made his first run for the Los Angeles mayoralty. After finishing a distant sixth, he practiced law and then returned to the state assembly in 1949. A year later, he ran for and won the U.S. House of Representatives seat that Helen Gahagan Douglas had vacated so that she could run for the Senate against Richard Nixon. Never satisfied with the office he had last won, he chose to vacate his House seat in 1954 to challenge Thomas Kuchel for the remaining two years of an unexpired Senate term to which the latter had been appointed. Despite losing by over 300,000 votes, Yorty chose to challenge Kuchel again two years later and was beaten even more soundly. Moreover, by opposing the state Democratic Party's chosen candidate in the primary, he alienated the party hierarchy. His standing with Democratic leaders worsened in 1960 when he publicly supported Republican presidential candidate Richard Nixon over John F. Kennedy. This event

Sam Yorty, 1971. JEFF ROBBINS/ASSOCIATED PRESS AP

may have helped to propel him back to the nominally nonpartisan arena of city politics.

Beginning as a decided underdog, Yorty narrowly won the 1961 Los Angeles mayoral election over longtime incumbent Norris Poulson, becoming the city's first mayor from the San Fernando Valley. His campaign included attacks on the "downtown machine," appeals to black voters who had been offended by public comments made by the chief of police, and opportunistic use of the "trash collection issue," as he railed at a city council ordinance requiring homeowners to separate their trash by "type" for multiple collections during the week.

From the outset, Yorty got along badly with the city council, but he won popularity by securing a lowering of property taxes and helping to bring new industry to the city. In his 1965 reelection campaign, many conservatives who had initially opposed him switched and supported him, and he won by a huge margin over several contenders.

Events in Yorty's second term permanently altered his image, as well as his brand of politics. In August 1965 the south central Los Angeles neighborhood known as Watts exploded in the first of the many inner-city riots that marked the "long, hot summers" of the late 1960s. Yorty's

reaction was to defend the conduct of the Los Angeles Police Department and condemn those responsible for the violence. He became even more controversial within his party and was publicly criticized by leading Democratic liberals, including Senator Robert F. Kennedy.

The 1969 mayoral contest was a nasty affair. Challenged by black city councilman Thomas Bradley, Yorty abandoned hope of winning over non-white voters and conjured up the specter of a dangerous "black block vote," charging ties between black community leaders and radical leftists. Race-baiting worked in the superheated political atmosphere, and Yorty succeeded in uniting the "white vote," winning by over 50,000. In his final term in any public office, Yorty exhibited little real interest in the daily demands of governing, taking numerous trips abroad. His travels may have been related to his next electoral goal—winning the U.S. Presidency in 1972. On a long shot, he took a stridently hawkish position on the Vietnam War, railed against "subversive organizations" that were undermining the nation, and called for reducing government spending to a minimum. He finished with only 0.5 percent of the overall Democratic primary vote. A year later, in a rematch with Bradley for reelection as mayor, he was soundly defeated, as black, Latino, and liberal Jewish voters turned out in far greater proportions than conservative whites.

Yorty's increasing political irrelevancy in the 1970s and 1980s did not deter him from running for almost any office that was available. In 1980, then a Republican, he ran unsuccessfully for a Senate nomination, and in the following year, when he tried once again to unseat Mayor Bradley, he lost even more decisively than in 1973. Out of political options, he retired to his home in Studio City, a part of Los Angeles, and busied himself for five years as host of a radio talk show. Disappointed not to be named to the 1984 Los Angeles Olympics Committee, Yorty spoke out publicly less frequently in his later years. He died at age eighty-eight at his home in Studio City, following a stroke. Per Yorty's instructions, no information was ever made public about his burial.

During the course of his political career, Yorty was a candidate in approximately twenty elections, winning about half. Glib and smooth, he was among the first politicians to take advantage of television. Of medium height and sandy-haired, he retained his wiry, athletic physique and had the ability to come across as both urbane and homespun. The adjectives most often applied to him, by friend and foe alike, were "colorful" and "maverick."

★

Yorty's official mayoral papers, covering all three terms and including scrapbooks for a longer period, are in the Los Angeles City Archives. Two biographies of Yorty have been published, one favorable and the other distinctly critical. Ed Ainsworth, *Maverick Mayor: A Biography of Sam Yorty of Los Angeles* (1966), is an admiring chronicle of Yorty's life, published during his second term as mayor. In contrast, John C. Bollens and Grant B. Geyer, *Yorty: Politics of a Constant Candidate* (1973), emphasizes the opportunism and shifting political perspective that characterized Yorty's career. A sound, detailed study of racial issues during Yorty's years in City Hall can be found in Raphael Sonenshein's *Politics in Black and White: Race and Power in Los Angeles* (1993). Another mid-career assessment can be found in *Current Biography* (1964). Informative obituaries of Yorty are in the *Los Angeles Times* and *New York Times* (both 6 June 1998).

GARY W. REICHARD

YOUNG, Coleman Alexander (*b.* 24 May 1918 in Tuscaloosa, Alabama; *d.* 29 November 1997 in Detroit, Michigan), first African-American mayor of Detroit, Michigan.

Young was the oldest of five children born to William Coleman Young, a tailor, and Ida Reese Jones, a teacher and homemaker. When Young was five years old, his family moved to Detroit's "Black Bottom" neighborhood where his father set up a tailor shop and also worked for the post office. Young attended St. Mary's Catholic School and the public Eastern High School, graduating with honors in 1934. In 1938 Young married his first wife, Marion. He worked for the Ford Motor Company's River Rouge plant in the early 1940s. Drafted into the army in February 1942, Young served in World War II as a second lieutenant and a bombardier-navigator.

Coleman A. Young, 1981. AP/WIDE WORLD PHOTOS

After the war Young worked as a union organizer for the Congress of Industrial Organizations (CIO) but was fired because of clashes with the union leader Walter Reuther. In 1951 he became the executive secretary of the National Negro Labor Council (NNLC), which the U.S. attorney general claimed was subversive and which was disbanded in 1954. Young held various other jobs in the 1950s, working as a spot cleaner in a laundry, running his own cleaning service, driving a taxi, and working as a butcher's assistant. Young and his first wife were divorced in 1954. The next year he married Nadine Drake, a secretary he had hired for the NNLC; they divorced in 1959. There were no surviving children from Young's two marriages. He then plunged into politics in 1960, winning a delegate's seat to the Michigan Constitutional Convention. He was elected to the Michigan Senate in 1964 and became a Democratic floor leader.

Young ran for mayor of Detroit in 1973 against John F. Nichols, a former police chief, in a bitterly contested election, winning by 233,000 votes to 216,000 votes. Detroit's racial balance reflected itself in the vote, with 92 percent of African Americans voting for Young and 91 percent of whites voting for Nichols, who campaigned on the need to make Detroit a safe place to live. Young attacked the police force as a "white and racist organization" upholding an "unjust racist society" and promised a quota system to increase the number of African-American officers. Once the election results confirmed Young's victory, the mayor-elect took a harder line on crime, hoping to end Detroit's reputation as "Murder City, USA." At a prayer breakfast meeting in December 1973, Young stated, "I issue an open warning now to all dope pushers, to all rip-off artists, to all muggers. It is time to leave Detroit. . . . Hit Eight-Mile Road and keep going." Eight-Mile Road was the entry to the suburbs, and whites reacted with terror, feeling Young was inviting crime and inner-city criminals to invade the suburbs.

Mayor Young's brave words may have been soothing to his core constituency, but turning around Detroit's downward slide as an aging industrial city required more than rhetoric. Young sought to revitalize the city's waterfront area and had high hopes for the Renaissance Center, which was under construction when he assumed office. A $377 million phoenix of high-rise towers, the center rose out of the dilapidated and decaying central business district and its grubby, vacant storefronts. The completed "Ren-Cen" failed to revitalize the central city, and Detroit lost its flagship department store, J. L. Hudson Co., which moved out. An exodus of industry and businesses, white flight, and abrasive race relations continued to plague Detroit.

Mayor Young was reelected for another four-year term in 1977. As the voting population grew increasingly African American, Young was easily reelected in 1981, 1985, and

1989. In total, he served for twenty years as Detroit's mayor. A rough-hewn, coarse, and blunt person, Young blistered the police with profanities for living in the suburbs. He suspended police officers living outside of the city limits, moved desk sergeants out into the streets, demoted others, promoted and hired large numbers of African Americans, and disbanded a special crime-fighting unit. Despite his efforts, crime rates continued to climb.

Unable to ignore the city's serious economic problems, Young finally asked the business community to help save Detroit, telling one reporter, "I don't give a goddamn about them making money so long as it is not excessive and so long as they have the city's interests at heart." With tax incentives and the use of public domain to condemn privately owned property, he was able to persuade General Motors and the Chrysler Corporation to stay in the city and build two medium-sized plants. He also used his mayoral influence and city zoning power to build a riverfront sports arena. Even so, the deindustrialization of Detroit continued as the city lost thousands of jobs and the population dropped in every decennial period. The city lost its professional football team, the Detroit Lions, which moved to a nearby suburb, as white flight continued and accelerated under Young's watch.

Some of these problems were beyond Mayor Young's control. A July 1974 U.S. Supreme Court decision mandating school busing in a system that was 70 percent African-American triggered an exodus of whites to the suburbs. By 1977 fiscal deficits forced layoffs of 4,500 city workers, a job and salary freeze, and the closing of two museums. Continued outbreaks of crime, such as an August 1976 rampage of young street toughs who robbed and assaulted patrons at a Cobo Hall rock concert, aggravated the city's problems and enraged the mayor. Young threatened a crackdown, called back laid-off policemen, and ordered a 10 P.M. curfew as well as arrests of street youth who ignored it.

Scandals began to plague the Young administration in 1984 when Charles Beckham, a close friend and aide to the mayor, was found guilty of "extortion, racketeering, and bribery" for awarding $6 million in city contracts to a businesswoman and friend of the mayor, Darralyn Bowers. Although Young was not indicted, tape recordings of the mayor's phone conversations indicated that he clearly condoned such bid rigging. In 1989 Young was the subject of a paternity suit brought by Ann Ivory Calvert. Young denied fatherhood, but blood tests established that he was indeed the father of Calvert's child. Despite the scandals, Young remained popular with African-American voters. In 1989 another appointee of Mayor Young's, Detroit's first African-American police chief, William Hart, was found guilty of stealing and misspending $2.3 million from a secret police fund and was sentenced to ten years in prison.

Young defended Hart by excusing him and saying that the "feds" were out to get him.

By Young's last term as mayor, which began in 1990, his personal and administrative scandals, his failure to check Detroit's civic and economic decline, and his profanity had begun to wear thin with voters. Young admitted in his 1994 autobiography that many of his supporters and staff members took "exception to my frequent use of [profanity]." During his last year in office, in February 1993, a *Detroit News* poll found that 82 percent of voters opposed Young's running for another term, and 75 percent said the city was worse off than it had been four years earlier. In a similar poll, a group of urban scholars and writers ranked Young as number twelve among the "twenty worst big-city mayors." Young decided not to run for reelection and endorsed a close follower and political friend, who lost to Dennis Archer, a pro-growth and racially conciliatory mayor.

Young, who suffered from emphysema, died of respiratory failure at age seventy-nine. He is buried in Detroit's Elmwood Cemetery.

In describing his political legacy, Young wrote, "Hell no. I don't think Detroit is better off now than it was when I became mayor in 1974." But he asserted it was better off than it would have been "without a mayor who will take on [anyone] who tries to mess with Detroit."

★

Young's autobiography, written with Lonnie Wheeler, *Hard Stuff: The Autobiography of Coleman Young* (1994), is surprisingly candid about the personal Young but not very analytical about his administration. Two other helpful sources are Wilbur C. Rich, *Coleman Young and Detroit Politics: From Social Activist to Power Broker* (1989), and Melvin G. Holli, *The American Mayor: The Best and the Worst Big-City Leaders* (1999). In addition, numerous other studies have examined Young's administrative policies, such as Marion Orr and Gerry Stoker, "Urban Regimes and Leadership in Detroit," *Urban Affairs Quarterly* (Sept. 1994), and Tamar Jacoby, "Mandate for Anarchy: Lessons from Detroit on How Not to Fix Ghetto Policing," *New Democrat* (May–June 1998). Obituaries are in the *Detroit Free Press* and *Detroit News* (both 30 Nov. 1997); see also their extensive coverage of Young's career and life in subsequent special issues (1–5 Dec. 1997).

MELVIN G. HOLLI

YOUNG, Robert George (*b.* 22 February 1907 in Chicago, Illinois; *d.* 21 July 1998 in Westlake Village, California), actor who played a variety of mostly sympathetic roles in films of the 1930s and 1940s.

Young was the son of Thomas Young, an Irish immigrant building manufacturer, and the fourth of five children.

Robert Young. AP/WIDE WORLD PHOTOS

When he was a boy, Young's family moved to Seattle, Washington, and then to Los Angeles, California, where he attended Lincoln High School. As a teenager, Young decided that he wanted to become an actor, and he began taking part in high school dramatics. After graduation, he studied and acted at night at the Pasadena Community Playhouse in California and worked with other theater groups there while also working in odd jobs, such as a drug store clerk and bank teller. Beginning in 1927, Young appeared in small roles in silent films.

During a stock company tour of a play called *The Ship* (1931), Young was spotted by a Metro-Goldwyn-Mayer (MGM) talent scout and signed to a long-term contract. His first movie with MGM, and his sound debut, was in a "Charlie Chan" mystery called *The Black Camel* (1931), shot on location in Honolulu, Hawaii. For the next four years Young was kept extraordinarily busy, usually appearing as a clean-cut young man in such films as *The Sin of Madelon Claudet* (1931), *Strange Interlude* (1932), *Today We Live* (1933), and *Tugboat Annie* (1933). Occasionally, he was loaned to other studios, as in RKO's *Spitfire* (1934, opposite Katharine Hepburn); Fox's *Stowaway* (1936, opposite Shirley Temple); and *Secret Agent* (1936), an Alfred Hitchcock spy melodrama filmed by Gaumont-British, in which Young was surprisingly cast as the villain. Young married his high school sweetheart, Elizabeth Louise "Betty" Henderson, in 1933; they had four children.

It was at MGM, however, that Young's career flourished, and throughout the 1930s into the 1940s, he was regularly cast opposite the studio's leading ladies, including Joan Crawford, Myrna Loy, Jean Harlow, Norma Shearer, and Greer Garson. He was also active in radio as a host or a guest on many programs. Although Young seldom achieved top billing, he was eventually given larger roles in such films as *Three Comrades* (1938), *Northwest Passage* (1940), and *The Mortal Storm* (1940), as well as the title roles in such films as *H. M. Pulham, Esq.* (1941) and *Joe Smith, American* (1942). Young also figured prominently as a newspaperman befriending a war orphan in *Journey for Margaret* (1942), the starring film debut of child actor Margaret O'Brien. At MGM and occasionally at other studios, the prolific actor sprinted from movie to movie, often making as many as seven in a single year.

It was only after Young's MGM contract terminated in 1945 that he could finally claim star status in roles that tested his acting skills. Among his most popular films in the 1940s were *Claudia* (1943), as the patient husband of a light-headed young wife; *The Enchanted Cottage* (1945), as an embittered, scarred war veteran who marries a drab spinster; *Crossfire* (1947), as a police lieutenant tracking down an anti-Semitic killer; and *Sitting Pretty* (1948), in which he played a suburban father who hires super-babysitter "Mr. Belvedere." Young was also effective in an uncharacteristic role as a scheming rogue in *They Won't Believe Me* (1947).

Young had also been working in radio, most prominently starring in the show "Western Union" on the Kate Smith Radio Hour in 1941. In 1949 NBC chose Young to star in *Father Knows Best*, a radio series about an average American family living in the Midwestern town of Springfield. When the show was turned into a comedy series for television in 1954, Young's "Jim Anderson" became an indelible cultural icon, the wise head of a clan that included Jane Wyatt as his wife, and Elinor Donahue, Billy Gray, and Lauren Chapin as his children. The idealized Anderson could always be counted on for sensible advice and solutions to not very pressing problems. The series, which won two Emmys (1957 and 1958) for Young, ran with original episodes until 1960 and continued into syndication for many years.

After attempting a second, short-lived situation comedy series called *Window on Main Street,* airing on CBS in 1961, Young retired from television for a number of years. He returned in 1969 to star in a successful ABC hour-long drama, *Marcus Welby, M.D.* (called *A Matter of Humanities* in syndication), in which he played a kindly, sagacious general practitioner in Santa Monica, California. The success of that play led to six seasons of *Marcus Welby, M.D.* (September 1969 to May 1976), in which "Dr. Welby" took an intensely personal view toward his patients, dispensing wisdom, compassion, and common sense along with the medicine. The program was esteemed by medical groups for its frank discussion of such topics as autism, drug addiction, and leukemia. Young won another Emmy, in the category outstanding continued performance by an actor in a leading role in a dramatic series, in 1970 for his performance in the role. Young later reappeared as "Dr. Welby" for two special television plays, *The Return of Marcus Welby, M.D.* in 1984, and *Marcus Welby, M.D.: A Holiday Affair* in 1988. Young continued to make television films for the rest of his life, including such titles as *Vanished* (1971), *All My Darling Daughters* (1972), *Little Women* (1978), and *Mercy or Murder?* (1987). In 1970 he was the host of the CBS special *Robert Young and the Family,* which satirized family life in America.

Despite his reassuring, silver-haired presence and air of authority, Young's life was anything but tranquil or untroubled. He had a long history of alcoholism and depression, admitting in a 1983 interview that his fight to overcome alcoholism was "an immensely slow, difficult process." He added, "After slipping back again and again, I at last made a giant step, and I was across the threshold to sanity." However, he attempted suicide in 1991, asserting that he had resumed drinking after asking his wife to form a suicide pact. She maintained that she had assumed he was "just rambling," and Young admitted himself to a hospital for psychiatric treatment.

Young died of respiratory failure at his home in Westlake Village, a suburb of Los Angeles. He is buried at Forest Lawn Memorial Park in Glendale, California.

Although he could not be called a charismatic film star, Robert Young was a consistently dependable actor who projected an image of quiet strength, especially on the television screen. In later years, despite the demons he battled in his personal life, he came to embody decency and integrity in several long-running television programs. In his acting, Young never revealed the troubling shadows that hovered over his private life, instead giving his best to every role.

★

Tributes to Young include Tom Shales, "America's Father Figure," *Washington Post* (23 July 1998); Ed Weiner, "Model Dad, Dream Doctor: Remembering Robert Young," *TV Guide* (8 Aug. 1998); and Giovanna Breu, Beth Karlin, and Champ Clark, "Father Figure," *People Weekly* (10 Aug. 1998). Obituaries are in the *New York Times, Los Angeles Times* (both 23 July 1998) and *Variety* (2 Aug. 1998).

TED SENNETT

YOUNGMAN, Henny (*b.* 16 March 1906, in London, England; *d.* 24 February 1998 in New York City), borscht belt comedian known as the "King of the One-Liners."

Though both parents were naturalized Americans, Youngman was born at London Jewish Hospital (some sources say Liverpool, England, and others put his birth date as 12 January). His Russian-born parents, Jacob Youngman (formerly Yonkel Jungman) and Olga Chetkin, met on New York's Lower East Side and married in 1904. They moved to England on their honeymoon, only returning after raising money for the trip a year and a half later, when Youngman was six months old.

The Youngmans lived in a top floor apartment at 223 Fifty-first Street in the Bay Ridge section of Brooklyn, New York, later moving to 281 Fifty-first Street, where Youngman and his younger brother Lester attended P.S. 2 on Forty-sixth Street. By all accounts, Youngman was a difficult student. While attending Manual Training High School, Youngman garnered his first comedy booking, at

Henny Youngman, 1986. © NEAL PRESTON/CORBIS

the Orpheum Theater. Hired by Solly Shore to fill in for Jewish comedians who refused to work on Yom Kippur, Youngman was halfway through his routine when a neighborhood police officer arrived and dragged him off the stage. His father forcibly brought him back to the synagogue for the end of the holiday services. He was expelled from school, but later studied printing at Brooklyn Vocational Trade School.

While attending the trade school, Youngman worked at Kresge's department store, where he printed business cards, letterhead, and joke cards. His friends at this time were his neighbor, would-be performer Jackie Gleason, and Milton Berle, who, having already established an act, often stopped by Kresge's after his gigs. Together, they frequented nearby vaudeville houses, and much of his early material came from the acts he saw in those venues. While working at Kresge's, he met Sadie Cohen. Despite his attraction to her, he was too nervous to speak to her early on. Eventually, however, he conquered his fear. The two began a relationship and were married four years later.

To supplement his income, Youngman started a band called the Swanee Syncopators. While trying to get a booking for his band, he asked Sadie to play a dance record to convince someone on the telephone that there was a band in the room. Youngman's combo was hired to play the dance hall in Coney Island. A Billboard review of that performance was positive, but the headline, "Hen Youngman and the Syncopators Play Coney Island Boardwalk," startled him. Seeing his nickname in print prompted him to change his name to Henny, a conglomeration of his nickname, "Hen," and Henry, the name on his birth certificate, because, as he said, "hens lay eggs."

He worked frequently at popular Jewish resorts in the Catskill Mountains, often at the Swan Lake Inn. Besides leading the band, Youngman served as a tummler, entertaining the guests and distracting them from the bad food and poor accommodations. His music career ended when his band was booked at the Nut Club in Pinedale, New Jersey. The headliners did not show up and the club's manager, having seen Youngman clowning around during rehearsals, asked him to do a set of comedy material. He was such a hit that he was hired as the house comic for the club for the next two weeks.

Other bookings followed. After his evening performances, Youngman went to Lindy's Restaurant, passing time with celebrities and newspaper columnists until the early hours of the morning. Anyone who was anybody was there, including radio broadcaster and nationally syndicated newspaper columnist Walter Winchell, who dubbed Youngman "the King of the One-Liners."

In 1936 Youngman was approached to appear at the Actor's Synagogue benefit. He not only won over the live audience but attracted the attention of Ted Collins, Kate Smith's manager, who promptly hired Youngman for weekly six-minute radio routines. His first broadcast was so good that Collins had him continue for four additional minutes. Youngman sought out more writers. Joe Quillen often provided the needed material. Other writers who got their start writing jokes for Youngman were Bill Manhoff, Harry Crane, Ray Singer, Bobby O'Brien, Snag Werris, Izzy Ellinson, Abe Burrows, and Danny Shapiro. Morey Amsterdam and Norman Lear also wrote for Youngman.

His signature line originated at this time, when his wife and several of her friends came backstage a few minutes before the broadcast was to begin. Still trying to learn his lines, he took Sadie by the elbow and walked her toward an usher. Directing the man to seat the group in the studio audience, he said, "Take my wife . . . please." At her request, he continued to use the line, even after her death in 1987.

Youngman began touring the country, averaging over 200 bookings a year for the next forty years. He eventually achieved success on television. In particular, *Rowan and Martin's Laugh-In* brought new appreciation for Youngman's brand of humor. He also appeared on *Hee-Haw, Hollywood Squares,* and *The Tonight Show Starring Johnny Carson.*

In 1974 Youngman recorded a half-hour of his material for the New York Telephone Company's new service, Dial-a-Joke. The strength of his popularity caused the service to receive 3,331,638 calls during its first month. Continuing his heavy performance schedule throughout the eighties and nineties, he appeared in television specials, performed at Radio City Music Hall for three separate performances of *Night of One Hundred Stars*, and worked with director Steven Spielberg on his animated television series, *Tiny Toons* (1991).

While performing two shows a night in San Francisco one week after Christmas in 1997, he came down with a cold that developed into pneumonia. Hospitalized on 2 January 1998, he died at age ninety-two at Mount Sinai Hospital in New York. A memorial was held at the Riverside Chapel in New York City on 27 February 1998, attended by several hundred mourners, including former mayors of New York Abraham D. Beame and David N. Dinkins. Also present were celebrities such as Alan King, Anne Meara, Jerry Stiller, Tony Bennett, and LeRoy Neiman. He is buried at the Mount Carmel Cemetery in Queens, New York.

Youngman's career spanned more than seventy years. He furthered the careers of many young comics and inspired those who came after him, most notably Red Buttons, Jack Carter, and Rodney Dangerfield. One of the most enduring of the borscht belt entertainers, entertainers associated with the Catskills' summer resorts, he brought the humor of the period to life for later generations. His many appearances in radio, television, and movies, including Martin Scorsese's *Goodfellas* (1990), rendered him an icon in American popular culture.

★

Youngman's autobiographies, *Take My Wife . . . Please! My Life and Laughs* (1973) and *Take My Life, Please!* (1991), provide accounts of his life and career. He also penned several collections of his jokes, notably *Henny Youngman's Greatest One-Liners* (1970), *Take My Jokes, Please!* (1983), *The Best of Henny Youngman* (1984), and *Henny Youngman's BIG Book of Insults* (1995); and recorded his jokes on album and tape, including *The World's Worst Jokes* (1987). Obituaries are in the *Los Angeles Times* and *Washington Post* (both 25 Feb. 1998) and the *New York Times* (26 Feb. 1998).

JOCELYN BERGER

Z

ZALE, Tony (*b.* 29 May 1913 in Gary, Indiana; *d.* 20 March 1997 in Portage, Indiana), middleweight champion and Hall of Fame boxer known as the "Man of Steel."

Zale was born as Anthony Florian Zaleski, the third of four sons born to the Polish immigrants Joseph Zaleski, a steelworker, and his wife Catherine Mazur. Zale was two years old when his father was struck by a car and killed while riding a bicycle. "I never got over it. With his death I became painfully bashful, withdrawn," he recalled more than fifty years later. His Roman Catholic family was deeply religious, and Zale's earliest ambition was to become a priest. By age fifteen, he had other interests. Two of his older brothers had outstanding careers as amateur boxers, and it was with their encouragement that he took up the sport. The Zale brothers set up a fight gym in their family garage. Zale, who combined speed and a powerful knockout punch, won the 1930 lightweight championship of the Indiana Golden Gloves tournament and won three other titles in his amateur career. Zale finished as the runner-up in the competition for a slot on the 1932 U.S. Olympic boxing team. "That was the disappointment of my life," he later reflected. "I had four matches. I won three of them. I was winning the fourth when I got a bad cut over my eye and they stopped the fight."

In 1934 Zale fought for the Inter-City Golden Gloves middleweight championship at Madison Square Garden in New York City, but was edged on points by Melio Bettina, a future world light-heavyweight champion. Zale won fifty of his ninety-five amateur fights by knockout and lost only eight times. On 11 June 1934 Zale made his professional debut in Chicago with a fourth-round knockout over Eddie Allen. After winning his first nine fights, Zale lost nine of his next seventeen fights and quit the ring. He later attributed these setbacks to mismanagement and overtraining. For the next two years he worked at the blast furnace of the Illinois Steel Mill and trained in fight gyms in the hope of reviving his career. "I knew I was a fighter. I kept in shape. I worked out fairly regular," he said.

Zale launched his comeback on 26 July 1937 with a four-round decision over Elby Johnson and won six out of seven fights over the next five months. In 1938 he signed to fight under the management of Chicago's Sam Pian and Art Winch, a team that had maneuvered Barney Ross to the lightweight and welterweight titles. Teaming up with these men marked the turning point in Zale's career. On 29 July 1940 Zale outpointed the hard-hitting National Boxing Association middleweight champion Al Hostak in a nontitle bout at Chicago Stadium. After this victory sportswriters dubbed Zale the "Man of Steel" because of his toughness and endurance. Hostak agreed to a 19 July 1940 rematch in his hometown of Seattle. Zale floored Hostak twice, then knocked him out in the thirteenth round. On 28 May 1941 they met again in Chicago and Zale retained the title with a second-round knockout.

Zale became the first undisputed middleweight cham-

Tony Zale looking at photos of his 10 June 1948 fight with Rocky Graziano. ASSOCIATED PRESS AP

pion in a decade on 28 November 1941 when he outpointed the number-one ranked Georgie Abrams in fifteen rounds at Madison Square Garden. Although Abrams won the first three rounds, Zale dominated the rest of the fight. Just nine days later, the United States entered World War II, and Zale's title was frozen for the duration. He lost a twelve-round decision to the heavyweight contender Billy Conn at Madison Square Garden on 13 February 1942. "No one who saw that Zale-Conn fight ever will forget how Tony stood up to the bigger man," Nat Fleischer wrote in *Ring*. Zale then enlisted in the U.S. Navy and served as a physical instructor at the Great Lakes Naval Center. He was offered a fortune to defend his title but declined on the grounds that it would be wrong to fight for personal gain during wartime.

Some doubted whether Zale could hold his own against younger challengers after serving for four years in the navy. In the first half of 1946 he knocked out six rivals in nontitle bouts. Even so, he was an underdog when he defended his title at Yankee Stadium on 27 September 1946 against the younger Rocky Graziano in the first of three epic fights. Zale broke his hand below the right thumb in the second round. Graziano hurt him with a barrage of punches in that round, but the champion was saved by the bell. Zale, trailing on points, stunned Graziano in the sixth round with a right to the midsection and then knocked him out with a left hook.

The Zale-Graziano trilogy set a new standard for boxing excitement. In 1981 the editors of *Ring* ranked Zale's first two clashes with Graziano among the ten greatest fights of all time. "They weren't fights," said the boxing historian Bert Randolph Sugar. "They were wars without survivors." Zale came on strong in the early rounds of his rematch with Graziano at Chicago Stadium on 16 July 1947, closing Graziano's eye and nearly ending the fight in the third and fourth rounds. But Graziano rallied, trapped Zale on the ropes in the sixth round, and pummeled him. Although Zale worked his way out of trouble, the referee stopped the fight and declared Graziano the winner by knockout. Zale, who felt cheated, did not contest the outcome. His managers had already signed a contract for a third fight.

On 10 June 1948 Zale dropped Graziano in the first round of their rubber match at an outdoor stadium in Newark, New Jersey. Graziano fought back in the second round with fierce combinations. But in the third round, Zale hit him with a right to the body and a smashing left hook to the jaw that ended the fight. Zale, who became the first middleweight champion in forty years to regain the title, fought Marcel Cerdan three months later and was knocked out in the twelfth round. It was Zale's last fight. "The arm was gone, and I knew it was over," he said.

In 1958 Zale was elected to the Boxing Hall of Fame. He won seventy of eighty-nine professional fights, forty-six by knockout. From 1949 to 1968 he ran the boxing program for Chicago's Catholic Youth Organization. He lived in New York from 1968 to 1971 and was a host at Gallagher's 33 restaurant. From 1971 to 1986 he was a boxing instructor for the Chicago Park District. In one of his final public appearances, Zale received the Presidential Citizens Medal on 16 October 1990 from President George Bush.

Zale married Adeline Richwalski in 1942, and they had two daughters. The couple divorced in 1952. On 19 September 1970 Zale married Philomena Theresa Gianfrancisco, a physical-education instructor and former professional baseball player. She died in 1992. Zale suffered from Parkinson's disease and Alzheimer's disease, and he died in a nursing home after his family suspended life support. He is buried in Calvary Cemetery in Portage, Indiana.

★

Zale was the subject of two cover profiles in *Ring* (Feb. 1942, Feb. 1947). Bert Randolph Sugar featured Zale in *The Great Fights: A Pictorial History of Boxing's Greatest Bouts* (1981), and *The 100 Greatest Boxers of All Time* (1984). An interview with Zale is included in Jack Cannon and Tom Cannon, eds., *Nobody Asked Me, But . . . : The World of Jimmy Cannon* (1978). Zale was the cover subject for an edition of the *Indianapolis Star* (14 July 1985). Obituaries are in the *Chicago Sun-Times* and *New York Times* (both 22 Mar. 1997).

STEVE NEAL

Fred Zinnemann, 1992. TIM ZINNEMANN

ZINNEMANN, Alfred ("Fred") (*b.* 29 April 1907 in Rzeszów, Poland; *d.* 14 March 1997 in London, England), motion picture director of such classics as *High Noon* (1952), *From Here to Eternity* (1953), *The Nun's Story* (1959), and *A Man for All Seasons* (1966).

Zinnemann was the elder of two sons of Oskar Zinnemann, a Vienna physician, and Anna Feiwel. After attending the Franz Josef Gymnasium, he studied law at the University of Vienna (1925–1927) but, inspired by the early film classics, sought to make movies instead. This inclination disturbed his bourgeois Jewish family, but eventually Oskar Zinnemann allowed his son to study filmmaking in Paris. Zinnemann enrolled at the brand-new École Technique de Photographie et Cinématographie in 1927 and thus became one of the first school-trained directors. Following the expiration of his visa, Zinnemann moved to Berlin in 1928. There his assistantships included work on a documentary-style film called *Menschen am Sonntag* (People on Sunday). Among his colleagues were Robert Siodmak, Billy Wilder, and Edgar Ulmer—all of whom later achieved success in Hollywood.

Zinnemann moved to the United States in 1929, arriving in New York City on the day of the October stock market crash. His education began with a weeklong bus ride across the country to Hollywood. There he was briefly an extra in the classic *All Quiet on the Western Front* (1930). More important, he was welcomed into the circle of the Austrian stage and film director Berthold Viertel, where he first gained the acquaintance of Hollywood's growing colony of European artists. There, too, he met the famous documentarian Robert Flaherty. He actually returned to Europe to help Flaherty prepare a documentary on Soviet Central Asia. The project was aborted, but Zinnemann considered this brief apprenticeship formative to his career.

It was a quasi-documentary project for the Mexican government that gave Zinnemann his first chance to direct. For *Los redes* (*The Wave*, 1934/1935), he spent months dramatizing the lives of a Yucatán fishing village in the company of the still photographer Paul Strand. Although this film achieved some renown, Zinnemann spent the next seven years in a kind of apprenticeship. From 1937 he was at the most rigidly hierarchical of studios, Metro-Goldwyn-Mayer (MGM). Honing his craft on low-budget shorts, Zinnemann directed dog stories, *Crime Does Not Pay* episodes, and an Academy Award–winning short about the conquest of puerperal fever (*That Mothers Might Live*, 1938). His first feature film was the B-picture *Kid Glove Killer* (1942). During this period Zinnemann met Renée

Bartlett, an English-born costumer. They married on 9 October 1936 and had one son, Tim Zinnemann, who became a film producer. Zinnemann was naturalized as a citizen of the United States in 1937.

Zinnemann considered *The Seventh Cross* (1944) to be the true start of his directing career. Based on a German novel by Anna Seghers, it told of a Nazi resister's struggle to survive with the aid of frightened friends and neighbors. It took some courage to tell of "good Germans" during World War II, but Zinnemann insisted on doing exactly that, and the picture was well received. *The Seventh Cross* established Zinnemann's pattern of celebrating men of conscience who struggle against oppressive institutions. Zinnemann himself felt oppressed by MGM's rigidity. He took leave of the studio in 1947 to make an independent movie about postwar refugees. *The Search* (1948) demonstrated his ability to meld documentary-style techniques with conventional storytelling. While the film introduced Montgomery Clift to the screen, it also featured many untrained refugee children whose demeanor amid the bombed-out locations gave the picture a terrible authenticity.

The Men (1950), about paraplegic veterans, introduced another great star, Marlon Brando, and again benefitted from naturalistic location filming in a veterans' hospital. *High Noon* (1952) vaulted Zinnemann to the top rank of Hollywood directors. Although Zinnemann came late to this rich collaboration with the producer Stanley Kramer and the screenwriter Carl Foreman, he gave the movie its bleak, realistic look as he skillfully developed the McCarthy-era parable of a lone righteous man in a town filled with cowards and opportunists. (The previous year Zinnemann had been involved in a bitter Directors Guild showdown over the demand for a loyalty oath.)

After a sensitive adaptation of Carson McCullers's *Member of the Wedding* (1952), Zinnemann scored his greatest triumph with *From Here to Eternity* (1953), which was considered a daring exposé of unrest and corruption in the U.S. Army on the eve of Pearl Harbor. Another story of loners bucking the system, it earned thirteen Academy Award nominations and eight Oscars, including best picture and best director. Zinnemann evoked performances of startling intensity from Deborah Kerr and the inexperienced Frank Sinatra. The moonlight swim of Kerr and Burt Lancaster has joined the scene of the showdown in *High Noon* in America's cultural memory.

Eclecticism marked Zinnemann's subsequent career. The giant 70-millimeter *Oklahoma* (1955) was an uncharacteristic musical comedy and a great popular success. *The Nun's Story* (1959) detailed the spiritual formation of a young Belgian woman (Audrey Hepburn) with extraordinary realism and then dramatized her inner struggles during medical missionary service in the Congo and wartime Europe. It remains Hollywood's most mature treatment of

a religious subject, and yet Zinnemann so humanized the material that the film was a great critical and popular success, earning eight Oscar nominations and a best director award from the New York Film Critics Circle. *The Sundowners* (1960) was a low-key family saga about Australian sheepherders. Other dramas were less successful, including *A Hatful of Rain* (1957), about drug addiction, and *Behold a Pale Horse* (1964), on the aftermath of the Spanish Civil War.

By the early 1960s Zinnemann had moved to London. Several Hollywood projects came to naught. But his low-budget drama of conscience about the sixteenth-century English statesman Sir Thomas More, *A Man for All Seasons* (1966), scored an unexpected triumph, including Zinnemann's second pair of Oscars for best picture and director. Three years later, however, his major production of *Man's Fate* was cancelled by MGM on the eve of shooting. The faltering company even attempted to bill Zinnemann for the picture's preparation costs.

Again Zinnemann bounced back, first with a realistic thriller about an attempt to assassinate the French president Charles de Gaulle (*The Day of the Jackal,* 1973) and then with *Julia* (1977), which dramatized the awakening conscience of the young American dramatist Lillian Hellman through a story of wartime friendship and political engagement. Zinnemann's last film, *Five Days One Summer* (1982), attempted a complex love story in an Alpine mountaineering setting (a favorite sport of the director's). The picture was not successful, and Zinnemann retired in London to enjoy a series of tributes and retrospectives. He was active in the struggle for filmmakers' "moral rights" to resist colorization and other distortions of their work. Honors came from the governments of America and France and from the city of Vienna, where decades earlier Zinnemann's parents and extended family had perished in the Nazi Holocaust.

Zinnemann died of a heart attack in London, and his ashes were scattered near Santa Monica, California. Among the most honored of postwar Hollywood filmmakers (four times named best director by the New York Film Critics Circle), he was later derided by auteurist critics as an "impersonal" realist. Although his work has been less studied than that of some contemporaries, his best films have endured in the popular imagination. A reserved gentleman of the old school, Zinnemann could show surprising tenacity and stubbornness in battling with a Hollywood system that ultimately came to honor him as one of its leading figures.

★

Zinnemann's papers are at the Margaret Herrick Library of the Academy of Motion Picture Arts and Sciences in Beverly Hills, California. His memoir, *A Life in the Movies* (1992), is anecdotal and heavily illustrated. The first critical anthology is Arthur Nolletti Jr., ed., *The Films of Fred Zinnemann: Critical Perspectives* (1999), with an interview and a useful bibliography. Interviews are in *Films and Filming* (Sept. 1964) and *American Film* 11 (Jan.–Feb. 1986). See also Alan Stanbrook, "A Man for All Movies," in *Films and Filming* (June 1967); John Howard Reid, "A Man for All Movies: The Films of Fred Zinnemann," in *Films and Filming* (May 1968); Gordon Gow, "Individualism Against Machinery," in *Films and Filming* (Feb. 1976); Michael Buckley, "Fred Zinnemann," in *Films in Review* 34 (1983): 1; and Gene D. Phillips, "Fred Zinnemann: Darkness at Noon," in his *Major Film Directors of the American and British Cinema* (1990). The hostile auteurist viewpoint is notoriously voiced by Andrew Sarris in *The American Cinema* (1968), qualified by his interview with Zinnemann in the *Village Voice* (16 Nov. 1982). Tim Zinnemann produced a film tribute to his father, *As I See It* (1997). Obituaries are in the *New York Times* and *Los Angeles Times* (both 15 Mar. 1997).

JOHN FITZPATRICK

ZOLL, Paul Maurice (*b.* 15 July 1911 in Boston, Massachusetts; *d.* 5 January 1999 in Chestnut Hill, Massachusetts), Harvard cardiologist and pioneer in the development of the heart monitors, pacemakers, and defibrillators used by millions of people around the world.

Zoll was the son of Hyman Zoll and Molly Homsky. A graduate of the Boston Latin School, he received an A.B. degree summa cum laude from Harvard University in 1932. He received an M.D. from Harvard Medical School in 1936. In his last year there he became engaged in research on the relationship of alcoholism to heart disease with a group headed by Dr. Soma Weiss. When he finished medical school, Zoll accepted a clinical internship at Beth Israel Hospital in Boston, followed by a year of residency at Bellevue Hospital in New York City. After his residency, he returned to Beth Israel in 1939 as a research fellow of the Josiah Macy Foundation, where he worked on the clinicopathologic correlations of coronary artery disease. On 28 October 1939 he married Janet Jones; they had two children.

During World War II Zoll served at the 160th U.S. Army Station Hospital in the United Kingdom, where he was cardiologist and chief of medicine. During that time he was dedicated to the unit dealing with thoracic problems. In 1944 he received the United States Army Legion of Merit Award. Zoll returned to Boston in 1945 and resumed his research activities on the pathophysiology of angina pectoris at Beth Israel Hospital, where he was chief of the cardiac clinic from 1947 to 1958. At that time the standard treatment for cardiac arrest was crude: a doctor would cut into the chest and squeeze the heart with his hand to

Paul M. Zoll, 1973. AP/WIDE WORLD PHOTOS

pump blood through the body. In 1950, borrowing an electrical stimulator, Zoll was able to produce ventricular extrasystoles in a dog. By 1952 Zoll and a team of other doctors in Boston were able to apply electric charges externally to the chest to resuscitate two human patients whose hearts had stopped. This was Zoll's fundamental discovery: finding that a single electrical stimulus to the surface of the chest could produce a heartbeat in patients with a condition known as heart block due to Stokes-Adams disease.

The first of these patients lived only twenty minutes. The second patient survived for eleven months, after fifty-two hours of electrical stimulation. Zoll's clinical experiments were published by the *New England Journal of Medicine* in 1952, but some of his colleagues either dismissed the importance of his achievement or considered his work "against the will of God." Zoll's discovery led to his development of external pacemakers to restore normal rhythms in patients whose hearts were beating erratically and dangerously. The electrical stimulation of the heart permitted fundamental studies of the physiologic and pharmacological behavior of the cardiac conduction system. His discovery and inventions played a significant role in the reduction of morbidity and mortality from heart disease in the second half of the twentieth century.

But Zoll continued to meet opposition from many fronts. External pacemakers, which kept patients tethered to large machines, were the main treatment for heart block. But the devices sometimes caused burns, involuntary muscle contractions, and intolerable pain. Optimal use of the new techniques from emergency resuscitation required quick diagnosis of cardiac arrest in a patient. In the early 1950s Zoll and his technical collaborators developed a practical monitoring device to display the electrical activity of the heart on an oscilloscopic screen. These cardiac monitors and programs for the management of cardiac arrest and arrhythmias form the foundation of modern coronary care units.

Between 1950 and 1960 Zoll and his colleagues developed a method for long-term direct electrical stimulation of the heart by an implanted pacemaker, effectively replacing the external one. Cardiac pacemakers have since played a significant role in the prevention of sudden death and in the rehabilitation of cardiac patients. It has been estimated that more than one million patients in the United States have implanted pacemakers.

Zoll published more than fifty papers on such topics as the electrical stimulation of the heart for resuscitation, the conversion of cardiac arrhythmias, long-term stimulation, and cardiac monitoring and physiological research. In 1977

Zoll retired but continued practicing and conducting research until 1993. Zoll was a member of the scientific review board of the *Journal of Medical Electronics* and associate editor of circulation for the same journal from 1956 to 1965. He was also part of the editorial board of the *Journal of Electrocardiology*. Zoll founded the Zoll Medical Corporation, a pioneer company in the manufacturing of defibrillators and other cardiac devices.

Zoll's wife, Janet, died in 1978, and on 2 January 1981 he married Ann Blumgart Gurewich. In his later years Zoll developed Alzheimer's disease. He died at age eighty-seven in the Heathwood Rehabilitation and Nursing Center in Chestnut Hill, Massachusetts, where he had lived for three years.

A serious and quiet man, Zoll was a pioneer in the field of cardiac pacing and electrophysiology. The many awards he received included the John Scott Award of the City of Philadelphia in 1967, the Albert Lasker Award for clinical medical research in 1973, the award for the Merit of the American Heart Association in 1974, and the Polytechnic/Wunsch Award in 1980 from the Polytechnic Institute in New York. He was a member of Phi Beta Kappa, Sigma XI, the American Heart Association, and the Association of American Physicians.

★

For information about Zoll's life and career, see *Biography Index,* a cumulative index to biographical material, vol. 24 (Sept. 1998–Aug. 1999). Obituaries are in the *New York Times* (8 Jan. 1999) and *Harvard Gazette* (28 Jan. 1999).

MARÍA PACHECO

DIRECTORY OF CONTRIBUTORS

AGNEW, BRAD
Northeastern State University, Tahlequah, Okla.
   Ashmore, Harry Scott
   Axton, Hoyt Wayne
ALEXANDER, THOMAS G.
Brigham Young University
   Arrington, Leonard James
ALLEN, HOWARD
Brooklyn College of the City University of New York
   (Retired)
   Weil, André
AMLER, JANE FRANCES
Manhattanville College
   Kennedy, John Fitzgerald, Jr.
   Marshall, E(dda) G(unnar)
ANDREWS, CHRISTINE A.
University of Chicago
   Sepkoski, J(oseph) John, Jr.
ARETAKIS, JONATHAN G.
Editorial East, Pembroke, Maine
   Farmer, Art(hur) Stewart
AURAND, HAROLD W., JR.
Pennsylvania State University, Schuylkill Campus
   Motley, Marion
BAKER, THERESE DUZINKIEWICZ
Western Kentucky University
   O'Sullivan, Maureen
BARBEAU, ART
West Liberty State College, West Virginia
   Barnett, A(rthur) Doak
   Randolph, Jennings
BAUER, BILL
Rutgers University
   Carter, Betty
BERGER, JOCELYN
Brooklyn College of the City University of New York
   Cafaro, William Michael
   Youngman, Henny
BOSKY, BERNADETTE LYNN
Gotham Writers' Workshop
   Applewhite, Marshall Herff, Jr. ("Herff"; "Do")
   Kane, Robert ("Bob")

BOYLES, MARY
University of North Carolina at Pembroke
   Amory, Cleveland ("Clip")
BRILEY, RON
Sandia Preparatory School, Albuquerque, N.Mex.
   Griffith, Calvin Robertson
   Pakula, Alan Jay
BRILLER, BERT R.
Vice Chairman, Editorial Board, Television Quarterly
   Goldenson, Leonard Harry
BYRNE, JOHN J.
Bronx Community College
   Bridges, Lloyd Vernet, Jr.
   Murray, Kathryn Hazel
CAMPBELL, JIM
Bucknell University (Retired)
   Hutson, Don(ald) Montgomery
   Turner, Clyde Douglas ("Bulldog")
CAREY, ROBERT B.
Empire State College, State University of New York
   Aserinsky, Eugene
   Kristeller, Paul Oskar
CARPENTER, BRIAN B.
Texas A&M University Libraries
   Swanson, Robert Arthur
CARR, DONALD ALAN
Pillsbury Winthrop LLP, Washington, D.C.
   Richardson, Elliot Lee
CARR, VIRGINIA SPENCER
Georgia State University
   Bowles, Paul Frederic(k)
CASTAÑEDA, JAMES AGUSTÍN
Rice University
   De Menil, Dominique Schlumberger
CHRONOPOULOS, THEMIS
Brown University
   Bird, Rose Elizabeth
CHURCH, GARY MASON
Montgomery College Library
   Johnson, Robert Samuel

CICARELLI, JAMES
Walter E. Heller College of Business Administration, Roosevelt University
Wallis, W(ilson) Allen
CICARELLI, JULIANNE
Freelance Writer, Arlington Heights, Ill.
Bunting-Smith, Mary Alice Ingraham ("Polly")
Jacobs, Helen Hull
Wills, Helen Newington
COCHRAN, CHARLES L.
U.S. Naval Academy
Taylor, Telford
COLBERT, THOMAS BURNELL
Marshalltown Community College
Fadiman, Clifton Paul
CRAWFORD, DESSA
Delaware County Community College
McCartney, Linda Louise Eastman
CROUSE, TIM MARTIN
MTV2
Byrd, Charlie Lee
CROWLEY, GWYNETH H.
Texas A&M University Libraries
Monroe, Rose Leigh Will
DALHOUSE, MARK TAYLOR
Washington and Lee University
Jones, Robert Reynolds, Jr. ("Bob")
DAMON, ALLAN L.
Horace Greeley High School, Chappaqua, N.Y.
Clifford, Clark McAdams
Kazin, Alfred
Kempton, (James) Murray
O'Dwyer, (Peter) Paul
DAVIDSON, ABRAHAM A.
Tyler School of Art, Temple University
Lichtenstein, Roy
DECKER, SHARON L.
State University of New York, Maritime College
Ogilvy, David Mackenzie
DIAZ, DAVID
University of Pennsylvania
Ray, James Earl
DICK, BERNARD F.
Fairleigh Dickinson University
Davis, Martin S.
DINNEEN, MARCIA B.
Bridgewater State College
McDowall, Roderick Andrew Anthony Jude ("Roddy")
Sherwood, Roberta
DINNERSTEIN, LEONARD
University of Arizona
Celebrezze, Anthony Joseph

DOBSON, MELISSA A.
Freelance Writer, Newport, R.I.
Calvin, Melvin
DOENECKE, JUSTUS D.
New College of Florida
Hughes, H(enry) Stuart
DOMIN, CHRISTOPHER
University of Arizona
Rudolph, Paul Marvin
DROBNICKI, JOHN A.
York College Library, City University of New York
Ewbank, Wilbur Charles ("Weeb")
DUBROW, MICKEY
Freelance Writer and Television Producer, Atlanta, Ga.
Bates, Clayton ("Peg Leg")
ECKSTEIN, PETER
Ann Arbor, Mich.
Adams, Charles Francis
ELLIS, MARION A.
Charlotte, N.C.
Sanford, (James) Terry
ENDERS, ERIC
Historian, Cooperstown, N.Y.
Leonard, Walter Fenner ("Buck")
ENGELBRECHT, LLOYD C.
Professor of Art History Emeritus, University of Cincinnati
Lerner, Nathan Bernard
EPSTEIN, MICHAEL M.
Southwestern University School of Law
Friendly, Fred W.
EVENSEN, BRUCE J.
DePaul University
Brickhouse, John Beasley ("Jack")
Mitchum, Robert Charles Durman
Payton, Walter Jerry
FAFOUTIS, DEAN
Salisbury State University, Md.
Chafee, John Hubbard
Fascell, Dante Bruno
FERRELL, ROBERT H.
Indiana University, Bloomington
Harriman, Pamela Beryl Digby Churchill Hayward
FEUERHERD, PETER
American Bible Society
Cherne, Leo
FINDLAY, RONALD E.
Columbia University
Lancaster, Kelvin John
FISCHEL, JACK
Millersville University
Holzman, William ("Red")
Hruska, Roman Lee
Shabazz, Betty Jean

FISCHER, WILLIAM E., JR.
U.S. Air Force
Wylie, Chalmers Pangburn

FITZPATRICK, JANE BRODSKY
Stephen B. Luce Library, State University of New York Maritime College
Lewis, Shari
Mann, Jonathan Max
Silverstein, Shel(don) Allan
West, Dorothy

FITZPATRICK, JOHN
Charles Scribner's Sons
Zinnemann, Alfred ("Fred")

FLYNN, JOSEPH G.
State University of New York College of Technology, Alfred
Bloom, Benjamin Samuel

FOLEY, MICHAEL S.
College of Staten Island, City University of New York
Lukas, J(ay) Anthony
Spock, Benjamin McLane ("Dr. Spock")

FRANCIS, BILL
National Baseball Hall of Fame
Ashburn, Don Richard ("Richie")
Wynn, Early, Jr. ("Gus")

FRIEDMAN, JOEL
Tulane Law School
Wisdom, John Minor

GARGAN, WILLIAM M.
Brooklyn College of the City University of New York
Ginsberg, (Irwin) Allen

GATES, JONATHAN A.
Nyack College
Quintero, José Benjamin

GENTILE, RICHARD H.
Independent Scholar, South Easton, Mass.
Peabody, Endicott ("Chub")
Tsongas, Paul Efthemios

GERBER, BARBARA L.
Brooklyn College of the City University of New York
Mars, Forrest Edward, Sr.
Whitney, Ruth Reinke

GETTLEMAN, MARVIN E.
Professor Emeritus, Brooklyn Polytechnic University
Murphy, Joseph Samson

GINTHER, KRISTAN
Writer, Los Angeles, Calif.
Hartman, Phil(ip) Edward

GOLDBERG, ROBERT ALAN
University of Utah
Goldwater, Barry Morris

GOOD, ELAINE MCMAHON
Nassau Community College, State University of New York
Bate, Walter Jackson

GOODBODY, JOAN
Sterling C. Evans Library, Texas A&M University
Abzug, Bella Savitzky
Arcaro, George Edward ("Eddie")

GORDON, NANCY M.
Independent Scholar, Amherst, Mass.
Cochran, Thomas Childs

GOTTLIEB, JANE
The Juilliard School
Menuhin, Yehudi
Solti, Georg

GRAFF, HENRY F.
Professor Emeritus, Columbia University
DiMaggio, Joseph Paul ("Joe")

GREENBERG, DAVID
Columbia University
Slate Magazine
Ehrlichman, John Daniel

GREENWALD, RICHARD A.
U.S. Merchant Marine Academy
Shanker, Albert

GREISING, DAVID
Chicago Tribune
Goizueta, Roberto Crispulo

GRIFFEN, CLYDE
Professor Emeritus, Vassar College
Simpson, Alan

GRIFFITH, JEAN W., JR.
Pittsburg State University
Bono, Salvatore Phillip ("Sonny")
Moore, Jack Carlton ("Clayton")

GUGLIELMO, TOM
University of Michigan
Notorious B.I.G. ("Biggie Smalls")

HACKNEY, SHELDON
University of Pennsylvania
Woodward, C(omer) Vann

HAGER, THOMAS
University of Oregon
Bowerman, William Jay ("Bill")
Hershey, Alfred Day

HANDLER, JESSICA
Atlanta, Ga.
Questel, Mae
Steel, Dawn Leslie
Wynette, Tammy

HARRINGTON, DANIEL
Weston Jesuit School of Theology, Cambridge, Mass.
Brown, Raymond Edward

HART, HENRY
College of William and Mary
Dickey, James Lafayette

HAWLEY, ELLIS W.
Professor Emeritus, University of Iowa
    Adams, Walter
    Stein, Herbert
HEALY, JOHN DAVID
Drew University
    Higginbotham, A(loysius) Leon, Jr.
    Leontief, Wassily
HEATH, FENNO F.
Director Emeritus, Yale Glee Club
    Shaw, Robert Lawson
HENRIQUES, DIANA B.
The New York Times
    Evans, Thomas Mellon
HODGES, GRAHAM RUSSELL
Colgate University
    Moore, Archie
HOLLADAY, HILARY
University of Massachusetts, Lowell
    Petry, Ann Lane
HOLLI, MELVIN G.
University of Illinois at Chicago
    Young, Coleman Alexander
HOOGENBOOM, LYNN
Copy Editor, New York Times News Service
    Leonard, Sheldon
IACULLO, MARIA T.
Brooklyn College of the City University of New York
    Mellon, Paul
    Stone, Lawrence
ISSEL, WILLIAM
San Francisco State University
    Alioto, Joseph Lawrence
JALENAK, NATALIE B.
Playhouse on the Square, Memphis, Tenn. (Retired)
    Greenfield, Mary Ellen ("Meg")
    Parker, Thomas Andrew ("Colonel")
JEBSEN, HARRY, JR.
Capital University, Columbus, Ohio
    Flood, Curt(is) Charles
JOHNSON, D. GALE
University of Chicago
    Schultz, Theodore William
JOLLY, J. CHRISTOPHER
Corvallis, Oreg.
    Bradbury, Norris Edwin
JUMONVILLE, NEIL
Florida State University
    Commager, Henry Steele
KALB, PETER R.
Middlebury College
    Feininger, Andreas Bernhard Lyonel

KALFATOVIC, MARY
Writer and Librarian, Arlington, Va.
    Kahn, Madeline Gail
KEEN, W. HUBERT
System Administration, State University of New York
    Gould, Samuel Brookner
    Wald, George David
KHATUN, SAIYEDA
University of Rhode Island
    Williams, Sherley Anne
KINYATTI, NJOKI-WA-
York College, City University of New York
    Clarke, John Henrik
    Weaver, Robert Clifton
KIRSHNER, RALPH
Independent Scholar, Chapel Hill, N.C.
    Rodbell, Martin
KNIGHT, CANDICE
Writer, Missoula, Mont.
    Griffith Joyner, Florence Delorez ("Flo Jo")
KNIGHT, CHRISTOPHER J.
University of Montana
    Gaddis, William
KOED, BETTY K.
United States Senate Historical Office
    Ribicoff, Abraham Alexander
KOTLOWSKI, DEAN J.
Salisbury State University, Maryland
    Exner, Judith Campbell
    Stans, Maurice Hubert
KREMPEL, DANIEL S.
Syracuse University
    Meisner, Sanford
    Meredith, (Oliver) Burgess
KRINGEN, TIMOTHY
Portland, Oreg.
    Jaffe, Leo
LaHOOD, MARVIN J.
Buffalo State College
    Powers, J(ames) F(arl)
LAKIN, PAMELA ARMSTRONG
Research Services Libraries, Harrick Libraries, Alfred University
    Wood, Beatrice
LANGRAN, ROBERT W.
Villanova University
    Powell, Lewis Franklin, Jr.
LANKEVICH, GEORGE J.
Professor of History Emeritus, City University of New York
    Batten, William Milford
LEAB, DANIEL J.
Seton Hall University
    Chandler, Dorothy Buffum

LEARY, WILLIAM M.
University of Georgia
   Carl, Marion Eugene
LEDDICK, DAVID
Writer, Miami Beach, Fla.
   Cadmus, Paul
LEVY, SHARONA A.
Borough of Manhattan Community College, City University
      of New York
   Klutznick, Philip M.
   Liman, Arthur Lawrence
LIGGETT, LUCY A.
Professor Emeritus, Eastern Michigan University
   Robbins, Harold
LITTLE, JOHN E.
Princeton University
   Link, Arthur Stanley
LO BRUTTO, VINCENT
Sohool of Visual Arts, New York City
   Kubrick, Stanley
LOUGHRAN, JAMES N.
St. Peter's College, Jersey City, N.J.
   Bradley, Thomas ("Tom")
LOVE, JOHNNIEQUE B.
University of Maryland Libraries
   Diggs, Charles Coles, Jr.
   Puzo, Mario
   Williams, Joe
McALPIN, MATTHEW
Chicago, Ill.
   McCormick, Kenneth Dale
MACAULAY, NEILL
Professor Emeritus, University of Florida
   Chiles, Lawton Mainor, Jr.
   Kirkland, (Joseph) Lane
   Lee, William Andrew
McBRIDE, CARRIE C.
Writer, New York City
   Rose, Frederick Phineas
McCAUGHEY, ROBERT A.
Barnard College
   Kirk, Grayson Louis
   McGill, William James
McLAUGHLIN, MARILYN SAUDER
Earhart Foundation, Ann Arbor, Mich.
   Ackley, H(ugh) Gardner
MacNIVEN, IAN S.
Independent Scholar, New York City
   Laughlin, James
MALONE, ELOISE F.
United States Naval Academy
   Turner, Francis Cutler ("Frank")
   Vernon, Raymond

MALONEY, WENDY HALL
Brooklyn College of the City University of New York
   Alferez, Enrique ("Rique")
   Smucker, Paul Highnam
MALONEY, WILLIAM J.
Writer, New York City
   Kalman, Tibor
   Stephens, Woodford Cefis ("Woody")
MARC, DAVID
Freelance Writer, Syracuse, N.Y.
   James, Dennis
   Skelton, Richard Bernard ("Red")
   Smith, Robert Emil ("Buffalo Bob")
MARKHAM, REED
Professor Emeritus, California State Polytechnic University
   Branscomb, (Bennett) Harvie
   Murray, James Patrick ("Jim")
MARKOE, LAUREN
Charlotte Observer
   Rosten, Leo Calvin
MARTEN, HARRY
Union College, Schenectady, N.Y.
   Levertov, Denise
MASON, KATHY S.
Southwest Missouri State University
   Douglas, Marjory Stoneman
   Lowe, Steward Alexander ("Alex")
MASSEY, DANNY
Freelance Writer, New York City
   Fasanella, Raphaele ("Ralph")
MAYO, LOUISE A.
County College of Morris, Randolph, N.J.
   Farmer, James Leonard, Jr.
   Strasberg, Susan Elizabeth
MEANOR, PATRICK H.
State University of New York, College at Oneonta
   Gill, Brendan
MECKNA, MICHAEL
Texas Christian University
   Hirt, Alois Maxwell ("Al")
MOBERG, VERNE
Columbia University
   Calderone, Mary Steichen
   Peterson, Esther
MORALES, RUBIL
Brooklyn, N.Y.
   Funt, Allen
MORAN, JOHN
Queens Borough Public Library, New York
   Rothwax, Harold J(ay)
MUGLESTON, WILLIAM F.
Floyd College, Rome, Ga.
   Morris, William Weaks ("Willie")

659

NASH, MADELEINE R.
Finkelstein Memorial Library
    Bancroft, Mary
NEAL, STEVE
Chicago Sun-Times
    Caray, Harry
    Luckman, Sid(ney)
    Royko, Mike
    Udall, Morris King
    Zale, Tony
NELSON, MARTHA E.
State University of Agriculture and Technology at Morrisville, N.Y.
    McCarty, Oseola ("Kelli")
NELSON, MURRY R.
Pennsylvania State University
    Chamberlain, Wilt(on) Norman
    Gates, William ("Pop")
NEWMAN, ROGER K.
School of Law, New York University
    Blackmun, Harry Andrew
    Brennan, William J., Jr.
OHL, JOHN KENNEDY
Mesa Community College
    Day, James Lewis
    Johnson, Leon William
O'KEEFE, KEVIN J.
Stetson University
    Rountree, Martha
OLSON, JAMES C.
President Emeritus, University of Missouri System
    Gellhorn, Martha Ellis
PACHECO, MARÍA
Buffalo State College
    Marston, Robert Quarles
    Nathans, Daniel
    Zoll, Paul Maurice
PARASCANDOLA, JOHN
U.S. Public Health Service
    Hitchings, George Herbert, Jr.
PETERS, SANDRA REDMOND
Southwest Missouri State University
    Farley, Chris(topher) Crosby
    Jackson, Walter Milton ("Milt"; "Bags")
PHILLIPS, LOUIS
New York City
    Espy, Willard Richard ("Wede")
PINSKER, SANDY
Shadek Professor of Humanities at Franklin and Marshall College
    Heller, Joseph
PISPECKY, ROBERT
Spotswood High School, New Jersey
    Lane, Burton

PORTER, DAVID L.
William Penn University
    Hunter, James Augustus ("Catfish")
    Reese, Harold Henry ("Pee Wee")
POTTER, BARRETT G.
State University of New York, College of Technology, Alfred
    Tormé, Mel(vin) Howard
POWERS, RICHARD GID
College of Staten Island, City University of New York
    Shepard, Alan Bartlett, Jr.
PUGH, WILLIAM WHITE TISON
University of Central Florida
    Crisp, Quentin
PULLE, FRANCES
State University of New York, Maritime College
    Garrity, W(endell) Arthur, Jr.
QUARATIELLO, ARLENE R.
Freelance Writer and Indexer, Atkinson, N.H.
    Buscaglia, Felice Leonardo ("Leo")
QUIGLEY, BRIAN
University of California, Berkeley
    Siskel, Eugene Kal ("Gene")
REICHARD, GARY W.
California State University, Long Beach
    Gore, Albert Arnold, Sr.
    Yorty, Samuel William
REYNOLDS, CLARK G.
College of Charleston, S.C.
    Forrest, Helen
    Norvo, Joseph Kenneth ("Red")
RIPPLE, RICHARD E.
Cornell University
    Perkins, James Alfred
RITCHIE, DONALD A.
U.S. Senate Historical Office
    Dickerson Whitehead, Nancy
    Drury, Allen Stuart
ROBERTS, PRISCILLA
University of Hong Kong
    Davies, John Paton, Jr.
ROBINSON, GREGORY K.
JazzTimes
    Snow, Clarence Eugene ("Hank")
ROCCO, JOHN
State University of New York, Maritime College
    Fuller, Samuel Michael
ROSEN, JEFFREY S.
Spotswood High School, New Jersey
    Mayfield, Curtis Lee
    Nitschke, Ray(mond) Ernest
ROUT, KATHLEEN KINSELLA
Michigan State University
    Cleaver, (Leroy) Eldridge

ROYCE, BRENDA SCOTT
Freelance Writer and Editor, Los Angeles, Calif.
    Delany, Sarah Louise ("Sadie")
RUHLMANN, WILLIAM J.
Writer, New York City
    Denver, John
    Perkins, Carl Lee
    Wilson, Carl Dean
SAMWAY, PATRICK
St. Joseph's University
    Dubus, Andre Jules
SAPIENZA, MADELINE
Independent Scholar, Washington, D.C.
    Bing, Franz Josef Rudolf
    Carberry, John Joseph
SCHERER, JOHN L.
Minneapolis, Minn.
    Anderson, (Helen) Eugenie Moore
    Lillehei, C(larence) Walton ("Walt")
SCHONDELMEYER, BRENT
Business Writer, Independence, Mo.
    Henson, Paul Harry
SCHRAG, ZACHARY M.
Ph.D. Candidate, Columbia University
    Weese, Harry Mohr
SCHROTH, RAYMOND A.
St. Peter's College, Jersey City, N.J.
Media Critic, National Catholic Reporter
    Rogers, Roy
SENNETT, TED
Author, Closter, N.J.
    Faye, Alice
    Kiley, Richard Paul
    Scott, George Campbell
    Sidney, Sylvia
    Stewart, James Maitland ("Jimmy")
    Young, Robert George
SHERWIN, MARTIN J.
Tufts University
    Hall, Theodore Alvin
    Hogan, William Benjamin ("Ben")
    Middlecoff, (Emmett) Cary ("Doc")
    Sarazen, Gene
    Stewart, (William) Payne
SHLOMO, ELKA TENNER
Texas A&M University
    Kanin, Garson
SITKOFF, HARVARD
Horton Social Science Center
University of New Hampshire
    Carmichael, Stokely (Kwame Touré)
SMALLS, F. ROMALL
Journalist and Media Consultant
    Nabrit, James Madison, Jr.

SMALLWOOD, JAMES M.
Oklahoma State University
    Mature, Victor John
    Smith, Ralph Corbett
    Walker, (Ewell) Doak, Jr.
SMITH, JAMES F.
Pennsylvania State University
    Sinatra, Francis Albert ("Frank")
SOLON, LEONARD R.
Physicist and Educator, Fort Pierce, Fla.
    Kendall, Henry Way
    Purcell, Edward Mills
    Reines, Frederick
    Schawlow, Arthur Leonard
    Seaborg, Glenn Theodore
    Wu, Chien-Shiung [Jianshiung]
SPATT, HARTLEY S.
State University of New York, Maritime College
    Edel, (Joseph) Leon
    Johnston, Alvin Melvin ("Tex")
    Postel, Jonathan Bruce
SPERLING, SUSAN
Chabot College and University of California,
    San Francisco
    Montagu, Ashley
ST. ANDRE, KENNETH E.
Phoenix Public Library
    Castaneda, Carlos César Salvador Arana
    Dixon, Jeane Lydia
STERTZ, STEPHEN A.
Dowling College
    Brozen, Yale
    Mas Canosa, Jorge
SU, DI
York College, City University of New York
    Schwann, William Joseph
SULLIVAN, JAMES J., III
State University of New York, Fashion Institute
    Brimsek, Francis Charles ("Frankie")
    Horst, Horst Paul
TAKOOSHIAN, HAROLD
Fordham University
    Whyte, William Hollingsworth, Jr.
TASSINARI, EDWARD J.
State University of New York, Maritime College
    Newhouser, Harold ("Prince Hal")
THOMPSON-FEUERHERD, JENNIFER
New York Institute of Technology, Old Westbury, N.Y.
    Pritzker, Jay Arthur
THORNTON, JOYCE K.
Texas A&M University Libraries
    Henry, Aaron Edd Jackson
    Holloway, Bruce Keener
    Reeder, Russell Potter, Jr. ("Red")

THORSEN, CONNIE
St. John's University, New York
 Tilberis, Elizabeth Jane Kelly ("Liz")
 Whitney, Betsey Maria Cushing

TODMAN, ANTHONY
St. John's University, New York
 Wilson, Flip

TOMA, YAN
Queens Borough Public Library, N.Y.
 Hornberger, H(iester) Richard, Jr. (Richard Hooker)

TOMASINO, ADRIANA C.
Ph.D. Candidate, City University of New York
 Cormack, Allan MacLeod
 Elion, Gertrude Belle ("Trudy")
 Huggins, Charles Brenton

TRIMBLE, PATRICK A.
Pennsylvania State University
 Dmytryk, Edward
 Tartikoff, Brandon

TRITTER, THORIN
Princeton University
 Helmsley, Henry Brakmann ("Harry")
 Trump, Frederick Christ

TSOUKAS, LIANN E.
University of Pittsburgh
 Bates, Daisy Lee Gatson
 Byrnes, Robert Francis
 Patterson, Louise Alone Thompson

TUTOROW, NORMAN
Visiting Fellow, Hoover Institution on War, Revolution,
 and Peace, Stanford University
 Fehrenbacher, Don Edward

TYTELL, JOHN
Queens College
 Burroughs, William Seward

UEBELHOR, TRACY STEVEN
University of Southern Indiana and Community College
 of Indiana
 Brown, George Edward, Jr.

VAILL, AMANDA
New York City
 Robbins, Jerome

VANDOREN, SANDRA SHAFFER
Archivist, Balch Institute for Ethnic Studies,
 Philadelphia
 Danilova, Alexandra Dionysievna ("Choura")

VINSON, BETTY B.
Freelance Writer, Mobile, Ala.
 Allin, John Maury
 Geneen, Harold Sydney

WALDMAN, MICAELA
Baruch College, City University of New York
 Chino, Wendell
 Paredes, Américo

WASHBURN, MARK
Charlotte Observer
 Tombaugh, Clyde William

WATSON, MARY ANN
Eastern Michigan University
 Kuralt, Charles Bishop

WEBB, SAMUEL
University of Alabama, Birmingham
 Wallace, George Corley

WEDGE, ELEANOR F.
Freelance Writer and Editor, New York City
 Bettmann, Otto Ludwig
 Castelli, Leo
 Michener, James Albert

WEIGOLD, MARILYN E.
Pace University, Pleasantville, N.Y.
 Bishop, Hazel Gladys
 Mason, (William) Birny J., Jr.

WEINSTEIN, HONORA RAPHAEL
Brooklyn College of the City University of New York
 Tracy, Arthur

WEISBLAT, LEIGH BULLARD
Independent Art Historian, New York City
 De Kooning, Willem
 Liberman, Alexander Semeonovitch

WEISBLAT, TINKY "DAKOTA"
Museum of Television and Radio
 Autry, (Orvon) Gene
 Graham, Virginia
 Rogers, Charles ("Buddy")
 Thompson, Kay

WELLS, WYATT
Auburn University, Montgomery
 Martin, William McChesney, Jr.

WEXLER, MOLLY JALENAK
Memphis Jewish Federation
 Steinberg, Saul

WHITMIRE, TIM
Charlotte Observer
 Caen, Herb Eugene
 Povich, Shirley Lewis

WRIGHT, ELIZABETH J.
Pennsylvania State University
 Dorris, Michael Anthony

YARBROUGH, TINSLEY E.
East Carolina University
 Johnson, Frank Minis, Jr.

OCCUPATIONS INDEX, VOLUMES 1–5

See also the Alphabetical List of Subjects beginning on p. 703.

	Volume
Stuart, Jesse Hilton	1
Sullivan, Walter Seager, Jr.	4
Swanberg, W(illiam) A(ndrew)	3
Taylor, Telford	5
Terry, Walter	1
Thomas, Lewis	3
Thompson, Kay	5
Trilling, Diana Rubin	4
Veeck, William Louis, Jr. ("Bill")	2
Wallace, Irving	2
Weil, André	5
Welch, Robert Henry Winborne, Jr.	1
Wellek, René	4
West, (Mary) Jessamyn	1
White, E(lwyn) B(rooks)	1
Whitehead, Don(ald) Ford	1
Whyte, William Hollingsworth, Jr.	5
Wojnarowicz, David Michael	3
Wood, Beatrice	5
Wright, Olgivanna Lloyd	1

Author (Poetry)

Armour, Richard Willard	2
Bowles, Paul Frederic(k)	5
Boyle, Katherine ("Kay")	3
Brautigan, Richard	1
Brodsky, Joseph	4
Bukowski, (Henry) Charles, Jr. ("Hank")	4
Carver, Raymond Clevie	2
Ciardi, John Anthony	2
Clampitt, Amy Kathleen	4
Cowley, (David) Malcolm	2
Dickey, James Lafayette	5
Duncan, Robert	2
Engle, Paul Hamilton	3
Espy, Willard Richard ("Wede")	5
Everson, William Oliver	4
Fitzgerald, Robert Stuart	1
Ginsberg, (Irwin) Allen	5
Guthrie, Alfred Bertram, Jr.	3
Holmes, John Clellon	2
Laughlin, James	5
Levertov, Denise	5
Lorde, Audre Geraldine	3
MacLeish, Archibald	1
Merriam, Eve	3
Merrill, James Ingram	4
Monette, Paul Landry	4
Nemerov, Howard	3
Oppen, George	1
Rexroth, Kenneth Charles Marion	1
Rice, Helen Steiner	1
Riding, Laura	3

	Volume
Rosten, Norman	4
Sarton, May	4
Schuyler, James Marcus	3
Silverstein, Shel(don) Allan	5
Stuart, Jesse Hilton	1
Warren, Robert Penn	2
Williams, Sherley Anne	5

Author (Science Fiction)

Zelazny, Roger Joseph	4

Author (Screenplays)

Bloch, Robert Albert	4
Brooks, Richard	3
Bukowski, (Henry) Charles, Jr. ("Hank")	4
Chayefsky, Sidney Aaron ("Paddy")	1
Clavell, James du Maresq	4
Foreman, Carl	1
Goodrich, Frances	1
Kanin, Garson	5
Lerner, Alan Jay	2
Maltz, Albert	1
Mankiewicz, Joseph Leo	3
Puzo, Mario	5
Roach, Harold Eugene ("Hal")	3
Roddenberry, Eugene Wesley ("Gene")	3
Ryskind, Morrie	1
Salt, Waldo	2
Southern, Terry	4
St. Johns, Adela Rogers	2

Author (Television)

Diamond, Selma	1
Moore, Garry	3

Author (Translation)

Bancroft, Mary	5
Bowles, Paul Frederic(k)	5
Fadiman, Clifton Paul	5
Fitzgerald, Robert Stuart	1
Hartdegen, Stephen Joseph	2
Howe, Irving	3
Isherwood, Christopher William	2
Levin, Meyer	1

Aviator

Boyington, Gregory ("Pappy")	2
Carl, Marion Eugene	5
Corrigan, Douglas ("Wrong-Way Corrigan")	4
Doolittle, James Harold	3
Gann, Ernest Kellogg	3
Hart, Marion Rice	2
Howard, James Howell	4
Johnson, Leon William	5
Johnson, Robert Samuel	5
Johnston, Alvin Melvin ("Tex")	5
Quesada, Elwood Richard ("Pete")	3

ALPHABETICAL LIST OF SUBJECTS, VOLUMES 1–5

See also the Occupations Index beginning on p. 663.

Subject	Volume	Subject	Volume
Faubus, Orval Eugene	4	Fowler, William Alfred	4
Faulk, John Henry	2	Foxx, Redd	3
Faye, Alice	5	France, William Henry Getty	3
Feather, Leonard Geoffrey	4	Francis, Sam(uel) Lewis	4
Fehrenbacher, Don Edward	5	Frederick, Pauline	2
Feininger, Andreas Bernhard Lyonel	5	Fredericks, Carlton	2
Feld, Irvin	1	Fredericks, Sara	2
Feldman, Morton	2	Freleng, Isadore ("Friz")	4
Fender, Clarence Leonidas ("Leo")	3	Freund, Paul Abraham	3
Fenwick, Millicent Hammond	3	Frick, Helen Clay	1
Ferguson, Homer Samuel	1	Friedman, Benjamin ("Benny")	1
Ferrer, José	3	Friedrich, Carl Joachim	1
Festinger, Leon	2	Friend, Charlotte	2
Fetchit, Stepin	1	Friendly, Fred W.	5
Feyerabend, Paul Karl	4	Friendly, Henry Jacob	2
Feynman, Richard Phillips	2	Frowick, Roy Halston. *See* Halston.	
Fidler, James Marion ("Jimmy")	2	Fulbright, J(ames) William	4
Fielding, Temple Hornaday	1	Fuller, R(ichard) Buckminster	1
Finch, Robert Hutchinson	4	Fuller, Samuel Michael	5
Fine, Reuben	3	Fuller, S. B.	2
Finkelstein, Louis	3	Funt, Allen	5
Finley, Charles Oscar ("Charlie")	4	Furcolo, (John) Foster	4
Finney, Walter Braden ("Jack")	4	Furness, Elizabeth Mary ("Betty")	4
Fish, Hamilton	3	Gabel, Hortense Wittstein	2
Fisher, Avery Robert	4	Gabor, Eva	4
Fisher, M(ary) F(rances) K(ennedy)	3	Gacy, John Wayne, Jr.	4
Fitzgerald, Ella Jane	4	Gaddis, William	5
Fitzgerald, Robert Stuart	1	Gaines, William Maxwell	3
Fitzsimmons, Frank Edward	1	Galarza, Ernesto, Jr.	1
Fixx, James Fuller	1	Gallo, Julio Robert	3
Flesch, Rudolf Franz	2	Gallup, George Horace	1
Fletcher, Harvey	1	Gann, Ernest Kellogg	3
Fletcher, Joseph Francis, III	3	Garbo, Greta	2
Flexner, Stuart Berg	2	Garcia, Hector Perez	4
Flood, Curt(is) Charles	5	Garcia, Jerome John ("Jerry")	4
Flory, Paul John	1	Gardner, Ava Lavinia	2
Folsom, James	2	Gardner, John Champlin, Jr.	1
Fonda, Henry Jaynes	1	Garrison, Jim	3
Foner, Philip Sheldon	4	Garrity, W(endell) Arthur, Jr.	5
Fontanne, Lynn	1	Garroway, David Cunningham	1
Foote, Emerson	3	Garson, Greer	4
Forbes, Malcolm Stevenson	2	Gates, John	3
Ford, Ernest Jennings ("Tennessee Ernie")	3	Gates, Thomas Sovereign, Jr.	1
Ford, Henry, II ("Hank the Deuce")	2	Gates, William ("Pop")	5
Foreman, Carl	1	Gavin, James Maurice	2
Forrest, Helen	5	Gaye, Marvin Pentz	1
Fortas, Abe	1	Gaynor, Janet	1
Forte, Fulvio Chester, Jr. ("Chet")	4	Gehringer, Charles Leonard ("Charlie")	3
Fosse, Robert Louis ("Bob")	2	Geisel, Theodor S. ("Dr. Seuss")	3
Fossey, Dian	1	Geldzahler, Henry	4
Foster, Vincent William, Jr.	3	Gellhorn, Martha Ellis	5

Subject	Volume	Subject	Volume
Harburg, Edgar Yipsel ("Yip")	1	Henson, James Maury ("Jim")	2
Haring, Keith Allen	2	Henson, Paul Harry	5
Harken, Dwight Emary	3	Hepburn, Audrey Kathleen	3
Harkness, Rebekah West	1	Herman, Floyd Caves ("Babe")	2
Harlow, Bryce Nathaniel	2	Herman, William Jennings ("Billy")	3
Harmon, Thomas Dudley	2	Herman, Woody	2
Harriman, Pamela Beryl Digby Churchill		Herrnstein, Richard Julius	4
Hayward	5	Hersey, John Richard	3
Harriman, W(illiam) Averell	2	Hershey, Alfred Day	5
Harrington, (Edward) Michael	2	Hexter, J. H. ("Jack")	4
Harris, Patricia Roberts Fitzgerald	1	Hickerson, John Dewey	2
Harris, Sydney Justin	2	Hicks, Granville	1
Harris, (Wanga) Phillip ("Phil")	4	Higginbotham, A(loysius) Leon, Jr.	5
Hart, Marion Rice	2	Highsmith, (Mary) Patricia	4
Hartdegen, Stephen Joseph	2	Hildreth, Horace Augustus	2
Hartline, Haldan Keffer	1	Hill, (Joseph) Lister	1
Hartman, Phil(ip) Edward	5	Hill, Julian Werner	4
Hartz, Louis	2	Hillcourt, William ("Green Bar Bill")	3
Hassenfeld, Stephen David	2	Himes, Chester Bomar	1
Hathaway, Starke Rosencrans	1	Hines, Earl Kenneth ("Fatha")	1
Haughton, Daniel Jeremiah	2	Hirshhorn, Joseph Herman	1
Haughton, William Robert ("Billy")	2	Hirt, Alois Maxwell ("Al")	5
Hawkins, Erskine Ramsay	3	Hiss, Alger	4
Hawkins, Frederick ("Erick")	4	Hitchings, George Herbert, Jr.	5
Hayakawa, S(amuel) I(chiye)	3	Hobby, Oveta Culp	4
Hayek, Friedrich August von	3	Hobson, Laura Kean Zametkin	2
Hayes, Helen	3	Hoffer, Eric	1
Hayes, Wayne Woodrow ("Woody")	2	Hoffman, Abbott ("Abbie")	2
Haynsworth, Clement Furman, Jr.	2	Hoffmann, Banesh	2
Hays, (Lawrence) Brooks	1	Hofheinz, Roy Mark	1
Hays, Lee	1	Hofstadter, Robert	2
Hays, Wayne Levere	2	Hogan, William Benjamin ("Ben")	5
Hayworth, Rita	2	Holden, William	1
Hazlitt, Henry Stuart	3	Holland, Jerome Heartwell ("Brud")	1
Head, Edith	1	Holley, Robert William	3
Healy, Timothy Stafford	3	Holloway, Bruce Keener	5
Hearst, William Randolph, Jr.	3	Holm, Hanya	3
Hecht, Harold	1	Holman, Nathan ("Nat")	4
Heidelberger, Michael	3	Holmes, John Clellon	2
Heifetz, Jascha	2	Holt, John Caldwell	1
Heinlein, Robert Anson	2	Holzman, William ("Red")	5
Heinz, Henry John, II ("Jack")	2	Hook, Sidney	2
Heinz, Henry John, III	3	Hooker, Evelyn Gentry	4
Heller, Joseph	5	Hopkins, Sam ("Lightnin'")	1
Heller, Walter Wolfgang	2	Hopper, Grace Brewster Murray	3
Hellman, Lillian Florence	1	Hornberger, H(iester) Richard, Jr. (Richard	
Helmsley, Henry Brakmann ("Harry")	5	Hooker)	5
Hemingway, Margaux	4	Horowitz, Vladimir	2
Hemingway, Mary Welsh	2	Horst, Horst Paul	5
Henderson, Leon	2	Horton, Mildred Helen McAfee	4
Henry, Aaron Edd Jackson	5	Houghton, Arthur Amory, Jr.	2

Subject	Volume	Subject	Volume
Kendrick, Alexander	3	Kurland, Philip B.	4
Kendricks, Eddie James	3	Kurtzman, Harvey	3
Kennedy, John Fitzgerald, Jr.	5	Kusch, Polykarp	3
Kennedy, Rose Elizabeth Fitzgerald	4	Kutner, Luis	3
Kennedy, William Jesse, Jr.	1	Kuznets, Simon Smith	1
Kent, Corita	2	Labouisse, Henry Richardson	2
Keppel, Francis	2	Ladd, George Eldon	1
Kerr, Walter Francis	4	Lamont, Corliss	4
Kertész, André (Andor)	1	Lamour, Dorothy	4
Keyserling, Leon Hirsch	2	L'Amour, Louis	2
Khaury, Herbert Butros. *See* Tiny Tim.		Lancaster, Burt(on) Stephen	4
Kienholz, Edward Ralph	4	Lancaster, Kelvin John	5
Kieran, John Francis	1	Lanchester, Elsa	2
Kiley, Richard Paul	5	Land, Edwin Herbert	3
Killian, James Rhyne, Jr.	2	Landon, Alf(red) Mossman	2
Kimball, Spencer Woolley	1	Landon, Margaret Dorothea Mortenson	3
Kinard, Frank Manning ("Bruiser")	1	Landon, Michael	3
King, Martin Luther, Sr. ("Daddy King")	1	Lane, Burton	5
Kirby, George	4	Lane, Frank Charles	1
Kirk, Grayson Louis	5	Langer, Susanne Katherina	1
Kirk, Russell Amos	4	Lansdale, Edward Geary	2
Kirkland, (Joseph) Lane	5	Lansky, Meyer	1
Kirstein, Lincoln	4	Lantz, Walter	4
Kirsten, Dorothy	3	Larson, Jonathan	4
Kistiakowsky, George Bogdan	1	Larson, (Lewis) Arthur	3
Kline, Nathan Schellenberg	1	Lasch, Christopher	4
Klopfer, Donald Simon	2	Lash, Joseph P.	2
Kluszewski, Theodore Bernard ("Ted"; "Big Klu")	2	Lasker, Mary Woodward	4
Klutznick, Philip M.	5	Lattimore, Owen	2
Knight, John Shively	1	Laughlin, James	5
Knight, Ted	2	Lausche, Frank John	2
Knopf, Alfred Abraham	1	Lawford, Peter Sydney Vaughn	1
Knott, Walter	1	Lay, Herman W.	1
Kohlberg, Lawrence	2	Layne, Robert Lawrence ("Bobby")	2
Koontz, Elizabeth Duncan	2	Lazar, Irving Paul ("Swifty")	3
Koopmans, Tjalling Charles	1	Lazarus, Ralph	2
Koresh, David	3	Leary, Timothy Francis	4
Korshak, Sidney Roy	4	Lebow, Fred	4
Kosinski, Jerzy Nikodem	3	Lee, J(oseph) Bracken ("Brack")	4
Kraft, Joseph	2	Lee, Pinky	3
Krasner, Lee	1	Lee, William Andrew	5
Kraus, Hans Peter	2	Le Gallienne, Eva	3
Krim, Arthur B.	4	Leinsdorf, Erich	3
Kristeller, Paul Oskar	5	Lekachman, Robert	2
Kroc, Ray(mond) Albert	1	Lelyveld, Arthur Joseph	4
Krol, John Joseph	4	LeMay, Curtis Emerson	2
Kubrick, Stanley	5	Lemnitzer, Lyman Louis	2
Kuhn, Margaret Eliza ("Maggie")	4	Lenya, Lotte	1
Kuhn, Thomas Samuel	4	Leonard, Sheldon	5
Kunstler, William Moses	4	Leonard, Walter Fenner ("Buck")	5
Kuralt, Charles Bishop	5	Leontief, Wassily	5

Subject	Volume
Magowan, Robert Anderson	1
Malamud, Bernard	2
Maleska, Eugene Thomas	3
Malone, Dumas	2
Maltz, Albert	1
Mamoulian, Rouben Zachary	2
Mancini, Henry Nicola	4
Mankiewicz, Joseph Leo	3
Mann, Jonathan Max	5
Manne, Sheldon ("Shelly")	1
Mannes, Marya	2
Manning, Timothy	2
Mantle, Mickey Charles	4
Mapplethorpe, Robert	2
Maravich, Peter Press ("Pistol Pete")	2
Marble, Alice	2
Marcello, Carlos	3
Margulies, Lazar	1
Maris, Roger Eugene	1
Mark, Herman Francis	3
Markham, Dewey ("Pigmeat")	1
Marks, John D. ("Johnny")	1
Marriott, J(ohn) Willard	1
Mars, Forrest Edward, Sr.	5
Marshall, E(dda) G(unnar)	5
Marshall, Thurgood	3
Marston, Robert Quarles	5
Martin, Alfred Manuel, Jr. ("Billy")	2
Martin, Dean	4
Martin, Freddy	1
Martin, John Bartlow	2
Martin, Mary Virginia	2
Martin, William McChesney, Jr.	5
Marvin, Lee	2
Mas Canosa, Jorge	5
Mason, (William) Birny J., Jr.	5
Massey, Raymond Hart	1
Matsunaga, Spark Masayuki ("Sparkie")	2
Matthews, Burnita Shelton	2
Mature, Victor John	5
Maxwell, Vera Huppé	4
May, Rollo Reece	4
Mayfield, Curtis Lee	5
Maynard, Robert Clyve	3
Mays, Benjamin Elijah	1
Meadows, Audrey	4
Means, Gardiner Coit	2
Medeiros, Humberto Sousa	1
Medina, Harold Raymond	2
Meeker, Ralph	2
Meisner, Sanford	5

Subject	Volume
Mellon, Paul	5
Menninger, Karl Augustus	2
Menuhin, Yehudi	5
Mercer, Mabel	1
Meredith, (Oliver) Burgess	5
Merman, Ethel	1
Merriam, Eve	3
Merrill, James Ingram	4
Merrill, John Putnam	1
Meyendorff, John	3
Meyner, Robert Baumle	2
Michener, James Albert	5
Middlecoff, (Emmett) Cary ("Doc")	5
Middleton, Drew	2
Milanov, Zinka	2
Milgram, Stanley	1
Milland, Ray	2
Millar, Kenneth. *See* Macdonald, Ross.	
Miller, Arnold Ray	1
Miller, Carl S.	2
Miller, Roger Dean	3
Miller, William Mosely	2
Mills, Wilbur Daigh	3
Milstein, Nathan	3
Minnelli, Vincente	2
Minnesota Fats (Rudolf Walter Wanderone, Jr.)	4
Mitchell, Joan	3
Mitchell, (John) Broadus	2
Mitchell, John James, Jr.	1
Mitchell, John Newton	2
Mitchell, Joseph Quincy	4
Mitchum, Robert Charles Durman	5
Mitford, Jessica ("Decca")	4
Mize, John Robert ("Johnny")	3
Mizener, Arthur Moore	2
Mohr, Charles Henry	2
Molnar, Charles Edwin	4
Monette, Paul Landry	4
Monk, Thelonious Sphere	1
Monroe, Marion	1
Monroe, Rose Leigh Will	5
Monroe, William Smith ("Bill")	4
Montagu, Ashley	5
Montgomery, Elizabeth	4
Montgomery, Robert	1
Moore, Archie	5
Moore, Garry	3
Moore, Jack Carlton ("Clayton")	5
Moore, Stanford	1
Moos, Malcolm Charles	1
Morgan, Henry (Lerner von Ost)	4

ISBN 0-684-80663-0

90000

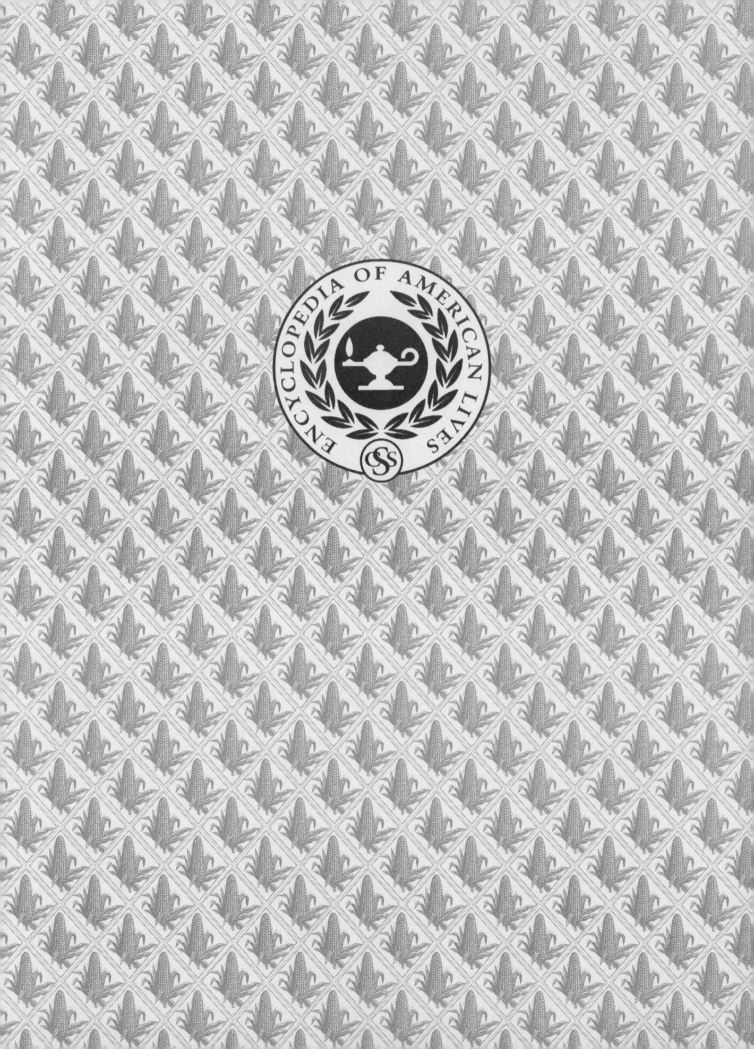